Child Rights in India

Child Rights in India

Law, Policy, and Practice

Third Edition

Asha Bajpai

OXFORD
UNIVERSITY PRESS

OXFORD
UNIVERSITY PRESS

Oxford University Press is a department of the University of Oxford.
It furthers the University's objective of excellence in research, scholarship,
and education by publishing worldwide. Oxford is a registered trademark of
Oxford University Press in the UK and in certain other countries

Published in India by
Oxford University Press
22 Workspace, 2nd Floor, 1/22 Asaf Ali Road, New Delhi 110002, India

First Edition published in 2003
Second Edition as Oxford India Paperbacks in 2006
Third Edition as Oxford India Paperbacks in 2017
Digitally Printed in 2024

ISBN-13: 978-0-19-947071-6
ISBN-10: 0-19-947071-5

Typeset in Adobe Garamond Pro 10.5/12.5
by The Graphics Solution, New Delhi 110092
Printed at Manipal Technologies Limited, Manipal

To my father,
Ram Manohar Bajpai—
my source of inspiration and strength

Contents

Abbreviations

AARTH	Action, Advocacy, Research and Training in Disability
AAY	Antyodaya Anna Yojan
ACASH	Association for Consumers Action on Safety and Health
ACHPR	African Charter on Human and Peoples Rights
ACPC	Area Child Protection Committee
ADR	Alternative Dispute Resolution
AFAA	Authorized Foreign Adoption Agency
AHTU	Anti-human Trafficking Unit
AI	Artificial Insemination
AIACHE	All India Association for Christian Higher Education
AIFTO	All India Federation of Teachers Organization
AIMPLB	All India Muslim Personal Law Board
AIPTF	All India Primary Teachers Federation
AISTF	All India Secondary Teachers Federation
ARC	Adoption Recommendation Committee
ARI	Acute Respiratory Infection
ART	Assisted Reproductive Technology
ASD	Action for Social Development
ASHA	Accredited Social Health Activist
AWC	Anganwadi Centre
AYUSH	Ayurveda, Yoga and Naturopathy, Unani, Siddha and Homoeopathy
BBBP	Beti Bachao, Beti Padhao
BBMP	Bruhat Bengaluru Bangalore Mahanagara Palike
BCG	Bacillus Calmette-Guerin
BLAST	Bangladesh Legal Aid and Services Trust
BLSAA	Bonded Labour System (Abolition) Act
BSY	Bal Sangopan Yojana
CA	Central Authority
CAA	Constitutional Amendment Act
CACL	Campaign against Child Labour
CAN	Child Abuse and Neglect
CARA	Central Adoption Resource Agency

CARE	Cooperative for Assistance and Relief Everywhere
CARINGS	Child Adoption Resource Information and Guidance System
CBO	Community Based Organization
CCTV	Closed-Circuit Television
CEDAW	Convention of the Elimination of All Forms of Discrimination against Women
CEDC	Children in Especially Difficult Circumstances
CEHAT	Center for Enquiry into Health and Allied Themes
CJM	Chief Judicial Magistrate
CLM	Child Labour Monitoring
CLPRA	Child Labour (Prohibition and Regulation) Act
CMAM	Community-Based Management of Acute Malnutrition
CMM	Chief Metropolitan Magistrate
CMPO	Child Marriage Protection Officer
CNCP	Children in Need of Care and Protection
CPC	Code of Civil Procedure
CPCR	Commission for Protection of Child Rights
CPCRA	Commission for Protection of Child Rights Act
CRH	Committee for Right to Housing
CrPC	Code of Criminal Procedure
CRPD	Convention on the Rights of Persons with Disabilities
CRY	Child Rights and You
CSA&E	Child Sexual Abuse and Exploitation
CSB	Central Supervisory Board
CSR	Child Sex Ratio
CVARA	Coordinating Voluntary Adoption Resource Agency
CWA	Child Workers in Asia
CWC	Child Welfare Committee
CYDA	Centre for Youth Development and Activities
DCI	Defence for Children International
DCPCR	Delhi Commission for Protection of Child Rights
DCPU	District Child Protection Unit
DDA	Delhi Development Authority
DLSA	Delhi Legal Services Authority
DOE	Director of Education
DPEP	District Primary Education Programme
DPSP	Directive Principles of State Policy
DPT	Diphtheria, Pertussis, and Tetanus
DRC	Declaration of the Rights of the Child
DWCD	Department of Women and Child Development
EBB	Educationally Backward Block
ECCD	Early Childhood Care and Development
ECCE	Early Childhood Care and Education
ECD	Early Childhood Development

ECDC	Early Childhood Development Center
ECHR	European Convention on Human Rights
ECPAT	End Child Prostitution in Asian Tourism
EDUSAT	Educational Satellite
EFA	Education for All
ENAP	Every Newborn Action Plan
ESC	European Social Charter
ESI	Employees' State Insurance
EWS	Economically Weaker Section
FAA	Foreign Adoption Agency
FACSE	Forum against Child Sexual Abuse
FAO	Food and Agriculture Organization
FASS	Forum against Sex Selection
FCA	Family Courts' Act
FCI	Food Corporation of India
FSC	Family Service Centre
FSSAI	Food Safety and Standards of India
FYP	Five Year Plan
GATT	General Agreement on Tariffs and Trade
GD	Government Department
GDP	Gross Domestic Product
GER	Gross Enrollment Ratio
GHARAUNDA	Group Home and Rehabilitation Activities under National Trust Act for Disabled Adults
GMA	Guardianship of Minors Act
GR	Government Resolution
GWA	Guardians and Wards Act
HAMA	Hindu Adoptions and Maintenance Act
HIV/AIDS	Human Immunodeficiency Virus/Acquired Immune Deficiency Syndrome
HLRN	Housing and Land Rights Network
HMA	Hindu Marriage Act
HMGA	Hindu Minority and Guardianship Act
HRAH	Human Right to Adequate Housing
HRARF	Human Rights Advocacy and Research Foundation
HSA	Hindu Succession Act
IAPA	Indian Association for Promotion of Adoption
IAY	Indira Awaas Yojana
IBRD	International Bank for Reconstruction and Development
ICA	Inter-country Adoption
ICARA	International Child Abduction Remedies Act
ICCPR	International Covenant on Civil and Political Rights
ICCW	Indian Council for Child Welfare
ICDS	Integrated Child Development Services
ICESCR	International Covenant on Economic, Social and Cultural Rights

ICMR	Indian Council of Medical Research
ICPS	Integrated Child Protection Scheme
ICSW	Indian Council for Social Welfare
ICT	Indian Contract Act
ICTC	Integrated Counselling and Testing Centre
IDA	Indian Divorce Act
IDM	Indian Diplomatic Mission
ILO	International Labor Organization
IMR	Infant Mortality Rate
IMRB	Indian Market Research Bureau
INA	Immigration and Nationality Act
INAP	India Newborn Action Plan
IO	Investigating Officer
IPC	Indian Penal Code
IPCA	International Parental Child Abductions
IQ	Intelligence Quotient
ISA	Indian Succession Act
ISPCAN	International Society for the Prevention of Child Abuse and Neglect
IT	Information Technology
ITPA	Immoral Traffick (Prevention) Act
IVD	Intravenous Drug
IVF	In-Vitro Fertilization
IYCF	Infant and Young Child Feeding
JICL	Juveniles in Conflict with Law
JJ Act	Juvenile Justice (Care and Protection of Children) Act
JJ Bill	Juvenile Justice (Care and Protection of Children) Bill
JJ Rules	Juvenile Justice (Care and Protection of Children) Rules
JJB	Juvenile Justice Board
JRY	Jawahar Rozgar Yojana
JSY	Janani Suraksha Yojana
JWO	Junior Welfare Officer
LAC	Latin America and the Caribbean
LLIN	Long Lasting Insecticide Treated Nets
LMIC	Low or Middle Income Country
MASUM	Mahila Sarvangeen Utkarsh Mandal
MCJM	Municipal Corporation of Greater Mumbai
MDC	Mentally Disabled Children
MDG	Millennium Development Goal
MDMS	Mid-Day Meal Scheme
MENA	Middle East and North Africa
MHADA	Maharashtra Housing and Area Development Authority
MHRD	Ministry of Human Resource Development
MMA	Medical Methods of Abortion
MMR	Maternal Mortality Ratio

MVA	Manual Vacuum Aspiration
MWCD	Ministry of Women and Child Development
NACO	National AIDS Control Organization
NAFRE	National Alliance for the Fundamental Right to quality Education and Equity
NAMS	National Academy of Medical Sciences
NCAG	National Coordination and Action Group
NCC	National Commission for Children
NCD	Non-communicable Disease
NCE	National Coalition for Education
NCF	National Curriculum Framework
NCHR	National Campaign for Housing Rights
NCLP	National Child Labour Project
NCPCR	National Commission for Protection of Child Rights
NCRB	National Crime Records Bureau
NDP	'No Detention' Policy
NDPS	Narcotic Drugs and Psychotropic Substances Act
NFBS	National Family Benefit Scheme
NFSA	National Food Security Act
NGO	Non-governmental Organization
NHM	National Health Mission
NHP	National Health Policy
NHRC	National Human Rights Commission
NIMC	National Inspection and Monitoring Committee
NIOS	National Institute of Open Schooling
NLM	National Literacy Mission
NMBS	National Maternity Benefit Scheme
NOAPS	National Old Age Pension Scheme
NOC	No Objection Certificate
NPAC	National Plan of Action for Children
NPCL	National Policy on Child Labour
NPE	National Policy on Education
NREP	National Rural Employment Programme
NRHM	National Rural Health Mission
NRI	Non-resident Indian
NSSO	National Sample Survey Organization
NUEPA	National University of Educational Planning and Administration
NUHM	National Urban Health Mission
NYP	National Youth Policy
OAS	Organization of American States
OAU	Organization of African Unity
OB	Operation Blackboard
OFCHR	United Nations High Commissioner for Human Rights
OHU	Observation Home, Umerkhadi

OOSC	Out-of-School Children
OP3 CRC	Optional Protocol to the CRC on a Communications Procedure
OPAC	Optional Protocol to the Convention on the Rights of the Child on the Involvement of Children in Armed Conflict
OPSC	Optional Protocol to the Convention on the Rights of the Child on the Sale of Children, Child Prostitution and Child Pornography
ORS	Oral Rehydration Salts
OSR	Overall Sex Ratio
PAP	Prospective Adoptive Parent
PCCSS	People's Campaign for Common School System
PCMA	Prohibition of Child Marriage Act
PCPNDT Act	Preconception and Prenatal Diagnostic Techniques (Prohibition of Sex Selection) Act
PDG	Prenatal Genetic Diagnosis
PDS	Public Distribution System
PHC	Primary Healthcare
PHFI	Public Health Foundation of India
PIL	Public Interest Litigation
PMDA	Parsi Marriage and Divorce Act
PMGA	Pradhan Mantri Gramodaya Yojana
PNDT Act	Prenatal Diagnostic Techniques (Regulation and Prevention of Misuse) Act
POCSO	Protection of Children against Sexual Offences
PPTCT	Prevention of Parent to Child Transmission
PTSD	Post-Traumatic Stress Disorder
PUCL	People's Union for Civil Liberties
PWD	Persons with Disability
PWDVA	Protection of Women from Domestic Violence Act
RBD	Registration of Births and Deaths
RBI	Reserve Bank of India
RCFCEA	Right of Children to Free and Compulsory Education Act
RCH programme	Reproductive and Child Health Programme
RDK	Rapid Diagnostic Kit
RGI	Registrar General of India
RGSEAG	Rajiv Gandhi Scheme for Empowerment of Adolescent Girls
RHCP	Registered Health Care Provider
RI	Routine Immunization
RIPA	Recognized Indian Placement Agency
RLEGP	Rural Landless Employment Guarantee Programme
RMNCH	Reproductive, Maternal, Newborn, and Child Health
RMP	Registered Medical Practitioner
RNTCP	Revised National Tuberculosis Control Program
RTE	Right to Free and Compulsory Education Act
RTI	Reproductive Tract Infection

SAA	Sarva Shiksha Abhiyan
SAARC	South Asian Association for Regional Cooperation
SAAs	Specialised Adoption Agencies
SARA	State Adoption Resource Agency
SCOSAC	Standing Committee on Sexually Abused Children
SCPCR	State Commissions for Protection of Child Rights
SCWLA	Supreme Court Women Lawyers Association
SD	Standard Deviation
SIF	Save Indian Family
SIPCOT	State Industries Promotion Corporation of Tamil Nadu
SIR	Social Investigation Report
SJPU	Special Juvenile Police Unit
SMA	Special Marriage Act
SNP	Supplementary Nutrition Programme
SRS	Sample Registration System
SSA	Sarva Shiksha Abhiyan
STF	Special Task Forces
TB	Tuberculosis
TFR	Total Fertility Rate
U5MR	Under-Five Mortality Rate
UCCJEA	Uniform Child Custody Jurisdiction and Enforcement Act
UDHR	Universal Declaration of Human Rights
U-DISE	Unified District Information System for Education
UEE	Universalization of Elementary Education
UIP	Universal Immunisation Programme
UIS	UNESCO Institute for Statistics
ULB	Urban Local Body
UMDA	Uniform Marriage and Divorce Act
UNCRC	United Nations Convention on the Rights of the Child
UNDP	United Nations Development Programme
UNESCO	United Nations Educational, Scientific, and Cultural Organization
UNFPA	United Nations Fund for Population Activities
UNICEF	United Nations Children's Fund
UNIFEM	United Nations Development Fund for Women
UOI	Union of India
UPE	Universal Primary Education
UT	Union Territory
VAK	Vikas Adhyayan Kendra
VCA	Voluntary Coordinating Agency
VIP	Very Important Person
WCD	(Ministry of) Women and Child Development
WHO	World Health Organization
UVA	Youth for Unity and Voluntary Action

Foreword to the Third Edition

Nationally as well as internationally, the idea of justice to the child has attracted the attention of all sections of the society ever since the turn of the century. While the law and policies have changed to become more child-friendly, practice has not changed to the desired degree. The increasing number of references brought before the judiciary on behalf of children is indicative of the persistence of traditional attitudes and approaches on the part of those entrusted with the implementation of laws and programmes introduced for the welfare of children. There is a need for change in mindset on the part of adults, generally, and those who are involved in protection of the rights of children, particularly. Asha Bajpai's book will certainly contribute to build up awareness on the part of adults who owe duties enforceable under law towards children.

In the context of India, there are three areas of child rights which deserve priority attention of all concerned. One, the right to free and compulsory primary education for all children, which is now a guaranteed fundamental right of every child. There are a dozen duty holders under the Right to Education Act (RTE), 2009 and the rules made under it. They include parents, guardians, teachers, managements of schools, government servants implementing the laws, parent–teacher associations, local bodies, state and central governments, and civil society organizations. No excuse, whatsoever, including scarcity of resources, is acceptable from the state for non-implementation of the RTE Act. Education is the key for enjoyment of all other rights, including equality and dignity. It is time to take up the implementation of the RTE Act in a mission mode involving the government and citizenry so that every child in this country gets quality education in the next 5 years, without fail.

Other issues of concern are health and nutrition as well as child trafficking and sex abuse.

Political leaders often talk of the demographic dividend referring to the large child population of India. But they do very little in actual terms to prepare the child citizens to take advantage of the situation. We need more and more studies on the status of children, like the present book, to focus public attention on the subject on a continuing basis. I am sure this revised third edition will also receive the same recognition from readers as the earlier two editions.

Now that there is ample study material readily available on the subject, the Bar Council of India should consider making Child Rights Law and Advocacy a compulsory subject for the LLB course. All lawyers and judges should be sufficiently informed of this branch of jurisprudence if rights of all children have to get adequate legal protection.

Prof. (Dr) N.R. Madhava Menon
Hony. Professor & IBA-CLE Chair, National Law School, Bengaluru, Karnataka, India
Hony. Director, MKN Academy for Continuing Legal Education, Kochi, Kerala, India

xx   Preface to the Third Edition

for her invaluable assistance in the research of new laws and the laws. Finally, my relations with
colleagues, students, and child rights professionals, and any of their works, have helped
shape the author. Very special thanks to my family—my mother, sister, and nieces for their
patience and understanding. They always encouraged my dreams and nurtured my decisions.

Preface to the Third Edition

This fully revised third edition provides the changes in national and international law, policy, and practice to promote and protect the rights of children. Since the last edition in 2005, several legal developments relating to child rights have taken place both nationally and internationally. A marked change in traditional thinking about child rights was promoted by the adoption of the United Nations Convention on the Rights of the Child (UNCRC) in 1989. Significantly, 20 November 2014 marked 25 years since the adoption of the UNCRC and the emergence of a different perspective on providing justice to children with a rights-based approach. This approach has been acquiring prominence in the child rights discourse across the world. It promotes justice, equality, participation, accountability, inclusion, and freedom for children.

This edition retains the earlier theoretical work of the original book and looks at laws and law reforms for providing justice to children in India with a child rights–based approach. There have been several legislations, progressive court judgments, and policy initiatives in India. This edition covers new developments in India, such as the Juvenile Justice (Care and Protection of Children) Act (JJ Act), 2015, the new Central Adoption Resource Agency guidelines; shared custody or joint parenting; international trends relating to joint custody, missing children, and out-of-school children; the Right of Children to Free and Compulsory Education (RTE) Act, 2009, and the National Food Security Act, 2013 (Right to Food Act). Thoroughly updated, each chapter is structured to include national laws, case laws, major policies and schemes of the government, international law, interventions and strategies by non-governmental organizations (NGOs) to protect and promote child rights, gaps in implementation of laws and policies, and recommendations for legislative reform in support of children.

It is my hope that this updated edition will be useful for child rights practitioners, social workers, governments and governmental agencies, policymakers, researchers, students, and international, regional, and national NGOs, among others, for using laws for improving the quality of children's lives and in their endeavour to promote and protect children's rights.

I am grateful to S. Parasuraman, Director of Tata Institute of Social Sciences (TISS), Mumbai, Maharashtra, India, who gave me the much-needed leave and inspiration to write this book. I would like to thank N.R. Madhava Menon for writing the foreword to this book. It has always been a pleasure working with the Oxford University Press, the publisher. I wish to thank the Research and Development Cell of TISS for its support. I really appreciate the prompt help from the librarian at TISS, Satish Kanamadi, and his team. I would like to acknowledge Arunima Jha for her invaluable assistance in the research of new laws and case laws. Finally, interactions with colleagues, students, and child rights professionals, and readings of their works, have helped shape this edition. Very special thanks to my family—my mother, sisters, and nieces for their patience and understanding. They always encouraged my dreams and trusted my decisions.

1 Rights of the Child

An Overview

The law, policy, and practice of child welfare have undergone a significant change from a historical perspective. Before 1839, there was the concept of authority and control. It was an established common law doctrine that the father had absolute rights over his children. After this, the welfare principle was reflected in the dominant ideology of the family. The Victorian judges, who developed the welfare principle, favoured one dominant family form. The Indian traditional view of welfare is based on *daya, dana, dakshina, bhiksha, ahimsa, samya-bhava, swadharma,* and *tyaga,* the essence of which were self-discipline, self-sacrifice, and consideration for others. It was believed that the well-being of children depended on these values.

Children were recipients of welfare measures. It was only during the twentieth century that the concept of children's rights emerged. This shift in focus from the 'welfare' to the 'rights' approach is significant. Rights are entitlements. They also imply obligations and goals. The rights approach is primarily concerned with issues of social justice, non-discrimination, equity, and empowerment. The rights perspective is embodied in the United Nations Convention on the Rights of the Child 1989 (UNCRC 1989), which is a landmark in international human rights legislation. India ratified the convention in December 1992.

India has the largest child population in the world. The number of children under the age of 18 years, which was 428 million in 2001 and rose to 430 million in 2006, is projected to remain above 400 million in the coming decade.[1] As per the 2011 Census, India has 158.7 million children in the age group of 0–6 years, comprising about 16 per cent of the total Indian population.[2] In the period 2008–13, 43 per cent of India's children under 5 years were underweight and 48 per cent had stunted growth.[3] According to a World Bank report published in 2013,[4] the mortality rate of children under 5 years of age is 53 per 1,000 live births and according to a 2013 United

---

[1] Ministry of Women and Child Development, *Third and Fourth Combined Periodic Report on the Convention on the Rights of the Child* (Government of India, 2011). Available at http://icds-wcd.nic.in/crc3n4/crc3n4_1r.pdf (accessed on 25 December 2015).

[2] Law Commission of India, *Early Childhood Development and Legal Entitlements*, Report No. 259, August, Government of India, 2015. Available at http://lawcommissionofindia.nic.in/reports/Report259.pdf (accessed on 24 October 2015).

[3] Law Commission of India, *Early Childhood Development.*

[4] World Bank, 'Mortality Rate, under-5 (per 1,000 Live Births)', n.d. Available at http://data.worldbank.org/indicator/SH.DYN.MORT (accessed on 24 January 2015).

Nations Children's Fund (UNICEF) Report,[5] more than 60 million children under 5 years are stunted. India ranked at the 112th position in 2012 in the child development index.[6]

The projected child population in India, by age group, up to 2016 is presented in Table 1.1.

Table 1.1   Projected Child Population by Age Group in India, from 1996 to 2016[7]

S. no.	Year	Child Population in the Age Group (Years)			
		0–4	5–9	10–14	0–14
1	1996	119,546	123,686	109,545	352,777
2	2001	108,494	116,145	122,905	347,544
3	2006	113,534	105,744	115,488	334,766
4	2011	119,530	110,968	105,206	335,704
5	2016	122,837	117,099	110,461	350,397

The Legal Definition of a Child

All cultures share the view that the younger the children, the more vulnerable they are physically and psychologically and the less they are able to fend for themselves. Age limits are a formal reflection of society's judgment about the evolution of children's capacities and responsibilities. Almost everywhere, age limits formally regulate children's activities: when they can leave school; when they can marry; when they can vote; when they can be treated as adults by the criminal justice system; when they can join the armed forces; and when they can work. But age limits differ from activity to activity and from country to country.[8]

The legal conception of a child has tended to vary depending upon the purpose. According to Article 1 of the UNCRC, 1989, 'a child means every human being below the age of eighteen years unless, under the law applicable to the child, majority is attained earlier'. The article thus grants the discretion to individual countries to determine by law whether childhood should cease at 12, 14, 16, or whatever age they find appropriate. In India, the age at which a person ceases to be a child varies in different laws. Some of the provisions relating to age are as follows.

Indian Majority Act, 1875

The Indian Majority Act, 1875 was enacted in order to bring about uniformity in the applicability of laws to persons of different religions.[9] Unless a particular personal law specifies otherwise, every

---

[5] UNICEF, *Improving Child Nutrition: The Achievable Imperative for Global Progress*, based on National Family Health Survey (NFHS), 2005–2006 and UNICEF Global Databases, 2013. Available at http://www.unicef.org/gambia/Improving_Child_Nutrition_-_the_achievable_imperative_for_global_progress.pdf (accessed on 24 January 2015).

[6] Law Commission of India, *Early Childhood Development*.

[7] Source: *Census of India*, 1991 (Government of India).

[8] UNICEF, *The State of the World's Children* (New York, USA: Oxford University Press, 1997). Available at http://www.unicef.org/publications/files/pub_sowc97_en.pdf (accessed on 24 January 2015).

[9] Indian Majority Act, 1875, Preamble.

person domiciled in India is deemed to have attained majority upon completion of 18 years of age. However, in case of a minor for whose person or property, or both, a guardian has been appointed or declared by any court of justice before the age of 18 years, and in case of every minor the superintendence of whose property has been assumed by the Court of Wards before the minor has attained that age, the age of majority will be 21 years and not 18.[10] The HMGA, 1956 defines a minor as a person who has not completed the age of 18 years.[11] The age of majority for the purposes of appointment of guardians of person and property of minors according to the Mohammedan law is also completion of 18 years.[12] Christians[13] and Parsis[14] also reach majority at 18 years. The age of marriage is 21 years for males and 18 years for females.[15]

For purposes of criminal responsibility, age limit is 7[16] and 12[17] under the Indian Penal Code (IPC), 1860. For purposes of protection against kidnapping, abduction, and related offences, age is fixed at 16 in the case of boys and 18 in the case of girls.[18] Under the Child Labour (Prohibition and Regulation) Act, 1986, child means a person who has not completed his 14th year of age.[19] For purposes of special treatment under the Juvenile Justice (Care and Protection of Children) Act (JJ Act), 2000, the age is 18 for both boys and girls.[20] Ages prescribed for majority under various legislations are presented in Table 1.2.

The word 'child' has been used in various legislations as a term denoting relationship, as a term indicating capacity, and as a term of special protection. Underlying these alternative specifications are very different concepts about the child. These include viewing children as a burden which invokes rights to maintenance and support; regarding children undergoing temporary disabilities making for rights to special treatment and special discrimination; treating children as specially vulnerable for ensuring rights to protection; and recognizing children as resources for the country's development necessitating their nurturing and advancement.

There does not appear to be any criteria or scientific parameters. In the criminal jurisprudence prevalent in India, the age of criminal responsibility of understanding the consequences of one's actions had been recognized as 12 years in the IPC. Referring to Section 82 of the IPC, it is pointed out that the same provides that nothing is an offence which is done by a child under 7 years of age. Section 83 of the IPC was also referred, which provides that nothing is an offence which is done by a child above 7 and under 12 years of age, who has not attained sufficient maturity of understanding to judge the nature and consequences of his conduct on a particular occasion.

---

[10] Indian Majority Act, 1875, Section 3.

[11] HMGA, 1956, Section 4(a).

[12] Dissolution of Muslim Marriage Act, 1939.

[13] Indian Divorce Act, 1860.

[14] Parsi Marriage and Divorce Act (PMDA), 1936.

[15] Prohibition of Child Marriage Act (PCMA), 2006, Section 2(a): 'child' means a person who, if a male, has not completed 21 years of age, and if a female, has not completed 18 years of age.

[16] IPC, 1860, Section 82.

[17] IPC, 1860, Section 83.

[18] The IPC deals with kidnapping from lawful guardianship, Section 361.

[19] Child Labour (Prohibition and Regulation) Act, 1986, Section 2(ii).

[20] JJ Act, 2000, Section 2(k).

Table 1.2 Age Prescribed for Majority under Various Laws[21]

Legislation	Provision
IPC, 1860	Nothing is an offence which is done by a child under the age of 7 years.[22] The age of criminal responsibility is raised to 12 years if the child is found to have not attained the ability to understand the nature and consequences of his/her act.[23] Attainment of 18 years of age for a girl is necessary for giving sexual consent. In case she is married, the prescribed age for sexual consent is not less than 15 years.
Factories Act, 1948	Child means a person who has not completed his 15th year of age.[24]
Indian Contract Act, 1870	A person below the age of 18 years has no capacity to enter into a contract.
Mines (Amendment) Act, 1952	No person below 18 years of age shall be allowed to work in any mine or any part thereof.
Apprentices Act, 1961	A person is qualified to be engaged as an apprentice only if he is not less than 14 years of age and satisfies such standards of education and physical fitness as may be prescribed.
Child Labour Prohibition and Regulation Act, 1986	No child below 14 years can work in any hazardous occupation or industry.
Constitution of India, 1950	Article 24 of the Constitution of India directs that no child below the age of 14 years shall be employed to work in any factory or mine or engaged in any other hazardous employment.
Constitution of India (Ninety-Third Amendment) Act, 2005	• Article 21A of the Constitution directs that the state shall provide free and compulsory education to all children of the age of 6–14 years in such a manner as the state may, by law, determine. • Article 45 of the Constitution directs that 'the State shall endeavour to provide early childhood care and education for all children until they complete the age of six years'. • Article 51(k) lays down a duty that the parents or guardians should provide opportunities for education to his child/ward between the age of 6 and 14 years.
PCMA, 2006	According to Section 2(a), 'child' means a person who, if a male, has not completed 21 years of age and, if a female, has not completed 18 years of age.

(Cont'd)

---

[21] Source: Compiled by the author.
[22] IPC, Section 82.
[23] IPC, Section 83.
[24] Factories Act, 1948, Section 2(c).

Table 1.2 (Cont'd)

Legislation	Provision
Right to Free and Compulsory Education Act (or the Right to Education [RTE] Act), 2009	Right to free and compulsory education for all children between the age of 6 and 14 years.
Protection of Children against Sexual Offences Act (POCSO Act), 2012	Child means any person below the age of 18 years.
Criminal Law (Amendment) Act, 2013	Attainment of 18 years of age for a girl is necessary for giving sexual consent.
JJ Act, 2015	• According to Section 2(12), 'child' means a person who has not completed 18 years of age. • According to Section 2(13), 'child in conflict with law' means a child who is alleged or found to have committed an offence and who has not completed 18 years of age on the date of commission of such offence. Juveniles in conflict with law in the age group of 16–18, involved in heinous offences,[25] can be tried as adults.
Army Head Quarters Regulations	The age of recruitment in the army is from 16 to 25 years. Persons, who are recruited at the age of 16 years undergo basic military training for up to 2½ years from the date of enrolment and are then inducted into regular service.

For instance, in some laws as in the PCMA, 2006, there is a difference between the age of the boy and that of the girl. The PCMA seeks to prohibit the solemnization of marriages of girls below the age of 18 years and boys below the age of 21 years.[26] There does not appear to be any rationale behind the difference in the age for a boy and that for a girl. The act prescribes penalties for the solemnization, prohibition, and allowing of child marriages. A male above 18 years of age can be punished under the act for contracting a marriage with a girl less than 18 years.[27] The PCMA is, however, silent on sexual relations in a child marriage. It extends legitimacy to children born of child marriages thus indirectly acknowledging sexual intercourse within a child marriage. Under IPC, 1860, sexual intercourse by a man with his wife above 15 years of age is an exception to rape.[28] The Criminal Law (Amendment) Act, 2013 raised the age of consent to 18 years but did not disturb this exception.[29]

Under IPC, sexual intercourse with a wife above 15 years of age and below 18 years of age will not amount to rape. The POCSO Act, 2012 was enacted to protect children from offences of sexual assault, sexual harassment, and pornography, and to provide a child-friendly system for

---

[25] Heinous offences are those which are punishable with imprisonment of 7 years or more.
[26] PCMA, 2006, Section 3.
[27] PCMA, 2006, Section 9.
[28] IPC, 1860, Section 375.
[29] Criminal Law (Amendment) Act, 2013.

the trial of these offences. Under the POCSO Act, the term 'child' has been defined to mean 'any person below the age of eighteen years'.[30] Further, under this act, children can also be held liable for committing sexual offences. As a result, sexual interactions or intimacies among or with children below the age of 18 years constitute an offence. These contradictions need to be addressed.

The Supreme Court of India[31] had requested the Law Commission for assistance with certain issues related to child marriage. The Supreme Court, in its order dated 27 March 2006, had also noted that different laws specify different ages while defining a child, and there were various contradictions between these legislations. The Writ Petition, which had been filed by the Delhi State Commission for Women and the National Commission for Women, had pointed out that while the word 'child' was defined as any person below the age of 18 in the Indian Majority Act and the JJ Act, 2000, the age of marriage was 18 for girls and 21 for boys. The Hindu Marriage Act (HMA), 1955 also prescribed the same minimum age for a marriage. The Writ Petition further stated that though the IPC contained no definition of the word 'child', the age of consent for the girl for sexual intercourse was 16 under Section 375 of the IPC, while in married couples the age of consent was presumed to be 15. According to the petitioner, the shariat allowed marriage at the age of 15. The petition further listed as a grievance the following: (i) Section 5 and 11 of the HMA did not authorize the court to declare a marriage void on the ground that either of the parties was underage. (ii) The exception to Section 375 of the IPC exempted a husband from the charge of rape if his wife was not under 15 years of age. The petition saw this as a direct contradiction to the Child Marriage Restraint Act of 1929, under which no child marriage was allowed. However the petition noticed that child marriages were not invalid under the Child Marriage Restraint Act, 1929. The petition, therefore, recommended that there should be a uniform definition of 'child' in all legislations for the sake of uniformity and for the sake of protecting children against child abuse. It argued that the legal minimum age for marriage was 18 under a number of ratified international agreements and the laws of many countries. It argued that all marriages under the age of 18 should be void. It further prayed that the Union of India should be directed to amend the laws relating to age of marriage and minimum age of giving sexual consent so that both were in conformity with each other. The petition hoped for deletion of the explanation under Section 375 of the IPC under which marital rape was not considered rape unless the wife was under 15 years of age.

The whole debate about who is a child, in a different context, came up again with the Supreme Court on 11 January 2016. The issue, as the apex court has observed, is the definition of 'child' under the IPC. At present, 'child' is defined in the IPC as 'any person below the age of 18' and there is no classification between children as young as 2 or 3 years and other minors in the context of rape. Noting that rape and sexual offences against infants and girl children below 10 years of age is nothing but 'brutal perversion', the Supreme Court on 11 January 2016 asked the Parliament to enact a separate offence of 'child rape' and provide rigorous punishment to offenders.[32] This is

---

[30] POCSO Act, 2012, Section 2(d).

[31] Writ Petition (Criminal) No. 81 of 2006.

[32] On 11 January 2016, the Supreme Court of India suggested that the Parliament should frame a separate law with a view to deal with cases related to child rape. The suggestion was offered after a writ petition was filed by Supreme Court Women Lawyers Association (SCWLA) in such respect. According to the prevailing provisions, there are no specific punishment for people who rape girls below the age of

the first time that the apex court has distinguished between minors and children below 10 years of age. The bench, led by Justice Dipak Misra, said that the Parliament has to separately define the word 'child' in terms of rape. 'The pain and distress caused to a child, including infants as young as 28 days old, who knows nothing about sex and rape is nothing but brutal perversion. When a society moves this way, it has to be stopped.' The court further directed that Section 376(i) of the IPC[33] only talks of 'woman below 16 years of age' and has no specific provision for girl children below 10 years of age and infants.[34] Attorney General Mukul Rohatgi said child rape can never be tolerated and agreed to highlight the court's order to the government for putting it up before the lawmakers for an appropriate legislation.

The JJ Act, 2000 defines a child or a juvenile as a person who has not completed 18 year of age.[35] On 16 December 2012, rape and murder of a young 21-year-old Nirbhaya in Delhi led to a huge public uproar. Among the convicts, there was a 17-year-old boy who was tried under the JJ Act, 2000 as per the law of the land and sent to a 'special home' for 3 years. He was released on 20 December 2015 after completing his 3-year term there. Again there was a public outrage because of his release. This apparently led to the passing of the JJ Act, 2015 on 22 December 2015. The JJ Act, 2015 came into force on 1 January 2016 after the president of India gave his assent to the bill on 31 December 2015. The act replaced the JJ Act, 2000.[36] The 2015 Act defines a child as anyone less than 18 years of age. However, a special provision has been inserted for the possibility of

---

10 or less. Therefore, an urgency to frame a law for such conditions has been shown after considering the growing cases of child rape in India. The SCWLA, in its petition, appealed the court to include castration as an additional punishment for those who commit child rape. Though the court abstained from directing castration as a punishment, as it is the ambit of the legislature, it suggested for a separate law to award more severe punishment in child rape cases. Further, the directive of the Supreme Court was also the first to make a distinction between infants and children below 10 and the general description of 'minors'. At present, Section 376(2)(f) of the IPC mentions rape of a woman below 12 years of age and has no specific mention of punishment for raping a girl below 10 and infants. See: In the Supreme Court of India Civil Original Jurisdiction Writ Petition (Civil) No. 4 of 2016, *Supreme Court Women Lawyers Association* v. *Union of India & Anr.* Available at http://supremecourtofindia.nic.in/FileServer/2016-01-12_1452592971.pdf (accessed on 30 January 2016)

[33] In the Supreme Court of India Civil Original Jurisdiction Writ Petition (Civil) No. 4 of 2016 *Supreme Court Women Lawyers Association* v. *Union of India & Anr.* Available at http://supremecourtofindia.nic.in/FileServer/2016-01-12_1452592971.pdf (accessed on 30 January 2016)

[34] IPC, 1860, Section 376 (1): Whoever, except in the cases provided for by Sub-section (2), commits rape shall be punished with imprisonment of either description for a term which shall not be less than seven years but which may be for life or for a term, which may extend to 10 years and shall also be liable to fine unless the women raped is his own wife and is not under 12 years of age, in which cases, he shall be punished with imprisonment of either description for a term which may extend to two years or with fine or with both, provided that the court may, for adequate and special reasons to be mentioned in the judgment, impose a sentence of imprisonment for a term of less than 7 years.

[35] Section 2 (k), JJ Act 2000.

[36] The Juvenile Justice Bill, 2014 introduced by the minister of women and child development, was passed by the Lok Sabha on 12 August 2014 and by the Rajya Sabha on 22 December 2015. It received presidential assent on 31 December 2015, and came into operation on 1 January 2016.

trying 16–18-year olds committing heinous offences, as adults.[37] A heinous offence is defined as one for which the minimum punishment under the IPC is 7 years.[38] The definition of a heinous crime is quite broad. It currently covers at least 46 offences. This classification does not seem to be based on any reasonable classification and violates the right to equality under Article 14 of the Constitution and the objective of protection under Article 15(3) of the Constitution.

It is necessary that the definition of 'child' be brought in conformity with the UNCRC, namely below 18 years of age, and the contradictions in the various legal provisions are addressed. Though one may like to have a uniform age limit legally prescribed for the status of childhood, it may perhaps not be possible or even desirable. Nevertheless, some rationalization is possible or some norms can be laid down, as some of the age limits in the laws appear to be arbitrary or based on socio-cultural perceptions. If the best interests of child interpretation were to be adopted, one can err on the side of a higher age limit for protective care and a lower age limit in respect of civil and cultural matters.

The Present Legal Framework

It is evident that legislation is one of the main weapons of empowerment of children. Even though appropriate legislation may not necessarily mean that the objectives of the legislation will be achieved, its very existence creates an enabling provision whereby the state can be compelled to take action. Legislation reflects the commitment of the state to promote an ideal and progressive value system. The notion of duty also applies to the state.

India follows an adversarial legal system with an in-built bias in favour of the accused who is presumed innocent till proved guilty. The Constitution of India, the fundamental law of the country, came into effect on 26 January 1950. It provides a protective umbrella for the rights of children. The Constitution of India, as of now, guarantees all the children certain rights which include

- right to free and compulsory elementary education for all children in the age group 6–14 years;[39]
- right to be protected from any hazardous employment till the age of 14 years;[40]
- right to be protected from being abused and forced by economic necessity to enter occupation unsuited to their age or strength;[41]
- right to equal opportunities and facilities to develop in a healthy manner and in condition of freedom and dignity and guaranteed protection of childhood and youth against exploitation and against moral and material abandonment.[42]

Besides, children have rights as equal as all other adult citizens of India, the important few of which are

[37] JJ Act, 2015, Section 15.
[38] JJ Act, 2015, Section 2(33).
[39] Article 21A of the Constitution of India.
[40] Article 24(iii) of the Constitution of India.
[41] Article 39(e)(iv) of the Constitution of India.
[42] Article 39(f) of the Constitution of India.

- right to equality;[43]
- right against discrimination;[44]
- right to personal liberty and due process of law;[45]
- right to being protected from being trafficked and forced into bonded labour;[46]
- right of weaker sections of people to be protected from social injustice and all forms of exploitations;[47]
- right to freedom including the freedom of speech and expression;[48]
- personal liberty and right to due process of law;[49]
- right against exploitation;[50]
- religious, cultural, educational rights;[51] and
- right to constitutional remedies.[52]

In addition to these basic rights, the Constitution of India provides affirmative or positive discrimination especially for children. These rights are necessary because of their physical and mental immaturity; the children are especially vulnerable and need special protection. The Constitution prohibits discrimination of citizens on the grounds of religion, race, caste, sex, place of birth, or any of them. But Subsection 3 adds: 'Nothing in this Article shall prevent the state from making any special provision for women and children.'[53] Therefore, laws can be made giving special protection to children. These rights are included in Parts III and IV of the Constitution. The fundamental rights in Part III are enforceable in courts whereas the directive principles of state policy in Part IV are guidelines and principles that are fundamental to the governance of the country. It is the duty of the state to apply these principles in making laws. If the fundamental rights are violated, a writ petition can be filed in the Supreme Court or the high court.[54]

Under the Constitution, it is the duty of the state to secure that children of tender age are not abused and forced by economic necessity to enter vocations unsuited to their age and strength,[55] and to ensure that children are given opportunities and facilities to develop in a healthy manner and in conditions of freedom and dignity.[56] The directive principles provide for maternity relief.[57] Rights provided under Part IV (directive principles) of the Constitution can be read into the

---

[43] Article 14 of the Constitution of India.
[44] Article 15 of the Constitution of India.
[45] Article 21 of the Constitution of India.
[46] Article 23 of the Constitution of India.
[47] Article 46 of the Constitution of India.
[48] Article 19(1)(a) of the Constitution of India.
[49] Article 21 of the Constitution of India.
[50] Article 23 of the Constitution of India.
[51] Article 29 of the Constitution of India.
[52] Article 32 of the Constitution of India.
[53] Article 15 of the Constitution of India.
[54] Articles 32 and 226 of the Constitution of India.
[55] Article 39(9)(e) of the Constitution of India.
[56] Article 39(f) of the Constitution of India.
[57] Article 42 of the Constitution of India.

fundamental rights provided in Part III and hence enforceable in courts. Due to judicial interpretation, many of the directive principles have now become enforceable through legal actions
brought before the courts (for example, the RTE Act). There are certain aspects relating to children that are dealt with in the state and concurrent lists of the Constitution of India.[58]

It is estimated that there are more than 250 central and state statutes under which the child is
covered in India. Some of the important, special legislations that deal with children are listed in
the following subsections.

Guardian and Wards Act, 1890

This act deals with the qualifications, appointment, and removal of guardians of children by the
courts and is applicable to all children irrespective of their religion.

Hindu Adoption and Maintenance Act, 1956

This codifies the law relating to adoption and maintenance among Hindus.

Hindu Minority and Guardianship Act, 1956

This provides for the appointment of guardians of minors among Hindus.

Young Persons Harmful Publications Act, 1956

This act prevents the dissemination of certain publications that are harmful to young persons.

Probation of Offenders Act, 1958

This law lays down the restrictions on imprisonment of offenders under 21 years of age.

Orphanages and Other Charitable Homes (Supervision and Control) Act, 1960

This act provides for the supervision and control of orphanages, homes for neglected women or
children and other like institutions

---

[58] List II—State list in Entry 4 includes prisons, reformatories, borstal institutions, and other institutions of a like nature and persons detained therein; also includes arrangements with other states for the use
of prisons and other institutions.

List III—Concurrent list in Entry 5 includes marriage and divorce, infants and minors, adoption, wills,
intestacy and succession, joint family and partition, all matters in respect of which parties in judicial proceedings were immediately before the commencement of this Constitution subject to their personal law.

Entry 30 includes vital statistics including registration of births and deaths.

Entry 41 includes custody, management, and disposal of property (including agricultural land) declared
by law to be evacuee property.

Apprentice Act, 1961

This lays down qualifications for persons above 14 years of age to undergo apprenticeship training in any designated trade.

Medical Termination of Pregnancy Act, 1971

This law stipulates when pregnancies may be terminated by registered medical practitioners.

Child Labour (Prohibition and Regulation) Act, 1986

This act prohibits the engagement of children in certain kinds of employment and regulates the conditions of work of children in certain other employments.

Children (Pledging of Labour) Act, 1933

This prohibits pledging the labour of children.

Infant Milk Substitutes, Feeding Bottles and Infant Foods (Regulation of Production, Supply and Distribution) Act, 1992

This act regulates the production, supply, and distribution of infant milk substitutes, feeding bottles, and infant feeds with a view to the protection and promotion of breastfeeding and ensuring the proper use of infant feeds and other incidental matters.

Pre-Conception and Pre-Natal Diagnostic Techniques (Prohibition of Sex Selection) Act, 1994

In order to stop prenatal sex determination leading to female foeticide, the Parliament enacted the Prenatal Diagnostic Techniques (Regulation and Prevention of Misuse) Act (PNDT Act), 1994. This act came into force on 1 January 1996 and was not completely implemented. There were virtually no cases of prosecution. In the meantime, new techniques had been developed that used preconception or during-conception sex selection. To bring these new technologies under the purview of the act and to ensure rigorous implementation, the law was amended in 2003. On 31 March 2003, the act was amended and titled as the Preconception and Prenatal Diagnostic Techniques (Prohibition of Sex Selection) Act (PCPNDT Act), 1994 effective from 14 February 2003. This act provides for the prohibition of sex selection before and after conception, and for regulation of prenatal diagnostic techniques appropriately as mentioned earlier, and for prevention of their misuse.

Prohibition of Child Marriages Act, 2006

The PCMA received the assent of the president of India on 10 January 2007. The act came into effect from 1 November 2007. The basic premise of the law is as follows:

- make a child go through a marriage is an offence;
- child or minor is a person up to 18 years in the case of girls and 21 years in the case of boys.

Right of Children to Free and Compulsory Education Act, 2009

The Constitution (Eighty-Sixth Amendment) Act, 2002 inserted Article 21-A in the Constitution of India to provide free and compulsory education of all children in the age group of 6 to 14 years as a fundamental right in such a manner as the state may, by law, determine. The RTE Act, 2009, which represents the consequential legislation envisaged under Article 21-A, means that every child has a right to full-time elementary education of satisfactory and equitable quality in a formal school which satisfies certain essential norms and standards. The RTE Act came into effect on 1 April 2010, upholding the right of children to free and compulsory education till completion of elementary education in a neighbourhood school in the 6 to 14 age group.

Protection of Children from Sexual Offences Act, 2012

The POCSO Act was formulated in order to effectively address sexual abuse and sexual exploitation of children. The act received the president's assent on 19 June 2012 and was notified in the Gazette of India on 20 June 2012. The POCSO Act, 2012 is a gender-neutral legislation. The act defines a child as any person below 18 years of age. It defines different forms of sexual abuse, including penetrative and non-penetrative assault, as well as sexual harassment and pornography. The POCSO Act further makes provisions for avoiding re-victimization and creating a child-friendly atmosphere through all stages of the judicial process, and gives paramount importance to the principle of 'best interest of the child'. It incorporates child-friendly mechanisms for reporting, recording of evidence, investigation, speedy trial of offences, and in-camera trial without revealing the identity of the child, through designated special courts. The act also provides for mandatory reporting of sexual offences.[59]

Besides these legislations mentioned here these special legislations that deal with children, there are provisions that concern children in various general statutes. Provisions relating to children have also developed in the areas of criminal law, family law, employment law, and other aspects of childcare and welfare. There are also specific rules which apply to minors engaged in civil or criminal proceedings or commercial matters. The Code of Criminal Procedure (CrPC), 1973 lays down various procedures to be followed in a criminal trial and provides for the machinery for the punishment of offenders. The Code of Civil Procedure, 1908 lays down the procedure to be followed in civil trials. The Indian Evidence Act, 1872 deals with the competency of the witness and the value of evidence given by children.[60]

Several criminal laws give special protection to children. These statutes include the IPC, 1860, Indian Evidence Act, 1872, and CrPC, 1973.

---

[59] Section 21(1) of POCSO Act.
[60] Section 112 of the Indian Evidence Act, 1872.

The Criminal Law (Amendment) Act, 2013 was passed by the Lok Sabha on 19 March 2013, and by the Rajya Sabha on 21 March 2013. It provides for amendment of the IPC, Indian Evidence Act, CrPC, and POCSO Act. The following are some important changes:

- Section 166(B) of the IPC[61] has been added, which states that that no hospital, whether private or public, whether centrally run or state-run, can deny treatment to a victim of rape. Any denial of this sort may result in imprisonment for a term which may extend up to one year.
- By the addition of Section 354(D) of the IPC,[62] voyeurism and stalking have been defined as separate offences. First-time offenders would be able to obtain a bail, but this would not be possible for repeat offenders.
- A new section was inserted by the amendment[63] and it says that cognizance shall not be taken of the offence punishable under Section 376-B of the IPC[64], that is, in marital rape unless the complaint is made by wife against the husband.
- Provision has been added that if any woman below the age of 18 years is alleged to be subjected to rape or sexual offence, then the court may take appropriate measures to ensure that she is not confronted by the accused and that the right of cross examination of the accused is also safeguarded.[65]
- A new section was inserted which says that the compensation payable by state government under Section 357-A of the CrPC shall be in addition to payment of fine to the victim under Section 326-A or Section 376-D of the IPC.[66]

The POCSO Act, 2012 criminalizes even consensual sex among those below 18 years, leading to a large number of rape cases being filed against boys mostly by girls' parents, who take undue advantage of the act to end a relationship they do not approve of. On the other hand, forced sex on married minor girls of ages above 15 by their husbands is condoned since the Criminal Law (Amendment) Act, 2013 does not recognize marital rape. The non-criminalization of sexual abuse of minor married girls above 15 'is inconsistent' with POCSO and must be amended.

The IPC, 1860 defines various categories of offences and the punishment for such offences. It has special provisions relating to the causing of miscarriages and injuries caused to the unborn child.[67] There are provisions for kidnapping, abduction, and buying of minors for the purposes of prostitution, slavery, and forced labour.[68]

The Immoral Traffic (Prevention) Act, 1956, which was amended in 1987, tries to curb trafficking in young persons, both boys and girls. There are provisions relating to children in the Cable Television Network (Regulation) Act, 1995 and the Prevention of Illicit Traffic in Narcotic Drugs and Psychotropic Substances Act, 1988.

---

[61] Section 166(B) of IPC, Inserted by Criminal Law (Amendment) Act, 2013 .
[62] 354(D) IPC of Criminal Law (Amendment) Act, 2013.
[63] Section 198-B of the CrPC.
[64] Section 273 of the CrPC.
[65] Section 273 of the CrPC.
[66] Section 357-B of the CrPC.
[67] Sections 312–18 of the IPC.
[68] Section 358–74 of the IPC.

In the area of family law, the personal laws are religion based. The rights of children born to Hindus are governed by the HMA, 1955 and the Hindu Succession Act (HSA), 1956. Christian children are governed by the Indian Divorce Act (IDA), 1860 and the Indian Succession Act (ISA), 1925. In matters of marriage, maintenance, custody, guardianship, adoption, succession, and inheritance, the Muslim children are governed by the Muslim personal law. The Parsi children are governed by the PMDA, 1936 and the ISA, 1925. An important provision in the CrPC, 1973 is the order for maintenance of children (Section 125).[69]

There are provisions relating to employment of children in the Factories Act, 1948, Minimum Wages Act, 1948, Plantations Labour Act, 1951, Mines Act, 1952, Merchant Shipping Act, 1958, Motor Transport Workers Act, 1961, Payment of Bonus Act, 1965, Beedi and Cigar Workers (Conditions of Employment) Act, 1966, Bonded Labour System (Abolition) Act, 1976, Trade Unions Act, 1926, and the various state shops and establishment acts. The Contract Act, 1872, Indian Partnership Act, 1932, and Indian Trust Act, 1882 contain provisions relating to civil and commercial rights and liabilities of minors.[70]

Juvenile Justice (Care and Protection of Children) Act, 2015

This act came into force 15 January 2016. It aims at ensuring protection, proper care, development, and social reintegration of children in difficult circumstances by adopting a child-friendly approach. One of the major controversial provisions in the new Act is the trial of some children between 16 and 18 years accused of heinous offences as adults, based on a preliminary assessment of their mental and physical capacity, circumstances in which the offence was allegedly committed and their ability to comprehend the consequences of the offence. The new law defines 'heinous offence' very broadly to include 'offences for which the minimum punishment under the Indian Penal Code (IPC) or any other law for the time being in force is imprisonment for seven years or more'. Based on this definition, there are at least 46 offences under which children in conflict with law can be tried as adults. This includes offences like trafficking, dowry deaths, acid attacks, robbery, or dacoity with an attempt to cause hurt or an armed weapon under the IPC. The minister of women and child development, Government of India has stated that 'crime in this segment of 16-18 has become the largest amount of crime and the victims of this group are only children. This will protect those seven-year-olds and three-year-olds and four-year-olds[71].' The act empowers JJBs to examine the nature of crime and decide whether it was committed as a child mind or as an adult mind. Based upon the preliminary inquiry of JJBs, a juvenile offender will be either sent for rehabilitation or will be tried as an adult. Child rights activists in India has described it as a 'dark moment in the history of Juvenile Jurisprudence in India that the battle fought over decades for a just system for adolescents and strides made in the

[69] CrPC, Section 125 provides for an order of maintenance of the legitimate or illegitimate child (not a married daughter) who has attained majority. Such a child, by reason of any physical or mental abnormality or injury, is unable to maintain itself.

[70] The enactments use the terms minor and minority, defined as below 18 years.

[71] *The Hindu*, 'Maneka Renews Plea to Amend Juvenile Justice Act', New Delhi, 17 December 2015. Available at http://www.thehindu.com/news/national/minister-for-women-and-child-development-maneka-gandhi-renews-plea-to-amend-juvenile-justice-act/article7997672.ece (accessed on 9 February 2016).

last decade to uphold rights of children, especially that of children in conflict with law have hit a dead end with the passing of the JJ Act 2015' and termed it as a 'regressive transfer system for juveniles in the age group 16–18 years'.

The 2015 Adoption of Children Guidelines

In 2015, adoption of children in India has gone online, and a 'waiting list' system has been put in place. The government has also launched a revamped information technology (IT) application for the purpose of adoption of children, called CARINGS—Child Adoption Resource Information and Guidance System. The new guidelines are aimed at strengthening regulations for adoption of orphans and abandoned and surrendered children, and is expected to bring more transparency and efficiency to the existing adoption system. The new guidelines will also make it possible for prospective adoptive parents (PAPs) to track the status of their applications. Here, CARINGS will contain a centralized databank of adoptable children and PAPs. It will also set timelines for domestic and inter-country adoption of children. Under the new system, PAPs in India need not approach adoption agencies for registration. Parents can register online and upload relevant documents to determine their eligibility. Home-study reports can be conducted by adoption agencies and uploaded online—an online referral to the PAPs—followed by a visit to adoption agencies by the PAPs. In cases of inter-country adoption also, all applications will be accepted online on CARINGS and requisite documents must be uploaded; post-adoption follow-up shall be posted online in CARINGS both in the case of domestic and international adoptions. On a periodic basis, CARINGS will generate reports online. The system will also supply real-time online information of children available in adoption agencies across the country.

Information Technology Act, 2000

Section 67A of the Information Technology Act, 2000[72] makes publication, transmission, and causing to be transmitted and published in electronic form any material containing sexually explicit act or conduct punishable with imprisonment up to 5 years and fine up to Rs 10 lakh. Browsing or downloading child pornography online is also a punishable offence under this act. Further, creating child pornography is punishable under the act. The act of collecting and storing cyber pornography is not an offence, but if the content involves minors, then it is punishable with imprisonment up to 5 years and fine up to Rs 10 lakh.

---

[72] Information Technology Act, 2000, Section 67A:

Punishment for publishing or transmitting of material containing sexually explicit act, etc., in electronic form. Whoever publishes or transmits or causes to be published or transmitted in the electronic form any material which contains sexually explicit act or conduct shall be punished on first conviction with imprisonment of either description for a term which may extend to five years and with fine which may extend to ten lakh rupees and in the event of second or subsequent conviction with imprisonment of either description for a term which may extend to seven years and also with fine which may extend to ten lakh rupees.

Policies and Plans Related to Children

A number of policy initiatives, plans, and programmes relating to children have been undertaken in India. The policy documents are reference points available for planning and other interventions. Some of the current major policy and plan documents are the following:

- National Policy on Education, 1986
- National Policy on Child Labour, 1987
- National Nutrition Policy, 1993
- National Health Policy (NHP), 2002
- National Charter for Children, 2003
- National Plan of Action for Children (NPAC), 2005
- National Policy for Persons with Disabilities, 2006
- National Policy for Children, 2013
- Child Rights in Five Year Plans

These policies, among others, are discussed in brief in the following subsections.

National Policy on Education, 1986 (Modified in 1992)

In several developed and developing countries, universal education was seen as a main factor in the development of a modern nation. The National Policy on Education in India was modified in 1992. Thereafter, the Parliament approved a programme of action which sought to launch the National Elementary Education Mission—Education for All—in 1993, and the District Primary Education Programme launched in 1994. Currently, the emphasis is on universal primary education.

National Child Labour Policy, 1987

The policy was formulated with the basic objective of suitably rehabilitating the children withdrawn from employment and reducing the incidence of child labour in areas where there is a known concentration of child labour. The policy consists of three main elements: the legal action plan, focus of central government programmes, and project-based plan of action.

National Plan for SAARC Decade of the Girl Child, 1991–2000

In 1992, the Government of India prepared a separate plan—National Plan for the Girl Child—for the period 1991–2000, identifying three major goals:

- Survival and protection of the girl child and safe motherhood.
- Overall development of the girl child.
- Special protection for vulnerable girl children in need of care and protection.

National Plan of Action for Children, 1992[73]

India joined the comity of nations in the successive reaffirmations of global commitment to the cause of children in 1989–90. The UNCRC in November 1989, the World Conference on Education for All at Jomtien (Thailand) in March 1990, the Global Consultation on Water and Sanitation in September 1990, the World Summit on Children in the autumn of 1990, and the SAARC (South Asian Association for Regional Cooperation) Summit on Children were all part of this reaffirmation process which transcended national barriers. India is a signatory to the World Declaration on the Survival, Protection, and Development of Children and the Plan of Action (September 1990) for implementing it.[74] The NPAC is a follow-up of the promises made by the global fraternity at the World Summit for Children. The NPAC identifies quantifiable targets in terms of major as well as supporting sectoral goals. Some of the major goals for 1990–2000 were:

- Reduction of infant mortality rate (IMR) to less than 10.
- Reduction of maternal mortality rate (MMR) by half.
- Reduction in severe and moderate malnutrition among under-5 children by half.
- Universal access to safe drinking water and improved access to sanitary means of excreta disposal.
- Universal enrolment, retention, minimum level of learning, reduction of disparities, and universalization of effective access of schooling.
- Achievement of adult literacy rate of 80 per cent in the age group of 15–35, with emphasis on female literacy.
- Improved protection of children in especially difficult circumstances.
- Assistance to children affected by one or more disabilities, having no access to proper rehabilitative services and, especially, upliftment of the status of those most marginalized.
- Removal of gender bias and improvement in the status of the girl child.
- Conservation and protection of the environment for the well-being of children.
- Promotion of advocacy and people's participation for the child.

National Nutrition Policy, 1993

The National Nutrition Policy reflects the understanding that malnutrition is not simply a matter of 'not enough food', but is most frequently caused by a combination of factors, including lack of time and attention to childcare, inadequate feeding of the child especially in the first year of life,

---

[73] Department of Women and Child Development, *Convention on the Rights of the Child Country Report India* (New Delhi: Ministry of Human Resources Development, Government of India, 1992). Available at http://icds-wcd.nic.in/CRCFEBmr.htm (accessed on 5 September 2016).

[74] Department of Women and Child Development, 'National Plan of Action: A Commitment to the Child', in *Convention on the Rights of the Child Country Report*, India, February 1997 (New Delhi: Government of India, 1992). Available at http://icds-wcd.nic.in/CRCFEBmr.htm (accessed on 5 September 2016).

poor health, unhygienic conditions, as well as the lack of purchasing power of poor families. An NPAC on Nutrition was formulated in 1995.

National Population Policy, 2000

The crux of the policy rests on denying state representation to the Parliament based on their population. In other words, the essence of the population policy is that by taking away the democratic rights of those states whose population is growing too fast, these states will somehow find a way of controlling their population. It simultaneously addresses the issues of child survival, maternal health, and contraception.

National Health Policy, 2001

The NHP, 1983 has now been revised and a new NHP, 2001 has been drafted. The main objective of NHP, 2001 is to achieve an acceptable standard of good health among the general population of the country. The approach would be to increase access to the decentralized public health system by establishing new infrastructure in deficient areas, and by upgrading the infrastructure in the existing institutions. Broadly, NHP, 2001 will endeavour to achieve time-bound goals in the areas of IMR, MMR, and so on.

National Policy for Children, 2013[75]

The Government of India adopted a new National Policy for Children, 2013 on 26 April 2013. The policy recognizes every person below the age of 18 years as a child and covers all children within the territory and jurisdiction of the country. It recognizes that a multisectoral and multi-dimensional approach is necessary to secure the rights of children. The policy has identified four key priority areas—survival; health and nutrition; education and development; and protection and participation—for focussed attention. As children's needs are multisectoral, interconnected, and require collective action, the policy calls for purposeful convergence and coordination across different sectors and levels of governance.

The National Policy for Children, 2013 aims to protect and encourage the rights of the children to survival, health, nutrition, education, development, protection, and participation. It has incorporated major inputs of various organizations regarding the needs of children with disabilities. Based on the new National Policy for Children, 2013, the Ministry of Women and Child Development developed a draft NPAC. The NPAC has been drafted in view of the existing schemes/programmes of various ministries. The purpose is to track and monitor the progress of what is already being done for children across ministries and sectors. The draft NPAC was circulated to all the key ministries/departments working for children, concerned institutions, and all the state governments and union territory administrations for comments and sugges-tions. The comments from all concerned have since been received. The draft NPAC is to be

[75] Ministry of Women and Child Development, Government of India.
Available at http://wcd.nic.in/policies/nationl-policy-children-2013 (accessed on 9 February 2016).

revised according to comments received from various ministries/departments, and the National Coordination and Action Group (NCAG) for Children is to be formed to monitor the progress of the implementation of the policy.[76]

Children in Five Year Plans[77]

The Indian economy is based in part on planning through its Five Year Plans (FYPs), which are developed, executed, and monitored by the erstwhile Planning Commission. The FYPs are centralized and integrated national economic programmes. The First Five Year Plan (1951–56) identified health, nutrition, and education as major areas of concern with regard to children. In 1953, the Central Social Welfare Board was set up to address the needs of children, women, and persons with disabilities.[78]

The Second Five Year Plan (1956–61) aimed at strengthening the child welfare systems. Welfare projects were extended to become the Coordinated Welfare Extension Projects in 1958 and the Children's Act was passed in 1960. Internationally, the Declaration of the Rights of the Child (DRC) came into being on 20 November 1959.[79]

During the Third Five Year Plan (1961–66), the child was recognized as a human being with special needs and special efforts were made to coordinate between sectors to ensure these needs. Nutrition programmes were set up. The Kothari Education Commission was set up in search of solutions to the lack of universal education for children.[80]

The Fourth Five Year Plan (1969–74) focussed on providing the basic services to children. Two major child policies came into existence—National Education Policy, in 1968 (as recommended by the Kothari Education Commission), and National Policy for Children, in 1974. The Fourth Five Year Plan also saw the establishment of Special Nutrition Programme, Balwadi Nutrition Programme, and Prophylaxis Scheme against Blindness due to Vitamin A Deficiency among Children.

The Fifth Five Year Plan (1974–79) saw a shift from child welfare to child development, where again coordination of services was the main agenda. A major accomplishment in 1975, which was a result of all plans so far, was the launching of the Integrated Child Development Scheme (ICDS). The year 1975 also saw the start of the Scheme of Creches/Day Care Centres for Children of Working and Ailing Mothers. Another major achievement was the setting up of the National Children's Fund in 1979.[81]

---

[76] Ministry of Women and Child Development, Government of India. Available at http://wcd.nic.in/policies/nationl-policy-children-2013 (accessed on 9 February 2016).

[77] Available at http://www.childlineindia.org.in/Working-Together-to-Reach-All-of-India-Children.htm (accessed on 23 January 2016).

[78] Available at http://www.childlineindia.org.in/Working-Together-to-Reach-All-of-India-Children.htm (accessed on 23 January 2016).

[79] Available at http://www.childlineindia.org.in/Working-Together-to-Reach-All-of-India-Children.htm (accessed on 23 January 2016).

[80] 'Child Related Policies and Child Rights Plans in Five Year Plans'. Available at http://www.childlineindia.org.in/Child-Rights-in-the-Five-Year-Plans.htm (accessed on 6 February 2016).

[81] 'Child Related Policies and Child Rights Plans in Five Year Plans'. Available at http://www.childlineindia.org.in/Child-Rights-in-the-Five-Year-Plans.htm (accessed on 6 February 2016).

The Sixth Five Year Plan (1980–85) was when, for the first time, the planning committee took into consideration the needs of working children. Programmes were undertaken to improve the health, nutrition, and educational status of working children. Health concerns of children also took priority in these plan years, with the introduction of the NHP, 1981 and the formulation of the Indian National Code for Protection and Promotion of Breast Feeding.[82]

The Seventh Five Year Plan (1985–90) saw the establishment of the Department of Women and Child Development in the Ministry of Human Resource Development. In 1986, the Government of India repealed the Children's Act and passed the JJ Act instead, and updated the National Education Policy. In 1987, the National Child Labour Project was started in areas that saw a high number of child labourers. Lastly, in 1990, the government set up CARA, to handle all concerns and issues regarding adoption. Internationally, this period was witness to the first comprehensive convention for child rights, the UNCRC.[83]

During the Eighth Five Year Plan (1992–97), India ratified the UNCRC, thereby making it a legal binding document. There was continued work in areas of day care, education, health, and so on. But this plan pays special focus also to the needs of the girl child. In 1992, the government adopted the National Plan of Action for the Girl Child. Some states also prepared similar documents and schemes for the girl child, for example, Haryana instituted the Apni Beti Apna Dhan scheme, Tamil Nadu initiated the Cradle Scheme, and Rajasthan introduced the Raj Lakshmi Scheme.[84]

The Ninth Five Year Plan (1997–2002) continued to address the plight of the girl child, concentrating on addressing the problem of the declining sex-ratio as well as female foeticide and infanticide. In the field of health, the government introduced the Reproductive and Child Health (RCH) programme. In the field of education, the government launched Sarva Shiksha Abhiyan (SSA) in 2001–02. The year 2000 also saw the adoption of the new JJ Act.

In the Tenth Five Year Plan (2002–07) the approach had shifted to a right-based one, ensuring the survival, development, and protection of children. Many goals were set out, such as reduction of IMR to 45 per 1,000 live births by 2007, and reduction of MMR to 2 per 1,000 live births by 2007. These goals were to be accomplished by expanding existing scheme such as ICDS, universal immunization, SSA, and so on. Major accomplishments have been a constitutional amendment making the RTE a fundamental right, the revision of the NHP to take into consideration more recent health concerns like human immunodeficiency virus/acquired immune deficiency syndrome (HIV/AIDS), the amendment of the JJ Act, and the adoption of the Goa Children's Act of 2003.

The Eleventh Five Year Plan (2007–12) marked the very first plan which earmarked child protection as its mandate. The Integrated Child Protection Scheme (ICPS) of the Ministry of Women and Child Development was approved in the Eleventh Five Year Plan but only commenced in the

[82] 'Child Related Policies and Child Rights Plans in Five Year Plans'. Available at http://www.child-lineindia.org.in/Child-Rights-in-the-Five-Year-Plans.htm (accessed on 6 February 2016).
[83] 'Child Related Policies and Child Rights Plans in Five Year Plans'. Available at http://www.child-lineindia.org.in/Child-Rights-in-the-Five-Year-Plans.htm (accessed on 6 February 2016).
[84] 'Child Related Policies and Child Rights Plans in Five Year Plans'. Available at http://www.child-lineindia.org.in/Child-Rights-in-the-Five-Year-Plans.htm (accessed on 6 February 2016).

third year of the plan period. The Twelfth Five Year Plan, therefore, has to see the ICPS effectively rolled out and implemented.

In the current Twelfth Five Year Plan (2012–17), the monitorable targets for children are to[85]

- reduce IMR to 25 and MMR to 1 per 1,000 live births;
- improve child sex ratio (0–6 years) to 950 by the end of the Twelfth Five Year Plan;
- reduce undernutrition among children aged 0–3 years to half of the NFHS-3 levels by the end of the plan; and
- ensure that all children receive a protective environment.

The Twelfth Five Year Plan strategy is[86]

- engendering development planning and making it child-centric; and
- calling for structural transformation not only in the direct policy and programme interventions for children but also in the policies and programmes of different sectors that impact children.

The Twelfth Five Year Plan interventions are[87]

- implementation of ICDS in mission mode;
- redesigning the Rajiv Gandhi National Crèche Scheme;
- strengthening and expanding the Rajiv Gandhi Scheme for Empowerment of Adolescent Girls (RGSEAG or Sabla scheme) for empowerment of adolescent girls and its linkage with education and skill development;
- consolidation of ICPS;
- expansion of childline services;
- design new child-participation interventions like baal panchayats;
- strengthening institutional mechanisms for the protection of child rights;
- ending discrimination against the girl child through institutional arrangements and interventions on promoting quality education for girls, prohibiting dowry and child marriages, incentive schemes for the girl child; and
- institutionalizing child budgeting.

These laws and policies tend to work in isolation. The right to education for instance is linked to issues of child labour, juvenile justice, child marriage, health, and nutrition. Moreover the policy perspectives relating to child and childhood are confused. Article 21A of the Constitution provides children between 6 and 14 years with the fundamental right to education. The Right

[85] 'Child Related Policies and Child Rights Plans in Five Year Plans'. Available at http://www.childlineindia.org.in/Child-Rights-in-the-Five-Year-Plans.htm (accessed on 6 February 2016).

[86] 'Child Related Policies and Child Rights Plans in Five Year Plans'. Available at http://www.childlineindia.org.in/Child-Rights-in-the-Five-Year-Plans.htm (accessed on 6 February 2016).

[87] Planning Commission, Government of India, Twelfth Five Year Plan, 2012–17. Available at http://planningcommission.nic.in/plans/planrel/fiveyr/welcome.html (accessed on 6 February 2016).

to Free and Compulsory Education (RTE) Act 2009 provides the the framework for the same. The JJ Act, 2015 identifies engaging a child (person below 18 years) and keeping him in bondage for the purpose of employment as punishable. The Child Labour (Prohibition and Regulation) Amendment Act, 2016 prohibits 'the engagement of children in all occupations and of adolescents in hazardous occupations and processes' wherein adolescents refers to those under 18 years; children to those under 14. So here the child is defined to be below 14 years. Section 3 in Clause 5 of this 2016 Act allows child labour in 'family or family enterprises' or allows the child to be 'an artist in an audio-visual entertainment industry. The clause does not define the hours of work; it simply states that children may work after school hours or during vacations. This is in contradiction of both RTE Act and JJ Act . According to the Prohibition of Child Marriage Act 2006, a child is a male who has not completed twenty one years of age and a female who has not completed eighteen years of age. This act does not declare a child marriage void ab initio but only under certain circumstances. The Persons with Disabilities (Equal Opportunities and Full Participation) Act Participation) Act 1995 is totally alienated from the education, health, and nutrition policies and the children in need of care and protection under the JJ Act 2016. The JJ Act 2016 has attempted to bring in adoption of all children under the act. But it is still not clear about adoption of children whose personal laws do not 'permit' adoption. Besides, the rights of children are inalienable and indivisible. They cannot work in isolation . The laws relating to children have to interlinked. Perhaps a single code on children can best protect the interests of the child. The laws and policies now have to conform to the international standards laid down in UNCRC , which India has ratified. The interpretation and enforcement of laws is not always in the best interest of the child.

International Law on the Rights of the Child

Law in the form of international conventions can contribute considerably. International instruments stress participation as a core value along with survival, protection, and development. Laws and legal strategies must be devised to encourage these values. In a recent judgment, the Supreme Court held that 'once signed, any international Treaty or Convention will be treated as a part of law unless otherwise stated'. The Indian government is thus bound in its obligation to implement any convention or treaty that is signed. India has ratified the UNCRC and the Convention on All Forms of Discrimination against Women.

Since the beginning of the twentieth century, the development of international law on the rights of the child has paralleled, in part, the development of the general body of international human rights law. The first stage was the recognition by the international community that all individuals, including children, were the objects of international law, requiring legal protection. The second stage, which is still evolving, is the granting of specific substantive rights to individuals, including children. The third stage, which is also still developing, is the acknowledgement that in order to ensure that individuals are able to enjoy the exercise of their fundamental rights, they must be acknowledged to possess the necessary procedural capacity to exercise and claim these rights and freedom.[88]

[88] Geraldine Van Bueren, *The International Law on the Rights of the Child* (Netherlands: Kluwer Academic Publishers, 1995).

Human Rights Instruments Specific to the Rights of the Child

The DRC, 1924, adopted by the Fifth Assembly of the League of Nations, can be seen as the first international instrument dealing with children's rights.[89] The declaration establishes the claim that 'mankind owes to the child the best it has to give'. The five principles that are enumerated are as follows:

- The child must be given the means requisite for its normal development, both materially and spiritually.
- The child who is hungry must be fed; the child who is sick must be nursed; the child who is backward must be helped; the delinquent child must be reclaimed; and the orphan and the 'waif' must be sheltered and succoured.
- The child must be the first to receive relief in times of distress.
- The child must be put in a position to earn a livelihood, and must be protected against every form of exploitation.
- The child must be brought up in the consciousness that its talents must be devoted to the service of its fellow men.

This declaration is important as it highlights the social and economic entitlements of children and establishes internationally the concept of the rights of the child, thereby laying the foundation for setting future international standards in the field of children's rights.[90]

Universal Declaration of Human Rights, 1948

The Universal Declaration of Human Rights, 1948 proclaims a catalogue of human rights which apply to all human beings and therefore, implicitly, to children (UNCRC, Article 1). It contains only two articles, which expressly refer to children—Article 25(2) on special care and assistance and Article 26 on education.

Article 25 emphasizes the rights of children to special care and assistance and it provides this through the direct protection of the rights of the child and indirectly through the protection of motherhood. Article 26 deals both with access to and the aims of education.

This is a non-binding resolution of the General Assembly, but it helped in laying down certain common standards for children worldwide.

Declaration of the Rights of the Child, 1959

The preamble describes the principles as enunciating rights and freedom, which governments should observe by legislative and other measures taken progressively. The DRC makes reference in its preamble to both the United Nations Charter and the Universal Declaration of Human Rights. The preamble also refers to the special safeguards and care, including appropriate legal protection

---

[89] Records of the Fifth Assembly, 1924, Supplement no. 23, *League of Nations Official Journal.*
[90] Van Bueren, *International Law.*

needed by children, and recalls the original recognition of those needs by the DRC, 1924 and in the statutes of specialized agencies and international organizations concerned with children. It reiterates the pledge that 'mankind owes to the child the best it has to give', and it places a specific duty upon voluntary organizations and local authorities to strive for the observance of these rights. The role of voluntary organizations is highlighted because of their instrumental role in persuading governments of the need for international legal protection of children's rights, and their recognized impartial expertise in the formulation of these rights.[91]

In accordance with the declaration, a child is entitled to a name and nationality[92], to adequate nutrition, housing, recreation, and medical services.[93] Attention is paid to the special needs of physically, mentally, and 'socially' handicapped children[94], and to children who are without a family.[95] The RTE is included, as is the right to play and recreation.[96] A noticeable departure from the principles of the 1924 Declaration is that the earlier declaration specified that 'children must be the first to receive relief', whereas the 1959 Declaration lays down that children shall be 'among the first' to receive protection and relief. This is a more realistic approach taking account of situations where more children's lives would be saved if relief is administered first to an appropriate adult such as a doctor.

The DRC enshrines the principle that children are entitled to 'special protection' and that such special protection should be implemented by reference to 'the best interests of the child', which 'shall be the paramount consideration'.[97] The declaration also contains a broad non-discrimination clause.[98]

International Covenant on Economic, Social, and Cultural Rights, 1966

It applies to all 'men and women' and therefore, by implication, to children.[99] The preamble recognizes that all human rights are interlinked and of equal importance. The covenant stresses that children 'deserve special measures of protection and assistance'.

The covenant specifically refers to children in Articles 10 and 12. In Article 10, the states recognize the family as the 'natural and fundamental group unit of society' and therefore accord the widest possible protection and assistance to the family. Article 10(3) contains a broad ambit of protection.

Special measures of protection and assistance should be taken on behalf of all children and young persons without any discrimination for reasons of parentage or other conditions. Children and young persons should be protected from economic and social exploitation.

---

[91] DRC, G.A. Res. 1386 (XIV), 14 U.N. GAOR Supp. (No. 16) at 19, U.N. Doc.A/4354 (1959). Available at http://www.cirp.org/library/ethics/UN-declaration/ (accessed on 5 September 2016).
[92] DRC, Principle 3.
[93] DRC, Principle 4.
[94] DRC, Principle 5.
[95] DRC, Principle 6.
[96] DRC, Principle 7.
[97] DRC, Principle 2.
[98] DRC, Principle 2.
[99] Van Bueren, *International Law*, p.19.

The International Covenant on Economic, Social, and Cultural Rights also enshrines in Article 13(1) the right of everyone to education and provides that primary education should be compulsory and free to all. States undertake the implementation of all the rights in the covenant. This covenant implicitly helped to raise the status of children in the resource allocation of the various countries.[100]

International Covenant on Civil and Political Rights, 1966

The International Covenant on Civil and Political Rights (ICCPR), 1966 complements the economic, social, and cultural covenant.[101] Children are implicitly entitled to benefit from all relevant rights contained in the covenant and in addition there are specific provisions for children. Article 14(1) provides an express exception to the right to a hearing in public, when it is in the interests of the juveniles or where it concerns the guardianship of children.

Article 14(3)(f) provides that criminal proceedings should take account of juveniles' age and their 'desirability of promoting their rehabilitation'. The covenant prohibits the imposition of death penalty for crimes committed by persons under 18 years of age.[102] Further, it obliges states to separate accused juveniles from accused adults and bring them as speedily as possible for adjudication[103] and accord them treatment according to their age and legal status.[104]

The family is recognized as being the natural and fundamental unit of society and as such is entitled to state protection.[105] Under the covenant, states are obliged to respect the liberty of parents to ensure the religious and moral education of children in accordance with their beliefs and, in the event of a dissolution of the marriage, provision shall be made for the protection of any children.[106] In addition to these specific rights, the ICCPR incorporates a specific article on children.[107]

Convention of the Elimination of All Forms of Discrimination against Women, 1979

Article 5(b) of the Convention of the Elimination of All Forms of Discrimination against Women (CEDAW), 1979 obligates states to take all appropriate measures to ensure that family education includes a proper understanding of maternity as a social function and the recognition of the common responsibility of men and women in the upbringing and development of their children, it being understood that *the interests of the children is the primordial consideration in all cases.* Article 16(1)(d) of the same convention provides that in all matters relating to marriage and

---

[100] Van Bueren, *International Law*

[101] See L. Henkin, ed., *The International Bill of Human Rights: The Covenant on Civil and Political Rights* (New York: Columbia University Press, 1981).

[102] UN Doc A/C 3/L 650. This was done at the initiative of Japan.

[103] This was a result of a proposal from Sri Lanka.

[104] ICCPR, Article 10(3).

[105] ICCPR, Article 23.

[106] ICCPR, Articles 18(4) and 24(4).

[107] ICCPR, Article 24.

family relations, *the interests of the children shall be paramount*.[108] This convention seems to restrict the best-interests principle in family relations and matters. The scope is not wide. But today, the principle needs wider applicability than custody and family matters.

United Nations Convention on the Rights of the Child, 1989

The UNCRC represents a turning point in the international movement on behalf of child rights. This comprehensive document contains a set of universal legal standards or norms for the protection and well-being of children. The range of rights can be summarized as the three Ps: provision, protection, and participation. Children have a right to be provided with certain services ranging from a name and nationality to heath care and education. They have a right to be protected from certain acts, such as torture, exploitation, abuse, arbitrary detention, and unwarranted removal from parental care; further, they have the right to participate in the decisions affecting their lives.

The UNCRC gives children their basic human rights—civil, economic, social, cultural, and political—which enable them to achieve their full potential.[109] The *civil rights* of children include the right to a name and a nationality, protection from torture and maltreatment, and special rules governing the circumstances and conditions under which children may be deprived of their liberty or separated from their parents, and so on. The *economic rights* under the UNCRC include the right to benefit from social security and the right to a standard of living adequate to ensure proper development and protection from exploitation at work. The *social rights* include the right to the highest attainable standard of health services, the right to social care for handicapped children, protection from sexual exploitation and abduction, and the regulation of adoption. Right to education, access to appropriate information, recreation and leisure, and participation in artistic and cultural activities are included in the *cultural rights* of the children under the UNCRC. It is unusual among human rights treaties because it is not only concerned with the granting and implementing of rights in times of peace, but is also concerned with the regulation of armed conflicts as they affect children as civilians and combatants.[110]

Broadly, the civil, political, social, economic, and cultural rights of every child can be grouped into the following four classes.

Right to Survival

This includes the right to life, the highest attainable standard of health and nutrition, and adequate standards of living. It also includes the right to a name and a nationality.

---

[108] In all matters relating to the placement of a child outside the care of the child's own parents, the best interests of the child, particularly his or her need for affection and right to security and continuing care, should be the paramount consideration.

[109] This is another way of classifying the rights under the UNCRC.

[110] Van Bueren, *International Law*, p.16.

Right to Protection

This includes freedom from all forms of exploitation, abuse, inhuman or degrading treatment, and neglect, including the right to special protection in situations of emergency and armed conflicts.

Right to Development

This includes the right to education, support for early childhood development and care, social security, and the right to leisure, recreation, and cultural activities.

Right to Participation

This includes respect for the views of the child, freedom of expression, access to appropriate information, and freedom of thought, conscience, and religion.

The UNCRC has identified a thematic clustering of child rights. The clustering is as follows:

- *General measures of implementation*: These are laid down in Articles 4, 42, and 44 of the UNCRC. This highlights the need to constantly review the relevance of reservations and the importance of bringing national legislation in conformity with the convention.
- *Definition of child*: Article 1[111] gives the definition of the age of the child. No minimum age is defined.[112]
- *General principles, civil rights, and freedoms*: In this theme, Articles 2, 3, 6, and 12 of UNCRC give the four general principles of the convention, that is, non-discrimination, best interests of the child, right to survival and development, and respect for the views of the child. Whereas, Articles 7, 8, 13–17, and 37(a) specify the civil rights and freedoms, which include the right to a name and nationality, freedom of expression and peaceful assembly, right not to be subjected to torture, and so on.
- *Family environment and basic health*: This theme includes Articles 5, 9–11, 18, 19, 21, 25, and 27, that deal with parental guidance and responsibilities, illicit transfer and non-return, unaccompanied minors and adoption, psycho-social recovery, and re-integration. It also includes provisions that address health, standard of living, and facilities for treatment and rehabilitation, in Articles 6, 18, 23, 24, 26, and 27.
- *Education, leisure, and special protection*: The theme stresses the importance of education, including vocational training and guidance, and also protection of refugee children, children in emergencies, children in the juvenile justice system, and children in danger of exploitation. In Articles 28, 29, and 31, it is laid down that education should be child-friendly, and leisure and culture should be provided. Physical and psychological recovery as well as social integration for children is given in Articles 22, 32–36, and 37–40.

---

[111] For the purpose of the present convention, a child means every human being below the age of 18 years unless, under the law applicable to the child, majority is attained earlier.

[112] This was done to avoid debate over abortion, which could have threatened the acceptance of the convention.

The UNCRC is guided by the principle of a *first call for children*—a principle that the essential needs of children should, at all times, be given priority in the allocation of resources at all times. The convention is derived from a core set of human values and ethical premises that recognize the inherent dignity and the equal and inalienable rights of all members of the human family as the foundation of freedom, justice, and peace in the world. Accordingly, the convention states that the rights shall be extended to all children without discrimination of any kind, irrespective of the child's or his or her parents' or legal guardian's race, nationality, colour, sex, language, religion, political or other opinion, social origin, property, disability, and birth or other status.[113] The convention also draws particular attention to the fact that such children need special consideration. It advocates measures for the protection and harmonious development of the child, which are consistent with the traditions and cultural values of different people. By providing safeguards against economic and other policies that have a negative effect on the well-being of children, the convention reaffirms a commitment to promote social progress that will ensure a better quality of life and greater freedom for people in general and children in particular. It also underscores the importance and potential of international cooperation for promoting and improving the living conditions of children in every country.[114]

Therefore, there are four general principles enshrined in the convention. These are meant to help with the interpretation of the convention as a whole and thereby guide national programmes of implementation. The four principles are formulated, in particular, in Articles 2, 3, 6, and 12.[115] These are:

- Non-discrimination (Article 2): State parties must ensure that all children within their jurisdiction enjoy their rights. No child should suffer discrimination. The essential message is equality of opportunity. Girls should be given the same opportunities as boys. Refugee children, children of foreign origin, or children of indigenous or minority groups should have the same rights as all others. Children with disabilities should be given the same opportunity to enjoy an adequate standard of living.
- Best interests of the child (Article 3): When the authorities of a state take decisions which affect children, the best interests of children must be a primary consideration. The principle relates to decisions by courts of law, administrative authorities, legislative bodies, and both public and private social-welfare institutions.
- The right to life, survival, and development (Article 6): The term 'development' in this context should be interpreted in a broad sense, adding a qualitative dimension—not only physical health but also mental, emotional, cognitive, social, and cultural development.
- The views of the child (Article 12): Children have the right to be heard and to have their views taken seriously, including any judicial or administrative proceedings affecting them.

An analysis of the UNCRC reveals that it attempts to accomplish five goals. First, it creates new rights under international law for children where no such rights existed, including the child's right to preserve his or her identity and the right of indigenous children to practice their own

---

[113] UNICEF, *The Right to Be a Child* (New Delhi, India, 1994).
[114] UNICEF, *The Right to Be a Child*.
[115] United Nations, *The Rights of the Child, Fact Sheet No. 10* (Geneva, 1996).

culture.[116] Second, the convention enshrines rights in a global treaty which had, until the convention's adoption, only been acknowledged or refined in case law under regional human rights treaties; for example, a child's right to be heard either directly or indirectly in any judicial or administrative proceedings affecting that child, and to have those views taken into account.[117] Third, the convention also creates binding standards in areas which, until the convention's entry into force, were only non-binding recommendations. These include safeguards in adoption procedures and the rights of mentally and physically disabled children.[118]

The convention also imposes new obligations in relation to the provision and protection of children. These include the obligation on a state to take effective measures to abolish traditional practices prejudicial to the health of children (although not mentioned expressly, this includes female circumcision) and to provide for rehabilitative measures for child victims of neglect, abuse, and exploitation.[119] Finally, the convention adds an additional express ground by which states are under a duty not to discriminate against children in their enjoyment of the convention's rights.[120]

Optional Protocols to United Nations Convention on the Rights of the Child

Optional protocols complement and add to the existing treaties. They are 'optional' because the obligations may be more demanding than those in the original convention; so states must independently choose whether or not to be bound by them. Optional protocols are treaties in their own right, and are open to signature, accession, or ratification by states that are party to the main treaty. To help stem the growing abuse and exploitation of children worldwide, the United Nations General Assembly, in 2000, adopted two Optional Protocols to the UNCRC to increase the protection of children from involvement in armed conflicts and from sexual exploitation. On 14 April 2014, a third Optional Protocol was adopted, allowing children to bring complaints directly to the UNCRC. The committee will then investigate the claims and can direct governments to take action.[121]

The three optional protocols are:

1. *The Optional Protocol to the Convention on the Rights of the Child on the Involvement of Children in Armed Conflict (OPAC)*[122]
   The optional protocol is a commitment for the following:

   - States will not recruit children under the age of 18 to send them to the battlefield.
   - States will not conscript soldiers below the age of 18.

---

[116] UNCRC, Articles 8 and 30.

[117] UNCRC, Article 12.

[118] UNCRC, Articles 21 and 23.

[119] UNCRC, Articles 28(3) and 39.

[120] UNCRC, Article 2(1).

[121] UNICEF, *Convention on the Rights of the Child*. Available at http://www.unicef.org/crc/index_protocols.html (accessed on 1 February 2016).

[122] The United Nations General Assembly adopted the treaty as a supplementary protocol to the UNCRC by Resolution 54/263 on 25 May 2000. Available at https://childrenandarmedconflict.un.org/mandate/opac/ (accessed on 7 September 2016).

- States should take all possible measures to prevent such recruitment—including legislation to prohibit and criminalize the recruitment of children under 18 and involve them in hostilities.
- States will demobilize anyone under 18 conscripted or used in hostilities and will provide physical and psychological recovery services and help their social re-integration.
- Armed groups distinct from the armed forces of a country should not, under any circumstances, recruit or use in hostilities anyone under 18. This protocol was ratified by India on 30 November 2005.

2. *Optional Protocol to the Convention on the Rights of the Child on the Sale of Children, Child Prostitution and Child Pornography (OPSC)*[123]

This protocol draws special attention to the criminalization of these serious violations of children's rights and emphasizes the importance of increased public awareness and international cooperation in the efforts to combat them. It supplements the convention by providing states with detailed requirements to end the sexual exploitation and abuse of children and also protects children from being sold for non-sexual purposes, such as other forms of forced labour, illegal adoption, and organ donation. The protocol provides definitions for the offences of 'sale of children', 'child prostitution', and 'child pornography'. It also creates obligations on governments to criminalize and punish activities related to these offences. It requires punishment not only for those offering or delivering children for the purposes of sexual exploitation, transfer of organs, or for profit or forced labour, but also for anyone accepting the children for these activities. The protocol also protects the rights and interests of child victims. Governments must provide legal and other support services to child victims. This obligation includes considering the best interests of the child in any interactions with the criminal justice system. Children must also be supported with necessary medical, psychological, logistical, and financial support to aid their rehabilitation and re-integration.[124] This protocol was ratified by India on 16 August 2005.

3. *The Optional Protocol to the UNCRC on a Communications Procedure (called OP3 CRC)*[125]

Optional Protocol 3 to the UNCRC on a Communications Procedure is an international human rights treaty that allows children, groups of children, or their representatives, who claim that their rights have been violated by their state to bring a communication, or complaint, before the UN committee on the rights of the child. It allows children to approach the UN if their rights are not being protected in their country and they have exhausted all domestic remedies to seek justice. It also allows any interested party to provide information about grave or systematic violations of child rights to the UN committee on the rights of the child (through the inquiry procedure). This protocol has not been ratified by India.

[123] Adopted and opened for signature, ratification, and accession by General Assembly Resolution A/RES/54/263 of 25 May 2000; entered into force on 18 January 2002. Ratified by India on 16 August 2005. Available at http://www.ohchr.org/EN/ProfessionalInterest/Pages/OPSCCRC.aspx (accessed on 1 February 2016).

[124] Available at http://www.ohchr.org/EN/ProfessionalInterest/Pages/OPSCCRC.aspx (accessed on 1 February 2016).

[125] Adopted and opened for signature, ratification, and accession by General Assembly Resolution A/RES/54/263 of 25 May 2000. Available at http://www.ohchr.org/EN/ProfessionalInterest/Pages/OPACCRC.aspx (accessed on 24 January 2015).

Hague Convention on Intercountry Adoption[126]

The Hague Convention on the Protection of Children and Co-operation in Respect of Inter-country Adoption (Convention), 1993 is an international agreement to safeguard inter-country adoptions. Concluded on 29 May 1993 in the Hague, the Netherlands, the convention establishes international standards of practices for inter-country adoptions. The convention aims to prevent the abduction of, sale of, or trafficking in children, and it works to ensure that inter-country adoptions are in the best interests of children. On 6 June 2003, India ratified the protocol and deposited its instrument of ratification.

Hague Convention on the Civil Aspects of International Child Abduction[127]

The Convention of 25 October 1980 on the Civil Aspects of International Child Abduction, 1980 seeks to combat parental child abduction by providing a system of cooperation between central authorities and a rapid procedure for the return of the child to the country of the child's habitual residence. The convention is based on a presumption that, save in exceptional circumstances, the wrongful removal or retention of a child across international boundaries is not in the interests of the child,[128] and that the return of the child to the state of habitual residence will promote his or her interests by vindicating the right of the child to have contact with both parents,[129] by supporting continuity in the child's life,[130] and by ensuring that any determination of the issue of custody or access is made by the most appropriate court having regard to the likely availability of relevant evidence. India has not signed the 1980 Hague Convention on the Civil Aspects of International Child Abduction. Parental child abduction is a criminal offence under the IPC.

Justice in Matters Involving Child Victims and Witnesses of Crime[131]

The guidelines represent good practice based on the consensus reflected in contemporary knowledge and relevant international and regional norms, standards, and principles, and are meant to provide a practical framework for achieving the following objectives:

---

[126] Convention of 29 May 1993 on Protection of Children and Co-operation in Respect of Intercountry Adoption. Available at https://www.hcch.net/en/instruments/conventions/full-text/?cid=69 (accessed on 26 January 2016).

[127] The Convention of 25 October 1980 on the Civil Aspects of International Child Abduction. Available at https://www.hcch.net/en/instruments/conventions/full-text/?cid=24 (accessed on 26 January 2016).

[128] Preamble. Also see Article 11 of the UNCRC.

[129] See UNCRC, Article 9.3: 'States Parties shall respect the right of the child who is separated from one or both parents to maintain personal relations and direct contact with both parents on a regular basis, except if it is contrary to the child's best interests.'

[130] See UNCRC, Article 8.

[131] United Nations Office on Drugs and Crime, UNICEF, United Nations, New York, 2009. Available at https://www.unodc.org/documents/justice-and-prison-reform/Justice_in_matters...pdf (accessed on 26 January 2016).

1. Assist in the design and review of national laws, procedures, and practices with a view to ensuring full respect for the rights of child victims and witnesses of crime, and to furthering the implementation of the UNCRC by the parties to that convention.
2. Assist governments, international organizations providing legal assistance to requesting states, public agencies, NGOs and community-based organizations, and other interested parties in designing and implementing legislation, policy, programmes, and practices that address key issues related to child victims and witnesses of crime.
3. Guide professionals and, where appropriate, volunteers working with child victims and witnesses of crime in their day-to-day practice in the adult and juvenile justice process at the national, regional, and international levels, consistent with the Declaration of Basic Principles of Justice for Victims of Crime and Abuse of Power.[132]
4. Assist and support those caring for children in dealing sensitively with child victims and witnesses of crime.

International Labour Organization Convention No. 182 on the Worst Forms of Child Labour[133]

Convention No. 182 on the Worst Forms of Child Labour was adopted in June 1999. It calls for the prohibition and the elimination of the worst forms of child labour, as a matter of urgency. Convention No. 182 defines the worst forms of child labour as follows:

• All types of slavery, including the sale and trafficking of children; forced labour to pay off a debt; any other type of forced labour, including using children in war and armed conflict.
• All activities which sexually exploit children, such as prostitution, pornography, or pornographic performances.
• Any involvement in illegal activities, especially the production or trafficking of drugs.
• Any work which could damage the health, safety, or well-being of children (so called 'hazardous work').

Convention on the Rights of Persons with Disabilities and its Optional Protocol[134]

The Convention on the Rights of Persons with Disabilities (CRPD) was adopted on 13 December 2006 at the United Nations (UN) Headquarters in New York. The purpose of the convention is to promote, protect, and ensure the full and equal enjoyment of all human rights and fundamental freedoms by all persons with disabilities. With their entering into force on 3 May 2006, they represent a significant paradigm shift in thinking on the place of persons with disability in the

---

[132] General Assembly Resolution 40/34.

[133] International Labour Organisation, Convention No. 182. Available at http://www.ilo.org/ipec/Campaignandadvocacy/Youthinaction/C182-Youth-orientated/C182Youth_Convention/lang--en/index.htm (accessed on 26 January 2016).

[134] Available at http://www.ohchr.org/EN/HRBodies/CRPD/Pages/OptionalProtocolRightsPersonsWithDisabilities.aspx (accessed on 1 February 2016).

society, articulating that they possess entitlements which are equal to those of the rest of society. The core elements of anti-discrimination, equal opportunities, and active inclusion measures are reflected in the convention, with provisions covering all policy fields such as access to justice, reasonable access, employment, IT, and access to social services.

Millennium Development Goals

In 2000, with the adoption of the Millennium Declaration, nearly 200 nations pledged to promote respect for human rights and to endeavour to protect and promote the full spectrum of rights in their territories. The Millennium Development Goals (MDGs), which include eradicating extreme poverty and hunger, achieving universal primary education, promoting gender equality and reducing child mortality, improving maternal health, and combating HIV/AIDS, malaria, and other diseases, provide a solid foundation upon which countries can build an environment that stimulates social justice, equity, liberty, development, and good governance. Among those committed to advancing the best interests of children in the context of the MDGs, legislative reforms have been of particular importance. Both the adoption and the effective implementation of laws and policies to protect children; promote their survival, education and development; eliminate inequalities and promote gender equality, and the empowerment of women are critical to help meet the MDGs.[135]

Regional Instruments for the Protection of Children

There are regional human rights instruments for the protection of children, adopted by the Council of Europe, the Organization of American States (OAS), and the Organization of African Unity (OAU).

European Convention on Human Rights, 1950

The convention adopts the term 'everyone' and children have successfully brought cases either on their own behalf or as co-applicants with their parents. The convention has thus been used as a valuable instrument for children. The Council of Europe has also adopted the European Social Charter, 1961. The charter contains a number of specific references to children. Part I enshrines the basic principle: 'Children and young persons have the right to special protection against the physical and moral hazards to which they are exposed.'[136]

---

[135] Available at www.unicef.org/publications/files/Children_and_the_MDGs.pdf (accessed on 7 September 2016).

[136] European Social Charter (revised), European Treaty Series No. 163, Strasbourg, 3.V.1996. Available at http://www.coe.int/en/web/conventions/full-list/-/conventions/rms/090000168007cf93 (accessed on 7 September 2016).

Enforcement of International Instruments in India

- The Government of India has ratified the UNCRC on 12 November 1992. It has also endorsed the 27 survival and development goals for the year 2000 laid down by the World Summit for Children. Article 73 of the Constitution states: 'Subject to the provisions of this Constitution, the executive power of the Union shall extend to the matters with respect to which Parliament has power to make laws; and to the exercise of such rights, authority and jurisdiction as are exercisable by the Government of India by virtue of any treaty or agreement.' Article 253 of the Constitution states that the 'Parliament has power to make any law for the whole or any part of the territory of India for implementing any treaty, agreement to Convention with any other country or countries or any decision made at any international conference, association or other body'. Therefore, international conventions like the UNCRC can be enforced in Indian courts without a statute. Any international convention consistent with the fundamental rights and in harmony with its spirit must be read into the provisions of the Constitution. Therefore, the provisions of the UNCRC in consonance with the fundamental rights can be enforced without a statute.
- This was clearly laid down in the case of *Mayanbhai Ishwarlal Patel* v. *Union of India*.[137] Again in the case of *Vishaka* v. *State of Rajasthan*,[138] the Supreme Court reiterated the principle that in the absence of a domestic law, the contents of international conventions and norms are relevant for the purpose of interpretation of the fundamental rights.
- It is significant to note that with the exception of the UNCRC, 1989, there is no other child-centred approach; also, the Asia region, which has the highest proportion of the world's children, does not have any similar regional human rights or child rights instrument. Many of them have ratified the UNCRC.

South Asian Association for Regional Cooperation Instruments

In South Asia, there is the SAARC Convention on Preventing and Combating Trafficking in Women and Children for Prostitution, 2002.[139] The purpose of this convention is to promote cooperation among the member states so that they may effectively deal with the various aspects of prevention, interdiction, and suppression of trafficking in women and children; the repatriation and rehabilitation of victims of trafficking; and prevent the use of women and children in international prostitution networks, particularly where the countries of the SAARC region are the countries of origin, transit, and destination.

In 2002, during the SAARC decade of the rights of the child, the SAARC countries adopted the Convention on Promotion of Child Welfare in South Asia. The purpose of the convention is to solidify the commitments that the South Asian countries have made at the world summit

---

[137] AIR 1969 SC 783.
[138] (1997) 6 SCC 241.
[139] The SAARC is a regional body of representatives from eight countries to promote mutual assistance in economic, agricultural, environmental, and other sectors. The SAARC countries are India, Bangladesh, Bhutan, Pakistan, Nepal, Sri Lanka, Afghanistan, and the Maldives.

and to other international bodies, by encouraging mutual cooperation and assistance. The aim is to protect the rights of the child while realizing the full potential of each child and their responsibilities and duties. According to the convention, this can be done by setting up regional arrangements to assist member states. The convention states that countries should recognize the rights of a child as laid out in the UNCRC and uphold the rights of the family as primary care-givers, and also recognize the best interests of the child. To achieve their goals, the states' regional priorities should be recognizing the need for essential services such as education and health, both preventive and curative, and providing appropriate legal and administrative safety nets such as national laws that protect the child from abuse, exploitation, neglect, violence, discrimination, trafficking, and child labour. [140]

Children and Courts

Rights are of limited value unless they can be asserted. One very significant structure of the legal system is represented by the courts. A court is a body which has an authority to take decisions. Provisions in various laws, which are presently in practice, guide these decisions. Children in India can come in direct contact with the courts and the legal system in various contexts, for example, as offenders and witness to crimes. Also, family matters like divorce, separation, adoption, and guardianship, among others, can bring a child to the courts. There are the ordinary civil and criminal courts based on the adversarial model. The system uses formal procedural justice to obtain binding decisions and remedies. The main laws that govern the criminal and civil justice systems include the Code of Civil Procedure, 1908, Indian Evidence Act, 1872, IPC, 1860, and CrPC, 1973. Beside these ordinary courts and legal procedures, there are also specialized courts. Two courts most commonly accessed by children are the juvenile courts or the JJBs[141] and family courts. Conciliation, counselling, and individualized treatment based on casework approach with expertise and inputs from law, psychiatry, and social work have been envisaged for these courts. Simplicity, informality, and flexibility have been attempted in these courts.

Children are unable, by definition, to petition the courts themselves; they have had to rely on the parens patriae role of the state. The courts have, on several occasions, responded to the needs of children through public interest litigation, especially in the areas of improvement of conditions of children in institutions, prisons, illegal confinement, treatment of physically and mentally disabled children, child labour, adoption, juvenile justice, prevention of trafficking of young girls, welfare of children of prostitutes, prohibition of corporal punishment in schools, and sex selection tests. Several of these issues were raised before the courts by social activists, journalists, newspaper reporters, or taken up suo motu by the courts. Some of the landmark decisions are mentioned next.

---

[140] Asha Bajpai, *Legislative Reform in Support of Children's Rights—Curriculum Framework* (New York: UNICEF, July 2012). Available at http://www.unicef.es/sites/www.unicef.es/files/recursos/legislative-re-form-in-support-of-children-rights.pdf (accessed on 1 February 2016).

[141] Juvenile courts have been replaced by the JJBs under the new JJ Act, 2000 for dealing with children in conflict with law.

M.C. Mehta v. State of Tamil Nadu[142]

This judgment passed elaborate directions to stop child labour in hazardous occupations and processes.

Sanjay Suri v. Delhi Administration[143]

The court ordered transfer of some guilty officers and laid down rules to protect children in jails.

Lakshmikant Pandey v. Union of India[144]

These were a series of decisions in which the Supreme Court laid down directions for inter-country adoption of children.

Gaurav Jain v. Union of India[145]

The Supreme Court held that segregating the children of prostitutes would not be in their interest.

People's Union for Democratic Rights v. Union of India[146]

Employment in construction work was held to be hazardous for children.

Vishal Jeet v. Union of India[147]

Several directions were issued to end sexual exploitation of children.

Dukhtar Jahan v. Mohammed Farooq[148]

The Supreme Court asked the husband to pay maintenance to the child even though he had divorced the wife. The allegation of the husband that the child was illegitimate was rejected.

---

[142] AIR 1997 SC 699.
[143] AIR 1986 SC 414.
[144] AIR 1984 SC 469; AIR 1986 SC 272; AIR 1992 SC 118.
[145] AIR 1990 SC 292.
[146] AIR 1982 SC 1473.
[147] AIR 1990 SC 1412.
[148] AIR 1987 SC 1049.

Sheela Barse v. the Secretary, Children's Aid Society & Ors[149]

The petition was filed in public interest with regard to improper functioning of childcare institutions in Mumbai, India. The Supreme Court directed that in no case should a child be kept in jail and a central law must be enacted to bring uniformity in the juvenile justice system.

Delhi Domestic Working Women's Forum v. Union of India & Ors[150]

The Supreme Court directed the setting up of the Criminal Injuries Compensation Board to award compensation to rape victims.

Sarita Sharma v. Sunita Sharma[151]

The court held that in the issue relating to custody of children, paramount consideration should be given to the welfare of the children.

Shantistar Builders v. Narayan Khimlal Totame[152]

The case dealt with the concept of suitable accommodation for a child.

Kishen Pattnayak v. State of Orissa[153]

Poor people were forced to sell children to buy food. The Orissa (now Odisha) government was compelled to take several welfare actions.

Unnikrishnan J.P. & Others v. State of Andhra Pradesh[154]

The court held that the right to education is implicit in the right to life.

The epistolary jurisdiction of the court, by which the Supreme Court entertains writs even on the basis of letters, has increased the access to courts. By liberalizing the principles of locus-standi, the court has enabled social activists, journalists, academicians, lawyers, and child welfare organizations to approach the highest court for redressal of injustice to children. During the past decade or so, affirmative action has been taken by the Supreme Court and the high courts to protect children's rights. There have been persistent efforts on the part of jurists and social activists to make law and the legal system a tool for social change.

---

[149] AIR 1987 SC 656.
[150] (1995) 1 SCC 14.
[151] (2000) 3 SCC 14.
[152] AIR 1990 SC 630.
[153] AIR 1989 SC 677.
[154] AIR 1993 SC 2178

Recently, in a case of an 'unwanted child' being born due to the doctor's negligence in performing the sterilization operation, the Supreme Court passed a judgment upholding that the woman was entitled to claim damages for bringing up the child. The High Court of Delhi upheld the death sentence on a couple for murdering a one-and-a-half-year-old girl during a witchcraft ritual. In another significant judgment, the Supreme Court held that the children of a Hindu father, born out of his illegal second marriage, were entitled to equal share in the property and assets left behind by him.

Pt. Parmananda Katara v. Union of India[155]

It has been held that it is the professional obligation of all doctors, whether government or private, to extend medical aid to the injured immediately to preserve life without waiting for legal formalities to be complied with by the police under the CrPC. Article 21 of the Constitution casts the obligation on the state to preserve life. No law or state action can intervene to delay the discharge of this paramount obligation of the members of the medical profession. The obligation being total, laws of procedure, whether in statutes or otherwise, which would interfere with the discharge of this obligation cannot be sustained and must, therefore, give way. This is a very significant ruling of the court. It is submitted that if this decision of the court is followed in its true spirit, it would help in saving the lives of many citizens who die in accidents because no immediate medical aid is given by the doctors on the ground that they are not authorized to treat medico-legal cases.

Nil Ratan Kundu v. Abhijit Kundu[156]

The Supreme Court has said that the welfare of a child is not to be measured merely by money or physical comfort, but the word 'welfare' must be taken in its widest sense, and the tie of affection cannot be disregarded.

Bachpan Bachao Andolan v. Union of India and Others[157]

Bachpan Bachao Andolan, an India-based movement, filed a public interest petition under Article 32 of the Constitution concerning the serious violations and abuse of children who are forcefully detained in circuses. The court ordered, among other things, that the employment of children in circuses be prohibited; raids be conducted in all circuses to liberate the children and examine the violations of their rights, and that the rescued children be kept in the care and protective homes until they are 18; the state talk to the parents of the children, and in case they are willing to take their children back to their homes, they may be directed to do so after proper verification; and the state frame a proper scheme for rehabilitation of rescued children from circuses.

---

[155] (1989) 4 SCC 286.
[156] AIR 2009 SC (Supp) 732.
[157] (2011) 5 SCC 1.

Pramati Educational & Cultural Trust & Others v. Union of India & Others[158]

The Supreme Court was dealing with the validity of Clause (5) of Article 15 of the Constitution, inserted by the Constitution (Ninety-Third Amendment) Act, 2005 with effect from 20 January 2006, and on the validity of Article 21A of the Constitution, inserted by the Constitution (Eighty-Sixth Amendment) Act, 2002 with effect from 1 April 2010. The Apex Court Bench held that none of the rights under Articles 14, 19(1)(g), and 21 of the Constitution have been revoked by Clause (5) of Article 15 of the Constitution. The court further held that the Constitution (Ninety-Third Amendment) Act, 2005 of the Constitution, inserting Clause (5) of Article 15 of the Constitution, is valid.

Salil Bali v. Union of India & ANR[159]

Seven writ petitions and one transferred case had been taken up together for consideration in view of the commonality of the grounds and reliefs prayed for therein. In the bill brought in the Parliament for the enactment of the JJ Act of 2000, it had been indicated that the same was being introduced to provide for the care, protection, treatment, development, and rehabilitation of neglected or delinquent juveniles and for the adjudication of certain matters relating to and disposition of delinquent juveniles. The essence of the JJ Act, 2000, and the rules framed under it in 2007, were restorative and not retributive, providing for rehabilitation and reintegration of children in conflict with law into mainstream society. The age of 18 had been fixed on account of the understanding of experts in child psychology and behavioural patterns that, till such an age, the children in conflict with law could still be redeemed and restored to mainstream society, instead of becoming hardened criminals in the future. There were, of course, exceptions where a child in the age group of 16 to 18 years may have developed criminal propensities, which would make it virtually impossible for him/her to be re-integrated into mainstream society; however, such examples were not of such proportions as to warrant any change in thinking, since it was probably better to try and re-integrate children with criminal propensities into mainstream society, rather than to allow them to develop into hardened criminals, which did not augur well for the future. This being the understanding of the government behind the enactment of the JJ Act, 2000, and the amendments brought into effect thereto in 2006, with the rules framed thereunder in 2007, and the data available with regard to the commission of heinous offences by children—within the meaning of Sections 2(k) and 2(l) of the JJ Act, 2000—the court did not think that any interference was necessary with the provisions of the statute till such a time as sufficient data was available to warrant any change in the provisions of the aforesaid act and the rules.[160] On the other hand, the implementation of the various enactments relating to children would possibly yield better results. Hence, the writ petitions and the transferred cases were, therefore, dismissed.

From the decisions of the courts it is significant that the child's interests are primarily the perceptions of the adults, and in cases of family disputes, the competing adult claimants. The

---

[158] Writ Petition (C) No. 416 of 2012.
[159] Writ Petition (C) No. 10 of 2013.
[160] AIR 2013 SC 37–43.

UNCRC lays down two principles of interpretation in international law, namely the best interests of the child and the evolving capacities of the child. The manner of application of the best interests principle[161] has transformed it from the traditional concept of welfarism. This is an umbrella provision for actions concerning children. The scope has been widened much beyond the custody area alone. Where judicial discretion is exercised, an understanding of the framework of rights can stimulate dynamic interpretations of law that will give the child access to justice through the court system and other methods of dispute settlement.[162] The courts in India have ensured the implementation of progressive laws and the interpretation of restrictive laws in the best interest of the child. The courts, in public interest litigation including suo motu petitions and in adversarial litigation, have passed orders in the interest of the child.

Monitoring Child Rights—Children's Commissions for Protection of Child Rights

The National Commission for Protection of Child Rights (NCPCR) was set up in March 2007 under the Commission for Protection of Child Rights (CPCR) Act, 2005, an Act of Parliament (December 2005). The Commission's Mandate is to ensure that all laws, policies, programmes, and administrative mechanisms are in consonance with the child rights perspective as enshrined in the Constitution of India and also the UNCRC. The child is defined as a person in the 0-to-18 years age group.

The commission visualizes a rights-based perspective flowing into national policies and programmes, along with nuanced responses at the state, district, and block levels, taking care of specificities and strengths of each region. In order to touch every child, it seeks a deeper penetration to communities and households and expects that the ground experiences gathered at the field are taken into consideration by all the authorities at the higher level. Thus, the commission sees an indispensable role for the state, sound institution-building processes, respect for decentralization at the local-bodies and community level, and larger societal concern for children and their well-being. The functions of the NCPCR, as laid out in the CPCR Act, 2005, are as follows:[163]

1. Examine and review the safeguards provided by or under any law for the time being in force for the protection of child rights and recommend measures for their effective implementation.[164]
2. Present to the central government, annually and at such other intervals as the commission may deem fit, reports upon working of those safeguards.[165]

[161] Article 3 of the UNCRC, 1989 states: 'In all actions concerning children, whether undertaken by public or private social welfare institutions, courts of law, administrative authorities or legislative bodies, the best interests of the child shall be a primary consideration.'

[162] Savitri Goonesekere, 'Children and Justice Integrating International Standards into the National Context', *The Child and the Law*, papers from the International Conference on Shaping the Future by Law Children, Environment and Human Health, UNICEF, New Delhi, 1994.

[163] Ministry of Women and Child Development, 'Citizen's Charter of the National Commission for Protection of Child Rights', Government of India. Available at http://ncpcr.gov.in/index1.php?lang=1&level=1&&sublinkid=5&lid=600 (accessed on 26 January 2016).

[164] CPCR Act, Section 13(1)(a).

[165] CPCR Act, Section 13(1)(b).

3. Inquire into violation of child rights and recommend initiation of proceedings in such cases.[166]
4. Examine all factors that inhibit the enjoyment of rights of children affected by terrorism, communal violence, riots, natural disaster, domestic violence, HIV/AIDS, trafficking, maltreatment, torture and exploitation, and pornography and prostitution, and recommend appropriate remedial measures.[167]
5. Look into the matter relating to the children in need of special care and protection, including children in distress, marginalized and disadvantaged children, children in conflict with law, juveniles without family, and children of prisoners, and recommend appropriate remedial measures.[168]
6. Study treaties and other international instruments and undertake periodical review of existing policies, programmes, and other activities on child rights and make recommendations for their effective implementation in the best interest of children.[169]
7. Undertake and promote research in the field of child rights.[170]
8. Spread child rights literacy among various sections of society and promote awareness of the safeguards available for protection of these rights through publications, the media, seminars, and other available means.[171]
9. Inspect or cause to be inspected any juveniles' custodial home, or any other place of residence or institution meant for children, under the control of the central government or any state government or any other authority, including any institution run by a social organization; where children are detained or lodged for the purpose of treatment, reformation, or protection, and take up with these authorities for remedial action, if found necessary.[172]

   a. Inquire into complaints and take suo motu notice of matter relating to deprivation and violation of child rights.[173]
   b. Inquire into non-implementation of laws providing for protection and development of children.
   c. Inquire into non-compliance of policy decisions, guidelines, or instructions aimed at mitigating hardships to ensure the welfare of and provide relief to such children.

   Alternatively, it needs to take up the issues arising out of such matters with appropriate authorities.

10. Such other functions as it may consider necessary for the promotion of child rights and any other matter incidental to the aforementioned function, a state commission, or any other commission duly constituted under any law for the time being in force.[174]

---

[166] CPCR Act, Section 13(1)(c).
[167] CPCR Act, Section 13(1)(d).
[168] CPCR Act, Section 13(1)(e).
[169] CPCR Act, Section 13(1)(f).
[170] CPCR Act, Section 13(1)(g).
[171] CPCR Act, Section 13(1)(h).
[172] CPCR Act, Section 13(1)(i).
[173] CPCR Act, Section 13(1)(j).
[174] CPCR Act, Section 13(1)(k).

11. The commission shall not enquire into any matter which is pending before a state commission or any other commission duly constituted under any law for the time being in force.[175]

12. Analyse existing law, policy, and practice to assess compliance with UNCRC, undertake inquiries and produce reports on any aspects of policy or practice affecting children, and comment on proposed new legislation related to child rights.[176]

13. Present to the central government annually and at such other intervals as the commission may deem fit, reports upon the working of those safeguards.[177]

14. Undertake formal investigation where concern has been expressed either by children themselves or by concerned persons on their behalf.[178]

15. Promote respect and serious consideration of the views of children in its work and in all government departments and organizations dealing with children.[179]

16. Produce and disseminate information about child rights.[180]

17. Compile and analyse data on children.[181]

18. Promote the incorporation of child rights into the school curriculum, training of teachers or personnel dealing with children.[182]

19. The State Commissions for Protection of Child Rights (SCPCR) were to be established in each state as per the provisions of the CPCR Act, 2005. The state commissions were set up to protect, promote, and defend child rights in each state. The commission consists of a chairperson and six members who are well versed in child welfare. At least one member should be a woman. The state commissions are required to submit an annual report to the state government as well as special reports when an issue needs immediate attention.[183] The functions of the commission are the same as those of the NCPCR.[184]

Government Programmes and Schemes[185]

There are several government documents, campaigns, and schemes that reaffirm the Government of India's commitment to the cause of children. Some of these programmes and schemes are also in cooperation with the non-governmental organizations (NGOs). These programmes and schemes focus on child labour, non-institutional services, health, nutrition, education, street children, children in institutions, child prostitutes, and disabled children. The Government of India is implementing several schemes and programmes for the welfare and development of

---

[175] CPCR Act, Section 13(2).

[176] NCPCR Rules, 2006, Rule 17.

[177] NCPCR Rules, 2006, Rule 17.

[178] NCPCR Rules, 2006, Rule 17.

[179] NCPCR Rules, 2006, Rule 17.

[180] NCPCR Rules, 2006, Rule 17.

[181] NCPCR Rules, 2006, Rule 17.

[182] NCPCR Rules, 2006, Rule 17.

[183] CPCR Act, Section 17.

[184] CPCR Act, Section 3.

[185] Ministry of Women and Child Development, Government of India. Available at http://wcd.nic.in/schemes-listing/2406 (accessed on 24 January 2015).

children and women, through more than 13 ministries and departments.[186] These programmes include the RCH programme for providing integrated quality health to women and children and the ICDS programme, which delivers health, nutrition, and preschool services through a single window. Two schemes under the latter programme are detailed as follows.

Integrated Child Development Services

The ICDS, a Government of India–sponsored programme, is India's primary social welfare scheme to tackle malnutrition and health problems in children below 6 years of age and pregnant and nursing mothers. The scheme is mainly focussed on reducing infant and child mortality and improving maternal health outcomes. Since malnutrition is closely linked to all of these MDGs, the interventions under the ICDS programme are expected to contribute towards the achievement of each of these long-term outcomes. Despite several achievements that the ICDS scheme has witnessed during its three decades of implementation, there remain some major challenges with regard to child malnutrition.

Integrated Child Protection Scheme[187]

The ICPS brings together multiple existing child protection schemes of the ministry under one comprehensive umbrella, and integrates additional interventions for protecting children and preventing harm. The ICPS, therefore, would institutionalize essential services and strengthen structures, enhance capacities at all levels, create database and knowledge base for child protection services, strengthen child protection at the family and community level, and ensure appropriate inter-sectoral response at all levels.

A point of significant concern is that there are various different ministries dealing with the issues of children.

Interventions and Strategies by Non-governmental Organizations

The NGOs have played a significant role and have been in the forefront, providing services to children. There has been a shift from the welfare approach to a thrust on development and empowerment in the interventions for children. The NGOs have developed several strategies based on child rights perspective to intervene on behalf of children and protect their rights. Many NGOs and grass-roots organizations have intervened with various approaches. Some of the interventions have been in the following kinds of activities:

1. Research and documentation
2. Advocacy at all levels to bring about structural and policy changes

---

[186] Department of Women and Child Development, *India Report on the World Summit for Children* (Ministry of Human Resource Development, Government of India, 2000).

[187] Ministry of Women and Child Development, Government of India. Available at http://icds-wcd. nic.in/icpsmon/ (accessed on 26 January 2016).

3. Preparing alternative reports on status of child rights
4. Promoting networking and coordination among NGOs to jointly advocate on issues which affect the rights of the child
5. Awareness building
6. Mobilization of public opinion
7. Intervening in special cases of violations
8. Providing a platform for expression of children's concerns
9. Direct action, like raids and liberation of children in servitude
10. Building pressure groups
11. Capacity building (building in the necessary skills, structures, attitudes, and knowledge), required to work better
12. Lobbying with the government to review existing schemes towards being more child-oriented
13. Running field action projects to reach out to children
14. Direct work with children and their communities

Role of International Organizations

Several international organizations like UNICEF, United Nations Development Programme (UNDP), United Nations Development Fund for Women (UNIFEM), World Health Organization (WHO), International Labour Organization (ILO), Food and Agriculture Organization (FAO), United Nations Educational, Scientific, and Cultural Organization (UNESCO), United Nations Fund for Population Activities (UNFPA), Cooperative for Assistance and Relief Everywhere (CARE), Save the Children, Canada, and the International Bank for Reconstruction and Development (IBRD) are actively involved in the development and protection of child rights. Some other important agencies, including Human Rights Watch, Defence for Children International (DCI), International Society for the Prevention of Child Abuse and Neglect (ISPCAN), and End Child Prostitution in Asian Tourism (ECPAT), work towards promoting the rights of the child

Challenges Ahead

Like many developing countries, India faces problems of infant mortality, child marriage, maternal mortality, and the phenomena of child widows, sex tourism, and child trafficking even across national borders for prostitution, child abuse, and child labour. There are several challenges ahead. Child marriages are still on. There is abuse and exploitation of children through international trafficking, through sex tourism, and even as instruments of amusement. The act itself is very weak and dilatory.[188] Child marriages are valid even though there is a prescribed minimum age of marriage. The procedures to prevent child marriages are very cumbersome and time consuming. Illiteracy and orthodoxy of the people have proved to be other stumbling blocks. There is a need for a uniform law of adoption so that the children of all religious communities can be adopted. Child sexual abuse needs a sensitive law. The disabled child needs special protection. Problems of

---

[188] AIR 2014 SC 2114.

street children need to be tackled. Drug abuse, HIV/AIDS, and environmental concerns place a huge obstacle in the way of children's rights to survival and development.

Liberalization has also aggravated emergency situations in rural and urban areas, which disrupt the major support systems of children such as family and school, thus exposing them to several vulnerabilities. Globalization has also led to expansion of international organized crime, enlarging the scope for exploitation of children.[189] Children are also victims of war, terrorism, poverty trap, environmental disasters, displacement due to development, and globalization.

Of all the demographic groups, the girl child is probably the most socially disadvantaged. At every stage of her lifecycle—from conception to adulthood—she is especially vulnerable to human rights abuses. In India, where every study points out the low utilization of health services, low coverage of ante-natal and post-natal care, and low levels of institutional deliveries, the utilization of the sophisticated modern technology for sex detection of the foetus on a large scale is a big surprise and a matter of concern. As per the 2011 Census, the child sex ratio (0–6 years) has shown a decline from 927 females per thousand males in 2001 to 919 females per thousand males in 2011. Some of the reasons for neglect of the girl child and low child sex ratio are preference for a boy child and the belief that it is only the son who can perform the last rites, lineage and inheritance runs through the male line, sons will look after parents in old age, men are the bread winners, and so on. Exorbitant demand for dowry is another reason for female foeticide/infanticide. A small-family norm, coupled with easy availability of sex determination tests, may be a catalyst in the declining child sex ratio, further facilitated by easy availability of pre-conception sex selection facilities.[190]

A child-focussed culture has to be developed. The legal system should interpret the laws in the context of the rights and standards given in the UNCRC. This will give the child access to justice through the court system. There has to be child-centred focus in legal proceedings. All the children's legislations need to be reviewed in the context of the UNCRC and its standards and there has to be linkages between them. The Indian legal system has to evolve a great deal for securing the rights of the child and providing justice to the child.

Legal reform alone cannot bring justice to the child. Inter-agency structures and systems need to be worked out, laying greater emphasis on prevention. Undoubtedly, the most effective preventive measure is awareness of such possible abuse and how to deal with it, among the various service providers—the doctors, teachers, lawyers, judges, police, volunteers, parents, trade unions, and social workers—so that they can significantly reduce the risk of abuse, if it does occur, by responding appropriately. Rights are of limited value unless they can be effectively asserted. Advocacy and lobbying in support of proposals for legal reform will also be necessary. The NGOs have assumed a significant role and they perform crucial tasks in the struggle for the realization of the rights of the child—a struggle in which law and rights prove to be important resources.

Implementation of law in its true spirit is necessary. Social legislations for vulnerable groups are difficult to enforce as the beneficiaries are unable to demand their rights. We have some very

[189] Murli Desai, 'Child Protection Current Status and Recommendations of Strategies for the India Country Programme for 2003–2007: A Consultancy Report for UNICEF India Country Office', New Delhi, December 2001.

[190] Ministry of Health and Family Welfare, Government of India, Press Information Bureau. Available at http://pib.nic.in/newsite/PrintRelease.aspx?relid=103437 (accessed on 26 January 2016).

good laws but the implementation is poor. There is also a lack of awareness of laws and rights among children.

Resource allocation for legislative and regulatory mechanisms to ensure the proper delivery of services is as much part of the legal reform as law. The development of the human person is the essence of development. If rights of the child are to be taken seriously, they must include rights to resource allocation for effective programmes on the education and cultural development of the child. Such resource allocation should be accompanied by the creation of participatory delivery mechanisms for the effective utilization of such resources through development processes which are humane and which foster self-reliance, dignity, and participation. The child's right to development is crucial, both to safeguard the right to a future as well as the rights of future children.[191]

This will require creative interaction between judges, lawyers, lawmakers, policy planners, law enforcers, intellectuals, government officials, social-work groups, child-rights activists, children's organizations, and child victims. It is also essential that issues relating to the rights of the child in the Third World have to be viewed not in isolation but within the context of development. And it is essential that the child is placed high on the political agenda of development.

These challenges have to be rapidly addressed. Above all, the core value of the universal legal principle—that policies be made, structures and processes be established, and actions be taken that are always and invariably in the best interests of the child—should be followed. The struggle for the realization of the rights of the child is indeed a long journey.

---

[191] Clarence Dias, 'The Child in the Developing World: Making Rights a Reality', Report of a Seminar on Rights of the Child, National Law School of India University, Bangalore, 1990.

2 Right to Family Environment

Adoption and Other Non-institutional Services

Adoption in History, Mythology, and Religion[1]

Adoption is the act of establishing a person as parent to one who is not in fact or in law his/her child. Thus, adoption signifies the means by which a status or legal relationship of parent and child between persons who are not related by nature is established or created.[2] The very purpose of any adoption proceeding is to affect this new status of relationship. As a result of a decree of adoption, the child, to all intents and purposes, becomes the child of the adoptive parent. Adoption is also defined as a process by which people take a child who was not born to them and raise him or her as a member of their family.[3]

Adoption is so widely recognized that it can be characterized as an almost worldwide institution with historical roots traceable into antiquity. Mythology also expresses the deepest needs of adoptive parents to treat the adopted child the same as if it were born to them. As quoted in James Frazer's *Golden Bough*, Diodorus Siculus describes Hera adopting Hercules: 'The Goddess got into bed and clasping the burly hero to her bosom, pushed him through her robes and let him fall to the ground in imitation of real birth.'[4]

Primitive tribes continue this practice to the present time.[5]

Four thousand years ago, his/her tongue would be cut out if an adoptee dared to openly say that he/she was not born to his/her parents. Moreover, if he/she went further in search of his/her biological family, he/she would be blinded in punishment. The Code of Hammurabi, a part of Babylonian Law, was clear in its strictures governing adoption: 'If a man takes a child in his name, adopts and rears him as a son, then the grown-up son may not be demanded back. If a man adopts a child as his son after he has taken him, he transgresses against his foster-father, that adopted son shall return to the house of his own father.'[6]

---

[1] Asha Bajpai, *Adoption Law and Justice to the Child* (Bangalore, India: National Law School of India University, 1996).

[2] Britannica Inc., *The New Encyclopaedia Britannica*, Vol. I, Fifteenth Edition (1991), p. 105.

[3] World Book Inc., *The World Book Encyclopaedia*, Vol. I (Chicago, Illinois: 1988), p. 66.

[4] T.G. Frazer, *The Golden Bough* (New York: Macmillan, 1922).

[5] S.B. Presser, 'The Historical Background of the American Law of Adoption', *Journal of Family Law II* (1972): 443–516.

[6] I. Kocourek and P. Wigmore, 'Evaluation of Law, Sources of Ancient and Primitive Laws', *Encyclopaedia Britannica*, Vol. II (1947), p. 135.

The meaning of the blood tie was so strong that the only acceptable method of initiating non-relatives was to make them 'artificially blood relatives' by adoption. Adoption into a group, therefore, meant complete severance from one's original family or group with the promise of allegiance and total loyalty to the new family. To seek one's origins or to question one's true identity was seen then as dangerous, ungrateful, and disloyal.[7]

The Egyptians and the Hebrews knew of adoption and chronicled the most famous example of all times. The daughter of the Pharaoh adopted a foundling as a son and called him Moses. It was the young adult Moses who returned to 'his people', the Jews, and led them out of their Egyptian bondage to their homeland. This was where he felt he truly belonged.[8]

Adoption in Hindu Mythology

Hindu mythology contains several 'visions' concerning adoption. Anthropologically and historically speaking, they represent attitudes and value systems of human history. They may not be adoptions but they represent the 'concept of adoption', that is, of bringing up someone else's child as one's own.

The myth of Shakuntala, found originally in the Mahabharata and later on artistically changed to suit the needs of Kalidasa, is among the most popular in this genre. The following is the conversation between Shakuntala and King Dushyant, who falls in love with her: 'Who art thou a fairest one? The bright-eyed one answered: "I am the daughter of the holy high-souled Kanwa." Said the king, "But Kanwa is chaste and celibate, nor can he have broken his rigid vow. How come is it that thou were the daughter of such a one?"

Then the maiden, who was Shakuntala, narrated to the king sage the secret of her birth. She revealed that her real sire was Vishwamitra, the holy sage who had been a Kshatriya and was made a Brahmin in reward for his austerities. It was said that Indra became alarmed at his growing power. So Indra commanded Menaka, the beautiful apsara, to disturb the meditation of the holy sage.... In time Menaka became the mother of a baby girl whom she left in the forest. Now the forest was full of lions and tigers, but a large bird protected her from harm.... Then Kanwa found and took pity on the child. He said: 'she will be mine, my own daughter.'[9]

The myth of Shakuntala assumes importance because it may be regarded as a case of female adoption, which was not much in favour in later times. It can be considered as a parable of humanity and fellow feeling.

Another myth relates to the origin of Agni and is found in a hymn from the Vedas. Matariyan brought Agni to Bhrigu as a gift, precious like wealth. Since this hymn relates to the Rig Veda, it is among the earliest sources in which the myth of miraculous origin is found. Here 'adoption' itself is an inference, strongly borne out by the reference to double birth. First is the birth as god, and second is the fact of Bhrigu establishing him among the clan of Ayu.

A myth relates to the birth of the mother of the Pandavas, Kunti (referred to as Pritha). King Pandu had two wives, Pritha and Madri. Pritha was of celestial origin, for her mother was a nymph and her brother (Vasudeva) was the father of Krishna. When she was a baby she had been

---

[7] L.A. Huard, 'The Law of Adoption, Ancient and Modern', *Vanderbilt Law Review* (1956), 9.743–63.

[8] Huard, 'The Law of Adoption', 9.743–63.

[9] Donald A. Mackenzie, *India—Myth and Legend* (London: Mystic Press, 1985), p. 159.

'adopted' by the Raja of Shuranyena, whose kingdom was among the Vindhya mountains. She was of pious heart and always showed reverence to holy men. The myth of Karna, found in the Mahabharata, is a tale of adoption and the consequent duties of a son. A classic example of foster care is that of Lord Krishna, who was the son of Devaki but was brought up by Yashoda.

The object of adoption was mainly to secure performance of funeral rites and to preserve the continuance of one's lineage.[10] A Dattak Homam made the relationship valid and gave full rights to name and inheritance to the son.[11] It has to be noted that adoption was a parent-oriented practice that mostly took place between families whereby the natural parents physically gave the child in adoption to the adopting couple, usually some kith or kin. Boys were given in adoption and a female could not take a child in adoption, excepting a widow, who could adopt a boy in the name of her late husband.[12] Adoption was a custom applicable to the Hindus. Christians, Muslims, Jews, and Parsis were out of its purview, though the Church accepted adoption as part of its canon law and gave the adopted child the full status of a biological child. On 21 December 1956, this custom of adoption among the Hindus was given a legal status through the enactment of the Hindu Adoption and Maintenance Act, 1956.

Adoption and Parsis

The laws of the ancient Zoroastrians are in the 21 nasks or holy books that were part of the Avesta.[13] During the Kirnian period[14] childlessness was considered the greatest calamity for a couple.

The Prophet sanctified childhood. Ahura Mazda holds the father of a family far above him who is childless. Sons were valued more than daughters as they were permanent economic assets and they commemorated the departed ones of their family. They also carried on the family line and perpetuated the father's name. A son could be adopted in case a man had none born to him.[15]

Chapter IX[16] of the *Digest of a Thousand Points of Law* deals with adoption of children and states that an instance of the concern of the ancient Iranians to see that no father neglected his natural duties towards his child or palmed them off on another individual is to be seen in the law, which allows a father to give his only minor child in adoption to some person. The father could appoint a guardian over his minor child, apparently to safeguard his interests in case of his death, but he could withdraw such guardianship whenever he found a proper reason for doing so.

This digest also mentions 'partial adoptions'. It has been pointed out that children were adopted not always because the adoptive parents had none of their own, for people having legitimate living children were also allowed to adopt children. This probably happened owing to people's desire to admit into their family more intelligent, more desirable, or more useful persons.

---

[10] *Inder Singh* v. *Kartar Singh*, AIR 1966 Punj 258.

[11] Manu, Chapter IX, 16.

[12] This principle is responsible for the doctrine of relation back.

[13] Sohrab Jamshedjee Bulsara, *The Laws of the Ancient Persians*, in *Digest of A Thousand Points of Law*, IX (Mumbai: Hosing Ankleshwaria, 1937), p. 38.

[14] 2000 BC–700 BC.

[15] Manekaji Nussurwanji Dhall, *Zoroastrian Civilisation* (1992), p. 38.

[16] Bulsara, 'The Laws of the Ancient Persians', pp. 56–7.

From a review of the ancient texts, the concept of adoption occupies a very important place in the religion of fire worshippers. The objective appears to be purely religious, that is, to deliver the father to the next world.

There is no legislation for the adoption of children by Parsis in India. The Parsis today recognize under their custom adoption in the forms of Palukaputra and Dharamaputra. The Palukaputra form of adoption is purely contractual and is determined at the option of either of the parties. A son or daughter can be adopted and created as their own and can be given certain property, that is, rights of inheritance or of performing religious ceremonies.[17]

When the Adoption of Children Bill, 1980 was introduced in the Parliament, some members of the Parsi Zoroastrian community formed a special committee, known as the Bombay Zoroastrian Jashan Committee, which declared that a very large part of their community was against the application of the bill to the Parsis in India, and they wanted the Parsi community to be exempted from the application of this bill.

Some members of the Parsi community who favoured this bill said that the Zoroastrian religion enjoins conversion. They quoted the statement of Justice Davar in his judgment.[18] Today, there appears a vast change among the Zoroastrian followers in India. It is now believed by many that any person, Zoroastrian or otherwise, is sent to heaven or hell solely on the basis of the balance of good deeds and bad deeds. Only Ahura Mazda decides the relative weights attached to the deeds committed. No funeral rites and ceremonies can affect the final judgment. Therefore, it is not absolutely necessary for a person to have a son or a descendant to perform his religious ceremonies.

In practice, it appears that adoption among Parsis is a question of personal preference. Nowadays, usually, a childless couple brings up the child of some relative. When it comes to distribution of property, a person's last words are usually respected. There are instances when certain priests have performed Navjot ceremony on children, of whose only one parent is a Parsi.

The concept of adoption, that is, looking after the welfare of someone else's child, can thus be regarded as prevalent among Parsis. Regarding the provision for such a child's security, many are of the view that a will made in his favour may prove sufficient.

Adoption and Muslims

Islam emerged in Arabia when the Iranian civilization was breathing its last. Islam gave the concept that the Almighty, the Creator of the universe, was supreme and man was his deputy on earth.

There is a story that Zaid was Prophet Mohammed's freedman and adopted son. Prophet Mohammed had seen and admired Zaid's wife Zainab and her husband at once offered to divorce her. Prophet Mohammed's marriage with Zainab occasioned much scandal among his contemporaries.[19]

---

[17] Paras Diwan, *Indian Personal Law II, Law of Adoption, Minority and Guardianship and Custody*, 2nd Edition (Allahabad, India: Wadhwa and Co., 1993), p. 4.

[18] (1909) Bom LR 95.

[19] The Holy Koran, revised and edited by the Presidency of Islamic Researchers, Ifta, Call of Guidance, 123.

During the time when this event took place, the Arabs used to consider their adopted children in the same light as real children of their body. In 'Surat'[20] XXXIII (Medinah) of the Koran, in the chapter on confederates, Prophet Mohammed forbade this practice and thus legalized his marriage with Zainab, the divorced wife of his freedman Zaid, who was also his adopted son.

There are certain Koranic injunctions relating to orphans:[21] Hedaya[22] contains very elaborate instructions for the faithful. The books of the Hedaya contain the laws relating to the rights of destitute children. Lakeet, in its primitive sense, signifies anything lifted from the ground: the term is chiefly used to denote an infant abandoned by some person on the highway.

It would, therefore, clearly appear that adoption in Islam would be permissible only if:

- the true identity of the child is disclosed to him where it is known; and
- the rights of inheritance of the natural heirs are not disturbed.

To provide security to the adopted child, one of the following methods or a combination of them could be adopted:

- Provide *kafala* (maintenance) for the child.
- Make a gift (always permissible under Muslim law) in favour of the child.[23]
- Bequeath up to one-third of the property in his favour[24] (also permissible under Muslim law).

Some Muslims have taken children as wards in India[25] under the Guardians and Wards Act (GWA), 1890 and then adopted them informally. In some Islamic countries such as Pakistan, Iran, Tunisia, and even some Arabic countries, substantial changes have been made in personal laws. Therefore, an attempt could be made again in India in the cause of justice to the destitute and orphaned children or lakeets.

---

[20] Verse.

[21] K.A. Majid (compiled), *Quaranic Injunctions Do and Do Not: The Code of Salvation*, extracts from the translation of A. Yusuf Ali (North Nizamabad, Karachi, Pakistan: Do and Don't Publishers, 1990), p. 21.

[22] The *Hedaya* (guide) was translated from the original Arabic by four Maulvis or Mohammedan lawyers and from Persian into English by Charles Hamilton by order of Warren Hastings, when he was Governor General of India.

[23] Under Mohammedan law a testamentary disposition is limited to one-third of the net estate.

[24] A Mohammedan cannot, by will, dispose of more than one-third of the surplus of his estate after payment of funeral expenses and debts. Bequests in excess of the legal third cannot take effect unless the heirs consent thereto after the death of testator. Law allows a man to give away the whole of his property during his lifetime but only one-third of it can be bequeathed by will.

[25] The Joint Committee of the Parliament introduced the Indian Adoption Bill in the Rajya Sabha in 1976. This bill was opposed by the Muslims on the ground that adoption was against the Koran. Another bill was introduced in the Lok Sabha on 16 December 1980. This bill exempted Muslims from its operation. This is Section 3(1) of the Adoption of Children Bill, 1980: 'No adoption order shall be made in respect of a Muslim child or for adoption by a Muslim of any child, whether a Muslim or not, under this Act.' This bill also lapsed when the Parliament was dissolved in 1984.

Adoption and Christians

Christians have not had any particular opposition to adoption. The very religion seems to have the 'concept of adoption' deeply embedded in it. If you look into the whole scheme of the Bible, there are several instances of adoption. The very birth of Jesus Christ took place in the following way.[26] It is said that when his mother Mary had been betrothed to Joseph before they came together, she was found to be with the child of the Holy Spirit, and her husband Joseph being a just man, unwilling to put her 'to shame', resolved to divorce her quietly. But as he considered this, an angel of the Lord appeared to him in a dream, saying, 'Joseph, Son of David, do not fear to take Mary, your wife for that which is conceived in her is of the Holy Spirit. She will bear a son and you shall call his name Jesus for he will save his people from their sins.' The reference to adoption in the canon law[27] of the Christians is in C-689 C3, which says that an adopted child can be baptized in the church, and C-110, which says that children who are adopted in accordance with the civil laws are to be considered the children of that person or persons who have adopted them.

Therefore, the canon law does not bar or prohibit Christians from adopting a child. But since there is no law on adoption for Christians in India, they have to resort to the GWA. The guardian has a fiduciary relationship with the child and this relationship would cease to exist on the death of the guardian, the marriage of the minor, or when the minor becomes a major.

A non-governmental organization (NGO) had come up with a bill on adoption, known as the Christian Adoption Bill, 1988. The main features of this bill were the following:

1. Adoption can be of children of either sex.
2. Adoption should be without court intervention.
3. Single males could also adopt; if adopting a girl, the age difference should be 21 years. The girl should not have completed the age of 15 years.

Under the Juvenile Justice (Care and Protection of Children) Act (JJ Act), 2000, persons of all religions including Hindus, Muslims, Christians, and Parsis could adopt a child under Section 41 of the act.[28]

---

[26] The New Testament, Mathew 1:18–23.

[27] The word 'canon' in its proper sense means a 'measuring rod'. But here it may be defined as the organized body of laws by which the pastoral ministry of the Church is guided and structures of the church defined.

[28] JJ Act, 2000, Section 41:

(1) The primary responsibility for providing care and protection to children shall be that of his family.
(2) Adoption shall be resorted to for the rehabilitation of the children who are orphan, abandoned, or surrendered through such a mechanism as may be prescribed.
(3) In keeping with the provisions of the various guidelines for adoption issued from time to time, by the state government, or the Central Adoption Resource Agency (CARA) and notified by the central government, children may be given in adoption by a court after satisfying itself regarding the investigations having been carried out as are required for giving such children in adoption.
(4) The state government shall recognize one or more of its institutions or voluntary organizations in each district as specialized adoption agencies (SAAs) in such a manner as may be prescribed for the placement of orphan, abandoned, or surrendered children for adoption in accordance with the guidelines

The JJ Act, 2015 came into force on 1 January 2016 after the president of India gave his assent to the bill on 31 December 2015. The 2015 Act repeals and replaces the JJ Act, 2000. The 2015 Act is a secular law and a person of any religion can adopt a child.[29]

The Present Status of Adoption

The traditional approach for adoption was institutionalization of destitute, neglected, marginalized children and children in especially difficult circumstances. This approach resulted in the child being separated from the family environment. The trend today is towards non-institutional services. During the last few decades, the significant role that a family plays in a child's nurture and his/her physical, psychological, mental, and social growth and development has been increasingly realized. The non-institutional approach to children in crisis is upheld globally as it meets the child's right to a family.[30] Every child has the right to a family. This can be achieved by strengthening the family as a unit, by providing counselling and support services. When the child's own family cannot look after him/her, substitute family-based care should be arranged. The final objective is towards de-institutionalization of the child. Some of the common family-based non-institutional services are adoption, foster care, and sponsorship programmes.

The concept and practice of adoption in India have changed significantly from the past. Adoptions in the earlier times were 'parent-centred'—the needs of the parents being the primary

---

notified under Subsection (3): Provided that the children's homes and the institutions run by the state government or a voluntary organization for children in need of care and protection, who are orphan, abandoned or surrendered, shall ensure that these children are declared free for adoption by the committee and all such cases shall be referred to the adoption agency in that district for placement of such children in adoption in accordance with the guidelines notified under Subsection (3).

(5) No child shall be offered for adoption—

   (a) until two members of the committee declare the child legally free for placement in the case of abandoned children;

   (b) till the 2 months period for reconsideration by the parent is over in the case of surrendered children; and

   (c) without his consent in the case of a child who can understand and express his consent.

(6) The court may allow a child to be given in adoption—

   (a) to a person irrespective of marital status;

   (b) to parents to adopt a child of same sex irrespective of the number of living biological sons or daughters; or

   (c) to childless couples.

[29] The JJ Act, 2015 has been passed by the Parliament of India. It replaces the JJ Act, 2000. The act came into force from 15 January 2016. It was passed on 7 May 2015 by the Lok Sabha and on 22 December 2015 by the Rajya Sabha. Available at http://www.wcd.nic.in/sites/default/files/JJAct2015.pdf (accessed on 20 September 2016).

[30] Article 9 of the United Nations Convention on the Rights of the Child (UNCRC) states that the child should be ideally brought up in a family environment that is secure, nurturing, and protects its rights.

consideration. The practice was to adopt children from within the family or kinship group. Beginning from the 1960s, changes have taken place at the social, legal, and practice levels of adoption. The traditional practice of institutional care being offered to an increasing number of orphaned, destitute children was replaced by non-institutional approaches of finding family-based alternatives. Adoption is considered the best alternative for children deprived of biological families. The practice of placing unrelated children in adoption through agency intervention began in the early 1970s. National and international instruments influenced this change, namely the National Policy for Children, 1974, the United Nations Declaration on the Rights of the Child, 1959, and most significantly, the UNCRC, 1989. Article 20 of the UNCRC states that children deprived of family environment be provided with alternative family care or institutional placement. The focus of adoption has now clearly shifted from the needs of parents to the rights of a child to a family.

Of the several million homeless children, only a few find homes through in-country adoption and inter-country adoption (ICA), as the data presented in Table 2.1 indicates.

Table 2.1.   Estimated Number of Adoptions in India (2010–15)[31,32]

Year	In-country Adoption	Inter-country Adoption
2010	5,693	628
2011–12 (January 2011 to March 2012)	5,964	629
2012–13 (April 2012 to March 2013)	4,694	308
2013–14 (April 2013 to March 2014)	3,924	430
2014–15 (April 2014 to March 2015)	3,988	374

Besides adoption, there are other non institutional services like foster care and sponsorship. Foster care provides temporary substitute care for children. It is different from adoption where the child severs all ties with his own natural parents. In foster care, the child is placed in another family for a short or extended period of time, depending on the circumstances. The child's own parents usually visit regularly and eventually, after the rehabilitation, the child may return home. When the family is undergoing a temporary crisis (like the death of a parent or sudden illness), children experience a lot of stress and tension. They may need to be removed from their natural home to prevent their neglect. These children can be placed in foster families till the crisis is over. Unwed mothers and single parents can also be helped through foster care. Services like foster care, though family-based, can be effectively implemented even while faced with large-scale natural calamities like earthquake or cyclone. The foster-care scheme must provide adequate financial support to the foster family in order to care for the child, as well as support to the natural parents towards rehabilitation so that they may take the child back, when possible.

Sponsorship provides supplementary support to families who are unable to meet educational and other needs of their children. The sponsorship assistance enables the family to send the child to school, provide medical aid, and at the same time, remain in touch with the family of birth.

[31] Source: CARA, Ministry of Social Justice and Empowerment, Government of India.

[32] For more details, see http://cara.nic.in/InnerContent.aspx?Id=90#Adoption%20Statistics (accessed on 12 August 2015).

Indian Adoption Laws

The practice of adoption is based on the enactments, directions, resolutions, judgments, and guidelines, along with social work inputs, to protect the rights of the child to family care and inheritance. The laws concerning adoption and guardianship of children that are popular in India are presented in Figure 2.1.

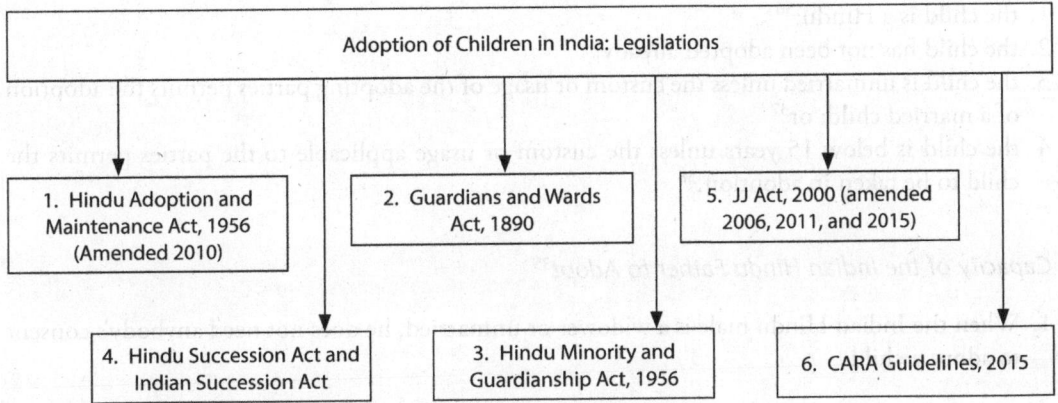

Figure 2.1. Adoption of Children—Indian Legislation

Hindu Adoptions and Maintenance Act, 1956—Significant Provisions

The statute of law governing adoption by Hindus[33] is the Hindu Adoptions and Maintenance Act (HAMA), 1956. Section 6[34] of the HAMA enumerates the requisites of a valid adoption. It lays down that no adoption shall be valid unless the person adopting has the capacity as also the right to take in adoption; the person giving in adoption has the capacity to do so; the person adopted

[33] HAMA, 1956, Section 2:

(1) This act applies—

 (a) to any person, who is a Hindu by religion in any of its forms or developments, including a Virashaiva, a Lingayat or a follower of the Brahmo, Prarthana, or Arya Samaj,

 (b) to any person who is a Buddhist, Jaina or Sikh by religion, and

 (c) to any other person who is not a Muslim, Christian, Parsi or Jew by religion unless it is proved that any such person would not have been governed by the Hindu law or by any custom or usage as part of that law in respect of any of the matters dealt with herein if this act had not been passed.

[34] HAMA, 1956, Section 6: Requisites of a valid adoption—No adoption shall be valid unless—

(1) the person adopting has the capacity, and also the right, to take in adoption;

(2) the person giving in adoption has the capacity to do so;

(3) the person adopted is capable of being taken in adoption; and

(4) the adoption is made in compliance with the other conditions mentioned in this chapter.

is capable of being taken in adoption; and the adoption is made in compliance with the other conditions mentioned under the act.

Who Can Be Adopted under the Hindu Adoptions and Maintenance Act

A child may be adopted under HAMA if[35]

1. the child is a Hindu;[36]
2. the child has not been adopted already;
3. the child is unmarried unless the custom or usage of the adopting parties permits the adoption of a married child; or[37]
4. the child is below 15 years unless the custom or usage applicable to the parties permits the child to be taken in adoption.[38]

Capacity of the Indian Hindu Father to Adopt[39]

1. When the Indian Hindu male is a widower or unmarried, he does not need anybody's consent to adopt a child.

---

[35] HAMA, 1956 (amended in 2010), Section 10.

[36] HMA, 1955, Section 2: This act applies—

(1) to any person who is a Hindu by religion in any of its forms or developments, including a Virashaiva, a Lingayat or a follower of the Brahmo, Prarthana, or Arya Samaj;
(2) to any person who is a Buddhist, Jaina, or Sikh by religion; and
(3) to any other person domiciled in the territories to which this act extends who is not a Muslim, Christian, Parsi, or Jew by religion, unless it is proved that any such person would not have been governed by the Hindu law or by any custom or usage as part of that law in respect of any of the matters dealt with herein if this act had not been passed.

Explanation—The following persons are Hindus, Buddhists, Jainas, or Sikhs by religion, as the case may be:

(1) any child, legitimate or illegitimate, both of whose parents are Hindus, Buddhists, Jainas, or Sikhs by religion;
(2) any child, legitimate or illegitimate, one of whose parents is a Hindu, Buddhist, Jaina, or Sikh by religion and who is brought up as a member of the tribe, community, group or family to which such parent belongs or belonged; and
(3) any person who is a convert or re-convert to the Hindu, Buddhist, Jaina, or Sikh religion.

[37] *Amar Singh* v. *Tej Ram* 1982 (84) Punj LR 2387.

[38] Existence of custom—be it family or tribal custom having its applicability to the parties concerned whereby the adoption of a person married or of the age of more than 15 years is permitted—is all that is required to be established by the provision of Section 10 so as to make adoption valid—(*Maya Ram* v. *Jai Narian* 1989 (1) HLR 352).

[39] HAMA, 1956, Section 7: Capacity of a male Hindu to take in adoption: Any male Hindu who is of sound mind and is not a minor has the capacity to take a son or a daughter in adoption 'provided that, if he has a wife living, he shall not adopt except with the consent of his wife unless the wife has completely

2. When the Indian Hindu male is married to an Indian Hindu female, he requires the consent of his wife unless

   a) the wife has ceased to be a Hindu;
   b) the wife has completely and finally renounced the world; or
   c) the wife has been declared to be of unsound mind by a court which has a competent jurisdiction.

3. When the Indian Hindu male is married to an Indian non-Hindu female, the wife's consent is not required under HAMA.

4. When the Indian Hindu male is a divorcee, he does not need anybody's consent if a decree of divorce has already been granted. However, wife's consent is needed if a petition for divorce is still pending before the divorce court.

5. A non-Indian Hindu male cannot adopt under the provisions of HAMA.

Other Conditions for a Valid Adoption[40]

1. If a Hindu male adopts a female child, there must be a difference of at least 21 years between the two.

2. The adoption must be real and not symbolic. The child must be actually given and taken in adoption by the respective parties. However, no specific *shastric* or religious ceremony is necessary for the purpose.

3. If a Hindu male wishes to adopt a male child, he must not already have any Hindu son, son's son, or son's son's son (whether by legitimate blood relationship or by adoption). Likewise,

---

and finally renounced the world or has ceased to be a Hindu or has been declared by a court of competent jurisdiction to be of unsound mind'.

[40] HAMA, 1956, Section 11: Other conditions for a valid adoption—In every adoption, the following conditions must be complied with:

(1) if any adoption is of a son, the adoptive father or mother by whom the adoption is made must not have a Hindu son, son's son or son's son's son (whether by legitimate blood relationship or by adoption) living at the time of adoption;

(2) if the adoption is of a daughter the adoptive father or mother by whom the adoption is made must not have a Hindu daughter or son's daughter (whether by legitimate blood relationship or by adoption) living at the time of adoption;

(3) if the adoption is by a male and the person to be adopted is a female, the adoptive father is at least 21 years older than the person to be adopted;

(4) if the adoption is by a female and the person to be adopted is a male, the adoptive mother is at least 21 years older than the person to be adopted;

(5) the same child may not be adopted simultaneously by two or more persons;

(6) the child to be adopted must be actually given and taken in adoption by the parents or guardian concerned or under their authority with intent to transfer the child from the family of its birth or in the case of an abandoned child or a child whose parentage is not known, from the place or family where it has been brought up to the family of its adoption, provided that the performance of datta homan, shall not be essential to the validity of an adoption.

if he wishes to adopt a female child, he must not have any Hindu daughter or son's daughter (whether by legitimate blood relationship or by adoption). This has some important implications :

a) If a Hindu male has a natural born son from his Hindu wife but the wife has divorced him and she has also been granted the custody of her son by a court of law, the Hindu male cannot adopt a son. The same rule applies to adoption of a daughter.

b) If a Hindu male does not have the capacity to beget a child, and he adopts a son with the consent of his wife, and subsequently his wife divorces him and is also granted the custody of the adopted son, the Hindu male cannot adopt another son.

c) If a Hindu male has a son from illegitimate relationship, but no legitimate son from his wife, he may adopt his own illegitimate son. If his wife is a non-Hindu, he does not even need her consent for adoption.

d) If he has a son from a non-Hindu wife who is raising this son as a non-Hindu, the Hindu male can adopt a Hindu child as his son without the consent of his non-Hindu wife. The same rule applies to the adoption of a daughter.

Adoption by a Hindu Woman[41]

A Hindu woman can also adopt a child if she is domiciled in India and is either unmarried or a widow or a divorcee. If she is married, only her husband has the capacity to adopt a child under HAMA; she has no capacity to do so. However, the following exceptions apply—

1. if the husband has been declared to be of unsound mind by a court of competent jurisdiction;
2. if the husband has completely and finally renounced the world; or
3. if the husband has ceased to be a Hindu.

She can adopt either an unmarried boy or a girl under 15 years of age. However, a married boy or girl and over the age of 15 years may be adopted provided custom or usage permit so, as in case of the adopting male. If a boy is adopted by the woman, the adopting mother must be at least 21 years older than him.

---

[41] HAMA, 1956, Section 8 (amended by HAMA Amendment Act, 2010): Capacity of a female Hindu to take in adoption: Any female Hindu

(1) who is of sound mind;

(2) who is not a minor; and

(3) who is not married, or if married, whose marriage has been dissolved or whose husband is dead or has completely and finally renounced the world or has ceased to be a Hindu or has been declared by a court of competent jurisdiction to be of unsound mind, has the capacity to take a son or daughter in adoption.

Equal Rights of Father and Mother to Adopt under the Hindu Adoptions and Maintenance Act[42]

Under HAMA, the father or the mother, if alive, shall have equal right to give a son or daughter in adoption. However, such a right shall not be exercised by either of them without the consent of the other unless one of them has completely and finally renounced the world or has ceased to be a Hindu or has been declared by a court of competent jurisdiction to be of unsound mind.[43]

Legal Effects of Adoption[44]

After adoption, the adopted child loses all its ties with the natural family and is treated like a natural born child in the adoptive family. The adopted child is conferred with all the rights and privileges of a natural born child in the adopting family. On the other hand, such a child loses all his rights and privileges of a natural born child in the natural family.[45]

However, all the restraints imposed upon him/her with respect to the degree of relationship under HMA, 1955 apply in both the natural and the adopted families.[46] Thus, he/she cannot

---

[42] HAMA, 1956 (amended in 2010), which serves the purpose of equality when it comes to taking consent of the spouse while adopting a child, Section 8. This section talks about the capacity of a female Hindu to take in adoption, which reads: 'Any female Hindu who is of sound mind and is not a minor has the capacity to take a son or daughter in adoption, provided that, if she has a husband living, she shall not adopt a son or daughter except with the consent of her husband unless the husband has completely and finally renounced the world or has ceased to be a Hindu or has been declared by a court of competent jurisdiction to be of unsound mind.'

[43] HAMA, 1965 (amended in 2010), Section 9(2): Subject to the provisions of Subsection (3) and Subsection (4), the father, if alive, shall alone have the right to give in adoption, but such a right shall not be exercised save with the consent of the mother unless the mother has completely and finally renounced the world or has ceased to be a Hindu or has been declared by a court of competent jurisdiction to be of unsound mind.

[44] HAMA, 1956, Section 12: Effect of adoptions—

An adopted child shall be deemed to be the child of his or her adoptive father or mother for all purposes with effect from the date of the adoption and from such date all the ties of the child in the family of his or her birth shall be deemed to be severed and replaced by those created by the adoption in the adoptive family, provided that—

(1) the child cannot marry any person whom he or she could not have married if he or she had continued in the family of his or her birth;

(2) any property which vested in the adopted child before the adoption shall continue to vest in such person subject to the obligations, if any, attaching to the ownership of such property, including the obligation to maintain relatives in the family of his or her birth;

(3) the adopted child shall not divest any person of any estate which vested in him or her before the adoption.

[45] HAMA, 1956, Section 12.

[46] HAMA, 1956, Section 12.

marry his/her siblings by birth as well as by adoption. As per HMA, 1955, two persons who are within the degree of prohibited relationship[47] and who are *Sapindas*[48] of each other cannot marry.

Once a valid adoption has been made, it cannot be revoked by the natural parent(s), the adopting parent(s), or the adopted child. Adopting parent(s) cannot give the child in adoption again.[49] Any agreement not to adopt is invalid irrespective of the parties involved.[50] Thus, if such an agreement is made between husband and wife, whether before getting married or after marriage, it is void, no matter the reasons for which it was made.[51] If adoption is made in consideration of some pecuniary rewards or property, the adoption is valid but the agreement with respect to the pecuniary reward or property is void and need not be performed.[52]

[47] HAMA, 1955, Section 3(g): Degrees of prohibited relationship: Two persons are said to be within the degrees of 'prohibited relationship'—

(1) if one is a lineal ascendant of the other; or
(2) if one was the wife or husband of a lineal ascendant or descendant of the other; or
(3) if one was the wife of the brother or of the father's or mother's brother or of the grandfather's or grandmother's brother of the other; or
(4) if the two are brother and sister, uncle and niece, aunt and nephew, or children of brother and sister or of two brothers or of two sisters.

Explanation: For the purposes of Clauses (f) and (g), relationship includes—

(1) relationship by half or uterine blood as well as by full blood;
(2) illegitimate blood relationship as well as legitimate;
(3) relationship by adoption as well as by blood;

and all terms of relationship in those clauses shall be construed accordingly.

[48] HAMA, 1955, Section 3(f):

(1) 'Sapinda relationship' with reference to any person extends as far as the third generation (inclusive) in the line of ascent through the mother, and the fifth (inclusive) in the line of ascent through the father, the line being traced upwards in each case from the person concerned, who is to be counted as the first generation.
(2) Two persons are said to be sapindas of each other if one is a lineal ascendant of the other within the limits of sapinda relationship, or if they have a common lineal ascendant who is within the limits of sapinda relationship with reference to each of them.

[49] HAMA, 1956, Section 15: Valid adoption not to be cancelled: No adoption which has been validly made can be cancelled by the adoptive father or mother or any other person, nor can the adopted child renounce his or her status as such and return to the family of his or her birth.

[50] Indian Contract Act (ICT), 1872, Section 23—What consideration and objects are lawful, and what not: The consideration or object of an agreement is lawful, unless—it is forbidden by law; or is of such nature that, if permitted it would defeat the provisions of any law or is fraudulent; or involves or implies, injury to the person or property of another; or the court regards it as immoral, or opposed to public policy.

In each of these cases, the consideration or object of an agreement is said to be unlawful. Every agreement of which the object or consideration is unlawful is void.

[51] ICA, 1872, Section 23.

[52] HAMA, 1956, Section 17: Prohibition of certain payments—

Effects of Marriage on Prior Adoption

If a bachelor or a widower Hindu adopts a child and subsequently marries, his wife shall be deemed to be the step-mother of the child.[53] It is not clear under HAMA as to the effects of remarriage by a divorced male. Logically deducing from HAMA, the legal position would be that the new wife of the adoptive father will be deemed to be step-mother of the adopted child. Similarly, if an unmarried, widowed, or divorced Hindu woman adopts a child and then marries, the husband would be deemed to be the step-father of the child.[54]

Under HAMA, the doctrine of relation back[55] does not apply as it used to under the classical Hindu law. Under the HAMA, the adopted child is deemed to have been born to the adopting family on the day of adoption for all legal consequences of adoption.[56]

Guardians and Wards Act, 1890

The GWA does not deal with adoption as such but mainly with guardianship, and is to be read along with the respective personal laws. This act is generally indirectly invoked by communities other than Hindus to become guardians of children during their minority. It may be indirectly invoked, in certain cases, to confer legal guardianship of children during their minority. But the process is not equivalent to adoption; it would only consider the child as the ward and not as son or daughter. The process makes the child a ward, not an adopted child. Under this law, when children turn 21 years of age, they no longer remain wards and assume individual identities. They do not have an automatic right of inheritance. These parents have to leave whatever they wish to bequeath to their children through a will, which can be contested by any 'blood' relative. Before the JJ Act of 2000, this was the only legislation that allowed non-Hindus in India to first take a

(1) No person shall receive or agree to receive any payment or other reward in consideration of the adoption of any person, and no person shall make or give or agree to make or give to any other person any payment or reward the receipt of which is prohibited by this section.

(2) If any person contravenes the provision of Subsection (1), he shall be punishable with imprisonment which may extend to 6 months, or with fine, or with both.

(3) No prosecution under this section shall be instituted without the previous sanction of the state government or an officer authorized by the state government on this behalf.

[53] HAMA, 1956, Section 14, Clause 3.

[54] HAMA, 1956, Section 14, Clause 4.

[55] The implications of this law can be understood from the situation wherein the boy belonging to a Joint Hindu Family dies and his widow adopts a son subsequently. Under classical Hindu law, the adoption of a son would have related back to the widow's deceased husband, with the result that some other relative would have been divested of his right to succeed to the property of the deceased. According to HAMA, if the death of the Hindu male resulted in inheritance of his property by a relative by virtue of being in the same Joint Hindu Family, a subsequent adoption by his widow will not divest that person's right of inheritance.

[56] HAMA, 1956, Section 12.

child as guardian and then adopt him/her. However, this act ended up being the first secular law that allowed for a child to be adopted in India.[57]

Following are the relevant provisions of the GWA, 1890, which are followed for facilitating adoption in India.

The GWA, 1890 applies to all minor children of any caste and creed, though in appointing or declaring a person as guardian the court will take into consideration the personal law of the minor.[58] But once a person is appointed or declared as guardian of a minor, irrespective of the fact whether the minor is a Hindu, or a Muslim, or subject to any personal law, such a guardian will be subject to the provisions of the GWA, 1890.

Section 7 of the GWA deals with the powers of the court to appoint or declare a person as guardian. The procedure under the GWA, 1890 is as follows.

Any person who claims or desires to be the guardian of the minor, or who is a relative or friend of the minor, or the collector of the district,[59] shall make an application to the district or family court where the minor ordinarily resides.[60] Under Section 19(b) of GWA, 1890, the court shall not appoint a guardian where the parents of the minor are alive and are physically and mentally fit to look after the interests of a minor, but the section excludes a married female.[61] On receipt of the application of a person, if the court comes to the conclusion that it would be for the welfare of the child to appoint a guardian of the person for the minor, it can appoint the guardian.[62] In considering what will be the welfare of the minor, the court shall take into account the age, sex, and religion of the minor, the character and capacity of the adopter, and the wishes of the deceased parent. If the minor is able to form an intelligent opinion, the court will consider his/her preference also.[63] The personal law of the minor is also to be taken into consideration along with the welfare of the child. The judicial attitude is fairly well settled that the welfare of the minor has been given greater significance than the rights of the parties under the personal law in deciding the question of guardianship under the act. Under Section 19(b) of the 1890 Act, the court shall not appoint a guardian where the parents of the minor are alive and are physically and mentally fit to look after the interests of a minor, but the section excludes a married female.[64] When the court

---

[57] Krishnamurthi Sangitha, 'Adoption Law in India', *The Alternative*, 19 December 2012. Available at http://www.thealternative.in/society/adoption-law-in-india/ (accessed on 26 August 2015).

[58] In effect, the procedural law regarding the appointment or declaration of the person as a guardian is laid down in the GWA, 1890, yet the substantive part is still the personal law. See Paras Diwan, *Law of Adoption: Minority, Custody and Guardianship* (Allahabad, India: Wadhwa and Co., 1989), p. 345.

[59] GWA, 1890, Section 8.

[60] GWA, 1890, Section 9.

[61] The Parliament has introduced the Personal Laws (Amendment) Bill, 2010, which aims to amend the GWA, 1890. The bill seeks to amend Section 19(b) of the 1890 Act and provides that the court shall not appoint a guardian where the parents of the minor are alive and are physically and mentally fit to look after the interests of a minor, but the section excludes a married female. The bill received the assent of the president and came into effect on 31 August 2010.

[62] GWA, 1890, Section 17.

[63] GWA, 1890, Section 17, Clause 3. Matters to be considered by the court in appointing: If minor is old enough to form an intelligent preference, the court may consider that preference.

[64] The Parliament has introduced the Personal Laws (Amendment) Bill, 2010, which aims to amend the GWA, 1890. The bill seeks to amend Section 19(b) of the 1890 Act and provides that the court shall

is satisfied that the appointment is for the welfare of the minor, an order appointing a guardian may be made in any one of the following three forms:[65]

- a simple order where no security is asked for;
- an order appointing a person as guardian and asking him to furnish security within a specified time; or
- an order appointing a guardian on the condition that he should furnish security.[66]

An order appointing a person as guardian under Section 7 amounts to the termination of the guardianship of all persons who have the care of the child, his person, or property. In passing the order for guardianship, the court may order or issue directions in respect to collateral matters also. A foreigner, therefore, wishing to take an Indian child for adoption, would have to use this very circuitous way under the GWA, 1890. The order would appoint the person as guardian of the child with leave to move the child out of India and take him/her to his own country for the purpose of adopting him/her, in accordance with the law of his country.

The procedure led to a lot of malpractice by social organizations and voluntary agencies engaged in the work of facilitating the adoption of Indian children by foreign parents. When the Supreme Court of India received a letter complaining of these malpractices and found that there was no legislation enacted by the Parliament for laying down the principles and norms which must be observed, and the procedure which must be followed in giving an Indian child in adoption to foreign parents, a writ petition was initiated on the basis of the letter. After hearing several social organizations and voluntary agencies engaged in placement of children in adoption, several judgments were passed, formulating the normative and procedural safeguards to be followed by other judgments clarifying and supplementing these norms and procedures. These were called the *Laxmikant Pandey* v. *Union of India* judgments.[67] The procedure for ICA laid down by these judgments can be summarized as follows.

The Supreme Court judgments have acknowledged ICA as a means to rehabilitate abandoned children. These guidelines attempted to put a stop to private adoptions. All ICAs were adoptions directly by foreign parents through governments recognized by them in both sending and receiving countries. The judgments attempted to make every party in the adoption process accountable. There were certain regulating agencies recommended in the judgments, like the Scrutinizing Agency, the Voluntary Coordinating Agency (VCA), the CARA, and the recognized Child

---

not appoint a guardian where the parents of the minor are alive and are physically and mentally fit to look after the interests of a minor, but the section excludes a married female. The bill received the assent of the President and came into effect on 31 August 2010.

[65] *Tuminra Khatun* v. *Ghariya Bibi*, AIR 1942 Cal. 281; *Mir* v. *Munji*, AIR 1952 Mad. 280, AIR 1983 J&K 70; *Bholanath* v. *Sharda Devi*, AIR 1954 Pat 489; *Smt Bhagwat Devi* v. *Muralidhar Sahu*, AIR 1943 PC106. In all these cases the court has stated that the principal matter to be considered is the welfare of the minor irrespective of the personal law of the child.

[66] The court has the discretion to ask for security from the guardian as prescribed by the state rules.

[67] *Laxmikant Pandey* v. *Union of India*, AIR 1984 SC 469, AIR 1986 SC 272, AIR 1987 SC 232, (1990) 4 SCC 513, AIR 1992 SC 118.

Welfare Agency (Placement Agency). The Child Welfare Agency processing the applications of the foreign parent had to place sufficient material before the court to satisfy it that the child is legally free for adoption.[68] After the enactment of the JJ Act, 2000, amended in 2006, 2011, and 2015, a person belonging to any religion, including a foreigner, can also adopt under the act.

The Hindu Minority and Guardianship Act, 1956

The Hindu Minority and Guardianship Act (HMGA), 1956 reforms and codifies the Hindu law relating to guardianship of minors and applies to all Hindus.[69] It deals with natural guardianship of the adopted child and provides that an adopted child is deemed to be the child of his or her adoptive father or mother for all purposes with effect from the date of the adoption, and from such date all the ties of the child in the family of his or her birth shall be deemed to be severed and replaced by those created by the adoption in the adoptive family. [70]

Succession and Inheritance Rights of Adoptive Children under the Hindu Succession Act, 1955 and the Indian Succession Act, 1925

These two acts—Hindu Succession Act (HSA) and Indian Succession Act (ISA)—govern succession and inheritance rights. The HSA, 1956 is a codified law dealing with the matters of succession of a deceased dying intestate and it applies to any person who is a Hindu by religion in any of its forms or development.[71] The act also applies to any person who is a Buddhist, Jaina, or Sikh by religion.[72] The general rules of succession under the HSA, 1956 for a male who dies intestate is that heirs known as Class-I heirs succeed in preference to heirs in other

---

[68] For details, see *Judgments of Laxmikant Pandey* v. *Union of India Relating to Inter-Country Adoption*, AIR 1985 Supp SCC 701 and 1984 (2) SCC 244, in this chapter.

[69] HMGA, 1956, Section 3(c): This act applies to any person domiciled in the territories to which this act extends who is not a Muslim, Christian, Parsi, or Jew by religion, unless it is proved that any such person would not have been governed by the Hindu law or by any custom or usage as part of that law in respect of any of the matters dealt with herein if this act had not been passed.

[70] HMGA, 1956, Section 7: Natural guardianship of adopted son: The natural guardianship of an adopted son who is a minor passes, on adoption, to the adoptive father and after him to the adoptive mother.

[71] HMGA, 1956, Section 2: Application of act—

(1)   This act applies—

  (a)   to any person, who is a Hindu by religion in any of its forms or developments including a Virashaiva, a Lingayat, or a follower of the Brahmo, Prarthana or Arya Samaj;

  (b)   to any person who is Buddhist, Jaina, or Sikh by religion; and

  (c)   to any other person who is not a Muslim, Christian, Parsi, or Jew by religion unless it is proved that any such person would not have been governed by the Hindu law or by any custom or usage as part of that law in respect of any of the matters dealt with herein if this Act had not been passed.

[72] *Arya Samaj Education Trust, Delhi and Ors.* v. *The Director of Education, Delhi Administration, Delhi and Ors*, AIR1976 Delhi 207.

classes.[73] The act was passed to govern intestate succession of Hindus. An adopted child under Hindu law is considered to be the child of the adoptive mother/father, like any other natural child, for all purposes including succession of property under HSA, 1956.[74] Hindu personal laws recognize adoption legally. All adopted children are treated as equals of the biological children of parents when it comes to inheritance and succession. Adopted children will not be entitled to a share in the assets of their biological parents or ancestors.[75]

The devolution of property of persons belonging to different religions married or registered under Special Marriage Act (SMA), 1954 is regulated by ISA, 1925 and a child born out of a void or voidable marriage under SMA, 1954 is deemed to be a legitimate child and is entitled to inherit in the same way as any other legitimate child.[76] The law of succession under the ISA, 1925 also does not provide a definition for the expression 'son'. Section 37 of the act (distribution where there are lineal descendants—where intestate has left child or children only) uses the expression 'children'. But it is without any qualification. Hence it is not clear whether it will include illegitimate children too.[77]

However, under the JJ Act, 2000, amended in 2006, which is applicable to all persons belonging to all religions, an adopted child gets all the rights and privileges like a natural-born child.[78] Though the JJ Act, 2000 grants the right to all Indian citizens, including Christians and Muslims, to adopt and confers the same rights as biological children have on the adopted child, it lacks clarity as to the application of succession law with respect to adopted children receiving inheritance rights in property[79]. This is an area for law reform and the position needs to be clarified.

The ISA, 1925 recognizes relationship only by consanguinity, that is, blood; therefore, an adopted child is not considered to be a 'child' under the act of 1925. The property of an intestate devolves upon those who are of the kindred of the deceased,[80] and kindred has been defined as the

---

[73] HSA, 1956 (amended in 2005), Schedule to Section 8: Son, daughter, widow, mother, son of a pre-deceased son, daughter of a pre-deceased son, son of a pre-deceased daughter, daughter of a pre-deceased daughter, widow of a pre-deceased son, son of pre-deceased son of a pre-deceased son, daughter of a pre-deceased son of a pre-deceased son, widow of a pre-deceased son of a pre-deceased son.

[74] HSA, 1956, makes no distinction between natural and adopted children. HSA, 1956, Section 1(a): 'agnate'—one person is said to be an 'agnate' of another if the two are related by blood or adoption wholly through males.

HSA, 1956, Section 1(c): 'cognate'—a person is said to be a 'cognate' of another if the two are related by blood or adoption but not wholly through males.

[75] HSA, 1956 and HMA, 1955.

[76] SMA, 1954, Section 26.

[77] Shanthakumar Lakshmi, 'Legitimacy of Bastardisation Law—A Critical Overview', *The Pratical Lawyer*, (2011) PL November S-8. Available at http://www.supremecourtcases.com/index2.php?option=com_content&itemid=5&do_pdf=1&id=22276 (accessed on 5 September 2015).

[78] JJ Act, 2000, Section 2(aa), inserted by the 2006 amendment.

[79] Archana Mishra, 'Bridging the Gap between the Juvenile Justice Act 2000 and Christian Personal Law—Inheritance Rights of Adopted and Illegitimate Children in India', *Australian Journal of Family Law* 29(2015): 43–64. Available at http://www.jgu.edu.in/sites/default/files/article/Mishra.pdf (accessed on 1 September 2015).

[80] ISA, 1925, Section 32: Devolution of such property: The property of an intestate devolves upon the wife or husband, or upon those who are of the kindred of the deceased, in the order and according to the rules hereinafter contained in this chapter.

connection or relation of the person descended from the stock or common ancestor.[81] The ISA, 1925 further provides that where the intestate dies leaving behind his child and no more lineal descendant, the property is to devolve on the surviving child. It is thus clear that ISA, 1925 does not contemplate an adopted child's share on intestacy.[82]

The issue of adoption by Christian parents under the JJ Act, 2000 came before the Madras High Court in *Re Christopher and Chandra*.[83] The petitioners had filed the application for a direction that the minor child, whom they had adopted as per Christian rites and customs under canon law and had also been declared by the court to be her legal guardian, was entitled to all legal rights including the right of inheritance, as if she were a biological child. The court, while allowing the application, held that the preamble to the JJ Act, 2000 and the act itself was enacted with a view to fulfilling India's international obligations as well as the Constitutional goal envisaged in Part IV of the Constitution.[84] Therefore, aspiring parents who intend to adopt children, without being inhibited by their personal laws, are entitled to adopt a child in terms of the provisions of the JJ Act, 2000. The view expressed in *Christopher* was endorsed by the Madurai Branch of the same high court in *Maria* (a minor, represented by her father and guardian Mohandas) v. *Accountant General Chennai*.[85] In 2014 a writ petition was filed in the Supreme Court in *Shabnam Hashmi* v. *Union of India* (UOI)[86] to elevate the right to adopt and to be adopted to the status of a fundamental right under Part III of the Constitution.[87] The writ petition also requested that the court lay down optional guidelines enabling the adoption of children by persons irrespective of religion, caste, creed, and so on. The court held that adoption under the legislation by prospective parents is optional. It does not contain an unavoidable imperative and cannot be stultified by principles of personal law which will continue to govern any person who chooses to so submit themselves to those personal laws. Such is the situation until such time as a uniform civil code is achieved. With respect to raising the right to adopt to the status of a fundamental right, the court applied judicial restraint by holding that it was not presently an appropriate time or stage for the right to adopt and the right to be adopted to be raised to the status of fundamental rights and/or to understand such rights to be encompassed by Article 21 of the Constitution. The court refused to recognize the right to adopt to be an integral part of Article 21, which guarantees the rights to life and liberty, on the ground that there are conflicting views and beliefs prevailing in the country which have hindered the goal of achieving a uniform civil code under Article 44.[88] But the bench observed that persons of any faith can adopt a child under the JJ Act, 2000 and

---

[81] ISA, 1925, Section 24: Kindred or consanguinity is the connection or relation of persons descended from the same stock or common ancestor.

[82] ISA, 1925, Section 37: Where the intestate has left surviving him a child or children, but no more remote lineal descendant through a deceased child, the property shall belong to his surviving child, if there is only one, or shall be equally divided among all his surviving children.

[83] 2009 (8) MLJ 309.

[84] The Constitution of India, Directive Principles of State Policy.

[85] WP(MD) No. 6823 of 2008, 14 September 2010.

[86] 2014 (2) SCALE 529.

[87] The Constitution of India, Fundamental Rights.

[88] Article 44 of the Constitution of India states that the state shall endeavour to secure for the citizens a uniform civil code throughout the territory of India.

this law will prevail until a uniform civil code is achieved. Rajan Gogai J. held that personal beliefs and faiths, though they must be honoured, cannot dictate the operation of the provisions of an enabling statute which grants superior status to enactments over personal beliefs. The court thus indirectly acknowledged that, if adoption rights have been granted statutorily to an individual who is guided by personal faith which does not recognize adoption, then the statute has preference over personal belief. By implication, the JJ Act, 2000 enables Christians and Muslims to adopt. But the court did not consider the rights of adopted children and the consequences of adoption. The question of devolution of property under the ISA, 1925 to adopted children who have been adopted by Christian parent(s) under the JJ Act, 2000 remains unanswered. It is high time for the legislature to amend the ISA, 1925 for devolution of property in relation to adopted children and for the judiciary to clearly rule on the devolution rights of adopted children under the JJ Act, 2000.[89]

Adoption under the Juvenile Justice (Care and Protection) of Children Act, 2000 (amended in 2006 and 2011)

The Chapter IV of the JJ Act clearly states that the rehabilitation and social reintegration of a child shall begin during the stay of the child in children's home or special home, but as the family is the best option to provide care and protection for children, adoption is the first alternative for rehabilitation and social reintegration of orphan, abandoned, or surrendered children.[90] The aim

---

[89] Mishra, 'Bridging the Gap'.

[90] JJ Act, 2000, Section 41: Adoption—

(1) The primary responsibility for providing care and protection to children shall be that of his family.

(2) Adoption shall be resorted to for the rehabilitation of the children who are orphan, abandoned, or surrendered through such mechanism as may be prescribed.

(3) In keeping with the provisions of the various guidelines for adoption issued from time to time, by the state government, or the CARA and notified by the central government, children may be given in adoption by a court after satisfying itself regarding the investigations having been carried out as are required for giving such children in adoption.

(4) The state government shall recognize one or more of its institutions or voluntary organizations in each district as SAAs in such manner as may be prescribed for the placement of orphan, abandoned, or surrendered children for adoption in accordance with the guidelines notified under Subsection (3): Provided that the children's homes and the institutions run by the state government or a voluntary organization for children in need of care and protection, who are orphan, abandoned, or surrendered, shall ensure that these children are declared free for adoption by the committee and all such cases shall be referred to the adoption agency in that district for placement of such children in adoption in accordance with the guidelines notified under Subsection (3).

(5) No child shall be offered for adoption—

  (a) until two members of the committee declare the child legally free for placement in the case of abandoned children,

  (b) till the two months period for reconsideration by the parent is over in the case of surrendered children, and

  (c) without his consent in the case of a child who can understand and express his consent.

of rehabilitation and social reintegration is to help children in restoring their dignity and self-worth and take them to the mainstream through rehabilitation within the family where possible, or otherwise, through alternative care programmes, and long-term institutional care should be of last resort.[91]

Under the JJ Act, 2000, institutionalization should be the last resort and the following non-institutional, family-based alternatives are provided:

1. adoption
2. foster care
3. sponsorship
4. after-care organizations

Under the JJ Act, adoption is recognized as a means of rehabilitation and social reintegration of a child and is defined as a process through which the adopted child is permanently separated from biological parents and becomes the legitimate child of his adoptive parents with all rights, privileges, and responsibilities that are attached to the relationship.[92] Sections 42,[93] 43,[94]

_____

(6) The court may allow a child to be given in adoption—

    (a)   to a person irrespective of marital status;

    (b)   to parents to adopt a child of same sex irrespective of the number of living biological sons or daughters; or

    (c)   to childless couples.

  [91] JJ Rules, 2007, Rule 32.

  [92] JJ Act, 2000, Section 2(aa), amended in 2006: 'adoption' means the process through which the adopted child is permanently separated from his biological parents and becomes the legitimate child of his adoptive parents with all the rights, privileges, and responsibilities that are attached to the relationship.

  [93] JJ Act, 2000, Section 42. Foster care—

(1) The foster care may be used for temporary placement of those infants who to be given for adoption.

(2) In foster care, the child may be placed in another family for a short or extended period of time, depending upon the circumstances where the child's own parents usually visit regularly and eventually after the rehabilitation, where the children may return to their own homes.

(3) The state government may make rules for purposes of carrying out the scheme of foster care programme of children.

  [94] JJ Act, 2000, Section 43. Sponsorship—

(1) The sponsorship programme may provide supplementary support to families, to children's homes, and to special homes to meet medical, nutritional, educational, and other needs of the children with a view to improving their quality of life.

(2) The state government may make rules for the purposes of carrying out various schemes of sponsorship of children, such as individual to individual sponsorship, group sponsorship, or community sponsorship.

and 44[95] of the JJ Act, 2000 deal with alternative methods of rehabilitation, namely foster care, sponsorship, and being looked after by an after-care organization.

There was no codified legislation dealing with the adoption of the abandoned, orphaned, and surrendered children. As a result, several irregularities appeared with respect of the custody, guardianship, or adoption of these types of children, which were prejudicial to the interest of the children. An attempt has been made in Chapter IV of the JJ Act.[96] This enactment deals with the concept of secular adoption whereby without any reference to the community or religious persuasions of the parents or the child concerned, a right appears to have been granted to all citizens to adopt. Under the JJ Act, 2000, amended in 2006, persons belonging to all religions including Hindus, Muslims, Christians, and Parsis can adopt.[97]

Section 41[98] of the JJ Act, 2000 was substantially amended in 2006 and for the first time the responsibility of giving in adoption was cast upon the court, which was defined by the JJ Rules,

[95] JJ Act, 2000, Section 44 . After-care organization—The state government may, by rules made under this act, provide—

(1) for the establishment or recognition of after-care organizations and the functions that may be performed by them under this act;
(2) for a scheme of after-care programme to be followed by such after-care organizations for the purpose of taking care of juveniles or the children after they leave special homes and children homes as well as for the purpose of enabling them to lead an honest, industrious, and useful life;
(3) for the preparation or submission of a report by the probation officer or any other officer appointed by that government in respect of each juvenile or the child prior to his discharge from a special home, children's home, regarding the necessity and nature of after-care of such juvenile or of a child, the period of such after-care, supervision thereof and for the submission of report by the probation officer or any other officer appointed for the purpose, on the progress of each juvenile or the child;
(4) for the standards and the nature of services to be maintained by such after-care organizations;
(5) for such other matters as may be necessary for the purpose of carrying out the scheme of after-care programme for the juvenile or the child: provided that any rule made under this section shall not provide for such juvenile or child to stay in the after-care organization for more than 3 years; provided further that a juvenile or child over 17 years of age but less than 18 years of age would stay in the after-care organization till he attains the age of 20 years.

[96] JJ Act, 2000, amended in 2006, Chapter IV: Rehabilitation and social reintegration of the juveniles—The amendment act of 2006 for the first time provides 'adoption' as one of the many means to rehabilitate and socially reintegrate children in conflict with the law and children in need of care and protection.

[97] *Shabnam Hashmi* v. *Union of India and Ors.*, AIR 2014 SC 1281.

[98] JJ Act, 2000, Section 41. Adoption—

(1) The primary responsibility for providing care and protection to children shall be that of his family.
(2) Adoption shall be resorted to for the rehabilitation of the children who are orphan, abandoned, or surrendered through such a mechanism as may be prescribed.
(3) In keeping with the provisions of the various guidelines for adoption issued from time to time, by the state government, or the CARA and notified by the central government, children may be given in adoption by a court after satisfying itself regarding the investigations having been carried out as are required for giving such children in adoption.

2007 to mean a civil court having jurisdiction in matters of adoption and guardianship, including the court of the district judge, family courts, and the city civil court.[99] The court is empowered to allow a child to be given in adoption to the following persons[100]:

- A person irrespective of his/her marital status
- The parents to adopt a child of the same sex irrespective of the number of existing biological sons or daughters
- The childless couple

If a child is abandoned, orphan, or surrendered, then the procedure of going through the Child Welfare Committee (CWC) will have to be followed before declaring a child legally free

---

(4)   The state government shall recognize one or more of its institutions or voluntary organizations in each district as SAAs in such a manner as may be prescribed for the placement of orphan, abandoned, or surrendered children for adoption in accordance with the guidelines notified under Subsection (3); provided that the children's homes and the institutions run by the state government or a voluntary organization for children in need of care and protection, who are orphan, abandoned or surrendered, shall ensure that these children are declared free for adoption by the committee and all such cases shall be referred to the adoption agency in that district for placement of such children in adoption in accordance with the guidelines notified under Subsection (3).

(5)   No child shall be offered for adoption—

(a)   until two members of the committee declare the child legally free for placement in the case of abandoned children;

(b)   till the two-month period for reconsideration by the parent is over in the case of surrendered children; and

(c)   without his consent in the case of a child who can understand and express his consent.

(6)   The court may allow a child to be given in adoption—

(a)   to a person irrespective of marital status;

(b)   to parents to adopt a child of same sex irrespective of the number of living biological sons or daughters; or

(c)   to childless couples.

[99] JJ Rules, 2007, Rule 33(5): For the purposes of Section 41 of the act, 'court' implies a civil court, which has jurisdiction in matters of adoption and guardianship and may include the court of the district judge, family courts, and city civil court.

[100] JJ Act, 2000, Section 41(6): The court may allow a child to be given in adoption—

(1)   to a person irrespective of marital status or;

(2)   to parents to adopt a child of same sex irrespective of the number of living biological sons or daughters; or

(3)   to childless couples.

for adoption. Section 41(5)[101] of JJ Act, 2000 provides that a child shall be offered for adoption by the CWC on fulfilment of the following requirements:[102]

- In case of an abandoned child, if two members of the CWC declare the child legally free for placement.
- In case of surrendered child, if the period of two months for reconsideration by the parents is lapsed.
- In case of a child who can understand and express his consent, if his/her consent is obtained in this regard.

It is significant to note that under Section 41(c) of the JJ Act, 2000, the child cannot be offered in adoption without his consent if he can understand and express his consent. This is an attempt to provide the right of participation to the child in an important decision of his/her life.

Juvenile Justice (Care and Protection of Children) Act, 2015[103]

The JJ Act, 2015[104] came into force on 1 January 2016 after the president of India gave his assent to the bill on 31 December 2015. The 2015 Act repeals and replaces the JJ Act, 2000. The act streamlines adoption[105] procedures for orphaned, abandoned, and surrendered children. The

---

[101] JJ Act, 2000, Section 41(5): No child shall be offered for adoption—

(1) until two members of the committee declare the child legally free for placement in the case of abandoned children,

(2) till the two-month period for reconsideration by the parent is over in the case of surrendered children, and

(3) without his consent in the case of a child who can understand and express his consent.

[102] JJ Act, 2000, Section 29 provides for the CWC. The committee has the sole authority to declare in need of care and protection the children who are orphan, abandoned, or surrendered free for adoption. The CWC shall determine legal status of all orphan, abandoned, and surrendered children. Functions and powers of the committee, procedure in relation to the committee, production of child before committee, procedure for inquiry, procedure related to orphan and abandoned children, and procedure related to surrendered children shall be governed as laid down in the amended JJ Act, 2006 and its rules. On clearance from CWC that a particular child is free for adoption, there will be termination of parental right.

[103] *Gazette of India*, 1 January 2016, available at http://wcd.nic.in/sites/default/files/JJ%20Act,%202015%20_0.pdf (accessed on 20 September 2016); JJ Act, 2015, available at http://www.wcd.nic.in/sites/default/files/JJAct2015.pdf (accessed on 25 September 2016).

[104] *Gazette of India*, 1 January 2016, available at http://wcd.nic.in/sites/default/files/JJ%20Act,%202015%20_0.pdf (accessed on 20 September 2016); JJ Act, 2015, available at http://www.wcd.nic.in/sites/default/files/JJAct2015.pdf (accessed on 25 September 2016).

[105] JJ Act, 2015, Section 2(2): 'adoption' means the process through which the adopted child is permanently separated from his biological parents and becomes the lawful child of his adoptive parents with all the rights, privileges and responsibilities that are attached to a biological child.

other non-institutional options include: sponsorship[106] and foster care[107] including group foster care[108] for placing children in a family environment which is other than child's biological family, which is to be selected, qualified, approved, and supervised for providing care to children. It also has several rehabilitation and social integration measures for institutional and non-institutional children

Some of the salient features of the JJ Act, 2015 relating to adoption are:

- The CARA is given the status of a statutory body to enable it to perform its function more effectively.[109] It primarily deals with adoption of orphan, abandoned and surrendered children through its associated/recognized adoption agencies.
- As per the very definition of adoption under JJ Act 2015, the adopted child is permanently separated from his biological parents and becomes the lawful child of his adoptive parents with all the rights, privileges and responsibilities that are attached to a biological child including succession and inheritance rights.
- The JJ Act, 2015 has tried to make the adoption process of orphaned, abandoned, and surrendered children more streamlined while adopting some of the concepts from the Hague Convention on Protection of Children and Cooperation in Respect of Inter-Country which India has ratified in 2003. Adoption shall be resorted to for ensuring right to family for the orphan, abandoned, and surrendered children.[110]
- Establishment for a state adoption resource agency (SARA) and the CARA which monitors, regulates, and make rules in regards to adoption of children.[111]
- Parents giving up their child for adoption will get 3 months to reconsider, compared to the earlier provision of 1 month.
- Adoptive parents should be financially and physically sound. A single or divorced person may adopt a child.
- A single male may not adopt a girl child.
- Disabled children will be given priority for adoption.
- Children in need of care and protection can allowed to be placed in foster care based on the orders of the CWC. The selection of the foster family is based on the family's ability, intent, capacity, and prior experience of taking care of children. Families will sign up for foster care

---

[106] JJ Act, 2015, Section 2(58): 'sponsorship' means provision of supplementary support, financial or otherwise, to the families to meet the medical, educational, and developmental needs of the child.

[107] JJ Act, 2015, Section 2(29): 'foster care' means placement of a child, by the committee for the purpose of alternate care in the domestic environment of a family, other than the child's biological family, that has been selected, qualified, approved and supervised for providing such care.

[108] JJ Act, 2015, Section 2(32): 'group foster care' means a family like care facility for children in need of care and protection who are without parental care, aiming on providing personalized care and fostering a sense of belonging and identity, through family like and community based solutions.

[109] The CARA is the nodal body for adoption of Indian children and is mandated to monitor and regulate in-country adoption and inter-country adoption (ICA). It is designated as the central authority (CA) to deal with ICAs in accordance with the provisions of the Hague Convention on Inter-country Adoption, 1993, ratified by Government of India in 2003.

[110] JJ Act, 2015, Section 56.

[111] JJ Act, 2015, Sections 67 and 68.

and abandoned, orphaned children, or those in conflict with the law will be sent to them. The selection of the foster family shall be based on family's ability, intent, capacity, and prior experience of taking care of children.[112] Such families will be monitored and shall receive financial aid from the state.[113] The foster family shall be responsible for providing education, health, and nutrition to the child and shall ensure the overall well-being of the child. No child regarded as adoptable by the committee shall be given for long-term foster care.[114]

- ICA is allowed when no Indian adoptive parents are available within 30 days of child being declared free for adoption.
- New offences including illegal adoption are also incorporated in the proposed legislation.[115]

Critique of Laws and Practice Related to Adoption[116]

The issue of 'gender injustice' is also evident in the practice of adoption. 'Childlessness' is not seen as a human problem, and the stigma of 'infertility' is attached only to the woman. The man is often forced to remarry and the male infertility factor is never under question. Patriarchal religious values are evident and implicit in the social practice of adoption as well as in the law of adoption. Research on Parliamentary debates shows that the objections raised by various religions towards the acceptance of a uniform adoption law are also based on the issue of succession, inheritance, and property rights. Considerable social consciousness bereft of any religious dogma among the masses and the social reformers and lawmakers is required for the evolution of a proper adoption law and its trouble-free practical implementation.

Critique of Hindu Adoption and Maintenance Act, 1956

The HAMA, 1956, is not a child-oriented legislation, but rather, parent-oriented. It is a religion-based law applicable only to Hindus. It is also not child-centred, since it is not a response of the society to the destitute, orphan, or abandoned child in an attempt to provide a 'home to the homeless'.

The HAMA is an attempt to de-emphasize the religious significance of adoption and put it on a secular basis. The performance of the religious ceremony Dattaka Homa is no longer essential.[117] But the physical act of giving and taking by the parties concerned is essential for its

---

[112] JJ Act, 2015, Section 44: The criteria for sponsorship shall include—

(1) where mother is a widow or divorced or abandoned by family;
(2) where children are orphan and are living with the extended family;
(3) where parents are victims of life threatening disease; or
(4) where parents are incapacitated due to accident and unable to take care of children both financially and physically.

[113] JJ Act, 2015, Section 44.

[114] JJ Act, 2015, Section 44.

[115] JJ Act, 2015, Section 80.

[116] Bajpai, *Adoption Law*.

[117] In *Madhusudhan Das* v. *Narayanibai*, 1983 SC 114, it was held that for a valid adoption the ceremony of giving and taking is an essential requisite on all adoptions, whatever the caste.

validity (HAMA, Section 11(iv)). Further, all the parties concerned—the natural parents, the adoptive parents, and the child—must be Hindus.[118]

Even today it is necessary to establish the religion of the child as Hindu if it is to be given or taken validly in adoption under the HAMA. Section 2(bb),[119] added in 1962 to cover abandoned children, states that such abandoned children shall be 'brought up' as Hindus. What it means to 'be brought up' as Hindus is still not very clear and needs to be defined. Such lack of clarity may give rise to contentious issues like the following:

- A Hindu male or female could have been allowed under the act to adopt a non-Hindu child also. Further, since on adoption the adopted child 'shall be deemed to be the child of his adoptive father or mother for all purposes', the child would then be a Hindu by religion.
- Under the HAMA, the court gets jurisdiction only in cases when a guardian other than the parents give the child in adoption. When the father or mother gives his/her child in adoption they need not go through the courts. This may lead to abuse and exploitation by the parents due to poverty and other causes. Therefore, all cases of adoption, whether by parents or guardians, should be through courts so that all in-country adoptions can be regulated and monitored.
- Under the HAMA, when an unmarried person or a widow/widower or divorcee adopts a child and subsequently marries, the other spouse is only the stepfather/stepmother of the child.[120]

Section 11(1) of the HAMA lays down that when a Hindu male or female desires to adopt a son, s/he can do so only when s/he has no Hindu son or son's son living at the time of adoption, whether by legitimate blood relation or by adoption. Similarly, no Hindu can adopt a daughter, if s/he already has a Hindu daughter or son's daughter living at the time of adoption. This provision seems to be discriminatory to illegitimate children and needs to be remedied. This means that the existence of an illegitimate son/daughter is no bar irrespective of the fact whether the adoption is by a male or female. In other words, if a woman has an illegitimate son, she can also adopt a son and if a Hindu male has an illegitimate son, he too can adopt a son. There could be a provision in the adoption law that the putative father can, by declaration before the proper legal forum, adopt his child as legitimate.[121]

Adoption is a specialized childcare service and needs to be handled by specialized courts—for instance, adoption cells in family courts could be established for this purpose, rather than civil courts.

---

[118] Therefore, Hindus could be by religion, by birth, and by negative definition, that is, by explaining who are not Hindus. Persons capable of giving and taking in adoption lose their capacity if they cease to be Hindus.

[119] See HAMA, 1956, Section 2(bb).

[120] HAMA, 1956, Section 14. Also see *Sitabai v. Ramchandra* (1969) 2 SCC 544, wherein it was held that when a widower or bachelor adopts a child and he gets married subsequent to the adoption, his wife becomes the stepmother of the adopted child. In case of there being two wives, the child becomes the adopted child of the senior wife in marriage and the junior wife becomes the stepmother of the adopted child.

[121] M.P.P. Pillai, *The Law of Adoption in India: Need for a Fresh Approach* (Bangalore, India: Rights of the Child, NLSIU, 1990).

The child, if he is capable of understanding, should be involved in the adoption process. There is no provision in the HAMA for it. The desire of the child should be ascertained before an adoption is made. The child should be counselled so that he/she is prepared to enter a new home.

The requirement under Section 10 of the HAMA, that the adoptee must not have completed the age of 15 years, does not appear to be reasonable. A minor child who has completed that age may still be in as much need of being adopted as one below that age.

Under Section 9 of the HAMA, if the father changes his religion, he loses his right to give his child in adoption and the right stands transferred to the mother, and if the mother changes her religion, she loses her right to be consulted and to prevent her child from being given in adoption without her consent. Thus, there is discrimination between a father and mother continuing to be Hindus and a father or mother ceasing to be a Hindu, based solely on religion, which violates Article 15(1) of the Constitution.[122]

According to the succession laws of India, an illegitimate child cannot inherit its father even if the genetic father is known. A father cannot cease to be a father simply because he is not lawfully wedded to the mother of the child. Therefore, an illegitimate child should be allowed to inherit the property of his putative/genetic father.

The adoptive parents are the natural guardians of their adopted minor child, first the father and then the mother. If the adopted child is less than 5 years, the adoptive mother will have preferential claim to the custody of the child.[123] This section should be amended as per the Law Commission recommendations. Mother should have the same and equal rights vis-à-vis father and the custody of the minor who has not completed 12 years of age shall ordinarily be with the mother.[124] This will be in the interest of the child.

The HMGA, 1956 (Sections 6 and 7) provides that a Hindu parent 'ceasing to be a Hindu' shall not 'be entitled to act as the natural guardian'. This provision has, therefore, classified Hindu

---

[122] Constitution of India, Article 15: Prohibition of discrimination on grounds of religion, race, caste, sex, or place of birth.

(1) The state shall not discriminate against any citizen on grounds only of religion, race, caste, sex, place of birth, or any of them.

[123] The provision contained in HMGA, 1956, Section 6(a).

[124] Some of the recommendations are: 'Mother' should have same and equal (and not inferior) rights vis à vis 'father'.

The provision contained in HMGA, 1956, Section 6(a), constituting the father as a natural guardian of a Hindu minor's person as well as in respect of his property in 'preference' to the mother, should be amended so as to constitute both the father and the mother as being natural guardians 'jointly and severally', having equal rights in respect of the minor. There is no justification for according a superior and preferential treatment to the father vis-à-vis the mother of the minor because it violates the spirit and conscience of Article 15 of the Constitution of India.

The custody of a minor who has not completed 12 years of age shall ordinarily be with the mother.

The proviso to Subsection (a) of HMGA, Section 6 deserves to be amended so that the custody of a boy or an unmarried girl who has not completed the age of 12 years (instead of the age limit of 5 years as prescribed at present) shall ordinarily be with the mother. Law Commission of India, *One Hundred Thirty-third Report on Removal of Discrimination against Women in Matters Relating to Guardianship and Custody of Minor Children and Elaboration of the Welfare Principle 1986.*

children into two categories—children whose parents continue to be Hindu and children whose parents have ceased to be Hindu—and has discriminated against the latter by providing for them the loss of their natural guardian. It is not at all fair and just to disrupt the parental home of the child solely because one of the parents has chosen to renounce his/her religion. This provision should be amended as it violates Article 15 of the Constitution.[125]

Under the HAMA, inheritance of property is automatic. Muslims, Christians, Parsis, and Jews have to resort to the GWA, 1890. The guardian–ward relationship does not have the force of law beyond the time when the child reaches the age of majority. The child does not gain automatically the privileges of permanent family linkages such as name, religion, properties, and inheritance, as in a legal adoption. This is again discrimination against children solely on the grounds of religion, and hence violates Article 15 of the Constitution.[126]

The definition of a 'child' varies under different legislations. The HAMA defines the child as not older than 15 years of age, and the GWA defines the child as not older than 18 years of age, unless it is a ward of the state. In the latter case, the age limit extends to 21 years. There should be uniformity regarding the minority of the child.

Any discrimination against the adopted child should be punishable by law. There is no provision regarding this under the HAMA.

- The focus of the adoption law is on the transfer of property, not on having a child, nor on enjoying parenthood.
- That adoption and maintenance matters are incorporated together under one law is also reflective of patriarchal biases.

The JJ Act is silent on the issue of ICA but in practice the adoption formalities have to be completed before the child is taken out of the country. This is a welcome move as earlier the child was taken as a ward with the hope that he would be adopted in the country of adoption as per the laws of that country, which may not always happen, and there were instances of malpractices and abuse. The functionaries in the juvenile justice system need training to carry out the provisions of the act in its true spirit.

Finally, there should have been a specific provision to make democratic institutions like Zilaa Parishads,[127] municipalities, or Panchayati Raj[128] responsible for the welfare of children.[129]

Under the JJ Act, 2015, foster care is restricted to children in need of care and protection. Also the definition of short or extended period is not specified. Sponsorship is not available to single

---

[125] Article 15(1): The state shall not discriminate against any citizen on grounds only of religion, race, caste, sex, place of birth, or any of them.

[126] For all practical purposes, however, guardianship placements are also treated like adoption. The child takes the guardian's family name and religion. With respect to a share in the family property, the guardian or any family member may make a will in favour of the child. Nevertheless, a guardianship placement will not stand the test of a legal challenge of adoption.

[127] District-level administrative structures.

[128] Village-level administrative structures.

[129] In England, according to the provisions of the Children Act, 1980, in the case of any person under 18 years who is a subject of a court order, it will be the duty of every local authority to make available such advice, guidance, and assistance as may promote the welfare of children.

fathers under this act. There are a lot of challenging responsibilities given to the CWC including declaring a child free for adoption. Many of them are temporary part-time members. At least some CWC members must be full-time salaried personnel.

Inter-country Adoption

Inter-country adoption (ICA) is the process by which you adopt a child from a country other than your own through permanent legal means and bring that child to your country of residence to live with you permanently. It consists of the legal transfer of parental rights and responsibilities from a child's birth parent(s) or other guardian to a new parent or parents. The ICA could be regarded as a lawful act when all measures have been exhausted by the state to keep the child with his/her family of origin, and if the child cannot remain with the original family, all measures have been exhausted by the state to provide for alternative care in the country of origin, and after paramount consideration of the best interest of the child, ICA as a measure of alternative childcare has been considered as a last resort.[130]

The concept of ICA is a relatively new concept in India. It did not find place in the top priorities of the legislators. There was not and still does not exist a legislation which primarily provides for ICA. But in the year 1984, the Honourable Supreme Court of India in a landmark case of *Laxmikant Pandey* v. *Union of India*,[131] laid down a few principles governing the rules for ICA. The case was instituted on the basis of a letter addressed to the court by a lawyer, Laxmikant Pandey, alleging that social organizations and voluntary agencies engaging in the work of offering Indian children to foreign parents are indulged in malpractices. It was alleged that these adopted children were not only exposed to long horrendous journey to distant foreign countries at the risk of their life, but they also ultimately become prostitutes and beggars. The Supreme Court, in this case, expressed its opinion and framed certain rules for ICA.

The Honourable Court asserted in Paragraph 8 of the judgment:

> [W]hile supporting Inter-Country adoption, it is necessary to bear in mind that the primary object of giving the child in adoption being the welfare of the people, great care has to be exercised in permitting the child to be given in adoption to foreign parents, lest the child may be neglected or abandoned by the adoptive parents in the foreign country or the adoptive parents may not be able provide to the child a life of moral and material security or the child may be subjected to moral and sexual abuse or forced labour or experimentation for medical or other research and may be placed in worse situation than that in his own country.

It further went on to give the prerequisites for foreign adoption. It stated:

> In the first place, every application from a foreigner desiring to adopt a child must be sponsored by social or child welfare agency recognized or licensed by the government of the country in which the foreigner is a resident. No application by a foreigner for taking a child in adoption should be

---

[130] R. Hodgkin and P. Newell, *Implementation Handbook for the Convention on the Rights of the Child* (Geneva: UNICEF, 2002), p. 298. Available at http://www.unicef.org/publications/files/Implementation_Handbook_for_the_Convention_on_the_Rights_of_the_Child.pdf (accessed on 11 September 2015).

[131] AIR 1984 SC 469.

entertained directly by any social welfare agency in India working in the area of Inter-Country adoption or by any institution or centre or home to which children are committed by the juvenile court.

The Supreme Court also insisted the age within which a child should be adopted in case of ICA: 'If a child is to be given in Inter-Country adoption, it would be desirable that it is given in such adoption before it completes the age of 3 years.' Such a ruling was delivered by the Supreme Court because it felt if a child is adopted by a foreign parent before he/she attains the age of 3, he/she has more chances of assimilating to the new environment and culture. Another important rule framed by the court during the course of judgment was that '[s]ince there is no statutory enactment in our country providing for adoption of a child by foreign parents or laying down the procedures which must be followed in such a case, resort had to be taken to the provisions of Guardian and Wards Act, 1890 for the purpose of felicitating such adoption.'

The Bombay High Court in *Re Jay Kevin Salerno*[132] iterated that 'where the custody of a child is with an institution, the child is kept in a private nursing home or with a private party for better individual care of the child; it does not mean that the institution ceases to have the custody of the child'. Therefore it may be submitted that in the absence of any explicit legislation on the subject, the Supreme Court has played a pivotal role in regulating the adoption of tender aged children to foreign parents.

A Hindu, even if he is a foreigner, that is, a national of another country, may adopt a Hindu child in India in accordance with the provisions of the HAMA. The only way in which a foreigner parent can take an Indian child in adoption is by becoming a guardian of the child under the GWA. The provisions of the GWA are applicable in case of ICA. Section 7[133] of the said act provides that, when the district court is satisfied that appointment of the guardian will be for the welfare of the minor, it appoints one. But the person appointed should come under any of the four categories mentioned in the act. These four categories are:[134]

[132] AIR 1988 BOM 139

[133] GWA, 1890, Section 7: Power of the court to make order as to guardianship—

(1) Where the court is satisfied that it is for the welfare of a minor that an order should be made—

   (a)   appointing a guardian of his person or property or both, or
   (b)   declaring a person to be such a guardian the Court may make an order accordingly.

(2) An order under this section shall imply the removal of any guardian who has not been appointed by will or other instrument or appointed or declared by the court.

(3) Where a guardian has been appointed by will or other instrument or appointed or declared by the court, an order under this section appointing or declaring another person to be guardian in his stead shall not be made until the powers of the guardian appointed or declared as aforesaid have ceased under the provisions of this act.

[134] GWA, 1890, Section 8: Persons entitled to apply for order—An order shall not be made under the last foregoing section except on the application of—

(1) the person desirous of being, or claiming to be, the guardian of the minor;
(2) any relative or friend of the minor;
(3) the collector of the district or other local area within which the minor ordinarily resides or in which he has property; or
(4) the collector having authority with respect to the class to which the minor belongs.

1. any person desirous of being guardian of the minor,
2. any relative or friend of the minor,
3. the collector of the district within whose jurisdiction the minor resides or in which he has property, or
4. the collector having authority with respect to the class to which the minor belongs.

The foreign parents desirous of adopting an Indian child makes an application to the court for being appointed guardian of the person and property of the child whom he wishes to take in adoption, and on being appointed the guardian, for leave of the court to take the child with him to his country for taking it in adoption.[135] As, since most of the children sought to be adopted are destitute and orphans, the notice under Section 11[136] of the act has no specific meaning. In their case, there is no agency which can look into the question whether the proposed adoption will be in their welfare or not. Thus, the High Court of Delhi rules provide that a notice should be sent to the Indian Council of Child Welfare, whereas the Bombay[137] and Gujarat[138] high courts rules provide for notice being sent to the Indian Council for Social Welfare (ICSW). Every child-welfare agency is required to get a license.[139] They are also required to maintain a register in which the names and particulars of all the children proposed to be given in ICA through it

[135] *Laxmikant Pandey* v. *Union Of India*, 1984 AIR 469.

[136] GWA, 1890, Section 11: Procedure on admission of application—

(1) If the court is satisfied that there is ground for proceeding on the application, it shall fix a day for the hearing thereof, and cause notice of the application and of the date fixed for the hearing—

    (a) to be served in the manner directed in the Code of Civil Procedure (CPC),1882 (14 of 1882)11 on—

        (i) the parents of the minor if they are residing in any state to which this act extends;

        (ii) the person, if any, named in the petition or letter as having the custody or possession of the person or property of the minor;

        (iii) the person proposed in the application or letter to be appointed or declared guardian, unless that person is himself the applicant; and

        (iv) any other person to whom, in the opinion of the court, special notice of the applicant should be given; and

    (b) to be posted on some conspicuous part of the court-house and of the residence of the minor, and otherwise published in such manner as the court, subject to any rules made by the high court under this act, thinks fit.

(2) The state government may, by general or special order, require that when any part of the property described in a petition under Section 10, Subsection (1), is land of which a Court of Wards could assume the superintendence, the court shall also cause a notice as aforesaid to be served on the collector in whose district the minor ordinarily resides and on every collector in whose district any portion of the land is situated, and the collector may cause the notice to be published in any manner he deems fit.

(3) No charge shall be made by the court or the collector for the service or publication of any notice served or published under Subsection (2).

[137] Rules of the High Court of Bombay (Original Side), 1957, Rule 361-B, notice dated 10 May 1972.

[138] *Re Rasiklal Chhaganlal Mehta*, AIR 1982 Guj 193.

[139] *Laxmikant Pandey* v. *Union of India*, 1984 AIR 469.

should be kept. The child welfare agency processing the adoption must place sufficient material before the court to satisfy that the child is legally available for adoption. It is imperative that the application for adoption of an Indian child by a foreigner should be sponsored by a social- or child-welfare agency recognized and licensed by the government of the country in which the foreigner is a resident.[140] There are three reasons for this:

1. It will reduce the possibility of profiteering and trafficking in children.
2. The court will not be able to satisfy itself about the eligibility of the parents unless it is backed by the agency of the country in which the foreigner resides.
3. In case adoption is made without the intervention of any agency, there would no authority or agency which could be made responsible for supervising the growth of the child.

These agencies are required to submit a home study report which includes, among others, the following:

1. source of referral,
2. schooling facilities,
3. current relationship between husband and wife, and so on.

Along with this report, the agency is also required to send a photograph of the family and a declaration stating that the family is willing to adopt the child in accordance with the law prevailing in their country. In case the child's biological parents exist, they should be properly assisted in making a decision about giving away the child in adoption to foreign parents by the child welfare agency to which the child is surrendered for making arrangement for its adoption. If the child is an orphan or destitute, then the agency must try to trace its biological parents before giving in adoption. If the agency is a non-registered agency, then it must contact a registered agency for giving in adoption. The district court is required to dispose of all the applications at the earliest, in no case later than two months from the date of filing of an application. Section 17[141] of the GWA provides that in appointing guardian of a minor, the court shall be guided by what, consistently with the law to which the minor is subject, appears in the circumstances to be for the welfare of the minor; and in considering what will be for the welfare of the minor, the court shall have regard

---

[140] CARA Guidelines, 2015, Para 38(13) authorize foreign adoption agencies (FAAs) to sponsor applications of NRIs or overseas citizen of India or foreign PAPs for ICA of Indian children.

[141] GWA, 1890, Section 17: Matters to be considered by the court in appointing guardian—

(1) In appointing or declaring the guardian of a minor, the court shall, subject to the provisions of this section, be guided by what, consistently with the law to which the minor is subject, appears in the circumstances to be for the welfare of the minor.

(2) In considering what will be for the welfare of the minor, the court shall have regard to the age, sex and religion of the minor, the character and capacity of the proposed guardian and his nearness of kin to the minor, the wishes, if any, of a deceased parent, and any existing or previous relations of the proposed guardian with the minor or his property.

(3) If minor is old enough to form an intelligent preference, the court may consider that preference.

(4) The court shall not appoint or declare any person to be a guardian against his will.

to the age, sex, and religion of the minor. The main function of the Council of Social Welfare or any other recognized agency in ICA is to help the court in finding what is for the welfare of the people. For this purpose the council prepares a report called *Child Study Report*. This report contains legal and social data regarding the child. The report should also contain an assessment of the child's behavioural pattern and its intellectual, emotional, and physical development. It should also contain a recent photograph of the child and information about the original parents.

Selecting an Agency

It is another aspect that needs to be taken care of when a person wants to adopt a kid from another country. It is always advisable to use a reputable agency with experience in ICA. Although the quality can vary, the adoption agencies are regulated by the state government. If the child is given in adoption without the help of the agency, then there are possibilities of involvement in the black market, loss of confidentiality, and infringements upon the child's right to privacy and permanency. Therefore, it is always desirable to give the child in adoption through a reputed adoption agency.

The GWA applies to all minor children of any caste and creed, though in appointing or declaring a person as guardian, the court will take into consideration the personal law of the minor.[142] But once a person is appointed or declared as guardian of a minor, irrespective of the fact whether the minor is a Hindu, or a Muslim, or subject to any personal law, such a guardian will be subject to the provisions of the GWA.

Section 7 of the GWA deals with the powers of the court to appoint or declare a person as guardian. The procedure under the GWA is as follows: Any person who claims or desires to be the guardian of the minor, or who is a relative or friend of the minor, or the collector (GWA, Section 8) of the district, shall make an application to the district or family court where the minor ordinarily resides (GWA, Section 9). On receipt of the application of a person if the court comes to the conclusion that it would be for the welfare of the child to appoint a guardian of the person of the minor, it can appoint the guardian.[143]

In considering what will be the welfare of the minor, the court shall take into account the age, sex, and religion of the minor; the character and capacity of the adopter; and the wishes of the deceased parent. If the minor is able to form an intelligent opinion, the court will consider his/her preference also.

Therefore, the personal law of the minor has to be taken into consideration at this time, along with the welfare of the child. The judicial attitude is fairly well settled that the welfare of the minor has been given greater significance than the rights of the parties under the personal law in deciding the question of guardianship under the act. When the court is satisfied that the appointment is for the welfare of the minor, an order appointing a guardian may be made in any one of the three forms:[144]

---

[142] In effect, the procedural law regarding the appointment or declaration of the person as a guardian is laid down in the GWA, yet the substantive part is still the personal law. Paras Diwan, *Law of Adoption, Minority, Custody and Guardianship* (Allahabad, India: Wadhwa and Co., 1989), p. 345.

[143] See GWA, 1890, Section 17.

[144] *Tuminra Khatun* v. *Ghariya Bibi*, AIR 1942 Cal. 281; *Mir* v. *Munji*, AIR 1952 Mad. 280, AIR 1983 J&K 70; *Bholanath* v. *Sharda Devi*, AIR 1954 Pat 489; *Smt Bhagwat Devi* v. *Muralidhar Sahu*, AIR 1943

- a simple order where no security is asked for;
- an order appointing a person as guardian and asking him to furnish security within a specified time; and
- an order appointing a guardian on the condition that he should furnish security.

An order appointing a person as guardian under Section 7 amounts to the termination of the guardianship of all persons who have the care of the child, his person, or property, as the case may be. In passing the order for guardianship, the court may order or issue directions in respect to collateral matters also.

A foreigner, therefore, wishing to take an Indian child for adoption, has to use the aforementioned very circuitous way under the GWA. The order would appoint the person as guardian of the child with leave to move the child out of India and take him/her to his own country for the purpose of adopting him/her, in accordance with the law of his/her country.

Role of Scrutinizing Agencies

The Supreme Court has recognized the Indian Council for Child Welfare (ICCW) and the ICSW as the agencies for the purpose of scrutiny of adoption cases.[145] Scrutinizing agencies are appointed by the court to facilitate the processing of applications as well as related documents with regard to the children being given in in-country adoption and ICA. The scrutinizing agency has to ascertain and verify whether[146]

- the giving institution is recognized by the Government of India to place children in foreign countries;
- the institution processing the cases in the receiving country has recognition from the Government of India; and
- the child is legally free for adoption.

In recent years, cases of abuses in the system of ICA have been frequently reported. There have been some significant ICA scandals in India. A public interest litigation (PIL) filed by an NGO called Advait Foundation in the Supreme Court of India revealed that by an estimate, about 600 to 800 Indian children are adopted by foreigners every year, despite allegations that these children are often abused after adoption and that large-scale rackets fraudulently obtain consent from parents whose children are taken away.[147] Some of the cases that were given a lot of media publicity were the *Preet Mandir* caseand the Andhra Pradesh adoption scandals.

PC 106. In all these cases the court has stated that the principal matter to be considered is the welfare of the minor irrespective of the personal law of the child.

[145] AIR 1986 SC 272.

[146] D. Paul Chowdhry, *Inter-country Adoption: Social and Legal Aspects* (New Delhi, ICCW, 1988), pp. 80–81.

[147] Harish V. Nair, *Mail Today*, New Delhi, 17 May 2015. Available at http://indiatoday.intoday.in/story/foreigners-adopting-indian-children-child-trafficking/1/438531.html (accessed on 22 August 2015).

Adoption Scandals

Inter-country adoptions generally envisage an image of happily married couples adopting orphaned and poor children or special children from India and giving them a home. However, these often result in many corrupt adoption scams abhorrently being run in the name of ICAs. Examples of two such scandals have been highlighted as follows.

Preet Mandir Scandal

Preet Mandir, a voluntary childcare and adoption organization, was founded in 1979 by the late Sardar Kartar Singh Anand. It was managed by the Balwant Kartar Anand Foundation, which is registered at Kanpur in Uttar Pradesh. In 1997, one of the founding trustees, Sardar Joginder Singh Bhasin (J.S. Bhasin), took over the management and started expanding Preet Mandir. The foundation ran several units and had planned projects in other states.[148]

In 1987, a PIL was filed against the state of Maharashtra, alleging that the conditions at a government-run home, Shishu Sadan, were appalling. As a result of this litigation, the Maharashtra government, on 15 July 2002, entrusted the overall management of this unit to Preet Mandir. Thereafter, new qualified staff consisting of a superintendent, 3 social workers, and 30 caretakers was engaged. The agreement was initially for only 1 year, but it has subsequently been extended.[149]

The first public sign that several things were wrong at Preet Mandir was a newspaper article in the *Indian Express* in early 1999.[150] The article surfaced, following a press conference at Preet Mandir concerning a controversy surrounding the child. Apparently, Preet Mandir had been under attack for allegedly offering money to the mother and for not making serious efforts to search for her.[151] Eventually, the child was reunited with his mother.[152] Preet Mandir, while describing the incidents as unfortunate, maintained that whatever it had done was within the confines of the law.[153]

In a complaint to CARA, Adoptions Centrum Sweden claimed that Preet Mandir was demanding $6,000 per child, in contravention of the CARA guidelines, which prescribed a maximum of $600 to $1,500. After a personal visit to Preet Mandir, the India Program for Adoptions Centrum Sweden concluded that 'the fee is too high, the care of the children bad and that the children are allocated too early for intercountry adoptions'. Adoptions Centrum informed other Nordic adoption agencies as well as Euradopt about this case.[154]

---

[148] Arun Dohle, 'Inside Story of an Adoption Scandal', *Cumberland Law Review* 39,1 (2009) (Birmingham). Available at https://www.brandeis.edu/investigate/adoption/docs/adoption_Dohle_cumb_final.pdf (accessed on 8 September 2015).

[149] Dohle, 'Inside Story'.

[150] *Indian Express*, 'Preet Mandir Says Its Hands Are Clean', 9 January 1999.

[151] *Indian Express*, 'Preet Mandir'.

[152] *Indian Express*, 'Preet Mandir'.

[153] *Indian Express*, 'Preet Mandir'.

[154] Dohle, 'Inside Story'.

The CARA sent a show cause notice to Preet Mandir, stating: 'The organization has not denied that a sum of $6,000 was suggested as expected payment for adoption of an Indian child, from an Irish couple … in contravention of CARA guidelines.' Consequently, the license of Preet Mandir was suspended until further orders on 25 August 2000.[155]

Following a complaint by Colonel Sukhdeo Singh, CARA requested the state government to conduct a detailed inquiry of the orphanage. At CARA's request, a team led by C.B. Turkar, Deputy Secretary, Ministry of Women and Children Development (WCD), investigated the matter. The investigation concluded the following:[156]

- Preet Mandir charged excessive fees in violation of CARA guidelines.
- The case files were not properly maintained. Some files did not even contain the *Home Study Report*, or the report was unsatisfactory. Many closed files did not have statements which proved or verified that the child had been handed over to the adoptive or biological parents.
- The register maintained for in-country adoption was incomplete. The addresses were incomplete, containing just the name of the state.
- The register maintained on non-resident Indian (NRI) parents was incomplete. Most addresses of NRI parents were Indian addresses, and their parents' addresses were missing.
- The agency had a license to house children up to 6 years of age. However, there were 22 children who were 6 years or older.
- The children housed in Unit 1 were found to be under-weight, and the medical files of the children hardly showed any increase in the weight of the children over time.[157]

The CARA inspection team was critical about the practices of Preet Mandir. Rooms were congested with children, with two to three lying in one cradle. Some 18 per cent of the children had died, and most had died within two months of birth and admission.[158] Many children were reported to have died of septicaemia, a widespread destruction of tissues due to absorption of disease, caused by bacteria or other toxins in the bloodstream. The team made the following overall observations regarding child care. Preet Mandir housed more than 300 children in all three of its units. These children were either committed or on remand. It also had a large strength of caretakers, nurses, professional social workers, and an adequate infrastructure to take care of children in need, but it required drastic improvements in functioning. Counselling to biological parents, adoptive parents, and promotional work seemed to be inadequate.[159] Social workers should have been more oriented towards providing assistance to parents, both biological and adoptive, and not dealing with them with a commercial objective. Efforts for placement of children in Indian adoption were limited. The data on adoption also indicated that the focus on in-country adoption was very low in comparison to inter-country and NRI adoption.[160] The committee suggested

---

[155] Dohle, 'Inside Story'.
[156] C.B Turkar's Report, Deputy Secretary, DWCD, Government of Maharashtra (4 July 2003).
[157] Turkar's Report.
[158] CARA Inspection Report, 20 May 2004.
[159] CARA Inspection Report.
[160] CARA Inspection Report.

that as an immediate measure, for the next three months, the agency should not propose ICA for any child less than 2 years of age except those with special needs or handicapped children. During this period, the agency should strengthen its in-country adoption programme to utilize the vast infrastructure and professional staff available to it; set up an advisory committee on child care, adoption matters, finance, and accounts; and also broad base the management of the organization.[161]

Andhra Pradesh Adoption Scandal

The Andhra Pradesh adoption scandal can be presented as a chronology of increasingly serious, cyclical adoption scandals. Although it is possible to begin the story earlier, it is convenient to begin with the events of 1995–96.[162] During that period, a particular individual working in the United States Embassy in Madras (now called Chennai) began to hold up ICAs based on suspicions of irregularities. The suspicions centred around an orphanage called Action for Social Development (ASD), run by Sanjeeva Rao. The PAPs generally responded by continuing to seek the adoption and emigration of 'their children'. It appeared that eventually the children whose adoptions had been held up by the United States Embassy were granted visas and allowed to travel to the United States. Some children were transferred away from ASD to other orphanages due to the allegations.[163]

The next phase of the scandal broke in March and April of 1999, and once again involved Sanjeeva Rao and his orphanage, ASD. This time, another individual, Peter Subbaiah, who ran the Good Samaritan Evangelical and Social Welfare Association, was also implicated.[164] The primary accusation concerned buying babies from a tribal group called the Lambada. The Lambada were a traditionally nomadic people, now settled into hamlets (called *tandas*) and surviving primarily through subsistence farming and farm labour, often under conditions of severe poverty. The Lambada had previously practised the custom of bride price, but had adopted the culturally predominant Indian dowry system, which requires the family of the bride to pay a substantial sum to the groom's family in order to arrange her marriage. In addition, the Lambada were said to believe that the third, sixth, and ninth child was, if a girl, 'inauspicious'.[165] They were allegedly prone both to female infanticide, and also to selling, for very modest sums, some of their female infants.[166] Press accounts in India referred to their 'fair complexion' as making

---

[161] Inspection Report conducted on the projects implemented by Preet Mandir, Pune, between 20 and 23 May 2004 (20 September 2006).

[162] David M. Smolin, 'Intercountry Adoption as Child Trafficking', *Valparaiso Law Review* 39, 2 (June 2005): 281–325 (Indiana). Available at http://works.bepress.com/david_smolin/3 (accessed on 22 August 2015).

[163] Smolin, 'Intercountry Adoption'.

[164] Smolin, 'Intercountry Adoption'.

[165] Rahman Azizur, 'Girls Pay Price of Being Born Poor', *Sydney Morning Herald*, Sydney, Australia, 7 May 2001.

[166] David M. Smolin, 'The Two Faces of Intercountry Adoption: The Significance of the Indian Adoption Scandals', *Seton Hall Law Review* 35, 403 (2005): 457.

them more attractive to foreign parents,[167] although it is not clear whether this reflected Indian, rather than American, prejudices.[168] The 1999 scandals began with the arrest of two women who were alleged to be acting as scouts or intermediaries in the purchase of children.[169] Although some reports styled these women as 'social workers',[170] they were charged with buying Lambada infants for relatively small sums ($15 to $45), and then receiving significantly larger sums ($220 to $440) from the orphanages for the children. Press reports indicated that the orphanages received $2,000 to $3,000 for each child placed in ICAs.[171] As a result of the 1999 scandals, Sanjeeva Rao and Peter Subbaiah were arrested and placed in prison. The government conducted dramatic raids to 'rescue' the children from the orphanages, taking 172 children from Rao's orphanage and 56 from Subbaiah's, the vast majority from each being female.[172] The 'rescue' of these children turned into a fiasco. It is reported that 10 children died shortly after being moved into government care.[173] While some claimed the children died from pre-existing conditions, others indicated that the fault was the government's. Some suggested that the parade of government officials 'visiting' the children had been a source of disease and infection.[174] Efforts to reunite the children with their birth parents were generally unsuccessful, and it appeared that the Lambada parents generally did not want their children back.[175] The government investigation allegedly revealed that most of the relinquishment documents were forged, with the signatures provided by thumb impressions of office attendants. The documents were alleged to be generally fraudulent in regard to the identities and original locations of the children.

The scandal caused a severe temporary slowdown of adoptions from Andhra Pradesh, but eventually the flow of adoptions from the state resumed. Sanjeeva Rao and Peter Subbiah were released from prison, apparently without ever being formally tried.[176]

Children of the World, the large Canadian adoption agency that had started an India programme in December 2000, reportedly had 15 couples in the process of adopting a child from the Bethany Orphanage when the scandal closed the orphanage.[177] Authorities subsequently

---

[167] Smolin, 'The Two Faces of Intercountry Adoption'.

[168] Indian sources clearly consider dark-complexioned children more difficult to place. For example, the Andhra Pradesh High Court noted, without embarrassment, that Indian parents rejected children for adoption who were reportedly 'black in complexion' (*John Clements* v. *All Concerned* (2003) 4 ANDHRA LAW TIMES 644, para. 35; Andhra Pradesh H.C, 2003 (3) ALD 597). The court was concerned with fraud that prospective Indian parents were shown a sick and dark-skinned child whom they would reject, and then that paperwork was attached to a different, more desirable child. The court did not seem to criticize the desire of Indian parents for light-skinned children. Similarly, the CARA website currently describes the special needs of one child as 'dark complexion squint eyes'. CARA, Ministry of Social Justice and Empowerment, *List of Special Needs Children Legally Free for Adoption*.

[169] Smolin, 'The Two Faces of Intercountry Adoption'.

[170] Smolin, 'The Two Faces of Intercountry Adoption'.

[171] Smolin, 'The Two Faces of Intercountry Adoption'.

[172] Smolin, 'The Two Faces of Intercountry Adoption'.

[173] Smolin, 'The Two Faces of Intercountry Adoption'.

[174] Smolin, 'The Two Faces of Intercountry Adoption'.

[175] Smolin, 'The Two Faces of Intercountry Adoption'.

[176] Smolin, 'Intercountry Adoption'.

[177] Smolin, 'Intercountry Adoption'.

arrested Sanjeeva Rao again, and raided his reopened ASD orphanage. Thirty-four children were taken from ASD; 22 were transferred to Sishu Vihar (the government orphanage), and 12 were hospitalized.[178]

The fallout of the Andhra Pradesh scandal continued into 2004, as Indian children continued to be subjects of custody battles between prospective foreign parents and the activists. Like other bitter custody disputes, the parties were often unwilling to compromise and yet each blamed the other for extending the struggle. The extension of the struggles were particularly unfortunate for the children, as it generally meant that they remained in either Sishu Vihar, or else in a private orphanage.[179] The unwillingness to compromise was likely heightened by each side's lack of authority to enter into a binding settlement determining the fate of the children. Unlike a traditional custody dispute, where a father and mother could agree on custody issues and be confident of court approval, neither the PAPs nor the activists had real authority to settle the cases. If the PAPs withdrew their petitions or failed to appeal, they would become legal strangers to the child they had sought to adopt, and would have no assurance that the child would be placed in a good home. The PAPs could reasonably fear that the children would be subject to political or bureaucratic delays dooming them to grow up in orphanages, or would be placed in inappropriate homes with those who came forward to adopt just to make a political point.[180]

From the experience of the Preet Mandir and the Andhra Pradesh scandals, it is clear that there is a need for a legal framework clearly defining 'trafficking' in the context of adoption in Indian law. The Immoral Trafficking and Prevention Act, 1956, and the IPC, 1860, deal only with matters related to prostitution/sexual exploitation, not trafficking. According to David Smolin, the term 'child laundering' expresses that the current ICA system frequently takes children illegally from birth parents, and then uses the official processes of the adoption and legal system to 'launder' them as 'legally' adopted children. Thus, the adoption system treats children in a manner analogous to a criminal organization engaged in money laundering, which obtains funds illegally but then 'launders' them through a legitimate business.[181]

In order to free children for ICAs, the authorities need to crosscheck whether the papers for the efforts made reflect the truth. In case of special needs children also, the normal rules must be followed. In many cases, children are labelled on paper as having special needs, though actually they may have only minor disabilities. Taking money in any form for adoption must be labelled as extortion. In the previously mentioned cases, the formal procedure which was designed to protect the children and their original families became a goal in itself and left behind parents who, when trying to fight the injustice done to them, found themselves totally powerless. But the implementation of laws by the government requires public pressure to make them effective.[182] In Andhra Pradesh, evidence was found that payments were directly made to birth families. Here,

---

[178] Women Development and Child Welfare Department, Government of Andhra Pradesh, *Action Taken Report on Adoption* (May 2001).

[179] Smolin, 'The Two Faces of Intercountry Adoption'.

[180] Smolin, 'The Two Faces of Intercountry Adoption'.

[181] David M. Smolin, 'Child Laundering: How the Intercountry Adoption System Legitimizes and Incentives the Practice of Buying, Trafficking, Kidnapping, and Stealing Children', *Wayne Law Review* 52 (2006), pp. 113, 115.

[182] Dohle, 'Inside Story'.

civil society took up the issue. After years of fighting by several women and child rights organizations, all involved in grassroots work for decades, ICA from Andhra Pradesh were stopped. The CARA continues to fine tune the adoption system and has brought the new 2015 guidelines, which address many of the issues. It will now depend on the implementation of these guidelines in its true spirit.

Inter-country Adoption under Juvenile Justice (Care & Protection of Children) Act, 2015

If an orphan or abandoned or surrendered child could not be placed with an Indian or NRI PAP despite the joint effort of the SAA and state agency within 60 days from the date the child has been declared legally free for adoption, such a child shall be free for ICA. Children with physical and mental disability, siblings and children above 5 years of age may be given preference over other children for such ICA, in accordance with the adoption regulations or guidelines framed by the CARA.[183]

Inter-country Adoption under CARA Guidelines, 2015

CARA Guidelines Governing Adoption of Orphan, Abandoned and Surrendered Children, 2015, read with JJ Act, 2000, amended in 2006 and 2011, and JJ Rules, 2007.

From 1 August 2015 the new Guidelines Governing Adoption of Children 2015[184] have come into effect. Along with it, the fully revamped IT application for the purpose of adoption of orphan, abandoned, or surrendered children. An online system, CARINGS, has also become operational.[185]

The guidelines draw support from:

1. JJ Act, 2000 and the rules framed thereunder;
2. Supreme Court judgment dated 8 February 2013 in the case of *Stephanie Joan Becker* v. *State and Anr.* (Civil Appeal No. 1053 of 2013);
3. Supreme Court judgment in the case of *L.K. Pandey* v. *Union of India* in WP (Crl.) No. 1171 of 1982;
4. UNCRC 1989;
5. the Hague Convention on Protection of Children and Co-operation in Respect of Inter-country Adoption 1993 (ratified by India on 6 June 2003 and brought into force on 1 December 2003).

---

[183] JJ Act, 2015, Section 59.

[184] Ministry of Women and Child Development, Government of India, Notification, New Delhi, dated 17 July 2015.

[185] Press Information Bureau, Government of India, Ministry of Women and Child Development, Notified on 1 August 2015. Available at http://pib.nic.in/newsite/PrintRelease.aspx?relid=124116 (accessed on 25 August 2015).

Among the new modification to the adoption process is the move towards online-based applications. The CARA[186] has put together a database of children available for adoption and it will allow prospective parents to register on their site; they can select the prospective children under categories such as age, language, and sex. The new guidelines are intended to provide regulation for adoption of orphan, abandoned, and surrendered children and would bring more transparency and efficiency in the adoption system. With the new guidelines, it would become possible for PAPs to track the status of their application, making the entire system more user-friendly.[187]

Fundamental Principles Governing Adoption[188]

As per the 2015 CARA guidelines, the following fundamental principles shall govern adoptions of children from India, namely

1. the child's best interests shall be of paramount consideration, while processing any adoption placement; and
2. preference shall be given to place the child in adoption with Indian citizens, with due regard to the principle of placement of the child in his own sociocultural environment, as far as possible.

The new rules have also mentioned certain criteria for prospective parents. Prospective parents will have to be in a stable marriage for at least a year to adopt and the minimum age difference between the child and either parent should not be less than 25 years. While single women can adopt either male or female children, single men will not be able to adopt a girl child.[189] When adopting a child aged 4 years or below, the parent cannot be older than 45 years and for children aged 8 years and above, the parent's age is capped at 55 years.[190]

The completely revamped CARINGS will facilitate the adoption of maximum number of adoptable children and ensure a smoother adoption process by curbing undue delays. CARINGS will contain a centralized data bank of adoptable children and PAPs. Clear-cut

---

[186] The CARA is an autonomous body under the Ministry of Women and Child Development, Government of India. It functions as the nodal body for adoption of Indian children and is mandated to monitor and regulate in-country adoption and ICAs. It is designated as the CA to deal with ICAs in accordance with the provisions of the Hague Convention on Inter-country Adoption, 1993, ratified by the Government of India in 2003. The CARA primarily deals with adoption of orphan, abandoned, and surrendered children through its associated/recognized adoption agencies.

[187] CARA Guidelines Governing Adoption of Children, 2015. For details, see http://cara.nic.in/InnerContent.aspx?Id=163#Guidelines%20-%202015 (accessed on 8 August 2015).

[188] Guideline 3 of the CARA Guidelines. For details, see http://cara.nic.in/InnerContent.aspx?Id=163#Guidelines%20-%202015 (accessed on 8 August 2015).

[189] Guideline 5 of the CARA Guidelines. For details, see http://cara.nic.in/InnerContent.aspx?Id=163#Guidelines%20-%202015 (accessed on 8 August 2015).

[190] Guideline 5 of the CARA Guidelines. For details, see http://cara.nic.in/InnerContent.aspx?Id=163#Guidelines%20-%202015 (accessed on 8 August 2015).

timelines for domestic adoption and ICA have been laid down to ensure early de-institutionalization of such children. The CARINGS will facilitate adoption with the help of the following features:[191]

1. The PAPs in India need not approach adoption agencies for registration. The parents can register online and upload relevant documents to determine their eligibility.
2. Home study reports are conducted by the adoption agencies and uploaded online.
3. There will be online referral to the PAPs followed by visit to adoption agencies.
4. In cases of ICA also, all applications are to be accepted online on CARINGS and requisite documents need to be uploaded in the system.
5. Both in domestic and in international adoption, post-adoption follow-up shall be posted online in CARINGS.
6. Real-time online report generation facility on periodic basis.
7. All SAAs are connected to CARA online for in-country adoption and ICA.
8. Centralized online receipt of application for ICA at CARA and distribution of applications to SAAs by CARA.
9. Real-time online information of children available in adoption agencies across the country.
10. The DCPUs are connected in CARINGS for monitoring adoption programmes at the district level.

Here, CARINGS would be instrumental to implement, supervise, monitor, and evaluate the child adoption programme in India in accordance with the Guidelines Governing Adoption of Children, 2015, issued by the Government of India.

To check many malpractices and to bring greater transparency and efficiency in the system, the new CARA Guidelines of 2015 governing adoption have come into effect from 1 August 2015. Under the 2015 guidelines, both the NRIs and the prospective Indian parent shall be treated equally while deciding the adoption of an Indian child.[192] Any NRI, overseas citizen of India, and foreign PAPs, living in a country which is a signatory to the Hague Adoption Convention and wishing to adopt an Indian child, can approach the concerned authorized foreign adoption agency (FAA) or the CA for preparation of their home study report and for further necessary action. In case there is no authorized FAA or CA in their country of residence, then the PAPs shall approach the concerned government department (GD) or Indian diplomatic mission (IDM) in that country for the purpose.[193]

---

[191] Press Information Bureau, Government of India, Ministry of Women and Child Development. Available at http://pib.nic.in/newsite/PrintRelease.aspx?relid=124116 (accessed on 23 August 2015).

[192] Para 15 of the CARA Guidelines: Non-resident Indian prospective adoptive parents shall be treated at par with Indians living in India in terms of priority for adoption of Indian orphan, abandoned or surrendered children. For details, see http://cara.nic.in/InnerContent.aspx?Id=163#Guidelines%20-%202015 (accessed on 8h August 2015).

[193] Para 16(2) of the CARA Guidelines: In case, there is no authorized FAA or CA in their country of residence, then the prospective adoptive parents shall approach the concerned GD or IDM in that country for the purpose. For details, see http://cara.nic.in/InnerContent.aspx?Id=163#Guidelines%20-%202015 (accessed on 8 August 2015).

There are three kinds of procedures recognized by CARA Guidelines 2015 for ICA:

1. Adoption by an NRI, overseas citizen of India, and foreign PAPs, living in a country which is a signatory to the Hague Adoption Convention.
2. Adoption by an overseas citizen of India or foreign national who is a citizen of a country that has ratified the Hague Convention and has been living in India for 1 year or more.
3. Adoption of a child from a foreign country by Indian citizens.

I. Adoption by a Non-resident Indian, Overseas Citizen of India, and Foreign Prospective Adoptive Parents, Living in a Country which Is a Signatory to the Hague Adoption Convention

The steps to be followed by an NRI, overseas citizen of India, and foreign PAPs living in a country which is a signatory to the Convention on Protection of Children and Co-Operation in Respect of Intercountry Adoption, 1993 are given in Figure 2.2.

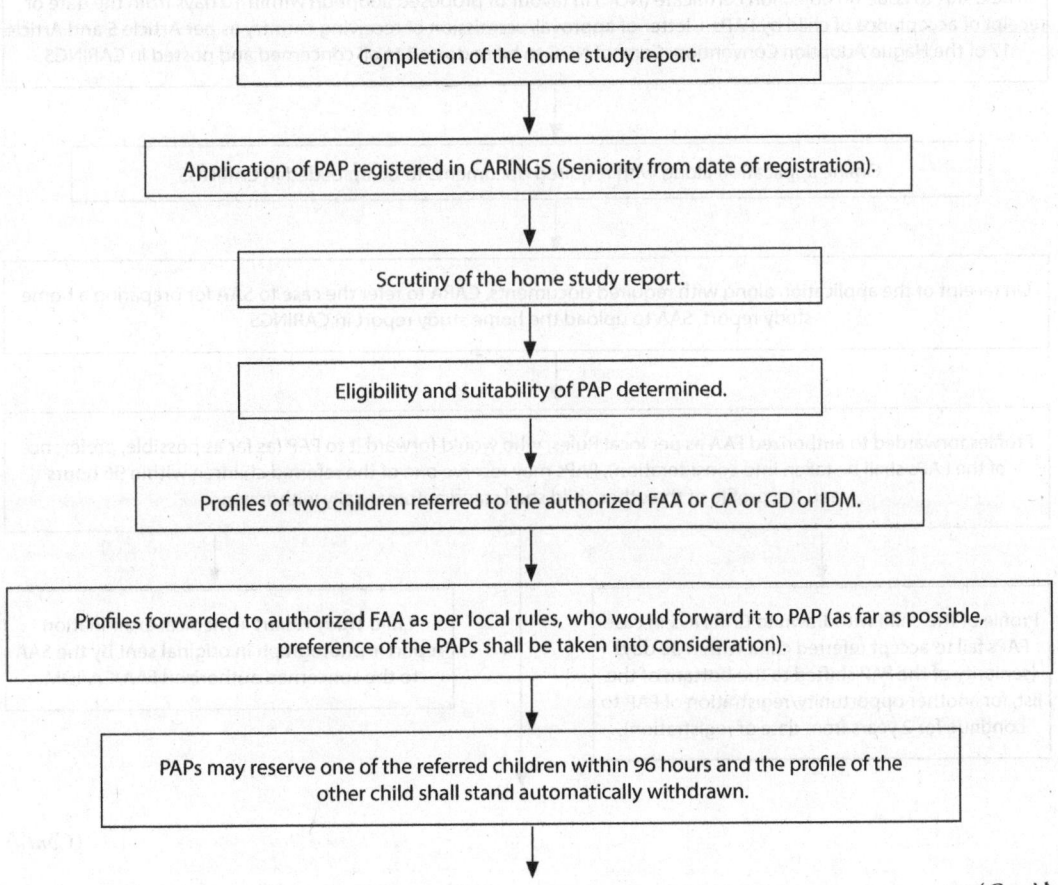

Completion of the home study report.

↓

Application of PAP registered in CARINGS (Seniority from date of registration).

↓

Scrutiny of the home study report.

↓

Eligibility and suitability of PAP determined.

↓

Profiles of two children referred to the authorized FAA or CA or GD or IDM.

↓

Profiles forwarded to authorized FAA as per local rules, who would forward it to PAP (as far as possible, preference of the PAPs shall be taken into consideration).

↓

PAPs may reserve one of the referred children within 96 hours and the profile of the other child shall stand automatically withdrawn.

↓

(Cont'd)

Child study report + medical examination report + photograph in original sent by the SAA to the concerned authorized FAA/CA/IDM.

↓

Profile of the child withdrawn to CARINGS in case PAPs fails to accept referred child within 30 days (seniority of the PAP shifted to the bottom of the list, for another opportunity/registration of PAP to continue for 2 years from date of registration).

↓

After the application is approved by CARA, the PAP may visit SAA to see the child and also get medical examination report of child reviewed.

↓

After the profile of the child is accepted by PAPs, FAA shall forward original documents of PAPs to concerned SAA.

↓

The CARA to issue no objection certificate (NOC) in favour of proposed adoption within 10 days from the date of receipt of acceptance of child by PAPs + letter of approval/permission of receiving country as per Article 5 and Article 17 of the Hague Adoption Convention. Copy of NOC to be endorsed to all concerned and posted in CARINGS.

↓

Online application along with required documents to be uploaded in CARINGS.

↓

On receipt of the application along with required documents, CARA to refer the case to SAA for preparing a home study report. SAA to upload the home study report in CARINGS.

↓

Profiles forwarded to authorized FAA as per local Rules, who would forward it to PAP (as far as possible, preference of the PAPs shall be taken into consideration), PAPs may reserve one of the referred children within 96 hours and the profile of the other child shall stand automatically withdrawn.

↓ ↓

Profile of the child withdrawn to CARINGS in case PAPs fail to accept referred child within 30 days (seniority of the PAP shifted to the bottom of the list, for another opportunity/registration of PAP to continue for 2 years from date of registration).

Child study report + medical examination report + photograph in original sent by the SAA to the concerned authorized FAA/CA/IDM.

(Cont'd)

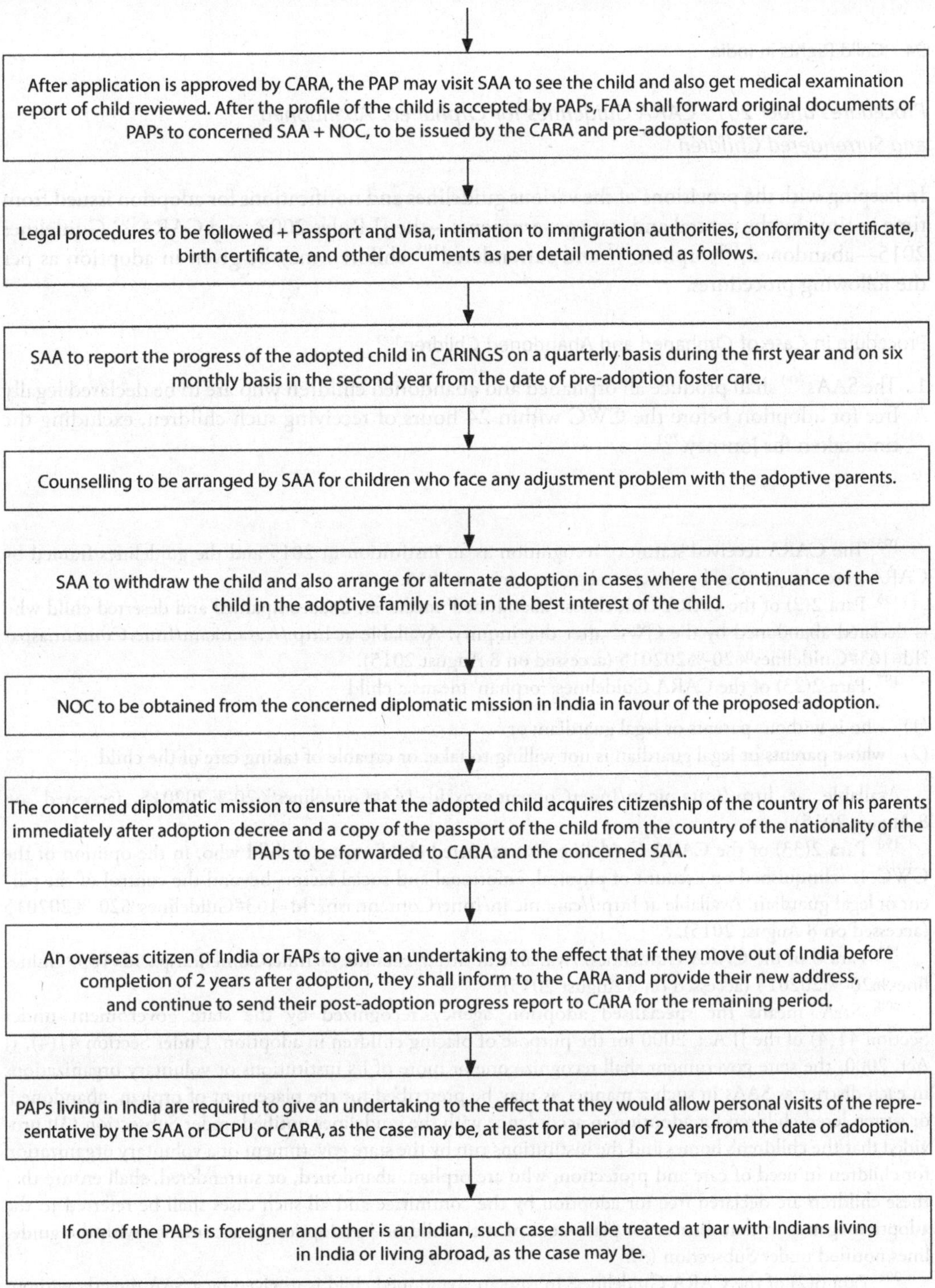

After application is approved by CARA, the PAP may visit SAA to see the child and also get medical examination report of child reviewed. After the profile of the child is accepted by PAPs, FAA shall forward original documents of PAPs to concerned SAA + NOC, to be issued by the CARA and pre-adoption foster care.

Legal procedures to be followed + Passport and Visa, intimation to immigration authorities, conformity certificate, birth certificate, and other documents as per detail mentioned as follows.

SAA to report the progress of the adopted child in CARINGS on a quarterly basis during the first year and on six monthly basis in the second year from the date of pre-adoption foster care.

Counselling to be arranged by SAA for children who face any adjustment problem with the adoptive parents.

SAA to withdraw the child and also arrange for alternate adoption in cases where the continuance of the child in the adoptive family is not in the best interest of the child.

NOC to be obtained from the concerned diplomatic mission in India in favour of the proposed adoption.

The concerned diplomatic mission to ensure that the adopted child acquires citizenship of the country of his parents immediately after adoption decree and a copy of the passport of the child from the country of the nationality of the PAPs to be forwarded to CARA and the concerned SAA.

An overseas citizen of India or FAPs to give an undertaking to the effect that if they move out of India before completion of 2 years after adoption, they shall inform to the CARA and provide their new address, and continue to send their post-adoption progress report to CARA for the remaining period.

PAPs living in India are required to give an undertaking to the effect that they would allow personal visits of the representative by the SAA or DCPU or CARA, as the case may be, at least for a period of 2 years from the date of adoption.

If one of the PAPs is foreigner and other is an Indian, such case shall be treated at par with Indians living in India or living abroad, as the case may be.

Figure 2.2 Adoption by a Non-resident Indian, Overseas Citizen of India, and Foreign PAPs, Living in a Country which Is a Signatory to the Hague Adoption Convention[194]

[194] Source: For details, see CARA Guidelines Governing Adoption of Children, 2015, available at http://cara.nic.in/InnerContent.aspx?Id=163#Guidelines – 2015 (accessed on 28 August 2015).

Procedures under 2015 CARA Guidelines for Orphaned, Abandoned, and Surrendered Children

In keeping with the provisions of the various guidelines and notifications for adoption issued from time to time by the central and state governments—the JJ Rules 2007, and CARA[195] Guidelines 2015—abandoned,[196] orphan,[197] and surrendered[198] children may be given in adoption as per the following procedures.

Procedure in Case of Orphaned and Abandoned Children[199]

1. The SAAs[200] shall produce all orphaned and abandoned children who are to be declared legally free for adoption before the CWC within 24 hours of receiving such children, excluding the time taken for journey.[201]

---

[195] The CARA received statutory recognition as an institution in 2015 and the guidelines framed by CARA were also notified by the central government in 2015.

[196] Para 2(2) of the CARA Guidelines: 'abandoned' means an unaccompanied and deserted child who is declared abandoned by the CWC after due inquiry. Available at http://cara.nic.in/InnerContent.aspx-?Id=163#Guidelines%20-%202015 (accessed on 8 August 2015).

[197] Para 2(23) of the CARA Guidelines: 'orphan' means a child

(1) who is without parents or legal guardian; or

(2) whose parents or legal guardian is not willing to take, or capable of taking care of the child.

Available at http://cara.nic.in/InnerContent.aspx?Id=163#Guidelines%20-%202015 (accessed on 8 August 2015).

[198] Para 2(33) of the CARA Guidelines: 'surrendered child' means a child who, in the opinion of the CWC, is relinquished on account of physical, emotional and social factors beyond the control of the parent or legal guardian. Available at http://cara.nic.in/InnerContent.aspx?Id=163#Guidelines%20-%202015 (accessed on 8 August 2015).

[199] Para 6 of the CARA Guidelines. Available at http://cara.nic.in/InnerContent.aspx?Id=163#Guidelines%20-%202015 (accessed on 8 August 2015).

[200] 'SAA' means the specialised adoption agency recognized by the state government under Section 41(4) of the JJ Act, 2000 for the purpose of placing children in adoption. Under Section 41(4), JJ Act, 2000, the state government shall recognize one or more of its institutions or voluntary organizations in each district as SAAs in such a manner as may be prescribed for the placement of orphan, abandoned, or surrendered children for adoption in accordance with the guidelines notified under Subsection (3): provided that the children's homes and the institutions run by the state government or a voluntary organization for children in need of care and protection, who are orphan, abandoned, or surrendered, shall ensure that these children are declared free for adoption by the committee and all such cases shall be referred to the adoption agency in that district for placement of such children in adoption in accordance with the guidelines notified under Subsection (3).

[201] Para 6(2) of the CARA Guidelines: In case an abandoned child is received by a SAA directly without the involvement of the CWC, such a child shall be produced before the CWC within 24 hours (excluding the time necessary for the journey) along with a report containing the particulars and photograph of the child as well as the circumstances in which the child was received and a copy of such report shall also be submitted by the SAA to the local police station within the same period.

2. A copy of the report should be filed with the police station in whose jurisdiction the child was found abandoned.[202]

3. A child becomes eligible for adoption when the CWC declares the child legally free for adoption after completion of its inquiry.[203] Such inquiry should be conducted by the probation officer or the child welfare officer, who shall produce report to the committee containing the findings within one month.[204]

4. On admission of the child, his details and photograph shall be entered online in CARINGS by the SAA within 72 hours of receiving the child, provided that the permission of CWC is obtained for the same, and the photograph of the child shall be changed by the SAA every 6 months in CARINGS.[205]

5. The SAA shall submit a report to the CWC immediately after 30 days from the date of production of the child before the CWC, as to whether any person has approached it to claim the child; the report may also include any information revealed by the child during his interim care.[206]

6. For tracing out the biological parents or the legal guardian(s), the DCPU[207] shall advertise the particulars and photograph of an abandoned child in a state-level newspaper with wide circulation within 72 hours from the time of receiving the child.[208]

---

[202] CARA Guidelines, Para 6(2).

[203] CARA Guidelines, Para 4: Any orphan or abandoned or surrendered child, declared legally free for adoption by the CWC is eligible for adoption. For details, see http://cara.nic.in/InnerContent.aspx?Id=163#Guidelines%20-%202015 (accessed on 8 August 2015).

[204] CARA Guidelines, Para 9(5): The home study report shall be completed in the format given in Schedule 6, within one month from the date of submission of requisite documents and shall be shared with the PAPs immediately, thereafter. For details, see http://cara.nic.in/InnerContent.aspx?Id=163#Guidelines%20-%202015 (accessed on 8 August 2015).

[205] CARA Guidelines, Para 6(4) : On admission of the child, his details and photograph shall be entered online in the Child Adoption Resource Information and Guidance System (CARINGS) in the prescribed format by the SAA within 72 hours of receiving the child, provided that the permission of CWC is obtained for the same and the photograph of the child shall be changed by the SAA every 6 months in CARINGS. For details, see http://cara.nic.in/InnerContent.aspx?Id=163#Guidelines%20-%202015 (accessed on 8 August 2015).

[206] CARA Guidelines, Para 6(10): The SAA shall submit a report to the CWC immediately after 30 days from the date of production of the child before the CWC as to whether any person has approached it to claim the child and the report may also include any information revealed by the child during his interim care. For more details, see http://cara.nic.in/InnerContent.aspx?Id=163#Guidelines%20-%202015 (accessed on 8 August 2015).

[207] CARA Guidelines, 2015, Para 2(13): District Child Protection Unit means the unit set up by the state government at the district level under Section 62A of the JJ Act, 2000. Available at http://cara.nic.in/InnerContent.aspx?Id=163#Guidelines%20-%202015 (accessed on 8 August 2015). For more details, see http://cara.nic.in/InnerContent.aspx?Id=163#Guidelines%20-%202015 (accessed on 8 August 2015).

[208] CARA Guidelines, 2015, Para 6(5): For tracing out the biological parents or the legal guardian(s), the DCPU shall advertise the particulars and photograph of an abandoned child in a state-level newspaper with wide circulation within 72 hours from the time of receiving the child. For details, see http://cara.nic.in/InnerContent.aspx?Id=163#Guidelines%20-%202015 (accessed on 8 August 2015).

7. In case the report from the local police regarding the non-traceability of the biological parents or legal guardian is not submitted despite reminders by the SAA or CWC, such a report shall be deemed to have been given, after expiry of two months in the case of an abandoned child less than 2 years of age and after the expiry of four months in the case of an abandoned child above 2 years of age.[209]

8. Subsequently, the CWC, after taking actions as per the provisions of the act and the rules made thereunder, shall issue an order declaring the abandoned or orphan child as legally free for adoption.[210]

Procedure in Case of Surrendered Children[211]

A surrendered child is one who has been declared as such after due process of inquiry by the CWC, and in order to be declared legally free for adoption, a surrendered child shall be any of these:

1. born as a consequence of non-consensual relationship;
2. born of an unwed mother or out of wedlock;
3. One of whose biological parents is dead and the living parent is incapacitated to take care; or
4. a child whose parents or guardians are compelled to relinquish him/her due to physical, emotional, and social factors beyond their control.

   a) The committee shall give effort for counselling of the parents, explaining the consequences of adoption, and exploring the possibilities of parents retaining the child,[212] and if the parents are unwilling to retain, then such children shall be kept initially in foster care or arrangements will be made for their sponsorship.

   b) If the surrender is inevitable, a deed of surrender shall be drawn in the presence of any two members of the CWC; but if the surrendering parent is an unmarried mother, the

---

[209] CARA Guidelines, 2015, Para 6(11): In case the report from the local police regarding the non-traceability of the biological parents or legal guardian is not submitted despite reminders by the SAA or CWC, such a report shall be deemed to have been given, after expiry of 2 months in the case of an abandoned child less than 2 years of age and after the expiry of 4 months in the case of an abandoned child above 2 years of age. For details, see http://cara.nic.in/InnerContent.aspx?Id=163#Guidelines%20-%202015 (accessed on 8 August 2015).

[210] CARA Guidelines, 2015, Para 6(12): The CWC, after taking actions as per the provisions of the act and the rules made thereunder, shall issue an order declaring the abandoned or orphan child as legally free for adoption in the format at Schedule – 1 and such order signed by any two members of the CWC shall be issued within a period of 2 months in case of a child up to 2 years of age and within 4 months for a child above 2 years of age, from the date of production of the child before the CWC. For details, see http://cara.nic.in/InnerContent.aspx?Id=163#Guidelines%20-%202015 (accessed on 8 August 2015).

[211] CARA Guidelines, 2015, Para 7. Available at http://cara.nic.in/InnerContent.aspx?Id=163#Guidelines%20-%202015 (accessed on 8 August 2015).

[212] CARA Guidelines, 2015, Para 7(4): To discourage surrender by biological parents, efforts shall be made by the SAA or the CWC for exploring the possibility of parents retaining the child, which shall include counselling and encouraging them to retain the child and explaining that the process of surrender is irrevocable. For details, see http://cara.nic.in/InnerContent.aspx?Id=163#Guidelines%20-%202015 (accessed on 8 August 2015).

deed may be executed in the presence of any single member, preferably female, of the CWC.[213]

c) In case of a surrendered child, two months' reconsideration time shall be given to the biological parent or parents after surrender before declaring the child legally free for adoption.[214]

Eligibility Criteria for Prospective Adoptive Parents under CARA Guidelines, 2015[215]

The eligibility criteria for PAPs under Guidelines Governing Adoption of Children, 2015 are:[216]

1. The PAPs should be physically, mentally, and emotionally stable; financially capable; motivated to adopt a child; and should not have any life-threatening medical condition.
2. Any PAP, irrespective of his marital status and whether or not he has his own biological son or daughter, can adopt a child.
3. Single female is eligible to adopt a child of any gender.
4. Single male person shall not be eligible to adopt a girl child.
5. In case of a couple, the consent of both spouses shall be required.
6. No child shall be given in adoption to a couple unless they have at least 2 years of stable marital relationship.
7. The age of PAPs as on the date of registration shall be counted for deciding the eligibility, and the eligibility of the PAPS to apply for children of different age groups shall be as shown in Table 2.2.

Table 2.2 The age of PAPs as on the date of registration[217]

Age of the Child	Maximum Composite Age of PAPs	Maximum Age of Single PAP
Up to 4 years	90 years	45 years
Above 4, up to 8 years	100 years	50 years
Above 8, up to 18 years	110 years	55 years

[213] CARA Guidelines, 2015, Para 7(6): If the surrender is inevitable, a deed of surrender, as provided in Schedule 4 shall be executed in the presence of any two members of the CWC: provided that if the surrendering parent is an unmarried mother, the deed may be executed in the presence of any single member, preferably female member of the CWC. For details, see http://cara.nic.in/InnerContent.aspx?Id=163#Guidelines%20-%202015 (accessed on 8 August 2015).

[214] CARA, 2015, Para 7(5): The SAA and the CWC shall ensure that the surrendering parents or the legal guardian is made aware that they can reclaim the surrendered child only within a period of 60 days from the date of surrender. For details, see http://cara.nic.in/InnerContent.aspx?Id=163#Guidelines%20-%202015 (accessed on 8 August 2015).

[215] CARA Guidelines, 2015. For details, see http://cara.nic.in/InnerContent.aspx?Id=163#Guidelines – 2015 (accessed on 26 August 2015).

[216] CARA, Ministry of Women and Child Development, Government of India. For details, see http://www.cara.nic.in/InnerContent.aspx?Id=141#Eligibility%20Criteria (accessed on 3 July 2015).

[217] Source: Central Adoption Resource Authority, Ministry of Women and Child Development, Government of India. Available at http://www.cara.nic.in/InnerContent.aspx?Id=141#Eligibility%20Criteria (accessed on 22 October 2016).

8. The minimum age difference between the child and either of the PAPS should not be less than 25 years.
9. The age for eligibility will be as on the date of registration of the PAPs.
10. Couples with more than four children shall not be considered for adoption.

Documents Required for Indian Adoption under Guidelines Governing Adoption of Children, 2015

The essential documents required are as follows[218]

1. One of the PAPs[219] shall have a Permanent Account Number (PAN) card and they have to upload PAN card in appropriate format.
2. The PAPs shall upload their own photograph/family photograph.
3. The PAPs shall provide an email account and mobile number.
4. After successful registration, the PAPs shall receive an online acknowledgement letter which will contain registration and credential details.
5. In case PAPs misplace their online acknowledgement letter, it can be regenerated using 'forgot password' link available in 'track status' page.
6. The following documents shall be uploaded at the time of registration:

   a) PAN card/passport,
   b) proof of residence (Aadhaar card/voter identity card/passport/driving license/current electricity bill/telephone bill),
   c) proof of income of last year (for example, salary slip/income certificate issued by a GD/income tax return),
   d) copy of marriage certificate and photograph,
   e) copy of divorce decree/death certificate of the spouse (if applicable),
   f) copy of birth certificate of the PAPs,
   g) certificate from a medical practitioner certifying that the PAPs do not suffer from any chronic, contagious, or fatal disease and they are fit to adopt,
   h) in case of a single parent, undertaking from a relative to take care of the child in case of mishap.

Home study report of the prospective adoptive parents for Indian residents[220]

Every resident Indian PAP who intends to adopt a child shall register online in CARINGS by filling up the application form and uploading the relevant documents. On receipt of the completed application form and required documents on CARINGS, the registration shall be complete and

---

[218] CARA, Ministry of Women and Child Development, Government of India. For details, see http://www.cara.nic.in/InnerContent.aspx?Id=144#Documents%20Required (accessed on 3 July 2015).

[219] CARA Guidelines, 2015, Para 2(24): 'prospective adoptive parents' (PAPs) means a person or persons eligible to adopt a child under the provisions of the act and these guidelines.

[220] CARA Guidelines, 2015, Para 9: Registration and home study of the prospective adoptive parents—

confirmed to the PAPs immediately. The PAPs shall then get their registration number from the acknowledgement slip and use it for viewing the progress of their case.

The home study report[221] of the PAP shall be prepared by the SAA in the state where the PAPs are located, through its social workers or through social workers from a panel maintained by the SARA or DCPU. The home study report shall be completed within one month from the date of submission of requisite documents and shall be shared with the PAPS immediately thereafter. As soon as it gets completed, the same shall be posted in the CARINGS by the SAA or DCPU or SARA, as the case may be.

The home study report will remain valid for 2 years and shall be the basis for adoption of a child by the PAP from anywhere in the country. The PAPs shall be declared eligible and suitable by the SAA based upon the home study report and supporting documents, and in case any PAP is not declared eligible or suitable, the reasons for the same shall be recorded in the CARINGS.

---

(1) Every resident Indian PAP, who intends to adopt a child, shall register online in CARINGS by filling up the application form as provided in Schedule 5 and uploading the relevant documents.

(2) The registration shall be complete and confirmed to the PAPs immediately on receipt of the completed application form and required documents on CARINGS.

(3) The PAPs shall get their registration number from the acknowledgement slip and use it for viewing the progress of their case.

(4) The home study report of the PAPs shall be prepared by the SAA in the state, where PAPs are located, through its social worker or through a social worker from a panel maintained by the SARA or DCPU, as the case may be.

(5) The home study report shall be completed in the format given in Schedule 6, within one month from the date of submission of requisite documents and shall be shared with the PAPs immediately, thereafter.

(6) The home study report shall be posted in the CARINGS by the SAA or DCPU or SARA as the case may be, as soon as it is complete.

(7) The home study report will remain valid for 2 years and shall be the basis for adoption of a child by the PAPs from anywhere in the country.

(8) The PAPs shall be declared eligible and suitable by the SAA based upon the home study report and supporting documents and in case any PAP is not declared eligible or suitable, the reasons for the same shall be recorded in the CARINGS.

(9) The PAPs can appeal against the decision of rejection to CARA.

(10) The appeal referred to Sub-paragraph (9) shall be disposed of within 15 days and the decision of CARA in this regard shall be binding.

(11) The DCPU shall facilitate online registration of PAPs, uploading of documents and also for addressing technical difficulties faced by the SAA.

These conditions apply under the provision that the adoption of a child by the PAPs, after completion of their registration and home study report, shall depend upon the availability of a suitable child.

For details, see http://cara.nic.in/InnerContent.aspx?Id=163#Guidelines%20-%202015 (accessed on 8 August 2015).

221 CARA Guidelines, 2015, Para 2(15) defines a home study report as a report containing details of the adoptive parents, which include social and economic status; family background; description of home; standard of living; compatibility between spouses and other family members; and health status. Available at http://cara.nic.in/InnerContent.aspx?Id=163#Guidelines%20-%202015 (accessed on 8 August 2015).

Adoption Leave[222]

Adoptive parents working in the offices under the control of the central government or the state government or the central or state public sector undertakings shall be entitled for adoption leave for proper care of the adoptee, as per the extant instructions of the concerned government or authority, and the benefit of this facility shall be available from the stage of pre-adoption foster care.[223]

Voice of the Child in Adoption Matters

It is significant to note that the right of the child to be heard in adoption matters is embodied in JJ Rules of 2007. Rule 33(g)[224] allows for the child's voice to be heard in adoption matters. It has to be borne in mind that it is only after attaining a certain age that even the law recognizes children as capable of expressing their opinion. According to Rule 33(g), children above 7 years who can understand and express their opinion shall not be declared free for adoption without their consent. Though the law guarantees child participation in the process of adoption, one needs to speculate the possibility of manipulation. Often abandoned children, orphans, and others, who are identified for adoption, are shown rosy pictures of being able to live a hassle-free life with parents who would provide them all comforts of life. But in reality, often, this picture is not true. Children should be informed about the true implications of adoption and counselled regarding the pros and cons of adoption.[225]

Legal Procedure for Getting the Adoption Order in Case of Inter-country Adoption as per CARA Guidelines, 2015

The SAA shall file an application in the competent court with relevant documents[226] within seven working days from the date of receipt of acceptance of the child by the PAPs for obtaining the adoption order from the court, and the SAA shall enclose the documents in original, along with the application.

In case the child is from a child-care institution which is located in another district, the SAA shall file the adoption petition in the concerned court of that district. The court will hold the adoption proceeding in-camera and dispose of the case within a period of two months from the date of filing of the adoption petition by the SAA. The SAA shall obtain a certified copy of the

[222] CARA Guidelines, 2015, Para 14. Available at http://cara.nic.in/InnerContent.aspx?Id=163#Guidelines – 2015 (accessed on 1 September 2014).

[223] CARA Guidelines, 2015, Para 2(26): 'pre–adoption foster care' means a stage when the custody of a child is given to PAPs, pending adoption order from the court. Available at http://cara.nic.in/InnerContent.aspx?Id=163#Guidelines – 2015 (accessed on 1 September 2014).

[224] JJ Rules, 2007, Rule 33(g)(vii): no child above 7 years who can understand and express his opinion shall be declared free for adoption without his consent.

[225] A.S. Shenoy , 'Child Adoption Policies in India—A Review Paper', Chair, International Relations Committee, Indian Council of Social Welfare (Nepal, 2007).

[226] CARA Guidelines, 2015, Schedule 8. For details, see www.cara.nic.in (accessed on 22 October 2016).

adoption order from the court and will forward it to the PAPs within 10 days, besides posting a copy of such an order and making necessary entries in the CARINGS.

Registration of a deed of adoption shall not be necessary. The SAA shall obtain the birth certificate of the child from the birth certificate issuing authority and provide it to the PAPs within 10 days from the date of availability of the adoption order, with the name of adoptive parents, as parents, and date of birth, as recorded in the adoption order.

Issuance of Passport and Visa, Intimation to Immigration Authorities, Conformity Certificate, Birth Certificate, and Other Documents

The CARA shall issue a conformity certificate[227] under Article 23 of the Hague Adoption Convention[228] within three working days from the date of availability of the adoption order in the CARINGS, in case the receiving country of the adopted child is a Hague Adoption Convention signatory.

The CARA shall inform the concerned immigration authorities and the foreigner regional registration office, or as the case may be, the foreigner registration office, about confirmation of adoption. To obtain Indian passport for the adopted child, the SAA shall submit the application to the regional passport officer within three working days from the date of receipt of a certified copy of the adoption order. The regional passport office shall issue passport for the adopted child within 10 days from the date of receipt of application.

In case the adopted child has been provided with a passport of the country of nationality of the PAPs by its diplomatic mission in India, the foreigner regional registration office or the foreigner registration office, as the case may be, shall issue exit visa to the adopted child within three working days from the date of online application for the same, along with all supporting documents by the PAPs.

The SAA shall also obtain birth certificate for the adopted child from the issuing authority within 10 days from the date of receipt of the adoption order, with the name of adoptive parents and date of birth as recorded in the adoption order. The adopted child shall be entitled to receive overseas citizen of India card, if found eligible. The adoptive parents shall come to India to take the adopted child to their country.

Follow Up of Progress of Adopted Child under CARA Guidelines

The authorized FAA or the CA or IDM or concerned GD, as the case may be, shall report the progress of the adopted child[229] online in the CARINGS, along with photographs of the child,

---

[227] Article 23 of Convention on Protection of Children and Co-Operation in Respect of Intercountry Adoption of 1993 states that an adoption certified by the competent authority of the state of the adoption as having been made in accordance with the convention.

[228] CARA Guidelines, 2015, Schedule 10. For details, see www.cara.nic.in (accessed on 22 October 2016).

[229] CARA Guidelines, 2015, Schedule 11. For details, see www.cara.nic.in (accessed on 22 October 2016).

on a quarterly basis during the first year and on six-monthly basis in the second year, from the date of arrival of the adopted child in the receiving country.

If an adjustment problem of the child with the adoptive parents comes to the notice of the authorized FAA or CA or the concerned GD in the receiving country on the basis of the progress report or in the course of post-adoption home visits, then, necessary counselling shall be arranged for the adoptive parents and for the adoptee, wherever applicable.[230]

If it is found that the child is unable to adjust in the adoptive family or that the continuance of the child in the adoptive family is not in the interest of the child, the authorized FAA or CA or the concerned GD in the receiving country or IDM, as the case may be, shall withdraw the child and provide necessary counselling and shall arrange for suitable alternate adoption or foster placement of the child in that country, in consultation with the IDM and CARA.[231]

In the event of adjustment problem of the child with the adoptive family, the child shall be entitled to receive care, protection, and rehabilitation through the child protection services of that country. The authorized FAA or CA or concerned GD, as the case may be, shall organize annual get-together of Indian adoptees and their adoptive parents and forward a report on the event to the CARA, and the IDMs shall facilitate such get-togethers.[232]

The PAPs shall furnish an undertaking to the effect that they would allow personal visits of the representative of authorized FAA, the foreign CA, or concerned GD, as the case may be, to ascertain the progress of the child with the adoptive parents/family at least for a period of 2 years from the date of arrival of the child in the receiving country.[233]

Adoption of a Child from a Foreign Country by Indian Citizens

Necessary formalities for adoption of a child from a foreign country by Indian citizens shall initially be completed in that country as per their law and procedure. The CARA shall issue approval, as required under Articles 5[234] and 17[235] of the Convention on Protection of Children

---

[230] CARA Guidelines, 2015, Para 20(2). Available at http://cara.nic.in/InnerContent.aspx?Id=163# Guidelines (accessed on 1 September 2014).

[231] CARA Guidelines, 2015, Para 20(3). Available at http://cara.nic.in/InnerContent.aspx?Id=163# Guidelines – 2015 (accessed on 1 September 2014).

[232] CARA Guidelines, 2015, Para 20(5). Available at http://cara.nic.in/InnerContent.aspx?Id=163# Guidelines – 2015 (accessed on 1 September 2014).

[233] CARA Guidelines, 2015, Para 20(6). Available at http://cara.nic.in/InnerContent.aspx?Id=163# Guidelines – 2015 (accessed on 1 September 2014).

[234] Article 5 of the Hague Convention, 1993: An adoption within the scope of the convention shall take place only if the competent authorities of the receiving state—

(1) have determined that the PAPs are eligible and suited to adopt;
(2) have ensured that the PAPs have been counselled as may be necessary; and
(3) have determined that the child is or will be authorized to enter and reside permanently in that state.

Ratified by India on 6 June 2003 and brought into force on 1 December 2003. Available at http://www.hcch.net/index_en.php?act=conventions.text&cid=69 (accessed on 11 September 2015).

[235] Article 17 of the Hague Convention, 1993: Any decision in the state of origin that a child should be entrusted to PAPs may only be made if—

and Co-operation in respect of Inter-country Adoption 1993, in the cases of adoption of children coming to India as a receiving country.

If the child adopted abroad by the Indian citizens has a foreign passport, then the child would require Indian visa to come to India and on submission of the visa application, the Indian mission in the country concerned may issue entry visa to the child after checking all the relevant documents to ensure that the adoption has been done following due procedure.

The immigration clearance for the child adopted abroad shall be obtained from the Foreigners' Division, Ministry of Home Affairs, Government of India, through the IDM to that country.

It is significant that the new CARA guidelines have addressed and clarified some concerns like searching for roots, adoption of special children, adoption of twin and siblings, adoption of older children, adoption expenses, and follow-up of ICA.

Root Search

In cases of root search, the concerned agencies or authorities (authorized FAA, CA, IDM, CARA, SARA, DCPU, or SAA), whenever contacted by any adoptee, shall facilitate his root search. In order to facilitate root search, the age and maturity of the child shall be taken into consideration.[236]

If the biological parents, at the time of surrender of the child, have specifically requested anonymity, then the consent of the parents should be taken by the SAA or CWC. In case of denial by the parents or if the parents are not traceable, the reasons and the circumstances under which the surrender took place shall be disclosed to the adoptee.[237]

In case of an orphan or abandoned child, information about his adoption, including the source and circumstances in which the child was admitted into the SAA, as well as the process followed for his adoption, may be disclosed to the adoptee by the SAA or the CWC.[238]

A root search by a third party shall not be permitted and the concerned agencies or authorities shall not make public any information relating to biological parents, adoptive parents, or

---

(1) the CA of that state has ensured that the PAPs agree;

(2) the CA of the receiving state has approved such decision, where such approval is required by the law of that state or by the central authority of the state of origin;

(3) the central authorities of both states have agreed that the adoption may proceed; and

(4) it has been determined, in accordance with Article 5, that the PAPs are eligible and suited to adopt and that the child is or will be authorized to enter and reside permanently in the receiving state.

Ratified by India on 6 June 2003, and brought into force on 1 December 2003. Available at http://www.hcch.net/index_en.php?act=conventions.text&cid=69 (accessed on 11 September 2015).

[236] CARA Guidelines, 2015, Paras 45(1), 45(2).

Available at http://cara.nic.in/InnerContent.aspx?Id=163#Guidelines (accessed on 1 September 2014).

[237] CARA Guidelines, 2015, Para 45(4).

Available at http://cara.nic.in/InnerContent.aspx?Id=163#Guidelines (last accessed on 1 September 2014).

[238] CARA Guidelines, 2015, Para 45(5).

Available at http://cara.nic.in/InnerContent.aspx?Id=163#Guidelines (accessed on 1 September 2014).

adopted child. The right of an adopted child shall not infringe the biological parents' right to privacy.[239]

Confidentiality of Adoption Records

All agencies or authorities involved in the adoption process shall ensure that confidentiality of adoption records is maintained, except as permitted under any other law for the time being in force.

Adoption Expenses

The PAPs shall bear the expenses for adoption.[240] The agency is not permitted to accept any donation in cash or kind, directly or indirectly, for adoption of a child from the PAPs.

Reporting of Adoptions

The SAA shall submit adoption data on CARINGS and also send quarterly reports[241] to SARA and CARA in the first week of every quarter.

Adoption of Children with Special Needs

The adoption process for children with special need shall be completed as expeditiously as possible by the concerned agencies or authorities, and the children shall be available for adoption by resident Indians and NRIs from the date they are declared legally free for adoption by the CWC. Such children with special needs shall be available for adoption by overseas citizens of India or foreign adoptive parents after 15 days from the date they are declared legally free for adoption.[242]

Special care must be taken while processing the cases for adoption of children with special need, so that the PAPs are aware of the real medical condition of the child and ready to provide extra care and attention that the child needs. The children with special need who were not adopted shall be provided with due care and protection by the SAA and if they do not have necessary facilities and the means for their long-term care, such children shall be shifted to any other specialized institutions run by any government or NGO.[243]

---

[239] CARA Guidelines, Para 45(7). Available at http://cara.nic.in/InnerContent.aspx?Id=163#Guidelines – 2015 (accessed on 1 September 2014).

[240] CARA Guidelines, Schedule 13. For details, see www.cara.nic.in (accessed on 1 September 2014).

[241] CARA Guidelines, 2015, Schedule 15. For details, see www.cara.nic.in (accessed on 1 September 2014).

[242] CARA Guidelines, 2015, Para 49(1). Available at http://cara.nic.in/InnerContent.aspx?Id=163# Guidelines (accessed on 1 September 2014).

[243] CARA Guidelines, 2015, Para 49(4). Available at http://cara.nic.in/InnerContent.aspx?Id=163# Guidelines (accessed on 1 September 2014).

Adoption of Older Children

A child who has completed 5 years of age shall be considered as an older child. Since it takes time for an older child to adjust with unrelated parents, it is important that the child and the PAPs are made familiar to each other before leaving the institution. Under the guidance of SAA or authorized FAA, the PAPs may have interactions with older children through video calls even before taking custody, and the PAPs may be encouraged to spend some quality time with the child before leaving the institution. The older children shall be deemed to be available for adoption by resident Indians and NRIs from the date they are declared legally free for adoption by the CWC, and they shall be available for adoption by overseas citizen of India or foreign PAPs after 30 days from the date they are declared legally free for adoption.[244]

Adoption of Twins and Siblings

Twins or siblings shall be available for adoption by resident Indians and NRIs from the date they are declared legally free for adoption by the CWC, and they shall be deemed to be available for adoption by overseas citizen of India or foreign PAPs after 30 days from the date they are declared legally free for adoption.[245]

- Any female of sound mind and who is not a minor has the capacity to adopt a child (HAMA, Section 8).[246]
- The father and the mother both shall have equal right to give a son or daughter in adoption but such a right shall not be exercised by either of them without the consent of the other unless one of them has finally renounced the world or has ceased to be a Hindu or has been declared by a court of competent jurisdiction to be of unsound mind (HAMA, Section 9).[247]

The CARA guidelines have certainly been simplified and some of the long-standing challenges and issues faced during adoption have been addressed and clarified. There will be transparency in the system as it would become possible for PAPs to track the status of their application, making the entire system more efficient and user friendly. However, adoption agencies have expressed concerns relating to the e-placement of children. The major concern is that wait-listed families in order of their registration get to 'reserve' a child online, from the details, including photos and medicals, of six children 'displayed' to them on CARINGS. According to several agencies in the field, this selection approach is reduced to an impersonal process, dictated by demand and supply, treating the child as an object to 'pick and choose'. Majority of the waiting children have medical conditions that require ongoing medical care, such as orthopaedic issues that may require multiple surgeries, serious heart issues, deafness or blindness, cerebral palsy, HIV, multiple conditions,

---

[244] CARA Guidelines, 2015, Para 50. Available at http://cara.nic.in/InnerContent.aspx?Id=163#Guidelines (accessed on 1 September 2014).

[245] CARA Guidelines, 2015, Para 51. Available at http://cara.nic.in/InnerContent.aspx?Id=163#Guidelines (accessed on 1 September 2014).

[246] Substituted by the Personal Laws (Amendment) Act, 2010, No. 30 of 2010.

[247] Personal Laws (Amendment) Act, 2010, No. 30 of 2010.

and other conditions in which they will best thrive with involved care over a span of years. As per the new computerized system, PAPs will lose out on the continued personalized counselling and handholding support during this most important decision of their life. There is also concern that this process may have no control on the way confidential information of the child, including photographs, might be treated. This can find its way on social media and websites, jeopardizing the 'best interest of the child'. It is 'unethical' and 'against rights of the child' to be exhibited along with his/her personalized details to prospective parents, to be chosen or rejected.[248]

Surrogacy

Surrogacy is a method of assisted reproduction, a contemporary practice, especially in a developing country like India. The word 'surrogate' has its origin in the Latin word 'surrogatus', meaning a substitute, that is, a person appointed to act in the place of another.[249] Hence, a surrogate mother is a woman who carries a child on behalf of another woman, either from her ovum or from the implantation in her womb of a fertilized egg from the other woman. *Black's Law Dictionary* defines surrogacy as the process of carrying and delivering a child for another person.[250] The *Britannica* defines 'surrogate motherhood' as the practice in which a woman bears a child for a couple unable to produce children in the usual way.[251]

The *Report of the Committee of Inquiry into Human Fertilization and Embryology*, or the Warnock Report (1984),[252] termed surrogacy as the practice whereby one woman carries a child for another with the intention that the child should be handed over after birth. A standard definition of 'surrogacy' is offered by the *American Law Reports*[253] as

> a contractual undertaking whereby the natural or surrogate mother, for a fee, agrees to conceive a child through artificial insemination with the sperm of the natural father, to bear and deliver the child to the natural father, and to terminate all of her parental rights subsequent to the child's birth.

Commercial surrogacy is currently legal in India. As costs of medical treatment are low in India, it is proving to be an attractive hub for foreigners to procure benefits of medical tourism,

---

[248] Anuradha Mascarehnas, 'Adoption Agencies Raise Concern over New e-Placement Guidelines', *Indian Express*, Pune, 4 September 2015. Available at http://indianexpress.com/article/cities/pune/adoption-agencies-raise-concern-over-new-e-placement-guidelines/ (accessed on 11 September 2015).

[249] Surrogacy in Latin. Available at http://www.latindictionary.org/surrogatus, http://en.wiktionary.org/wiki/surrogatus (accessed on 6 September 2015).

[250] R.E. Oliphant, *Surrogacy in Black Law Dictionary. Family Law* (New York: Aspen Publishers, 2007), p. 349.

[251] Surrogacy in *New Encyclopedia, Britannica*. Available at http://www.britannica.com/EBchecked/topic/575390/surrogate-motherhood (accessed on 6 September 2015).

[252] Department of Health and Social Security, *Report of the Committee of Inquiry into Human Fertilisation and Embryology*, Chairman: Dame Mary Warnock DBE, Her Majesty's Stationery Office LONDON, U.K., 1988. Available at http://www.hfea.gov.uk/docs/Warnock_Report_of_the_Committee_of_Inquiry_into_Human_Fertilisation_and_Embryology_1984.pdf (accessed on 10 September 2016).

[253] Danny R. Veilleux, 'Annotation, Validity and Construction of Surrogate Parenting Agreement', *American Law Reports* 77 ALR 4th 70 (1989).

especially surrogacy.[254] Commercial surrogacy is emerging and doctors and surrogate mothers are engaging in profiteering, as evident from numerous newspaper accounts of surrogate women citing money as the main reason for engaging in such arrangements. Surrogacy in India is legitimate because no Indian law prohibits it.[255] Assisted Reproductive Technology (ART) is a term used to refer to advanced and innovative medical interventions that help people realize their dream of giving birth to a child. It includes a number of scientific techniques that assist reproduction, for example, artificial insemination (AI), in-vitro fertilization (IVF), and so on.[256]

The guidelines help regulate ART procedures. They include the following:[257]

- Surrogacy arrangement to be governed by a contract among parties, which will contain all the terms requiring consent of the surrogate mother to bear the child, agreement of her husband and other family members for the same, medical procedures of AI, reimbursement of all reasonable expenses for carrying the child to full term, willingness to hand over the child born to the commissioning parent(s), and so on.
- A surrogacy arrangement should provide for financial support for the surrogate child in the event of death of the commissioning couple or individual before delivery of the child, or divorce between the intended parents and subsequent willingness of none to take delivery of the child.
- A surrogate mother should not be over 45 years of age. Before accepting a woman as a possible surrogate for a particular couple's child, the ART clinic must ensure that the woman satisfies all treatable criteria to go through a successful full-term pregnancy.
- A surrogacy contract should necessarily take care of life insurance cover for the surrogate mother.
- One of the intended parents should be a donor as well, because the bond of love and affection with a child primarily emanates from biological relationship. Also, the chances of various kinds of child abuse, which have been noticed in cases of adoptions, will be reduced.
- In case the intended parent is single, he or she should be a donor to be able to have a surrogate child. Otherwise, adoption is the way to have a child which is resorted to if biological (natural) parents and adoptive parents are different. Legislation itself should recognize a surrogate child

[254] 'Medical Tourism Booms in India', *Economic Times*, New Delhi, 7 February 2006. Available at http://articles.economictimes.indiatimes.com/2006-02-07/news/27443329_1_medical-tourism-cost-advantage-number-of-overseas-patients (accessed on 4 September 2015).

[255] Law Commission of India, *228th Report on 'Need for Legislation to Regulate Assisted Reproductive Technology Clinics As Well As Rights and Obligations of Parties to a Surrogacy'*, submitted to the Union Minister of Law and Justice, Government of India by Dr. Justice A.R. Lakshmanan, Chairman, Law Commission of India, on the 5th day of August, 2009, New Delhi.

[256] 'Wanna Rent a Womb, Come to Anand', *Times of India*, Ahmedabad, 11 February 2006. Available at http://timesofindia.indiatimes.com/city/ahmedabad/Wanna-rent-a-womb-come-to-Anand/articleshow/1410939.cms (accessed on 4 September 2015).

[257] 'Surrogacy in India: Indian Council of Medical Research (ICMR) Guidelines', *Sensible Surrogacy*. Available at http://www.sensiblesurrogacy.com/surrogacy-in-india-guidelines/ (accessed on 6 September 2015).

to be the legitimate child of the commissioning parent(s) without any need for adoption or even declaration of guardianship.

- The birth certificate of the surrogate child should contain the name(s) of the commissioning parent(s) only.
- Right to privacy of donor as well as surrogate mother should be protected. Sex-selective surrogacy should be prohibited.
- Cases of abortions should be governed by the Medical Termination of Pregnancy Act, 1971 only.

In India, according to the National Guidelines for Accreditation, Supervision and Regulation of ART Clinics, evolved in 2005 by the ICMR and the National Academy of Medical Sciences (NAMS), the surrogate mother is not considered to be the legal mother.[258] The birth certificate is made in the name of the genetic parents. The US position as per the Gestational Surrogacy Act, 2004 is similar to that of India.[259] The National Guidelines for Accreditation, Supervision and Regulation of ART Clinics, 2005 are non-statutory, have no legal sanctity, and are not binding. This means is that surrogate mothers need to sign a 'contract' with the childless couple. There are no stipulations as to what will happen if this 'contract' is violated.

To determine the legality of surrogacy agreements, the ICA, 1872[260] would apply and thereafter the enforceability of any such agreement would be within the domain of Section 9 of the CPC.[261] Alternatively, the biological parent/s can also move an application under the GWA for seeking an order of appointment or a declaration as the guardian of the surrogate child.[262]

Surrogacy arrangement is, therefore, made as a result of an agreement between the parties.[263] This agreement is written down and every aspect related to the parties is specifically addressed. The rights and liabilities of the parties are specifically laid down. The parties cannot on a later date, after signing the contract, claim that the intention of the parties was any different from what is mentioned in the surrogacy contract.[264]

---

[258] ICMR/NAMS, 'Code of Practice, Ethical Considerations and Legal Issues', Chapter 3, *Guidelines for ART Clinics in India.* Available at http://icmr.nic.in/art/Chapter_3.pdf (accessed on 4 September 2015).

[259] Malathy Iyer, 'Draft Law Tightens Surrogacy Norms', *Times of India*, Mumbai, 2008. Available at http:// articles.timesofindia.indiatimes.com (accessed on 11 September 2015).

[260] ICA, 1872, Section 2(h) defines a contract as: 'a contract is an agreement enforceable by law'. Thus, a contract is an agreement made between two or more parties which the law will enforce, whereas an agreement is defined under Section 2(e) as every promise and every set of promises, forming consideration for each other. When a proposal is accepted it becomes a promise. Thus an agreement is an accepted proposal. Therefore, in order to form an agreement there must be a proposal or an offer by one party and its acceptance by other party.'

[261] CPC, 1908, Section 9: Courts to try all civil suits unless barred—The courts shall (subject to the provisions herein contained) have jurisdiction to try all Suits of a civil nature excepting suits of which their cognizance is either expressly or impliedly barred.

[262] Law Commission of India, *228th Report on 'Need for Legislation'.*

[263] ICA, 1872, Section 2(e): Every promise and every set of promises, forming the consideration for each other, is an agreement.

[264] Indian Surrogacy Law Centre Blog, 'Legal Review of the Surrogacy Contract'. Available at http:// indiansurrogacylaw.com/legal-review-of-the-surrogacy-contract.html (accessed on 4 September 2015).

In the event that the surrogate mother decides to repudiate[265] the contract, it is not only logical but also ethical that the contracting father should not be forced to pay child support and the surrogate mother should be held liable. However, what such a logical argument does not take into account is the welfare of the child, who may then face financial hardships that are the consequences of a decision or a contract to which they were never a party.[266] With regard to the surrogate mother, she should be made to restitute[267] any payments made to her by the contracting parents to prevent unjust enrichment by repudiation of the contract, in consonance with Section 65 of the 1872 Act,[268] which states that no person should be allowed to receive advantage under a void agreement[269] or under a contract that becomes void. This would also discourage opportunistic behaviour on the part of the surrogate mothers.

Legally, a surrogacy arrangement has been defined by the Indian Supreme Court as an agreement whereby a woman agrees to become pregnant for the purpose of gestating and giving birth to a child she will not raise, but hand over to a contracted party.[270] Often it is done with the intention of entering into a contract; at times the intention of the parties can be inferred from the transaction. In common parlance, the term refers to arrangement made between the two parties under which a woman (surrogate mother) agrees to (i) donate the egg and by AI, carry a foetus in the embryo of her own and give birth; (ii) carry the term of pregnancy with the help of fertilized egg.

In the case of surrogacy, a woman undertakes to bear a child for a childless couple and agrees to relinquish all parental rights at the birth of the child for a payment or other consideration, which becomes void for its contravention of statutory enactments, since the contract involves bartering of human lives, and also infringes public policy.

As per the provisions of the ICA, 1872, legal contracts can be either general contracts,[271] or special contracts,[272] or specific contracts.[273] Thus, contracts can be classified into different heads depending upon their subject matter or purpose. With respect to surrogacy, it is difficult to decide

---

[265] According to ICA, 1872, Section 39: 'Any intimation whether by words or by conduct that the party declines to continue with the contract is repudiation, if the result is likely to deprive the innocent party of substantial the benefit of the contract.'

[266] ICA, 1872, Section 39.

[267] ICA, 1872, Section 65 states: 'When an agreement is discovered to be void, or when a contract becomes void, any person who has received any advantage under such agreement or contract is bound to restore, it, or to make compensation for it, to the person from whom he received it.'

[268] ICA, 1872, Section 65.

[269] ICA, 1872, Section 2(g) states that 'an agreement not enforceable by law is said to be void'.

[270] J. Arijit Pasayat in *Baby Manji Yamada* v. *Union of India*, AIR 2009 SC 84.

[271] Those set of contracts the purpose of which can be anything but must be legal, for example, contract to supply goods. Sections 1–75 deal with general contracts.

[272] There are certain contracts the subject matter or purpose of which is special and different from usual contracts, for example, Contract of Indemnity. Sections 124–147 of the ICA, 1872 deal with such contracts. Bailment and pledge are special classes of contract. Chapter IX (Sections 148–181) of the ICA, 1872 deals with the contract of bailment and pledge.

[273] Mostly, such contracts are extended forms of general forms contract where it is compulsory for a particular transaction to be preceded by a usual contract, for example, Transfer of Property. Sections 124–238 of the ICA, 1872 deal with specific kinds of contracts.

under which type or under which head it falls. If surrogacy transactions were to be considered legal, then it must fall in the category of either specific or special contract. However, for them to be legal, they must satisfy all the requirements of a contract as laid down under the ICA. Under Section 10[274] of the ICA, all agreements are contracts, if they are made:

1. by the free consent,
2. of parties competent to contract,
3. for a lawful consideration and a lawful object, and
4. are not expressly declared to be void.

Section 10 further provides that if a contract has to be to be in writing under the provisions of any other law, then it must also be in writing. All the aforementioned requirements of a valid contract must be present in every case. In other words, these requirements are conjunctive, and not disjunctive. All of them must coexist in every case.

Apart from the contractual point of view, surrogacy may be treated as a statutory transaction. However, this requires a particular statute which can govern such transactions. In such a scenario, the question of legality of a surrogacy contract may not arise, as it would then be backed by statutes governing the surrogacy relationship.

In 2002, the Supreme Court of India held that commercial surrogacy was legal in India.[275] In *Jan Balaz* v. *Union of India*,[276] the Gujarat High Court conferred Indian citizenship on two twin babies fathered through compensated surrogacy by a German national in Anand district.

However, in the absence of a statute governing surrogacy, several issues arise:

1. Surrogacy is neither protected by law, nor prohibited by law. There is no separate statute dealing with surrogacy and nor does the current legal system support it.[277]
2. Despite absence of any statutes or position in the legal system, surrogacy transactions are being extensively entered into in some parts of India.[278]
3. The subject matter of surrogacy contract, that is, the surrogate child, is a human being and as such cannot be the subject matter or object of contract.[279]

---

[274] ICA, 1872, Section10: All agreements are contracts if they are made by the free consent of parties competent to contract, for a lawful consideration and with a lawful object, and are not hereby expressly declared to be void.

[275] AIR 2009 SC 84.

[276] AIR 2010 Guj 21.

[277] *Jan Balaz* v. *Anand Municipality*, AIR 2010 Guj 21 at Section 14.

[278] Lakshmi Ajay, 'A Hub of Rent-a-Womb Industry in India', *Indian Express*, Gujarat, 13 February 2014. Available at http://indianexpress.com/article/india/india-others/gujarat-a-hub-of-rent-a-womb-in-dustry-in-india/ (accessed on 4 September 2015).

[279] *Nutan Kumar* v. *IInd Additional District Judge*, AIR 1994 All 298: 'Though the expression "object" is not defined in the ICA, 1872, it has held to mean a "purpose" or "design" of the contract. If the object is opposed to public policy or tends to defeat any provisions of law, it becomes unlawful and thereby it is void under Section 23 of the Act.'

To legalize surrogacy, the Law Commission of India submitted the 228th report on ART procedures, titled *Need for Legislation to Regulate Assisted Reproductive Technology Clinics As Well As Rights and Obligations of Parties to a Surrogacy*, discussing the importance and need for surrogacy, and also the steps taken to control surrogacy arrangements. The following observations had been made by the Law Commission:[280]

1. Surrogacy arrangement will continue to be governed by contract among parties, which will contain all the terms requiring consent of surrogate mother to bear child, agreement of her husband and other family members for the same, medical procedures of artificial insemination, reimbursement of all reasonable expenses for carrying child to full term, willingness to hand over the child born to the commissioning parent(s), and so on. But such an arrangement should not be for commercial purposes.

2. A surrogacy arrangement should provide for financial support for the surrogate child in the event of death of the commissioning couple or individual before delivery of the child, or divorce between the intended parents and subsequent willingness of none to take delivery of the child.

3. A surrogacy contract should necessarily take care of life insurance cover for the surrogate mother.

4. One of the intended parents should be a donor as well, because the bond of love and affection with a child primarily emanates from biological relationship. Also, the chances of various kinds of child abuse, which have been noticed in cases of adoptions, will be reduced. In case the intended parent is single, he or she should be a donor to be able to have a surrogate child. Otherwise, adoption is the way to have a child which is resorted to if biological (natural) parents and adoptive parents are different.

5. Legislation itself should recognize a surrogate child to be the legitimate child of the commissioning parent(s) without there being any need for adoption or even declaration of guardian.

6. The birth certificate of the surrogate child should contain the name(s) of the commissioning parent(s) only.

7. Right to privacy of donor as well as surrogate mother should be protected.

8. Sex-selective surrogacy should be prohibited.

9. Cases of abortions should be governed by the Medical Termination of Pregnancy Act, 1971 only.

Developed nations like the United Kingdom and Canada prohibit commercial surrogacy. Majority of the countries prohibit commercial surrogacy. In this context, the state in its regulatory role is attempting to legalize commercial surrogacy in India.[281] India is possibly the only country in the world to legalize commercial surrogacy by virtue of the ART Bill, 2010.[282]

As far as the legality of the concept of surrogacy is concerned, Article 16.1 of the Universal Declaration of Human Rights (UDHR), 1948 says that 'men and women of full age without

---

280 Law Commission of India, *228th Report on 'Need for Legislation'*.

281 Law Commission of India, *228th Report on 'Need for Legislation'*.

282 Tanzeem Fatima and Tasleem Fatima, 'Surrogacy: Legal Issues and Challenges', *Excellence International Journal of Education and Research (Multi- subject journal)* 2, 3 (Uttar Pradesh:March 2014).

any limitation due to race, nationality or religion have the right to marry and found a family'. In England, surrogacy arrangements are legal and the Surrogacy Arrangements Act, 1985 prohibits advertising and other aspects of commercial surrogacy. In the United States also, commercial surrogacy seems prohibited in many states. In the famous *Baby M* case,[283] the New Jersey Supreme Court, though allowed custody to commissioning parents in the 'best interest of the child', came to the conclusion that surrogacy contract is against public policy. It must be noted that in the United States, surrogacy laws are different in different states. In Australia, commercial surrogacy is illegal, contracts in relation to surrogacy arrangement unenforceable, and any payment for soliciting a surrogacy arrangement is illegal. Majority of the countries prohibit commercial surrogacy. It is an ongoing war of morals and ethics versus technological advances.[284]

Bill No. 61 of 2014, named the Surrogacy (Regulation) Bill, 2014,[285] was introduced in the Lok Sabha on 8 August 2014. The important provisions of the bill are as follows.

- This bill deals with surrogacy arrangements alone and not with ART as such.
- The bill provides to allow commercial surrogacy arrangements for couples from abroad if they have an appointed guardian in India.
- The bill provides that insurance for the surrogate mother must be sponsored by the commissioning couple.
- The bill provides for surrogacy for gay couples, after same-sex relations are allowed in India.
- The bill does not discuss ART Banks, whereby surrogate mothers and egg donors can be identified.

Surrogacy (Regulation) Bill, 2016[286]

The Surrogacy (Regulation) Bill, 2016 proposes to regulate surrogacy in India by establishing national surrogacy board at the central level as well as state surrogacy boards and appropriate authorities in states and union territories. The proposed legislation ensures effective regulation of surrogacy, prohibits commercial surrogacy, and allows ethical surrogacy to the needy infertile Indian couples.

The major objectives of the bill are to regulate surrogacy services in the country, provide altruistic ethical surrogacy to the needy infertile Indian couples, prohibit commercial surrogacy including sale and purchase of human embryo and gametes, prevent commercialization of surrogacy, prohibit potential exploitation of surrogate mothers, and protect the rights of children born through surrogacy. The salient features of the bill are follows:

---

[283] *Re Baby M*, 537 A.2d 1227; 109 N.J. 396 (N.J. 1988).

[284] Sarkar Arunima, 'Articulating Various Facets of Female Reproduction Laws: Issues And Challenges', *Indian Journal Of Legal Philosophy* 2, 1 (Andhra Pradesh: March 2014).

[285] The Surrogacy (Regulation) Bill, 2014, by Kirit Premjibhai Solanki, M.P. A. Bill to provide for regulation of surrogacy and for matters connected therewith or incidental thereto.

[286] Press Information Bureau, Government of India. Available at http://pib.nic.in/newsite/PrintRelease. aspx?relid=149186 (accessed on 6 October 2016).

- To allow altruistic ethical surrogacy to intending infertile couple between the age of 23 and 50 years and 26 and 55 years for female and male, respectively.
- The intending couples should be legally married for at least 5 years and should be Indian citizens.
- The intending couples should not have any surviving child biologically or through adoption or through surrogacy earlier except when they have a child and who is mentally or physically challenged or suffer from life-threatening disorder with no permanent cure.
- The intending couples shall not abandon the child born out of a surrogacy procedure under any condition.
- The child born through surrogacy will have the same rights as are available for the biological child.
- The surrogate mother should be a close relative of the intending couple and should be between the age of 25 and 35 years. She can act as a surrogate mother only once.
- The surrogate mother will carry a child which is genetically related to the intending couple.
- An order concerning the parentage and custody of the child to be born through surrogacy is to be passed by a court of the magistrate of the first class.
- An insurance coverage of reasonable and adequate amount shall be ensured in favour of the surrogate mother.
- National Surrogacy Board shall exercise the powers and shall perform functions conferred on the board under this act.
- The board shall consist of the minister in-charge of the Ministry of Health and Family Welfare as the chairperson, secretary to the Government of India in-charge of the department dealing with the surrogacy matter, as vice-chairperson, and three women members of the Parliament, of whom two shall be elected by the house of the people and one by the council of state as members.
- The National Surrogacy Board and state surrogacy board shall be the policy-making bodies and an appropriate authority will be the implementation body for the act.
- The appropriate authority shall comprise an officer of or above the rank of the joint director of Health and Family Welfare Department, as chairperson, an eminent woman representing women's organization, as member, an officer of the law department of the state or the union territory concerned not below the rank of a deputy secretary, as member and an eminent registered medical practitioner, as a member.
- The surrogacy clinics shall be registered under this act after the appropriate authority is satisfied that such clinics are in a position to provide facilities and can maintain equipments and standards including specialised manpower, physical infrastructure, and diagnostic facilities as may be prescribed in the rules and regulations.
- No person, organization, surrogacy clinic, laboratory, or clinical establishment of any kind shall undertake commercial surrogacy, abandon the child, exploit the surrogate mother, sell human embryo or import embryo for the purpose of surrogacy. Violation to the said provision shall be an offence punishable with imprisonment for a term which shall not be less than 10 years and with a fine which may extend to Rs 10 lakh.
- The surrogacy clinics shall have to maintain all records for a period of 25 years.
- Transitional provision: Subject to the provisions of this act, there shall be provided a gestation period of 10 months from the date of coming into force of this act to protect the well-being of already existing surrogate mothers.

The Surrogacy (Regulation) Bill, 2016, was cleared by the Indian Cabinet, on 24 August 2016. The bill bans commercial surrogacy, and bars single people, married couples who have biological/adopted children, live-in partners, and homosexuals from opting for surrogacy. The bill allows only childless couples who have married for at least 5 years to opt for 'altruistic' surrogacy. The surrogate mother should be a close relative of the couple, should be married, and have borne a child. Foreigners, NRIs, and persons of Indian origin (PIOs) who hold Overseas Citizens of India cards have been barred from opting for surrogacy. According to the new bill, a married woman who has at least one child of her own can be a surrogate mother only once in her lifetime. Childless or unmarried women are not allowed to carry somebody else's child.[287]

International Laws Relating to Adoption and Surrogacy

Children are on the international agenda today in a way that they have never been before. There are now some universally accepted basic rights which are essential to any child's harmonious and full development, even if there is a diversity of the nations' socio-economic, religious, and cultural perceptions of childhood and the child's role in the family and society at large.

Inter-country or international adoptions, in which the adopter and the adoptee are of different nationality or different domicile, are becoming increasingly frequent in the modern world. Many countries, particularly in Europe and America, no longer have a sufficient number of children available for adoption. Conversely, countries in which there are numerous children who may be adopted rarely have a large number of prospective adopters.[288] It is intended as a protection measure when in-country care for a child who cannot remain with his or her family is not available, but its escalation has been so rapid and often uncontrolled that countries of origin have been hard-pressed to ensure that the best interests of the children concerned are being upheld.

Every state has the right to regulate the manner in which an adoption may be affected and there are, therefore, a great many ways in which a person may be adopted. However, there are some international conventions that attempt to harmonize national rules regarding adoptions. The needs for special safeguards and care, including appropriate legal protection for a child, have been stated in the Geneva Declaration of the Rights of the Child 1924.[289] This declaration stated that 'mankind owes to the child the best that it has to give'. This declaration was the first step towards protecting children's rights in the broadest sense.

---

[287] Available at http://indianexpress.com/article/india/india-news-india/surrogacy-bill-sushma-swaraj-married-couples-can-now-opt-homosexuals/ (accessed on 28 September 2016).

[288] I. Delupis, *International Adoptions and the Conflict of Laws* (Uppsala: Almqvist & Wiksell, 1975), p. 11.

[289] It was drafted by the Save the Children International Union, an NGO established by Eglantyne Jebb to respond to the needs of children during the aftermath of World War I. The declaration was adopted by the League of Nations in 1924.

Evolution of United Nations Instruments Relating to Adoption

In 1959, the United Nations (UN) gave official recognition to the human rights of children by adopting the Declaration of the Rights of the Child, 1959, a 10-principle document. The declaration set out certain principles relating to the rights of a child to a name and nationality and to be protected from practices which may foster religious discriminations.[290] Besides, there were several general declarations, covenants, and conventions, which stated the rights of children.[291] The Declaration of Social and Legal Principles relating to the Protection and Welfare of Children with Special Reference to Foster Placement and Adoption Nationally and Internationally, 1986 also recognized that the primary aim of adoption is to provide the child who cannot be cared for by his or her own parents with a permanent family. It can be stated that foster placement should also be regulated by law.[292]

The various declarations on the rights of the child were not binding on the governments of the world. Therefore, an idea emerged about drafting a treaty between the governments, on the rights of the child, which would be more binding. Second, it was realized that the interests of children were not necessarily identical with those of their guardians. The project to draft a convention started within the UN Commission of Human Rights; a special working group was set up for the purpose under that body.[293]

During the second reading of the draft convention, four areas emerged as what might be called highly controversial issues. These were the rights of the unborn child, the right to foster care and adoption, freedom of religion, and the minimum age for participation in armed conflict.[294]

[290] Every child, without any exception whatsoever, shall be entitled to these rights, without distinction or discrimination on account of race, colour, sex, language, religion, political or other opinion, national or social origin, property, birth or other status, whether of himself or of his family. Principle 1, United Nations Declaration of the Rights of the Child 1959.

The child shall be entitled from his birth to a name and a nationality. Principle 3, United Nations Declaration of the Rights of the Child 1959.

The child shall be protected from practices which may foster racial, religious, and any other form of discrimination. He shall be brought up in a spirit of understanding, tolerance, friendship among people, peace, and universal brotherhood, and in full consciousness that his energy and talents should be directed to the service of the fellow men. Principle 10, United Nations Declaration of the Rights of the Child 1959.

[291] UDHR, 1948, the International Covenant on Economic, Social, and Cultural Rights, 1976, the International Convention on the Elimination of All Forms of Racial Discrimination 1966, and the Convention on the Elimination of All Forms of Discrimination against Women 1979.

[292] Declaration on Social and Legal Principles relating to the Protection and Welfare of Children, with Special Reference to Foster Placement and Adoption Nationally and Internationally, 1986, Article 10: Foster placement should be regulated by law.

[293] It was in commemoration of the twentieth anniversary of the Declaration of the Rights of the Child 1959, that 1979 was designated as the International Year of the Child (IYC). As part of this celebration, Poland proposed that an international treaty be drafted which would put into legally binding language the principles set forth in the 1959 Declaration. The working group established by the Commission in 1979 completed its first draft of the convention in February 1988.

[294] C.P. Cohen, *United Nations: Convention on the Rights of the Child*, 28 ILM 1448, 1989.

Objections to the freedom of religion and to adoption and foster care were launched by the Islamic delegations, which found articles relating to them in conflict with the Koran and with their national legislations.[295] The final text of the articles guaranteeing freedom of religion and the right to adoption and foster care is the result of very difficult and delicate negotiations.[296]

The principles, that children have equal values as human beings, that the best interest of the child should be of primary consideration, that due weight should be given to the child's opinion, and that each child has rights, are all of great importance.[297]

The convention also has recognized the right of a child to have an identity and to grow up in a family environment. It also states that the parties to the convention that permit the system of adoption must ensure that the best interests of the child shall be the paramount consideration. The convention also provides that there should be no discrimination of any kind, irrespective of the child's or his/her parents' or legal guardian's race, colour, sex, language, religion, birth, or other status.

Under the convention, a committee is established to monitor the implementation and all state parties have to submit their first report to the committee within 2 years of ratification. There is also a link between reports by the states and discussions about assistance. On 11 December 1992, India ratified the convention[298] and acquired an obligation to ensure that the rights enshrined under the convention are protected in the country. It is the Government of India that is responsible for ensuring that the norms laid down in the convention are adhered to in actual practice by enacting laws. International treaties do not automatically become part of the national law. They have to be incorporated into the legal system by appropriate law.[299] Article 4 of the convention provides that the state parties should review its legislation and ensure that the laws are consistent with the convention.[300]

Therefore, we now have to make laws for adoption of all children without any discrimination. The various rights under the convention are not ranked in order of importance, but the

---

[295] According to Islamic law it is not possible for a child to be able to choose a religion or to change his or her religious faith. This is a privilege available only to adults. Similarly, the Islamic religion does not recognize the right to adoption. In part, this position is based on a concept of consanguinity and inheritance within the interrelated extended family, which cannot and should not be altered or affected by the act of bringing an outsider into the family structure. Instead, the Islamic countries substitute the concept of adoption with the concept of Kafala as a method of caring for abandoned or orphaned children. Under Kafala, a family may take a child to live with them on a permanent legal basis, but that child is not entitled to use the family's name or to inherit from the family. The practice of Kafala would seem to be somewhat akin to permanent foster care.

[296] I.A. Huard, 'The Law of Adoption, Ancient and Modern', *Vanderbilt Law Review* ix (1956): 243–63.

[297] T. Hammerberg, 'Making Reality of the Rights of the Child', *Legal Perspectives*, File No. 33, 1993, p. 9.

[298] By the end of 1992, 117 countries have ratified the CRC. By 1996 it was raised to 185. Recently, Somalia also ratified. Only the USA has not ratified it as of now.

[299] The Constitution of India, Article 253: Parliament has the power to make any law for the whole or any part of the territory of India for implementing any treaty agreement or convention with any other country.

[300] See CRC, Article 4.

convention has an integrated approach and they interact with one another to form part of the same wholeness.

India has also become a signatory to the Declaration of the World Summit for Children, setting up goals for survival and child development for the year 2000. The survival and development goals of the World Summit for Children provide substance to the commitment to implement the provisions of the convention.[301]

United Nations Convention on the Rights of the Child 1989
(Ratified by India on 11 December 1992):

The Convention on the Rights of the Child, adopted by the General Assembly of the United Nations on 20 November 1989 and ratified by India in 1992, recognizes that each child should grow up in a family environment, in an atmosphere of happiness, love, and understanding, and a child, by reason of his physical and mental immaturity, needs special safeguards and care, including appropriate legal protection, before as well as after birth.[302] In fact, the UNCRC recognizes family as the fundamental group of the society and the natural environment for growth and well-being of all its members, particularly children. In accordance with Article 3[303] of the UNCRC, the best interests of the child shall be the primary consideration in all actions

---

[301] The National Plan of Action for the Child formulated by the Government of India incorporates immediate as well as long-term goals for the year 2000 and outlines a time-bound strategy for achieving the targets.

[302] CRC, Article 20:

(1) A child temporarily or permanently deprived of his or her family environment, or in whose own best interests cannot be allowed to remain in that environment, shall be entitled to special protection and assistance provided by the state.

(2) States parties shall in accordance with their national laws ensure alternative care for such a child.

(3) Such care could include, inter alia, foster placement, kafalah of Islamic law, adoption or if necessary placement in suitable institutions for the care of children. When considering solutions, due regard shall be paid to the desirability of continuity in a child's upbringing and to the child's ethnic, religious, cultural, and linguistic background.

[303] CRC, 1989, Article 3:

(1) In all actions concerning children, whether undertaken by public or private social welfare institutions, courts of law, administrative authorities, or legislative bodies, the best interests of the child shall be a primary consideration.

(2) States parties undertake to ensure the child such protection and care as is necessary for his or her well-being, taking into account the rights and duties of his or her parents, legal guardians, or other individuals legally responsible for him or her, and, to this end, shall take all appropriate legislative and administrative measures.

(3) States parties shall ensure that the institutions, services, and facilities responsible for the care or protection of children shall conform with the standards established by competent authorities, particularly in the areas of safety, health, in the number and suitability of their staff, as well as competent supervision.

concerning children, whether undertaken by public or private social welfare institutions, courts of law, administrative authorities or legislative bodies. This principle, reiterated in article 21[304] UNCRC in relation to adoption, implies a case-by-case appreciation of the interest of the child, and conflicts with a general approach which considers the adoption of a child as beneficial for him in all cases. Articles 18[305] and 27[306] of UNCRC confirm the importance of the responsibility

[304] UNCRC, 1989, Article 21:

States parties that recognize and/or permit the system of adoption shall ensure that the best interests of the child shall be the paramount consideration and they shall:

(1) Ensure that the adoption of a child is authorized only by competent authorities who determine, in accordance with applicable law and procedures and on the basis of all pertinent and reliable information, that the adoption is permissible in view of the child's status concerning parents, relatives, and legal guardians and that, if required, the persons concerned have given their informed consent to the adoption on the basis of such counselling as may be necessary.

(2) Recognize that ICA may be considered as an alternative means of child's care, if the child cannot be placed in a foster or an adoptive family or cannot in any suitable manner be cared for in the child's country of origin.

(3) Ensure that the child concerned by ICA enjoys safeguards and standards equivalent to those existing in the case of national adoption;

(4) Take all appropriate measures to ensure that, in ICA, the placement does not result in improper financial gain for those involved in it;

(5) Promote, where appropriate, the objectives of the present article by concluding bilateral or multilateral arrangements or agreements, and endeavour, within this framework, to ensure that the placement of the child in another country is carried out by competent authorities or organs.

[305] CRC, 1989, Article 1:

(1) States parties shall use their best efforts to ensure recognition of the principle that both parents have common responsibilities for the upbringing and development of the child. Parents or, as the case may be, legal guardians, have the primary responsibility for the upbringing and development of the child. The best interests of the child will be their basic concern.

(2) For the purpose of guaranteeing and promoting the rights set forth in the present convention, states parties shall render appropriate assistance to parents and legal guardians in the performance of their child-rearing responsibilities and shall ensure the development of institutions, facilities and services for the care of children.

(3) States parties shall take all appropriate measures to ensure that children of working parents have the right to benefit from child-care services and facilities for which they are eligible.

[306] CRC, 1989, Article 27:

(1) States parties recognize the right of every child to a standard of living adequate for the child's physical, mental, spiritual, moral, and social development.

(2) The parent(s) or others responsible for the child have the primary responsibility to secure, within their abilities and financial capacities, the conditions of living necessary for the child's development.

(3) States parties, in accordance with national conditions and within their means, shall take appropriate measures to assist parents and others responsible for the child to implement this right and shall in case of need provide material assistance and support programmes, particularly with regard to nutrition, clothing, and housing.

of parents for the upbringing of their children, but at the same time, the UNCRC requires the state parties to provide necessary assistance to parents (or other caretakers) in the performance of their parental responsibilities.

Convention on Protection of Children and Co-Operation in Respect of Inter-country Adoption 1993 (Ratified by India on 6 June 2003 and brought into force on 1 December 2003) (Hague Convention)

The ICA is a relatively new phenomenon, emerging only in the aftermath of the Second World War as a 'humanitarian' response, and expanding dramatically in the 1970s, with few international safeguards in place until the advent of the 1993 Hague Convention. The Convention on Protection of Children and Cooperation in Respect of Inter-country Adoption was adopted at the seventeenth session of the Hague Conference on Private International Law. India was also a participant at the deliberations.[307] The convention is to cover all inter-country adoptions between countries becoming parties to it, whether those adoptions are partly parent-initiated or arranged by public authorities, adoption agencies, or by private providers of adoption services. The convention sets a framework of internationally agreed minimum norms and procedures that are to be complied with in order to protect the children involved and the interests of their parents and adoptive parents. Contracting states are free to maintain or impose requirements and prohibitions additional to those set out in the convention.

India signed the Hague Convention on the Protection of Children and International Cooperation in Inter-country Adoption (1993) on 9 January 2003 and ratified the same on 6 June 2003, with a view to strengthening international cooperation and protection of Indian children placed in ICA. For the purpose of implementation of the convention in the country, the Ministry of WCD functions as the administrative ministry and the CARA as the central authority.[308]

The purpose of the Hague Convention was to reform pre-Hague ICA practice, which was viewed as 'chaotic', 'incoherent', and particularly subject to the abuse of child laundering/child trafficking. The primary mechanism for this reform was a system of Central Authorities who would provide the necessary supervision and accountability for all significant functions, persons,

---

(4) States parties shall take all appropriate measures to secure the recovery of maintenance for the child from the parents or other persons having financial responsibility for the child, both within the state party and from abroad. In particular, where the person having financial responsibility for the child lives in a state different from that of the child, states parties shall promote the accession to international agreements or the conclusion of such agreements, as well as the making of other appropriate arrangements.

[307] This conference was convened at the Hague on 10 March 1993 at the invitation of the Government of Netherlands and was attended by government delegates of nearly 69 countries, including India. At the conclusion of the seventeenth session of the Hague Conference, the participating states adopted the final text of the convention.

[308] Convention on Protection of Children and Co-Operation in Respect of Intercountry Adoption, Article 6(1): A contracting state shall designate a central authority to discharge the duties which are imposed by the convention upon such authorities.

and organizations involved in ICA, under minimum standards delineated in the convention.[309] The system of central authorities was also intended to facilitate the necessary international cooperation. Inadequate implementation of the convention poses severe challenges to the development of an ethical and orderly ICA system.[310]

In order to implement the norms, principle and procedure relating to adoption of children laid down by the Hague Convention on ICA, India must have an enabling legislation.

Salient Features of the Hague Convention

The convention's objects are as follows:[311]

- To establish safeguards to ensure that ICAs take place in the best interests of the child and with respect to his/her fundamental rights.
- To ensure a system of cooperation among contracting states so that the safeguards are respected and thereby there is a prevention of abduction, sale, or trafficking of children, and to secure the recognition of adoptions made in accordance with the convention. The convention is to apply to all adoptions between contracting states that create a permanent parent–child relationship.[312]

Requirement for ICA are set out in Articles 4 and 5 of the convention. The convention also requires every contracting state to establish central authorities and accredited bodies related to ICAs. The procedural requirements in ICAs are set out in the convention.

Article 14 of the convention requires that PAPs, habitually resident in one contracting state and wishing to adopt a child habitually resident in another, must apply to the central authority in the state of their habitual residence, or by reason of Article 22, to an accredited agency in that state. Under Article 22(5), the home study report on the PAPs finding them eligible and suited to adopt, and the report on the child, are to be prepared 'under the responsibility of the respective state's Central Authority or other public authority or an accredited body'. Chapter V of the convention deals with the recognition and effects of adoption. It ensures that adoptions certified as made in accordance with the convention shall be recognized by operation of law in both the contracting states.

Chapter VI of the convention contains a number of provisions of general application. Articles 30 and 32 deal with the preservation of information concerning the child's origin, identity of his/her parents, and his/her medical history. Article 33 deals with the reporting of actual or possible responsibility for ensuring that appropriate measures are taken. No reservations are permitted under Article 40 of the convention.

---

[309] David M. Smolin, *Abduction, Sale and Traffic in Children in the Context of Intercountry Adoption*, Information Document No. 1 for the Attention of the Special Commission of June 2010 on the practical operation of the Hague Convention of 29 May 1993 on Protection of Children and Co-operation in Respect of Intercountry Adoption, Permanent Bureau, The Hague, Netherlands, 2010.

[310] Smolin, *Abduction, Sale and Traffic.*

[311] Hague Convention, Article 1.

[312] Hague Convention, Article 2.

Article 21[313] of the convention deals with safeguards pertaining to ICAs. It also emphasizes on priority to in-country adoption, and ensures that status of children in ICA are equivalent to national adoptions, the placement of children has no improper financial gain, and the placement of children in ICA involve competent authorities of both the countries.

Significance and Relevance of the Hague Convention to India

The objectives and provisions of the convention reiterate and elaborate what is clearly contained in the Constitution of India, the National Policy for Children 1974, the UNCRC, the Supreme Court guidelines for ICA laid down in the *Laxmikant Pandey* judgments,[314] and the GWA. For instance, Article 4 of the Hague Convention states that an adoption within the scope of the convention will take place only after the possibilities for placement of the child within the state of origin of the child have been given due consideration. It also provides for consent of the child where possible, and counselling of the child and the parents, and ensures that such consent has not been induced by payment or compensation of any kind.

Article 6 of the Hague Convention states that there should be a designated central authority to discharge the duties which are imposed by the convention. In India, the CARA has also been set up with similar functions.[315] The CARA Guidelines 2015 have been formulated to ensure the implementation of what has been stated in the Hague Convention.

Articles 10, 11, 12, and 13 of the Hague Convention provide for accreditation to the competent bodies and norms for registration of agencies for ICAs. Under the prevalent Supreme Court guidelines, directions have been given to the Ministry of Social Welfare of the Government of India and of the states to recognize and license suitable agencies within the country. These could be further streamlined to ensure that the right kinds of agencies are involved.

Every application from a foreigner desiring to adopt a child from India must be sponsored by a social worker or child welfare agency recognized or licensed by the government of the country in which the foreigner is a resident.[316] Article 15 of the Hague Convention provides what we call the home study report, which has to accompany every application of the foreigner. There are similar provisions laid down in the Supreme Court guidelines and the guidelines of the task force.[317]

---

[313] Convention on Protection of Children and Cooperation in Respect of Inter-country Adoption, 1993, Article 21.

[314] *Laxmikant Pandey* v. *Union of India*, AIR 1984 SC 4699; AIR 1986 SC 273; AIR 1987 SC 232.

[315] CARA Guidelines, 2015. Available at http://cara.nic.in/InnerContent.aspx?Id=163#Guidelines (accessed on 5 September 2015).

[316] Hague Convention, Article 14.

[317] In *Laxmikant Pandey* v. *Union of India* (1984 SCR (2) 795), the Supreme Court had laid down the normative and procedural safeguards to be followed in the matter of inter-country and in-country adoptions. Pursuant to the judgment, the Ministry of Welfare, Government of India had issued certain guidelines in 1989. These guidelines were subsequently revised in 1995 pursuant to the recommendations made by a task force constituted by the Government of India under the chairmanship of Justice P.N. Bhagwati, former chief justice of India. The object of the revised guidelines was to provide a sound basis for adoption within the framework of the norms and principles laid down by the Supreme Court of India in a series of orders passed in Laxmikant Pandey's case. Under the revised guidelines, the Government of India in the

Article 24 of the Hague Convention states that the recognition of adoption may be refused in a contracting state only if the adoption is manifestly contrary to its public policy, taking into account the best interests of the child. This clause is the general escape clause, which allows any of the convention's provisions to be disregarded when observance would be manifestly contrary to the public policy. This clause probably adds a little to the power of exception which any of the contracting states would already have under the general rules of public policy, which operate over and above the framework of the convention. This convention is compatible with Indian laws both in letter and spirit, and we now need a law on ICA based on Supreme Court judgments, CARA guidelines, and the Hague Convention.

Protocol to Prevent, Suppress and Punish Trafficking in Persons, Especially Women and Children, 2000

The first major international instrument dealing with the trafficking of children is part of the 2000 United Nations Palermo protocols, titled the Protocol to Prevent, Suppress and Punish Trafficking in Persons, especially Women and Children. Article 3(a) of this document defines child trafficking as the 'recruitment, transportation, transfer, harboring and/or receipt' of a child for the purpose of exploitation.[318]

It creates a global language and legislation to define trafficking in persons, especially women and children; assist victims of trafficking; and prevent trafficking in persons. The trafficking in persons protocol also establishes the parameters of judicial cooperation and exchange of information among countries.[319] Although the protocol anticipates accomplishing what national legislation cannot do on its own, it is also intended to jumpstart national laws and to harmonize regional legislation against the trafficking in women and children. In December 2000, 148 countries gathered in Palermo, Italy, to attend a high-level conference opening the new United Nations Convention against Transnational Organized Crime to states signature. Of the 148 countries present, 121 signed the new United Nations Convention against Transnational Organized Crime, and over 80 countries signed one of its supplementary protocols—the Protocol to Prevent, Suppress and Punish Trafficking in Persons, Especially Women and Children. Another supplementary Protocol against the Smuggling of Migrants by Land, Sea and Air was also open for states signature, and a third Protocol on the Illicit Manufacturing of and Trafficking in Firearms was expected to be completed at the end of 2001.[320] The new UN convention and its supplementary protocol on trafficking in persons have to be ratified by 40 countries before they become instruments of

---

Ministry of Welfare had set up CARA to act as a clearing house of information with regard to children available for in-country and ICA and to regulate, monitor, and develop programmes for the rehabilitation of children through adoption.

[318] UN (2000),'U.N. Protocol to Prevent, Suppress and Punish Trafficking in Persons, especially Women and Children'.

[319] Janice G. Raymond, *Guide to the New UN Trafficking Protocol* (North Amherst, United States: European Women's Lobby, 2001). Available at http://www.no-trafficking.org/content/pdf/guide_to_the_new_un_trafficking_protocol.pdf (accessed on 5 September 2015).

[320] Raymond, *Guide to the New UN Trafficking Protocol.*

international law. The protocol promises to contest the world's organized crime networks and combat the trade in human beings and transnational prostitution. In an age of globalization of capital, information, and technology, organized trafficking operates as a transnational industry not contained by national borders.[321] The Protocol to Prevent, Suppress and Punish Trafficking in Persons, Especially Women and Children, commonly referred to as the Trafficking in Persons Protocol, specifically addresses the trade in human beings for purposes of the exploitation of prostitution and other forms of sexual exploitation, forced labour or services, slavery or practices similar to slavery, servitude, and the removal of organs.[322]

The exploitation of children has taken on a transnational character, frequently involving organized criminal groups and networks. Today, the most profitable activities of international organized crime are trafficking of arms, drugs, and human beings, including children. Trafficking of children is most often connected to the sale of children, child prostitution, and child pornography, as well as to child labour, child soldiering, illegal adoption, and other forms of exploitation.[323]

As a result of the growing globalization of child exploitation, the international community took immediate action. Using the same information technologies that facilitate the exploitation of children, people dedicated to child protection have attempted to increase global awareness. The explosive growth in circulation of information about old and new forms of child exploitation led to an innovative global movement to fight the practice.[324]

Highlights of the Trafficking in Persons Protocol

- That trafficked persons, especially women in prostitution and child labourers, are no longer viewed as criminals but as victims of a crime.[325]
- That global trafficking will be answered with a global response. Although organized criminals such as traffickers, smugglers, pimps, brothel keepers, forced labour lords, enforcers, and gangs are powerful forces, organized cooperation by police, immigration authorities, social service agencies, and NGOs is encouraged by this protocol.[326]
- That there is now an accepted international definition of trafficking and an agreed-upon set of prosecution, protection, and prevention mechanism on which to base national legislation against trafficking, and which can serve as a basis for harmonizing various country laws.[327]
- That all victims of trafficking in persons are protected, not just those who can prove having been forced.[328]

---

[321] Raymond, *Guide to the New UN Trafficking Protocol.*

[322] Raymond, *Guide to the New UN Trafficking Protocol.*

[323] UNICEF, *Handbook on the Optional Protocol on the Sale of Children, Child Prostitution and Child Pornography* (Italy: UNICEF Innocenti Research Centre, February, 2009). Available at http://www.unicef-irc.org/publications/pdf/optional_protocol_eng.pdf (accessed on 5 September 2015).

[324] UNICEF, *Handbook on the Optional Protocol on the Sale Of Children.*

[325] Raymond, *Guide to the New UN Trafficking Protocol.*

[326] The Trafficking in Persons, Article 10.

[327] Raymond, *Guide to the New UN Trafficking Protocol.*

[328] The Trafficking in Persons, Articles 3(a) and 3(b).

- That the consent of a victim of trafficking is irrelevant.[329]
- That the definition provides a comprehensive coverage of criminal means by which trafficking takes place, including not only force, coercion, abduction, deception, or abuse of power, but also less explicit means, such as abuse of a victim's vulnerability.[330]
- That this new international definition of trafficking helps ensure that victims of trafficking will not bear the burden of proof.[331]
- That the exploitation of prostitution and trafficking cannot be separated. The protocol acknowledges that much trafficking is for the purpose of prostitution and for other forms of sexual exploitation.[332]
- That it is not necessary for a victim to cross a border, so that women and children who are domestically trafficked for prostitution and forced labour within their own countries are also protected, subject to provisions listed in Article 3 of the main convention.[333]
- That the key element in the trafficking process is the exploitative purpose, rather than the movement across a border.[334]
- That this protocol is the first UN instrument to address the demand which results in women and children being trafficked, calling upon countries to take or strengthen legislative or other measures to discourage this demand that fosters all forms of exploitation of women and children.[335]

The process for adopting a child from another country (ICA) changed in significant ways with the ratification of the Hague Convention by various countries. Countries who are parties to the Hague Adoption Convention are referred to as Convention Countries. ICAs between the Convention Countries are governed by Hague adoption procedures. Countries who are not parties to the Hague Adoption Convention are referred to as non-Convention countries.

International Law Relating To Surrogacy

The importance of the family is laid down in international instruments. The UDHR[336] states that the family is the natural and fundamental group unit of society and is entitled to protection by society and the state.[337] The Convention for the Protection of Human Rights and Fundamental Freedoms, usually referred to as European Convention on Human Rights (ECHR), is an international treaty by which signatory states oblige themselves to secure certain rights to persons within their jurisdiction.[338]

Various countries have their own laws on surrogacy, discussed as follows.

---

[329] The Trafficking in Persons, Article 3(b).
[330] The Trafficking in Persons, Article 3(a).
[331] The Trafficking in Persons, Article 3(b).
[332] The Trafficking in Persons, Article 3(a).
[333] Raymond, *Guide to the New UN Trafficking Protocol.*
[334] The Trafficking in Persons, Article 3(a).
[335] The Trafficking in Persons, Article 9.5.
[336] UDHR. Available at www.un.org/Overview/rights.htm (accessed on 7 September 2015).
[337] UDHR, Article 16.
[338] ECHR, Article 1: Persons who consider that a state has breached its obligations under the convention and who have exhausted domestic remedies can seek redress before the European Court of Human Rights. Available at http://echr-online.info/echr-introduction/ (accessed on 7 September 2015).

Belgium[339]

Altruistic surrogacy is legal in Belgium, but commercial surrogacy is illegal. Further, although altruistic surrogacy is technically legal, there is only one hospital taking in couples and there are extremely strict rules to get in. This makes a lot of couples seek treatment outside Belgium.

France[340]

In France, Article 17/6 of the Civil Code makes void any agreement with a third party relating to procreation or gestation. In the *Mennesson* case, the highest court in France, the Cour de Cassation, ruled that that it was contrary to public policy to give effect to foreign surrogacy agreements. An appeal is currently being prepared by the intending parents for submission to the European Court of Human Rights. Likewise, the French Embassy's website in Kyiv strongly warns its citizens against the practice, saying those who fail to comply with the ban may encounter 'serious judicial and administrative problems', including possible criminal sanction.[341]

On the other hand, the Conseil d'Etat, the highest administrative court, provided an administrative means of recognizing foreign surrogacy agreements by overturning a decision of the French Consulate in India not to issue travel documents. The Conseil d'Etat has no jurisdiction over matters of parentage but nevertheless made an order which effectively made lawful a surrogacy agreement entered into overseas.[342]

Germany

The German courts have held that surrogacy is a breach of Article 1 of the Constitution, which states that human dignity is inviolable. To make a human being the subject of a contract is impermissible under German law, including the use of a third party's body for the purposes of reproduction. The strict definition of motherhood under the German Civil Code also makes surrogacy arrangements impermissible.[343]

The Netherlands

The popular image of the Netherlands as a liberal bastion does not as yet extend to its approach to surrogacy. Altruistic surrogacy is legal in the Netherlands, but commercial surrogacy is illegal.

---

[339] Available at http://www.familylaw.com.ua/index.php?option=com_content&view=article&id=69&Itemid=99&lang=en (accessed on 1 August 2015).

[340] French Civil Code.

[341] Available at http://www.familylaw.com.ua/index.php?option=com_content&view=article&id=69&Itemid=99&lang=en (accessed on 1 August 2015).

[342] Available at http://www.familylaw.com.ua/index.php?option=com_content&view=article&id=69&Itemid=99&lang=en (accessed on 1 August 2015).

[343] Available at http://www.familylaw.com.ua/index.php?option=com_content&view=article&id=69&Itemid=99&lang=en (accessed on 1 August 2015).

Entering or attempting to enter a surrogacy arrangement can be punished with imprisonment. Moreover, although altruistic surrogacy is technically legal, there are very few hospitals taking in couples and there are extremely strict rules to get in. This makes a lot of couples seek their treatment outside the Netherlands.[344]

Sweden

Surrogacy is banned in Sweden, but the country recently took a step toward a possible lifting of its ban on surrogate motherhood, when the Riksdag's Committee on Social Affairs recently voted by a wide majority to authorize the government to carry out an inquiry into surrogate motherhood.[345] Surrogacy in Sweden is on the right track, but still a very long way from liberalization.[346]

United Kingdom

Commercial surrogacy arrangements are not legal in the UK. Such arrangements were prohibited by the Surrogacy Arrangements Act 1985,[347] making it illegal to pay more than the expenses for a surrogacy. Regardless of contractual or financial consideration for expenses, surrogacy arrangements are not legally enforceable within the UK. A surrogate mother still maintains the legal right of determination for the child, even if they are genetically unrelated. Unless a parental order or adoption order is made, the surrogate mother remains the legal mother of the child.[348]

The UK's approach makes it very difficult for the intending parents to enter into commercial surrogacy arrangements. For example, it is unlawful for intending parents to advertise for a surrogate, or for a woman to advertise a willingness to become a surrogate. Section 2(1) of the Surrogacy Arrangements Act, 1985 prevents a third party (though not a surrogate or intending parents) from initiating or taking part in negotiations, offering or agreeing to negotiate, or compiling any information with a view to its use in making, or negotiating the making of, surrogacy arrangements.[349]

Since the Human Fertilisation and Embryology Act, 1990 came into force, intending parents have been able to acquire legal parenthood of their child to the exclusion of the surrogate (and, if applicable, her husband) by a parental order. The criteria for a parental order are now contained in Section 54 of the Human Fertilisation and Embryology Act, 2008. A parental order will usually be granted by the English courts, provided that the criteria set out in Section 54 are met and it is in the child's best interests to make the order. Although the act provides that no more

---

[344] Available at http://www.familylaw.com.ua/index.php?option=com_content&view=article&id=69& Itemid=99&lang=en (accessed on 1 August 2015).

[345] *The Local Se*, 'Sweden Mulls Legalizing Surrogate Motherhood', 13 March 2012.

[346] *The Local Se*, 'Sweden Mulls Legalizing Surrogate Motherhood'.

[347] D. Brahams, The Hasty British Ban on Commercial Surrogacy, *The Hastings Center Report* 17, 1(February 1987): 16–19, New York.

[348] Available at http://www.familylaw.com.ua/index.php?option=com_content&view=article&id=69& Itemid=99&lang=en (accessed on 1 August 2015).

[349] Available at http://www.familylaw.com.ua/index.php?option=com_content&view=article&id=69& Itemid=99&lang=en (accessed on 1 August 2015).

than 'reasonable expenses' should be paid to the surrogate, the English courts have retrospectively approved surrogacy payments made overseas which go beyond reasonable expenses. In any case, the couple must provide the English court with detailed documentation of all payments made to the surrogate mother.

United States

Issuance of a US citizenship at birth to a child born abroad is governed by the Immigration and Nationality Act (INA), 1952, Sections 301 and/or 309. The determination of citizenship to children born overseas to a US parent falls within jurisdiction of the US Department of State, which requires a US citizen to have a biological connection to a child in order to transmit US citizenship to such a child.[350]

Some states have written legislation, while others have developed common law regimes for dealing with surrogacy issues. Some states facilitate surrogacy and surrogacy contracts, others simply refuse to enforce them, and some penalize commercial surrogacy. Surrogacy-friendly states tend to enforce both commercial and altruistic surrogacy contracts and facilitate straightforward ways for the intended parents to be recognized as the child's legal parents. Some relatively surrogacy-friendly states only offer support for married heterosexual couples. Generally, only gestational surrogacy is supported and traditional surrogacy finds little to no legal support.

States generally considered to be surrogacy-friendly include California,[351] Illinois,[352] Arkansas,[353] Maryland,[354] and New Hampshire,[355] among others.

Important Judgments Relating to Adoption and Surrogacy

Important Judgments Relating to In-Country Adoption

Re Manuel Theodore D'souza and Mrs. Lourdes D'souza[356]

Facts

This was a matter of appointment of guardian of a female minor. Two couples who were Indian citizens and professing the Christian faith applied to the Mumbai High Court for being appointed

---

[350] Available at http://www.familylaw.com.ua/index.php?option=com_content&view=article&id=69& Itemid=99&lang=en (accessed on 1 August 2015).

[351] Available at http://digitalcommons.law.ggu.edu/cgi/viewcontent.cgi?article=1522&context=ggulrev (accessed on 1 August 2015).

[352] H. Joseph Gitlin, Illinois Becomes Surrogacy Friendly. Available at http://www.aaml.org/sites/default/files/Illinois%20Becomes%20Surrogacy%20Friendly.pdf (accessed on 1 August 2015).

[353] *Arkansas Democrat Gazette*, Sunday, 5 August 2007, reproduced on Simple Surrogacy. Available at https://www.simplesurrogacy.com/news/65-surrogates- families-find-state-eases-way.html (accessed on 1 August 2015).

[354] Available at http://www.inciid.org/printpage.php?cat=thirdparty&id=782, (accessed on 1 August 2015).

[355] Law Office of Catherine Tucker, 'FAQs about Surrogacy in New Hampshire'. Available at http://tuckerlegal.com/faqs-surrogacy-new-hampshire/ (accessed on 1 August 2015).

[356] (2000) 3 BCR 243.

as guardians under the GWA. In the course of the proceedings, they amended their petition to seek a prayer that the child be given to them in adoption.

The main issues before the court were:

- In the absence of legislation, whether the court has powers of giving an abandoned, orphaned, or destitute child in adoption.
- Does an abandoned, orphaned, or destitute child has a right to a family, a name, and nationality as a part of the right to life.
- Is the right of being adopted a fundamental right guaranteed to a child by Article 21 of the Constitution.
- Can the state deny to an orphaned or destitute child the right to be adopted because of its constitutional failure to enact legislation to give effect to Entry 5 of List III of the Seventh Schedule to the Constitution of India.
- Whether a married, childless couple has the fundamental right to adopt a child.
- Is adoption purely a part of personal law.
- If the right to adopt is a fundamental right, can civil courts enforce this right in the absence of legislation and/or administrative instructions having the force of law.
- Can this court, in exercise of the power conferred on it under Clause 17 of the amended letters patent, give a child in adoption.

Held

It was held by the court that the abandoned, orphaned, destitute, or a similarly situated child has the right to be adopted as a part of his fundamental right to life, as embodied in Article 21 of the Constitution. The fundamental right to life of these children includes the right to be adopted by willing parent/parents and to have a name and nationality. The right to be adopted, therefore, is an enforceable civil right which is justiciable in a civil court.

In the absence of any legislation setting out who can adopt, a person or persons who has or have taken a child in guardianship under the GWA will have the right to petition the courts to adopt the child.

As jurisdiction to pass orders on guardianship is in the district court and/or a high court having jurisdiction under its letters patent, pending legislation, it will be these courts which will have the right to give the child in adoption by way of a miscellaneous application in the petition for guardianship.

The court, before giving the child in adoption, must satisfy itself that it is in the best interest of the child that the person or persons seeking the guardianship of the child is or are suitable parent or parents.

A period of 2 years must elapse before the court considers the petition for adoption from the date the court passes the order of guardianship. Before making an order of adoption, the following conditions will have to be satisfied:

- A home study should be available which must contain, among other information, the following:

  ◆ The financial status of the adoptive parent or parents and their capacity to look after the needs of the child.

- ◆ The health and the medical report of the adoptive parent/parents.
- ◆ The opinions formed by the interviewer after interviewing the parent/parents and the child, if possible.
- ◆ Progress report of the child after having been given in guardianship, including state of health.

- The cost of preparing the report shall be borne by the adoptive parent/parents.
- Before passing final orders on the petition, the views of the Indian Council of Social Work (ICSW) shall be heard. The costs of ICSW will be borne by the adoptive parent/parents. The adoptive parent/parents will have to deposit a sum of Rs 500/- initially. Any additional expenses will be reimbursed by the adoptive parent(s).

As a child can be given in guardianship to person/persons eligible under the GWA and as they also have been given the right to adopt, the issue whether a childless couple has a fundamental right to adopt need not be answered, though prima facie it may be possible to arrive at that conclusion.

A guardian/guardians who has/have been appointed by courts in the post and whose guardianship continues, can apply for adoption if a period of 2 years has elapsed since the date of order of appointment of guardianship.

The legal consequences of an order of adoption will be that the personal law of the adoptive parent(s) would be applicable to the child, whose right of inheritance will be the same as that of a natural-born child.

As a consequence of adoption, the adoptive parent(s) will have the right to apply and get rectified the register of births showing the adoptive parent/parents as parents of the adopted child and bearing their name and surname, if so desired by the adoptive parents.

The court held these directions binding and they were issued to all state governments and authorities in the states and union territories within the territorial jurisdiction of the Mumbai High Court, under Articles 225 and 226 of the Constitution of India as parens patriae.

Vinay Pathak and His Wife, Indian Adoption Petition[357]

Facts

The petitioners, who are Hindus, were married. Both of them were actors by profession, though the second petitioner, with two young children to look after, was on a sabbatical. In a Guardianship Petition instituted under the GWA before the court on 13 April 2005, the petitioners sought their appointment as guardians of a female child. The child was born on 12 November 2004. The biological mother of the child and her spouse executed a declaration on 16 November 2004, four days after the child was born, recording the circumstances in which they had decided to surrender the child at the nursing home where the child was born. The declaration stated that the mother and her spouse had been counselled by a social worker at Bal Vikas, which is a placement agency recognized by the Government of India, and that they had voluntarily agreed to surrender the

---

[357] (2009) 111 BOM LR 3816.

child. At the foot of the declaration, a Scrutiny Officer of the ICSW made an endorsement of having counselled the parents of the contents of the document and of making the mother aware of the fact that she had a period of two months to reclaim the child, failing which the child may be placed either in adoption or guardianship. The parents did not come forth to claim the child. An affidavit was filed before the court on 13 April 2005,[358] in which the managing trustee of Bal Vikas certified the facts and recorded an opinion that it would be in the interest of the child to place her under guardianship.

By an order dated 8 June 2005, the petitioners were appointed guardians of the child. The child had since lived with the petitioners for over 4 years. A petition was filed seeking a declaration that the petitioners are the adoptive parents of the child with consequential rights, privileges, and responsibilities under the law.

The issue which arose before the court was whether a Hindu couple governed by the HAMA, with a child of their own, can adopt a child of the same gender under the provisions of the JJ Act.

Held

The court held that the JJ Act is viewed as amending the conflicting provisions of the HAMA. The JJ Act creates an exception in the case of adoption of an abandoned child. The focus of the legislation is on the condition of the child taken in adoption and its provisions are secular in character, not restricted to any religious or social group. Embargo under the HAMA, that a Hindu having a biological child cannot adopt a child of the same gender, is thus lifted by the JJ Act. The child of whom the petitioners assumed guardianship of did fit the description of a child in need of care and protection under Section 2(d)(v) of the JJ Act and of a surrendered child under Subsection (2) of Section 41, and in the interest and welfare of the child, the petition for adoption was allowed.

Ratio Decidendi

When the child to be adopted is an orphaned, abandoned, or surrendered child, or a child in need of care and protection as defined in JJ Act, the bar imposed by Section 11 (i) and (ii) of the HAMA does not bar a Hindu parent having a biological child from adopting the child of the same gender. The JJ Act comes into play.

Shabnam Hashmi v. Union of India[359]

Facts

The issue of common adoption of children irrespective of religion, race, or class came before the apex court in the aforementioned writ petition, wherein the petitioner sought for guidelines for the same and also urged the apex court to issue directions to the Union of India to enact an optional law with the prime focus on the child, in which considerations like religion would take a hind seat.

---

[358] 'Guardianship Petition', 83 of 2001.
[359] AIR 2014 SC 128.1

The petitioner, Shabnam Hashmi, had moved this court back in 2005 after she was told that she had only guardianship rights over a young girl she had brought home from an adoption home. Being a Muslim, she was subject to the Muslim Shariat Law which did not recognize an adopted child to be on par with a biological child. In her plea, Hashmi wanted the right to adopt and the right to be adopted to be recognized as fundamental rights. The bench, however, rejected the plea by stating that the sphere of practices and beliefs in the country reflected a conflicting thought process among the people.

Held

The court stated that adoption was a matter of personal choice and there was no compulsion on any person to adopt a child. The JJ Act defines adoption in Section 2(aa).[360] It confers upon the adoptive parents and the child all rights, privileges, and responsibilities that are attached to a normal parent–child relationship.

The three-judge bench consisting of Chief Justice P. Sathasivam and Justices Ranjan Gogoi and Shiv Kirti Singh, however, maintained that personal laws would continue to govern any person who chooses to submit himself until such time that the vision of a uniform civil code is achieved.

With this declaration, prospective parents, irrespective of their religious background, would be free to access the provisions of the JJ Act—a secular act—for adoption of children after following the procedure prescribed. The petitioner, Shabnam Hashmi, could treat the child like her own daughter.

This is a landmark judgment by the Supreme Court that has ruled that any person can adopt a child under the JJ Act, irrespective of the religion he or she follows, even if the personal laws of the particular religion do not permit it. The Supreme Court stated that '[t]he JJ Act 2000 is a secular law enabling any person, irrespective of the religion he professes, to take a child in adoption. It is akin to the Special Marriage Act 1954, which enables any person living in India to get married under that Act, irrespective of the religion he follows. Personal beliefs and faiths, though must be honoured, cannot dictate the operation of the provisions of an enabling statute.'

The ruling assumes significance as there are over 12 million orphaned children in India, but on an average only 4,000 get adopted every year. Till now, Muslims, Christians, Jews, and those from the Parsi community only had the power of guardianship, in which one possesses only legal right on the child till he or she turns an adult. The biological parents have a right to intervene during that period. Adoption makes one a natural parent and the child also gets all rights akin to a naturally born child and even inherits property rights.

The court, however, turned down the plea for declaring the right of a child to be adopted and right of a parent to adopt a fundamental right under the Constitution, saying that such an order cannot be passed at this stage in view of conflicting practices and beliefs. Terming the JJ Act a 'small step towards formation of a uniform civil code', the court said: 'A person is always free to adopt or choose not to do so and, instead, he follows dictates of the personal law. To us, the JJ Act is a small step in reaching the goal enshrined by Article 44 of the Constitution which prescribes a uniform civil code.'

---

[360] JJ Act, 2000, Section 2(aa): 'adoption' means the process through which the adopted child is permanently separated from his biological parents and becomes the legitimate child of his adoptive parents with all the rights, privileges, and responsibilities that are attached to the relationship.

Reportedly, the All India Muslim Personal Law Board (AIMPLB) had registered its protest against the PIL, terming it a covert attempt to slip in a uniform code by the backdoor, which would infringe the Shariat law. 'We have our own personal law and no step should be taken to covertly formulate a uniform adoption code without taking into account our stand on the issue', AIMPLB said before the apex court.[361]

Important Judgments on Inter-Country Adoptions

Laxmikant Pandey v. Union of India[362]

Facts

This writ petition was initiated on the basis of a letter addressed by one Laxmikant Pandey, an advocate, complaining of malpractices indulged in by social organizations and voluntary agencies engaged in the work of offering Indian children in adoption to foreign parents. The petitioner, accordingly, sought relief, restraining India-based private agencies 'from carrying out further activity of routing children for adoption abroad', and directing the Government of India, the ICCW, and the ICSW to carry out their obligations in the matter of adoption of Indian children by foreign parents. This letter was treated as a writ petition and, by an order, the court issued notice to the Union of India, the ICCW, and the ICSW to appear in answer to the writ petition and assist the court in laying down principles and norms which should be followed in determining whether a child should be allowed to be adopted by foreign parents and, if so, the procedure to be followed for that purpose, with the object of ensuring the welfare of the child.

Held

In the absence of a law providing for adoption of an Indian child by a foreign parent, the only way in which such adoption can be effectuated is by making it in accordance with the law of the country in which the foreign parents reside. Therefore, the only way in which a foreign parent could take an Indian child in adoption was by making an application to the court under whose jurisdiction the child ordinarily resided, for being appointed guardian of the person of the child under the GWA, with leave to remove the child out of India and take it to his own country for the purpose of adopting it in accordance with the law of his country. It was opined that such ICA should be permitted after exhausting the possibility of adoption within the country by the Indian parents.

The concern in this case was not the cases of adoption of children living with their biological parents, for in such class of cases, the biological parents would be the best persons to decide whether to give their child in adoption to foreign parents. It was only in those cases where the children sought to be taken in adoption are destitute or abandoned or are living in social or child welfare centres that it was necessary to consider that normative and procedural safeguards should be forged for protecting their interest and promoting their welfare.

The requirements to be insisted upon, so far as a foreigner wishing to take a child in adoption is concerned, were laid down. A summary of the requirements is as follows.

---

[361] Available at http://www.dailymail.co.uk/indiahome/indianews/article-2563303/Muslims-right-adopt-historic-Supreme-Court-ruling.html#ixzz3jXVbYk5E

[362] (1984) 2 SCC 244.

- Every application from a foreigner desiring to adopt a child must be sponsored by a social or child welfare agency recognized by the government of the country in which the foreigner is resident, and every application for taking a child in adoption must be accompanied by a home study report prepared by a professional social worker, and other documents.
- The Government of India shall prepare a list of social or child welfare agencies licensed or recognized for ICA by the government of each foreign country where the children from India are to be taken in adoption, and the list shall be prepared after getting the necessary information from the government of each foreign country and the IDMs in that foreign country.
- If the biological parents are known, they should be properly assisted in making a decision about relinquishing the child for adoption, by the institution or centre or home for childcare or social or child welfare agency to which the child is being surrendered. It was also pointed out that the biological parents should be induced or encouraged or even permitted to take a decision in regard to giving a child in adoption before the birth of the child or within a period of three months from the date of (accessed on 5 January 2017) birth.
- But where the child is an orphan, destitute, or abandoned child and its parents are not known, the institution or centre or home for childcare or social or child welfare agency in whose care the child has come, must try to trace the biological parents of the child. If the biological parents can be traced and it is found that they do not want to take back the child, the adoption process may continue. But if for any reason the biological parents cannot be traced, there can be no question of taking their consent or consulting them.
- Every recognized social or child welfare agency must maintain a register with the names and particulars of all children proposed to be given in ICA through it. The recognized social or child welfare agency must prepare a child study report through a professional social worker, giving all relevant information in regard to the child so as to help the foreigner to come to a decision whether or not to adopt the child, and to understand the child if he decides to adopt it; as also to assist the court in coming to a decision whether it will be for the welfare of the child to be given in adoption to the foreigner wishing to adopt it.
- The Government of India should set up a CARA with regional branches at a few centres, which are active in ICAs. Such an agency can act as a clearing house of information in regard to children available for ICA, and all applications by foreigners for taking Indian children for adoption can then be forwarded by the social or child welfare agency in the foreign country to the CARA, and the latter can in turn forward them to any of the recognized social or child welfare agencies in the country.

Laxmikant Pandey v. Union of India and Another[363]

Facts

This writ petition was initiated on the basis of a letter addressed by the petitioner, complaining of malpractices indulged in by social organizations and voluntary agencies engaged in the work of offering Indian children in adoption to foreign parents.

[363] AIR 1985 Supp SCC 701.

Held

1. The scrutinizing agency appointed by the court for the purpose of assisting it in reaching the conclusion whether it would be in the interest of the child to be given in adoption to foreign parents, must not in any manner be involved in placement of children in adoption.

2. The social or child welfare agency sponsoring the application must undertake that in case of disruption of the family of the foreigner before adoption can be effected, it will take care of the child and find a suitable alternative placement for it with the approval of the social or child welfare agency concerned in India and report such alternative placement to the court handling the guardianship proceedings, and such information shall be passed on both by the court as also by the social or child welfare agency concerned in India to the secretary, Ministry of Social Welfare, Government of India.

3. In the event of disruption of the family of the foreigner before adoption can be affected, the agency shall give intimation of this fact to the Indian Embassy or High Commission, as the case may be, and the Indian Embassy or High Commission shall also be kept informed about the whereabouts of the child so that they can take the necessary steps for ensuring that the child is properly taken care of and a suitable alternative placement for it is found. The primary responsibility for ensuring that the child is legally free for adoption must be that of the social or child welfare agency processing the application of the foreigner for guardianship of the child.

4. No court in a state will entertain an application for appointment of a foreigner as guardian of a child which has been brought from another state, and if there is a social or child welfare agency in that other state which has been recognized by the Government of India for ICA. If there is no recognized social or child welfare agency in the state where the child is found or obtained, the child shall be transferred to a recognized social or child welfare agency at the nearest place in the immediate neighbouring state.

5. Progress reports shall be submitted by the social or child welfare agency sponsoring the application of the foreigner until adoption is affected.

6. A foreign social or child welfare agency having a representative in India should have such a representative who is an Indian citizen with a degree or diploma in social work, coupled with experience in child welfare.

7. The execution of a bond would ordinarily be sufficient. The bond should be by way of security for repatriation of the child to India in case it becomes necessary to do so, as also for ensuring adoption of the child within a period of 2 years.

8. Where it is not possible for the foreigner to complete the adoption process within 2 years, an application should be made to the court for extension of time for making the adoption and the court may grant appropriate extension of time.

9. Notice of the application for guardianship of a child should in no case be published in the newspapers, because then the biological parents would come to know who is the person taking the child in adoption.

10. The recognized social or child welfare agency processing the application must also be entitled to recover from the foreigner who has sought to be appointed guardian of the child, costs incurred in preparing and filing the application, and processing it in court.

11. The court recommended the setting up of a VCA in each state and if circumstances so require, there may even be more than one VCA in a state. Where there is a VCA or any other centralized agency which maintains a register of children available for adoption as also

a register of Indian adoptive parents, it would be enough to wait for a period of three to four weeks.

Bengt Ingmar Eriksson v. Jamnibai Sukharya Dhangda[364]

Facts

One J and her husband, labourers of a village in Bassein taluk, had two minor daughters, G and L. Returning home late one evening, J found both the minor daughters missing from home, and unable to trace them till next morning, lodged a missing report at Bassein police station. Next evening, two minor girls were found crying on the street in Bombay city (now Mumbai) and at night both these girls were sent to a remand home at Dongri. The metropolitan magistrate, after receiving a report that it was not possible to trace the parents of the minor girls at Bassein, detained the girls in the observation home. One Mrs. M, a representative of the Family Association for Inter-country Adoption incorporated in Sweden, approached the juvenile court for permission to ascertain whether any child in the remand home could be considered for being given in foreign adoption, and thereafter, as a constituted attorney of one Mr. E, a national of Sweden, filed two miscellaneous petitions on the original side of the Bombay High Court for appointment as guardian of girls G and L, in accordance with the provisions of Section 9 of the GWA. One petition in respect of girl G was dismissed by the high court on the ground that G and L were siblings and they could not be separated, and thereafter, the petition in respect of L was withdrawn. Prior to the disposal of the said petitions, the juvenile court had passed an order declaring both the girls G and L to be destitute under Section 45 of the Bombay Children Act, 1948. Later, Mrs. M, as constituted attorney of E, the national of Sweden, again filed one miscellaneous petition for appointment of E as guardian of both minor girls G and L. After completion of other formalities, a notice of the application was given by the high court to representatives of the ICSW and after receiving their representation, the high court allowed the petition and granted leave to remove both the girls G and L to Sweden. On application to the juvenile court to hand over custody of the two girls G and L, the custody was handed over to Mr. E and his wife in February 1981. In July 1981, a court in Sweden granted permission for adoption of both the girls in favour of their national E and his wife, and that decree of adoption became final. Swedish citizenship was thereafter granted to the adopted children and they were given Swedish names. J, the mother, who was making inquiries for over 2 years, made an application in February 1982, claiming custody of the girls G and L to the juvenile court, but it disposed these applications expressing inability as the two girls had already left for Sweden in pursuance of the orders of the high court. After about 2 years, J addressed a letter through her advocate to the ICSW, seeking information about the two girls G and L. A year later, J took out a notice of motion, claiming that she should be added as a party, a respondent to the miscellaneous petition in which E was appointed as guardian and was permitted to take the two girls G and L to Sweden for adoption. J further prayed for reopening the case and setting aside the order passed in favour of E. The principal relief she claimed was directing E to produce

---

[364] Decided 8 June 1987. Notice of Motion No. 1738 of 1985 in Misc. Petition No. 570 of 1980 (Bom. Original Side).

and hand over the two girls to her as their mother and natural guardian, and by way of interim relief, sought a direction that the two girls G and L be brought back to Bombay for meeting the natural parents. J also took out a motion of notice for contempt proceedings against Mr. E and his constituted attorney in India, Mrs. M.

Held

- That the submission that the natural mother had a legal right to the custody of the children and that right could not be deprived for any reasons whatsoever was totally untenable. It was well settled that whenever a question pertaining to custody of a minor child arose before a court, the matter had to be decided not on consideration of legal rights of parties but on the sole and predominant criteria of what would best serve the interest and welfare of the minor.[365]
- That having regard to all the circumstances in the case including the time interval, it was in the interest and welfare of girls G and L that they should continue to have their status of adopted children and live in Sweden in their adoptive homes.
- That in spite of the sympathy one might feel for the natural mother, the effect of removing the girls G and L from the care and control of the adoptive parents would lead to disastrous consequences which must be avoided, and that it was not in the interest of the children to grant any relief sought in the motion.

This decision laid down several directions relating to the adopted children:

- The principle that the best interest of the child was of paramount consideration was reiterated.
- It was also not possible to grant the relief because the two girls G and L were no longer Indian nationals but had acquired Swedish nationality after passing of the adoption decrees by the Swedish court. An adopted child must be treated in law as if it had been born to the adopters in wedlock and since an adoption affected the status traditionally, the law of the domicile had a paramount controlling influence over the creation of status. Consequently, on adoption decree being passed, the law of their domicile would determine the rights of care and custody in respect of the two girls, and that was the Swedish law. In view of these developments, it was not possible for the high court to have any control over the two girls and it was not permissible to pass any order directing Mr. E, a Swedish national, to bring back the two girls who were also Swedish nationals.
- The undertaking given to the high court at the time of passing of the order appointing Mr. E as guardian, that the minor girls would be repatriated to India as and when it became necessary, could not be availed of after passing of the decree of adoption by the Swedish court. Once the girls became Swedish nationals and were duly adopted, the undertaking to repatriate them came to an end and could not be enforced.
- Irrespective of the fact whether a child was adopted in a foreign country or in India, the court should be extremely reluctant and slow in either setting aside the adoption or in ignoring it as

---

[365] *Mrs Elzabeth Dinshaw* v. *Arvand M. Dinshaw*, AIR 1987 SC 3; *J v. C*, 1967 Ch. Div. 761; re E(D)1970 AC 669.

it would lead to serious consequences both to the adopter and to the adopted child. The court might exercise its jurisdiction in exceptional cases, where it was established that the adoption was secured by fraud or misrepresentation and such fraud or misrepresentation was at the instance of the adopter.

- No directions could be issued to the adoptive parents in respect of upbringing of the daughters G and L and making them learn any Indian languages and it would be appropriate to leave it to the good sense of the adoptive parents to determine whether the girls should maintain any contact with the natural parents in India, and if so, in what form.

- More precautions were required to be taken before declaring a child as a destitute. It was desirable that the state government should immediately issue the following instructions to the police so that such occasions would not be repeated when, in spite of a complaint having been lodged about a missing child, the police authorities fail to give any assistance to the unfortunate parents:

  a) A separate register of missing children should be maintained at each police station.

  b) An entry should be made immediately on production of any missing child at the police station and the child's photograph kept in the register.

  c) Copies of the entries in the register with the copies of the photograph should be forwarded at the end of each month by each police station to the commissioner of police in Greater Bombay and a central register should be maintained in the office of the commissioner of police. In the rural areas, copies should be forwarded to the office of the district superintendent of police and a central register should be maintained at each district headquarters.

  d) The state government should give wide publicity to the fact of recovery of missing children in local newspapers, on the radio, and on the television. This publicity should be given within a period of fifteen days from the date of production of the child before the juvenile court.

Re Jay Kevin Salerno[366]

Facts

In this petition, Pooja, a minor, was abandoned by her natural mother in the care of Bal Asha Trust, an institution. This institution is not recognized for ICA. Hence, the secretary of the trust requested St Joseph's Home and Nursery to admit the minor to that institution for the purpose of ICA. After the child was accepted and registered at St Joseph's Home, she was kept in a private nursing home for better care. The child was thus not physically kept at St Joseph's Home. As per the direction of the Supreme Court, a child has to be in the custody of a recognized agency for at least a month. This was to prevent a recognized institution from acting merely as a post office or conduit pipe.

It was held that the term 'custody' cannot be interpreted as actual physical custody. Interpreting the Supreme Court direction given in the case of Laxmikant Pandey too literally would also cause

---

[366] Misc. Petition No. 490 of 1987 (Bom. Original Side). Decided 7 October 1987.

harm to a child in a given case; for example, it may not be desirable to move the child physically from familiar surroundings to another place for a period of one month merely for the preparation of a child study report. The custody, therefore, of a recognized institution should be broadly interpreted to mean not physical custody but custody in the sense of supervision and control over the child so that the institution can arrange for a child's individual care or medical treatment (whenever required).

Laxmikant Pandey v. Union of India and Others[367]

In this judgment, further directions were given regarding the adoption of children by foreign parents:

- It was not agreed that Indian citizenship should continue until the adopted child attains the age of majority and is legally competent to opt. Such a step would run counter to the need of quick assimilation and may often stand as a barrier to the requirements of the early cementing of the adopted child into the adoptive family. With regard to the issue of the birth certificate of the adopted child, it was opined that such a certificate should be obtained on the basis of application of the society sponsoring adoption. In most of these cases the registration of birth may not be available because that would not have been done.
- The licensing authority should ordinarily ensure that the registered agency has proper child-care facilities.
- An escalation of 30 per cent was allowed for expenses to be recovered from the adoptive parents by the agency offering placement, for maintaining the child. But the escalation of 10 per cent each year was not agreed to. The matter would be reviewed once in 3 years so far as escalation of expenses was concerned.
- About the transfer of children from statutory homes to recognized agencies for placement, it was directed that as and when such a request is received from recognized agencies, the juvenile court or the board set up under the JJ Act may consider the feasibility of such transfer and make appropriate order keeping the interests of the child in view, as also other relevant factors like the possibility of an adoption within a short period and the facilities available in the recognized agency.

Smt. Anokha v. State of Rajasthan[368]

Facts

A couple who were Italian nationals adopted a female child from its biological mother after the father of the biological child, known to them for 20 years, died in a road traffic accident. The district judge before whom a petition was filed under Sections 7, 10, and 17 of the GWA, 1890

---

[367] 1991 (2) Scale, Order dated 14 August 1991 in Criminal Misc. Petition Nos. 3352, 3475, 2045, 5704, 8661, 8842, 9122 of 1990, and 2838 of 1991 in Writ Petition (Criminal) No. 1171 of 1986.

[368] (2004) 1 SCC 382.

dismissed the same on the ground that the guidelines prescribed by the Ministry of Welfare, Government of India, would have to be followed and that unless an authorized agency in Italy submitted an enquiry report and an NOC was issued by the Ministry of Welfare, the application for appointment of foreigners as guardians could not be accepted. The district judge, while holding so, took the view that the guidelines would apply irrespective of whether the child's biological parents were alive or not. The high court also affirmed the said view.

Held

While reversing the decisions of the district court and the high court, the Supreme Court referred to the decision in L.K. Pandey[369] and held as follows.

The decision (has referred to three classes of children):

1. children who are orphaned and destitute or whose biological parents cannot be traced;
2. children whose biological parents are traceable but have relinquished or surrendered them for adoption; and
3. children living with their biological parents. The third category has been expressly excluded from consideration as far as the decision was concerned, for in such cases, the biological parents would be the best persons to decide whether to give their child in adoption to foreign parents.

The reason is obvious. Normally, no parent with whom the child is living would agree to give a child in adoption unless he or she is satisfied that it would be in the best interest of the child. That is the greatest safeguard.

The guidelines prescribed for 'Adoption of Indian Children' issued by the Ministry of Welfare, Government of India, have been formulated from various directives as given by this court in the several decisions and do not relate to regulation of the adoption procedure to be followed in respect of the third category of children, namely, children with their biological parents who are sought to be given in adoption to a known couple, as is the situation in this case. It is only where there is a need to impersonalized attention of a placement of authority that there is a need to closely monitor the process, including obtaining of an NOC from the CARA, Ministry of Welfare. Indeed, CARA has been set up under the guidelines for the purpose of eliminating the malpractices indulged in by some unscrupulous placement agencies, particularly the trafficking in children.

Under the CARA Guidelines, the home study report is to be enclosed, with a copy to CARA, with an application for adoption, which must be routed through a foreign and enlisted agency, which in turn must be an enlisted agency in India. The home study report is required to contain the following particulars:

1. Social status and family background.
2. Description of home.
3. Standard of living as it appears in the home.

---

[369] (1984) 2 SCC 244.

4. Current relationship between husband and wife.
5. Current relationship between the parents and children (if any children).
6. Development of already adopted children (if any).
7. Current relationship between the couple and the members of each other's family.
8. Employment status of the couple.
9. Health details such as clinical test, heart condition, past illness, and so on (medical certificates and other documents).
10. Economic status of the couple.
11. Accommodation for the child.
12. Schooling facilities.
13. Amenities in the home.
14. Reasons for wanting to adopt an Indian child.
15. Attitude of grandparents and relatives towards adoption.
16. Anticipated plans for the adoptive child.
17. Legal status of the prospective adopting parents.

The report is required to be notarized, which must in turn be attested either by an officer of the Ministry of External Affairs or an officer of the justice or social welfare department of the foreign country concerned, or by an officer of the Indian Embassy or High Commission or Consulate in that country.

The Supreme Court further held that none of these provisions impinge upon the rights and choice of an individual to give his or her child in adoption to named persons, who may be of foreign origin. The Court, in such cases, has to deal with the application under Section 7 of the GWA and dispose of the same after being satisfied that the child is being given in adoption voluntarily after being aware of the implication of adoption, namely that the child would legally belong to the adoptive parents' family, not influenced by any extraneous reasons such as the receipt of money or other factors, that the adoptive parents have produced evidence in support of their suitability, and finally, that the arrangement would be in the best interest of the child.

St. Theresa's Tender Loving Care Home and Ors. v. State of Andhra Pradesh[370]

Facts

The appellants were residents of USA and were married. They had earlier adopted one son, but wanted to adopt a female child from India. The minor child Sahiti was stated to be the daughter of an unmarried mother by name Esther, a native of Hyderabad, and earning a livelihood as a labourer. Due to social stigma, she had relinquished the child in favour of the appellants and permission of the family court was sought. The mother had executed the relinquishment deed in favour of the appellant. The state of Andhra Pradesh resisted the claim of the appellant as the state government had banned relinquishment of children because of child trafficking indulged in by some unscrupulous organisations. An inquiry was directed to be conducted by the crime branch

[370] AIR 2005 SC 4375.

of CID. After enquiry, the CID reported that the relinquishment deed was a fake and fabricated document.

The central government also requested the CARA to initiate action against appellants for the false claim. The family court rejected the application, holding that the VCA issued the NOC on the ground that the Indian parents had refused to adopt the child because she was suffering from skin disease. The family court was of the view that the so-called reasons did not merit. The child study report was also referred to, which indicated that the child did not suffer from any ailment. The view of the family court was affirmed by the high court.

Held

The court held that it should be ensured that behind the mask of social service or upliftment, the evil design of child trafficking is not lurking. It was further held that it is the duty of the state to ensure a safe roof over an abandoned child. Keeping in view the welfare of the child, all possible efforts should be made by the state governments to explore the possibility of adoption under the supervision of the designated agency. In the background of what was noticed by the family court and the high court, it was crystal clear that the orders passed do not suffer from any infirmity to warrant interference. Dismissing the appeal, the appellant was also prosecuted for offences punishable under various provisions of the IPC. The accusations related to cheating and manipulation/fabrication of documents.

Aniruddha M. Railkar and Anr. v. Indian Council for Social Welfare and Anr.[371]

Facts

The appellants are foreign nationals of Indian origin residing in the USA. They desired to adopt an Indian child. They initially applied to the US agency Adoptions from the Heart. Their home study report was done. They were approved for adoption. Since they desired to adopt an Indian child, they obtained information from the website of the CARA,. They came to learn, inter alia, of an NGO called Preet Mandir. They were given a match for a male child that they desired. The CARA gave the clearance for the adoption in 2005. Accordingly, the appellants executed the acceptance deed and accepted the child. Meanwhile, recognition granted to the NGO got suspended.

The appellants filed a petition for appointment as guardian of the said child. However, the family court, Pune, heard and rejected the appellants' petition on the ground that the recognition to Preet Mandir for granting ICA was suspended. Hence, the appellants filed an appeal at the High Court of Bombay.

Held

The high court held that the consideration by the family court about the suspension of the licence and issue framed thereon was misconceived. Such applications are to be dealt with expeditiously, as any delay on the part of any authority, including judicial officers, results in delayed bonding of the child with their adoptive families, causing their overall welfare to be prejudicially affected. Courts are required only to oversee and supervise work already done by the recognized NGOs and CARA. Further, the courts have to ensure that adoptive parents are reasonably settled and able to take care of the children.

Any adverse report against any recognized and accredited agency or NGO calls for necessary action to be taken against its errant officers only, and should not lead to rejection of adoption of a child who is not even responsible for any illegal act of the agency. Hence, the impugned order was not sustainable. The court, accordingly disposing of the appeal, declared the appellants as guardians, and allowed them to take custody of the minor child.

Ratio Decidendi

By virtue of Section 7 of the GWA, the only consideration for appointing a guardian is the welfare of child. The court, while disposing such petitions, is required to consider financial and cultural background of the adoptive parents.

Robert Heijkamp v. Bal Sadan Rescue Home[372]

Facts

The petitioners—husband and wife—were Dutch nationals. They were sponsored as suitable adoptive parents by their government agency. They applied to the Dutch sponsoring agency for adoption and through it applied to the respondents (Bal Anand World Children Welfare Trust). The respondent was a trust recognized by the government as a child welfare organization.

The petitioners sought an order for their appointment as guardians of the person of the child now in the custody of the respondents. The petitioners submitted their documents to CARA. As per the certificate issued by the CWC dated 13 September 2006, the child's mother was an inmate of the Beggar's Home for Women. The child was born on 13 November 2004, when her mother was an inmate of the Beggar's Home. The mother was stated to be suffering from psychosis and therefore was not in a position to take care of her child. The child was brought before the CWC by the probation officer of the Beggar's Home for Women, and was placed in the custody of the respondents for her further care. Even after publication in newspapers, no one came forward to claim the child. The CWC, therefore, declared the child legally free for adoption and recorded its no objection for her suitable rehabilitation. The VCA, by its certificate, stated the medical problems of the child and that no suitable Indian family was willing to adopt her. The CARA also issued an NOC stating that it was satisfied that the necessary procedure had been properly followed.

Held

It would be necessary for the CWC to satisfy itself clearly in each case whether the abandonment is likely to be only temporary or whether it is likely to be of a longer duration. Indeed, even this

[372] (2008) 1 Bom CR 719.

conclusion would be subject to the decision of the court in such matters. The CWC cannot, on its own, come to this conclusion. The mental illness of a person can only be determined under the provisions of the Mental Health Act, 1987 or any other statutory enactment providing for such determination. There is no provision in the JJ Act or in any other law which confers any power, statutory or otherwise, on the CWC to determine whether a person is mentally ill or not. If, therefore, for instance, the court, under the Mental Health Act, records the finding that the parent of a child is mentally ill, the CWC would be justified in coming to the conclusion that the child is abandoned and therefore declare the child of such person legally free for placement/adoption. If again, for instance, the court, in exercise of powers under the Mental Health Act, returns a finding that the alleged mentally ill person is likely to be cured of his illness, the CWC may or may not declare the child of such person legally free for placement/adoption. Therefore, this petition was dismissed with liberty to the petitioners to file the petitions afresh, after complying with the aforementioned requirements.

Craig Allen Coates v. State[373]

Facts

The child, Anil, was found abandoned by police officials of New Delhi, and was transferred to the respondent's institution in the year 2006. The child was declared as an abandoned child and was certified legally free for adoption by the CWC. The Coordinating Voluntary Adoption Resource Agency (CVARA) and the CARA gave their clearance for ICA of the child. In this case, the child to be adopted was found to have developmental delays and difficulties with respect to learning and expressing, and required special care for learning needs. The medical board at the All India Institute of Medical Sciences (AIIMS) opined that such a child would benefit from family-based care and nurturance, rather than institutional care.

The board examined Ms. Coates (the lady applying for adoption), her intentions, her professional experience, and her proposed education of the child. She had extended experience in home-based nursing and in a respite home where she had given personal care to patients with neuro-muscular disorders, cognitive impairments, and other handicaps. Her experience in home health and her sensitivity towards multicultural issues was evident in her interactions. She presented a clear vision of the family, school, and community resources she needed to mobilize in order to make the adoption successful. She was found to be committed to providing physical therapy, occupational therapy, speech therapy, and special education to her adopted child. She had adequate financial and emotional resources to provide for the adopted child. The board also viewed the recently recorded video made with the child's current setup where the child's interaction within the group was observed. The reciprocity in the relationship between Ms. Coates and the child became apparent during the interview. The board was of the opinion that the petitioners should be allowed to adopt the minor male child.

[373] (2010) 11 SCR 102.

Held

The Supreme Court, after considering the report of the medical board of AIIMS and considering the experience of the appellants therein in home nursing, found her the proper person to whom the child could be given in adoption.

The court also directed that for ICAs, the procedure followed could include a reference to an expert committee on the lines constituted in this case to ensure that ICAs are allowed only after full and proper satisfaction is recorded by all the agencies, including a committee of experts, wherever reference to such a committee is considered necessary.

The court further held that CARA should request the director of AIIMS to constitute a committee of experts to be headed by professor and head of the department of psychiatry, AIIMS and in order to facilitate references to them in regard to children who may be living at distant places from Delhi, CARA may have similar expert committees constituted in other states too.

Mr. Frank M. Costanzo v. Regional Passport Officer[374]

Facts

The adoptive parents filed a petition under Sections 7 and 10 of the GWA before the family court at Puducherry. The biological parents recorded no objection and the family court passed an order appointing the foreign nationals as guardians. Thereafter, they also filed another application under Section 17 read with Section 26, seeking permission to take the child to the USA. The government pleader, who represented the Union of India, Social Welfare Department, endorsed no objection and the petition was allowed, granting permission to the adoptive parents to take the child to the USA. But when they applied for the issuance of a passport to the adopted son, the regional passport officer rejected the request on the ground that the adoption was not done in accordance with the procedures and guidelines framed by the Supreme Court and incorporated into the rules. The regional passport officer consequently demanded an NOC from CARA. Challenging the said decision, a writ petition was filed by the adoptive parents.

Held

A question arose as to whether the regional passport officer could insist upon an NOC from the CARA for the issuance of a passport to a child adopted by foreign nationals. After referring to the decisions of the Supreme Court in *Laxmikant Pandey*[375] and *Smt. Anokha*,[376] the high court held that in the case of adoption from biological parents, the guidelines would not apply. Consequently, the court came to the conclusion that the regional passport officer was not entitled to insist upon an NOC from the CARA.

---

[374] W.P. No. 14880 of 2010, Madras High Court.
[375] (1984) 2 SCC 244.
[376] (2004) 1 SCC 382.

Maria Chaya Schupp, a German National represented by her Constituted Attorney, Smt. Geeta Menon v. the Director General of Police and Ors.[377]

Facts

The petitioner, a 32-year old German national, approached the respondents for finding out details of her biological mother. The petitioner claimed that as a child she was an inmate of the respondent's institution known as Society for Sisters of Charity Nirmala Social Welfare Centre, a child welfare agency. The petitioner claimed that she recollects having grown up at the said centre and when the petitioner was 6 years old, she was given up for ICA by the respondents to Shri Wolfgang Schupp and Smt. Ingrid Schupp of Germany in March 1981. The petitioner suspected that she was possibly kidnapped and then given up for adoption with the active assistance of the respondents. The petitioner stated that she had in her possession two documents indicating her date of birth differently. These documents were provided to her adoptive parents by the German Agency Pro Infante, before her adoption. Therefore, she was not sure whether her date of birth was 24 March 1976 or 8 December 1975.

The petitioner's plight and her search for details of her mother were widely reported in several newspapers. The petitioner claimed that she had psychological reasons for the urge to know about her biological mother and a person's right to know of one's biological parents is well entrenched in law in most civilized countries around the world.

The respondents refused to give any information to the petitioner. The petitioner contended that the refusal to release any information regarding the biological mother of the petitioner was only in order to cover up the respondent's nefarious and illegal role in kidnapping and placing the petitioner for ICA. The petitioner was thus deprived of her right to secure valid information and hence the intervention of the court was needed. The denial of information to the petitioner, though a German Citizen, is a denial of her right to life under Article 21 of the Constitution of India. Hence, the present petition was filed.

Held

The court held that the petitioner possessed documents indicating her date of birth differently, which was furnished to her adoptive parents by German agency Pro Infante prior to her adoption. It was found that prior to 1984; no formal recognition or licence was required by institutions to engage in adoption work. Further, material documents on which the petitioner relied to hold that the respondent—the Society for Sisters of Charity Nirmala Social Welfare Centre, which had her custody—could be aware of particulars of her birth and existence or otherwise of her biological mother, were undated. Thus, records so produced to and by the petitioner were vague and established inconsistent history of the petitioner's birth. Therefore, the court dismissed this petition.

What is significant in the matter is that the right to search for roots, as such, was not rejected.

---

[377] 2010 Cri LJ 883.

In Re: Mr. Tim Cecil and Mrs. Steffi Cecil[378]

Facts

A petition was filed in the High Court of Madras under Sections 3[379] and 7 to 10[380,381,382,383] of the GWA, by a couple from Germany, seeking their appointment as guardians of an infant girl

---

[378] High Court of Madras, O.P. No. 247 of 2011.

[379] GWA, 1890, Section 3: Saving of jurisdiction of Courts of Wards and Chartered High Courts—This act shall be read subject to every enactment heretofore or hereafter passed relating to any Court of Wards by any competent Legislature, authority or person in any state to which this act extends; and nothing in this act shall be construed to effect or in any way derogate from, the jurisdiction or authority of any Court of Wards, or to take away any power possessed by any High Court.

[380] GWA, 1890, Section 7: Power of the court to make order as to guardianship—

(1) Where the court is satisfied that it is for the welfare of a minor that an order should be made—(a) appointing a guardian of his person or property or both, or (b) declaring a person to be such a guardian—the court may make an order accordingly.
(2) An order under this section shall imply the removal of any guardian who has not been appointed by will or other instrument or appointed or declared by the court.
(3) Where a guardian has been appointed by will or other instrument or appointed or declared by the court, an order under this section appointing or declaring another person to be guardian in his stead shall not be made until the powers of the guardian appointed or declared as aforesaid have ceased under the provisions of this act.

[381] GWA, 1890, Section 8: Persons entitled to apply for order—An order shall not be made under the last foregoing section except on the application of

(1) the person desirous of being, or claiming to be, the guardian of the minor;
(2) any relative or friend of the minor;
(3) the collector of the district or other local area within which the minor ordinarily resides or in which he has property; or
(4) the collector having authority with respect to the class to which the minor belongs.

[382] GWA, 1890, Section 9: Court having jurisdiction to entertain application—

(1) If the application is with respect to the guardianship of the person of the minor, it shall be made to the district court having jurisdiction in the place where the minor ordinarily resides.
(2) If the application is with respect to the guardianship of the property of the minor, it may be made either to the district court having jurisdiction in the place where the minor ordinarily resides, or to a district court having jurisdiction in a place where he has property.
(3) If the application with respect to the guardianship of the property of a minor is made to a district court other than that having jurisdiction in the place where the minor ordinarily resides, the court may return the application if in its opinion the application would be disposed of more justly or conveniently by any other district court having jurisdiction.

[383] GWA, 1890, Section 10: Form of application—

(1) If the application is not made by the collector, it shall be by petition signed and verified in manner prescribed by the CPC, 1882 (14 of 1882), for the signing and verification of a plaint, and stating, so far as can be ascertained,

aged about 8 months. This case was filed with the consent of the biological parents, without being processed through a recognized agency from either of the countries involved. It was argued by the petitioners that sponsorship by an agency and a home study report are necessary only in cases of adoption of abandoned children and that the same need not be insisted upon in cases where the biological parents themselves willingly give their child in adoption. In this case the biological parents themselves were giving the child in adoption.

Held

The court, in light of the mandate contained in the UNCRC and the Hague Convention—both of which had been ratified by India—and also in light of provisions of the JJ Act, 2000 as amended in 2006, held that the primary responsibility of providing care and protection to children was that of his birth family. Since the child had a fundamental right to be protected against any kind of exploitation, biological parents could not be held to have an absolute and unfettered right to give their children in adoption or for foster care to foreign nationals. Therefore, the same could not, as on date, enable biological parents to contend that their rights to give their children in adoption to foreign nationals was absolute and unfettered. In such circumstances, despite the fact that the parties involved in this case appeared to be genuine, the court was unable to order the original petition as prayed for unconditionally, without even a home study report. Hence, the minimum safeguard

<hr>

(a)   the name, sex, religion, date of birth and ordinary residence of the minor;

(b)   where the minor is a female, whether she is married, and if so, the name and age of her husband;

(c)   the nature, situation, and approximate value of the property, if any, of the minor;

(d)   the name and residence of the person having the custody or possession of the person or property of the minor;

(e)   what near relations the minor has, and where they reside;

(f)   whether a guardian of the person or property or both, of the minor has been appointed by any person entitled or claiming to be entitled by the law to which the minor is subject to make such an appointment;

(g)   whether an application has at any time been made to the Court or to any other Court with respect to the guardianship of the person or property or both, of the minor, and if so, when, to what Court and with what result;

(h)   whether the application is for the appointment or declaration of a guardian of the person of the minor, or of his property, or of both;

(i)   where the application is to appoint a guardian, the qualifications of the proposed guardian;

(j)   where the application is to declare a person to be a guardian, the grounds on which that person claims;

(k)   the causes which have led to the making of the application; and

(l)   such other particulars, if any, as may be prescribed or as the nature of the application renders it necessary to state.

(2)   If the application is made by the collector, it shall be by letter addressed to the court and forwarded by post or in such other manner as may be found convenient, and shall state as far as possible the particulars mentioned in Subsection (1).

(3)   The application must be accompanied by a declaration of the willingness of the proposed guardian to act, and the declaration must be signed by him and attested by at least two witnesses.

that could be adopted was to call for a home study report, if not a sponsorship through an agency, so that the decision taken by the biological parents to hand over their child to the petitioners could be accepted to be a decision taken in the best interest of the child. In view of this, a direction was issued to the CARA to engage services of a recognized and approved agency in Germany and have a home study conducted in respect of the petitioners, and submit the same to the court to enable the court to allow the original petition, as prayed for. All that was required was that CARA should request an approved agency in Germany to conduct a home study and send a report, which could be forwarded by the concerned authority to this court within the period stipulated. Therefore, the original petition before the court shall be filed or immediately upon receipt of a report from CARA, whichever was earlier. With this direction, the petition was disposed of.

In this case the court assured that the minimum safeguard of a home study report was at least required relating to adoption even where the child was not abandoned and the birth parents were there.

Stephanie Joan Becker v. State and Ors.[384]

Facts

By the application filed under Section 7 of the GWA, the appellant had sought for an order of the court appointing her as the guardian of a female orphan child aged about 10 years. Whereas by the second application filed under Section 26 of the GWA, the appellant had sought permission of the court to take the child, Tina, out of the country for the purpose of adoption.

The application was rejected by the trial court on a sole and solitary ground, namely that the appellant, being a single PAP, was aged about 53 years at the relevant point of time, whereas for a single adoptive parent the maximum permissible age as prescribed by the Government of India guidelines in force was 45. Though a no objection, which contained an implicit relaxation of the rigour of the guidelines with regard to age, had been granted by the CARA, the High Court of Delhi did not interfere with the trial court's order. The appellant, thereafter, filed an appeal at the Supreme Court of India, thereby challenging the impugned order made by the High Court of Delhi by its order dated 9 July 2012 in FAO No. 425 of 2010.

Held

The Supreme Court held that the appellant was appointed as the legal guardian of the female child with necessary directions. Each and every norm of the adoption process spelt out under the guidelines of 2006, as well as the guidelines of 2011, has been adhered to. It was found that the apprehension raised by the intervener, though perhaps founded on good reasons, had proved themselves wholly unsubstantiated in the case. If the foreign adoptive parent was otherwise suitable and willing, and consent of the child had also been taken (as in this case), and the expert bodies engaged in the field were of the view that in the present case the adoption process would end in a successful blending of the child in the family of the appellant in the USA, it could not be seen as to how the appellant could be understood to be disqualified or disentitled to the relief(s)

---

[384]   AIR 2013 SC 3495.

sought by her in the proceedings in question. Therefore, having regard to the totality of the facts of the case, the proposed adoption would be beneficial to the child apart from being consistent with the legal entitlement of the foreign adoptive parent.

The court held that since the adoption process adhered to the guidelines, and expert bodies were also in favour of adoption of the child, the appellant could not be disqualified or disentitled to the relief sought by him/her, and set aside the impugned order.

Varsha Sanjay Shindey v. The Society of Friends of the Sassoon Hospitals and Ors[385]

Facts

The petitioners got married in 2001 and, unfortunately, were not blessed with becoming parents of their biological child; therefore, they decided to adopt a child. Petitioners registered their names with the respondent to adopt a child. According to the petitioners, in May 2013, a detailed home study of the petitioners was done and they were invited by the respondents to visit them and select a baby. Accordingly, the petitioners visited the respondents and saw three babies, and decided to adopt a baby, Isha; this decision was communicated to the respondents, and the same was also communicated in written form on the next day.

Then a Mysore family, which was a foreign couple of Indian origin residing in the USA, was registered for adoption with the US-based adoption agency (Authorized Foreign Adoption Agency [AFAA]) in March 2010. The Screening Committee of CARA examined prima facie suitability of the PAPs of the Mysore family. In the year 2013, baby Isha was accepted by the Mysore family and all necessary formalities were initiated.

The petitioners were later informed that baby Isha had been shown to the foreign couple and they had decided to adopt her. A pre-adoption counselling meeting was organized by the respondents and a list of 13 babies of special needs were sent to the petitioner. The petitioners, however, informed that they wanted to adopt the same baby girl, Isha. Being aggrieved by the decision of the respondents to give baby Isha to the intervenors, namely Mrs. Rachel Mathew and her husband Mr. Raj Narayan Mysore, the petitioners filed a writ petition at the High Court of Mumbai.

Held

The high court observed that there appeared a conflict between SARA[386] and ARC,[387] on the one hand and the CARA and Recognized Indian Placement Agency (RIPA)[388] on the

---

[385] 2014 (5) ALL MR 297.

[386] The SARA is being set up in every state/union territory as a unit under the state child protection society (SCPS) and headed by the concerned secretary of the state government/union territory administration to promote in-country adoption and regulate ICA. The SARA coordinates, monitors, and develops the work of adoption and renders secretarial and administrative assistance to the Advisory Committee on Adoption, Ministry of Women and Child Development, Government of India, available at http://wcd.nic.in/icpsmon/st_aicps45.htm (accessed on 11 September 2015).

[387] The Adoption Recommendation Committee.

[388] RIPA: Such agencies are recognized by CARA to undertake ICA.

other, and this resulted in creating a bottleneck in the process of adoption. The documents on record clearly established that the overseas Indian couple had already approved the child and hence there was no question of showing the child again to the Indian parents. Therefore, the petitioners, in this case, cannot claim any right or priority to get the child in adoption merely because they are Indian parents who should be given preference over overseas Indians or foreign couples.

Though the main issue involved in the petition was disposed of, the court kept the petition pending in order to see the compliance of the directions given by the high court to the respondents, CARA, SARA, and ARC, first in respect of giving the child Isha in adoption to the Mysore family and, second, to ensure that the petitioners also get the child in adoption expeditiously. The court further proposed to lay down the following guidelines for in-country adoption and ICAs:

1. All the concerned agencies, namely RIPA, SAAs, SARA, ARC, and AFAA should scrupulously follow the guidelines which have been laid down in 2011.
2. The RIPA and SAAs were directed to complete the home study report within a stipulated time as prescribed under the rules. The court proposed that the ratio of 80:20 should be adhered to and preference should be given to Indian parents first, and if the Indian parents decline to accept the child in adoption, only then the child may be shown to foreign parents.
3. Though there was no specific number mentioned in the guidelines as to the number of Indian parents to whom the child should be shown, the court was of the view that within a period of 3–4 weeks, the child should be shown to as many Indian parents as possible and, second, at a time, the child should be shown only to one parent and not multiple number of parents, as had been done in this case.
4. If the child is not accepted by Indian parents, and the adoption agencies, on account of their experience, come to the conclusion that the child is not likely to be taken in adoption by Indian parents, only in that case is the child to be shown to foreign parents.
5. When the child is shown to the foreign parents, it should be shown in the list of priorities which are mentioned in the said guidelines, namely: initially it should be shown to NRIs, then overseas Indian parents, and only thereafter to foreigners.
6. The ARC should give a recommendatory letter within five days in respect of the children with special needs and within 15 days in respect of other children. This should be strictly adhered to. Non-compliance of the said guideline should be strictly viewed and action, if necessary, may be taken against the concerned authorities, ARC, or SARA who do not follow the said schedule. The ARC and SARA should work not in conflict but in coordination with CARA, it being the centralized nodal agency.

Some important judgments on adoption are mentioned in Table 2.3.

Table 2.3 Important Judgments on Adoption

S. no	Judgment name	Ratio decidendi
	Important judgments on in-country adoptions	
1.	Re Manuel Theodore D'souza and Mrs. Lourdes D'souza [2000 (3) BCR 243]	It was held by the court that the abandoned, orphaned, destitute, or a similarly situated child has a right to be adopted as a part of his fundamental right to life, as embodied in Article 21 of the Constitution. The fundamental right to life of these children includes the right to be adopted by willing parent/parents and to have a name and nationality. The right to be adopted, therefore, is an enforceable civil right which is justiciable in a civil court.
2.	Vinay Pathak and His Wife, Indian Adoption Petition (2009 (111) BOMLR 3816	When the child to be adopted is an orphaned, abandoned, or surrendered child or a child in need of care and protection as defined in the JJ Act, Section 11(i) and (ii) of the HAMA does not impose a bar on the Hindu having a biological child from adopting the child of same gender.
3.	*Shabnam Hashmi* v. *Union of India* (AIR 2014 SC 1281)	The honourable court maintained that personal laws would continue to govern any person who chooses to submit himself until such time that the vision of a uniform civil code is achieved. With this declaration, the court held that the prospective parents, irrespective of their religious background, would be free to access the provisions of the JJ Act—a secular act—for adoption of children after following the procedure prescribed. The right to adopt was not declared a fundamental right.
	Important judgments on inter-country adoptions	
1.	*Laxmikant Pandey* v. *Union of India* [(1984) 2 SCC 244].	In the absence of a law providing for adoption of an Indian child by a foreign parent, the only way in which such adoption can be effectuated is by making it in accordance with the law of the country in which the foreign parents reside. Therefore, the only way in which a foreign parent could take an Indian child in adoption was by making an application to the court under whose jurisdiction the child ordinarily resided, for being appointed guardian of the person of the child under the GWA, and with leave to remove the child out of India and take it to his/her own country for the purpose of adopting it in accordance with the law of his/her country. It was opined that such ICA should be permitted after exhausting the possibility of adoption by Indian parents within the country.

(Cont'd)

Table 2.3   *(Cont'd)*

S. no	Judgment name	Ratio decidendi
2.	*Laxmikant Pandey v. Union of India & Another* (AIR 1985 Supp SCC 701).	The Court recommended the setting up of such a VCA in each state and if circumstances so require, there may even be more than one VCA in a state. Where there is a VCA or any other centralized agency which maintains a register of children available for adoption as also a register of Indian adoptive parents, it would be enough to wait for a period of three to four weeks.
3.	*Bengt Ingmar Eriksson v. Jamnibai Sukharya Dhangda* [Notice of Motion No. 1738 of 1985 in Misc. Petition No. 570 of 1980 (Bom. Original Side)]	The principle that the best interest of the child was of paramount consideration was reiterated. The best interest of the child in this case was that the biological parents would be the best persons to decide whether or not to give their child in adoption to foreign parents.
4.	Re Jay Kevin Salerno [Misc. Petition No. 490 of 1987 (Bom. Original Side)]	It was held that the term 'custody' cannot be interpreted as actual physical custody. Interpreting the Supreme Court direction given in the case of Laxmikant Pandey too literally would also cause harm to a child in a given case, for example, it may not be desirable to move the child physically from familiar surroundings to another place for a period of one month merely for the preparation of a child study report. The custody, therefore, of a recognized institution should be broadly interpreted to mean not physical custody but custody in the sense of supervision and control over the child so that the institution can arrange for a child's individual care or medical treatment (whenever required).
5.	*Laxmikant Pandey v. Union of India & Others* [1991 (2) Scale].	It was not agreed that Indian citizenship should continue until the adopted child attains the age of majority and is legally competent to opt. Such a step would run counter to the need of quick assimilation and may often stand as a barrier to the requirements of the early cementing of the adopted child into the adoptive family. In regard to the issue of the birth certificate of the adopted child, it was opined that such certificate should be obtained on the basis of application of the society sponsoring adoption. In most of these cases the registration of birth may not be available because that would not have been done.
6.	*Smt Anokha v. State of Rajasthan* [2004 (1) SCC 382]	The Supreme Court referred to the decision in L.K Pandey and further held that none of these provisions formulated by various court directions would impinge upon the rights and

(Cont'd)

Table 2.3   *(Cont'd)*

S. no	Judgment name	Ratio decidendi
		choice of an individual to give his or her child in adoption to named persons, who may be of foreign origin. The court, in such cases, has to deal with the application under Section 7 of the GWA and dispose of the same after being satisfied that the child is being given in adoption voluntarily after being aware of the implication of adoption, namely that the child would legally belong to the adoptive parents' family, not influenced by any extraneous reasons such as the receipt of money and other reasons; that the adoptive parents have produced evidence in support of their suitability; and finally that the arrangement would be in the best interest of the child.
7.	*St. Theresa's Tender Loving Care Home & Ors.* v. *State of Andhra Pradesh* (AIR 2005 SC 4375)	The court held that it should be ensured that behind the mask of social service or upliftment, the evil design of child trafficking is not lurking. It was further held that it is the duty of the state to ensure a safe roof over an abandoned child. Keeping the welfare of the child in view, all possible efforts should be made by the state governments to explore the possibility of adoption under the supervision of the designated agency.
8.	*Aniruddha M. Railkar and Anr.* v. *Indian Council for Social Welfare and Anr.* [2007 (109) BOMLR 839]	By virtue of Section 7 of the GWA, the only consideration for appointing a guardian is the welfare of child. The court, while disposing such petitions, requires to consider financial and cultural background of the adoptive parents.
9.	*Robert Heijkamp* v. *Bal Sadan Rescue Home* (FAP [foreign adoption petition] No. 89,98,108 of 2007)	It would be necessary for the CWC to satisfy itself clearly in each case whether the abandonment is likely to be only temporary or whether it is likely to be of a longer duration. Indeed, even this conclusion would be subject to the decision of the court in such matters. The CWC cannot, on its own, come to this conclusion. The mental illness of a person can only be determined under the provisions of the Mental Health Act or any other statutory enactment providing for such determination. There is no provision in the JJ Act or in any other law which confers any power, statutory or otherwise, on the CWC to determine whether a person is mentally ill or not.
10.	*Mr. Frank M. Costanzo* v. *Regional Passport Officer* (W.P. No.14880 of 2010, Madras High Court)	A question arose as to whether the regional passport officer could insist upon an NOC from the CARA for the issue of a passport to a child adopted by foreign nationals. After referring to the decisions of the Supreme Court in *Laxmikant*

(Cont'd)

Table 2.3 *(Cont'd)*

S. no	Judgment name	Ratio decidendi
		Pandey and *Smt. Anokha*, the high court held that in the case of adoption from biological parents, the guidelines would not apply. Consequently, the court came to the conclusion that the regional passport officer was not entitled to insist upon an NOC from CARA.
11.	*Maria Chaya Schupp, a German National represented by her Constituted Attorney, Smt. Geeta Menon* v. *the Director General of Police and Ors.* (2010 Cri LJ 883)	The right to know one's origins is a dimension of the broader right to ascertain and preserve one's identity. Identity is a complex concept which, unsurprisingly, has never been defined legally. In a nutshell, identity is 'what we know and what we feel'. However, the scope of this writ petition can only be confined to how best the Court could intervene to help the petitioner in her root search and whether directions issued to any of the respondents would result in the petitioner being able to reach her goal. Hence, the larger issues sought to be raised, of possible child trafficking and the need for better safeguards and policing the abuse of inter-country adoptions of Indian children, are not addressed. The court directed to scrupulously follow guidelines issued in *Laxmikant Pandey* (AIR 1986 SC 274, AIR 1987 SC 232, AIR 1992 SC 118) with respect to the vile practices, involving children, indulged in by institutions, as has been reiterated by the apex court time and again.
12.	*Craig Allen Coates* v. *State* [2010 (11) SCR 102]	The court also directed that for ICAs the procedure followed in various states could include a reference to an expert committee on the lines constituted in that particular case to ensure that ICAs are allowed only after full and proper satisfaction is recorded by all the agencies, including a committee of experts, wherever reference to such a committee is considered necessary.
13.	In Re: Mr. Tim Cecil and Mrs. Steffi Cecil (HIGH COURT OF MADRAS, O.P. No. 247 of 2011)	The court, in light of the mandate contained in the UNCRC and the Hague Convention, both of which had been ratified by India, and also in light of the provisions of JJ Act, 2000, as amended by JJ Act, 2006, held that the primary responsibility of providing care and protection to children was that of the birth family. Since the child had a fundamental right to be protected against any kind of exploitation, biological parents could not be held to have an absolute and unfettered right to give their children in adoption or for foster care to foreign nationals.

(Cont'd)

Table 2.3   *(Cont'd)*

S. no	Judgment name	Ratio decidendi
14.	*Stephanie Joan Becker* v. *State and Ors.* (AIR 2013 SC 3495)	If the foreign adoptive parent is otherwise suitable and willing, and consent of the child has also been taken (as in the present case) and the expert bodies engaged in the field are of the view that the adoption process would end in a successful blending of the child in the family, then the foreign adoptive parents could not be disqualified or disentitled to adopt.
15.	*Varsha Sanjay Shindey v. The Society of Friends of the Sassoon Hospitals and Ors.* [2014 (5) ALL MR 297]	The high court observed that there appeared a conflict between SARA and ARC on the one hand and the CARA and RIPA on the other, and this resulted in creating a bottleneck in the process of adoption. The documents on record clearly established that the overseas Indian couple had already approved the child and hence there was no question of showing the child again to Indian parents. Therefore, the petitioners cannot claim any right or priority to get the child in adoption merely because they are Indian parents and that preference should be given to Indian parents over overseas Indians or foreign couples. The court further proposed certain guidelines for in-country adoption and ICAs.

Important Judgments on Surrogacy

Baby Manji Yamada v. Union of India and Anr.[389]

Facts

The petition was filed by the grandmother of the appellant under Article 32[390] of the Constitution, against directions of the high court. The biological parents, Dr. Yuki Yamada

---

[389] AIR 2009 SC 84.

[390] Article 32: Remedies for enforcement of rights conferred by this part—

(1) The right to move the Supreme Court by appropriate proceedings for the enforcement of the rights conferred by this part is guaranteed.

(2) The Supreme Court shall have power to issue directions or orders or writs, including writs in the nature of habeas corpus, mandamus, prohibition, quo warrant, and certiorari, whichever may be appropriate, for the enforcement of any of the rights conferred by this part.

(3) Without prejudice to the powers conferred on the Supreme Court by Clauses (1) and (2), Parliament may by law empower any other court to exercise within the local limits of its jurisdiction ill or any of the powers exercisable by the Supreme Court under Clause (2).

(4) The right guaranteed by this article shall not be suspended except as otherwise provided for by this Constitution.

and Dr. Ikufumi Yamada, had come to India in 2007 and chosen a surrogate mother in Anand, Gujarat, and a surrogacy agreement was entered into between the biological father and biological mother on one side and the surrogate mother on the other. It appears from some of the statements made that there were matrimonial discords between the biological parents. The child was born on 25 July 2008. On 3 August 2008 the child was moved to Arya Hospital in Jaipur following a law and order situation in Gujarat, and she was being provided with much needed care, including being breastfed by a woman. It is stated by the petitioner that the genetic father Dr. Ifukumi Yamada had to return to Japan due to expiration of his visa. It is also stated that the Municipality at Anand had issued a birth certificate indicating the name of the genetic father.

The stand of the respondent was that there is no law governing surrogacy in India and lots of irregularities are being committed in the name of surrogacy . According to it, a money-making racket is being perpetuated in the name of surrogacy. It is also the stand of the said respondent that the Union of India should enforce stringent laws relating to surrogacy. The petitioner questioned the locus standi of the respondent to file a habeas corpus petition. It is contended that though custody of the child was being asked for, there was not even an indication as to in whose alleged illegal custody the child was. It was also contended by the respondent that though the petition before the high court was styled as a PIL, there was no element of public interest involved.

The learned counsel for the respondent, with reference to the counter-affidavit filed in the court, had highlighted certain aspects relating to surrogacy. The learned solicitor general had taken exception to certain statements made in the said counter-affidavit by the respondent and submitted that the petition before the high court was not in good faith and was certainly not in public interest.

Held

The court insisted on constitution of national and state commissions for protection of child rights and children courts for providing speedy justice in offences against children and related matters, provided under the Commission for Protection of Child Rights Act (CPCRA), 2005. In the present case, if any action is to be taken, it has to be taken by the commission. It has a right to inquire into complaints and even to take suo moto notice of matters relating to (a) deprivation and violation of child rights; (b) non-implementation of laws providing for protection and development of children; and (c) non-compliance of policy decisions, guidelines, or instructions aimed at mitigating hardships of and ensuring welfare of the children and to provide relief to such children, or take up the issues arising out of such matters with appropriate authorities. No complaint was made by anybody relating to the child. Direction was given to any aggrieved person to approach the commission constituted under CPCRA. Accordingly, the writ petition was disposed of.

Ratio Decidendi

The commission constituted under CPCRA has the right to inquire into complaints or take suo motu action relating to violation of child rights and development of children and provide relief in such matters with appropriate authorities.

Amy Antoinette Mcgregor & Anr. v. Directorate of Family Welfare
Govt. of NCT of Delhi & Anr.[391]

Facts

This writ petition was filed by two petitioners, residents of Sydney, Australia. The first petitioner was the wife and the second was the husband. It appears that due to some medical problem the first petitioner could not physically conceive a child. After medical examination by best doctors and taking medical advice, they found that the cause was some 'lupus' and it was an immuno-suppressive stipulation which does not physically and practically allow the embryos to thrive and properly flourish in the mother's body. The doctors, therefore, advised her to proceed with a gestational surrogacy. It is a procedure by which one woman, the surrogate mother, carries a fertilized donor egg or embryo for the first petitioner. It basically involves IVF, which involves mixing of eggs and sperms outside the uterus, followed by implanting the fertilized eggs into the uterus, where the embryo will grow and develop into a baby. This is available, apart from India, in only two countries throughout the world, namely Thailand and America, which offer an assured and medically secure IVF process. For a long time, the petitioners had a desire to have a child but because of the medical problem they could not conceive. Now they thought of using the aforementioned technique to get a child. However, for the sake of family balancing, they intended to have one girl child and one boy child and for this purpose, in the surrogacy procedure for the petitioners, the prenatal techniques play an essential and important role. According to the petitioners, though they want a child, yet they do not want two children of the same sex in view of their principle of balanced family, and accordingly they want to prevent two births of the same sex by using advanced prenatal techniques. For this purpose, it appears that the petitioners made an application to the first respondent, seeking to forward it to the concerned department, and in that application they made a request that the provisions of the Pre-Conception and Pre-Natal Diagnostic Techniques (Prohibition of Sex Selection) Act, 1994 cannot be made applicable to them, and it was also further stated that couples who have no children and wish to have a male or female child should be allowed to make use of the prenatal diagnostic techniques to have children of both sexes to balance their family. So these couples cannot be treated at par with the couples who choose the sex of foetus in order to have a male child, leading to imbalance in male to female ratio.

The present writ petition was, therefore, filed seeking the following reliefs:

1. Issue a writ of mandamus or any other appropriate writ, order, or direction directing the first respondent to grant a 'no objection' to the petitioners with reference to their application pending disposal in their office.
2. Issue a writ of mandamus or any other appropriate writ, order, or direction, thereby directing that the Pre-Natal Diagnostic Techniques Act as ultra vires with respect to its applicability to the surrogacy process.

---

[391] 205 (2013) DLT 96.

Held

The legislative purpose of the Pre-Natal Diagnostic Techniques (Regulation and Prevention of Misuse) Amendment Act, 2002 reads as under:

> An Act to provide for the prohibition of sex selection, before or after conception, and for regulation of pre-natal diagnostic techniques for the purposes of detecting genetic abnormalities or metabolic disorders or chromosomal abnormalities or certain congenital malformations or sex-linked disorders and for the prevention of their misuse for sex determination leading to female foeticide and for matters connected therewith or incidental thereto.

The intention was, therefore, clear that one of the integral purposes of the legislation is prevention of misuse of prenatal diagnosis for sex determination, since such a determination is legislatively perceived to lead to female foeticide. From a reading of the writ petition filed by the petitioners, it was clear that the assumption and the reason given are speculative and factually misconceived. The assumption of the petitioners that it is possible to identify the gender of the foetus before impregnation has no basis in the science of genetics or any currently established principle of sexual reproduction.

The challenge to the provisions of the act on the ground of hostile discrimination and unreasonable classification is, therefore, misconceived. The writ petition was, accordingly, dismissed.

Hema Vijay Menon v. State of Maharashtra and Ors.[392]

Facts

The petitioner was a highly qualified lecturer and had participated in several national and international seminars and symposiums in law, and was often invited as a guest faculty at several institutions to deliver lectures on various subjects of law. In 2010, the petitioner lost her only son, who was 15 years of age. The petitioner and her husband suffered severe mental trauma due to the loss of their only son and decided to bear a child. The petitioner went through five cycles of IVF procedures at Jaslok Hospital, Mumbai, to conceive the child. However, due to certain ailments, the petitioner was incapacitated to bear the child and the attempts were unsuccessful. Upon the failure of IVF procedures at Jaslok Hospital at Mumbai, the petitioner was asked by an eminent doctor at the Jaslok Hospital to opt for the surrogacy procedure. After consultation with her husband, the petitioner decided to have a child through surrogacy arrangement. In furtherance of the said desire, in March 2013, an embryo was successfully transplanted in the womb of a surrogate mother. In 2014, the surrogate mother went into labour and the petitioner and her husband rushed to Mumbai. The surrogate mother delivered a baby boy and the said child was immediately placed in the hands of the petitioner and her husband. It is worthwhile to mention that the petitioner had spent an amount of Rs. 45,00,000/- for the surrogacy procedure. With a view to look after the newly born baby, the petitioner applied for maternity/child care leave to the principal of the respondent college as according to the petitioner, the petitioner was entitled to maternity leave in view of the provisions of Maharashtra Civil Services (Leave) Rules, 1981, which recognize the right of a woman to maternity leave and are applicable to lecturers

---

[392] Writ Petition No. 3288 of 2015.

like the petitioner. The petitioner also sought support from the government resolution dated 28 July 1995, which provides for maternity leave to the adoptive mother in the same manner as is available to a natural mother. The principal of the respondent college approved the leave and the proposal was forwarded to the joint director of higher education for necessary action. To the surprise of the petitioner, the joint director of higher education, Nagpur, informed the respondent principal of the college by the impugned communication that there was no provision in the government resolution dated 28 July 1995 for granting maternity leave to a mother who begets a child through surrogacy procedure. The petitioner challenged the communication by this petition.

Held

The court held that as rightly pointed out on behalf of the petitioner, there is nothing in Rule 74 of the Maharashtra Civil Services (Leave) Rules, 1961, which would disentitle a woman who has attained motherhood through the surrogacy procedure to maternity leave. Rule 74 provides for maternity leave to a female government employee. The court did not find anything in Rule 74 which disentitles the petitioner to maternity leave, like any other female government servant, only because she has attained motherhood through the route of surrogacy procedure. It is worthwhile to note that by the government resolution dated 28 July 1995, maternity leave is not only provided to a natural mother but is also provided to an adoptive mother, who adopts a child on its birth. The only reason for refusing maternity leave to the petitioner is that there is nothing in the government resolution dated 28 July 1995 for providing maternity leave to the mother who begets the child through surrogacy. If the government resolution dated 28 July 1995 provides maternity leave to an adoptive mother, it is difficult to gauge why maternity leave should be refused to the mother who secures the child through surrogacy. In the court's view, there could not be any distinction whatsoever between an adoptive mother that adopts a child and a mother that begets a child through a surrogate mother, after implanting an embryo in the womb of the surrogate mother. In our view, the case of the mother who begets a child through the surrogacy procedure, by implanting an embryo created by using either the eggs or sperm of the intended parents in the womb of the surrogate mother, would stand on a better footing than the case of an adoptive mother. At least, there cannot be any distinction between the two. Right to life, under Article 21 of the Constitution of India, includes the right to motherhood and also the right of every child to full development. If the government can provide maternity leave to an adoptive mother, it is difficult to digest the refusal on the part of the government to provide maternity leave to a mother who begets a child through the surrogacy procedure. The court did not find any propriety in the action on the part of the joint director of higher education, Nagpur, of rejecting the claim of the petitioner for maternity leave. The action of the respondents were clearly arbitrary, discriminatory, and violative of the provisions of Articles 14 and 21 of the Constitution of India. Hence, for the reasons aforesaid, the writ petition was allowed.

Law Reform in Adoption and Surrogacy

There are serious and urgent concerns in various areas of adoption and surrogacy, in which there is a need for law reform.

Searching for Roots

Adoption is an emotional experience. It is also a physical, biological, and psychological experience. The child's best welfare and interest should be the paramount consideration in all questions relating to his/her adoption. Searching for roots, that is, searching for birth family relatives, is a sensitive and emotional process.[393] A person's right to know her biological or genetic origins raises some of the hardest legal and ethical issues that we have had to face in the last several years. This question arises not only in the case of adopted children, but also in cases of abandoned or displaced children, children conceived by AI artificial insemination, or children born out of wedlock. It opens up, in the words of Geraldine van Beuren, a whole Pandora's Box—the principle of the best interests of the child and his/her right to know very often conflicts with other competing rights such as the mother's right to privacy and autonomy and the rights of the adoptive parents.[394]

Children who seek information of the identity of their biological parents articulate this need as a right to know their origins. The right to know one's origins means the right to know one's parentage, that is, one's biological family and ascendance and one's conditions of birth. Internationally, this right is widely perceived as the right to know, and is considered as an integral part of one's right to life and right to privacy. It protects each individual's interest to identify where he/she came from. The right to know one's identity has also been guaranteed in the UNCRC,[395] the Hague Convention,[396] and recent case law of the European Court of Human Rights.[397] This psychological need to know one's identity has been articulated as a right in Articles 7[398] and 8 of

---

[393] Jagannath Pati, Deputy Director, CARA (Indian Central Authority), *Root Search By Adopted Children: Issues And Challenges*, India, Inter-Country Adoption New Zealand, New Zealand. Available at http://www.icanz.gen.nz/index.php/resources-a-links/birth-family-search/an-indian-view-of-search# (accessed on 11 September 2015).

[394] G. Van Beuren, 'Children's Access to Adoption Records: State Discretion or an Enforceable International Right', 58 *Modern Law Review* 37 (1995).

[395] CRC, 1989, Article 8:

(1) States parties undertake to respect the right of the child to preserve his or her identity, including nationality, name and family relations as recognized by law without unlawful interference.

(2) Where a child is illegally deprived of some or all of the elements of his or her identity, states parties shall provide appropriate assistance and protection, with a view to re-establishing speedily his or her identity.

[396] Hague Convention, 1993, Article 30:

(1) The competent authorities of a Contracting State shall ensure that information held by them concerning the child's origin, in particular information concerning the identity of his or her parents, as well as the medical history, is preserved.

(2) They shall ensure that the child or his or her representative has access to such information, under appropriate guidance, in so far as is permitted by the law of that state.

[397] S. Besson, 'Enforcing the Child's Right to Know her Origins: Contrasting Approaches under the Convention on the Rights of the Child and the European Convention on Human Rights', *International Journal of Law, Policy and the Family* 21, 2(2007): 137–59.

[398] Article 7:

(1) The child shall be registered immediately after birth and shall have the right from birth to a name, the right to acquire a nationality and, as far as possible, the right to know and be cared for by his or her parents.

the CRC.[399] The CRC, for the first time, protects this right to know for a child and not just as an adult.[400] The state needs to provide assistance to a child to find its identity.

In addition to the CRC, the child's right to know her identity is also protected in the Hague Convention, which India has ratified. In Article 30,[401] it requires state authorities to ensure that information held by them concerning the child's origin, in particular information concerning the identity of his or her parents, as well as the medical history, is preserved and that the child or his or her representative has access to such information, under appropriate guidance, in so far as it is permitted by law in that state. Thus, Article 30 provides that even a child or his/her representative can have access to information relating to her identity, as far as it is permitted by law of the state. India has ratified this convention and the existing law governing adoption under the Supreme Court guidelines clearly permit the release of such information to an adopted child when s/he is mature.

The child's right to know his or her origin is derived from the general right to privacy, guaranteed under Article 17[402] of the International Covenant on Civil and Political Rights, 1966.

The right to privacy would include the right to know and receive information of one's family and private life and guarantees against arbitrary interference with the same. The right to privacy and family life is also guaranteed under Article 8[403] of the ECHR.

---

(2) States parties shall ensure the implementation of these rights in accordance with their national law and their obligations under the relevant international instruments in this field, in particular where the child would otherwise be stateless.

[399] Article 8:

(1) States parties undertake to respect the right of the child to preserve his or her identity, including nationality, name and family relations as recognized by law without unlawful interference.

(2) Where the child is illegally deprived of some or all of the elements of his or her identity, states parties shall provide appropriate assistance and protection, with a view to re-establishing speedily his or her identity.

[400] Jayna Kothari, 'The Child's Right to Identity: Do Adopted Children have the Right to Know Their Parentage?' For details, see http://www.cry.org/resources/pdf/ncrrf/ncrrf_reportby_jayna.pdf (accessed on 29 June 2015).

[401] Article 30:

(1) The competent authorities of a contracting state shall ensure that information held by them concerning the child's origin, in particular information concerning the identity of his or her parents, as well as the medical history, is preserved.

(2) They shall ensure that the child or his or her representative has access to such information, under appropriate guidance, in so far as is permitted by the law of that state.

[402] Article 17:

(1) No one shall be subjected to arbitrary or unlawful interference with his privacy, family, home, or correspondence, nor to unlawful attacks on his honour and reputation.

(2) Everyone has the right to the protection of the law against such interference or attacks.

[403] Article 8: Right to respect for private and family life—

(1) Everyone has the right to respect for his private and family life, his home and his correspondence.

The contact between a child placed in adoption and its biological mother is a distant reality in case of India, as the biological mother hardly resides in the place/address given in the surrender deed because of social stigma. Getting to know more about the social background of the biological mother may be quite meaningful in the sense that it may yield positive results in terms of improved self-concept, self-esteem, and ability to relate to others.[404]

The need to know one's parentage and background is crucial to children and adults who do not have this information. This right to know one's origins means having the information and identity of one's biological parents and conditions of birth. The right to know stems from the desire to know the identity of the self.[405] Social scientists have considered the meaning of identity to be determined by three main aspects: self-definition, coherence of personality, and a sense of continuity over time.[406] Identity is thus seen as essentially 'self-in-context'.[407]

This means that identity is often determined by social changes and one's definition of self is affected by how a relationship is seen in the social context. As Yngves on commented, 'adoption transgresses our notions of identity',[408] and the journey of identity development is complex and problematic for adopted persons.[409] Since adoption is governed by different kinds of social arrangements, these arrangements have implications on the development of the identity of the child.[410]

The quest for the right to identity is based on the child's right to privacy or respect for her private life, autonomy, and freedom of expression.[411] Under the Indian Constitution, Article 21 protects the right to life for every citizen. Article 21 states: 'No one shall be deprived of his life or personal liberty except according to procedure established by law.' The right to life has been expanded considerably to include the right to privacy.[412]

---

(2)   There shall be no interference by a public authority with the exercise of this right except such as is in accordance with the law and is necessary in a democratic society in the interests of national security, public safety or the economic well-being of the country, for the prevention of disorder or crime, for the protection of health or morals, or for the protection of the rights and freedoms of others. And finally, this need of the child to know about her background was recognized in the Declaration on Social and Legal Principles relating to the Protection and Welfare of Children, with Special Reference to Foster Placement and Adoption Nationally and Internationally in Article 9 which states that the need of a foster or an adopted child to know about his or her background should be recognized by persons responsible for the child's care, unless this is contrary to the child's best interests.

[404]   Pati, *Root Search By Adopted Children*.

[405]   H.D. Grotevant, N. Dunbar, J.K. Kohler, and A.L. Esau, 'Adoptive Identity: How Contexts Within and Beyond the Family Shape Developmental Pathways', *Family Relations* 49 (2000): 379–87.

[406]   Grotevant et al., 'Adoptive Identity'.

[407]   Grotevant et al., 'Adoptive Identity'.

[408]   B. Yngvesson, 'Geographies of Identity in Transnational Adoption' (Mine, Yours, Ours & Theirs-Adoption and Changing Kinship and Family Patterns Conference, Oslo, May 1999).

[409]   Grotevant et al. (n. 18).

[410]   Grotevant et al. (n. 18).

[411]   Besson, *Enforcing the Child's Right to Know her Origins*.

[412]   *Kharak Singh* v. *State of Uttar Pradesh* (AIR 1963 SC 1295); *Sunil Batra* v. *Delhi Administration* (1980 AIR 1579).

This is similar to Article 8 of the ECHR, which guarantees the right to respect for private and family life, home, and correspondence. The right to know one's origins has been held to be an essential part of the right to respect for one's private life.

Thus, the right to know one's parents can be understood in relation to the right to one's family and generally the right to preserve one's identity. As Samantha Besson argues, the right to family should be interpreted more broadly to include not only one's social or legal parents but also one's biological or genetic parents, to give a true meaning to the child's right to identity and privacy.[413] Such an interpretation of Article 21 of the Constitution would not only be in consonance with the current jurisprudence on the right to privacy, but would also be in consonance with the international acceptance of the right to identity. Articles 7 and 8 of the UNCRC clearly guarantee the right to identity for children.

For adoptive parents, it has often been held that confidentiality also must be promoted to protect the right of the adopting parents.[414] Adoptive parents could have a similar interest to protect their ties to the child and would not want any interference by identification of the child's biological parents.[415] In addition to the competing rights of the biological parents and adoptive parents, several American courts have held that the public has a strong interest, too, in preserving the confidentiality of adoption records, and public attitudes towards illegitimacy and parents who neglect or abuse children have not changed sufficiently to warrant disclosure of the circumstances leading to adoption.[416]

Such public policy considerations include a fear, as Geraldine Van Beuren articulates, 'that if access is allowed, children will be abandoned rather than given up for adoption and that such access to the birth records may have a negative effect on the willingness of parents to adopt'.[417] However, none of these assumptions have been factually proven.

The Karnataka High Court's precedent-setting order recognizing the right of an adoptee to know the identity of her birth mother underscored the need for laying down some law or guidelines for this.[418] This judgment is the legal recognition of the adoptee's right to know, which has been widely accepted in many jurisdictions but was not clarified in the Indian context at all. The 2015 CARA guidelines have laid down some guidelines for roots search and confidentiality of records, but what is required is a law in this area.

---

[413] Besson, *Enforcing the Child's Right to Know her Origins*.

[414] In *re Roger B.*, 418N.E.2d751 (Ill. App. 1981); In *re Christine*, 397 A.2d 511 (1979); In *re Sage* (1978), 21 Wn. App. 803, 806, 586 P.2d 1201, 1203; *Mills* v. *Atlantic City Department of Vital Statistics* (1977), 148 N.J. Super. 302, 307–08, 372 A.2d 646, 649; In *re Adoption of Spinks* (1977), 32 N.C. App. 422, 427, 232 S.E.2d 479, 483.)

[415] Besson *Enforcing the Child's Right to Know her Origins*.

[416] In *Re Roger B* (n 54); Confidentiality is perceived to promote the efficacy of the adoption process in states, where the statutes provide for sealed birth records *Alma Society, Inc.* v. *Mellon* (2d Cir. 1979), 601 F.2d 1225, 1235.

[417] Van Beuren, 'Children's Access to Adoption Records'.

[418] Jayna Kothari, 'A Difficult Road to Her Roots', *The Hindu*, 30 March 2013. Available at http://www.thehindu.com/opinion/op-ed/a-difficult-road-to-her-roots/article4562334.ece (accessed on 9 September 2015).

Juvenile Justice (Care and Protection of Children) Bill, 2014[419]

A new Juvenile Justice (Care and Protection of Children) Bill (JJ Bill), 2014 was passed by the cabinet to replace the JJ Act, 2000. This bill seeks to bring in much awaited adoption reforms in the country.[420] Eligibility of adoptive parents and the procedure for adoption have been included in the bill. The bill proposes that the CARA will frame regulations on adoption. These regulations will be implemented by state and district agencies. The PAPs should be physically and financially sound. A single or divorced person may adopt a child. A single male may not adopt a girl child. The bill also provides for ICA.[421] Under the JJ Bill of 2014, ICA is allowed if the adoption cannot take place within the country within 30 days of the child being declared legally free for adoption.[422] Under the JJ Act, 2000, the biological family could be allowed to visit a child in temporary placement with a family for a short/extended period of time before being given for adoption. The JJ Bill, 2014 provides for the same with an addition of a new provision for monthly checks on the foster family by the CWC.[423]

In addition to other major changes, this bill expressly grants inheritance rights to the adopted child who, after adoption, becomes the child of adoptive parents for all purposes. The bill makes adoption a secular act by explicitly making the religion of the person immaterial when adopting a child. At the same time, it excludes it from the operation of the HAMA. A Parliamentary Standing Committee which submitted a report on the bill[424] found that the emphasis of the proposed legislation is on non-institutional care of children by strengthening the status and role of CARA, which is envisaged to be an apex body for adoption. The CARA is mandated to monitor and regulate in-country adoption and ICAs through various modes. The committee welcomed this initiative and hoped that this would lead to streamlining the adoption procedure and removing the present complexities involved therein. The progression of recognizing the need and granting the right to adopt such a child, rather than restricting the right under personal law, is evidence that rules of personal law based on religion may be reformed in order to bring them into conformity with social and legal change.[425]

---

[419] The Lok Sabha, on 7 May 2015, passed the JJ Bill, 2014.

[420] Abantika Ghosh, 'Govt likely to keep new adoption rules out of Juvenile Justice Act', *Indian Express*, New Delhi, 30 June 2015. Available at see http://indianexpress.com/article/india/india-others/govt-likely-to-keep-new-adoption-rules-out-of-juvenile-justice-act/#sthash.BTFFkXRB.dpuf (accessed on 24 July 2015).

[421] JJ Bill, 2014, PRS Legislative Research. For details, see http://www.prsindia.org/billtrack/the-juvenile-justice-care-and-protection-of-children-bill-2014-3362/ (accessed on 24 July 2015).

[422] JJ Bill, 2014, PRS Legislative Research. For details, see http://www.prsindia.org/billtrack/the-juvenile-justice-care-and-protection-of-children-bill-2014-3362/ (accessed on 24 July 2015).

[423] JJ Bill, 2014, PRS Legislative Research. For details, see http://www.prsindia.org/billtrack/the-juvenile-justice-care-and-protection-of-children-bill-2014-3362/ (accessed on 24 July 2015).

[424] The Parliamentary Standing Committee on Human Resource Development, Rajya Sabha (Upper House of Parliament of India), 264th Report on The Juvenile Justice (Care and Protection of Children) Bill, 2014.

[425] Mishra, 'Bridging the Gap'.

The CARA guidelines, 2015, which have come into effect from 1 August 2015, have included several of these provisions.[426]

Enabling Legislation for Implementing the Hague Convention

India has ratified the Hague Convention on ICA of children. The CARA guidelines, 2015 have been adopted to implement the convention. However, guidelines are not the appropriate instruments because they do not address the main concerns and are not binding. What is required is an enabling legislation to implement the Hague Convention. The enabling legislation will comply with the international standards set out in the Convention. There is a need to introduce many changes in some of the national legislations to criminalize the act of obtaining improper gains from ICA. Excessive 'bureaucratization' of adoption process needs to be prevented.

Code of Ethics

A field like the rehabilitation of abandoned, orphaned, and destitute children calls for total dedication to the highest standards of professionalism, competence, integrity, and social vision. A code of ethics and professional conduct thus becomes imperative. Among the non-institutional services, adoption is the most appropriate form of rehabilitation for the orphaned and destitute child since it ensures the child's right to family. It also meets the needs of persons who are considering parenthood through adoption. There is a growing recognition the world over that the main purpose behind placing a child in adoption is to serve the child's best interest.[427]

International adoption consortiums foundation has developed a protocol of 'Ethics in Adoption' that serves as the standard. The Hague Convention's Articles on International Adoption represent a cross-section of divergent beliefs and personages amalgamated into a 'oneness', all towards the betterment of the child of adoption. Members of the International Adoption Consortium agree to abide by the code of ethics demonstrated as follows.[428]

1. Members recognize that they have moral and ethical obligations to the adoption community, their clients, and to the association.
2. Members strive to follow a professional and ethical standard of practice which has core values of trust and honesty.
3. Members follow International Adoption Consortium code of ethics, laws, and regulations. Members educate themselves to the laws regarding adoptions internationally and adhere to those laws.
4. Members will provide to their customers information that is accurate and complete. Members will be aware of the laws of all countries where they are doing business and will make the families aware of those laws as they relate to their adoption.

[426] See Cara Guidelines, available at http://www.cara.nic.in/InnerContent.aspx?Id=163#Guidelines – 2015 (accessed on 9 September 2015).

[427] Pati Jagannath, *Adoption: Global perspective and ethical issues* (India: Concept Publishing Company, 2007), p. 198.

[428] Pati, *Adoption*, p. 198.

5. All members shall:[429]

   a) Disclose to customers and prospective customers, clearly, conspicuously, and in easy-to-understand language, accurate information about the adoption process, fees involved, and the time when the fees are to be paid.

   b) Disclose all fees involved with an adoption, giving a detailed listing of fees charged by the member and any fees charged by any agents or contracted agents hired by the member.

   c) Disclose when any money is being sent directly to another party and if so, how much and for what services.

   d) Disclose all estimates of fees that may be incurred but not paid directly to the adoption professional, such as estimated travel, gifts, room, and board fees.

   e) Not engage in deceptive or misleading trade practices including false advertising and marketing.

   f) Adhere to confidentiality rules and regulations as required by state adoption licensing and based on fair information principles.

   g) Strive to make adoption a positive experience and seek to resolve disputes that are raised by their clients in a timely and responsive manner.

   h) Abide by all laws of the community, and state and federal government.

   i) Assure that their customers are aware of the adoption laws and regulations in the country, state, or region they are adopting from.

   j) Follow all local, state adoption licensing regulations.

   k) Agree to cooperate in any compliance assessment and resolution of conflicts or disputes.

   l) Abide by any decisions made to resolve a conflict or dispute.

These code of ethics need to be included in the laws of adoption.
It is significant to note:

Conventions, Regulations and Guidelines are not the appropriate instruments because they do not address the main concerns.... The formal controlling process is counterproductive. Instead of taking away threats, it takes away transparency and causes a mystification of reality. The more adoption is regulated and monitored, the more politically correct objectives get distanced from daily practices and employees in the field are transformed into gatekeepers, protecting dossiers and covering up politically unwelcome facts.'[430]

Towards a Common Secular, Uniform Law on Adoption

Religion has played a very dominant role in India and religion is the basis of various personal rights, including adoption. The Constitution has itself recognized the existence of various personal laws in operation in our country. When the Constitution was being adopted and enacted, it had, in Article 44, directed that the state shall endeavour to secure for the citizens a uniform civil code throughout the territory of India. In 1949, when this article was enacted, we already had uniform codes covering every aspect of legal relationship excepting only those matters in which

---

[429] Pati, *Adoption*, p. 198.
[430] Arun, 'Inside Story'.

we were governed by the various personal laws. The laws of contracts, of transfer of property, of sale of goods, partnership, companies and negotiable instruments, of civil procedure, arbitration, and limitation of crimes and criminal procedures, and a host of other statutory laws were uniform civil codes applying throughout the country. As Dr. B.R. Ambedkar observed during the debates in the Constituent Assembly on the draft Article 35 (subsequently enacted as Article 44), the only area which was not covered by any uniform civil code was marriage and succession, and it was the intention of those who enacted Article 44 as part of the Constitution to bring about that change. In fact, Article 44 could have only the different personal laws in view, the rest of the areas having mostly been covered by uniform civil codes. The article, therefore, appears to be a demonstration of the conviction on the part of its framers that the existence of the different religion-oriented personal laws of ours is not in tune with egalitarian philosophy.

About Article 44 in particular, it has been observed by Chief Justice Gajendragadkar that 'in any event, the non-implementation of the provisions contained in Article 44 amounts to a grave failure of Indian democracy and the sooner we take suitable action in that behalf, the better'.[431] In 1985, the Supreme Court regretted in the unanimous decision of the five-judge bench in the Shah Bano case that Article 44 of our Constitution has remained a dead letter and that 'a beginning has to be made if the Constitution is to have any meaning'.[432] In another decision in that year, a two-judge bench of the Supreme Court relied on these observations and reiterated that 'the time has come for the intervention of the Legislature in these matters to provide for a uniform code'.[433]

The comments of K.M. Munshi in the Constituent Assembly debates still hold good today in the interest of social justice to the child.[434] Munshi pointed out that as regards the right to freedom of religion guaranteed under Article 25 of the Constitution, it was subject to reasonable restriction by the state, and the Parliament could make laws regulating and restricting...any secular activity which may be associated with religious practices. Hence, if a religious practice or secular activity falls within the field of social welfare, it would be open to the Parliament to make laws about it and such a law would not violate any fundamental rights. The object of this provision, he said, was that as and when the Parliament thinks proper, an attempt may be made to unify the personal laws of the country. Munshi, talking about the argument relating to minority rights, pointed out that even in the most advanced Islamic countries, the personal law of each minority has not been recognized as so sacrosanct as to prevent the enactment of a uniform civil code. He said: 'When you want to consolidate a community, you have to take into consideration the benefit which may accrue to the whole community and not to the customs of a part of it.'

Article 44 is contained in Part IV of our Constitution, captioned 'Directive Principles of State Policy', and Article 37 declares that though the provisions contained in Part IV are not enforceable in or by any court as the provisions relating to fundamental rights in Part III are, yet 'the principles therein laid down are nevertheless fundamental in the governance of the country and it shall be the duty of the State to apply these principles in making laws.' Therefore, the provisions of Part IV are mandatory in letter and spirit and if that is so, the non-implementation of these

---

[431] P.B. Gajendragadkar, *Secularism and the Constitution of India* (Pralhad Balacharya, University of Bombay, Bombay, 1971).

[432] *Mohd. Ahmed Khan* v. *Shah Bano Begum And Ors* 1985 AIR SC 945, 1985 SCR (3) 844.

[433] *Ms. Jordan Diengdeh* v. *S.S. Chopra* AIR 1985 SC 935.

[434] Constituent Assembly Debates, 1949, Vol. VII.

provisions would deviously amount to a breach of trust with which we have entrusted ourselves by our Constitution.

The question of a uniform civil code has again sprung into prominence because of the judgment delivered by Justice Kuldeep Singh and Justice Sahai in the case of *Sarla Mudgal* v. *Union of India*, on 10 May 1995.

The main issues involved were:

- whether a Hindu husband married under the Hindu law, by embracing Islam, can solemnize a second marriage;
- whether such a marriage without having the first marriage dissolved under the law would be valid; and
- whether the converted husband would be guilty of bigamy under Section 494 of the IPC.

It was held by the Supreme Court that the second marriage of the Hindu husband after embracing Islam violates the principles of justice, equity, and good conscience and would be void on the ground of natural justice.

While delivering the judgment, the Supreme Court requested the government to have a 'fresh look' at Article 44 of the Constitution of India and 'retrieve Article 44 from the cold storage' where it has been lying since 1949. The court also observed that successive governments till date had been wholly remiss in implementing Article 44.

The court stated that Article 44 is based on the concept that there is no necessary connection between religion and personal law in a civilized society. Article 25 guarantees religious freedom, whereas Article 44 seeks to divert religion from social relations and personal law. Marriage, succession, and like matters of a secular character cannot be brought within the guarantee enshrined under Articles 25, 26, and 27.

This judgment generated a renewed debate on the uniform civil code. The oral observation on 11 August 1995, of Justice Kuldeep Singh (Justice Sahai had already retired) that their observations on the uniform civil code were obiter dicta and not binding, were perhaps meant to stem the debate under judicial restraint. The oral observation from the bench does not, and in law cannot, value away the direction of the two judges to the Union government.

On 9 August 1995, the Maharashtra Legislative Assembly passed a bill called the Maharashtra Adoption Act, 1995 to provide for adoption of children, which applied to every person adopting a child in the state of Maharashtra, irrespective of the person's religion, caste, race, and sex. The Government of Maharashtra declared that this legislation was for giving effect to the policy of the state towards securing the principles specified in Article 44 of the Constitution of India.

Some of the salient features of the proposed act were:

- The age of the person adopting the child has to be 25 years or more.
- A married Hindu woman whose husband is alive will be able to adopt with her husband's consent.
- Twins will be able to be adopted at the same time.
- Adoption will be done in the jurisdiction of the district courts in which the person adopting the child resides.

This bill did not receive the presidential assent. An attempt has also been made in Kerala for a uniform law on adoption. The proposed bill envisages giving full legal status to the adopted children at par with the biological children, irrespective of the religious status of the adoptive parents.[435]

But, whatever the controversy, adoption of children is not an issue of Hindu law or Muslim law or any other theological system, but an issue of justice to the child and the best interests of the child. If the Maharashtra bill had in its preamble stressed on the aspect of the justice to the child rather than the uniform civil code, it would perhaps have had a better chance of being enacted into a law. The proposed common secular law on adoption would perhaps be acceptable to all communities if its main focus was on the welfare of the destitute and orphan child and it did not interfere with the inheritance laws, which are of divine origin in some communities. But, for the safety and security of the adopted child, the following could be considered.

- All the parents who have adopted a child would be deemed to have willed away one-third of their property to their adopted child out of love and affection, unless a wish to the contrary has been expressed in writing, along with reasons, to be recorded, which would facilitate the application of the mind and prudence of the court.
- In case there is no property, usufructuary rights and other heritable rights like tenancy, cultivation, and so on could be shared at least to the extent of one third of the property.
- In case of joint Hindu family property/Wakf property/Parsi, Jewish, or Christian trusts, the adopted child should become a beneficiary in the corpus of the property to the extent of one-third of the property.
- Perhaps a form of contract could be provided which gives the rights and duties of the adoptive parents and adopted children along with a remedy of breach of specific performance.

The absence of a secular law not only affects Indians, but it also affects the foreign nationals who come to India with the desire of adopting a child. In the case of *Shabnam Hashmi* v. *Union of India*,[436] when Shabnam Hashmi visited her first adoption centre in New Delhi's suburbs, she was told that they did not have any Muslim children. Shabman Hashmi, who had a son, wanted to adopt a daughter to make a complete family. However, she learnt that Muslims cannot adopt or be adopted and if they want to do so it can only be done by virtue of the GWA, which does not give the legal status of biological parents nor does the adoptee have any rights of inheritance. She filed a writ petition at the Supreme Court in 2005 to give Muslim adoptive parents the same status as that of a biological parent and to recognize adoption as a fundamental right under Article 21. A prayer was also made, requesting the court to lay down optional guidelines enabling adoption of children by persons irrespective of religion, caste, creed, and so on, and further for a direction to the respondent, Union of India, to enact an optional law for facilitation of adoption

---

[435] K. Telang, *Sharing*, Newsletter of the Indian Association for the Promotion of Adoption, Vol. II, No.1, July–October 2000.

[436] (2014) 2 SCALE 529.

irrespective of religious considerations. The court disposed the matter on 19 February 2014 without issuing any such direction, but it emphasized that the provisions relating to adoption under the JJ Act, 2000 can be availed by any person notwithstanding the position of adoption under the personal law.[437]

In this case, the Supreme Court did not recognize adoption as a fundamental right under Article 21 and claimed self-restraint. The court's refusing to recognize the right to adoption as a fundamental right guaranteed under Article 21, which guarantees the right to life and liberty, is a major setback as far as the best interest of children is concerned.

India ratified the CRC on 11 December 1992, which would imply that they have to be incorporated into the legal system. Article 4 of the convention provides that the state parties should review their legislation and ensure that the laws are consistent with the convention. Principle 1 of the convention reads 'every child, without any exception whatsoever, shall be entitled to these rights without distinction or discrimination on account of race, language, religion'. A child shall be protected from practices which may foster racial, religious, or any other form of discrimination. The convention's object clearly states that the convention is to apply to all adoptions between contracting states that create a permanent parent–child relation. So, discrimination relating to adoption of children on the grounds of religion is not valid.

Article 25 of the Constitution of India protects only such practices which are essential and integral to any religion.[438] This right to freedom of religion is not an absolute right. Therefore, a uniform law governing adoption cannot be declared unconstitutional. The first and the most important priority is the enactment of a common or special adoption law that will be applicable to all people of India, irrespective of their religion. This would be an enabling legislation and ensure the best interests of the child.

Need for Surrogacy Legislation in India

The moral issues associated with surrogacy include the criticism that surrogacy leads to commoditization of the child, breaks the bond between the mother and the child, interferes with nature, and leads to exploitation of poor women in underdeveloped countries who sell their bodies for money.[439] Sometimes, psychological considerations may come in the way of a successful surrogacy arrangement. As far as the legality of the concept of surrogacy is concerned, it would be worthwhile to mention that Article 16.1 of the UDHR, 1948 says, inter alia, that 'men and

---

[437] JJ Act, 2000, Section 41 contemplates adoption though it makes it clear that the primary responsibility for providing care and protection to a child is of his immediate family. Sections 42, 43, and 44 of the act deal with the alternative methods of rehabilitation, namely foster care, sponsorship, and being looked after by an after-care organization. The JJ Act, 2000, however, did not define 'adoption' and it is only by the amendment of 2006 that the meaning thereof came to be expressed in the following terms: Section 2(aa)—'adoption' means the process through which the adopted child is permanently separated from his biological parents and become the legitimate child of his adoptive parents with all the rights, privileges, and responsibilities that are attached to the relationship.

[438] Constitution of India, Article 25 provides for freedom of conscience and free profession, practice, and propagation of religion.

[439] Constitution of India, Article 25.

women of full age without any limitation due to race, nationality or religion have the right to marry and found a family'.[440]

We need a separate statute governing surrogacy.[441] Surrogacy cannot be dealt with under the ICA, as the subject matter of surrogacy contract, that is, a surrogate child, is a human being and as such cannot be the subject matter or object of contract.[442]

The Law Commission recommended that commercial surrogacy needs to be prohibited. This means that only those reasonable expenses incurred by the surrogate mother to bear the child shall be given by the intended parents. To legalize surrogacy, the Law Commission of India submitted the 228th report titled *Need for Legislation to Regulate Assisted Reproductive Technology Clinics As well As Rights and Obligations of Parties to a Surrogacy* on ART procedures.[443] The following observations had been made by the Law Commission:

1. Surrogacy arrangement will continue to be governed by contract among parties, which will contain all the terms requiring consent of the surrogate mother to bear child, agreement of her husband and other family members for the same, medical procedures of AI, reimbursement of all reasonable expenses for carrying child to full term, willingness to handover the child born to the commissioning parent(s), and so on. But such an arrangement should not be for commercial purposes.

2. A surrogacy arrangement should provide for financial support for the surrogate child in the event of death of the commissioning couple or individual before delivery of the child, or divorce between the intended parents and subsequent willingness of none to take delivery of the child.

3. A surrogacy contract should necessarily take care of life insurance cover for the surrogate mother.

4. One of the intended parents should be a donor as well, because the bond of love and affection with a child primarily emanates from biological relationship. Also, the chances of various kinds of child abuse, which have been noticed in cases of adoptions, will be reduced. In case the intended parent is single, he or she should be a donor to be able to have a surrogate child. Otherwise, adoption is the way to have a child which is resorted to if biological (natural) parents and adoptive parents are different.

5. Legislation itself should recognize a surrogate child to be the legitimate child of the commissioning parent(s) without there being any need for adoption or even declaration of guardian.

6. The birth certificate of the surrogate child should contain the name(s) of the commissioning parent(s) only.

[440] Law Commission of India, *28th Report on 'Need for Legislation'*.

[441] Lakshmi Ajay, 'Gujarat, a Hub of Rent-a-Womb Industry in India', *Indian Express*, 13 February 2014. Available at http://indianexpress.com/article/india/india-others/gujarat-a-hub-of-rent-a-womb-in-dustry-in-india/ (accessed on 4 September 2015).

[442] Though the expression 'object' is not defined in the ICA, 1872, it has held to mean a 'purpose' or 'design' of the contract. If the object is opposed to public policy or tends to defeat any provisions of law, it becomes unlawful and thereby it is void under Section 23 of the act: *Nutan Kumar* v. *IInd Additional District Judge*, AIR 1994 All 298.

[443] Law Commission of India, *228th Report on 'Need for Legislation'*.

7. Right to privacy of the donor as well as the surrogate mother should be protected.
8. Sex-selective surrogacy should be prohibited.
9. Cases of abortion should be governed by the Medical Termination of Pregnancy Act, 1971 only.[444]

The aforementioned Law Commission report does not include the international aspects of surrogacy. Surrogacy law in India must include the nationality and paternity issues of the child.[445] The proposed legislation on surrogacy must address not only the domestic but also the international requirements of surrogacy. India has made a mark in the recent times for surrogacy at the international level, and is required to address this need of its new-found importance.[446] A legislation on surrogacy which does not cater to the needs of the international arena is merely incomplete.[447] There is a need for the proposed law to include regulation of medical institutions. It also needs to harmonize the law in conformity with the existing legislations like the Indian Evidence Act, 1872.[448] The proposed legislation must include the rights of the child in case there is a breach of the agreement and also maintenance and restitution rights of the child and the mother in surrogacy agreements.[449]

Non-governmental Organization and Government Initiatives, Programmes, and Schemes

Family Service Centre[450]

A family service centre (FSC) is a non-profit organization whose mission is '[e]mpowering the family, the core unit of society, by creating an enabling and supportive environment, providing counseling and developing positive human values'. The FSC nurtures individual, family, and

---

[444] Law Commission of India, *228th Report on 'Need for Legislation'*.

[445] Hari G. Ramasubramanian, *Indian Surrogacy Law Centre Review of 228th Report of Law Commission of India on Surrogacy*, 2009. Available at http://blog.indiansurrogacylaw.com/indian-surrogacy-law-centre-review-228th-report-law-commission-india/ (accessed on 9 September 2015).

[446] Ramasubramanian, *Indian Surrogacy Law Centre Review*.

[447] Ramasubramanian, *Indian Surrogacy Law Centre Review*.

[448] Ramasubramanian, *Indian Surrogacy Law Centre Review*.

[449] The Surrogacy (Regulation) Bill, 2016, was cleared by the Indian Cabinet, on 24 August 2016. The bill bans commercial surrogacy, and bars single people, married couples who have biological/adopted children, live-in partners, and homosexuals from opting for surrogacy. The bill allows only allows childless couples who have married for at least 5 years to opt for 'altruistic' surrogacy. The surrogate mother should be a close relative of the couple, should be married, and should have borne a child. Foreigners, NRIs, and PIOs who hold overseas citizens of India cards have been barred from opting for surrogacy. According to the new bill, a married woman who has at least one child of her own can be a surrogate mother only once in her lifetime. Childless or unmarried women are not allowed to carry somebody else's child. Available at http://indianexpress.com/article/india/india-news-india/surrogacy-bill-sushma-swaraj-married-couples-can-now-opt-homosexuals/ (accessed on 28 September 2016).

[450] Available at www.fscmumbai.org/ (accessed on 29 July 2015).

community empowerment through numerous programmes. The sponsorship programme provides financial support to families to meet educational, medical, nutritional, and other needs of the children with a view to improving their quality of life. Apart from financial assistance, extensive and in-depth efforts are put in by the social workers using various tools of social work—individual counselling, group sessions, school and home visits, recreational and educational activities, and so on, thereby paving a path for holistic development of the child. The FSC is one of the pioneer adoption agencies in Mumbai. It is also a forerunner of the concept of foster care for children awaiting adoption, as we believe that child requires a family care from birth. The agency provides hand-holding of PAPs and helps them through the process of documentation, home study, placement, and follow ups. They are also provided a common platform for exchange of thoughts, feelings, and experiences through orientation meetings, parenting sessions, and support groups. Simultaneously, extensive counselling is done with the *birth mothers* to enable them to deal with their emotions, trauma, legal adoption procedure, and many-a-times, even rehabilitation. On the other hand, utmost care is provided to the *children* in terms of family environment, and physical, psychological, and social well-being. The FSC is also involved in foster-care programmes. The supportive atmosphere of a foster home enables a child to develop healthy self-esteem, values, and behaviours. It also ensures that a child's psychological, emotional, and physical needs are met and helps nurture familial, cultural, and social bonds.

Indian Association for Promotion of Adoption and Child Welfare[451]

The Indian Association for Promotion of Adoption and Child Welfare (IAPA) is a non-profit voluntary organization, started in 1970. The founders were a group of professional social workers, adoptive parents, and lawyers who were then concerned with the problems involved in the adoption of abandoned and destitute children. Their concern related to their direct experience of the problems either as parents trying to adopt an unrelated child or as professionals helping pre-adoptive parents and promoting the concept of adoption among Indians. The direct service programmes have been focused on securing permanent family through adoption, preserving those families that are in crisis, and strengthening the disadvantaged to brighten the child's future. Simultaneously, the activities have been directed towards raising awareness, advocacy, and upgradation of the standards in serving the child. The services include:

- Pre-adoption foster family care for the orphaned/abandoned child and placement in adoption. Pre-adoption and post-adoption counselling.
- Promotion of adoption.
- Care of the child in crisis situation through family assistance or through foster family care within the community.
- Facilitate education and enrichment of the underprivileged children through financial support and other allied programmes.

---

[451] Available at http://www.iapacw.org/projects.aspx (accessed on 7 September 2015).

Maharashtra Government Foster Care Schemes (Bal Sangopan Yojna)[452]

The state of Maharashtra, in joint initiative with UNICEF, took a lead in introducing Bal Sangopan Yojana (BSY) in February 1995. This was followed in Karnataka mainly for de-institutionalization of children, and by *Mamta Grihas* in Orissa, and foster family care in Gujarat.[453] The foster care scheme is based on the belief that a family is the best environment for raising a child. A foster family is a temporary family for a child whose birth family is unwilling or unable to assume full responsibility for the child. The goal of foster care is to return the child to his or her own family as soon as possible. It is, thus, a programme whereby substitute family care is provided for a temporary period to children whose parents are unable to care for them because of illness, death, separation or desertion of one parent, or any other crisis. Since every child needs and has the right to be cared for in a family, foster care is a programme whereby a home is provided for the child for a short or extended period. A grant per child per month is given by the government to the foster parent(s) through an NGO for meeting the basic expenses of the child. The implementing NGO is given a supporting grant per month per child to meet administrative expenses, including home visits. The supportive atmosphere of a foster home enables a child to develop healthy self-esteem, values, and behaviours. Foster parents play an important role in providing a child in care a home and in supporting children through the hardship associated with separation and loss of family. Foster parents also ensure that a child's psychological, emotional, and physical needs are met, and help nurture familial, cultural, social, and religious bonds.

SOS Children's Villages of India[454]

SOS Children's Villages of India are committed to the welfare of orphaned and abandoned children—often throughout the whole of their childhood—and to strengthening families and communities as a preventive measure in the fight against child abandonment and social neglect. The following are two of their programmes:

- Family Based Care is a curative programme of SOS Children's Villages of India. It reaches out to over 6,500 once parentless or abandoned girls and boys in 32 SOS Children's Villages across India. Each children's village has 12–15 family homes, with every home consisting of 10 children on an average, along with an SOS mother. All-round development, including education, nutrition, health, and psychological development, is taken care of till the children are settled in their lives.
- Family Strengthening Programme is a preventive community intervention programme, covering over 17,000 children at 33 locations across India. Designed to prevent children from losing parental care or being abandoned, this programme runs in slums and rural areas, within

[452] Available at https://womenchild.maharashtra.gov.in/Sitemap/womenchild/pdf/fostercare.pdf (accessed on 7 September 2015).

[453] Telang, *Sharing*.

[454] Available at http://www.soschildrensvillages.in/about-us/what-we-do/child-care (accessed on 5 January 2017).

a 30-km radius of an SOS Children's Village. Taking a child rights-based approach, this programme attempts to assist and empower parents or caregivers in taking care of children in their natural families and communities. In the process, it strengthens not only the families and their children whose uplift it basically aims at, but also creates a vibrant network within the community that will last much longer and become sustainable in caring for the vulnerable families for a very long period.

3 Right to Parental Care
Custody and Guardianship

Historical Evolution

The legal relationship of a parent and a child is composed of rights and duties. Parents have parental rights by virtue of being natural guardians of their children. The term guardianship, in its fullest sense, embraces a 'bundle of rights' or, to be more exact, a 'bundle of powers' which a parent has over the child—that is, the full parental rights which constitute the parent–child relationship. These normally include the right to determine the child's upbringing 'as regards religion, education, and other matters'. The word 'custody' is normally used in India to denote the right to physical possession of the child, that is, charge of the minor's person. In Hindu law, the concept of guardianship appears to date back to the Vedic age, when for all practical purposes, the Hindu family was a patriarchal one, with considerable powers resting with the head of the family. Infants were considered as the property of the father. Acquisition or holding of independent separate property was not possible for them and the properties belonged to the father.[1] Gradually, the son's right to separate self-acquired property was recognized by law.

The ancient Hindu law vested the supreme guardianship of all in the broad principle of the king as parens patriae.[2] Sage Narada[3] mentioned the father and mother as guardians. The minor children mostly lived in the joint family and were always under the protection of the *karta* or the head of the family. Even if the child did not belong to a joint family but if he belonged to the first three varnas, he had to go to a guru's ashram to study and was under the protection of the guru.[4] Thus there was no need for the law of guardianship of the person.[5] The question of guardianship of the minor's property would have arisen only in those cases where the child was not a member of any joint family and had no parents. In respect of such children, the king was the supreme guardian who protected all such children and their property.[6]

---

[1] A.N. Saha, *Guardians and Wards Act*, 13th Edition (Eastern Law House, 1998).
[2] *Manu Smriti*, VII, 27; *Gautama Smriti*, 10, 48.
[3] *Narada Smriti*, XIII, 28–29.
[4] 'Guru' means teacher.
[5] Paras Diwan, *Modern Hindu Law* (Uttar Pradesh: Allahabad Law Agency, 1992), 239.
[6] Paras Diwan, *Modern Hindu Law* (Uttar Prashesh: Allahabad Law Agency, 13th edition, 1998).

In the ancient texts, the following are the references to custody and guardianship. A text of Manu[7] states: 'The king shall protect the inherited (and other) property of a minor until he has returned (from his teacher's home) or until he has passed his minority.' Sage Gautama[8] also declared: 'The king should protect till he has attained majority or has completed his education.' According to Vasishtha:[9] 'The king might entrust others with the minor's affairs.' Narada stated: 'The father has the first claim and after him comes the elder brother. His powers as guardian will be determined as may be deemed justly required for the benefit of the infant.'[10]

It is significant here that the concept of benefit of the minor was prevalent even in Narada's text. It is also to be noted that with the exception of Narada, who alone mentions the father, the mother, and the elder brother as guardians, all other sages merely declare the king to be the guardian of the minor's[11] property. But none of the ancient text writers have spoken of the guardianship of the person of the minor. All of them mention about the guardianship of the property of the minor. It seems that the guru or the teacher was the guardian of his pupil and because of joint family system, the children in the family were under the protection of the karta or the head of the joint family property. Under Hindu law, since the joint family was like a perpetual corporation, after the death of the father or karta the issue of guardianship did not arise at all.[12]

Till the passing of the Hindu Minority and Guardianship Act (HMGA), 1956, the traditional Hindu Law remained in force throughout British India and most of the Indian states.[13] The main feature that emerged in these laws was the predominant position of the father in respect of guardianship. The HMGA reformed and codified the Hindu law of guardianship and minority. Under the act, the supremacy of the paternal right during the lifetime of the father remained intact. So long as he was alive, he was the sole guardian and after his death or if he was unfit, the mother was the natural guardian of her minor children.

During the British period, the courts developed the law of guardianship. The Guardians and Wards Act (GWA) was passed in 1890 and conferred on the district courts the power of appointing guardians of minor children belonging to any community. A guardian is thus a person who has rights and duties with respect to the care and control of a minor's person or property. Guardianship includes the right to make decisions about the minor's upbringing, disposal of his/her property, and so on.[14] The word used in defining guardian is 'care'. 'Care' implies looking-after in a wider senses than 'custody', which is simply 'physical keeping'. Custody refers to the physical care and control of a minor. Custody is thus the right to the physical presence of the child. It includes the right to take day-to-day decisions regarding the child's education, medical treatment, and general movement. Custody can only be of the person of the minor but not of its property.[15]

[7] *Manu Smriti*, VII, 27.

[8] *Gautama Smriti*, 10, 48.

[9] *Vasishtha Smriti*, 16, 7–8.

[10] *Narada Smriti*, XIII, 28–29.

[11] Paras Diwan, *Law of Adoption, Minority, Guardianship of Custody* (Delhi: Universal Law Publishing Co. Pvt. Ltd., 2000).

[12] Diwan, *Law of Adoption*.

[13] Diwan, *Law of Adoption*.

[14] GWA, Section 4(2).

[15] Lawyers' Collective, *Legal Aid Handbook 2, Custody and Guardianship of Minors* (Delhi: Lawyers Collective and Kali for Women, 1995).

The Present Legal Regime

The law of guardianship and custody of minors is governed by the following:

1. The GWA, 1890.
2. The HMGA, 1956 and the unmodified Muslim law of custody and guardianship.
3. The personal matrimonial laws of Hindus, Parsis, and Christians, which lay down the principles relating to the custody and guardianship of children during matrimonial proceedings: Hindu Marriage Act (HMA), 1956, Special Marriage Act (SMA), 1954, Indian Divorce Act (IDA), 1869, and Parsi Marriage and Divorce Act (PMDA), 1936.
4. Section 7(g) of the Family Courts' Act (FCA), 1984 provides for the jurisdiction of the family court in adjudicating matter concerning or relating to the guardianship of the person or the custody of, or access to, any minor.
5. Protection of Women from Domestic Violence Act (PWDVA), 2005

Section 2(b)[16] of the PWDVA defines child as 'any person below the age of 18 years and includes any adopted, step or foster child'. Section 21[17] lays down that notwithstanding anything contained in any other law for the time being in force, the magistrate, at any stage of hearing of the application for grant of any relief, may grant temporary custody of any child to the aggrieved person or to the person making an application on her/his behalf and specify the arrangements for visit of such child by the respondent. However, the magistrate may refuse to allow such visits if in his opinion such visits may be harmful to the interests of the child. In the matters relating to custody, education, and maintenance of children, the court is invested with a very wide discretion and broad powers. In the welfare of children, the court can pass any orders, since the act states that the court may pass any order 'as it may deem just and proper'. Justness or properness of the order is to be looked at from the interest of the children, as it is their interest which should be uppermost in the mind of the court.

It is certainly not the interest of any party, innocent or otherwise. It is also not a mere question of balance of convenience. The court has power to pass any order in respect of children, by placing them into the custody of either parents or of a third person or of an institution. It may give custody to one parent and care and control to the other. It may pass any interim or permanent orders and may vary them, change them, or rescind them at any time. Similarly, orders can be passed in regard to maintenance and education of children. The court has the power to refuse to exercise the jurisdiction but it would do so only in very exceptional cases.

---

[16] PWDVA, Section 2(b): 'child' means any person below the age of 18 years and includes any adopted, step, or foster child.

[17] PWDVA, Section 21: Custody orders—Notwithstanding anything contained in any other law for the time being in force, the magistrate may, at any stage of hearing of the application for protection order or for any other relief under this act grant temporary custody of any child or children to the aggrieved person or the person making an application on her behalf and specify, if necessary, the arrangements for visit of such child or children by the respondent, provided that if the magistrate is of the opinion that any visit of the respondent may be harmful to the interests of the child or children, the magistrate shall refuse to allow such visit.

In deciding the question of custody, the court would take into consideration the following:

1. Welfare of the child, which is of paramount consideration.
2. Wishes of the parents.
3. Wishes of the child.
4. Age and sex of the child.

The court is also free to consider any other matter which helps it to determine the question in the interest of the child. Whenever a question arises before the court pertaining to the custody of a minor child, the matter is to be decided not on consideration of legal rights of parties but on the sole and predominant criterion of what would best serve the interest and welfare of the minor.

The English and Indian decisions are replete with such statements that (i) the children of tender years should be committed to the custody of the mother, (ii) older boys should be in the custody of the father, and (iii) older girls should be in the custody of the mother. But these are judicial statements of general nature and there is no hard-and-fast rule. As to the children of tender years, it is now a firmly established practice that the mother should have their custody since father cannot provide the material care and affection which are essential for their proper growth. It is now also accepted that for proper psychological development of a child of tender years, mother's care is indispensable.

Whenever the question of custody of a minor child is a concern, it is the adopted approach that it is given in favour of the mother unless it is brought on record that the mother suffers from some disqualification by virtue of her character, total inability to take care of the child, or such other handicap. The question of custody of minor children is never a static problem and the issue can be reexamined at any stage.

Code of Civil Procedure, 1908

Rule 3 of Order XXXIIA of the Code of Civil Procedure, 1908 (also referred to as the Civil Procedure Code or CPC) states that, in suits or proceedings relating to matters concerning the family, where it is possible to do so in consistence with the nature and circumstances of the case, the court has a duty to assist the parties in arriving at a settlement. Also, if at any stage, it appears to the court that there is a reasonable possibility of a settlement between the parties, the court may adjourn the proceeding for such period as it thinks fit to enable attempts to be made to effect such a settlement.[18] India amended the CPC to include the process of mediation. All civil judges, when they try a civil suit including a suit relating to child custody, are first supposed to explore the possibility of adopting alternate dispute resolution mechanisms before they actually decide the suit. If, through alternate dispute resolution, an amicable solution can be found, the judge is competent to pass a decree in terms of the amicable solution.[19]

[18] Code of Civil Procedure (Amendment) Act, 1908, Order XXXII-A, Rule 3.
[19] Section 89: Settlement of disputes outside the court—

(1) Where it appears to the court that there exist elements of a settlement which may be acceptable to the parties, the court shall formulate the terms of settlement and give them to the parties for their

Habeas Corpus Proceedings

A writ of habeas corpus in custody proceedings is a court order that requires the person or agency who has unlawful custody of a child to return the child to the person who has lawful custody. The writ could be directed at a parent, who has lawfully or unlawfully taken the child and refused to return the child, at an agency who wrongfully removed the child from the custody of the parent, or at any other person who is keeping the child from the person with lawful custody.

The full name of the writ is 'habeas corpus ad subjiciendum'. Habeas corpus means that you have the body. Habeas corpus ad subjiciendum means 'that you have the body to submit or answer'. This is a prerogative process for securing the liberty of the subject by affording an effective means of immediate release from unlawful detention, whether in state or in private custody. By it, the court commands the production of the subject and enquires into the cause of his detention. If there is no legal justification for the detention, the party is ordered to be released. The writ is applicable as a remedy in all cases of wrongful deprivation of personal liberty. The principal aim of the writ is to provide for a swift judicial review of alleged unlawful restraint on the liberty of a subject.[20] The writ is a writ of right and is granted ex debito justitiae. It is not, however, a writ of course. Both at common law and by statute, the writ of habeas corpus may be granted only upon ground for its issue being shown. The writ may not, in general, be refused

observations and after receiving the observations of the parties, the court may reformulate the terms of a possible settlement and refer the same for

    (a)   arbitration;
    (b)   conciliation;
    (c)   judicial settlement including settlement through Lok Adalat; or
    (d)   mediation.

(2)   Where a dispute has been referred

    (a)   for arbitration or conciliation, the provisions of the Arbitration and Conciliation Act, 1996 (26 of 1996) shall apply as if the proceedings for arbitration or conciliation were referred for settlement under the provisions of that act;

    (b)   to Lok Adalat, the court shall refer the same to the Lok Adalat in accordance with the provisions of Subsection (1) of Section 20 of the Legal Services Authority Act, 1987 (39 of 1987) and all other provisions of that act shall apply in respect of the dispute so referred to the Lok Adalat;

    (c)   for judicial settlement, the court shall refer the same to a suitable institution or person and such institution or person shall be deemed to be a Lok Adalat and all the provisions of the Legal Services Authority Act, 1987 (39 of 1987) shall apply as if the dispute were referred to a Lok Adalat under the provisions of that act;

    (d)   for mediation, the court shall effect a compromise between the parties and shall follow such procedure as may be prescribed.

(3) (a)   In every suit or proceeding to which this order applies, an endeavour shall be made by the court in the first instance, where it is possible to do so consistent with the nature and circumstances of the case, to assist the parties in arriving at a settlement in respect of the subject-matter of the suit.

[20] *Miss. Atya Shamim* v. *Deputy Commissioner/Collector*, AIR 1999 JK 140.

merely because there exists an alternative remedy by which the validity of the detention can be questioned.[21]

In Halsbury's *Laws of England*, Fourth Edition,[22] it has been stated: 'Sometimes, a writ of habeas corpus is sought for custody of a minor child. In such cases also, the paramount consideration which is required to be kept in view by a writ-Court is "welfare of the child".'

In Habeas Corpus, Bailey[23] states: 'It is further observed that an incidental aspect, which has a bearing on the question, may also be adverted to. In determining whether it will be for the best interests of a *child* to grant its *custody* to the father or mother, the Court may properly consult the *child*, if it has sufficient judgment.'

It is well established that in issuing the writ of habeas corpus in the case of infants, the jurisdiction which the court exercises is an inherent jurisdiction distinct from a statutory jurisdiction conferred by any particular provision in any special statute. In other words, the employment of the writ of habeas corpus in child-custody cases is not pursuant to, but independent of, statute. The jurisdiction exercised by the court rests in such cases on its inherent equitable powers and exerts the force of the state, as parens patriae, for the protection of its infant ward, and the very nature and scope of the inquiry and the result sought to be accomplished call for the exercise of the jurisdiction of a court of equity. The primary object of a habeas corpus petition, as applied to infants, is to determine in whose custody the best interests of the child will probably be advanced. In a habeas corpus proceeding brought by one parent against the other for the custody of their child, the court has before it the question of the rights of the parties as between themselves, and also has before it, if presented by the pleadings and the evidence, the question of the interest which the state, as parens patriae, has in promoting the best interests of the child. In such cases due weight must be given to the circumstances such as a child's ordinary comfort, contentment, intellectual, moral and physical development, his health, education, general maintenance, and favourable surroundings.[24]

The employment of the forms of habeas corpus in a child custody case is not for the purpose of testing the legality of a confinement or restraint as contemplated by the ancient common law writ, or by statute, but the primary purpose is to furnish a means by which the court, in the exercise of its judicial discretion, may determine what is best for the welfare of the child, and the decision is reached by a consideration of the equities involved in the welfare of the child, against which the legal rights of no one, including the parents, are allowed to militate.[25]

In Clarke,[26] it has been stated: 'But with respect to a child under guardianship for nurture, the child is supposed to be unlawfully imprisoned when unlawfully detained from the custody of the guardian; and when delivered to him, the child is supposed to be set at liberty.'

The rights or interests to be considered in a habeas corpus proceeding involving the custody of a child are those of the child, parent, and those who have for years discharged all the obligations of parents; but the paramount considerations are the welfare and interest of the child, and the

---

[21] *Halsbury Laws of England*, Vol. II, Paragraph 1455, Fourth Edition (UK: Lexis Nexis).

[22] Vol. 24, Para 511, p. 217.

[23] Vol. I, p. 581

[24] *Kamla Devi v. State Of Himachal Pradesh And Ors.*, AIR 1987 HP 34.

[25] *Howarth v. Northcott*, 152 Conn 460, 208 A 2d and 540, 17 ALR3d 758.

[26] (1857) 7 El & Bl l86, 119 ER 1217.

court may consider the question of interest which the state, as parens patriae, has to promote the child's best interest, particularly if the matter is raised by the pleadings.[27]

It has been held that the natural right of the parent is an important consideration and that, in the absence of special circumstances, the child should be awarded to the parent as against more distant relatives or third persons. However, the legal right of the parent is secondary to the best interest of the child, and such right will not be enforced where it is not advantageous to the child, although it has also been held that in the absence of a finding that the parent is unfit to have custody, the mere fact that it is not to the best interest of the child to be in his parents' custody is not controlling.[28]

Ordinarily, a parent who is a fit and proper person to have custody of the child and who has not for any reason forfeited the right to custody, may be awarded custody notwithstanding the wishes or desires of the child. However, the court may consider the wishes of child, where the child is sufficiently mature in mind to form a judgment, and other conditions being equal, the wishes of the child may well be the controlling consideration.[29]

The fact that the child has been well cared for over a long period and has become attached to the environment may warrant giving custody of the child to the person who has cared for it, even as against the parents; but the parent's right will not be denied unless the foster alliance was protracted and acquiesced in a spirit of abandonment and a severance will be disadvantageous to the child. In determining the custody to the child, the court is not bound to respect the mother's possession of the child, where such possession was obtained by unlawful means.[30]

Besides the efficacy of the writ of habeas corpus in liberating the subject from illegal confinement in public prison, it also extends its influence to remove every unlawful restraint of personal freedom in private life, availing for instance, to restore children to the lawful custody.[31]

Guardians and Wards Act, 1890

The GWA, 1890 was among the earliest statutes enacted by the British Indian legislature, relating to minors. The charters of the high courts and the High Court Act of 1861 conferred special jurisdiction on the high courts in regard to minor children. Before 1890, there were scattered statutes and regulations enacted by the presidencies of Madras, Bombay, and Bengal.[32] The GWA was a consolidating and amending statute. All the provisions of the earlier scattered statutes have been consolidated under the present act. It is a complete code defining the rights and remedies of guardians and wards. All matters relating to guardianship, their rights and obligations, the removal and replacement of the guardian, and remedies available to the wards are regulated by the provisions of the act. This act applies to all minor children of any caste and creed, though in appointing or declaring a person as guardian of the minor, the court will take into consideration the personal law of the minor (Section 19). The GWA deals with the guardian of the person and property of the

---

[27] *Corpus Juris Secundum*, Vol. 39 (1976), p. 914.
[28] *Corpus Juris Secundum*, p. 922.
[29] *Corpus Juris Secundum*, p. 924.
[30] *Corpus Juris Secundum*, p. 926.
[31] *Wharton's Law Lexicon*, Fourteenth Edition (1938), p. 462.
[32] Diwan, *Law of Adoption*.

minor. But once a person is appointed or declared as guardian of a minor, irrespective of the fact whether the minor is a Hindu, Muslim, or subject to any other personal law, such a guardian will be subject to the provisions of the act. Once a certified guardian is appointed or declared, the powers of natural or testamentary guardian under the personal law stand suspended.[33] But if the personal law is not in conflict with any provision of the act, the personal law will apply.[34]

Courts have exercised the power of appointing guardians from a very early time. Whenever a matter of guardianship or custody of a child is brought before them, the courts assume the charge of the child and endeavour to see that the child is brought up in the same manner as the natural parents would have done. The guardian court usually discharges the function by appointing a suitable guardian. A guardian appointed by the court is under the supervision and control of the court and he cannot take any steps, except the routine ones, without the prior permission of the court. The court may be called upon to appoint a guardian of the person of the minor or of his property or of both. The procedure for appointing guardians is prescribed under this act.

The natural guardian of a minor is the person who is legally presumed to have a natural right of guardianship over it and consequently is presumed to make ultimate decisions about his/her welfare. The natural guardian has the legal right to act as a minor's guardian, unless that right is taken away by a court in a proceeding under the GWA or unless a testamentary guardian has been properly appointed by will. The natural guardian does not have to go to court to be appointed guardian. A person cannot surrender to another party his or her duty to act as a guardian, although custody of a minor may be given to another.

Under Section 20 of the GWA, the relationship between a guardian and the ward is a fiduciary relationship. This means that guardians cannot profit from their guardianship and must act only with the wards' welfare in mind. There are two types of guardians: of the minor's person and of the minor's property. A guardian of a minor's person is expected to take custody of the minor and is obliged to provide financial support, healthcare, and education. If a court has appointed the guardian of the person, he or she is not permitted to remove the ward from the jurisdiction of that court without the court's permission.

Guardians of property have an obligation to deal with the minor's property as if it were his or her own and can act to protect or enhance the property. Guardians of property who are appointed by the court cannot mortgage, transfer, or dispose of immovable property, or lease it without prior approval from the court. Transfer in violation of this restriction is void. Generally, the powers of guardians that are appointed by a will can be further restrained by the will, and the powers of guardians of property are contained in the GWA.

Welfare of the Child under the Guardians and Wards Act, 1890

Section 17 of the GWA deals with the power of the court to appoint or declare a person as guardian. Whenever the court, on the application of a person, comes to the conclusion that it would be for the welfare of the child to appoint a guardian of the person or property or both of the minor, it can appoint a guardian. Section 17 lays down the various factors which would help the court in finding out the welfare of the child.

[33] *A.R. Krishnan Chetty* v. *Valliachani*, AIR 1914 Mad 648.
[34] *Siddigunnisa Bibi* v. *Nizamuddin*, AIR 1932 All 215.

Section 7(1) lays down the cardinal rule in the matter of guardianship and custody of children. It states that the court should appoint a guardian only when it is satisfied that the appointment of guardian is necessary for the welfare of the child. In considering what will be for the welfare of the minor, the following factors have been mentioned, all of which are contained in Section 17(2):

- age of the minor;
- sex of the minor;
- religion of the minor;
- character and capacity of the proposed guardian;
- nearness of kin to the minor;
- wishes, if any, of the deceased parent;
- any existing or previous relations of the proposed guardian with the minor or his property; or
- if the minor is old enough to form an intelligent preference, the court may consider that preference.

These are the guiding factors laid down by the GWA to determine the welfare of the child. Section 7, read with Section 17, can be interpreted as stating that the welfare of the minor should be consistent with the personal law of the minor. It is significant to note that the personal law of the minor is a very important consideration.

Also, Section 17(5) states that the court shall not appoint or declare any person to be a guardian against his/her will. This means that the guardian appointed by the court must accept his/her appointment. His/her will appears to be more important than the welfare of the child. Even if he is the most suitable person for the welfare of the child, if he does not accept his appointment, he cannot be appointed. This provision clearly subordinates the welfare of the child as the paramount consideration. From the wordings of the provision of the GWA, it thus appears that the welfare of the minor should conform to the personal law of the minor and the willingness of the guardian.

The other considerations, such as age, sex, character, and capacity of the guardian, nearness of kin, wishes of the deceased parent, and wishes of the child, may help the court in determining the welfare of the child. From the reading of Sections 7(1) and 17, it has not been specifically mentioned that the *welfare of the child is the paramount consideration*. The principle of the best interests of the child has not been actually laid down. But decisions of the Supreme Court and high courts have interpreted that the welfare of the child should be of paramount consideration.

Under Section 7, the district court or the family court has the power to appoint or declare a person as guardian of a minor's person or property and once it decides to make such an appointment or declaration, Section 17 comes into operation, as the court would appoint a guardian after considering these factors. These factors assist the court in determining what is for the welfare of the child.

Hindu Minority and Guardianship Act, 1956

Under the HMGA, the father is the natural guardian of the person and property of legitimate children, and after him,[35] the guardianship vests in the mother (Section 6). The Supreme Court

---

[35] For the latest interpretation of 'after him', see *Githa Hariharan & Another* v. *Reserve Bank of India and Another* and *Vandana Shiva* v. *Jayanta Bandhopadhyaya & Another,* (99) 2 SCC 228.

has now made the mother also the natural guardian.[36] The undivided share of the minor in the joint family property is excluded from the purview of guardianship. The father cannot now deprive the mother of guardianship after his death by appointing a guardian by will. Even during the lifetime of the father, the mother is entitled to the custody of her children below the age of 5 years. It is suggested that this age needs to be increased.

Under the act, the mother is the natural guardian of her illegitimate children and after her death, the putative father is the natural guardian. The adoptive father, and after him the adoptive mother, is the natural guardian of an adopted child. Under the HMGA, both the parents have been given the power of appointing testamentary guardians. Parents have power of testamentary appointment in all those cases where they are competent to act as natural guardians.

However, a Hindu father cannot appoint a guardian of his minor illegitimate children, even when he is entitled to act as their natural guardian. The guardianship of a minor girl comes to an end on her marriage and it cannot be revised even if she becomes a widow during her minority. In that event, the guardianship would belong to the nearest *sapinda* (near kinsmen) of her husband.

Qualifications Regarding Natural Guardians

Although Section 6(a) of the HMGA declares that in the case of a boy or an unmarried girl, the natural guardians of a Hindu minor are the father, and after him, the mother, that proposition is subject to two qualifications, enumerated as follows:

- The proviso to Section 6 lays down that the custody of a minor who has not completed the age of 5 years shall ordinarily be with the mother; and
- Section 13(1) lays down that in the appointment or declaration of any person as guardian of a Hindu minor by a court, the welfare of the minor shall be the paramount consideration. By Subsection (2) of the same section, it is provided, inter alia, that no person is entitled to guardianship by virtue of the provisions of this act if the court is of the opinion that his or her guardianship will not be for the welfare of the minor.

It is thus fairly clear that if the case comes before the court, the court must look to the welfare of the minor and not merely to the legal provisions relating to guardianship. In this sense, Section 6 is subject to Section 13, whereby welfare of the minor is to be of paramount consideration (HMGA, Section 13). This is the legal position under the HMGA which is supplemental to the GWA as regards Hindu children. The provisions for the appointment or declaration of guardians are given in the GWA.

Section 13(1) makes the welfare of the minor paramount or the sole consideration in the appointment and declaration of the guardian. Section 13(2) says that no person is entitled to guardianship by virtue of the provisions of this statute or any other law if it is not for the welfare of the child. Thus, all guardians—natural, testamentary, certificated, or marriage guardians—are subject to the principle of paramountcy of the welfare of children.

---

[36] See *Githa Hariharan* v. *Reserve Bank of India*, (99) 2 SCC 228.

Custody and Guardianship during Matrimonial Proceedings

The matrimonial courts/family courts may be called upon to decide questions of passing orders relating to custody, education, and maintenance of children at any one of the following stages of matrimonial proceedings:

- Pending matrimonial proceedings, that is, between the period of filing of the petition and final disposal of the petition. These orders are known as interim orders or temporary orders.
- At the time of the passing of the decree granting the petition. These are known as permanent orders.
- Subsequent to the passing of the decree granting the petition. At this stage the question may come up in either of the following two ways:

  ♦ When in the matrimonial proceedings, no application was made for custody, education, and maintenance of children and therefore, after the decree, an altogether fresh petition may be made for the same.
  ♦ When the court had already passed a permanent order of custody, education, or maintenance, an application may be made to get that order modified, rescinded, or changed.

Section 26 of the HMA, 1955[37] deals with custody of the children. Section 38 of the SMA, 1954 is substantially the same as Section 26 of the HMA. Dealing with the same subject, Section 49 of the PMDA, 1936[38] is slightly differently worded. The difference between the two provisions is in two respects:

- Under the former statute, the age of children for whom such orders can be made is 18 years, while under the latter, the age is 16, that is, the ages of children in regard to whom such orders can be made should be below the age of 18 years under the PMDA.
- Under the HMA and the SMA, the wishes of children are to be considered, but there is no such provision under the PMDA, though in practice the courts do consult the wishes of the children if they are intelligent enough to express the same (though the courts are not bound to follow them).

The IDA, 1869 deals with the subject in Part XI (Sections 41 to 44), under the title 'Custody of Children'. Interim matters relating to custody, education, and maintenance of children are dealt with in Section 41 (judicial separation proceedings) and Section 43 (nullity and divorce proceedings), while matters relating to permanent custody and other related issues are dealt with in Section 42 (judicial separation proceedings) and Section 44 (nullity and divorce proceedings). In fact, the provisions are substantially the same as under the PMDA. The IDA does not deal with the question of custody, maintenance, and education of children in restitution proceedings. The

---

[37] HMA, Section 26.
[38] PMDA, Section 49.

age of children is their minority, that is, below the age of 18 years under the IDA. In the interest of children, it is recommended that this provision should be uniformly incorporated under all the statutes. Further, the age of children in respect of whom orders of custody, maintenance, and education can be made should be the age of minority.[39]

Jurisdiction of the Court

Permanent orders for custody, education, or maintenance can be made only if the court passes a decree granting the relief. If the petition is dismissed, the proceedings relating to children also fall through and the court has no power to make any orders for custody, education, or maintenance of children. Thus, in matters relating to custody, maintenance, and education of children the court exercises jurisdiction only if it has jurisdiction in the main petition.

The question relating to custody, education, or maintenance of children may come before the court in any one of the following situations:

- Interim orders for custody, education, or maintenance of children. Interim orders may be passed at any time from the date of filing of the proceedings and before the final disposal of the proceedings.
- Permanent orders of custody, education, or maintenance of children. Such orders may be passed:
  - At the time of passing of the decree granting the relief in a matrimonial case.
  - Subsequent to the passing of the decree in a matrimonial case. The question may come up in the following two situations:
  - If at the time of the passing of the decree or earlier no prayer was made for custody, education, or maintenance, of children, a fresh application by petition may be made subsequently at any time after the passing of the decree.
  - When orders for custody, education, or maintenance have already been made, an application may be made for revoking, suspending, or varying such orders.

In these matters, the court is invested with a very wide discretion and broad powers. In the welfare of children it has power to pass any order. It is now a very well-established principle that in all proceedings in respect of children, their welfare is the paramount consideration, though the court may also take into consideration such matters as age, sex, wishes of the child, and the fitness of the parent to whom custody is to be committed.

The court has power to revoke, suspend, or vary any order of custody, education, or maintenance of children at any time subsequent to making of the order, whenever the circumstances of the case require it to do so. This applies to both interim and final orders of custody, education, maintenance, and access. For variation of the order, the party seeking to do so must establish a case justifying revocation, suspension, or rescinding of the order.

---

[39] Diwan, *Law of Adoption*.

Muslim Personal Law of Custody and Guardianship

The Muslim law of custody and guardianship is based on certain verses in the Koran[40] and a few *Hadis*.[41] These verses speak of the guardianship of the property of the minor, but very little has been said about the guardianship of the person of the minor.[42]

On the failure of the natural guardian and testamentary guardian, the matter is governed by the GWA. The power of appointing or declaring any person as guardian is conferred on the district court. The district court may appoint or declare any person as guardian of a minor child's person as well as property whenever it considers it necessary for the welfare of the minor, taking into consideration the age, sex, wishes of the child, and the personal law of the minor.[43]

Section 2 of the Muslim Personal Law (Shariat) Application Act, 1937 includes guardianship among the issues where the Muslim Personal Law (Shariat) will apply. Under Muslim law, guardians are of three types:[44]

- natural guardians
- testamentary guardians
- guardians appointed by the court

[40] The following verses in the Koran (IV, 2, 5, 6) are considered to be the foundation of the law of guardianship:

> Give unto orphans their substance and give them not the bad in exchange for the good and devour not their substance by adding it to your own substance. Verily that would be a great sin. Give not unto the weak of understanding, the substance which God has appointed you to preserve for them but provide them therewith and clothe them and speak to them with kindly speech. Provide orphans until they attain the age of marriage, then if ye perceive that they are able to manage their affairs well, then deliver unto them their substance and devour it not wastefully or hastily for they are growing up. Let him that is rich abstain generously (entirely from taking the property of orphans) and that who is poor let him take thereof in reason. And when ye deliver up their substance unto orphans, have (the transaction) witnessed in their presence.

Another verse runs as: 'Come not near the wealth of the orphans save with that which is better, till he comes to strength' (The Koran XVIII, 34; iv, 153).

The Koran permits a guardian of property of minor to take reasonable recompense for the trouble of looking after the affairs of an infant (iv, 5).

[41] The following *Hadis* trace the history of the obligation and liability of guardians of minor children (Misccat ul-Messabib, Book XIII, Chapter XVII, Part 3):

> When these revelations came down, viz., meddle not with the substance of the orphan, otherwise than for improving thereof and surely they who devour the possessions of the orphans unjustly, shall swallow down nothing but fire into their bellies and shall broil in ragging flames, all those who have orphans in their care went home and they separated their own food from orphans and also their water, fearful lest they might be mixed. Then when the orphans left any of their meat or drink, it was taken care of for them to eat afterwards. Then this method was unpleasant to the orphans, and they mentioned it to the Prophet, the God sent down this revelation, of Mohammed, they will ask concerning the orphans, answer to deal righteously with them is best and if ye mix your things with theirs, verily, they are your brethren. Then they mixed their meat and drink together.

[42] Diwan, *Law of Adoption*.
[43] GWA, Section 17.
[44] Diwan, *Law of Adoption*.

Natural Guardians

The father's right of guardianship is recognized in all schools of Muslim law. Even when the custody is with the mother or any other female entitled to custody, the father's right of general supervision and control exists.[45]

Testamentary Guardian

The father, as natural guardian, has full powers of appointing a guardian for his children by his will. In the absence of the father and his executor, the grandfather can also appoint a guardian by his will. A mother can be appointed as a testamentary guardian or executor of the person as well as of the property of her minor children. But the Muslim mother has no power to appoint testamentary guardian of the property of her minor children.

Guardians Appointed by the Court

Guardians can be appointed by the court under the procedures prescribed in the GWA.

Hizanat (custody)—Right of the Mother

All Muslim authorities recognize the mother's right of *hizanat* or custody. According to the *Rudd-ul-Muhtar*, 'the right of the mother to the custody of her child is recognized whether she be a *mosalman*, or a *kitabia* or a *majoosia*, even though she be separated from her husband. But it does not belong to one who is an apostage'.[46] The *Fatwai Alamgiri* puts it thus: 'The mother is of all persons the best entitled to the custody of her infant children during connubial relationship as well as after its dissolution.'[47] The term hizanat is applied to the woman to whom belongs the right of rearing up a child.

Of all the persons, the first and foremost right to have the custody of children belongs to the mother, and she cannot be deprived of her right so long as she is not found guilty of misconduct.[48] The mother has the right of custody and care of children during the period laid down in Muslim law. Hizanat is recognized in the sense that it can be enforced against the father or any other person. But it is a right to which obligations are attached. The mother's right of hizanat is, in fact, a right of rearing of children. If she is not found suitable to bring up the child, or her custody is not conducive to the physical, moral, and intellectual welfare of the child, she can be deprived of it.

Since Muslim law considers the right of hizanat as no more than the right of rearing up the children, it terminates at an early age of the child. In this regard, Muslim law makes a distinction

---

[45] The father's right to control the religion of his children is recognized even if the mother is a non-Muslim. He also has the right to control the education, general upbringing, and movements of his children. In the absence of the father, the same right can be exercised by the grandfather or executor, whoever is entitled to guardianship.

[46] *Rudd-ul-Muhtar*, 11, 1041.

[47] *Fatwai Alamgiri*, I.728.

[48] *Md Shafi* v. *Shamim*, AIR 1979 Bom 16.

between the son and the daughter. According to the *Fatwai Alamgiri*, the mother is entitled to the custody of a boy until he is independent of her care, that is, until he is 7 years old.[49] According to the Hanafis, it is an established rule that the mother's right of hizanat over her son terminates on the latter's completing the age of 7 years.[50]

The Shias hold the view that the mother is entitled to the custody of her son until he is weaned[51] (this is considered to be on the completion of 2 years) and that during this period the mother cannot be deprived of the custody of her son under any circumstances whatever, except with her own consent.[52] On the completion of the age of 2 by the son, the mother's right of custody terminates.

According to the Malikis, the mother's right of hizanat over her son continues till the child attains puberty.[53] The rule among the Shafis and the Hanbalis is the same as among the Hanafis. But these schools hold the view that on completion of the age of 7 years, the child is given a choice of living with either parent. But in every case, the father is entitled to the custody of his son when he attains puberty.[54]

Among the Hanafis, the mother is entitled to the custody of daughters till they attain the age of puberty.[55] Among the Malikis, the Shafiis, and the Hanbalis, the mother's right of custody over her daughters continues till they are married.[56] On the other hand, under the Ithana Ashari law, the mother is entitled to the custody of her daughters till they attain the age of 7.[57] In all the schools of Muslim law, the mother has the right to the custody of her married daughters below the age of puberty in preference to the husband.[58] The mother has the right of her children up to the ages specified in each school, irrespective of the fact whether the child is legitimate or illegitimate.

Other Females Entitled to Hizanat

Among the Hanafis, the following females are, after the mother, entitled to *hizanat* of the minor children of the age up to which the mother is entitled to it:[59]

[49] 'The Hedaya, or Guide: A Commentary on the Mussulman Laws' in Alī ibn Abī Bakr Marghīnānī, *Making of Modern Law: Foreign, Comparative and International Law, 1600-1926*, second edition, edited by Standish Grove Grady, translated by Charles Hamilton (W. H. Allen, 1870). See also *Imtiaz* v. *Masood*, AIR 1979 All 25.

[50] *Farjanb* v. *Aynu*, AIR 1989 Bom 357.

[51] See *Sharaya-ul-Islam*.

[52] *Sherkhan* v. *Ajbhoi*, 11 Bom LR 75.

[53] *Sautayra*, 1, 348.

[54] *Fatwai Alamgiri*, I. 730; *Fatwai Kazi Khan*, I. 478. For details see Diwan, *Law of Adoption*.

[55] *Fatwai Alamgiri*, I. 730; *Fatwai Kazi Khan*, I. 478. For details see Diwan, *Law of Adoption*.

[56] *Rudd-ul-Muhtar*, II. 1054.

[57] Baillie, II, 95.

[58] In the matter of *Khatija Bibi* ILR (1870) 5 Bom LR 557. In the matter of *Mohim Bibi* (1874) 13 BLR.

[59] Tayabji and Ameer Ali give a different list. The rule is that among the females, the nearer excludes the remoter.

- mother's mother, howsoever high[60]
- father's mother, howsoever high[61]
- full sister
- consanguine sister[62]
- uterine sister's daughter
- consanguine sister's daughter
- full sister's daughter
- maternal aunts, in like order as sisters
- paternal aunts, in like order as sisters[63]

Under the Shia school, after the mother, the hizanat belongs to the father. In the absence of both the parents, or on their being disqualified, the grandfather is entitled to the custody.[64] Among the Malikis, the following are entitled to the custody of a minor in the absence of the mother:

- maternal grandmother
- maternal great grandmother
- maternal aunt and grand-aunt
- full sister
- uterine sister
- consanguine sister
- paternal aunt

All the schools of Muslim law recognize the right of the father to the custody of his minor children in the following two cases:

- On the completion of the age by the child up to which the mother or other females are entitled to its custody.
- In the absence of the mother or other females who have the right to hizanat of minor children.

---

[60] *Fatima* v. *Shaik Peda*, AIR 1941 Mad 944; *Nur Begum* v. *Begum*, AIR 1934 Lah 274; In re *Ghulam Md*, AIR 1924 Sind 154.

[61] *Boocha* v. *Elahi Bux*, ILR 11 Cal 574.

[62] In the *Hedaya* and the *Fatwai Alamgiri* the consanguine sister is not mentioned. Mulla holds the view that the omission is purely accidental, since the paternal aunt is expressly mentioned. Ameer Ali puts her after full sister's daughter and uterine sister's daughter (II, 253.). See Diwan, *Law of Adoption*.

[63] Diwan, *Law of Adoption*.

[64] Authorities are not clear as to who is entitled to the custody after the grandfather. Some Shia authorities have laid down certain rules of preference, on the basis of which the textbook writers have compiled a list of persons who are entitled to the custody of minor children in the absence of the grandfather. Ameer Ali holds the view that after the grandfather, *hizanat* belongs to the grandmother, after her it belongs to the ascendants, then to collaterals within the prohibited degrees, the nearer excluding the remoter. For details see Diwan, *Law of Adoption*.

The father cannot be deprived of the right of hizanat of his male child of 7 years if he is not found to be unfit.[65]

The cardinal principle of hizanat in Muslim law also is the welfare of the child. This is the reason why Muslim law gave preference to the mother over the father in the matter of custody of children of tender age. The Muslim law of hizanat states that every other consideration is subordinated to the welfare of the child. A woman who is unworthy of credit may still retain the custody of the child, if welfare of the child so requires.

Custody and Guardianship of Children in Family Courts

Marriage dissolution leaves many problems to be resolved and family disputes, especially custody disputes, by their very nature, call for solutions which must be arrived at with speed and simplicity, and at low cost, guided mainly by conciliation proceedings. A suit or proceeding in relation to the guardianship of the person or custody of, or access to, any minor is dealt with by family courts, or by district courts where there are no family courts.[66] The family court has provided for the association of family counsellors, conciliators, and social service organizations in the process of settlement of disputes through conciliation. Thus, the family court is a specialized court.[67] In any matrimonial conflict which is heading towards a divorce or separation inevitably, questions of custody and maintenance of children will arise. In such situations, the family courts are required to make a decision based on the best interests of the child.

Under Section 10(3)[68] of the FCA, the principal judge has the power to frame rules. When making a parenting order in relation to a child, the court must apply a presumption that it is in the best interests of the child for the child's parents to have equal, shared parental responsibility for the child. While determining the best interests of the child, the primary considerations are:

1. Ensuring benefit to the child of having spent equal or substantial or significant time to develop a meaningful relationship with both the child's parents and to ensure an implementation of overnight access so that the child gets love and affection of not only both the parents but also

---

[65] Diwan, *Law of Adoption*.
[66] FCA, Section 2.
[67] FCA, Section 6.
[68] FCA, Section 10: Procedure generally—

(1) Subject to the other provisions of this act and rules, the provisions of the Code of Civil Procedure, 1908 (5 of 1908), and of any other law for the time being in force shall apply to the suits and proceedings other than the proceedings under Chapter IX of the Code of Criminal Procedure (CrPC), 1973 (2 of 1974), before a family court and for the purpose of the said provisions of the code, a family court shall be deemed to be a civil court and shall have all the powers of such court.

(2) Subject to the other provisions of this act and the rules, the provisions of the CrPC, 1973 (2 of 1974), or the rules made thereunder, shall apply to the proceedings under Chapter IX of the code before a family court.

(3) Nothing in Subsection (1) or Subsection (2) shall prevent a family court from laying down its own procedure with a view to arrive at a settlement in respect of the subject matter of the suit or proceedings or at the truth of the facts alleged by the one party and denied by the other.

of grandparents, uncles, aunties, cousins, and other family members, thereby ensuring that the family heritage is maintained.
2. Ensuring the need to protect the child from physical or psychological harm from being subjected to, or exposed to, abuse, neglect, or family violence.

Under Section 12[69] of the FCA, the court is empowered to secure the services of medical experts; the scope of Section 12 envisages the following:

1. For settling a problem the judge of the family court cannot merely take his own personal decision. Under this section, he has to rely and consult an expert as while deciding the dispute between husband and wife, the fate and future of innocent children, if there are any, have to be kept in mind. The judge, therefore, will have to act as all-in-one. If either or both litigants are quarrelsome, the altercations definitely lead to litigation on various grounds and their children will be the worst sufferers. In such cases the opinion of medical and welfare experts will be of much use.
2. The family court, either on an application by one of the litigant or the court suo motto, while exercising its discretion to conduct a psychiatric/psychological evaluation of both the parents including the child in order to ensure that custody is given to the emotionally and mentally fit parent, must ensure welfare of the child. Procedure for such psychological evaluation shall be as per procedure prescribed.
3. Failure in marriages is sometimes due to lack of awareness or realization among the litigants where often one of the partners suffers from a personality disorder and/or adjustment disorder which can be easily diagnosed through psychological evaluation.
4. The child/children are psychologically evaluated (by play therapy) to determine stress, depression level, and also any bad tutoring or poisoning of mind to alienate the child from one of the two parents. On diagnosis, if confirmed, the child is assisted through intervention of psychological counselling.

A review of the petitions/orders passed by the family courts in Mumbai in which children's interests were involved reveal:[70]

• Children's concerns are never the primary or major concerns in any petition. The facts always concentrate on the matrimonial disputes and children are merely mentioned for an ancillary relief along with the parents.
• There is no follow-up of the orders relating to children.
• There is no set of standards/guidelines laid down to deal with children in family courts.

[69] FCA, Section12 : Assistance of medical and welfare experts—In every suit or proceedings, it shall be open to a family court to secure the services of a medical expert or such person (preferably a woman where available), whether related to the parties or not, including a person professionally engaged in promoting the welfare of the family as the court may think fit, for the purposes of assisting the family court in discharging the functions imposed by this act.

[70] Asha Bajpai, 'A Study of Children and Courts in Mumbai', unpublished research study in Mumbai, sponsored by BRS and TISS, 1999.

- The judges, lawyers, counsellors, and other court personnel are not trained to adopt a 'child-centred approach'.
- The orders depend on the perception of individual judges as to what constitutes the 'best interest of the child'. Some judges interview the child personally; others leave it to the counsellors.

Child interviews are conducted in family courts in cases of custody and access of children. Children find the atmosphere of a family court intimidating when they are brought to the court for an interview. They are bewildered and confused. The judges' chambers do not have 'child-friendly' environment. Children are often the least considered. Children also need behavioural expertise and services. Associations between marital conflict and adjustment problems in children are now well established. Children's distress and behavioural irregularities increase due to marital conflict. In fact, marital conflict is related to the children's negative outcomes in homes that are characterized as disturbed for other reasons. There is no direct provision in the FCA for the psychological recovery and social re-integration of the child. The links with social service agencies and childcare professionals are inadequate. The workload in the family courts is so high that in many instances it is not possible to consider the child's special concerns and needs.

A child's perceptions are very different. The jurisprudence of rights and obligations developed in the conventional mould is not appropriate for the delivery of justice to the child. Children, by themselves, are unable to avail of legal rights and entitlements because of physical and mental immaturity.

There are several legal, social, and ethical issues involved. Several rival considerations compete for recognition while dealing with the welfare of the child within a legal regime. There are independent power centres—the courts, police, and social services—that are involved in an ad hoc manner, without any coordination between the various agencies.

The voices of children need to be heard in the family courts. A guardian ad litem or a representative or a counsel in the family court should aid the child. This service should have absolute freedom from hierarchical and functional interference. It has to be able to promote the child's interest authoritatively. Human behavioural scientists and experts should necessarily be associated whenever a child is involved. This service must also have a direct link between the children and the courts and become the ultimate point of reference. This can be provided for within the existing framework of the FCA. Training has to be provided to the judges, lawyers, police, counsellors, and other court personnel to develop child-centred competencies.[71]

Children and women of minority communities should also get the benefits of counselling and informal forum and speedy settlement of disputes in family courts. When the FCA transferred the jurisdiction of the district court to family court, it did not expressly transfer the matrimonial jurisdiction of the high court to the family court. Whereas, under the IDA, GWA, PMDA, Dissolution of Muslim Marriages Act, 1939, and for matrimonial issues concerning the Jewish community, the jurisdiction continues to be with the high court. This needs to be rectified so that all children get the benefit of the FCA.[72]

[71] See Asha Bajpai, *Towards Equity and Empowerment of Children, 1989–1999: A Decade of Family Court* (Mumbai: Family Court Bar Association, 1999).

[72] Flavia Agnes, 'Contesting Rights Over Children, Custody and Guardianship in Matrimonial Disputes', *Manushi*, no. 114.

Areas of Concern

The court is invested with a very wide discretion and broad powers in matters of custody, education, or maintenance of children. The expression generally used in the matrimonial statutes is 'if the court thinks fit'. Although the matrimonial statutes do not directly mention that in these proceedings the welfare of children is of paramount consideration, the courts have always taken the welfare of the children as the paramount consideration in determining matters relating to custody of children. The custody is given to a person only if it is for the welfare of the child. The court may look into other matters such as age, sex, or wishes of the child, but the welfare of the child will override all these considerations.

An area of concern is that if the court dismisses the matrimonial proceedings, proceedings relating to children terminate automatically. The court exercises jurisdiction over children only if it has jurisdiction in the main petition.

Orders in respect of children, whether temporary or permanent, are never final. The court may, on the application of either party, alter, rescind, or modify any order at any stage of the proceedings, or subsequently at any time after the passing of the decree till the child attains majority.

When parents separate from each other, the court gives custody of children to one of the parents and access to the other parent is usually allowed so that children grow up under the full awareness and affection of both parents.

While deciding what is best for the child, many varying factors need to be considered by the courts: the child, parents, relationship between child and parents, surroundings of the family, educational possibilities, future prospects of the children and their parents, wishes of parents and children, and so on. When studying the orders of the family courts it was evident that the concept of the best interests of the child or the welfare of the child is not at all mentioned in the decisions.[73] The best interest of the child may have been considered, but there was no evidence. The courts do not give any information about the factors they have considered or the reasons for awarding custody. The orders just mention whom the custody was given to in a particular case. If the case is dismissed for any reason, the custody issue is also dismissed without looking at the welfare of the child. It all appears to be a question of 'negotiations'. The party who can 'negotiate' well will get the decision tilted in his/her favour. The courts have neither the time nor the resources to evaluate the various factors. It is also important to understand the additional factors that lead to the custody decision rather than just the surface problems as stated by the parties, and try to find a solution that is truly in the child's best interests.

In fact, it appears that orders relating to children are just disposed of as secondary matters. Judges in family courts, in many cases, depend on the counsellors to understand the dynamics of family relationship and children's wishes. Judges need multi-disciplinary social help in making decisions based on legal, social, and psychological principles. The services of mental health experts and childcare experts are not used in the family courts in all custody cases. The judges in the family courts are not sufficiently trained to be aware of the psychological pitfalls implicit in making children choose and reject a parent.[74]

---

[73] Asha Bajpai, 'The Legal System and the Principle of the Best Interest of the Child', unpublished research study in Mumbai, 1998.

[74] Bajpai, *Legal System*.

Judicial interviews with children in chambers can be traumatic. The child's wish may also be a result of deliberate or subconscious influence on the part of one of the parents. It may also be difficult to prove what the child really wants. The child may be in the middle of conflicting loyalties and will not want to hurt either of the parents. Each custody decision has to be a concrete evaluation of the facts of the particular case. But in practice the family courts are not equipped to determine the best interests of the child. Judges and other personnel handling a large number of assigned cases obviously have less time to hear each case. They suffer due to high caseloads, lack of specific training and experience, rapid turnover, and low status.

The divorce proceedings are turned into a 'battleground' by parents to settle scores with each other and the children are often turned into instruments. One of the easiest ways to poison a child's mind is to malign the mother and label her as 'adulterous' and 'promiscuous'. The child may not know what it means, but s/he is scared. Instigated in several cases by the father and his relatives, s/he rejects the mother without even knowing her. A teenage girl instigated by her grandparents screamed at her widowed mother for being friendly with a man. The daughter was convinced that her mother had committed a 'sin'.[75]

In order to have an upper hand, a lawyer or adviser may advise one of the spouses to strike when the other is most vulnerable. In one case, the husband served the petition when the wife was in the seventh month of pregnancy. Due to the trauma, the wife delivered prematurely, which endangered the child's life. In another case, the wife served the petition on her husband during the daughter's annual examination. The father took it well but the daughter's performance in the examination was affected. Making the child the centre of legal battles always affects the very core of the child. A husband will find a new wife and a wife will find a new husband but the child will lose the parents and will never find 'new' parents.[76]

The parents play upon the child's psyche and pass on their own prejudices regarding their spouses to the child. It is impossible for 'warring' parents to accept that even while one spouse has failed the children, s/he could be a good parent to them. Hurt by their spouse, they put venom in the mind of their children about the other parent. They fail to comprehend to what extent it would affect the child's personality. Not only is the child deprived of the other parent's association, but is also tutored to view the other parent through a tinted glass. A distorted image of the other parent is projected while their emotions may pull them in the opposite direction. This dichotomy of emotions carries through to their adult life. The changes in the child are slow, subtle, and silent. Most parents put the blame on the other parent and abdicate their responsibility. Nobody tries to heal the scars of this child torn between two warring parents.

The phenomenon of the father/mother not possessing any resources or income to provide for the child is very common. Clearly, it is obvious that when the parent appears before the family courts, there is 'nothing in their name'. This adversely affects the child.

The trauma of the child is never taken into consideration. The parents are busy taking care of their own interests. Even within a conflicting situation of divorce, it is necessary for the parents to examine their motives and assess the consequences of their actions on their children. Sometimes the parent does not see the child for years nor contribute anything towards the child's upkeep.

---

[75] Gheewala, *Towards Equity and Empowerment of Children, 1989–1999: A Decade of Family Court* (Mumbai: Family Court Bar Association, 1999).

[76] Gheewala, *Towards Equity and Empowerment.*

Then all of a sudden, when the child is well settled in the new surroundings, the parent may come to stake a claim and assert ownership over the child without pausing to question the implications of such a move upon the child. Is remarriage of the spouse disturbing them? Are they consumed by jealousy? Is it hurting their ego? Why in the first place did they not see the child for years? What pleasure would they get by shattering the secure life of the child? In custody 'battles' it is necessary to set limits on the demands of parents, examine their motives closely, and evaluate their contributions towards the child before consenting to any rights. The time has come for parents to realize that the child is not their 'property' for exercising their ownership rights.

There is no legal representation of the child's interests in the family courts. The husband and wife may know what they want and be able to hire lawyers to help them get it, but no one speaks for the children, even though they have at least as much at stake in the divorce as do their parents. The adults are most likely to be preoccupied with their own problems and to be in a position where what is best for them is not necessarily best for the children. Moreover, the emotional stress during the last days of a dying marriage can be such that the parents do not really know what is best for themselves, let alone for anyone else.

Almost by default, the courts have been given the responsibility to see that children are not the innocent casualties of matrimonial warfare. If the children have been injured by conflict between their parents, the court is expected to heal the wounds. Unfortunately, it rarely does so, nor does it have the expertise or resources to do so.

In family courts, much effort is being made these days towards saving marriages. But what has to be saved is not solely the form of marriage, but its spirit. A marriage can be saved at too great a cost, especially for children. It is the children who pay the heaviest price, for they pay not only in present unhappiness but also in future maladjustment and perhaps also in their own marriages to come. Thus, the child's interests should be represented by a counsel or a representative.

In the best interests of the child it is absolutely necessary that experienced and able judges preside over the family courts. They ought to have some training in handling the delicate matters and being child-friendly.

When everybody is trying to save time in view of pendency of large number of litigations in various courts, it is a sad commentary that even in joint petitions under Section 13-B of the HMA, the parties are sent to marriage counsellors and a lot of time is wasted. In such cases only the best interests of the child need to be looked into when children are involved.

Not only in regard to the matrimonial petitions but also in all litigations, wherever they are pending, much time is consumed by the unnecessary procedure of filing affidavit of documents, giving inspection, and such formalities. It is common knowledge that unless the last stage is reached, this formality is not to be complied with. Consequently, there is much avoidable delay. Particularly in case of family courts, which are constituted for quick and speedy disposal of such matters, any application, however complicated, should not be allowed to be on the file of the family court for more than a couple of years.

The judge should take the help of experts in every child-custody matter. Family courts must be equipped with legal, social, economic, medical, and psychological experts. Section 9 of the FCA contemplates the judges' role as one of assistance and persuasion to settle the matter. For that purpose, the court may follow such procedure as it may deem fit. The same power is repeated in Section 10(3) of the act, where the scope is wider, in as much as the procedure can be devised for arriving at the truth of the facts alleged by one and denied by the other. But in the absence of clear rules laid down by the high court in this regard, the judges very often hesitate to experiment with any innovative procedure. The result is that the cases are handled in a routine way to avoid any criticism or censure when the matter goes to the high court in appeal.

Under the law, appeals from the family court go the high court. Very often, judges who have no experience whatsoever of dealing with family disputes in a humane and child-friendly way deal with the matter. In the interests of the child, the high court should be able to have the same special approach to deal with the case in a humane way, as is supposed to be done in the family court, since appeals should also follow the same standards. It is therefore necessary that there should be a separate division in the high court where children's issues are dealt with in a sensitive manner. Another alternative could be a second appeal in the family court itself, before a division bench.

Other issues that call for consideration in this regard include the following:

- The family courts should also have a supervisory role.
- In cases of mutual consent, the judge/counsellors should strike down those clauses which are against the welfare of the child.
- There should be proper follow-up of orders relating to children and the family courts must carry on the consequences of the decisions.
- Decisions of the family court reflect the stereotyped beliefs of the judges and counsellors themselves about what is in a child's best interests. These beliefs may or may not fit with the empirical findings. The court needs expertise from various fields.

In the family court the principles of law, the conscience of the community, and the social sciences, particularly those dealing with human behaviour and personal relationships, must work together.

Some Emerging Trends in Custody Matters

While interpreting the principle of the best interest of the child in family courts, several legal, social, and ethical issues are involved. Several rival considerations compete for recognition while dealing with the welfare of the child or the best interests of the child. This principle of the welfare of the child or the best interests of the child has been applied largely in relation to family affairs, especially relating to disputes concerning custody, adoption, and maintenance. This principle guides decisions generally in custody cases at present. An underlying assumption in social policy is that parents or their surrogates in the families are responsible for their own children. Recently, there has been a well-documented increase in the divorce rate in India and the largest number of circumstances in which the law of child custody applies is on the divorce of the child's parents. The presence of children adds to the family complexity and complicates a divorce considerably. Child-related issues such as custody, visitation, and child support appear to be particular catalysts for litigation. The custody orders may nevertheless also be passed in cases of judicial separation of parents, restitution of conjugal rights, nullity of marriages, and other cases.[77]

---

[77] Asha Bajpai, 'The Principle of the Best Interest of the Child and the Indian Legal System', unpublished manuscript, Mumbai.

The principle of child's welfare reflects a modern belief that while parents may choose divorce for themselves and must face the consequences of their own decisions, children need legal protection against their parents' actions. The legal justification for the fundamental intrusion into parental autonomy in the interests of the children is on the premise that children will be 'damaged' by their parent's divorce and that it is the responsibility of the courts to protect them against such 'damage'.

The child's welfare depends entirely on the current understanding (of adults) of what is best for children. The posing of the issue as a choice between parents is itself problematic, since although the ultimate decision dictates such a choice, the process of decision-making involves other direct or indirect considerations. The welfare of the child holds the central position in the custody disputes. Whatever the practice, the laws place the child's protection or nurturance philosophy at the centre of the decision-making process and whatever interpretations are given to the welfare principle, nowadays, the prominence of the child-centred approach receives universal support. Every case involves different facts and circumstances; therefore, previous decisions could only provide guidelines or indicators as to what was regarded as the best interests of the child.

Shared Custody or Joint Parenting

Although joint custody is not specifically provided for in Indian law, it is reported by lawyers that family court judges do use this concept at times to decide custody disputes. Two examples of attempts to institutionalize shared parenting in India in recent times are noted as follows. A set of guidelines on 'child access and child custody,' prepared by the Child Rights Foundation, a Mumbai-based non-governmental organization (NGO), understands joint custody in the following manner: 'Child may reside alternately, one week with the custodial parent and one week with non-custodial parent, and that both custodial and non-custodial parent share joint responsibility for decisions involving child's long term care, welfare and development.'[78]

Although the guidelines state that this understanding of joint custody is consistent with the United Nations Convention on the Rights of the Child (UNCRC), 1992, it must be noted that there can be no straitjacket formula that can be applied universally to all cases of custody. The second example of joint custody is found in a 2011 judgment of the Karnataka High Court, which used the concept to resolve a custody dispute involving a 12-year-old boy. In *K.M. Vinaya* v. *B. Srinivas*,[79] a two-judge bench ruled that both parents are entitled to get custody 'for the sustainable growth of the minor child'. Joint custody was effected in the following manner:

- The minor child was directed to be with the father from 1 January to 30 June and with the mother from 1 July to 31 December of every year.
- The parents were directed to share equally the education and other expenditures of the child. Each parent was given visitation rights on Saturdays and Sundays when the child was living with the other parent.

---

[78] Child Rights Foundation, 'Child Access and Custody Guidelines' (2011). Available at http://www.mphc.in/pdf/ChildAccess-040312.pdf, p. 24 (accessed on 17 July 2015).

[79] MFA No. 1729/ 2011, Karnataka High Court, judgment dated 13 September 2013.

- The child was to be allowed to use telephone or video conferencing with each parent while living with the other.

In addition to the aforementioned examples, there has been a growing demand to institute shared custody in India, from 'father's rights' groups, who argue that the Indian family laws, including the law of custody, are biased towards the mothers. Consequently, these groups demand that fathers must have 'equal rights' over custody of children. This assertion about the law being biased towards the mothers is not only factually incorrect, but the demand is also based on a faulty understanding of equality in our constitutional and legal framework. As we have discussed in the following pages, the father is still deemed the natural guardian under both religious and secular family laws, while the mother is not. Further, in our society, equality in conjugal and family life is still a distant dream. A large number of women continue to disproportionately bear the burden of housework and childcare, even when they have a paid employment outside the home. Thus, when during the subsistence of marriage, there is no equality in parental and care-giving responsibilities, then on what ground can one claim equality in parental rights over children after the dissolution of the marriage? Our Constitution and the legal framework direct the state to pursue substantive equality. Substantive equality recognizes the difference in the socio-economic position of the sexes within the home and outside of it, and aspires to achieve equality of results.[80]

Non-resident Indian Battles

When non-resident Indian (NRI) marriages break down, it brings many aspects to be dealt with, like child custody and maintenance. Many girls married from India find it difficult to get maintenance mainly because of the lack of awareness of their rights.

On the other hand, we can have a different perspective of child custody through the recent Norway case, where both the parents jointly had a fight for the custody of their children. Eventually, custody was given to the grandparents; this case brought to light how the foreign land governs situations from a different perspective than that of India, and how Indian couples have fallen prey to this.

The Uniform Child Custody Jurisdiction and Enforcement Act (UCCJEA) is concerned with determining which state will have the original jurisdiction regarding child custody.

Inter-parental Child Removal[81]

Although the Indian legal system treats inter- and intra-state child abduction in India as a crime, Inter-Parental Child Removal across international borders is not defined in any Indian

---

[80] Government of India, Law Commission of India, Report No.257, 'Reforms in Guardianship and Custody Laws in India', May 2015.

[81] Anil Malhotra, *India's Dilemma on Inter-Parental Child Removal* (International Family Law, Jordan Publishing). Available at http://www.jordanpublishing.co.uk/practice-areas/international-family-law/news_and_comment/indian-dilemma-on-inter-parental-child-removal#.V9vN2Yh97IU (accessed on 16 September 2016).

legislation and is not specified as an offence under any statutory law. The problem is compounded by the fact that India is not a signatory to the Hague Convention on Civil Aspects of International Child Abduction, 1980 (referred to as the 'Hague Convention, 1980' and the '1980 Convention' later in this chapter), which is signed by 80 countries worldwide. Hence, inter-parental child custody conflicts are invariably decided by Indian courts supposedly on the principle of the welfare of the abducted child as being the paramount consideration, and can take an average of 8 years, by which time the child attains majority during his/her illegal detention in India. The abducted child is generally a foreign citizen by birth and the abductor can be an Indian citizen or a foreign citizen, and there may be pre-existing custody orders from competent courts in the child's country of habitual residence. The prerogative writ of habeas corpus as an expedient remedy is thus consistently invoked, being the most effective, emergent, and efficacious one to a distressed parent whose child has been removed to India from foreign borders or vice-versa. The foreign court custody order forms the basis of invoking this extraordinary constitutional remedy. A case law analysis reveals that till 1997, Indian courts perpetually exercised a power of summary return of a removed child to the country of habitual residence in compliance with a foreign court order to restore parental rights of an aggrieved parent. However, 1998 onwards, the Supreme Court has held that a custody order of a foreign court shall be only one of the many consideration while determining the matter on merits, where the welfare-of-the-child principle will be the clinching factor. As a result, whenever any habeas corpus petition seeks summary return of an abducted child to a foreign country, the court invariably opines that it needs further determination by requiring evidence to be led by warring spouses, and the parties are relegated to conventional court custody proceedings. Due to the huge backlog of cases in the Indian courts, a protracted, time-consuming, expensive, and tedious custody petition results, and the unfortunate removed child is fought over as a trophy to be won in a battle of egos of one or both litigating parents.

Sometimes, the love and affection of the abducted child is hijacked by the abductor with a psychological disorder, to such an extent that the child's tender mind gets permeated with ill-will towards the other parent who, for no fault, is denied access to his loved one.

Need for an International Legal Instrument in India

With the increasing number of NRIs abroad and the rise of multiple problems leading to family conflicts, inter-parental child removal to India now needs to be resolved on an international platform. It is no longer a local problem. The phenomenon is global. Most of the international parental child abductions (IPCA) from the UK, Australia, Canada, and the USA are to India. It is a matter of national shame that India has acquired the dubious distinction of being classed a safe haven for perpetuators of international inter-parental child abduction. Steps have to be taken by joining hands globally to resolve these conflicts through the medium of courts interacting with each other. Until India becomes a signatory to the Hague Convention, 1980, this may not be possible. The time has now come where it is not possible for the Indian courts to stretch their limits to adapt to different foreign court orders arising from different jurisdictions. It is equally important that to create a uniform policy of law, some clear, authentic, and universal child custody law is enacted within India by adhering to the principles laid down in the Hague Convention, 1980. Divergent views emerging at different times may not be able to cope with the rising number of such cases, which come up from time to time for interpretation.

There is a need for an expeditious acceptance and implementation of the international principles of inter-parental child removal, which are couched in the Hague Convention. Today, removal of children across borders has also acquired a dual carriageway dimension. Earlier, cases of foreign children brought to India against parental consent were common citations. Now, the reverse is also true and child removal from India makes it a two-way street. How would Indian courts deal with situations where Indian children were removed to foreign jurisdictions in violation of local court orders or parental wishes? Which law would apply and how would it extend to a foreign country?

Clearly, there is no international legal instrument that can be invoked and the only remedy with the aggrieved parent would be to invoke the national law of the foreign country where the child is wrongfully retained. However, it is easier said than done: visa formalities, travelling expenses, litigation costs, and above all, foreign court procedures would be insurmountable deterrents. Such a problem would defy solutions and workable remedies.

Universal Concern

The universal solution to both domestic and international problems of our global NRI community in the matter of inter-parental child conflicts cannot be resolved on a universal platform until India becomes a part of the global family of contracting countries who are signatories to the Hague Convention. There was an Indian endeavour to do so by the framing of the Civil Aspects of International Child Abduction Bill, 2007. But, alas, it was never tabled before the Parliament and it never saw the light of the day. India cannot be a beneficiary of an international conclave unless it joins the table with the convention countries by acceding to the convention. The child should not suffer. A law must be put in place forthwith for the cause of the child.

The weight of the evidence suggests overwhelmingly that child abduction starts at home. A way forward can be found only when society begins to ask itself the painful question of why this abuse and abduction is so prevalent in NRI marriages, and why families, that ought to be safe havens for children, are so indifferent to the needs of their children and the effects that their disintegration causes on their children.

In the absence of any Indian legislation on the subject, there is no uniform pattern of decisions to resolve issues of custody and contact which arise when parents are separated and live in different countries.

A few recent decisions of various cases of IPCA show that the time has now come for some international perspective in this regard. There are certain situations when parents move the court and seek habeas corpus relief, and the parent with the child abroad moves the court there and gets a restraint order. Both the parents get equipped with the judicial orders and the dual-continental custody battle takes place in two jurisdictions.

It is, therefore, the gravest need of the hour that the Indian legislature may consider enacting some legislation to protect the rights of the abducted child and to resolve the clash between the rule of domicile and the nationality rule. Maybe, till this is done, the Supreme Court of India could well lay down some uniform guidelines to be consistently followed in IPCA from foreign jurisdictions.[82]

Review and Analysis of Some Reported Major Judicial Decisions[83]

Gohar Begum v. Suggi alias Nazma Begum[84]

The child was the illegitimate daughter of the appellant who was a Muslim woman. The mother was the mistress of the father who was then living with the respondent. The father had sworn an affidavit acknowledging the paternity of the child and undertaking to bring her up properly. He had sufficient means. The appellant applied for the custody of the daughter under Section 491 of the CrPC, 1973 (illegal detention by the respondent).

The high court held that the child was not illegally and improperly detained by the respondent. It held that it was not the function of the court, in an application under Section 491, to record findings on such controversial facts like paternity of the child, and that the mother should apply for custody under the GWA. The court held that it did not appear to be in the interest and welfare of the minor to grant custody to the mother. It did not give any reason for this view. On appeal, the Supreme Court held that the mother was entitled to custody of the child. The fact that the mother had a right under the GWA to recover custody of the child is no justification for denying rights under Section 491 of the CrPC.

The court held that under Mohammedan law, the custody of an illegitimate child, no matter who the father is, should be with the mother. With respect to a child under guardianship for nurture, the child is supposed to be unlawfully imprisoned when unlawfully detained from the custody of the guardian, and when delivered to him, the child is supposed to be set at liberty.

The technicalities of the law appear to come in the way of the best interest of the child. It is to be noted with concern that the concept of illegitimacy of children is still prevalent in the Indian laws.

Jijabai Gajre v. Pathan Khan and Ors[85]

The father and the mother of the appellant, Jijabai, lived separately. The appellant had obtained properties from her father under a gift deed dated September 1944. She served notice, dated 31 March 1962, on the tenant to terminate his tenancy and to surrender possession, or in the alternative, to be allowed to recover at least half of the land. The tenant pleaded that the appellant was a minor and her claim barred by limitation. As the father was alive, notice by the mother on behalf of the minor was invalid.

---

[82] Lakshay Soni and Anubhuti Seth, 'Legal Issues and Response Child Custody Law', Symbiosis Law School, Noida. This essay has been submitted to Uni Assignment Centre as an assignment. Available at http://www.uniassignment.com/essay-samples/law/legal-issues-and-response-child-custody-law-family-essay.php (accessed on 16 September 2016).

[83] Bajpai, 'Principle of the Best Interest of the Child'.

[84] AIR 1960 SC 93.

[85] (1970) 2 SCC 717.

The Naib Tehsildar held that as the father of the appellant was alive and was, in law, her natural guardian, the lease executed was not legal and valid, as the mother was not entitled to represent her.

The high court held the mother to be considered the natural guardian, as the father was not interested.

The Supreme Court held that the father was alive but was not taking any interest in the affairs of the minor and it was as good as if he was non-existent, so far as the minor was concerned. Therefore, in this case, the mother can be considered the natural guardian of the minor daughter.

A prolonged litigation had to be carried on, which itself was against the interest of the child. In this case, the Tehsildar's court just looked at the technicalities of law.

Rosy Jacob v. Jacob A.[86]

The Supreme Court considered a Christian father's application to obtain custody of his children under Section 25 of the GWA. The court was entrusted with a judicial decision to order return of the ward to the custody of the guardian. The court held that Section 25 of the GWA is attracted only if a ward leaves or is removed from custody of a guardian of his person and the court is empowered to make an order for the return of the ward to his guardian if it is of the opinion that it will be for the welfare of the ward to return to the custody of his guardian.

Under the IDA (Section 3(5), the sons of native fathers cease to be minors on attaining 16 years of age and the daughters cease to be minors on attaining 13 years of age. The court held that Section 25 of the GWA contemplates not only actual physical custody but also constructive custody of the guardian, which includes all categories of guardians. It was further held that Section 25 of the GWA demands reasonable and liberal interpretation. The court also held that the discretion under Section 25 is to be exercised judiciously.

The court went on to pronounce the presumption that a minor's parents would do their very best to promote the child's welfare and would not grudge any sacrifice of their own personal interest. The father's fitness is to be considered, determined, and weighed in terms of the welfare of the minor. If the custody of the father cannot promote the welfare of the child equally or better than the custody with the mother, the father cannot claim indefeasible right to custody under Section 25 of the GWA.

The court stated that in disputes between a mother and a father, a 'just and proper balance' must be struck between the child's welfare and the parents' rights, even though the child's welfare must ultimately be considered more important. In considering this application, the court declared that 'the controlling consideration governing the custody of the children is the welfare of the children concerned and not the rights of their parents'.

Thrity Hoshie Dolikuka v. H.S. Dolikuka[87]

In this case both the parents were working and the child was with the father. The mother wanted to remove the child from the father's home and place her in a boarding school.

---

[86] AIR 1973 SC 2090.
[87] AIR 1982 SC 1276.

The high court had refused custody of the daughter to the mother mainly on the ground that the mother was a 'working girl'. The Supreme Court held that the father cannot be considered to be a fit person to be given the custody of the child. The mother was given the custody of the minor daughter till she reached the age of 16 years. The child was allowed to continue her education at the boarding school. The parents were given liberty to meet the daughter alternately in accordance with the rules and regulations of the school. The father was given the first opportunity.

During vacations, the girl would live with the father for the first half and with the mother for the second half. After the vacation, the girl had to be taken back to the boarding school and entrusted to the custody of the principal.

The court stated that there was no duty or obligation of the court to send for the minor and interview her to ascertain her wishes, before deciding the question of her custody. The father was obsessed with the idea of obtaining exclusive control of the daughter and keeping the daughter with him in his house. The mother had no self-interest or obsession and had the best interest and welfare of the daughter in mind and was prepared to make any necessary sacrifice for the daughter. Custody was given to the mother.

Bhagyalakshmi v. K. Narayanna Rao,[88] *Thrity Hoshie Dolikuka v. Hoshiam S. Dolikuka,*[89] and *Jaswant Kaur v. Manjit Singh*[90]

In the first case the wife left the husband and took with her three minor children aged 14, 12, and 9. After 3 years, the father sued for custody. In the second case, the 11-year-old girl was with the father. In the third case, the mother gave birth to the child at her parent's house and the child remained in their custody. When the boy was 10, the father sued the maternal grandparents for custody. In all these three cases, the issue involved custody of growing children.

The court granted custody to the father in the first case, viewing the minors' welfare, including material as well as spiritual well-being. The father was better off financially, while the mother's father was in debt. Besides, a 14-year-old son needed his father's advice, hence the father was given custody. In the second case, the 11-year-old daughter needed her mother's guidance, hence the mother was given custody (partly on this ground). A 10-year-old boy needed his father's 'control', hence the father was given custody in the third case despite the fact that the child had been in the continuous care of his grandparents. The court viewed the minor's welfare, including material as well as spiritual well-being. Importance was given to the financial capacity of the father.

Sumitra Devi v. Bhikan Choudhary[91]

Application for maintenance under Section 125 of the CrPC was filed by a woman for herself and her minor daughter. She asserted that the child was from her marriage but the husband denied

---

[88] AIR 1983 Mad 9.
[89] AIR 1982 SC 1277.
[90] AIR 1985 Del 159.
[91] AIR 1985 SC 765.

this. She alleged that the husband was already married once and that was not known to her at the time of marriage. The husband alleged that she was already 3 months pregnant at the time of their marriage and therefore the marriage was void on the grounds of fraud. He also said that there were no religious rites. After 10 years of marriage, the relationship strained on these grounds and she sought maintenance from her husband. The magistrate granted maintenance both to her and to her child. The sessions judge reversed the order. The Patna High Court approved the sessions court order. So the mother appealed to the Supreme Court.

The Supreme Court chastized the lower courts for not examining the witnesses properly. The case was remanded to the magistrate for a proper examination within 3 months, as already a lot of time was lost due to the improper conduct of the case by her lawyers and the courts. The Supreme Court reminded the magistrate that under Section 125 of the CrPC, even an illegitimate minor child was entitled to maintenance. The Supreme Court said the lawyers and magistrates had not devoted proper attention to the case. The lower courts did not refer to the fact that the couple were living together for 10 years and their names appeared in the voters' list as 'husband and wife'. Witnesses also confirmed it. The evidence regarding the religious ceremonies were not complete. Therefore, the case was remanded for a fresh enquiry. The Supreme Court said that the role of the court in this type of cases is not that of a silent spectator or of a passive agency. It must take genuine interest to find out the truth. If the right questions were put to the witnesses, facts would have come out and the prolonged litigation could have been avoided.

Elizabeth Dinshaw v. Arvand Dinshaw[92]

The petitioner and her husband were living in the USA. They were divorced and the child (minor) continued to live with the mother, pursuant to a divorce decree. The father was given visitation rights on weekends and it was specifically directed in the decree that if the father wished to travel with the minor child outside the territorial limits of the USA, he shall bring a petition to the court, setting forth the conditions under which he intends to leave the country with the minor child.

Taking advantage of the weekend visitation rights granted to him by the aforementioned decree, the father picked up his minor son and secretly left the USA, not intimating the court about the intention to take him out of the country; nor had he given the slightest indication to the petitioner about his intention to leave the USA permanently for India. The conduct of the father in taking the child from the custody of the person to whom it had been entrusted by the court was undoubtedly most reprehensible.

The court, after going into the facts and circumstances of the case, looked into what would best serve the interest and welfare of the minor and opined that in the interest and welfare of the child, he should return to the USA and continue his education there under the guardianship and custody of the mother to whom the guardianship and custody had been entrusted by a competent court. The court held that the minor child should go back with his mother to the USA and continue there as a ward of the concerned court having jurisdiction in the state of Michigan. The father had tendered an unconditional apology for this illegal act.

---

[92] (1987) 1 SCC 42.

The court further held that the father cannot claim advantage of the wrongful act of abduction. Whenever a question arises before the court pertaining to the custody of a minor child, the matter is to be decided not on the considerations of the legal rights of the parties but on the sole and predominant criterion of what should serve the interest and welfare of the minor. The court was satisfied that the petitioner, who is the mother, was full of genuine love and affection for the child and could solely be trusted to look after him, educate him, and attend to his proper upbringing in every possible way.

Poonam Datta v. Krishnlal Datta[93]

On the death of the minor's father, the mother was living separately from her in-laws. Money received from the employer of the deceased father was kept in a fixed deposit in a bank. The minor was studying in a school in which his mother was a teacher. The grandfather wanted custody of the child.

The court directed that the child be kept in custody of her mother and continue to study in the same school. But the grandfather was permitted to take the child and keep him in the company of his family every weekend. Money was to remain in deposit and the interest thereof payable to the mother and the grandfather in equal share. This arrangement was to continue until either of the parties moved for the appropriate guardianship proceedings and got a declaration. The case was under Section 6 of the HMGA and Sections 12 and 17 of the GWA. The court directed the parties to consider the interest of the child as paramount.

Kirtikumar Maheshankar Joshi v. Pradipkumar Karunashankar Joshi[94]

After the unnatural death of their mother, the children were living with their maternal uncle. The father was facing charge under Section 498 of the Indian Penal Code (IPC). Before the Supreme Court, the children expressed their willingness to remain with their maternal uncle, who, according to them, was looking after them very well. In the interest and welfare of the children, custody was handed over to the maternal uncle instead of the father. In the welfare of the child, the legal rights were superseded.

Chandrakala Menon v. Capt Vipin Menon and Another[95]

The appellant married the respondent. A girl was born to them in 1985 and 2 years later, both went to the USA, leaving the girl with her maternal grandparents at Bangalore. After 2 years, the girl went to live in the USA and was sent back to live with her maternal grandparents a year later. Differences arose between the husband and the wife and they filed a joint petition for divorce by mutual consent. While the girl was residing with her maternal grandparents in Bangalore, the respondent came to see the daughter and took her away to Bombay. A case of kidnapping was

[93] (1989) Supp. (1) SCC 587.
[94] (1992) 3 SCC 573.
[95] (1993) 2 SCC 6.

registered against the respondent. The high court held that the respondent, being a natural guardian of the girl, could not be charged with the offence of kidnapping. This appeal by Chandrakala was against the order of the high court.

The Supreme Court dissolved the marriage by mutual consent under Section 13B of the HMA. Regarding custody of the child, the judges gathered her wishes and sentiments in their chambers and found that she had ample love and affection for both her parents and also her maternal grandparents. The court granted custody to the mother Chandrakala and the father was given visitation rights.

The principle reiterated in this case is that the question regarding the custody of a minor child cannot be decided on the basis of the legal rights of the parties. The custody of the child has to be decided on the sole and predominant criterion of what would serve the interest and welfare of the minor.

Pannilal v. Rajinder Singh[96]

Land owned by the respondents was sold, while they were still minors, by their mother, acting as their guardian. On attaining majority, the respondents sued Pannilal for possession on the ground that the sale was made without permission of the court though the sale deed was signed by the mother and attested by the father.

The trial court held that there was no reliable evidence on record to show that the alienation in dispute had been made for the legal necessity or for the benefit of the minors.

The high court held that there was no evidence to show that the father of the respondents was not taking any interest in their affairs or that they were in the keeping and care of the mother to the exclusion of the father. The sale by the mother was held to be void. The Supreme Court also held that there was no evidence to show that the father was not taking an interest in their affairs. Sale by the mother was not sale by the father, who was the natural guardian.

Anjali Anil Rangari v. Anil Rangari[97]

This writ petition was filed by the appellant—a mother of two minor children, a daughter and a son, aged 9 and 5 years respectively. The father averred in the application before the chief judicial magistrate's (CJM) court that the mother left the matrimonial home along with two children for Delhi, where her parents reside, without informing him as well as his parents. The children were in illegal custody and were in wrongful confinement by the mother. The Nagpur police went to Delhi and fetched the children from the custody of the mother and produced them before the CJM, who passed an order directing that custody be given to the father. The Supreme Court held that the custody of the children with the mother was neither unlawful nor were they wrongfully confined by the mother in Delhi. The father was directed to hand over the custody of both the children to the mother.

---

96 (1993) 4 SCC 38.
97 (1997) 10 SCC 342.

Dhanwanti Joshi v. Madhav Unde[98]

The respondent married the appellant (who was then in the USA) in 1982. On 19 June 1982, a separate marriage ceremony as per Hindu rituals was performed. Nine months later, a boy was born to them in the USA. The appellant left the respondent when the child was 35 days old. The respondent continued to live in the USA and the appellant and her son were living in India. The parties have been involved in civil and criminal litigation both in the USA and in India for 14 years.

The petition was filed for custody and divorce. The family court granted custody to the father. The high court held that the custody is to be given to the father who has acquired citizenship in the USA and will provide a comparatively superior upbringing.

The Supreme Court gave the custody to the mother and visitation rights to the father when he is in India. Whatever may be the disputes between the parties, in proceedings under the GWA, the courts have to consider what is in the interest of the minor child. The paramount interest of the boy, aged 14 years of age, is definitely his future education and career. The further education of a boy aged 14 years of age will be comparatively superior to other legal technicalities, the high court opined.

Both the family court and the high court based their decisions on the sole circumstance, that is, the financial capacity of the father to give better education to the boy in USA. The welfare of the child is not to be measured by money alone, nor by physical comfort only. The word 'welfare' must be taken in its widest sense. The moral and religious welfare must be considered as well as physical well-being. Nor can the ties of affection be disregarded.[99] More important are the stability and the security, the loving and understanding care and guidance, and the warm and compassionate relationship that are essential for the full development of the child's own character, personality, and talents.[100]

Githa Hariharan & Another v. Reserve Bank of India and Another and *Vandana Shiva v. Jayanta Bandhopadhyaya & Another*[101]

The petitioner, Githa Hariharan, applied to the Reserve Bank of India (RBI) in 1984 for 9 per cent relief bond to be held in the name of her minor son, along with an intimation that the mother would act as the natural guardian for the purposes of investment. The application was sent back by the RBI, advising her to produce the application signed by the father, and in the alternative, the bank informed that a certificate of guardianship from a competent authority would be necessary.

In the second instance, the writ petition (WP [c] 1016 of 1991) by Vandana Shiva was a prayer for custody of her minor son, who was staying with her. The father had shown total apathy

---

[98] 1997 (9) *Judgements Today* 220.

[99] See L.J. Lindley in *Re v. Mc Grath* 1893 [1] Ch. 143.

[100] Hardy Boys J of New Zealand court in *Walker v. Walker and Hanuson* 1981 NZ Recent Law 257, cited by British Law Commission Working Paper No. 96—quoted by the Supreme Court.

[101] AIR 1999 SC 1149.

towards the child and was not interested in his welfare and benefit, except the right to be a natural guardian without, however, discharging any corresponding obligation.

Both the petitions prayed for the declaration of the provision of Section 6(a) of the HMGA, read with Section 19(b) of the GWA, as violative of Articles 14 and 15 of the Constitution. The father and mother are natural guardians in terms of the provisions of Section (6) read with Section 4(c) of the HMGA.

The court held that Section 6(a) itself recognizes that both the father and mother ought to be treated as natural guardians and the expression 'after' should be read and interpreted in a manner so as not to defeat the true intent of legislature.

The word 'after' in Section 6 of the HMGA shall have to be given a meaning which would serve the need of the situation, namely the welfare of the minor. The word 'after' does not necessarily mean after the death of the father. On the contrary, it depicts an intent so as to ascribe the meaning as in the absence of, be it temporary or otherwise, or total apathy of the father towards the child, or even inability of the father by reason of ailment or otherwise, and it is only in the event of such a meaning being ascribed to the word 'after', as used in Section 6, that the same would be in accordance with the intent of the legislation, namely the welfare of child. A rigid incidence of strict statutory interpretation may not be conducive to the growth of the child, and welfare being the predominant criterion, it would be a plain exercise of judicial power of interpreting the law so as to be otherwise conducive to a fuller and better development and growth of the child. The whole tenor of the HMGA is to protect the welfare of the child, and as such, any interpretation ought to be in consonance with the legislative intent.

S.N. Nirmala v. Nelson Jayakumar[102]

The division bench of the Gujarat High Court denied the mother visiting rights to her minor daughter while dismissing her appeal against the single judge's order conferring custody to the father. The Supreme Court held that the mother should not be denied visiting rights in relation to the minor daughter in the custody of the father without adequate justification.

Kumar V. Jahgirdar v. Chethana Ramatheertha[103]

In these two appeals, the subject matter of dispute between the married couple, now separated by decree of divorce obtained on mutual consent under the provisions of the HMA, is their rival claim to the exclusive custody of their daughter Aaruni, who is now a little over 9 years old and is pursuing her education in a well-known school in the city of Bangalore, where the parties reside.

After obtaining divorce on mutual consent, the wife, Chethana Ramatheertha, was re-married to Anil Kumble, a cricketer of national and international repute. The family court of Bangalore, by its judgment dated 20 April 2002, after considering the evidence led by the parents of the child, came to the conclusion that as the wife is re-married to a famous cricketer and is leading a different style of life involving frequent tours with her second husband for attending cricket

---

[102] (1999) 3 SCC 126.
[103] Special Leave Petition (Civil) 4230–4231 of 2003.

events, there is likelihood of the child developing distance and dislike for her natural father. The exclusive custody of the child was directed to be given to the natural father with only right of visitations to the mother on every week, on Sundays between 10 a.m. and 8 p.m., and to keep the child with her overnight on two Sundays in a month, with prior intimation to her former husband.

The high court, in appeal, by its impugned judgment dated 27 January 2003, however, took a different view and reversed the judgment of the family court. On the basis of evidence on record, the division bench of the high court formed an opinion that in the absence of compelling reasons and circumstances, the mother cannot be deprived of the company of the child to the detriment of the interest of the child. The high court, therefore, set aside the judgment of the family court and directed that the mother should continue to retain exclusive custody of the child, with visitation rights to her former husband. The former husband was allowed to keep the child on weekends, either on Saturday or Sunday, from morning till evening, and he could also be with the child during half the period of school vacations. The stay of the child with each of them during half of the vacations was to be shared by the two parents under mutual agreement. The father was also allowed to visit the child as and when he liked, with prior intimation and mutual arrangements with the mother. The parties were also given liberty to seek necessary modifications in the arrangement evolved by the high court.

Without going into the allegations, counter-allegations, and misapprehensions expressed against each other, on the paramount consideration of best safeguarding the interest of the child, the judgment of the high court giving exclusive custody of the child to the mother and visitation rights to the natural father was maintained with little modification for the following reasons.

The child was 9 years of age and on advent of puberty. This is the age in which she requires more care and attention of the mother. The mother, at this age of the child, deserves to continue to keep the custody of the female child. She is reported to have given up her service and leading the life of a house-wife. The progress report of Aaruni from Sophia High School, Bangalore, indicated that she is very good at studies and has a bright educational career.

The prospect of arrival of the second child in the family of the wife was another circumstance which would be in favour of the present child.

The petitioner lived alone with his father. There were no female members living jointly with him, although he may have female relations in the city, but that would not ensure constant company, care, and attention to the female child.

The petitioner/natural father was a busy stock broker reportedly carrying on his business with the aid of online computer, but it could not be said that in the course of his business, he would not have to remain out of residence for attending his office and other business engagements.

The apprehension expressed against the second husband, that he might poison the mind of the child and create ill-will towards the natural father, was not borne out from the evidence on record. On the contrary, the second husband, in his deposition, had made statements evincing a very cooperative and humane attitude on his part towards the problem of the estranged couple and the child. The court found that the apprehension expressed against the second husband was without foundation. The parents of the child had separated by mutual consent without making any vicious allegation against each other. They also agreed under the express terms of the consent decree of divorce to take responsibility of bringing up their child as her joint guardians. This gesture of decency and cooperation in jointly looking after the child had to continue. In this mutual agreement of the separated couple, on behalf of the second husband, it was assured that he would continue to give his unreserved cooperation and help and would do nothing to spoil the relationship or intimacy of the child with the natural father.

The visitation rights given to the natural father, in the present circumstances, also did not require any modification because with the passage of time, the growing child should eagerly wait for the company of his father as a happy and enjoyable moment rather than treat it as a part of empty ritual or duty. To make visitation rights of the natural father effective and meaningful for proper growth of the child, active cooperation of both the parents and her step-father was expected and it was hoped that none would fail in this regard.

Since the mother of the child was married to a famous cricketer, as and when she left the country on tour with her husband during school days or vacation period of the child without taking the child with her, the custody of the child during her absence from her home was to be given to the natural father instead of leaving the child to the care and custody of some other member of the family.

With this observations and modification, the Supreme Court maintained the judgment of the high court. The two appeals were, thus, disposed of.

Ashish Ranjan v. Anupam Tandon[104]

In the instant contempt case, Ashish Ranjan, the appellant, was aggrieved that a consent order—passed on 3 May 2008 by the Lok Adalat held in the Supreme Court—that he and his parents must have visitation rights to see his minor son Kislay Ranjan, was wilfully violated by his ex-wife, Anupama Tandon. Disposing of the contempt petition, the bench said: 'The applicant could not get the benefit of his visitation rights. During our conversation with the child we could clearly note that the child had been tutored by the respondents to make him completely hostile towards his father and that he could not meet his son.'

On the respondents' contention that no further relief should be granted since a final order had been passed, the bench said: 'A mere technicality cannot prevent the Court from doing justice in exercise of its inherent powers. The power under Article 142 of the Constitution can be exercised by this Court to do complete justice between the parties, wherever it is just and equitable to do so and must be exercised to prevent any obstruction to the stream of justice. Thus, doctrine of res judicata is not applicable in matters of child custody.'

The bench further said: 'If the instant case is considered in totality, the child, Kislay, has been tutored by the respondents and he has adopted a hostile attitude towards the applicant. In such a fact-situation the applicant is fully justified in seeking review/modification of the said order. The Bench granted liberty to the applicant to approach the appropriate court/forum for seeking custody of the child, Kislay, or any other appropriate relief in this regard.'

---

[104] Contempt Petition (Civil) No. 394 of 2009, Transfer Petition (Civil) No. 195 of 2008.

Giving this ruling, a bench of Justices P. Sathasivam and B.S. Chauhan said: 'While considering the welfare of the child, the moral and ethical welfare of the child must also weigh with the court as well as his physical wellbeing. The child cannot be treated as a property or a commodity and therefore, such issues have to be handled by the court with care, caution, love, and affection and applying a human touch to the problem.'

Writing the judgment, Justice Chauhan said: 'Statutory provisions dealing with the custody of the child under any personal law cannot and must not supersede the paramount consideration as to what is conducive to the welfare of the minor. In fact, no statute on the subject, can ignore, eschew or obliterate the vital factor of the welfare of the minor.'

While determining the question as to which parent should be given the care and control of a child, the paramount consideration remains the welfare and interest of the child and not the rights of the parents under the statute, the Supreme Court held.

Ruchi Majoo v. Sanjeev Majoo[105]

The Supreme Court had to decide conclusively in this case, the custody of an 11-year-old child, born to expatriate parents in the USA, the couple having separated and the wife having returned to India. The husband, however, did not take this lying down and filed a case in the Supreme Court of California alleging, inter alia, that the wife had illegally abducted the child. The matter proceeding ex parte, the husband got an order in his favour, which he promptly used to get a red corner notice issued against the wife.

The wife, too, was prompt in getting the decree of an Indian court in her favour, which declared her as the natural guardian of the boy. Soon after, the Delhi High Court set aside the order, stating that the district court did not have jurisdiction under the GWA. Leaving aside all the various proceedings and counter-proceedings, three issues came up for decision before the Supreme Court, which were:

1. Whether the district court had jurisdiction under Section 9 of the GWA, that is, was the child 'ordinarily resident' in the USA or India.
2. Whether the high court was right in declining to exercise extraordinary jurisdiction under Section 151 of the CPC on the sole ground of the 'principle of comity of courts'.
3. Whether the district court order granting custody to the mother required modification to the extent of granting the husband visitation rights.

The canswered the questions 1 and 3 in the affirmative, stating that the Indian courts did have jurisdiction and that the father should, in any event, have the right of visitation.

It answered question 2 in the negative, while touching upon several complex issues of private international law and making the assertion that India could not blindly subscribe to the rules of private international law of other nations and regards must be had to its peculiar and unique socio-political context while formulating its rules of private international law.

---

[105] Criminal Appeal No. 1184 of 2011 (Arising out of SLP [Crl.] No.10362 of 2010).

K.M Vinaya v. B Srinivas[106]

A two-judge bench ruled that both parents are entitled to get custody 'for the sustainable growth of the minor child'. Joint custody was effected in the following manner:

1. The minor child was directed to be with the father from 1 January to 30 June and with the mother from 1 July to 31 December of every year.
2. The parents were directed to share equally the education and other expenditures of the child.
3. Each parent was given visitation rights on Saturdays and Sundays when the child was living with the other parent.
4. The child was to be allowed to use telephone or video conferencing with each parent while living with the other.

Roxann Sharma v. Arun Sharma[107]

In a remarkable judgment dealing with interim custody, visitation rights, and guardianship of a child suffering in its parents' matrimonial disputes, , a two-judge bench of the Supreme Court laid down various propositions of law while awarding the interim custody till final disposal by the trial court to the mother. The bench, speaking through Justice Vikramjit Sen, lay down very sharp observations and examined various definitions of a 'guardian', 'visitation rights', and tested the issue from the angle of provisions of the HMA and the GWA. In a custody battle between estranged parents, a minor child who has not completed 5 years of age shall be allowed to remain with the mother, the Supreme Court ruled, saying that in such cases the child should not be treated as a 'chattel'. The court said that under the HMGA, a father can be guardian of the property of the minor child but not the guardian of his person if the child is less than 5 years old.

The court said that there can be no cavil that when a court is confronted by conflicting claims of custody, there are no rights of the parents which have to be enforced; the child is not a chattel or a ball that is bounced to and fro between the parents. It is only the child's welfare which is the focal point for consideration. The Parliament rightly thinks that the custody of a child less than 5 years of age should ordinarily be with the mother and this expectation can be deviated from only if there are strong reasons.

The apex court quashed the order of the Bombay High Court, which granted custody of a 2-year-old child to the father on the ground that the mother had not established her suitability to be granted interim custody of the infant.

The HMGA postulates that the custody of an infant or a tender-aged child should be given to his/her mother unless the father discloses cogent reasons that are indicative of and presage the livelihood of the welfare and interest of the child being undermined or jeopardized if the custody is retained by the mother. Section 6(a) of the act, therefore, preserves the right of the father to be the guardian of the property of the minor child but not the guardian of his person while the child is less than 5 years old. It carves out the exception of interim custody, in contradistinction of guardianship, and then specifies that custody should be given to the mother so long as the child is below 5 years in age. The court said that the act placed the onus on the father to prove that it was not in the welfare of the infant child to be placed in the custody of the mother, and high court

---

[106] MFA No. 1729/ 2011, Karnataka High Court, Judgment dated 13 September 2013.
[107] Civil Appeal No. 1966 of 2015.

order virtually nullifies the spirit of the enactment. The act immediately provides that the custody of a minor who has not completed the age of 5 years shall ordinarily be with the mother. The use of the word 'ordinarily' cannot be over-emphasized. It ordains a presumption, albeit a rebuttable one, in favour of the mother.

Summarily, the law laid down by the judgment restricting itself to interim custody can be summarized as follows:

1. Three separate definitions of 'guardianship', 'custody', and 'visitation' have been examined in paragraph 5 from Black's Law Dictionary.
2. Visitation rights have been ascribed the meaning: 'In a dissolution or custody suit, permission granted to a parent to visit children. In domestic relations matters, the right of one parent to visit children of the marriage under order of the court.'
3. In paragraph 9, though the mother is a Christian by religion, applicability of the HMGA has been relaxed, contrary to the law mentioning that it was not disputed. The custody of a minor shall ordinarily be with the mother. However, the use of the word 'ordinarily' cannot be overstretched.
4. Paragraph 10: ' We must immediately clarify that this Section [Section 6] or for that matter any other provision including those contained in the GWA, does not disqualify the mother to have custody of the child even after the latter's crossing the age of five years.'
5. Paragraph 13: 'We must again clarify that the father's suitability to custody is not relevant where the child whose custody is in dispute is below 5 years since the mother is per se best suited to care for the infant during his tender age. It is for the Father to plead and prove the Mother's unsuitability since Thalbir is below 5 years of age. In these considerations the father's character and background will also become relevant but only once the Court strongly and firmly doubts the mother's suitability; only then and even then would the comparative characteristic of the parents come into play.'
6. Frequent visitation does not mean continuous visitation.
7. Whether one has permanent residence in India or not is not so important a factor.
8. The focal point for consideration in such cases is welfare of the child.
9. Considering that global relocation is a well-known legal concept now, the entitlement as to custody by the left behind spouse has to be jurally investigated.
10. Forum shopping or court shopping by parties to litigation must be dealt with firmly.
11. Also, co-ordinate benches of high courts must respect prior orders.
12. The parent who does not have interim custody should be allowed to visit the child without removing him/her from the custody of the other parent. Spending more time than is allowed amounts to temporary transfer of custody which is impermissible.

Judgments Relating to Guardianship Rights of Unwed Mothers

Nil Ratan Kundu & Another v. Abhijit Kundu[108]

Honourable Apex Court observed in the instant case: 'The principles in relation to custody of minor child are well settled. In determining the question as to who should be given

[108] (2009) 9 SCC 413.

custody of minor child the paramount consideration is the welfare child and not rights of the parents.'

As per pronouncement made by Honourable Apex Court and Honourable high court, though custody of minor with the mother is safer than father but it shall not be the straight jacket formula that in every case mother's custody is advisable and father should be deprived from that. It depends upon case to case how the discretion should be exercised in favour of mother or father. It enjoins duty on the court to see welfare of the child while allowing custody.

ABC v. The State (The NCT of Delhi)[109]

The appellant, who adheres to the Christian faith, was well educated, gainfully employed, and financially secure. She gave birth to her son in 2010, and subsequently raised him without any assistance from or involvement of his putative father. Desirous of making her son her nominee in all her savings and other insurance policies, she took steps in this direction, but was informed that she must either declare the name of the father or get a guardianship/adoption certificate from the court. She thereupon filed an application under Section 7 of the GWA[110] (henceforth referred to as the act) before the guardian court for declaring her the sole guardian of her son. Section 11[111]

---

[109] Civil Appeal No. 5003 of 2015 (Arising out of SLP (Civil) No. 28367 of 2011)

[110] Section 7: Power of the court to make order as to guardianship—

(1) Where the court is satisfied that it is for the welfare of a minor that an order should be made—

    (a) appointing a guardian of his person or property or both, or

    (b) declaring a person to be such a guardian, the court may make an order accordingly.

(2) An order under this section shall imply the removal of any guardian who has not been appointed by will or other instrument or appointed or declared by the court.

(3) Where a guardian has been appointed by will or other instrument or appointed or declared by the court, an order under this section appointing or declaring another person to be guardian in his stead shall not be made until the powers of the guardian appointed or declared as aforesaid have ceased under the provisions of this act.

[111] Section 11: Procedure on admission of application—

(1) If the court is satisfied that there is ground for proceeding on the application, it shall fix a day for the hearing thereof, and cause notice of the application and of the date fixed for the hearing—

    (a) to be served in the manner directed in the Code of Civil Procedure, 1882 (14 of 1882) on—

        (i) the parents of the minor if they are residing in [any state to which this act extends];

        (ii) the person, if any, named in the petition or letter as having the custody or possession of the person or property of the minor;

        (iii) the person proposed in the application or letter to be appointed or declared guardian, unless that person is himself the applicant; and

        (iv) any other person to whom, in the opinion of the court special notice of the applicant should be given; and

of the act requires a notice to be sent to the parents of the child before a guardian is appointed. The appellant published a notice of the petition in a daily newspaper, namely Vir Arjun, Delhi edition, but was strongly averse to naming the father. She filed an affidavit stating that if at any time in the future the father of her son raised any objections regarding his guardianship, the same could be revoked or altered as the situation might require. However, the guardian court directed her to reveal the name and whereabouts of the father and consequent to her refusal to do so, dismissed her guardianship application on 19 April 2011. The appellant's appeal before the high court was dismissed in limine, on the reasoning that her claim that she is a single mother could only be decided after notice was issued to the father; that a natural father could have an interest in the welfare and custody of his child even if there is no marriage; and that no case can be decided in the absence of a necessary party.

It was argued on behalf of the appellant that her fundamental right of privacy would be violated if she was forced to disclose the name and particulars of the father of her child.

The court stated that any responsible man would keep track of his offspring and be concerned for the welfare of the child he has brought into the world; this does not appear to be so in the present case, on a perusal of the pleading as they presently portray. Furthermore, Christian unwed mothers in India are disadvantaged when compared to their Hindu counterparts, who are the natural guardians of their illegitimate children by virtue of their maternity alone, without the requirement of any notice to the putative fathers. It would be apposite for us to underscore that our directive principles envision the existence of a uniform civil code, but this remains an unaddressed constitutional expectation.

The court further stated that Section 11[112] is purely procedural; and there lies no harm or mischief in relaxing its requirements to attain the intendment of the act. Given that the term 'parent' is not defined in the act, the court interpreted it, in the case of illegitimate children whose sole caregiver is one of his/her parents, to principally mean that parent alone. Guardianship or custody orders never attain permanence or finality and can be questioned at any time, by any person genuinely concerned for the minor child, if the child's welfare is in peril. The uninvolved parent is therefore not precluded from approaching the guardian court to quash, vary, or modify its orders if the best interests of the child so indicate. There is thus no mandatory and inflexible procedural requirement of notice to be served to the putative father in connection with a guardianship or custody petition preferred by the natural mother of the child, of whom she is the sole caregiver.

(b) to be posted on some conspicuous part of the court-house and of the residence of the minor, and otherwise published in such manner as the court, subject to any rules made by the high court under this act, thinks fit.

(2) The state government may, by general or special order, require that when any part of the property described in a petition under Section 10, Subsection (1), is land of which a court of wards could assume the superintendence, the court shall also cause a notice as aforesaid to be served on the collector in whose district the minor ordinarily resides and on every collector in whose district any portion of the land is situate, and the collector may cause the notice to be published in any manner he deems fit.

(3) No charge shall be made by the court or the collector for the service or publication of any notice served or published under Subsection (2).

[112] GWA, Section 11.

However, the court was greatly perturbed by the fact that the appellant had not obtained a birth certificate for her son and stated that it is bound to create problems for the child in the future.

Accordingly, the court directed that if a single parent/unwed mother applies for the issuance of a birth certificate for a child born from her womb, the authorities concerned may only require her to furnish an affidavit to this effect, and must thereupon issue the birth certificate, unless there is a court direction to the contrary. Trite though it is, yet the court emphasized that it is the responsibility of the state to ensure that no citizen suffers any inconvenience or disadvantage merely because the parents fail or neglect to register the birth. Nay, it is the duty of the state to take requisite steps for recording every birth of every citizen.

The Honourable Supreme Court allowed the appeal and thus directed the guardian court to consider the appellant's application for guardianship expeditiously, without requiring notice to be given to the putative father of the child.

Judgments on Non-resident Indians' Custodial Battles

Marggarate Pulparampil v. Dr. Chacko Pulparampil[113]

It is one of the earliest cases before an Indian court involving the issue of children's custody in NRI marriage. In this judgment the high court of Kerala not only recognized the important principle of 'real and substantial connection' to establish the court's jurisdiction to decide custody issue, but also recognized the availability of the remedy of writ of habeas corpus to claim custody of a child who has been illegally removed by a parent. Here the Court allowed the child to be moved back to the mother in Germany even though that meant allowing the child to be moved out of the Indian court's jurisdiction, as the court felt that the interests of the child were of paramount consideration and in this case made it necessary to give the custody to the mother in Germany. The court also laid down the safeguards for ensuring that the parental rights of the father in India were not totally compromised in the process, by passing a series of directions to balance the conflicting interests, mentioned as follows.

1. The petitioner will execute a bond to the court to produce the children whenever ordered by this court to do so.
2. An undertaking from the German Consulate authority in Madras that they will render all assistance possible for the implementation of any order passed by this court from time to time within the framework of the German Law will be produced by the petitioner.
3. The petitioner will obtain and send a report from the Parish Priest within the Parish in which they propose to live every three months to the court, giving sufficient details about the children, their health and welfare, and send a copy thereof to the father.
4. The petitioner will inform the registrar of the court the address of her residence from time to time, and any change of address will be immediately notified.
5. She will not take the children outside West Germany without obtaining the previous orders of the court, excepting when they are brought to India as directed in this order.

---

[113] AIR 1970 Ker 1.

6. Once in 3 years, she must bring the children to this country for a minimum period of one month at her own expense. At that time, the father will have access to the children on terms and conditions to be directed by this court when the children have reached this country. The 3 years' period will be determined from the date on which the children are taken by the mother from this country. They will be brought to India earlier as directed by the court at the instance of the father, provided that it is not within a year from today, if the father is willing to meet the expenses for the trip from Germany to India and back for the mother and children.

7. The father, if he is visiting Germany, will be allowed access to the children on terms and conditions as ordered by this court on motion by the father intimating his desire to go and see the children and requesting for permission for access.

8. When the children are brought to India at the end of 3 years the whole question of custody may be reviewed suo motu by this court or at the instance of the father or mother and the present order maintained, modified, altered or cancelled.

Surinder Kaur Sandhu v. Harbax Singh Sandhu[114]

In the instant case, the Supreme Court had to decide the custody of the wife/mother in circumstances where while the wife was still in England, the husband had clandestinely taken away the children to India to his parents' place, even as the English Court had already passed an order on the children's custody in England. The court looked into all the relevant facts of the case to decide what was in the best interest of the children and ultimately, on the basis of this consideration, directed the custody of the children to be given to the mother.

Sarita Sharma v. Sushil Sharma[115]

In the instant case, the petitioner's husband had filed a case for divorce in American courts and while the legal battle for custody was still on, both the parties having been appointed as managing conservators of the children, the wife brought the children to India, allegedly without even informing the husband. It was alleged by the husband that the children were in illegal custody of Sarita Sharma, and the high court had allowed the petition and directed Sarita to restore the custody of two (21) children to the husband. The passports of the two children had also been ordered to be handed over to him. In the appeal, the Supreme Court held that the decree passed by the foreign court may be a relevant factor but it cannot override the consideration of welfare of minor children, and expressed doubt whether respondent husband would be in position to take proper care of children because of his bad habits and also because he lived with his aged mother in the USA, with no other family support. It further added that ordinarily the female child should be allowed to remain with the mother so that she can be properly looked after and that it is not desirable to separate two children from each other, and that, therefore, custody of the mother in India was not illegal custody.

---

[114] AIR 1984 SC 1224.
[115] [2000] 1 SCR 915.

Leeladhar Kachroo v. Umang Bhat Kachroo[116]

Upholding the order of a Canadian court granting custody of the younger son to the mother and allowing him to go back to Canada, the Indian court upheld the contention and that it has the jurisdiction to order the travelling out of the minor child with one of the parents and the mere possibility of losing jurisdiction would not dissuade the court from permitting the departure of the child with the determined parent in the interest of the child. Hence, the court held that it was empowered to entrust the custody of a child to a parent who resides outside its jurisdiction, if it is conducive to the welfare of the child.

Mandy Jane Collins v. James Michael Collins[117]

Between a 62-year old American father and 39-year old British mother resident in Ireland, who were litigating over the custody of their 8-year old minor daughter said to be illegally detained in Goa by the father, the court, declining the issuance of a writ of habeas corpus, held that the parties could pursue their remedies in normal civil proceedings in Goa. The court, dismissing the mother's plea for custody, concluded that the question of permitting the child to be taken to Ireland without first adjudicating upon the rival contentions of the parents in normal civil proceedings in Goa is not possible, and directed that status quo be observed. This, in effect, meant that the 8-year old minor girl continue to live in Goa without her mother or any other female family member in the father's house. In a challenge to this decision by the mother before the Supreme Court of India, the appeal was dismissed on 21 August 2006, leaving it open to the parties to move the appropriate forum for the custody of the child, which, if done, was directed by the Supreme Court to be decided within a period of three months with earlier visitation rights continuing to the mother.

V. Ravi Chandran v. Union of India & Ors[118]

V. Ravi, an American citizen, married Vijayashree in December 2000, in Tirupati, India, according to Hindu rites. In July 2002, their son Adithya was born in the US. In July 2003, Vijayashree approached the New York State Supreme Court for a divorce. On 18 April 2005, the court passed a consent order granting joint custody to the parents. The marriage was dissolved in September 2005, incorporating the 18 April 2005 order. On 18 June 2007, a consent order with regard to the joint custody awarded, specifying details of residence, time sharing, and holidays, was made by the family court of the state of New York.

On 28 June 2007, Vijayashree brought Adithya to India, telling his father that she would henceforth be living with her parents in Chennai. The father moved the family court in New York and was granted temporary sole legal and physical custody of Adithya. Vijayashree was directed to turn over the child and his passport to the father. Further, the New York court

---

[116] (2005) 2 Hindu Law Reporter, Delhi 449.
[117] (2006) 2 Hindu Law Reporter Bombay 446.
[118] (2009) 14 Scale 27.

suspended custodial time granted to the mother and issued non-bailable child abuse warrants against her.

Adithya's father filed a petition in the Supreme Court of India for his son to be produced. But both mother and child could not be traced for over 2 years, until the Central Bureau of Invstigation (CBI) finally located them and produced them in court in October 2009.

The Supreme Court declared that while dealing with the custody case of a child removed by a parent from one country to another, in contravention of the orders of the court where the parties had set up their matrimonial home, the court in India had to consider whether to conduct a summary inquiry or an elaborate inquiry into the question of child custody.

In the case of a summary inquiry, the court would return custody to the country from which the child had been removed, unless such return is shown to be harmful to the child. In case of order of summary return, all aspects of the child's welfare would be investigated by the court where the matrimonial home was situated.

In the event of an elaborate inquiry, the court could ignore the order of the foreign court (or treat the fact of the child's removal from another country as one of the circumstances), go into the merits, and decide the issue of custody from the standpoint of the child's permanent welfare. If the court took the view that an elaborate inquiry was necessary, the court was bound to consider the welfare and happiness of the child as paramount. It would go into all relevant aspects of the child's welfare, including stability and security, a loving and understanding environment, and full development of the child's character, personality, and talents.

The issue of a summary or elaborate inquiry is to be decided from the standpoint of the best interests of the minor. The summary jurisdiction to return the child is exercised if, for example, the child is removed to another country where his native language is not spoken, or the child is divorced from the social customs and contacts to which he is accustomed, or education in the native land is interrupted and the child is subjected to a foreign system of education that could psychologically disturb him. Summary jurisdiction is to be exercised only if the court is moved quickly and promptly, that is, before the child develops roots in the country to which he has been removed.

Alternatively, the court can think about conducting an elaborate inquiry taking into account other facts such as the time that has lapsed after the removal, and it could be considered that it would be in the best interests of the child for him not to be sent back to the country from which he was removed. In that case, the unauthorized removal of the child from his native country would not come in the way; the court can ignore the removal and independently consider whether sending the child back is in his best interests.

The court observed that the matter of custody of a minor child was not to be decided on considerations of the legal rights of the parties but on the sole and predominant criterion of the best interests of a minor.

The Supreme Court applied this declared law and examined whether, in the facts of the present case, an elaborate inquiry or a summary inquiry should be conducted by the court in India. It observed that the minor child Adithya was an American citizen, born and brought up in the USA, and that Adithya's natural environment was America. Keeping in view the best interests and welfare of the child, the mother and father had obtained a series of consent orders regarding custody/parenting rights and maintenance from the courts in America. That, in June 2007, both parties had agreed to a comprehensive arrangement with respect to shared joint legal and physical custody of Adithya.

Vijayashree alleged before the Supreme Court of India past denial of basic rights to the child by the father. She said the father had failed to give the child medication, denied him education, did not provide a stable environment, and abused the child. The court observed that in view of the fact that all orders with regard to custody of Adithya had been passed by courts in America, with the consent of both parties, the mother's present allegations had no substance.

The submission that the American courts had no jurisdiction, and that the orders passed were inconsistent with Indian laws and could not be executed, was rejected. The court observed that the mother had been staying in India for 2 years and had not pursued any legal proceedings for sole custody of the child or for a declaration that the orders passed by the American courts were null, void, and without jurisdiction. In fact, she did initiate proceedings under the GWA but later withdrew the case. The judgment noted that there is nothing to even remotely suggest that it would be harmful for the child to return to his native country.

Next, the court examined the issue of the child developing roots in the country to which he had been removed, and prompt application for return/custody of the child. The court observed that Adithya was not receiving an education in any one place in India. He had moved from one school to another—first in Dehra Dun and then, in a few months, to Chennai. Indeed, both mother and son could not be traced for 2 years after the court issued a notice because they were moving from one state to another. Vijayashree's parents denied any knowledge of their daughter's whereabouts since September 2007. The court held that under these circumstances, there had been no occasion for the child to develop roots in India. It also noted that the father had moved for custody without delay, and that the child could not be produced for 2 years as the mother was constantly on the move.

The court added that the father was prepared to pay all the travel expenses and make living arrangements for the mother in the USA till the courts in America passed the necessary orders. Also, that he would comply with the earlier joint custody order passed by the American courts with the consent of both parties. And, he would request the American courts to drop all warrants issued against the mother and would not pursue criminal charges against her. The fact of confirmation of admission for Adithya in a school in the US was also noted by the court.

The Supreme Court concluded that it would be in Adithya's best interests to return to the US. Vijayashree was ordered to return to the USA with Adithya within 15 days.

Shilpa Aggarwal (Ms.) v. Aviral Mittal & Anr.[119]

This case arose out of a habeas corpus petition before the high court of Delhi, filed by the father of the child. The high court had directed the return of the child to England to join the proceedings before the courts of England and Wales, failing which the child had to be handed over to the petitioner, the father, to be taken to England as a measure of interim custody, leaving it for the court in that country to determine which parent would be best suited to have the custody of the child. That direction was upheld by this Court with the observation that since the question as to what is in the interest of the minor had to be considered by the court in the UK in terms of the order passed by the high court directing return of the child to the jurisdiction of the said court did not call for any interference.

[119] (2010) 1 SCC 591.

Gurmeet Kaur Batth v. State of Punjab[120]

The high court held that it can exercise jurisdiction vested in it under Article 226 of the Constitution of India by issue of the writ of habeas corpus in cases of international inter-parental child abduction. The Canadian court order in favour of the petitioner mother was relied upon and enforced. In *Vikram Vir Vohra* v. *Shalini Bhalla*,[121] the Supreme Court of India upheld the ultimate consideration of betterment of the child and held that that child custody orders are interlocutory in nature and can be altered for the welfare of the child. Consequently, the Supreme Court permitted the mother to take her minor son, aged about 10 years, to Australia in accordance with the wishes of the child to stay with the mother, upholding the welfare of the child as a paramount consideration.

Arathi Bandi v. Bandi Jagadrakshaka Rao[122]

In the instant case, the marriage between the parties was solemnized according to Hindu rights in the USA. After marriage they had settled down in the USA and a minor child was born there, who was a US citizen by birth. The husband or the father filed a petition for dissolution of marriage in a court in the USA. In these proceedings, an order was passed restraining the wife from leaving the State of Washington. The wife/mother was found suitable for custody in view of the problems of the husband/father at the work place, but limited visitation rights were granted to the father. The motion of the wife for relocation to India was denied. However, in violation of the orders of the court, the wife travelled to India with the minor child on 17 July 2008. Since the wife did not return with the child, the husband moved an application seeking modification of the final parenting plan and interference. The husband was made custodial parent and the wife was granted visitation rights. The court of Washington also issued a writ of habeas corpus, directing the state and its officers to locate and take the minor child into immediate custody. Since the wife did not return with the child, the husband filed a habeas corpus petition in the Indian high court. The high court issued a non-bailable warrant against the wife. The high court directed the wife to return the child to the USA. The Supreme Court upheld the directions issued by the high court and directed the husband to make necessary arrangement for the stay of his wife and child on their landing in the USA.

Judgments on Joint Custody or Shared Parenting

Eugenia Archetti Abdullah v. State of Kerala[123]

The facts of the case are as follows.

The petitioner wife, the respondent husband, and the children were all US citizens in this case. The petitioner wife had approached the court with a habeas corpus petition seeking a direction

---

[120] (2009) 2 Punjab Law Reporter 250 (Punjab and Haryana).
[121] (2010) 3 Judgments Today 213.
[122] Crl A. Nos. 934–936 of 2013; decided on 16 July 2013 (SC).
[123] (2005) 1 HLR Ker 34.

or commanding respondents numbers 2 to 4 to produce two infants named Roshan and Nishant before the Hon'ble Court and to handover their custody, with their passports, to the petitioner, their mother. The two infant twins were less than 3 years old. The petitioner and the respondent got married while in the United States, after which they moved to Bahrain where the petitioner gave birth to the said two children. Because of a shift of employment they went back to the state of Texas in the USA and settled there. According to the petitioner, their married life was not happy, which led to domestic violence from part of the second respondent. This resulted in a criminal case. Finally, the matter was settled.

The respondent lost his employment in Texas and both them, with their children, visited India and came to Kozhikode in the state of Kerala, where the second respondent (husband) had his roots. While there, according to the petitioner, there was again ill-treatment on part of the second respondent and she was thrown out of the residential house, and finally she had to fly back to the United States without the children. According to her, the custody of the children with the respondent was an act of illegal custody, and hence they were illegally detained.

The petitioner wife had already moved a petition for custody of the children as well as for the dissolution of the marriage with the second respondent, in accordance of the family law applicable in the State of Texas in United States.

In light of the facts and circumstances of the case, the court, while granting custody of the children to the petitioner wife, laid down rigorous conditions, one of them being shared custody/visitation rights for a period of seven days from the time of the court order to the time the petitioner wife left India. Further, it allowed continued access/visitation rights to the respondent spouse to meet up with his minor children for three hours every day, although quite limited and laying down contingency measures in the event of violation of the said conditions by the petitioner wife.

Mausami Ganguli v. Jayant Ganguli[124]

Hon'ble Supreme Court held in the instant case that the idea of shared parenting is still new to Indian custody jurisprudence. While the old principle of the father as the natural guardian has been laid to rest, in its place the best interest of the child principle is applied to custody disputes. It was further held by the court that the custody orders can be applied under Section 21 of the PWDVA only in addition to applications for protection or other orders. This means that where there is domestic violence and a woman wants a protection or other similar order, she can also apply for temporary custody. The magistrate can give orders of temporary custody of children only. This will not prevent the other party from going to an appropriate forum and seeking permanent custody or joint custody of the children. If a matter with regard to custody of children is pending in a court, an application under the PWDVA for temporary custody of children can be made in the same court.

Analysis of Case Laws

From the survey of rulings of the high courts and the Supreme Court in India, some of the trends and issues that affect the custody decision are discussed as follows.

---

[124] (2008) 7 SCC 673.

Restoration of Minor to Lawful Custody by a Writ of Habeas Corpus

A habeas corpus proceeds on the fact of illegal restraint. Article 226 of the Constitution[125] is frequently resorted to in order to obtain the custody of the child from a person who has unlawfully detained him/her, as it is a speedy remedy. The underlying principle of every writ of habeas corpus in reference to the child has been to ensure the protection and well-being of the child brought before the court under the writ.[126]

Tender Years Doctrine

In the interest of the child, a special provision for children of tender years has been made. Section 6(a) of the HMGA lays down that ordinarily the custody of children of tender years will be with the mother. The tender age is considered to be up to 5 years. This is a mandatory provision. But the courts have considered children from birth up to the age of 13 years to be of 'tender years'.

The courts have laid down the following:

1. A child of tender years should be in the custody of the mother.[127]
2. A boy of 7 years would be much better off living with his mother than with his father.[128]
3. If the mother is a suitable person to take charge of the child, it is quite impossible to find an adequate substitute for a child of tender years.[129]
4. The mother's lap is 'God's own cradle' for a child of this age.[130]
5. The conversion of a mother[131] or her being an outcaste[132] does not matter. A non-Hindu mother of a Hindu child of tender age is entitled to its custody. It is significant to note that in these cases the religion of the parties is not a factor. The same views have been expressed by the courts irrespective of the fact whether the parties were Hindus, Muslims, Christians, or Parsis. (Also see *Rajkumar Gupta* v. *Barbara Gupta*, AIR 1989 Cal 165).

It appears to be a universally recognized rule now that a parent cannot be deprived of the custody of his/her children merely because he/she happens to be poor.[133] Many court decisions have given custody to the party who has taken care of the child even if he/she is financially/economically less well off than the other. This trend has favoured women as custodians and if

---

[125] Article 226 of the Constitution of India empowers high courts to issue orders, directions, and rulings in the nature of certain writs.

[126] Diwan, *Law of Adoption*.

[127] *Ahmed* v. *Dehnatton*, (1917) 40 IC 1070.

[128] *Tara Bai* v. *Mohan Lal*, AIR 1932 Bom 405.

[129] *Saraswatibai* v. *Sripad*, AIR 1941 Bom 103.

[130] *Re Kamal Rudra* ILR (1949) 2 Cal 374.

[131] *Budhan* v. *Bahadur Khan*, AIR 1942 Pesh 41.

[132] *Kaulesra* v. *Jorai Kasudhan*, ILR, (1905) 28 AII 233.

[133] Diwan, *Law of Adoption*, p. 444.

a mother is financially/economically less well off than the father, courts still consider giving her custody on the grounds that the father can be ordered to pay her maintenance.[134]

Abdication and Abandonment

In a case where the father had given custody of his three children to their grandfather under an agreement and then after 7 years asked for their custody, the court held that the father must be held to have lost his right to the guardianship of his children, not merely because he allowed them to be maintained and educated by the grandfather, but also because at this stage, to alter the course of their life would be detrimental to their interest.[135]

Mother Also a Natural Guardian

The Supreme Court has held that[136] the mother is also the natural guardian of her minor child in the absence of the father. The landmark judgment is hailed as historic, as no longer will women live in fear of losing custody of their children on the ground that they are not the natural guardians of their children. The validity of any transaction cannot now be called into question on the ground that it has been entered into by the mother and not the father. Local bodies like schools, banks, passport offices, immigration officials, and government institutions will be obliged to enter into transactions with the mother without insisting that the father alone can apply on behalf of the child. Clearly, this judgment is in the interest of the child. But the court has unfortunately stopped short of giving equal status to the mother as a natural guardian.

Paternal Rights and Welfare of Children

Section 19 of the GWA provides for the supremacy of paternal rights whereas Section 17 provides for the welfare of the child. In many cases, the courts have to decide between these two contending issues.

Before 1950, the courts have generally given importance to the father's right as the natural guardian and legal guardian. The courts have held in several cases that before the father can be deprived of the custody of the child, it must be established that he is unfit to act as a guardian because of any act or conduct.[137] From 1950 onwards, there appears a general change in judicial thinking,[138] and in a series of cases the Madras high court held that the welfare of the child is paramount and the father can be deprived of custody even though he is not found unfit, if circumstances show that in the welfare of the child, the custody should be given to someone else.

---

[134] Lawyers Collective, *Legal Aid Handbook 2.*

[135] *Baldeo* v. *Dhannaram*, AIR 1927 Nag 314.

[136] See *Githa Hariharan & Another* v. *Reserve Bank of India and Another*, and *Vandana Shiva* v. *Jayanta Bandhopadhyaya & Another*, AIR 1999.

[137] See *Queen* v. *Nisbet, Perry* OC 103; *Re Callor Nariuswamy*, Mayne's PCS, 391; *Re Hanumath Boe*; *Reade* v. *Krishna*, (1886) ILR Mad 391; *Re Andiappa* v. *Nallendrian*, (1915) ILR 39 Mad 473.

[138] Diwan, *Law of Adoption.*

Wishes of the Child

This is an important factor to be taken into consideration by the courts. The Indian courts have in some cases given effect to the wishes of children of 10 years, and in some others, they have declined to give them effect. Whereas, in some cases, the court has gone against the wishes of a child of 16 years. As is evident, some courts take the orthodox view that the father's right of custody, being an absolute right, is enforceable against the wishes of the children, whatever be their age. Under the present law, in many cases, the courts have disregarded the wishes of older children who are capable of expressing their preference whenever the courts were of the view that the wishes of the children must be disregarded for their own welfare.

Two questions can be raised here:

1. Is it in the interest of the child to stay with somebody with whom he does not wish to stay?
2. Do children actually give their own preferences to the courts? Do their custodian's interests and wishes influence their wishes?

At present judges and courts are not equipped and trained to determine the actual wishes of the child and see through the other external influences and reasons. But in the best interests of the child, they have to be equipped to deal with such issues. Scientific evaluation techniques are available for this.

Critique of the Present Law

It is thus evident from the analysis of the case laws that the welfare principle has quite often not been properly appreciated or has been overlooked by the trial court, and the mother has had to approach the higher court at considerable cost of time and money. Many cases do not reach the higher courts for lack of resources and in these cases the interest of the child suffers. Second, due to long legal battles, the custody of the child remains with a person with whom it should perhaps not remain. The right of the child to speedy trial is also violated. The trial courts have to be sensitized to the rights of the child and to be more child-friendly. Besides, these are the following lacunae:

1. The personnel working in family courts are not sensitive to child rights.
2. There are no provisions for follow-up of cases after the court has given custody and access to parents.
3. The prevailing assumption in the present custody and guardianship laws is that the child's interests are identical to those of the parent's interest, but this may not always be true. Children may have interests independent of their parents.
4. There has to be provision for legal counsel in every case where children are involved.
5. There is no enforcement of child maintenance and support orders. There has to be enforcement mechanism/body.
6. The child, in these contests, does not have full party status. They are not regarded as independent third parties. This has to be provided.
7. There is no concept of available alternatives/options for the child while determining the orders.

8. In matrimonial proceedings the question of custody is treated as ancillary proceeding. When matrimonial proceedings are filed between the parties, the relationship is usually strained and the home is virtually broken. The parties may not be living together. The position in law is that if the main proceedings are dismissed, the proceedings in respect of children are not continued. The children have to go back to the tense environment. There is a need to protect the interests of children at this stage. Even if the main petition fails, arrangements need to be made in the best interests of the child.

9. There is no law on parental responsibility. There is a need for such a law.

10. After the Githa Hariharan Case, the mother has been given the status of natural guardian in the HMGA, but in all other laws, the father still has the superior position as a natural guardian. This is discrimination against children as a class.

11. Tender years of children are generally till 5 years. This needs to be reviewed. The Law Commission recommendations in the 83rd and 133rd reports need to be considered.

12. The maintenance orders need to be enforced stringently.

13. The non-custodial parent, in many cases, should not automatically be given access or visitation rights.

14. The children are often shuttled back and forth from parent to parent on a regular basis.

15. Orders are passed without making adequate arrangements for children.

16. There is no provision to understand or handle the trauma that a child is undergoing during the custody battle between the parents.

17. The concept of illegitimacy of children is still prevalent in laws. This outdated concept needs to be removed.

The number of cases related to inter-parental child custody conflicts has gone up sharply. As more and more marriages fall apart, NRI parents often remove their children to India or to foreign jurisdictions either in violation of a foreign court custody order, or in infringement of the other spouse's parental rights.[139]

Indian law provides for the recognition and enforcement of judgments delivered by foreign courts. Section 13 of the CPC of India provides that 'a foreign judgment shall be conclusive as to any matter thereby directly adjudicated upon between the same parties or between parties under whom they or any of them claim litigating under the same title except:

1. Where it has not been pronounced by a court of competent jurisdiction;

2. Where it has not been given on the merits of the case;

3. Where it appears on the face of the proceedings to be founded on an incorrect view of international law or a refusal to recognise the law of India in cases in which such law is applicable;

4. Where the proceedings in which judgment was obtained are opposed to natural justice;

5. Where it has been obtained by fraud;

6. Where it sustains the claim founded on breach of any law enforced in India.'

---

[139] See Gangadhar S Patil, 'Law Commission to Suggest Amendment to Guardians and Wards Act', *Economic Times*, ET Bureau, 30 October 2014.

Further, Section 14 of the CPC provides that the courts shall presume, upon the production of any document purporting to be a certified copy of a foreign judgment, that such judgment was pronounced by a court of competent jurisdiction, unless the country appears on the record. But such presumption may be displaced by proving want of jurisdiction. However, it may be noted that it is for the parties to approach the court to get such recognition of foreign judgments.

India has also entered into reciprocal arrangements for the execution of decrees passed by courts under Section 44A[140] of the the CPC.[141]

A Comparative Survey of International Laws

Australian Law

Under the Family Law Act (FLA), 1975, the family court was set up to administer the law. It was envisaged as a 'helping court' and was to operate as a 'closed court' with limited formality, simplified procedures, and with the assistance of specialist counselling and welfare staff.

The act directed that in custody and other proceedings concerning children, the paramount consideration should be the welfare of the child. The main innovations in custodial matters were: provision for parents to attend conferences with welfare officers to discuss the welfare of children and endeavour to resolve differences; provision for the wishes of children concerned to be ascertained and observed; and an attempt to provide more effective enforcement procedures.

Paramount Consideration—The Welfare of the Child

In common law, a father had sole custody of his legitimate children. By the FLA, the father and the mother, *subject to* any *court order, have joint custody of children of the marriage under the age of eighteen.* In exceptional circumstances, the family court may order that the disputing parents

---

[140] CPA, Section 44A: Execution of decrees passed by courts in reciprocating territory—

(1) Where a certified copy of a decree of any of the superior courts of any reciprocating territory has been filed in a district court, the decree may be executed in India as if it had been passed by the district court.

(2) Together with the certified copy of the decree shall be filed a certificate from such superior court stating the extent, if any, to which the decree has been satisfied or adjusted and such certificate shall, for the purposes of proceedings under this section, be conclusive proof of the extent of such satisfaction or adjustment.

(3) The provisions of Section 47 shall as from the filing of the certified copy of the decree apply to the proceedings of a district court executing a decree under this section, and the district court shall refuse execution of any such decree, if it is shown to the satisfaction of the court that the decree falls within any of the exceptions specified in Clauses (a) to (f) of section 13.

[141] Prem Kumar Malhotra, Additional Secretary, Government of India, Ministry of Law & Justice, New Delhi; the Honourable Justice Vikramjit Sen, High Court of Delhi, New Delhi; the Honourable Justice Manmohan, High Court of Delhi, New Delhi; *The Judges' Newsletter on International Child Protection* XVI (Spring 2010), Special Focus, Theme 1, India.

have joint custody, with care and control to one party. The most common order is a grant of sole custody to one parent, with the other parent given access to the child.

The concern of the legislation in this area is to promote the interests of the child, which may often be overlooked by the parents themselves, embroiled as they may be in a bitter dispute. The act states that in custody proceedings the court shall regard the welfare of the child as the paramount consideration. This test was also applied under the Matrimonial Causes Act, 1959. There are no principles of law providing a decisive test as to the welfare of the child. Rather, *this is a question to be determined from case to case on the particular and unique facts.*

The Wishes of the Child

In addition to emphasizing the welfare of the child, the act directs that except in special circumstances the court shall not make a custody order contrary to the wishes of any child of 14 or over. If the child is under 14, the court may take into account his or her wishes.

The Japanese Law—The Family Court in Japan and the Best Interests of the Child

The family court in Japan is a specialized court dealing with family affairs cases and juvenile delinquency cases. Through its basic objectives of maintaining the welfare of families and seeking the sound upbringing of juveniles, it tries to answer the modern demand for justice fitted to the needs of society. It is a court in which the principles of law, the conscience of the community, and the social sciences, particularly those dealing with human behaviour and personal relationships, work together. Practically, the function of the court is to deal, within the scope defined by law, with actual problems of families and delinquent juveniles.

Jurisdiction of the Family Court

The family court has a very broad jurisdiction encompassing all disputes and conflicts within the family as well as all related domestic affairs, which are of legal significance.

The juvenile division of the family court handles cases involving delinquent juveniles under 20 years of age and adults who have in some way brought about an injury to the welfare of juveniles. 'Delinquent juveniles' include not only minors who have committed criminal offences under the penal laws, but juveniles whose tendencies indicate that they might commit offences in future as well. The court has primary jurisdiction in regard to all juvenile offences, whether they are felonies such as homicide or arson, or misdemeanours such as traffic offences and violation of administrative control laws. Thus, all criminal cases concerning minors primarily are sent to the family court for investigation and hearing.

Jurisdiction over Adult Criminal Cases

Adults who have committed acts injurious to the welfare of juveniles are also subject to the family court's jurisdiction. Various specific offenses are set down in the Child Welfare Law, the Labour

Standards Law, and the School Education Law, among others. Such offences as the inducement of obscene acts, cruel treatment, and employment of children at extremely late hours are examples. The foundation of the jurisdiction over the offences is the protection of juveniles and the maintenance of their basic human rights. However, neither desertion nor neglect of the duty of support by parents or guardians constitutes an offence justifying the jurisdiction of the family court in Japanese juvenile law. Support is considered to be a family law problem and therefore is subject to determination and conciliation procedure of the family affairs division, while desertion, if sufficient to constitute an offence under the penal code, is handled by a regular criminal court.

The French Legal System Relating to Custody of Children

The court which has exclusive jurisdiction on matters of divorce and its consequences is the Tribunal de Grande Instance. One of the judges of the Tribunal is appointed to deal with matrimonial matters. *He is especially in charge of the duty of safeguarding the interest of minor children.* He is also exclusively competent to decide on the custody of children and on the modification of the alimony, whatever the ground for divorce. The trial on the grounds or consequences of divorce and the interim relief are held in camera.[142]

Consequences of Divorce on the Children

The general principle is that divorce leaves intact the rights and duties of the father and mother with regard to their children. However, the custody of the children is given to either of the spouses. In exceptional cases such custody may be given to a third person chosen preferably among the relatives or, when this is not possible, to an educational institution.

The spouse who has been deprived of the custody of the children has the right to watch the way in which they are brought up and educated. S/he also has the duty to contribute, proportionately to his/her income, to the expenses. S/he has also the right to visit and to receive them in his/her residence. Such a right can be denied only for grave reasons. Notwithstanding the normal provisions to the contrary, in law, the spouse who is denied the custody of the children may be entrusted with the task of administering, under judicial control, all or part of the estate of the children, if the interest of a good administration of such estate so requires.

The decision on the grant of custody of the children and on the mode of exercise of parental authority is taken at the request of one of the spouses or of a member of the family or of the Procureur de la Republique. For reaching a decision, the judge has to take into account:

1. the agreements entered into between the spouses;
2. the information collected during the inquiry and counter-inquiry; and
3. the feelings expressed by the minor children. They will be heard if it appears necessary and when no inconvenience is likely to be caused to them.

[142] See David J. Annoswamy, *The French Legal System and its Indian Connection* (NLSIU, Bangalore: Institute of Comparative Law, 1996).

The spouse who has been denied custody of the children will contribute for their mainte-nance and education in the form of alimony paid to the person who has been entrusted with their custody. The form of such alimony and the guarantee for its payment are fixed by the judgment, or in case of divorce, on joint request by the agreement between the spouses, as approved by the judge.

When the nature and the assets of the spouse liable to pay permits, the liability for alimony may be discharged, in whole or in part:

1. by depositing certain amount of money with an accredited organization with a charge to pay to the children a periodical allowance indexed to the cost of living;
2. by granting usufructuary right over some properties; or
3. by allotting some income yielding properties.

When the capital thus constituted becomes insufficient to cover the needs of the children, the person who has the custody may ask for grant of supplement in the form of alimony. The parent who is mainly in charge of the major children, who are unable to provide themselves for their needs, may ask the other spouse to pay him a contribution for their maintenance and education.

The Law in the United States of America

In USA, the interests of the child, the parents, and the state balance delicately. The natural rights of parents have a constitutional basis in American law and cover such areas as control over reli-gious training, medical decisions, and mental health. Parental rights are not absolute. The child's interests are protected by the state through the parens patriae power. The state uses guardians' ad litem and special child advocates to protect many children whose parents' rights are questioned. Each advocate is appointed individually to act, often in a voluntary capacity, to represent children in court or to make recommendations to the court that are in the best interest of the child. The principle of the best interest of the child is the basic guideline governing civil cases involving chil-dren. In broad terms, it means that a court must operate in such a manner as to further justice, while at the same time promoting the welfare and well-being of the child. The best interest princi-ple is used in a variety of situations in the US: mental health commitments; delinquency hearing; abuse, neglect, or dependency hearings; and custody determination following a divorce. In cases wherein the parents' rights and responsibilities are balanced against the child's best interest, above all other considerations, the child's interests are paramount in the eyes of the judge. But to enforce the rights of the child above those of the parents, the parents' rights first must be overcome.

The Best or Least Worst Interest of the Child

The term *best interest* also refers to the goal of the judicial determination in abuse, neglect, and dependency actions in juvenile court. The courts are charged with discovering and putting into place dispositions that will meet the child's best interest. This phrase, though neither advocated nor invented by the courts, came into popular use after publication of the series of books by Professor Joseph Goldstein, Dr Anna Freud, and Dr Albert Solnit—*Beyond the Best Interest of the Child* (1973), *Before the Best Interest of the Child* (1979), and *In the Best Interest of the Child*

(1986). These books are an examination of information derived from the Yale University Child Study Center and the Hampstead Child Therapy Clinic. In these books, the authors question the value and ability of any person's attempts to determine and put into effect the best interest of a child. The case goal that is offered by these authors to supplant the so-called best interest goal is 'the least detrimental harm'.

Another author, Coyne (1992) of the University of Nebraska at Omaha, has used a different phrase—'finding the least worst solution'. Although the least worst solution may not be readily apparent to the lawyers and the judge in a particular case, focusing on the least worst solution, Coyne says, will force the lawyers or judge to confront the perils in the other choices available, thereby avoiding or mitigating them. A more productive goal than seeking the best interest, which may be unknowable, is to seek the least worst solution, which would help the professionals involved in the case avoid doing greater harm to a child who is already the subject of an abuse, neglect, or dependency action.

The need for reform in the United States was expressed earlier. In the early nineteenth century, the view of families as patriarchal entities gave way to the newer ideal of democracies populated by individuals with inalienable rights and obligations.[143]

By 1830, a Maryland court was ready to give open support to the notion that a child had an important interest in remaining in his or her mother's care. In *Helms* v. *Franciscus* (1830), the court gave custody of a child of tender years to the mother after she had been granted a legal separation on the basis that her husband had been living in open adultery with another woman. The innocent injured spouse received custody of the infant of the marriage, but again the father's right to the older children was upheld despite the fact that the man was an adulterer. The right of a father to ownership of his children was recognized, but the court acknowledged that the laws of nature require that a child not be snatched from a mother in infancy. A child should stay with the breastfeeding mother. Here, the emphasis is not on a woman's right to companionship of her child, but rather on the interests of a breastfeeding child.

The tender years rule was the first appearance of legal consideration of the needs of very young children; as such, it was a best interest standard. Once the tender years rule was fully accepted by the US divorce courts, fathers found the tables completely turned. For almost a century, the only way a father could gain custody over the children of the marriage, on legal separation or divorce, was to prove the mother's unfitness. During the peak of the tender years rule, the law was as gender-biased against men as it had been in favour of them before.

The gender bias was declared unconstitutional by many states in the wake of the first gains of the women's movement. In *Ex parte Devine* (1981), for example, the Alabama Supreme Court declared the gender-based 'tender years rule' over when it found the doctrine to be unconstitutional. Similarly, a few years earlier, in *State ex rel. Watts* v. *Watts* (1973), New York's highest court, its Court of Appeals, found that any legal presumption against fathers was unconstitutional.

Other courts have found otherwise. Oklahoma's Supreme Court, in *Gordon* v. *Gordon* (1978), upheld that state's statutory preference for maternal custody, 'other things being equal'; in that case, the US Supreme Court refused to hear an appeal against the state court's ruling (1978), in effect refusing to disapprove the state court's decision.

---

[143] Nancy E. Walker, Catherine M. Brooks, Lawrence S. Wrightsman, *Children's Rights in the United States* (New Delhi: Sage, 1999).

West Virginia's high court, however, has held the tender years rule to be constitutional on the basis of the following:

1. Men and women are not similarly situated when it comes to parenting, at least when the child is very young (e.g. breastfeeding).
2. The presumption in favour of mothers may be an appropriate offset to the historic disadvantages they suffered (*J.B.* v. *V.B.*, 1978).

As state courts dropped the tender years rule and its explicit preference for mothers, they retained the spirit of it in the name of 'the best interest of the child standard'. In essence, the tender years doctrine, which was aimed at meeting the needs of children, became gender-neutral without losing the goal of appropriately addressing children's needs. Currently, the courts are asked to carry out evaluations about the child's best welfare. A judge is not required to follow the psychologist's recommendations. In fact, judges' decisions may reflect their own stereotyped beliefs about what is in a child's best interests, beliefs that may or may not fit in with empirical findings.[144]

The Uniform Marriage and Divorce Act (UMDA), 1979, which has had a significant impact on the statutory reforms of many states, describes the following as among the factors a judge may consider in reaching a custody decision:

1. The mental and physical health of all individuals involved;
2. The child's adjustment to home, school, and community;
3. Each parent's ability to provide food, clothing, medication, and other remedial care and material benefits to the child;
4. The interaction and interrelationship of the child with parents or other individuals who might affect the child's best interests (thus, in a general sense, the parent's lifestyle and the child's individual needs);
5. The wishes of the parents and the child.

It is with respect to the last factor that children's rights to self-determination are beginning to emerge. At least twenty states permit children beyond a specified age to state which parent they prefer for custody. Some states specify age, typically 12 or 14; others consider the maturity of the child's cognitive or emotional development. For instance, in the case *In re Marriage of Rosson* (1986), the court concluded that a child of a sufficient age and capacity to reason well enough to form an intelligent custody preference does have the right to have that preference seriously considered. But consensus is lacking on how much weight is to be given to the child's preferences.

Laws in the United Kingdom

The term 'child' means a person who has not reached his or her eighteenth birthday. This broad definition grants agencies and courts great discretion when dealing with young people. In English law, the word 'custody' has been used in a wider sense so as to include practically all the rights of

---

[144] Walker, Brooks, and Wrightsma, *Children's Rights*.

guardianship, as well as in a narrow sense, so as to include only 'care and control'. The history of the law relating to the custody of a child in the United Kingdom shows two important trends, as will be evident from the following.

The Guardianship of Minors Act (GMA), 1971 repealed the Guardianship of Infants Act, 1925. It made no changes in the substantive law.

General Principles

A dispute over custody may take one of the two forms: it may be a dispute between the father and the mother; or it may be a dispute between one parent and a stranger, for example, a testamentary guardian appointed by the other parent, or a person who has obtained de facto control of the child either with the parent's consent or as a result of his having abandoned it.

As the House of Lords held in *J. v. C.*,[145] the principle laid down in Section 1 of the GMA, that the welfare of the child is to be regarded as the first and paramount consideration, applies equally whether the dispute is between the parents, or between one or both parents and a stranger. In this case, however, the wishes of an unimpeachable parent stand high among the remaining considerations: to give effect to the blood tie will itself normally be for the child's benefit and usually he should be with his natural parents. But there is no presumption that the natural parents should have custody; in the words of Lord Macdermott:[146] [W]hen all the relevant facts, relationships, claims and wishes of parents, risks, choices and other circumstances are taken into account and weighed, the course to be followed will be that which is most in the interests of the child's welfare as that term has now to be understood.

If all considerations are equal, however, the court will give effect to this relationship and grant custody to a parent rather than to a stranger. This was not the case in *J. v. C.* The parents of the child were Spanish nationals resident in Spain, but the child, who was then aged 10 years, had spent the whole of his life, except for 18 months, with foster parents in England. He had been brought up as an English boy, spoke little Spanish, and scarcely knew his natural parents. The House of Lords refused to interfere with the order of the trial judge who left custody, care, and control with the foster parents and refused to give it to the natural parents on the ground that they 'would' be quite unable to cope with the problems of adjustment or with consequential maladjustment and suffering, and that the father's character would inflame the difficulties' if the boy were to go to live with them in Spain.

The one statutory exception to this rule is to be found in Section 3 of the Custody of Children Act, 1891. This section provides that where a parent has abandoned or deserted his child or allowed it to be brought up by, and at the expense of, another person, school, institution, or local authority, in such circumstances as to show that he was unmindful of his parental duties, no order is to be made giving him the custody of the child unless he proves that he is a fit person to have it. But in order to bring this section into play, the parent's conduct must show some degree of moral turpitude. If he relinquishes control temporarily because this is the best that he can do for the child in the circumstances, the court ought not, on this ground alone, to deprive him of custody. In practice, this section is rarely invoked.

[145] (1969), All ER 788.
[146] (1969), All ER 788, p. 821.

Power of Appellate Courts

It will be seen that the court must always be guided by the interests of the child and, as the House of Lords emphasized in *J. v. C.*,[147] a court of first instance has a discretion with which no appellate court will interfere, unless it is satisfied that the lower court has clearly acted under a misapprehension of fact, or gave weight to irrelevant or unproved matters, or failed to take relevant matters into account.[148] On the other hand, an appellate court is not entitled to allow an appeal and substitute its own discretion merely because it would have come to a different conclusion on the evidence.[149] Difficulty arises because in some cases appellate courts are so convinced that the lower court exercised its discretion wrongly, that they will reverse the decision even though the latter purported to apply the right principles in reaching it.[150] On hearing an appeal, a court is apparently entitled to consider the relative weight which the lower court attached to the various facts which it had to take into account, and to conclude that the court acted on the wrong principles if it disagrees with the weighting.[151]

Children's Act, 1989, Section 1, provides: 'When a court determines any question with respect to:

- upbringing of a child or
- the administration of the child's property or the application of any income arising form it, the child's welfare shall be the court's paramount consideration.'

The welfare principle in Section 1 applies only to courts, but parents, local authorities, and children themselves must also have regard of children's welfare. Decisions by parents which conflict with welfare may be reviewed by the courts, and thus it has been said that parents must apply the welfare principle. The same could be said of children.[152] Local authority decisions, which do not require court approval, are generally immune from review on the merits, but local authorities are under a duty to safeguard and promote the welfare of children in need, and those they are looking after.[153] The word 'first' was thought by the Law Commission to suggest that the child's welfare should be balanced with other factors.[154]

The leading case on the welfare principle is *J. v. C*,[155] where the courts considered whether a 10-year-old boy should be returned to his parents (Spanish nationals resident in Spain) or remain with English foster parents who had looked after him for all, except 18 months, of his life. The

---

[147] As in *Re Thin*, [1926], Ch. 676, CA.

[148] See *Re O'Hara*, [1900] 2 IR 232 at pp. 238, 243, 251; *Re Carroll*, [1931] 1 KB 317, 360–3, CA; *R. v. Bolton Union*, (1892) 36 Sol. J. 255.

[149] [1969]t All ER 788, H.L.; [1970] AC 668.

[150] *B.(B.) v. B. (M)*, [1969] I All E.R. 891, 961; [1969] P 103, 115.

[151] If evidence is available to the appellate court, which was not available before the lower court.

[152] *Re O* (1971) 2 WLR 784 CA.

[153] Cf. *Re O* (1962) 2 All ER 10 CA.

[154] Law Com 96 para 6, 9. Law Com No. 172, Review of Child Law Guardianship and Custody (1988) HC 594 para.

[155] 1990 AC 668.

House of Lords upheld the decision of the trial judge and the court of Appeal that he should stay in England. Lord Macdermott stated that paramountcy of welfare means:

> [T]he child's welfare is to be treated as the top item in a list of items relevant to the matter in question. [The words] connote a process whereby, when all the relevant facts, relationships claims and wishes of parents, risks, choices and other circumstances are taken into account and weighed, the course to be followed will be that which is most in the interests of the child's welfare as that term is now understood....... It is the paramount consideration because it rules upon or determines the course to be followed.[156]

The boy's welfare necessitated that he remain with the parent figures he was attached to, the more so since his natural parents would have been unable to cope with his consequent maladjustment. Against these considerations, the claims of 'unimpeachable' natural parents could not prevail. The court came to a different conclusion in a similar case in 1996.

The Children's Act, 1989 did not create a unified family court but it reformed the magistrate's court, renaming the domestic court the 'family proceedings court' and giving it jurisdiction over all civil matters concerning the upbringing of children.

The act created four orders relating to children. These are:

1. residence order which states where the child should live,
2. the contact order which requires a carer to allow someone to have contact with the child,
3. the prohibited steps order which restricts the exercise of parental responsibility, and
4. the specific issue order which determines how parental responsibility is to be exercised.

Together exercised, these are known as the 'Section 8' orders.

International Law on Unwed Mothers

In the United Kingdom, the Children Act, 1989 allocates parental responsibility, which includes all rights, duties, powers, responsibilities, and authority of a parent over the child and his/her property. According to Section 2(2) of that act, parental custody of a child born of unwed parents is with the mother in all cases, and additionally with the father, provided he has acquired responsibility in accordance with the provisions of the act. To acquire responsibility, he would have to register as the child's father, execute a parental responsibility agreement with the mother, or obtain a Court order giving him parental responsibility over the child.

In the USA, each State has different child custody laws, but predominantly, the mother has full legal and physical custody from the time the child is born. Unless an unmarried father establishes his paternity over the child, it is generally difficult for him to defeat or overwhelm the preferential claims of the mother to the custody. However, some States assume that both parents who sign the child's birth certificate have joint custody, regardless of whether they are married or not.

In Ireland, Section 6(4) of the Guardianship of Infants Act, 1964 ordains: 'The mother of an illegitimate infant shall be guardian of the infant'. Unless the mother agrees to sign a statutory

---

[156] 1990 AC 668, at 710–11.

declaration, an unmarried father must apply to the court in order to become a legal guardian of his child.

Article 176 of the Family Code of the Philippines explicitly provides that 'illegitimate children shall use the surname and shall be under the parental authority of their mother, and shall be entitled to support in conformity with this Code'. This position obtains regardless of whether the father admits paternity. In 2004, the Supreme Court of the Philippines, in *Joey D. Briones* v. *Maricel P. Miguel*,[157] held that an illegitimate child is under the sole parental authority of the mother.

The law in New Zealand, as laid out in Section 17 of the Care of Children Act, 2004, is that the mother of a child is the sole guardian if she is not married to, or in civil union with, or living as a de facto partner with the father of the child at any time during the period beginning with the conception of the child and ending with the birth of the child.

In South Africa, according to the Children's Act No. 38 of 2005, parental responsibility includes the responsibility and the right—

1. to care for the child;
2. to maintain contact with the child;
3. to act as guardian of the child; and
4. to contribute to the maintenance of the child. The biological mother of a child, whether married or unmarried, has full parental responsibilities and rights in respect of the child. The father has full parental responsibility if he is married to the mother, or if he was married to her at the time of the child's conception, or at the time of the child's birth or any time in between, or if at the time of the child's birth he was living with the mother in a permanent life-partnership, or if he

   a) consents to be identified or successfully applies in terms of Section 26 to be identified as the child's father or pays damages in terms of customary law;
   b) contributes or has attempted in good faith to contribute to the child's upbringing for a reasonable period; and
   c) contributes or has attempted in good faith to contribute towards expenses in connection with the maintenance of the child for a reasonable period.

This conspectus indicates the preponderant position that it is the unwed mother who possesses primary custodial and guardianship rights with regard to her children, and that the father is not conferred with an equal position merely by virtue of his having fathered the child.

It is thus abundantly clear that the predominant legal thought in different civil and common law jurisdictions spanning the globe, as well as in different statutes within India, is to bestow guardianship and related rights to the mother of a child born outside of wedlock.

---

[157] Joey D. Briones, *Petitioner* v. Maricel P. Miguel, Francisca P. Miguel and Loreta P. Miguel, *Respondents*. G.R. No. 156343, 18 October 2004. Available at http://sc.judiciary.gov.ph/jurisprudence/2004/oct2004/156343.htm (accessed on 26 September 2016).

International Judgments on Child Custody

In re the Marriage of Moyne v. Moyne[158]

The Moynes were married in 2003, and lived in Minnesota until 2010. In October of that year, the father, a French citizen, relocated to France. The mother joined Father in France with their two children from mid-April through June of 2011, allegedly with the intention of relocating to France. The mother ultimately returned to Minnesota and filed for divorce in September 2011, while the children were still residing with her in Minnesota. The children returned to France shortly thereafter, and the father refused to return them to Minnesota despite court orders that he do so (a case for their return was pending before France's highest court).

After an evidentiary hearing to address the issue of jurisdiction and a full trial on custody and parenting time, the district court found that it had jurisdiction over the divorce, custody, and child support matters, and awarded sole legal and physical custody to the mother. The father appealed, arguing, among other things, that the court lacked subject-matter jurisdiction to decide the case because the mother had not been a resident of Minnesota for 180 days prior to filing for divorce (see Minn. Stat. 518.07) and because Minnesota was not the children's home state (see Minn. Stat. 518D.201 and 518C.101).

The court of Appeals affirmed in an opinion that provides a useful primer on all three subject-matter jurisdiction statutes. Reviewing the record, the court of Appeals found the evidence sufficient to support the district court's conclusion that the mother did not lose her Minnesota residence by traveling to France. The court focused here on whether the mother truly established an 'intent to abandon [her] old home [in Minnesota]' where Mother retained her Minnesota driver's license, had close family connections to Minnesota, did not send all her belongings to France, and looked for a realtor but never listed the Minnesota home for sale. The court also noted that the mother is neither fluent in French nor a French citizen, and traveled to France out of financial dependence on the father.

The court also affirmed the lower Court's ruling that Minnesota was the children's home state (giving Minnesota jurisdiction to decide custody and child support matters), reasoning that the record supported a finding that the children's travel to France was merely a 'visit'. The court was also careful to note that the mother's alleged intent to relocate the children to France was irrelevant because 'the children's home state analysis focuses on where the children lived, not where their parents intended to reside'.

Perhaps unsurprisingly in light of the father's refusal to return the children to Minnesota, the court of Appeals also affirmed the grant of sole physical and legal custody to the mother.

International Trends Relating to Joint Custody[159]

Joint custody systems vary widely across the globe. A comparative review of different countries reveals a vast diversity of approaches. The term 'joint custody" can refer to several different things: joint legal custody, joint physical custody, or a combination of both.

---

[158] A13-2077 (Minn. Ct. App. 12 May 2014).
[159] 257 *Law Commission Report.*

The Definition in the State of Virginia recognizes this:

'Joint custody' means (i) joint legal custody where both parents retain joint responsibility for the care and control of the child and joint authority to make decisions concerning the child even though the child's primary residence may be with only one parent, (ii) joint physical custody where both parents share physical and custodial care of the child, or (iii) any combination of joint legal and joint physical custody which the court deems to be in the best interest of the child.[160]

Similarly, the State of Georgia defines joint custody as 'joint legal custody, joint physical custody, or both joint legal custody and joint physical custody'.[161]

There is a similar distinction between sole legal custody and sole physical custody, although some States (including Virginia) combine them together.[162] The State of California has the following definitions:

1. 'Sole legal custody' means that one parent shall have the right and the responsibility to make the decisions relating to the health, education, and welfare of a child.[163]
2. 'Sole physical custody' means that a child shall reside with and be under the supervision of one parent, subject to the power of the court to order visitation.[164]

One of the unifying themes across the different shared parenting systems is the importance given to the best interest of the child.[165] However, jurisdictions differ on how they apply this standard. Some have a presumption that shared parenting is in the best interest of the child—Australia's Family Law Act, for example, states that 'When making a parenting order in relation to a child, the court must apply a presumption that it is in the best interests of the child for the child's parents to have equal shared parental responsibility for the child'.[166] Other jurisdictions allow for shared parenting but do not contain this presumption. Minnesota law explicitly states that 'There is no presumption for or against joint physical custody' with certain exceptions.[167] Canada, South Africa, the UK, and Kenya also have no presumption for or against joint custody.[168]

---

[160] VA Code Ann., section 20–124.1.

[161] Ga. Code Ann., section 19–9–6(4).

[162] VA Code Ann., section 20–124.1 ('Sole custody' means that one person retains responsibility for the care and control of a child and has primary authority to make decisions concerning the child.)

[163] West's Ann. Cal. Fam. Code, section 3006.

[164] West's Ann. Cal. Fam. Code, section 3007.

[165] See, for example, Canada Divorce Act, 1985, Section 16(8) ('In making an order under this section, the court shall take into consideration only the best interests of the child.'); Australia Family Law Act, 1975, Section 65AA (as amended in 2006) ('[I]n deciding whether to make a particular parenting order in relation to a child, a court must regard the best interests of the child as the paramount consideration.'); South Africa Children's Act, No. 38 of 2005, section 9; U.K. Children's Act, 1989, section 1(1).

[166] Australia Family Law Act, 1975, section 61DA (as amended); see also Idaho Code Ann., section 32-717B(4) ('[T]here shall be a presumption that joint custody is in the best interests of a minor child or children'.)

[167] M.S.A., section 518.17(2)(a).

[168] Canada Divorce Act, R.S.C., 1985, c. 3 (2nd Supp.), section 16(4), (8); South Africa Children's Act, No. 38 of 2005, sections 22, 23, 30; U.K. Children's Act, 1989, sections 8, 11(4); Kenya Children's Act, sections 82(1), 83(1).

Many countries that allow (or even have a statutory preference for) shared parenting do not allow it in some cases. Where there is domestic violence or any sort of abuse, most jurisdictions have a presumption against shared parenting.[169] Shared parenting is also disfavoured where parents have a particularly contentious relationship. As a US Court of Appeals noted in *Braiman* v. *Braiman*: *Joint custody is encouraged primarily as a voluntary alternative for relatively stable, amicable parents behaving in mature civilized fashion. As a court-ordered arrangement imposed upon already embattled and embittered parents, accusing one another of serious vices and wrongs, it can only enhance familial chaos.*[170]

Practical considerations are also relevant. Some jurisdictions consider geographical proximity when deciding an award of shared parenting.[171] Family courts in South Africa, for example, do not frequently award joint physical custody of children on the basis that such an arrangement would be disruptive for the child, particularly in cases where the parents live far apart.[172] Also, the de facto living situation of the child can be relevant—in the United Kingdom, shared residence orders 'may be regarded as appropriate where it provides legal confirmation of the factual reality of a child's life'.[173]

A number of jurisdictions recognize the distinction between legal custody (the right to make major decisions for a child, such as decisions involving education, medical and dental care, religion, and travel arrangements)[174] and physical custody (the right to provide routine daily care and control of the child).[175] This distinction parallels the distinction between guardianship and

---

[169] Id. St. 32–717B(5) ('There shall be a presumption that joint custody is not in the best interests of a minor child if one (1) of the parents is found by the court to be a habitual perpetrator of domestic violence.') (Idaho); Australia Family Law Act, 1975 (as amended), Section 61DA(2) (Presumption that equal parental responsibility is in the best interest of the child does not apply if there are reasonable ground to believe that a parent has engaged in abuse or family violence.)

[170] *Braiman* v. *Braiman*, 44 NY 2d 584 (1978) (citations omitted); see also *Padgen and Padgen* (1991) FLC 92-231 (Austr.) (setting preconditions for shared custody, including compatible parenting, mutual trust, cooperation, and good communication).

[171] *Padgen and Padgen* (1991) FLC 92-231 (Austr.).

[172] A. Barrat and S. Burman, 'Deciding the Best Interests of the Child', 118 *South African Law Journal* (2001).

[173] *In re A,* [2008] EWCA Civ 867, para 66.

[174] See V.A.M.S. 452.375(1)(2) ('Joint legal custody' means that the parents share the decision-making rights, responsibilities, and authority relating to the health, education and welfare of the child, and, unless allocated, apportioned, or decreed, the parents shall confer with one another in the exercise of decision-making rights, responsibilities, and authority.'); 15 V.S.A., Section 664(1)(A) ("Legal responsibility" means the rights and responsibilities to determine and control various matters affecting a child's welfare and upbringing, other than routine daily care and control of the child. These matters include but are not limited to education, medical and dental care, religion and travel arrangements. Legal responsibility may be held solely or may be divided or shared.')

[175] See VA Code Ann., section 20-124.1 ('Joint custody' means ... (ii) joint physical custody where both parents share physical and custodial care of the child.'); 15 V.S.A., section 664(1)(B) ("Physical responsibility" means the rights and responsibilities to provide routine daily care and control of the child subject to the right of the other parent to have contact with the child. Physical responsibility may be held solely or may be divided or shared.'); Ga. Code Ann., Section 19–9–6(3) ("Joint physical custody" means

custody in India. Some jurisdictions use other terms for this distinction. In Australia, for example, 'parental responsibility'—defined as 'the duties, powers, responsibilities and authority which, by law, parents have in relation to children'—is distinct from the amount of time the child spends with each of the parents.[176] Similarly in France, 'parental authority', which refers to 'a set of rights and duties whose finality is the welfare of the child',[177] is distinct from a parent's right of access and lodging. Kenya distinguishes between 'legal custody' and 'actual custody'.

United Nations Convention on the Rights of the Child, 1989

The UNCRC is an internationally recognized agreement between nations which establishes a comprehensive set of goals for individual nations to achieve on behalf of their children.

In general, the convention calls for

1. freedom from violence, abuse, hazardous employment, exploitation, abduction or sale;
2. adequate nutrition;
3. free compulsory primary education;
4. adequate health care;
5. equal treatment regardless of gender, race, or cultural background;
6. the right to express opinions and freedom of thought in matters affecting them;
7. safe exposure/access to leisure, play, culture, and art.

Recognizing the special vulnerability of children, all of these goals are expressed with respect to a child's age and evolving capacities—the child's best interests are always the paramount concern. The convention repeatedly emphasizes the primacy and importance of the role, authority, and responsibility of parents and family; it is neutral on abortion; and is consistent with the principles contained in the Bill of Rights.

The UNCRC is the most complete statement of children's rights and is the first to give these rights the force of international law. A child is defined in the convention as a person under the age of 18, unless national laws mandate an earlier age of majority.

Article 41 provides that nothing in the convention is to affect provisions in a State's laws which are more conducive to the realization of the rights of the child than the provisions of the convention.

Article 9 gives a right not to be separated from parents except in certain limited circumstances, for example, 'where the parents are living separately and a decision must be made as to the child's place of residence'.

---

that physical custody is shared by the parents in such a way as to assure the child of substantially equal time and contact with both parents.')

[176] Cf. Australia Family Law Act 1975, section 61B ('In this part, parental responsibility, in relation to a child, means all the duties, powers, responsibilities and authority which, by law, parents have in relation to children.'), *with* Australia Family Law Act, 1975, Section 61DA (the presumption that parents have equal responsibility 'does not provide for a presumption about the amount of time the child spends with each of the parents').

[177] France Civil Code, Article 371-71.

Article 9(3) provides that 'State parties shall respect the right of the child who is separated from one or both parents to maintain personal relations and direct contact with both parents on a regular basis, except if it is contrary to the child's best interests'.

The convention refers to one of the provisions of the Declaration of the Rights of the Child which provides that the child, by reason of his physical and mental immaturity, needs special safeguards and care, including appropriate legal protection.

Article 3(1) of the convention provides, 'in all actions concerning children, whether undertaken by public or private social welfare institutions, courts of law, administrative authorities or legislative bodies, the best interests of the child shall be a primary consideration'.

Article 18(1) obliges State Parties to use their best efforts to ensure recognition of the role of parents in protecting the interests of children and that *both* parents have common responsibilities for the upbringing and development of the child. This also applies to legal guardians.

Article 12 recognizes that a child does have views which should be given weight in accordance with his age and maturity.

Article 12(2) provides: 'for this purpose, the child shall in particular be provided the opportunity to be heard in any judicial and administrative proceedings affecting the child, either directly or through a representative or an appropriate body, in a manner consistent with the procedural rules of national law.'

The convention directs the state parties to ensure that 'both parents have common responsibilities for the upbringing and development of the child'.[178] The UNCRC provides that a child should be separated from his or her parents if there is 'abuse or neglect of the child by the parents, or where the parents are living separately and a decision must be made as to the child's place of residence'.[179] Welfare of the child, as a criterion for decision, is generally flexible, adaptable, and reflective of contemporary social attitudes regarding the family.[180]

The Committee on the Rights of the Child has provided additional guidance regarding the best interest standard in its General Comment 14.[181] The committee stated that it is 'useful to draw up a non-exhaustive and non-hierarchical list of elements that could be included in a best-interests assessment by any decision-maker having to determine a child's best interests'.[182] The committee suggested that the following considerations can be relevant: the child's views; the child's identity (such as sex, sexual orientation, national origin, religion and beliefs, cultural identity, and personality); preservation of the family environment and maintaining relations (including, where appropriate, extended family or community); the care, protection, and safety of the child; any situation of vulnerability (disability, minority status, homelessness, abuse, and so on); and the child's right to health and right to education.[183] However, there are two main criticisms of the best interest standard when applied to custody issues.

[178] UNCRC, Article 18.

[179] UNCRC, Article 9.

[180] Stephen Gilmore, *Great Debates: Family Law* (Palgrave Macmillian, 2014), pp. 76–83.

[181] Committee on the Rights of the Child, General Comment No. 14 on the Right of the Child to Have His or Her Best Interests Taken as a Primary Consideration (art. 3, para. 1), U.N. Doc. CRC/C/GC/14 (29 May 2013).

[182] Committee on the Rights of the Child, General Comment 14, at para 50.

[183] Committee on the Rights of the Child, General Comment 14, at paras 52–79.

First, it is unpredictable and information intensive. Parents who are divorcing are left guessing as to how the courts will make custody decisions; this can lead to unnecessary pre-court bargaining that may be harmful to both the child and the parents.[184] This can be resolved by a more predictable rule-based standard which delineates the content of the best interest standard. On the other hand, a rule-based standard is likely to be rigid and not consider the individual circumstances of each case.[185] Second, the best interest standard primarily focuses on the predicaments of the child alone and does not take into consideration the feelings and interests of the parents. The parents are also actors within the family who have rights, and any legal framework must account for their welfare as well.[186] Thus, it is an open question whether the best interest of the child standard is an adequate legal tool to resolve child custody decisions, or whether it needs to be supplemented with further legislative guidelines.

The Hague Convention on the Civil Aspects of International Child Abduction, 1980[187]

The Hague Convention, 1980 encompasses nearly all European countries, including some of the former Soviet and Yugoslav republics, and other westernized countries around the world. Members also include a few countries in Africa, South America, and the pro-Western margins of the Middle East. As of July 2015, 93 states are party to the convention.[188]

The United States Congress enacted the International Child Abduction Remedies Act (ICARA)[189] as the implementing legislation for the Hague Convention, 1980. The ICARA establishes the convention as the law of the USA, provides definitions, sets forth jurisdiction, and addresses certain details regarding how the USA will enforce the provisions of the treaty. The ICARA explicitly states that its provisions are in addition to, and not in lieu of, the Hague Convention, 1980.[190]

The Hague Convention, 1980 provides for immediate return of children who are taken from their country of 'habitual residence' in violation of 'custody rights'.[191] It is not concerned with substantive custody questions or even with jurisdiction; its purpose is to send children back to their primary residence where they came from after making a determination about a very limited set of factual questions. It is a sort of extradition, but should not be confused with it.

---

[184] Committee on the Rights of the Child, General Comment 14, at paras 52–79.

[185] Committee on the Rights of the Child, General Comment 14, at paras 52–79.

[186] Committee on the Rights of the Child, General Comment 14, at paras 52–79.

[187] Concluded on 25 October 1980 and entered into force between the signatories on 1 December 1983.

[188] 'Status Table: Convention of 25 October 1980 on the Civil Aspects of International Child Abduction', Hague Conference on Private International Law, 14 June 2011. Available at https://www.hcch.net/en/instruments/conventions/status-table/?cid=24 (accessed on 17 July 2015).

[189] Pub. L. No. 100-300, 102 Stat. 437 (1988) (ICARA). The ICARA is codified at 42 U.S.C., sections 11601–11611. The ICARA was created to deal with the international abduction of children and to allow a petitioner to assert his or her rights in exigent circumstances. See *Distler* v. *Distler*, 26 F. Supp. 2d 723, 727 (D.N.J. 1998).

[190] See 42 U.S.C., Section 11601(b)(2).

[191] The Hague Convention, Article 4.

Article 16 of the convention specifically bars courts in countries to which children have been abducted from considering the merits of custody once they receive notice of the wrongful removal or retention of the children.

The Hague Convention, 1980 provides that all Contracting States, as well as any judicial and administrative bodies of those Contracting States, 'shall act expeditiously in all proceedings seeking the return of a children' and that those institutions shall use the most expeditious procedures available to the end that final decision be made within six weeks from the date of commencement of the proceedings.[192]

The convention provides that if the petitioner successfully proves a prima facie case, the child must be returned unless the respondent can prove that an affirmative defence applies. The petitioner must demonstrate a prima facie case by a preponderance of the evidence.[193]

The elements of a prima facie case are enumerated in Articles 3[194] and 4[195] of the Hague Convention, 1980. Courts have recognized that the petitioner establishes a prima facie case if he or she proves three elements:

1. prior to removal or wrongful retention, the child was habitually resident in a foreign country;
2. the removal or retention was in breach of custody rights under the foreign country's law; and
3. the petitioner actually was exercising custody rights at the time of the removal or wrongful retention.[196]

If the petitioner establishes a prima facie case, the abducted child must be returned to the country of habitual residence unless the respondent can prove that one of the designated affirmative defences applies.[197]

Although most decisions recite these three elements as establishing a prima facie case, technically there is at least one more element: proving that the abducted child is under the age of 16. This is a critical element of the Hague Convention case because, as discussed further below,

---

[192] The Hague Convention, Article 11.

[193] 42 U.S.C., Section 11603(e).

[194] The Hague Convention, Article 3:

The removal or the retention of a child is to be considered wrongful where

(1) it is in breach of rights of custody attributed to a person, an institution or any other body, either jointly or alone, under the law of the state in which the child was habitually resident immediately before the removal or retention; and

(2) at the time of removal or retention those rights were actually exercised, either jointly or alone, or would have been so exercised but for the removal or retention. The rights of custody mentioned in subparagraph (1) above, may arise in particular by operation of law or by reason of a judicial or administrative decision, or by reason of an agreement having legal effect under the law of that state.

[195] The Hague Convention, Article 4: 'The Convention shall apply to any child who was habitually resident in a Contracting State immediately before any breach of custody or access rights. The Convention shall cease to apply when the child attains the age of 16 years.'

[196] The Hague Conventions, Articles 3 and 4.

[197] *Furnes* v. *Reeves*, 362 F.3d 702, 722 (11th Cir. 2004).

Article 4 of the convention explicitly states: 'The Convention shall cease to apply when the child attains the age of 16 years.'[198] Even if a child is under 16 at the time of the wrongful removal or retention as well as when the convention is invoked, the convention ceases to apply when the child reaches 16.[199] Thus, once a child reaches the age of 16, the child cannot be returned under the convention, even if the child was less than 16 years old at the time of wrongful removal, and even if the petition was filed when the child was less than 16 years old.[200]

In addition, although not part of the petitioner's prima facie case, if the petitioner can demonstrate that the petition is filed within 1 year of the wrongful removal or retention, then the well-settled affirmative defence in Article 12 of the Hague Convention, 1980[201] does not apply. Thus, while technically not part of the petitioner's prima facie case, proving that the petition was filed within 1 year of wrongful removal or retention is critically important.

Important features of the convention include:

1. For the Hague Convention, 1980 to apply, the abducted child must have been 'habitually resident in a Contracting State immediately before any breach of custody or access rights'.[202]
2. To be actionable under the Hague Convention, 1980, child abduction and retention cases must be international, and the involved countries must be recognized by the USA as signatories to the convention.[203]

---

[198] The Hague Convention, Article 4.

[199] The Hague International Child Abduction Convention: Text and Legal Analysis, 51 Fed. Reg. 10494 (1986) (Public Notice 957).

[200] Articles 18, 29, and 34 make clear that the convention is a non-exclusive remedy in cases of international child abduction. Article 18 provides that the convention does not limit the power of a judicial authority to order return of a child at any time, presumably under other laws, procedures, or comity, irrespective of the child's age. Article 29 permits the person who claims a breach of custody or access rights, as defined by Articles 3 and 21, to bypass the convention completely by invoking any applicable laws or procedures to secure the child's return. Likewise, Article 34 provides that the convention shall not restrict the application of any law in the state addressed for purposes of obtaining the child's return or for organizing visitation rights. Assuming such laws are not restricted to children under 16, a child 16 or over may be returned pursuant to their provisions.

[201] The Hague Convention, Article 12:

Where a child has been wrongfully removed or retained in terms of Article 3 and, at the date of the commencement of the proceedings before the judicial or administrative authority of the Contracting State where the child is, a period of less than 1 year has elapsed from the date of the wrongful removal or retention, the authority concerned shall order the return of the child forthwith. The judicial or administrative authority, even where the proceedings have been commenced after the expiration of the period of 1 year referred to in the preceding paragraph, shall also order the return of the child, unless it is demonstrated that the child is now settled in its new environment. Where the judicial or administrative authority in the requested State has reason to believe that the child has been taken to another State, it may stay the proceedings or dismiss the application for the return of the child.

[202] The Hague Convention, Article 4.

[203] The Hague International Child Abduction Convention: Text and Legal Analysis, 51 Fed. Reg. 10494 (1986) (Public Notice 957).

3. The determination of habitual residence also is important because the parents' custody rights are governed by the laws of the country of habitual residence.[204]

4. A valid petition must allege that removal or retention of the child was wrongful. As is true for all other elements of a prima facie case, the petitioner must prove this element by a preponderance of the evidence.[205]

5. In addition to possessing custody rights under the laws of the country where the child habitually resides, the petitioner also must exercise those rights.[206]

Exceptions to a Country's Obligation to Return a Child

Under the convention, a country may refuse to return an abducted child or grant access to the child if one of the following exceptions apply:

1. The child has become well-settled in the new surroundings.[207]

2. The petitioners consented to or acquiesced in the removal or retention.[208]

3. There is a grave risk that the child would be exposed to physical or psychological harm or otherwise placed in an intolerable situation in his or her country of habitual residence.[209]

4. The child objects to being returned and has reached an age and degree of maturity at which the court can take account of the child's views.[210]

5. The return would violate the fundamental principles of human rights and freedoms of the country where the child is being held.[211]

Access or visitation: Partners to the convention also agree to respect the rights of custody and access/visitation from other partner countries. One can apply through the convention to establish or enforce the access/visitation rights to one's children living in other partner countries.

---

[204] The Hague Convention, Article 3(a).

[205] 42 U.S.C., Section 11603(e).

[206] Courts have required that the petitioner demonstrate, by a preponderance of the evidence, that he or she actually was exercising custody rights at the time of removal; *Krefter* v. *Wills*, 623 F. Supp. 2d 125, 135 (D. Mass. 2009); or immediately prior to the removal or retention; the Hague Convention, Article 3; *Nicolson* v. *Pappalardo*, 674 F. Supp. 2d 295, 298 (D. Me. 2009); cf. *Olguin* v. *Cruz Santana*, No. 03 CV 6299 (JG), 2004 WL 1752444, at *4 (E.D.N.Y. Aug. 5, 2004) (holding that the respondent bore the burden of proving by a preponderance of the evidence her claim that petitioners were not actually exercising custody rights at the time of the removal) and *Morrison-Dietz* v. *Dietz*, No. 07-1398, 2008 WL 4280030, at *6 (W.D. La. 17 September 2008) (holding that 'the party opposing the return has a burden of proving, by a preponderance of the evidence, that the other party was not actually exercising custody rights') (citations omitted), aff'd, 349 F. App'x 930 (5th Cir. 2009).

[207] The Hague Convention, Article 12.

[208] The Hague Convention, Article 13(a).

[209] 42 U.S.C., Section 11603(e)(2).

[210] The Hague Convention, Article 13.

[211] The Hague Convention, Article 20.

India and the Hague Convention on Civil Aspects of International Child Abduction 1980

As of now, India is not a party to the Hague Convention, 1980. Other than the statutory provisions of law quoted above, in which matters of child custody are agitated in different courts in different proceedings, the principles of the convention cannot be enforced in Indian Courts. Different recent decisions indicate a trend that Indian courts generally tend to decide the inter-parental child custody disputes on the paramount consideration of the welfare of the child and the best interest of the child. A foreign court custody order is only one of the considerations in adjudicating any such child custody dispute between parents. Foreign court orders of child custody are no longer mechanically enforced and normally the Indian courts go into the merits of the matter to decide the best interest of the child, irrespective of any foreign court custody order. Hence, the position of law in India varies on a case to case basis and there is no uniform precedent which can be quoted or cited as a universal rule. Due to India not being a signatory to the Hague Convention of 1980, questions regarding the custody of such children are now considered by the Indian courts on the merits of each case bearing the welfare of the child to be of paramount importance, while considering the order made by the foreign court to be only one of the relevant factors in such decision.

***

The area of private international law is at its infancy stage in India. Due to the lack of legislative developments in this regard, both at the international and domestic levels, the sole refuge can be sought before the judiciary. Similar is the situation in the cases of inter-parental child abduction in India. Although the judiciary has been showing remarkable creativity in dealing with a plethora of such cases, the temporary nature of this solution cannot be disputed. As such, a more consistent and permanent legal response is awaited. The first step that can be taken in this direction is the signing of the 1980 Convention. Further, adoption of the convention by the legislature should follow. Besides, bilateral agreements should be signed with the other non-signatory countries in this regard.

Some Legal Developments and Trends of Comparative Law

When the needs of children cannot be met by those responsible for their care, the state recognizes its responsibility to intervene and assure their care, development, and safety. A survey of comparative legal interventions in custody and guardianship proceedings reveal that the practice of democratic legal systems has accepted, on a wide front, the challenge of individualization. Wide powers have been given to the courts to make decisions based on the welfare of children during marital proceedings.

1. Growth of the child-welfare professions and the desire to reach better and more justifiable decisions in children's cases have shifted the reasoning in these cases towards arguments based on theories of child development. The courts rely on the evidence of experts and reports from welfare officers. But the 'child welfare science' is reconstructed by the legal process.
2. As a general rule, children are represented by a next friend or guardian ad litem. A child who wishes to proceed without a guardian ad litem must seek leave of the court.

3. The definition of the child in developed countries is a person who is under the age of 18.

4. The opinion of the minor is considered in deciding custody. In Hong Kong, the age is above 10 years and in Australia it is 14 years or over.

5. The welfare principle applies not only to courts but also to parents, local authorities, and children themselves.

6. Evaluators get involved in a family's legal dispute and the custody and visitation of the family's minor children. The evaluators help the courts understand the family dynamics in a way that will allow for the development of an appropriate plan for custody and visitation of minor children.

7. In developed countries it is a well-settled law that the religion of the minor is not at all a relevant factor in determining the custody of the child. In developing countries, the law is still to be settled. However, the trends are changing through case laws.

8. The law imposes duty on children to support and assist their parents.

9. There has been an arbitration of awards by courts.

10. The child's interests are represented in matrimonial disputes.

11. The arbitration option is given to the parties in dispute.

12. Conciliation counselling in an attempt to bring about an agreement.

13. Mediation has become an important option.

14. Alternative dispute resolution (ADR) techniques in custody disputes.

15. Unified family courts bring together under one-court custody and guardianship disputes, as well as juvenile justice matters.

16. Strong evidence is needed to justify a change of custody.

17. Third parties, relatives, and friends may stand as sureties for the implementation of schemes relating to children.

18. The maintenance amount for children can be deposited with an accredited organization charged with paying the children periodical allowances.

19. Finding the least worst solution will force the lawyers and judges to confront the perils in other choices available.

20. The gender-based tender years doctrine was found unconstitutional by some US courts, but it was retained in the best interest of the child.

21. In the tender-years doctrine, the emphasis is not on women's rights to companionship of the child, but on the tender years interest of a breast-feeding the child.

22. Consensus is lacking on how much weight is to be given to the child's preference.

23. Scientific evaluations of child-custody decisions are carried out.

24. A continuing conflict-riddled relationship between parents can be determinant in joint custody arrangement.

25. Today, custody mediations are being questioned because of their 'non-legal' character.

26. In-service training is being given to develop professional ability and skill.

27. The family court clinic is an auxiliary organ of the court for scientific examination and diagnosis of parties and juveniles.

28. Senior citizens and volunteers from the public are involved.

29. Attendants are appointed as defence counsel for a child.

30. One of the judges of the matrimonial court is exclusively appointed to take charge of safeguarding the interests of minor children.

31. The child's wishes are presented in an affidavit.
32. Access is a right of the child which promotes its welfare and should be denied only in exceptional circumstances.
33. Casework method is used to diagnose the cause of a particular trouble and to prescribe a reasonable remedy.
34. The court plays a supervisory role for the protection of the welfare of families.
35. Judges and probation officers are expected to use wide professional skills in the field of medicine, psychology, pedagogy, sociology, and other sciences related to human beings.
36. Welfare conferences to discuss the welfare of the child should be held.
37. Judicial interviews should be sparingly used.
38. The child's counsel should make submissions on the welfare of the child and put forward the wishes of the child.
39. Paramountcy of welfare is a principle whereby all the relevant facts, relationships, claims, and wishes of the parents, risks, choices, and other circumstances are taken into account and weighed.
40. A list of factors of the welfare checklist from various countries include

    • the mental and physical health of all individuals involved;
    • age of the child;
    • sex of the child;
    • mental sturdiness of the child;
    • the child's adjustment to home, school, and community;
    • each parent's ability to provide food, clothing, medication, and other benefits to the child;
    • parent's lifestyle;
    • wishes of the child;
    • needs of the child;
    • separation of siblings;
    • moral guilt of parents;
    • characteristics of parents;
    • continuity principle;
    • housing conditions;
    • school situation;
    • playmates for the child;
    • remarriage of parents;
    • wishes of the parents;
    • religion or faith of parents;
    • views of experts;
    • representation of the child's interests;
    • health or financial difficulties of parties;
    • priority to parties who can no longer have any children;
    • a parent who lives with the child longer than the other parent and where a clearly negative impact would be experienced by the child as a result of change of environment;
    • healthy growth of the child;
    • he relations between the child and parents;

- lifestyle of parents (conventional morality);
- religious convictions;
- detailed future scheme which would be put into action to ensure the maintenance and education of children, along with sureties for its implementation;
- consequences of the court's decision;
- least detrimental solution.

Legislations include a duty to minimize delay because of the damage the uncertainty of litigation could do to children, and the existence of a legal culture where delay is acceptable. Decision-making processes should take account of the child's sense of time. The paramountcy of the child's welfare and the speed with which young children develop attachments mean that delay often benefits one of the adults and harms the child.

Above all, the trend is to view the family divorce through the eyes of children, understand how children feel, what they fear and wish, and what makes conflict resolution difficult to be achieved. We need to stay focused on the needs of the children who have the most to lose, and finally, we must reduce the pain for the children—the real pawns in the game of their parents' divorce.

Law Commission's Report on 'Best Interest of the Child' in International Human Rights Law[212]

While the 'welfare of the child' principle dominates the domestic legal framework, a comparable legal standard is found in international human rights law. According to the UNCRC, 'in all actions concerning children, whether undertaken by public or private social welfare institutions, courts of law, administrative authorities or legislative bodies, the best interests of the child shall be a primary consideration'.[213]

The convention directs the State Parties to ensure that 'both parents have common responsibilities for the upbringing and development of the child'.[214] The UNCRC provides that a child should be separated from his or her parents if there is 'abuse or neglect of the child by the parents, or where the parents are living separately and a decision must be made as to the child's place of residence'.[215] Welfare of the child, as a criterion for decision, is generally flexible, adaptable, and reflective of contemporary attitudes regarding family within society.[216]

The Committee on the Rights of the Child has provided additional guidance regarding the best interest standard in its General Comment 14.9. The Committee stated that it is 'useful to draw up a non-exhaustive and non-hierarchical list of elements that could be included in a best-interests assessment by any decision-maker having to determine a child's best interests'.[217] The Committee suggested that the following considerations can be relevant: the child's views;

---

[212] Law Commission of India, Report No. 257 on proposed 'Reforms in Guardianship and Custody Laws in India'.

[213] UNCRC, Article 3 (1989).

[214] UNCRC, Article 18 (1989).

[215] UNCRC, Article 9 (1989).

[216] Gilmore, *Great Debates*, pp. 76–83.

[217] General Comment 14, at para 50.

the child's identity (such as sex, sexual orientation, national origin, religion and beliefs, cultural identity, and personality); preservation of the family environment and maintaining relations (including, where appropriate, extended family or community); the care, protection, and safety of the child; any situation of vulnerability (disability, minority status, homelessness, abuse, and so on); and the child's right to health and right to education.[218] However, there are two main criticisms of the best-interest standard when applied to custody issues.

First, it is unpredictable and information intensive. Parents who are divorcing are left guessing as to how the courts will make custody decisions; this can lead to unnecessary pre-court bargaining that may be harmful to both the child and the parents.[219] This could be resolved by a more predictable rule-based standard, which delineates the content of the best interest standard. On the other hand, a rule-based standard is likely to be rigid and not consider the individual circumstances of each case.[220] Second, the best-interest standard primarily focuses on the predicaments of the child alone and does not take into consideration the feelings and interests of the parents. The parents are also actors within the family who have rights and any legal framework must account for their welfare as well.[221] Thus, it is an open question whether the best-interest standard is an adequate legal tool to resolve child custody decisions, or whether it needs to be supplemented with further legislative guidelines.

Discussion

It is clear that rulings granting custody are affected by issues like poverty, character, adultery, immorality, religion, sex, age, abandonment, remarriage, wishes of parents and children, and nearness of kin.[222] These are the factors that are taken into account by the courts while determining the best interests of the child.

There are no hard-and-fast rules or precedents; in fact, there cannot be. Decisions are based on the facts and circumstances of each case. Courts often prefer not to disturb the status quo and generally place the child in the custody of the person who has already exercised custody at the time of petition. Courts have also, in recent times, rejected the arguments relating working women to economic well-being, but in some cases orthodox views still persist. Issues like child abuse and cruelty to children have not come up frequently. The child's interests are fashioned primarily on the perspective, needs, and wishes of competing adult claimants, or to protect the general policies of childcare, or what the adults perceive to be the best interest of the child. Wherever possible, the courts have taken the wishes of children into account, but many children can be easily tutored by the undue influence of the non-custodial parent against the absentee parent.

Clearly, the best-interest standard gives judges tremendous discretion. The background of judges and their understanding as to what is the best interest of the child play an important role. It is still a question of 'proved' and 'not proved', based on the facts presented before the courts. There also appears to be tension between the apparent meaning of the best interest standard and

---

[218] General Comment 14, at paras 52–79.
[219] General Comment 14, at paras 52–79.
[220] General Comment 14, at paras 52–79.
[221] General Comment 14, at paras 52–79.
[222] Paras Diwan, *Muslim Law in Modern India* (Delhi: Wadhwa and Co., 1987), pp. 128, 129.

its construction in legislative and court decisions. There are also risks to the child due to delays and adjournments that are a regular feature of the legal system.

Since the child is not represented in the Indian courts, it is up to the judge to ensure that the child's interests are not harmed or negated. The judges are not trained or sensitized to be friendly. Besides, even in those cases where the courts have managed to determine the best interests of the child, the social, administrative, and enforcement machinery is not sensitive enough to implement them.

Child sexual abuse cases have now started coming up in custody matters brought before courts. Orders granting custody of children to one parent are invariably accompanied by an order granting visitation rights to the non-custodial parent. Courts are of the view that it is essential for the healthy emotional development of the children to have continued contact with the non-custodial parent. But the visitation rights to the non-custodial parent do not always serve the best interest of the child. There is now a need for the non-custodial parent to justify and the courts to determine whether visitation rights and access are in the best interest of the child. The non-custodial parent could interfere with the quality of relationship between the child and the custodial parent.

Some courts recognize joint custody. Joint legal custody entitles both parents to share equally in all decisions relating to the child's upbringing, medical care, and attention. However, the quality of the child–parent relationship appears to be a function of the degree of conflict rather than the custody arrangement; the ex-partners displaying the most bitterness also have the most conflictual relationship with their children, even when the children are in joint custody.[223]

Assessing the 'Parent–Child Goodness of Fit'

Courts in India have recognized the welfare principle, but many aspects of the legal and judicial framework remain wanting. Courts tend to grant custody of a child to either one parent or another, presuming that it is for the welfare of the child. Joint-custody arrangements, where both parents have custody of the child, are rarely considered. Problems in court decisions are compounded by inconsistencies in the law. For instance, the HMGA regards the welfare of the child as being of paramount consideration, but the GWA contains no such provision. Similarly, the HMGA does not treat the mother on an equal footing with the father as the natural guardian of her child. Further, custody battles are among the most fiercely fought in courts, because there is no agreement or understanding about what constitutes the welfare of the child. As a result, it is impossible to ensure that the interests of the child are actually protected. The legal framework also contains no guidelines about the manner and process by which custody issues should be handled.[224]

Children constitute an arena for parental power struggles. The toughest part of custodial decisions occurs in assessing this 'parent–child goodness of fit'. It involves gathering of data from several sources—interviews, reports, psychological testing, projective techniques, and direct

[223] P.R. Amato and S.J. Rezac, 'Contact with Non-residential Parents, Interparental Conflict, and Children's Behaviour', *Journal of Family Issues* 15 (1994): 191–207.

[224] Law Commission of India, 'Reforms in Guardianship and Custody Laws in India'.

observation of each parent, both individually and with children. After gathering the data, it has to be integrated and assigned weights to the relative meaning of each fact before making a responsible, fact-based decision. It is a unique and speculated skill of extrapolating meaningful recommendations, from a decision-making strategy that combines data from a variety of sources along a variety of different behavioural dimensions, into a coherent whole. This requires the involvement of several experts along with the judge. In the superior courts, there have been instances as in Thrity Dolikukas case, where the Supreme Court has appointed independent experts, but there is no such instance at the trial-courts level. Many of the trial courts and even high courts have erred in their decision-making and the child has had to go through unnecessary trauma and further litigation. No court has looked into the lifelong trauma of the child. There can never be any compensation for such trauma, but a provision to this effect can go a long way in creating awareness on this aspect. There is also a need for follow-up of the custody decisions.

The courts have considered the wishes of the child, but children whose parents are separated or are in conflict situations may be predicated to demonstrate some behaviour of distress or confusion more often than many children in intact families. The wishes expressed to the court may not always be their own. They may not want to 'hurt' the feelings of the custodial parent or their wishes can be 'influenced' by several factors, which might not have come up before the court.

How can courts make routine decisions in cases of custody? Custody cases have to be treated differently. It is a parental tug-of-war in which each parent claims his or her legal rights while tearing the child apart. Rarely is it a simple process to evaluate both parents and the child and determine the best interests of the child. Finally, it is undoubtedly true that the best parenting is achieved with two parents.

Originally, unless the father was unfit, he had an absolute 'right to the custody and control' of a child. Later, the decisions swung to the presumption that a child of tender years should be placed with the mother.

In the legal process the courts usually consider children through a paternalistic discourse. Whether the talk is of 'needs', 'welfare', or 'best interest' of the child, it is adults who interpret this. Analysis of the process reveals that the focus of law is inevitably drawn to competing adults. This is so whether they are seeking possession of the child as object or are engaged in a power struggle over the child. The discourse of judges and lawyers who claim to take into account only the interest of the child (as opposed to the interests of each of the parents) can be countered by showing that when they speak of the child, they are inevitably speaking of something else—the father, the mother, the family. Courts also rested the issue of custody solely on the welfare of the child.

Law Reform

Law Reform in the Best Interest of the Child

The welfare of the child as the sole consideration or paramount consideration is the principle, found at present only in the substantive laws on custody and guardianship. The other substantive and procedural laws are silent on this issue. In fact, the best-interest principle should be included in all the substantive and procedural laws including the matrimonial laws, the CPC, and the CrPC.

There is a lot of emphasis on the age of the child, which is arbitrarily fixed in many legislations. The best interest interpretation needs to be adopted on this issue and one can err on the side of higher age limit for protective care, and lower age limit for special rights in respect of civil and cultural matters, as the courts and the enforcement authorities are at present interpreting it very technically and narrowly.

Determining the best interests of the child demands that medical justice, educational justice, recreational justice, nutritional justice, and participatory justice are included. The courts need new institutional arrangements and involvement of professional services before passing an order.

The 133rd Law Commission Report[225] made several recommendations in the existing laws relating to custody and guardianship of children. These amendments need to be incorporated in the laws relating to custody and guardianship. A summary of the recommendations is as follows.

The mother should have same and equal (and not inferior) rights vis-à-vis the father

The provision contained in Section 6(a) of the HMGA, constituting the father as a natural guardian of a Hindu minor's person as well as in respect of his property in preference to the mother, should be amended so as to constitute both the father and the mother as being natural guardians 'jointly and severally'—having equal rights in respect of the minor—because there is no jurisdiction for according a superior and preferential treatment to the father vis-à-vis the mother of the minor, and besides, it violates Article 15 of the Constitution of India.

The custody of a minor who has not completed 12 years of age shall ordinarily be with the mother

The proviso to Subsection (a) of Section 6 of the HMGA needs to be amended so that the custody of a boy or an unmarried girl who has not completed the age of 12 years (instead of the age limit of 5 years as prescribed at present) shall ordinarily be with the mother.

The third amendment lays down some important considerations in the application of the welfare principle

The welfare principle projected in Section 13 of the HMGA and Section 17 of the GWA needs to be amplified and spelt out so as to make the following explicit.

1. Where the father has remarried, the custody of the minor, irrespective of the minor's age, shall ordinarily be with the mother. The minor should not be obliged to live with his or her stepmother unless there are exceptional circumstances which shall be recorded in writing.
2. Where the mother has remarried, a female child should not be made to live with her stepfather in order to guard against possible sexual abuse and harassment. The court may consider

---

[225] Government of India, Ministry of Law, Justice and Company Affairs, the 133rd Law Commission Report, 'Removal of Discrimination against Women in Matters Relating to Guardianship and Custody of Minor Children' (New Delhi: 1989).

whether the paternal or maternal grandparents should be entrusted with the custody of the female child on merits.

3. Where the mother has remarried but the father has not, ordinarily the minor, even if a male child, should not be made to live with the stepfather.

4. Where both the father and mother have remarried, the court may determine whether to entrust the guardianship and/or custody to the father, the mother, or the grandparents, depending on what the court considers to be conducive to the maximum welfare of the minor in the light of the facts of each case.

5. A mother shall not be denied the custody of the minor merely on the ground that the father is in more affluent circumstances or that the mother's economic circumstances are not as good as those of the father.

6. In applying the welfare principle, the court shall have due regard to the fact that the minor needs emotional support and warmth of the mother, who is ordinarily better equipped than the father to impart such emotional support and warmth which are essential for building up a balanced personality.

Grandparents shall have equal claim in the matter of appointment of guardian of a minor, irrespective of whether they are paternal grandparents or maternal grandparents

In considering the question of appointment of guardian of the person and the property of a minor and entrustment of the custody of a minor, the circumstances whether the grandparents are from the paternal side or maternal side should be disregarded. The paternal grandparents on the one hand, and maternal grandparents on the other, shall be treated at par, having equal claim to be appointed in this behalf, subject to the paramount consideration regarding the welfare of the minor.

It should be recognized that both father and mother have a claim to the exclusion of others to be appointed a guardian of a minor unless considered unfit by the court

Section 19(b) of the GWA, which inter alia provides that the court will be authorized to appoint the guardian of the person of a minor whose father is living and is not, in the opinion of the court, unfit to be the guardian of the person of the minor, deserves to be amended so as to accord equal treatment to the mother by incorporating a reference to the mother along with that to the father. It should be provided that the court will not be authorized to appoint the guardian of the person of a minor whose *father or mother* is living and is, in the opinion of the court, not unfit to be the guardian of the person of the minor, for there is no rational basis for discriminating between the father of a minor on the one hand and the mother of a minor on the other, in the context of this provision. A consequential amendment also needs to be made in Section 41(e) by substituting the words 'father or mother' in place of the word 'father', wherever it occurs therein.

Section 7 of the Hindu Minority and Guardianship Act relating to guardianship of an adopted son should be amended

As at present, Section 7 of the HMGA is applicable in the context of natural guardianship of an adopted son. In view of the enactment of the law, which now enables a daughter also to be adopted, the aforementioned provision requires to be recast so as to be made applicable also to the guardianship of an adopted daughter who is a minor. So also, the phrase 'to the adoptive father and after him to the adoptive mother' needs to be substituted by the phrase 'to the adoptive father and the adoptive mother jointly and severally', for the sake of removing discrimination against women.

The laws have to clearly state that the guardianship and custody are not to be looked at from the point of view of anybody's right; they have to be looked at from the point of view of the welfare of the child and his best interest. In every case, irrespective of age, sex, religion, caste, and other factors, the best interest of the child shall prevail and shall be the only and sole criterion overriding all other considerations.

The Law Commission of India submitted its Report No. 257 on 'Reforms in Guardianship and Custody Laws in India'[226] to the union minister of law and justice on 22 June 2015. The report suggests amendments to existing laws to emphasize the 'welfare of the child' in custody and guardianship matters, and introduces the concept of joint custody as an option to be considered in certain cases. Children are the worst affected in proceedings of divorce and family breakdowns. Often, parents use children as pawns to strike their own bargains, without considering the emotional, social, and mental upheavals that the children may face. The Commission believes this imbalanced situation can be addressed in some measure through changes to the law that will place a duty upon the court to uphold the child's welfare in each and every case. This will ensure that the child's future is safe and protected, regardless of changing familial circumstances.[227]

The key aspects of the legislative recommendations are as follows:[228]

1. *Welfare principle:* The draft law strengthens the welfare principle in the GWA with a continuous emphasis on its relevance in each aspect of decision-making related to guardianship and custody.
2. *Abolition of preference:* The draft law removes the preference for the father as the natural guardian under Hindu law, and both parents are granted equal legal status with respect to guardianship and custody.
3. *Joint custody:* The draft law empowers courts to award joint custody to both parents in circumstances conducive to the welfare of the child, or award sole custody to one parent with visitation rights to the other.
4. *Mediation:* Parties to a custody matter must ordinarily consider expert-led and time-bound mediation which can not only promote better outcomes for parents and children, but also reduce the strain on the overburdened court system.
5. *Child support:* The draft law empowers courts to fix an amount specifically for child support, to meet basic living expenses of the child. Financial resources of parents and the standard of living of the child must be considered when fixing such amounts. Child support must continue till

---

226 Press Information Bureau, Government of India, Ministry of Law and Justice, 22 May 2015. Available at http://pib.nic.in/newsite/PrintRelease.aspx?relid=121932 (accessed on 17 July 2015).

227 Law Commission of India, 'Reforms in Guardianship and Custody Laws in India'.

228 Press Information Bureau, Government of India, Ministry of Law and Justice, 22 May 2015. Available at http://pib.nic.in/newsite/PrintRelease.aspx?relid=121932 (accessed on 17 July 2015).

the child turns 18, but may be extended till 25 or longer, in case of a child with mental or physical disability.

6. *Guidelines:* The draft law includes detailed guidelines to help courts, parents, and other stake-holders arrive at the best arrangement to serve the welfare of the child. The guidelines introduce several new concepts in this regard, including parenting plans, grand-parenting time, visitation rights, and relocation of parents. They also elaborate the position on related aspects such as determining the intelligent preference of a child, access to records of the child, and mediation.

Proposed Amendments to Reforms in Guardianship and Custody Laws in India by the Law Commission of India

Amendments to the Hindu Minority and Guardianship Act, 1956

1. Amendment in Section 6(a) regarding both the mother and the father as the natural guardians of a minor.

2. Removal of the anomalies vis-à-vis the GWA, relating to limitation on the court's power to appoint a guardian only when a minor's father is alive, so as to include the mother in the same vein.

3. Amendment in the proviso of Section 6(a) to ensure flexibility in cases where joint custody is awarded.

4. Amendment in Section 7 to the effect that the natural guardianship of an adopted child (in place of adopted son) who is a minor will pass, upon adoption, to the adoptive mother and father.

Amendments to the Guardians and Wards Act, 1890

1. Amendment in Sections 17 and 19 to lay stress on the welfare principle and reaffirm the rec-ommendations of the 83rd Report of the Law Commission, wherein during the appointment or declaration of a guardian, the welfare of the minor shall be the paramount consideration.

2. Amendment in Section 25

   a) Drafting of a substitute section replacing 'arrest' with the requirement to return the ward to the custody of his or her guardian.

   b) The language of the provision to clarify that the section is applicable to cases where the child is not in the custody of the guardian, though the latter is entitled to such custody.

   c) While giving an order under this section, the wishes of a child (14 years or above) shall be taken into consideration. Where a minor above 14 years has left or been removed from custody, the court is to consider the preference of that child.

3. Insertion of New Chapter IIA covering issues like custody of the child, child support, and visitation issues.

   a) Insertion of Section 19A: The objectives require that the welfare of a child be given the topmost priority. Other aspects to be considered include recognizing the changing emo-tional, intellectual, and physical needs of the child; maintaining a healthy and continuing relationship with both parents, society, and siblings; recognizing the prior and future ability and commitment of the parents to participate in the growth of the child; protecting the child from violence of any kind, and so on.

b) Insertion of Section 19B: To provide for detailed considerations in matters of custody and child support. The provisions will be in addition to the powers of the court under the IDA, the PMDA, and the HMA.

c) Insertion of Section 19C: To provide definition of joint custody and sole custody.

d) Insertion of Section 19D: To empower the courts to pass different custody orders. The court should be able to retain the power to modify the orders, provided that such modifications remain in the welfare of the child, and the reasons for the same are recorded.

e) Insertion of Section 19E: To grant additional power to Courts to enforce custody.

f) Insertion of Section 19F: Parties are recommended to go for mediation before the proceedings begin. Parties should be given opportunity to participate with trained mediators. The court should have the power to obtain independent psychological evaluation of the child in order to determine various related issues. The mediation must be time bound and must conclude within 60 days of being so ordered.

g) Insertion of Section 19G: While calculating child support, the court must take into account the financial resources of the parents, the standard of living of the child, the physical and emotional condition of the child, and other such factors. The court should have the power to continue child support even after a child attains the age of 18, and this period may extend till the age of 25 if appropriate, and not thereafter. If a child has mental or physical disability, then child support should be provided beyond 25 years of age. Further, the courts should have the power to order for the liability of the estate of a parent who dies during or after an order for child support is passed.

h) Insertion of Schedule (Guidelines): The guidelines are to discuss issues like factors to be considered when granting joint custody; determining the preference of a child; access to a child's records; parenting plan; grand-parenting time; mediation; visitation; decision-making, and relocation.

Joint Custody

The face of child-custody arrangements is changing. A number of countries across the globe have adopted a preference for shared parenting systems over sole custody as a post-divorce arrangement with respect to children. In the West, this trend has arisen largely in response to changing familial roles (male caretakers taking on more child rearing responsibilities), as well as psychological studies revealing that the involvement of both parents in child rearing is preferable to sole custody arrangements.[229] Studies indicate that children generally fare better when parents share custody, and some jurisdictions in some countries have a legally prescribed presumption of joint custody.[230] However, scholars and courts also caution that a presumption of joint custody can

[229] Government of India, 'Reforms in Guardianship and Custody Laws in India', Report No. 257, May 2015, p. 7. Available at http://lawcommissionofindia.nic.in/reports/Report%20No.257%20Custody%20 Laws.pdf (accessed on 23 September 2016).

[230] Several states in the USA have this. See, for example, Idaho Code Ann., section 32–717B(4) ('Except as provided in subsection (5), of this section, absent a preponderance of the evidence to the contrary, there

run contrary to the best-interest standard, especially in cases of domestic violence, where battered women may agree to joint custody out of fear of further violence.[231]

In November 2014, the Law Commission of India issued the 'Consultation Paper on Adopting a Shared Parenting System in India'.[232] It surveyed shared parenting.

Reasons for Adopting Joint Custody in India

First, with rapid social and economic change, conjugal and familial relationships are becoming more complex and so are the conditions of their dissolution. As these social changes that affect family life escalate, we need to update the laws governing the family relationships, during and after the marriage.[233] At present, our legal framework for custody is based on the assumption that custody can be vested with either one of the contesting parties and suitability is determined in a comparative manner. But, just as the basis for dissolving marriage has shifted over time, from fault-based divorce to mutual-consent divorce, we need to think about custody differently and provide for a broader framework within which divorcing parents and children can decide what custodial arrangement works best for them.

Second, the judicial attitude towards custody matters has evolved considerably. As legal scholar and activist Flavia Agnes notes:

> In modern day custody battles, neither the father, as the traditional natural guardian, nor the mother, as the biologically equipped parent to care for the child of tender age, are routinely awarded custody. The principle, best interest of the child takes into consideration the existing living arrangements and home environment of the child.... Each case will be decided on its own merit, taking into account the overall social, educational and emotional needs, of the child.[234]

---

shall be a presumption that joint custody is in the best interests of a minor child or children.'); Minn. Stat. Ann., section 518.17(2)(b) ('The court shall use a rebuttable presumption that upon request of either or both parties, joint legal custody is in the best interests of the child.')

[231] Botts K. Jennifer and Nestor C. Lauren, *Child Custody: Background and Policy Implications of a Joint Custody Presumption* (2011) ('Advocates for victims of domestic violence argue vehemently against placing a presumption of joint custody in the law.'). This report was prepared in response to continuing legislative interest in creating a presumption of joint custody as the standard for courts to apply when making child custody decisions. The report discusses the current law in Maryland, other states' laws, the findings of a recent study by a Minnesota commission convened to examine the issue, and arguments for and against creating a presumption of joint custody. The final report was reviewed by Susan H. Russell.

[232] The paper is available at http://lawcommissionofindia.nic.in/Consultation%20Paper%20on%20 Shared%20Parentage.pdf (accessed on 17 July 2015).

[233] Swati Deshpande, 'Divorced Dads Unite for Custody Rights', *Times of India*, 9 September 2009. Available at http://timesofindia.indiatimes.com/india/Divorced-dads-unite-for-custody-rights/articleshow/ 4988614.cms (accessed on 19 November 2016): 'Their experience is that family courts often swing totally one way or the other as child-custody battles usually end with one parent getting full control over the minor; the other parent is allowed only partial access during weekends or school holidays.')

[234] Agnes, *Family Law II*, p. 255.

Despite this development in judicial attitude, we have ignored the idea that under certain favourable circumstances, the best interest of the child could also result from simultaneous association with both the parents. Since there is no inherent contradiction between pursuing the best interest of the child and the concept of shared custody, the law needs to provide for this option, provided certain basic conditions are met.

Third, as already mentioned, a number of institutions, including the judiciary, have already started engaging with the idea of shared custody. We have earlier referred to some of these recent developments. But currently, this idea is being put into practice in a haphazard manner. There are several components to the idea of shared custody, such as clear determinants of the best interest of the child standard, the role of judges and mediators, parenting plans, and so on. These must be laid down in the law, in order for shared custody to be a viable option that facilitates divorcing parents to mutually agree on the preferred custodial arrangement, without compromising on the welfare of the child.

In the legal systems of several Western countries that we have reviewed in this chapter, there is a presumption in favour of joint custody, and sole custody is awarded only in exceptional circumstances. We have already referred to the inequalities in parental roles, responsibilities, and expectations that exists in our country. Therefore, we are not in favour of the law placing a presumption in favour of joint custody. As opposed to the case of guardianship, where we have recommended shared and equal guardianship for both parents, in this case, we are of the view that joint custody must be provided as an option that a decision-maker can award, if the decision-maker is convinced that it shall further the welfare of the child.

Mediation in Child Custody Cases

Mediation refers to a method of non-binding dispute resolution with the assistance of a neutral third party who tries to help the disputing parties to arrive at a negotiated settlement.[235] In the context of child custody, the focus of mediation is not to determine who is right or wrong, but rather to establish a solution that meets a family's needs and is in the best interest of the child.[236] The benefits of mediating a child-custody dispute are that both parents have input in determining custody and access arrangements for their children; the children feel more secure knowing that their parents are willing to continue working together to resolve family problems; parents are in the best position to decide what their children need; it helps parents develop some trust in each other, which allows for future negotiation on issues that arise; it is easier to work with a plan that parents have formulated themselves, rather than one that is imposed by the court; and it can help avoid a long and costly court battle.[237] Mediation reportedly produces better outcomes for children after divorce.[238]

[235] *Afcons Infra. Ltd.* v. *Cherian Varkey Constn.*, (2010) 8 SCC 24, para 8.

[236] Terri Garner, *Child Custody Mediation: A Proposed Alternative to Litigation*, 1989 J. DISP. RES. 139, 139–40.

[237] *Family Conciliation Services—Frequently Asked Questions*, Manitoba Family Services. Available at http://www.gov.mb.ca/fs/childfam/family_conciliation_faq.html (accessed on 17 July 2015).

[238] Danielle Gauvreau, 'Mediation Versus Litigation: Examining Differences in Outcomes amongst the Children of Divorce', *Riverdale Mediation*. Available at http://www.riverdalemediation.com/wp-content/uploads/2009/07/Gauvreau-Mediation-vs-litigation.pdf (accessed on 23 March 2015).

Current Legal Framework for Mediation in India

Section 89 of the CPC provides that a court can formulate terms of a settlement and give them to the parties for their observation and, after receiving the observation of the parties, reformulate the terms and refer the same for arbitration, conciliation, judicial settlement (including settlement through Lok Adalat), or mediation. Rule 3 of Order XXXIIA of the CPC states that in suits or proceedings relating to matters concerning the family, where it is possible to do so consistently with the nature and circumstances of the case, the court has a duty to assist the parties in arriving at a settlement. Also, if at any stage, it appears to the court that there is a reasonable possibility of a settlement between the parties, the court may adjourn the proceeding for such period as it thinks fit to enable attempts to be made to effect such a settlement.

There is a growing need of mediation for matrimonial disputes in India. In *K. Srinivas Rao* v. *D.A. Deepa*,[239] the Supreme Court stated that:

> Quite often, the cause of the misunderstanding in a matrimonial dispute is trivial and can be sorted. Mediation as a method of alternative dispute resolution has got legal recognition now. We have referred several matrimonial disputes to mediation centres. Our experience shows that about 10 to 15% of matrimonial disputes get settled in this Court through various mediation centres. We, therefore, feel that at the earliest stage i.e. when the dispute is taken up by the Family Court or by the court of first instance for hearing, it must be referred to mediation centres. Matrimonial disputes particularly those relating to custody of child, maintenance, etc. are preeminently fit for mediation.

Furthermore, the Mediation Training Manual,[240] circulated by the Mediation and Conciliation Project Committee of the Supreme Court, states that all cases arising from strained or soured relationships—including disputes relating to matrimonial causes, maintenance, and custody of children—are normally suitable for alternative dispute resolution processes.[241]

International Approaches to Mediation in Child Custody

Despite many differences in the law regulating divorce and child custody worldwide, there is a broad awareness that the best way to reorganize a family after separation involves a consensual/extrajudicial solution that minimizes conflict and encourages collaborative parenting.[242]

Virginia law specifies that 'Mediation shall be used as an alternative to litigation where appropriate'.[243] The goals of mediation 'may include development of a proposal addressing the child's residential schedule and care arrangements, and how disputes between the parents will be handled in the future'.[244] However, in assessing the appropriateness of a referral for mediation, the court

---

[239]   AIR 2013 SC 2176.

[240]   The manual is available at http://supremecourtofindia.nic.in/MEDIATION%20TRAINING%20MANUAL%20OF%20INDIA.pdf (accessed on 17 July 2015).

[241]   *Mediation Training Manual*, p. 67.

[242]   Giancarlo Tamanza et al., 'Separation and Divorce in Italy: Parenthood, Children's Custody, and Family Mediation', 51(4) *Family Court Rev.*, 557, 557 (2013).

[243]   VA Code Ann., section 20–124.2(A).

[244]   VA Code Ann., section 20–124.2(A).

shall ascertain upon motion of a party whether there is a history of family abuse.[245] The fee paid to a mediator is set by statute and is paid by the government.[246] Although the statutory scheme does not expressly say so, it appears that courts have the obligation to ensure that a mediated agreement is in the best interest on the child.[247]

South African law also encourages mediation. It states that, in any matter concerning a child, 'an approach which is conducive to conciliation and problem-solving should be followed and a confrontational approach should be avoided'.[248] More specifically, a children's court may order mediation before deciding an issue, but it must consider several factors before doing so: the vulnerability of the child, the ability of the child to participate in the proceedings, the power relationships within the family, and the nature of any allegations made by the parties.[249] Mediation cannot be used in a matter involving the alleged abuse of a child.[250] Where parents reach an agreement through mediation, the court must confirm that the agreement is in the best interests on the child.[251] Also, when divorced parents who are co-holders of parental rights and responsibilities are experiencing difficulties in the exercise of their rights, they must attempt to agree on a parenting plan before seeking the court's assistance.[252] In developing a parenting plan, the parents must either seek assistance from certain specified people (e.g., a social worker) or go through mediation.[253]

In China, a court dealing with a divorce case 'shall carry out mediation'.[254] However, mandatory mediation has been criticized as problematic in cases of domestic violence—mediated agreements in such cases will not be the product of negotiations between parties of equal bargaining power.[255]

In Canada, family mediation is widely promoted as an alternative to litigation.[256] The Divorce Act, 1985 requires every lawyer or advocate acting on behalf of a divorcing spouse to

[245] VA Code Ann., section 20–124.4.

[246] VA Code Ann., section 20–124.4 ('The fee of a mediator appointed in any custody, support or visitation case shall be $100 per appointment and shall be paid by the Commonwealth from the funds appropriated for payment of appointments made pursuant to subsection B of Section 16.1–267.')

[247] See Va. Prac. Family Law, section 15:14(i) (2014 ed.) (citing a case where 'a trial judge concluded that it would be contrary to public policy to simply enforce an arbitrator's award without determining whether the award is in the best interests of the child, and, while the arbitrator's decision could be given weight, it could not be used to deprive the court of its jurisdiction to determine the child's best interests'.)

[248] Children's Act, No. 38 of 2005, Section 6(4).

[249] Children's Act, No. 38 of 2005, Section 49.

[250] Children's Act, No. 38 of 2005, Section 71(2).

[251] Children's Act, No. 38 of 2005, Section 72.

[252] Children's Act, No. 38 of 2005, Section 33(2).

[253] Children's Act, No. 38 of 2005, Section 33(5).

[254] Marriage Law of the People's Republic of China (1980), Article 32.

[255] Charlotte Germane, Margaret Johnson, and Nancy Lemon, 'Mandatory Custody Mediation and Joint Custody Orders in California: The Danger for Victims of Domestic Violence', *Berkeley Journal of Gender, Law & Justice*, 1(1): 175, 176 (2013); see generally Dennis P. Saccuzzo, Nancy E. Johnson, and Wendy J. Koen, 'Mandatory Custody Mediation: Empirical Evidence of Increased Risk for Domestic Violence Victims and Their Children' (2003). Available at https://www.ncjrs.gov/pdffiles1/nij/grants/195422.pdf (accessed on 14 November 2016).

[256] Francine Cyr, Gessica Di Stefano, and Bertrand Desjardins, *Family Life, Parental Separation, and Child Custody in Canada: A Focus on Quebec, Family Court Review.*, 51(4): 522, 528 (2013).

discuss with the spouse the advisability of negotiating the matters that may be the subject of a support order or a custody order and to inform the spouse of mediation facilities that might be able to assist with this.[257] A lawyer must submit a certification to the court that he or she has discussed this with the client.[258] In addition, Canadian family law provides that parents who cannot agree must attend a mediation information session prior to appearing before a judge.[259] The session provides information on the mediation process, including the nature and objectives of mediation, the steps involved in the process, the role of the mediator, and the roles played by the spouses.[260] After attending this session, the spouses can proceed with mediation or continue legal proceedings. Provincial laws also provide for mediation.[261] In the province of Quebec, for example, divorcing couples that have children can obtain the services of a professional mediator during the negotiation and settlement of their application for separation, divorce, dissolution of the civil union, child custody, spousal or child support, or the review of an existing decision.[262] Five hours are paid by the Family Mediation Service and another 2.5 hours can be added when a revision of an existing court judegment is needed.[263] Some provincial laws also specify the duties of dispute resolution professionals[264] and the required qualifications for family mediators.[265]

Suggested Amendments by the National Commission for Women

Section 4: Definition—For Sub-clause (ii) of Clause (b) of Section 4, the following shall be substituted: 'a guardian appointed by the will of minor's last surviving parent'. After Clause (c) of Section 4 a new Clause (d) shall be inserted—'Parent includes both mother and father or survivor'.

Section 6: For Section 6 the following shall be substituted: 'The natural guardian of a Hindu minor, in respect of the minor's person as well as in respect of the minor's property (excluding his or her undivided interest in joint family property) are both the parents; ie. mother and father, provided that no person shall be entitled to act as the natural guardian of a minor under the provisions of this section a) if he ceased to be Hindu or if he has completely and finally renounced the world by becoming a hermit or ascetic. Explanation: in the section the 'expression parents' does not include a step father and a step mother.

---

[257] Divorce Act, 1985, Section 9(2).

[258] Divorce Act, 1985, Section 9(3).

[259] Francine Cyr et al., *Family Life.*

[260] Francine Cyr et al., *Family Life.*

[261] Francine Cyr et al., *Family Life.*

[262] Francine Cyr et al., *Family Life.*

[263] Francine Cyr et al., *Family Life.*

[264] See, for example, British Columbia Family Law Act, Section 8. Available at http://www.bclaws.ca/EPLibraries/bclaws_new/document/ID/freeside/00_11025_01 (accessed on 17 July 2015).

[265] See, for example, British Columbia Family Law Act Regulations, B.C. Reg. 347/2012, Sections 4 and 5. Available at http://www.bclaws.ca/civix/document/id/complete/statreg/331105891 (accessed on 17 July 2015).

Section 7: Natural guardianship of adopted son. For Section 7 the following shall be substituted: 'natural guardianship of adopted child'. The natural guardianship of an adopted child passes, on adoption, to the adoptive parent/parents.

Section 8: Powers of natural guardian. In Subsection 6 of Section 8, at the end after the words the property is situated, the words or where the minor normally resides shall be added -This will read as 'In this section 'Court' means the city civil court or a district court or a Court empowered under section 4A of the Guardian and Wards Act, 1890, within the local limits of whose jurisdiction the immovable property in respect of which the application is made is situated, and where the immovable property is situated within the jurisdiction of more than one such court, means the court within the local limits of whose jurisdiction any portion of the property is situated or where the minor normally resides.

Section 9: Testimentary guardians and their powers. For Subsection 1 of Section 8 the following shall be substituted—'A Hindu parent entitled to act as natural guardian of her/his minor children, may, by will, appoint a guardian for any of them in respect of the minor's person or in respect of the minor's property (other than the undivided interest referred in section 12) or in respect both'. For Subsection 2 of Section 9 the following shall be substituted 'An appointment made under Subsection (1) shall have no effect if there is a surviving parent dies without appointing by will, any person as guardian'. Section 9 (3) should be deleted. Section 9 (4) should be deleted. Section 9 (6) should be deleted.

Section 13: Welfare of minor to be paramount consideration. After Subsection 2 of Section 13, a new Subsection 3 shall be added—'Where the court has seen the question of fitness of guardian to act as such, regard may be had to the wishes of the person.'

Justification

Section 4: Definition—Consequential amendments in respect of the amendment suggested in Sub-clause ii of Clause b of the Section.

Section 6: Natural guardians of a Hindu Minor. There is no clear-cut categorical statement of law in the statute that the mother and father are both natural guardians of the child at all times and for all purposes.

Section 7: Natural guardianship of adopted son. To remove the discriminatory provision against daughter.

Section 8: Powers of natural guardian. In Subsection 6 of Section 8—For the sake of convenience of the minor and his/her guardian.

Section 9: Subsection (1) of Section 9—To give equal rights to both the parents to act as natural guardian. Subsection (2) of Section 9—Consequential amendment in respect to Subsection (1. Section 9(3)—Consequential amendment. Section 9(4)—Consequential amendment. Section 9(6)—Consequential amendment.

Need to Accede to the Hague Convention on the Civil Aspects of International Child Abduction 1980

The Law Commission has already recommended in its 218th Report the need to sign the convention. It went a step further in the 219th report titled 'Need for Family Law Legislations for Non-resident Indians'. The Commission recognized the lack of legal framework in India regarding such issues and recommended that India be a signatory to the Hague Convention of 1980. This may not happen spontaneously, and India being a country following dualist approach of International Law, enforcing of the treaty by enacting legislation may take some time. Till then, foreign missions should be set up in India in the states with high population of NRIs. These missions could assist the courts to ensure return of children to the country of their foreign residence if they are removed in violation of foreign court orders. This would be an excellent step to enhance global integration with regard to such cases in India till the Hague Convention of 1980 is enforced. Second, uniform guidelines should be established to assist the wronged parents in such cases to pursue legal remedy against the abduction. This would help the foreign parents with limited knowledge of the Indian legal system to enforce their rights.

Owing to the advent of technology with the establishment of easier and economic forms of travel and communication, national boundaries have increasingly become irrelevant for the purposes of cultural exchanges.[266]

The globe has shrunk to such an extent that cultural taboos do not hold back anybody from going in search of greater achievements. This brings in a package of both desirable and undesirable effects. Every employment opportunity, especially the ones established under the modern technological umbrella, comes with a lot of responsibility and financial benefits, with the after-effect being increasing independence of individuals and ego inflations, which paves the way for undesirable familial problems.[267]

Earlier, spousal and inter-parental conflicts were simply equated with divorce, or with various measures of marital dissatisfaction, hostile attitudes, and physical aggression. This failure to distinguish among types of conflict has confounded the debate about the extent to which different kinds of divorce conflicts are normal and functional. A divorce conflict has at least three important dimensions which should be considered when assessing its incidence and its effects on children. First, the conflict has a domain dimension, which can refer to disagreements over a series of divorce issues such as financial support, property, division, custody, and access to the children, or to values and methods of child-rearing. Second, the conflict has a tactics dimension, which can refer to the manner in which divorcing couples informally try to resolve disagreements, or it can refer to ways in which divorce disputes are formally resolved by the use of attorney negotiation, mediation, litigation, or arbitration by a judge. Third, conflict has an attitudinal dimension, referring to the degree of negative emotional feeling or hostility directed by divorcing parties towards each other, which may be covertly or overtly expressed.[268]

Statistics show that the number of divorce cases and custody disputes has increased ever since the advent of globalization and technological development leading to a very busy life-style and work culture. The international parental child abduction/child removal finds its root here.[269] International parental child abduction or removal can be defined as the removal of a child by one parent from one country to another without the approval of the other parent. Child removal, in

---

[266] Justice A.R. Lakshmanan, 'International Child Abduction—Parental Removal' (2008) 48 IJIL 427.

[267] Lakshmanan, 'International Child Abduction'.

[268] Lakshmanan, 'International Child Abduction'.

[269] Lakshmanan, 'International Child Abduction'.

this context, encompasses an interference with the parental rights or right to contact with the removed child. These acts by a parent when brought before a court of law have in the past created considerable amount of confusion specifically in the area of competence of courts with regard to jurisdictional aspects.[270]

The international community acted to solve this crisis by adopting on 25 October 1980 an International Convention on the Civil Aspects of International Child Abduction which entered into force on 1 December 1983. This convention seeks to protect children from harmful effects of abduction and retention across international boundaries by providing a procedure to bring about their prompt return. The main objects of the convention are:

a)   to secure the prompt return of children wrongfully removed to or retained in any contracting state; and

b)   to ensure that rights of custody and of access under the law of one contracting state are effectively respected in the other contracting states.

Many states of the world have become signatory to this convention. Some states like Australia have brought about amendments in their family law legislations to make the Hague Convention operative in their nation. India, however, is not a signatory to this convention.[271]

The Indian courts while deciding cases pertaining to minor children have not followed a uniform pattern. There also is an absence of progressive development in the subject. If some matters are decided with prime importance placed on the welfare of the child, some are based on the technicalities of various provisions of law and jurisdictional tiffs. The reason cited for this can be the absence of any law that governs this aspect. This will only affect both the physical and emotional condition of the child, who is caught in the fire of shattered relationships.[272]

This situation only shows that the time has come for some international perspective in this regard. The fact of India not being a signatory to the Hague Convention on the Civil Aspects of International Child Abduction may have a negative influence on a foreign judge who is deciding on the custody of a child. Without the guarantee afforded by the Hague Convention to the effect that the child will be swiftly returned to the country of origin, the foreign judge may be reluctant to give permission for the child to travel to India. As a logical upshot, India should become a signatory to the Hague Convention and this will, in turn, bring the prospect of achieving the return to India of children who have their homes in India.[273]

India should keep pace and change according to the changing needs of the society. The Law Commission of India, therefore, recommended that the Government may consider that India should become a signatory to the Hague Convention which will in turn bring the prospects of achieving the return to India of children who have their homes in India.[274]

At a symposium organized in India by the British High Commission, the participants, including British Deputy High Commissioner to India Julian Evans, Head of International Family

---

270   Lakshmanan, 'International Child Abduction'.
271   Lakshmanan, 'International Child Abduction'.
272   Lakshmanan, 'International Child Abduction'.
273   Lakshmanan, 'International Child Abduction'.
274   Lakshmanan, 'International Child Abduction'.

Justice for England and Wales Lord Justice Mathew Thorpe, Chief Justice of the Family Court of Australia Diana Bryant, and the former Attorney-General of India, Soli Sorabjee, urged India to sign the convention. The discussion was moderated by advocate Anil Malhotra. Experts from the office of children's issues, U.S. State department, Hague Permanent Bureau, the National Commission for Protection of Child Rights, and the National Judicial Academy also attended the symposium. The participants said, 'given the increased international mobility, there has been a steady rise in cross-border parental child removal cases. Last year, India was second only to Pakistan as a destination for children removed from the United Kingdom alone by one parent against the wishes of the other.'[275]

Non-Governmental Organizations' Interventions

The role of NGOs and voluntary agencies in India has been very important. In situations of widespread poverty and deprivation, exploitation, and discrimination, the State has not been in a position to ameliorate everything. The NGOs have stepped in to provide basic health and child care services, runnings home for the destitute and distressed and providing education and training opportunities. At the same time, these NGOs have also been working towards building a more humane society free from exploitation and want. The partnership between NGOs and the government has been of mutual benefit. The NGOs are a necessary corollary to the democratic machinery of the government; they are the means of democratic empowerment of those who are less powerful and less advantaged, as the government machinery and its authorized institutions are not always sufficient to guarantee the protection of human rights. Some examples are mentioned as follows:

SARTHI[276]

SARTHI is an NGO that participates in outreach efforts on a wide range of issues that confront children in difficult circumstances throughout Bihar. Located just to the west of Bengal, Bihar is one of India's poorest and most underdeveloped regions. SARTHI's most central work is the protection and rehabilitation of children placed in Bihar's government homes for minors. SARTHI does not discriminate in its efforts to help all children within this sizeable and diverse population, which includes children from broken or abusive families, orphaned children, street children, handicapped children, and juvenile offenders. SARTHI's mission is 'to work with children to protect and promote the rights of the children for their holistic development with community involvement. We try to create a child-friendly society by empowering children and generating mass awareness with the help of different stakeholders.' SARTHI's work is guided by the UNCRC, setting out the civil, political, economic, social, and cultural rights of children. SARTHI believes all children should understand their right to survival, protection, development, and participation.

---

[275] *The Hindu*, 'Jurists Want India to Sign Hague Convention on International Child Abduction', 14 May 2013.

[276] Available at http://www.sarthi-bihar.org/#!home/c1kk0 (accessed on 14 November 2016).

Save Indian Family[277]

Save Indian Family (SIF) is a movement, a group of non-funded, non-profit NGOs in India. SIF is a movement which promotes and associates with formation of various NGOs which intend to work for men's welfare and strongly believe in replacing the word 'men'/'women' by 'person' and 'husband'/'wife' by 'spouse' in any government law/policy. SIF takes pride in stating that it has an effective force of over 100,000 members on ground and more the 10,000 on the internet who are fighting this legal terrorism like commandos. SIF is a strong team of dedicated families comprising victims of misuse of various laws like Section 498A, dowry death, and many other similar sections of the IPC; various sections of the Dowry Prohibition Act, 1961; Protection of Women from Domestic Violence Act, 2005; Section 125 of CrPC; all the Marriage Acts (Hindu, Muslim, Christian, and SMA); the GWA; and gender-biased laws in India, including those against rape, sexual harassment at work place, and so on. The SIF team includes NRIs and senior citizens who campaign and create awareness about gross injustice and abuse that happen in the Indian legal system. SIF gives a message to society about gender equality and family harmony.

Aims and Objectives

1. To promote marital and family harmony.
2. To actively work for creating a dowry-free society without adversely affecting the institution of marriage, family structure, and implication of innocents.
3. To provide a platform for fighting against misuse of dowry laws.
4. To create awareness about current dowry/cruelty/harassment related laws and their detrimental effects on family members including husband, wife, children, and relatives.
5. To provide legal, psycho-social, and emotional support to the innocent persons who are affected by malicious implication through dowry laws. To provide legal aid to families from weaker and needy sections of society.
6. To demote cultural changes like single parenting and live-in relationships, to safeguard child welfare and integrity of Indian family.
7. To safeguard interests of elders and their respect in society and discourage elder-abuse through dowry related laws.
8. To promote deterrents against false complaints and arrests without investigation. To discourage malicious prosecutions in matrimonial cases.
9. Pursue amendments/reforms in existing laws and legal procedures, so that all sections of society enjoy equal rights for justice, irrespective of their race, age, religion, and gender. To promote gender equality and reduce gender discrimination.
10. To work to ensure speedy trial and justice to all.
11. To take up issues related to human rights violations and violation of fundamental rights as per the Indian constitution, and raise these issues at appropriate platforms.

---

[277] Available at http://www.saveindianfamily.in/ (accessed on 14 November 2016).

12. To collaborate with different sections of society, other organizations working towards similar goals, women's organizations, government bodies, legal authorities, and others for the betterment of Indian society.

13. To perform all such acts as may be necessary for the achievement and accomplishment of the above-mentioned aims and objectives.

4 Right against Economic Exploitation
Child Labour

What Is Child Labour?

Child labour is a complex and a controversial issue. Unfortunately, it is a global phenomenon. In almost all societies, children work in some way, though the types of work they do and the forms of their involvement vary. But many millions of children work under abusive and exploitative conditions that are clearly dangerous to them. They are found working in the following situations, among others:

- In agriculture, performing heavy work and exposed to the many hazards associated with the introduction of modern machinery and chemicals.
- In dangerous industries and occupations, such as glass making, construction, mining, and carpet weaving.
- In domestic service, carrying out arduous work under conditions of isolation, over excessively long hours, and with physical and sexual abuse.
- On the streets, working as rag pickers, vendors, and child prostitutes, often under threat of violence from street gangs and the police, and with exposure to life-threatening diseases.
- In small industrial workshops and service establishments.
- At home, tending younger children or helping in family farms and business, working such long hours that it is impossible to play or attend school.
- As bonded labourers in outright slavery.
- In predominantly export-oriented industries, such as textiles, clothing, carpets, and footwear.

Child labour includes children prematurely leading adult lives, working long hours for low wages, under conditions damaging to their health and to their physical and mental development, sometimes separated from their families, frequently deprived of meaningful education and training opportunities that could open up a better future for them.[1] Child labour is, therefore, all work that places children at risk.[2]

---

[1] Francis Blanchard. 1983. 'Introduction', in *ILO: Report of the Director-General, International Labour Conference*, 69th Session, Geneva, pp. 3–4.

[2] Blanchard, 'Introduction', pp. 3–4.

When the business of wage earning or of participation in self or family support conflicts directly or indirectly with the business of growth and education, the result is child labour.[3] Any non–school-going child is a child labourer.[4] A recent International Labour Organization (ILO) report on child labour used the term 'child labour' to cover all economic activities carried out by persons less than 15 years of age, regardless of their occupational status (wage earners, own-account workers, unpaid family workers, and so on), but not household work performed by them in their parents' home, except where such work can be assimilated to an economic activity—as for example, when a child must devote his or her entire time to the work, so that his or her parents can be employed outside the home, due to which the child is deprived of the possibility of going to school.

The term 'child labour' is often defined by ILO as work that deprives children of their childhood, their potential, and their dignity, and is harmful to physical and mental development.[5] It refers to work that:

- is mentally, physically, socially, or morally dangerous and harmful to children; and
- interferes with their schooling by:
  - deprives them of the opportunity to attend school;
  - obliges them to leave school prematurely; or
  - requires them to attempt to combine school attendance with excessively long and heavy work.[6]

This includes children working in any sector, occupation, or process, including the formal and non-formal, organized and unorganized, within or outside the family.[7] Child labour also includes:

- child labour in bondage;
- child labour within and with families (including domestic child labour);
- girl child labour;
- child labour separated from families; and
- child labour which is itinerant.

Child labour can be broadly classified into the following categories:

- child labour covered by legislation;
- child labour falling outside the legislative framework;

---

[3] Edwin Robert and Anderson Seligman, *Encyclopaedia of the Social Sciences*, Volume 6 (USA: Macmillan, 1959).

[4] Child labor defined as 'all children out of school' by MV Foundation, NGO in Hyderabad. Available at http://mvfindia.in/approach/ (accessed on 26 September 2016).

[5] ILO, 'What Is Child Labour?', International Programme on the Elimination of Child Labour (IPEC). Available at http://www.ilo.org/ipec/facts/lang--en/index.htm (accessed on 4 July 2015).

[6] ILO, 'What Is Child Labour?'.

[7] Campaign against Child Labour (CACL)—A network of over 5,400 anti-child labour groups spread over 12 states in India.

- agriculture and allied activities; and
- informal, unorganized, semi-urban, and urban sector.[8]

Magnitude of Child Labour

The estimates on the magnitude of child labour vary due to multiplicity of definitions, different methods of computation, and the collection of data at different points of time. Statistics on child labour are, therefore, elusive not only because of the special and practical difficulties involved in the design and implementation of child surveys, but also because of differences in perception about what constitutes a child, or child work, or child labour. Despite these shortcomings, certain figures and estimates have been produced and these highlight a very concerning global scenario.

Earlier estimates based on very limited statistical information obtained from about a hundred countries indicated that there were 73 million working children between 10 and 14 years of age in these countries in 1995. However, recent experimental surveys carried out by the ILO's Governance and Tripartism Department in a number of countries indicate that this figure is a gross underestimation. Child labour is much more common in poorer households, but is not limited to poor households.[9] Work within the family unit accounts for the largest share of children's employment in most South Asian countries, with the exception of Bangladesh and the Maldives. For 7–14-year-old children in employment, the proportion of children working in the agricultural sector ranges from 92 per cent in Nepal, 75 per cent in Pakistan, 66 per cent in Sri Lanka, to 54 per cent each in Bhutan and India. From country-level statistics'[10] it is apparent that there are substantial numbers of child labourers from households in the higher income quintiles in most developing countries.[11]

Globally, during 2000–12, children in the 5–11 years age group accounted for by far the largest share of all child labourers: 73 million, or 44 per cent of the total child labour population.[12] Regional differences in involvement in child labour are considerable.

New estimates by the ILO suggest that the number of child labourers worldwide has dropped by a third between 2000 and 2012, from 245 million to 168 million. In the same period, the number of children doing hazardous work more than halved, to just over 85 million. Child labour fell at its fastest rate between 2008 and 2012. In the year 2008, the ILO estimated that there were 215 million child labourers worldwide. While the drop is positive, the figure 168 million

[8] Public Hearing and Second National Convention of Child Labourers: Reference Kit, Campaign against Child Labour, March 1997.

[9] ILO–IPEC, 'World Report on Child Labour: Economic Vulnerability, Social Protection and the Fight Against Child Labour' (Geneva: ILO, 2013).

[10] ILO–IPEC, *Marking Progress against Child Labour—Global Estimates and Trends 2000–2012* (Geneva: ILO, 2013).

[11] UCW Country Statistics Database on Child Labour. Available at www.ucw-project.org/Pages/ChildLabIndicator.aspx (accessed on 4 July 2015).

[12] ILO–IPEC, *Marking Progress.*

suggests that over one in ten children worldwide will still fall under the ILO's definition of a child labourer.[13]

For the overall 5–17-years age group, child labourers number some 77.7 million in Asia and the Pacific, 59 million in Sub-Saharan Africa, 12.5 million in Latin America and the Caribbean (LAC), and 9.2 million in the Middle East and North Africa (MENA). The largest absolute number of child labourers is found in the Asia and the Pacific region, while Sub-Saharan Africa is the region with the highest rate of child labour.[14] Seen in relative terms, however, the biggest concern remains the Sub-Saharan Africa region.[15] In that region, more than one in five children (21 per cent of the children) in the 5–17-years age group are in child labour. Seen in relative terms, however, the biggest concern remains the Sub-Saharan Africa region.[16] There, more than one in five children (21 per cent of child labour) in the 5–17-years age group are child labour.[17] This compares with 9 per cent in Asia and the Pacific and LAC and 8 per cent in MENA. The Asia and the Pacific region registered by far the largest absolute decline in child labour among 5–17 year olds for the 2008–12 period, from 114 million to 78 million.[18] The number of child labourers in the same age group also decreased in Sub-Saharan Africa by 6 million, and modestly in LAC (by 1.6 million). According to the ILO, the decline in child labourers in the Sub-Saharan Africa region, unlike the other regions, occurred against the backdrop of a significant increase in child population. This means that the decline was entirely attributable to a fall in child labour incidence, rather than to demographic factors.[19] The net impact of these changes is that the worldwide population of child labourers has become more concentrated in the Sub Saharan Africa region. While Sub-Saharan Africa accounted for 30 per cent of all 5–17 year olds in child labour in 2008, 4 years later this figure had risen to 35 per cent.[20]

Child Labour in India

India is a no exception where basic rights of many children are seen being snatched away commonly on streets, restaurants, agricultural fields, or perhaps every nook and corner that can be associated with the labour work. Globally, around 215 million children under the age of 18 are target of child labour,[21] while India contributes more than 2 per cent share in the world's child labour population—almost equal to its present contribution in the world's GDP(1.67 per cent). India has the highest population of child labourers in the world. [22]

[13] *The Guardian*, 'Child Labour Drops Worldwide: Explore the Data', 24 September 2013. Available at http://www.theguardian.com/news/datablog/2013/sep/24/child-labour-drops-worldwide-data (accessed on 27 June 2015).

[14] ILO–IPEC, *Marking Progress*.

[15] ILO–IPEC, *Marking Progress*.

[16] ILO–IPEC, *Marking Progress*.

[17] ILO–IPEC, *Marking Progress*.

[18] ILO–IPEC, *Marking Progress*.

[19] ILO–IPEC, *Marking Progress*.

[20] ILO–IPEC, *Marking Progress*.

[21] ILO, 'What Is Child Labour?'.

[22] Census of India. 2001. Available at http://www.unicef.org/india/children.html (accessed on 25 June 2015).

One of the disconcerting aspects of child labour is that children are sent to work at the expense of education. Child labour, thus, prejudices children's education and adversely affects their health and safety.[23]

Table 4.1 shows the work Participation (main and marginal) rate of children in different age groups in the total labour force, according to the study done by the National Commission for Protection of Child Rights (NCPCR) in 2014.[24] It shows that in India, according to the 2011 census, there are 6,052,763 working children in the age group 10–14 years and 2,175,718 working children in the age group 5–9 years. We have children as young as 5 years working.

Table 4.1   Child Labour in India[25]

All India Child Labour Population according to 2011 Census				
	Age Group	Main Workers	Marginal Workers	Total
All India Total	5–9	1,108,808	1,066,910	2,175,718
Total	10–14	3,244,439	2,808,324	6,052,763
Total		4,353,247	3,875,234	8,228,481

As per the Global Report on Child Labour published by the ILO in the year 2013, the activity rate of children in the age group of 5–14 years is 5.1 per cent in the LAC region, which is the lowest in the world. In the Asia-Pacific Region, it is 18.8 per cent. In comparison to that, the activity rate of children in India, as per the 2001, census is 5 per cent.[26] As per the National Sample Survey Office (NSSO) survey of 2009–10, the working children are estimated at 4.984 million, which shows a declining trend. Table 4.2 shows year-wise details of working children, as per the NSSO survey.

Table 4.2   NSSO Estimate of the Magnitude of Child Labour in India, 1993–2009/10 (in Millions)[27]

Year	Boys	Girls	All
1993–4	7.35	6.0	13.3
1999–2000	5.4	4.8	10.2
2004–05	4.76	3.9	8.6
2009–10	3.1	1.8	4.9

Table 4.3 gives the data on the magnitude of child labour in India from different sources. While the 2011 national census gives the figure of child labour as 10.12 million, the United Nations Children's Fund (UNICEF)–NSSO data says 4.98 million. There is a vast difference between the two figures.

[23] Government of India, Planning Commission, Working Group for Social inclusion of Vulnerable Group like Child Labour and Bonded and Migrant Labour in the 12th Five Year Plan (2012–17).

[24] NCPCR, 2014. Available at http://ncpcr.gov.in/showfile.php?lid=930 (accessed on 27 June 2015).

[25] Source: NCPCR, 2014. Available at http://ncpcr.gov.in/showfile.php?lid=930 (accessed on 14 November 2016).

[26] Government of India, Ministry of Labour and Employment, *Annual Report 2012–13*, p. 91.

[27] Source: NSSO, various rounds, 'Employment and Unemployment Situation in India'.

Table 4.3   Child Labour in India from Various Data Sources[28]

Source	Number of Working Children
2011 National Census	10.12 million
National Sample Survey, 2009–10	4.98 million

Major Sectors where Children Work

Much of India's child employment is concentrated in agriculture and allied activities. Accounting for over two-thirds of child employment, agriculture is the single largest sector of the concentration of child labour in India.[29] This is followed by manufacturing, wherein 16.55 per cent are found to be engaged in manufacturing commodities. Trade, hotels, and restaurants account for the next significant share of child workers, with 8.45 per cent. Most of the children engaged in agriculture work as part of the farm household unit. However, a significant proportion of them also work as paid casual labour at a wage rate mostly half that of adults.[30]

Agricultural work is hazardous. With the increasing use of fertilizers and pesticides in agriculture, the nature of work is increasingly becoming more hazardous. Similarly, in the manufacturing sector, the second largest sector of child employment, most of the children are engaged in the informal sector with near absence of any provisions related to work hours, overtime, basic social security, and representation of voice. It is common to see children extensively engaged in hotels and restaurants, where they are paid measly wages and made to work under distressing conditions.[31]

Whether in a farm-field or a manufacturing unit, child labourers are extensively engaged on casual basis and deprived of decent wages. Almost one-fourth of all child workers engaged in manufacturing are found to be employed in the manufacture of textile products. Wood products followed by food and beverage production appear to account for the single largest share of child workers, at 13 and 12 per cent respectively. Tobacco production and apparel, on the other hand, account for around one-tenth each in child employment. Some of the other prominent industries in which child workers are engaged are related to fabricated and other non-metallic manufacturing, which together account for nearly 14 per cent of the total manufacturing employment.[32]

From figure 4.1, it is very clear that the maximum number of children work in the agricultural sector, followed by manufacturing sector. Children working in the agricultural sector constitute two-third of all child labour force in India and their percentage in rural child labour force is more than 75 per cent. According to the NSSO estimates of 2004–5, there are around 5.6 million children working in agriculture, of which 2.75 million are girls. Much of agricultural work can be hazardous, especially when health and safety standards are low, and can cause sickness, injury, or even death. Children are particularly at risk as their bodies and minds are still developing,

[28] Sources: Census of India, 2011; UNICEF; and NSSO Data 2009–10.

[29] Anoop K. Satpathy, Helen R. Sekar, and Anup K. Karan, *Rehabilitation of Child Labour in India, Lessons Learnt from the Evaluation of NCLPs* (Noida: V. V. Giri National Labour Institute, 2010).

[30] Satpathy, Sekar, and Karan, *Rehabilitation of Child Labour.*

[31] Satpathy, Sekar, and Karan, *Rehabilitation of Child Labour.*

[32] Satpathy, Sekar, and Karan, *Rehabilitation of Child Labour.*

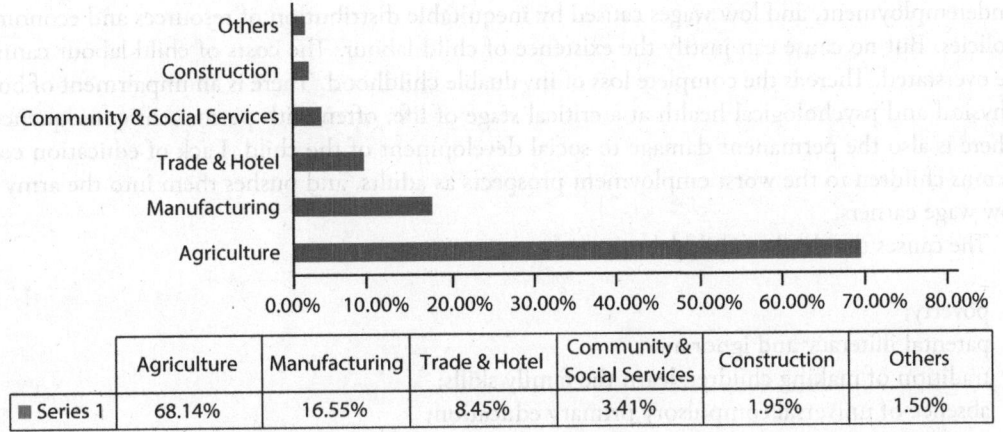

	Agriculture	Manufacturing	Trade & Hotel	Community & Social Services	Construction	Others
■ Series 1	68.14%	16.55%	8.45%	3.41%	1.95%	1.50%

Figure 4.1: Percentage Distribution of Child Labour by Sectors of Employment, All-India (2004–05)[33]

and they are more vulnerable to hazards such as pesticides. The negative health consequences of their work can last into adulthood.[34] The agricultural sector is not included in the list of hazardous industries under the law, and hence children work in this sector. The current Child Labour (Prohibition and Regulation) Act, 1986 does not prohibit or even regulate the conditions of work in the agriculture and cultivation sector, except those 'processes in agriculture where tractors, threshing and harvesting machines are used and chaff cutting'. By excluding all those sectors where a large number of children are engaged in work, the law provides a justification for continuance of child labour in such a hazardous sector.

The state with the highest child labour population in India, in the age group of 5–14 years, is Uttar Pradesh, which has 896,301 working children as per the 2011 census. Other states where child labour population is more than 0.4 million are Maharashtra (496,916), Bihar (451,590), and Andhra Pradesh (404,851).[35]

Causes and Consequences of Child Labour

It is often assumed that the nature and extent of poverty in a country determines the number of its child labour. Studies that have been undertaken in various countries around the world, particularly those that are relatively underdeveloped economically, do show that child labour and poverty are intimately linked. However, it is also clear that the specific circumstances of child labour are influenced by many other factors. No single cause can be isolated for the prevalence of child labour. It is a combination of several factors. It is inherent in the cycle of poverty, unemployment,

[33] Source: NSSO Data, 2004–05, calculated from unit records. Available at http://planningcommission.nic.in/reports/sereport/ser/ser_nclp1709.pdf (accessed on 14 November 2016).

[34] ILO–FAO, 'Child Labour in Agriculture', Agriculture and Decent Work working paper. Available at http://www.fao-ilo.org/fao-ilo-child/ (accessed on 6 April 2015).

[35] Census of India, 2011, Government of India.

underemployment, and low wages caused by inequitable distribution of resources and economic policies. But no cause can justify the existence of child labour. The costs of child labour cannot be overstated. There is the complete loss of invaluable childhood. There is an impairment of both physical and psychological health at a critical stage of life, often with permanent consequences. There is also the permanent damage to social development of the child. Lack of education condemns children to the worst employment prospects as adults, and pushes them into the army of low wage earners.

The causes that lead to child labour are:[36]

- poverty;
- parental illiteracy and ignorance;
- tradition of making children learn the family skills;
- absence of universal compulsory primary education;
- non-availability of and non-accessibility to schools;
- irrelevant and non-attractive school curriculum;
- social and cultural environment;
- 'informalization' of production;
- employers' preference to children for their cheap labour and inability to organize against exploitation;
- family work;
- level of technology;
- apathy of trade unions; and
- ineffective enforcement of the legal provisions pertaining to child labour.

Child labour often creates a vicious cycle of poverty, as a child coming from an impoverished family surviving harsh conditions becomes an unskilled, debilitated adult who is not employed even in the industry that exploited him/her earlier. Furthermore, child labourers receive low, negligible income and often no wages at all. They have no rights as workers and cannot join trade unions. Child labour also depresses adult labour and keeps adults unemployed.[37]

Girl Child Labour[38]

The girl child requires a special mention in the context of child labour. Although the labour of young children of both sexes is exploited, the plight of the girl child labourer is worse off. She is a child, a girl, and a labourer, and she faces discrimination on all counts, in almost all areas—rural

---

[36] Helen Sekar, *Ensuring Their Childhood* (New Delhi: V.V. Giri National Labour Institute, 2001).

[37] Vikas Adhyayan Kendra, *Facts against Myths*, Vol. III, 8, 1996, p. 2. This is bi-monthly factsheet of Vikas Adhyayan Kendra (VAK), a secular voluntary organization established in 1981 to expose and dispel the prevailing myths, stereotypes and propaganda perpetuated by the ruling bloc with particular reference to the prevailing hegemonic discourse of the neo-liberal paradigm, communal, caste and other divisive ideologies and practices.

[38] Asha Bajpai, *Recommendations given to the National Commission for Women, New Delhi, for Amending the Child Labour (Prohibition and Regulation) Act, 1986* (unpublished).

and urban. There are many reports of girls being allocated tasks that are more tedious or arduous, more damaging to education, less paid, and requiring a fairly longer working day than boys.[39] Girl child labour is prevalent in the following areas:

- Household work: Girls between the ages of 6 and 11 sweep, wash, collect water and firewood, and mind younger siblings and livestock.
- Agriculture work: Young girls work long hours in the fields.
- Home-based piece-rate work: Girls toil in this kind of work. Their existence as economic entities is rarely known to anybody. Large numbers of home-based girls are employed in rolling beedis,[40] the carpet industry, lock making, and gem polishing. Poverty forces them to work but cultural tradition prevents them from seeking work in the organized sector. Therefore, in their case there is no legal protection at all. Their work is seen as part of their mothers' labour. The patriarchal value system that operates in the family justifies the unequal labour of boys and girls.
- Bonded labour: During drought, famine, or natural calamities, they may be given away as bonded labour to moneylenders or sold into beggary or prostitution. The red light areas of India's major cities are full of female child prostitutes who have been sold by families or lured away. Some communities institutionalize prostitution by dedicating their young girls as *devadasi*s.
- Domestic servants: Girl children are forced to work for long duration, without wages, or on low wages. In return, they have no opportunity for acquiring any skill. They have to face rampant and systematic physical and sexual exploitation.

Therefore, the significant characteristics of girl child labour are:

- Invisible work—not recognized as economic activity. They do not come under the purview of law.
- No identifiable employer.
- Long working hours and poor conditions that prevent them from attending any school.
- No skill formation.
- Low pay and low status.
- Physical abuse.
- Sexual harassment and abuse.

Girls are particularly vulnerable to the negative impacts of child labour; they constitute a majority of the children in some of the most dangerous forms of child labour, including forced and bonded labour, commercial sexual exploitation, and domestic work outside of their home. Four South Asian countries have the highest gender disparities globally. Pakistan (82 girls:100 boys) and Afghanistan (71:100) have high disparities at the expense of girls; Bangladesh (94 boys:

[39] Assefa Bequele and Jo Boyden, eds, *Combating Child Labour* (Geneva: ILO, 1988).

[40] A beedi is a thin, Indian cigarette filled with tobacco flakes and wrapped in a *tendu* leaf or possibly even *Piliostigma racemosum* leaf tied with a string at one end. The name is derived from the Marwari word *beeda*—a mixture of betel nuts, herbs, and spices wrapped in a leaf.

100 girls), Nepal (92:100) have high disparities at the expense of boys.[41] The activity status of children in South Asia differs considerably by gender. More boys are reported in employment in Bangladesh, India, and Sri Lanka and more girls in Bhutan, Maldives, and Pakistan. Gender differences begin to emerge more clearly in the 15–17 years age range, driven by the different cul- turally-dictated paths that boys and girls take when leaving education.[42] Specifically, larger shares of girls in this age range are reported 'inactive' (that is, out of school and out of employment) (Bhutan is an exception). Sectoral composition of South Asian children's employment shows variation by sex, although patterns are less clear across countries.[43]

An ILO study of 16 countries found that although roughly the same percentage of girls are involved in economic activity as boys, girls engage in more non-economic household chores and work longer total hours (economic and non-economic) than boys.[44] Girls also constitute a majority of the children in some of the most dangerous forms of child labour, including forced and bonded labour, commercial sexual exploitation, and domestic work outside of their home.[45] A 2009 study found that girls in India between 7 and 14 years were more than fifteen times as likely as male peers to report their primary activity as housework.[46] In India, researchers found that the rate of rural child marriage for 12-to-17-year-old girls is strongly correlated with hours spent doing household chores.[47]

Domestic Girl Child Labour

Here are a few real-life instances of inhuman torture and exploitation of domestic child labour:

- Nirmala, a 13-year-old maid working with a couple, was beaten with iron rods for braking a glass. This incident brought to light many such cases of violence against domestic workers in Delhi.
- Nayaagamma witnessed the torture of her 13-year-old daughter Kaveri, a domestic servant, by the local police. She was suspected of stealing some jewellery from her employer's house. Unable to bear the shame and sight of the brutal torture of her innocent daughter, she com- mitted suicide in Bengaluru on 29 April 1997.
- Mary Gracy Ekka, 25, was murdered on 24 July 1995 inside the kitchen of the home she worked in, in broad daylight in Bandra, one of the busiest suburbs of the city of Mumbai.

---

[41] Sherin Khan and Scott Lyon, 'Measuring Children's Work in South Asia—Perspectives from NHhousehold Surveys', ILO Understanding Children's Work (UCW), first published 2015. Available at http://www.ucw-project.org/attachment/wcms_35937120150414_124838.pdf (accessed on 4 July 2015).

[42] Khan and Lyon, 'Measuring Children's Work'.

[43] Khan and Lyon, 'Measuring Children's Work'.

[44] ILO, *Give Girls a Chance: Tackling Child Labour, a Key to the Future*, a report, 2009, p. 20.

[45] ILO, *Accelerating Action against Child Labour*, Global Report under the Follow-up to the ILO Declaration on Fundamental Principles and Rights at Work, International Labour Conference, 99th Session.

[46] ILO, 'Accelerating Action'.

[47] ILO, 'Accelerating Action'.

The certificate permitting burial stated in one simple sentence: 'shock and haemorrhage, due to injuries to vital organs'.

• In 2012, a 15-year-old girl attempted suicide because of the ill-treatment meted out to her by her employers. Her parents, believing domestic labour was the best job for her, had sent her to work with this family who tortured and abused her, which led her to attempt suicide.[48]

Such aforementioned testimonies are endless.[49]

There is a growing phenomenon of rampant and systematic exploitation of children in domestic work in urban areas. In many cases, such children have been forced to work for long durations, without food, and/or have worked for very low wages. Many of the live-in domestic workers are in a situation of near slavery. With the violation of their human rights, not only are living and working conditions sub-human, but even blatant injustice like non-payment of wages as well as criminal acts of physical, sexual, and psychological violence amounting to torture have been documented. A task force was set up by four non-governmental organizations (NGOs)/networks working with child labourers and on child rights issues and domestic work in Mumbai, primarily to obtain first-hand detailed information on the causes of death of three child workers, Cherry, Radha, and Asha. The interim fact-finding report of the task force pointed out the following common features derived from all the three cases:

• The employers have been inflicting injuries and battering them repeatedly, over weeks and months.
• The employers have amply demonstrated the extent of their disturbed mentality, going by the gruesome third-degree battering of the children.
• The employers are all professionals, two among them being government employees, who have been treated leniently by the respective government departments.
• The child domestic workers have had no recourse to help or were working in conditions of absolute bondage and slavery.
• These children constituted a force that is predominantly invisible and silent, and hence subject to a higher degree of exploitation and abuse.
• The children were continuously locked in the homes and had no opportunity to share/express their anguish and pain, and this proved to be a critical psychological hazard.
• The employers did have their own children who had been well protected, which clearly demonstrates that the employers had exploited the class background of the domestic workers to abuse them.
• In India, the share of girls in agriculture is much larger than boys, while in Bangladesh, the share of boys is much higher in agriculture.[50]

---

[48] Dev, 'Family Thought Maid's Job was Best Bet for Daughter', *Times of India*, 11 July 2012 available at http://articles.timesofindia.indiatimes.com/2012-07-11/bangalore/32631985_1_lakshmi-thambi-rajesh-jain (accessed on 11 July 2011).

[49] The RALLY. 'The Hidden "Live-In" Slaves, The Domestic Workers', May Day Message, April 1998.

[50] Arun Dev, 'Family Thought Maid's Job Was Best Best for Daughter'.

Bonded Child Labour

The South Asian Task Force on Bonded Child Labour defines a bonded child labourer as:

> a child (below 18 years of age as defined in the UNCRC) working against debt taken by himself/ herself or his/her family members, or working against any social obligation (e.g., caste factor, ethnic or religious practices, etc.) without or with the child's consent, under conditions that restrain his/ her freedom and development, making him/her vulnerable to physical and other forms of abuse and depriving him/her of his/ her basic rights.[51]

Bonded labour system is a modern form of slavery which combines feudal values, traditions, and practices, with contemporary exploitative labour relations. Almost all South Asian societies bear the brunt of this, one way or the other. However, it is more prevalent in India, Pakistan, and Nepal.[52]

Bonded child labour refers to the phenomenon of children working in conditions of servitude in order to pay off a debt that binds them to their relatives or guardians—usually a parent. The creditors-cum-employers offer 'loans' to destitute parents in an effort to secure the labour of a child, which is always cheap, but even cheaper under a situation of bondage.[53] The parents, on their part, accept the loans. Bondage is a traditional worker–employer relationship, and the parents need the money, perhaps to pay for the costs of a medical treatment, perhaps to provide a dowry to a marrying child, or perhaps—as is often the case—to help put food on the table.[54] The children who are sold to these bond masters work long hours over many years in an attempt to pay off these debts. Due to the astronomically high rates of interest charged and the abysmally low wages paid, they are usually unsuccessful.[55] As they reach maturity, some of them may be released by the employer in favour of a newly-indebted and younger sibling, back to their parent, or even to their own children.[56]

Human Rights Watch,[57] based on a survey of 100 bonded children in five states (Rajasthan, Tamil Nadu, Karnataka, Maharashtra, and Uttar Pradesh), has identified bonded child labour in a number of occupations and workplaces including agriculture, brick kilns, stone quarries, carpet weaving, beedi rolling, rearing of silk cocoons, production of silk sarees, silver jewellery, synthetic

---

[51] William F. Stafford, Jr., 'Understanding Bonded Child Labour in Asia, An Introduction to the Nature of the Problem and How to Address It' (Child Workers in Asia [CWA] Task Force on Bonded Child Labour, 2007).

[52] 'Child Workers in Asia'. Available at http://www.globaladvocacy.com/Bonded_Child_Labour.html (accessed on 8 July 2015).

[53] Human Rights Watch Children's Rights Project, The Small Hands of Slavery: Bonded Child Labour in India (New York: Human Rights Watch, 1996). Available at http://hrw.org/reports/1996/India3.htm (accessed on 14 November 2016).

[54] Human Rights Watch Children's Rights Project, Small Hands of Slavery.

[55] Human Rights Watch Children's Rights Project, Small Hands of Slavery.

[56] Human Rights Watch Children's Rights Project, Small Hands of Slavery.

[57] Human Rights Watch is a non-profit, non-governmental human rights organization made up of roughly 400 staff members around the globe. Its staff consists of human rights professionals including country experts, lawyers, journalists, and academics of diverse backgrounds and nationalities. See more at https://www.hrw.org/about (accessed on 9 November 2015).

gemstones, precious gem cutting, diamond cutting, leather products, and so on.[58] The problem also exists in a number of sectors including carpet weaving, agriculture, salt-making, fireworks and matches, glass, silver works, gemstones, and leather. There have been reports of bonded child labour in other industries such as circuses, fisheries, shops and tailoring establishments, and domestic work.[59]

Out of School Children, Child Labour, and Education

According to Article 6 of the Universal Declaration of Human Rights (UDHR), everyone has the right to education. Education shall be free, at least in the elementary and fundamental stages. Elementary education shall be compulsory. Again, Article 8 of the United Nations Convention on the Rights of the Child (UNCRC) recognizes 'the right of children to education, and with a view to achieving this right progressively and on the basis of equal opportunity'. Basic education is a human right, and yet there are millions of out-of-school children around the world today. Many are children from vulnerable and marginalized communities, the majority of whom are girls. Child labour denies children their right to a full-time, formal, quality education.

New data from the UNESCO Institute for Statistics (UIS) show that the global number of children and young adolescents out of school is rising at the same time that the international community is setting a new sustainable development goal that includes universal secondary education.[60] According to UIS data for the school year ending in 2013, 124 million children and young adolescents roughly between the ages of 6 and 15 years have either never started school or have dropped out, compared to 122 million in 2011. The data serves as a grim reminder that the world has yet to fulfill its original promise to provide every child with a primary education.[61]

The newly released UNESCO eAtlas on out-of-school children (OOSC) provides worrying evidence not only of the low priority being accorded to basic education across developing countries, but also by the developed world in terms of the aid given to education.[62] The rise in the number of children who are out of school around the world closely mirrors the situation in India, where public education is slowly falling off the policy map of the government. The massive cuts in the last budget and the recently released policy document of the Rajasthan government inviting

---

[58] Human Rights Watch Children's Rights Project, *Small Hands of Slavery*.

[59] Ravi S. Srivastava, *Bonded Labour in India: Its Incidence and Pattern* (Geneva: International Labour Office, June 2005).

[60] UNESCO Institute for Statistics and the Education for All Global Monitoring Report, 'A Growing Number of Children and Adolescents Are Out of School As Aid Fails to Meet the Mark', July 2015. Available at http://www.uis.unesco.org/Education/Documents/fs-31-out-of-school-children-en.pdf (accessed on 9 November 2015).

[61] UNESCO eAtlas of Out-of-School Children, 'Global Trends on Out-of-School Children'. For more information, see http://www.uis.unesco.org/data/atlas-out-of-school-children/en (accessed on 14 November 2016).

[62] Kiran Bhatty, 'The UN Report on Out-of-School Kids is Bad News for India: The Real Picture May Be Worse', *The Wire*, 7 July 2015. Available at http://thewire.in/2015/07/07/the-un-report-on-out-of-school-kids-is-bad-news-for-india-but-the-real-picture-is-worse/ (accessed on 8 July 2015).

the private sector to take over government schools are important indicators of the new policy thrust.[63]

Parents want to send their children to school. The demand for basic education, especially among the poorer sections of the population, has increased while the state's commitment to providing the opportunity to help this section move up the economic ladder has decreased. This is evident from the fact that the share of gross domestic product (GDP) to education in India has remained at a very low and constant level over the last decade or so, hovering below 4 per cent.[64] This is among the lowest in the world. The situation has been worsened by the decline in foreign aid to education over the same period. This is the result of a worldwide trend as indicated by UNESCO, but in the Indian case, also of the perception that India does not need the aid—a perception projected by the Indian state as well. Without the government itself stepping in to make up for the loss in foreign funds, the result is a growing neglect of this crucial sector.[65]

The child labour phenomenon is closely related to that of OOSC. The majority of children not in school are engaged in some form of work activity, and, for children in school, involvement in work makes them more susceptible to premature drop-out. There is a consensus emerging that when a child is not attending school, he/she would be part of the labour pool. There is evidence to show that child labour depresses school enrolment rates, negatively affects school achievement, decreases graduation rates, and increases drop-out rates. Household poverty forces millions of children out of school and into paying jobs, or especially for young girls, domestic chores.[66]

At the national level, during 2014, out of an estimated 204.1 million children in the age group of 6–13 years, an estimated 6.064 million children were out of school. This accounts for 2.97 per cent of the total children in the said age group across all states and Union Terrotories in India. Percentage of OOSC in the 6–13 years age group has reduced considerably from 2009 (4.53 per cent) and 2005 (6.94 per cent). Disaggregation reveals that a higher percentage of children in the rural areas (3.13 per cent) are out of school as compared to those in the urban areas (2.54 per cent). This is found to be in line with the trend observed in the previous two rounds in 2005 and 2009. The findings from 2014 round reveal that in the age group of 6–13 years, an estimated 4.695 million children are out of school in rural India, and an estimated 1.369 million children are out of school in urban India.[67] The Indian Market Research Bureau (IMRB) survey conducted in 2009 indicated that the number of OOSC declined from 13.45 million in 2005–06 to 8.15 million in 2009–10. These surveys indicated that the percentage of OOSC to total population in the age group 6–14 years has decreased from 6.94 per cent in 2005–06 to 4.28 per cent in 2009–10.[68]

[63] Bhatty, 'UN Report on Out-of-School Kids'.

[64] Bhatty, 'UN Report on Out-of-School Kids'.

[65] Bhatty, 'UN Report on Out-of-School Kids'.

[66] Global March against Child Labour, 'Policy Paper—Out of School Children and Child Labour', 2014. Available at http://globalmarch.org/sites/default/files/Policy-Paper.pdf (accessed on 14 November 2016).

[67] 'National Sample Survey of Estimation of Out-of-School Children in the Age 6–13 in India', 2014, Draft Report Submitted by Social & Rural Research Institute. Also available at: http://ssa.nic.in/pabminutes-documents/NS.pdf (accessed on 8 July 2015).

[68] NSSO data.

According to a UNESCO report, India, with 1.4 million children, ranks among the top five nations with kids aged six to 11 out of school (in 2014).[69]

A gender-wise disaggregation reveals that 3.166 million males and 2.898 million females are estimated to be out of school. In proportion, 2.77 per cent of the estimated male population (114.4 million) and 3.23 per cent of the estimated female population (89.7 million) are out of school, that is, a higher percentage of females (as compared to males) are out of school in the 6–13 years age group.[70]

Among the two age groups, that is, 6–10 years and 11–13 years, it is observed that estimated percentage of OOSC is higher in the age group 11–13 years (3.28 per cent), as compared to 6–10 years (2.77 per cent).[71] All of them are to be considered as part of the labour force.

The Second National Labour Commission Report (2002) established the link between child labour and education and stated:

> All out of school children must be treated as child labourers or as those who have the potential to become child labourers ... Thus, all work done by children, irrespective of where it is done, must be considered as child labour. Only then girls and children working within the family become a part of the strategy to eliminate child labour, and significant headway will be made towards achieving the goal of eliminating child labour.[72]

As per Census 2011, the total number of working children in the country has declined from 12.6 million as per the Census of 2001, to 4.353 million as per Census of 2011, which is a reduction of 65 per cent.[73] This decline owes credit to the Right to Education Act, 2005 (RTE),[74] which promises free and compulsory education to all aged between 6 and 14 years. There are five main components that the act puts forth:

- In India, every child is entitled to free and compulsory full-time elementary education (first to eighth grade) as facilitated by the Right of Children to Free and Compulsory Education Act, 2009 (RCFCEA). This means elementary education of satisfactory and equitable quality in a formal school run with certain essential standards.
- Parents of children covered under the RTE are not liable to pay for school fees, uniforms, textbooks, mid-day meals, transportation, ad so on until the elementary education is complete.
- If a child has not managed to secure admission in a school according to age, it will be the government's responsibility to get the child admitted in an age-appropriate class. Schools will have to organize training sessions to allow such a child to catch up with others.

[69] NSSO data.

[70] NSSO data.

[71] NSSO data.

[72] Second National Commission on Labour, *Report of the Study Group on Women and Child Labour*, 2002, Section viii—'Recommendations', p. 220.

[73] Press Information Bureau, Ministry of Labour and Employment, Government of India, 'Rehabilitation of Freed Child Labourers' 23 July 2014. Available at http://pib.nic.in/newsite/PrintRelease.aspx?relid=107275 (accessed on 8 July 2015).

[74] See Chapter 7 for details of the RTE Act.

- No child shall be held back (failed) or expelled until the completion of elementary education.
- Not following the RTE rules can invite a penalty of Rs. 25,000.

There are contradictions in the constitutional mandate as well as the child labour laws. Article 24 of the Constitution of India states that no child below 14 years can work in any hazardous occupation or industry.[75] This implies that children below 14 years can work in any non-hazardous occupation or industry. On the other hand, Article 21A of the Constitution of India provides for free and compulsory education to all children aged 6 to 14 years.[76] The RTE Act, which came into force on 1 April 2010, guarantees the right to every child between the ages of six and 14 to free and compulsory elementary education, whereas the Child Labour (Prohibition and Regulation) Act (CLPRA), 1986 makes a distinction between hazardous and non-hazardous categories of work for children under 14 years. Under the 1986 Act, only employment of child labour in hazardous occupations is a cognizable offence.[77] Many children continue to be employed in non-hazardous occupations like agriculture and household work. Hence, a vast majority of them remain out of school even though the RTE Act envisages education for each and every child.

All OOSC must be treated as child labourers or as those who have the potential to become child labourers. Thus, all work done by children, irrespective of where it is done, must be considered as child labour. Only then will girls and children working within the family become a part of the strategy to eliminate child labour, and significant headway will be made towards achieving the goal of eliminating child labour.[78]

The contradiction can be addressed by amending the constitutional provisions and amending or repealing the CLPRA. In linking child labour to education, the tasks of eliminating child labour and of universalizing education become synonymous. One cannot be achieved without the other. The task of withdrawing a child from work, therefore, becomes the same as inducting the child into school.[79] Children must be in schools and not at work, so that they access their right to education and all their entitlements to recreation, play, health, and nutrition. All children

[75] Article 24 in the Constitution of India, 1949: Prohibition of employment of children in factories, among others. No child below the age of 14 years shall be employed to work in any factory or mine or engaged in any other hazardous employment provided that nothing in this subclause shall authorize the detention of any person beyond the maximum period prescribed by any law made by Parliament under Subclause (b) of Clause (7); or such person is detained in accordance with the provisions of any law made by Parliament under Subclauses (a) and (b) of Clause (7).

[76] Article 21 in the Constitution of India 1949: Protection of life and personal liberty. No person shall be deprived of his life or personal liberty except according to procedure established by law.

[77] Standing Committee on Labour, *The Child Labour (Prohibition and Regulation) Amendment Bill, 2012*, Fortieth Report, Fifteenth Lok Sabha (India: Ministry of Labour and Employment, Government of India, 2013–2014). Available at http://164.100.47.134/lsscommittee/Labour/15_Labour_40.pdf (accessed on 9 November 2015).

[78] National Commission on Labour, *Report of the Study Group on Women and Child Labour* (2001), p. 220.

[79] National Commission for Protection of Child Rights (NCPCR), 'Abolition of Child Labour and Making Education a Reality for Every Child as a Right' (New Delhi, 2008). Available at http://ncpcr.gov.in/showfile.php?lid=68 (accessed on 9 November 2015).

must be guaranteed full-time formal day school. The CLPRA must be aligned to ensure legal provisions of RTE Act and ensure right to quality education. All children must have a right to quality education. Improving access to schooling is essential, but is only a part of the answer. There is also a general need to improve school quality in order for schooling to be seen by parents as a worthwhile alternative to child labour.[80] Corporal punishment also needs to be eliminated to encourage children to go to school, and above all, remain there.

Evolution of Policy on Child Labour

National Policy on Child Labour

The National Policy on Child Labour (NPCL)[81] is a landmark endeavour in the progressive elimination of child labour in India. A National Policy on Child Labour has been formulated in conjunction with the legal measures to address the socio-economic issues having a bearing on child labour and to provide a framework for a concrete programme of action. The policy attempts to deal with the situation where the children work, or are compelled to work, on a regular or a continuous basis to earn wages for themselves and/or their families, and where their conditions of work result in there being severely disadvantaged and exploited, and where abuses connected with such factors impacting on wage-employed children need to be given close attention by the state for rectification, amelioration, and regulation through specific legal and administrative instruments and measures. The policy encompasses action in the fields of education, health, nutrition, integrated child development, and employment.[82] Figure 4.3 details the evolution of the policy on child labour in India.

The NPCL is set under the following three heads:

- The Legislative Action Plan.
- Focusing of general programmes for benefiting child labour wherever possible.
- Project-based plan of action in areas of high concentration of child labour engaged in wage/quasi-wage employment.

Legislative Action Plan

Under the Legislative Action Plan, emphasis is laid on strict and effective enforcement of the provisions of the CLPA Act, the Factories Act, 1948, the Mines Act, 1952, the Plantation Labour Act, 1951, and other acts containing provisions relating to the employment of children.

---

[80] Lorenzo Guarcello, Scott Lyon, and Furio Rosati, 'Child Labour and Out of School Children: Evidence from 25 Developing Countries', Understanding Children's Work (UCW) Programme, Background Paper for Fixing the Broken Promise of Education for All (UNICEF and UNESCO Institute of Statistics, 2014). Available at http://allinschool.org/wp-content/uploads/2015/01/OOSC-2014-Child-labour-final.pdf (accessed on 2 July 2015).

[81] Government of India, National Policy on Child Labour, 1987.

[82] Ashok Narayan, *Child Labour Policies and Programmes: The Indian Experience* (New Delhi: Government of India, Ministry of Labour and Employment, 1988).

Table 4.4   The Evolution of Child Labour Policy in India[83]

S. No	Event	Date	Details
1.	Ratification of ILO, Night Work of Young Persons (Industry) Convention 1919 (No. 6).	July 1921	Night work by young persons in any public or private industrial undertaking prohibited.
2.	Ratification of ILO, Minimum Age of Trimmers and Stokers Convention 1921 (No. 15).	November 1922	Employment of young persons as trimmers and stokers in vessels or ports prohibited.
3.	Ratification of ILO, Medical Examination of Young Persons (Sea) Convention 1921 (No. 16).	November 1922	Compulsory medical examination of children and young persons employed at sea provided for.
4.	Enactment of Children (Pledging of Labour) Act, 1933.	February 1933	Pledging of labour of children prohibited and penalty for parents/guardians pledging child labour prescribed. Employment of children below 15 years prohibited in certain occupations.
5.	Enactment of Employment of Children Act, 1938.	February 1938	Employment of children below 15 years prohibited in certain occupations.
6.	Adoption and Enactment of the Constitution of India Act by the Constituent Assembly.	1949	Prohibition of employment of children below 14 years of age in factories, mines, and hazardous employment in terms of a fundamental right; and directive principles laid down against the abuse of the tender age of the children and for free and compulsory education for children up to 14 years of age.
7.	Ratification of ILO, Night Work of Young Persons (Industry) Convention (Revised) 1948 (No. 90).	July 1950	Night work by children and young persons abolished.
8.	Ratification of ILO, Minimum Age (Industry) Convention 1919 (No. 5).	September 1955	Employment of children under 14 years of age in public or private industrial undertaking prohibited.
9.	Report of the National Labour Commission.	1969	Recommended combination of work with education and flexible employment hours, which would not inhibit education.
10.	Ratification of ILO, Minimum Age (Underground Work) Convention 1965 (No. 123).	March 1975	Employment of persons below 16 years of age for work underground in mines prohibited.

[83] Source: Compiled by author from various sources.

Table 4.4   (Cont'd)

S. No	Event	Date	Details
11.	Report of Gurupadaswamy Committee.	1979	Recommended setting up of Child Labour Advisory Board; fixation of minimum age of entry to any establishment; strengthening of enforcement machinery; and formulation of effective educational policy with emphasis on integration of educational requirements with local crafts.
12.	Establishment of the Central Child Labour Advisory Board with labour minister as chairman.	March 1981	To review implementation of existing laws; to suggest legislative and welfare measures for working children; and to recommend industries where child labour should be eliminated.
13.	Enactment of Child Labour (Prohibition and Regulation) Act, 1986.	December 1986	Employment of children below 14 years of age prohibited in specific occupations and processes; procedure for modification of schedule of banned occupations or processes laid down; regulation of working conditions for children in non-prohibited employment provided for; penalties for violation of the law provided for; and uniformity in definition of 'child' in related laws provided for.
14.	Adoption of the National Child Labour Policy, 1987.	August 1987	Provided for a legislative action plan; focusing of general development programmes for the benefit of working children as well; and formulation of project-based action plain in areas of high concentration of child labour.
15.	Report of the Task Force on Child Labour set up by the Child Labour Advisory Board under the Chairmanship of Dr L.M. Singhvi.	December 1989	Recommended amendments to child labour laws and NPCL.
16.	Report of the National Commission on Rural Labour.	July 1991	Recommended enactments of compulsory Primary Education Acts by states; creation of non-formal education centres; enhancement of outlays for elementary education guaranteed; wage employment for parents of working children; universal prohibition of child labour; media publicity against child labour.
17.	Report of the study group on women and children of the II National Commission on Labour.	2002	Recommended the enactment of Child Labour (Prohibition and Education) Bill, 2000.

(Cont'd)

Table 4.4   (Cont'd)

S. No	Event	Date	Details
18.	Child Labour (Prohibition and Regulation) Amendment Bill, 2012.	Passed by the Cabinet on 13 May 2015	Attempting to strike a balance between the need for education for a child and the reality of the socio-economic condition and social fabric in the country, the Cabinet has approved that a child can help his family or family enterprise, which is other than any hazardous occupation or process, after his school hours or during vacation. Also, an exception has been made for a child working as artist in an audio-visual entertainment industry, except the circus, provided that the school education of the child is not affected; a new definition of adolescent has been introduced in the CLPR Act and employment of adolescents (14 to 18 years of age) has been prohibited in hazardous occupations and processes; stricter punishment for employers for violation of the act has been proposed to act as a deterrent; offence of employing any child or adolescent in contravention of the act by an employer has been made cognizable; taking a realistic view of the socio-economic conditions of the parents/guardians, there would be no punishment in case of a first offence by the parents/guardians and in case of a second and subsequent offence, the penalty would be a fine which may extend to Rs 10,000; constitution of Child and Adolescent Labour Rehabilitation Fund for one or more districts for the rehabilitation of the child or adolescent rescued. Thus, the act itself will provide for a fund to carry out rehabilitation activities.
19.	The Child Labour (Prohibition and Regulation) Amendment Act, 2016	The act received the assent of the President on 29 July 2016	The act is called the Child and Adolescent Labour (Prohibition and Regulation) Act, 1986. The act provides for ban of employment of children below 14 in all occupations and enterprises, except those run by his or her own family. It defines children between 14 and 18 years as adolescents and bars their employment in any hazardous occupations. It makes child labour a cognizable offence attracting a jail term of up to 2 years and penalty up to Rs 50,000. The act has a provision of creating rehabilitation fund has also been made for the rehabilitation of children.

Focusing of General Programmes for Benefiting Child Labour

Various national development programmes exist in the areas of education, health, nutrition, integrated child development, and income and employment generation for the poor. These programmes will be utilized to create socio-economic conditions in which the compulsions to send the children to work diminish and the children are encouraged to attend school rather than take up wage employment.

Project Based Plan of Action in Areas of High Concentration of Child Labour

This involves launching of projects for the welfare of working children in areas of high concentration of child labour. These projects withdraw children from hazardous employment and ensure their rehabilitation through education in special schools.[84] The Government of India has been implementing the National Child Labour Project (NCLP) scheme for rehabilitation of child labour since 1988 in the areas of high concentration. Under this scheme, all children in the age group of 9–14 years are rescued from hazardous occupations and processes and enrolled in NCLP Special Training Centres which have a provision for bridge education, vocational training, mid-day meal stipend, and other facilities, before being mainstreamed into formal education system. At present, the scheme is approved for 270 districts in 20 states of the country through approximately 6,000 Special Training Centres with enrolment of more than 250,000 children.[85] In 2011–12, 1,25,716 children were brought into the mainstream against a figure of 64,050 in 2013–14.[86]

The Legal Regime Relating to Child Labour and Bonded Child Labour in India

Laws to Prohibit and Regulate Child Labour in India

The Constitution of India[87] has laid down that no child under the age of 14 years shall be employed in any mine or engaged in any other hazardous employment[88] and any contravention of this provision shall be an offence punishable in accordance with law. The directive principles of state policy, in Article 39(e), provide that the health and strength of workers, men and women, and the tender age of children are not abused and that citizens are not forced by economic necessity to enter avocations unsuited to their age or strength. Article 39(f) directs that the children

---

[84]Department of Women and Child Development, *India Report on the World Summit for Children*, (Ministry of Human Resource Development, Government of India, 2000).

[85] Press Information Bureau, 'Rehabilitation of Freed Child Labourers' (Ministry of Labour and Employment, Government of India). Available at http://pib.nic.in/newsite/PrintRelease.aspx?relid=107275 (accessed on 9 November 2015).

[86] Vishnu Deo Sai, 'Number of child Labourer Has Declined: Govt', *Day and Night News*, 4 July 2015. For more, see http://www.dayandnightnews.com/2014/07/number-of-child-labourer-has-declined-govt/ (accessed on 4 July 2015).

[87] See the Constitution of India, Parts III and IV. The fundamental rights are embodied in Part III of the Constitution and the directive principles are in Part IV.

[88] Constitution of India, Article 24.

are given opportunities and facilities to develop in a healthy manner and in conditions of freedom and dignity, and that childhood and youth are protected against exploitation and moral and material abandonment. It has been made a duty of the state to raise the level of nutrition and the standard of living and to improve public health. Article 21A of the Constitution of India provides for free and compulsory education for all children between 6 and 14 years.[89]

Legislation to control and regulate child labour in India has existed for several decades. A resume of the history of legislation relating to child labour and some salient features are presented below.[90]

Factories Act, 1881

- Minimum age (7 years);
- successive employment (employment in two factories on the same day) prohibited;
- duration of employment (working hours not to exceed nine hours a day and at least four holidays to be given in a month); and
- factories employing 100 or more persons were covered by this act.

The Factories Act, 1881 was revised in 1891 with respect to the following matters:

- minimum age (increased to 9 years); and
- hours of work (maximum seven hours per day, with prohibition of work at night between 8 p.m. and 5 a.m.).

Mines Act, 1901

This act prohibited employment of children under 12 years of age.

Factories Act, 1911

Provisions of this act are:

- work between 7 p.m. and 5.30 a.m. prohibited;
- work in certain dangerous processes prohibited; and
- certificate of age and fitness required.

[89] The Constitution (86th Amendment) Act, 2002 inserted Article 21A in the Constitution of India to provide free and compulsory education for all children in the age group of 6 to 14 years as a fundamental right in such a manner as the state may, by law, determine. The RTE Act, which represents the consequential legislation envisaged under Article 21A, means that every child has a right to full-time elementary education of satisfactory and equitable quality in a formal school which satisfies certain essential norms and standards. Article 21A and the RTE Act came into effect on 1 April 2010.

[90] A.P. Verma, 'Child Labour in India: An Overview', *Award Digest: Journal of Labour Legislation* XX, nos 7–12 (July–December 1994).

Factory (Amendment) Act, 1922

To implement the ILO Convention (No. 5) 1919, the amendment provided for changes such as:

- minimum age (15 years in general);
- working hours (maximum six hours, and also an interval of half an hour if children are employed for more than five-and-a-half hours);
- establishments employing 20 or more persons with mechanical processes were covered under this act, with power vested in the local government to exclude the applications of provisions to premises employing 10 or more persons;
- prohibition of employment of children below 18 and women in certain processes; and
- provision for medical certificate and also certificate of re-examination for continuing work.

Indian Mines Act, 1923

This act raised the minimum age for employment from 12 to 13 years.

Factories (Amendment) Act, 1926

This act imposed certain penalties on the parents and guardians for allowing their children to work in two separate factories on the same day.

Indian Ports (Amendment) Act, 1931

This act laid down 12 years as the minimum age that could be prescribed for handling goods in ports. The report of the Royal Commission on Labour (1931) had an impact on legislation pertaining to child labour during the period between 1931 and 1949.

Tea Districts' (Emigration Labour) Act, 1932

This was passed to check migration of labourers to districts in Assam. It provided that no under-age child was employed or allowed to migrate unless the child was accompanied by his or her parents or adults on whom the child was dependent.

Children (Pledging of Labour) Act, 1933

This act prohibited pledging of children, that is, taking of advances by parents and guardians in return for bonds, pledging the labour of their children—a system akin to the bonded labour system. The Royal Commission noticed this practice of pledging of labour of children in areas such as Amritsar, Ahmedabad, and Madras, among others, and in carpet and beedi factories. The children in these situations were found to be working under extremely unsatisfactory conditions.

Factories (Amendment) Act, 1934

This act had elaborate provisions for regulating the employment of children of various age groups in the factories, such as:

1. employment of children between 12 and 15 years was generally prohibited in certain areas;
2. employment of children under 12 and 15 years was restricted to five hours a day in other areas; and
3. for employment of children between 15 and 17 years, certain restrictions were imposed.

Mines (Amendment) Act, 1935

This also introduced division of children according to age groups, and the position which emerged was as follows:

1. Employment of children less than 15 years old in mines was prohibited.
2. Underground employment was permitted only on production of certificate of physical fitness granted by a qualified medical practitioner for persons between 15 and 17 years.
3. Working time restricted to a maximum of ten hours a day and fifty-four hours a week for work above the ground, and nine hours a day for work underground.

Employment of Children Act, 1938

This act was passed to implement the Convention adopted by the 23rd session of ILO (1937), which inserted a special article on India:

> Children under the age of thirteen years shall not be employed or work in the transport of passengers, or goods, or mails, by rail, or in handling of goods at docks, quays, or wharves, but excluding transport by hand. Children under the age of fifteen years shall not be employed or work...in occupations to which this Article applies which are scheduled as dangerous or unhealthy by the competent authority.

This act:

- prohibited employment of children under 15 years in occupations connected with transportation of goods, passengers, and mails, or in the railways;
- raised the minimum age of handling goods on docks from 12 to 14 years; and
- provided for the requirement of a certificate of age.

Factories Act, 1948

This act raised minimum age for employment in factories to 14 years.

Employment of Children (Amendment) Act, 1949

This act raised the minimum age to 14 years for employment in establishments governed by the act.

Employment of Children (Amendment) Act, 1951

As a result of the ILO Convention relating to night work of young persons, this act prohibited the employment of children between 15 and 17 years at night in the railways and ports, and also provided for requirement of maintaining a register for children under 17 years.

Plantations Labour Act, 1951

This act prohibited the employment of children under 12 years in plantations.

Mines Act, 1952

This act prohibited the employment of children less than 15 years in mines. The act stipulated two conditions for underground work:

- requirement to have completed 16 years of age; and
- requirement to obtain a certificate of physical fitness from a surgeon.

The act prohibits employment of persons (below 18 years) in any mine or part thereof (Section 40) and also their presence in any part of the mine above ground where any operation connected with or incidental to any mining operation is being carried out (Section 45). The act prescribes punishment of fine up to Rs 500 in case of employment of persons below 18 years (Section 68). For contravention of any other provision of the act, there is provision of imprisonment up to three months or fine up to Rs 1,000 or both (Section 73).

Factories (Amendment) Act, 1954

This includes prohibition of employment of persons under 17 years at night. ('Night' was defined as a period of 12 consecutive hours which included hours between 10 p.m. and 7 a.m.).

The Merchant Shipping Act, 1958

This prohibits children under 15 from being engaged to work in any capacity in any ship, except in certain specified cases.

The Motor Transport Workers Act, 1961

This act prohibits the employment of children less than 15 years old in any motor transport undertaking.

The Apprentices Act, 1961

This prohibits the apprenticeship/training of a person less than 14 years old.

The Beedi and Cigar Workers (Conditions of Employment) Act, 1966

This act prohibits:

* the employment of children under 14 years in any industrial premises manufacturing beedis or cigars; and
* persons between 14 and 18 years from working at night between 7 p.m. and 6 a.m.

Employment of Children (Amendment) Act, 1978

This act prohibits employment of a child below 15 years in occupations in railway premises such as cinder picking or clearing of ash pit or building operations, in catering establishments, and in any other work which is carried on in close proximity to or between the railway lines.

The Child Labour (Prohibition and Regulation) Act, 1986

The CLPRA, 1986 is an outcome of various recommendations made by a series of committees.[91] From a reading of the recommendations made by various committees, there was a national consensus in favour of a uniform comprehensive legislation to prohibit the engagement of children in certain other employment. To achieve this goal, the Parliament enacted the CLPRA, which came into force on 23 December 1986.

Legislative history in India has traversed a long way since 1881 by progressively extending legal protection to the working children. Provisions relating to child labour under various enactments have concentrated mainly on aspects such as minimizing working hours, increasing minimum age, and prohibition of employment of children in occupations and processes detrimental to the health and welfare of children of tender age.[92] The Employment of Children Act, 1938, which was the first enactment on child labour, was repealed by the CLPRA.

---

[91] National Commission on Labour, 1969, Committee on Child Labour, 1979, Gurupadswamy Committee on Child Labour, 1976, and Sanat Mehta Committee, 1984.

[92] M. Gupta, 'Special Problems of Enforcement of Child Labour Laws and Regulations', *Awards Digest: Journal of Labour Legislation*, XX, no. 7–12.

Objectives of the Child Labour (Prohibition and Regulation) Act, 1986

The objectives of the CLPRA are:

- banning the employment of children, that is, those who have not completed their 14th year, in specified occupations and processes;
- laying down procedures to decide modifications to the schedule of banned occupations or processes; and
- regulating the conditions of work of children in employment where they are not prohibited from working.

Significant Provisions of the CLPRA

The preamble to the act states that it is an act to prohibit the employment of children in certain occupations and to regulate the conditions of work of children in certain other occupations. The act prohibits the employment of any person who has not completed his 14th year of age[93] in occupations and processes set forth in Part A[94] and Part B[95] of the schedule of the act.

[93] CLPRA, Section 3: 'No child shall be employed or permitted to work in any of the occupations set forth in Part A of the Schedule or in any workshop wherein, any of the processes set forth in Part B of the Schedule is carried on.'

[94] Part A lists... out the occupations connected with

(1) transport of passengers, goods or mails by railway; (2) cinder picking, clearing or an ash pit or building operation in the railway premises; (3) work in a catering establishment at a railway station, involving the movement of a vendor or any other employee of the establishment from one platform to another or into or out of a moving train; (4) work relating to the construction of a railway station or with any other work where such work is done in close proximity to or between the railway lines; (5) a port authority within the limits of any port; (6) work relating to selling of crackers and fireworks in shops with temporary licences; (7) abattoirs/slaughter houses; (8) automobile workshops and garages; (9) foundries; (10) handling of toxic or inflammable substances or explosives; (11) handloom and power loom industry; (12) mines (underground and underwater) and collieries; and (13) plastic units and fibreglass workshops; (13) plastic units and fibreglass workshops; (14) domestic workers or servants; (15) dhabas (roadside eateries), restaurants, hotels, motels, tea shops, resorts, spas or other recreational centres; (16) diving; (17) caring of elephant; (18) working in the circus.

[95] Part B lists out the following processes:

Beedi making; carpet weaving; cement manufacture, including bagging of cement; cloth printing, dyeing, and weaving; manufacture of matches, explosives, and fireworks; mica cutting and splitting; shellac manufacture; soap manufacture; tanning; wool cleaning; building and construction industry; manufacture of slate pencils (including packing); manufacturing of products from agate; manufacturing process using toxic metals and substances such as lead, mercury, manganese, chromium, cadmium, benzene, pesticides, and asbestos; hazardous processes as defined in Section 2(cb) and 'dangerous operations' as notified in rules made under Section 87 of the Factories Act 1948 (Act 63 of 1948); printing as defined in Section 2(k) (iv) of the Factories Act 1948 (Act 63 of 1948); cashew and cashew nut desiccating and processing; soldering processes in electronic industries; agarbatti manufacturing; automobile repairs and maintenance including processes incidental thereto, namely, welding, lathe work, dent beating and painting; brick kilns and roof tiles units; cotton ginning and processing and production of hosiery goods; detergent manufacturing;

The act thus classifies all establishments in two categories:

- those in which employment of child labour is prohibited, and
- those in which the working conditions of child labour shall be regulated.

The Central Government has the power to amend the schedule.[96] The Central Government may, by notification in the official gazette, constitute an advisory committee called the Child Labour Technical Advisory Committee for the purpose of addition of occupations and processes to the Schedule (CLPRA, Section 5). While several occupations and processes have been added, some more have to be included. Work in the entertainment industry involves performance work, for example, acting, appearing in promotional events, dancing, doing voice-overs, modelling, including photographic modelling, playing a musical instrument, or singing. Work supporting the entertainment industry, such as working front-of-house or backstage, is not considered as child labour.[97] Children also have to undergo rigorous training for the sake of their parents who

---

fabrication workshops (ferrous and non-ferrous); gem cutting and polishing; handling of chromate and manganese ores; jute textile manufacture and coir making; lime kilns and manufacture of lime; lock making; manufacturing processes having exposure to lead such as primary and secondary smelting, welding and cutting of lead-painted metal constructions, welding of galvanized or zinc silicate and polyvinyl chloride, mixing (by hand) of crystal glass mass, sanding or scraping of lead paint, burning of lead in enamelling workshops, lead mining, plumbing, cable making, wire patenting, lead casting, type founding in printing shops, store type setting, assembling of cars, shot making and lead glass blowing; manufacture of cement pipes, cement products, and other related work; manufacture of glass, glassware including bangles, fluorescent tubes, bulbs, and other similar glass products; manufacture of dyes and dye stuff; manufacturing or handling of pesticides and insecticides; manufacturing or processing and handling of corrosive and toxic substances; metal cleaning and photo engraving and soldering processes in electronic industry; production of burning coal and coal briquettes; manufacturing of sports goods involving exposure to synthetic materials, chemicals, and leather; moulding and processing of fibreglass and plastic; oil expelling and refinery; paper making; potteries and ceramic industry; polishing, moulding, cutting, welding, and manufacture of brass goods in all forms; processes in agriculture where tractors and threshing and harvesting machines are used, and chaff cutting; saw mill—all processes; sericulture processing; skinning, dyeing, and processing for the manufacture of leather and leather products; stone breaking and stone crushing; tobacco processing including manufacture of tobacco and tobacco paste and handling of tobacco in any form; tyre making, repairing, retreading, and graphite benefaction; utensils making, polishing, and metal buffing; zari making (all processes), electroplating, graphite powdering and incidental processing, grinding or glazing of metals, diamond cutting and polishing, extraction of slate from mines, rag picking and scavenging, processes involving exposure to excessive heat (e.g. working near furnace) and cold, merchandised fishing, food processing, beverage industry, timber handling and loading, mechanical lumbering, warehousing, processes involving exposure to free silica such as slate, pencil industry, stone grinding, slate stone mining, stone quarries, agate industry.

[96] CLPRA, Section 4.

[97] Sharmistha Bhattacharjee, 'Sophisticated Work Done By Children: Is Child Labour: An Overview Of Children Working In Industries', *International Journal of Research in Humanities, Arts and Literature*, 2, no. 6. Available at https://www.google.co.in/url?sa=t&rct=j&q=&esrc=s&source=web&cd=1&cad=rja&uact=8&ved=0ahUKEwjmoeej6ZrPAhULS2MKHVrNDxUQFggcMAA&url=http%3A%2F%2Fwww.impactjournals.us%2Fdownload.php%3Ffname%3D2-11-1402121407-7.%2520Humanities-Sophisticate

want to register their child's name in record books such as *Limca Book of Records*. Children in the sphere of sports are engaged as jockeys in camel races. These races, being very risky, seriously injure children.[98]

The prohibition of employment of children is not applicable to any workshop wherein any process is carried on by the occupier with the aid of his family, or to any school established by or receiving assistance or recognition from the government.[99]

Part III of the act provides for regulation of conditions of work of children in establishments in which none of the occupations or processes referred to in the Schedule are carried out. It provides for the hours and period of work and weekly holidays for the children. The period of work of the child on each day shall be so fixed that no period shall exceed three hours and that no child shall work for more than three hours before he has had an interval for rest for at least one hour.[100] The total period of work, inclusive of the interval for rest, should be not more than six hours. The child is not permitted to work between 7 p.m. and 8 a.m. or overtime. Double employment of a child is banned.[101] The act also empowers the appropriate government to make rules for the health and the safety of the children employed or permitted to work in any establishment or class of establishments.[102]

Procedure for Prosecution of Offences

The procedure laid down in the act relating to the prosecution of offences is as follows:

- Any person, police officer, or inspector may file a complaint of the commission of an offence under this act in any court of competent jurisdiction.
- Every certificate as to the age of a child which has been granted by a prescribed medical authority shall, for the purposes of this act, be conclusive evidence as to the age of the child to whom it relates.[103]
- No court inferior to that of a metropolitan magistrate or a magistrate of the first class shall try any offence under this act.

Penalties Under the Act

The penalties under this act are relatively more stringent than the earlier acts and violating the provisions relating to child labour in certain other acts results in a penalty under this act.[104]

---

d%2520work%2520done%2520by%2520children%2520Is%2520child%2520labour-Sharmistha%2520B-hattacharjee.pdf&usg=AFQjCNEsxT5SJyKHsqZpIrs7FeNsK_9KWA&sig2=LDufAIwbK9kIMEmG-FLDOLg&bvm=bv.133178914,d.dGo (accessed on 19 September 2016).

98 Bhattacharjee, 'Sophisticated Work Done By Children'.

99 CLPRA, Proviso to Section 3.

100 CLPRA, Section 7(1), (2), (3), (4), (5), (6).

101 CLPRA, Section 7(1), (2), (3), (4), (5), (6).

102 CLPRA, Section 13.

103 CLPRA, Section 10.

104 CLPRA, Section 15.

The penalties[105] under this act are as follows:

- Whoever employs any child or permits any child to work in any hazardous employment shall be punishable with imprisonment for a term which shall not be less than three months but which may extend to 1 year, or with fine which shall not be less than ten thousand rupees but which may extend to twenty thousand rupees, or with both.[106] For a repeat offence, the punishment is imprisonment for a term which shall not be less than six months but which may extend to 2 years.[107]
- For failing to give notice to the inspector as required by Section 9, or failing to maintain a register as required by Section 11, or making any false entry in the register, or failing to display an abstract of Section 3,[108] or failing to comply with any other provisions of this act or rules, the punishment is imprisonment which may extend to one month, or with fine which may extend to Rs 10,000, or both.[109]

It is to be noted that the act provides for both fines as well as imprisonment. But in practice, in those few instances where the employer is prosecuted, s/he is generally fined.

Positive Features of the Act

- It increases and makes the penalties more stringent for employing child labour in violation of the law for factories, mines, merchant shipping, and motor transport [Section 15(1) and (2)].
- It defines 'family' and thereby makes it more explicit, thus precluding the possibility of its abuse.
- It empowers the Union government to bring into force provisions that regulate conditions of work of children in non-hazardous employment, and also empowers state governments to make rules for further regulation. It provides the machinery, that is, the Child Labour Technical Advisory Committee, for adding to the list of occupations and processes in which the employment of child labour is prohibited. (This was not possible in the Employment of Children Act, 1938).
- It permits any person, besides a police officer or inspector, to file a complaint against anyone employing or permitting a child below 14 in the prohibited occupations and processes.
- It makes the display of Sections 3 and 14 of CLPRA a mandatory requirement for the railway administration, the port authority, and the occupier.

---

[105] CLPRA, Section 14.

[106] CLPRA, Section 14(1).

[107] CLPRA, Section 14(2).

[108] CLPRA, Section 12: 'Every railway administration, every port authority, and every occupier shall cause to be displayed in a conspicuous and accessible place at every station, its railway or within the limits of a port or at the place of work, as the case may be, a notice in the local language and in the English language containing an abstract of Sections 3 and 14'.

[109] CLPRA, Section 14(3).

[110] Long title substituted through CLPR Amendment Act, 2016, Section 2.

The Child Labour (Prohibition and Regulation) Amendment Act, 2016

Salient Features

The short title of 'The Child Labour (Prohibition and Regulation) Act, 1986' will be changed to 'The Child and Adolescent Labour (Prohibition and Regulation) Act, 1986'.[110]

1. Some important definitions in the new 2016 act are (see Table 4.5):

   a) The definition of 'adolescent' inserted in Section 2(a) clause is: 'A person who has completed 14th years of age but has not completed his 18th year.'[111] No adolescent shall be employed or permitted to work in any of the hazardous occupations or processes set forth in the schedule.[112]

   b) Under this act, a 'child' means a person who has not completed his 14th year of age or such age as may be specified in the Right of Children to Free and Compulsory Education Act, 2009, whichever is more.[113] There is a linkage between the age in Right to Education Act, 2009 and the age of child labour under the amended act.

   c) 'Family', in relation to an occupier, means the individual, the wife or husband, as the case may be, of such individual, and their children, brother or sister of such individual.[114]

   d) 'Artist' means a child who performs or practices any work as a hobby or profession directly involving him as an actor, singer, sports person, or in such other activity relating to the entertainment or sports activities falling under clause (b) of Subsection (2) of CLPRAA 2016.

2. No child shall be employed or permitted to work in any occupation or process. But the exceptions are:

   a) if he helps his family or family enterprise, which is other than any hazardous occupations, after his school hours or during vacations;

   b) works as an artist in an audio-visual entertainment industry, including advertisement, films, television serials or any such other entertainment or sports activities except the circus, subject to prescribed conditions and safety measures, and no such work shall effect the school education of the child.[115] It prohibits the engagement of children in all occupations and of adolescents in hazardous occupations and processes with the exception of family enterprises if it does not affect their school.

3. No adolescent shall be employed or permitted to work in any of the hazardous occupations or processes set forth in the schedule.[116] The central government may, by notification, specify the nature of the non-hazardous work to which an adolescent may be permitted to work

---

[111] Substituted by CLPR Amendment Act, 2016, Section 5.

[112] Section 3A inserted in the CLPR Amendment Act, 2016.

[113] Substituted by CLPR Amendment Act, 2016, Section 4(b).

[114] Substituted by CLPR Amendment Act, 2016, Section 5.

[115] Substituted by CLPR Amendment Act, 2016, Section 5.

[116] Substituted by CLPR Amendment Act, 2016, Section 22.

under this act.[117] The Schedule to the 2016 Act includes only (1) mines, (2) inflammable substances or explosives, and (3) hazardous process. 'Hazardous process' has the meaning assigned to it in clause (cb) of the Factories Act, 1948.[118] The list of hazardous occupations for children from 83 under the new act is now only (2), that is, mining, explosives, and occupations as mentioned in the Factories Act. This means that work in chemical mixing units, cotton farms, battery recycling units, and brick kilns, among others, have not been included. Further, even the ones listed as hazardous can be removed, according to Section 4—not by Parliament but by government authorities at their own discretion.[119]

4. Their conditions of work, including working hours, leave, weekly holiday, health and safety, among others, will be regulated.

5. Constitution of Child and Adolescent Labour Rehabilitation Fund to which the amount of the fine realized from the employer of the child and adolescent, within the jurisdiction of each district shall be credited. The amount deposited or invested, under this fund and the interest accrued on it, shall be paid to the child or adolescent in whose favour such amount is credited.[120]

Table 4.5   Penalties under the New Act[121]

S. No.	Type of Offence	Penalties
1.	Employment of children in any occupation and process[122]	Imprisonment for a term which shall not be less than six months but which may extend to 2 years, or with fine which shall not be less than Rs 20,000 but which may extend to Rs 50,000, or with both, provided that the parents or guardians of such children shall not be

[117] Section 3A inserted in the CLPR Amendment Act, 2016.

[118] Substituted by CLPR Amendment Act, 2016, Section 22 . Under Section 2(cb) of the Factories Act, 'hazardous process' means any process or activity in relation to an industry specified in the

[f]irst Schedule where, unless special care is taken, raw materials used in it or the intermediate or finished products, bye-products, wastes or effluents thereof would—(i) cause material impairment to the health of the persons engaged in or connected with it or (ii) result in the pollution of the general environment: Provided that the state government may, by notification in the Official Gazette, amend the First Schedule by way of addition, omission or variation of any industry specified in the said Schedule.

[119] Substituted by CLPR Amendment Act, 2016, Section 7.

[120] Inserted under CLPR Amendment Act, 2016, Section 19.

[121] Substituted by Section 18(a) of the CLPR Amendment Act, 2016.

[122] Child Labour (Prohibition And Regulation) Amendment Act, 2016, Section 3:

(1) No child shall be employed or permitted to work in any occupation or process.

(2) Nothing in Subsection (1) shall apply where the child,—

(a) helps his family or family enterprise, which is other than any hazardous occupations or processes set forth in the Schedule, after his school hours or during vacations;

(b) works as an artist in an audio-visual entertainment industry, including advertisement, films, television serials or any such other entertainment or sports activities except the circus, subject to such

Table 4.5   (Cont'd)

S. No.	Type of Offence	Penalties
		punished unless they permit such child for commercial purposes in contravention of the provisions of the act.[123]
2.	Employment of adolescents in certain hazardous occupations and processes[124]	Punishable with imprisonment for a term which shall not be less than six months but which may extend to 2 years or with fine which shall not be less than Rs 20,000 but which may extend to Rs 50,000, or with both, provided that the parents or guardians of such adolescent shall not be punished unless they permit such adolescent to work in contravention of the provisions of Section 3A.
3.	Having been convicted of an offence under Section 3 or Section 3A commits a like offence afterwards[125]	Punishable with imprisonment for a term which shall not be less than 1 year but which may extend to 3 years.
4.	Fails to comply with or contravenes any other provisions of this act or the rules made thereunder	Punishable with simple imprisonment which may extend to one month or with fine which may extend to ten thousand rupees or with both.

conditions and safety measures, as may be prescribed, provided that no such work under this clause shall effect the school education of the child.

[123] Child Labour (Prohibition and Regulation) Amendment Act, 2016, Section 3.

[124] Child Labour (Prohibition and Regulation) Amendment Act, 2016, Section 3A: No adolescent shall be employed or permitted to work in any of the hazardous occupations or processes set forth in the schedule, provided that the Central Government may, by notification, specify the nature of the non-hazardous work to which an adolescent may be permitted to work under this act.

[125] Child Labour (Prohibition and Regulation) Amendment Act, 2016, Section 14: Penalties—

(1) Whoever employs any child or permits any child to work in contravention of the provisions of Section 3 shall be punishable with imprisonment for a term which shall not be less than 3 months but which may extend to 1 year or with fine which shall not be less than Rs 10,000 but which may extend to Rs 20,000 or with both.

(2) Whoever, having been convicted of an offence under Section 3, commits a like offence afterwards, he shall be punishable with imprisonment for a term which shall not be less than 6 months but which may extend to 2 years.

(3) Whoever—

    (a) fails to give notice as required by Section 9; or

    (b) fails to maintain a register as required by Section 11 or makes any false entry in any such register; or

    (c) fails to display a notice containing an abstract of section 3 and this section as required by Section 12; or

    (d) fails to comply with or contravenes any other provisions of this act or the rules made thereunder

shall be punishable with simple imprisonment which may extend to one month or with fine which may extend to Rs 10,000 or with both.

Certain other relevant changes brought in by the amendment act are:

- Offences by employer have been made cognizable and compoundable.[126]
- Provision for rehabilitation of rescued child or adolescent under Section 14C.[127]
- Duties conferred on district magistrates, to ensure that the provisions of this act are properly carried out and the district magistrate may specify the officer, subordinate to him, who shall exercise all or any of the powers, and perform all or any of the duties.[128]

The Juvenile Justice (Care and Protection of Children) Act, 2015

Section 79 of the JJ Act 2015, provides punishment for exploitation of a child employee. If any person ostensibly engages a child and keeps him in bondage for the purpose of employment or withholds his earnings or uses such earning for his own purposes shall be punishable with rigorous imprisonment for a term which may extend to 5 years and shall also be liable to fine of one lakh rupees. In this section, the term 'employment' includes selling goods and services, and entertainment in public places for economic gain.

Laws Relating to Bonded Child Labour

Article 23 of the Constitution of India prohibits the practice of debt bondage and other forms of slavery, both modern and ancient.[129] Along with the CLPRA and other labour laws, the following laws provide legal protection to bonded child labourers.

---

[126] Child Labour (Prohibition And Regulation) Amendment Act, 2016, Section 14A: Notwithstanding anything contained in the Code of Criminal Procedure, 1973, any offence committed by an employer and punishable under Section 3 or Section 3A shall be cognizable.

[127] Child Labour (Prohibition And Regulation) Amendment Act, 2016, Section 14C: The child or adolescent, who is employed in contravention of the provisions of this act and rescued, shall be rehabilitated in accordance with the laws for the time being in force.

[128] Child Labour (Prohibition And Regulation) Amendment Act, 2016, Section 14D:

(1) Notwithstanding anything contained in the Code of Criminal Procedure, 1973, the district magistrate may, on the application of the accused person, compound any offence committed for the first time by him, under Subsection (3) of Section 14 or any offence committed by an accused person being parent or a guardian, in such manner and on payment of such amount to the appropriate government, as may be prescribed.
(2) If the accused fails to pay such amount for composition of the offence, then, the proceedings shall be continued against such person in accordance with the provisions of this act.
(3) Where any offence is compounded before the institution of any prosecution, no prosecution shall be instituted in relation to such offence, against the offender in relation to whom the offence is so compounded.
(4) Where the composition of any offence is made after the institution of any prosecution, such composition shall be brought in writing, to the notice of the court in which the prosecution is pending and on the approval of the composition of the offence being given, the person against whom the offence is so compounded, shall be discharged.

[129] *People's Union for Democratic Rights* v. *Union of India* [Asiad Workers' Case], AIR 1982 SC 1473, para 1486.

Bonded Labour System (Abolition) Act, 1976

The object of the act is to provide for the abolition of bonded labour system with a view to preventing the economic and physical exploitation of the weaker sections of the society. In this act, bonded labour system is defined in Section 2(g) as the system of forced, or partly forced, labour which a creditor extracts from a debtor by virtue of an agreement between the two. The Bonded Labour System (Abolition) Act (BLSAA) aims to abolish all debt agreements and obligations. It is the legislative fulfilment of the Indian Constitution's mandate against *begar* and forced labour.[130] It frees all bonded labourers, cancels any outstanding debts against them, prohibits the creation of new bondage agreements, and orders the economic rehabilitation of freed bonded labour.

The aggrieved person or any person on his behalf can approach the District Magistrate, who is Chairman of the Vigilance Committee constituted under the act, and has been entrusted with certain duties and responsibilities for implementing the provisions of the act. The matter can also be brought to the notice of the Sub-Divisional Magistrate of the area or any other person who is a member of the Vigilance Committee of the District or Sub-division. [131] The bonded labour is to be immediately released from the bondage. His liability to repay bonded debt is deemed to have been extinguished. The freed bonded labour shall not be evicted from his homesteads or other residential premises which he was occupying, as part of consideration for the bonded labour. A rehabilitation grant of Rs 20,000 to each of the bonded labourers is to be granted and assistance for his rehabilitation provided.[132] The offence under the act is cognizable and bailable.

[130] Consequently, post-act social action litigation on behalf of bonded labours is brought under both the BLSAA and the Constitution of India. For a discussion of cases, see Y.R. Haragopal Reddy, *Bonded Labour System in India* (New Delhi: Deep and Deep Publications, Chapter 4).

[131] Section 13: Vigilance Committees—(i) Every state government shall by notification in the Official Gazette constitute such number of vigilance committees in each district and each sub-division as it may think fit. (ii) Each vigilance committee, constituted for a district, shall consist of the following members, namely, (a) the district magistrate, or a person nominate by him, who shall be the chairman; (b) three persons belonging to the scheduled castes or scheduled tribes and residing in the district, to be nominated by the district magistrate; and (c) two social workers, resident in the district, to be nominated by the district magistrate. Explanation: Not more than three persons to represent the official or non-official agencies in the district connected with rural development, to be nominated by the state government; (d) one person to represent the financial and credit institutions in the district, to be nominated by the district magistrate; (iii) Each vigilance committee, constituted for a sub-division, shall consist of the following members, namely, (a) the sub-divisional magistrate, or person nominated by him, who shall be the chairman; (b) three persons belonging to the scheduled casts or scheduled tribes and residing in the sub-division, to be nominated by the sub-divisional magistrate; (c) two social workers, resident in the sub-division, to be nominated by the sub-divisional magistrate; (d) not more than three persons to represent the official or non-official agencies in the sub-division connected with rural development to be nominated by the district magistrate; and (e) one person to represent the financial and credit institutions in the sub-division, to be nominated by the sub-divisional magistrate.

[132] Press Information Bureau, 'Release and Rehabilitation of Bonded Labourers' (Government of India, Ministry of Labour and Employment, 21 December 2011). Available at http://pib.nic.in/newsite/PrintRelease.aspx?relid=79122 (accessed on 8 July 2015).

The responsibility for rehabilitating the freed bonded labourers lies with the respective State Governments. In order to assist the State Governments in the task of rehabilitation of identified and released bonded

Any person who contravenes provisions of the act is punishable with imprisonment for a term which may extend to 3 years and also with a fine which may extend to two thousand rupees. [133]

Children (Pledging of Labour) Act, 1933

This act predates independence but remains in force. It is rarely used and rarely mentioned in discussions of bonded labour and child labour, probably because the more recent laws carry penalties that, while lenient themselves, are none the less stiffer than those of the Children (Pledging of Labour) Act.

The act calls for penalties to be levied against any parent, middleman, or employer involved in making or executing a pledge of child's labour. Such a pledge is defined as an 'agreement written or oral, express or implied, whereby the parent or guardian of a child, in return for any payment or benefit received or to be received by him, undertakes to cause or allow the services of the child to be utilized in any employment'.[134] Lawful labour agreements are limited to those made in consideration of reasonable wages and terminable at seven days' or less notice. The fines for violating this law are Rs 50 against parents and Rs 200 against either the middleman or employer.

Critique of the Laws

The CLPRA needs to be amended for better implementation and enforcement. The following are the areas of concern that need legal reform:

- CLPRA covers only 10 per cent of the total working children. Moreover, the agricultural sector, which constitutes more than 75 per cent of child employment, is not covered by the act. The CLPRA is not easy to enforce in the unorganized sector because the units are numerous and unregistered. The employer–employee relationship is continuously changing, and frequently, the unit is a tiny family-based one. Most of these units spring up and disappear overnight and are very difficult to keep track of, in the absence of any requirement of registration.
- Section 3 of the CLPRA[135] keeps the occupation, work, or process that is carried on by the occupier with the aid of his family out of the purview of the act. The intention of the act is to exempt a family enterprise in which all or several of the members of the family are involved. It was not intended to exempt farmed out, piece-rate work, where the home merely replaces the factory premises. This proviso is abused by employing children in respect of families and work

---

labourers, a Centrally Sponsored Plan Scheme for Rehabilitation of Bonded Labour is in operation since May, 1978. Under the scheme, rehabilitation assistance at Rs 20,000 per bonded labour is provided which is equally shared by the central and state government.

[133] BLSAA, Sections 4, 5, 6, and 14.

[134] Children (Pledging of Labour) Act 1933, Section 2: 'Child' is a person less than 15 years old.

[135] Section 3 proviso: Provided that nothing in this section shall apply to any workshop wherein any process is carried on by the occupier with the aid of his family or to any school established by or receiving assistance or recognition from Government.

experience acquired by children. This provision helps employers to 'pose as family members' of the children working in their premises, and thus continue to exploit the children. When any action is taken against any employer for employing a child, the excuses given are that 'the child is a relative and is helping in housework', or 'the child is being trained for a family trade', and so on. Therefore, there is a need to add to the provision that 'it shall be presumed that occupier is also the employer for the purpose of the act and the onus to prove that the child is a member of his or her family would rest on the occupier'.

- In the CLPRA, the definition of 'workshop'[136] in Section 2(x) is to be amended to include all places of work/occupation in which children are employed. Section 3 of the act should be amended to include the factories as registered under the Factories Act, 1948 and the Mines Act.

- The word 'occupier'[137] in Section 2(vi) is not clearly defined and, therefore, it may not have check on the employers' agents and the contractors who play a vital role in the employment of children.

- The word 'hazardous' is not clearly defined and it is left to the Technical Advisory Committee[138] to define hazardous occupations and processes. The word at present appears to take into consideration only the physical harm to the children. The emotional and psychological aspects have also to be taken into consideration. In fact, there should be prohibition of all forms of child labour since all occupations are hazardous to children as they affect the development of the child. If the child is denied primary, elementary education because of the need to work, it is a hazard.[139] Besides, there are occupations that are not included in the hazardous list but the children involved in them are subject to the grossest forms of physical, emotional, and sexual abuse within the four walls of a home. Even though the child comes into direct contact with harmful pesticides and fertilizers in agricultural processes, the agricultural sector is kept out of the purview of the act. The definition of 'hazardous' process in the Factories Act, 1948 could be considered.[140] There should be a provision for public mechanisms and participation in the functioning of the Technical Advisory Committee. Children in hazardous employment should be given top priority in all developmental efforts. The principle of every right for every child calls for elimination of all forms of child labour, so that no child is discriminated against

---

[136] CLPRA, Section 2(x): Workshop means any premises (including the precincts thereof) wherein any industrial process is carried on, but does not include any premises to which provisions of Section 67 of the Factories Act, 1948 for the time being apply.

[137] CLPRA, Section 2(vi) defines 'occupier' in relation to an establishment or a workshop as the person who has the ultimate control over the affairs of the establishment or workshop.

[138] CLPRA, Section 4.

[139] Ossie Fernandes, 'Towards Amendments/Restructuring of the Child Labour Prohibition and Regulation Act 1986', a draft note prepared on behalf of the Legal Working Group, Campaign Against Child Labour (CACL).

[140] Factories Act, Section 2(cb) defines hazardous process as any process or activity in relation to an industry specified in the First Schedule where, unless special care is taken, raw materials used therein or the intermediate or finished products, by-products, wastes, or effluents thereof would cause material impairment to the health of the persons engaged in or connected therewith, or result in the pollution of the general environment. The First Schedule of the Factories Act contains a list of industries involving hazardous processes.

and deprived of childhood and corresponding rights. While more and more sectors are being added to the list of hazardous occupations and processes where employment of children under 14 years of age is banned, children continue to work in non-hazardous sectors and are thus denied their basic human rights.[141]

- There is no preventive mechanism under the act to prevent child labour. Under the National Child Labour Projects (NCLP), only a certain number of children working in some notified sectors have been targeted. Hence, only some children may have been rescued while new children continue to enter the labour force. In practice, many girl children are left out from this project. Prevention needs to be an important aspect of the law. Besides, under NCLP, there is no formal schooling, which is the right of every child.
- It is clear that child labour and education are linked. But there is absolutely no linkage to education in the Child Labour Act. In fact, all OOSC can be termed as child labour. All children must go to formal schools.
- The dual policy of regulation and prohibition is itself faulty. After the enactment of the Right to Free and Compulsory Education Act, 2009, there is absolutely no question of regulation. All children must be in school and all forms of child labour that interferes with formal school education must be banned.
- Non-implementation of the laws is an area of concern. It is required to go through a lengthy and complex process in order to enforce the law. Law enforcement calls for a strong political will and vigilance among civil society members and a simple, quick mechanism to report non-compliance. The BLSAA is outdated and needs a review.

Laws Relating to Domestic Child Labour

The Central Government amended the Central Civil Service Conduct rules to prohibit any government official/civil servants from employing children below the age of 14 years as domestic workers. Indian law prohibits the employment of children below 14 years age in certain occupations, in accordance to the CLPRA.[142] Domestic child labour is hazardous and has been included in the hazardous list of occupations in the Schedule to the CLPRA. Hence, from 10 October 2006, there has been a ban on child labour in domestic work. So, no child below 14 years labours in household work.[143]

---

[141] Enakshi Ganguli Thukral and Parul Thukral, *India Child Rights Index* (HAQ, Centre for Child Rights, 2011).

[142] Press Information Bureau, 'Employment of Children as Domestic Servants and in Dhabas Banned from October 2006', 1 August 2006'. Available at http://pib.nic.in/newsite/erelease.aspx (accessed on 8 July 2015):

> The government has decided to prohibit employment of children as domestic servants or servants or in dhabas (roadside eateries), restaurants, hotels, motels, teashops, resorts, spas or in other recreational centres. The ban has been imposed under the Child Labour (Prohibition & Regulation) Act, 1986 and will be effective from 10th October 2006. The Ministry of Labour and Employment has recently issued a notification to this effect, giving three-month mandatory notice.

[143] Press Information Bureau, 'Employment of Children'.

Besides, there have been several efforts by some state governments to prevent domestic child labour. The Karnataka government passed the Minimum Wage Act for Domestic workers on 1 April 2004. Notifications for Minimum Wage Act for Domestic Workers were passed in the following state governments: Kerala (23 May 2005), Andhra Pradesh (24 April 2007), and Rajasthan (4 July 2007).

The Government of Tamil Nadu in India, included domestic workers in their unorganized workers group. The Tamil Nadu Domestic Workers Welfare Board was constituted on 22 January 2007. The notification for the Minimum Wage Act for Domestic Workers was passed in August 2007.

Enforcement of the Child Labour and Bonded Child Labour Legislation

In spite of the laws, child labour continues to exist in prohibited industries and areas of employment, and is subject to very little regulation and control in non-prohibited industries and areas of employment. Table 4.6 shows the position regarding the number of prosecutions and convictions under the CLPRA from 1992 to 1999.[144]

Table 4.6 Prosecutions and Convictions under CLPRA during 2009–13: Enforcement Figures on Child Labour (Prohibition and Regulation) Act, 1986 for the Last 5 Years[145]

Year	Inspections	Violations	Prosecutions	Convictions
2009	328,077	8,709	5,633	1,489
2010	255,176	11,182	4,570	1,536
2011	150,771	14,411	6,011	976
2012	164,453	12,019	5,018	1,144
2013	174,994	8,859	3,486	1,041
Total	1073,471	55,180	24,718	6,186

Table 4.6 clearly shows that the number of convictions is very low. Out of 55,180 violations in 5 years, only 6,186 have been convicted, which is nearly 11 per cent conviction(2009–2013). Most employers were acquitted by the courts as the prosecution failed to prove the offence due to the casual approach of the prosecution witnesses and inability to produce independent witnesses. Even if the employer was convicted, he was normally let off with a fine. It is rare that any employer has undergone imprisonment for violating the CLPRA. Studies in child labour reveal that enforcement of child labour legislation faces a number of problems. Broadly, the difficulties fall into the following categories:[146]

[144] Meena Gupta, 'Special Problems of Enforcement of Child Labour Laws and Regulations', *Award Digest, Journal of Labour Legislation* XX, nos 7–12.

[145] *Source*: Ministry of Labour and Employment, Government of India. Available at http://labour.nic.in/content/division/directions-of-supreme-court.php (accessed on 26 June 2015).

[146] Gupta, 'Special Problems'.

- *Enforcement of social legislations*: Social legislations are often difficult to enforce, as the law enforcers do not understand the spirit of the law. Neither the employers of child labour, nor the parents, nor the law enforcers perceive child labour as an undesirable thing.
- *Informalization of child labour*: Due to 'informalization of child labour', namely work involving child labour moving out of the factories and large establishments into small cottage and home-based units, from out of the organized sector to the unorganized sector, it has become difficult to enforce the act. This requires a large increase in the labour enforcement machinery. Other labour laws are applicable only to the organized sector. Besides, no records are maintained of the child workers.
- *No successful conviction*: Where an inspector manages to find children working in an establishment in violation of the law, the prosecution does not lead to successful conviction. The reasons for acquittal in many cases are:[147]

  - Delay in filing the case: Courts rely on evidence and the inspectors fail to produce evidence in courts. Many employers, especially from small units, are often let off because they claim that the children are their family members. The proviso to Section 3 of the CLPRA helps them in this claim.[148] In larger units, the employers generally claim that the children had come to meet their parents or to provide lunch to their parents and were not working there.[149] There is, therefore, no evidence that the child was working in the premises and the courts let off the employers. The offence should be made cognizable. The burden of proof should be shifted on the employer.
  - Another reason for failure of prosecution is lack of evidence relating to the age of the child. The child's age has to be proved in the courts. Usually, in rural areas, the children do not have birth certificates. There is therefore no reliable evidence to prove the age of the child. In such cases, the inspector is supposed to get the child medically examined at the expense of the employer. This leads to further delay. There should be severe punishment for giving wrong certificates. In case of certain groups, the statement of the mother regarding the age of child should be valid.
  - Courts tend to pass lighter sentences in child labour matters. This is also due to the insensitivity of the judiciary.
  - The implementation of child labour legislation is entrusted to inspectors of factories. The inspectors are overburdened and the enforcement of the CLPRA is not their 'priority'. It is commonly believed that there is rampant corruption in the enforcement machinery. Besides, the inspectors are not sensitized towards the problem of child labour. They have no responsibility for implementing the act. Even in a progressive state like Maharashtra, no inspector appointed under the CLPRA has been punished or even asked to explain why he did not implement the act. Community participation and accountability have to be introduced.

[147] E. Illamathian, 'Micro-Lab on Case Studies', paper presented at the workshop on 'Enforcement of Child Labour Laws in Match and Fireworks in Tamilnadu', organized by Tamilnadu Institute of Labour Studies, 8–9 December 1992.

[148] 'Provided that nothing in this section shall apply to any workshop wherein any process is carried on by the occupier with the aid of his family.'

[149] Gupta, 'Special Problems'.

Bonded child labour is a problem defined by the social, cultural, and political histories of a particular community. This issue is complex, and the fight against it needs an integrated approach and multi-pronged strategy. Interventions remain incomplete unless land, parents, employment, education, health, and gender issues are tackled simultaneously. Official statistics relating to the enforcement of the BLSAA are difficult to obtain. Up to 1988, there were 7,000 prosecutions under the act throughout India, of which only 700 resulted in convictions.[150] The main obstacles to enforcement are:

- Apathy among government officials: Vigilance committees, which form the core of the enforcement of the act, have to be functional. Collectors are too overburdened to implement the act.
- There is corruption, lack of accountability, and a caste and class bias in the enforcement.
- There are no linkages between the various applicable acts.

Judicial Response Relating to Child Labour and Bonded Labour

Important Case Laws Relating to Child Labour

The judiciary in the country has shown its great concern for the working children by bringing occupations or processes under the judicial scrutiny by directly applying the constitutional provisions relating to children.

In *People's Union for Democratic Rights* v. *Union of India*[151] the court held: But apart from the requirement of ILO Convention No. 59, we have Article 24 of the Constitution which even if not followed up by appropriate legislation must operate *proprio vigore* and construction work being plainly and undoubtedly a hazardous employment, it is clear that by reason of constitutional prohibition no child below 14 years can be allowed to be engaged in construction work. There can, therefore, be no doubt that notwithstanding the absence of specification of construction industry in the Schedule to the Employment of Children Act, 1938, no child below 14 years can be employed in construction work and the Union of India as also every state government must ensure that this constitutional mandate is not violated in any part of the country.

The Supreme Court has suggested that it is the duty of the government to ensure education of children of parents who are working in construction sites.

Labourers Working on Salal Hydro Project v. State of Jammu and Kashmir and Others[152]

The Supreme Court directed that whenever the Central Government undertakes a construction project which is likely to last for a considerable period of time, it should ensure that children of construction workers who are living at or near the project site are given facilities for schooling. The Court also specified that this may be done either by the Central Government itself or if the

---

[150] Reddy, *Bonded Labour System in India*, p. 171.
[151] AIR 1982 SC 1480.
[152] 1983 Lah IC 542.

Central Government entrusts the project work or any part thereof to a contractor, necessary provision to this effect may be made in the contract with the contractor.

M.C. Mehta v. State of Tamil Nadu and Others[153]

In this case, the Supreme Court allowed children to work in a prohibited occupation like fireworks. According to Justice Ranganath Mishra and Justice M.H. Kania, the provision of Article 45 in the Directive Principles of State Policy still remained a far cry and though according to this provision all children up to the age of 14 years are supposed to be in school, economic necessity forces grown-up children to seek employment. Children can, therefore, be employed in the process of packing of fireworks, but packing should be done in an area away from the place of manufacture to avoid exposure to accidents.

Rajangam, Secretary, District Beedi Workers Union v. State of Tamil Nadu and Others[154]

The Supreme Court opined that tobacco manufacturing was indeed hazardous to health. Child labour in this trade should therefore be prohibited as far as possible, and employment of child labour should be stopped either immediately or in a phased manner, which is to be decided by the state government, but it should be within a period not exceeding 3 years.

M.C. Mehta v. State of Tamil Nadu and Others[155]

When news about an accident in one of the Sivakasi cracker factories was published in the media wherein several children were reported dead, the court took suo motu cognizance of it. The court gave certain directions regarding the payment of compensation. An Advocates' Committee was also constituted to visit the area and report on the various aspects of the matter.[156]

A three-judge Bench of the Supreme Court comprising Justice Kuldip Singh, Justice B.L. Hansaria, and Justice S.B. Majumdar delivered a landmark judgment on 10 December 1996. This judgment is of considerable important and is a progressive advancement in public interest litigation and child jurisprudence. The decision has attempted to tackle the problem of child labour.

M.C. Mehta, a lawyer, filed a writ under Article 32 of the Constitution of India, as the fundamental right of children against exploitation (Article 24) was being grossly violated in the match and fireworks industries in Sivakasi, where children were employed. The court then noted that the manufacturing process of matches and fireworks is hazardous, giving rise to accidents, including fatal cases. Therefore, keeping in view the provisions contained in Articles 39(f) and 45 of the

---

[153] (1991) SC 283.

[154] (1992) 1 SCC 221.

[155] AIR 1997 SC 699.

[156] The committee consisting of Shri R.K. Jain, a senior advocate, Indira Jaisingh, another senior advocate, and Shri K.C. Dua, advocate, submitted its report on 11 November 1991.

Constitution, it gave directions as to how the quality of life of children employed in the factories could be improved.

Social action through law and the struggle for children's rights got a new impetus with the passing of these directions. This ruling has certainly succeeded in generating a lot of enthusiasm relating to the elimination of child labour among the concerned agencies and state governments. Since labour is on the concurrent list of the Constitution, there has to be coordination between both the Central and the state governments. Besides the labour ministry, the education ministry also needs to be involved as more schools, teachers, and staff will be required. Teachers and staff will have to be oriented and mobilized to integrate child labourers entering their schools. It requires an inter-sectoral action. Massive additional funds will be required to comply with the judgment. Rules will have to be immediately framed by the state governments for implementing the directions of the court.

Child labour has been made expensive and thereby deterrent to both the employer and the government. An important dimension is the award of compensation granted to the affected parties, that is, the children. This implies that it is the obligation or a social duty of the state to protect the fundamental rights of children.

A tremendous responsibility has been placed on the inspectors appointed under the CLPRA. But many of these inspectors are themselves responsible for the tardy implementation of the act. Therefore, there is a need for orientation and training of these inspectors and the other staff concerned. A question that arises is how these inspectors will ensure that, in non-hazardous industries, the child receives education for at least two hours each day at the cost of the employer.

Certain aspects that need to be considered are:

- Greater involvement of voluntary agencies concerned with child welfare.
- Access to adequate schooling facilities as, in our country, schools are simply not available in many areas.
- Accountability of enforcement officers involved.
- Review and amendment of the CLPRA, the Primary Education Act, the JJ Act, and the rules made under them.
- The invisibility of the girl child, especially those who work as helpers of adult workers.

The judgment certainly holds out hopes for the future. These hopes should turn out to be true in the cause of justice to the child, and they should not become another 'lucrative' option for the enforcement officials and parents. Perhaps, an independent enforcing body can monitor the enforcement of this judgment.

A. Srirama Babu v. Chief Secretary Government of Karnataka[157]

The High Court of Karnataka looked at the issue of eradication of child labour in the sericulture industry, especially in weaving of silk saris, where children in the age group of five to eight were engaged in huge numbers. While the schedule to the CLPRA is silent about this industry, the

---

[157] ILR 1997 Kar 2269.

court enunciated the criterion of hazardous work. To be hazardous, the work should be either inherently injurious to the children or the conditions of work harmful to their health.

The court held that all employments which cripple the health of a child and which disable him from being a healthy member of the society should be treated as hazardous industries. It directed the Commissioner of Labour to issue notices to the deviant establishments for appropriate action.

Haria Ginning and Pressing Factory v. Mamlatdar and Ors.[158]

The Mamlatdar-cum-ex officio Labour Inspector made inspections in the factory premises of the petitioners and observed that each of the owners/management of the factories was engaging young boys below 14 years of age, and their engagement was contrary to the provisions of the CLPRA. Hence, the Additional Labour Commissioner, Gandhidham, Kutch, directed the petitioners to deposit a sum of Rs 20,000 for each child labour employed by them, failing which, the petitioners were liable to face appropriate legal action.

The petitioners submitted that four persons employed by them were above 14 years of age, while five other children had come to serve tiffin to the labours/workmen. They submitted that they had not committed any wrong and that the Assistant Labour Commissioner and the Mamlatdar acted absolutely illegally in issuing such directions.

In the present matter, it was held by the Court that:

Assuming that power is conferred upon the Inspector or the Mamlatdar or the Assistant Labour Commissioner to make recoveries from such person, who is alleged to have committed violations of the provisions of the act, the Inspector, Mamlatdar or Assistant Labour Commissioner could not act on basis of their whims, caprice or arbitrariness. They cannot simply say that the written statement/show cause notice does not satisfy them, therefore, the recovery would be made. In cases like the present, an inquiry is required to be made and the inquiry must include production of oral, so also documentary, evidence. When a person comes before the authority and makes a submission that he had not committed any wrong and his defence was that as many as four persons were above the age of 14 years and other five had come to serve the tiffin upon the workers, then the matter is of disputed facts. It is to be seen that for other four, the defence was accepted, but, for the remaining five, the Assistant Labour Commissioner filed a false affidavit to mislead this Court. In absence of any document on record to reveal that the child labour was brought by the other industry, who had given job-work to the establishment, he could not have said that the child labour was brought by other workers who had come to complete the job-work of the third parties. In the matters like present, the defense cannot be rejected holding it to be prima facie bogus or worth rejection, the authority cannot reject the defense on the ground that such authority was not satisfied. The satisfaction of the authority or the Court though is a perception of that authority, but, the authority or the Court cannot simply hold in two lines that they were not satisfied, therefore, they were rejecting the defenses. Some order to be a legal order must have tenets of legal order; they must consider the case of both the sides, arguments raised by both the sides and the reasons for rejecting or accepting the arguments of one or the other side. The authority yet is not given jurisdiction to pick up one view and say that other is wrong. Before rejecting the view or defense, the authority or Court is required to hold that for further reasons, such defense is not palatable.

[158] (2008) ILLJ 432 Guj.

The Court accepted the defence of the petitioner that the four persons employed by them were above 14 years of age and were not were illegally engaged as labourers. The Court further held that the approach of the Mamlatdar/Assistant Labour Commissioner could not be protected and thus the orders passed by Mamlatdar/Inspector and Assistant Labour Commissioner were quashed and the petition was allowed.

Court on its own Motion and with Other Writ Petitions WP 9767/2009[159]

In this case, the Delhi High Court referred the matter to the National Commission for Protection of Child Rights to evolve a Plan of Action to eliminate the menace of child labour and to effectuate the mandate of Articles 23, 24, 39, 45, and 47 of the Constitution. The Supreme Court had given a large number of mandatory directions in *M.C. Mehta* v. *State of Tamil Nadu*, reported in AIR 1997 SC 699. One of the important directions was to direct an employer to pay a compensation of Rs 20, 000 for having employed a child below the age of 14 years in hazardous work in contravention of the CLPRA. The appropriate Government was also directed to contribute a grant/deposit of Rs 5,000 for each such child employed in a hazardous job. The said sum of Rs 25,000 was to be deposited in a fund to be known as Child Labour Rehabilitation-cum-Welfare Fund, and the income from such corpus was to be used for rehabilitation of the rescued child. As the constitutional mandate and statutory provisions with regard to children were not being vigorously implemented and there was lack of coordination between different agencies of the Government of NCT of Delhi and other authorities, the Delhi High Court, vide a detailed order dated 24 September 2008, directed the NCPCR to formulate a detailed Action Plan for strict enforcement and implementation of CLPRA and other related legislations, and to suggest measures regarding education, health, and financial support to the rescued children. The National Commission was also directed to suggest measures for timely recovery and proper utilization of funds collected under the Supreme Court's direction in the aforesaid M.C. Mehta's case. The National Commission, after holding consultation with various stakeholders and after conducting research and survey, submitted to the Court a Delhi Action Plan for Total Abolition of Child Labour. According to the NCPCR, the child labour profile in Delhi is of two types, namely OOSC living with their parents in Delhi, and migrant children from other states who have left their families behind. The Action Plan for Total Abolition of Child Labour was based on two strategies. The first strategy was an 'Area Based Approach' for elimination of child labour, wherein all children in the age group of 6 to 14 years would be covered, whether they were in school or out-of-school. The National Commission had proposed that this approach be initiated as a pilot project in North-West District of Delhi. The second strategy was an approach to be adopted in the context of migrant child labour. It involved a process of identification, rescue, repatriation, and rehabilitation of child labour. This strategy was proposed to be implemented as a pilot project in South Delhi District. Both the strategies, in essence, implemented the CLPRA, Delhi Shops and Establishment Act, 1954, the JJ Act, and the BLSAA. The Strategy for Unaccompanied Migrant Child Labourers in Delhi was based on the Protocol on Prevention, Rescue, Repatriation and Rehabilitation of Trafficked and Migrant Child Labour, issued by Ministry of Labour and

[159] (2009) ILR 6 Delhi 663.

Employment, Government of India, in 2008. According to the Action Plan, trafficked and migrant child labourers were primarily engaged in prohibited occupations such as zari, bulb manufacturing, auto workshop units, and domestic households, among others. This strategy contemplated constitution of a Steering Committee on Child Labour at the state level, and a Task Force on Child Labour at the district level. The Delhi Action Plan provided for a detailed procedure to be adopted at the pre-rescue and actual rescue stage. The pre-rescue plan dealt with how information was to be collected and verified, the composition of the rescue team, as well as what training was to be imparted in advance to the members of the rescue team. The pre-rescue plan provided for prior preparation of residential centres through RBC (Residential Bridge Course), JJ Homes, and NGO shelters for accommodating the child labour proposed to be rescued. The Delhi Action Plan provided a detailed procedure for interim care and protection of the rescued children. It provided for immediate medical examination of the children and gave directions on how investigation was to be conducted and charge sheet was to be prepared. The strategy for Unaccompanied Migrant Children also provided for assessment and verification of the child's background and intra-state as well as interstate repatriation.

The Action Plan provided for detailed procedure for rehabilitation and social integration of the child labour as well as training and capacity building of duty bearers. In a bid to ensure proper coordination among different agencies of the Government of NCT subsequent to the filing of the aforesaid Action Plan, the Labour Department of Government of NCT of Delhi had raised some issues. According to the Labour Department, CLPRA prohibited employment of children only in certain scheduled occupations and processes. Consequently, according to the Labour Department, child workers employed in non-hazardous jobs could not be rescued. The Labour Department had further urged that in the Action Plan it had been stipulated that all children between the age of 14 and 18 years had to be liberated and handed over to the police, even though the CLPRA defined child as a person who had not completed 14 years of age. On a perusal of CLPRA, the Labour Department[160] was of the view that under the said act, only child workers employed in scheduled occupation and processes could be liberated and children employed above the age of 14 years could not be rescued. Delhi High Court stated that the JJ Act would apply to children between the age of 14 and 18 years as well as to those children below the age of 14 years employed in non-scheduled occupations and processes. Consequently, the said children would be governed by the JJ Act as well as the BLSAA, if applicable, and not by the CLPRA, as stipulated in the Delhi Action Plan prepared by the National Commission. Moreover, at the request of the Labour Department, the Delhi High Court directed that the responsibility of lodging a police complaint against an employer employing child labour would lie with the Delhi Police and not the Labour Department, as directed in the Delhi Action Plan. Delhi High Court further clarified that the authority to take action under the BLSAA would be the Deputy Commissioner of District concerned and not the Labour Department. It was further clarified that the recoveries of fine of Rs 20,000, as stipulated by the Supreme Court in M.C. Mehta's case, will not have to await a conviction order of the offending employer. The said amount would be recovered as arrears of land revenue and the said amount would be utilized for the educational needs of the rescued child even if the child has subsequently crossed the age of 14 years.

---

[160] Ministry of Labour and Employment, Government of India. Available at http://labour.gov.in/content/ (accessed on 9 November 2015).

Bachpan Bachao Andolan (BBA) v. Union of India[161]

In February and March 2004, the Petitioner BBA, an NGO, received complaints from many Nepalese parents, whose children had been trapped in circuses for more than 10 years and had never been allowed to meet them even after repeated requests to the circus owners. Majority of the complaints were for the children in the Great Indian Circus, which was found to be located in Palakkad, Kerala. The Petitioner found that the life of these children began at dawn with training and abuse, merciless beating, and two biscuits and a cup of tea. After three to five shows and facing sexual harassment from the crowds, the young girls were allowed to go back to their tents around midnight. Even then, if any child complained about the inadequate amount of food or the leaking tent in the rain, he/she would be scolded and ill-treated by the managers or employers, and sometimes even beaten. Children were found to be frequently abused physically, emotionally, and sexually in these places. There was perpetual sexual harassment and violation of the JJ Act and all international treaties and conventions related to human rights and child rights where India is a signatory. The Petitioner complained about living and working conditions of the children and enumerated the following broad categories.

Insufficient Space

In almost all the circuses visited by the research team, the living conditions were deplorable. Usually five to 10, and sometimes even more people were crammed into a single tent. Thus most of the child artists complained of insufficient space and lack of personal space and privacy.

Meals

Most of the circuses provided two meals—lunch and dinner—to the artists and tea was provided twice daily from the canteen run by the management. Most often, the food was inadequate to satisfy the appetite of young growing children.

Sleep Timings

Sleep timings were also very erratic, depending upon the nature of the work being performed by the child artists, though on a general trend most went to bed at midnight after the last show was over, to be woken up at dawn for practice.

Poor Sanitation

There were no proper toilets and bathrooms. Make-shift toilets were created on the circus ground near the tents and all the company girls had to share it; the stench around them was unbearable. In general, condition of sanitation in circuses was pathetic. It also precipitated unhygienic conditions that could lead to diseases.

No Healthcare Personnel

There were no healthcare personnel to look into their day-to-day healthcare needs as well as the accidents that were common in circuses. The manager or the keeper usually provided medication

[161] AIR 2011 SC 3361.

for common ailments such as fever, cold, and so on and looked into the first aid needs of the artists. For a serious medical condition or an accident during training or performance, the trainer or the manager usually accompanied the patient to the nearest medical help. The management used to bear the charges of the treatment during that time, but later deducted it from the salary of the incumbent. Overall, it could be said that the living conditions inside the premises of the circus arena were squalid and deplorable, with no facilities and basic amenities being provided to the circus artists.

High Risk Factor

The nature of the activities in circuses was such that the risk factor for the artists was very high, as accidents and mishaps during practise sessions and shows were common phenomenon. On top of that, there were no healthcare personnel employed by the circuses to look into the healthcare needs of the artists, even at the time of emergency. It was found that the lives of the children were endangered due to the risk factor involved in the circuses, especially of those who were involved in items like ring of death, well of death, sword items, rope dance, and so on. Moreover, some circuses either failed to or were ignorant about taking the necessary precautions, which further heightened the risk involved.

Remuneration

Besides paying meagre salaries to the children, the management of some circuses held back the salaries of the children, saying that the money would be paid only to their parents when they visit them, which rarely happened. Salary accounts were often manipulated and the loss due to accidents or mishaps was not compensated.

Bound by Contract

The child artists were brought to the circuses to be contracted for three to 10 years and once the contract was signed/agreed upon by the parents or guardians of the children, the ignorant children were bound and indebted to the circus management and were unable to break away from the circus.

Daily Routine Hindering Their All-round Development

In the circus, there was no education, no play, no recreation for the children, and their life was confined to the circus without any exposure to the outside world. All this prohibited them from knowing the other opportunities available. Due to the cruel and inhuman attitude of the management in some circuses, which imposed restrictions on the children for meeting their folks, and also due to the travelling nature of the troupe, most of the children ended up losing contact with their parents, especially those across the border or residing at far-off places even within the country. Consequently, they were exposed to a world which hindered their psychological, spiritual, and socio-economic development, with no knowledge of their rights, duties, and scope for a better future, and thus, left with no other option but to continue working in the circuses for the rest of their lives. Instability in life due to the circus's nomadic existence made it difficult for them to pursue formal education, resulting in a large number of illiterate children and adults in circuses.

The Petitioner contended that employment of children in circus involved many legal complications, and in that respect the major complications were as mentioned below.[162]

1. Deprivation of the children from getting educated, thereby violating their Fundamental Right for education, enshrined under Article 21A of the Constitution.
2. Deprivation of the children from playing and expression of thoughts and feelings, thereby violating the Fundamental Right to freedom of expression.
3. Competency to enter into contract for working in circus.
4. Violation of statutory provisions of law like Employment of Children's Act, 1938, the Children (Pledging of Labour) Act, 1933, the CLPRA, the Minimum Wages Act, 1976, the Prevention of Immoral Traffic Act, the Equal Remuneration Act, 1976 and Rules made thereunder, and the BLSAA read with rules made thereunder, the Factories Act, 1948, Motor Transport Workers Act, 1961, and so on.
5. Existing labour laws and legitimacy of contracts of employment for children.
6. The legitimacy of contracts of employment for children and working conditions.

The Ministry of Women and Child Development identified the shortcomings and gaps in existing child protection institutions. They identified the reasons for limitations in effective implementation of programmes. The reasons identified were as follows:[163]

1. Lack of Prevention: Policies, programmes, and structures to prevent children from falling into difficult circumstances were mostly lacking.
2. Poor planning and coordination:

   a) Poor implementation of existing laws and legislations;
   b) Lack of linkages with essential lateral services for children, for example, education, health, police, judiciary, and services for the disabled, among others;
   c) No mapping had been done of the children in need of care and protection or of the services available for them at the district, city, and state levels;
   d) Lack of coordination and convergence of programmes/services;
   e) Weak supervision, monitoring, and evaluation of the juvenile justice system.

2. Services were negligible relative to the needs:

   a) Most of the children in need of care and protection, as well as their families, did not get any support and services;
   b) Resources for child protection were meagre and their utilization was extremely uneven across India;
   c) Inadequate outreach and funding of existing programmes resulted in marginal coverage even of children in extremely difficult situations;

---

[162] *Bachpan Bachao Andolan* v. *Union Of India & Others* (Writ Petition [C] No. 51 of 2006).

[163] Compiled by Walsh Vincent, *Supreme Court on Children*, 2nd edition (New Delhi: Human Rights Law Network Vision [HRLN], Socio Legal Information Centre, August 2011).

d) Ongoing large-scale rural–urban migration created an enormous variety and number of problems related to social dislocation, severe lack of shelter, and rampant poverty, most of which were not addressed at all;

e) Lack of services addressing the issues like child marriage, female foeticide, discrimination against the girl child, and so on;

f) Little interventions for children affected by HIV/AIDs, drug abuse, militancy, disasters (both manmade and natural), abused and exploited children, and children of vulnerable groups like commercial sex workers, prisoners, migrant population, and other socially vulnerable groups;

g) Little interventions for children with special needs, particularly mentally challenged children.

3. Poor infrastructure:

a) Structures mandated by legislation are often inadequate;

b) Lack of institutional infrastructure to deal with child protection;

c) Inadequate number of child welfare committees (CWCs) and juvenile justice boards (JJBs).

d) Existing CWCs and JJBs not provided with requisite facilities for their efficient functioning, resulting in delayed enquiries and disposal of cases.

5. Inadequate human resources:

a) Inappropriate appointments to key child protection services, leading to inefficient and non-responsive services;

b) Lack of training and capacity building of personnel working in the child protection system;

c) Inadequate sensitization and capacity building of allied systems including police, judiciary, healthcare professions, and others;

d) Lack of proactive involvement of the voluntary sectors in child protection service delivery by the state/union territory administrations;

e) Large number of vacancies in existing child protection institutions.

6. Serious service gaps:

a) Improper use of institutions in contravention to government guidelines;

b) Lack of support services to families at risk, making children vulnerable;

c) Overbearing focus on institutional (residential) care, with non-institutional (that is, non-residential) services neglected;

d) Inter-state and intrastate transfer of children, especially for their restoration to families, not provided for in the existing schemes;

e) Lack of standards of care (accommodation, sanitation, leisure, food, and so on) in all institutions due to lower funding;

f) Lack of supervision and commitment to implement and monitor standards of care in institutions;

g) Most 24-hour shelters did not provide all the basic facilities required, especially shelter, food, and mainstream education;

h) Not all programmes addressed issues of drug abuse, HIV/AIDS, and sexual abuse-related vulnerabilities of children;

i) None of the existing schemes addressed the needs of child beggars or children used for begging;

j) Minimal use of non-institutional care options like adoption, foster care, and sponsorship to children without home and family ties;

k) No mechanism for child protection at the community level or involvement of communities and local bodies in programmes and services;

l) Serious services and infrastructure gaps, leading to few adoptions;

m) Cumbersome and time-consuming adoption services;

n) Lack of rehabilitation services for old children not adopted through regular adoption processes;

o) Aftercare and rehabilitation programmes for children above 18 years were not available in all states, and where they did exist, they were run as any other institution under the JJ Act.

The Supreme Court observed that by virtue of Section 3 of the RCFCEA, every child of the age 6–14 years shall have a right to free and compulsory education in a neighbourhood school till the completion of elementary education. Further, the court pointed out that Chapter 6 of the RCFCEA had special provisions for protection of the right of children. The NCPCR had been constituted and enjoyed a statutory status by virtue of this act. The court said that it was, therefore, necessary that a coordinated effort be made by the three agencies, namely the Commission, the ministry, and the state governments.

The court stipulated that in the state/union territory, the responsibility must vest either on the chief secretary or a secretary in charge of children, women, and family welfare. It would be open to the state government in appropriate cases to nominate for the said purpose a special officer not lower than the rank of a secretary to the state government.

The court said that it was abundantly clear that the Government of India was fully aware about the problems of children working in various places, particularly in circuses. The Court further added that the right of children to free and compulsory education had been made a Fundamental Right under Article 21A of the Constitution and, therefore, every child of the age of 6 to 14 years had the right to free elementary education in a neighbourhood school.

The court gave the following directions.

1. In order to implement the Fundamental Right of children under Article 21A, the Central Government was directed to issue suitable notifications prohibiting the employment of children in circuses within two months from the date of the judgment.

2. The Respondents were directed to conduct simultaneous raids in all the circuses to liberate the children and check the violation of Fundamental Rights of the children. The rescued children were to be kept in the care and protective homes till they attained the age of 18 years.

3. The Respondents were also directed to send the children back to their parents after proper verification, in case they are willing to take their children back.

4. The Respondents were directed to frame a proper scheme of rehabilitation of children rescued from circuses.

Manilal Dayal Ji & Company v. Respondent: Competent Authority and Inspector, Child Labour and Ors[164]

This batch of writ petitions was filed by two beedi manufacturers. In the course of a survey, the members of the Survey Team, that is, the Inspectors, found that the petitioner had engaged child labour and the said child labour was found rolling beedis at the time of survey. On finding that the child found working in the house was aged less than 14 years, the inspector sent a notice to the petitioners, asking him to deposit Rs. 20,000 towards the Child Labour-cum-Rehabilitation Fund. After submission of reply by the petitioners, the statement of the inspectors was recorded and thereafter the Assistant Labour Commissioner passed the order directing issuance of revenue recovery certificate for recovery of Rs. 20,000 in each of the cases.

The parents of the child involved in each of the writ petitions were working as *gharkhata* workers[165] and their names were submitted to the different authorities under the Beedi and Cigar Workers (Conditions of Employment) Act, 1966, and the Employees Provident Funds and Miscellaneous Provisions Acts, 1952. In some of the cases the petitioners had filed the form submitted before the Provident Fund Commissioner, wherein the name of the concerned child was mentioned as the child dependent upon the employee who is engaged by the petitioner. Thus, there appeared to be no dispute whatsoever that the employee engaged by the petitioner was a gharkhata worker.[166]

The Court held that the petitioners, who were beedi manufacturers, had employed gharkhata workers and the said gharkhata workers had engaged their minor sons/daughters/family members below the age of 14 years for rolling beedis. Thus, the manufacturers were protected under the proviso to section 3 of the CLPRA as the provisions of the act would not apply in cases where the concerned child labour was a family member of the gharkhata workers.

Some Significant Court Rulings Related to Bonded Child Labour

People's Union for Democratic Rights v. Union of India [167]

The Supreme Court in this case provided a rule to determine what situations constitute forced labour. The court held: 'Where a person provides labour or service to another for remuneration which is less than the minimum wage, the labour or service provided by him clearly falls within the scope and ambit of forced labour'.

---

[164] (2015) 144 FLR 1063.

[165] Gharkhata beedi worker is a home-based unorganized worker who rolls beedis in his/her home. Home-based work refers to any type of production activity that is carried out at home; the home is also the work place. But the very fact of the home being the workplace makes these workers invisible and hence they are often not counted as workers in spite of spending many hours in economically productive activity.

[166] In *Chhotabhai Purushottam Patel* v. *The State Of Maharashtra* (AIR 1971 Bom 244), the Bombay High Court has defined the gharkhata system in para 9 as one in which the worker takes the tobacco and beedi leaves home, cuts the beedi leaves at his residence, and delivers the prepared beedis at the workplace or the shop or the stock factory of the employer.

[167] (1982) 3 SCC 235.

The Supreme Court of India ruled: Any factor, which deprives a person of choice of alternatives and compels him to adapt one particular course of action may properly be regarded as 'force' and any labour or service which is compelled as a result of such 'force', it would be 'forced labour'.

It further stated: Where a person provides labour or service to another for remuneration which is less than minimum wage, the labour or service provided by him clearly falls within the scope and ambit of the word 'forced labour' ... as described in Article 23 of the Indian Constitution.

Bandhua Mukti Morcha[168] v. Union of India and Ors.[169]

The court emphasized that when the allegations revealed that the workers were being held in bondage without basic amenities like shelter, drinking water, or two square meals a day, it was a violation of the fundamental rights, as in this country everyone has a right to live with dignity and freedom from exploitation. The court also ruled that its power under Article 32 is very wide and it can adopt any 'appropriate' proceedings.

The Supreme Court of India ruled: Whenever it is shown that a labour is made to provide forced labour, the court would raise a presumption that he is required to do so in consideration of an advance or other economic considerations received by him and is, therefore, a bonded labour.

Neeraja Chaudhary v. State of Madhya Pradesh[170]

This case was on behalf of a group of bonded quarry workers in the early 1980s. A letter was sent to the Supreme Court, referring to an article written by the petitioner. The reporter had visited three of the villages in Madhya Pradesh where released bonded labourers were returned after the Court had ordered their release in a case filed by Bandhua Mukti Morcha.[171] All the 75 released bonded labourers from these villages were from tribal communities and they had not been rehabilitated six months after their release. The Supreme Court stated that it was imperative that the freed bonded labourers are properly rehabilitated after their identification and release. The Supreme Court also ruled:

> it is the plainest requirement of Articles 21 and 23 of the Constitution that bonded labourers must be identified and released and on release they must be suitably rehabilitated. Any failure of action on the part of the State Government(s) in implementing the provisions of the Bonded Labour System (Abolition) Act would be the clearest violation of Article 21 and Article 23 of the Constitution.

Bandhua Mukti Morcha v. Union of India[172]

In this judgment the court directed the Central Government to convene a meeting of the concerned ministers from different states to evolve policies for the progressive elimination of child

---

[168] Bandhua Mukti Morcha is an organization working for the release of bonded labourers.

[169] AIR 1984 SC 802; (1984) 3 SCC 161.

[170] (1984) 3 SCC 243.

[171] See *Bandhua Mukti Morcha* v. *Union of India and Others* in the previous para.

[172] AIR 1997 SC 2218.

labour. Some of the areas pointed out were compulsory education of children, vocational training, health check-ups, and nutritious food.

Bachpan Bachao and Ors. v. Union of India and Ors.; Shramjeevi Mahila Samiti v. State and Ors.; and Kalpana Pandit v. State[173]

This case dealt with three writ petitions pertaining to the problems of child trafficking and forced child labour and the regulation of placement agencies.

Petition filed by Kalpana Pandit

The first petition was filed by a poor domestic servant, Kalpana Pandit, after her daughter went missing when she was provided employment by a placement agency as a domestic help. This petition brought to the forefront the issue of exploitation of children working as domestic help and children going missing in the process. It was noted by the court that many placement agencies would place children initially at some residence as domestic help, but such children would ultimately be forced into the flesh trade. Therefore, the court also deemed it proper to address this issue, treating the petition as public interest litigation.

Petition filed by Bachpan Bachao Andolan

The second petition was filed by BBA, an NGO. The petition highlighted the problem of several thousand minors being kidnapped and trafficked from various states and brought to Delhi and sold for the purposes of prostitution, begging, drug peddling, slavery, forced labour, and various other crimes. The petitioner prayed to the court to direct the government to:

1. take appropriate measures for the immediate rescue and release of all such minor children;
2. protect the fundamental rights of such children;
3. take steps for the proper rehabilitation, social reintegration and education for the children who are released from various illegal placement agencies and other places in the NCT of Delhi; and
4. formulate and to bring into immediate effect a specific and stringent law to deal with such illegal placement agencies.

Petition filed by Shramjeevi Mahila Samiti

The third petition was filed by Shramjeevi Mahila Samiti, an NGO operating in Kolkata, West Bengal, on the similar problem of trafficking, kidnapping, forced labour, and bondage of 298 women and children. The petition brought to light the cases of women and children who were brought to Delhi from their villages and employed in various houses. Their place of employment was constantly changed so that their families were unable to contact them. Wages were not paid and they were confined against their wishes. There were instances of physical and sexual abuse as well.

---

[173] WP (Crl.) No. 82 of 2009, WP (Crl.) No. 619 of 2002, and WP (Crl.) No. 879 of 2007. Decided on 24 December 2010.

Observations made by the court

In this case, the Delhi High Court observed that trafficking in women and children was the gravest form of abuse and exploitation of human beings and further made the following observations:

- Poverty and lack of opportunity pave the way for trafficking. Child trafficking typically begins with a private arrangement between a trafficker and a family member, driven by the family's economic plight and the trafficker's desire for profit and cheap labour. Some crimes that are commonly concurrent with child trafficking include domestic violence, child abuse or neglect, child sexual abuse, and child pornography.
- The main laws dealing with child trafficking in India include the Immoral Trafficking Prevention Act, 1956, the JJ Act, and the Indian Penal Code, 1850 (IPC). The UN Protocol to Prevent, Suppress and Punish Trafficking in Persons, also referred to as the Palermo Protocol on Trafficking, deals with the problem of trafficking internationally.

The Court issued the following directions and suggestions to various stakeholders.

Directions with regard to placement agencies

- The court observed that there are as many as 123 such agencies functioning in Delhi, engaged in placement of children in various establishments, including as domestic help. There is no statutory control over the functioning of these agencies. The result is that children who are either picked up from the streets or brought from various other states to Delhi are first placed as domestic help and later shifted to other more hazardous work, with some even pushed into prostitution. This defeats the very spirit of the JJ Act. The CWCs formed under the act and vested with extensive powers have, in the absence of appropriate rules and regulations for the exercise of that power, been rendered hollow. As a result, the court gave various directions in its order dated 4 October 2004.
- The court directed the CWCs in Delhi to submit a detailed report regarding the complaints received by them about child abuse in cases where children are placed with households to work as domestic servants, and the action taken by the committees.
- The court also directed the Secretary, Social Welfare Department, Government of Delhi, to indicate whether any rules have been framed or can be framed under the JJ Act to regulate the exercise of powers by committees and also to regulate the functioning of the placement agencies dealing with domestic child labour.
- The state government submitted a report stating that it was not possible to frame guidelines for monitoring the placement agencies under the JJ Act. Instead, it was suggested that steps be taken for making registration under the Delhi Shops and Establishments Act, 1954 (DSEA) mandatory, whereby the placement agencies could also be regulated. The necessary amendment in the aforesaid act has since been made.

Suggestions for the regulation of placement agencies

In order to regulate the manner in which placement agencies work, the counsel for Kalpana Pandit made the following suggestions.

Domestic workers who are placed by the agencies can be classified as children and adults. Children will be in the age group of 14 to 18 years and the adults above 18. The government must:

- Register the placement agencies both under the DSEA as and when registration becomes mandatory, and under the Inter-state Migrant Workmen (Regulation of Employment and Conditions of Service) Act, 1979 (ISMW Act), with immediate effect.
- Direct the licensing authorities under the ISMW Act to grant licenses to the placement agencies as 'contractors' for a specified period of time and make them furnish records as per the requirements under the act.
- Direct the inspectors appointed under the CLPRA to ensure that children below 14 are not employed as domestic help, and regulate the conditions of employment of children in the age group of 14–18.
- Direct the licensing authority under the ISMW Act to supply a copy of their records to the CWCs, who, in turn, will ensure that children who are placed by these contractors are cared for properly.
- Ensure that the CWCs are duly enabled by framing model rules with respect to working children and their rehabilitation needs.
- Direct that children below 14 who are rescued are either repatriated, reintegrated, or rehabilitated by the intervention of the CWCs.
- Ensure that in cases of abuse which are covered by the IPC, these agencies either collectively or individually help prosecute the perpetrator.

Suggestions Given by the Solicitor General

- The Solicitor General emphasized that every state government must have a set of guidelines for NGOs that want to assist in inquiries/fact-finding and rescue operations. The guidelines published in Bernard Boetoen's *An NGO's Practical Guide in the Fight against Child Trafficking* should be adopted.
- The police must also follow certain guidelines in conducting fact-finding and rescue operations to ensure confidentiality of the child and provide adequate care to the child through provision of basic necessities such as food and drinking water in the police station. It is important that no child be kept in the police station.

Directions Issued by the Court

Framing of comprehensive law: The court observed that there was no comprehensive legislation to take care of the problem. Multiple statutes with multiple authorities, due to lack of coordination and disconnect among them, are not able to tackle the issue effectively. Therefore, there is a need to study the feasibility of having a single legislation to regulate the problem of employment of children and adult women as domestic helps. Until that is achieved, the government must ensure that various enforcement agencies of different statutes work in a coordinated and cooperative manner. Necessary guidelines should be issued or rules framed in this behalf. A single-window enforcement agency should be created.

Registration of placement agencies

1. The Labour Department will register all placement agencies. The registration process will be within a finite period of time. Failure to register within that prescribed time should invite penal action, which can be prescribed by this court.
2. The registration process should not only be for agencies located in Delhi but also for all the agencies that place women and children in homes located in Delhi.
3. The registration information should require:

    a) details of the agencies;
    b) number of persons who are employed through the agencies, their names, ages, and addresses;
    c) details of salaries fixed for each person;
    d) addresses of the employers;
    e) period of employment;
    f) nature of work;
    g) details of the commissions received from the employers.

4. The information should be available for easy access by the CWCs as well as the Delhi Commission for Women. The information should be put up on the Labour Department website. Until such time as this is done, the records should be made available to the Commission and the committees.

Duties of the Commission of Women and Children and Delhi Commission for Women

1. To go through the records provided by the Labour Department;
2. To verify the information and to seek further information where information is found to be inadequate, by summoning the placement agencies;
3. Use the services of Childline, a service set up by the Ministry of Women and Child Development, Union of India, to verify the information in appropriate cases;
4. Entertain complaints made by the domestic worker himself/herself or through a guardian, an NGO, the employer, or the police in appropriate cases;
5. Decide the complaints made within a period of 30 days;
6. To hear the following types of cases:

    a) withholding of agreed wages;
    b) harassment, including harassment by the employer or at the hands of the placement agencies;
    c) harassment and abuse by placement agency proprietor/staff at their premises or at workplace;
    d) non-compliance with the agreed terms;
    e) abusive working conditions that are beyond the physical capacity of the child in cases where persons between ages 14 and 18 are employed;
    f) long hours of work;
    g) lack of basic facilities including medical care and food.

Powers of the Committee/Commission:

1. Summon the placement agencies or the employer on receiving a complaint;
2. Direct payment of wages as per agreed terms, and impose fines in appropriate cases;
3. Direct payment of compensation in cases where severe injuries are caused to the domestic worker during the course of work;
4. Direct medical assistance;
5. Direct the placement agency to comply with the agreement with the employer or return the commission where the terms are not complied with;
6. Impose fines on the placement agencies where it is found that terms of the agreement are not followed;
7. Direct legal aid to the child/woman where a criminal offence has happened;
8. Direct employers to inform the local police or the committee/commission within 24 hours in cases where the domestic worker is missing;
9. In cases where a domestic worker has been placed in a home against her wishes, enable her to leave her employment and direct the agency to return the commission paid by the employer back to the employer.
10. Directions to the police: The court also directed the police to fulfill its obligations under the Police Circular issued by the Deputy Commissioner of Police, Headquarters, New Delhi, which requires the Delhi Police to:

    a) Regulate the functioning of placement agencies;
    b) Ensure proper screening of domestic workers being recruited by placement agencies, by maintaining the register of all such agencies;
    c) Ensure that the agencies enroll applicants on the basis of formal applications containing full details, including photographs and contact addresses of the applicants, the details of previous employers, and so on. The court directed the administration at the highest level in Delhi Police to reconsider the feasibility of implementation of these instructions.

International Legal Interventions, Strategies, and Movements

The ILO's policy considers the abolition of child labour as the objective, based on the recognition that total abolition will take a long time and that a start has necessarily to be made. It has defined priority areas to this end. It has launched a global project, the IPEC. The UNICEF acknowledges the need to tackle the problem of child labour in order to implement the CRC. International standards, especially those laid down by the ILO and the United Nations (UN), have had impact on our law-making process. One of the most important tools available to the ILO and the UN for improving the legislation and international standards concerning child labour is the set of large numbers of international treaties, declarations, covenants, and conventions. Some of them, relating to child labour, are as follows.

1919: Minimum Age (Industry) Convention No. 5

Adopted at the first session of the ILO and ratified by 72 countries, the convention established 14 years as the minimum age for children to be employed in industry. It was the first international effort to regulate children's participation in the workplace and was followed by numerous ILO instruments applicable to other economic sectors.

1930: Forced Labour Convention No. 29

This convention provides for the suppression of the use of forced or compulsory labour in all its forms. The term 'forced or compulsory labour' is considered to mean all work or service exacted from any people under the threat of penalty and for which they have not offered themselves voluntarily.

1948: Convention No. 87[174]

Convention No. 87 concerning Freedom of Association and Protection of the Right to Organize provides for the right of workers and employers, without any distinction, to establish and join organizations of their own choosing without previous authorization. Their organizations have the right to form or join federations and confederations, including those at the international level.

1966: International Covenant on Civil and Political Rights

Adopted by the UN General Assembly in 1966 and brought into force in 1976, it reaffirms the principles of the UDHR with regard to civil and political rights and commits state parties to take action to realize these rights. Article 8 states that no one should be kept in slavery or servitude or be required to perform forced or compulsory labour.

1966: International Covenant on Economic, Social, and Cultural Rights

Adopted by the UN General Assembly in 1966 and brought into force in 1976, it reaffirms the principles of the UDHR with regard to economic, social, and cultural rights. Article 10 enjoins state parties to protect young people from economic exploitation and from employment in work likely to hamper their morals, their health, or their lives, or likely to hamper their normal development. It also commits state parties to set age limits below which the paid employment of child labour should be prohibited and punishable by law.

1973: ILO Minimum Age Convention No. 138[175]

The ILO Convention No. 138 concerning Minimum Age for Entry to Employment and Work supersedes prior instruments applicable to limited economic sectors. The convention obliges

[174] India and ILO, Ministry of Labour and Employment, Government of India. Available at http://labour.nic.in/upload/uploadfiles/files/Divisions/childlabour/Website%20-%20Copy%20(1)%20gyanesh.pdf (accessed on 10 July 2015).

[175] India and ILO, Ministry of Labour and Employment, Government of India. Available at http://labour.nic.in/upload/uploadfiles/files/Divisions/childlabour/Website%20-%20Copy%20(1)%20gyanesh.pdf (accessed on 10 July 2015).

member states to pursue a national policy designed to ensure effective abolition of child labour. In this connection, it establishes that no child can be employed in any economic sector below the age designated for the completion of compulsory schooling—and not less than 15 years. The minimum age for admission to any work likely to jeopardize health, safety, or morals is 18 years.

The convention was adopted by the ILO at its 58th Session in June 1973. This is one of the eight Core Conventions of the ILO, referred to as Fundamental or basic Human Rights Conventions, and the ILO has been very active in promoting its ratification. Each country ratifying this convention undertakes to:

1. Pursue a national policy designed to ensure the effective abolition of child labour;
2. Specify a minimum age for entry to employment or work, which will not be less than the ages of completion of compulsory schooling;
3. To raise this progressively to a level consistent with the fullest physical and mental development of young people;
4. Guarantee that the minimum age of entry to any type of employment or work, which is likely to compromise health, safety, or morals of young person, shall not be less than 18 years.

Table 4.7 The Minimum Age of Admission to Employment and Work under ILO's Convention No. 138[176]

	The Minimum Age at Which Children Can Start Work	Possible Exceptions for Developing Countries
Hazardous Work: Any work which is likely to jeopardize children's health, safety, or morals should not be done by anyone under the age of 18.	18 (16 under strict conditions)	18 (16 under strict conditions)
Basic Minimum Age: The minimum age for work should not be below the age for finishing compulsory schooling, which is generally 15.	15	14
Light Work: Children between the ages of 13 and 15 years may do light work, as long as it does not threaten their health and safety, or hinder their education or vocational orientation and training.	13–15	12–14

1973: Minimum Age Recommendation No. 146

This calls on states to raise the minimum age of employment to 16 years. While not legally binding, it nonetheless is a strong call to action on the part of member states. Convention No. 138 and this recommendation are regarded as the most comprehensive international instruments and statements on child labour.

[176] Source: ILO Convention No. 138 on the minimum age for admission to employment and work.

1989: United Nations Convention on the Rights of the Child

This enshrines as interdependent and indivisible the full range of the civil, political, economic, social, and cultural rights of all children that are vital to their survival, development, protection, and participation in the lives of their societies. Because of this connection between children's rights and their survival and development, virtually all the convention's articles address issues—such as education, health, nutrition, rest and relaxation, social security, the responsibilities of parents—that are related to child labour and its effects on children. One of the tenets of the convention is that in all actions concerning children, their best interests should be taken fully into account. Article 32 recognizes the children's right to be protected from work that threatens their health, education, or development, and enjoins state parties to set minimum ages for employment and to regulate working conditions.

1999: Convention No. 182 Concerning the Prohibition and Immediate Action for the Elimination of the Worst Forms of Child Labour[177]

This ILO convention was adopted on 17 June 1999. This convention defines for the first time what constitutes the 'worst forms of child labour', and includes a ban on forced or compulsory recruitment of child soldiers. It calls for international cooperation on social and economic development, poverty eradication, and education to realize its terms, and provides for broad consultations among governments, workers, and employers—the 'social partners' in the ILO's tripartite structure. It defines the worst forms of child labour as:

1. all forms of slavery or practices similar to slavery, such as the sale and trafficking of children, debt bondage, serfdom, and forced or compulsory labour;
2. forced or compulsory recruitment of children for use in armed conflict;
3. use of a child for prostitution, production of pornography, or pornographic performances;
4. use, procuring, or offering of a child for illicit activities, in particular for the production and trafficking of drugs; and
5. work which is likely to harm the health, safety, or morals of children.

The convention requires ratifying States to 'design and implement programmes of action' to eliminate the worst forms of child labour as a priority and to 'establish or designate appropriate mechanisms' for monitoring implementation of the convention, in consultation with employers' and workers' organizations. It also says that the ratifying States should 'provide support for the removal of children from the worst forms of child labour, and their rehabilitation; ensure access to free basic education or vocational training for all children freed from the worst forms of child labour; identify children at special risk; and take into account the special situation of girls'.

An accompanying recommendation defines 'hazardous work' as:

---

[177] Adopted by the General Conference of the ILO at its 87th Session, Geneva, 17 June 1999.

work which exposes children to physical, psychological or sexual abuse; work underground, under water, at dangerous heights or in confined spaces; work with dangerous machinery or tools, or which involves heavy loads; work in unhealthy environments which may expose children to hazardous substances, temperature, noise or vibrations; and work under particularly difficult conditions such as long hours, during the night or where a child is confined to the premises of the employers.[178]

Strategies for Effective Implementation of International Conventions[179]

All conventions so far have paid very little heed to the 'strategies', and this is the gap that needs to be urgently filled. Any new convention, no matter how narrow or focused the area of intervention may be, will fail if sufficient attention is not paid to the operational aspects.

The urgent need is to focus energy and resources on preparing a well-defined plan of action which clearly identifies each actor and his responsibilities. These actors are first and foremost accountable to working children and their immediate communities. Viable alternatives should be evolved on the basis of the following principles:

1. All actions should be child-centred and in the best interest of working children. Interventions should have a positive short-term and long-term effect on the children themselves, first and foremost.
2. All interventions should improve the quality of life of the children, their families, and their communities.
3. Organized representation of working children and their centrality has to be recognized and respected. No decisions or actions which have an impact on working children, should be taken without consulting them.[180]
4. The immediate and long-term impacts of all actions on 'working children' have to be monitored and assessed. It should be mandatory that the monitoring mechanisms should include working children and NGOs.
5. A comprehensive strategy has to be designed to address the basic causes that create and perpetuate child labour. An action plan—that identifies a set of specific interventions that will have an impact on the basic causes of child labour and create alternatives that improve the quality of life of child workers and their communities—will have to be formulated. This will have a spin-off effect on working children outside the target group as well.
6. All strategies should place special emphasis not only on the problems of girls but also of all marginalized groups, including backward castes and tribes.
7. Short-term strategies should always be steps towards long-term goals and not limit themselves to removing the scum from the top of a boiling pot. Long-term strategies should concern

---

[178] International Labour Conference (1999), *World of Work*, 30, 5.

[179] The Concerned for Working Children, 'Child Labour—The New ILO Convention, A Position Paper', Bengaluru, India.

[180] This point received special mention in the Amsterdam Child Labour Conference.

themselves with the root causes of child labour and its perpetuation. These strategies should recognize that policies such as globalization, structural adjustment, and the General Agreement on Tariffs and Trade (GATT) have further marginalized large sections of our societies. A strategy to successfully address child labour has to include mechanisms to counter policies which are anti-poor and anti-children.

8. The implementation of the convention has to be monitored by children and local communities who are nearest to the reality at the grass roots and who are the first ones to experience the real impact of the conventions on children. The authority to ensure implementation and monitoring of relevant instruments should be decentralized and vested with local authorities/governments. Local task forces should be formed to monitor the implementation of the intervention, and these should mandatorily include working children and NGOs. Such a body should be primarily concerned with monitoring and evaluating the short-term and long-term impacts on the working children themselves.[181]

International Initiatives and Movements

Child labour was sharply reduced in Western countries at the beginning of the twentieth century, in part by combining legislation and its enforcement with compulsory primary education. Other important factors included a rise in family incomes and technological improvements that made children's labour less useful to employers. But legislation had an undeniable impact far beyond deterrence. It set new standards and changed attitudes across society. These in turn provided, and still provide, the best insurance against a return to high levels of child labour in industrialized countries.[182] Hong Kong, which is completely urban and has a thriving economy, has provided a notable success story, having eliminated child labour through:

1. regular and persistent inspections by the labour department;
2. special annual campaigns to detect child employment;
3. requiring all young workers to carry identity cards with their photographs, thus facilitating enforcement; and
4. introducing welfare benefits, especially social assistance, to poor families, which assured a minimum income and removed the need to rely on child labour.[183]

Child labour legislation can also be a means of educating people and promoting debate on the issue. An example of legislation being used in this educative way comes from Brazil, where children working on the street were considered a social welfare or public security problem and

---

[181] UNESCO, 'Recommendation on the Development of Adult Education', 26 November 1976. Available at http://portal.unesco.org/en/ev.php-URL_ID=13096&URL_DO=DO_TOPIC&URL_SECTION=201.html (accessed on 9 November 2015).

[182] UNICEF, 'The State of the World's Children', 1997. Available at http://www.unicef.org/sowc97/ (accessed on 14 November 2016).

[183] UNICEF, 'The State of the World's Children'.

deemed 'delinquents'. Child-centred policies were developed and street children began to be seen as active and responsible agents of their own destinies.[184]

The new Article of the Constitution of Brazil[185] states that it is the duty of the family, of society, and of the State to assure children and adolescents, with absolute priority, of the right to life, health, nutrition, education, recreation, vocational preparation, culture, dignity, respect, liberty, and family and community solidarity, over and beyond making them safe from neglect, discrimination, exploitation, cruelty, and oppression.[186] This was followed by the passing of the statute on children and adolescents in July 1990, which set child labour in the context of child rights by clearly stating that the welfare of the child must take precedence over all competing interests, including those of the family. The principle established is 'children first'.

The ILO's International Programme on the Elimination of Child Labour, 1992[187]

The IPEC, established in 1992, has played a key role in promoting international and national action to eliminate child labour. The IPEC has supported more than 250 child labour surveys, 60 of which were national in scope, and since 2000, has published regular global and regional child labour reports and analytical studies.[188] Through policy-focused work at the national level in more than 100 countries, IPEC has also encouraged the development of appropriate legal and policy frameworks in line with international standards on child labour. At the same time, IPEC-supported projects at the community level have provided models of good practice for removing children from child labour by equipping them with education and skills.[189]

In 2006, 6 years after the ILO Convention No. 182 on the Worst Forms of Child Labour came into force, the ILO constituency set the goal of eliminating all the worst forms of child labour by 2016. A global action plan was subsequently agreed upon by the ILO constituents to provide a strategic framework and action plan for the ILO, and in particular IPEC, in the period up to 2016. By endorsing the plan and the 2016 target, the ILO Governing Body reconfirmed its commitment to the elimination of child labour as one of the Organization's highest priorities. This commitment was reinforced in 2012 when the ILO Governing Body approved a new plan of action on the fundamental principles and rights at work.[190] The plan of action emphasizes the universal nature of these rights, their interrelated and mutually reinforcing qualities, and their significance as enabling rights for the achievement of all the ILO strategic objectives related to fundamental principles and rights at work, employment, social protection, and social dialogue.[191]

---

[184] Jo Boyden and William Myers, 'Exploring Alternative Approaches to Combating Child Labour: Case Studies from Developing Countries', Innocenti Occasional Papers, Child Rights Series No. 8, UNICEF International Child Development Centre, Florence (1995), p. 20.

[185] Passed by the Brazilian Congress in October 1988.

[186] Boyden and Myers, 'Exploring Alternative Approaches', p. 20–23.

[187] Available at http://www.ilo.org/ipec/lang--en/index.htm (accessed on 9 November 2015).

[188] Available at http://www.ilo.org/ipec/lang--en/index.htm (accessed on 9 November 2015).

[189] Available at http://www.ilo.org/ipec/lang--en/index.htm (accessed on 9 November 2015).

[190] The ILO's Fundamental Principles and Rights at Work Action Plan address child labour, freedom of association and collective bargaining, forced labour, and discrimination.

[191] ILO, 'Decent Work', Report of the Director-General, 87th Session, Geneva, June 1999. Available at http://www.ilo.org/public/english/standards/relm/ilc/ilc87/rep-i.htm (accessed on 9 November 2015).

Given that nearly 60 per cent of child labour takes place in agriculture, the Food and Agriculture Organization of the United Nations (FAO) supports agricultural stakeholders through policy support and programmes to prevent and reduce child labour in agriculture and rural areas. FAO also works with partners to address the root causes of child labour, in particular with the ILO, the International Fund for Agricultural Development (IFAD), the International Union of Food workers (IUF), the International Food Policy Research Institute (IFPRI), and Consultative Group on International Agricultural Research (CGIAR),[192] through the International Partnership for Cooperation on Child Labour in Agriculture, that was established in 2007.[193]

The Roadmap for Achieving the Elimination of the Worst Forms of Child Labour by 2016 was adopted at The Hague Global Child Labour Conference of 2010 and subsequently endorsed by the ILO's Governing Body in recognition of the need for a 'new momentum' if the world is to attain the ambitious 2016 target. In the Roadmap, Conference participants—representatives from governments, employers' and workers' organizations, non-governmental and other civil society organizations, regional and international organizations—highlighted the urgent need to upscale and accelerate country-level actions against child labour in the lead-up to 2016.[194] The 2012 action plan adopted by the ILO Governing Body specifically calls for support to member states in implementing the Roadmap. Policy priorities identified in the Roadmap include national legislation and enforcement, education and training, social protection, and, of particular relevance for the current Report, labour markets. In the area of labour markets, the Roadmap identifies, inter alia, the following as key priorities:[195]

1. taking action to foster a well-functioning labour market, as well as access to vocational training for adults and young people of working age that corresponds with the current and future needs of the labour market so as to facilitate the school-to-work transition;
2. supporting employment creation and promoting decent and productive work for adults and young people of working age, that is consistent with the fundamental principles and rights at work; and
3. working towards regulating and formalizing the informal economy where most instances of the worst forms of child labour occur, including through the strengthening of state labour inspection and enforcement systems and capacities.

[192] The CGIAR is a global partnership that unites organizations engaged in research for a food-secure future.

[193] ILO–FAO, 'International Partnership for Cooperation on Child Labour in Agriculture', Geneva, 2013. Available at http://www.fao-ilo.org/fao-ilo-child/international-partnership-for-cooperation-on-child-labour-in-agriculture (accessed on 9 November 2015).

[194] ILO, 'World Report on Child Labour: Paving the Way to Decent Work for Young People', Geneva, 2015.

[195] ILO, 'Implementing the Roadmap for Achieving the Elimination of the Worst Forms of Child Labour By 2016—A Training Guide for Policy Makers, IPEC (Geneva: ILO, 2013). Available at https://www.google.co.in/url?sa=t&rct=j&q=&esrc=s&source=web&cd=1&cad=rja&uact=8&ved=0ahUKEwih6Jyq6prPAhVW-mMKHa_8CRMQFggcMAA&url=http%3A%2F%2Fwww.ilo.org%2Fipecinfo%2Fproduct%2Fdownload.do%3Ftype%3Ddocument%26id%3D22055&usg=AFQjCNEXnUDflYfDVXCL-TJ4Ztm6CCbfKA&sig2=nNW0DLnI6zNU-sdqN_WqoA&bvm=bv.133178914,d.dGo (accessed on 9 November 2015).

In 2013, the Brazilian Government, following on from the conference in The Hague, hosted the Global Conference on Child Labour.[196] The conference provided an opportunity for governments, social partners, and civil society to reflect on the progress made since the previous global conference was held in The Hague in 2010, and to discuss ways to step up global efforts against child labour—especially its worst forms. In the Conference outcome document,[197] participants reiterated their commitment to fully implement The Hague Roadmap, and acknowledge the need for reinforced national and international action in this regard.

One of the most potent means of addressing child labour is to regularly check the places where girls and boys may be working. Child labour monitoring (CLM) is the active process that ensures that such observation is put in place and is coordinated in an appropriate manner. Its overall objective is to ensure that children and young legally employed workers are safe from exploitation and hazards at work as a consequence of monitoring. The active scrutiny of child labour at the local level is supported by a referral system which establishes a link between appropriate services and ex-child labourers.[198] In practice, CLM involves the identification, referral, protection, and prevention of child labourers through the development of a coordinated multi-sector monitoring and referral process that aims to cover all children living in a given geographical area. Its principal activities include regularly repeated direct observations to identify child labourers and to determine risks to which they are exposed, referral of these children to services, verification that they have been removed, and tracking them afterwards to ensure that they have satisfactory alternatives.[199]

Applicable International Law on Bonded Children

The practice of bonded child labour violates the following international human rights conventions; India is a party to all of them, and as such is legally bound to comply with their terms.

1926: Convention on the Suppression of Slave Trade and Slavery

This convention requires signatories to 'prevent and suppress the slave trade' and 'to bring about, progressively and as soon as possible, the complete abolition of slavery in all forms'. It also

---

[196] III Global Child Labour Conference, 'Towards a Child Labour-Free World', Brasilia, 8–10 October 2013.

[197] ILO and the Ministry of Social Affairs and Employment of the Netherlands, The Hague Global Child Labour Conference 2010—Towards a World without Child Labour, Mapping the Road to 2016, Conference Report, ILO, IPEC (Geneva, 2010). Available at https://www.google.co.in/url?sa=t&rct=j&q=&esrc=s&source=web&cd=1&cad=rja&uact=8&ved=0ahUKEwidqrSD6prPAhUQw2MKHYwPAwgQFggcMAA&url=http%3A%2F%2Fwww.ilo.org%2Fipecinfo%2Fproduct%2Fdownload.do%3Ftype%3Ddocument%26id%3D14575&usg=AFQjCNF3TB52_sJM636gmo9TBjq-vN-mrIg&sig2=_bRP3jct9eLdKTPZaNajPg&bvm=bv.133178914,d.dGo (accessed on 9 November 2015).

[198] ILO, 'Child Labour Monitoring (CLM)'. Available at http://www.ilo.org/ipec/Action/Childlabourmonitoring/lang--en/index.htm (accessed on 9 November 2015).

[199] ILO, 'Child labour monitoring (CLM)'.

obligates to 'take all necessary measures to prevent compulsory or forced labour from developing into conditions analogous to slavery'.[200]

1956: Supplementary Convention on the Abolition of Slavery, the Slave Trade, and Institutions and Practices Similar to Slavery

The supplementary convention on slavery offers further clarification of prohibited practices and refers specifically to debt bondage and child servitude as institutions similar to slavery. It requires state parties to take all practicable and necessary legislative and other measures to bring about progressively and as soon as possible the complete abolition of ... debt bondage ... [and] any institution or practice whereby a child or young person under the age of 18 years, is delivered by either or both of his natural parents or by his guardian to another person, whether for reward or not, with a view to the exploitation of the child or young person or his labour.[201]

The convention defines debt bondage as follows.

> Debt bondage, that is to say, the status or condition arising from a pledge by a debtor of his personal services or those of a person under his control as security for a debt, if the value of those services as reasonably assessed is not applied towards the liquidation of the debt or the length and nature of those services are not respectively limited and defined.[202]

1989: Convention on the Rights of the Child

Articles 32 (child labour)[203], 35 (Abduction, sale and trafficking)[204], and 36 (other forms of exploitation)[205] of the CRC mandate protections that are particularly relevant for the bonded child labour.

---

[200] Convention on the Suppression of Slave Trade and Slavery was signed at Geneva on 25 September 1926; the Protocol amending the Slavery Convention, done at New York, was entered into force on 7 December 1953; the Supplementary Convention on the Abolition of Slavery, the Slave Trade, and Institutions and Practices similar to Slavery was entered into force on 30 April 1957.

[201] The Supplementary Convention on the Abolition of Slavery, the Slave Trade, and Institutions and Practices Similar to Slavery, Adopted by a Conference of Plenipotentiaries convened by Economic and Social Council resolution 608(XXI) of 30 April 1956 and done at Geneva on 7 September 1956. Entry into force: 30 April 1957, in accordance with Article 13. Available at http://www.ohchr.org/EN/ProfessionalInterest/Pages/SupplementaryConventionAbolitionOfSlavery.aspx (accessed on 14 November 2016).

[202] Supplementary Convention on the Abolition of Slavery.

[203] CRC, Article 32: The government should protect children from work that is dangerous or might harm their health or their education.

[204] CRC, Article 35: The government should take all measures possible to make sure that children are not abducted, sold, or trafficked. This provision in the convention is augmented by the Optional Protocol on the sale of children, child prostitution, and child pornography.

[205] CRC, Article 36: Children should be protected from any activity that takes advantage of them or could harm their welfare and development.

India and International Law on Child Labour

India ratified the CRC with a declaration on Article 32.[206] The Government of India ratified the convention in December 1992, but with the solitary rider in relation to article 32 stating that due to wide spread poverty and illiteracy which are some of the reason beyond its control, the economic, social and cultural rights can only be progressively implemented in a developing country like India, subject to the extent of available resources. The implementation of the CRC, which recognizes the right of the child (understood to be up to 18 years old) to be protected from economic exploitation and from performing any work that is likely to be hazardous or to interfere with the child's education, or to be harmful to the child's health or physical, mental, spiritual, moral, and social development, is thus stalled by the Government.[207]

Justifying the continuation of India's declaration that has been made on Article 32, the Initial Report by the Government of India to the CRC Committee opened by stating that undesirable child labour still persists in the country due to socio-economic compulsions, and cited various policies and programmes.[208] It quoted its efforts to implement the judgment in *MC Mehta* v. *State of Tamil Nadu*,[209] that were initiated by the government for the protection of children from work. However, the government admitted that 'the number of working children covered by the special school is minuscule compared to the total number of children waiting to be released and rehabilitated'.[210]

In its First Periodic Report,[211] the Government of India admitted that the non-availability of accurate, authentic, and up-to-date data on child labour has been a major handicap in 'planned intervention for eradication of this social evil'. It further stated that this does not minimize the urgency and importance of drawing up concrete programmes for identification, release, and rehabilitation of working children. While the Report identified poverty as a major factor compelling parents to send their children to work, it also stated that the correlation between child labour and regional poverty in India does not necessarily indicate a causal relationship. It further stated that

[206] CRC, Article 32: (1) States parties recognize the right of the child to be protected from economic exploitation and from performing any work that is likely to be hazardous or to interfere with the child's education, or to be harmful to the child's health or physical, mental, spiritual, moral, or social development. (2) States parties shall take legislative, administrative, social and educational measures to ensure the implementation of the present article. To this end, and having regard to the relevant provisions of other international instruments, states parties shall in particular: (a) Provide for a minimum age or minimum ages for admission to employment; (b) Provide for appropriate regulation of the hours and conditions of employment; (c) Provide for appropriate penalties or other sanctions to ensure the effective enforcement of the present article.

[207] Memorandum: 'A Plea to Government of India for Urgent Measures to Implement the Convention on the Rights of the Child and the Constitutional Commitments'. Available at http://www.childrensright-sindia.org/pdf/CRC%2020%20BS%20MEMORANDUM.pdf (accessed on 9 November 2015).

[208] Ministry of Women and Child Development, Government of India, 'Convention on the Rights of the Child, India First Periodic Report—2001',. Available at http://wcd.nic.in/crc.htm (accessed on 8 July 2015).

[209] (1996) RD-SC 1576.

[210] HAQ: Centre for Child Rights, *Twenty Years of CRC: A Balance Sheet*, Volume I (New Delhi, 2011).

[211] 'Convention on the Rights of the Child, India First periodic Report—2001'.

ineffective enforcement of child labour-related laws and the lack of awareness and educational opportunity contribute to the existence and acceptance of this social evil.[212]

Government of India's Stand on ILO Convention 182[213]

Regarding the implementation of the Convention on Prohibition and Immediate Action for the Elimination of the Worst Forms of Child Labour, the Government of India has taken the following stand:

The worst forms of child labour are already prohibited under various acts, namely:

1. Slavery, Debt Bondage and Forced or Compulsory Labour through Bonded Labour System (Abolition) Act, 1976.
2. Prostitution, Pornography and Pornographic performances banned through IPC, Immoral Trafficking Prevention Act, 1956.
3. Production and trafficking of drugs has been banned by Narcotic Drugs and Psychotropic Substances Act, 1985.
4. Child labour below 14 years in hazardous occupation is prohibited under the CLPRA.[214]

The Government of India stated that it agreed with the principles of the convention. The convention could not be ratified so far because it mandates the age of 18 years for prohibition of children from employment in specified hazardous occupations, whereas according to the CLPRA, the minimum specified age for employment in the hazardous occupations is 14 years. The Government of India further stated that it follows the policy of ratifying ILO conventions only when the existing laws and practices are in conformity with the provisions of the said convention. The Union Cabinet has approved the proposal of the Ministry of Labour and Employment for amending the CLPRA, which is in line with the ratification of Convention No. 182.

The Child Labour (Prohibition and Regulation) Amendment Bill, 2012 was introduced in the Rajya Sabha during the Winter Session of Parliament in 2012.[215] The Rajya Sabha has referred the Amendment Bill to the Parliamentary Standing Committee on Labour, and presently the Bill is under examination of the Standing Committee.[216] The Amendment Bill covers:

---

[212] HAQ: Centre for Child Rights, *Twenty Years of CRC*.

[213] India and ILO, Ministry of Labour and Employment, Government of India. Available at http://labour.nic.in/upload/uploadfiles/files/Divisions/childlabour/Website%20-%20Copy%20(1)%20gyanesh.pdf (accessed on 10 July 2015).

[214] Press Information Bureau, Government of India. Available at http://pib.nic.in/newsite/PrintRelease.aspx?relid=121636 (accessed on 9 November 2015).

[215] PRS Legislative Research (PRS), 'Child Labour (Prohibition and Regulation) Amendment Bill, 2012'. Available at http://www.prsindia.org/billtrack/the-child-labour-prohibition-and-regulation-amendment-act-2012-2553/ (accessed on 9 November 2015).

[216] PRS, 'Standing Committee Report Summary: The Child Labour (Prohibition and Regulation) Amendment Bill, 2012'. Available at http://www.prsindia.org/uploads/media/Child%20Labour/SC%20summary%20-%20Child%20Labour%20_A_%20Bill.pdf (accessed on 9 November 2015).

1. Complete prohibition on employment of children below 14 years and linking the age of the prohibition with the age under the Right to Free and Compulsory Education Act.
2. Prohibition of working of adolescents (14 to 18 years) in mines, explosives and hazardous occupations set forth in the Factories Act, 1948.
3. Stricter punishment to the offenders and making the offences cognizable under the act.

The process of ratification of ILO Convention 182 would be taken up only after the amendments were finalized.[217]

A look at Table 4.8 on the ratification status of international instruments on child labour would give us an understanding of the Government of India's position on relevant international instruments to which it is a state party.

Table 4.8   Ratification Status of International Instruments on Child Labour[218]

International Legal Instruments	Status of Ratification/Signature/Adoption
1. ILO Convention No. 29 (Forced Labour, 1930)	Ratified on 30 November 1954
2. ILO Convention No. 87 (Freedom of Association and Protection of Rights, 1948)	Not ratified
3. ILO Convention No. 98 (Right to Organise and Collective Bargaining Convention, 1949)	Not ratified
4. ILO Convention No. 100 (Equal Remuneration Convention, 1951)	Ratified on 25 September 1958
5. ILO Convention No. 105 (Abolition of Forced Labour, 1957)	Ratified on 18 May 2000
6. ILO Convention No. 111 (Discrimination, Employment and Occupation Convention, 1958)	Ratified on 3 June 1960
7. ILO Convention No. 138 (Minimum Age Convention, 1973)	Not ratified
8. ILO Convention No. 182 (Worst Forms of Child Labour, 1999)	Not ratified
9. International Convention on Protection of Rights of All Migrant Workers and Members of their Families, 1990	Not ratified

It is clear that India still has to conform to several international standards relating to child labour, like ILO Convention No. 87 (Freedom of Association and Protection of Rights, 1948) and ILO Convention No. 98 (Right to Organise and Collective Bargaining Convention, 1949).

[217] PRS, 'Standing Committee Report Summary'.
[218] Source: Ministry of Labour and Employment. Available at http://labour.nic.in/content/ (accessed on 10 July 2015); NHRC. Available at nhrc.nic.in/ (accessed on 10 July 2015).

This implies that child labourers cannot form unions. India has not ratified ILO Convention No. 138 (Minimum Age Convention, 1973) also. Our child labour laws do not stipulate any minimum age of working. The child labourers cannot form associations. We still have to ratify ILO Convention No. 182 (Worst Forms of Child Labour, 1999) and the International Convention on Protection of Rights of All Migrant Workers and Members of their Families 1990. Our reservation about Article 32 of the CRC is still there.

Non-governmental Organization and Government Initiatives, Programmes, and Schemes in India

Non-governmental Organizations' Interventions

The non-governmental organizations (NGOs) have played an active and vital role in making child labour visible, raising levels of public concern, and protecting the working children. They have monitored the conditions in which the children work and helped launch the long, indispensable process of changing public attitudes, providing alternatives, and ensuring access to justice. A number of NGOs have taken up the issue of child labour and bonded labour and carried out programmes to throw light on this issue. The interventions are in the areas of counselling, awareness raising, social mobilization, encouraging community participation, releasing children from work, providing vocational training, enrolling children in schools and ensuring their retention, monitoring the functioning of schools, bringing children into the formal mainstream schooling system, preparing educational kits, and facilitating interaction between the various stakeholders like government officials, teachers, employers, and others. Some such interventions are presented as follows.

The Mammipuddi Venkatarangaiya Foundation[219]

The Mammipuddi Venkatarangaiya Foundation (MVF) is based in Hyderabad, in Andhra Pradesh in southern India. The foundation has developed an innovative and successful approach to dealing with the issue of child labour, which is based on a firm conviction that all children must be in school. It recognizes the inextricable link between universal education and the abolition of all forms of child labour. With community participation and action, the MVF seeks to remove all barriers to ensure that every child goes to school and stays in school. The MVF's activities focus on the twin task of abolition of child labour and strengthening of schools. The MVF believes that every child has a right to a childhood and an opportunity to develop to his/her full potential, and that every form of work done by a child interferes with this right. According to the Foundation, the essence of any programme to eliminate child labour is, first of all, to create a norm within communities that no child should work and that all children should be in formal schools. When child labourers are withdrawn from work, they are enrolled in 'bridge schools'. The purpose of these schools is to allow children to catch up on the education they have missed, and after this, they can enroll in the formal education system in the class that is most appropriate for their age.

[219] Available at www.mvfindia.in (accessed on 15 November 2016).

The Concerned for Working Children[220]

The Concerned for Working Children is a development agency based in Bengaluru, India. Active since the late 1970s, it works in partnership with children and their communities, local governments, and national and international agencies to implement viable, comprehensive, and appropriate solutions to address the various problems that children and their communities face, and is committed to empowering children and ensuring their democratic participation in all matters that affect them. Through their advocacy and research programmes, they have contributed extensively to policy debates around child labour and children's rights at the national and international level. The CWC's work is grounded in the principles of children's rights. The organization has facilitated formation of unions by children, worked to increase children's participation in governance, and conducted work helping children carry out research and information management. Bhima Sangha, a union of working children, was formed in 1990, and expanded with the formation of the International Movement of Working Children in 1996 and the National Movement of Working Children in 1999. More recently, CWC has become active in facilitating school children's organizations to bring some of the benefits of self-organization to school-going children.

Bachpan Bachao Andolan[221]

Bachpan Bachao Andolan (BBA) symbolizes India's largest grass roots movement for the protection of children, ensuring their quality education. As on October 2014, BBA has rescued more than 83,500 victims of trafficking, slavery, and child labour, and has helped them re-establish trust in society and find promising futures for themselves. Since its establishment by the Indian children's rights activist Kailash Satyarthi in 1980, BBA has led the world's largest civil society campaign in the form of the Global March against Child Labour, and has been at the forefront of laying down laws against child labour and trafficking in India.

Campaign against Child Labour[222]

Campaign against Child Labour (CACL), launched in 1992 as a network of a few organizations initially, has grown over the years. At present, the campaign consists of a network of over 6,000 anti-child labour groups spread over 19 states in India. It involves active women groups, trade unions, academic institutions, media agencies, child right and human right organizations, research bodies. Corporate houses, student volunteers, and eminent citizens also constitute an integral part of the campaign. The CACL is committed to the eradication of child labour through building public opinion, investigation of abuse/exploitation, advocacy, lobbying, and monitoring of national and international developments. The campaign believes in networking and alliance building with other like-minded groups. It intervenes in specific cases of violation of child rights and abuse of children and initiates relevant advocacy and lobbying to restore justice and rights of the child.

---

[220] Available at http://www.concernedforworkingchildren.org/about/ (accessed on 15 November 2016).
[221] Available at http://www.bba.org.in/?q=content/about-us (accessed on 15 November 2016).
[222] Available at www.caclindia.org (accessed on 15 November 2016).

Government of India Initiatives and Schemes

Child labour is a socio-economic problem whose solution needs sustained efforts over a long period of time. Considering the nature and magnitude of the problem, the Government of India is following a sequential approach of first covering children working in hazardous occupations/processes. The government has adopted a multi-pronged strategy for eradication of child labour, as elaborated next:[223]

- A legislative action plan in the form of the CLPRA.
- Project-based action plan in areas of high concentration of child labour under the NCLP Scheme.
- Focus on general development programmes for the benefit of the families of child labourers.

The Government of India has been implementing the CLPRA over the years. Based on the advice of the Technical Advisory Committee on Child Labour, two additional occupations, namely caring of elephants and working in the circus, has been added to schedule of banned occupations during 2011. At present there are 18 occupations and 65 processes prohibited under the CLPRA.[224] The enforcement of the act is poor. There is a need for joint inspections with the civil society for stricter enforcement.

The Government of India has implemented NCLP for rehabilitation of children withdrawn from work. Under the Project, children withdrawn from work are enrolled in special schools where they are provided with bridge education, vocational training, nutrition, stipend, healthcare, and so on before being mainstreamed into the formal education system.[225]

Besides this, the government has made the right to education a Fundamental Right for children under the Constitution. Every child in the age group of 6–14 years is to be provided free and compulsory education The Right of Children to Free and Compulsory Education Act (Right to Education Act, or RTE Act) came into force on 1 April 2010 to facilitate implementation of this right. The Government is contemplating certain amendments in the CLPRA which are in line with Right to Free and Compulsory Education Act, 2009. [226]

The Cabinet has approved the proposal of Ministry of Labour and Employment for amending the CLPRA in an attempt to bring it in line with the ratification of ILO Convention No. 138. The Child Labour (Prohibition and Regulation) Amendment Bill, 2012 has been introduced in the Parliament to prohibit employment of children below the age of 14 years in all occupations

[223] M. Anjan Kumar Yadav, 'Campaign Against Indian Products', Ministry of Labour and Employment, Government of India. Available at http://164.100.47.132/LssNew/psearch/QResult15.aspx?qref=105001 (accessed on 9 November 2015).

[224] Ministry of Labour and Employment, Government of India, Thirty Sixth Session of the Tripartite Committee on Conventions, New Delhi, 2012. Available at http://labour.gov.in/upload/uploadfiles/files/latest_update/what_new/5056a62160211Agendaof36thCOCNIC.pdf (accessed on 9 November 2015).

[225] Press Information Bureau, Ministry of Labour and Employment, Government of India, 'Steps to Implement The Child Labour Protection Act'. Available at http://pib.nic.in/newsite/PrintRelease.aspx?relid=86710 (accessed on 9 November 2015).

[226] Ministry of Labour and Employment, 'Thirty Sixth Session of the Tripartite Committee On Conventions'.

and processes. The Bill also proposes to prohibit the employment of adolescents between the age of 14 and 18 years in hazardous occupations and processes specified in the schedule to the proposed amendment Bill. These amendments, when approved, would enable India to ratify ILO Conventions 138 and 182.[227]

Besides, the government emphasizes convergence of services and support from different departments to the families of these children so that the circumstances compelling these children to work are mitigated.

National Child Labour Project Scheme

The largest and most structured intervention in the area of child labour in India is the NCLP. The basic objective of the National Child Labour Project (NCLP) is 'suitably rehabilitating the children withdrawn from employment thereby, reducing the incidence of child labour in areas of known concentration'. The NCLP Scheme targets children below 14 years of age working in specific areas of hazardous work which are mentioned in the Schedule to the CLPRA. Under the Scheme, a survey of child labour engaged in hazardous occupations/processes is conducted, following which the children are withdrawn from work and admitted to special schools in order to enable them to be mainstreamed into the formal schooling system. These schools are often referred to as 'bridge centres', underscoring their inherent temporary function and their their ultimate objective—mainstreaming children into schools.[228]

The programme, centrally managed by the Ministry of Labour and Emplpyment, was launched in nine districts in 1987 and has been expanded in January 2005 to 250 districts in 21 different states of the country. So far, 400,200 working children have been covered under the scheme and about 308,000 children have been mainstreamed into formal education system.[229]

Children in NCLP bridge schools are taught according to a condensed syllabus for a maximum period of 3 years, during which time the children are expected to complete the level of Class 5 and be ready to join the formal stream of education in Class 6. Children who are able to complete their course in less than 3 years are encouraged to enter the formal school earlier.[230] It is not only access to education, but rather ensuring their retention in schools, that can make the long-lasting difference in improving the lives of working children and preventing them from returning to the workforce. The economic challenges faced by many families in keeping children released from work in school, as well as the lack of perception of education as a valuable investment for their future, can easily lead former child labourers to drop out from rehabilitation programmes shortly after enrolment.[231]

---

[227] Ministry of Labour and Employment, Government of India. Available at http://labour.gov.in/upload/uploadfiles/files/Divisions/childlabour/Website%20-%20Copy%20(1)%20gyanesh.pdf (accessed on 9 November 2015).

[228] UNICEF India, 'Developing a Tracking System to Follow up Children in the National Child Labour Projects Scheme (NCLP)'. Available at http://unicef.in/Story/760/Developing-a-tracking-system-to-follow-up-children-in-the-National-Child-Labour-Projects-Scheme-NCLP-#sthash.kz67vEeb.dpuf (accessed on 9 November 2015).

[229] UNICEF India, 'Developing a Tracking System'.

[230] UNICEF India, 'Developing a Tracking System'.

[231] UNICEF India, 'Developing a Tracking System'.

Regular monitoring of children, both in bridge schools and after mainstreaming, becomes, therefore, crucial. Moreover, collecting information on the child after withdrawal from work is essential not only to follow up on his or her educational progress, but also to better understand the multiple vulnerabilities surrounding the phenomenon of child labour and to adjust the existing rehabilitation mechanisms accordingly to ensure the programme's efficiency and maximum benefit for the child. To address this issue, UNICEF is supporting the Central Ministry of Labour and Employment, Government of India, in the development of a child tracking system to monitor the progress of children involved in NCLP.[232]

The attempt of NCLP must aim to mainstream these children in regular formal schools rather than in non-formal education. The various poverty alleviation programmes must reach the families of these children simultaneously. Strengthening of families of child labourers and rehabilitating them must go hand in hand. All child labourers must be rehabilitated and sent to schools rather than remain in selected occupations, processes, and target areas.

INDO-USDOL Child Labour Project[233]

The INDUS Child Labour Project was a Technical Cooperation Project of the Ministry of Labour and Employment and Directorate of Education of the Government of India, and the United States Department of Labour (USDOL), between 1 January 2003 and 31 March 2009, within the framework of a Joint Statement of Enhanced Indo-US Co-operation on Elimination of Child Labour.[234]

The Project aimed to contribute to the prevention and elimination of hazardous child labour by enhancing the human, social, and physical capacity of target communities and improving compliance with child labour policy and legislation in the target districts. The project's uniqueness was based on a partnership agreement between the US and India, based on equal financial contribution from the two partners. The Project was implemented in 10 hazardous sectors in 21 districts across five states—Maharashtra, Madhya Pradesh, Tamil Nadu, Uttar Pradesh, and Delhi.[235]

The major components of the project were:

- identifying children working in hazardous occupations by means of a detailed survey;
- withdrawing children in the age group 8–14 from hazardous occupations and providing them meaningful transitional education and social support to prevent relapse;
- making provision for systematic vocational education/training of adolescents withdrawn from hazardous work;

[232] UNICEF India, 'Developing a Tracking System'.

[233] ILO, 'INDO-USDOL Child Labour Project for Preventing and Eliminating Child Labour in Identified Hazardous Sector'. Available at http://www.ilo.org/newdelhi/whatwedo/projects/WCMS_124679/lang--en/index.htm (Last accessed on 9 November 2015).

[234] ILO, INDO-USDOL Child Labour Project.

[235] Ministry of Labour and Employment, Government of India. Available at http://labour.nic.in/content/division/indus.php (accessed on 9 November 2015).

- increased economic security of families who withdraw their children from hazardous work by encouraging savings and development of alternative livelihoods;
- access to quality education provided for children to prevent their entering or re-entering hazardous work;
- monitoring and tracking of children released from hazardous work to ensure that their situation has improved;
- public support and momentum created against child labour in the target districts and in favour of educational opportunities;
- strengthening capacity of national, state, district, and local institutions so they can function as ongoing support for eliminating hazardous child labour; and
- raising interest towards action against hazardous child labour in other states.[236]

Law Reform

The CLPRA was enacted to deal with the problem of child labour and protect the children from economic exploitation. However, as with the earlier acts, the 1986 Act also operated within a regulatory framework with the wrong belief that child labour could not be abolished as long as poverty existed. As a consequence, the law has revealed several legal and procedural loopholes.[237] The law is limited in scope. It does not cover all hazardous occupations and processes where children are working. It excludes children working in family-based enterprises. The law is based on the poverty argument and on the premise that the decision on whether children should work, especially within the family or household, is that of the parents. Another premise is that so long as the child is not forced to work in an exploitative environment, the State should not take any legal action. Thirdly, it presupposes an employer–employee relationship where child labour is engaged, and assumes that exploitation of children is not possible within the family premises, even though the processes or occupations are, otherwise, hazardous.[238] These beliefs and premises on which the Child Labour Act is based are incorrect. It is clear that once the child is employed in enterprises and industries outside the home, or at home, for wages or to help in domestic chores or family occupations, it does result in the forfeiture of opportunities for education and development for the child.[239] The CLPRA is silent on the Right to Education of the child, thus violating the Constitutional mandate given in Article 21A. It violates the CRC provisions on right to education, health, nutrition, and development. Any hazardous occupation or process remains hazardous whether done by a child within the family or outside. There is no rights-based approach in the act. The law does not recognize the child as an independent rights holder who should be the focus of the act. Instead, the focus of the act is on the establishment, employer,

---

[236] ILO, 'INDO-USDOL Child Labour Project'.

[237] Alok Kumar, Asha Pathak, Sandeep Kumar, Pooja Rastogi, and Prateek Rastogi, 'The Problem of Child Sexual Abuse in India: Laws, Legal Lacuna and the Bill', *Journal of Indian Academy of Forensic Medicine*, 34, no. 2 (April–June 2012). Available at http://medind.nic.in/jal/t12/i2/jalt12i2p170.pdf (accessed on 9 November 2015).

[238] Kumar et al., 'The Problem of Child Sexual Abuse'.

[239] Ashok Agarwal, 'Compulsory Schooling and Child Labour'. Available at http://www.karmayog.org/childlabour/childlabour_18517.htm (accessed on 9 November 2015).

administration, and procedures, with no provisions for the child's rehabilitation. It does not say what should happen to the child labourer after rescue or once the employer is prosecuted. The act is silent on the rehabilitation and reintegration of the child. It was only after the landmark judgment of the Supreme Court in the *M.C. Mehta* v. *Tamil Nadu*[240] case that the government set up a Child Labour Rehabilitation and Welfare Fund.

The CLPRA prohibits the employment of children in certain hazardous industries and processes, but it does not define what constitutes hazardous work. It only provides a list of hazardous occupations/processes. As a result, it leaves a loophole for employment of children in unidentified hazardous occupations and processes, and the use of hazardous materials.[241] The CLPRA does not cover agriculture and allied activities which account for the highest incidence of child labour. Agricultural work is hazardous to the health of the child due to the pesticides prevalent in the farms and fields. In fact, any work that interferes with a child's right to education, health, and development must be considered hazardous.

The RTE Act is for children between 6 and 14 years only. The implementation of the act is poor and the problem is further compounded by absence of schools/infrastructure and the falling budgetary allocation for education. Even where schools are present, the poor quality of education provided in these institutions is a major concern. Corporal punishment is another major barrier. The laws effectively cover only a small proportion of children, and leave little or no scope for the participation of people in the enforcement and monitoring of these laws and programmes. The laws have failed to take advantage of the 73rd and 74th Constitutional Amendments which provide significant opportunities for local community involvement in the elimination of child labour and the universalization of primary education.[242]

The National Policy on Education talks of universal elementary education, but education has not become compulsory up to 14 years of age in terms of law. Pre-primary education is not legislated upon. Non-formal education, rehabilitation, and general development programmes are talked about in the NPCL but are not made a part of law. Laws on education ignore street children and disabled children.[243]

Linkages between education and the prevalence of child labour demand a convergence of laws on education and child labour. Today, there are a number of fragmented laws on these issues. While laws on child labour speak about penalizing employers who employ child labour, they do not speak of education.

Poverty can no longer be an excuse for continuance of child labour. Financial conditions of families of child labourers need to be strengthened. Poverty alleviation programmes of the government must reach the families. In the *M.C. Mehta* judgment, the court had observed:

1. providing an alternative source of income to the family is a pre-requisite for the eradication of child labour;

---

[240] AIR 1997 SC 699.

[241] *The Report of The Second Indian National Labour Commission–2002.* Available at http://www.prsindia.org/uploads/media/1237548159/NLCII-report.pdf (accessed on 30 June 2015).

[242] *Report of the Second Indian National Labour Commission.*

[243] *Report of The Second Indian National Labour Commission.*

2. employers of children must pay a compensation of Rs. 20,000 as per the provisions of the CLPRA, for every child employed;
3. the fine should be deposited in a Child Labour Rehabilitation-cum-Welfare Fund;
4. employment should be provided to an adult in the family in lieu of the child working in a factory or mine or any other hazardous place of work; that in the absence of alternative employment, the parent/guardian will be paid the income earned on the Corpus Fund, the suggested amount being fixed at Rs 25,000 for each child;
5. payment will cease if the child is not sent for education. In cases of non-hazardous employment, the employer will bear the cost of education; and
6. State's contribution/grant, fixed at Rs 5,000 for each child employed in a factory or mine or any other hazardous employment, should be deposited in the corpus fund and the district will be the unit for collection.

Providing alternate source of income to the family and sending the child to school can be considered as a legislative strategy to combat the problem of child labour.

The implementation of the act depends entirely on the state's bureaucratic machinery. It assumes that the bureaucracy, poorly staffed and ill-equipped as it is today, will be able to ensure that children do not work in hazardous processes and occupations, and that conditions of work in non-hazardous settings will be upgraded.[244] The bureaucracy is also expected to determine whether a child is working in a non-hazardous process or a hazardous occupation and also gather evidence against the employer. In many cases it is not possible to gather witnesses against the employer. Many times the children are shown to be family members of the employer. Many a times the labour inspectors do not get cooperation from the community also. Thus, it is necessary that the community be involved in inspections. Under the CLPRA, the employer is supposed to notify the Labour Department whether any children are working in his establishment. This means that one expects those who may be guilty or proven guilty and prosecuted, to volunteer to notify their improprieties or illegal acts to the authorities—which is highly unlikely. Moreover, the onus of proving the age of the child lies with the prosecutor, and not the offender.[245] The determination of the age of the child is a difficult issue as many children do not have birth certificates or school leaving certificates.

The main thrust of the NCLP is to reduce the incidence of child labour in project areas, thereby encouraging the elimination of child labour progressively. Under these projects, attempts are to be made to integrate elements of various development programmes to benefit working children.[246] This Project is for select children in select sectors, and for non-formal education. Every child must have a right to formal education up to 18 years of age.[247] A major recommendation given

---

[244] *Report of the Second Indian National Labour Commission.*

[245] *Report of the Second Indian National Labour Commission.*

[246] Activities in project areas include: (a) stepping up the enforcement of child labour laws; (b) raising public awareness to educate people about the undesirable aspects of child labour; (c) setting up special schools/centres for working children with provision for education, vocational training, supplementary nutrition, healthcare, and so on; (d) strengthening the formal education structure; (e) including families of working children as beneficiaries in poverty alleviation and income-generating programmes.

[247] Satpathy, Sekar, and Karan, *Rehabilitation of Child Labour in India.*

by the study on evaluation of the NCLP Scheme for the overall success of the Project includes convergence of services from different government departments as well as NGOs, improving the quality of education, and reviewing the curriculum.[248]

The Study Group on Women and Children of the Second National Commission on Labour appointed by the Ministry of Labour and Employment, Government of India, recommended convergence of laws and schemes on child labour and education. It recommended a draft for discussion. The draft Bill was known as The Child Labour (Prohibition and Education) Bill, 2001. The Bill intended to ensure that no child would be deprived of a future by being deprived of an education and having to spend his childhood working. It recognized every child out of school as child labour or potential child labour. It sought to tackle the problem of child labour by ensuring universal education. It also sought to ensure that children do not work in situations where they are exploited and deprived of a future. The Commission felt that the child labour legislation should not only be regulatory but also developmental.[249]

For the Twelfth Five Year Plan (2012–17), the Planning Commission of the Government of India constituted a Working Group on the subject of Labour Laws and Other Labour Regulations. According to the Report submitted by the group on the CLPRA, it was recommended to make employment of a child below the age of 14 years illegal in the employment code to support the implementation of the RTE Act. Alternately, more number of activities was recommended to be included under the CLPRA schedule of jobs prohibited for children. Prohibition of child labour from 'meat shop'/abattoir was strongly recommended. [250]

Although estimates differ on the number of child workers in India, the number is reportedly the largest in the world. There is a need for policy and law reform. The dual policy of prohibition and regulation has failed to reduce child labour. All OOSC are child labourers. There must be no distinction between hazardous (worst) and non-hazardous forms of labour. This has to be based on the premise that all children must be in school in compliance with the RTE Act and any labour that denies children this right is hazardous and a violation. There must be linkages between the CLPRA and the RTE Act. Both cannot work in mutual isolation. The NCPCR also called for a consonance between the CLPRA and the RTE Act, which guarantees education as a fundamental right to all children in the 6–14 years age group.[251]

Moreover, the CLPRA itself was not fully implemented. The Department of Labour, with its limited mandate, does not have the capacity to implement it effectively. The goal must not be just to rescue children from situations of labour but to ensure their education, training, and rehabilitation; this issue needs to be taken away from the Department of Labour and put as a responsibility of the Ministry of Women and Child Development, so that the protective and rehabilitative services of the JJ Act are automatically made available to rescued children who

---

[248] Satpathy, Sekar, and Karan, *Rehabilitation of Child Labour in India*.

[249] *Report of the Second Indian National Labour Commission*.

[250] Ministry of Labour and Employment, Government of India, *Report of the Working Group on 'Labour Laws & Other Regulations' for the Twelfth Five Year Plan (2012–17)*. Available at http://planningcommission.gov.in/aboutus/committee/wrkgrp12/wg_labour_laws.pdf (accessed on 9 November 2015).

[251] Shanta Sinha, 'Monitoring Children's Rights: National Commission for Protection of Child Rights'. Available at http://www.ohchr.org/Documents/Issues/ViolenceAgstChildren/Shanta_Shinha_NCPCR_India.pdf (accessed on 14 November 2016).

need it. With the notification of some industries as hazardous for children, work in hazardous industries has shifted from visible workplaces to less visible home settings. The definition of 'child labour' must encompass children working for the families in their own homes, children in agriculture work, work rendered by girl children and all other forms of work that deprives them of their right to education in a full-time formal school. The definition of 'child labour' must be inclusive, recognize all forms of child labour as prohibitive, and include children up to 18 years of age. The JJ Act lists children in labour as children in need of care and protection, and also makes exploitation of children a cognizable offence—something which the CLPRA does not, and must do.

The CLPRA needs to be amended and also aligned to the RTE Act and other laws. It must have a child rights-based approach. Some of the recommendations are as follows.

- The current CLPRA does not specify the minimum age of employment of children in occupations and processes other than the prohibited ones. Most laws and legal provisions relating to child labour specify the minimum age for employment to be 14 years. Nevertheless, the United Nations CRC, in Article 1, sets the standard concerning the definition of a child—a child means every human being below the age of 18, unless, under the law applicable to the child, majority is attained earlier. This standard age of the child should be adhered to in all legislations including the CLPRA. Determining the age of the child is a big problem. In a country like India, many children do not have birth certificates. This procedure needs to be simplified. Besides, it is recommended that till such time as age is determined, the benefit of doubt should be in favour of the child.

- There is no provision for the education of working children. In many countries, occupations and processes are not prohibited. In fact, the CLPRA stands in direct contradiction to the fundamental right to free and compulsory education, as mandated by the Constitution in the RTE Act.[252]

- There is no specific provision in the 1986 Act for applying the provisions of other laws like the Industrial Disputes Act, the Shops and Commercial Establishments Act, the Minimum Wages Act, and other laws. A child who has a dispute relating to his wages, salaries, and other employment benefits in the permissible areas of work has to approach the adult dispute resolution mechanism. However, the child labourers in the prohibited areas of work cannot even approach the adult dispute settlement machinery as their employment is 'illegal' under the act.[253] There should be a provision in the act for a dispute resolution mechanism for the protection of wages or other employment benefits. Special courts could be set up for a speedier and more effective trial of violations under this act.

- Elimination of child labour should be statutory on the part of all local self-government bodies, both rural and urban. There should immediately be a provision for elimination of child labour, whether directly or indirectly, in all government organizations.

- It is necessary to establish an in-depth monitoring agency at the state and national level to oversee enforcement of the BLSAA. For full implementation of the act, this body should be

[252] Thukral and Thukral, 'India Child Rights Index'.

[253] Ossie Fernandes, 'Towards Amendments/Restructuring of the Child Labour (Prohibition and Regulation) Act 1986'.

statutorily empowered to receive and address complaints of act violations and complaints of official misconduct. In the BLSAA, there should be more provisions for rehabilitation of children and their needs should be specifically addressed.

- The rules relating to the CLPRA in various states need to be immediately amended for better implementation of the CLPRA.
- The present definition of establishment has considerable scope for extension and enlargement.[254]
- The CLPRA should be amended to prohibit the employment of children up to the age of 18 in all sectors, including employment carried on with the aid of the family. Because of the dispersed nature of work, all sorts of child labour are passed off as family labour. This provision is widely abused by employers
- The Supreme Court judgment in *M.C. Mehta* v. *the State of Tamil Nadu*[255] should be strictly enforced and citizens' groups be actively involved.
- The distinction between hazardous and non-hazardous occupations in the 1986 Act and in the Government policy should be done away with, as all employment of children per se is hazardous to their health and education. The dual policy of regulation and prohibition should be abandoned.
- An adequate and effective social security system should be put in place as a measured step towards preventing children from being driven into child labour. Poverty alleviation pro-grammes of the Government of India must be extended to the families of children who have to work.
- There should be community involvement in the measures for the development of the child and the elimination of child labour at the level of the panchayats.[256]
- Economic exploitation of children must be a cognizable offence under the CLPRA.
- The CLPRA is not in conformity with the ILO Conventions 138 and 182, which provide for minimum age of entry into employment and prohibition of employment of persons below 18 years, in work which is likely to harm health, safety, and morals of children.[257]
- District magistrates—called district collectors or deputy commissioners in some states—are responsible for the enforcement of the BLSAA. The district magistrate is to constitute and participate in the functioning of a district-level 'vigilance committee'. Very few such vigilance committees have been formed or are operative.
- References to rehabilitation of freed bonded labourers occur twice in the BLSAA—once in reference to the district magistrate's duty to 'secure and protect the economic interests' of the bonded labourer (Section 11) and once in stipulating the vigilance committees' duty to provide for their 'economic and social rehabilitation' (Section 14). The act itself does not specify what this rehabilitation should consist of and has left the implementation to the state governments.

[254] CLPRA, Section 2(iv) defines establishment as a shop, commercial establishment, workshop, farm, residential hotel, restaurant, eating house, theatre, or other place of public amusement or entertainment.

[255] AIR 1997 SC 699.

[256] Village councils.

[257] Available at http://www.firstpost.com/printpage.php?idno=2242120&sr_no=0 (accessed on 14 November 2016).

- The extent to which the bonded labourers have been identified, released, and rehabilitated by the government officials is negligible.[258]
- The Children (Pledging of Labour) Act, 1933 is outdated and needs to be amended. The penalty provided under the act for a serious action like making an agreement to pledge the labour of a child is as meager as Rs 200 (Section 6).
- India must ratify ILO Minimum Age Convention 138 and the worst form of child labour convention.

The Child Labour (Prohibition and Regulation) Amendment Bill, 2012 was introduced in the Rajya Sabha on 4 December 2012. The Bill seeks to amend the CLPRA, which prohibits the engagement of children in certain types of occupations and regulates the condition of work of children in other occupations. The act prohibits employment of children below 14 years in certain occupations such as automobile workshops, beedi-making, carpet weaving, handloom and power loom industry, mines, and domestic work. In light of the RTE Act, the Bill seeks to prohibit employment of children below 14 years in all occupations except where the child helps his/her family after school hours. The Bill adds a new category of persons called 'adolescent', which means a person between 14 and 18 years of age. The Bill prohibits employment of adolescents in hazardous occupations as specified (mines, inflammable substance, and hazardous processes). The central government may add or omit any hazardous occupation from the list included in the Bill. The Bill enhances the punishment for employing any child in an occupation. It also includes penalty for employing an adolescent in a hazardous occupation. The penalty for employing a child was increased to imprisonment between 6 months and 2 years (from 3 months to 1 year), or a fine of Rs 20,000 to Rs 50,000 (from Rs 10,000–20,000), or both. The penalty for employing an adolescent in hazardous occupation is imprisonment between 6 months and 2 years, or a fine of Rs 20,000 to Rs 50,000, or both. The government may confer powers on a District Magistrate to ensure that the provisions of the law are properly carried out. The Bill empowers the government to make periodic inspection of places at which employment of children and adolescents are prohibited.[259]

On 13 May 2015, the Union Cabinet approved a complete ban on employment of children below 14 years, except for some family businesses, entertainment, and sports activities, while raising the punishment for violations to up to 3 years of jail.[260] Other provisions approved in the Bill include:

- Making child labour a cognizable offence, the fine has also been increased to up to Rs 50,000 for the employers.

[258] Human Rights Watch, Children's Rights Projects, *The Small Hands of Slavery, Bonded Child Labour in India* (USA: Human Rights Watch, 1996).

[259] PRS, 'Bill Summary: The Child Labour (Prohibition and Regulation) Amendment Bill, 2012'. Available at http://www.prsindia.org/uploads/media/Child%20Labour/Bill%20Summary%20-%20Child%20Labour%20_Prohibition_%20amendment%20Bill,%202012.pdf (accessed on 15 November 2016).

[260] Press Trust of India, 'Cabinet Approves Changes to Child Labour Laws', *Economic Times*, 13 May 2015. Available at http://articles.economictimes.indiatimes.com/2015-05-13/news/62124383_1_child-labour-employment-union-cabinet (accessed on 15 November 2016).

- The amendments to the Child Labour (Prohibition & Regulation) Bill has, however, relaxed the penal provisions for parents or guardians, who were earlier subjected to same punishments as applicable to the employer of the child. It provides that there would be no punishment for parents or guardians in case of first offence, while a maximum penalty of Rs 10,000 can be levied in case of the second and subsequent offences.
- Imprisonment for violations have been enhanced. This has been enhanced to imprisonment of 6 months to 2 years and fine of Rs 20,000–50,000 for the first offence. For the second offence, the jail provision has been increased from 6-24 months to 12-36 months.
- The new bill provides that employment of children below 14 years will be prohibited in all occupations and processes. Besides, the age of prohibition of employment will be linked to age under Right of Children to Free and Compulsory Education Act, 2009.
- The Bill also provides for the setting up of a Child and Adolescent Labour Rehabilitation Fund for one or more districts for rehabilitation of children or adolescents rescued. Thus, the law itself will provide for a fund to carry out rehabilitation activities.
- The age of prohibition of employment has been linked to age under Right of Children to Free and Compulsory Education Act, 2009.
- Children between 14 and 18 years will not be allowed to work in hazardous industries. Exceptions have, however, been made in case of works in which the child helps the family or family enterprises. Besides a new definition of adolescent has been introduced in the Child Labour (Prohibition and Regulation) Bill and employment of adolescents (14 to 18 years of age) has been prohibited in hazardous occupations and processes. The condition is that such enterprises should not involved any hazardous occupation. Another condition set forth is that they should work after school hours or during vacations. Moreover, exemption has also been given where the child works as an artist in an audio-visual entertainment industry, including advertisement, films, television serials or any such other entertainment or sports activities except the circus. This exemption is also conditional and stipulates taking up prescribed safety measures.

The new amendments are criticized on the ground that permitting child labour in families will again provide a loophole to the employers. Second, the age of the child has been maintained as 14 years. The problem lies in the inclusion of this proviso in the law, especially since it is a known fact that the notion of family is very wide and ambiguous in India. This is exactly the kind of legal loophole that has led to the continuation of child labour till now. Past experience of implementation of the law, that had a similar proviso (Section 3 of the CLPRA, 1986),[261] has shown that this was the one way in which children were tied to home-based work and exploited.

---

[261] CLPRA, Section 3, Prohibition of employment of children in certain occupations and processes:

No child shall be employed or permitted to work in any of the occupations set forth in Part A of the Schedule or in any workshop wherein any of the processes set forth in Part B of the Schedule is carried on, provided that nothing in this section shall apply to any workshop wherein any process is carried on by the occupier with the aid of his family or to any school established by, or receiving assistance or recognition from government.

On the other hand, on the exceptions made in the new laws proposed, the Government states:

> While considering a total prohibition on the employment of child, it would be prudent to also keep in mind the country's social fabric and socio-economic conditions. In a large number of families, children help their parents in their occupations like agriculture, artisanship etc and while helping the parents, children also learn the basics of occupations. Therefore, striking a balance between the need for education for a child and the reality of the socio-economic condition and social fabric in the country, the Cabinet has approved that a child can help his family or family enterprise, which is other than any hazardous occupation or process, after his school hours or during vacation.

The aforementioned amendment bill was passed by both Houses of Parliament.[262] The Child Labour (Prohibition and Regulation) Amendment Act, 2016 was notified in the official Gazette of India on 30 July 2016.[263]

Critique of the Child Labour (Prohibition and Regulation) Amendment Act, 2016.

The amended 2016 Act prohibits children under the age of 14 from working but the problem is the exception for 'family businesses'. Children below 14 will be allowed to work in family businesses, outside school hours and during holidays. Children between 15 and 18 years now defined as adolescents will be permitted to work except in mines and industries. It has also drastically reduced the number of hazardous jobs from 83 to 3, which 15–18 year olds are banned from doing. The act seems to have brought in a new concept of part-time student, part time child labour along with part-time teachers.[264] The government says the law will help poor families earn a living and give children a chance to acquire skills. Now, some children will go to school, come back, study, play, learn, relax and otherwise enjoy life. But 'some other poor children' must wake up early in the morning, work before going to school, then run to school and come back and work again at home and sleep late in the night? They will have no leisure, no time to play, or to study leading to serious short- and long-term physical, psychological, and social consequences. These tired, sleepy, unhealthy children may soon drop out from school. Is this joyful learning, quality education, a happy childhood? Will it not perpetuate a labour force of children and adolescents that will be cheap and vulnerable working in cottage industry, small-scale industry, manufacturing units operating out of residential areas claiming to be family enterprises, unorganized sector, which can now flourish unregulated as family enterprise and work in hazardous units.[265]

---

[262] Rajya Sabha Passes Child Labour Bill That Allows Work In Family Business. Available at http://www.ndtv.com/india-news/rajya-sabha-passes-child-labour-bill-that-allows-work-in-family-businesses-1434074 (accessed on 5 October 2016).

[263] Ministry of Law and Justice, Government of India. Available at http://uphome.gov.in/writereadd-ata/Portal/Images/The-Child-Labour(Prohibition_and_Regulation)Amendment-Act,2015.pdf (accessed on 5 October 2016).

[264] Asha Bajpai, 'Proposed Amendments to Child Labour Act Need Review', *The Hindu*, Mumbai, 11 August 2016. Available at http://www.thehindu.com/news/cities/mumbai/proposed-amendments-to-child-labour-act-need-review/article8972381.ece (accessed on 5 October 2016).

[265] Bajpai, 'Proposed Amendments'.

Census 2011 shows 33.9 million children are out of school and hence vulnerable to labour. Around 1.01 crore children in the 5–14 age group earn for their families.[266] They will not be protected under the new law. Why this discrimination among children? Is it only because he or she is poor? Many poor families themselves send their children to work. Poverty has made parents to sell children, send them for begging, and force them to child labour. The very premise that children can work in families is deeply flawed. Making children work is not the solution. There is a need to strengthen their families through dedicated poverty alleviation programs.

How will the government enforce this new law? Which will be the implementing and monitoring agency? Under the current 1985 Child Labour Act, when labour inspectors used to visit factories children working there all became the 'relatives' of the factory owner. There were practically no prosecutions of any violation of existing laws pertaining to child labour. The owners in many cases could not be prosecuted because there were no witnesses. Corruption among government officials charged with enforcement of labour laws is notorious and widespread. Labour inspectors, medical officers, local *tehsildars*, police, and magistrates are known to be susceptible to bribery.

Education is the most important component in reducing child labour. There must have been linkages between child labour law and education laws. They cannot work in isolation. There is a need for Constitutional amendment of Article 24 that mandates that no child below the age of 14 years shall be employed to work in any factory or mine or engaged in any other hazardous employment. That implies that children below 14 can work in non-hazardous industries. Article 24 is in contrast to Article 21A which provides free and compulsory education for all children between 6 and 14 years. Article 24 must be amended to prohibit all children from working in any industry including family enterprises. The ILO Convention 182 on the worst forms of child labour and Convention 138 on the minimum age to work—have still not been ratified by India. We need to establish an independent implementing and monitoring agency to oversee the enforcement of the Child Labour law. This is a block in the development agenda. Child labour is not a labour law issue but an issue of child rights and child protection. Education, play, sport, leisure, and rest are not luxuries reserved for only a few.[267]

***

In 1986 and 1987, the Government of India adopted a new set of policies towards working children. The policy of the government is to ban the employment of children below the age of 14 years in factories, mines, and other hazardous employment in accordance with the provisions of the Constitution and to regulate the working condition of children in non-hazardous occupations and processes. The government would also endeavour to provide voluntary part-time, non-formal education for working children, rather than press for compulsory universal primary education.[268] Besides, the present CLPRA does not deal with the causes in political economy which give rise to child labour, nor does it provide for any mandatory time frame for the gradual prohibition of child labour. This policy has to change now. No longer can the dual policy of prohibition and regulation along with non-formal, part-time education continue. A firm and a

---

266 Bajpai, 'Proposed Amendments'.

267 Bajpai, 'Proposed Amendments'.

268 Myron Weiner, *The Child and the State in India* (New Delhi: Oxford University Press, 1991).

clear policy stand has to be taken, that the place of children is at school and not in the workplace. Basic, full-time, formal primary education for all children is a keystone of these rights, and in some ways a condition for the exercise of other rights.

Several socio-economic and political factors are responsible for the existence and perpetuation of child labour. Although poverty and inequality are the main factors influencing the number of child workers, they are not the only causes. Child labour is not purely an economic question and we have to opt for a model that will continuously generate employment, but 'poverty can no longer be an excuse for child labour'. Poverty has not prevented governments of other developing countries from expanding mass education or making primary education compulsory. In many countries, the diffusion of mass literacy preceded the industrial revolution and governments often introduced compulsory education when levels of poverty were high. Poverty has to be addressed as one of the causes, not the sole cause.

The governments of all developed countries and many developing countries have removed children from the labour force and ensured that they attend school. They believe that employers should not be permitted to employ child labour, and parents, no matter how poor, should not be allowed to keep their children out of school. Modern states regard education as a legal duty, not merely a right—parents are required to send their children to school, children are required to attend school, and the state is obligated to enforce compulsory education. Compulsory primary education is the policy instrument by which the state effectively removes children from the labour force. The State thus stands as the ultimate guardian of children, protecting them against both parents and would-be employers.[269] Therefore, poverty cannot prevent India from providing education to all children. The 93rd constitutional amendment, despite its inadequacies,[270] can be a good beginning. This amendment has inserted Article 21A,[271] which provides for free and compulsory education to all children of the age of 6–14 years in such manner as the State may by law determine. This can be interpreted to mean that any work, whether hazardous or non-hazardous, that blocks children's access to education violates Article 21A. Every state has to enact a comprehensive legislation to implement the provisions of the Constitution and to provide adequate budget.

In our country, law has a crucial role to play in social transformation. It is evident that legislation is one of the main weapons, and the process is still incomplete. Child labour is a complex issue. It needs a multi-sectoral, integrated approach. It is not only the concern of any particular ministry; the Ministry of Labour and Employment, or the Department of Women and Child Development or family welfare, or the Ministries of Human Resource, Finance, Health, Social Justice and Empowerment, and Agriculture all have to work together. A legal strategy could be a combination of several legislations. The related acts and the rules made thereunder need to be reviewed and amended to conform and be linked to the child labour legislation.

The main focus should now be on enforcement and implementation. Compulsory education laws normally precede child labour laws and their enforcement. It has been experienced that enforcing compulsory education laws, though by no means simple, is easier than enforcing child

---

[269] Weiner, *Child and the State*.

[270] See Chapter 7, the section on education.

[271] The Constitution of India, Article 21A: The state shall provide free and compulsory education to all children of the age of 6 to 14 years in such manner as the state, by law may determine.

labour laws and factory laws. The enforcement of compulsory education laws was facilitated by the system of compulsory birth registration. Of course, the societal coalitions have proved to be crucial in introducing and extending compulsory education laws and banning the employment of children. Church groups, religious leaders, trade unionists, schoolteachers and educational officials, philanthropists, and social reformers have played significant roles.[272]

Modern States regard education as a legal duty and not merely a right.[273] The notion of the duty denies parents the right to choose. Parents are told by the State that no matter how great their need is for child labour or income, they must relinquish their child to school for a part of the day. The notion of duty also applies to the State. Education needs more of our funds, it also needs our creative thinking about how to develop schools relevant to the needs of actual and potential child workers. Schools must be able to draw and retain children. Schools must teach useful skills that are seen as relevant by both children and parents.

It is also clear that any programme of eliminating child labour has to provide reasonable alternatives for the child workers it ousts out of the workplace they had entered due to extreme poverty. The CRC explicitly specifies in Article 28 that parties must promote and encourage international cooperation in support of developing countries' efforts to ensure access to education for all children.

The best guarantee that the government will take its responsibilities seriously is when all sectors of society become involved in the genuine national movement against child labour. As the implications of child rights and the principle of the CRC start to permeate society, attitudes, assumptions, and values will correspondingly change. And with greater community awareness comes greater involvement, leading to a powerful, if informal, labour inspectorate—of families and neighbours, strangers and friends. Such a development represents the best chance of protecting all children, but especially those farthest from official scrutiny, who are working in the informal sector and in rural areas.

The UNICEF State of the World's Children Report of 2011[274] catalogues the array of dangers faced by adolescents aged 10 to 19 years, including early pregnancy and childbirth, educational and economic marginalization, as well as workplace abuse and exploitation, and argues for policies aimed at turning this vulnerable age into an age of opportunity. The UNESCO Education for All Global Monitoring Report of 2012[275] emphasizes the central importance of education in preparing young persons for life and in giving them opportunities for decent work. The ILO report for The Hague Global Child Labour Conference of 2010[276] stresses the importance of addressing youth employment alongside other issues such as education, social protection, and poverty in an integrated policy respond to child labour. [277] India should have, by now, withdrawn

---

[272] Weiner, *Child and the State*.

[273] The Constitution of India, Article 51A, 93rd Constitution Amendment Act: A parent or guardian has a fundamental duty to provide opportunities for education to his child or, as the case may be, ward between the age of 6 and 14 years.

[274] UNICEF, —'The State of the World's Children 2011: Adolescence: An Age of Opportunity', New York, 2011.

[275] UNESCO, 'Youth and Skills: Putting education to work— Education For All', Global Monitoring Report of 2012, Paris, 2012.

[276] The Hague Global Child Labour Conference, 'Towards a World without Child Labour'.

[277] The Hague Global Child Labour Conference, 'Towards a World without Child Labour'.

the Declaration on Article 32 to the CRC, reviewed the CLPRA, and enacted a new law prohibiting child labour in all sectors up to 18 years of age, and sending all children to school till that age. All children out of school are child labourers. The RTE Act and Rules thereunder are a step forward for children in the age group of 6–14 years in government (state) and government-aided schools. But the Constitutional Amendment and the RTE Act fail to enshrine the rights of children aged 0–6 years for early learning, care, and development, and also fail to guarantee this right for children in the age group 14–18 years. Non-aided schools (private education institutions) are largely left out of the purview of the RTE Act, with only special reservation of 25 per cent being provided for the weaker sections/disadvantaged groups. It is urgently required to enact an amendment to Article 21A, ensuing the fundamental right to early childhood care, development, and education (0–6 years) and enlarging the scope of Article 21A to cover children in all schools in the age group 15–18, guaranteeing them also the right to free, compulsory, equitable, and quality education. In India, child labour has been a direct function of adult unemployment and underemployment, with the child as a supplementary (and sometimes even primary) source of income. With the increase in employment in the unorganized sectors, child labour may increase. With the new amendments, this is the right time for the Government to ratify the ILO Convention 138 on minimum age of employment and ILO Convention 182 on worst forms of child labour, and also withdraw its reservation on Article 32 of the CRC.

5 Right to Protection against Sexual Abuse and Exploitation

Child sexual abuse (CSA) and exploitation is not new—the extent of the problem is that children are sold, rented out, and sexually abused by adults everywhere. While it is almost impossible to obtain accurate figures, it is a fact that millions of girls and boys worldwide are being used in prostitution, pornography, trafficking, and other forms of sexual abuse and exploitation. There is no uniformly accepted definition of child abuse. There have been a number of definitions of the phrase 'child sexual abuse'. It could be defined as an activity relating to sex organs engaged in for sexual gratification, which takes advantage of, violates, or deceives children or young people. Furthermore, their plight has a multiplier effect since research has shown that frequently abused and exploited adolescents are abusers and exploiters themselves as adults.

The CSA has been defined as any kind of physical or mental violation of a child with sexual intent usually by a person who is in a position of trust or power vis-à-vis the child. The CSA is also defined as any sexual behaviour directed at a person under 16, without informed consent.

The Standing Committee on Sexually Abused Children[1] (SCOSAC) has defined CSA as follows:

> Any child below the age of consent may be deemed to have been sexually abused when a sexually mature person has by design or by neglect of their usual societal or specific responsibilities in relation to the child engaged or permitted engagement of that child in activity of a sexual nature, which is intended to lead to the sexual gratification of the sexually mature person. This definition pertains whether or not it involves genital or physical contact, whether or not initiated by the child and whether or not there is a discernible harmful outcome in the short run.

The Children's Act, 1989 of Great Britain defines 'sexual abuse' as the involvement of dependent, developmentally immature children and adolescents in sexual activities they do not normally comprehend, to which they are unable to give informed consent, or that which violate the social taboos of family roles. This definition introduced the concepts of 'informed consent' and 'dependent'. It is the dependent nature of child and young people that make CSA a particular problem.

In Australia, CSA refers to a variety of behaviour ranging from enthusiasm to intercourse, from intimate kissing and cuddling to penetration with an object. The penetration may be oral,

[1] SCOSAC, 1984.

vaginal, or anal.[2] In 1988, a National Seminar on Child Abuse in India[3] recognized the need for defining afresh the term 'child abuse' in the Indian context. The committee concerned evolved the following definition.

Child abuse and neglect (CAN) is the intentional, non-accidental injury and maltreatment of children by parents, caretakers, employers, or others including those individuals representing government/non-government bodies, which may lead to temporary or permanent impairment of their physical, mental, psycho-social development, disability, or death.

The problem of CSA is, for feminists, the problem of masculine sexuality. Sakshi[4] defines CSA as any behaviour directed at a person under 16, without that person's informed consent.[5] According to Sakshi, CSA is the physical or mental violation of a child with sexual intent, usually by an older person, who is in some position of power and/or trust vis-à-vis the child. The CSA includes an adult exposing his or her genitals to a child or persuading the child to do the same; an adult touching a child's genitals or making the child touch the adult's genitalia; an adult involving a child in pornography; an adult having oral, vaginal, or anal intercourse with a child; any verbal or other sexual suggestions made to a child by an adult; and so on. Sexual abuse of children can take place in the family, in the neighbourhood, in school, in institutions, and on the street. The abuser, generally a male, usually violates a relationship of trust with the child, taking advantage of his power and position.[6]

The United Nations has defined CSA as contacts or interactions between a child and an older or more knowledgeable child or adult (a stranger, sibling, or person in a position of authority, such as a parent or a caretaker), when the child is being used as an object of gratification for the older child's or adult's sexual needs. These contacts or interactions are carried out against the child using force, trickery, bribes, threats, or pressure.[7]

Some other definitions describe it as any kind of physical or mental violation of a child with a sexual intent, usually by an older person who is in possession of trust or power vis-à-vis the child. The list is not exhaustive.

The CSA becomes exploitation when a third party benefits through a profit. Commercial sexual exploitation of children commonly refers to using a child for sexual purposes in exchange for cash or favours in kind between the client/customer and the intermediary or agent who profits from such trade in children. Those who profit may be from a wide range of persons, including parents, family member, procurers/agents, community members—largely men, but also women.[8] Commercial exploitation includes child prostitution through trafficking, child sex tourism, and child pornography.

Child sexual abuse and exploitation (CSA&E) covers the sexual maltreatment of both children and young people. The sexual exploitation of children is a multi-billion-dollar industry of

---

[2] See Australian Report Commissioned by the Law Reform Commission of Victoria.

[3] Institute of Public Cooperation and Child Development, New Delhi, 2–24 June 1988.

[4] A non-governmental organization (NGO) in New Delhi.

[5] See Sakshi, 'Child Sexual Abuse—A Draft Manual', unpublished.

[6] Sakshi, *Child Sexual Abuse: Beyond Fear Secrecy and Shame* (New Delhi: 1999).

[7] UNICEF, 2001. Available at https://www.unicef.org/rosa/commercial.pdf (accessed on 12 January 2016).

[8] UNICEF, 2001. Available at https://www.unicef.org/rosa/commercial.pdf (accessed on 12 January 2016).

international proportions. It is an abuse of power and violation of human rights and, in many cases, a contemporary form of slavery. The perpetrator can be anyone who exploits the child's vulnerability to gain sexual gratification. The CSA&E involves mental, physical, and emotional abuse of a child through overt and covert sexual acts, gestures, and disposition when informed consent or resistance by the child victim to such acts is not possible. It can also include activities which do not involve direct touching. Sexual abuse and exploitation takes different forms, as elaborated next.

1. Child labourers and young domestic workers are frequently used for the sexual gratification of the employers and other adults.
2. Children are sexually abused within the family. Rape within a family has its own alarming numbers.
3. With the advent of human immunodeficiency virus/acquired immune deficiency syndrome (HIV/AIDS), there is an increased demand for younger child prostitutes.
4. Children are used as attractions in sex tourism. Children are victims of a globally organized sex trade. In some countries, this helps in attracting much-needed foreign exchange.
5. Children are abused within the context of cultural or traditional practices such as child marriages.
6. Children in institutions are vulnerable to sexual abuse from those who are supposed to take care of them.
7. Children in situations of conflicts, and displaced, migrant, and refugee children are particularly vulnerable to all forms of sexual exploitation.
8. Child pornography is reaching alarming proportions, especially with the help of high-tech mediums.

Disabled children with problems of communication and comprehension are particularly vulnerable to sexual abuse. Sexual abuse and exploitation include:

1. fondling, touching, and kissing;
2. exhibitionism and voyeurism;
3. oral, anal, or vaginal sexual intercourse;
4. photography/filming children for sexual purposes;
5. persuading a child to touch or fondle the sexual parts of any other person (child or adult); and
6. masturbating (using the child as a sexual object).[9]

There are occurrences of sexual abuse and exploitation of children within families and homes. The law generally presumes that guardians of the child are innocent and it takes a lot of professional commitment to establish an offence against such guardians.

Impact of Sexual Abuse/Exploitation

The sexual exploitation of children not only has damaging and long-term impact on the victim, but also affects the families, communities, and society at large. Like any crime that continues to go unchecked, the sexual exploitation of children—both within the homes and as an organized

---

[9] Sakshi, 'Child Sexual Abuse'.

trafficking racket—directly suggests the health of a society as a whole. Children who have been sexually abused suffer severe trauma or damage which can be physical, mental, emotional, or psychological. The trauma may last a lifetime if the process of healing does not take place. Sexually transmitted diseases or HIV or pregnancy at an early age can be some of the disastrous outcomes of CSA. With the family support system getting destroyed, the child can face social isolation and social stigmatization. Very often, the child is blamed for being sexually exploited, for 'affecting the honour of the family'. The child is made to feel guilty for what happened and a deep sense of worthlessness develops. Children may also feel powerless, angry, frightened, and lonely. Depression, isolation, and self-destructiveness are also some of the short-term and long-term impacts of sexual abuse.

Part A: Child Sexual Abuse in India

A research study by the Special Cell for Women and Children of the Tata Institute of Social Sciences, Mumbai,[10] revealed that a total of 1,176 cases of CSA were registered during 1990–95 in Mumbai, and a total of 57 reported cases (in Mumbai during 1994–95) on sexually abused girls below the age of 10 years were studied from police records. Some of the findings of this study were significant.

1. The offender is often known to the child and her family.
2. A large number of children (40.4 per cent) have been abused or assaulted in the offender's house. In 35 per cent cases the child was sexually abused in public places such as a garden, creek, building halls, common areas in chawls,[11] public toilets, and so on.
3. Only serious cases have been reported to the police.
4. More than half the accused arrested were not granted bail. Out of the 22 accused who were granted bail, 15 were below the age of 18 years and hence the bail was granted through the juvenile courts.
5. The age of consent of abuse is around 3 years and it shows increased vulnerability at around seven years of age.
6. Men of all ages can be abusers. In this study, the ages of the accused were in the range of 12 years to 62 years. The data also showed that 17 of the abusers were below 18 years of age.
7. About 30.4 per cent of the offenders (that is 17 out of 57 cases) were aged less than 18 years.
8. A large number of cases in the study show that the offender was a neighbour of the child. Sometimes, the offenders were older children in the community. Some of the offenders were in fact popular among children.
9. Sexual abuse could involve both touching as well as non-contact abuse.
10. Statements taken by investigating officers mostly revolve around one episode of CSA, and no history is therefore looked at or questioned.

---

[10] Nahida Shaikh and T. Panchal, 'Documentation of Police Cases of Sexually Abused Girls in Mumbai City between 1994–95 by the Special Cell for Women & Children', Tata Institute of Social Sciences, Mumbai, 1997.

[11] A cluster of tiny homes.

A study was conducted by the Ministry of Women and Child Development (MWCD), Government of India, on child abuse in India in 2007.[12] In order to examine the incidence of sexual abuse among children, a questionnaire was administered to 12,447 children belonging to the five different categories, including children in family environment, children in schools, children in institutions, children at work, and street children. For the purpose of the study, sexual abuse was defined as severe forms of sexual abuse[13] and other forms of sexual abuse.[14] Major findings of the study were:

i. Across the country, every second child was being subjected to other forms of sexual abuse and every fifth child was facing severe forms of sexual abuse. Out of the children questioned, 5.69 per cent reported being sexually assaulted. Children on streets, children at work, and children in institutional care reported the highest incidence of sexual assault. 72.1 per cent children did not report the matter to anyone. 50 per cent of the abusers were cousins, uncles, and friends and class fellows.

1. About 77 per cent children who were forced to touch private parts of the body, did not report the matter to anyone. Children on streets, children at work, and children in institutional care reported the highest incidence. Out of the total child respondents, 14.5 per cent reported incidences when someone made them fondle or touch their private body parts.

2. More than 80 per cent children forced to exhibit private body parts chose to keep quiet. The highest percentage of children reporting that they were forced to exhibit private body parts reported that such abuse was perpetrated by friends and class fellows, followed by uncles and neighbours.

3. Out of the total child respondents, 4.6 per cent reported being photographed in the nude. About 72 per cent children did not report the matter to anyone.

4. Regarding other forms of abuse, the friends or class fellows and the uncles or neighbours emerged as the main abusers in this category, which was similar to the trends of abuse reported in severe forms of sexual abuse. The high percentage (21.06 per cent) of children in family environment reporting forcible kissing is a cause of concern. More girls faced sexual abuse of the form of rubbing private body parts against the shoulder of the child and other such acts during travel, as compared to boys. The highest percentage (33.09 per cent) of the aforementioned form of abuse was reported among children at work. 16.97 per cent out of the total child respondents admitted to being forced to view private body parts of abusers. Almost 79 per cent children chose to keep quiet when forced to see private body parts. The highest percentage of children reported such abuses by friends and class fellows, followed by uncles and neighbours. About 30.22 per cent of the total number of child respondents reported that someone had exposed them to pornographic pictures. An

---

[12] MWCD, 'Study on Child Abuse India', prepared by Loveleen Kacker, Government of India, 2007.

[13] Severe forms of sexual abuse include: (a) assault, including rape and sodomy; (b) touching or fondling a child; (c) exhibitionism—forcing a child to exhibit his/her private body parts; and (d) photographing a child in the nude.

[14] Other forms of sexual abuse include: (a) forcible kissing; (b) sexual advances towards a child during travel; (c) sexual advances towards a child during marriage situations; (d) exhibitionism—exhibiting before a child; (e) exposing a child to pornographic material.

overwhelming majority of child respondents (66.1 per cent) were shown dirty pictures by their friends or class fellows, followed by uncles and neighbours (13.1 per cent).

According to official statistics reported in 'Crime in India, 2014',[15] the incidents involving children reported (classified on the basis of crime heads) during 2011, 2012, 2013, and 2014 are presented in Table 5.1.

Table 5.1   Crimes Committed against Children[16]

S. No.	Crime Head	Year			
		2011 (1)	2012 (2)	2013 (3)	2014
1.	Murder	1,451	1,597	1,657	1,817
2.	Infanticide	63	81	82	121
3.	Rape	7,112	8,541	12,363	13,766
4.	Kidnapping and abduction	15,284	18,266	28,167	37,854
5.	Foeticide	132	210	221	107
6.	Abetment of suicide	61	144	215	56
7.	Exposure and abandonment	700	821	930	983
8.	Procuration of minor girls	862	809	1,224	2020
9.	Buying of girls for prostitution	27	15	6	14
10.	Selling of girls for prostitution	113	108	100	82
11.	Other crimes (including Prohibition of Child Marriage Act [PCMA], 2006)	7,293	7,580	13,259	8484
12.	Total	33,098	38,172	58,224	65304

Child rape continues to be reported significantly from various states and union territories (UTs). Table 5.2 provides the detailed information on child rape victims and their proportion in the total rape victims during the year 2014.

Table 5.2.   Age-group-wise Victims of Rape Cases (Total) (Section 376 of the Indian Penal Code [IPC]) during 2014[17]

S. No.	State/UT	No. of Cases Reported	No. of Victims				
			Below 6 Years	6 Years and above, below 12 Years	12 Years and above, below 16 Years	16 Years and above, below 18 Years	Total Victims
	Total (All India)	674	23	84	211	115	433

[15] National Crime Records Bureau (NCRB), 'Crime in India, 2014', Ministry of Home Affairs, Government of India.

[16] Source: NCRB, 'Crime in India, 2014'.

[17] Source: NCRB, 'Crime in India 2014'.

A total of 12,363 cases of child rape were reported in the country during 2013, as compared to 8,541 in 2012, accounting for an increase of 44.7 per cent. Maximum of the child rape cases were reported in Madhya Pradesh (2,112 cases), followed by Maharashtra (1,546 cases) and Uttar Pradesh (1,381 cases). These three states together accounted for 40.8 per cent of the total child rape cases reported in the country.[18]

On an average, three children out of one hundred thousand are victims of rape. For every one hundred thousand children population, maximum of such incidents were reported in Mizoram and Andaman and Nicobar Islands (16 children each), followed by Delhi (14 children), Sikkim, and Goa (12 children each).[19]

From Table 5.2, it is clear that the maximum number of cases of abuse were reported in the age group of 14–18 years, followed by the group 10–14 years. This implies that the most vulnerable age for sexual abuse is between 14 and 18 years.

Child Sexual Abuse in Institutions

There has been a significant increase in the number of cases of CSA in institutions. The sexual assault case of a deaf and mute girl in the Observation Home, Umerkhadi (OHU), Mumbai, referred to as 'Billa No. 31' in all available documents pertaining to her case, is an example of lapses that occur in dealing with such cases under the present system.[20]

The medical examination for investigation of sexual assault, ordered by the superintendent on 22 September 1997 and conducted by the doctor on duty at OHU, was inconclusive because it was incomplete. No attempt was made to collect any forensic evidence other than from the clothes she was wearing. The doctor appeared to be unaware of the procedures to be followed while investigating a case of sexual assault. There was no facility to help the victim to cope with the physical and emotional trauma. There was a lapse of 20 days between the date of assault and the report to the police. There was no efficient and timely communication mechanism. Evidence was, in fact, suppressed.

Many such cases of institutional abuse have come to light. In 2010 *Mumbai Mirror*, a local daily in Mumbai, reported that five children died of malnutrition in an orphanage in Kavadas village near Mumbai and five other children were on the brink of death due to severe malnutrition and unhygienic living conditions.[21] In 2011, it came to light that five mentally challenged girls were raped and 15 others were physically abused, all aged between 14 and 18 years, at the Kalyani Mahila and Balak Seva Sansthan in New Panvel. Four of the five girls raped were 'deaf and mute'. The girls were visited by men from outside the shelter home and taken to the terrace of the home and raped. Nineteen girls from the home were examined at Panvel Rural Hospital. The reports confirmed that five girls had been raped and the rest of the girls too had been physically abused. This shelter home ran without any formal licence between 2006 and 2009, and no action was

---

[18] NCRB, 'Crime in India, 2014'.

[19] NCRB, 'Crime in India, 2014'.

[20] Report of the investigation done by the Forum against Child Sexual Exploitation (FACSE) team.

[21] Yogesh Sadhwani and Bapu Deedwania, 'Orphanage Hell', *Mumbai Mirror*, 23 August 2010. Available at http://www.mumbaimirror.com/index.aspx?page=article&sectid=2&contentid=2010082320 100823033006642ddc20bb0 (accessed on 14 November 2016).

taken against it.[22] Similarly, 13 boys and 5 girls were found to have suffered rape, starvation, regular thrashing, and sexual assault at an orphanage in Kavdas. The horrors in the orphanage extended from pitiable living conditions, almost no food, and physical abuse, going right up to violent rape of the girls, and sodomy of the boys. Alcohol was often forced down their throats while their tormentors abused them.[23]

After the publication of the article 'Orphanage Hell' in *Mumbai Mirror*, the Bombay High Court took suo motu cognizance of this article and a public interest litigation (PIL 182/2010) was initiated.[24] The Bombay High Court appointed the Maharashtra State Coordination Committee for Child Protection[25]. The Committee surveyed the institutions for the mentally challenged in Maharashtra and submitted a report titled 'The Status of Mentally Deficient Children's (MDC) Homes in Maharashtra' to the Mumbai High Court.

Some of the significant findings of the committee with regard to homes for MDCs across Maharashtra were:[26]

1. Haphazard and ad hoc distribution of homes across the state. Fewer MDC homes for girls as compared to boys. Only one MDC home in Maharashtra is fully funded by the government.
2. Vacancies of staff in MDC homes in Maharashtra.
3. Several adult persons in MDC homes for children. No rehabilitation or reintegration plan for those persons above 18 anywhere in the entire state.
4. The MDC homes in Maharashtra being used as hostels.
5. Children inappropriately sent to MDC homes. Some of them not mentally challenged.
6. Inadequate understanding and improper use of intelligence quotient (IQ) tests by the authorities.
7. Over 59 per cent of MDC homes in the state are not registered under the Juvenile Justice (Care and Protection of Children) Act (JJ Act), 2000.
8. No quality care provided to children.
9. Nearly 60 per cent of MDC homes are managed by trusts that do not meet the requirements of the Department of Women and Child Development (DWCD).

[22] Bapu Deedwania and Yogesh Sadhwani, '19 Mentally-Challenged Abused in Shelter Home', *Mumbai Mirror*, 5 March 2011. Available at http://www.mumbaimirror.com/article/2/2011030520110305075700 241778894a1/19-mentallychallenged-abused-in-shelter-home.html (accessed on 15 November 2016).

[23] Yogesh Sadhwani, 'Girls, Boys Raped Daily, Alcohol Forced Down Their Throats', *Mumbai Mirror*, 28 July 2011. Available at http://www.mumbaimirror.com/article/2/2011072820110728041923 3825d2 6d16b/Girls-boys-raped-daily-alcohol-forced-down-their-throats.html (accessed on 15 November 2016).

In a similar case, an 11-year-old girl who had been repeatedly raped and sodomized died in January 2012 due to severe diarrhoea and incessant vomiting in an orphanage in Delhi. (Neeraj Chauhan, 'Orphanage Horror: Girl Dies, Autopsy Says Rape' *Times of India*, 26 January 2012. Available at http://articles.time-sofindia.indiatimes.com/2012-01-26/delhi/30666267_1_orphanage-autopsy-report-girl (accessed on 15 November 2016).)

[24] Asha Bajpai, the author of this book, was appointed as the amicus curiae in PIL 182/2010.

[25] The committee consisted of Asha Bajpai as chairperson and Harish Shetty, Sarita Shankaran, Chitra Acharya, and Pramod Nigudkar as members.

[26] Maharashtra State Coordination Committee for Child Protection, *Status Report of Homes for Mentally Deficient Children in Maharashtra*, committee appointed by the Mumbai High Court, dated 27 July 2011.

10. Records of children (CWC orders, IQ records, medical records, case files) are inadequately maintained across the state.
11. Basic infrastructure is not in place in a majority of homes.
12. No Right to Play for the children in MDC homes in Maharashtra.
13. No Right to Education for children in MDC homes in Maharashtra.
14. No Home is equipped to understand and deal with CSA.
15. Not a single MDC home in the state employs the number and kind of staff specified under the DWCD rules.
16. The CWC members are ignorant and unaware of their responsibilities or the rights of children.
17. Transfer of children is not done keeping the best interest of the child in focus.
18. Inconsistencies across ministries dealing with children with disabilities.
19. Child labour and corporal punishment were observed.

There were no procedures or protocols laid down to deal with such cases of abuse within the institutions. In several cases the 'carers', that is, those who are supposed to take care of the children in the institutions, themselves are the abusers.[27] There are several cases which go unreported. Doctors who are the first to come in contact with such victims are not trained to deal with such cases. Often, doctors are not equipped to examine rape victims. The trauma caused to the child victim of sexual assault finds no mention in any report. The medical reports are incomplete and vague in many cases. The medical or psychiatric assessment needs to be sensitively carried out. The staff in the hospitals or institutions are not equipped or trained to deal with such cases.

From the police point of view, child rape and indecent assault are peripheral crimes. The police also have practically no training in dealing with cases of CSA. Besides, investigation of such cases requires a different kind of expertise, which is lacking. There is a wide communication gap between the child's statement and the recordings of the police and the language of the courts. A stereotypical pattern of investigation is followed, without any sensitivity.

Several important directions in the interest of children have been passed by the Mumbai High Court in PIL 182/2010. Some of them are as follows.

1. The procedure of granting licenses to MDC homes shall take due care to ensure that all applications are carefully scrutinized in order to verify the expertise of the persons involved in submitting the proposal. Norms shall be framed in regard to infrastructural facilities which must be made available, and finances that must be available to run the home.[28]
2. Government hospitals in Maharashtra must reserve beds in pediatric departments for treatment of mentally challenged child victims of sexual abuse and other child victims.[29]

[27] See Yogesh Sadhwani, 'Monsters!' *Mumbai Mirror*, 4 May 2011. Available at http://www.mumbaimirror.scom/article/15/20110504201105040606631397213c4972/Monsters.html (accessed on 14 November 2016).

[28] Judgment dated 16 September 2010, Mumbai High Court, in PIL 182/2010, D.Y. Chandrachud and R.P. Sondur Baldota, JJ.

[29] Judgment dated 16 October 2010, Mumbai High Court, in PIL 182/2010, Mohit. S. Shah, and D.Y. Chandrachud.

3. The Department of Social Welfare, through the Commissioner of Disabilities, runs schools and educational centres for children with disabilities, providing services of speech therapy and vocational training. Such services should be made available to the inmates of the MDC homes so that the development of such mentally as well as physically disabled children would be much faster.[30]

4. The Principal District Judge shall nominate a judicial officer of the rank of District Judge when the home is in District Headquarters, or Civil Judge, Junior Division/junior magistrate of first class where the home is in Taluka headquarters or a remote place (preferably a lady judicial officer in either case), to submit reports about the manner in which the concerned MDC homes are run in their respective jurisdictions.[31]

5. Guidelines for cases of sexual abuse/assault/sexual offences against MDC need to be followed by all stakeholders in a coordinated manner.[32]

A government resolution (GR) had been issued by the state government of Maharashtra on 30 May 2012, under which the children in the MDC homes in Maharashtra are to be transferred from the DWCD to the Social Justice Department. The following provisions of the Persons with Disabilities (Equal Opportunities, Protection of Rights and Full Participation) Act (PWD Act), 1995 should be complied in every MDC Home:[33]

a. every child with disability has access to free education (Section 26 a);
b. setting up of special schools (Section 26 c);
c. vocational training facilities (Section 26 d);
d. part-time classes;
e. government to provide aids and appliances to persons with disabilities (Section 42);
f. to undertake rehabilitation (Section 66);
g. disability certificate to be issued to all children (Rule 4).

6. Twenty-five children from MDC Home Mankhurd are attending normal school under the Inclusive Education Program of Sarva Shiksha Abhiyan[34] (SSA).[35]

---

[30] Judgment dated 5 Februaury 2011, Mumbai High Court, in PIL 182/2010, Mohit S. Shah, C.J. and D.Y. Chandrachud, J.

[31] Judgment dated 11 March 2011, Mumbai High Court, in PIL 182/2010, Mohit S. Shah, C.J. and D.Y. Chandrachud, J.

[32] Judgment dated 29 July 2011, Mumbai High Court, in PIL 182/2010, Mohit S. Shah, C.J. and D.Y. Chandrachud, J.

[33] Judgment dated 5 July 2012, Mumbai High Court, in PIL 182/2010, D.Y. Chandrachud and M.S. Sanklecha, J.J.

[34] The SSA is the Government of India's flagship programme for achievement of Universalization of Elementary Education (UEE) in a time-bound manner, as mandated by 86th amendment to the Constitution of India, making free and compulsory education to the children of 6–14 years age group a fundamental right.

The SSA is being implemented in partnership with state governments to cover the entire country and address the needs of 192 million children in 1.1 million habitations.

[35] Judgment dated 24 June 2013, Mumbai High Court, in PIL 182/2010, D.Y. Chandrachud and A.A. Sayed, J.J.

7. The state government should ensure that male wardens should not be kept in homes for mentally challenged children that include girls and whenever girls are taken to the toilets, they should be accompanied by a female staff and not by male staff.[36]

8. Children in MDC homes who are above 14 years old should be permitted to continue their education till the age of 18 years under the SSA.[37] This exception has been made to children in MDC homes.

9. The Principal Secretary, Department of Women and Child Development, should determine the compensation for victims of sexual abuse payable to these children.[38]

10. The state and district SSA to take steps to ensure that the Right of Children to Free and Compulsory Education Act (RTE Act), 2009 is implemented immediately for children in MDC homes in Maharashtra. The Education Inspector's Office, School Education Department, Government of Maharashtra, should link National Institute of Open Schooling (NIOS) accredited institutions to the MDC homes.[39]

11. Under the National Trust Act, 1999, a provision is made for health insurance scheme for the welfare of persons with autism, mental retardation, cerebral palsy, and multiple disabilities. The Chairperson of the National Trust should ensure that health insurance is provided to the children in MDC homes in Maharashtra.[40]

12. The state government should ensure that medical officers are appointed in every home, and if this is not possible immediately, then it should at least ensure that medical officers from a nearby hospital pays weekly visits to these homes immediately from the next week.[41]

13. The Principal Secretary, Department of Women and Child Welfare, and the Social Justice Department should ensure that the Chunauti rehabilitation model is replicated in all the MDC Homes in Maharashtra.[42]

The National Legal Regime

The Constitution of India contains provisions for the protection of children. Under the Constitution, it is the duty of the state to ensure that children of tender age are not abused and forced by economic necessity to enter vocations unsuited to their age and strength [Article 39(e)], and to ensure that children are given opportunities and facilities to develop in a healthy manner in conditions of freedom and dignity [Article 39(f)]. According to Article 23 of the Constitution, trafficking in women for immoral purposes is prohibited. The Constitution directs the state to enact special legislations and policies for protecting children and youth against exploitation of

[36] Judgment dated 12 June 2014, Mumbai High Court, in PIL 182/2010, V.M. Kanade and P.D. Kode, J.J.

[37] Judgment dated 18 September 2014, Mumbai High Court, in PIL 182/2010, V.M. Kanade and P.D Kode, J.J.

[38] Judgment dated 20 March 2015, Mumbai High Court, in PIL 182/2010, V.M. Kanade and A.R. Joshi, J.

[39] Judgment dated 20 March 2015, in PIL 182/2010.

[40] Judgment dated 20 March 2015, in PIL 182/2010.

[41] Judgment dated 20 March 2015, in PIL 182/2010.

[42] Judgment dated 20 March 2015, in PIL 182/2010.

moral and material abandonment. In India, there was no comprehensive law on CSA till 2012. Legal intervention was in the form of investigations which start with registration of offences under the earlier Juvenile Justice Act, 1986, or the present JJ Act, 2000, or the IPC, 1860,[43] or the Immoral Traffic (Prevention) Act (ITPA), 1956 (amended in 1986).

The JJ Act was enacted to provide for the care, protection, treatment, development, and reha-bilitation of neglected or delinquent children. The act did not directly deal with CSA, but the definition of a neglected juvenile included a juvenile who lived in a brothel or with a prostitute or frequently went to any place used for the purpose of prostitution or was found to associate with any prostitute or who was being or was likely to be abused or exploited for immoral or illegal purposes. Such neglected children were produced before a Juvenile Welfare Board who would, after an inquiry, send the child to a juvenile home for care, protection, and rehabilitation.

Under the JJ Act, 1986, a sex worker's child was automatically considered a neglected child. The magistrate had the power to segregate the prostitute from her child and place the child in a corrective institution. Besides, under the act, while males above 18 years were considered adults, the age was reduced to 16 years for females. The Juvenile Welfare Boards generally were not equipped to deal with cases of CSA. The observation homes could not provide special care and treatment for such victimized children.

Juvenile Justice (Care and Protection of Children) Act, 2000 (amended 2000, 2006, 2011)[44]

Since the JJ Act, 1986 has been replaced by the JJ Act, such children are now being produced before the CWCs which have replaced the Juvenile Welfare Boards.[45] In practice, at present, it appears that there has been a change only in the nomenclature. The actual functioning of the earlier Boards and the present Committees remain almost the same. An abused child is regarded as a child in need of care and protection.

---

[43] IPC, Section 375: A man is said to commit 'rape' who, except in the case hereinafter has sexual inter-course with a woman under circumstances falling under any of the six following descriptions:

- First—Against her will.
- Second—With her consent, when her consent has been obtained by putting her or any person in whom she is interested in fear of death or of hurt.
- Third—With her consent, when the man knows that he is not her husband, and that her consent is given because she believes that he is another man to whom she is or believes herself to be lawfully married.
- Explanation—Penetration is sufficient to constitute the sexual intercourse necessary to the offence of rape. Exception—Sexual intercourse by a man with his own wife, the wife not being under 15 years of age, is not rape.
- Imprisonment not less than 7 years and may extend to life (Section 376).
- IPC, Section 377: Whoever voluntarily has carnal intercourse against the order of nature with any man, woman or animal, shall be punished with imprisonment for life, or with imprisonment of either descrip-tion for a term which may extend to 10 years, and shall also be liable to fine.
- Explanation: Penetration is sufficient to constitute the carnal intercourse.

[44] Amended in 2006 and 2013.
[45] See Chapter 6 on Juvenile Justice.

Juvenile Justice (Care and Protection of Children) Act 2015

The JJ Act, 2015 replaced the aforementioned JJ Act, 2000 and came into force on 15 January 2016. Children in need of care and protection include those children who have been or are being or are likely to be abused, tortured or exploited for the purpose of sexual abuse or illegal acts. Such children have to be produced before the Child Welfare Committees.

Immoral Traffic (Prevention) Act, 1986

Under Section 8, children, both girls and boys, are given protection from sexual abuse. There are also provisions against brothel keepers and against keeping minor girls in brothels. Discretionary powers have been given to magistrates for interim placement of children who are housed in institutions.

Inadequacies in Law

Before 2012, under the IPC, 1860, if a child was sexually abused, a case could be filed for statutory rape or 'outraging the modesty of the woman' in the case of girls (Section 375), and for 'unnatural sexual offence' (Section 377) in the case of boys. The ordinary criminal laws were totally inadequate to protect the children who were victims of sexual abuse. These legislations did not include the common forms of CSA, nor their impact on the children.

The discretionary power given under the former Section 376[46] of the IPC to decrease the sentence of the accused had been used in many cases to the detriment of the victims. For instance, in *Raju* v.

---

[46]   IPC, Section 376: Punishment for rape—

(1)   Whoever, except in the cases provided for by Subsection (2), commits rape shall be punished with imprisonment of either description for a term which shall not be less than 7 years but which may be for life or for a term which may extend to 10 years and shall also be liable to fine unless the women raped is his own wife and is not under 12 years of age, in which cases, he shall be punished with imprisonment of either description for a term which may extend to 2 years or with fine or with both, provided that the court may, for adequate and special reasons to be mentioned in the judgment, impose a sentence of imprisonment for a term of less than 7 years.

(2)   Whoever—

(a)   being a police officer commits rape—

(i)   within the limits of the police station to which he is appointed; or

(ii)   in the premises of any station house whether or not situated in the police station to which he is appointed; or

(iii)   on a woman in his custody or in the custody of a police officer subordinate to him; or

(b)   being a public servant, takes advantage of his official position and commits rape on a woman in his custody as such public servant or in the custody of a public servant subordinate to him; or

(c)   being on the management or on the staff of a jail, remand home or other place of custody established by or under any law for the time being in force or of a woman's or children's institution takes advantage of his official position and commits rape on any inmate of such jail, remand home, place or institution; or

State of Karnataka,[47] considering the young age of the accused persons, one being 24 and the other being 21, and the long lapse of time during which they suffered disrepute, the sentence was reduced from 7 years of rigorous imprisonment to three. In a case reported in 1987, an 11-year-old girl was raped and she was pinned down to the floor and gagged. The session's court convicted the accused with 5 years' imprisonment. In an appeal, to enhance the sentence, the Madhya Pradesh High Court held that 'increasing cases of personal violence and crime rate cannot justify a severe sentence on young offenders'.[48] There are several such insensitive judgments. This discretionary power has been deleted by the CLA Act, 2013.[49]

The restrictive interpretation of 'penetration' in the Explanation to Section 375 of the IPC[50] was an obstacle to cases of CSA. Explanation to Section 375 did not treat forced sexual intercourse

---

(d) being on the management or on the staff of a hospital, takes advantage of his official position and commits rape on a woman in that hospital; or

(e) commits rape on a woman knowing her to be pregnant; or

(f) commits rape on a woman when she is under 12 years of age; or

(g) commits gang rape, shall be punished with rigorous imprisonment for a term which shall not be less than 10 years but which may be for life and shall also be liable to fine, provided that the Court may, for adequate and special reasons to be mentioned in the judgment, impose a sentence of imprisonment of either description for a term of less than 10 years. Explanation 1—Where a woman is raped by one or more in a group of persons acting in furtherance of their common intention, each of the persons shall be deemed to have committed gang rape within the meaning of this subsection. Explanation 2—'Women's or children's institution' means an institution, whether called an orphanage or a home for neglected woman or children or a widows' home or by any other name, which is established and maintained for the reception and care of woman or children. Explanation 3—'Hospital' means the precincts of the hospital and includes the precincts of any institution for the reception and treatment of persons during convalescence or of persons requiring medical attention or rehabilitation.

[47] (1994) 1 SSC 453.

[48] *Vinod Kumar & Anr.* v. *State of Madhya Pradesh*, 1987 Cr LJ 1541.

[49] The CLA Act has deleted proviso to Section 376(2).

[50] IPC, Section 375: Rape—A man is said to commit 'rape' who, except in the case hereinafter excepted, has sexual intercourse with a woman under circumstances falling under any of the six following descriptions:

- First—Against her will.
- Second—Without her consent.
- Third—With her consent, when her consent has been obtained by putting her or any person in whom she is interested in fear of death or of hurt.
- Fourth—With her consent, when the man knows that he is not her husband, and that her consent is given because she believes that he is another man to whom she is or believes herself to be lawfully married.
- Fifth—With her consent, when, at the time of giving such consent, by reason of unsoundness of mind or intoxication or the administration by him personally or through another of any stupefying or unwholesome substance, she is unable to understand the nature and consequences of that to which she gives consent.
- Sixth—With or without her consent, when she is under 16 years of age. Explanation.—Penetration is sufficient to constitute the sexual intercourse necessary to the offence of rape.

by a husband against the wife (above 15 years) as an offence. Section 376-A[51] also had the same reasoning.

The classification of penetrative abuse of a child below the age of 12 as unnatural offence under Section 377[52] or as outraging the modesty of a woman under Section 354 of the IPC,[53] only depending on the type of penetration, was wrong. It ignored the 'impact' of the abuse on the child and focused more on technicalities. There was no provision to deal with the trauma of the child.

The CWCs were not equipped to deal with children who are victims of sexual abuse. The observation homes set up under the JJ Act, 1986 do not provide special care and treatment for victimized children. The structures under the JJ Act, 2000 are yet to be put in place in some states.

Clearly, an urgent need was felt for recognition of children's human rights and their necessity of legally mandated protection. The legal notion of sexual abuse of children was outdated. There were no procedural provisions concerned with ensuring successful prosecution of protecting the best interests of the child. The provisions under the IPC before 2012 did not really provide relief to a child who had been sexually abused because of their built-in problems of a limited perspective and insensitive procedures.[54]

Protection of Children from Sexual Offences Act, 2012

Until 2012, various provisions of the IPC were used to deal with sexual offences against children as the law did not make a distinction between an adult and a child. The Protection of Children from Sexual Offences Act (POCSO Act), 2012 was passed by the Lok Sabha on 22 May 2012 and the Rajya Sabha on 10 May 2012. The act is a special law to protect children from sexual abuse and exploitation.[55] It provides protection to children below the age of 18 years[56] from offences of sexual assault, sexual harassment, and pornography and provides a child-friendly system for the

---

- Exception—Sexual intercourse by a man with his own wife, the wife not being under 15 years of age, is not rape.

[51] Section 376A: Intercourse by a man with his wife during separation—Whoever has sexual intercourse with his own wife, who is living separately from him under a decree of separation or under any custom or usage without her consent shall be punished with imprisonment of either description for a term which may extend to 2 years and shall also be liable to fine

[52] Section 377: Unnatural offences—Whoever voluntarily has carnal intercourse against the order of nature with any man, woman or animal, shall be punished with imprisonment for life, or with imprisonment of either description for a term which may extend to 10 years, and shall also be liable to fine. Explanation—Penetration is sufficient to constitute the carnal intercourse necessary to the offence described in this section.

[53] Section 354: Assault or criminal force to woman with intent to outrage her modesty—Whoever assaults or uses criminal force to any woman, intending to outrage or knowing it to be likely that he will thereby outrage her modesty, shall be punished with imprisonment of either description for a term which may extend to 2 years, or with fine, or with both.

[54] P.D. Mathew, 'Sexual Abuse of Children and the Law', *Legal News and Views*, May 1996.

[55] The act, along with the rules, has come into effect from 14 November 2012.

[56] Section 2(d): 'Child' means any person below the age of 18 years.

trial of these offences. The act provides for stringent punishments which have been graded as per the gravity of the offence. The POCSO Act provides for the establishment of Special Courts for trial of offences under the act, keeping the best interest of the child of paramount importance at every stage of the judicial process (Section 28).[57]

The POCSO Act has consolidated the various Supreme Court and High Court guidelines and directions relating to child victims and witnesses and strengthened the legal provisions for the protection of children from sexual abuse and exploitation. It incorporates child-friendly mechanisms and procedures for reporting, medical examination, recording of child statement, investigation, maintaining respect and dignity of child victims during trial in courts , and ensuring care and protection to the child at every stage of the legal process.[58]

Any person (including the child) who has an apprehension that an offence under the POCSO Act is likely to be committed, or has knowledge that an offence has been committed, has a mandatory obligation to report the matter.[59] An express obligation has also been vested upon media personnel, and the staff of hotels, lodges, hospitals, clubs, studios, or photographic

---

[57] Designation of special courts:

(1) For the purposes of providing a speedy trial, the state government shall in consultation with the Chief Justice of the High Court, by notification in the Official Gazette, designate for each district, a court of session to be a special court to try the offences under the act, provided that if a Court of Session is notified as a children's court under the Commissions for Protection of Child Rights Act, 2005 or a Special Court designated for similar purposes under any other law for the time being in force, then, such court shall be deemed to be a Special Court under this section.

(2) While trying an offence under this act, a special court shall also try an offence [other than the offence referred to in Subsection (1)], with which the accused may, under the Code of Criminal Procedure (CrPC), 1973, be charged at the same trial.

(3) The special court constituted under this act, notwithstanding anything in the Information Technology Act (ITA), 2000, shall have jurisdiction to try offences under Section 67B of that act in so far as it relates to publication or transmission of sexually explicit material depicting children in any act, or conduct or manner or facilitates abuse of children online.

[58] Manoharan Arlene, ed., Swagata Raha, Geeta Sajjanshetty, *Frequently Asked Questions on the Protection of Children from Sexual Offences Act, 2012* (Bangalore, India: Center for Child and Law, NLSIU, 2013).

[59] POCSO Act, Section 19: Reporting of offences—

(1) Notwithstanding anything contained in the CrPC, 1973, any person (including the child), who has apprehension that an offence under this act is likely to be committed or has knowledge that such an offence has been committed, he shall provide such information to (a) the special juvenile police unit (SJPU); or (b) the local police.

(2) Every report given under Subsection (1) shall be

(a) ascribed an entry number and recorded in writing;
(b) be read over to the informant;
(c) shall be entered in a book to be kept by the police unit.

(3) Where the report under Subsection (1) is given by a child, the same shall be recorded under Subsection (2) in a simple language so that the child understands contents being recorded.

(4) In case contents are being recorded in the language not understood by the child or wherever it is deemed necessary, a translator or an interpreter, having such qualifications, experience and on payment of such fees as may be prescribed, shall be provided to the child if he fails to understand the same.

facilities, to report a case if they come across material or objects that are sexually exploitative of children.[60] Failure to report the offence under the POCSO Act is punishable with imprisonment of up to six months or fine or both. This penalty is, however, not applicable to a child. The act also makes it an offence to report false information, when such a report is made other than in good faith.[61]

A case must be reported to the SJPU or the local police, who must then record the report in writing, ascribe an entry number, read the report over to the informant for verification, and enter it in a book. A first information report (FIR) must be registered and its copy must be handed to the informant free of charge. If a case is reported by a child, it must be recorded in simple language so that the child understands what is being recorded. If it is being recorded in a language that the child does not understand, a qualified translator or interpreter must be provided to the child.

Some significant provisions under the POCSO Act are as follows.

1. Establishment of Special Courts. A sessions court in every district to be designated as special court by the state government in consultation with chief justice; the special court will give the best interest of the child paramount importance at every stage of the judicial process.[62]

---

(5) Where the SJPU or local police is satisfied that the child against whom an offence has been committed is in need of care and protection, then, it shall, after recording the reasons in writing, make immediate arrangement to give him such care and protection (including admitting the child into shelter home or to the nearest hospital) within twenty-four hours of the report, as may be prescribed.

(6) The SJPU or local police shall, without unnecessary delay but within a period of 24 hours, report the matter to the CWC and the special court or where no special court has been designated, to the Court of Session, including need of the child for care and protection and steps taken in this regard.

(7) No person shall incur any liability, whether civil or criminal, for giving the information in good faith for the purpose of Subsection (1).

[60] POCSO Act, Section 20—Obligation of media, studio and photographic facilities to report cases.

Any personnel of the media or hotel or lodge or hospital or club or studio or photographic facilities, by whatever name called, irrespective of the number of persons employed therein, shall, on coming across any material or object which is sexually exploitative of the child (including pornographic, sexually-related or making obscene representation of a child or children) through the use of any medium, shall provide such information to the SJPU, or to the local police, as the case may be.

[61] POCSO Act, Section 21: Punishment for failure to report or record a case—

(1) Any person, who fails to report the commission of an offence under Subsection (1) of Section 19 or Section 20 or who fails to record such offence under Subsection (2) of Section 19 shall be punished with imprisonment of either description which may extend to six months or with fine or with both.

(2) Any person, being in-charge of any company or an institution (by whatever name called) who fails to report the commission of an offence under Subsection (1) of Section 19 in respect of a subordinate under his control, shall be punished with imprisonment for a term which may extend to 1 year and with fine.

(3) The provisions of Subsection (1) shall not apply to a child under this act.

[62] POCSO, Section 28: Designation of Special Courts.

a) The special court should take cognizance of offences without the accused being committed to it for trial.[63]

2. Special public prosecutor to be appointed.[64]

3. Ensuring that the identity of the child is not disclosed at any time during investigation or trial. Disclosure with the special court's permission, if found to be in interest of child.

4. Before any medical examination, consent by or on behalf of the child must be obtained. Medical examination irrespective of whether a FIR/complaint has been filed under Section 27 of the POCSO Act. Privacy of the child must be respected and medical examination conducted in the presence of parent/guardian/person the child trusts. If such a person is not available then the

[63] POCSO Act, Section 33: Procedure and powers of special court—

(1) A special court may take cognizance of any offence, without the accused being committed to it for trial, upon receiving a complaint of facts which constitute such offence, or upon a police report of such facts.

(2) The special public prosecutor, or as the case may be, the counsel appearing for the accused shall, while recording the examination-in-chief, cross-examination or re-examination of the child, communicate the questions to be put to the child to the special court which shall in turn put those questions to the child.

(3) The special court may, if it considers necessary, permit frequent breaks for the child during the trial.

(4) The special court shall create a child-friendly atmosphere by allowing a family member, a guardian, a friend or a relative, in whom the child has trust or confidence, to be present in the court.

(5) The special court shall ensure that the child is not called repeatedly to testify in the court.

(6) The special court shall not permit aggressive questioning or character assassination of the child and ensure that dignity of the child is maintained at all times during the trial.

(7) The special court shall ensure that the identity of the child is not disclosed at any time during the course of investigation or trial, provided that for reasons to be recorded in writing, the special court may permit such disclosure, if in its opinion such disclosure is in the interest of the child.

Explanation. For the purposes of this subsection, the identity of the child shall include the identity of the child's family, school, relatives, neighbourhood, or any other information by which the identity of the child may be revealed.

(8) In appropriate cases, the special court may, in addition to the punishment, direct payment of such compensation as may be prescribed to the child for any physical or mental trauma caused to him or for immediate rehabilitation of such child.

(9) Subject to the provisions of this act, a special court shall, for the purpose of the trial of any offence under this act, have all the powers of a court of session and shall try such offence as if it were a court of session, and as far as may be, in accordance with the procedure specified in the CrPC, 1973 for trial before a court of session.

[64] POCSO Act, Section 32: Special Public Prosecutors—

(1) The state government shall, by notification in the Official Gazette, appoint a special public prosecutor for every special court for conducting cases only under the provisions of this act.

(2) A person shall be eligible to be appointed as a special public prosecutor under Subsection (1) only if he had been in practice for not less than 7 years as an advocate.

(3) Every person appointed as a special public prosecutor under this section shall be deemed to be a public prosecutor within the meaning of clause (u) of Section 2 of the CrPC, 1973 and provision of that Code shall have effect accordingly.

examination must be conducted in the presence of a woman nominated by the head of a medical institution. If the victim is a girl, examination should be conducted by a woman doctor.[65]

a) The police must record the statement of the child at the child's residence or where the child usually resides or a place of the child's choice, as far as practicable, by woman police personnel not below the rank of sub-inspector. Police personnel should not be in uniform. The statement should be recorded in simple language so that child comprehends what is recorded. Assistance of translator or interpreter should be taken if the child does not understand the language in which the statement is recorded. In case of the child having mental or physical disability, assistance of a special educator, and a person familiar with manner of the child's communication, or an expert, should be present. During examination of the child, police personnel should ensure that the child does not come in contact 'in any way with the accused'.

Wherever possible, statement should also be recorded by audio-video electronic means.[66]

1. Recording of statement by a Magistrate under Section 164 of the CrPC, 1973.[67] The magistrate must record the statement as spoken by the child. The presence of the advocate of the accused not required when statement is being recorded by audio-video electronic means.

[65] POCSO Act, Section 27: Medical examination of a child—

(1) The medical examination of a child in respect of whom any offence has been committed under this act, shall, notwithstanding that a first information report or complaint has not been registered for the offences under this act, be conducted in accordance with Section 164A of the CrPC, 1973.
(2) In case the victim is a girl child, the medical examination shall be conducted by a woman doctor.
(3) The medical examination shall be conducted in the presence of the parent of the child or any other person in whom the child reposes trust or confidence.
(4) Where, in case the parent of the child or other person referred to in Subsection (3) cannot be present, for any reason, during the medical examination of the child, the medical examination shall be conducted in the presence of a woman nominated by the head of the medical institution.

[66] POCSO Act, Section 24: Recording of statement of a child.

(1) The statement of the child shall be recorded at the residence of the child or at a place where he usually resides or at the place of his choice and as far as practicable by a woman police officer not below the rank of sub-inspector.
(2) The police officer while recording the statement of the child shall not be in uniform.
(3) The police officer making the investigation, shall, while examining the child, ensure that at no point of time the child come in the contact in any way with the accused.
(4) No child shall be detained in the police station in the night for any reason.
(5) The police officer shall ensure that the identity of the child is protected from the public media, unless otherwise directed by the special court in the interest of the child.

[67] CrPC, Section 164: Recording of confessions and statements—

1) Any metropolitan magistrate or judicial magistrate may, whether or not he has jurisdiction in the case, record any confession or statement made to him in the course of an investigation under this chapter or under any other law for the time being in force, or at any time afterwards before the commencement of the inquiry or trial, provided that any confession or statement made under this subsection may also be recorded by audio-video electronic means in the presence of the advocate of the person accused of an

a) There has to be an in-camera trial in the presence of family member, guardian, relative, or friend in whom the child has trust or confidence. The child should not be called repeatedly to testify. To ensure speedy trial Special Public Prosecutor and the advocate of the accused shall communicate questions to be asked of the child to the Special Court, and the Special Court shall in turn put them to the child. No aggressive questioning or character assassination is

---

offence; provided further that no confession shall be recorded by a police officer on whom any power of a magistrate has been conferred under any law for the time being in force.

2) The magistrate shall, before recording any such confession, explain to the person making it that he is not bound to make a confession and that, if he does so, it may be used as evidence against him; and the magistrate shall not record any such confession unless, upon questioning the person making it, he has reason to believe that it is being made voluntarily.

3) If at any time before the confession is recorded, the person appearing before the magistrate states that he is not willing to make the confession, the magistrate shall not authorize the detention of such person in police custody.

4) Any such confession shall be recorded in the manner provided in Section 281 for recording the examination of an accused person and shall be signed by the person making the confession; and the magistrate shall make a memorandum at the foot of such record to the following effect:

I have explained to (name) that he is not bound to make a confession and that, if he does so, any confession he may make may be used as evidence against him and I believe that this confession was voluntarily made. It was taken in my presence and hearing, and was read over to the person making it and admitted by him to be correct, and it contains a full and true account of the statement made by him. (Signed) A.B. Magistrate.

5) Any statement (other than a confession) made under Subsection (1) shall be recorded in such manner hereinafter provided for the recording of evidence as is, in the opinion of the magistrate, best fitted to the circumstances of the case; and the magistrate shall have power to administer oath to the person whose statement is so recorded. (5A)—

   1. In cases punishable under Section 354, Section 354A, Section 354B, Section 354C, Section 354D, Subsection (1) or Subsection (2) of Section 376, Section 376A, Section 376B, Section 376C, Section 376D, Section 376E or Section 509 of the IPC, the judicial magistrate shall record the statement of the person against whom such offence has been committed in the manner prescribed in Subsection (5), as soon as the commission of the offence is brought to the notice of the police, provided that if the person making the statement is temporarily or permanently mentally or physically disabled, the magistrate shall take the assistance of an interpreter or a special educator in recording the statement, provided further that if the person making the statement is temporarily or permanently mentally or physically disabled, the statement made by the person, with the assistance of an interpreter or a special educator, shall be videographed.

   2. A statement recorded under Clause (a) of a person, who is temporarily or permanently mentally or physically disabled, shall be considered a statement in lieu of examination-in-chief, as specified in Section 137 of the IEA, 1872 such that the maker of the statement can be cross-examined on such statement, without the need for recording the same at the time of trial.

6) The magistrate recording a confession or statement under this section shall forward it to the magistrate by whom the case is to be inquired into or tried.

allowed. The child's dignity is to be maintained at the time of trial.[68] Frequent breaks must be given to the testifying child, when found necessary. Evidence should be recorded within 30 days of cognizance being taken by the Special Court, that is, final report being filed; in case of delay, the Special Court is to record reasons. The trial should be completed [as far as possible] within 1 year of cognizance being taken by the Special Court. The Special Court should ensure that the child is not exposed 'in any way to the accused at the time of recording of the evidence'. The accused should be able to hear the testimony of the child and communicate with his lawyer. The evidence of a child may be recorded through video-conferencing, one-way mirror, curtain, or any other device.[69]

Section 27 provides the procedure for conducting the medical examination of a child in respect of whom any offence has been committed under the act. The specific provisions are:

1. In case the victim is a girl child, the medical examination has to be conducted by a woman doctor.
2. The medical examination must be conducted in the presence of the parent of the child or any other person in whom the child reposes trust or confidence.

Section 33 provides for the procedure to be adopted by the Special Court.

1. If required, the Special Court should permit frequent breaks for the child during the trial.
2. The special court should create a child-friendly atmosphere by allowing a family member, a guardian, a friend, or a relative, in whom the child has trust or confidence, to be present in the court.
3. The special court should ensure that the child is not called repeatedly to testify in the court.
4. The special court is not to permit aggressive questioning or character assassination of the child and must ensure that dignity of the child is maintained at all times during the trial.
5. The special court must ensure that the identity of the child is not disclosed at any time during the course of investigation or trial, unless it believes that such disclosure is in the interest of the child.

[68] POCSO Act, Section 34: Procedure in case of commission of offence by child and determination of age by special court—

(1) Where any offence under this act is committed by a child, such child shall be dealt with under the provisions of the JJ Act, 2000.
(2) If any question arises in any proceeding before the special court whether a person is a child or not, such question shall be determined by the special court after satisfying itself about the age of such person and it shall record in writing its reasons for such determination.
(3) No order made by the special court shall be deemed to be invalid merely by any subsequent proof that the age of a person as determined by it under Subsection (2) was not the correct age of that person.

[69] POCSO Act, Section 36: Child not to see accused at the time of testifying—

(1) The special court shall ensure that the child is not exposed in any way to the accused at the time of recording of the evidence, while at the same time ensuring that the accused is in a position to hear the statement of the child and communicate with his advocate. (2) For the purposes of Subsection (1), the special court may record the statement of a child through video conferencing or by utilizing single visibility mirrors or curtains or any other device.

Section 35 prescribes the period within which the evidence is to be recorded and the case is to be disposed and states:

1. The evidence of the child should be recorded within a period of 30 days of the special court taking cognizance of the offence.
2. The special court shall complete the trial within a period of 1 year from the date of taking cognizance of the offence.

Section 36 stipulates that the Special Court shall ensure that the child is not exposed in any way to the accused at the time of recording of the evidence.

Section 37 of the POCSO Act requires the special court to try cases *in camera* and in the presence of the parents of the child or any other person in whom the child has trust or confidence.

Section 38 also provides for the court to take the assistance of a translator or interpreter or a special educator as per the circumstances.

To provide for relief and rehabilitation of the child, as soon as the complaint is made to the SJPU or local police, they are required to make immediate arrangements to give the child care and protection such as admitting the child into a shelter home or the nearest hospital within 24 hours of the report. The SJPU or the local police are also required to report the matter to the CWC within 24 hours of recording the complaint, for long-term rehabilitation of the child (Sections 19[5] and 19[6]).[70]

The act casts a duty on the central and state governments to spread awareness through media, including the television, radio, and the print media, at regular intervals to make the general public, children, as well as their parents and guardians aware of the provisions of this act (Section 43).[71] The punishment for breaching this provision by the media may be prison terms ranging from 6 months to 1 year (Section 23).[72]

---

[70] Section 19(5): Where the SJPU or local police is satisfied that the child against whom an offence has been committed is in need of care and protection, then, it shall, after recording the reasons in writing, make immediate arrangement to give him such care and protection (including admitting the child into shelter home or to the nearest hospital) within twenty-four hours of the report, as may be prescribed.

Section 19(6): The SJPU or local police shall, without unnecessary delay but within a period of 24 hours, report the matter to the CWC and the special court or where no special court has been designated, to the court of session, including need of the child for care and protection and steps taken in this regard.

[71] Public awareness about the act: The central government and every state government, shall take all measures to ensure that—

(a) the provisions of this act are given wide publicity through media including the television, radio and the print media at regular intervals to make the general public, children as well as their parents and guardians aware of the provisions of this act;
(b) the officers of the central government and the state governments and other concerned persons (including the police officers) are imparted periodic training on the matters relating to the implementation of the provisions of the act.

[72] Procedure for media:

(1) No person shall make any report or present comments on any child from any form of media or studio or photographic facilities without having complete and authentic information, which may have the effect of lowering his reputation or infringing upon his privacy.

Table 5.3 Punishments for Offences Covered in the Act[73]

S. No.	Crime Head	Minimum Penalty	Maximum Penalty	Fine
1.	Penetrative sexual assault, Section 4[74]	7 years of imprisonment.	Imprisonment for life	Yes
2.	Aggravated penetrative sexual assault, Section 6[75]	10 years of rigorous imprisonment.	Rigorous imprisonment for life.	Yes
3.	Sexual assault, Section 8[76]	Imprisonment for 3 years.	Imprisonment for 5 years.	Yes
4.	Aggravated sexual assault, Section 10 (a)[77]	Imprisonment for a term of 5 years.	Imprisonment for a term of 7 years.	Yes
5.	Sexual harassment, Section 12[78]	Imprisonment of either description for a term.	Imprisonment for 3 years.	Yes
6.	Using a child for pornographic purposes, Section 14[79]	Imprisonment of either description.	Imprisonment for 5 years. In cases of second conviction it may extend for 7 years.	

(Cont'd)

(2) No reports in any media shall under the act, may permit such disclosure, if in its opinion such disclosure is in the interest of the child.

(3) The publisher or owner of the media or studio or photographic facilities shall be jointly and severally liable for the acts and omissions of his employee.

(4) Any person who contravenes the provisions of Subsection (1) or Subsection (2) shall be liable to be punished with imprisonment of either description for a period which shall not be less than six months but which may extend to 1 year or with fine or with both. disclose, the identity of a child including his name, address, photograph, family details, school, neighbourhood or any other particulars which may lead to disclosure of identity of the child, provided that for reasons to be recorded in writing, the Special Court, competent to try the case.

[73] Source: POCSO Act, 2012.

[74] Punishment for penetrative sexual assault—Whoever commits penetrative sexual assault shall be punished with imprisonment of either description for a term which shall not be less than 7 years but which may extend to imprisonment for life, and shall also be liable to fine.

[75] Punishment for aggravated penetrative sexual assault—Whoever commits aggravated penetrative sexual assault shall be punished with rigorous imprisonment for a term which shall not be less than 10 years but which may extend to imprisonment for life and shall also be liable to fine.

[76] Whoever, commits sexual assault, shall be punished with imprisonment of either description for a term which shall not be less than 3 years but which may extend to 5 years, and shall also be liable to fine.

[77] Whoever, commits aggravated sexual assault, shall be punished with imprisonment of either description for a term which shall not be less than 5 years but which may extend to 7 years, and shall also be liable to fine.

[78] Whoever, commits sexual harassment upon a child shall be punished with imprisonment of either description for a term which may extend to 3 years and shall also be liable to fine.

[79] (1) Whoever, uses a child or children for pornographic purposes shall be punished with imprisonment of either description which may extend to 5 years and shall also be liable to fine and in the event of

Table 5.3   (Cont'd)

S. No.	Crime Head	Minimum Penalty	Maximum Penalty	Fine
7.	Storage of pornographic material involving children, Section 15[80]	Imprisonment of either description for a term.	Imprisonment for 3 years.	Yes
8.	Abetment, Section 17[81]	Shall be punished with punishment provided for that offence.	N.A	N.A
9.	Attempt to commit an offence, Section 18[82]	Imprisonment of any description provided for the offence.	Term may extend to one half of the imprisonment for life or, as the case may be, one-half of the longest term of imprisonment provided for that offence.	Yes

(Cont'd)

second or subsequent conviction with imprisonment of either description for a term which may extend to 7 years and also be liable to fine.

(2) If the person using the child for pornographic purposes commits an offence referred to in Section 3, by directly participating in pornographic acts, he shall be punished with imprisonment of either description for a term which shall not be less than 10 years but which may extend to imprisonment for life, and shall also be liable to fine.

(3) If the person using the child for pornographic purposes commits an offence referred to in Section 5, by directly participating in pornographic acts, he shall be punished for rigorous imprisonment for life and shall also be liable to fine.

(4) If the person using the child for pornographic purposes commits an offence referred to in Section 7, by directly participating in pornographic acts, he shall be punished with imprisonment of either description for a term which shall not be less than 6 years but which may extend to 8 years, and shall also be liable to fine.

(5) If the person using the child for pornographic purposes commits an offence referred to in Section 9, by directly participating in pornographic acts, he shall be punished with imprisonment of either description for a term which shall not be less than 8 years but which may extend to 10 years, and shall also be liable to fine.

[80] Punishment for storage of pornographic material involving child—Any person, who stores, for commercial purposes any pornographic material in any form involving a child shall be punished with imprisonment of either description which may extend to 3 years or with fine or with both.

[81] Punishment for abetment—Whoever abets any offence under this act, if the act abetted is committed in consequence of the abetment, shall be punished with punishment provided for that offence. Explanation—An act or offence is said to be committed in consequence of abetment, when it is committed in consequence of the instigation, or in pursuance of the conspiracy or with the aid, which constitutes the abetment.

[82] Punishment for attempt to commit an offence: Whoever attempts to commit any offence punishable under this act or to cause such an offence to be committed, and in such attempt, does any act towards the commission of the offence, shall be punished with imprisonment of any description provided for the offence, for a term which may extend to one-half of the imprisonment for life or, as the case may be, one-half of the longest term of imprisonment provided for that offence or with fine or with both.

Table 5.3   (Cont'd)

S. No.	Crime Head	Minimum Penalty	Maximum Penalty	Fine
10.	Failure to report or record a case, Section 21[83]	Imprisonment of either description.	May extend to six months, and in case of any person in charge of any company or an institution, for a term of 1 year.	Yes
11.	False complaint or false information, Section 22[84]	Imprisonment for a term.	Six months, and in case of victimizing the child, it may extend to 1 year.	Yes

Implementation of the POCSO Act

For effective and better implementation, on the directions of the Ministry of Women and Child Development (MWCD) at various levels, the state governments/UTs have initiated action to set up the Special Courts/Children's Courts. As a result, as per information available so far, 18 states/UTs have designated Special Courts/Children's Court to try offences under the act.[85]

As the National Commission for Protection of Child Rights (NCPCR) and State Commissions for Protection of Child Rights (SCPCR) have been designated the role of

[83] Punishment for failure to report or record a case—

(1) Any person, who fails to report the commission of an offence under Subsection (1) of section 19 or section 20 or who fails to record such offence under Subsection (2) of Section 19 shall be punished with imprisonment of either description which may extend to six months or with fine or with both.

(2) Any person, being in-charge of any company or an institution (by whatever name called) who fails to report the commission of an offence under Subsection (1) of Section 19 in respect of a subordinate under his control, shall be punished with imprisonment for a term which may extend to 1 year and with fine.

(3) The provisions of Subsection (1) shall not apply to a child under this act.

[84] Punishment for false complaint or false information:

(1) Any person, who makes false complaint or provides false information against any person, in respect of an offence committed under Section 3, 5, 7 and Section 9, solely with the intention to humiliate, extort or threaten or defame him, shall be punished with imprisonment for a term which may extend to six months or with fine or with both.

(2) Where a false complaint has been made or false information has been provided by a child, no punishment shall be imposed on such child.

(3) Whoever, not being a child, makes a false complaint or provides false information against a child, knowing it to be false, thereby victimizing such child in any of the offences under this act, shall be punished with imprisonment which may extend to 1 year or with fine or with both.

[85] Available at http://www.dnaindia.com/analysis/editorial-dna-edit-the-c-in-pocso-1949876, (accessed on 13 January 2014).

monitoring authority under the act, the Ministry has been following up with state governments to expedite the process of formation of SCPCRs in their states. As a result, SCPCRs have been set up in 26 states/UTs.

Section 39 of the POCSO Act requires the state government to prepare guidelines for use of NGOs, professionals, and experts or persons to be associate with the pre-trial and trial stage to assist the child. On request from several state governments, model guidelines have also been issued to all the state governments/UT administrations, which can be adopted or adapted by them for better implementation of the act.

Section 39 of the POCSO Act reads:

> Subject to such rules as may be made in this behalf, the State Government shall prepare guidelines for use of non-governmental organisations, professionals and experts or persons having knowledge of psychology, social work, physical health, mental health and child development to be associated with the pre-trial and trial stage to assist the child.

In consonance with this section, the MWCD in September 2013 issued the Guidelines for Professional and Experts under the POCSO Act. These guidelines are based on the fundamental principles laid down in the Preamble of the act which include best interest of the child; right to life and survival; right to be treated with dignity and compassion; right to be protected from discrimination; right to be informed; right to participation; right to safety; right to compensation, and so on.

The guidelines have chapters on a broad range of topics, ranging from how to interview a child, to guidelines for dealing with a CSA victim by medical and health professionals, psychologists and mental health experts, social workers and support persons, child development experts, and legal representatives, and elucidates the importance of mandatory reporting.

These guidelines seem to complement the law in place and make it effective in creating a child-friendly approach, fulfilling the objectives of the act.[86]

Criminal Law Amendment Act, 2013 and POCSO

The CLA Act, 2013[87] provides for amendment of the IPC,[88] the CrPC,[89] the Indian Evidence Act (IEA), 1872[90], and the POCSO Act.[91] The 2013 act expands the definition of rape to include oral sex as well as the insertion of an object or any other body part into a woman's vagina, urethra, or

---

[86] Model Guidelines under Section 39 of the Protection of Children from Sexual Offences Act, 2012. Available at http://wcd.nic.in/act/POCSO%20-%20Model%20Guidelines.pdf (accessed on 16 November 2016).

[87] 'The Criminal Law (Amendment) Act, 2013'. Available at http://www.ycce.edu/admin/pdf/Anti-rape_bill_2013.pdf (accessed on 13 April 2015).

[88] Amends Sections 100, 228A, 354, 370, 370A, 375, 376, 376A, 376B, 376C, 376D, and 509 of the IPC. It also inserts new Sections 166A, 166B, 326A, 326B, 354A, 354B, 354C, and 354D in the IPC.

[89] Amends Sections 26, 54A, 154, 160, 161, 164, 173, 197, 273, 309, 327 and First Schedule of the CrPC. It also inserts new Sections 357B and 357C in the CrPC.

[90] Amends Sections 114, 119, and 146 of the IEA. It also inserts the new Section 53A in the act.

[91] Amends Section 42 of the POCSO Act.

anus.[92] The punishment for rape is 7 years at the least, and may extend up to life imprisonment. Any man who is a police officer, medical officer, army personnel, jail officer, public officer, or public servant, and found guilty of rape, may be imprisoned for at least 10 years. A punishment of life imprisonment extending to death has been prescribed for situations where the rape concludes with the death of the victim, or the victim entering into a vegetative state. Gang rape has been prescribed a punishment of at least 20 years under the newly amended sections. Marital rape is an exception to Section 375, provided that the wife is not under 15 years of age. Unless the wife is below 15 years of age, it is not rape. Thus, age of consent for wives has been reduced to 15, while for unmarried girls it is 18.[93]

As stated above, the IPC provides for a marital rape exception, which states that 'sexual intercourse or sexual acts by a man with his own wife, the wife not being under 15 years of age, is not rape'. No such exception has been grafted into the POCSO Act, under which an act of sexual intercourse with a person under 18 is an offence irrespective of the gender or age of the victim or the accused. Further, one of the grounds of aggravated penetrative sexual assault is penetrative sexual assault by 'a relative of the child through blood or adoption or marriage or guardianship or in foster care or having a domestic relationship with a parent of the child or who is living in the same or shared household with the child commits penetrative sexual assault on such child'. This is punishable with a fine and a minimum term of 10 years imprisonment, which may extend to life imprisonment. It is clear that under the POCSO Act, a spouse of a person below the age of 18 years can be prosecuted. Irrespective of whether the marriage has been contracted voluntarily, a person having sexual contact with a person under 18 years can be punished. Further, it is now mandatory for those who have information about the commission of a sexual offence to report it to the local police. Section 42A of the POCSO Act was introduced by the CLA Act,[94] Which implies that in case of conflict between the provisions of the POCSO Act and any other law, the former will override. Owing to Section 42A of the POCSO Act, the exception under the IPC will not apply.[95]

---

[92] Section 375—Under the new section, a man is said to commit rape if there is:

- Penetration of penis into vagina, urethra, mouth or anus of any person, or making any other person to do so with him or any other person;
- Insertion of any object or any body part, not being penis, into vagina, urethra, mouth or anus of any person, or making any other person to do so with him or any other person;
- Manipulation of any body part so as to cause penetration of vagina, urethra, mouth or anus or any body part of such person or makes the person to do so with him or any other person;
- Application of mouth to the penis, vagina, anus, urethra of another person or makes such person to do so with him or any other person;
- Touching the vagina, penis, anus or breast of the person or making the person touch the vagina, penis, anus or breast of that person or any other person.

[93] The Centre for Child and the Law (CCL)–NLSIU, 2013. This note has been prepared by Swagata Raha with inputs from Anuroopa Giliyal from the CCL, NLSIU.

[94] POCSO Act, Section 42A: Act not in derogation of any other law—The provisions of this act shall be in addition to and not in derogation of the provisions of any other law for the time being in force and, in case of any inconsistency, the provisions of this act shall have overriding effect on the provisions of any such law to the extent of its inconsistency.

[95] CCL-NLSIU, 2013.

It is imperative to note that the CLA Act has deleted the proviso to Section 376(2) of IPC,[96] that gave the discretion to the courts to reduce the period of sentence than the minimum required.

Child Marriages

Child Marriage can be regarded as a form of sexual abuse of children. Ameena, a child bride married to a 60-year-old man, was rescued by an alert flight attendant who noticed her sobbing during a flight between Hyderabad and New Delhi.[97] The bridegroom was arrested and sent to prison for marrying a minor without consent and later released on bail.

In Rajasthan, on the day of Akshay Tritiya, which is popularly known as Akha Teej, hundreds of child marriages are openly performed. Akha Teej is regarded as the most auspicious day for celebrating marriages. On this day even infants who have just been born or are only a few years old and cannot even sit or walk, are married. The child brides or the bridegroom do not understand

---

[96] Section 376(2): Whoever—

(a) being a police officer commits rape—

    (i) within the limits of the police station to which he is appointed; or
    (ii) in the premises of any station house whether or not situated in the police station to which he is appointed; or
    (iii) on a woman in his custody or in the custody of a police officer subordinate to him; or

(b) being a public servant, takes advantage of his official position and commits rape on a woman in his custody as such public servant or in the custody of a public servant subordinate to him; or

(c) being on the management or on the staff of a jail, remand home or other place of custody established by or under any law for the time being in force or of a woman's or children's institution takes advantage of his official position and commits rape on any inmate of such jail, remand home, place or institution; or

(d) being on the management or on the staff of a hospital, takes advantage of his official position and commits rape on a woman in that hospital; or

(e) commits rape on a woman knowing her to be pregnant; or

(f) commits rape on a woman when she is under 12 years of age; or

(g) commits gang rape, shall be punished with rigorous imprisonment for a term which shall not be less than 10 years but which may be for life and shall also be liable to fine, provided that the court may, for adequate and special reasons to be mentioned in the judgment, impose a sentence of imprisonment of either description for a term of less than 10 years. Explanation 1—Where a woman is raped by one or more in a group of persons acting in furtherance of their common intention, each of the persons shall be deemed to have committed gang rape within the meaning of this subsection. Explanation 2—'Women's or children's institution' means an institution, whether called an orphanage or a home for neglected woman or children or a widows' home or by any other name, which is established and maintained for the reception and care of woman or children. Explanation 3—'Hospital' means the precincts of the hospital and includes the precincts of any institution for the reception and treatment of persons during convalescence or of persons requiring medical attention or rehabilitation.

[97] Later, the battles for Ameena's custody were fought as much in news reports, opinion columns, and letters to the editor of newspapers as in courts. Questions were raised especially about Ameena's age, the validity of her marriage, and the applicability of secular laws to minority communities.

Table 5.4 Age at First Marriage Percentage Analysis of Specific Exact Age and Median Age at First Marriage, and Median Age at First Cohabitation with Spouse, According to Current Age, India, 2005–06

Current Age	Percentage Figures for Exact Age at First Marriage				Number of Respondents	Median Age at First Marriage	Median Age at First Cohabitation
	15	18	20	21			
15–19	11.9	N.A.	N.A.	N.A.	24,811	a*	a*
20–24	18.2	47.4	64.4	Na	22,779	18.3	18.5
25–29	25.4	55.4	72.4	78.6	20,417	17.4	17.8
30–34	28.5	61.2	76.5	82.0	17,656	16.8	17.4
35–39	31.0	63.4	79.1	84.3	15,866	16.6	17.2
40–44	32.4	64.6	79.8	85.5	13,049	16.5	17.1
45–49	32.9	64.2	79.1	85.1	9,807	16.5	17.3

Notes: a* = Omitted because less than 50 per cent of the women or men were married or began living with their spouse for the first time before reaching the beginning of the age group.

the solemnity of these ceremonies, but for elders it is the safest and most tested way of keeping property and money within the family and of preserving the 'chastity' of their daughters.

As can be seen from Table 5.4 (figures sourced from National Family Health Survey, 2005–06), more than half women are married before the legal minimum age of 18. Among women aged 20–49, the median age at first marriage is 17.2 years. By contrast, men in the same age group get married 6 years later, at a median age of 23.4 years. Sixteen percent of men aged 20–49 are married by age 18, 28 percent by age 20, and 58 percent by age 25. Women today are waiting slightly longer to marry. In the late 1990s, the median age at first marriage was 16.7 years, six months earlier than it is now. The median age at first marriage in India is almost 2 years higher for women aged 20–24 than for women aged 40–49. Urban women marry more than 2 years later than rural women; the median age at marriage among urban women aged 20–49 is 18.8 years, compared to 16.4 years among their rural counterparts.[98] The actual figures are probably much higher, as correct information is not often available. One of the major reasons for this incorrect information is that registration of marriages is not compulsory in many states and even where this is compulsory, this is not done because of several socio-cultural practices.

Early marriage is a form of sexual abuse of the girl child as they have to become mothers. Early motherhood denies the girl an opportunity for development and increases the risk of higher numbers of low-birth-weight babies, child deaths and disabilities, maternal deaths, gynecological problems, and an increased number of pregnancies to replace the lost children. Early marriage also deprives the girls of the opportunities of schooling; they are made to assume domestic and childcare responsibilities early, which hampers their intellectual and personality development.[99] The age at marriage is, therefore, indicative of the status of women.

[98] National Family Health Survey, 2005–06.

[99] Shanti Ghosh, 'Girl Child: A Lifetime of Deprivation and Discrimination', *Indian Journal of Social Work* II, no. 1 (January 1991).

Child marriages are currently dealing with by the PCMA, 2006 and by the various personal laws. The Indian Majority Act (IMA), 1875 lays down the age of majority as 18 years (Section 3). But in case of marriage, dower, divorce, and adoption, personal laws of parties regulate the age of majority. In 1929, the pressure exerted by social reformers had forced the British government to pass laws relating to child marriages. Taking into consideration the popular traditions and practices, the British government enacted the Child Marriage Restraint Act (CMRA), 1929, popularly known as the Sharda Act. This was an act to restrain the solemnization of child marriages. It was applicable to all Indians—Hindus, Muslims, and Christians. It prescribed the minimum age for marriage for both boys and girls. In 1929, the minimum age of marriage for girls was 15 and for boys it was 18. This position was maintained by the Hindu Marriage Act (HMA), 1955, which prescribed the same minimum age of marriage. This act prohibited the solemnization of child marriages but it did not declare these marriages either void or illegal. The punishment under the act was very mild. This was a weak legislation and could not achieve the desired result.[100] Child marriages were deeply entrenched in the society as a custom and the Sharda Act failed to make any dent in this practice.

The Child Marriage Restraint (Amendment) Act, 1978 was passed to provide more teeth to the act and to raise the minimum age of marriage. This amended act raised the minimum age of marriage by 3 years to make it 18 years for girls and 21 for boys.[101] This was still not considered enough and the PCMA was notified on 10 January 2007, thereby repealing the CMRA, to overcome the constraints of the former legislations in effectively dealing with the problem of child marriages in India and to put in place a comprehensive mechanism.[102]

Under JJ Act, 2015, a child in need of care and protection includes a child below 18 years, who is at imminent risk of marriage before attaining the age of marriage, and whose parents, family members, guardians, or any other person are likely to be responsible for solemnization of such a marriage.

Salient Features of the Prohibition of Child Marriage Act, 2006

1. To make a provision to declare child marriage as voidable at the option of the contracting party to the marriage, who was a child.
2. To provide a provision requiring the husband or, if he is a minor at the material time, his guardian to pay maintenance to the minor girl until her remarriage.
3. To make a provision for the custody and maintenance of children born of child marriages.
4. To provide that notwithstanding annulment of a child marriage by a decree of nullity under the proposed Section 3, every child born of such marriage, whether before or after the commencement of the proposed legislation, shall be legitimate for all purposes.
5. To empower the district court to add to, modify, or revoke any order relating to maintenance of the female petitioner and her residence and custody or maintenance of children, and so on.

[100] S. Saxena, 'Child Marriages in Rajasthan: A Challenge to Child Marriage Restraint Act', *A.I.R. Journal*, 2000.

[101] CMRA, Section 2(a) defines a child as a person who, if a male, has not completed 21 years of age, and if a female, has not completed 18 years of age.

[102] Government of India: MWCD, 'The Prohibition of Child Marriage Act, 2006', UNICEF. Available at http://www.unicef.org/india/Child_Marriage_handbook.pdf (accessed on 16 November 2016).

6. To make a provision for declaring the child marriage as void in certain circumstances.
7. To empower the courts to issue injunctions prohibiting solemnization of marriages in contravention of the provisions of the proposed legislation.
8. To make the offences under the proposed legislation cognizable for the purpose of investigation and for other purposes.
9. To provide for appointment of Child Marriage Prevention Officers by the state governments.
10. To empower the state governments to make rules for effectively administering the legislation.[103]

Under this law, the definition of child remains the same as the old law, that is, a child is a male under 21 years of age and a female under 18 years of age.[104]

Voidable Marriages

Section 3 of this act states that 'child marriages shall be voidable at the option of the contracting party who was a child at the time of the marriage'. It allows filing of a petition declaring the marriage void within 2 years of the child attaining majority. This means that a boy and/or girl who was a minor at the time of his/her marriage has the option of approaching the courts to declare the marriage null and void within 2 years of attaining adulthood.[105]

Rights of Children

Following the United Nations Convention on the Rights of the Child (UNCRC) and the national JJ Act, the PCMA declares that all children born are legitimate, including those born in void or voidable marriages.[106] The act further provides for appropriate orders for custody of any child born from the marriage, taking welfare and best interests of the child into consideration.[107]

Punishment

All the punishments for contracting a child marriage have been enhanced. The PCMA provides that any male adult above 18 years of age who marries a minor shall be punished with rigorous imprisonment of up to 2 years or with fine up to one hundred thousand rupees or with both.[108] Similar punishment of rigorous imprisonment and fine is prescribed for anyone who performs, conducts, directs, abets, promotes, permits the solemnization of, or negligently fails to prevent any child marriage. However, no woman can be punished with imprisonment.[109]

[103] The Statement of Objects and Reasons of the PCM Act, 2006.
[104] PCMA, Section 2(a).
[105] Law Commission of India, 'proposal to amend the Prohibition of Child Marriage Act, 2006, and Other Allied Laws', Report No. 205, February 2008.
[106] PCMA, Section 6.
[107] PCMA, Section 5.
[108] PCMA, Section 9.
[109] PCMA, Sections 10 and 11.

Injunctions

The act allows for injunctions to prohibit child marriages, including ex parte interim injunctions. While minors have an option of coming out of a marriage that is not of their choice, the act mandates the issuance of an injunction order to parties solemnizing the child marriage. However, the injunction order can only be given after the Court has issued a written notice and given adequate opportunity to the concerned parties to show cause against the issue of the injunction. At the same time, the act also provides that in case of any urgency, the Court shall have the power to issue an interim injunction without giving any notice under this section, and allows ex parte injunctions as well.[110]

The child marriage that has been solemnized in contravention of the injunction order is void ab initio, which means that it is void right in its inception.

Void Marriage

Section 12 provides that the marriage of a minor will be declared null and void in certain circumstances. These situations include where a child is a) taken or enticed out of the keeping of the lawful guardian; or (b) by force compelled, or by any deceitful means induced to go from any place; or (c) is sold for the purpose of marriage, and made to go through a form of marriage, or if the minor is married, after which the minor is sold or trafficked or used for immoral purposes. Further, Section 14 provides that any child marriage solemnized in contravention of injunction orders issued under Section 13, whether interim or final, shall be void ab initio.

Age of Marriage under Various Personal Laws

The personal laws in India are based on religion. Marriages among the Hindus[111] are regulated by the provisions of the HMA, 1955. A valid marriage between two Hindus can take place where the bridegroom has completed the age of 21 years and the bride has completed the age of 18 years, apart from other conditions like not having a living spouse, not being of unsound mind, and so on. Thus, neither party to a marriage amongst Hindus can any longer be of a child's age, that is, of less than 18 years of age, which is the age of majority. Any marriage made in contravention of the age limits has not been declared to be void or violable under other provisions of the act, but such marriages have been made punishable with simple imprisonment up to 15 days and fine up to one thousand rupees or with both. Both the bride and bridegroom are punishable if they marry before their eligible age. Since marriage can be solemnized only between two major persons, there is no question of obtaining consent of the guardian of the persons for the purpose of marriage under the act. But if the marriage of a girl has been solemnized before she attained the age of 15 years, she can repudiate

---

[110] Ruchira Goswami, 'Child Marriage in India: Mapping the Trajectory of Legal Reforms', 23 March 2010. Available at http://sanhati.com/excerpted/2207/ (accessed on 16 November 2016).

[111] The act applies to any person who is a Hindu by religion in any of its forms or developments (including a Virashaiva or a Lingayat or follower of the Brahma, Prarthana, or Arya Samaj), to any person who is Buddhist, Jain, or Sikh by religion, and to any person who is not a Muslim, Christian, Parsi, or Jew by religion.

the marriage after attaining 15 years but before attaining the age of 18, whether or not the marriage has been consummated. She can also seek divorce thereafter from her husband through the court.

In Muslim law, it is essential that parties at the time of marriage should have attained puberty, which is a biological fact to be ascertained by evidence. Puberty is generally taken to come at the age of 15 years. According to the Hanafi School of Law, the earliest stage of puberty is 12 years for boys and 9 years for girls. The marriage of a person below the age of puberty is to be solemnized by a guardian and such marriage is not void. A marriage arranged by the father or parental grandfather binds the minor. The minor cannot annul such marriage on attaining puberty if the guardian had acted in the interest of the minor. If a guardian other than the father or grandfather arranges the marriage, the minor can exercise the 'option of puberty' and repudiate the marriage within a reasonable time if it is not consummated.

Christian Marriage Act, 1872

As per the Christian Marriage Act (CMA), a valid marriage amongst Christians requires the boy to have completed 21 years and the girl to have completed 18 years. Further, a minor has been defined as a person who has not completed the age of 21 years and who is not a widower or widow. A minor under the act can marry with the consent of the father and, if he is dead, with the consent of the guardian, and if there is no guardian, with the consent of the mother.

Parsi Marriage and Divorce Act, 1936

As per the Parsi Marriage and Divorce Act (PMDA), a valid marriage amongst Parsis can take place between a boy who has completed the age of 21 years and a girl who has completed the age of 18 years. Since only major persons can marry under the Parsi law, there cannot be any child marriage among Parsis.

Special Marriage Act, 1954

As per the Special Marriage Act (SMA), the age of marriage under this act is 21 years for males and 18 years for females. Any marriage solemnized in contravention of the age requirement will be null and void and can be nullified by the court.

Foreign Marriage Act, 1969

Under this act a valid marriage can be effected in a foreign country or in a foreign ship in foreign territorial water between a boy who has completed the age of 21 years and a girl who has completed the age of 18 years at the time of the marriage.

Validity of Child Marriages

The marriages, if performed under the personal laws, are not void. The marriages are void only under the SMA and the PMDA, but under all the other personal laws, that is, under the HMA,

CMA, and the Muslim law, the marriages are valid. Marriage below the age of consent is valid under Christian law, provided it is with the consent of the guardians. Under Muslim law, every Muslim of sound mind, who has attained puberty, may be validly contracted in marriage by their guardians.[112] The persons concerned, as provided under Sections 3, 4, 5, and 6 of the act, can be punished but the marriage remains valid. If such child marriages had been rendered void, the sufferer would have been the bride as a stigma of 'already once married' would have been attached to her, and because the marriage would be illegal, she would not receive any maintenance.

Repudiation of Child Marriages

The HMA gives an option to the girl to opt out of a child marriage and repudiate it if her marriage was performed when she was below 15 years old. However, this has to be done before she attains the age of 18 years. The boys are not given such an option. Under Muslim law, a parent or guardian can validly arrange for the marriage of the child but the child has the option to repudiate the marriage on attainment of puberty. In the absence of evidence, puberty is generally assumed to be at 15 years.[113] A minor whose marriage has been contracted by any guardian other than the father or father's father has the option to repudiate the marriage on attaining puberty. The mere exercise of the option of repudiating such a marriage on attaining puberty does not act as dissolution of the marriage unless the act of repudiation has the approval of the court.[114]

Guidelines for Dealing with the Issue of Child Sexual Abuse

The National Human Rights Commission (NHRC) has laid down the following guidelines for the media in addressing the issue of dealing with CSA:[115]

1. The media should bring the issue of CSA into the realm of public knowledge and public debate. It is important that the issue of sexual abuse is presented as a serious violation of rights, not only as an offence against children.
2. The media should, through sensitive and meaningful projection and coverage of the issue, be instrumental in creating a sense of moral indignation and outrage over incidents of CSA. The media should also take care to ascertain the facts, context, and circumstances. A report on such sensitive issues should not be filed based on superficial interviews with persons supposedly witness to the incident.

[112] *Baillie*, Digest of Muhammedan Law, London, Pt 1 (1865), Pt II (1869), p. 50. Under the Shafei, Ithna Ashari, and Ismaili laws, the father or father's father can act as the marriage guardian for a minor. In so far as Hanafi law is concerned, the list is not so restricted and includes other relations.

[113] *Baillie*, p. 50. The lowest age of puberty according to its natural signs is 12 in males and 19 in females. When the signs do not appear both the sexes are held to be adult when they have completed their 15th year. See *Fatwa Alamgiri*, V, p. 93; *Md Idris* v. *State of Bihar*, 1980 Cr LJ 764.

[114] *Baillie*, p. 51. It has been held that no formal decree is required to confirm the exercise of option of repudiation by a spouse. However, an order of judge is necessary to give it the force of law. See *Mafizuddin Mondol* v. *Rahima Bibi*, (1933) 58 Cal LJ 73, 1934 AC 104; *Pirmahommad* v. *State of Madhya Pradesh*, AIR 1960 MP 24.

[115] Available at nhrc.nic.in/Documents/Guidelinesforthemedia.pdf (accessed on 16 November 2016).

3. The media should desist from the temptation to sensationalize or exaggerate a particular incident of child abuse.

4. When the media reports an incident of sexual abuse it should also report subsequently on actions taken by concerned authorities and continue to report till action is taken to punish the abusers.

5. The media should not unwittingly glorify the act of sexual abuse by giving undue prominence to the perpetrator.

6. The victim should not be further victimized or made to relive the trauma he/she has been through.

7. Under no circumstances should the media disclose or reveal the identity of the victim. Masking techniques should be used wherever the victim is made to give a first person account of his/her experience. The victim, relatives, and concerned persons must be assured of confidentiality.

8. The media should not create a prurient interest in the sexuality of the child by image or innuendo.

9. The child should not come across as a passive entity.

10. Besides drawing attention to the problem of CSA, the media also needs to enlighten the public on what can be done to prevent such incidents and what needs to be and must be done if such an incident has taken place, including providing information on legal or other remedies.

11. The media should provide its target audience with full knowledge about the rights of the child and the legal remedies available to a child in the unfortunate event of a case of CSA.

12. The media needs to develop a system wherein viewers/audience can comment/evaluate on the quality and impact of the programmes being aired and telecast.

13. The media should document and widely disseminate best practices on prevention of CSA, action taken against abusers, work of selected NGOs, and so on.

14. In all reporting, the media must be guarded by the principle of best interest of the child, as required in the CRC.[116]

Some Initiatives Relating to Child Victims and Witnesses of Sexual Offences

In the past it was noticed that the testimonies of the child victims were not being recorded sensitively by the police/judge/prosecutor/magistrate. The recording of the statements of child victims required a special provision in the CrPC. There was no such provision before 2012. Trained personnel were needed to interview the victimized children. The language of the child had to be understood by the legal system. Before 2012, the natural habitat of the victim was generally disturbed, which was a source of trauma to the child. The delays in the system at every stage further added to the trauma of the child victim. There were several cases pending in the courts as the trials went on for years. In several cases the girls had become adults by the time the final judgment came through. The investigation of trial of sexual offences had to be made time-bound. Special courts needed to be set up.

---

[116] Available at nhrc.nic.in/Documents/Guidelinesforthemedia.pdf (accessed on 16 November 2016).

The minor child was required to give his/her evidence in the presence of the accused as well as several 'strangers' in the court. In the jurisprudence of fair trial in India, exceptions of hearsay evidence were accepted in cases of dying declaration, and some other cases. Therefore, in case of a child victim's testimony, such an exception needed to be made. A guardian ad litem or a representative of the child's interest could be appointed to help the child in court proceedings and to look after the best interest of the child.

Courts have held that a child witness, if found competent and reliable to depose to the facts and such evidence, could be the basis of conviction. In other words, even in the absence of oath, the evidence of a child witness can be considered under Section 118 of the IEA, provided that such witness is able to understand the questions. Therefore, the evidence of a child witness and his/her credibility would depend upon the circumstances of each case. The only precaution that the Court should bear in mind while assessing the evidence of a child witness is that the witness must be a reliable one and his/her demeanour must be like any other competent witness, so that there is no likelihood of the child being tutored.

Further, Section 118 of the IEA envisages that all persons shall be competent to testify, unless the Court considers that they are prevented from understanding the questions put to them or from giving rational answers to these questions, because of tender years, extreme old age, disease—whether of mind, or any other cause of the same kind.[117] However, a child of tender age can be allowed to testify if s/he has the intellectual capacity to understand questions and give rational answers. Recently, the Mumbai High Court upheld the testimony of a 12-year old in a murder case, as the lone eyewitness account of the 12-year old grandson helped nail the two murder accused. The court held that the 'child witness was a witness of truth'. The court reiterated yet again that depositions by children who have the capacity to understand things and their consequences cannot be discarded as evidence in a criminal trial. The child's testimony was corroborated by other evidence of strangulation marks and stone injury.

While the law recognizes the child as a competent witness, a child particularly at a tender age, say of 6 years, who is unable to form a proper opinion about the nature of the incident because of immaturity of understanding, is not considered by the court to be a witness whose sole testimony can be relied upon without other corroborative evidence. The evidence of the child is required to be evaluated carefully because s/he is an easy prey to tutoring. Therefore, the court looks for adequate corroboration to his testimony from other evidence.

United Nations Guidelines on Justice in matters involving Child Victims and Witnesses of Crime 2005 recognize that children are particularly vulnerable and need special protection, assistance, and support appropriate to their age, level of maturity, and unique needs in order to prevent further hardship and trauma that may result from their participation in the criminal justice process. The UN Guidelines further state that girls are particularly vulnerable and may face

---

[117]   IEA, Section 118: Who may testify—

All persons shall be competent to testify unless the Court considers that they are prevented from understanding the questions put to them, or from giving rational answers to those questions, by tender years, extreme old age, disease, whether of body or mind, or any other cause of the same kind. Explanation—A lunatic is not incompetent to testify, unless he is prevented by his lunacy from understanding the questions put to him and giving rational answers to them.

discrimination at all stages of the judicial system. The UN Guidelines stress the importance of ensuring dignity, including physical, mental, and moral integrity of the child witness; the judicial process should be sensitive to the child's age, wishes, understanding, gender, sexual orientation, ethnic, cultural, religious, linguistic and social background, caste, socio-economic condition, as well as special needs of the child including health, ability, and capacities.

So far as examination of the testimony of witnesses, including child witnesses, in cases involving sexual offences are concerned, the same has been the subject matter for consideration before the Supreme Court of India as well as High Courts in several cases. Extensive guidelines have been laid down by the Supreme Court as well as the Delhi High Court in several judgments with regard to every stage of a criminal investigation as well as the trials. These guidelines in cases regarding sexual offences laid down judicial precedents; additional guidelines have been compiled in the decision dated 29 September 2009 in Crl.A.No.121/2008, *Virender v. The State of NCT of Delhi*.[118]

The directions from various judgments of the Supreme Court and High Courts are as follows:

1. To create a child-friendly environment, separate rooms be provided within the Court precincts where the statement of the child victim can be recorded (Ref: *Court On Its Own Motion* v. *State & Anr*[119]).

2. In case of any disability of the victim or witness involving or impairing communication skills, assistance of an independent person who is in a position to relate to and communicate with such disability requires to be taken.

3. The trials into allegations of commission of rape must invariably be in-camera. No request in this behalf is necessary (Ref: *State of Punjab* v. *Gurmit Singh*[120]).

4. The Committal Court shall commit such cases to the Court of Sessions preferably within 15 days after the filing of the charge-sheet (Ref: *Court On Its Own Motion* v. *State & Anr*[121]).

5. The child witness should be permitted to testify from a place in the courtroom which is other than the one normally reserved for other witnesses.

6. To minimize the trauma of a child victim or witness, the testimony may be recorded through video conferencing or by way of a closed-circuit television (CCTV). If this is not possible, a screen or some arrangement may be made so that the victims or the child witness do not have to undergo seeing the body or face of the accused. The screen which should be used for the examination of the child witness or a victim should be effective and installed in such manner that the witness is visible to the trial judge so that he may notice the demeanour of the witness. Single visibility mirrors may be utilized which, while protecting the sensibilities of the child, shall ensure that the defendant's right to cross examination is not impaired (Ref: *Sakshi* v. *UOI*[122]).

7. Competency of the child witness should be evaluated and order be recorded thereon.

---

[118] (2009) 4 JCC 2721.

[119] (2010) ILR 6 Delhi 193.

[120] AIR 1996 SC 1393.

[121] (2007) 4 JCC 2680.

[122] AIR 2004 SC 3566.

8. The trial court is required to be satisfied and ought to record its satisfaction that the child witness understands the obligation to speak the truth in the witness box. In addition to the above, the court is required to be satisfied about the mental capacity of the child at the time of the occurrence concerning which s/he is to testify, as well as about the ability to receive an accurate impression thereof. The court must be satisfied that the child witness has sufficient memory to retain an independent recollection of the occurrence and a capacity to express in words or otherwise his or her memory of the same. The court has to be satisfied that the child witness has the capacity to understand simple questions which are put to it about the occurrence. There can be no manner of doubt that record of the evidence of the child witness must contain such satisfaction of the court.

9. As far as possible, avoid disclosing the name of the prosecutrix in the court orders to save further embarrassment to the victim of the crime; anonymity of the victim of the crime must be maintained as far as possible throughout.

10. The statement of the child victim shall be recorded promptly and at the earliest by the concerned Magistrate and any adjournment shall be avoided and in case the same is unavoidable, reasons are to be recorded in writing (Ref: *Court on Its Own Motion* v. *State of N.C.T. of Delhi*[123]).

11. The court should be satisfied that the victim is not scared and is able to reveal what has happened to her when she is subjected to examination during the recording of her evidence. The court must ensure that the child is not concealing portions of the evidence for the reason that she is bashful or ashamed of what has happened to her.

12. It should be ensured that the victim who is appearing as a witness is at ease so as to improve upon the quality of his/her evidence and enable his/her to shed hesitancy to depose frankly, so that the truth is not camouflaged on account of embarrassment and the shame being felt by the victim at detailing the occurrence.

13. Questions should be put to a victim or to the child witness which are not connected to the case to make him/her comfortable and to depose without any fear or pressure.

14. The trial judge may permit, if deemed desirable, to have a social worker or other friendly, independent, or neutral adult in whom the child has confidence to accompany the child who is testifying (Ref: *Sudesh Jakhu* v. *K.C.J. & Ors*[124]).

   a. This may include an expert supportive of the victim or child witness in whom the witness is able to develop confidence; this person should be permitted to be present and accessible to the child at all times during his/her testimony. Care should be taken that such person does not influence the child's testimony.

15. Persons not necessary for proceedings, including extra court staff, to be excluded from the courtroom during the hearing.

16. Unless absolutely imperative, repeated appearance of the child witness should be prevented. It should be ensured that questions which are put in cross examination are not designed to embarrass or confuse victims of rape and sexual abuse (Ref: *Sakshi* v. *UOI*[125]).

[123] W.P. (C) 9767/2009, decided by the Delhi High Court on 15 July 2009.
[124] 62 (1996) DLT 563.
[125] 62 (1996) DLT 563.

17. Questions to be put in cross examination on behalf of the accused, in so far as they relate directly to the offence, should be given in writing to the presiding officer of the court, who may put them to the victim or witnesses in a language which is clear and is not embarrassing (Ref: *Sakshi* v. *UOI*[126]).

18. The examination and cross examination of a child witness should be carefully monitored by the presiding judge to avoid any attempt to harass or intimidate the child witness.

19. It is the duty of the court to arrive at the truth and subserve the ends of justice. The courts have to take a participatory role in the trial and not act as mere tape recorders to record whatever is being stated by the witnesses. The judge has to monitor the proceedings in aid of justice in a manner that something which is not relevant is not unnecessarily brought into record. Even if the prosecutor is remiss in some ways, the court can control the proceedings effectively so that the ultimate objective, that is, the truth, is arrived at. The court must be conscious of serious pitfalls and dereliction of duty on the part of the prosecuting agency. Upon failure of the prosecuting agency showing indifference or adopting an attitude of aloofness, the judge must exercise the vast powers conferred under Section 165 of the IEA and Section 311 of the CrPC to elicit all necessary materials by playing an active role in the evidence collecting process (Ref: *Zahira Habibulla H. Sheikh & Anr.* v. *State of Gujarat & Ors.*[127]).

20. The judge is expected to actively participate in the trial and elicit necessary materials from the witnesses at the appropriate context which he feels necessary for reaching the correct conclusion. The judge has uninhibited power to put questions to the witness either during chief examination or cross examination or even during re-examination for this purpose. If a judge feels that a witness has committed an error or slip, it is the duty of the judge to ascertain whether it was so, for, to err is human and the chances of erring may accelerate under stress of nervousness during cross examination. (Ref: *State of Rajasthan* v. *Ani alias Hanif & Ors.*[128]).

21. The court should ensure that the embarrassment and reservations of all those concerned with the proceedings, which includes the prosecutrix, witnesses, and counsels, does not result in camouflaging the ingredients of the offence. The judge has to be conscious of these factors and rise above any such reservations on account of embarrassment to ensure that they do not cloud the truth and the real actions which are attributable to the accused persons.

22. The court should ascertain the spoken language of the witness as well as range of vocabulary before recording the deposition. In making the record of the evidence the court should avoid use of innuendos or such expressions which may be variably construed. For instance—*gandi harkatein* or *batamezein* have no definite meaning. Therefore, even if it is necessary to record the words of the prosecutrix, it is essential that what those words mean to her and what is intended to be conveyed are sensitively brought out.

23. The court should ensure that there is no use of aggressive, sarcastic language or a gruelling or sexually explicit examination or cross examination of the victim or child witness. The court should come down heavily to discourage efforts to promote specifics and/or illustration,

---

[126] 62 (1996) DLT 563.
[127] AIR 2006 SC 1367.
[128] AIR 1997 SC 1023.

by any of the means, of the offending acts, which would traumatize the victim or child witness and affect their testimony. The court should ensure that no element of vulgarity is introduced into the court room by any person or the record of the proceedings.

24. In order to elicit complete evidence, a child witness may use gestures. The courts must carefully translate such explanation or description into written record.

25. The victim of child abuse or rape or a child witness, while giving testimony in court, should be allowed sufficient breaks as and when required (Ref: *Sakshi* v. *UOI*).[129]

26. Cases of sexual assaults on females should be placed before lady judges wherever available (Ref: *State of Punjab* v. *Gurmit Singh*[130]).

27. To the extent possible, efforts should be made that the staff in the courtroom concerned with such cases are also of the same gender.

28. The judge should be balanced, humane, and should ensure protection of the dignity of the vulnerable victim. There should be no expression of gender bias in the proceedings. No humiliation of the witness should be permitted either in the examination-in-chief or the cross-examination.

29. A case involving a child victim or child witness should be prioritized and appropriate action taken to ensure a speedy trial to minimize the length of the time for which the child must endure the stress of involvement in a court proceeding. While considering any request for an adjournment, it is imperative that the court considers and gives weight to any adverse impact which the delay or the adjournment or continuance of the trial would have on the welfare of the child.

In addition, certain general guidelines have been mandated, which read as follows:[131]

1. Effort should be made to ensure that there is continuity of persons who are handling all aspects of the case involving a child victim or witness, including such proceedings which may be out of the criminal justice system. This may involve all steps commencing from the investigation to appointment of the prosecutor to whom the case is assigned as well as the judge who is to conduct the trial.

2. The police and the judge must ascertain the language with which the child is conversant and make every effort to put questions in such language. If the language is not known to the court, efforts to bring an independent translator in the proceedings, especially at the stage of deposition, should be made.

3. It must be ensured that the number of times a child victim or witness is required to recount the occurrence is minimized to the absolutely essential. For this purpose, right at the inception, a multidisciplinary team involving the investigating officer and the police, social services resource personnel, as well as the prosecutor should be created and utilized in the investigation

---

[129] AIR 1997 SC 1023.

[130] AIR 1997 SC 1023.

[131] *State* v. *Rahul*, CRL. L.P. 250/2012, date of decision: 15 April 2013, by Honourable Ms. Justice Gita Mittal, Honourable Mr. Justice J.R. Midha.

[132] *State* v. *Rahul*.

and prosecution of such cases involving a child either as a victim or a witness. This would create and inspire a feeling of confidence and trust in the child.

4. The child victim shall not be separated from his/her parents/guardians nor taken out from his/her environment on the ground of 'Ascertaining voluntary nature of statement' unless the parents/guardian are reported to be abusive or the Magistrate thinks it appropriate in the interest of justice (Ref: *Court on Its Own Motion* v. *State of N.C.T. of Delhi*[132]).

5. Courts in foreign countries have evolved several tools including anatomically correct illustrations and figures (as dolls). No instance of such assistance has been pointed out in this court. Extensive literature with regard to such aids being used by foreign courts is available. Subject to assistance from experts, it requires to be scrutinized whether such tools can be utilized in this country during the recording of the testimony of a child victim witness so as to accommodate the difficulty and diffidence faced. This aspect deserves serious attention of all concerned as the same may be a valuable tool in the proceedings to ensure that the complete truth is brought out.

6. No court shall detain a child in an institution meant for adults (Ref: *Court on Its Own Motion* v. *State of N.C.T. of Delhi*[133]). This would apply to investigating agencies as well.

7. The judge should ensure that there is no media reporting of the in-camera proceedings. In any case, sensationalization of such cases should not be permitted.

All these concerns apply to all stages of a child witness's court appearance, including the competency examination of the child and evaluation of his/her response thereto. The best interest of the child must be the complete focus of every action, especially court proceedings, and the decision must be considered.[134]

There have been several initiatives and best practices relating to child victims and witnesses, as mentioned next.

Vulnerable Victims and Witness Court in Delhi[135]

The protocol captioned as Guidelines for Recording of Evidence of Vulnerable Witnesses in Criminal Matters is in vogue for the operationalization of the Child Victim Court Room in the District Courts in Delhi. Currently, these guidelines are being applied in the Child Witnesses Court Room in the District Courts at Karkardooma. Delhi has now become the first city in the country to have its own 'Vulnerable Witness Deposition Complex' which has been designed 'to provide protection, privacy, confidentiality and comfort to vulnerable witnesses in an in-camera atmosphere' in cases of sexual offences. Delhi has also laid down guidelines for recording of evidence of vulnerable witnesses.[136] The objectives of the guidelines are:

---

[133]   *State* v. *Rahul.*

[134]   *State* v. *Rahul.*

[135]   Aneesha Mathur, 'City Anchor: A Courthouse to Allow Child Witnesses to Depose without Fear', *Indian Express.* Available at http://www.indianexpress.com/news/city-anchor-a-courthouse-to-allow-child-witnesses-to-depose-without-fear/1003530 (accessed on 16 November 2016).

[136]   Delhi High Court, Delhi Committee.

1. securing best interests of the child;
2. eliciting complete, accurate, and reliable evidence;
3. minimizing harm or secondary traumatization of the witness;
4. ensuring rights of the accused to a fair trial.

Special Children's Court in Goa[137]

In Goa, the matters related to sexual abuse are dealt with in-camera so as to protect the victim from the alleged offender. The atmosphere in the court room is free and informal, the President does not wear a black coat or a gown, and advocates and police appear in civil dress. The court has the power to award compensation to child victims. The victims and witnesses are helped in getting familiarized with the court settings, be comfortable with the court proceedings, and also informed about the roles that would be played by key persons in the Court, namely the Judge, defense lawyer, prosecutor, and others. The court ensures that the questioning is short and clear so as to not confuse the child witnesses. Child witnesses below 8 years are permitted to respond to leading questions facilitated by social workers. Aggressive questioning of child witnesses during cross examination is avoided and permission to ask direct questions to children below 10 years in cross-examination is denied. Such questions are asked through the Presiding Officer or a person with whom the child is comfortable with. Views of the child witnesses are allowed to be heard and respected, their privacy is respected, and inconvenience to them is minimized. The President sees to it that the child is prepared for the testimony and is capable as a witness. The Prosecutor is given sufficient time to prepare the child witness and adjournment is given when the child is found to be uncomfortable. The testimony of the child is recorded soon after charges are framed and the identity of the victim is protected.

The challenges in the Goa courts are:

1. The need to change the negative mindset of the Presiding Officer, Prosecutor, Police, advocates, and parents of child victims.
2. Effective protection of child victims, lack of infrastructure, lack of space for the child to sit with the family till the testimony is recorded, lack of place for witnesses to sit till they are called in the Court, lack of regular Presiding Officers to conduct the matters, and the lack of training for the Presiding Officer and the Prosecutor.[138]

Intellectually Challenged Children before the Criminal Justice System as Victims and Witnesses—A *Chunauti*[139]

Children with mental and other developmental disabilities, living in institutions, are perfect targets for neglect, sexual abuse, and assault. A sexual assault is a severe, heinous breach of

---

[137] *Report of Judicial Colloquium on Children's Court*, organized by CCL–NLSIU, Bangalore, in collaboration with the Law Commission of India, with the support of UNICEF India Country Office, New Delhi, 26 February 2012.

[138] *Report of Judicial Colloquium on Children's Court.*

[139] Chunauti means 'challenge'.

trust and faith for the mentally deficient victim children, by persons who are their 'caretakers'. What happened at Kavdas, Kalyani, and Mamta Homes and other homes throughout the state of Maharashtra in India, is an abdication of responsibility and dereliction of duty by the duty bearers including the state, the DWCD, the CWCs, the inspection authorities, the state advisory boards, and other caretakers of the most vulnerable and marginalized unfortunates of our society, our MDC. It was a collective failure of the structures and system. The children saw the institution as a 'place of refuge'. They put complete faith and trust in the *Babas*, *Pappas*, and *Mummys*, but it resulted in abuse, starvation, and also deaths.

Project Chunauti, is a field action project working for the rehabilitation and reintegration of 93 victims of abuse. Project Chunauti is a unique partnership project between several stakeholders. The activities done through the project include:

1. assessment of the children's immediate needs and providing them services;
2. counselling to address trauma and behavioural issues;
3. life skill education;
4. therapeutic inputs—dance therapy;
5. providing therapeutic toys;
6. vocational inputs—gardening and mehendi;
7. occupational therapy;
8. sending children to a regular school through SSA;
9. special education;
10. developing care plans;
11. regular monitoring and reporting to the High Court;
12. capacity building of staff;
13. advocacy for policy changes.

After 2 years of these interventions, the children have calmed down and settled into the Home. They are slowly overcoming their trauma and negative experiences of the past. These victims and witnesses gave evidence in court during the criminal proceedings. This was a landmark event setting a precedent for mentally challenged and hearing and speech impaired children to give evidence.

On 31 March 2013, six accused were convicted. Death sentence was awarded to the founder of the orphanage for murder of an inmate and gang rape of five mentally challenged girls, including three minors. The others were sentenced to imprisonment ranging from life to 7 years.[140] On 6 December 2013, the Thane judgment was given. Six accused were held guilty of charges ranging from rape, sodomy, attempt-to-murder, and culpable homicide, to torture and neglect. Their sentences ranged from 5 years to life in prison. Delivering the judgment, the Principal Sessions Judge said: 'The children were subject to such form of tortures that they could not raise their voice against the people torturing them. This sentence should send correct message in the society.'[141]

---

[140] See also http://www.mid-day.com/articles/panvel-orphanage-founder-gets-death-sentence-in-girls-gang-rape-case/205292#sthash.zO8EJISc.dpuf (accessed on 16 November 2016).

[141] Available at http://ibnlive.in.com/news/kavdas-orphanage-case-six-convicted-two-acquitted/437997-3-237.html (accessed on 16 November 2016).

On appeal to the High Court of Mumbai, the death sentence to the founder was commuted but the conviction for rape by the lower court was upheld. Of the 10 accused, 5 were acquitted of all charges.

Children are gradually coming out of the trauma. They have expressed their interests in the areas of education and vocational skills. This has led to the Project developing further linkages to provide these skills to the children.

Judicial Trends

Judgments Relating to Child Marriages

P. Venkataramana v. State[142]

The question placed before the Full Bench was 'whether a Hindu marriage governed by the provisions of the HMA, 1955, where the parties to the marriage or either of them are below their respective ages as set out in Clause (iii) of Section 5 to the HMA, is void ab initio and is no marriage in the eye of law'.

It was held that clause (iv) inserted in Subsection (2) of Section 13 clearly indicates the mind of the legislature that the violation of clause (iii) of Section 5 is not to render the marriage either void or voidable; but in case the bride was below the age of 15 years at the time of solemnization of the marriage and she has repudiated the marriage after attaining the age of 18 years, a decree for divorce can be obtained whether the marriage was consummated or not. If the marriage performed in contravention of clause (iii) of Section 5 was void ab initio, there was no necessity to insert clause (iv) in Subsection (2) of Section 13. It may be pointed out that, by insertion of this clause (iv), the legislature has given to the Hindus an option of what is known in Mohammedan law as Khyar-ul-bulugh (option of puberty). But the legislature has not proceeded on the footing that the marriage between the spouses, when it is performed in violation of clause (iii) of Section 5, is void ab initio. This amendment reinforces and confirms the view that we are taking on a pure interpretation of the different provisions of the HMA even as it stood prior to its amendment by the Marriage Laws (Amendment) Act, 1976.

It was held for these reasons that the decision of the Division Bench of the High Court in *P.A. Saramma v. Ganapatulu*[143] does not lay down the correct law and that any marriage solemnized in contravention of clause (iii) of Section 5 is neither void nor voidable, the only consequence being that the persons concerned are liable for punishment under Section 18, and further, if the requirements of clause (iv) of Subsection (2) of Section 13, as inserted by the 1976 Act are satisfied, at the instance of the bride, a decree for divorce can be granted. Barring these two consequences, one arising under Section 18 and the other arising under clause (iv) of Subsection (2) of Section 13, after the enactment of the 1976 Act, there is no other consequences whatsoever resulting from the contravention of the provisions of clause (iii) of Section 5.

---

[142] AIR 1977 AP 43 (FB).
[143] AIR 1975 AP 193.

Smt Sushila Gothala v. State of Rajasthan and Others[144]

This petition was a PIL. The petitioner had approached the court under Article 226 of the Constitution of India for issuance of direction to the respondents to immediately stop the menace of child marriage in Rajasthan in an effective manner, and further for a direction to punish the officer who was responsible for not prohibiting the child marriages, as per the provisions of the CMRA. On the occasion of Akha Teej[145] every year, child marriages are performed in contravention of the act as it is considered an auspicious day for performing marriages.

The writ petition was disposed of with the observation that this social evil can be eradicated only if the people of Rajasthan themselves revolt against this age-old custom, which is primitive in nature and cannot be justified by any civilized society. The court further held that as per Section 13 of the act, if the child marriage prevention officers have not been appointed, the government should consider the feasibility of making the provisions of the act more stringent, and punishment for contravention of the act should be severe.

William Rebello v. Agnelo Vaz And Another[146]

An application was filed for dispensing with the age limit of the marriage and to give necessary directions to the civil registration authority to register the marriage of the applicants. As Applicant No. 1 was not 21 years of age and could not marry, the court was requested to remove the impediment as both the parents had given consent for such marriage. In the application, it was also contended that as a result of friendship between Applicants No. 1 and 2, Applicant No. 2 had become pregnant and the pregnancy was 20 weeks old.

The application for the removal of the impediment was entertained under the provisions of Article 5 of the Portuguese Civil Code and the trial judge, on the basis of the submissions made, considered the application and thought it fit to remove the impediment, and accordingly allowed the application.

The Director, Tamil Nadu State Judicial Academy v. State Of Tamil Nadu[147]

In the instant case, the High Court of Madras gave various directions to different authorities, including those to judicial magistrates, juvenile justice boards, and legal services authorities.

1. Trials of cases of trafficking should generally be *in-camera* and the Magistrate/Board should avoid disclosing the name of the prosecutrix and their orders, to save embarrassment to the victim, and anonymity of the victim of the crime should be maintained throughout.

[144] AIR 1995 Rajasthan 90.

[145] The festival of Akha Teej is observed every year in the state of Rajasthan. It falls sometimes in the month of April and sometimes in the month of May.

[146] AIR 1996 Bombay 204.

[147] Writ Petition No. 36807 of 2006.

2. The evidence of the child should be taken *in-camera*, as per Section 327[148] of the CrPC; and translators should be provided if the child is from another state and does not speak the local language. It should be ensured that the Special Courts/ Boards have a child-friendly and supportive atmosphere while taking the child's evidence. Preferably, an elder woman who inspires the confidence of the child may be present.

Sheeba Abidi v. State And Another[149]

The instant case laid down the following:

1. It permitted the judge to use a videotaped statement of the child (taped in the presence of a child-support person).
2. The child was allowed testifying via CCTV or from behind a screen to obtain a full and candid account of the acts complained of.
3. Cross-examination of a minor should only be carried out by the judge based on written questions submitted by the defence upon perusal of the minor's testimony.
4. Whenever a child is required to give testimony, sufficient breaks should be allowed as and when required by the child.

Jitender Kumar Sharma v. State and Another[150]

In this case, both the boy and the girl who were minors had fallen in love, eloped together, and gotten married as per Hindu rites and ceremonies.

---

[148] Section 327. Court to be open.

(1) The place in which any criminal court is held for the purpose of inquiring into or trying any offence shall be deemed to be an open one

   1.   Subs. by Act 45 of 1978, s. 27, for Magistrate (w. e. f. 18- 12- 1978).
   2.   Subs. by s. 27 ibid. fpr Certain words (w. e. f. 18. 12. 1978).
   3.   Renumbered by Act of 1983, s. 4.
      Court, to which the public generally may have access, so far as the same can conveniently contain them, provided that the presiding Judge or Magistrate may, if he thinks fit, order at any stage of any inquiry into, or trial of, any particular case, that the public generally, or any particular person, shall not have access to, or be or remain in, the room or building used by the Court.

(2) Notwithstanding anything contained in Subsection (1), the inquiry into and trial of rape or an offence under Section 376, Section 376A, Section 376B, Section 376C, or Section 376D of the IPC shall be conducted in camera: Provided that the presiding judge may, if he thinks fit, or on an application made by either of the parties, allow any particular person to have access to, or be or remain in, the room or building used by the court.

(3) Where any proceedings are held under Subsection (2), it shall not be lawful for any person to print or publish any matter in relation to any such proceedings, except with' the previous permission of the court.]

[149] *Sheeba Abidi* v. *State, National Capital Territory (nct) of Delhi & Anr.* =113 (2004) Delhi Law Times.
[150] 171 (2010) DLT 543.

The Division Bench of the Delhi High Court considered the issue of validity of such a marriage. The Court opined that a Hindu marriage which is not void under the HMA would continue to be valid, provided the provisions of Section 12 of the PCMA[151] are not attracted. A marriage in contravention of Clause (3) of Section 5 of the HMA was neither void nor voidable. However, Section 3[152] of the PCMA had introduced the concept of a voidable marriage. Since this was a secular law, it would override the provisions of the HMA. In view of Section 3 thereof, which made child marriages voidable at the option of the contracting party being a child, the Court observed that the position contained in Clause (3) of Section 5 of the HMA, holding that such a marriage was neither void nor voidable, was the legal position prior to the enactment and enforcement of the PCMA, and after this enactment the marriage in contravention of Clause (3) of Section 5 of the HMA would not be ipso facto void but could be void if any of the circumstances enumerated in Section 12 of the PCMA was triggered. The legislature made a specific provision for void marriages under certain circumstances but did not render all child marriages void. It also introduced the concept of a voidable child marriage, clearly indicating that all child marriages are not void.

Kammu v. State of Haryana and Others[153]

In this case, the question of the custody of a Muslim girl of 15 years was raised before the Punjab and Haryana High Court. The Petitioners argued that according to Section 12(a) of the PCMA[154]

---

[151] Section 12: Marriage of a minor child to be void in certain circumstances—Where a child, being a minor

(a) is taken or enticed out of the keeping of the lawful guardian; or
(b) by force compelled, or by any deceitful means induced to go from any place; or
(c) is sold for the purpose of marriage; and made to go through a form of marriage or if the minor is married after which the minor is sold or trafficked or used for immoral purposes, such marriage shall be null and void.

[152] Section 3: Child marriages to be voidable at the option of contracting party being a child—

(1) Every child marriage, whether solemnized before or after the commencement of this act, shall be voidable at the option of the contracting party who was a child at the time of the marriage, provided that a petition for annulling a child marriage by a decree of nullity may be filed in the district court only by a contracting party to the marriage who was a child at the time of the marriage.
(2) If at the time of filing a petition, the petitioner is a minor, the petition may be filed through his or her guardian or next friend along with the child marriage prohibition officer (CMPO).
(3) The petition under this section may be filed at any time but before the child filing the petition completes 2 years of attaining majority.
(4) While granting a decree of nullity under this section, the district court shall make an order directing both the parties to the marriage and their parents or their guardians to return to the other party, his or her parents or guardian, as the case may be, the money, valuables, ornaments and other gifts received on the occasion of the marriage by them from the other side, or an amount equal to the value of such valuables, ornaments, other gifts and money:
       Provided that no order under this section shall be passed unless the concerned parties have been given notices to appear before the district court and show cause why such order should not be passed.
[153] Crl. Writ Petition No. 623 of 2009 (O&M), decided on 16 February 2010.
[154] Section 12: Marriage of a minor child to be void in certain circumstances—Where a child, being a minor (a) is taken or enticed out of the keeping of the lawful guardian.

the marriage of the minor child was void because the girl was enticed away by the Respondent from the lawful custody of the father.

The Punjab and Haryana High Court held that the matter was to be seen in reference to the application of the law to Muslims. As per Section 2 of the Muslim Personal Law (Shariat) Application Act (MPLSA Act), 1937[155], only the Muslim Personal Law (MPL) would apply to Muslims in case of marriage and guardianship. The Court further stated, 'It is apparent that the rule of decision in cases where the parties are Muslims shall be the Muslim Personal Law (Shariat) that would be applicable for the purpose of marriage and dissolution of marriage etc ... No doubt that as per the Prohibition of Child Marriage Act, 2006, marriage of minor is void in certain circumstances and specially as per Section 12(a) of the act if the child is taken or enticed out of the keeping of the lawful guardian and the same is applicable to all Citizens of India. It nevertheless did not repeal the Muslim Law.'[156]

The Court then held that the MPLSA Act is a special act, whereas the PCMA, is a general act. The general provisions would have to yield to specific provisions. It is a well-settled proposition of law that the special act would have predominance over the general act.

In the present case, however, it was stated that the said marriage was without the consent of the father. According to Mohammedan law, if the girl is less than 15 years old, the consent of the father is necessary and in the absence of the same, the marriage is void. The factum of this marriage was not denied. The only assertion was that the said marriage was without the consent of her guardian, that is, her Wali. But in this case, since the girl was over the age of 15 years, she could choose to marry without the consent of her natural guardian.

By holding that Personal Law would supersede the PCMA, which is a secular law, the Punjab and Haryana High Court failed to recognize the legislative intent to curb the social evil of child marriage. However, luckily, the other High Courts have interpreted the conflict between personal laws and the PCMA differently.

Court on its Own Motion (Lajja Devi) v. State[157]

In this case the Delhi High Court discussed the plight of girls subjected to child marriage and observed:

---

[155] Section 2: Application of Personal Law to Muslim—Notwithstanding any customs usage to the contrary, in all questions (save questions relating to agricultural land) regarding intestate succession, special property of females, including personal property inherited or obtained under contract of gift or any other provision of Personal Law, marriage, dissolution of marriage, including talaq, illa, zihar, lian, khula and mubaraa, maintenance, dower, guardianship gifts, trusts and trust properties, and wakfs (other than charities and charitable institutions and charitable and religious endowments) the rule of decision in cases where the parties are Muslims shall be the Muslim Personal Law (Shariat).

[156] Section 21: Repeal and savings—

(1) The CMRA, 1929 (19 of 1929) is hereby repealed.
(2) Notwithstanding such repeal, all cases and other proceedings pending or continued under the said act at the commencement of this act shall be continued and disposed of in accordance with the provisions of the repealed act, as if this act had not been passed.

[157] W.P. (Crl.) No. 338/2008, Crl. M.C. No. 1001/2011, Crl. M.A. No. 3737/2011, W.P. (Crl.) No. 821/2008, Crl. M.A. No.8765/2008, and WP (Crl.) No. 566/2010.

The purpose and rationale behind the Prohibition of Child Marriage Act, 2006 is that there should not be a marriage of a child at a tender age as he/she is neither psychologically nor physically fit to get married. There could be various psychological and other implications of such marriage, particularly if the child happens to be a girl. In actuality, child marriage is a violation of human rights, compromising the development of girls and often resulting in early pregnancy and social isolation, with little education and poor vocational training reinforcing the gendered nature of poverty. Young married girls are a unique, though often invisible, group. Required to perform heavy amounts of domestic work, under pressure to demonstrate fertility, and responsible for raising children while still children themselves, married girls and child mothers face constrained decision making and reduced life choices. Where a girl lives with a man and takes on the role of caregiver for him, the assumption is often that she has become an adult woman, even if she has not yet reached the age of 18.

Some of the ill-effects of child marriage were summarized by the High Court as:

1. Girls who get married at an early age are often more susceptible to the health risks associated with early sexual initiation and childbearing, including HIV and obstetric fistula. Obstetric fistula can also be caused by the early sexual relations associated with child marriage, which take place sometimes even before menarche.
2. Young girls who lack agency, status, personal autonomy, power, and maturity are often subjected to domestic violence, sexual abuse including rape, and social isolation.
3. Early marriage almost always deprives girls of their education or meaningful work, which contributes to persistent poverty. A lack of education also means that young brides often lack knowledge about sexual relations, their bodies, and reproduction, exacerbated by the cultural silence surrounding these subjects.
4. Child marriage denies the girl the ability to make informed decisions about sexual relations, planning a family, and her health. It perpetuates an unrelenting cycle of gender inequality, sickness, and poverty.
5. Getting the girls married at an early age when they are not physically mature leads to highest rates of maternal and child mortality.
6. Early marriages are also linked to wife abandonment and increased levels of divorce or separation, and child brides also face the risk of being widowed by their husbands who are often considerably older. In these instances, the wife is likely to suffer additional discrimination as in many cultures divorced, abandoned, or widowed women suffer a loss of status, and may be ostracized by society and denied property rights.

The Court then lamented at the state of the legal position regarding child marriages in India, and said:

It is distressing to note that the IPC, 1860 acquiesces child marriage. The exception to Section 375 specifically lays down that sexual intercourse of man with his own wife, the wife not being under 15 years of age is not rape, thus ruling out the possibility of marital rape when the age of wife is above 15 years. On the other hand, if the girl is not the wife of the man, but is below sixteen, then the sexual intercourse even with the consent of the girl amounts to rape? It is rather shocking to note the specific relaxation is given to a husband who rapes his wife, when she happens to be between 15–16 years. This provision in the IPC, 1860 is a specific illustration of legislative endorsement and sanction to child marriages. Thus by keeping a lower age of consent for marital intercourse, it seems that the legislature has legitimized the concept of child marriage.

With regard to the other statutory provisions related to child marriage, the Court noted, '... the Indian Majority Act, 1875 lays down 18 years as the age of majority but the non-obstante clause excludes marriage, divorce, dowry, and adoption from the operation of the act with the result that the age of majority of an individual in these matters is governed by the personal law to which he is a subject.' This saving clause silently approves of the child marriage, which is in accordance with the personal law and customs of the religion. The Dowry Prohibition Act (DPA), 1961 also contains provisions, which give implied validity to minor's marriages. The words 'when the woman was minor' used in Section 6(1)(c) reflects the implied legislative acceptance of the child marriage. Criminal Procedure Code, 1973 also contains a provision, which incorporates the legislative endorsement of child marriage. The code makes it obligatory for the father of the minor married female child to provide maintenance to her in case her husband lacks sufficient means to maintain her. The insertion of option of dissolution of marriage by a female under Section 13(2)(iv) to the HMA through an amendment in 1976 indicates the silent acceptance of child marriages. The option of puberty provides a special ground for divorce for a girl who gets married before attaining 15 years of age and who repudiates the marriage between 15 and 18 years.

The court said that the holding of a child marriage as voidable and not void by the PCMA leads to an anomalous situation where on the one hand child marriage is treated as an offence which is punishable under law, and on the other hand, it still treats this marriage as valid, that is, voidable till it is declared as void.

The court further held that these provisions containing legal validity provide an assurance to the parents and guardians that the legal rights of the married minors are secured. The acceptance and acknowledgement of such legal rights itself, and providing a validity of child marriage, defeats the legislative intention to curb the social evil of child marriage. Thus, even after the passing of the new act, certain loopholes still remain; the legislations are weak, as they do not actually prohibit child marriage. It can be said that though the practice of child marriage has been discouraged by the legislations, it has not been completely banned.

T. Sivakumar v. the Inspector of Police[158]

In this case five issues were raised for answers, mentioned as follows.

1. Whether a marriage contracted by a person with a female of less than 18 years could be said to be valid marriage and the custody of the said girl be given to the husband (if he is not in custody)?
2. Whether a minor can be said to have reached the age of discretion and thereby walk away from the lawful guardianship of her parents and refuse to go in their custody?
3. If yes, can she be kept in the protective custody of the state?
4. Whether in view of the provisions of JJ Act, a minor girl who claims to have solemnized her marriage with another person, would not be a juvenile in conflict with law, and whether the Court, dealing with a writ of habeas corpus, has the power, in violation of the procedure mandated by the JJ Act, to entrust the custody of the minor girl to a person who contracted

---

[158] (2011) 5 CTC 689.

the marriage with the minor girl and thereby committed an offence punishable under Section 18 of the HMA and Section 9 of the PCMA?

5. Whether the principles of Section 17 and 19(a) of the Guardians and Wards Act, 1890 could be imported to a case arising out of the alleged marriage of a minor girl, admittedly in contravention of the provisions of the HMA?

The Madras High Court referred to the provisions of HMA and the PCMA. It observed that the position under the HMA as well as the CMRA was that these acts do not declare marriage of a minor either as void or voidable, and such marriages are treated as valid. In this legal scenario, the Hindu Minority and Guardianship Act, 1956 also provided that the husband of a wife is her natural guardian. After taking note of this legal position, the Court discussed the reason for enacting the PCMA, and noted, 'It is manifestly clear that this Act is secular in nature which has crossed all barriers of personal laws'. Section 3 of this act makes child marriages voidable at the option of the contracting party being a child. The Court noted that this was a significant departure from the position in the HMA. By declaring that the PCMA shall apply to all citizens, the Parliament has intended to allow the PCMA to override the provisions of the HMA to the extent of inconsistencies between these two enactments. This is manifest from the statement of Objects and Reasons of the PCMA, which reads as follows.

1. The CMRA, 1929 was enacted with a view to restraining solemnisation of child marriages. The act was subsequently amended in 1949 and 1978 in order, inter alia, to raise the age limit of the male and female persons for the purpose of marriage. The act, though restrains solemnization of child marriages yet it does not declare them to be void or invalid. The solemnization of child marriage is punishable under the act.

2. There has been a growing demand for making the provisions of the act more effective and the punishment thereunder more stringent so as to eradicate or effectively prevent the evil practice of solemnization of child marriages in the country. This will enhance the health of children and the status of women. The National Commission for Women in its Annual Report for the year 1995–96 recommended that the Government should appoint Child Marriage Prevention Officers immediately. It further recommended that –

   a. the punishment provided under the act should be made more stringent;
   b. marriages performed in contravention of the act should be made void; and
   c. the offences under the act should be made cognizable.

3. The NHRC undertook a comprehensive review of the existing act and made recommendations for comprehensive amendments therein vide its Annual Report 2001–2002. The central government, after consulting the state governments and union territory administrations on the recommendations of the National Commission for Women and the NHRC, had decided to accept almost all the recommendations and give effect to them by repealing and re-enacting the CMRA, 1929.

The Madras High Court was of the view that the PCMA, being a special law, will have overriding effect over the HMA to the extent of any inconsistency between the two enactments. Therefore, the Court decided that Section 3 of this act would have overriding effect over the HMA and the marriage with a minor child would not be valid but voidable and would become valid if after attaining the age of majority both parties to the marriage elect to accept the marriage, or if within 2 years from the date of attaining 18 years in the case of the female and 21 years in the case of the male, a petition is not filed before the District Court under Section 3(1) of the PCMA for annulling the marriage. Until such an event of acceptance of the marriage or lapse of limitation period, the marriage shall continue to remain voidable. If the marriage is annulled as per Section 3(1) of the PCMA, the same shall take effect from the date of marriage and, in such an event, in the eye of law there shall be no marriage at all between the parties at any point of time.

Judgments on Other Non-commercial Forms of Child Sexual Abuse

Ghanshyam Mishra v. The State[159]

The High Court, in this case, had enhanced the sentence as the perpetrator of the offence had taken advantage of the teacher–student relationship he shared with the victim.

Tukaram & Another v. The State of Maharashtra (Mathura's Case)[160]

Mathura, a girl aged between 14 and 16 years, was raped by two policemen of Desaigunj police station where she had gone along with others to register a complaint. The sessions court held that the prosecution had failed to prove its case, and that Mathura was a 'shocking liar' whose testimony is riddled with falsehood and improbabilities and that, of her own free will, she had surrendered her body to a police constable. The medical examination showed old injuries on the hymen, and no semen stains were traced.

In an appeal, the High Court, while convicting the accused, observed:

> Mere passive or helpless surrender of the body and its resignation to the other's lust induced by threats or fear cannot be equated with the desire or will, nor can it furnish an answer by the mere fact that the sexual act was not in opposition to such desire or violation. On the other hand, taking advantage of the fact that Mathura was involved in a complaint filed by her brother and that she was alone at the police station at the dead of the night, it is more probable that the initiative for satisfying sexual desire must have proceeded from the accused and that the victim Mathura must not have been a willing party to the act of sexual intercourse. Her subsequent conduct in making a statement immediately not only to her relatives but also to the members of the crowd leave no manner of doubt that she was subjected to forcible sexual intercourse.

The Supreme Court set aside this conviction on the grounds that sexual intercourse was not proved to amount to rape in the present case and that no offence was brought home. It further held that there were no circumstances available which made out a case of fear on the part of the girl and there was no finding that she was put into fear of death or hurt. Therefore, Section 375(3) of the IPC did not apply. This judgment was severely criticized by women's organizations and led to the amendments of rape laws in India. Section 155(4) of the IEA, which permitted the previous sexual history/character of the victim to be adduced as evidence to establish consent or otherwise, was repealed as a consequence to this judgment.

---

[159] AIR 1957 Orissa 78.
[160] (1979) 2 SCC 143, AIR 1979 SC 185.

Gorakh Daji Ghadge v. The State of Maharashtra[161]

This was a case where a father had raped his 13-year-old daughter in their home. The Mumbai High Court held that seminal emission is not necessary to establish rape. What is necessary to establish rape is that there must be penetration. The High Court has also dealt with the father–daughter relationship and stated that: 'Crimes in which women are victims need to be severely dealt with and in extreme cases such as this when the accused, who is the father of the victim girl, has thought it fit to "deflower" his own daughter of tender years to gratify his lust, then only a deterrent sentence can meet the ends of justice.'

Yashwant Rao v. State of MP[162]

There was a rape of a minor girl aged around 7 or 8 years. It was held that there was no legal compulsion to look for corroboration of the evidence.

The trends of these decisions reflect that the approach and the attitude towards the rights of the child are gradually progressing beyond mere technicalities. But, there is still a long way to go.

In one of the most outstanding cases of CSA,[163] the Delhi High Court held that when a father, in perverted company, sexually molested and abused his daughter over a period of time, his acts amounted to acts against the order of nature, and charges could be framed under Section 377 of the IPC along with Sections 354 and 100 of the IPC, though not under Section 376. This decision was reached after considering comparable legislation of Western Australia, Canada, Washington State, Massachusetts, the Michigan Statute, British law, and others. The Court, after observing on the inadequacies of our archaic system of examination in court, laid down specific guidelines and directions for the trial judge to follow while hearing the case to avoid harassment, anxiety, and embarrassment to the child psyche.[164]

In another case, a 4-year-old girl was subjected to oral sex, rape, and sodomy, which resulted in her death. The Delhi High Court set aside the judgment of the trial court of culpable homicide not amounting to murder. This judgment was appealed in the Supreme Court and the Supreme Court imposed a life sentence upon both the accused for the offence of culpable homicide not amounting to murder.[165]

The Supreme Court set aside the Delhi High Court order of acquittal, holding that the report of the doctor, who conducted the autopsy with meticulous precision, and the evidence of the investigating officer about recovery of articles, require to be believed unless shown to be unreliable. The trial of sexual abuse cases is conducted in such an insensitive manner that a sexually abused child, rather than being treated for her own trauma, has to fight the adversarial system and end up being further traumatized.[166]

---

[161] 1980 Cr LJ 1380.
[162] 1993 (Suppl 1) SCC 520.
[163] *Smt. Sudesh Jhaku v. K.C.J. and Others*, (1998) Cr LJ 2428.
[164] *Smt. Sudesh Jhaku v. K.C.J. and Others*.
[165] 1120, 1998.
[166] *State, Government of NCT of Delhi v. Sunil and Another Appeal*.

The child has to be cross-examined by the defence lawyer who may use different strategies to get the answers desired. Lack of proper understanding of the law among the judges and insensitivity to child rights has resulted in the accused being discharged in several CSA cases. The judges do not at all consider the issue of the child's trauma. Besides, the offences of sexual assault are generally tried by the criminal justice system under three different sections, namely rape, attempt to rape, and molestation, depending upon the proximity of molestation.[167]

Narayanamma v. State of Karnataka[168]

The Supreme Court did not enhance the sentence of 3 years rigorous imprisonment passed by the trial court. It was held that merely because the prosecutrix was simple enough to repose confidence in the accused persons and stayed with them in a room in a hotel, it cannot be held that she was a consenting party.

Delhi Domestic Working Women's Forum v. UoI[169]

The Supreme Court laid broad parameters in this case in assisting rape victims. The Court indicated the inherent defects in the present system as:

1. complaints are being handled roughly and not given due attention;
2. the victims are, more often than not, humiliated by the police; and
3. the experience of furnishing evidence in court has been negative and destructive.

The guiding principles suggested by the Court are summarized next.

The complainant of sexual assault is to be provided with legal representation; it being important to secure continuity of assistance by ensuring that the same person who looked after the complainant's interest in the police station represents her up to the end of the case.

1. Legal assistance is to be provided at the police station as the victim would be in a state of distress.
2. The police should be under a duty to inform the victim of her right to representation before any questions are asked of her and the police report should state so.
3. Victims who do not have their own lawyers should be provided with a list of advocates at the police station.
4. The Court, upon application, shall appoint the advocate by the police at the earliest convenient moment.
5. In all rape trials anonymity of victims must be maintained as far as necessary.
6. It is necessary, with regard to the Directive Principles contained under Article 38(1) of the Constitution, that victims are awarded compensation by the court on conviction of the offender.

---

[167] *State, Government of NCT of Delhi v. Sunil and Another Appeal.*
[168] (1994) 1 SSC 728.
[169] (1995) 1 SCC 14, 18–21.

State of Punjab v. Gurmit Singh[170]

This case was with regard to the gang rape of a girl under 16 years of age. The Supreme Court, in this case, settled several important points of law. First, it stated that the courts cannot overlook the fact that in case of sexual offences, the delay in lodging an FIR can be due to a variety of reasons, partly because of the reluctance of the prosecutrix and her family members to go to the police and complain about an incident which concerns the reputation of the prosecutrix and the honour of her family. Secondly, it also held that there is no requirement of law to insist upon corroboration of the statement of the prosecutrix for conviction of an accused and that corroborative evidence is not an imperative component of judicial credence in every case of rape.

While dealing with the importance of in-camera trial in rape cases, the Supreme Court observed that a trial in camera would not only be in keeping with the self-respect of the victim of the crime and in tune with the legislative intent, but it is also likely to improve the quality of the evidence of a prosecutrix because she would not be so hesitant or bashful to depose frankly as she may be in an open court under the gaze of the public.

Childline India Foundation & Anr v. Alan John Waters & Ors (The Anchorage Case)[171]

Duncan Grant set up the Anchorage Shelter Home in Mumbai in 1995, that Alan Waters visited frequently. Police investigation revealed that two British nationals, Grant and Waters, used to run the Anchorage Shelters, which housed a large number of street children aged between 8 and 18 years. William Michael D'Souza, an Indian, and a former pimp for homosexual tourists, was the manager of the Shelters. The investigation revealed that Grant and Waters were sexually abusing the children under their care and that a large number of foreign paedophiles were regularly visiting the Shelters and taking the children to Goa, where also the children were being sexually abused. The acts of abuse documented by the police investigation were: (a) oral sex forcibly performed on the boys; (b) forced manipulation of the boys' penis; (c) boys made to forcibly manipulate the accused's penis; (d) sadistic beatings of the boys; (e) biting of the boys for perverse pleasure; and so on.[172]

The Sessions Court Case

In March 2006, Justice Paranjape of a Mumbai Sessions Court sentenced Grant and Waters to 6 years in prison on the charge of sodomy and sexually abusing five minor boys at the Anchorage Shelter Home. Justice Paranjape fined Grant and Waters a fine of Rs. 3.2 million each. Of this sum, Rs 500,000 each was to be used for the rehabilitation of two boys who were residents of

---

[170] AIR 1996 SC 1393.

[171] *Childline India Foundation & Anr.* v. *Alan John Waters & Ors*, on 18 March 2011, Bench: P. Sathasivam, B.S. Chauhan, Supreme Court of India, Criminal Appellate Jurisdiction, Criminal Appeal Nos. 1208–1210 of 2008.

[172] Available at http://www.childlineindia.org.in/anchorage-case-history-updated.htm (accessed on 16 November 2016).

Anchorage and whose testimony in court was crucial to the case. The two boys spoke in clear terms about the prolonged abuse they suffered at the hands of the accused, the nature of the sexual acts perpetrated on them, and their desperation and poverty, which prevented them from leaving the shelter or filing a complaint. The court also convicted William Michael D'Souza, manager of the shelter, for assaulting the children and abetting in the conspiracy, and sentenced him to 3 years of rigorous imprisonment and a fine of Rs 6,500.[173] The Sessions Court stated that a deterrent punishment was being imposed in order to help 'wipe out the name of India from the map of sex tourism. Let paedophiles all over the world know that India should not be their destination in future.' Lawyers, academics, and the public hailed this judgment as a landmark judgment in its field.[174]

Grant and Waters then challenged the conviction in the Bombay High Court, which acquitted them in 2008.

The Bombay High Court Case

Allan Waters and Duncan Grant filed an appeal at the Bombay High Court against the state. In their judgment, the honourable judges stated:

1. The testimony of the two boys, which was the basis for the Trial Court's judgment, cannot be considered reliable as their testimonies recorded by the Police subsequent to the FIR was not consistent with what they recorded with Meher Pestonjee, freelance journalist, and Maharukh Adenwala prior to the FIR being lodged. The Court said that this amounted to improving the testimony and was not corroborative, as contended by the Prosecution.
2. The acts that the boys' testimony reported were ruled to not indicate a definitive crime under Section 377.

The accused were therefore acquitted of all charges.

This judgment was highly criticized on the following grounds:

1. The learned judges ignored the settled position of law as to how evidence of child victims of sexual violence is to be appreciated. Instead, they applied a completely unrealistic yardstick in evaluating that evidence. The judges had not considered that the victims were illiterate street children and could not be put to the same test as an educated adult.
2. The learned judges had also held that since no complaint was made for a long time, the FIR was delayed, and the child witnesses did not run away from the shelter though they were free to do so, it suggested that that no sexual abuse took place. The learned judges completely ignored the fact that the victims of sexual abuse were vulnerable and defenceless street children who were so desperate to get a roof over their heads that they were prepared to put up sexual abuse.

---

[173] Available at http://www.hindu.com/2006/03/19/stories/2006031904371000.htm (accessed on 16 November 2016).

[174] Available at http://www.childlineindia.org.in/anchorage-case-history-updated.htm (accessed on 16 November 2016).

3. The CSA in institutions is widespread, and yet prosecutions are notoriously rare and convictions are rarer still. The victims are under the control of the paedophiles; they are vulnerable and embarrassed by what has happened to them; they are scared that if they complain they will lose their shelter and food which they need to survive in the cities; they lack support, and ultimately do not depose in court, either because they are too scared to do so, or because they have been bribed/pressurized by the accused. Most victims are illiterate, which only compounds the problems of gathering evidence and putting up a strong case. Most of these problems are systemic and endemic to this situation. However, in the few cases where these problems have been overcome, the courts have let the people down by disbelieving the victims on minor technical grounds. Unless this changes, the most vulnerable category of our people will continue to be exploited and paedophiles will never be brought to justice.

The Supreme Court Judgment

An appeal was filed by the Maharashtra Government against the Mumbai High Court judgment in the Anchorage case.

The Supreme Court rejected the arguments of Duncan and Waters and sentenced them to finish their time in jail. In a landmark order, the Supreme Court said, 'Children are the greatest gift to humanity. The sexual abuse of children is one of the most heinous crimes.' The Supreme Court also confirmed the conviction and sentence of 3-year jail awarded by the trial court to another accused, William D'Souza, who had already served the term.[175]

Govind Shripat Maraskolhe v. The State of Maharashtra[176]

The complainant registered a complaint of kidnapping of his daughter, aged about 14 years, by the accused/appellant, aged about 25 years, and offence was registered under Sections 363 and 366 of the IPC. The victim was traced and brought to the police station and her statement was recorded, which revealed that the accused had a sexual affair with her. Thus, offence punishable under Section 376 of the IPC was added to the report already lodged.

The Appellant argued that he had a love affair with the prosecutrix and she was a consenting party to the relationship. He submitted that the prosecutrix did not resist being taken away by him and was a willing party.

The Bombay High Court held that the prosecutrix in the present case was below the age of 16 years at the time of incident and thus the Appellant could not claim benefit of her alleged consent for his sexual advances towards her. When an accused cohabits with a girl below the age of 16, her consent, even if spelt out by circumstances, is immaterial or irrelevant. Even if consent exists, the nature of such consent cannot absolve the accused from guilt. The Court went on to observe, 'Child rape cases are cases of perverse lust for sex where even innocent children are not spared in pursuit of sexual pleasure. It should, therefore, be considered a crime against humanity.'

---

[175] Available at http://www.childlineindia.org.in/anchorage-case-history-updated.htm (accessed on 16 November 2016).

[176] (2010) ALL MR (Cri) 907.

The court then upheld the sentence whereby the appellant was convicted for offences punishable under Sections 376, 363, and 366 of the IPC and sentenced to rigorous imprisonment for 7 years.

Judgments on POCSO

1. Delhi High Court, Court on Its Own Motion v. State and Anr. on 14 August 2007[177]

The Honourable High Court of Delhi had issued the following directions to be followed by investigating officers while probing cases of CSA.

The children, by reason of their physical and mental status, need special safeguards and care. Child victims of sexual abuse are to be treated with compassion and dignity. All concerned associated with Criminal justice System need to be sensitized about their protective role to prevent further victimization of child victims. To secure this end it is rendered imperative to lay down certain guidelines, which we do and direct as follows:-

Police

1. On a complaint of a cognizable offence involving a child victim being made, concerned police officer shall record the complaint promptly and accurately.
2. The investigation of the case shall be referred to an officer not below the rank of Sub-Inspector, preferably a lady officer, sensitized by imparting appropriate training to deal with child victims of sexual crime.
3. The statement of the victim shall be recorded verbatim.
4. The officer recording the statement of the child victim should not be in police uniform.
5. The statement of the child victim shall be recorded at the residence of the victim or at any other place where the victim can make a statement freely without fear.
6. The statement should be recorded promptly without any loss of time.
7. The parents of the child or any other person in whom the child reposes trust and confidence will be allowed to remain present.
8. The investigation officer to insure that at no point should the child victim come in contact with the accused.
9. The child victim shall not be kept in the police station overnight on any pretext, whatsoever, including medical examination.
10. The investigating officer recording the statement of the child victim shall ensure that the victim is made comfortable before proceeding to record the statement and that the statement carries accurate narration of the incident covering all relevant aspects of the case.
11. In the event the investigating officer should so feel the necessity, he may take the assistance of psychiatrist.
12. The investigating officer shall ensure that the child victim is medically examined at the earliest preferably within twenty four hours (in accordance with Section 164-A Cr.P.C.) at the nearest government hospital or hospital recognized by the government.

---

[177] W.P. (Crl.) No. 930/2007.

13. The investigating officer shall ensure that the investigating team visits the site of the crime at the earliest to secure and collect all incriminating evidence available.

14. The investigating officer shall promptly refer for forensic examination clothing and articles necessary to be examined, to the forensic laboratory which shall deal with such cases on priority basis to make its report available at an early date.

15. The investigation of the cases involving sexually abused child may be investigated on a priority basis and completed preferably within 90 days of the registration of the case. The investigation shall be periodically supervised by senior officer(s).

16. The investigating officer shall ensure that the identity of the child victim is protected from publicity.

Delhi Commission for Women v. Delhi Police[178]

The Honourable High Court of Delhi passed comprehensive guidelines to be followed by the police, hospitals/doctors, CWCs, courts, prosecutors, and other authorities. This includes setting up of Crisis Intervention Centres by the Delhi Commission of Women (DCW). The Honourable High Court of Delhi defined a Crises 108 Intervention Centre as an agency recognized by the Delhi Police and DCW for responding to calls received at the police stations complaining of sexual assault, to provide counseling and other support services to victims of rape. The districts have been associating with various NGOs, including Swanchetan, for the purpose. However, it needs to be noted that NGOs which have not been recognized by the DCW do not meet with the directions/requirements of the Honourable High Court of Delhi.

State v. Aas Mohammad[179]

A 14-year-old girl was in a sexual relationship with her landlord. A complaint was filed by the mother on discovering that the girl was six months pregnant. In court, the girl admitted that the matter was reported only because the man had refused to marry her. During the proceedings, the accused offered to marry the girl, deposit a sum of Rs 30,000 in her name, and provide shelter for her mother. The couple got married when he was released on bail. The judge ensured compliance with the undertaking and acquitted the accused as the girl and her mother retracted their statements.

The above ruling is in contradiction with the spirit of the POCSO Act. This act means to protect children from offences of sexual assault, sexual harassment, and child pornography; not to give legality to child marriage or any such acts which are clearly illegal in India. The marriage of an underage is a mockery of justice and the resilience of the court on such matter is a grave wrong.

State v. Iskhar Ahmed[180]

Judge Shalini Nagpal, Chandigarh Special Court, held that '[h]aving a love affair with the prosecutrix and having conversations with her, would not give a license to the accused to commit

---

[178] W.P. (Crl) 696/2008.

[179] Decided on 13 August 2013 by Judge T.S. Kashyap. SC No. 78/2013.

[180] Decided on 3 December 2013 by Shalini Singh Nagpal, Judge, Special Court, Chandigarh. SC No. 0300064 of 2013.

rape on her person or even to have sexual intercourse with her consent, as consent of the child to penetrative sexual assault is immaterial'. This implies that the liability that exists in the POCSO Act is strict liability, that is, the doctrine of mens rea is not taken into consideration.

In Reference v. Firoz Khan[181]

In this case the appellant Rakesh Choudhary went with an unknown person to the house of the complainant on the pretext that the said unknown person was a friend of the complainant's brother and asked that he be given some space in the house. The complainant's mother refused to provide space to that unknown person, and therefore Rakesh Choudhary and his companion left the premises. After sometime it was found that the deceased-prosecutrix, aged 4 years, was missing. An FIR was lodged before the police. Later, some visitors found that one girl child was lying unconscious in the field. The child was unconscious and she was not able to give any evidence. It was confirmed that rape was committed with the deceased-prosecutrix, and therefore the case was registered. Thereafter, the deceased-prosecutrix was sent to the Care Hospital Nagpur so that her life could be saved, but she expired on her way there. The doctor who treated the deceased-prosecutrix found that due to pressure caused on the mouth and throat of the deceased, oxygen could not reach her brain, and that, due to contusion in the private parts of the deceased-prosecutrix, she died due to cardio-respiratory arrest. The various samples were sent to the Forensic Science Laboratory and the incident was probed by the investigation officer. After much effort, the appellant Mohd. Firoz was arrested. The case was duly committed to the Sessions Judge, Seoni being Special Judge under the POCSO Act .

After considering the evidence adduced by the parties before the trial Court, death sentence was directed to the appellant Mohd. Firoz. Therefore, a reference was made to High Court of Madhya Pradesh.

The Honourable High Court held that the crime committed by the appellant Mohd. Firoz satisfies the test of a 'rare of rarest case' and, therefore, upheld the death sentence and also other sentences imposed upon the appellant by the trial Court.

Upon the NCPCR petitioning the High Court, in a path breaking judgment rendered on 9 April 2013, it has been directed that the states of Punjab and Haryana as well as Union Territory of Chandigarh shall ensure that SCPCRs, each headed by a Chairperson who should be an ex-Judge of the High Court shall become fully functional by appointing the said Chairpersons and six members through a transparent selection process. The High Court has further directed mandatory registration of all children's homes, constitution and notification of children's courts, and appointment of special public prosecutors, besides constituting a proper selection committee to make further selections of various committees to be set up for child welfare. Hence, the entire machinery of monitoring child rights has been galvanized. A further direction has been issued that the national commission and the state commissions shall start discharging their functions under POCSO for implementing its provisions and modules/training programmes for sensitizing all stakeholders on child rights, and for dealing with cases in children's court be also initiated in the Chandigarh Judicial Academy. It is now for the state governments to implement this

---

[181] Criminal Reference No. 9/2013.

beneficial mandate and create an effective machinery to check heinous crimes of gross sexual abuse against children by enlightening all concerned about it.

Judgments on the Two-Finger Test

There have been some significant judgments relating to the banning of the two-finger test.

Narayanamma (Kum) v. State Of Karnataka and Ors[182]

The Court held that fact of admission of two fingers and hymen rupture does not give a clear indication that the prosecutrix is habitual to sexual intercourse. The doctor has to opine as to whether the hymen stood ruptured much earlier or carried an old tear. The factum of admission of two fingers could not be held adverse to the prosecutrix, as it would also depend upon the size of the fingers inserted. The doctor must give his clear opinion as to whether it was painful and bleeding on touch, for the reason that such conditions obviously relate to the hymen.

Lillu @ Rajesh & Anr v. State of Haryana[183]

The two-finger test is an age-old practice which is considered barbaric and sexist by most developed nations, but continues to be used in Indian hospitals to 'predict' if a girl was raped or if the sex was consensual. It is performed by a doctor who inserts a finger in the female's vagina to check the level of vaginal laxity, which is used to determine if she is 'habituated to sexual intercourse'. The efficacy of this test has been questioned because neither vaginal laxity and/or the absence of a hymen are any indicator of sexual activity. Also, it is not anyone's business who the victims were having consensual sex with. A woman who sleeps with another man is not 'fair game'. She is a human being who has the unequivocal right to say 'Yes' or 'No' to sex with a person. It is shocking that a test like this was carried out in medical facilities in a democracy.

In the present case involving a 13-year-old who was raped, the Supreme Court said the two-finger test was immaterial as the question of consent does not arise at all. The Supreme Court went on to denigrate the practice, saying it 'violates the privacy, physical and mental integrity and dignity' of rape victims. 'Medical procedures should not be carried out in a manner that constitutes cruel, inhuman or degrading treatment,' the Court said. 'A rapist not only causes physical injuries, but also leaves behind a scar on her dignity, honour, reputation and chastity.'

'This test, even if the report is affirmative, cannot ipso facto, be given rise to presumption of consent,' the bench of justices B.S. Chauhan and F.M.I. Kalifulla ruled. The Justice Verma Committee had also spoken out against the test. 'Such tests are not only inhumane, but they also shatter the girl, who is already traumatised, to another round of humiliation.'

In view of International Covenant on Economic, Social, and Cultural Rights 1966 and the United Nations Declaration of Basic Principles of Justice for Victims of Crime and Abuse of Power 1985, rape survivors are entitled to legal recourse that does not re-traumatize them or

---

[182] (1994) 5 SCC 728.
[183] AIR 2013 SC.

violate their physical or mental integrity and dignity. They are also entitled to medical procedures conducted in a manner that respects their right to consent. Medical procedures should not be carried out in a manner that constitutes cruel, inhuman, or degrading treatment and health should be of paramount consideration while dealing with gender-based violence. The state is under an obligation to make such services available to survivors of sexual violence. Proper measures should be taken to ensure their safety and there should be no arbitrary or unlawful interference with their privacy.

Held that undoubtedly, the two-finger test and its interpretation violates the right of rape survivors to privacy, physical and mental integrity, and dignity. Thus, this test, even if the report is affirmative, cannot ipso facto be given rise to presumption of consent.

Important International Legal Initiatives

The CRC, which has been ratified by several countries including India, gives a common, cross-national, comprehensive foundation standard for all the world's children. Article 11 prohibits the illegal transfer of children abroad. Article 19 refers to the state's obligation to protect children from all forms of physical or mental violence, injury or abuse, negligent treatment, maltreatment, or exploitation, including sexual abuse, perpetrated by parents or others responsible for their care. Article 34 enjoins the state parties to protect the child from all forms of sexual exploitation and abuse.

Some International Best Practices

Working Together to Deal with Child Sexual Abuse

Interdisciplinary and inter-agency work is an essential process in the task of protecting children from abuse. Local systems for inter-agency cooperation have been set up throughout England and Wales. The experience gained by professionals in working and training together has succeeded in bringing about a greater mutual understanding of the roles of the various professions and agencies and a greater ability to combine their skills in the interest of abused children and their families. In every local authority area, there is a close working relationship between social services departments, the police service, medical practitioners, community health workers, the education service, and others who share a common aim to protect the child at risk. Cooperation at the level of individual cases is supported by joint agency and management policies for child protection, consistent with their policies and plans for related service provision. There is a recognized joint forum for developing, monitoring, and reviewing child protection policies. This forum is known as the Area Child Protection Committee (ACPC) in the UK. A similar multidisciplinary forum in the USA is the Child Protection Services. The Dutch Child Protection Boards[184] are a public service under the control of the Ministry of Justice in the Netherlands. The Boards receive reports from mental health agencies, schools, the confidential doctors, the police, and so on, and

---

[184] Bette L. Bottoms and Gail S. Goodman, eds, *International Perspectives on Child Abuse and Children's Testimony: Psychological Research and Law* (New York: SAGE Publications Inc., 1996).

investigate whether the rights of the child are being violated and how that violation influences the child's normal development. They also seek to determine the causes of the violation and the measures necessary to restore the rights of the child.[185] Investigations are carried out by social workers, but contrary to usual practice in the USA and the UK, the social workers of the Child Protection Boards usually do not interview a child about alleged sexual abuse.

Mandatory Reporting Laws

In India, until the POCSO Act was enacted, there were no mandatory reporting systems of cases relating to CSA. The USA has detailed statutory provisions to deal with the issue of detection and prevention. All the states have enacted child abuse reporting statutes by 1967, with the following basic elements:

1. a definition of conditions worthy of reporting,
2. list of persons that required reporting,
3. the degree of certainty required warranting reporting the suspected abuse,
4. penalties imposed for failure to report, and
5. delineation of the reporting procedures.

TV Link Courts (Closed-Circuit Television)

A child is competent to testify if it can understand the question and give rational answers. The right to confrontation requires the accused to see the witness and vice versa. In case of CSA, the child victim is the main witness. In *Coy* v. *Lowa* (487 US1012 [1988]), the court held that there could be exceptions to this rule where it is required to further an important public policy such as the protection of children. In *Maryland* v. *Craig* (497 US805 [1990]), a CCTV was used at the stage of recording the testimony of an alleged victim of child abuse, as the child was under serious emotional distress and found it difficult to communicate. The Supreme Court of the USA has held that, 'The State's interest in the physical and psychological well-being of child abuse victims may be sufficiently important to outweigh a defendant's right to face-to-face confrontation since the State has a competing interest in protecting minor victims of sex crimes from further trauma and embarrassment.'[186]

Under Sections 32 and 32A of the Criminal Justice Act, 1988, in the Crown Court or in the youth courts in the UK, a child may, at the discretion of the court, give evidence-in-chief by means of a video and/or be questioned during the trial via a live CCTV link. These provisions apply to child witnesses under the age of 14 years in the case of offences of violence or cruelty, and to child witnesses under 17 years of age in the case sexual offences. The provisions apply to any child witness (with prosecution and defence) other than the accused. Under-represented

[185] T. Veldkamp, 'De toekomst van de kinderbescherming [The Future of Child Protection]', in Kinderen Beschermen en jeugd hulp verlenen [Protecting and Helping Children], eds A. Groen and A. van Montfoort (Arnhem, the Netherlands: Gouda Quint, 1993), pp. 93–113.

[186] Bottoms and Goodman, *International Perspectives on Child Abuse*.

defendants are also prohibited, under Section 34A of the 1988 Act, from cross examining child witnesses, or a witness who is to be cross-examined following the admission of video evidence. Other measures such as the use of screens or the removal of wigs and gowns, can be used at the court's discretion on a non-statutory basis.

Legislation allowing the use of CCTVs for child witnesses has been enacted in most Australian states. For example, the Evidence (Closed-Circuit Television) Act, 1991 provides that a court may order the use of a CCTV. The legislation provides that the court is not to make an order if it considers that to do so would be unfair to any disability in the child, as well as the importance of the matters on which the child is called upon to give evidence. It can be seen that the CCTV is not an automatic right, with the court needing to be satisfied in each case that its use would be an advantage over the ordinary method of testifying.

Legal Interviewing

Legal interviews of the child victims must be conducted by experts in the field of children. Different strategies may be utilized in different circumstances to obtain an appropriate response from the child.[187] These include:

1. Open questions, that is, questions that allow the child to narrate their own point of view.
2. Closed questions, that is, questions that can be answered only with a 'yes' or 'no'.
3. Choice questions, that is, questions that suggest one of two given possibilities.
4. Hypothetical questions, that is, questions that raise a topic introduced by the interviewer.

A specially trained and skilled interviewer interviews a child and it is this interviewer who interprets the child's narrative and presents it before the court. It is the interviewer and not the child who gives evidence and faces cross-examination under the law of Israel. Under Texan law, an out-of-court statement of a child witness is admissible as evidence without producing the child for cross-examination, if the totality of the circumstances render the statement reliable, and the facts of a particular case indicate that use of out of-court testimony is necessary to protect the child. Under the Magistrate's Courts Act, a child is not to be normally called as witness for the prosecution; any statement made in writing by a child should be treated as admissible in evidence in any matter in which his/her oral testimony would be admissible. The Report of the Advisory Group on Video Evidence in 1989 recommended that both examination-in-chief, that is, the interview, and cross-examination should be video-recorded and produced before the court as evidence. Though, under the British law, the procedure adopted is the replacing of examination-in-chief by the video-recorded interview of the child.

Assistance to Victims

Payment of compensation may be awarded to the victim in both civil and criminal proceedings. Compensation is necessary as often the harm suffered by the child limits his/her ability to acquire

---

[187] Maharukh Adenwalla, *Child Sexual Abuse and the Law* (Mumbai: India Centre for Human Rights and Law, 2000).

an education and earn a living. The payment of compensation is in addition to penal sentences in criminal proceedings. Criminal Inquiries Compensation Boards have been constituted under the Children's Act, 1989 (UK) for payment of compensation to victims of child abuse who have sustained physical injury as a result of a crime of violence. The Juvenile Justice Coalition and the Victim Assistance Programme have been set up under the American law to assist victims of CSA. The Juvenile Justice Coalition includes service providers, mental health professionals, doctors, and lawyers. They assist the child in dealing with legal procedures. The Victim Assistance Programme assists sexually abused children after the indictment has been obtained. In the Delhi Domestic Working Women's Forum case,[188] the Supreme Court has directed the establishment of Criminal Injuries Compensation Board for awarding compensation to rape survivors. These Boards have to be set up immediately.

Delayed Discovery Statute

A provision requires to be incorporated under the law to extend the limitation period for survivors of CSA. Extension of statute of limitation will ensure that crimes against children can be initiated even several years after the offence has been committed. The period of limitation runs from attaining majority or from the child victim becoming aware of the incident. Victims of CSA often suffer from repressed memory or post-traumatic stress disorder (PTSD). The law perceives these as constituting 'insanity', and therefore, the period of limitation will run once the disability is removed. Under the Alaskan law, a criminal prosecution for sexual offences against a victim less than 18 years of age may be commenced at any time. The law prevailing in New Hampshire allows a criminal prosecution to be brought up to 22 years after the victim has attained 18 years of age. Under the California Code of Civil Procedure, the Delayed Discovery Statute applies to perpetuators of the offence as well as liable third parties, that is, a person/entity who owes a duty of due care to the victim. Several adult survivors of CSA will benefit from such a statute.

Witness Support System

In the UK, child witnesses are entitled to assistance to prepare for the court experience.[189] The child witness supporter should ask children if they would like the parent or carer, or some other supportive adult who is close to the child, to be present during preparation sessions. Such people can play a critical role in the child's ability to cope with the court case and in reinforcing messages.

Child Witness Code[190]

In the USA, there is a Child Witness Code. The code draws heavily on the existing law in the USA and several other countries. The purpose of this code is to ascertain the truth, reduce trauma

---

[188] (1995) 1 SCC 14.

[189] National Society for the Prevention of Cruelty to Children (NSPCC) and Childline, *Preparing Young Witnesses for Court—A Handbook for Child Witness Supporters* (NSPCC/Childline, 1998).

[190] Bottoms and Goodman, *International Perspectives on Child Abuse*.

to children, create conditions that will allow children to provide reliable and complete evidence, increase the number of children who are able to testify in legal proceedings, and protect the rights of persons accused of crime. The salient features of the code are mentioned below.

1. The court shall give docket priority for a speedy trial to any criminal case involving a child victim.
2. Programmes designed to prepare children to testify serve the interests of justice and are encouraged.
3. Making provisions for a waiting area for child witnesses.
4. The court shall appoint a guardian ad litem for a child who has been a victim of or a witness to a crime, to protect the best interests of the child.
5. A child satisfying a judicial proceeding or deposition shall have the right to be accompanied by up to two persons of the child's own choosing.
6. Every child, irrespective of age, is qualified to be a witness unless the child lacks the ability to communicate, remember, distinguish truth from falsehood, or appreciate the duty to tell the truth in court.
7. Appointment of an interpreter for child.
8. While testifying, a child shall be allowed to have a comfort item of the child's own choosing, such as a blanket, toy, or a doll.
9. Provision for rearranging the courtroom to make the child comfortable.
10. Leading questions can be asked during direct examination.
11. Live link television testimony.
12. The courtroom may be closed during proceedings.
13. Videotape deposition.
14. Screens and other devices to shield the child from the defendant.
15. Protection of child's privacy and safety.
16. Child hearsay exception.
17. Multidisciplinary team investigation and interviewing.
18. Videotaping and audiotaping investigative interviews.

International Convention on Child Victim and Witnesses

Considering the obligations under the CRC,[191] which was adopted by the General Assembly in its resolution 44/25 of 20 November 1989 and entered into force on 2 September 1990, and the Optional Protocols thereto,[192] as well as other relevant international legal instruments, considering in particular Economic and Social Council resolution 2005/20 of 22 July 2005, which includes as an annex the Guidelines on Justice in Matters involving Child Victims and Witnesses of Crime (the 'Guidelines'), considering also that every child victim or witness of crime has the right to have his or her best interests given primary consideration, while safe-guarding the rights of accused persons and convicted offenders, the following rights of child

---

[191] United Nations, Treaty Series, vol. 1577, No. 27531.
[192] United Nations, Treaty Series, vols. 2171 and 2173, No. 27531.

victims and witnesses of crime, in particular those contained in the CRC and in the Guidelines need to be kept in mind.

1. The right to be treated with dignity and compassion;
2. The right to be protected from discrimination;
3. The right to be informed;
4. The right to be heard and to express views and concerns;
5. The right to effective assistance;
6. The right to privacy;
7. The right to be protected from hardship during the justice process;
8. The right to safety;
9. The right to special preventive measures;
10. The right to reparation, considering that improved responses for child victims and witnesses of crime can make children and their families more willing to disclose instances of victimization and more supportive of the justice process.

The rights in this convention need to be specifically adopted for the protection of child victims and witnesses.

Guidelines for Medico-legal Care for Survivors of Sexual Abuse, World Health Organization, 2003[193]

The WHO guidelines contain a separate chapter on CSA, noting the fact that victims of CSA are more likely to experience depression, substance abuse, PTSD, and suicide in later life than their non-abused counterparts. The guidelines observe that the dynamics of CSA differ from those of adult sexual abuse. In particular, children rarely disclose sexual abuse immediately after the event. Moreover, the disclosure seems to be a process rather than a single episode and is often initiated following a physical complaint or a change in behaviour. Therefore, the evaluation of children requires special skills and techniques in history taking, forensic interviewing, and examination; the examiner may also need to address specific issues related to consent and reporting of CSA.[194]

The Convention on Consent to Marriage, Minimum Age for Marriage and Registration of Marriages

This convention (referred to as the Convention on Minimum Age of Marriage later in this chapter) came into force in December 1964. It obligates states parties to:

---

[193] Available at http://whqlibdoc.who.int/publications/2004/924154628x.pdf (accessed on 16 November 2016).

[194] WHO, *Guidelines for Medico-legal Care for Victims of Sexual Violence* (Geneva, 2003).

1. specify a minimum age for marriage;
2. prohibit legal acceptance of any marriage without the full and free consent of both parties;
3. register all marriages.

India is still not a signatory to this convention and must ratify it.

The recent UN Resolution on Child, Early and Forced Marriage[195] was adopted unanimously and India too is now a party to it. However, there has been much criticism about India not being a co-sponsor to the resolution and the Indian delegates giving official statements to the effect about India not being in a position to eliminate child marriage completely due to high poverty levels.

1. Poverty cannot be an excuse. Poverty needs to be addressed and it is not only poverty that is the cause of child marriages.
2. This resolution needs to be sponsored by India.

Role Played by NGOs and the Government in Child Sexual Abuse Cases

Interventions in CSA cases are generally in the form of bringing cases of such abuse to the notice of the police and the court, helping the police and the courts in investigating these cases sensitively. The Forum against Child Sexual Abuse (FACSE) is a group of interested activists. The group has brought to light several cases of CSA. Trauma counselling is also provided by the Forum to the victims of CSA and exploitation in institutions. The Maharashtra State Monitoring Committee on Juvenile Justice, set up by the Mumbai High Court,[196] has also investigated and sent reports to the Mumbai High Court on cases of CSA. The Court has issued directions to the authorities concerned to follow up these cases.

The legal processes involved in the entire prosecution of CSA have to be seen in the best interest of the child right from the stage of the decision to file a complaint, to the registration of the FIR and filing of a charge sheet, making the decision to commence trial proceedings, and of course, to the trial in the courts. There is thus a need to amend both the substantive and procedural laws to ensure successful prosecution and protect the best interests of the child. Law reform alone cannot bring about justice to the child. Inter-agency structures and systems need to be worked out, laying great emphasis on prevention. Undoubtedly, the most effective prevention

---

[195] A landmark resolution calling for a ban on child marriage was agreed on 21 November, during the 69th session of the General Assembly. The resolution marks the first time that UN Member States have agreed upon substantive recommendations for the steps that countries, international organizations, and others must take to address the problem of child, early, and forced marriage.

The UN Resolution on Child, Early and Forced Marriage, supported by 116 Member States, was introduced and led by the Governments of Canada and Zambia and built on the previous year's resolutions in the General Assembly and Human Rights Council, which were procedural resolutions calling for reports and further consideration of the issue. Read the full resolution at http://www.who.int/pmnch/media/events/2014/child_marriage.pdf?ua=1 (accessed on 12 January 2016).

[196] See the decision in the case of *Krist Pereira* v. *State of Maharashtra & Ors*, Crim. Writ Petition No. 1107 of 1996, Mumbai High Court.

measure is awareness of such possible abuse and of how to deal with it, among the various service providers—doctors, teachers, lawyers, judges, police, volunteers, parents, and social workers—so that they can significantly reduce the risk of abuse and respond appropriately, if it does occur.[197]

Arpan[198]

Arpan is a registered NGO based in Mumbai and the largest in the world among those active on the issue of CSA, with a team of dedicated and skilled professionals working since 2006. Arpan has reached out to over 85,000 children and adults directly and over 211,000 individuals indirectly since its inception.

Arpan is currently working in Mumbai and Thane in Maharashtra with a child-centric model of intervention in the area of CSA, with a balanced emphasis on prevention and healing components. While the focus is on children, Arpan also understands the need for reaching out to adult survivors of CSA in order to support them in an adequate manner and prevent any further re-victimization, as well as to enable them to heal from the impact of CSA.

Arpan empowers children, teachers, parents, NGO professionals, and other caregivers in multiple settings like schools, NGO set-ups, institutions, and elsewhere with knowledge, skills, and attitude to prevent instances of CSA and provide adequate support to children who have been victims. Along with empowering relevant stakeholders, Arpan also offers psychotherapeutic support through trained, qualified therapists to children and adult survivors of sexual abuse, and their families.

Tulir[199]

Tulir—Centre for the Prevention and Healing of Child Sexual Abuse (CPHCSA) is a registered, non-governmental, non-profit organization committed to working against CSA in India. Its objeives are:

1. To support and participate in local, national, and international efforts to promote and protect the rights of the child.
2. To raise awareness on CSA.
3. To work towards improving policy and advancing practice to prevent and address cases of CSA with a special emphasis on the psychosocial well-being of children.
4. To provide direct intervention services in the areas of prevention and healing of CSA.
5. To undertake research, documentation, and dissemination of information on CSA.

   Its activities include:

1. personal safety education;
2. training and consultancy;

---

[197] Asha Bajpai, 'The Sexual Abuse and Exploitation of Children', *One India, One People*, September 1999.

[198] Available at http://arpan.org.in/ (accessed on 16 November 2016).

[199] Available at http://www.tulir.org/ (accessed on 16 November 2016).

3. healing and intervention;
4. research and documentation;
5. resource development;
6. advocacy and networking.

Law Reform

Law Reform Relating to the Protection of Children from Sexual Offences Act, 2012

The POCSO Act has adopted some of the international best practices in the interest of the child and has tried to make the legal system more child-friendly, but there are gaps in the law and there is a need for law reform. For the first time, we have a law that relates to children as victims, and the procedures adopted are to protect child victims and to see that they are not further victimized. The POCSO Act requires all stakeholders within the legal system to deal with the child victims of sexual offences. Police officials, doctors, judges, lawyers, and prosecutors must be trained to understand children's vocabulary, language, and developmental maturity in order to pose age-appropriate questions to them; to assess the value of their statements; and to help them in securing justice.[200] Most states have not yet notified special courts or appointed special public prosecutors. Cases of offences against children are, therefore, still being brought before regular criminal courts, thus denying children their right to a child-friendly system and structure.

Despite POCSO laying down that the Central and state governments shall take measures to give wide publicity through media—including television, radio, and print media—and impart periodic training to all stakeholders on the matters relating to implementation of provisions of the POCSO Act, the act is relatively unknown. Most CSA cases are not booked under the act. Child sex offenders get away despite a stringent law. The act is unknown. Indoctrination, training, familiarization, and actual application by police officers and other stakeholders still remains a far cry.[201]

Some of the Provisions of the POCSO Act That Need Reform

Age of Consent

Under the POCSO Act, sexual activity with children below the age of 18 years has come to be treated as a crime, the question of consent has no meaning in the case of children, and even in a case of a 'valid child marriage', the boy can be penalized under the provisions of the act. The CLA Act of 2013, drafted in much haste after the 16 December (2012) gang rape case in Delhi, causes confusion on the question of consent and sexual activity between minors in a valid marriage. On one hand it makes consent immaterial in the case of victims of rape below the age of 18 years, on the other, it declares sexual intercourse by a husband with his wife as statutory rape only if

---

[200] Note prepared by Anuroopa Giliyal, Geeta Sajjanashetty, and Swagata Raha, lawyers, CCL, NLSIU, Bangalore.

[201] Anil Malhotra, 'POCSO—A Child Law in Oblivion'. Available at LU JUNE 2013.html (accessed on 16 November 2016).

the wife is below the age of 15 years. When these laws were being drafted, several voices had demanded that the age of sexual consent be lowered to 16 years so that consensual sexual activity among young people does not get criminalized. Even the fact that a child marriage is per se valid but under the PCMA, and therefore sexual activity between young married couples should be not criminalized, went unheard. These confusions must be removed to ensure that protections required by young people are not denied because of confusion in existing laws.

Section 42A, read with the definition of child and the offences under the act, has the potential to lead to unintended consequences—the most severe of which could be the resort to child marriage in order to evade criminal prosecution.[202] The case law on PCMA reveals that there have been several cases in which girls between the ages of 16 and 18 years have left their homes on their own with a man of their choice. In such cases, parents of the girl generally rush to file a case against the man, alleging kidnapping from lawful guardianship, rape, and sexual assault. Even prior to the enactment of the POCSO Act, there have been such cases. They were known as 'love cases'. Under the POCSO Act criminal consequences can follow in cases where girls elope with and/or marry a man they claim to love.[203] The NCPCR Bill, 2010 proposed that any consensual sexual act that may constitute penetrative sexual assault should not be an offence when it is between two children who are both above 14 years of age and are either of the same age or the difference in age is not more than 3 years.[204] It is imperative that the POCSO Act be amended to address this anomaly.

The draft bill submitted by the NCPCR had set the age limit for consensual sex at 16; the Standing Committee constituted by the parliament raised the age to 18. The Committee, while justifying the move, argued that most laws regard a child as a person below the age of 18 in adherence to the CRC. But the Standing Committee failed to review provisions of Article 5, CRC, which lays stress on the crucial aspect of a child's evolving capacities, and the need for the law to realize that growing up is a complex process which is not marked by a single rite of passage but by a series of staged transitions characterized by the acquisition of growing responsibility and self sufficiency. This age is at variance with various other laws such as the IPC and the PCMA.

Implementation of POCSO

State governments will have to ensure that all the requirements specified under the law are in place and all key stakeholders will have to internalize the core principles of child rights in the spirit of the act in order for the law to work.[205] There is a need for greater awareness and sensitization among law enforcement officials, child protection agencies, the judiciary, and society at large. The POCSO Act does not offer support to persons like counsellors to the child victim and the family at the police stations. Presently, the child has to be produced before a CWC which will then offer a support person to the victim. This support needs to be included. Victim-protection scheme needs to be included in the POCSO Act.

---

[202] Note prepared by Giliyal et al.
[203] Note prepared by Giliyal et al.
[204] NCPCR Draft Bill on Protection of Children from Sexual offences.
[205] NCPCR Draft Bill.

Child-Friendly Court Rooms

Many court rooms continue to be formidable with the judge on a high podium and the small child witness far below, from where her voice is barely audible to the judge. Delhi has now become the first city in the country to have its own Vulnerable Witness Deposition Complex, which has been designed 'to provide protection, privacy, confidentiality and comfort to vulnerable witnesses in an in-camera atmosphere' in cases of sexual offences.

Mandatory Reporting

The act calls for mandatory reporting to the designated authorities by any person who 'apprehends' that an offence might be committed under the act or knows that such an offence has been committed any time in the past. Failure to report the same is considered a criminal offence punishable with imprisonment. The mandatory nature will encourage moral policing and even consensual intimate behaviour which may lead to complaints by disapproving family members and others, leading to harassment of young adults.[206]

After the POCSO Act was passed with the provision of mandatory reporting, reportedly, there does not appear to be any increase in reporting of cases. People are extremely wary of reporting cases or even coming to service delivery agencies because it is mandatory to report these crimes. Doctors reportedly refuse to examine children and school managements are reluctant to report. Some schools have stopped awareness sessions on CSA. Even NGOs hesitate to bring cases.[207] This affects prevention of the abuse. For example, when a teenage girl approaches a doctor to terminate her pregnancy which could have been due to consensual sex, the doctor is mandated by law to report it as a case of sexual abuse. Similarly, situations where children, out of curiosity, are exploring each other sexually in a one-off instance or in socially sanctioned situations, such as child marriage, are far from criminal acts; however, non-reporting of such instances will attract punishment under the act. Also in cases of 'privileged communication', such as information obtained through lawyer–client discussions, doctor–patient, counsellor–client, teacher–student, psychotherapy, or in ceremony of confession (reconciliation) to Catholic priests, will be correct to follow the procedure.[208] According to mental health professionals, it is the reporting of minor offences that could result in a paradoxical situation where the solution is worse than the crime. Especially, a situation which could have been handled through family sessions would call for mandatory involvement of the police under the new dispensation, resulting in the arrest of the sexual offender, and in a long-drawn criminal case. This, in turn, would trigger complications that could compromise the earning capacity of the family if the offender is an earning member, induce guilt in the victim, provoke resentment in the family against the victim, and split the family apart if sides are taken; all of which are serious matters that can have long-lasting repercussions. The law is silent on these and many more situations like these.

---

[206] Geeta Ramasheshan, 'Law and the Age of Innocence', (19 June 2012). Available at http://www.the-hindu.com/opinion/op-ed/law-and-the-age-of-innocence/article3543940.ece) (accessed on 16 November 2016).

[207] Available at www.tulir.org (accessed on 16 November 2016).

[208] Ramasheshan, 'Law and the Age of Innocence'.

On the other hand, penalizing a person for not reporting may prove counter-productive, given the social stigma attached to the issue.[209] Although the act provides for protection of the victim, it is silent on the protection of the person who reports of such abuse. In reality, the obligation to report, without providing protection for the same, dissuades people from reporting.[210]

Social Audit, Monitoring, and Review of the Act

There is a also a need for rigorous monitoring and review of the act, and personnel not performing their mandatory duties must be held accountable and punished. The Justice Verma Committee Report,[211] in one of its conclusions on CSA, holds: 'there is an urgent need to audit the performance of all institutions of governance and law and order. It is indeed necessary that we must now have external social audit for the sake of transparency. We also wish to make it clear that every case of a missing child must be registered as FIR.' The Committee further makes suggestions of constituting 'an oversight mechanism' through the High Court, special training needs programmes, sensitizing officials on sexual abuse of children, and strict implementation of provisions of various child laws. The Government must create the machinery to implement the POCSO Act in true letter and spirit and educate its officers, besides all stakeholders, on what it contains.

Marital Rape

The POCSO Act defines a 'child' as 'any person below the age of 18 years' and raises the age of consent from 16 years under the IPC to 18 years. Unlike the IPC, which treats sexual intercourse by a man with his wife above the age of 15 years as an exception to rape, the POCSO Act does not permit any exception. In fact, penetrative sexual assault and non-penetrative sexual assault by a person who is related to a child through marriage constitutes an aggravated offence. As per the provisions of the POCSO Act, any person can be prosecuted for engaging in a sexual act with a child, irrespective of whether the latter consented. A husband/wife can be prosecuted for engaging in a sexual act with his/her spouse below the age of 18 years. The act does not recognize consensual sexual acts among children or between a child and an adult.[212]

Conflicting Provisions between the POCSO, the IPC, and the PCMA

The PCMA forbids marriage below the age of 18 for girls and 21 for boys; but it makes such marriage neither null nor void unless, of course, either of the parties seeks annulment. Such a provision in the PCMA brings it in direct conflict with the POCSO Act, as it has created a situation wherein the existence of child marriages is tolerated on one hand, while any form of sexual relations which emanate from such relations has been made punishable. Under the IPC, vide

---

[209] Kaushiki Sanyal, 'Standing Committee Report Summary: The Protection of Children from Sexual Offences Bill, 2011', 14 March 2012.

[210] Sanyal, 'Standing Committee Report Summary'.

[211] Available at http://www.prsindia.org/parliamenttrack/report-summaries/justice-verma-committee-report-summary-2628/ (accessed on 2 May 2015).

[212] Note prepared by Giliyal et al.

Section 375, having intercourse with one's wife under the age of 16, irrespective of her consent, is regarded as rape. Therefore, there will be no relief if the wife is above 15 years of age, although she comes under the definition of 'child' prescribed by the act. But the act is silent on the issue of marital rape. However, it must be noted that the CLA Act has increased the scope of definition of 'rape' to incorporate "sexual assault'. Yet, the amendment has left the present conflict unresolved as the proposed law would still contain an exemption for married couples.

Compensation

Compensation for the psychological trauma suffered by the child due to child marriage, loss of education, loss of health, involvement in child labour, and sexual exploitation, must also be included in the POCSO Act.

Preventive Measures

The POCSO Act only deals with actions to be taken after the child has suffered sexual violence. There are no preventive measures included in the act.

Period of Limitation

The act does not mention any statute of limitation. This increases the scope of reporting of the crime, and even an act which was committed 20 or 50 years ago can be reported.

Law Reform Relating to Child Marriages Laws

The PCMA does not make a child marriage void. It declares that an underage child marriage is voidable at the opinion of a contracting party who was a child at the time of the marriage. No provision is there in the PCMA to stop a child bride from living with her husband and being sexually abused. There are anomalies in law which need to be amended. The IPC acquiesces child marriage. The exception to Section 375 specifically lays down that sexual intercourse of man with his own wife, the wife not being under 15 years of age, is not rape, thus ruling out the possibility of marital rape when the age of wife is above 15 years. On the other hand, if the girl is not the wife of the man, but is below 16, then the sexual intercourse even with the consent of the girl amounts to rape. Specific relaxation is given to a husband who rapes his wife, when she happens to be between 15 and 16 years of age. This provision in the IPC is a specific illustration of legislative endorsement and sanction to child marriage. Thus, by keeping a lower age of consent for marital intercourse, it seems that the legislature has legitimized the concept of child marriage. The IMA lays down 18 years as the age of majority but the non obstante clause excludes marriage, divorce, dower, and adoption from the operation of the act, with the result that the age of majority of an individual in these matters is governed by the personal law to which he is a subject. This saving clause silently approves of child marriage, which is in accordance with the personal law and customs of religion. The DPA also contains provisions which give implied validity to minor's marriages. The words 'when the woman was minor' used in Section 6(1)(c) reflects the implied legislative acceptance of child marriage.

Holding of a child marriage as voidable and not void by the PCMA leads to an anomalous situation where on the one hand child marriage is treated as an offence which is punishable under law, and on the other hand, it is still treated as valid, that is, voidable till it is declared as void.

The practice of child marriage has been discouraged by the legislations but it has not been completely banned. Presently, child marriages are seen more as a welfare issue, a social evil, rather than a child protection issue. The concerned department responsible for implementation of the child marriage law and related programmes and schemes fall in the women's welfare section of the MWCD, and the focus of government interventions on elimination of child marriages lies more in terms of addressing it within the realm of reproductive health, nutrition, and education programmes for adolescent girls.[213] Clearly, it is a child protection issue. It violates the child's right to development, education, protection from sexual abuse and exploitation, protection from economic exploitation, right to nutrition and health, and right to leisure.

Law reform relating to child marriages cannot be looked into in isolation. Child marriage does not only constitute a single rights violation but also endangers the survival and well-being of women and girls by exposing them to sexual violence at an early stage, unplanned and frequent pregnancies, a denial of educational opportunities, and isolation from society. Therefore, laws relating to child labour, sexual offences against children, right to education, domestic violence, and abortion must be seen in the context of law reform to prevent and protect children from child marriages.

There must be a dedicated cadre of officers exclusively dealing with prohibition and prevention of child marriage and enforcing of the PCMA, besides the child protection committees. Child protection committees must be established along with CMPOs and civil society groups to empower community groups to play a key role in preventing and prosecuting child marriages. There is confusion because of some child marriages being declared void and some voidable. Marriage of a minor solemnized by use of force, fraud, deception, enticement, selling and buying or trafficking, is a void marriage, while all other child marriages are voidable at the option of the parties to the marriage, and hence valid marriages, until they are nullified by the court. This must be demystified and clarified.

The following amendments need to be incorporated in the PCMA:

1. There must be uniform age of 18 years for both boys and girls. The difference in ages reinforces patriarchal norms and gender biases.
2. The PCMA, which is the national law against child marriage, does not allow the question of consent in case of minors and treats child marriage as a punishable offence. This anomaly in the law must be rectified. If the law does not attribute consent to a child, it must render all child marriages void, as all child marriages then become marriages that have taken place either through some form of coercion or use of fraud, trafficking, and such other illegal means, or by influencing the mind of the child.[214]
3. On 23 July 2007, the Supreme Court of India reiterated its earlier judgment of 14 February 2006, that marriages of all citizens of India, irrespective of their religion, have to be compulsorily registered in the states where the marriage is solemnized. This was a major step forward

---

[213] 'Child Marriage in India: Achievements, Gaps and Challenges, Response to Questions for OHCHR Report on Preventing Child, Early and Forced Marriages for Twenty-Sixth Session of the Human Rights Council', HAQ—Centre for Child Rights, New Delhi, India.

[214] 'Child Marriage in India: Achievements, Gaps and Challenges'.

to prevent child marriage, as it makes it mandatory to declare age at the time of marriage. Some states have enacted this law on registration of marriages. Some states' specific marriage registration laws talk about registration of every marriage, including a child marriage. Such a provision further reinforces the practice of child marriage because on being registered, it is not only viewed by society as a valid marriage but also as a valid practice. There must be a national law ensuring compulsory registration of marriages. It must be ensured that the registrars of marriage do not register a child marriage and are provided the means to ascertain the age of the couple before the marriage is finally registered.[215]

4. Birth certificates are the most authentic documents of identity. It must be ensured that there is 100 per cent birth registration, along with ensuring that birth registration necessarily leads to possession of a birth certificate also.

5. Registration of Births and Deaths (Amendment) Bill, 2012 was introduced in the Rajya Sabha on 7 May 2012 after a series of efforts being made since 2007, primarily to include registration of marriages within its purview. This Bill needs to be pursued.

6. Section 42A of the POCSO Act, which was introduced by the CLA Act[216] states that this act shall be in addition to and not in derogation of the provisions of any other law for the time being in force and, in case of any inconsistency, the provisions of this act shall have overriding effect on the provisions of any such law to the extent of its inconsistency. The provision essentially implies that in case of conflict between the provisions of the POCSO Act and any other law, the former will override. Owing to Section 42A of the POCSO Act, the exception under the IPC will not apply. Thus, in all cases of child marriage where the bride or groom is below 18 years of age, a charge of aggravated penetrative sexual assault can lie against them under the POCSO Act.

One recommendation is that all child marriages must be declared void and the PCMA, the IPC, the IMA, and the DPA must be amended accordingly.[217] However, concerns were expressed by the society that this may lead to stigmatization of the girl child. A middle path has been recommended by the Law Commission of India.[218] It recommends that all child marriages below a certain age, that is, 16 years of age, be made void. However, all the sections relating to maintenance in Section 4 of the PCMA, regarding maintenance to the female party to the marriage till her remarriage, and the provisions relating to child custody and legitimacy of the children in Sections 5 and 6 of the PCMA, be made applicable to cases of void marriages also, the Commision recommended.

---

[215] 'Child Marriage in India: Achievements, Gaps and Challenges'.

[216] Section 42A: Act not in derogation of any other law—The provisions of this act shall be in addition to and not in derogation of the provisions of any other law for the time being in force and, in case of any inconsistency, the provisions of this act shall have overriding effect on the provisions of any such law to the extent of its inconsistency.

[217] The Law Commission of India, Report No. 205, 'Proposal to Amend the Prohibition of Child Marriage Act, 2006 and Other Allied Laws Presented to the Union Minister for Law and Justice, Ministry of Law and Justice, Government of India by Dr. Justice AR. Lakshmanan, Chairman, Law Commission of India, on 5th day of February, 2008'.

[218] Law Commission of India, Report No. 205.

All marriages between 16 and 18 should be made voidable at the option of either party. The sections relating to maintenance, child custody, and legitimacy in Sections 4, 5, and 6 should be applicable to voidable marriages as they are at present. Consequently, Sections 3(1) and 3(3) of the PCMA should be amended to incorporate the above-mentioned changes, as explained next.

3(1) (i) Any marriage of a child below 16 years of age solemnized after the commencement of this Act will be null and void and may, on a petition be presented by either party thereto against the other party be so declared by a decree of nullity. (ii) Every marriage of a child between the ages of 16 and 18, whether solemnized before or after the commencement of this Act, shall be voidable at the option of the contracting party who was a child at the time of the marriage. Section 3(3) should be amended to read as under:– '(3) The petition under Section 3(1)(ii) may be filed at any time till the person contracting a child marriage attains 20 years of age'. iii) the exception to the rape Section 375 of the Indian Penal Code be deleted. This would ensure that the age of consent for sexual intercourse for all girls, whether married or not, is 16. The 172nd Report of the Law Commission had recommended increasing the age of consent for all girls to 16.[219]

Amendment to the Right to Education Act, 2005

The right to free and compulsory education under the RTE Act is limited to children in the 6–14 age category. Unless it is extended to all children up to the age of 18 years, attempts made to delay the age of marriage are likely to fail.

Amendment to the Child Labour (Prohibition and Regulation) Act, 1986

The Child Labour (Prohibition and Regulation) Act (CLPRA) permitted children under the age of 14 to work in 'non-hazardous industries' including some agricultural work, in contravention of the RTE Act, which says that all children between 6 and 14 must be in school. Anyone over the age of 14 can be employed for hazardous work and below 14 in non-hazardous work. In other words, employment of children from 14 to 21 years of age is legal and permitted. It implies that a child can attain majority at 14 to stop education and start working or get married. If children are sent to school, it will delay child marriages. A constitutional amendment is necessary. The Second National Labour Commission Report (2002) established the link between child labour and education and stated:

All out of school children must be treated as child labourers or those who have the potential to become child labourers. All work done by children, irrespective of where it is done, must be considered as child labour. Only then girls and children working within the family become a part of the strategy to eliminate child labour, and significant headway will be made towards achieving the goal of eliminating child labour. The age of 18 must be prescribed for abolition of child labour and provision of compulsory education and age of marriage for both boys and girls. Child marriages stop the education of the child hence it can be considered as child labour. Child brides and grooms treated as children in need of care and protection. There must be Rehabilitation Schemes for families and children in their homes who resort to child marriages.

[219] Law Commission of India, Report No. 205.

Child Marriage Can Be Considered As an Offence of Trafficking for Marriage

Under Section 366 of the IPC, kidnapping/abduction of a woman to compel her for marriage or for illicit intercourse and use of criminal intimidation or any other method of compulsion is a punishable offence. Section 496, IPC, makes going through the marriage ceremony with fraudulent intention a punishable offence. With an amendment to the criminal law in April 2013, Section 370 of the IPC now contains specific provisions to deal with human trafficking for purposes of sexual exploitation, slavery, and servitude. This provision can be used to book a case of trafficking for marriage also, though marriage is not mentioned in it explicitly.

Domestic Violence and Child Marriages

Domestic violence is more common among women who had been married as children. India has the highest rate of domestic violence among women married by 18 years, with a rate of 67 per cent. The Protection of Women against Domestic Violence Act (PWDA), 2005 must provide for more stringent punishments and extra protection in cases of child marriages. The PCMA must also include this as an offence.

Law Reform Relating to Child Victims and Witnesses

We have a long way to go to further improve the status of child victims and witnesses through law, in keeping with constitutional mandate and the international law. In fact, it is time for reform. We need to review the very adversarial legal system in India as far as child victims and witnesses are concerned. Many children of varying ages, different intellectual and physical abilities, speaking different languages, or some not being able to speak at all, are victims and witnesses of crime and have to go through the trauma of this adversarial system in India. Child victims and witnesses should no longer have to give evidence or be cross-examined in court. Advances in video technology could also be exploited to spare victims of sexual offences the ordeal of appearing in a courtroom. Their physical presence itself in a criminal trial and while undergoing forensic procedures must be dispensed with.

The child victim of crime being an important player in the whole process of the criminal justice system, much attention needs be given to their rights, privileges, and protection. Since the testimony of the victim is a very important piece of evidence in a criminal trial, it is essential that the victim should be able to give his/her testimony freely and without any fear or pressure, for the purpose of securing the ends of justice. There is a need for legislative, procedural, and even constitutional reform for child victims and witnesses.

The Convention on Minimum Age of Marriage must be ratified and guidelines to victims and witnesses must be adopted in our laws.

Part B: Commercial Sexual Exploitation and Trafficking of Children

The nightmare of child abuse takes a more alarming turn when placed in the context of organized exploitation for commercial gain. Sexual exploitation of children involves the use of children for sexual activities for material gains to the children themselves or others. Child prostitution is a term in popular usage but is inaccurate because it implies consent. A child does not consent. Sexual exploitation of a child occurs at an age when consent has no meaning. S/he is rather victimized into sexual slavery for profit. Child sexual exploitation involves power relations and social structures.

Cutting across class, caste, and gender there is an emerging scenario of child vulnerability per se. The groups at risk and the areas prone to commercial sexual exploitation of children can be identified as follows:[220]

Children in general are at risk but the high-risk groups of children can be identified as:

- children living in brothels;
- children living in communities where religious and cultural norms force them into prostitution, such as *jogins, devadasi, basavis, bedias, bancharas, dommaras, venkatasanis, etc.;*
- street children, slum children, and children without shelter;
- children of alcoholic parents and drug traffickers;
- children who have been sexually abused, raped, molested, and stigmatized;
- child widows and those deserted by husbands;
- children employed as domestic help;
- children born to AIDS victims;
- children detained in custodial and educational institutions away from families;
- children affected by terrorism and natural calamities;
- children of families affected by displacement and sickness in industries;
- children affected by transitory poverty in families;
- children in refugee camps;
- children of bonded labourers;
- children of low-skilled or unemployed labour;
- children of broken and disturbed families; and
- migrant children.

The vulnerable areas are

- state and national highways;
- areas from where locals displaced due to big projects and ventures are forced to migrate and settle without proper rehabilitation, for example, tribal areas;
- areas experiencing closure or failure of industry;
- residential schools, childcare institutions, and jails where children are illegally detained;
- beauty parlours, massage homes, health clubs, and casinos;
- areas prone to natural disasters such as floods and drought;
- inhospitable terrain such as deserts and mountainous areas and arid zones;
- quarry and construction sites;
- industries involving child labour; and
- coastal belt, especially tourist resorts where children become victims of paedophiles.

---

[220] *Report on the Six Regional Consultations on Sexual Exploitation and Trafficking of Children*, sponsored by the DWCD, Government of India, and UNICEF, India.

The origin of child sexual exploitation lies only in the circumstances in which a young victim is gainfully subjected to sell his/her body to satiate the sexual urges of another person. The sexual exploitation of children does not occur in a vacuum but involves a more widespread exploitation, sexual or otherwise. Sexual exploiters include not only 'users' but also 'suppliers', namely, pimps, brothel owners, and parents, among others, and the 'protectors', namely, government officials, local politicians, and police, among others. Poverty and ignorance are the underlying causes of this worldwide phenomenon, as families rely on their youngest members to contribute to the household income.

The propelling factor which actualizes commercial sex exploitation of children is the role played by traffickers. The traffickers, through various modus operandi, take the children through unknown and unfamiliar routes to make retracing practically impossible, and they cut off the children from their roots and alienate and isolate them. 'Trafficking' as a phenomenon has been defined by the UN General Assembly in 1994 as 'the illicit and clandestine movement of persons across national and international borders, largely from developing countries, with the end goal of forcing women and girl children into economically oppressive and exploitative situations for the profit of recruiters, traffickers, and crime syndicates as well as other illegal activities such as forced domestic labour, false marriage, clandestine employment, and forced adoption'. The element of migration, with or without consent, to an alien exploitative environment is an essential component of the concept of trafficking. Globalization, liberalization, and feminization of poverty have only aggravated the situation. Though there are no comprehensive and absolutely reliable statistics to that effect, it is a known and acknowledged fact that trafficking women and girls for labour and commercial sexual exploitation is on the rise in India. This includes not merely cross border trafficking but also transportation of victims from less developed rural areas to urban markets where there is a rising demand. There are now many routes by which children are being moved from one country to another by criminal networks. Children are trafficked (on the supply side) for prostitution, begging, organ transplant, pornographic and other unlawful sexual activities, child brides, camel races, and for supposedly good jobs that lead to prostitution. The demand for children to be trafficked comes from the clients, pimps, procurers, brothel owners, police, guardians, and parents. There is a pervasive and powerful alliance, always adult-dominant, in society which originates, perpetuates, and proliferates this demand. Perfect market conditions exist in the sex trade, where there is unfailing supply of children to meet the burgeoning demand. The definition of trafficking by the UN General Assembly clearly indicates that trafficking has the distinct components of recruitment, movement through transportation, forced or slavery like labour, and third-party profit.

At the time of recruitment, it is possible that all or some of the members of the family are instrumental, or at least aware of the trafficking. In fact, this assumes importance from the point of view of action. The issue is of the person in authority taking advantage of the vulnerability of the individual to be trafficked. The traffickers are generally more than one individual and often change hands to avoid getting caught during transit. Different kinds of traffickers have been identified, like nexus-organized crime gangs, police, pimps, and even politicians. Unfortunately, peer trafficking too occurs in cases where children themselves are used to force or entice other children.

The transportation routes normally used are the existing roads, railway lines, river routes, and open borders. Needless to say, those earning third-party profit are the least affected by the altered social situation. Figure 5.1 in previous page illustrates the different aspects of trafficking in a flow diagram.

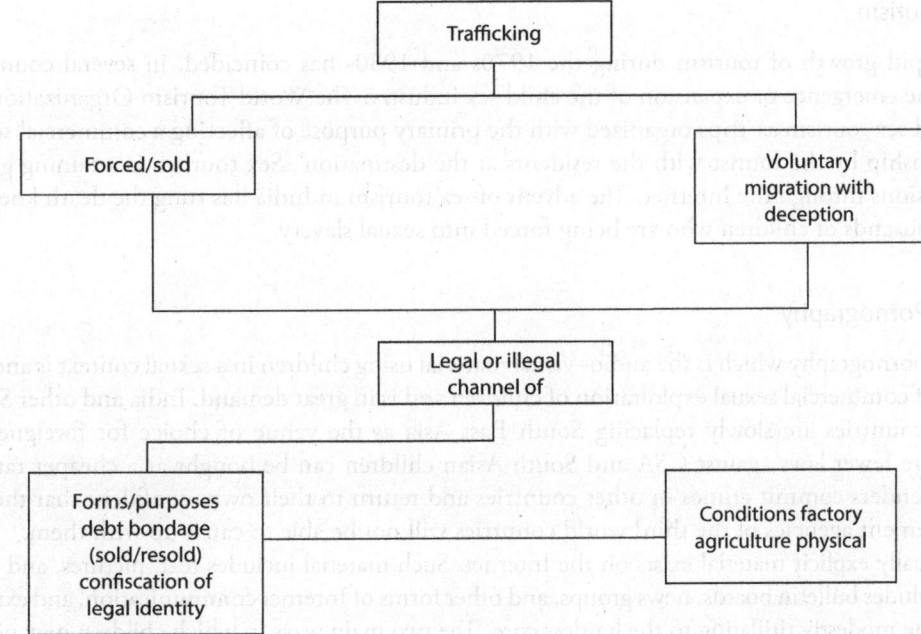

Figure 5.1   Trafficking[221]

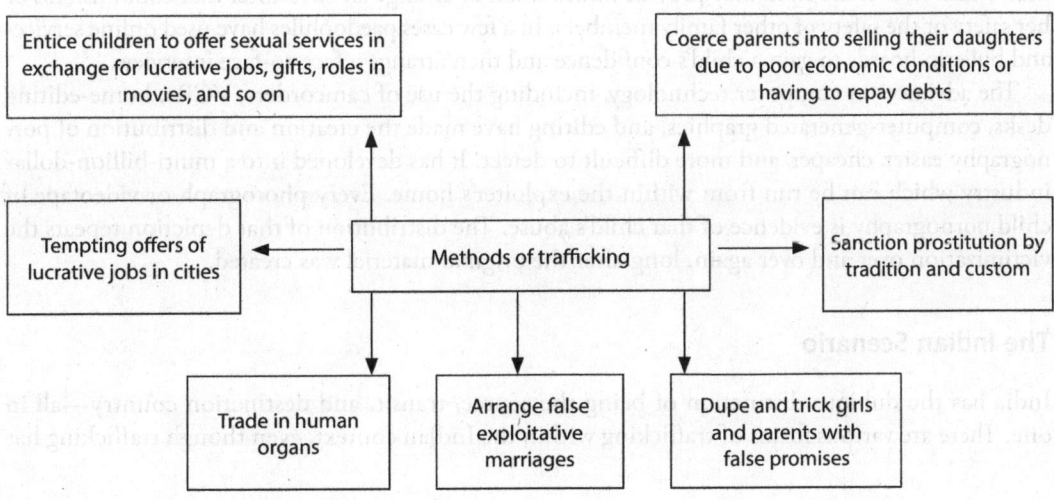

Figure 5.2   Methods of Trafficking

221   Source for Figure 5.1 and Figure 5.2: Global Alliance against Traffic in Women.

Sex Tourism

The rapid growth of tourism during the 1970s and 1980s has coincided, in several countries, with the emergence or expansion of the child sex industry. The World Tourism Organization has defined sex tourism as 'trips organized with the primary purpose of affecting a commercial sexual relationship by the tourist with the residents at the destination'. Sex tourism is attaining global dimensions through the Internet. The advent of sex tourism in India has rung the death knell for the thousands of children who are being forced into sexual slavery.

Child Pornography

Child pornography which is the audio–visual material using children in a sexual context is another form of commercial sexual exploitation of children and is in great demand. India and other South Asian countries are slowly replacing South East Asia as the venue of choice for foreigners as there are fewer laws against CSA and South Asian children can be bought at a cheaper rate.[222] Sex offenders commit crimes in other countries and return to their own, confident that the law enforcement agencies of the third world countries will not be able to catch up with them.

Sexually explicit material exists on the Internet. Such material includes text, pictures, and chat, and includes bulletin boards, news groups, and other forms of Internet communication, and extends from the modestly titillating to the hardest core. The two main ways in which children may potentially be harmed by child pornography are by being exposed to pornography and by being filmed or photographed or made the subjects themselves in some other way. Teenagers are particularly at risk because they often use the computer unsupervised and because they are more likely than younger ones to participate in online discussions regarding companionship, relationship, or sexual activity. These risks include exposure to inappropriate material of a sexual or violent nature, or encountering email or bulletin-board messages that are demeaning or belligerent. Another risk is the possibility that, while online, the child may provide information or arrange an encounter that could risk his or her safety or the safety of other family members. In a few cases paedophiles have used online services and bulletin boards to gain a child's confidence and then arrange a face-to-face interview.

The advances in computer technology, including the use of camcorders, VCRs, home-editing desks, computer-generated graphics, and editing have made the creation and distribution of pornography easier, cheaper, and more difficult to detect. It has developed into a multi-billion-dollar industry which can be run from within the exploiter's home. Every photograph or videotape of child pornography is evidence of that child's abuse. The distribution of that depiction repeats the victimization over and over again, long after the original material was created.

The Indian Scenario

India has the dubious distinction of being the source, transit, and destination country—all in one. There are various forms of trafficking within the Indian context, even though trafficking has

---

[222] Young Men's Christian Association (YMCA), End Child Prostitution in Asian Tourism (ECPAT), and UNICEF. 1995. *Child Prostitution—The Ultimate Abuse*, Report on The National Consultation on Child Prostitution, 18–20 November, New Delhi.

most often been linked to prostitution. Clearly, trafficking takes place for a range of purposes. Prostitution is but the most visible form of this abusive and degrading trade of women and children. At the same time, trafficking of children also takes place for labour such as work at construction sites, work in the carpet industry, domestic work, pushing children into bonded bondage, begging, marriage, to provide jockeys for camel races in the Gulf countries, and for pornography. The number of victims of trafficking and the purpose, to which they are put, depend on global trading patterns and the demand and supply trends of a particular economy.[223] The issues of forced marriage for labour and other forms of forced labour in agriculture as well as industry, domestic service, begging, camel jockeying, organ transplant, among others, cannot be ignored. Entry and consolidation of major crime syndicates in the sphere of trafficking makes it difficult to probe and intervene into specific cases. Evidence of trafficking for forced begging, marriage, and labour in informal work ghettoes are on the rise within the Indian context. There are some evident forms of trafficking with religious or community sanction—the Bassanis, Joginis, Bhogam Vandhis, and Venkatesinis in Andhra Pradesh; the Muralis, Aradhinis, and Tamasha girls in Maharashtra; the Thevadiyars in Tamil Nadu; the Bedia, Bachhda, and Sansi communities in Madhya Pradesh; and the Nat community in Uttar Pradesh. The community justifies and legitimizes the practice and, ultimately, many of the victims get trafficked into prostitution.

In India, traditional systems of children in prostitution varied as the devdasi or the Jogini, and the trafficking system that moves young girls across South Asia and into urban centres reveal the active exploitation and the socio-economic realities that make such exploitation possible. In the last few years, increasing number of instances of commercial sexual exploitation of children have also come to light in popular tourist destinations like Goa. A survey sponsored by the Central Social Welfare Board (CSWB) in 1991 in six metropolitan cities of India indicated that the population of women and child victims of commercial sexual exploitation would be between 70,000 and 100,000. It also revealed that about 30 per cent of them are below 18 years of age. The major contributory factors for the commercial sexual exploitation of women and children are poverty and unemployment or lack of appropriate rehabilitation. About 70 per cent of them are illiterates; 43 per cent of them desire to be rescued. Most of those who want to leave have given the reasons like desire to save their children from commercial sexual exploitation, protection of the future of their children, and fear of diseases. The others continue to be exploited due to absence of alternative sources of income, social non-acceptability, family customs, poverty, ill health, and their despondence.[224]

Table 5.5 gives the official statistics relating to various crimes under trafficking of minor children.

As represented in the table, a total of 1,224 cases were reported in the year 2013 as compared to 809 such cases in 2012, showing an increase of 51.3 per cent over 2012. West Bengal has

[223] 'Child Trafficking in India'. Available at http://www.haqcrc.org/sites/default/files/Child%20 Trafficking%20in%20India-A%20Situational%20Analysis.pdf (accessed on on 25 May 2015).

[224] UNICEF Regional Office Save the Children Alliance. 1999. *Trafficking of Women and Children in South Asia: Taking Stock and Moving Ahead: A Broad Assessment of Anti-Trafficking Initiatives in Nepal, Bangladesh and India*, a report, 21 November.

Table 5.5 Crime Head-wise Incidence of Various Crimes under Human Trafficking during 2009–13 and Percentage Variation in 2013 over 2012[225]

S. No.	Crime Head	Year					Percentage Variation in 2013 over 2012
		2009	2010	2011	2012	2013	
1.	Procuration of minor girls (Section 366-A IPC)	237	679	862	809	1,224	51.3
2.	Importation of girls from foreign country (Section 366-B IPC)	48	36	80	59	31	−47.5
3.	Selling of girls for prostitution (Section 372 IPC)	57	130	113	108	100	−7.4
4.	Buying of girls for prostitution (Section 373 IPC)	32	78	27	15	6	−60.0
5.	ITPA	2,474	2,499	2,435	2,563	2,579	0.6
	Total	2,848	3,422	3,517	3,554	3,940	10.9

reported 486 such cases indicating a share of 39.7 per cent at the national level followed by Bihar (193 cases) (15.8 per cent) and Assam (129 cases) (10.5 per cent).

The US Government's 2014 *Trafficking in Persons Report* (TIP Report) clearly refers to the existing situation of human exploitation and trafficking that involves men, women, and children in India. According to the report, over 90 per cent of the trafficking is done within the borders and 10 per cent is from overseas. The problem is spread over various forms of exploitation. Trafficking of women and young girls from Nepal and Bangladesh into India for sexual exploitation is the most common. These girls from poor families and often in the age group of 9–14 years are brought into India and sold to brothel owners in Kolkata, Mumbai, and Delhi, amongst several other cities. Not all are kidnapped or forced out of their homes in their native lands. Many are sold by their parents or close relatives to get away from abject poverty.[226]

A lot of young boys are trafficked into India for work as bonded labour in industries like coal, brick kilns, handloom and embroidery, rice mills, and agriculture. They are made to work up to

[225] Source: UNICEF's *Manual for Social Workers: Dealing with Child Victims of Trafficking and Commercial Sex Exploitation*, Government of India, Department of Women and Child Development. Available at http://www.bettercarenetwork.org/sites/default/files/Manual%20for%20Social%20Workers%20-%20Dealing%20with%20Child%20Victims%20of%20Trafficking%20and%20Commerical%20Sexual%20Exploitation.pdf (accessed on 11 October 2016).

[226] Government of USA, *2014 Trafficking in Person Report*.

16 hours a day in return for subsistence food and very little or no money. These children are often sexually exploited by their owners and beaten or tortured in cases of non-compliance.[227]

Several young boys from Bihar find their way to factories in Nepal, while young girls from Nepal are brought through transit points of Raxaul and Gorakhpur to be sold to traffickers in India. Kolkata is a major transit point and destination for girls and women coming from Nepal and Bangladesh. The trafficking network is well established with deep involvement of government officials, police at the borders and within the states and in some cases politicians, all of whom profit from this activity that has now taken the shape of an industry.[228]

India is also a transit point for young boys who are sent to Dubai and other Middle East countries for camel racing. Very often these young boys are sexually exploited and kept as bonded labourers. Another area where children are frequently sent to is Saudi Arabia, where begging is an organized billion dollar industry, especially during Haj. In India, begging syndicates often maim children and put them on to streets to get maximum collection from them.[229]

According to the NHRC of India, over 40,000 children are reported missing every year of which over 11,000 remain untraced. It is in this backdrop, that the recent discovery of child trafficking into Kerala has got the government's attention. Children from various states were being brought into Kerala by train. At the station, they were stopped and the persons who were escorting them could not come up with an acceptable reason as to why they were being brought in to Kerala. All escorting adults were arrested and now the Kerala High Court has ordered a Central Bureau of Investigation (CBI) investigation into the matter.[230]

Trafficking for sex and other purposes has always existed in India, but now there is trafficking children for domestic slavery. This is due to rising demand for domestic maids due to rising income in urban areas and wide scale poverty in rural areas. This trafficking shows the rise of massive inequality in India.[231]

There are so many human rights violations that take place on trafficked person. The list includes the following:[232]

1. Deprivation of the right to life (slave-like conditions).
2. Deprivation of the right to security.
3. Deprivation of dignity.
4. Deprivation of the right to access to justice and redressal of grievances.
5. Denial of access to health services.
6. Denial of right to self-determination (for example, when the victim is retrafficked).
7. Denial of right to return to own community.

---

[227] Government of USA, *2014 TIP*.

[228] Government of USA, *2014 TIP*.

[229] Government of USA, *2014 TIP*.

[230] Government of USA, *2014 TIP*.

[231] See http://www.theguardian.com/global-development/2015/apr/28/child-trafficking-india-domestic-labour-chhattisgarh (accessed on 25 May 2015).

[232] P.M. Nair, *Trafficking of Women and Children for Sexual Exploitation*, handbook for law enforcement agencies in India (New Delhi: UNODC, 2007).

8. Double jeopardy (for example, a person trafficked across a border is sometimes convicted for non-possession of passport/visa and is simultaneously punished for 'soliciting').
9. Denial of right to representation.
10. Denial of right to be heard before decision making

Indian Laws Dealing with Commercial Sexual Exploitation of Children and Trafficking

According to Article 23 of the Constitution of India, trafficking in women and children for immoral purposes is prohibited. Articles 39(e) and (f) of the directive principles of state policy state that it is the duty of the state to secure that the tender age of children are not abused and forced by economic necessity to enter vocations unsuited to their age and strength and directs the state to ensure that the children are given opportunities to develop in a healthy manner and in conditions of freedom and dignity.

Trafficking was first dealt with by the Suppression of Immoral Traffic in Women and Girls Act (SITA), 1956, which was passed on 31 December 1956. The legislation was enacted in pursuance of the UN Convention of 1950.[233] This act had several loopholes. Some of the drawbacks were:[234]

- The act did not conform fully to the international convention on the subject.
- The definition of prostitution was unsatisfactory.
- No provision for dealing with policing and punishment of criminals who have set up interstate and international networks to procure children.
- No specific provisions to deal with prostitution of children.
- No provision for dealing with sexual exploitation of boys.
- Lesser sentence compared to that in the IPC to offenders who induct children and women into prostitution.
- Customer not made accountable.
- Protective homes set up under the act were mainly custody homes and not properly staffed.
- No provision for the children of prostitutes.
- No accountability placed on the superintendent of the protective homes.

Immoral Traffic (Prevention) Act, 1956

The SITA, 1956, proved to be inadequate to combat the increasing commercialization of trafficking. Parliament amended the law in 1970 and later in 1986. The act was amended by the following:

---

[233] UN Convention for the Suppression of Traffic in Persons and of Exploitation of the Prostitution of Others. This was approved by the General Assembly resolution 317(iv) of 2 December 1949. In 1950, the Government of India ratified this convention.

[234] Sheela Barse, *A Critique of the Suppression of Immoral Traffic in Women and Girls Act 1956* (Mumbai, India: Neer Gaurav Research and Development Foundation).

- The SITA, 1978 (46 of 1978) with effect from 2 October 1979
- The SITA, 1986 (44 of 1986) with effect from 26 January 1987.

As a result of substitution of the words (ITPA) 'Immoral Traffic (Prevention) Act' for the words 'Suppression of Immoral Traffic in Women and Girls Act' made by Section 3 of the Amending Act No. 44 of 1986, the principal act was short titled as the Immoral Traffic (Prevention) Act, 1956. The ITPA was enacted to bring into effect the 'UN Convention for the Suppression of the Traffic in Persons and of the Exploitation of the Prostitution of Others, 1950'. Moreover, it was aimed to give effect to Constitutional mandate in Article 23—Article 23 of the Constitution, which provides for prohibition of traffic in human beings and forced labour, clearly mandates that traffic in human beings, beggary and other similar forms of forced labour, are prohibited and any contravention of this provision shall be an offence punishable in accordance with law.

Prostitution under this act means the sexual exploitation or abuse of persons for commercial purposes and the expression 'prostitute' should be construed accordingly.[235] This definition is wider and includes sexual exploitation and abuse of any person—female, eunuch, or male—for commercial purposes. The act has introduced the concept of child[236] victims as against minors[237] and majors[238] and imposes higher degree of criminality to sexual exploiters of children.

By the use of presumptions, the burden of the prosecution is lightened by the ITPA, 1986. There are certain presumptions under the act in favour of the child victims. These are as follows:

- If a child is found in a brothel or under suspicious circumstances in the custody of a person, other than the parent or lawful guardian who is unable to explain satisfactorily the presence of such a child, that person shall be presumed to have procured the child for the purposes of prostitution (Section 6(2) and 6(2A)).
- A report in a newspaper on the use of certain premises as a brothel is deemed to be sufficient proof of the landlord, occupier, or tenant knowingly allowing such use (Section 3(2A) (a)).
- If a child is found accompanying, in suspicious circumstances,[239] a person who is neither its parent nor lawful guardian and who is leaving the country, that person is committing the offence of immoral trafficking.

The ITPA does not make prostitution per se a criminal offence or punish a person because the person prostitutes himself or herself. The purpose of the enactment is to inhibit or abolish commercialized sexual abuse and exploitation and the traffic in persons as an organized means of living. The object is attempted to be achieved by two major strategies, namely, by punishing

---

[235] ITPA, 1986, Section 2(f).

[236] Section 2(aa), ITPA, 1986: 'Child' means a person who has not completed the age of 16 years.

[237] Section 2(cb), ITPA, 1986: 'Minor' means a person who has completed the age of 16 years but has not completed the age of 18 years.

[238] Section 2(ca), ITPA, 1986: 'Major' means a person who has completed the age of 18 years.

[239] Suspicious circumstances in this section includes situations in which (i) the mother tongue of the accused is different from that of the child or the language is different from that generally spoken in the locality, (ii) where the child is wrongfully confined without access to others, and (iii) where the child is married to a foreigner.

those who are guilty of such conduct and by rescuing and rehabilitating the victims of such exploitation.[240] The act criminalizes the procurers, traffickers, and profiteers of the trade but in no way does it define trafficking per se in human beings.

The ITPA, 1956 did not define trafficking comprehensively since it only criminalized trafficking for the purpose of prostitution. It does not criminalize the employment of a trafficked person. The ITPA, being a special legislation, has comprehensive, stringent, and effective provisions to address the issues in trafficking and consequent exploitation. However, there is no bar in utilizing the provisions of ITPA along with IPC. In any given context, the investigating police officer can file charge-sheet against the accused under the graver sections of all laws which are applicable. The ITPA provisions can be included along with IPC, JJ Act, and other legislations which would apply to the facts and circumstances of the case under investigation.[241]

Section 8 of ITPA is generally subjected to abuse. The women and children who are subjected to the offences under the act are firstly 'arrested' as 'prostitutes' for 'soliciting' prostitution and prosecuted. This is a typical case of the survivor of an offence ultimately becomes the convict.[242] A trafficked woman must not be victimized under Section 8 of ITPA or any other section of any law. When investigation reveals that she has been sexually exploited against her informed consent, charge sheet be filed against all her exploiters not only under ITPA, but also under the relevant sections of IPC, dealing with sexual assault (376 and 377, among others). Consent obtained under lure, deceit, duress, coercion, compulsion, and force is not 'consent' in the legal sense. Furthermore, if the victim is a girl child, the offence is complete even if there was consent.[243]

Rescue and Rehabilitation of Children and Minors under the ITPA, 1986

Where a magistrate has reason to believe from information received from the police or from any other person authorized by the state government that any person is living on, or is carrying on, or is being made to carry on prostitution in a brothel, he may direct a police officer not below the rank of a sub-inspector to enter such brothel and to remove such person and produce him/her before the judge (Section 16). A minor or a child rescued under this act is treated as a neglected child (Section 2(d) (vi)) under the JJ Act, 2000, and has to be produced before the Juvenile Welfare Board (Section 4(1)), now the CWC (Section 32) for reception and rehabilitation, and placing in safe custody. There is a provision for providing for intermediate custody in a shelter, children's home, or corrective institution (Section 2(b)) 33(1)) after rescue pending detailed inquiry.

---

[240] N.R.M. Menon, *Prevention of Immoral Traffic and Restoration of Human Dignity, Select Materials on Public Legal Education* (Bangalore: Legal Services Clinic, National Law of India University, 1991).

[241] Nair, *Trafficking of Women and Children*.

[242] *Justice Verma Committee Report Recommendations*. Available at http://nlrd.org/resources-womens-rights/anti-trafficking/anti-trafficking-schemespolicy-document/verma-committee-report-on-trafficking-in-india (accessed on 28 May 2015).

[243] *Justice Verma Committee Report Recommendations*. Available at http://nlrd.org/resources-womens-rights/anti-trafficking/anti-trafficking-schemespolicy-document/verma-committee-report-on-trafficking-in-india (accessed on 28 May 2015).

The Supreme Court observed in the Bachpan Bachao Andolan (BBA) decision:[244]

Trafficking in women and children has become an increasingly lucrative business especially since the risk of being prosecuted is very low. Women and children do not usually come to the brothels on their own will, but are brought through highly systematic, organized and illegal trafficking networks run by experienced individuals who buy, transport and sell children into prostitution. Traffickers tend to work in groups and children being trafficked often change hands to ensure that neither the trafficker nor the child gets caught during transit. Different groups of traffickers include gang members, police, pimps and even politicians, all working as a nexus. Trafficking networks are well organized and have linkages both within the country and in the neighbouring countries. Most traffickers are men. The role of women in this business is restricted to recruitment at the brothels.

The ITPA, 1986 needs amendment to bring in the social realities and curb the complex, organized crime.

Indian Penal Code, 1860

A trafficked minor is subjected to the following violations of the IPC, 1860 provisions:

1. Displaced from his/her community, which tantamount to kidnapping/abduction (Sections 361, 362, 365, 366 IPC may apply).
2. Procured illegally (Section 366A IPC).
3. Sold by somebody (Section 372 IPC).
4. Bought by somebody (Section 373 IPC).
5. Imported from a foreign country (if she hails from a foreign country, or even from J&K state, and is under 21 years of age (Section 366B IPC)).
6. Wrongfully restrained (Section 339 IPC).
7. Wrongfully confined (Section 340 IPC).
8. Physically tortured/injured (Section 327, 329 IPC).
9. Subjected to criminal force (Section 350 IPC).
10. Mentally tortured/harassed/assaulted (Section 351 IPC).
11. Criminally intimidated (Section 506 IPC).
12. Outraged of her modesty (Section 354 IPC).[245]
13. Raped/gang raped/repeatedly raped (Section 375, Section 376 IPC).
14. Subjected to perverse sexual exploitation ('unnatural offences') (Section 377 IPC).
15. Defamed (Section 499 IPC).

Additionally, under the CLA Act, 2013, Sections 370 and 370A have been added to the IPC.[246] The new Section 370 defines the offence of trafficking thus replacing the prior Section 370 IPC,

[244] 2011 5 SCC 1.
[245] Amended by the CLA Act, 2013.
[246] The CLA Act, 2013 was passed by the Lok Sabha on 19 March 2013, and by the Rajya Sabha on 21 March 2013, which provides for amendment of IPL, Indian Evidence Act, and Civil procedure Code on

which dealt with the buying or disposing of any person as a slave. The IPC now has a provision on trafficking, which can be used to prosecute traffickers in a range of labour sectors, including India's brick kilns, rice mills, farms, embroidery factories, mines, stone quarries, homes, and carpet factories, and not only sex work. The definition of trafficking can be represented as given in Table 5.6.

Table 5.6   Indian Penal Code, Section 370

Statute	Section	Act	Means	End (Exploitation)
IPC	370 Whoever for the purpose of exploitation	Recruits	Using threat	Physical exploitation
		Transports	Using force or any other form of coercion	Sexual exploitation
		Harbours	Abduction	Slavery
		Transfers	Practicing fraud, or deception	Practices similar to slavery
		Receives	Abuse of power	Servitude
			Inducement	Forced removal of organs

The new Section 370 criminalizes anyone who recruits, transports, harbours, transfers, or receives a person using certain means (including threats, force, coercion, fraud, deception, abduction, abuse of power, or inducement) for purposes of exploitation. Exploitation in turn is not defined but is said to include any act of physical exploitation or any form of sexual exploitation, slavery, or practices similar to slavery, servitude, or the forced removal of organs. Punishment ranges from 7 to 10 years' rigorous imprisonment with fine.[247] This is further enhanced and graded depending on whether the victim is an adult or minor, if more than one person or minor is trafficked, if the trafficker is a repeat offender and whether the trafficker is a police officer or public servant. This definition of trafficking recognizes the fact that targeting the demand for trafficked labour is often crucial in the fight against trafficking. This definition is also in line with the international definition of trafficking.[248]

---

laws related to sexual offences. The bill received Presidential assent on 2 April 2013 and deemed to come into force from 3 April 2013. It was originally an ordinance promulgated by the President of India, Pranab Mukherjee, on 3 April 2013, in light of the protests in the 2012 Delhi gang rape case.

[247] Whoever, knowingly or having reason to believe that a minor has been trafficked, engages such minor for sexual exploitation in any manner, shall be punished with rigorous imprisonment for a term which shall not be less than 5 years, but which may extend to 7 years, and shall also be liable to fine.

Whoever, knowingly by or having reason to believe that a person has been trafficked, engages such person for sexual exploitation in any manner, shall be punished with rigorous imprisonment for a term which shall not be less than 3 years, but which may extend to 5 years, and shall also be liable to fine

[248] Definition of trafficking in Article 3 of the United Nations Protocol to Prevent, Suppress and Punish Trafficking against Persons, Especially Women and Children supplementing the 2000 United Nations Convention against Transnational Organized Crime. India signed the UN Protocol on 12 December 2002 and ratified it in May 2011.

This definition links traditional offences under the IPC to the composite offence of 'trafficking in persons' and this inexorable link will put an additional burden on the police to lodge an FIR and investigate it in accordance with law. Phrases like 'abuse of power or a position of vulnerability' and 'giving or receiving benefits to achieve the consent of a person having control of another person' are per se not offences in the eyes of our law. It is therefore imperative that these actions be linked to the offence of 'trafficking' so as to make them culpable. This definition has been adopted in the Goa Children's Act, 2003.[249]

This provision also includes organ trade. As the explanation further clarifies 'exploitation' would also include prostitution. This is in addition to the ITP Act, 1956. The intention of the legislature in including 'other forms of sexual exploitation' and 'forced labour or services' can be read to address situations where the trafficked persons are used for pornographic purposes or in services like massage parlours. The new section also ensures that persons involved at each and every stage of trafficking chain are brought within the criminal justice system. Also by specifically including that if a person is brought with his/her consent, where such consent is obtained through force, coercion, fraud, deception, or under abuse of power, the same will amount to trafficking, the law has been substantially strengthened. This will cover all situations where girls who happen to be major are duped with promises of marriage and willingly accompany the traffickers who exploit them in various ways. It has also been specifically added in the provision that consent of the victim is immaterial for the determination of the offence.[250]

The new section also differentiates the instances of trafficking major persons from minor persons. This differentiation is brought about by providing separate penalty for each with higher minimum sentence for trafficking minor persons. While earlier no minimum imprisonment term was provided, now, the minimum (rigorous) imprisonment term is fixed. In addition the section also provides for enhanced punishment for repeated offender as well as where the offender traffics more than one person at the same time. By providing that trafficking in minor persons on a repeated conviction will attract imprisonment for life (meaning the remaining natural life) the law has been substantially changed. This will surely act as a big deterrent. Involvement of a public servant including a police officer shall entitle him to life imprisonment which shall mean the remaining natural life.[251]

---

[249] *Justice Verma Committee Report Recommendation*. On 23 December 2012, a three-member committee headed by Justice J.S. Verma, former Chief Justice of the Supreme Court, was constituted to recommend amendments to the Criminal Law so as to provide for quicker trial and enhanced punishment for criminals accused of committing sexual assault against women. The other members on the Committee were Justice Leila Seth, former judge of the High Court and Gopal Subramanium, former Solicitor General of India. The Committee submitted its report on 23 January 2013. It made recommendations on laws related to rape, sexual harassment, trafficking, and CSA, medical examination of victims, police, electoral and educational reforms. Available at http://nlrd.org/resources-womens-rights/anti-trafficking/anti-trafficking-schemespolicy-document/verma-committee-report-on-trafficking-in-india (accessed on 28 May 2015).

[250] *Justice Verma Committee Report Recommendation*.

[251] *Justice Verma Committee Report Recommendation*.

Changes Brought About By Criminal Law Amendment, 2013

The recent CLA Act, 2013 recognizes trafficking as an offence in the Section 370 of the IPC. This is on similar lines as the Palermo Protocol, ratified by India in May 2011, following a Supreme Court judgment defining trafficking in PIL filed by BBA in 2011. The amendment targets the entire process that leads to trafficking of a person and also makes the employment of a trafficked person and subsequent sexual exploitation a specific offence under Section 370A.[252] While the old Section 370 of IPC dealt with only buying or disposing of any person as a slave the new section will take in its purview buying or disposing of any person for various kinds of exploitation including slavery. This provision includes organ trade as well. As the explanation further clarifies 'exploitation' would also include prostitution. This is in addition to the ITP Act, 1956.

The new section also ensures that persons involved at each and every stage of trafficking chain are brought within the criminal justice system. Also, by specifically including that if a person is brought with his/her consent, where such consent is obtained through force, coercion, fraud, deception, or under abuse of power, the same will amount to trafficking, the law has been substantially strengthened. This will cover all situations where girls who happen to be major are duped with promises of marriage and willingly accompany the traffickers who exploit them in various ways. It has also been specifically added in the provision that consent of the victim is immaterial for the determination of the offence.[253]

The new section also differentiates the instances of trafficking major persons from minor persons. This differentiation is brought about by providing separate penalty for each with higher minimum sentence for trafficking minor persons. In addition, the section also provides for enhanced punishment for repeated offender as well as where the offender traffics more than one person at the same time (Table 5.7). By providing that trafficking in minor persons on a repeated conviction will attract imprisonment for life (meaning the remaining natural life) the law has been substantially changed.[254] Involvement of a public servant including a police officer shall entitle him to life imprisonment which shall mean the remaining natural life.[255] Section 370A further adds strength to trafficking related law by criminalizing employment of a trafficked (major/minor) person. A person who has reason to believe or apprehension that the minor/major person employed by them has been trafficked will make them criminally liable. This places a huge responsibility on the employers who were till now, let off easily under the not so strict provisions of the child labour laws and juvenile related laws. Here also a higher minimum prison term is prescribed where a minor person is involved. Also important is the fact that irrespective of age of

[252] India Prohibits All Forms of Trafficking, 21 March 2013, Bachpan Bachao Andolan. Available at http://www.bba.org.in/news/210313.php (accessed on 17 November 2016).

[253] Garima Tiwari, *Children as Victims of Trafficking in India*. Available at http://acontrarioicl.com/2013/05/27/children-as-victims-of-trafficking-in-india/ (accessed on 17 November 2016).

[254] 'Piecemeal Approach'. Available at http://www.frontline.in/social-issues/general-issues/piecemeal-approach/article4431434.ece (accessed on 17 November 2016).

[255] Rajul Jain, *Human Trafficking and Law: Understanding Criminal Law (Amendment) Ordinance, 2013*. Available at http://nlrd.org/resources-womens-rights/anti-trafficking/anti-trafficking-government-notificationsadvisories/human-trafficking-and-law-understanding-criminal-law-amendment-ordinance-2013 (accessed on 17 November 2016).

the person employed, simply employing a trafficked person is an offence. This provision will go a long way in ensuring that people verify the antecedents of the placement agencies as also get the police verification of the persons employed. This will also aide in curbing the huge demand for labour who are victims of unsafe migration[256].

Table 5.7 Criminal Procedure Code—Amendments[257]

Classification under Schedule 1 CrPC		
Offence		**Punishment/Imprisonment /Fine**
Exploitation of a trafficked child		5 to 7 years + Fine
Exploitation of a trafficked person		3 to 5 years + Fine
Cognizance	**Bail**	**Triable By**
Cognizable	Non-bailable	Court of session

Provisions in Other Laws Relating to Trafficking of Minors[258]

The provisions in the laws below may also be applicable in cases of trafficking of minors, as trafficking also results in child labour, bonded labour, trafficking for removal of human organs, illegal migration.

Juvenile Justice (Care and Protection of Children) Act, 2015

Under JJ Act, 2015, a juvenile or child means a person who is under 18 years of age. It prohibits exploitation of child employee. If anybody ostensibly engages a child and keeps him in bondage for the purpose of employment or withholds his/her earnings or uses such earning for his/her own purposes shall be punishable with rigorous imprisonment for a term which may extend to 5 years and shall also be liable to fine of Rs 1 lakh.[259] It includes any forms of forced labour and sexual exploitation. This provision can be used against people who traffic children for the purpose of labour and against those who employ such trafficked children. It is essential for the law enforcement agencies to note that such children must neither be treated as accused nor be arrested and that they must be produced before the CWC.[260]

---

[256] Jain, *Human Trafficking and Law.*

[257] Prepared by the author on the basis of CLA Act, 2013.

[258] See https://asiafoundation.org/resources/pdfs/StanfordHumanTraffickingIndiaBackground.pdf (accessed on 28 May 2015).

[259] JJ Act, 2015, Section 79.

[260] JJ Act 2015 , Section 2(ix): Child in need of care and protection is a child who is found vulnerable and is likely to be inducted into drug abuse or trafficking.

Bonded Labour (Abolition) Act, 1976

The act prohibits anyone from making any advance or compelling any person to render any bonded labour and states further that any agreement or custom requiring any person to do work as a bonded labourer is void and provides for punishment for anyone who compels any person to render bonded labour or even advance any bonded debt.[261] Punishment in both cases of enforcing bonded labour and advancing bonded debt is imprisonment up to 3 years and fine up to Rs 2,000. The bonded labourers are to be treated as victims and not offenders.

Child Labour (Prohibition and Regulation) Act, 1986

This act defines a 'child' to be a person who has not completed 14 years of age and lays down the industries in which children should not be employed apart from laying down a few safety measures and other requirements which shall be met irrespective of what is stated in the other labour legislations.[262]

However, this act does not apply to any employment that is undertaken with the help of family members in one's own residence. Any person, police officer, or (labour) inspector may file a complaint of the commission of an offence under this act in a court not lower than metropolitan magistrate or a magistrate of the first class.[263] The trafficked children are to be treated as victims and not as offenders, and may be treated as 'children in need of care and protection' under the JJ Act, 2000. The act provides for penalties to the employer if children are found employed in prohibited employments.

Scheduled Castes and Scheduled Tribes (Prevention of Atrocities) Act, 1989

Many victims of trafficking belong to marginalized groups. Traffickers target such areas, as they are vulnerable socially and economically. This act provides an additional tool to safeguard women and young girls belonging to scheduled castes and scheduled tribes and also to create a greater burden on the trafficker/offender to prove his lack of complicity in the matter.[264] This can be effective if the offender knows the status of victims. It specifically covers certain forms of trafficking such as forced or bonded labour (Clause vi) and sexual exploitation of women (Clauses xi, xii).

A minimum punishment of 6 months is provided which could extend up to 5 years in any offence covered Section 3.

Transplantation of Human Organs Act, 1994

The shocking exploitation of abject poverty of many donors for even small sums of money appears to have provided the foundation for enacting the act. This act deals with criminal responsibility

---

[261] UNODC, *Resource Book on the Legal Framework on Anti Human Trafficking*, Government of India (2008), p. 99.

[262] UNODC, *Resource Book on the Legal Framework on Anti Human Trafficking*, p. 98.

[263] Section 16(I)

[264] UNODC, *Resource Book on the Legal Framework on Anti Human Trafficking*.

in cases of harvesting of organs and trafficking of persons for this purpose includes traffickers, procurers, brokers, intermediaries, hospital/nursing staff, and medical laboratory technicians involved in the illegal transplant procedure.[265]

Section 11 declares prohibition of removal or transplantation of human organs for any purpose other than therapeutic purposes. Section 18 provides for punishment for removal of human organs without authority. Section 19 provides for punishment for commercial dealings in human organs. The authorization committee under the act has to be satisfied that the authorization for removal is not for commercial consideration. Since some amount of urgency has to be exhibited because of the need for transplantation, expeditious disposal of the application would be appropriate. The penalty incurred for organ trade is also very high. This law does not allow exchange of money between the donor and the recipient

Section 19 clarifies that it punishes those who seek willing people or offer to supply organs; it should be punishable with imprisonment for a term which shall not be less than 2 years but which may extend to 7 years and shall be liable to fine which shall not be less than Rs 10,000 but may extend to Rs 20,000.

The CLA Act, 2013 recognizes trafficking as an offence in the Section 370 of the IPC. This is on the similar lines as the Palermo Protocol, also ratified by India in May 2011, following a Supreme Court judgment defining trafficking in a PIL field by BBA in 2011. While the old Section 370 of IPC dealt with only buying or disposing of any person as a slave the new section will take in its purview buying or disposing of any person for various kinds of exploitation including slavery. This provision includes organ trade as well.

Immigration (Carrier's Liability) Act, 2000

The Immigration Act can be used to prosecute those who indulge in the illegal transport of human beings from other countries. In its definition 'carrier' means a person who is engaged in the business of transporting passengers by water or air and includes any association of persons, whether incorporated or not, by whom the aircraft or the ship is owned or chartered. This act applies only to carriers by air or by sea.

The carrier may be punished by the competent authority under the Passport Act, by imposing a penalty of Rs 1,000.

Prohibition of Child Marriage Act, 2006

This act defines marriage of a minor child to be void in certain circumstances. Section 12 defines that marriages where the minor has been taken out of lawful guardianship, or is by force compelled, or by any deceitful means induced to go from any place; or sold, or trafficked or used for immoral purposes are null and void.

The CMPOs are notified by the state government and such officers have the duty of preventing child marriages as well as collection of evidence for prosecution (Section 16).

However there is no specific section for the punishment.

[265] UNODC, *Resource Book on the Legal Framework on Anti Human Trafficking*, p. 125.

Missing Children and Linkages to Trafficking for Abuse and Exploitation

Missing children are often in a number of high-risk situations and their links to trafficking and child labour is of very great significance. A countless number of children go missing every year. The category of missing children include a number of problems including abduction or kidnapping of children by family members and by non-family members, run-away children or those forced to run away by family and surrounding circumstances, children who are in a difficult or aggressive environment, trafficked children, and lost children.[266] Due to this wide array of problems, it is hard to survey the number of missing children. Often cases are not reported to the police. Children who go missing may be exploited and abused for various purposes from camel jockeys in the Gulf countries to victims of organ trade and even grotesque cannibalism as reported at the Nithari village in Noida, Uttar Pradesh. There are also a large number of children who run away from homes after dropping out of school or facing difficulties at home. They usually run away to the glamorous big cities where they fall prey to exploiters and are employed in tea stalls, brothels, and forced to beg. Most of the children come from poorer families who do not have access to police services or whose reports are not taken seriously.[267]

As defined by Supreme Court in the judgment of *Bachpan Bachao Andolan* v. *Union of India & Ors*[268] and the advisory of Ministry of Home Affairs, a missing child is a person below 18 years of age whose whereabouts are not known to the parents, legal guardians, and any other persons, who may or may not be legally entrusted with the custody of the child, whatever may be the circumstances/causes of disappearance. The child will be considered missing and in need of care and protection, until located and/or his/her safety/well-being is established.[269]

The first comprehensive information in India on missing children was the collection of information by NCRB which started in 1953. A report on child prostitution[270] wherein the hidden linkage of 'missing children' to child trafficking was detailed was one of the first efforts on the issue. A more liberal approach to expand the issue was taken by the NHRC in its research on trafficking of women and children in India in 2004. Nevertheless, the figure of 44,000 missing children as estimated by NHRC in 2004–05[271] and the figure of 1,17,480 missing children (in 392 districts), as reflected by the BBA report is just the tip of the iceberg.[272]

As per official government data, in India, during the period from 2009 to 2011, the numbers of children that have gone missing are 2,36,014 and out of them 75,808 are still untraced. However,

---

[266] Available at http://www.childlineindia.org.in/missing-children-india.htm (accessed on 27 May 2015).

[267] Available at http://www.childlineindia.org.in/missing-children-india.htm (accessed on 27 May 2015).

[268] Writ Petition (Civil) No. 75 of 2012.

[269] Available at http://www.childlineindia.org.in/missing-children-india.htm (accessed on 27 May 2015).

[270] B. Bhamati for UNICEF in 1996.

[271] National Human Rights Commission. 2005. *Action Research on Trafficking in Women and Children in India* (New Delhi).

[272] *Missing Children in India*, a study by Bachpan Bachao Andolan. Available at www.bba.org (accessed on 17 November 2016).

only 34,899 FIRs have been registered in all.[273] Between 2013 and 2014, at least 67,000 children in India went missing, of whom 45 per cent were minors trafficked into prostitution. According to the NCRB, a girl is abducted every eight minutes in India. A US report on human trafficking states that India is one of the world's main hubs for child sex trafficking.[274]

Earlier, when a child went missing, there was no FIR filed as there was no cognizable offence committed. Hence only an entry was made into the General Station Diary at the concerned police office. Information of the missing child was forwarded to the chief of police as well as locally police officers generate awareness through the media. The police headquarters of each state has a missing person bureau. A database of missing persons is maintained by the Missing Persons Wing at the NCRB in New Delhi.[275]

Some Recommendations/Suggestions of the NHRC Committee[276]

1. Priorty Issue: The problem of 'missing children' is a grave matter which is also a human rights issue. Therefore, this issue needs to be made a 'priority issue' by all stakeholders, especially the law-enforcement agencies. The directors general of police of states should take appropriate steps to issue police orders/circulars/standing instructions, sensitize all officers in this regard, and make them accountable.[277]

2. Missing Persons Squad/Desk in Police Stations: The committee recommends that every police station across the country should have special squad/missing persons desk to trace missing children. This squad/desk should have a registering officer who should be made responsible of registering complaints of missing children. The Juvenile Aid Police Unit (JAPU) can, if required, be utilized for addressing the issue of missing children, even though the children who are missing can never be labeled as juveniles, but are, in fact, children in need of care and attention.[278]

3. Court Directives: There is a need to reiterate the implementation of the Supreme Court Guidelines given on 14 November 2002 in Writ Petition (Cri.) No 610 of 1996 filed by *Horilal* v. *Commissioner of Police, Delhi & Ors.* in all police stations across the country. This would entail prompt and effective steps for tracing missing children. As per the directions given by the Delhi High Court, a cell relating to missing persons/children was set up in the

---

[273] See also http://bba.org.in/?q=content/supreme-court-india-directs-registration-over-75000-cases-missing-children#sthash.qch3hqcy.dpuf (accessed on 17 November 2016).

[274] Available at http://scroll.in/article/677280/half-the-67000-children-who-went-missing-in-india-last-year-were-sold-into-prostitution, (accessed on 27 May 2015).

[275] Available at http://nlrd.org/childs-rights-initiative/latest-advisories-notifications-child-rights-initiative/nhrc-guidelines-on-missing-children (accessed on 25 May 2015).

[276] *Report of NHRC Committee on Missing Children 2007.* Available at nhrc.nic.in/Documents/Reports/misc_MCRReport.doc (accessed on 25 May 2015).

[277] *Report of NHRC Committee on Missing Children 2007.* Available at nhrc.nic.in/Documents/Reports/misc_MCRReport.doc (accessed on 25 May 2015).

[278] *Report of NHRC Committee on Missing Children 2007.* Available at nhrc.nic.in/Documents/Reports/misc_MCRReport.doc (accessed on 25 May 2015).

CBI. This cell has been functioning ever since but due to lack of adequate resources, desired results could not be achieved. Since the CBI is a central investigating agency having powers and jurisdiction to take up cases of inter-state and international ramifications, it would be desirable to strengthen this cell to enhance its capacity to coordinate and investigate criminal cases relating to missing children and persons.[279]

4. Role of District Administration: The legislation enjoins upon the district administration in the country to get places where children are employed periodically inspected. Again, it is a matter of concern that in the identified cases of child labour and bonded labour in which prosecutions are launched against the employer the conviction rate is not even 1 per cent which obviously has resulted due to lack of supervision. Such apathy towards this vital issue has to be curbed in favour of a proactive approach. The committee urges the authorities concerned to hold district administration accountable for dereliction in discharging this responsibility. The committee is of the opinion that this exercise of regular inspections, if undertaken with all earnest, will ensure linking back a large number of children missing from their homes.[280]

5. Mandatory Reporting: The state police headquarters should evolve a system of mandatory reporting whereby all incidents of missing children across the country should be reported to the newly constituted NCPCR within 24 hours of occurrence. Failure to report promptly would give rise to the presumption that there was an attempt to suppress the incident. The reporting should be done promptly and the procedure could be the same as is being followed by the concerned authorities for reporting custodial death cases to the NHRC.[281]

6. Involving Institutions Such As the Panchayat Raj Institutions (PRIs): In order to make the investigative procedures concerning missing children more transparent and user-friendly, it would be preferable for the police investigating team to involve the community at large, such as representatives of panchayati raj institutions, municipal committees, neighbourhood committees, and resident welfare associations in addition to existing helplines.[282]

7. Involving NGOs: In places where vulnerable groups of children are found in large numbers, there is need for enforcement agencies to evolve some kind of a mechanism in partnership with NGOs and social workers, whereby apart from rendering counseling to them, aware-ness raising activities are also carried out.[283]

8. National Database and Monitoring: The NCRB should establish a National Tracking System that would encompass the grass roots level in locating and tracing missing children. There should be prompt reporting of not only missing children cases, but also of return/rescue/

[279] *Report of NHRC Committee on Missing Children 2007.* Available at nhrc.nic.in/Documents/Reports/ misc_MCRReport.doc (accessed on 25 May 2015).

[280] *Report of NHRC Committee on Missing Children 2007.* Available at nhrc.nic.in/Documents/Reports/ misc_MCRReport.doc (accessed on 25 May 2015).

[281] *Report of NHRC Committee on Missing Children 2007.* Available at nhrc.nic.in/Documents/Reports/ misc_MCRReport.doc (accessed on 25 May 2015).

[282] *Report of NHRC Committee on Missing Children 2007.* Available at nhrc.nic.in/Documents/Reports/ misc_MCRReport.doc (accessed on 25 May 2015).

[283] *Report of NHRC Committee on Missing Children 2007.* Available at nhrc.nic.in/Documents/Reports/ misc_MCRReport.doc (accessed on 25 May 2015).

recovery. All instances where children are rescued from places of exploitation including places of sexual exploitation and also exploitative labour, should be dovetailed into the NCRB database. The database should be updated on a regular and systematic basis.[284]

9. State Crime Records Bureau/District Crime Records Bureau: There is an urgent need to revive the State Crime Records Bureau (SCRB) and District Crime Records Bureau (DCRB). The database on missing persons, their return, and the processes involved should be properly documented. The State Missing Person's Bureau (MPB) needs to be revamped, made functional and strengthened.[285]

10. Helpline: There is a need to establish a child helpline through NGOs/PRIs/other agencies with adequate support from government in all the districts. The DWCD, Government of India, may take the initiative to set up such a national network.[286]

11. Outsourcing Preliminary Inquiry to NGOs: The NHRC committee came to know about several instances where NGOs are actively functional, delivering the best results, in tracing missing children and also documenting them. Such efforts and initiatives have supplemented the work of the law-enforcement agencies.[287]

12. Cognizability of the Evidence: As of now the issue of missing children is not a cognizable offence and the very fact of missing of a child does not convey occurrence of a crime. However, some states like Andhra Pradesh and Tamil Nadu allow the police to register FIRs and take up investigation. In order to facilitate proper enquiry/investigation, it is advisable that an FIR is registered by the police with respect to the issue of missing children. However, experience shows that in many cases a child may not have gone missing and the panic reaction of the parents or wards lead to such reporting. Therefore, all such issues may not warrant registration of an FIR immediately. Nevertheless, it is advisable to register FIR if a missing child does not come back or is not traced within a reasonable time. The state governments are advised to consider issue of appropriate directions to the law-enforcement agencies to set a time limit of 15 days from the date of reporting that if a missing child is not traced back within 15 days, a presumption may be made of some malafide and an FIR registered with respect to all such issues of missing children.[288]

13. Sensitization of Stakeholders: There is a need to sensitize all ranks of police personnel and other stakeholders to the issue of missing children.[289]

[284] Report of NHRC Committee on Missing Children 2007. Available at nhrc.nic.in/Documents/Reports/misc_MCRReport.doc (accessed on 25 May 2015).

[285] Report of NHRC Committee on Missing Children 2007. Available at nhrc.nic.in/Documents/Reports/misc_MCRReport.doc (accessed on 25 May 2015).

[286] Report of NHRC Committee on Missing Children 2007. Available at nhrc.nic.in/Documents/Reports/misc_MCRReport.doc (accessed on 25 May 2015).

[287] Report of NHRC Committee on Missing Children 2007. Available at nhrc.nic.in/Documents/Reports/misc_MCRReport.doc (accessed on 25 May 2015).

[288] Report of NHRC Committee on Missing Children 2007. Available at nhrc.nic.in/Documents/Reports/misc_MCRReport.doc (accessed on 25 May 2015).

[289] Report of NHRC Committee on Missing Children 2007. Available at nhrc.nic.in/Documents/Reports/misc_MCRReport.doc (accessed on 25 May 2015).

14. Rescue of Children in Need of Care and Attention: There is a need to identify 'run away children', 'abandoned children', 'neglected children', and such 'vulnerable children' who are often found roaming around places where they are particularly exposed to abuse and exploitation such as railway stations and traffic junctions. Their vulnerability increases due to a lack of support structures—family or otherwise. Proper identification, provision of care and support, and a 'safe place' is vital for them.[290]

15. I-Card for Children: The local administration should facilitate the schools to keep a watch on their children, especially when they become untraced or become dropouts. Schools and old teaching institutions should introduce photo identity cards of children, so that tracing is possible. All such photos with identity particulars be documented and database be developed urgently. The state governments and the central government should take initiatives in this regard. Schools should embark on a programme of empowering the children on their rights, legal strengths, and defence mechanisms in case of need.[291]

16. Poverty Alleviation Measures: It is acknowledged that poverty is one of the main factors in pushing children into inhospitable conditions and making them vulnerable for exploitation. The central and state governments have introduced several schemes to be implemented at gram panchayat level with the object of providing job opportunities to the poor and the disadvantaged and elevating them from the poverty line.[292]

17. Role of State Commissions: There is a need to involve state human rights commissions and women commission of state or centre in regard to the issue of missing children.[293]

18. Role of Media: The media can play an important role in increasing public awareness of missing children and the plight of the thousands of hapless families whose children are listed as untraced.[294]

19. Missing Children from across Border: This is a grey area, which largely remains unaddressed. It has been reported that several foreign children who have been trafficked into India have been punished as illegal immigrants and are made to suffer. The NHRC recommends the state governments to undertake review of all such cases and provide relief to such children, as all trafficked children, irrespective of their nationality, are children in need of care and attention. Moreover, there is a need to develop a protocol on this issue.[295]

20. Survey and Research: The existing legislation requires the state and district authorities to periodically carry out inspections/surveys of places where children are employed with a view

---

[290] Report of NHRC Committee on Missing Children 2007. Available at nhrc.nic.in/Documents/Reports/misc_MCRReport.doc (accessed on 25 May 2015).

[291] Report of NHRC Committee on Missing Children 2007. Available at nhrc.nic.in/Documents/Reports/misc_MCRReport.doc (accessed on 25 May 2015).

[292] Report of NHRC Committee on Missing Children 2007. Available at nhrc.nic.in/Documents/Reports/misc_MCRReport.doc (accessed on 25 May 2015).

[293]vReport of NHRC Committee on Missing Children 2007. Available at nhrc.nic.in/Documents/Reports/misc_MCRReport.doc (accessed on 25 May 2015).

[294] Report of NHRC Committee on Missing Children 2007. Available at nhrc.nic.in/Documents/Reports/misc_MCRReport.doc (accessed on 25 May 2015).

[295] Report of NHRC Committee on Missing Children 2007. Available at nhrc.nic.in/Documents/Reports/misc_MCRReport.doc (accessed on 25 May 2015).

to identifying missing children and those engaged in bonded labour/child labour. This task has remained a low priority area. There is an urgent need for the state administration to undertake micro studies especially at the places.[296]

Significant Findings of a Study on Missing Children by Bachpan Bachao Andolan[297]

The genesis of this research study arose from the case of missing children in Nithari in 2006 when BBA was involved in organizing initiatives to bring the matter into public limelight. The case demonstrated the worst forms of abuse and exploitation of children, with more than 30 children having gone missing and brutally murdered.[298]

Some of the most significant findings of this study are:

- No clear-cut definition of missing children as per legal system, which leads to confusion as to how the cases should be treated.
- No provision on addressing the issue of missing children in the Indian legal system.
- No comprehensive statements of purpose/protocols for addressing the issue of missing children at the national level, involving all states/UTs and other stakeholders.
- No proper mechanism to document and update the database and information on the number of registered, traced, and untraced cases of missing children.
- Lack of coordination between the agencies dealing with the missing children, for example, police, NCRB, SCRB, NGOs, and CSOs.
- Urban centres have high number of children reported missing.
- Areas with better connectivity and facility of transport and communications have high number of missing children.
- States and districts with international borders also have large number of children registered missing.
- Regions with migratory population, including slums, are registering more missing children.
- Children and families from socially and economically poorer background formed the majority of victims.

Based on its research, BBA recommended that defining a missing child is very important to help investigating agencies to deal with the phenomenon. It is important to have a clear policy guideline on definitions of trafficking and missing children. For example, the SOPs developed by the Delhi Police has defined a missing child as:

A child (a person who is below 18 years of the age) whose whereabouts are not known to the parents, legal guardians or any other person who may be legally entrusted with knowing whereabouts/well

---

[296] Report of NHRC Committee on Missing Children 2007. Available at nhrc.nic.in/Documents/Reports/misc_MCRReport.doc (accessed on 25 May 2015).

[297] *Missing Children in India*, a study by Bachpan Bachao Andolan. Available at www.bba.org (accessed on 17 November 2016).

[298] Available at http://bba.org.in/?q=content/missing-children-india-synopsis (accessed on 17 November 2016).

being of the child whatever may be the circumstances/causes of disappearance. Further recommendations included:

- The child in need of care and protection will be considered missing until located and/or his/her safety/well-being is established.
- Compulsory registration and investigation of all cases in case of missing children.
- The SOPs should be carefully drafted to support investigation.
- Creation of a highly skilled investigation and rapid response agency/task force on missing children. This agency will comprise highly skilled and trained individuals from various disciplines.
- The government should establish a National Centre for Missing and Exploited Children (NACMEC).
- Nodal officers on missing children in every district should be appointed. S/he should be notified by the respective state governments and the official should be made accountable to take all steps to trace/give care and protection to the missing child.
- Adequate legal administrative/financial support should be provided by the state government.
- Each state government should set up an advisory body including all government departments concerned as well as appropriate NGOs working in the field of missing children, trafficked children, and child labour. The body should be given statutory powers to ensure monitoring of the enforcement of law.
- Childline to have national linkage.
- Training and capacity building of police officers, prosecutors/judicial officers, executive magistrate, labour department officials, welfare department officials, officials of other departments concerned, counsellors/care providers, forensic department, media, NGOs working in the same field, PRI representatives and other stakeholders.
- Developing tools and knowledge products like handbooks, SOPs, films, and posters for capacity building.
- The NACMEC, when established, will be the repository of all the data including collation, collection, analysis, interpretation, documentation, and dissemination.
- Creation of a comprehensive plan for rehabilitation of rescued children who need rehabilitation or other assistance. Nationwide awareness generation programmes on the issue of missing children and trafficking

Laws Relating to Child Pornography

Child pornography is any photograph, videotape, film, or other reproduction, whether electronic or otherwise, of any sexual performance involving a child under the age of 18 years.

Young Persons (Harmful Publications) Act, 1956

In this act (Section 2(c)), young person means a person under the age of 20 years. It is an offence to sell, let, hire, distribute, or publicly exhibit harmful publications (Section 3(1)).

Information Technology Act, 2000

Under Section 67 of the ITA, 2000 (Amended vide Information Technology (Amendment) Act [ITAA], 2008),[299] publication and transmission of pornography is an offence. Section 67A of the ITA, 2008 provides for punishment of 5 years on the first conviction and punishment of 7 years for subsequent convictions for publishing or transmitting of material containing sexually explicit act, for example, in an electronic form.[300] Section 67B prescribes for punishment for publishing or transmitting of material depicting children in sexually explicit act in electronic form. It provides that whoever

(a) publishes or transmits or causes to be published or transmitted material in any electronic form which depicts children engaged in sexually explicit act or conduct; or

(b) creates text or digital images, collects, seeks, browses, downloads, advertises, promotes, exchanges, or distributes material in any electronic form depicting children in obscene or indecent or sexually explicit manner; or

(c) cultivates, entices, or induces children to online relationship with one or more children for and on sexually explicit act or in a manner that may offend a reasonable adult on the computer resource; or

(d) facilitates abusing children online; or

(e) records in any electronic form own abuse or that of others pertaining to sexually explicit act with children, shall be punished on first conviction with imprisonment of either description for a term which may extend to 5 years and with a fine which may extend to Rs 10,00,000 and in the event of second or subsequent conviction with imprisonment of either description for a term which may extend to 7 years and also with fine which may extend to Rs 10,00,000.

---

[299] Punishment for publishing or transmitting obscene material in electronic form

Whoever publishes or transmits or causes to be published in the electronic form, any material which is lascivious or appeals to the prurient interest or if its effect is such as to tend to deprave and corrupt persons who are likely, having regard to all relevant circumstances, to read, see or hear the matter contained or embodied in it, shall be punished on first conviction with imprisonment of either description for a term which may extend to two-three years and with fine which may extend to five lakh rupees and in the event of a second or subsequent conviction with imprisonment of either description for a term which may extend to five years and also with fine which may extend to ten lakh rupees.

[300] Punishment for publishing or transmitting of material containing sexually explicit act, etc. in electronic form (inserted vide ITAA 2008):

Whoever publishes or transmits or causes to be published or transmitted in the electronic form any material which contains sexually explicit act or conduct shall be punished on first conviction with imprisonment of either description for a term which may extend to five years and with fine which may extend to ten lakh rupees and in the event of second or subsequent conviction with imprisonment of either description for a term which may extend to seven years and also with fine which may extend to ten lakh rupees.

Regulation of Cyber Cafés

Attempts to regulate cyber pornography are being made. For instance, the Government of Maharashtra and Mumbai Police have attempted to bring cyber cafés within the purview of the Rules for Licensing and Controlling Places of Public Amusement (Other than Cinemas) and Performances for Public Amusement Including Cabaret Performances, Melas and Teammates Rules 1960 ('the Amusement Rules') framed under Section 13 of the Mumbai Police Act, 1951.

The ITA empowers the government to prescribe standards for intermediaries, including cyber cafés. If a cyber café does not comply with the rules, it would be liable for any misuse by the customer.

- Under the rules, all cyber cafés have to register with the registration agency notified by the government. The rules require cyber cafés to maintain records of users' identity, contact details and websites accessed for a minimum period of 1 year. Cyber cafés are required to disclose the records to inspecting officers on their demand.
- The rules also provide requirements for seating and lay out. Cyber cafés shall display a board, clearly visible to the users, prohibiting them from viewing pornographic sites and downloading information prohibited under the law.[301]

Judgments

Trafficking of Minors for Sexual Abuse and Exploitation

Vishal Jeet v. Union of India[302]

This was a PIL wherein the Supreme Court issued directions that all state governments must direct their law-enforcing authorities to take appropriate speedy steps against the evil and directed to set up advisory committees with experts from all fields to make suggestions regarding measures for eradicating child prostitution, for care and rehabilitation of rescued girls, for setting up of rehabilitative homes, and for a survey of the devadasi and jogin traditions.

Dhananjaya Chatterjee v. State of West Bengal[303]

It was a case of rape and murder of a helpless and defenseless schoolgirl of 8 years by a security guard. Death sentence imposed by the trial court was subsequently confirmed by the high court. It was held that the offence was not only inhuman and barbaric, but a totally ruthless crime of rape followed by cold-blooded murder and it was an affront to human dignity.

---

[301] Cyber Café Rules, 2011.
[302] *Vishal Jeet v. Union of India*, AIR 1990 SC 1412.
[303] [1994(2) SCC 220].

Amrita Ahluwalia v. Union of India and Ors.[304] *on 12 December 1991 (Ameena's Case)*[305]

On 11 August 1991 the newspapers announced the dramatic 'rescue' of a 'child bride' on the previous day. On the flight from Hyderabad to Delhi (en route to Riyadh), Ameena, the child bride, 10 or 11 years old, had been spotted crying bitterly by several passengers, who had reported the matter to the airhostess. Ameena then told the airhostess that the old man beside her, Yahya Mohammed al-Sageih, a 60-year-old Saudi Arabian national, was taking her away after having forcibly married her in Hyderabad (her native town) only a few days before. She wept throughout the flight. As soon as the plane landed in Delhi, al-Sageih was arrested by the city police, and Ameena was produced before the metropolitan magistrate, who temporarily entrusted her to the local Nari Niketan (destitute women's home). The parents, in Hyderabad, were also subsequently arrested. After months of legal dispute over her custody, during which she was moved to a children's home, the Delhi High Court ordered her restoration to her family. Al-Sageih was released on bail but with orders to cooperate with the investigation and not leave the country until the case had been dismissed. He was accommodated in the Saudi Arabian embassy. Ameena underwent a checkup at the government hospital. According to the information on her passport and the nikhanama (marriage certificate) produced by al-Sageih, her age was 35; her parents claimed she was 18; her own statement and her medical examination suggested she was 11 or 12. According to the preliminary reports, al-Sageih had arrived in Bombay on 28 July and met Ameena's family in Hyderabad on 7 August through a marriage broker who arranged such matches. The wedding had taken place the following day. Al-Sageih reportedly paid the father, Badruddin, Rs 6,000 as mehr (marriage settlement). Badruddin is an autorickshaw (three-wheeler scooter) driver with 8 children; Ameena is the second of five daughters. The Shakkargun locality of Hyderabad city where the family live is a Muslim ghetto, poor and torn by frequent communal strife. In Delhi, airhostess Ahluwalia passionately pleaded for Ameena's release from the Nari Niketan and outlined her plans for her future if granted custody. She gave several other interviews of a similar kind to the press and on television ('give my Ameena back', among other requests). Women's organizations—Saheli and the Janwadi Mahila Samiti—also protested Ameena's stay in a Nari Niketan and applied for custody of her. Their application was refused, but Ameena was produced in court on 13 August and moved to a 'short stay' at home in response to the outrage over her confinement in a Nari Niketan. The court also refused to admit Ahluwalia's petition, through Saheli, for custody of Ameena. Instead, it directed the Juvenile Justice Court to decide on an appropriate residence for Ameena. At this stage, Ameena expressed a wish to return to her parents. The city police filed criminal charges against both al-Sageih and Ameena's parents under various sections of the IPC: Sections 366 (abduction), 420 (cheating and forgery), 467, 471, and 486 (using forged documents), 372 (sale of minor for prostitution), 373 (purchase of minor for prostitution), 120B (entering into a conspiracy to commit all the above offenses), and Section 4 of the CMRA, 1929 (as amended in 1978). Ameena's parents were released on bail on the basis of bonds provided by two local residents on 3 January 1992. On 29 August, the arrival of

---

[304] 1992 CriLJ 1906.
[305] Rajeswari Sunder Rajan, *The Scandal of the State* (Duke University Press, 2003).

Ameena's parents in Delhi to meet their daughter and file a petition for her restoration to them was occasion for another furor. In interviews, Badruddin, Ameena's father, defended the marriage as being in accordance with Muslim custom and expressed resentment at the 'interference of outsiders'. On 5 September the court rejected all the petitions for custody of Ameena and ordered her to be kept in a home for children for 3 months. On 5 December, her 3-month state custody got over, her case came up for review again, but the Juvenile Justice Board had not arrived at any decision. On 21 February, a division bench of the Delhi High Court, expressing dissatisfaction with the Juvenile Justice Board's lethargy in the matter, ordered Ameena to be presented to them the following week in order to formally 'ascertain her wishes' on the matter. They then ordered the Juvenile Board to speed up its decision but reserved final judgment over the matter.[306] Meanwhile the case against al-Sageih and Ameena's parents was proceeding independently of the custody case. On 21 February 1992, the court was packed when the three accused appeared before the metropolitan magistrate to face the charges against them. The public prosecutor asked for a trial in the Sessions Court, and the case was adjourned for further hearing. In the custody issue the Juvenile Board, finding the parents 'unfit', ordered (on 4 March) that Ameena be transferred to a service home in Hyderabad for 3 years. The decision of the Juvenile Board was subject to review by the high court.

On 11 March 1992 Ameena appeared before the division bench of the high court, comprising B.N. Kirpal and Santosh Duggal. She reiterated her wish to go home. The judges examined Badruddin at length to ascertain his fitness and willingness to take charge of Ameena. Badruddin produced three affidavits given on his behalf by respectable Hyderabad citizens. The following day, the judges ordered Ameena's restoration to her parents but stipulated that she be first presented to a metropolitan magistrate in Hyderabad. They also directed the magistrate's court to verify the state government's arrangements for monitoring Ameena's welfare once she was back at her parents' home. Kirpal said: 'With the passing of this order we hope a nightmarish chapter in the young life of Ameena will hopefully come to a satisfactory end.' In a sense, the Ameena custody issue comes to a close here. Later in the year, on 9 September, the prosecution case against al-Sageih and the Badruddins was resumed in court. Al-Sageih's defense advocate, Irshad Ullah Khan, argued that Ameena had never stated in court that she had been coerced into marriage. He also invoked the MPL, which allowed the marriage of a legally minor girl if she had attained puberty, which might happen at an age as early as 9 years. The court, however, ruled that al-Sageih be tried on all the charges listed against him, including abduction and violation of CMRA. The chief issue here was, clearly, the conflict between the CMRA and the MPL. This controversy over which system of laws applies—the uniform civil and criminal laws or the differentiated religious personal law requires some elaboration. India's dual law structure is an inheritance from colonial jurisprudence. The CMRA is a civil law, applicable to Indians of all religions. It was first passed in 1929 and was revised in 1978, stipulating an increase in the minimum legal age of marriage, which is at present 18 for women and 21 for men. Any case filed against the marriage of underage children makes the bridegroom (if over 21) and the parents or guardians liable to prosecution under the CMRA. The Shariat Act states that the MPL will prevail over custom or usages that are contrary to it, but nowhere does it say that the MPL

---

[306] *Amrita Ahluwalia* v. *Union of India and Others* on 12 December 1991. Equivalent citations: 1992 CriLJ 1906.

will outweigh any legislation clashing with it. So legislations like the Contract Act, Criminal Procedure Act, and the CMRA outweigh the MPL. It was argued that Ameena's marriage had after all been performed 'openly'. Ameena's testimony against the accused, also, was conflicting. The case went on, with several witnesses appearing for the prosecution; but the crucial testimony was Ameena's. On 17 November, when Ameena appeared in court, she formally withdrew her charges. Weeping, she told the Sessions judge, that the marriage had taken place with her consent. Her evidence was taken in the judge's chambers to save her the ordeal of testifying in open court. The state prosecutor confronted her with her very different statement to the police the previous year, soon after she had been 'rescued'. Ameena denied the earlier statement and her signature. She gave her age as 16 or 17 years, not 12 as earlier claimed (but she did not know her date of birth). She said she did not remember what she had said earlier to her interlocutors on the plane and to the police. Ameena's testimony obviously weakened the state's case considerably, though charges were not officially dropped.

In July 1993 the newspapers reported that al-Sageih had jumped bail in February and left the country. His sureties paid up the bail amount.

Public at Large v. State of Maharashtra and Others[307]

This petition arose due to suo motu notice taken by the court of a newspaper article which indicated that minor girls were illegally confined and forced to be sex workers. The respondents were directed by the court to show cause as to why action had not been taken under Sections 336 and 366 of the IPC and Sections 5 and 6 of the SITA, 1956. The court passed directions as under:

- To frame a proper scheme so that the women including minors who are produced for sexual slavery are released from the confinement of their procurers;
- For implementing this scheme, a proper cell, also involving social workers, be created so that by regular checking, minors and others can be released and rehabilitated in the society; and
- Considering the spread of the dreaded disease of AIDS, the state of Maharashtra shall frame a proper scheme with the active assistance of the Municipal Corporation of Greater Mumbai for carrying out HIV tests for the willing sex workers so that the disease may not spread like wildfire in the city.

On the basis of the directions passed by the court, raids were carried out and about 473 minor girls and child sex workers were rescued by the police and kept in the custody of juvenile homes. The respondents pointed out in their affidavit that a majority of the girls had come to Mumbai from the neighbouring states of Karnataka, Kerala, Tamil Nadu, and Andhra Pradesh, the Northeastern states such as Assam, and also from countries like Nepal and Bangladesh. The court constituted a committee for the rehabilitation of the rescued girls. The court gave the following directions:

[307] 1997 (4) Bom CP 171.

The respondents, state government, to see that strict vigilance is maintained in the areas where sex workers normally operate and to rescue the child sex workers. Further, adequate steps should be taken to see that those who indulge in trafficking of women should be suitably punished. For this purpose, appropriate directions should be issued to the investigating agencies to take immediate steps. Sometimes, it is noticed that a police officer who detects this type of activity does not take immediate action on the ground that such duty is assigned to some other officer. In the view of the court, this was not the proper approach because all police officers are bound to take immediate action in those cases where cognizable offences are committed. They may not investigate those cases but they can certainly report them to the proper officer and during such time take preventive measures. Section 107 of the IPC, 1860 provides that a person abets the doing of a thing if he intentionally aids, by any or illegal commission, the doing of that thing.

It is high time that the state governments take serious steps to prevent forcible pushing of women and young girls into prostitution and to prevent the trafficking in women, that is, buying and selling of young girls. These girls may be victims of kidnapping, they may be victims of various deprivations, and they may be victims of circumstances beyond their control. For this purpose, regular raids should be carried out in the area where sex workers operate. On numerous occasions, it is reported in newspapers that persons from social organizations who dare to rescue these girls are manhandled, beaten, or threatened. To prevent such situations, for the time being, the government must have a squad of police officers who can take immediate action.

The state government shall set up an advisory committee, if not already set up, within four weeks from the date of the order in terms of Direction No. 2 of Paragraph 15 of the judgment of the apex court in the case of *Vishal Jeet*[308] to comply with the objects set out therein and to further take steps to implement the suggestions made by the advisory committee.

The state is to set up homes for rehabilitation of rescued sex workers including children so as to enable these rescued sex workers to acquire alternative skills in order to enable them to have alternative source of employment. In a civilized state, it is the duty of the state to take preventive measures to eradicate child prostitution without giving room for any complaint of culpable indifference. One should not forget that these rescued girls are also fellow human beings who require some support and treatment for getting out of the immoral activities.

To regularly carry out AIDS awareness programmes in the areas where sex workers normally operate.

The state government is to submit periodic reports, by taking out notice of motion, either through the learned advocate-general or the learned government pleader, stating what steps are taken pursuant to the aforesaid directions and how many girls are rescued from the clutches of middlemen, whether medical treatment is given, and whether rehabilitation facilities are made available to them. Even recent newspaper reports indicate that pimps or middlemen are raising their muscle strength to prevent NGOs from receiving illegally confined girls.

The state government is further to place before the court the compliance report of these directions.

---

[308] AIR 1990 SC 1413.

Public at Large v. State of Maharashtra and Others[309]

This petition was relating to the rehabilitation of rescued girls. After hearing the various parties and the representations on behalf of various women's social organizations, consensus on the following points was arrived at:

- There was unanimity on the point that the rescued girls should not be subjected to HIV test.
- If HIV tests have already been carried out on some of the girls, their identity should not be disclosed and they should not be informed of the result of the test.
- All the rescued girls must be subjected to medical examination for finding out their age and also given treatment if they are suffering from any other diseases.
- If the girls are found to be adult and are not covered by the JJ Act, and if they do not desire to remain in the present institutes, they must be allowed to leave the said homes.
- The other state governments should be contacted and if those state governments were ready and willing to make arrangements for reception of these girls, the chairman, Juvenile Justice Board would pass necessary orders. The police should give them necessary escort and the girls must be handed over to the respective states on receipt of the request made by such states.
- Rehabilitation of these girls is possible if they are segregated in groups of ten or fifteen and thereafter counselling work is done.
- Parents of four minor girls who have been traced and who have been pleading that the police have wrongly taken them in custody should be released.
- Until the girls are sent back to their respective states, the state government will direct adequate number of probation officers to carry out the counselling job. The management in charge will permit the police to record statements of the girls. The police should trace the belongings of the girls and restore the same to them.

State v. Shri Freddie Peats and Others[310]

The accused Freddie Peats, then 66 years old, claimed to be a man of God ('Father' Peats), a medical doctor and social worker who ran a 'boarding' or 'orphanage' for boys generally from broken homes and deprived families. Peats used to sexually abuse and assault the boys. On his arrest there were 2,305 photographs found in his flat. These photographs recorded different acts of sexual assault, abuse, exploitation, repulsive remarks, and other brute and silent violence against the children and their privacy. These photographs covered a period of about 17 years and were of boys from the neighbourhood and from schools all over Goa. Some of them were of foreign visitors. Apart from photographs, there were negatives, drugs, syringes, torture paraphernalia, several passports, and bankbooks. In many photographs, the man in the criminal act of sexual assault on children was Peats himself.

The sessions court held Freddie Peats guilty of offences punishable under Sections 292, 293, 342, 355, 328, 337, 323, and 337 of the IPC; Sections 20 and 43 of the JJ Act; Section 9 of

[309] Writ petition No. 112 of 1996.
[310] Sessions case No. 24/1992, Criminal Appeal No. 4/1996.

ITPA, 1956; Section 27 of the Drugs and Cosmetics Act 1940. Freddie Peats was ordered life imprisonment and fine. He appealed against the order but the appeal was dismissed.

Due to the intervention of child rights activist Sheela Barse, the trial in the Freddy Peats Case followed some child friendly procedures like the following:

- Trial was held in camera in the chamber of the sessions judge. Similarly, examination of child victim/witnesses were also conducted in camera so that the witnesses are not 'awed' by the court atmosphere.
- All persons in the trial were in informal dress.
- No police officer was present inside the chamber or at the place where the trial was conducted.
- While recording evidence, the child was directed to face the judge so that he will not have occasion to look at the accused and be frightened.

Similar procedures need to be followed in other CSA trials under the present legal system.

Gaurav Jain v. Union of India[311]

The court took judicial notice of the fact that a large number of women enter flesh trade under various circumstances and observed:

> Prostitution is not confined, as in the ITP Act, to offering of the body to a person for promiscuous sexual intercourse. Normally, the word 'prostitution' means an act of promiscuous sexual intercourse for hire or offer or agreement to perform an act of sexual intercourse or any unlawful sexual act for hire as was the connotation of the Act. By amendment the act of a female and exploitation of her person by an act or process of exploitation for commercial purpose making use of or working up for exploitation of the person of the women taking unjust and unlawful advantage of trapped women for one's benefit or sexual intercourse has been brought within its frame. The word 'abuse' has a very wide meaning—everything which is contrary to good order established by usage amounts to abuse. Physical or mental maltreatment also is an abuse. An injury to genital organs in an attempt of sexual intercourse also amounts to sexual abuse. Any injury to private parts of a girl constitutes abuse under the JJ Act.... Three Cs, viz., counselling, cajoling and coercion are necessary to effectively enforce the provisions of ITP Act and JJ Act.

The Supreme Court passed an order directing the constitution of a committee to make an in-depth study of the problem. In 1998, the central government, pursuant to the directions issued by the Supreme Court constituted Committee on Prostitution, Children Prostitutes and Children of Prostitutes and Plan of Action to Combat Trafficking and Commercial Sexual Exploitation of Women and Children.

The committee opined that the problem of child prostitution does not stand by itself and is a component of overall phenomenon in the country. The committee found that though the problem of prostitution is mainly found in large cities, but in the urban areas and some rural areas also, it poses to be a prevalent problem. Amongst the sex workers, the child prostitutes constitute

[311] AIR 1997 SC 3021.

a major bulk of the component. Child prostitutes constitute 12 to 15 per cent of prostitutes in any area. On account of the social sanctions, women are exploited by the customs of devdasis, jogins, and venkatans known by other names in different parts of the country. They are highly prevalent in Karnataka, Maharashtra, and Andhra Pradesh. The number of red light areas having increased in recent times, brothel-based prostitution is on the vane but there is an increasing trend towards decentralized mode of prostitution.

The major reasons for induction of prostitution are poverty and unemployment or lack of appropriate rehabilitation. Many of these women hail from Andhra Pradesh, Karnataka, Tamil Nadu West Bengal, Bihar, Maharashtra, Uttar Pradesh, Assam, Gujarat, Goa, Madhya Pradesh, Kerala, Meghalaya, Orissa, Punjab, Rajasthan, and Delhi. Delhi receives prostitutes from about 70 districts in the country, Bombay from 40 districts, Bengaluru from 70 districts, Kolkata from 11 districts, and Hyderabad from 3 districts.

The committee also identified 10 types of prostitutes like street walkers, religious prostitutes, prostitutes in brothel, singing and dancing girls, bar nude, massage parlour, and call girls. The committee found that these women enter into prostitution between the age of 16 and 19 years and lose market by the time they became 35 years of age. Thereafter such persons either manage brothels or develop contact with high leads and the vicious cycle continues.

The Supreme Court also held that women found in flesh trade should be viewed more as victims of adverse socio-economic circumstances rather than offenders in our society. The court said that it is the duty of the state and all voluntary NGOs and public spirited persons to come in to their aid to retrieve them from prostitution, rehabilitate them with a helping hand to lead a life with dignity of person, self-employment through provisions of education, financial support, developed marketing facilities as some of major avenues in this behalf. Marriage is another object to give them a real status in the society. Acceptance by the family is also another important input to rekindle the faith of self-respect and self-confidence. Housing, legal aid, free counselling assistance, and all other similar aids and services are meaningful measures to ensure that these unfortunate women do not again fall into the trap of red light area contaminated with foul atmosphere. Law is a social engineer. The courts are part of the state steering by way of judicial review. Judicial statesmanship is required to help regaining social order and stability. Interpretation is effective armory in its bow to steer clear the social malady, economic reorganization as effective instruments remove disunity, and prevent frustration of the disadvantaged, deprived and denied social segments in the efficacy of law, and pragmatic direction pave way for social stability, peace and order. This process sustains faith of the people in rule of law and the democracy becomes useful means to the common man to realize his meaningful right to life guaranteed by Article 21.

Prerna v. State of Maharashtra and Others[312]

Prerna, the petitioner is a registered organization which works in the red light areas of Mumbai and Navi Mumbai with the object of preventing the trafficking of women and children and rehabilitating the victims of forced prostitution. This petition was filed in public interest to protect

[312] Criminal Writ Petition No. 788 of 2002, Mumbai High Court.

children and minor girls rescued from the flesh trade against the pimps and brothel keepers keen on re-acquiring possession of the girls. On 16 May 2002, the social service branch of the Mumbai police raided a brothel at Santacruz. Four persons who are alleged to be brothel keepers/pimps were arrested. Twenty four females were rescued. On conducting an ossification test, 10 of them were found to be minors. In this case, the Mumbai High Court passed the following directions which are of great significance for the children rescued from the brothels:

• No magistrate can exercise jurisdiction over any person under 18 years of age whether that person is a juvenile in conflict with law or a child in need of care and protection, as defined by Sections 2(1) and 2(d) of the JJ Act, 2000. At the first possible instance, the magistrate must take steps to ascertain the age of a person who seems to be under 18 years of age. When such a person is found to be under 18 years of age, the magistrate must transfer the case to the Juvenile Justice Board if such a person is a juvenile in conflict with law, or to the CWC if such a person is a child in need or care and protection.

• A magistrate before whom persons rescued under ITPA, 1956 or found soliciting in a public place are produced should, under Section 17(2) or the said act, have their ages ascertained the very first time they are produced before him. When such a person is found to be less than 18 years of age, the magistrate must transfer the case to the Juvenile Justice Board if such person is a juvenile in conflict with law or to the CWC if such a person is a child in need of care and protection.

• Any juvenile rescued from a brothel under ITPA, 1956 or found soliciting in a public place should only be released after an inquiry has been completed by the probation officer.

• The said juvenile should be released only to the care and custody of a parent/guardian after such parent/guardian has been found fit by the CWC, to have the care and custody or the rescued juvenile.

• If the parent/guardian is found unfit to have the care and custody of the rescued juvenile, the procedure laid down under the JJ Act, 2000 should be followed for the rehabilitation of the rescued child.

• No advocate can appear before the CWC on behalf of a juvenile produced before the CWC after being rescued under ITPA, 1956 or found soliciting in a public place. Only the parents/guardian of such juvenile should be permitted to make representations before the CWC through themselves or through an advocate appointed for such purpose.

• An advocate appearing for a pimp or brothel keeper is barred from appearing in the same case for the victims rescued under ITPA, 1956.

Bachpan Bachao Andolan v. Union of India and Others[313]

The petitioner sought application of the provisions of the JJ Act, 2000 and intra-state trafficking of young children, their bondage and forcible confinements, regular sexual harassment and abuses was suggested to be made cognizable offences under the IPC, 1860. There was violation of various laws concerning child labour and their abuse and traffic. Concerns of child and

---

[313] Writ Petition (C) No.51 of 2006.

the paradigm of child rights had been addressed suitably in various international conventions and standards on child protection including the UNCRC, 1989. India ratified the UNCRC in 1992. Convention prescribes standards to be adhered by all state parties in securing the best interest of the child. Integrated Child Protection Scheme seeks to create database and knowledge base for child protection services; it needs to strengthen child protection at family and community level.

The court held that Government of India was fully aware about problems of children working in various places particularly in circuses. The RTE had been made fundamental right under Article 21A of the Constitution. Hence, every child of the age of 6 to 14 years has right to have free education in neighbourhood school till elementary education. Therefore, court in order to implement fundamental right of children under Article 21A directed that central government must issue suitable notifications prohibiting the employment of children in circuses and also directed respondents to conduct simultaneous raids in all circuses to liberate the children and check the violation of fundamental rights of children. They were also directed to frame proper scheme of rehabilitation of rescued children.

Prajwala v. Union of India[314]

In this petition, a demand was made for a 'victim protection protocol' with detailed national guidelines with regard to the pre-rescue, rescue, and post-rescue stages involved in the rehabilitation of women and children trafficked for commercial sexual exploitation.

Orissa Patita Udhar Samiti v. State of Orissa and Others[315]

A writ application was filed by an NGO taking up the cause of the commercial sex workers residing in Mallisahi at Bhubaneswar. It was averred in the writ application that more than 40,000 of such commercial sex workers were living in the state capital. They were living in certain red light areas in a distress condition and Mallisahi situated in Unit-III, Kharavelanagar, Bhubaneswar, among others. Though they were living in the slums at Mallisahi on government land, no amenities were being provided to them by the Bhubaneswar Municipal Corporation for which they are leading a life of misery and were being repeatedly threatened by the authorities to be forcibly evicted from their residential houses in which they are residing since almost for last more than four decades. According to the petitioner, the State Mahila Commission in a report had highlighted the exploitation to which some inhabitants of Mallisahi were being subjected to. The petitioner further contended that they had approached the Bhubaneswar Municipal Authorities for rehabilitation of such commercial sex workers residing at Mallisahi by making construction of habitable house and allotting the same to them as a measure of rehabilitation thereby eradicating some of the maladies of the said inhabitants.

In a report prepared by the DWCD under the Ministry of Human Resources Development of the Union of India, various suggestions were made to improve the situation which should

---

[314] 2006 (9) SCALE 531.
[315] 2007(1)OLR150.

be taken up by the state government and a draft plan of action was also formulated in the report recommending prevention of trafficking in women, awareness generation and social mobilization, healthcare services, education and child-care amenities, housing, shelter and civil amenities, economic empowerment, legal reforms and law enforcement, rescue and rehabilitation, institutional machinery and methodology. The objective of such plan of action was to mainstream, to reintegrate women and child victims of commercial sexual exploitation in society and to provide specialized services to enable such victims to access existing schemes and services.

However, no return whatsoever was filed by the state to show to the court what steps it had taken for evolving procedures and principles to ensure that the commercial sex workers also enjoy their fundamental and human rights.

Therefore, The Orissa High Court issued a direction to the state of Odisha to take immediate measures in accordance with the *Gaurav Jain* decision and the DWCD *Report* so as to rehabilitate the commercial sex workers residing at Mallisahi in Bhubaneswar by providing minimum amenities such as water supply and electricity by undertaking awareness camps to make such victims aware of their rights under the Constitution, providing minimum education to the children of such victims, providing healthcare so as to prevent spreading of AIDS and providing alternate accommodation to them. The court further held that in the event it is decided to evict the said inhabitants of Mallisahi, without complying with the aforesaid direction, such victims/ commercial sex workers residing over government land would not be evicted from their place of residence.

Bachpan Bachao Andolan v. Union of India[316]

In this case, the Solicitor General of India provided a detailed report on the issue of child trafficking in India. He further submitted that each state government must identify an officer who is responsible for implementation of schemes in relation to children. There must be a parallel linkage between a point of contact of the collectorate/executive administration with a point in legal aid, that is, the executive chairman of the State Legal Services Authority and a point in the NGO sector/civil society. Similarly, points must be identified in each zila parishad and panchayat samiti and gram panchayats. In fact, the presiding officers of the gram *nyayalaya*s may also be encouraged to identify children who are vulnerable and who need protection. In view of the performance of the present NCPCR, which has taken pioneering efforts, it is expected that on a close interface between the NCPCR, the state governments and the MWCD, positive outcomes should actually be worked out.

The court while appreciating the research paper submitted by the Solicitor General stated:

> It is, therefore, necessary that a coordinated effort must be made by the three agencies, namely, the Commission, the Ministry and the State Governments. Learned Solicitor General submitted that the recommendations be implemented by the concerned agencies. In the State/Union Territory, the responsibility must be vest either on the Chief Secretary or a Secretary Incharge of Children,

---

[316] (2011) 5 SCC 1.

Women and Family Welfare. It would be open to the State Government in appropriate cases to nominate a special officer for the said purpose not lower than the rank of a Secretary to the State Government. Each State must issue a circular effectively indicating how the recommendations will be implemented. We accept the submissions of the learned Solicitor General and direct that the said circular shall be issued within 4 weeks from today and a compliance report be filed by the Chief Secretary of each State to this Court.

The court further ruled:

submissions made by the learned Solicitor General it is abundantly clear that the Government of India is fully aware about the problems of children working in various places particularly in circuses. It may be pertinent to mention that the RTE has been made a fundamental right under Article 21A of the Constitution. Now every child of the age of 6 to 14 years has right to have free education in neighbourhood school till elementary education.

Munni v. State of Mahrashtra[317]

The court stated that the menace of sexual abuse by immoral trafficking of children to force them somehow to enter in the business of prostitution is age-old phenomenon and needs to be tackled by central as well as state government with utmost care and precaution. Poverty, illiteracy, or helplessness of parents may make the minor girl vulnerable to sexual abuse/exploitation. Protecting children against any perceived or real danger/risk to their life, their person-hood and childhood is necessary. It is about reducing their vulnerability to any kind of harm or harmful situations. It is also about protecting children against social, psychological, and emotional insecurity and distress. It must ensure that no child falls out of the social security and safety net and those who do, receive necessary care and protection to be brought back into the safety net by child-friendly measures.

The CWC, constituted under the act, can do commendable service to fight against child abuse and to protect children from child abuse of various forms. The decision as to protective custody of the child in need of care and protection with a view to rehabilitate the rescued minor child can be left best to be considered by the competent quasi-judicial authority like CWC created under the said act as it can pass appropriate orders to protect the dignity of the child as well as its best interest. Welfare of the child is paramount factor. Section 29 of the act provides constituting five members district (administrative unit in India) level quasi-judicial bodies CWCs in which one of the members is designated as chairperson and at least one of the members shall be woman. The committee shall have the final authority to dispose of cases for the care, protection, treatment, development, and rehabilitation of the Children in Need of Care and Protection as well as to provide for their basic needs and protection of human rights. The CWCs have the final say to dispose of the cases for the care, protection, treatment, development, and rehabilitation of the children as well as to provide for their basic needs, protection and restoration to their family.

---

[317] Criminal Writ Petition No. 227/2011(Bombay High Court).

Judgments Relating to Missing Children

Hori Lal v. Commissioner of Police, Delhi and Others[318]

The Supreme Court of India gave detailed guidelines on 14 November 2002, while hearing the writ with regards to effective and emergency steps to be taken in case of tracing out the missing women and children. The court held that for having effective search of the kidnapped minor girls, following steps shall be taken by the investigation officer in all the states:

1) Publish photographs of the missing persons in the newspaper, telecast them on television promptly, and in case not later than one week of the receipt of the complaint. Photographs of a missing person shall be given wide publicity at all the prominent outlets of the city/town/village concerned that is at the railway stations, interstate bus stands, airport, regional passport office and through law enforcement personnel at border checkpoints. This should be done promptly and in any case not later than one week of the receipt of the complaint. But in case of a minor/major girl such photographs shall not be published without the written consent of the parents/guardians.

2) Make inquiries in the neighbourhood, the place of work/study of the missing girl from friends, colleagues, acquaintance, and relatives immediately. Equally all the clues from the papers and belongings of the missing person should be promptly investigated.

3) Contact the principal, class teacher, and students at the missing person's most recent school/educational institutions. If the missing girl or woman is employed somewhere, then to contact the most recent employer and her colleagues at the place of employment.

4) Conduct an inquiry into the whereabouts from the extended family of relatives, neighbours, school teachers including school friends of the missing girl or woman.

5) Make necessary inquiries whether there have been past incidents or reports of violence in the family. Thereafter the investigation officer/agency shall take the following steps:

   a) Diligently follow up to ensure that the records requested from the parents are obtained and examine them for clues;

   b) Search the hospitals and mortuaries immediately after receiving the complaint

   c) Announce the reward for furnishing clues about missing person within a month of her disappearance.

   d) Equally hue and cry notices shall be given within a month.

   e) The investigation should be made through women police officers as far as possible.

   f) The concerned police commissioner or the DIG/IG of the state police would find out the feasibility of establishing a multitask force for locating girl children women.

   g) Further, in the metropolitan cities such as Delhi, Mumbai, Kolkata, and Chennai, the investigating officer should immediately verify the red light areas and try to find out the minor girls. If any minor girl (may or may not be recently brought there) is found her permission be taken and she may be taken to the children's home (Section 34 of the JJ Act, 2000, and the investigating officer to take appropriate steps that all medical/other facilities are provided to her. The registry is directed to communicate this order to the

---

[318] Writ Petition (Crl) No. 610 of 1996 decided on 14 November 2002.

chief secretaries of all the state governments and the UTs for taking effective steps for implementation.

Nithari Judgment[319]

Several children had gone missing in and around the area in quick succession and there were reports galore made by respective relations/parents about missing of their children from Sector 31, Noida and Nithari Village, Gautam Budh Nagar from the year 2005 onwards. Rimpa had gone missing from her home in the neighbourhood of Pandher's Noida residence in early 2005. On 20 July 2005, a written complaint was made by one Anil Haldar about missing of his daughter Rimpa Haldar at Police Station Sector 20, Noida and the said report was entered in the general diary. Another girl Payal also mysteriously disappeared and on the complaint made by Nand Lal, the father of missing girl, the Chief Judicial Magistrate Gautam Budh Nagar ordered registration of FIR. In observance of the order of Chief Judicial Magistrate, a case at case crime No. 838 of 2006 was registered at Police Station Sector 20, Noida, under Section 363, 366 IPC about Payal missing.

The case of Nithari serial killings came to light towards the fag end of December 2006, following discovery of human remains from a drain behind Pandher's house in Noida. A subsequent and thorough search of the drain had kept yielding human remains and skeletons for over a week. The case was initially probed by the Noida police but was later handed over to the CBI, which had registered a total of 19 FIRs related to the serial killing.

Koli was sentenced to death along with Pandher by the Ghaziabad court on 13 February 2009, and the Allahabad High Court had confirmed Koli's death sentence on 11 September 2009 while acquitting Pandher of the charges. Aggrieved, victim Rimpa's father Anil Haldar had filed the appeal challenging Pandher's acquittal and sought restoration of the death sentence awarded to him by the Sessions court.

The Honourable Supreme Court upheld the death sentence to Nithari serial killer Surendra Kohli saying that the killings by the Appellant Surendra Koli are horrifying and barbaric.[320] He used a definite methodology in committing these murders. He would see small girls passing by the house, and taking advantage of their weakness lure them inside the house and there he would strangulate them and after killing them, he tried to have sex with the body and would then cut off their body parts and eat them. Some parts of the body were disposed of by throwing them in the passage gallery and drain (*nala*) beside the house. The bench confirmed the death sentence to 39-year-old Koli, who has also been awarded capital punishment by the trial court in three other cases of rape and killing of young women and children in Nithari village near Noida on the outskirts of the National Capital. While confirming Koli's death sentence, the Supreme Court kept pending with itself the CBI appeal against acquittal of Pandher, saying any order passed against him or in his favour can have a bearing on remaining cases which are at the trial stage.

---

[319] Criminal (Capital) Appeal No. 1475 of 2009 (from Jail), Reference No. 3 of 2009, *Moninder Singh Pandher and Surendra Koli (Appellants)* v. *State of U.P. (Respondent)*. Honourable Imtiyaz Murtaza J. Honourable K.N.Pandey, J. (Delivered by Honourable Imtiyaz Murtaza J.).

[320] AIR2011SC970.

Koli, thereafter filed his mercy petition before the governor of Uttar Pradesh on 7 May 2011, which was rejected 23 months later, on 2 April 2013. The mercy petition was thereafter forwarded to the union home ministry on 19 July 2013 and it was turned down by the President on 20 July 2014. The Allahabad court had agreed to hear the PIL disagreeing with the centre's preliminary objection, as follows:

> [T]he convict (Koli) had not filed a petition (at the time of filing of the PIL) challenging the rejection of his mercy petition. The proceeding which has been instituted before this court is not in the nature of an appeal on merits against the order of conviction. The petition seeks to question the constitutionality of the execution of the sentence of death in the present case, on the ground of a delay on the part of constitutional authorities in disposing of the mercy petitions.[321]

The Allahabad High Court on 28 January 2015 commuted the death sentence of Surinder Koli to life imprisonment in the case relating to the serial Nithari killings in Noida, a few kilometres away from the National Capital.[322]

Bachpan Bachao Andolan v. Union of India and Others[323]

In a petition filed by BBA, the Honourable Supreme Court of India passed a landmark judgment on the issue of missing children.[324] The bench headed by Honourable Chief Justice of India Justice Altamas Kabir comprising Honourable Justice Vikramajit Sen and Honourable Justice Sharad Arvind Bobde has taken the issue of missing children very seriously in the light of the facts presented before it by the BBA. The Honourable Court took into cognisance that in 2011 alone 90,654 children went missing with 34,406 children still remaining untraced. However, only 15,284 FIRs were registered and investigations were launched.

The Honourable Supreme Court issued the following directions:

1. Compulsory registration of cases by police of missing children with the assumption that they are victims of kidnapping and trafficking.
2. Compulsory registration of cases by police of all those children who are still untraced (in 2011, 34,406 children are still untraced).
3. Doctrine of presumption of crime of trafficking or kidnapping in all missing children cases.
4. SOP on investigation of missing children cases to be formulated.
5. National portal on tracing missing children to be formulated and implemented.
6. Appointment and training of special child welfare officers in every police station to deal with the cases of missing children.
7. Police will maintain records of recovered children along with photographs and ministry of home affairs to facilitate the maintenance of records of missing children.

---

[321] Available at http://timesofindia.indiatimes.com/india/Nithari-serial-killings-case-Hearing-concludes-on-Kolis-petition-in-HC/articleshow/46033075.cms (accessed on 28 May 2015).

[322] Available at http://www.thehindu.com/news/national/nithari-killings-convict-surinder-kolis-death-sentence-commuted-to-life/article6830342.ece (accessed on 17 November 2016).

[323] WP (Crl) 75 of 2012.

[324] Order issued in May 2013 (Writ Petition (Civil) No. 75 of 2012).

The Honourable Court has defined missing children as 'a person below 18 years of age whose whereabouts are not known to the parents, legal guardians or any other person who may be legally entrusted with the custody of knowing the whereabouts/well-being of the child whatever may be the circumstances/ causes of disappearance. The child will be considered missing and in need of care and protection, until located and/or his/her safety/well-being is established.'

Commenting upon many other suggestions made by NHRC and National Legal Service Authority (NALSA), the bench remarked: 'A specific investigation should be conducted if a missing child is recovered to ascertain the involvement of organized gang in trafficking and child labour.'

Bachpan Bachao Andolan—Petitioner(s) v. Union of India and Others[325]

This matter was listed pursuant to the direction given on 26 April 2013, when the contempt petition filed in the writ petition by the petitioner, complaining of the manner in which a complaint made regarding a missing child was sought to be handled by the concerned police station, was being considered. It has also come up on account of the other directions which had been given for implementing the various provisions of the JJ Act, 2000, as amended in 2006. On 17 January 2013, when this matter came up for consideration, the court had given an interim direction that in case a complaint with regard to any missing children was made in a police station, the same should be reduced into an FIR and appropriate steps should be taken to see that follow-up investigation was taken up immediately thereafter. An element of doubt had been raised on behalf of the state of Madhya Pradesh regarding the recording of the FIR relating to a missing child, having regard to the provisions of Section 154 of the CrPC, 1973, which relates to information in cognizable cases. It was made clear that, in case of every missing child reported, there will be an initial presumption of either abduction or trafficking, unless, in the investigation, the same is proved otherwise. Accordingly, whenever any complaint is filed before the police authorities regarding a missing child, the same must be entertained under Section 154 of the CrPC. However, even in respect of complaints made otherwise with regard to a child, which may come within the scope of Section 155 CrPC, upon making an entry in the book to be maintained for the purposes of Section 155 CrPC, and after referring the information to the magistrate concerned, continue with the inquiry into the complaint. The magistrate, upon receipt of the information recorded under Section 155 CrPC, shall proceed, in the meantime, to take appropriate action under Sub-section (2), especially, if the complaint relates to a child and, in particular, a girl child.

The court accepted the suggestion that there should be, in shifts, a special juvenile officer on duty in the police station to ensure that the directions contained in this order are duly implemented. To add a further safeguard, the court directed the NLSA that the para-legal volunteers who have been recruited by NLSA should be utilized so that there is, at least, one paralegal volunteer, in shifts, in the police station to keep a watch over the manner in which the complaints regarding missing children and other offences against children, are dealt with.

---

[325] In the Supreme Court of India Civil Original Jurisdiction Writ Petition (C) No.75 oF 2012 Bachpan Bachao Andolan. *Petitioner(s)* v *Union of India & Ors.* Respondent(s) with Contempt Petition (C) No.186/2013 in Writ Petition (C) No.75/2012 order.

The court directed that the suggestion regarding a computerized programme, which would create a network between the Central Child Protection Unit as the head of the organization and all State Child Protection Units, District Child Protection Units, City Child Protection Units, Block Level Child Protection Units, all SJPUs, all police stations, all Juvenile Justice Boards and all CWCs, should be seriously taken up and explored by the NLSA with the MWCD. Once introduced, the website link should also be made known to the public at large. The State Legal Services Authorities should also work out a network of NGOs, whose services could also be availed of at all levels for the purpose of tracing and reintegrating missing children with their families which, in fact, should be the prime object, when a missing child is recovered. The court added that as suggested on behalf of the NALSA, every found/recovered child must be immediately photographed by the police for purposes of advertisement and to make people aware of the missing child. Photographs of the recovered child should be published on the website and through the newspapers and even on TV so that the parents of the missing child could locate their missing child and recover him or her from the custody of the police. The Ministry of Home Affairs shall provide whatever additional support by way of costs that may be necessary for the purpose of installing such photographic material and equipment in the police stations.

International Instruments for Combating Trafficking

International law is a powerful tool for combating human trafficking. The instruments of international law that have laid down provisions as to how to define, prevent, and prosecute human trafficking are the United Nations Convention against Transnational Organized Crime and its two related protocols: the United Nations Protocol to Prevent, Suppress, and Punish Trafficking in Persons, Especially Women and Children, and the United Nations Protocol against the Smuggling of Migrants by Land, Sea, and Air, which entered into force in 2003–04. The United Nations Office on Drugs and Crime (UNODC) created these conventions, which have supported international law's ability to combat human trafficking. In support of enforcing these instruments, the UNODC established the United Nations Global Initiative to Fight Human Trafficking (UN.GIFT) in 2007. Instruments that have dealt with human trafficking date back to the abolition of slavery. They include provisions within the Slavery Convention, 1926 and the Supplementary Convention on the Abolition of Slavery, the Slave Trade, and Institutions and Practices Similar to Slavery, 1956. Additional tools of international law that include segments against the trafficking of persons include the Universal Declaration of Human Rights, 1948, the International Covenants on Civil and Political Rights, 1966, the United Nations Convention for the Suppression of the Traffic in Persons and of the Exploitation of the Prostitution of Others, 1949, and the Convention on the Elimination of all Forms of Discrimination Against Women, 1979.[326]

The United Nations Human Rights Council also issues mandates to thematic working groups, special rapporteurs, and country rapporteurs, which help to monitor compliance with or abuses

---

[326] King Lindsey, 'International Law and Human Trafficking', *Topical Research Digest: Human Rights and Human Trafficking*, 2014. Available at http://endslavery.salvos.org.au/wp-content/uploads/2014/09/10.-InternationalLaw.pdf (accessed on 17 November 2016).

of certain treaties. The Trafficking Protocol is unique from other treaties because it was created as a law enforcement instrument, which, in theory, gives it more influence than agreements. Provisions within the Trafficking Protocol state that parties must take action to penalize trafficking, protect victims of trafficking, and grant victims temporary or permanent residence in the countries of destination. Therefore, if a state is a party to the convention and its protocols, it has an obligation to create legislation that supports these provisions at the domestic level.[327]

The Universal Declaration of Human Rights, 1948

Though not a legally binding document, this sets the stage for most of the international instruments. Article 4 of the declaration states that no one shall be held in slavery or servitude. Slavery and the slave trade shall be prohibited in all its forms. Article 5 provides that no one shall be subjected to torture or to cruel, inhuman, or degrading treatment or punishment.

Tourism Bill of Rights and the Tourist Code, 1985

This was adopted by the World Trade Organization (WTO). It enjoins that the states should prevent any possibility of using tourism to exploit others for prostitution purposes. The Tourist Code enjoins tourists to refrain from exploiting others for prostitution purposes.

These covenants and conventions which India has ratified, unless they infringe on the fundamental rights, do not need legislative measures to enforce them in the courts of India.

The SAARC Regional Convention on Combating the Crime of Trafficking in Women and Children for Prostitution

The Male Declaration adopted by SAARC member states at the close of the Ninth SAARC Summit called for a Regional Convention on Combating the Crime of Trafficking. Some of the significant features of this convention agreed to by the parties are as follows:

Trafficking in women and children for prostitution is a crime against human dignity and as such effective measures, including legal, socioeconomic, and administrative, to be taken to effectively prevent trafficking in women and children.

- To specify in their national legislation, the procurement, enticing, or taking away of another person for the purposes of prostitution and exploitation even with consent, as a serious offence.
- To provide in their national legislation, punishments for any person who keeps or manages or knowingly finances or takes part in the financing of a brothel or rents out a building or a place or any part thereof for the purposes of prostitution.
- In a spirit of cooperation among themselves, the parties agree to assist and coordinate the various aspects of trafficking in women and children inside and outside their countries.

---

[327] Available at http://endslavery.salvos.org.au/wp-content/uploads/2014/09/10.-InternationalLaw.pdf (accessed on 1 June 2015).

The Convention for the Suppression of Trafficking in Persons and
of the Exploitation of the Prostitution of Others, 1949

The preamble to the convention states that prostitution and the accompanying evil of the traffic in person for the purpose of prostitution are incompatible with the dignity and worth of the human person and endanger the welfare of the individual, the family, and the community. The salient features of the convention are as follows:

- Any person, who in order to gratify the passions of another, procures, entices, or leads away for the purpose of prostitution another person, even if with such person's consent, or exploits the prostitution of another person, even if with such person's consent, is liable for punishment (Article 1).
- Any person who keeps or manages or knowingly finances a brothel or knowingly lets or rents a building or other place or any part thereof for the prostitution of another is liable for punishment (Article 2).
- The aforementioned offences shall be regarded as extraditable offences in any extradition treaty entered into between state parties to this convention (Articles 8 and 9).
- Each state party to this convention shall establish or maintain a service to coordinate and centralize results of investigation of offences under the convention, and such service should compile all information for facilitation of prevention and punishment of offences, and such service should be in close touch with corresponding services of other state parties (Article 14).
- The service so established should furnish particulars of an offence or an attempt to commit such offence to services established by other state parties. The information so furnished should include the description of the offender, fingerprints, photographs, method of operation, police record, and record of conviction (Article 15).
- The state parties should take measures for the prevention of prostitution and for the rehabilitation and social adjustment of the victims of prostitution (Article 16).
- The state parties shall undertake with immigration and emigration authorities such measures as are required to check the traffic in persons of either sex for the purpose of prostitution (Article 17).
- The state parties shall, pending the completion of the procedure for repatriation, make suitable arrangements for the temporary care and maintenance of destitute victims of international traffic. Repatriation should take place only with the consent of the victim or the person claiming such victim and after agreement is reached with the state of destination (Article 19).
- The state parties are to communicate to the secretary general of the United Nations such laws and regulations that have been promulgated in their respective states, and each year thereafter, such laws and regulations that have been promulgated and measures taken by the state parties concerning the applicability of the convention (Article 21).

Supplementary Convention on the Abolition of Slavery, Slave Trade,
and Institutions and Practices Similar to Slavery, 1956[328]

This convention resulted in an update of the 1926 Convention to Suppress the Slave Trade and Slavery preceded it.

---

[328] Entered into force on 30 April 1957, Articles 1, 3, 6, and 7. Available at http://www.unicri.it/wwd/ trafficking/minors/docs_ilr/supplementary_convention_on_the_abolition_of _slavery.pdf (accessed on 29 January 2010).

The updated document included the criminalization of debt bondage, serfdom, servile marriage, and child servitude.[329]

International Covenant on Civil and Political Rights, 1966[330]

This covenant lays down that every child, without any discrimination, has the right to such measures of protection as are required by his status as a minor on the part of his family, society, and the state.

Convention on the Elimination of all Forms of Discrimination against Women, 1979[331]

This enjoins state parties to take all appropriate measures, including legalization, to suppress all forms of traffic in women and exploitation or prostitution of women.[332]

India has ratified all the aforementioned instruments and therefore is bound to make laws in consonance with the aforementioned provisions.

The United Nations Convention against Torture and Other Cruel, Inhuman or Degrading Treatment or Punishment, 1984

The monitoring body under this convention is the Committee against Torture. The convention states that there should be no expulsion or return of a person to another state if there are substantial grounds for believing that s/he would be in danger of torture. The alleged victims of torture have the right to complain to and have his/her case promptly and impartially examined by competent authorities. Complainant and witnesses shall be protected against any consequential ill treatment or intimidation. There is also a provision for redress and right to compensation.

International Labour Organization Convention No. 29 on Forced Labour,[333] 1930

Under this convention, the states have to suppress use of forced or compulsory labour within the shortest possible period. The officials shall not constrain any person to work for private individuals, companies, or associations. The monitoring body, as of all ILO conventions, is the Committee of Experts on the Application of Conventions and Recommendations.

[329] *Supplementary Convention on the Abolition of Slavery, the Slave Trade, and Institutions and Practices Similar to Slavery*, 1956.

[330] Entered into force on 23 March 1976. Articles 8, 24. Available at http://www.unicri.it/wwd/trafficking/minors/docs_ilr/international_covenant_on_civil_and_political_rights.pdf (accessed on 29 January 2010).

[331] Entered into force on 3 September 1981. Articles 1, 3, 5, 6, 10, 11. Available at http://www.unicri.it/wwd/trafficking/minors/docs_ilr/1979_cedaw.pdf (accessed on 29 January 2010).

[332] CEDAW, Article 6.

[333] Under this convention, 'forced or compulsory labour' means all work or service which is exacted from any person under the menace of any penalty and for which the said person has not offered himself voluntarily.

International Covenant for Economic, Social and Cultural Rights, 1966[334]

The International Covenant on Economic, Social and Cultural Rights (ICESCR) makes up the International Bill on Human Rights, by recognizing that the ideal of human beings to be free can be achieved only if conditions are created whereby everyone may enjoy his civil and political rights, as well as his economic, social, and cultural rights.[335]

Article 10.3 states that 'special measure of protection and assistance should be taken on behalf of all children and young person without any discrimination for reasons of parentage or other conditions'.

Children and young person should be protected from economic and social exploitation. Their employment in work harmful to their morals or health, dangerous to life, or likely to hamper their normal development should be punishable by law. States should also set age limits below which the paid employment of child labour should be prohibited and punishable by law.

United Nations Convention on the Rights of the Child, 1989

The UNCRC,[336] which has been ratified by several countries including India, gives a common, cross-national, comprehensive foundation standard for all the world's children. Article 6 enjoins all state parties to take appropriate measures to suppress all forms of traffic in women and exploitation of prostitution of women. Article 11 prohibits the illegal transfer of children abroad. Article 19 is also relevant. It refers to the states' obligation to protect children from all forms of physical or mental violence, injury or abuse, neglect or negligent treatment, maltreatment, or exploitation including sexual abuse perpetrated by parents or others responsible for their care. Articles 34 and 35 lay down the obligations of the state to protect the child from all forms of sexual exploitation and sexual abuse. For these purposes, state parties shall, in particular, take all appropriate national, bilateral, and unilateral measures to prevent:

• the inducement or coercion of a child to engage in any unlawful sexual activity.
• the exploitative use of children in prostitution or other unlawful sexual practices.

On the exploitative use of children in pornographic performance and materials, Article 35 enjoins the state parties to take all appropriate national, bilateral, and multilateral measures to prevent the abduction or the sale of or traffic in children for any purpose or in any form. Article 39 ensures that states take all appropriate measures to promote the physical and psychological recovery and social reintegration of a child victim from any form of neglect, abuse, torture, or any other form of cruel, inhuman, or degrading treatment or punishment or armed conflict.

---

[334] Entered into force on 3 January 1976. Article 10.3 Available at http://www.unicri.it/wwd/trafficking/minors/docs_ilr/international_covenant_on_economic.pdf (accessed on 29 January 2010).

[335] UNODC, *Resource Book on the Legal Framework on Anti Human Trafficking*, p.138.

[336] Ratified by India on 11 December 1992.

ILO Convention on the Worst Form of Child Labour (Convention No. 182)

The international standard in the elimination of child labour was set in the year 1999 when the ILO member states unanimously adopted the ILO Convention concerning the Prohibition and Immediate Action for the Elimination of the Worst Forms of Child Labour, 1999 (No. 182). This convention prohibits the following categories of child labour terming them 'worst forms of child labour' which should not be tolerated by any country—(a) slavery (and all its forms), debt bondage, serfdom, and forced or compulsory labour; (b) child prostitution or pornography; (c) production or trafficking of drugs; and (d) work likely to harm the health, safety, or morals of children.

The U.S. Trafficking Victims Protection Act, 2000

This law sets out minimum standards government must follow to fight trafficking.

While sanctions form part of the retaliation against underperformers, political considerations have prevented sanctions from being applied to India.[337]

Optional Protocol to the Convention on the Rights of the Child on the Sale of Children, Child Prostitution, and Child Pornography, 2000[338]

The important articles of this protocol (adopted by the UN General Assembly) are as follows.

- To prohibit sale of children, child prostitution, and child pornography[339]
  - Sale of children has been defined as any act or transaction whereby a child is transferred by any person/s to another for remuneration or other consideration.[340]
  - Child prostitution has been defined as use of a child in sexual activities for remuneration or other consideration.
  - Child pornography has been defined as any representation of a child engaged in real or simulated explicit sexual activities or any representation of the sexual parts of a child for primarily sexual purposes.
- Criminal or penal law to be made to cover sale of children including offering, delivering, or accepting a child for purposes of sexual exploitation, transfer of organs for profit of forced labour.[341]
- To protect rights of child victims in criminal justice process keeping the best interest of the child in view.
- Protection of rights of child victims in the criminal justice process: In recognizing their special needs, especially as witness; in keeping them informed at all times of all things; providing support services.

---

[337] B. Skinner, *Crime So Monstrous: Face to Face with Modern Day Slavery* (New York: Free Press, 2008).
[338] Ratified by India on 16 August 2005.
[339] Optional Protocol to the CRC Article 1.
[340] Optional Protocol to the CRC Article 2.
[341] Optional Protocol to the CRC Article 3.

♦ Protecting privacy and identity of the child; providing for their safety and that of their family where appropriate; and avoiding unnecessary delay in granting compensation.
♦ Best interests of the child shall be a primary consideration.

• To ensure appropriate training for persons working with child victims.

The ILO Convention No. 182 Concerning the Prohibition and Immediate Action for the Elimination of the Worst Form of Child Labour
This convention includes:

• Use of child for prostitution, production of pornography, or pornographic performances.
• Use, procuring, or offering of a child for illicit activities, in particular for the production and trafficking of drugs.

An accompanying recommendation[342] defines 'hazardous work' as 'work which exposes children to physical, psychological or sexual abuse'. Paragraph 11 recommends how countries may cooperate with each other to deal with criminals and criminal networks, such as those involved in the trafficking of children and child pornography.

United Nations Convention against Transnational Organized Crime and Its Two Related Protocols[343]

A. The United Nations Protocol to Prevent, Suppress, and Punish Trafficking in Persons, Especially Women and Children
B. The United Nations Protocol against the Smuggling of Migrants by Land, Sea, and Air, which entered into force in 2003–04.

United Nations Convention against Transnational Organized Crime (UNTOC) is a 2000 United Nations-sponsored multilateral treaty against transnational organized crime. The convention was adopted by a resolution of the United Nations General Assembly on 15 November 2000. It is also called the Palermo Convention, and its following protocols (the Palermo Protocols).

Transnational crime has emerged in recent years as an important security issue on the international agenda, presenting considerable challenges to policymakers, researchers, and agents combating these crimes. The convention can be divided into four main areas: criminalization, international cooperation, technical cooperation, and implementation. The convention establishes four offences: (a) participation in an organized criminal group; (b) money laundering; (c) corruption; and (d) obstruction of justice.

---

[342] Paragraph 4 of the recommendation.

[343] Dimitri Vlassis, *Overview of the Provisions of the United Nations Convention against Transnational Organized Crime and its Protocols*, Crime Prevention and Criminal Justice Officer, Secretary of the AD HOC Committee for the Elaboration of the United Nations Convention against Transnational Organized Crime, United Nations Centre For International Crime Prevention (United Nations). Available at http://www.unafei.or.jp/english/pdf/RS_No59/No59_32VE_Vlassis1.pdfzs83 (accessed on 17 November 2016).

The convention creates numerous obligations for countries, which range from updating or adopting new legislation to upgrading the capacity of their law enforcement authorities and their criminal justice systems in general. The convention will apply to the prevention, investigation and prosecution of (a) the offences established in accordance with (the convention); and (b) serious crime as defined (by the convention), when the offence is transnational in nature and involves an organized criminal group. The convention also defines transnationality. An offence is transnational in nature if it is committed in more than one state; it is committed in one state but a substantial part of its preparation, planning, direction, or control takes place in another state; it is committed in one state but involves an organized criminal group that engages in criminal activities in more than one state; or it is committed in one state but has substantial effects in another state. In addition, the provisions on extradition and mutual legal assistance contain specific and very carefully negotiated language to permit application of these articles in order to establish both the transnationality and the involvement of an organized criminal group.

This convention consists of 41 articles that require states parties to criminalize, inter alia, participation in an organized group (Article 5), the laundering of the proceeds of crime (Article 6), and corruption (Article 8). States parties are additionally obligated to adopt measures for the prosecution of offenders (Articles 10 and 11), and for the confiscation and seizure of, inter alia, the proceeds of such crimes (Articles 12 to 14). The United Nations Office on Drugs and Crime (UNODC) acts as custodian of the UNTOC and its protocols.

Protocol to Prevent, Suppress and Punish Trafficking in Persons, Especially Women and Children, Supplementing the United Nations Convention against Transnational Organized Crime

The Protocol to Prevent, Suppress and Punish Trafficking in Persons, Especially Women and Children entered into force on 25 December 2003. It is the first global legally binding instrument with an agreed definition on trafficking in persons. The intention behind this definition is to facilitate convergence in national approaches with regard to the establishment of domestic criminal offences that would support efficient international cooperation in investigating and prosecuting trafficking in persons. An additional objective of the Protocol is to protect and assist the victims of trafficking in persons with full respect for their human rights.[344]

The protocol, inter alia covers the following.[345]

Definition of trafficking in persons: 'Trafficking in persons' shall mean the recruitment, transportation, transfer, harbouring or receipt of persons, by means of the threat or use of force or other forms of coercion, of abduction, of fraud, of deception, of the abuse of power or of a position of vulnerability or of the giving or receiving of payments or benefits to achieve the consent of a person having control over another person, for the purpose of exploitation. Exploitation shall include, at a minimum, the exploitation of the prostitution of others or other forms of sexual exploitation, forced labour or services, slavery or practices similar to slavery, servitude or the removal of organs. The recruitment, transportation, transfer, harbouring, or receipt of a child for

---

[344] Available at http://www.unodc.org/unodc/en/treaties/CTOC/ (accessed on 17 November 2016).
[345] Available at http://www.unodc.org/unodc/en/treaties/CTOC/ (accessed on 17 November 2016).

the purpose of exploitation shall be considered 'trafficking in persons' even if this does not involve any of the means set forth here.

This protocol supplements the United Nations Convention against Transnational Organized Crime. It has to be interpreted together with the convention. The provisions of the convention apply, mutatis mutandis, to this protocol unless otherwise provided. The offences established in accordance with Article 5 of this protocol shall be regarded as offences established in accordance with the convention. The purposes of this protocol are

a) to prevent and combat trafficking in persons, paying particular attention to women and children;
b) to protect and assist the victims of such trafficking, with full respect for their human rights; and
c) to promote cooperation among states parties in order to meet those objectives.[346]

All protocol offences are also regarded as convention offences, which makes all convention provisions (for example, legal assistance, applicable to cases which involve only protocol offences). The protocol is intended to 'prevent and combat' trafficking in persons and facilitate international cooperation against such trafficking. It applies to the 'prevention, investigation and prosecution' of protocol offences, but only where these are 'transnational in nature' and involve an 'organized criminal group', as those terms are defined by the convention. It provides for protection of trafficked persons (Articles 6–8). The negotiation of the protocols against Trafficking in Persons and the Smuggling of Migrants both found it necessary to deal with the fact that the primary subject matter, while often treated as a commodity by smugglers and traffickers, consists of human beings whose rights must be respected and who must be protected from various forms of harm.[347]

The Protocol against the Smuggling of Migrants by Land, Air, and Sea

The protocol supplements the convention, and provisions of the two should be interpreted together. Provisions of the convention apply to the protocol mutatis mutandis unless otherwise specified or the protocol Article 2 expresses three purposes: preventing and combating smuggling, promoting cooperation among states parties, and protecting the rights of smuggled migrants. The scope of application of the instrument (Article 4) applies both to combating smuggling and protecting rights, but limits both to offences which are transnational in nature and involve an organized criminal group as defined by the convention. The protocol applies only to the prevention, investigation or prosecution of such offences and the protection of the rights of persons who have been the objects of such offences. The phrase 'persons who have been the object of such (that is, trafficking) offences' in this and other protocol provisions is intended to clarify that smuggled migrants, while sometimes exploited or endangered by smugglers, are not 'victims' of the primary protocol offence. The obligations placed on states concerning return or repatriation are the same in this instrument as in the Protocol against Trafficking in Persons. The basic obligation on states parties is to 'facilitate and accept' the return of nationals or specified residents without undue

---

[346] Available at http://www.unodc.org/unodc/en/treaties/CTOC/ (accessed on 17 November 2016).
[347] Available at http://www.unodc.org/unodc/en/treaties/CTOC/ (accessed on 17 November 2016).

delay and to verify without delay whether illegal migrants in other countries are in fact their nationals or residents (Art. 18(1), (3)). This includes the obligation to issue any necessary travel documents such as passports, entry or transit visas.[348]

International Initiatives to Prevent Child Pornography on the Internet

In the Netherlands the hotline for child pornography on the Internet was created by the Foundation for Internet Providers, Internet users, the National Criminal Intelligence Service, the National Bureau against Racial Discrimination, and a psychologist (Table 5.8). Like other national hotlines that are starting to be set up, it operates by asking Internet users to report any child pornography that they find. The Netherlands hotline tries to have a preventive attitude towards the problem, in that once a site is reported, the website provider will ask the issuer of the material, if he can be traced, to remove it from the Internet, and will report that person to the police if he or she fails to do so.

Singapore has attempted to regulate the content of the Internet as far as possible, through a Class Licence Scheme, where Internet service providers and Internet content providers are required to block out objectionable sites as directed by the Singapore Broadcasting Authority. Schools, libraries, and other providers of Internet access to children are required to institute a tighter level of control, although options as to how this could be implemented have not yet been identified.

In China, Internet users must register with the police, and it is reported that a company in Massachusetts, USA, is investing in technology designed to allow the Government of China to censor the Internet.

The Internet Society of New Zealand and the Internal Affairs Department set up a joint working group to tackle pornography on the Internet in December 1996. This followed several high-profile raids and monitoring exercises by the authorities. The society is also developing a code of practice for Internet service providers.

The UK police were involved in Operation Starbust, an international investigation of a paedophiles ring thought to be using the Internet to distribute graphic pictures of child pornography, and the biggest operation so far carried out in the UK. Nine British men were arrested as a result of the operation which involved other arrests in Europe, America, South Africa, and the Far East. The Operation identified 37 men worldwide.

Table 5.8   Status of Ratification of International Instruments Related to Trafficking by India[349]

Name of the Instrument	Status
The Convention for the Suppression of Trafficking in Persons and of the Exploitation of the Prostitution of Others, 1949.	India acceded to the convention on 9 May 1950.

(Cont'd)

---

[348] Available at http://www.unodc.org/unodc/en/treaties/CTOC/ (accessed on 17 November 2016).

[349] Source: United Nations Human Rights: Office of the High Commissioner for Human Rights. Available at http://www.ohchr.org/ (accessed on 17 November 2016).

Table 5.8 *(Cont'd)*

Name of the Instrument	Status
Supplementary Convention on the Abolition of Slavery, Slave Trade, and Institutions and Practices Similar to Slavery, 1956.	India ratified it on 23 June 1960.
The International Covenant on Civil and Political Rights (ICCPR), 1966.	India acceded to the convention on 10 April 1979
The International Covenant for Economic, Social and Cultural Rights (ICESCR), 1966.	India acceded to the convention on 10 April 1979.
UNCRC, 1989	India acceded to the convention on 11 December 1992.
The ILO Convention on the Worst Form of Child Labour (Convention No. 182)	Not yet ratified by India.
Optional Protocol to the Convention on the Rights of the Child on the Sale of Children, Child Prostitution, and Child Pornography, 2000	India ratified the Optional Protocol on 16 August 2005.
United Nations Convention against Transnational Organized Crime and its two related protocols: A. Protocol to Prevent, Suppress and Punish Trafficking in Persons, Especially Women and Children, supplementing the United Nations Convention against Transnational Organized Crime. B. The Protocol against the Smuggling of Migrants by Land, Air and Sea.	India ratified it on 5 May 2011.
SAARC Convention on Preventing and Combating Trafficking in Women and Children for Prostitution, 2002	India ratified it in 2002

Government/Non-governmental Organization Interventions in the Area of Exploitation and Trafficking in India

The National Plan of Action for Children (1992) includes children of prostitutes in the category of children in especially difficult circumstances, but does not suggest any goals or activities for them. Based on a Supreme Court judgment in July 1997, a committee was formed to make an in-depth study of the problems of prostitution, child prostitutes, and children of prostitutes, with the secretariat of the Department of Women and Child Development (DWCD) as its chairperson. The report of this committee[350] includes a plan of action to combat trafficking and commercial sexual exploitation of women and children, aiming at bringing to the mainstream and reintegrating these women and child victims in the society. The plan includes action points such

---

[350] DWCD, Government of India, 1998.

as prevention of trafficking, awareness generation and social mobilization, healthcare services, education and childcare, housing shelter and civic amenities, economic empowerment, legal reforms and law enforcement, rescue and rehabilitation, and so on. It recommends setting up of night-care shelter, education support programme, institutionalization, Anganwadi-cum-day-care centres or Balwadi, non-formal education, formation of self-help groups by women victims, and community education based on experience of the Devadasi Rehabilitation Programme in Karnataka and Prerana in Mumbai. The DWCD has prepared guidelines for proposals for projects to combat trafficking of women and children through prevention, rescue, and rehabilitation in destination and source areas, including trafficking under sanction of tradition.

The National Plan of Action for Children, 2005 is by far the most comprehensive planning document concerning children. Its value is that it clearly outlines goals, objectives, and strategies to achieve the objectives outlined and recognizes the needs of all children up to the age of eighteen. It is divided into four basic child right categories as per the UNCRC: child survival, child development, child protection, and child participation—to protect children from trafficking the government needs to address root causes of vulnerability, sensitize police, medical facilities and media about the issue, create mechanisms to track, investigate and prevent trafficking; and to protect child labourers it is first important to understand the number of working children in India through the census survey, strengthen formal school systems, properly implement child labour laws.[351]

The NGO initiatives in India have been restricted primarily to networking, lobbying/advocacy, and welfare services to the victims and their children. There are some organizations which have tackled the issue of trafficking for prostitution but in a different perspective, like sensitizing and taking preventive measures among caste-based communities of prostitutes, through programmes for their children, specially the girl child. There are many such organizations like Abhivday Ashram, Morena, Sanlaap in Kolkata, Satya Sohan Ashram, Sagar, and Vimochana at Athni. Vocational training is imparted along with education to the girl child so that she does not become a prey to the traffickers. They also conduct community sensitization programmes. Sangram in Sangli, Maharashtra, conducts awareness generation programmes among the community where the devadasi practice is common. Gram Niyojan Kendra runs awareness generation and skill-training programmes in Rajasthan and Uttar Pradesh.

Organizations such as Prerana in Bombay and Joint Women's Programme in Delhi and Allahabad run balwadis and healthcare centres for children of prostitutes. Intervention by NGOs and women's groups on the issue of trafficking take the following forms:

- Advocacy for the rights of those who are trafficked for the purpose of prostitution.
- Advocacy for the rights of migratory labour or for those who are trafficked for labour.
- Networking for united action to prevent trafficking by like-minded groups.
- Lobbying for changes in legislation.
- Advocacy for rights of women in prostitution.
- Providing welfare services for health, education, and childcare.
- Running of shelter/safe homes.

---

[351] Available at http://www.childlineindia.org.in/National-Plan-of-Action-2005.htm (accessed on 2 June 2015).

- Facilitation of rehabilitation and repatriation.
- Providing information about laws, policies, and programmes.

There are some networks and organizations that work in the areas of trafficking. These include the following.

End Child Prostitution in Asian Tourism

This has been monitoring and acting against sex tourism in Asia and, in recent times, elsewhere. The ECPAT promotes transactional governmental cooperation and extraterritorial legislation, which allows governments to bring their nationals to trial for crimes committed in other countries, and draws public attention to the arrest, detention, and conviction of paedophiles engaged in sex tourism. The ECPAT also engages the interest and commitment of world tourism authorities, travel agents, holiday guide publishers, and tour promoters in actively working against sex tourism.

Action against Trafficking and Sexual Exploitation of Children

Action against Trafficking and Sexual Exploitation of Children (ATSEC) is a network that deals with cross-border activities between West Bengal and Bangladesh to facilitate advocacy, research, social mobilization, technical assistance, and programme support at the national and regional levels. It also aims to develop capacity of the government organizations and NGOs to plan and implement advocacy programmes.

The Network against Child Sexual Exploitation and Trafficking (NACSET)

The Network against Child Sexual Exploitation and Trafficking (NACSET) is a network against commercial sexual exploitation and trafficking. As the prevention of trafficking and CSE is a major orientation and thrust of NACSET, it has given adequate importance to approaching organizations which can play a crucial role on this front. For example, village-based organizations engaged in water conservation, drought relief, soil conservation work in the perennially drought-prone areas along with women's organizations and youth organizations are encouraged to join the network. The NACSET believes effective prevention can be achieved primarily by expanding in this manner to all the relevant organizations and social forces.

Action Aid

Action Aid is working to curb the trafficking of women and children. The Action Aid India campaign, aimed at promoting coordinated action against trafficking, looks closely at interventions at the grass roots and links it to policies and action at state, national, and international levels. Prevention at source is attempted by using strong systems and a community-based approach through exact mapping and tracking of the vulnerable areas from where trafficking takes place. A comprehensive analysis of the situation on the ground with respect to trafficking has been carried out. In the course of conducting sensitization and training exercises, a training manual has been developed for use by those doing prevention work. An assessment tool has been designed to go with the training manual. Rehabilitation and reintegration of trafficked persons is attempted through interventions which are sensitive to the situation of the trafficked persons and in keeping with their aspirations. Support has been given to create an organization of trafficked persons themselves to have self-regulatory boards to prevent children from being trafficked into prostitution.

Save Our Sisters Movement

The Save Our Sisters (SOS) Movement, recently launched by Save the Children India, Mumbai, has a major goal to seek out the feasibilities of establishing working partnerships among NGOs working at the city, state, and national levels, corporate sector, media, government, and the judiciary to combat the problem. Its objectives are grouped under advocacy, prevention, rehabilitation, and legislation. It has started holding regional workshops, developing awareness booklets, collecting resource material for a Central Resource and Documentation Centre, conducting a survey of various rehabilitation homes for the reused children in Maharashtra, mapping of the trafficked-prone areas, and so on.

Campaign against Child Trafficking

The Campaign against Child Trafficking (CACT) has been initiated by Terre des Hommes aiming at developing a national strategy for combating child trafficking using three broad dimensions for addressing the problem: awareness generation, legal interventions, and projects at the grass roots creating and strengthening a region-specific intervention through database and building local strategies; and building partnership with the appropriate groups like decision-makers, media, and citizens to ensure implementation of international conventions, initiating national legislative processes, and aiding its conversion into enforceable law.

Sanlaap

As an obvious outcome, a major focus of Sanlaap's activities is centred in and on the red-light areas of Kolkata and its suburbs. Sanlaap is particularly engaged in lobbying with the government, judiciary, and police to get access to the rescued children commercially abused in prostitution, who are in custody, and the children of the prostitutes, to support them with necessary counselling and care. An effort is also made to rehabilitate the young girls trafficked from suburban and rural areas of West Bengal, Nepal, and Bangladesh.

Bachpan Bachhao Andolan

The BBA symbolizes India's largest grassroots movement for the protection of children, ensuring their quality education. As on October 2014, BBA has rescued more than 83,500 victims of trafficking, slavery, abuse, and child labour and has helped them re-establish trust in society and find promising futures for themselves. Its mission is to identify, liberate, rehabilitate, and educate children in servitude through direct intervention, child and community participation, coalition building, consumer action, promoting ethical trade practices, and mass mobilization.[352]

Prajwala, Hyderabad[353]

The philosophy of Prajwala evolved based on the need of women and children who are victims of trafficking. Prajwala emerged as an anti-trafficking organization, which believes in preventing women and children from entering prostitution, which is the worst form of sexual slavery.

The Anti-Human Trafficking Unit[354]

Trafficking of women and children is one of the gravest organized crimes, extending beyond boundaries and jurisdictions. Combating and preventing human trafficking requires a holistic approach by all stakeholders and integrated action on prevention, protection, and prosecution. Keeping this philosophy in mind, Project IND/S16 of the United Nations Office on Drugs and Crime, which is a joint initiative of UNODC and the Government of India and funded by the US Government, was launched in April 2006 in India. The Anti-Human trafficking Unit (AHTU) project is focused on 'strengthening the law-enforcement response in India against trafficking in persons, through training and capacity building'. The major activities in the project are training of police officials and prosecutors, setting up integrated AHTU, establishing networks amongst law-enforcement agencies and civil society partners as well as developing appropriate tools including protocols, manuals, SOPs, compendiums and other training aids. The AHTUs were set up by UNODC in 2007 in certain states, by involving police, prosecutors, other government officials and NGOs and by providing non-expendable and expendable resources as well as protocols, is a classic example of integrated, multi-stakeholder synergy in anti-trafficking.[355]

Law Reform Relating to Trafficking

Trafficking is a complex crime with innumerable constituents. The Indian law has many effective provisions to deal with trafficking. They are scattered in different statutes like the ITPA, JJ Act and the IPC, Trade in Human Organs Act, Bonded Labour Act. However, due to lack of coordination and synergies, these provisions remain underused and in many cases abused.

The ITPA does not achieve the objective it is meant to achieve, primarily since it did not define 'trafficking', and is hence reduced to a legislation dealing with prostitution. While actual numbers are difficult to obtain, government and NGO reports suggest that hundreds of thousands to millions of women and girls are prostituted in India (median age of entry is 11 years), many of whom are victims of sex trafficking. However, despite the high prevalence, very few cases of sex

---

[352] Available at http://www.bba.org.in/ (accessed on 14 April 2015).

[353] Available at http://www.prajwalaindia.com/home.html (accessed on 17 November 2016).

[354] *A Compendium of Best Practices on Anti-human Trafficking by NGOs* (New Delhi: Compiled by HAQ Center for Child Rights, United Nations Office on Drugs and Crime Regional Office for South Asia, 2008).

[355] *Compendium of Best Practices.*

trafficking are actually reported and prosecuted. India reviewed its ITPA and includes provisions to better prevent trafficking and provide support services for survivors

The Immoral Traffic (Prevention) Amendment Bill, 2006[356] was introduced in the Lok Sabha on 22 May 2006. The highlights of the bill included the following:

- The Immoral Traffic (Prevention) Amendment Bill, 2006 amends the ITPA, 1956 to combat trafficking and sexual exploitation for commercial purposes.
- The bill deletes provisions that penalized prostitutes for soliciting clients. It penalizes any person visiting a brothel for the purpose of sexual exploitation of trafficked victims.
- All offences listed in the bill would be tried in camera, that is, the public would be excluded from attending the trial.
- The term 'trafficking in persons' has been defined with a provision for punishing any person who is guilty of the offence of trafficking in persons for the purpose of prostitution.
- The bill constitutes authorities at the centre and state levels to combat trafficking.

Gaps in the bill:

- While prostitution is not an offence, practicing it in a brothel or within 200 metres of any public place is illegal. There seems to be a lack of clarity on whether prostitution ought to be a legitimate way of earning a living if entered into by choice.
- Penalizing clients who visit prostitutes could drive this sector underground, preventing legal channels of support to victims of trafficking.
- This bill punishes trafficking for the purpose of prostitution. Trafficking for other purposes (such as bonded labour and domestic work) are not covered by the bill.
- The rank of special police officer, who would enforce the act, is lowered from inspector to sub-inspector. Such powers delegated to junior officers could lead to greater harassment.
- The bill constitutes authorities at the centre and state level to combat trafficking. However, it does not elaborate on the role, function, and composition of these authorities.

Owing to a lack of consensus, the Union Cabinet referred the Immoral Traffic (Prevention) Amendment Bill, 2007 ('revised bill') to a Group of Ministers (GOM) for further consideration. The stringent criticism on legal, political, and public health grounds resulted in divergence of opinion within the government. Consequently, the ITPA Amendment Bill lapsed in February, 2009.

The Ministry of Women and Child Development, Government of India has drafted the Trafficking of Persons (Prevention, Protection, Rehabilitation) Bill, 2016 to create a unifying law on trafficking. However, the present version of the 2016 Bill raises several concerns. Broadly, the 2016 Bill, fails to define or provide guidance on key terms like trafficking, prevention, protection, and rehabilitation; lacks enforcement mechanisms for measures it proposes such as the anti-trafficking committees; lacks clarity regarding the functioning and coordination of the various laws which provide protection against trafficking in India including the Immoral

---

[356] Available at http://www.prsindia.org/billtrack/the-immoral-traffic-prevention-amendment-bill-2006-143/ (accessed on 17 November 2016).

Traffic Prevention Act, 1956, Juvenile Justice (Care and Protection of Children) Act, 2015, Bonded Labour System (Abolition) Act, 1976, Inter-State Migrant Workmen Act (Regulation of Employment and Conditions of Service) Act, 1979, among others, and the proposed TIP Bill, 2016; and lacks clarity regarding financial commitments from the government to enforce the provisions 2016 Bill. What is required is a comprehensive law.

As India reviews its ITPA and include provisions to better prevent trafficking and provide support services for survivors, it is also called on India to 'address the root causes of trafficking' and to 'ensure the effective investigation, prosecution and punishment of traffickers'.

Section 5 of the ITPA makes 'procuring, inducing or taking a person for the sake of prostitution' as a punishable offence. However the records show that this is one of the most underused provisions of the act with an abysmal rate of prosecution and conviction. On the other hand, one of the prime examples for the abuse of law is Section 8 of the same act. The women and children who are subjected to the offences under the act are firstly 'arrested' as 'prostitutes'. Young children and women who are supposed to be protected by the act are 'arrested' under the very same law. The result is that women and children are arrested for the act of 'soliciting' prostitution and prosecuted. This is a typical case of the survivor (we prefer the term to 'victim') of an offence ultimately becomes the convict. We recommend that the law needs to be sensitized and overhauled lest it degrades into a tool to stigmatize girls and women for the rest of their lives.[357]

In practice the law enforcement reveals the following gaps:

• Under ITPA, 1986, almost 75 per cent of those arrested are females. It is evident that the spirit of the act has not been followed as the victims are being harassed.

• There have been several instances of occurrences of sexual abuse and exploitation of children within families and homes. The law generally presumes that guardians of the child are innocent and it takes a lot of professional commitment to establish such an offence against such guardians.

• Law relating to paedophiles' is inadequate. Therefore, the police are generally ineffective when it comes to registering the crimes, especially when it actually comes to registering the cases against foreign tourists where passport officers and international links are involved. The judiciary and the police are not aware of the laws and rights of the children.

• The laws governing prostitution are biased against the prostitute. Under ITPA, 1986, the customer is not an offender. For a fixed sum of money, a man is able to obtain women or girls to satisfy his sexual needs, with or without her consent. In other words, what constitutes rape outside the brothel is converted to prostitution inside the brothel and both children and women are deprived of their rights.

On the recommendation of the Justice Verma Committee Report, the Government of India recently adopted anti-trafficking provisions in the IPC through the CLA Act of 2013, to conform to the internationally-recognized definition of the crime of trafficking as outlined in the

---

[357] *Justice Verma Committee Report.* Available at http://nlrd.org/resources-womens-rights/anti-trafficking/anti-trafficking-schemespolicy-document/verma-committee-report-on-trafficking-in-india   (accessed on 17 November 2016).

Palermo Protocol. However, India's other anti-trafficking legislation, like the ITPA of 1956, has not been changed in nearly 30 years working to empower girls and women to resist and end sex trafficking[358]

As per the suggestions of the Verma Committee Report, the following amendments are required in the ITPA, 1986:[359]

The new law on trafficking of minors must be a gender neutral and an enabling and empowering legislation[360]

- The ITPA of 1956 must be changed in consonance with the 2013 Constitutional law amendment. The definition of trafficking must be as per the Palermo Protocol.
- Addressing the gender based violence against women and children with a right based perspective and within the framework of rights given in the constitution of India, CRC and CEDAW. The rights-based framework sees violence as a breach of language which sees sexual crimes as a breach of bodily integrity and sexual autonomy rather than in terms of modesty and morality.
- Include provisions for rehabilitation, counselling, and support services and assistance to survivors of violence, which include both male and female's professional training.
- Stringent punishment for the accused but no capital punishment with provision for correctional services for reformation.
- Classification of offences as per POCSO Act must be considered. The distinctions between sexual assault and aggravated sexual assault must be maintained.[361]
- Amend the ITPA by including specific provisions that will improve anti-trafficking efforts, protect children and survivors and address other shortcomings still remaining. Amending this act will put India in line with its international legal obligations under the protocol. The provisions are:
  - ◆ Legal protection and removal of criminal sanctions from women and children in prostitution.
  - ◆ Criminalization of pimps and brothel keepers, not women or children in prostitution.
  - ◆ Punishment for those who pay for sex.
  - ◆ Strict liability for traffickers and buyers of a minor regardless of whether the perpetrators knew the victim's age.
  - ◆ Establishment of a fully government-funded Trafficking Victims Rehabilitation and Welfare Fund.

- Establish a protocol for verifying the age of the survivors leads to prevent the exploitation of loopholes in the ITPA and JJ Act. The survivors, if they are below the age of 18 are sent

[358] Available at http://www.equalitynow.org/take_action/sex_trafficking_action491 (accessed on 17 November 2016).

[359] *Verma Committee Report*. Available at http://nlrd.org/resources-womens-rights/anti-trafficking/ anti-trafficking-schemespolicy-document/verma-committee-report-on-trafficking-in-india (accessed on 17 November 2016).

[360] Available at http://ohrh.law.ox.ac.uk/to-whomsoever-it-may-concern-the-case-of-criminal-law-amendment-act-2013/ (accessed on 17 November 2016).

[361] Available at http://ohrh.law.ox.ac.uk/to-whomsoever-it-may-concern-the-case-of-criminal-law-amendment-act-2013/ (accessed on 17 November 206).

to CWC as prescribed in the JJ Act. However, since most of the trafficked persons do not have adequate records to prove their age, they are shown as adults using falsified documents presented mostly by pimps and middlemen. It is shown from studies that in most cases, the survivors are 'bailed out' by pimps and middlemen. A standardized protocol has to be put in place whereby the age of survivors is objectively assessed by a body of experts using well recognized tests like the ossification test.

- A specialized police force to deal with trafficking since it has inter alia trans-border connections as well. It is a sophisticated crime which needs a specialized law-enforcement agency to tackle.

- The following directions need to be followed by the magistrates while dealing with trafficking offences:

    a) Every magistrate before whom a child is brought must be conscious of the provisions of the JJ Act, 2000.

    b) He must find out whether the child is below the age of 18 years.

    c) If it is so, he cannot be accused of an offence under Section 7 or 8 of ITPA.

    d) The child will then have to be protected under Juvenile Justice Authority.

    e) The magistrate has a responsibility to ascertain and confirm that the person produced before her or him is a child by accurate medical examination.

    f) The definition of a child in Section 2(k) means a juvenile or a child as a person who has not completed 18 years of age.

    g) Once the age test is passed under Section 17(2) establishes that the child is a child/minor less than 18 years of age, the magistrate/sessions judge while framing charges must also take into account whether any offence has been committed under Sections 342, 366, 366A, 366B, 367, 368, 370, 371, 372, 373, 375 and if so, he or she must also frame charges additionally.

    h) The child should be considered as a child in the protection of the Child Welfare act.

    i) The child should be handed over to the CWC to take care of the child. The performance of the CWC must be reviewed by the high court with a committee of not less than three Honourable Judges and two psychiatrists.

    j) A child must not be charged with any offence under ITPA or IPC.

    k) A minor trafficked victim must be classified as a child in need of care and protection. Further, the magistrate must also order for intermediate custody of minor under Section 17(3) of ITPA, 1956.

    l) There should not be any joint proceedings of a juvenile and a person who is not a juvenile on account of Section 18 of the JJ Act, 2000.

    m) It is necessary that courts must be directed that the same lawyer must not represent the trafficker as well as the trafficked minor.

    n) Evidence of child should be taken in camera.

    o) Courts must protect the dignity of children. The children's best interest should be the priority.

- Special courts need to be set up as provided under Section 22A of the ITPA to deal with the offence of trafficking,

- Comprehensive code to deal with 'Trafficking and Sexual Exploitation (both commercial and otherwise)'. This code ought to be complemented with specialized judicial mechanism to prosecute offender while protecting the survivors.[362]

The enforcement of law in India has been weak in dealing with abusers, exploiters, and traffickers of children. There have been several gaps in implementation. To strengthen the implementation and enforcement of laws, following are some recommendations:

- To prevent secondary victimization during interrogation/examination by investigating agencies as well as during court procedure, where a child is made to recall minute details of the sexual acts and experience, and is grilled in getting proof, a model code of conduct[363] should be evolved. There should be a standardized questionnaire for examination of the prosecutrix, indicating the parameters for supervision.
- Examination of the victim/witnesses should be in the presence of social workers/women police/parents or others who have the trust or confidence of the child. Examinations should also be done in a familiar atmosphere and not in police stations.
- Age and other tests of the rescued victim should also be done in the presence of child-supporting individuals and preferably in the homes where the children are lodged after rescue. The homes should therefore, be provided with these facilities.
- Questioning should be done mostly by women police officers. The mental health aspects of the children have to be kept in mind. There should not be too much pressure on the child to speak all the details of the traumatic incident.
- Adopting a multidisciplinary approach to the crime should be attempted by co-opting additional members into the investigating team so as to include doctors, social workers, co-opting mental health exerts counsellors, or anyone who would be useful in the overall rehabilitation of the child.
- Investigation should necessarily be conducted into the trafficking angle in all cases of missing persons, procurement of minor girls, buying and selling, child marriages, and all cases of kidnapping and abduction.
- Police officers should not be in uniform while examining the child and specially trained child-friendly police officers should examine the child. The venue of the trial should be a safe place other than the usual court buildings.
- Law and order and VIP duties are of high priority for police, whereas CSA cases are low priority crimes. This should be rectified.
- Criminal Compensation Injuries Board should be set up.
- Special courts, within a certain time frame, should handle all cases involving sexual abuse of children.
- The burden of proof should be shifted to the accused.
- Formation of a nodal cell at the state level to deal with interstate and inter-country dimensions of abuse may be tried.
- The age of the child in applicable acts varies. The JJ Act defines child as below 18 years of age. The PCMA also specifies 18 years as the cut-off age for restraining child marriage. Section 375

---

[362] *Verma Committee Report.*

[363] *Report on the Six Regional Consultations on Sexual Exploitation and Trafficking of Children*, sponsored by Department of Women and Child Development, Government of India, and UNICEF, India.

of the IPC identifies wife as not being under 15 years of age and Section 376(2)(f) as not under 12 years of age. The ITPA sees a female child as not exceeding 16 years of age, while a minor is up to 18. The age of the child should be uniformly defined as up to 18 years. There should be a proper mechanism to determine the age of the child.

- The laws governing prostitution are biased against the prostitute. Under the ITPA, the customer is not an offender. Under the IPC, transmitting a sexually transmitted disease is an offence. The prostitute can be isolated compulsorily if she is found to have AIDS. The rescue operations have led to a spate of glaring human rights abuses of the prostitutes including right to freedom from violence, right to shelter and residence, right to seek legal help, right to family, right to information and right to representation.

- The ITPA, 1986, to be more effective, needs the following measures:

    ◆ Notification of public place.
    ◆ Closure of brothels keeping minors.
    ◆ Setting up of special courts for speedy trials.
    ◆ Rescue operations to be more humanely and sensitively carried out along with a rehabilitation plan protecting the human rights of the prostitutes.
    ◆ Age verification of the rescued children to be immediately carried out. In fact it should be linked to the rescue operations.

The ministry of women and child development has proposed an anti-trafficking bill called the Trafficking of Persons (Prevention, Protection and Rehabilitation) Bill, 2016. The bill envisages creating district- and state-level anti-trafficking committees with government officers and NGO representatives to mobilize efforts to prevent, rescue, protect, and rehabilitate victims of trafficking, in addition to providing medical care, psychological assistance, and skill development. The government is to formulate programmes for rehabilitation, support, after-care, and reintegration services. The state governments are to form specialized schemes for women in prostitution or who have been the victims of other forms of commercial sexual exploitation. A Central Anti-Trafficking Advisory Board will advise the government on the bill's implementation.

The bill creates new offences. It criminalizes using a narcotic substance, alcohol, or psychotropic substance for trafficking (Section 16), administering any chemical substance or hormone to a trafficked woman or child to enable early sexual maturity (Section 17), and revealing the identity of a victim or witness to a crime of trafficking. If such information is published in the media, the offending individual and owner of the media venture are both liable to be punished. The bill also penalizes the contravention of the registration requirements for protection homes, special homes, and placement agencies.

Monitoring of Cyber Pornography

A committee appointed by the Mumbai High Court[364] laid down several restrictions on cyber cafés to provide for an adequate degree of supervision and control so that minors are protected from being exposed to pornographic sites on the Internet in the cyber cafés. The committee has

---

[364] *Jayesh Thakker & Another* v. *State of Maharashtra & Others and Internet Users Association of India (Intervenors)*, Suo Motu, Writ Petition 1611 of 2001, Mumbai High Court.

given recommendations to make a child-friendly or child-safe 'cyber zone' where minors could safely access and use the Internet for information, education, communication, and entertainment. The committee's recommendations include:

- A suggested definition of cyber cafés to be included in the rules under the Mumbai Police act.
- Procedures for licensing cyber cafés.
- Regulations requiring cyber café operators to demand photo ID cards (of any kind) from all users.
- Requiring that minors be restricted to using machines in the common open space of cyber cafés (that is, not in cubicles).
- Requiring that these machines be fitted with software filters.
- Email and website information to be provided by the Internet service providers informing the public about the hazards and possible solutions.
- Setting up a hotline to the cyber crime investigation cell.
- Taking steps to increase awareness about cyber crime in general.

Extra-Territorial Jurisdiction

Several instances of CSA&E have come to light in India involving foreigners. The objective of extra-territorial jurisdiction is to apply the domestic criminal law to crimes committed by nationals in other territories. Jurisdictional lines must not be allowed to come in the way of apprehending and convicting adults who prey upon children. There is an urgent need for such legislation to effectively tackle sex tourism and trafficking of children for commercial sexual exploitation. Under the Swedish Penal Code, a Swedish citizen who has committed an offence outside of Sweden, which is an offence in Sweden and in the country in which it was committed, is liable under the Swedish law and can be tried by the Swedish court. The Crimes (Child Sex Tourism) Amendment Act, 1994 is an Australian law that prohibits and criminalizes sexual acts overseas with children less than 16 years of age. Australian courts have adopted the procedure of video-link evidence whereby the court is able to hear evidence directly from witnesses who are in overseas locations.

Law Reform Relating to Missing Children

An advisory issued by the Ministry of Home Affairs dated 31 January 2012 reveals that Government of India is aware of the seriousness of the problem of missing children. The advisory states:

> The issue of missing and untraced children, based on police records, is a matter of deep concern to the Government of India. It requires a concerted and systematic attention of Central and State Governments. As missing children are exposed to high risk situations, they are vulnerable and fall prey to crimes of exploitation, abuse, including human trafficking. It is, therefore, necessary that effective steps be taken for investigation of cases relating to missing children and tracing of these children.[365]

365 This advisory is in continuation of the advisories dated 09 September 2009, 14 July 2010, 02 December 2011 and 4 January 2012 issued by this ministry to all the states/UTs on similar/related lines.

Need for Correct Data on Missing Children

The data on missing children is a big gap. Whether these missing children land up in begging rings, flesh trade, paedophilic net and organ trade or end up getting exported for camel jockeying, amongst others, it is always an organized crime. There is a great difficulty in getting the correct numbers of untraced women and children. There is no correlation between the number of children who are missing, the number of complaints or FIRs registered and the number children who are traced and supposedly rehabilitated. Every district magistrate in the country must report with the help of all his officers, supervised by a judicial officer to the high court the total number of missing children in every district. Thereafter, the FIR should be registered. The high courts in all states must monitor the investigation of all these cases.

The data from various websites and agencies must be regularly updated and matched, for example the data from the state and district/city police control room/local police net, ZIP NET, www.trackthemissingchild.gov.in, www.childlineindia.org.in, and www.stoptrafficking.into should be updated and shared regularly.

Nodal Officer for Every State and Union Territory for Missing Children

An officer not below the rank of a DIG should be declared nodal officer for every state/UT for handling the cases of missing children. Supervision of investigation of such cases by senior police officers of the level of deputy superintendent/additional superintendent may be ensured. When, any heinous crime or organized crime on missing children, such as, victims of rape, sexual abuse, child pornography, and organ trade, is reported, the investigation of such cases should be taken over by the CID of the states/UTs to expedite the investigation and to ensure prosecution of the offenders. State crime branch should maintain close links with District Missing Children Unit (DMCU) and ensure that uploading of data and matching of missing children with UIDBs/ Children found is carried out effectively.

Record of Profiles of all traffickers

Profile of all traffickers who facilitate such trafficking should be maintained at Police station level in Gang Registers. All police officers and men, especially the team of officers handling investigation into these cases need to be trained and sensitized on an ongoing basis to the issues concerned.

Training and Sensitization of law enforcement

The issues of missing children, human trafficking along with JJ Act may be made part of syllabus in the state police training colleges and all law enforcement training institutes to sensitize the police force. When training, they must be oriented to undertake all preventive steps including steps to identify children in distress, watch of suspicious persons, special attention at transit points, namely, border areas, ICPs, railway stations, bus stations, airports, ports etc., identify vulnerable population/places and take steps to address the vulnerability on time. The border security force (BSF)/ Indo-Tibetan Border Police (ITBP)/ Sashastra Seema Bal Sashastra Seema Bal (SSB) personnel in outposts on borders should be trained to look-out for trafficked children on the borders.

Inclusion of Children in shelter Homes and Institutions

Missing Persons Bureau in the state should have a centralized data on children lodged in these shelter homes run by the government/non-governmental agencies in the state with mechanism to update the data on regular basis.

Involvement of Child line

Child line helpline number 1098 is running in various states and districts. They need to be strengthened for missing children. There should be at least one dedicated police personnel at this helpline on 24×7 basis with proper monitoring mechanism and networking with identified civil society organizations

Identity Cards for Children in All Schools

Schools must issue identity cards to all children.

Coordination and networking between agencies

Coordination and networking between agencies dealing with missing children include the police, the SJPU, the designated police officers in some police stations, Home Department, Police Department, Social Welfare Department, Women and Child Welfare Department, Juvenile Justice Department, CWCs, Labour Department, Health Department, Tourism Department as well as other agencies like State Human Rights Commission, State Women's Commission, SCPCR, railways, RPF, BSF, SSB, ITBP, among others. State governments must institutionalize a coordinating mechanism among all these agencies through an SOP clearly mandating the roles and responsibilities of each of these agencies. All police stations and CWCs in the country must be connected.

Comprehensive Uniform Standard Operating protocol for the country for missing children

There are Standard Operating procedures in some states. A comprehensive uniform protocol was directed by the Supreme Court which has been reportedly submitted.[366]

Mandatory Registration of Missing complaints of Any Minor by Police

On 16 September 2009, the Delhi High Court on its own Motion116 has taken suo motu cognizance pertaining to missing children. One of the first directions is that Delhi Police will, without any delay, register all complaints of missing children as FIRs and that the Delhi Police will strictly follow the Supreme Court's directions in Horilal.[367] The Supreme Court, on 17 January 2013,

---

[366] *Bachpan Bachao Andolan* v. *Union of India*, Writ Petition (Civil) No. 75 of 2012.
[367] Writ Petition (Crl) No. 610 of 1996, decided on 14 November 2002.

has directed police stations across the country to compulsorily register missing complaints of any missing minor and appoint a special police officer to handle complaints of juveniles. Such police personnel should be stationed at every police station in plain clothes. These directions must be monitored and enforced

Strengthening and Operational Zing AHTUs throughout the Country

The AHTUs must be provided with resources and infrastructure and funding strengthened throughout the country

Placement Agencies in the States

A framework must be provided within which the placement agencies, that provide employment to children, could be regulated and monitored

Law Reform Relating to Trade in Human Organs of Children

Organized crime groups lure people with false promises and convince or force them to sell their organs for a low price. The recipients of the organs pay a much higher price than the donors receive. This part benefits the traffickers who are part of an organized criminal network. The trafficked organs can be acquired in many different and terrible ways. People may be kidnapped, killed and sold, especially children, for their organs. Other ways for the brokers to procure the organs are through deception or coercion. There have been cases where a victim will go to a doctor or hospital for an unrelated illness or accident, but in the hospital, the person's kidney is removed without their knowledge or consent.

Organ trafficking can be distinguished from other forms of trafficking, since the traffickers and organ 'brokers' involved are often from decent and respected industry sectors. Doctors and other healthcare practitioners, ambulance drivers, and mortuary workers are often involved in organ trafficking in addition to those involved in other human trafficking networks.[368]

According to the BBA secretary 'while trying to locate missing children, many times he has found dead bodies of children without their vital organs. 'What was shocking was that their kidneys or other vital organs were missing. In many cases, police just says the body was lying in a stream, where some animal must have eaten the child's organ.' It is much easier to file a case of kidnapping and murder against unknown persons. If you accept the organs were missing, you have to do a thorough investigation. So, the details in such cases get murkier.'

On the issue of illegal extraction of organs, the Supreme Court of India[369] observed that they find that only three cases have been registered by the CBI—one is a case in the year 2007 against one Mahender Singh Goldi. The allegation was that the kidneys of boys and girls were being

---

[368] Available at http://www.unric.org/en/human-trafficking/27447-organs-for-sale (accessed on 17 November 2016).

[369] *Bachman Bache Angolan* v. *Union of India & Ors*, Writ Petition (C) No. 51 of 2006 Supreme Court of India.

extracted and they were being sold by deceiving them. A charge sheet was filed against 9 persons and the case is still pending at the stage of prosecution evidence. In respect of a third complaint, a closure report was filed. These three are enough for us to arouse a suspicion that there exists a huge racket of extraction and sale of human organs and in view of the statement made by the Director General of Health Services and in the context of trafficking of children whose numbers are not available, we draw an adverse inference against all the state police departments, who have failed to respond to the data sheet which this Committee had requested. We come to the conclusion that there appears to be organized networks and gangs which are operating which through middlemen are inducing and abducting children including female children and with the connivance of police is actually selling them, abducting them, subjecting them to sexual assault and possibly extraction of organs.[370].'

The Transplantation of Human Organs Act, 1994, has failed miserably in achieving its objectives. There are organized gangs, at national and international levels, which are operating through middlemen who are inducing and abducting children including female children is actually selling them, abducting them, subjecting them to sexual assault and possibly extraction of organs. It is a very grave crime akin to drug trafficking and must be taken very seriously by the law makers and law enforcement agencies. The definition needs an amendment. The punishments need to make more deterrent as it violates fiduciary relationship. Protocols need to be developed for proper implementation of the act. Organ trafficking involves societal and global issues that must be discussed within the broader paradigm of global injustices. International law enforcers must cooperate across borders in order to address organ-related crimes.

---

[370]   *Bachman Bache Angolan* v. *Union of India & Ors*, Writ Petition (C) No. 51 of 2006 Supreme Court of India.

6 Juvenile Justice
Administration and Implementation

Vulnerable Children

Care of the child is primarily the responsibility of parents and elders in the family. In traditional India, children in need of care and protection (CNCP) were looked after in the joint family, caste group, village community, and religious institutions. To be born in a happy and comfortable home is a privilege that not many children are destined to enjoy. With the spread of urbanization and industrialization, breakdown of family structures and religious sanctions, population explosion, prospects of adventure and excitement in cities, the conditions of children deteriorated.

The vast majority of the children are impoverished. This has given rise to children in especially difficult circumstances (CEDC) who are vulnerable, marginalized, destitute, and neglected, and are quite frequently deprived of their basic rights to family care, protection, shelter, food, health, and education. According to an estimate, there are around 340 million deprived children in India. The vulnerable group of deprived children can be categorized as orphans, abandoned and destitute, working and street children, victims of natural calamities, emergencies or man-made disasters, children with disability, AIDS-affected children, children engaged in substance abuse, children of sex workers, juvenile offenders or children in conflict with law, children of families 'at risk' like refugees, migrants and construction workers, chronically and terminally ill, prisoners or lifers, single parents, and the girl child.

Among the vulnerable groups of children, India has the largest population of street children in the world.[1] At least 18 million children live or work on the streets of urban India.[2] According to a definition by United Nations Children's Fund (UNICEF), street children are those for whom the street (in the widest sense of the word)—more than their family—has become their real home, a situation where there is no protection, supervision, or direction from responsible adults.

Another group of vulnerable children is that of the child labourers. According to a survey conducted by 7th All India Education Survey (2002), currently, there are 17 million child labourers

---

[1] United Nations Development Programme (UNDP), *Human Development Report, 1993* (New York: Oxford University Press, 1993).

[2] Abhinav Singh and Purohit Bharathi, 'Street Children as a Public Health Fiasco', *Peace Review: A Journal of Social Justice*, 23, no. 1, 2011

in India.[3] These children are exposed to physical and mental abuse, besides hazardous work and unsafe working conditions. Underage sex workers are those who have been forced into prostitution. Torture and exploitation are a cruel reality these children have to face. Many of them are also badly affected by drug abuse and are being used by organized crime groups in drug trafficking and peddling. Most Indian children are disabled because of poverty and it is correlated. Protein malnutrition, iodine deficiency, and Vitamin A deficiency are the major causes of mental retardation and blindness.

Exodus to cities like Mumbai has led to expansion of slums and pavement dwellings. Children of such migrant workers suffer from abuse, neglect, and exploitation. Children also become orphans and destitute due to natural calamities like floods, droughts, earthquakes, and environmental disasters. Children are also the most innocent victims of terrorism, armed conflicts, and other political reasons. India is a country that traditionally idolizes sons. Girl children, especially in rural areas, remain deprived of adequate access to basic healthcare, nutrition, and education.

The CEDC can be further classified, as shown in Figure 6.1.

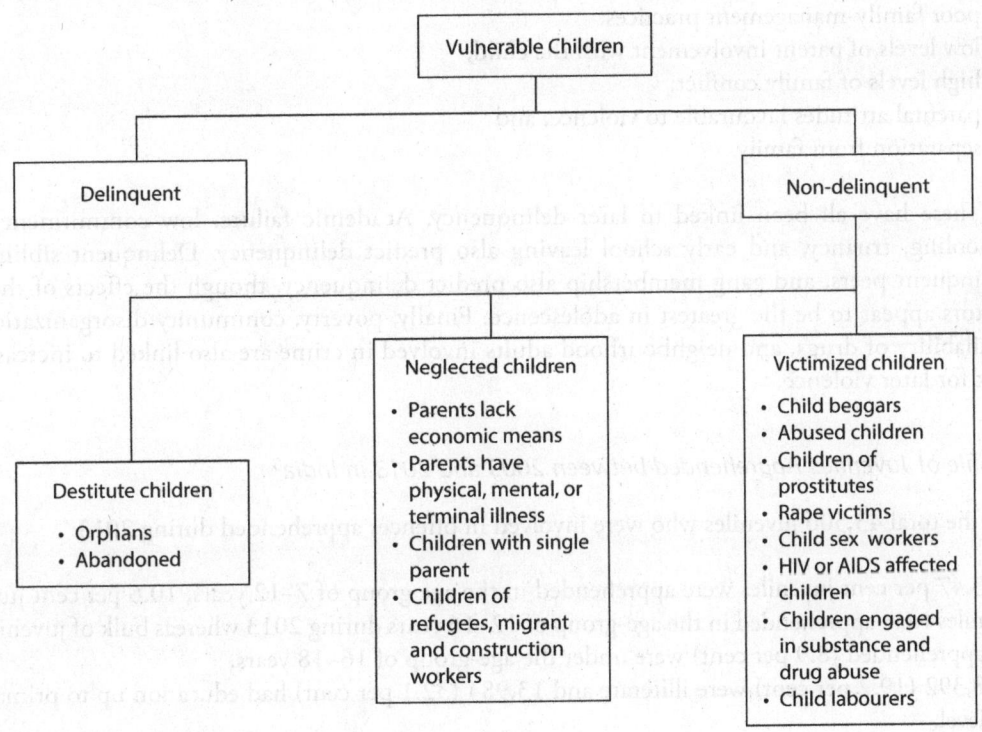

Figure 6.1   Children in Especially Difficult Circumstances

---

[3] Department of Educational Surveys and Data Processing, National Council of Educational Research and Training, New Delhi, 2002.

Delinquency

Delinquency is any act, course of conduct, or situation, which might be brought before the court and adjudicated whether in fact it comes to be treated there, or by some other resources or indeed remains untreated. The juvenile delinquent or a child in conflict with law is thus a person who has been adjudicated as such by a court of proper jurisdiction though he may be no different, at any rate, up and until the time of court contact and adjudication, from masses of children who are not delinquents. Juvenile delinquency is an act or omission by a child or young fantasy which is punishable by law under the legal system. A Brazilian activist had rightly said: 'A juvenile delinquent is nothing more than a poor child caught red-handed in the struggle for survival.'

Studies indicate that juvenile delinquency is a result of the interactions of contextual, individual, and situational factors.[4] Some of these factors within a family are

- living with criminal parents,
- harsh discipline,
- physical abuse and neglect,
- poor family-management practices,
- low levels of parent involvement with the child,
- high levels of family conflict,
- parental attitudes favourable to violence, and
- separation from family.

These have all been linked to later delinquency. Academic failure, low commitment to schooling, truancy, and early school leaving also predict delinquency. Delinquent siblings, delinquent peers, and gang membership also predict delinquency, though the effects of these factors appear to be the greatest in adolescence. Finally, poverty, community disorganization, availability of drugs, and neighbourhood adults involved in crime are also linked to increased risk for later violence.

Profile of Juveniles Apprehended between 2003 and 2013 in India[5]

Of the total 43,506 juveniles who were involved in offences apprehended during 2013:

- 3.47 per cent juveniles were apprehended in the age group of 7–12 years, 10.6 per cent juveniles were apprehended in the age-group of 12–16 years during 2013 whereas bulk of juveniles apprehended (8.9 per cent) were under the age-group of 16–18 years.
- 8,392 (19.2 per cent) were illiterate and 13,984 (32.1 per cent) had education up to primary level.

---

[4] Rolf Loeber and David Farrington, eds, *Serious and Violent Juvenile Offenders* (SAGE Publications Inc., 1998).

[5] National Crime Records Bureau, 'Crime in India 2013'. Available at http://ncrb.nic.in/StatPublications/CII/CII2013/Home.asp (accessed on 14 October 2016).

- Children living with parents (35,244) have accounted for 81.0 per cent of the total juveniles apprehended.
- The share of homeless children (2,462) who were involved in various crimes was just 5.7 per cent (see Table 6.1).

Table 6.1 Incidence and Rate of Juveniles in Conflict with Law under the Indian Penal Code (IPC) (2003–13)

| S. no. | Year | Incidence of | | Percentage of juvenile crimes to total crimes | Estimated mid-year population* (in lakh) | Rate of crime by juveniles |
		juvenile crimes	total cognizable crimes			
(1)	(2)	(3)	(4)	(5)	(6)	(7)
1	2003	1,789	17,16,120	1.0	10,682	1.7
2	2004	19,229	18,32,015	1.0	10,856	1.8
3	2005	18,939	18,22,602	1.0	11,028	1.7
4	2006	21,088	18,78,293	1.1	11,198	1.9
5	2007	22,865	19,89,673	1.1	11,366	2.0
6	2008	24,535	20,93,379	1.2	11,531	2.1
7	2009	23,926	21,21,345	1.1	11,694	2.0
8	2010	22,740	22,24,831	1.0	11,858	1.9
9	2011	25,125	23,25,575	1.1	12,102	2.1
10	2012	27,936	23,87,188	1.2	12,134	2.3
11	2013	31,725	26,47,722	1.2	12,288	2.6

Source: National Crime Records Bureau, Ministry of Affairs, Government of India, Crime in India 2013.

Figure 6.2 presents a classification by attributes of juveniles apprehended during 2013. Of the total number of 43,506 arrested and sent to court in 2013[6]

- 15.2 per cent (6,613) juveniles were disposed of after advice or admonition;
- 19.8 per cent (8,599) were placed under care of parents/guardians;
- 3.9 per cent (1,689) were sent to institutions;
- 21.9 per cent (9,549) were sent to special homes;
- 4.0 per cent (1,756) were dealt with fine;
- 7.4 per cent (3,198) were either acquitted or their cases were otherwise disposed of; and
- percentage of juveniles awaiting trial at the end of 2013 was 27.8 per cent (12,102 out of 43,506)

---

[6] National Crime Records Bureau, 'Crime in India 2013'.

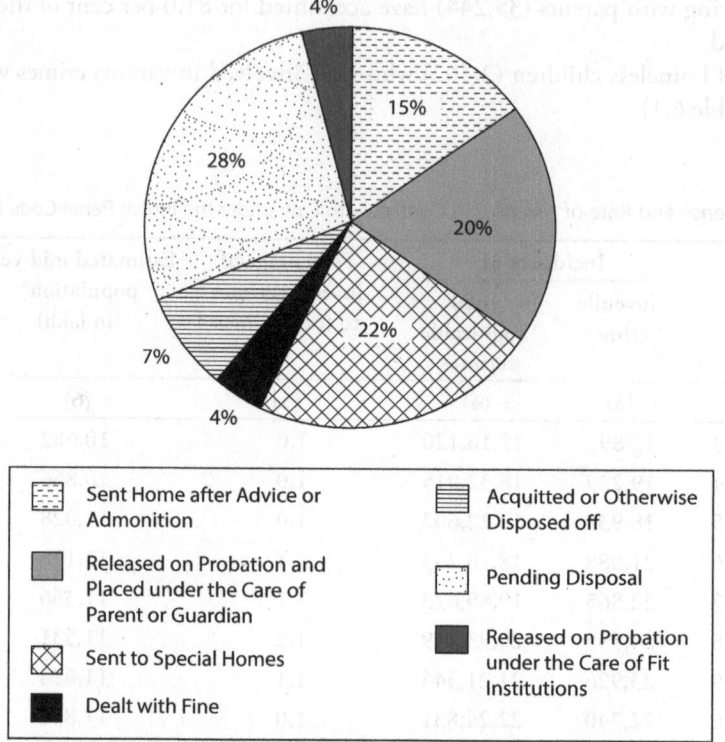

Figure 6.2   Disposal of Juveniles Apprehended during 2013[7]

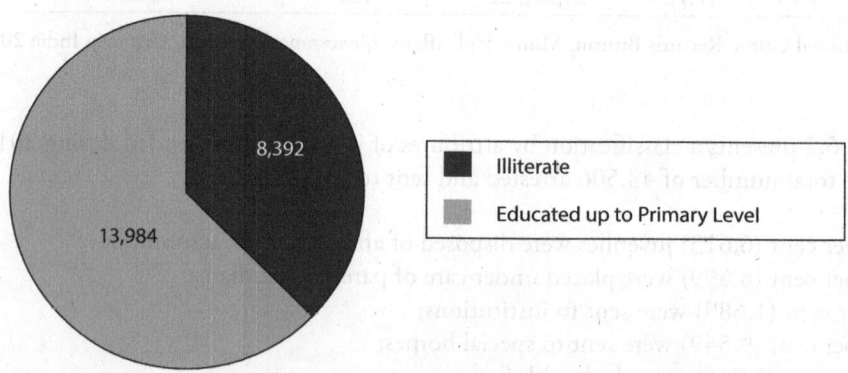

Figure 6.3   Classification by Attributes of Juveniles Apprehended during 2013[8]

---

[7] Source: National Crime Records Bureau, Ministry of Home Affairs, Government of India, Crime in India 2013. Available at http://ncrb.nic.in/StatPublications/CII/CII2013/Home.asp (accessed on 14 October 2016).

[8] Source: National Crime Records Bureau, Ministry of Home Affairs, Government of India, Crime in India 2013. Available at http://ncrb.nic.in/StatPublications/CII/CII2013/Home.asp (accessed on 14 October 2016).

Classification of Juveniles Arrested by Attributes during 2013

As per the National Crime Records Bureau, Ministry of Affairs, Government of India, Crime in India 2013, the classification of juveniles arrested by attributes during 2013 is as follows:[9]

- 8,392 (19.2 per cent): Illiterate
- 13,984 (32.1 per cent): Educated up to primary level

It is significant to note that a large number of juveniles are sent home, that is, back to the same family and neighbourhood that have most likely contributed to their delinquent behaviour. Therefore, families, schools, and neighbourhoods are the primary socializing agents to bring up children into non-delinquent individuals and need to be strengthened. Another area of concern is the large number of cases pending disposal. As can be seen in Figure 6.2, around 51.3 per cent juveniles apprehended have been poorly educated.

Brief History of the Juvenile Justice Legislation

After Independence, many of the then states like Uttar Pradesh, Hyderabad, Mysore, West Bengal, and Saurashtra developed their separate acts whereas the centrally governed states (union territories) were covered under the Central Children Act, 1960 which was amended in 1978. In 1969, Assam, Madhya Pradesh, and Rajasthan developed their separate acts. As Gujarat was a part of Maharashtra, the Mumbai Children Act was implemented in areas other than Saurashtra. Similar Children's Acts were passed at different times. Himachal Pradesh passed it in 1979 and Haryana in 1984.

By and large, some of the common features of these acts were as follows:

- The acts covered neglected, delinquent, and victimized children.
- Initially, there was only one agency to deal with children, namely, the juvenile court. The Central Children Act for the first time introduced a separate agency, namely the Child Welfare Board, for handling neglected children and leaving the juvenile court to deal with delinquent children.
- Appointment of a separate probation officer to deal with the child and proper aftercare services for his/her rehabilitation in the society were provided for in the acts of all the states, though in practice they were hardly taken care of by the states.
- There were no provisions for special qualification, training, or knowledge of child psychology for persons dealing with juvenile cases.
- There was no uniformity in all these acts as to the age of the child.
- Different states followed different practices and procedures.

Hence there was a need for a uniform legislation for the entire country.

[9] National Crime Records Bureau, Ministry of Home Affairs, Government of India, Crime in India 2013. Available at http://ncrb.nic.in/StatPublications/CII/CII2013/Home.asp (accessed on 14 October 2016).

Juvenile Justice Act, 1986

The Juvenile Justice Act (JJ Act), 1986 (herein referred to by the abbreviations 'JJ Act') replaced the Children's Acts, formerly in operation in the states and the union territories (UTs). It came into force in 1987 on a uniform basis for the whole country. The preamble of the JJ Act, 1986 states that the act is to provide for the care, protection, treatment, development, and rehabilitation of neglected and delinquent juveniles and adjudication of certain matters relating to disposition of delinquent juveniles.

The objectives of JJ Act 1986 were the following:

- To lay down a uniform framework for juvenile justice in the country so as to ensure that no child under any circumstances is lodged in jail or police lock-up.
- To provide for a specialized approach towards the prevention and treatment of juvenile delinquency.
- To spell out the machinery and infrastructure required for the care, protection, treatment, development, and rehabilitation of various categories of children coming within the purview of the juvenile justice system.
- To establish norms and standards for the administration of juvenile justice.
- To develop appropriate linkages and coordination between the formal system of juvenile justice and voluntary agencies.
- To constitute special offences in relation to juveniles.
- To bring the operation of the juvenile justice system in conformity with the United Nations Standard Minimum Rules for the Administration of Juvenile Justice.

Under JJ Act, juvenile meant a boy who had not attained the age of 16 years or a girl who had not attained the age of 18 years [Section 2(h)]. The juveniles were further classified into neglected juveniles and delinquent juveniles. A neglected juvenile [Section 2(i)] was a very wide term and included a juvenile who was found begging [Section 2(a)], or who had no home and was a destitute, or who had unfit parents, or who lived in a brothel or with a prostitute, or who led an immoral life, or a juvenile who was being abused or there was a possibility that in future he may be abused for immoral purposes. A delinquent juvenile[10] was one who had committed an offence under any law of the land and came in conflict with law. The Juvenile Welfare Board dealt with neglected juveniles whereas the delinquent juveniles were brought before the juvenile court.[11]

Machinery for Implementing the 1986 Act

The act has provided for the classification and separation of delinquents on the basis of their age, the kind of their delinquency, and the nature of offences committed by them. The four types of institutions under the act were as follows:

---

[10] JJ Act 1986, Section 2(e): 'Delinquent juvenile' means a juvenile who has been found to have committed an offence.

[11] JJ Act, 1986, Section 2(i): 'Juvenile court' means a court constituted under Section 5.

- Observation homes: These were for temporary reception of juveniles during the pendency of any inquiry regarding them under this act [Section 11].
- Juvenile homes: A neglected juvenile was sent for accommodation, maintenance, and facilities for education, vocational training, and rehabilitation [Section 9].
- Special homes: A delinquent juvenile was sent for accommodation, maintenance, and facilities for education, vocational training, and rehabilitation [Section 10].
- After-care organizations: These were for the purpose of taking care of juveniles after they left juvenile homes or special homes and for the purpose of enabling them to lead an honest, industrious, and useful life [Section 12].

Procedure in Case of a Neglected Juvenile under 1986 Act

The procedure in brief [Sections 13 and 14] can be represented as shown in Figure 6.4.

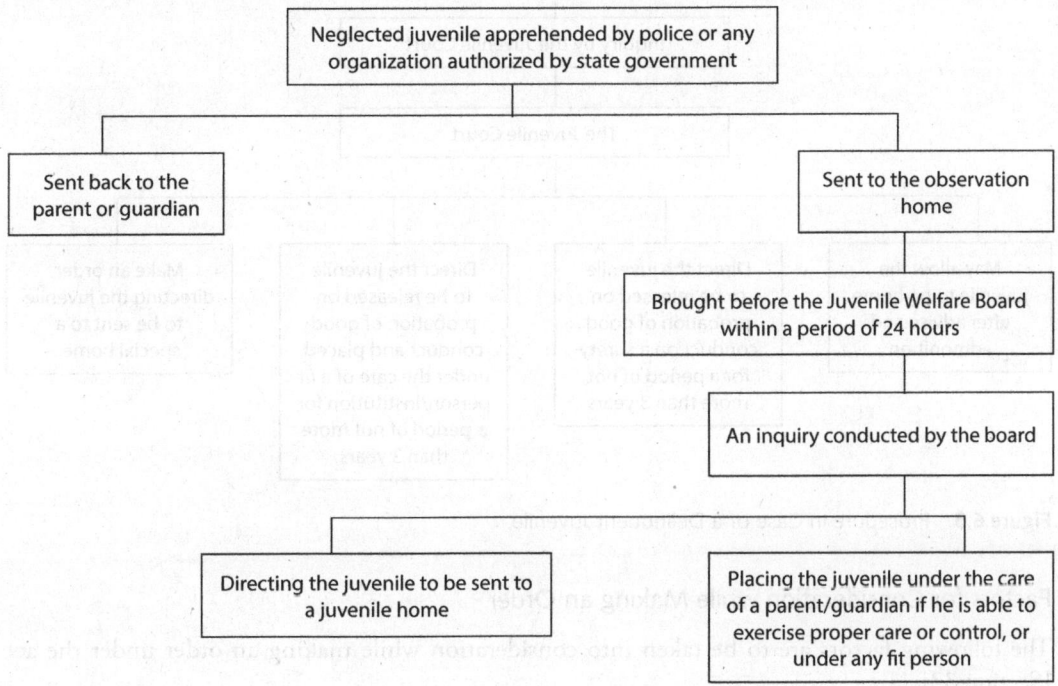

Figure 6.4   Procedure in Case of a Neglected Juvenile

Procedure in Case of a Delinquent Juvenile under 1986 Act

The procedure in brief [Sections 18, 19, and 20) can be represented as shown in Figure 6.5.

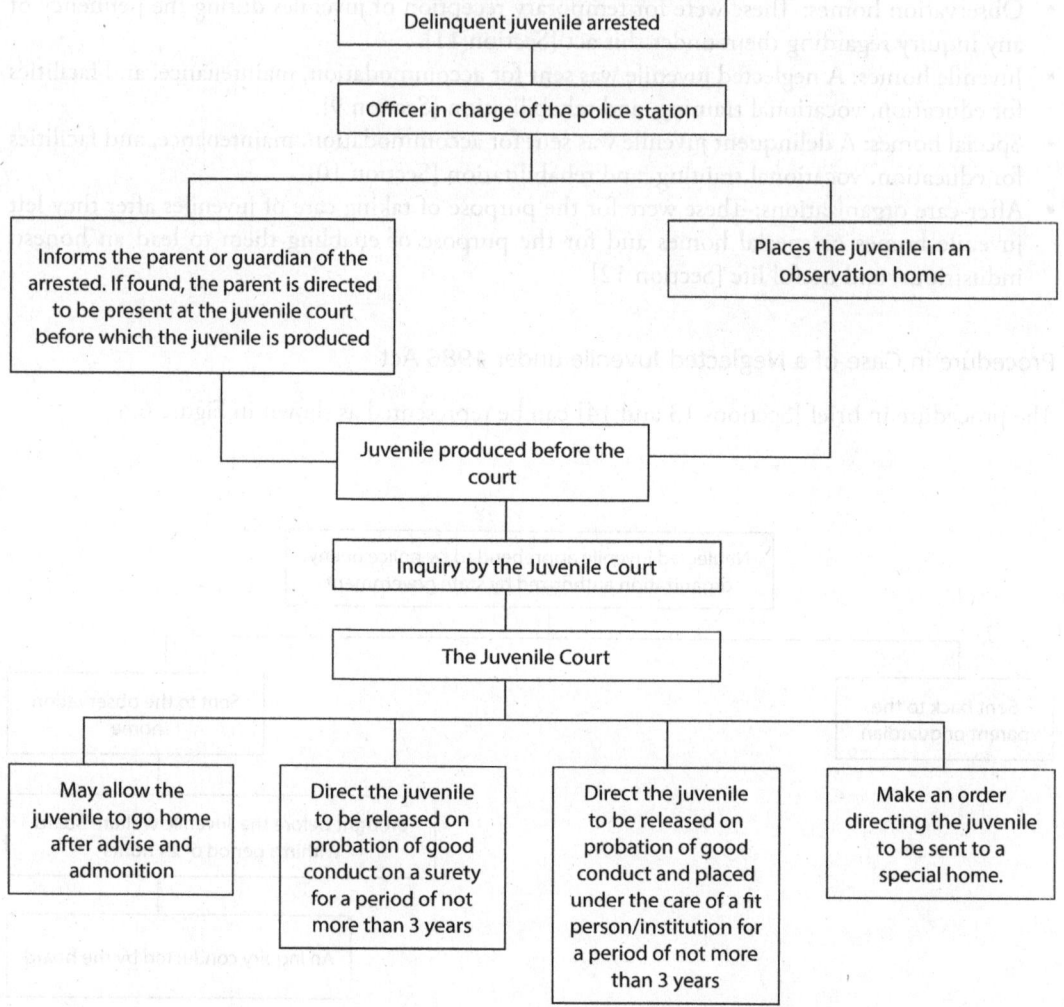

Figure 6.5 Procedure in Case of a Delinquent Juvenile

Factors for Consideration while Making an Order

The following factors are to be taken into consideration while making an order under the act [Section 33]:

- age of the juvenile,
- state of physical and mental health of the juvenile,
- circumstances under which the juvenile lives,
- report made by the probation officer,
- religion of the juvenile, and
- any other circumstances to be taken into consideration in the welfare of the juvenile.

Special Offences in Respect of Juveniles

Chapter VI of JJ Act, 1986 provides for punishment for certain special offences in respect of the juvenile [Sections 41, 42, 43, 44, and 45]. These offences and their corresponding punishments are listed in Table 6.2.

Table 6.2 Punishment for Special Offences in Respect of Juvenile, JJ Act, 1986

Special Offences	Punishment
1. Cruelty to juveniles (assault, abandoning, and others)	1. Imprisonment up to six months or fine or both
2. Employment of juveniles for begging	2. Imprisonment up to 3 years and fine
3. Giving intoxicating or narcotic drugs or psychotropic substances to a juvenile	3. Imprisonment up to 3 years and fine
4. Exploitation of juvenile employees	4. Imprisonment up to 3 years and fine

Sanctions By the Juvenile Court [Section 21]

Under the 1986 Act, the court could order any of the following dispositions after explaining to the juvenile and the parent or guardian under whose care the juvenile has been placed, the terms and conditions of the order:

- Direct the juvenile to be released on probation of good conduct and placed under the care and custody of any parent, guardian, or other fit person executing a bond with or without surety as required by the court for the well-being and good behaviour of the juvenile for a period not exceeding 3 years.
- Direct the juvenile to be released on probation of good conduct and placed under the care of any fit institution for the good behaviour and well-being of the juvenile for any period not exceeding 3 years.
- Order the juvenile to pay a fine if over 14 years of age and earning money.
- Order the juvenile to be released on probation of good conduct and placed under the supervision of a probation officer for any period not exceeding 3 years.

If none of these aforementioned alternatives were feasible, the court could order the juvenile to be sent to a special home, established or recognized within the state. A delinquent boy above 14 years of age or a delinquent girl above 16 years of age must be sent to a special home for a minimum period of 3 years. The juvenile delinquents below this specified age should be sent to a special home till they cease to be children.

There are provisions relating to appeal by an aggrieved person against an order made by a competent authority under the act. Only one appeal to the court of sessions has been permitted [Section 37] but in majority of the cases, the children have no resources for appeal and so there are not many appeals against the orders of the juvenile courts.

Administration and Implementation of the Juvenile Justice Act, 1986

The history of the implementation of the JJ Act, 1986 is a history of hopes unrealized and promises unfulfilled. The judges, the law enforcers, the police, the probation officers, and other staff, have not carried the spirit of the act.

One of the objectives of the act was to lay down a uniform framework and to ensure that no child was lodged in jail or police lock-up. The act fulfilled the long-felt need of bringing about a uniform legislation for the whole of India. Though the act was a central legislation but the implementation was left to the state governments. Section 1(3) also made provision for appointing different dates for bringing into force the different provisions of the act. It was done on different dates by different states. Therefore, even in the new millennium there were states which have still had to set up the machinery under the act.

A study done on the implementation of the JJ Act, 1986 revealed that in practice, there were the following areas of concern in the administration and implementation of the 1986 Act:[12]

- Arbitrary detention is illegal under Articles 21 and 22 of the Constitution of India. Articles 50, 56, and 57 of the Code of Criminal Procedure (CrPC) mandate that no person can be detained in custody without knowing the grounds of arrest and that a detainee must be presented before a magistrate within 24 hours of his arrest. Section 160 of the CrPC prohibits the detention of males under the age of 15 or females of any age for the purpose of investigation or questioning by the police. Article 9 of the International Covenant on Civil and Political Rights and Article 37 of the UN Convention on Rights of Child prohibit arbitrary detention. Both the Beijing Rules and the UN Rules for juveniles deprived of their liberty state that the human rights of juveniles should be protected and respected while in custody. India has ratified both these instruments. The JJ Act, 1986 also prohibited the detention of juveniles in either police stations or jails. But in spite of all these mandates, there were several instances where children had been taken overnight for interrogation by the police and tortured and later released next morning. There was no record of their arrest. It was alleged that this normally happened when big thefts occurred. Then, there were complaints that the police did not produce the child within 24 hours after they had been arrested. Moreover, pressure was put on the child to tell the judge the wrong time of the pick-up. Many children preferred to go to adult lock-ups rather than observation homes. Therefore, when picked up by the police, they would say that they were 18 years so that they are taken to the lock-up where they will be released earlier rather than being confined to institutions. The magistrate generally did not send them for age verification. In rural areas, if the child was well-built, he was treated like an adult offender and taken to the police station. If later on his parents managed to come with evidence of age (which was very rare) he was released, otherwise the procedures of ordinary criminal law were followed.
- Juvenile courts were generally situated at district headquarters. Many children and their parents had to travel long distances at considerable trouble and expense to reach the courts on

[12] Asha Bajpai, 'Juvenile Justice in Maharashtra—Administration and Implementation', a study sponsored by UNICEF, 1998 (unpublished).

the date of the hearing and after reaching there, many times they would have to return due to adjournments. The juvenile court had all the semblance of an adult criminal court. The juvenile courts used the words 'arrest', 'charge sheet', 'offence', 'offender', 'criminal', 'bail', 'bond', among others. The police, judge, magistrate, advocate, lawyer, public prosecutor, stamp fee, and other such factors were very much present in the juvenile justice system. The juvenile courts set up under JJ Act, 1986 could be called 'special courts' but the personnel in those courts were not aware of the specialized approach. The atmosphere in the juvenile court was generally very intimidating. The judges sat in the front of the table and the child stood like an 'accused' in front of them. The child was not made comfortable or made to sit down. The child was petrified and did not know what was happening to him/her or what was going to happen when he appeared before them. Therefore, the adult criminal justice system, terminology, functioning style, and attitudes were prevalent in practice. On days the juvenile courts did not sit, children in many states were taken to the premises of the ordinary courts for remand. In many instances, the police had arrested a juvenile without enough evidence. The bail application formats in some of the juvenile courts were in English. Petitions in juvenile court also had to bear a nominal stamp fee. In the juvenile courts, the court fee, the application, and the bail procedure were a source of harassment to the poor parents. The Mumbai High Court in a judgment has suggested the waiver of court fees. Cases were piling up in the juvenile courts mainly due to delay in filing charge sheets by the police, non-appearance of the investigating officer (IO), and other such factors.[13]

- Juvenile courts had turned into second-class criminal courts. To a large extent differences were due to court organization and resources. The lack of clear laws, rules, and standards articulating how the court process was supposed to work had also contributed to the problem. The 'best interests' principle requires an individual assessment in each case. But the caseload of the judges and probation officers was so high in the juvenile courts, especially in metropolitan cities like Mumbai, that there was no time for such assessment.[14] The assistant public prosecutor was present but there was nobody to present the interests of the child before the courts. A duty counsel had been recently appointed in the juvenile court in Mumbai but there was a need to appoint such duty counsels in all the juvenile courts to represent the interests of children.

- The definition of juvenile delinquency was very legalistic and, restrictive and as a matter of fact, it did not take into consideration all actions that lead to the act of 'offence' but those acts are often by themselves not an offence. Exclusion of these acts had a far-reaching consequence and often made the whole juvenile justice system meaningless. For example, absenteeism, act of defiance to lawful authority, all these can be symptoms of a child gradually turning into a criminal unless treated early. But unfortunately, due to restrictive and legalistic definition of juvenile delinquency, these symptoms are neglected so long as the child does not completely turn criminal by committing an act of crime.[15] The IPC defines offences with an adult

---

[13] Asha Bajpai, 'A Pilot Study of Children and Courts in Mumbai', sponsored by Board of Research Studies, TISS, Mumbai, 2000.

[14] Bajpai, 'Juvenile Justice in Maharashtra'.

[15] N.L. Mitra, *Juvenile Delinquency and the Indian Justice System* (New Delhi: Deep and Deep Publication, 1988), p. 34.

perspective. As far as children are concerned, the offences cannot be treated similarly as is the practice today. All borderline sub-delinquency and pre-delinquency acts can be included; for instance, in a school code non-formal authorities be given the power to take correctional steps.[16] The juvenile justice system should be the last resort and petty acts should not come before the courts. Such acts can be dealt within the community.

- An issue to be noted was the motivation of the personnel involved in the system. There were several pressures at work that influenced their behaviour, like the poor pay, the inadequate staff, the desire to succeed, the need to release acute feelings of frustration, and other overwhelming emotions.

- The IO, under the 1986 juvenile justice system, was a police officer and he had practically no experience of dealing with CEDC. Besides, dealing with children was not considered as mainstream work. It was a low-priority job. Their priority was *bandobust*, law and order, and investigating the so-called high-profile crimes like dacoities, extortions, and murders. Many a times, the cases in the juvenile courts were adjourned, as the IO was absent. The repatriation orders for children were pending for months and years because the police was busy with law and order, VIP bandobust, duties during festivals like Ganpati and Navratri. Many IOs were unaware of either the objectives of the JJ Act or its provisions, or whether the children are neglected or delinquent, or whether they are lost or vulnerable. The policemen at the grass roots like the havaldar and the constable were unaware of this law. A very senior police official commented that as far as children are concerned, we are aware of only three things— they should not be handcuffed, police should not be in uniform, and they should be produced before the juvenile court. This was the level of awareness at the highest level. The juvenile justice law forms almost negligible portion of the police-training curriculum. The investigation of these issues required a different kind of expertise which was absolutely lacking. There was a stereotype pattern of investigation which was carried on without any sensitivity or follow-up.

- A child in extremely difficult circumstances, who is already a victim of his/her circumstances, when s/he came in conflict with the prevalent system, was subjected to secondary, in fact multiple, victimization. The detention, investigation, trial, and institutionalization processes further contribute to his/her victimization. The insensitive and untrained functionaries concerned, which included the police, the Juvenile Welfare Boards, the juvenile courts, the children's homes, further perpetuated the trauma. The core staff like caretakers, cooks, and guards who were directly in contact with the children were not trained at all. The delays in the system at every stage further added to the trauma of the child. The issue of the child's trauma was not at all considered by the legal system. The insensitivity of the functionaries led to the children being scared of the system. A terrified child stood before the court or the board, not knowing what was happening. Some children were seen clinging to the table at the Juvenile Welfare Board for support but were rudely told to take their hands off the table. Children were also sometimes labelled by the insensitive staff as 'thief', 'criminal', 'insect', among others.[17]

[16] Mitra, *Juvenile Delinquency*.

[17] Asha Bajpai, *Juvenile Justice in Maharashtra, Administration and Implementation*, a study sponsored by UNICEF, 1998.

- The JJ Act, 1986 classified children into neglected and delinquent, with the intention of providing different structures to deal with them. One with a 'welfare approach' and the other with a 'justice approach'. The term 'juvenile' has a stigma attached to it. It is very difficult to differentiate between a neglected juvenile and a delinquent juvenile. One is the cause of the other. Neglect leads to delinquency and vice versa. The categorization is, therefore, vague and artificial. Besides, in the observation home both categories of children were kept together for long periods of time and both were dealt with similarly.
- The Juvenile Welfare Boards were the backbone of the entire juvenile justice system as they handled 80 per cent of the children. The members were part-time honourary workers, whereas this is a full-time job which requires total commitment.
- The JJ Act, 1986 did not directly deal with child sexual abuse but the definition of a neglected juvenile includes a juvenile who lived in a brothel or with a prostitute or frequently went to any place used for the purpose of prostitution or was found to associate with any prostitute or who was being or was likely to be abused or exploited for immoral or illegal purposes. Such neglected children were produced before a Juvenile Welfare Board who may, after an inquiry, send the child to a juvenile home for care, protection, and rehabilitation. Under the JJ Act, 1986, a prostitute's child was also automatically regarded a neglected child. The magistrate had the power to segregate the prostitute from her child and place the child in a corrective institution. Besides, under the 1986 Act while males above 18 years were considered adults, the age was reduced to 16 years for females. The juvenile welfare boards were generally not equipped to deal with cases of child sexual abuse. The observation homes could provide special care and treatment for such victimized children.
- The JJ Act, 1986 bound itself only to matters regarding the relationship between the government and the children. Parents, relatives, school, and community did not have any role in the care and nurture of the child.

Problems with Institutional Care in Juvenile Justice Act, 1986

The legal response was 'institutionalization' in several cases. The JJ Act, 1986 did not clearly specify that institutionalization should be the last resort and that non-institutional, family-based, preventive services should be explored and made mandatory. Although JJ Act did not mention about non-institutional services, there were some non-institutional services that were being carried out in some parts of the country. Some juvenile welfare boards took the initiative of linking non-institutional services.

Institutional care is expensive and includes infrastructure costs. This is not cost-effective and hence it is important to promote more cost-effective and child-friendly non-institutional care.[18] The closed institutions are shrouded in their own mysterious goings-on. Children are at the mercy of caretakers who are untrained. Stories of beatings, sodomy, rape, and corruption filter through the homes. In this age of satellite communication, children at the institutions were

---

[18] Nilima Mehta, *Non-Institutional Services for Children in Especially Difficult Circumstances*, a manual supported by UNICEF, Maharashtra, and compiled for the directorate of women and child development, Government of Maharashtra, July 1996.

learning to make brooms and chalks.[19] After-care homes in practice were absolute failures; they had turned into boarding and lodging places. There was no system of investigation or monitoring. The visitors' body did not exist and the advisory board was only on paper.[20] Appointments of staff to these institutions were done by the government which was itself a defaulter in the system.[21] Training was on ad hoc basis. The core staff which is actually in direct contact with the children is untrained. There are no ongoing intensive training programmes. The issue of missing and runaway children is very important as the major chunk of neglected children fall in this category. The parents of missing children have to run from pillar to post to trace their children. There is a need for a centralized agency that can give information relating to missing children.

- The classification committee was not there in majority of the institutions. In some institutions where it was present, it had become a mere formality.
- In case of children of substance abuse there is a need for specialized treatment and approach which was lacking.
- Children who were utilized in the workshops in the institutions and for selling the products sold were not paid any remuneration.
- The inspection of the institution was mostly a formality looking into written records, weights, and quantity, rather than looking at the quality of childcare and the interests of children.
- There was no interim/periodical assessment and review of children who are in the institutions. Once committed by the court, the child remains in the institution till his/her period is over.
- No child was informed of his/her rights, especially the right to free legal aid.
- There was no proper facility for development of character and abilities.
- Escape of children was treated as on offence and punished.

Non-institutional Services

Institutionalization should be the last resort; non-institutional services must be explored first. Non-institutional services are family-based, family-like services for children. Non-institutional services have the following major objectives:

- To ensure the child's right to a family.
- To strengthen the family as a unit and prevent family disintegration.
- To develop preventive, supportive, community-based, family-oriented outreach programmes for the CEDC.
- To provide the necessary support and strength to families 'at risk' in order to prevent abandonment and institutionalization of the child due to social and economic circumstances.
- To arrange for substitute family care when the child's own family of origin cannot look after him/her due to special circumstances.
- To work towards de-institutionalizing the child and reinstate/rehabilitate him/her in his/her own biological family or a substitute adoptive or foster family.

[19] Bajpai, *Juvenile Justice in Maharashtra*.
[20] Bajpai, *Juvenile Justice in Maharashtra*.
[21] Bajpai, *Juvenile Justice in Maharashtra*.

- To mobilize resources within the local community so that the innate capacities of the people are developed, leading to their participation.

Non-institutional services include adoption,[22] foster care,[23] sponsorship,[24] daycare/night shelter,[25] family assistance,[26] school social work,[27] and community centres.[28] The following observations were made:

- The need for non-institutional services is greater among families 'at risk' who belong to the lower socio-economic strata.
- Children in nuclear families are more vulnerable to the effects of family disintegration than extended families/joint families.
- Families are willing to help children of relatives and friends, or children from the same socio-economic strata if support is provided to them.
- In child welfare interventions, if the family as a unit is assisted rather than the child in isolation, the process of rehabilitation can be more effective.
- The rehabilitation and integration of the institutionalized child into the mainstream of society is difficult because of the deprivation and psychological trauma experienced in early childhood, which are sometimes irreversible.
- De-institutionalization with careful supervision of children as part of an early rehabilitation plan has proved to be an effective strategy.

---

[22] Adoption provides substitute family care for abandoned, destitute, and orphan children. No child should be deprived of care by biological parents solely because of economic reasons. Such families should be given economic support. But when the biological parents relinquish a child permanently due to circumstances beyond their control, or the child is declared a destitute, adoption is the best non-institutional service. First option should be in-country and after all possible efforts have failed, the child can be given in inter-country adoption. After adoption the child severs all ties with his natural parents and should get all the rights of a natural child in the adoptive family.

[23] Foster care provides temporary substitute care for children. When the family is undergoing a temporary crisis (like a death of a parent or sudden illness) children experience a lot of stress and tension. They may need to be removed from their natural home to prevent their neglect. These unfortunate children can be placed in foster families till the crisis is over. Unwed mothers or single parents could also be helped by this scheme by giving financial support.

[24] This programme provides supplementary support to families who are unable to meet educational and other needs of their children. Sponsorship enables the family to send the child to school, provide medical aid, and at the same time, remain with the birth family

[25] Here the child is placed in a substitute family only during the day or night. This kind of service would enable working mothers or single parents to keep the child within the family and continue their work.

[26] This scheme provides the families with opportunities for self-employment so that they become financially independent. This is especially useful for families to help them to overcome temporary crisis situations like unemployment or serious family illness.

[27] These are multipurpose counselling centres and are very effective in controlling juvenile delinquency and family breaks.

[28] Supportive services in government and municipal schools through a school counsellor or a social worker are very effective in preventing drop-outs and providing counselling and other support services.

Amendments Suggested in Juvenile Justice Act, 1986

The study on administration and implementation of JJ Act, 1986[29] suggested the following amendments to JJ Act, 1986.

While planning child welfare interventions, services have to be in the context of the socio-economic, political, cultural realities, so that there is a child-in-situation approach rather than a child-removed-from-situation approach. The following issues are required to be taken care of by the government, the lawmakers, the NGOs, and the society at large:

- The entire juvenile justice system should be 'child-friendly' with a focus on the empowerment of the child.
- The juvenile court remains the venue with the most hope of rehabilitating society's troubled families and youths. To function well, it needs qualified and committed staff, funds, and effective dispositional options along with community support.
- Children are to be made aware of their rights.
- A grievance mechanism is to be provided in all institutions or homes wherein children can have access.
- Clear rules are to be laid down to deal with the staff who physically and sexually abuse children. Health, nutrition, education, and vocational training facilities are to be updated for CEDC.
- All accredited journalists, public interest litigation lawyers, researchers, academicians, and legal aid organizations need to be given the right to visit any institution and interview any inmate.
- Social audits by independent bodies are to be made mandatory for the institutions wherein CEDC are lodged.
- Media should be friendly towards child rights and highlight pending cases, missing children, facilities in homes, and children's grievances and views.
- Trained social workers are to be attached to the courts as per the JJ Act.
- Institutionalization should be the last resort. Closed institutions should be gradually eliminated. Only open institutions with family-type environment should be allowed in future. Partnership between government-run institutions and voluntary organizations is essential so that there is no situation of either/or, but a relation of complementarity between institutional and non-institutional services. Existing institutional infrastructure should be utilized as a base for initiating the non-institutional services so that there is a gradual phasing out of institutional care. A linkage should be established between both the approaches.
- Non-institutional services should be given statutory recognition. The JJ Act, 1986 should clearly mention that institutionalization should be the last resort and the courts should opt for rehabilitation within the families and the communities. The functionaries and staff of the institutions, when reoriented and sensitized to the needs of children and the advantages of non-institutional services, would support the de-institutionalization of the child in a phased manner.
- The JJ Act, should contain special provisions to reflect the new approaches relating to child care. The act should be liberally constructed so that each child under the jurisdiction of the juvenile court shall receive, preferably in the child's own home, the care, guidance, and control

[29] Bajpai, *Juvenile Justice in Maharashtra.*

that will serve the child's welfare and its best interests. The court's intervention should build on the family strengths and be responsive to the family needs.

- The JJ Act, should be suitably amended to provide that representatives of all non-institutional services are present at the entry point, that is, at the Juvenile Welfare Boards and Juvenile Courts to prevent institutionalization of children.
- Rights of the girl child relating to arrest, interrogation, and release should be protected.
- Standards should be set for quality services in childcare standards for recreation, rehabilitation, and counselling. Standards of childcare should be laid down as per the Convention on the Rights of the Child. Inspection should be done on the quality of these services provided to the children.
- Only violent, serious offences are to be regarded as 'offence' as far as children are concerned. Needy, dependent, neglected children and CEDC are to be kept out of the judicial system. Schemes and welfare measures for their protection and empowerment need to be formulated. Families of such children are to be empowered.
- There should be a separate and exclusive investigating agency for children.
- Appointments of personnel in the juvenile justice system should be made by an independent body. Schemes for rewards and incentive along with punishment should be formulated for the personnel. Accountability of functionaries is to be taken into consideration. Quality education and vocational training for children should be arranged in consonance with the present market requirements.
- Mentally and physically disabled children are to be provided with special residential facilities and education.
- Special treatment for victimized and sexually abused children should be provided.
- Grants to organizations should depend on the ratings of the quality of services provided to children and not on the number of children as is being done now.
- There should be reservation of seats in higher education and jobs for children from the institutions.
- More involvement of the community, NGOs, and child welfare agencies should be encouraged.
- Training of all the functionaries to be made continuous and ongoing. Special focus should be on the core staffs who directly deal with the children, like attendants, caretakers, security staff, cooks, probation officers, and superintendents.
- Inspection and monitoring of the institutions and organizations are to be conducted by an independent agency.
- There should be periodic evaluation of programmes that are conducted in the institutions.
- A separate department for missing/runaway children with extensive links with the print and television media should be organized.
- The juvenile should participate in decision-making process in the issues affecting him/her.
- Judges should visit the place of detention for necessary observations and review of their orders.
- Records relating to children have to be properly maintained.
- Interaction and sharing of expenses between juvenile court and juvenile welfare board and institutions should be encouraged.
- A guardian ad litem or a representative of the child's interest could be appointed to help the child in court proceedings. It will be his job to look after the best interest of the child and convey the same to the court. Legal aid and legal representation should be provided to the child. The medical and psychiatric assessment and treatment need to be humanely and more sensitively carried out.

Juvenile Justice (Care and Protection of Children) Act, 2000[30] (Amended in 2006 and 2011)

The ratification of the Convention on the Rights of the Child, 1989 by India in 1992 and the changing social attitudes towards criminality by children reflected in Supreme Court decisions like *Amrutlal Someshwar Joshi*,[31] *Ramdeo Chauhan*,[32] and *Arnit Das*,[33] and the need for a more child-friendly juvenile justice system were some of the factors that led to the passing of the JJ Act, 2000. The preamble to the act states that it is an act to consolidate the law relating to juveniles in conflict with law (JICL) and CNCP, by providing for proper care, protection, and treatment, by catering to their development needs, and by adopting a child-friendly approach in the adjudication and disposition of matters in the best interest of children and for their ultimate rehabilitation through their various established institutions under this enactment. It is clearly stated that the provisions of this act shall apply to all cases involving detention, prosecution, penalty, or sentence of imprisonment of JICL (Figure 6.6).[34] Chapter II of the act deals with JICL. Chapter III provides for CNCP, and Chapter IV deals with rehabilitation and social integration of both the categories of children. Chapter V is for miscellaneous measures.

In this act, 'juvenile' or 'child' means a person who has not completed 18 years of age [Section 2(k)] whereas JICL means a person who is alleged to have committed an offence and has not completed 18th year of age as on the date of the commission of such an offence[35] [Section 2(l)]. Thus there are two distinct categories of children under this act:

- 'juvenile' for children in conflict with law and
- 'child' for CNCP [Section 2(d)].

The 2000 Act expands the definition of the 'neglected juvenile' by adding new categories of children. This category of children includes: mentally and physically disabled children; sick children or children suffering from terminal diseases or incurable diseases having no one to support or look after them; children who are abused or tortured or likely to be abused or tortured; children likely to be inducted in drug abuse, and children victimized by armed conflict or natural calamity. It also includes a child who is found begging, or who is either a street child or a working child,[36] a child who does not have a parent, and no one is willing to take care of him/her or whose

---

[30] Received the assent of the president on 30 December 2000.

[31] (1994) 6 SCC 488.

[32] (2000) 7 SCC 455.

[33] (2000) 5 SCC 488.

[34] JJ Act, 2000, Section 2(4), Inserted by the Juvenile Justice (Care and Protection of Children) Amendment Act, 2006 with effect from 22 August 2006.

[35] JJ Act, 2000, Section 2(l), Inserted by the Juvenile Justice (Care and Protection of Children) Amendment Act, 2006 with effect from 22 August 2006.

[36] JJ Act, 2000, Section 2(ia), Inserted by the Juvenile Justice (Care and Protection of Children) Amendment Act, 2006 with effect from 22 August 2006.

parents have abandoned or surrendered him[37] or who is missing and runaway child and whose parents cannot be found after reasonable inquiry.

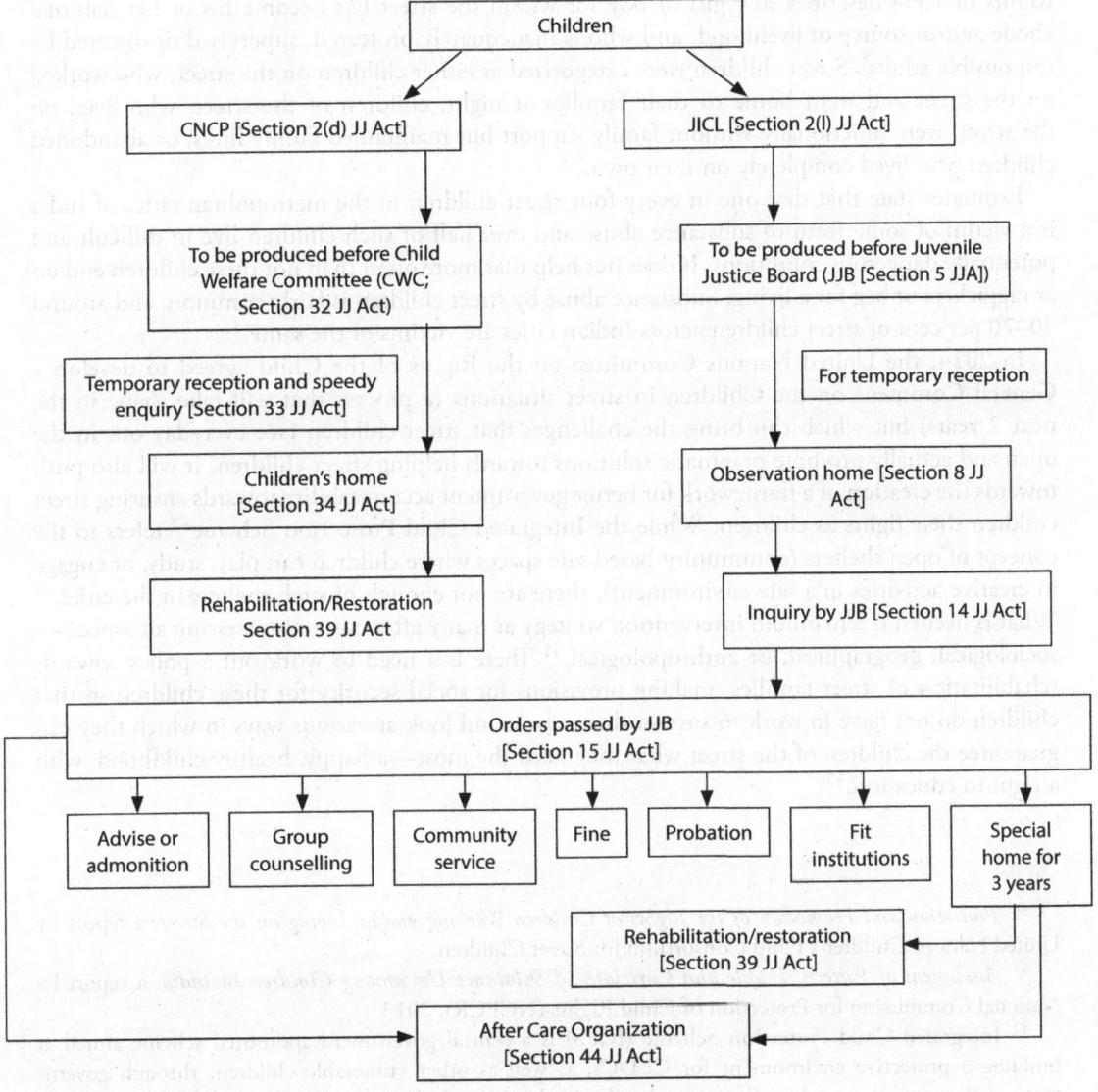

Figure 6.6 Procedure Relating to CNCP[38] and JICL under JJ Act, 2000[39]

---

[37] JJ Act, 2000, Section 2(v): Inserted by the Juvenile Justice (Care and Protection of Children) Amendment Act, 2006 with effect from 22 August 2006.

[38] JJ Act, 2000, Section 32.

[39] JJ Act, 2000, Section 7. Figure data compiled by the author based on various provisions of the JJ Act, 1986.

Street Children

Street children are generally CNCP. The term 'street child' used by the Commission on Human Rights in 1994 describes 'any girl or boy for whom the street has become his or her habitual abode and/or source of livelihood, and who is inadequately protected, supervised or directed by responsible adults'. Street children were categorized as either children on the street, who worked on the street and went home to their families at night; children of the street, who lived on the street, were functionally without family support but maintained family links; or abandoned children who lived completely on their own.[40]

Estimates state that that one in every four street children in the metropolitan cities of India is a victim of some form of substance abuse and over half of such children live in difficult and potentially dangerous conditions. It does not help that more often than not these children end up as ragpickers or beg for a living. Substance abuse by street children is fairly common, and around 40–70 per cent of street children across Indian cities are victims of the same.[41]

In 2014, the United Nations Committee on the Rights of the Child agreed to develop a General Comment on the Children in street situations (a process that will take shape in the next 2 years) but which can bring the challenges that street children face everyday out in the open and actually promote pragmatic solutions towards helping street children. It will also push towards the creation of a framework for better government accountability towards ensuring street children their rights as children. While the Integrated Child Protection Scheme[42] refers to the concept of open shelters (community-based safe spaces where children can play, study, or engage in creative activities in a safe environment), there are not enough of such shelters in the cities.[43] What is needed is a manifold intervention strategy at many after correctly assessing all aspects— sociological, geographical, or anthropological.[44] There is a need to work out a policy towards rehabilitation of street families, making provisions for social security for these children so that children do not have to work to sustain themselves, and look at various ways in which they can guarantee the children of the street what they need the most—a happy, healthy childhood, with a right to education.[45]

---

[40] *Protection and Promotion of the Rights of Children Working and/or Living on the Street*, a report by United Nations Children's Fund Consortium for Street Children.

[41] *Assessment of Pattern, Profile and Correlates of Substance Use among Children in India*, a report by National Commission for Protection of Child Rights (NCPCR), 2013.

[42] Integrated Child Protection Scheme (ICPS) is a central government sponsored scheme aimed at building a protective environment for CEDCs, as well as other vulnerable children, through government-civil society partnership. For more details visit http://wcd.nic.in/icpsmon/home1.aspx (accessed on 17 November 2016).

[43] Available at http://www.huffingtonpost.in/suma-ravi-/nobodys-child_b_7434444.html (accessed on 18 June 2015).

[44] Available at http://www.huffingtonpost.in/suma-ravi-/nobodys-child_b_7434444.html (accessed on 18 June 2015).

[45] Available at http://www.huffingtonpost.in/suma-ravi-/nobodys-child_b_7434444.html (accessed on 18 June 2015).

Provisions Relating to Juveniles in Conflict with Law

The JICL has been defined as a juvenile who is alleged to have committed an offence and has completed 18th year of age as on the date of commission of such offence.[46]

Nothing is an offence done by a child under 7 years of age.[47] In other words no child below 7 years can be prosecuted. Children between 7 and 12 years having sufficient maturity of understanding that he knew what he was doing was wrong are responsible under JJ Act.[48] Children between 12 and 18 years are responsible under JJ Act, 2000. The best evidence of age proof is the birth certificate or the school-leaving certificate. Age in ration card, election card, and identity card is not considered as proof by courts. Medical examination must be done in a public or private hospital. The hospitals do the ossification test (examination of teeth, height, weight, ossification of bones). An error of 2 years on either side is allowed.[49]

In practice, police incorrectly depict a JICL as adult and retain custody. In many cases magistrates and judges have no time to ascertain it, are too busy to notice it, and thus continue as is. The juvenile himself/herself is not aware to raise plea of juvenility. In many cases the accused juvenile, due to monetary constraints, has no legal representation till the trial stage when a legal aid lawyer is appointed.

Whenever a claim of juvenility is raised before any court or a court is of the opinion that an accused person was a juvenile on the date of the commission of the offence, the court shall make an inquiry, take such evidence as may be necessary (but not an affidavit) so as to determine the age of the person, and shall record a finding whether the person is a juvenile or a child or not, stating his age as close as may be.[50]

There are two provisos under Section 7A:

1. The claim of juvenility may be raised before any court and it shall be recognized at any stage, even after the final disposal of the case, and such a claim shall be determined in terms of the provisions contained in this act, even if the juvenile has ceased to be so on or before the commencement of this act.
2. If the court finds a person to be juvenile on the date of commission of the offence and it shall forward the juvenile to the board for passing appropriate order, and the sentence, if any, passed by a court shall be deemed to have no effect.

---

[46] JJ Act, 2000, Section 2(l): Inserted by the Juvenile Justice (Care and Protection of Children) Amendment Act, 2006 with effect from 22 August 2006.

[47] IPC, 1860, Section 82.

[48] IPC, 1860, Section 83.

[49] In *Jaya Mala* v. *Home Secretary, Government of India*: On 29 July 1982, AIR 1982 SC 1297. It was held that one can take judicial notice that the margin of error in age ascertained by radiological examination is 2 years on either side.

[50] JJ Act, 2000, Section 7A: Inserted by the Juvenile Justice (Care and Protection of Children) Amendment Act, 2006 with effect from 22 August 2006.

Constitution of Juvenile Justice Boards

The state government is empowered to constitute JJBs for every district[51] within a period of 1 year[52] to deal with JICL [Section 4(1)]. The board shall consist of a bench of a metropolitan magistrate or a judicial magistrate of the first class and two social workers of whom at least one has to be a woman [Section 4(2)]. The magistrate appointed to the bench shall have special knowledge or training in child psychology or child welfare and he shall be designated as the principal magistrate. The social workers appointed to the bench shall be actively involved in health, education, or welfare activities pertaining to children for at least 7 years [Section 4(3)].

Production for the Juvenile in Conflict with Law

A juvenile in conflict with law has to be produced before the JJB. When the board is not sitting, such a juvenile may be produced before an individual member [Section 5(2)]. The order made by the board shall not be invalid in the absence of any member during any stage of the proceedings provided there are at least two members, including the principal magistrate, present at the time of the final disposal of the case [Section 5(3)]. If there is any difference of opinion among the members of the board, the opinion of the majority shall prevail and where there is no majority, the opinion of the principal magistrate shall prevail [Section 5(4)].

Apprehension of Juveniles in Conflict with Law

As soon as a juvenile in conflict with law is apprehended by the police, he shall be placed under the charge of the special juvenile police unit (SJPU; Section 2(d)(4))[53] or the designated police officer who shall immediately report the matter to a member of the board without any loss of time but within a period of 24 hours of his apprehension excluding the time necessary for the journey.

---

[51] JJ Act 2000, Section 4(1): Inserted by the Juvenile Justice (Care and Protection of Children) Amendment Act 2006 with effect from 22 August 2006.

[52] From the date of commencement of the Juvenile Justice (Care and Protection of Children) Amendment Act, 2006.

[53] The SJPU means a unit of the police force of a state designated for handling of juveniles or children under Section 63.

JJ Act, 2000, Section 63: Special juvenile police unit—

(1) In order to enable the police officers who frequently or exclusively deal with juveniles or are primarily engaged in the prevention of juvenile crime or handling of the juveniles or children under this Act to perform their functions more effectively, they shall be specially instructed and trained.

(2) In every police station at least one officer with aptitude and appropriate training and orientation may be designated as the 'juvenile or the child welfare officer' who will handle the juvenile or the child in coordination with the police.

(3) Special juvenile police unit, of which all police officers designated as above, to handle juveniles or children will be members, may be created in every district and city to coordinate and to upgrade the police treatment of the juveniles and the children.

No juvenile in conflict with law shall be placed in police lock-up or lodged in a jail [Section 10].[54] After the juvenile is placed under the charge:

- the officer in charge of the police station or the special juvenile police shall inform the parent or guardian of the juvenile, if found, and direct him to be present at the board; and
- the probation officer [Section 2(s)] has to obtain information regarding the antecedents and family background and other matters [Section 13].

When such a juvenile who is accused of a bailable or non-bailable offence appears before the board, such a person shall be released on bail with or without surety or placed under the supervision of a probation officer or under the care of any institution of fit person[55] unless there are reasonable grounds for believing that the release is not in the interest of the juvenile [Section 12(1)]. The board shall hold an inquiry, which has to be completed within a period of four months from the date of its commencement unless there are special circumstances to be recorded in writing [Section 14]. The Chief Judicial Magistrate or the Chief Metropolitan Magistrate shall review the pendency of cases of the board at every six months, and shall direct the board to increase the frequency of its sittings or may cause the constitution of additional boards.[56]

Orders That May Be Passed Regarding the Juvenile in Conflict with Law [Section 15]

The scope of the orders have been widened. The board shall have to obtain the social investigation report on the juvenile either through a probation officer or a recognized voluntary organization and, after taking into account the findings, pass an order. Where a Board is satisfied that a juvenile has committed an offence, it can pass the following orders:

- Allow the juvenile to go home after advice and admonition and counselling.
- Direct the juvenile to participate in group counselling and similar activities.
- Order the juvenile to perform community service.
- Order the parent of the juvenile or the juvenile himself to pay a fine, if he is over 14 years of age and earns money, or in the interest of the juvenile, impose necessary conditions and order that the juvenile remain under the supervision of a probation officer for a period not exceeding 3 years.
- Direct the juvenile to be released on probation of good conduct and placed under the care of any parent, guardian, or other fit person [Section 2(1)] after executing a bond with or without surety for any period not exceeding 3 years, or in the interest of the juvenile, impose necessary conditions and order that the juvenile remain under the supervision of a probation officer for a period not exceeding 3 years [Section 15(3)].

[54] JJ Act, 2000, Section 10: Inserted by the Juvenile Justice (Care and Protection of Children) Amendment Act, 2006 with effect from 22 August 2006.

[55] JJ Act, 2000, Section 12(1): Inserted by the Juvenile Justice (Care and Protection of Children) Amendment Act, 2006 with effect from 22 August 2006.

[56] JJ Act, 2000, Section 14(2): Inserted by the Juvenile Justice (Care and Protection of Children) Amendment Act, 2006 with effect from 22 August 2006.

- Direct the juvenile to be released on probation of good conduct under the care of any fit institution for a period not exceeding 3 years, or in the interest of the juvenile, impose necessary conditions and order that the juvenile remain under the supervision of a probation officer for a period not exceeding 3 years.
- Make an order directing the juvenile to be sent to a special home for a period of 3 years. If the JJB is satisfied that having regard to the nature of the offence and the circumstances of the case it is expedient so to do, for reasons to be recorded, reduce the period of stay to such period as it thinks fit.[57]

Orders That May Not Be Passed Against the Juvenile

It has been specifically provided that no JICL shall be sentenced to death or imprisonment for any term which may extend to imprisonment for life[58], or committed to prison in default of payment of fine or in default of furnishing security [Section 16(1)]. The act also states that if none of the above provisions are suitable or sufficient, the board may order the JICL to be kept in a place of safety and report it to the state government who may provide for protective custody provided that the period of detention so ordered shall not exceed in any case the maximum period of 3 years[59] [Section 16(2)]. The board also has powers to make an order directing that the relevant records of conviction shall be removed after the expiry of the period of appeal or a reasonable period [Section 19(2)].

Dealing with Pending Cases in Respect of a Juvenile

All proceedings in respect of a juvenile pending in any court in any area on the date on which this 2000 Act[60] comes into force in that area, shall be continued in that court as if this act had not been passed and if the court finds that the juvenile has committed an offence, it shall record such finding and instead of passing any sentence in respect of the juvenile in accordance with the provisions of this act as if it had been satisfied on inquiry under this act that a juvenile has committed that offence. The board may, for an adequate and special reason to be mentioned in the order, review the case and pass appropriate order in the interest of such juvenile.[61]

In all pending cases including trial, revision, appeal, or any other criminal proceedings in respect of a JICL, in any court, the determination of juvenility of such juvenile shall be in terms of a juvenile who is alleged to have committed an offence and has not completed 18 years of age

[57] JJ Act, 2000, Section 15(1)(g): Inserted by the Juvenile Justice (Care and Protection of Children) Amendment Act, 2006 with effect from 22 August 2006.

[58] JJ Act, 2000, Section 16(1): Inserted by the Juvenile Justice (Care and Protection of Children) Amendment Act, 2006 with effect from 22 August 2006.

[59] As provided in JJ Act, 2000, Section 15(2): Inserted by the Juvenile Justice (Care and Protection of Children) Amendment Act, 2006 with effect from 22 August 2006.

[60] Amended in 2006 and 2011.

[61] JJ Act, 2000, Section 20: Inserted by the Juvenile Justice (Care and Protection of Children) Amendment Act, 2006 with effect from 22 August 2006.

as on the date of commission of offence, even if the juvenile is above 18 years and the provisions of this act would apply retrospectively.[62]

Homes to Be Established under the Act

Observation homes and special homes have to be established under this act for the JICLs by the state government in or under an agreement with voluntary organizations in every district or a group of districts [Section 9(1)].

The observation homes are for the temporary reception of any JICL during the pendency of any inquiry regarding them under this act. The observation home will have a reception unit where the juvenile who is not placed under the charge of a parent or guardian will be initially kept for preliminary inquiries, care, and classification. The classification has to be done according to the age groups such as 7–12 years, 12–16 years, and 16–18 years. While doing such a classification, due consideration has to be given to physical and mental status and degree of offence committed, for further induction of the juvenile into observation home [Section 8(4)].

Provision in Respect of Escaped Juveniles

Any police officer can take charge without warrant of a JICL who has escaped from a special home or an observation home or from the care of a person under whom he was placed under this act. The juvenile should be sent back to the home or person from where or whom he has escaped and no proceedings should be instituted against him for such escape. The board that passed the order in respect of the juvenile should be informed [Section 22].

Prohibition of Publication of Personal Information of Juvenile Involved in any Proceedings under the Act

There is a prohibition on publication of any report in any newspaper, magazine, news-sheet, or any other visual media of any inquiry regarding a juvenile in conflict or CNCP[63] under this act. Unless it is in the interest of the juvenile, the name, address, or any other particulars that will lead to the identification of the juvenile cannot be published [Section 21].

Any person who contravenes this provision will be punished with a penalty which may extend to Rs 25,000.[64]

Penalties and Punishment of Special Offences against the Juvenile under the Act

There are certain special offences under the act which are cognizable (Table 6.3).

---

[62] Explanation to JJ Act, 2000, Section 20: Inserted by the Juvenile Justice (Care and Protection of Children) Amendment Act, 2006 with effect from 22 August 2006.

[63] JJ Act, 2000, Section 21(1): Inserted by the Juvenile Justice (Care and Protection of Children) Amendment Act, 2006 with effect from 22 August 2006.

[64] JJ Act, 2000, Section 21(2): Inserted by the Juvenile Justice (Care and Protection of Children) Amendment Act, 2006 with effect from 22 August 2006.

Table 6.3   Special Offences

Offences	Punishment
Assaulting, abandoning, exposing, or willfully neglecting the juvenile or causing or procuring him to be assaulted, abandoned, exposed, or neglected in a manner that is likely to cause such juvenile mental or physical suffering by a person who has actual charge of the juvenile [Section 23].	Imprisonment for a term which may extend to six months or fine or both.
Employment or use of juvenile or the child for the purpose of begging or causing him to beg [Section 24(1)].	Imprisonment for a term which may extend to 3 years and fine.
Abetment of the above offence by a person who has actual charge of the juvenile [Section 24(2)].	Imprisonment for a term which may extend to 1 year and fine.
Giving or causing to give a juvenile or a child intoxicating liquor in public places or any narcotic drug or psychotropic substance except upon the order of a duly qualified medical practitioner or in case of sickness [Section 25].	Imprisonment for a term which may extend to 3 years and fine.
Ostensibly procuring a juvenile or the child for the purpose of any hazardous employment, keeps him in bondage and withholds his earnings or uses such earnings for his own purpose [Section 26].	Imprisonment for a term which may extend for 3 years and fine.

Rehabilitation and Social Reintegration

Chapter IV of JJ Act, 2000 provides for the rehabilitation and social reintegration of the child in the children's home or special home.[65]

The act provides for non-institutional services like

- adoption [Section 41(2)];
- foster care [Section 42(a)];
- sponsorship [Section 43(1)]; and
- sending the child to an after-care organization [Section 44].

Adoption means the process through which the adopted child is permanently separated from his biological parents, and become the child of his adoptive parents with all the rights, privileges, and responsibilities that are attached to the relationship.[66] Adoption shall be resorted to for the rehabilitation of the children who are orphan, abandoned, or surrendered.[67] In keeping with the

---

[65] JJ Act, 2000, Section 40.

[66] JJ Act, 2000, Section 2(aa): Inserted by the Juvenile Justice (Care and Protection of Children) Amendment Act, 2006 with effect from 22 August 2006.

[67] JJ Act, 2000, Section 41(2): Inserted by the Juvenile Justice (Care and Protection of Children) Amendment Act, 2006 with effect from 22 August 2006.

provisions of the various guidelines for adoption issued from time to time by the state government or the Central Adoption Resource Agency (CARA) and notified by the central government, children may be given in adoption by a court after it satisfies itself that the investigations having been carried out, as required for giving such children in adoption.[68]

Under the act, the state government shall recognize one or more of its institutions or voluntary organizations in each district as specialized adoption agencies for the placement of orphan, abandoned, or surrendered children for adoption in accordance with the guidelines notified under Subsection (3).[69]

Before handing over for adoption, the children's homes and the institutions run by the state government or a voluntary organization for CNCP, who are orphan, abandoned or surrendered, shall ensure that these children are declared free for adoption by the committee and all such cases shall be referred to the adoption agency in that district for placement of such children in adoption.

The act provided that no child shall be offered for adoption[70]

- until two members of the committee declare the child legally free for placement in the case of abandoned children;
- till the two months' period for reconsideration by the parent is over in the case of surrendered children; and
- without his/her consent in the case of a child who can understand and express his/her consent.

The court may allow a child to be given in adoption to[71]

- a person irrespective of marital status;
- parents to adopt a child of same sex irrespective of the number of living biological sons or daughters; or
- childless couples.

Appeals, Revisions, and Confidentiality

The JJ Act, 2000 also has provisions for appeal to the court of sessions [Section 52]. The high court has the power to call for the record of the proceedings of the court of sessions or the competent authority [Section 53]. All the reports of the social worker and the competent authority have to be kept confidential [Section 51].

[68] JJ Act, Section 41(3): Inserted by the Juvenile Justice (Care and Protection of Children) Amendment Act, 2006 with effect from 22 August 2006.

[69] JJ Act, 2000, Section 41(4): Inserted by the Juvenile Justice (Care and Protection of Children) Amendment Act, 2006 with effect from 22 August 2006.

[70] JJ Act, 2000, Section 41(5).

[71] JJ Act, 2000, Section 41(6): Inserted by the Juvenile Justice (Care and Protection of Children) Amendment Act, 2006 with effect from 22 August 2006.

Creation of a Fund [Section 61]

The state government can create a fund for the welfare and rehabilitation of the juvenile or child.

Advisory Boards [Section 62]

There is a provision for the creation of central, state, district, and city advisory boards for advising the government on matters relating to the children under this act.

Constitution of Child Protection Unit Responsible for Implementation of the Act [Section 62-A][72]

Every state government shall constitute a Child Protection Unit for the state and every district, consisting of officers and other employees as may be appointed by that government, to take up matters relating to CNCP and JICL with a view to ensure the implementation of this act including the establishment and maintenance of homes, notification of competent authorities in relation to these children and their rehabilitation, and coordination with various official and non-official agencies concerned.

Children Who Are Mentally Ill or Addicted to Drugs (Section 58)[73]

Where it appears to the competent authority that any juvenile or child kept in a special home, an observation home, a children's home, a shelter home, or in an institution in pursuance of this act is a mentally ill person or addicted to alcohol or other drugs which lead to behavioural changes in a person, the competent authority may order his removal to a psychiatric hospital or psychiatric nursing home in accordance with the provisions of the Mental Health Act, 1987.

In case the juvenile or child had been removed to a psychiatric hospital or psychiatric nursing home, the competent authority may, on the basis of the advice given in the certificate of discharge of the psychiatric hospital or psychiatric nursing home, order to remove such juvenile or child to an Integrated Rehabilitation Centre for Addicts or similar centres maintained by the state government for mentally ill persons (including the persons addicted to any narcotic drug or psychotropic substance) and such removal shall be only for the period required for the in-patient treatment of such juvenile or child.[74]

---

[72] JJ Act, 2000, Section 62-A: Inserted by the Juvenile Justice (Care and Protection of Children) Amendment Act, 2006 with effect from 22 August 2006.

[73] JJ Act, 2000, Section 58: Inserted by the Juvenile Justice (Care and Protection of Children) Amendment Act, 2006 with effect from 22 August 2006.

[74] Explanation to Section 58—For the purposes of this subsection—

(1) Integrated Rehabilitation Centre for Addicts shall have the meaning assigned to it under the scheme called Central Sector Scheme of Assistance for prevention of Alcoholism and Substance (Drugs) Abuse and for Social Defence Services made by the Government of India in the Ministry of Social Justice and Empowerment or any other corresponding scheme for the time being in force;

Significant Changes Brought about by the Juvenile Justice Act, 2000

The JJ Act, 2000[75] has brought in some significant changes in an attempt to make the system more child-friendly. These are:

- The act defines a child as a person who has not completed 18 years of age. There is now no discrimination in the age of boys and girls and the age conforms to the United Nations Convention of the Rights of Children (UNCRC).
- Use of distinct terms such as 'juvenile' for children in conflict with law and 'child' for CNCP has been introduced.
- The JJB is to replace juvenile courts and CWCs to replace the existing Juvenile Welfare Boards.
- The JJ Act 2000 empowers the board to give a child in adoption.
- The JJ Act 2000 requires that the child's consent be taken into account before the adoption is completed.
- The new JJ Act allows parents to adopt a child of the same sex irrespective of the number of living biological sons or daughters.
- Rehabilitation and social integration of a child is an important part of the act.
- Non-institutional services are provided as alternatives to institutionalization.
- Non-governmental organizations have been involved in the act.
- There is a provision for juveniles being placed under the charge of special juvenile police unit.
- The act provides for reception, classification, and pre-trial detention of juveniles.
- New dispositional alternatives such as group counselling and community service have been provided to the JJBs.
- There are provisions for children's homes or shelter homes for CNCP.
- Provision for monitoring and evaluation of children's home and shelter homes by the central and state governments has been incorporated.
- Restoration of child to the family is now considered as the prime objective of any children's home or shelter home.

Rules under the Juvenile Justice (Care and Protection of Children) Act, 2000 (56 of 2000) and the Amendment Act 33 (of 2006)

The Ministry of Women and Child Development at New Delhi, on 26 October 2007, notified the Model Rules under the JJ Act, 2000 and the Amendment Act, 2006 to be administered by the states for better implementation and administration of the provisions of the act in its true spirit and substance. The rules related specifically to management of the homes, standards to be

---

(2) 'mentally ill person' shall have the meaning assigned to it in Clause (I) of Section 2 of the Mental Health Act, 1987.

(3) 'psychiatric hospital' or 'psychiatric nursing home' shall have the meaning assigned to it in Clause (q) of Section 2 of the Mental Health Act, 1987.

[75] Amended in 2006 and 2011

adhered to, roles and responsibilities of the JJ functionaries, procedures and functioning of the competent authorities, rehabilitation mechanism, and operation of the JJ Fund.[76]

Significantly, the Juvenile Justice Rules have established certain fundamental principles, which are to be followed in administration of juvenile justice. These are:

1. **Principle of presumption of innocence:** A JICL is presumed to be innocent of any criminal intent up to the age of 18 years. Any unlawful conduct of a juvenile or a child or a JICL which is done for survival, or is due to environmental or situational factors or is done under control of adults, or peer groups, is ought to be covered by the principles of innocence.

2. **Principle of dignity and worth:** This principle reflects the fundamental human right enshrined in Article 1 of the Universal Declaration of Human Rights that all human beings are born free and equal in dignity and rights. Respect of dignity includes not being humiliated, personal identity, boundaries and space being respected, not being labelled and stigmatized, being offered information and choices, and not being blamed for their acts.

3. **Principle of right to be heard:** This principle provides for every child's right to express his views freely in all matters affecting his interest in every stage in the process of juvenile justice.

4. **Principle of best interest:** The principle of best interest of the juvenile or child shall mean that the traditional objectives of criminal justice, retribution and repression, must give way to rehabilitative and restorative objectives of juvenile justice.

5. **Principle of family responsibility:** This principle provides that the primary responsibility of bringing up children, providing care, support, and protection shall be with the biological parents. However, in exceptional situations, this responsibility may be bestowed on willing adoptive or foster parents.

6. **Principle of safety (no harm, no abuse, no neglect, no exploitation, and no maltreatment):** This principle says that right from the initial contact till such time a child or a juvenile remains in contact with the care and protection system, and thereafter, he shall not be subjected to any harm, abuse, neglect, maltreatment, corporal punishment or solitary or otherwise any confinement in jails and extreme care shall be taken to avoid any harm to the sensitivity of the juvenile or the child.

7. **Positive measures:** This principle states that provisions must be made to enable positive measures that involve the full mobilization of all possible resources, including the family, volunteers, and other community groups, as well as schools and other mainstream community institutions or processes, for the purpose of promoting the well-being of the juvenile or child through individual care plans carefully worked out.

8. **Principle of non-stigmatizing semantics, decisions, and actions:** This principle states that the use of adversarial or accusatory words, such as, arrest, remand, accused, charge sheet, trial, prosecution, warrant, summons, conviction, inmate, delinquent, neglected, custody,

---

[76] These rules called the Juvenile Justice (Care and Protection of Children) Rules, 2007 have come into force on the date of its publication in the Official Gazette and these rules will be conformed to until the concerned state government formulates rules specific for the state with effect to implementation of the JJ Act.

or jail are prohibited in the processes pertaining to the child or juvenile in conflict with law under the act.

9. **Principle of non-waiver of rights:** This principle states that no child or juvenile in conflict with law, whether by himself or the competent authority or anyone acting or claiming to act on behalf of the juvenile or child can waive his/her right under the act.

10. **Principle of equality and non-discrimination:** There shall be no discrimination against a child or juvenile in conflict with law on the basis of age, sex, place of birth, disability, health, status, race, ethnicity, religion, caste, cultural practices, work, activity, or behaviour of the juvenile or child or that of his parents or guardians, or the civil and political status of the juvenile or child, and every child shall be guaranteed equality in treatment under the act.

11. **Principle of right to privacy and confidentiality:** This principle provides that the juvenile's or child's right to privacy and confidentiality shall be protected by all means and through all the stages of the proceedings and care and protection processes.

12. **Principle of last resort:** This principle provides that institutionalization of a child or juvenile in conflict with law shall be a step of the last resort after reasonable inquiry and that too for the minimum possible duration.

13. **Principle of repatriation and restoration:** This principle states that every juvenile or child has the right to be reunited with his/her family and restored back to the same socio-economic and cultural status that such juvenile or child enjoyed before coming within the purview of the act.

14. **Principle of fresh start:** The principle of fresh start promotes new beginning for the child or juvenile in conflict with law by ensuring erasure of his/her past records.

When these principles are adhered to in letter and spirit, it would certainly ensure that every child who comes into contact with the JJ system is assured safety, care, protection, and justice.

Critique of the Juvenile Justice (Care and Protection of Children) Act, 2000[77]

- The act has expanded the definition of the CNCP very significantly. It could lead to undue interference in the lives of several poor children and their families by the 'system'. Adequate safeguards need to be provided or there should be two distinctly separate legislation.
- The act fails to expressly lay down the age of innocence, that is, the minimum age below which this act would not be applicable.
- The act retains a high degree of dependence on adult criminal justice agencies like the police, the magistrate, and the lawyers, and also on procedures.
- The problem of special care and needs of the disabled children who may be before the juvenile justice system have been ignored. The education, training, and recreation of children have not been provided for. Besides basic or school education, even higher education and training of these children have to be considered. Open school and open university education system should be made accessible to these children.

[77] Amended in 2006 and 2011.

- The health and nutrition of the children have to be provided for. Permanent posts of residential nurses and doctors are very important.
- The CWCs will be playing a very important role under the new act. It should have been specifically provided that these posts should no longer be on honorary, part-time, or voluntary basis.
- The dispositional alternatives provided for CNCP are very limited considering the wide scope of the act. These should be increased.
- The act is silent on inter-country adoption.
- There is no linkage between the JJ Act 2000 and the other related legal provisions relating to children, for instance, child labour, primary education, sexual abuse, adoption, disabilities, and health.
- There is a need for a provision relating to the kind of inspections required for the smooth functioning of the homes. The inspections should include physical facilities, cleanliness, nutrition, behavioural problems and disabilities, disciplinary practices, and physical and emotional health of the staff and children.
- Section 16 of the act provides for segregation of a juvenile who has attained the age of 16 years and has committed a serious offence. This has to be removed as segregation and solitary confinement will violate the right to development of the child.
- Punishment for cruelty to a juvenile or child, or exploitation of juvenile employees as provided in Sections 23, 24, 25, and 26 is imprisonment and fine. These are serious offences and punishment should be further enhanced. There should also be a provision for compensation to be paid to the victim.
- All institutions/homes established under this act should obtain a certificate of recognition from the Board of Control established under the Orphanages and Other Charitable Homes Act, 1960.
- Many states have still not complied with the provisions of the 1986 act. A mandatory time frame should be set up to comply with the provisions of the 2000 act.
- Often a JICL remains in the Observation Home despite passing of bail order as he is unable to furnish surety. There is no provision in the act for the JJB to modify the conditions of bail to be able to ensure that a juvenile is able to avail of bail and be released from the observation home.
- The Board has the discretion to pass any order stipulated under Section 15(1), but often the order does not show as to why a particular option has been identified above all others as the most appropriate by the board in respect to that JICL. There is no provision in the act for the board to show as to why it chose a particular option vis-à-vis all the others and this causes confusion and lack of clarity. There should be a provision to mention the reason for having passed that particular order.
- The act makes no provision for the CWC at the time of passing orders on completion of inquiry to give reasons as to why a particular order was passed. The CWC should give reasoned orders so as to assess whether the order passed is reasonable and is in the best interest of the child.
- There is no provision for inspection and social auditing for Special Homes and Observation Homes.
- The Right of Children to Free and Compulsory Education Act or Right to Education (RTE) Act makes education of every child between the age of 6 and 14 compulsory. But there is no

provision for education in the JJ Act. Children spend many months in Observation Homes and Children Homes without access to education.

- Place of safety has been defined as 'any place or institution (not being a police lock-up or jail), the person in-charge of which is willing temporarily to receive and take care of the juvenile and which, in the opinion of the competent authority, may be a place of safety for the juvenile'. But in reality, no proper institutions have been set up which can effectively act as places of safety. The JJB is therefore many times at a loss regarding where to send a person who committed an offence as a juvenile but has ceased to be so when the matter comes up for hearing.
- The JJ Act, 2000 does not contain any provisions for the diversion of children away from the formal system. All children who are arrested by the police are to be brought before the JJB for a formal determination of guilt and disposition.
- The after-care homes have become a farce and turned into mere hostels with no rehabilitation or reintegration plans. They are also very few in number.

Trends of Judicial Response to Juvenile Justice

Krishna Bhagwan v. State of Bihar[78]

Facts

Krishna Bhagwan was convicted of murder by a session's judge and sentenced to life imprisonment. No plea was taken that he was a 'child' under the Children Act at the time of committing the offence. If it was done, the session's judge could not have tried him. The plea of age was taken for the first time in the high court. The bench, which heard it, placed it before a larger bench. It referred two questions for answer. First, whether the Children Act would be applicable if the convict was a child (a boy below 16 years) at the time of the offence but has crossed that age at the time of the sentence? Second, whether the plea of age can be taken at the time of the appeal and what procedure should be adopted to determine the age of the convict at the time of the offence?

Held

The high court stated that the various provisions of the Children Act and the JJ Act showed that extraordinary procedure has been prescribed for enquiring into offences committed by a child. The basic approach is curative and reformative, not punitive.

Answering the first question, the high court quoted Sections 3 and 56 of the JJ Act and stated that even if a child accused has ceased to be a child, the inquiry may be continued and orders may be made as if the accused had continued to be a juvenile. The lawmakers were aware of the possibility that while undergoing trial, a child accused may cease to be a juvenile. They introduced a 'deeming fiction' which requires the courts to treat the accused as a child. This provision is made, treating children as a class, as they are of tender age and immature mind. Even if the

---

[78] AIR 1989 Patna 217.

crime is abhorrent, there shall be no imprisonment or death sentence. They shall be kept only in safe custody.

Regarding the question whether the question of age can be raised at the appellate stage, the high court held that it could be done at the appellate stage, in the case of children. But the court should be alert to the misuse of such a plea when a convict is sentenced.

Sanjay Suri v. Delhi Administration[79]

Facts

A news report described the ill treatment meted out to minors in the Tihar Jail in Delhi in connivance with the jail staff. The writers of this report then moved the Supreme Court seeking the relief on behalf of the child prisoners. The court then appointed the district judge to make an inquiry and report to it. His report 'disclosed a shocking state of affairs', according to the judgment. Adult prisoners subjected children to sexual assault. They feared that if their names were disclosed, they would be victimized.

Held

The court passed several orders based on the report. Some juvenile undertrial prisoners were ordered to be released immediately. Some convicted minors were freed on parole for one month. The judgment stressed the need to generate a sense of humanism in jail administration.

The court passed certain orders to protect children. It called upon the magistrates and trial judges to specify the age of the person ordered to be detained. 'We call upon the authorities in the jails throughout India not to accept any warrant of detention as a valid one unless the age of the detainee is shown therein', the judgment emphasized. Thus, the jail authorities can refuse to honour a warrant if the age of the person remanded to jail custody is not indicated. The warrant may be returned to the issuing court for rectifying the defect. The age is to be shown so that the detainee could be directed to an adult prison or a juvenile jail. The youth shall not be assigned any work in the same area where regular prisoners are made to work. Care should be taken to ensure that there is no scope for their meeting and having contact. Wardens should be shifted every 3 years. The visitors' board should consist of a cross-section of society, the judgment said.

Jayendra v. State of U.P.[80]

Facts

The offence was committed in 1974. Jayendra was convicted by the trial court which was confirmed by the Allahabad High Court. Under Section 2 of UP Children's Act, a child was defined as one who is below 16 years. Section 27 of the act said that notwithstanding anything to the

---

[79] AIR 1986 SC 414.
[80] AIR 1982 SC 685.

contrary in law, no court shall sentence a child to imprisonment for life or to any term of imprisonment. If a child was found to have committed an offence punishable with imprisonment, the court may order him to be sent to an approved school till the age of 18 years. However, the high court sent the convict to jail. This was challenged before the Supreme Court.

Held

The Supreme Court called for a report from the doctor in charge of the jail hospital as regards the age wherein the age of the convict based on various tests was found to be about 23 years at the time of the report (in 1981). That would mean that in 1974, at the time of the offence, he was about 16 years and 4 months old. The judgment stated that in the normal course, the court would have sent the convict to an approved school but in view of the fact that he was by now 23 years old, it could not be done. Therefore, the conviction was upheld but the sentence of imprisonment was quashed. The court directed the immediate release of the youth.

Munna v. State of UP[81]

Facts

A public interest petition was filed both in the Allahabad High Court and the Supreme Court when reports of sexual abuse in Kanpur Central Jail appeared in newspaper based on a social activist's findings. The high court asked the sessions judge of Kanpur to visit the jail and find out whether boys below sixteen are detained in the Central Jail and whether they are maltreated. The jail authorities meanwhile released a large number of boys. Therefore, when the sessions judge visited the jail, there were only some six children there. But there were eighty-four undertrials who were between 16 and 21 years of age. The judge also reported that there was general ignorance about the UP Children's Act among the jail authorities. There were parallel proceedings on the same issue in the high court and the Supreme Court.

Held

The high court orders are not available, but the Supreme Court passed certain general directions regarding children in jails. The Supreme Court stated that if the allegations were true, it showed 'to what utter depths of depravity man can sink'. A court cannot abdicate its constitutional duty of ensuring human dignity to the juvenile undertrial prisoners. Declaring that the court must investigate into the allegations, it said that even if it was found that the youths were guilty, they could not be maltreated. 'They do not shed their fundamental right when they enter the jail. Moreover, the object of punishment being reformation, we fail to see what social objective can be gained by sending juveniles to jails where they would come into contact with hardened criminals and lose whatever sensitivity they may have to finer and nobler sentiments', the court said.

---

[81] AIR 1982 SC 806.

Bhoop Ram v. State of UP[82]

Facts

The appellant and five others were convicted by the sessions judge of Bareilly for murder and other offences and were sentenced to life imprisonment. The appellant appealed to the Supreme Court arguing that he should have been treated as a 'child' within the meaning of Section 2(4) of the Children Act and sent to an approved school for detention till he attained the age of 18 years instead of being sentenced to life imprisonment. He said he was less than 16 years when the offence was committed, and showed his school certificate as evidence. The sessions judge had rejected the certificate as evidence and stated that since he was below 18 years he was given life sentence and not capital punishment. When the appeal was heard, the Supreme Court asked the sessions judge to have the convict examined by the chief medical officer of the state to ascertain his age. The medical report, after radiological and physical tests, showed that the convict was above 16 years at the time of commission of the offence. The sessions judge rejected the school certificate as 'it is not unusual that in schools, ages are understated by 1 or 2 years for future benefits'. It was argued by the convict that the court should go by the school certificate and the opinions of the medical officer and sessions judge about the age were subjective.

Held

The Supreme Court ordered his immediate release as it ruled that at the time of the commission of the offence the man was below 16 years according to the school certificate. It followed an earlier Supreme Court order in similar circumstances.[83] This is because the convict should have been sent to an approved school in the first place. Since there was miscarriage of justice, the conviction was sustained, but the sentence was set aside. The Supreme Court held that the school certificate should be taken as valid, as there was no material evidence contradicting the age given in it.

The medical opinion cannot replace the fact given in the certificate. The sessions judge went by his surmise that many parents give false age to gain benefits. The medical opinion cannot be foolproof. Therefore, the convict should have been treated as a 'child' under the act, said the Supreme Court while quashing the sentence and releasing him.

Sheela Barse v. Secretary, Children's Aid Society[84]

Facts

The petitioner, a freelance journalist, sent a letter to the Bombay High Court making certain allegations about the observation homes managed by the Children's Aid Society. The society was regarded as a public trust and given state funds. The letter was treated as a writ petition and the high court passed certain orders. The main grievances in her letter-petition were:

[82] AIR1987 SC 1329.
[83] *Jayendra and Another v. State of Uttar Pradesh* AIR 1982 SC 685.
[84] AIR 1989 SC 1278.

- delay in restoration of children to their parents;
- non-application of mind in the matter of taking children into custody and directing production before the juvenile court;
- absence of proper follow-up action after admission of the children in the homes; and
- detention being illegal, it amounts to harassment of children.

The society denied the allegations in the high court, producing documents as evidence. The high court accepted some charges and rejected others. It then passed seven procedural directions. The petitioner was not satisfied with them and appealed against the high court.

Held

The Supreme Court held that children should not be made to stay in the observation homes for too long. As long as they were there, they should be kept occupied. The occupations should be congenial and intended to bring about adaptability in life, self-confidence, and development of human values.

Dedicated workers must be found and, after training, they alone should be employed in the children's homes. The juvenile court has to be manned by a judicial officer with some special training.

Krist Pereira v. the State of Maharashtra and Others[85]

Facts

This was a public interest litigation, which was filed after the death of a child in a remand home in Bhiwandi under mysterious circumstances. The Mumbai High Court constituted a committee of experts to examine the conditions in different juvenile remand homes, children's homes, and special homes in the state of Maharashtra and to make appropriate recommendations for improving their standards. The report of the committee brought to light the extremely distressing and pathetic conditions prevailing in the various homes in the state.

Held

The high court constituted the State Committee on Juvenile Justice which shall be consulted in matters of appointments as well as removal of personnel in the remand homes. The other significant directions were:

- establishment of more juvenile and special homes;
- establishment of rehabilitation committees in districts;
- appointment of at least one social worker in each juvenile court;
- appointment of duty counsellors and visitors;

[85] Criminal writ petition no. 1107 of 1996, Mumbai High Court.

- superintendent of institutions to be given powers to suspend caretakers and other members of the staff for misbehavior; and
- training programmes for judges and other staff.

Umesh Singh v. State of Bihar[86]

Facts

In the instant case one of the accused Arvind Singh was charged for murder under Section 302, IPC read with Section 149, IPC and for causing hurt by dangerous weapons under Section 324, IPC read with Section 148 IPC and under Section 27 of the Arms Act 1959 for using arms and ammunitions without license. He was 13 years on the date of occurrence of the crime. His trial was conducted along with other accused who were not children and the Court found them guilty of the offence.

Held

In this case the opinion of the Medical Board was that the age of the accused would be about 16½ years, on the date of occurrence. The Chief Judicial Magistrate assessed the age as 17 years. The Sessions Judge took the view that Medical Board can merely make an estimate of the age of the person and held that the age of the person ascertained by the medical opinion cannot be preferred over the age ascertained through the evidence.

Arnit Das v. State of Bihar[87]

Facts

According to the FIR,[88] one Abhishek was shot dead on that day. On 13 September 1998, the petitioner was arrested in connection with the said offence. On 14 September 1998 the petitioner was produced before the additional chief judicial magistrate (ACJM), Patna, who after recording his statement under Section 164 of the CrPC remanded him to juvenile home, Patna. The petitioner claimed to have been born on 18 September 1982 and therefore a juvenile entitled to protection of the JJ Act, 1986. The petitioner's claim was disputed on behalf of the prosecution. The ACJM directed an inquiry to be held under Section 32 of the JJ Act. A medical board referred the petitioner to examination. On receipt of the report of the medical board and on receiving such other evidence as was adduced on behalf of the petitioner, the ACJM concluded that the petitioner was above 16 years of age on the date of the occurrence and therefore, was not required to be tried by a juvenile court. The sessions court in appeal and the high court in revision had

---

[86] 1999 (2) BLJ 108 (Pat).

[87] AIR 2000 SC 2264.

[88] On 5 October 1998 Crime No. 574/98 under Section 302 IPC was registered at police station Kadamkuan, Patna.

upheld the finding. The petitioner had filed this petition seeking leave to appeal. The leave was granted.

Issues

Two questions were considered by the Supreme Court:

- By reference to which date, the age of the petitioners is required to be determined for finding out whether he is a juvenile or not. Is it the date of offence which is crucial for determining the age of the person claiming to be juvenile or is it the date on which the person is brought before the competent authority.
- Whether the finding as to age, as arrived at by the courts below and maintained by the High Court, can be sustained.

Held

So far as the present context was concerned, it was held that the crucial date for determining the question whether a person is juvenile is the date when he is brought before the competent authority. So far as the finding regarding the age of the appellant was concerned it was based on appreciation of evidence and arrived at after taking into consideration the material available on record and valid reasons being assigned for it. The finding arrived at by the learned ACJM had been maintained by the sessions court in appeal and the high court in revision. The Supreme Court found no case for interfering with that finding. The appeal in this case was dismissed.

The age of the child is a matter of great concern. The issue has come up before the courts several times and in practice there are children lodged in adult jails because they had no evidence to prove their age. In such cases, it is recommended that the benefit of doubt should always be in favour of the child.

In another case of *Raj Singh* v. *State of Haryana*,[89] the Supreme Court held that the trial of the delinquent juvenile in the court of sessions stands vitiated as at the time of occurrence of the offence, the accused was a juvenile. In the case of *Arnit Das* v. *State of Bihar* the Supreme Court overruled this judgment and held that the 'date of commission of the offence is irrelevant for finding out whether the person is a juvenile'. Further, that 'the crucial date for determining whether a person is a juvenile is the date when he is brought before the competent authority'. The decision in the *Arnit Das* case is being criticized as the concern of the court in this decision seems to be more on the offence than on the best interest of the child. Many juveniles continue to languish in jails for long periods of time because their age is not determined. The magistrates who are not empowered to exercise the powers of the JJBs should send the accused who claims or appears to be a juvenile for immediate determination of age.

89 2000(6)SCC 759.

Ram Deo Chauhan @ Raj Nath v. State of Assam[90]

Facts

The appellant was charged under Sections 302 and 326 of the IPC for having caused the death of four persons of a family. He was also charged to have caused injuries with the sharp edged weapon to the mother of the deceased and the neighbour of the deceased. On proof of charges, the Trial Court convicted the appellant of the offences. During the trial, the appellant was examined for determination of his age.

The Trial Court, after referring to various judgments, concluded that 'the murder was committed in the most brutal manner with severe cruelty inflicting number of injuries on each victim including a female baby hardly of 2½ years of age and two helpless women. It is rarest of the rare cases which are of exceptional nature which warrants the awarding of maximum penalty under the law to the accused/appellant.'

Hence, the Trial Court sentenced the accused to death under Section 302 of the IPC.

Not satisfied with the impugned judgment of the Trial Court, the appellant filed an appeal in the High Court. The conviction of sentence passed by the Trial Court was confirmed by the High Court.

However, review was sought on the ground that the accused was below 16 years of age on the date of occurrence and ought to have been tried by Juvenile Court.

Held

In the instant case the Supreme Court opined that the statement of a doctor was not more than the opinion. The court has to form its conclusion on the basis of all the facts and circumstances disclosed in conjunction with such oral testimony as may be available. Too much reliance cannot be placed on text books on Medical Jurisprudence and Toxicology while determining the age of the accused. An x-ray ossification test may provide a surer basis than the medical opinion of the doctor. Hence the sentence passed by the Trial and High Court were upheld.

Pratap Singh v. State of Jharkhand and Anr.[91]

Facts

The appellant was alleged as one of the conspirators to have caused the death of the deceased by poisoning. On the basis of the FIR, the appellant was arrested and produced before the chief judicial magistrate (CJM) Chas. On production, the learned CJM assessed the age of the appellant to be around 18 years.

A petition was filed on behalf of the appellant claiming that he was a minor on the date of occurrence of crime, whereupon the learned CJM transmitted the case to the Juvenile Court.

[90]   2001 Cr LJ 2902 (SC)
[91]   AIR 2005 SC 2731.

The appellant was produced in the Juvenile Court. On his production, the Juvenile Court assessed the age of the appellant by appearance to be between 15 and 16 years and directed the civil surgeon to constitute a medical board for the purpose of assessing the age of the appellant by scientific examination and submit a report. No such medical board was constituted. Thus, the learned ACJM asked the parties to adduce evidence and on examining the school leaving certificate and mark sheet of Central Board of Secondary Education came to the finding that the appellant was below 16 years of age recorded in the aforesaid certificate. The appellant was then released on bail.

The question which required authoritative decision was whether the date of occurrence would be the reckoning date for determining the age of the alleged offender as juvenile offender or the date when he is produced in the court/competent authority.

Held

The JJ Act is not only a beneficent legislation, but also a remedial one. The act aims at grant of care, protection, and rehabilitation of a juvenile vis-à-vis the adult criminals. Having regard to Rule 4 of United Nations Standard Minimum Rules for the Administration of Juvenile Justice, it must also be borne in mind that the moral and psychological components of criminal responsibility was also one of the factors in defining a juvenile. The meaning of the expression 'juvenile' used in a statute by reason of its very nature has to be assigned with reference to a definite date. The term 'juvenile' must be given a definite connotation. A person cannot be a juvenile for one purpose and an adult for other purpose. It was, having regard to the constitutional and statutory scheme, not necessary for the Parliament to specifically state that the age of juvenile must be determined as on the date of commission of the offence. The same is in-built in the statutory scheme. The statute must be construed having regard to the scheme and the ordinary state of affairs and consequences flowing therefrom. The modern approach is to consider whether a child can live up to the moral and psychological components of criminal responsibility, that is, whether a child, by virtue of his or her individual discernment and understanding can be held responsible for essentially anti-social behaviour.

Any law mandating the court to take into consideration certain documents over others in determining an issue must be provided for only by law. Only a validly made law can take away the power of the court to appreciate evidence for the purpose of determination of such a question in the light of Section 35 of the Indian Evidence Act.[92] The court, therefore, must determine the age of the juvenile as on the date of occurrence and not the date on which he was produced before the board.

---

[92] Indian Evidence Act, Section 35: Relevancy of entry in public (record or an electronic record) made in performance of duty—

An entry in any public or other official book, register or [record or an electronic record], stating a fact in issue or relevant fact, and made by a public servant in the discharge of his official duty, or by any other person in performance of a duty specially enjoined by the law of the country in which such book, register, or [record or an electronic record] is kept, is itself a relevant fact.

Gurpreet Singh v. State of Punjab[93]

Facts

In this case, Kuljit Singh was a student of BA Part I in Arya College, Ludhiana and he was a witness in a case filed for prosecution of the accused Gurpreet Singh under Section 307 IPC[94] which was pending. One evening, Kuljit Singh along with his brother and friends was returning to his house from college after attending classes and when they reached near Oriental Public School, the appellants along with the accused, Meharban Singh, who were present there armed with kirpans, confronted him. Gurpreet Singh shouted that Kuljit Singh should be done to death and he attacked him with kirpan on his head. Thereafter, Mohinder Pal Singh inflicted kirpan blow in the abdomen of Kuljit Singh. Accused Meharban Singh assaulted him with kirpan on the temporal region whereupon Kuljit Singh fell down. In the meantime, accused Harbhajan Singh who too was armed with kirpan came there and also dealt a kirpan blow on the forehead of Kuljit Singh. All the aforesaid accused persons thereafter inflicted several injuries upon Kuljit Singh even after he fell down. In the process of inflicting injuries, Gurpreet Singh also received injuries at the hands of one of the co-accused. On *halla* being raised, people of the locality arrived, whereafter the accused persons fled away. Kuljit Singh was taken to the hospital where the doctor declared him dead. After registering the case, the police took up investigation and on completion thereof submitted a charge sheet against the accused persons, on receipt whereof, the learned magistrate took cognizance and committed all the aforesaid accused persons, including the appellants, to the court of sessions to face trial. As accused Meharban Singh died during trial, the same proceeded against the remaining three accused persons. On appeal being filed by the appellants, the High Court confirmed their conviction and sentence. Therefore, appeal was filed in the Supreme Court of India. It was argued on behalf of appellant Mohinder Pal Singh that on the date of the alleged occurrence, he was a juvenile within the meaning of Section 2(h) of the JJ Act, 1986 (hereinafter referred to as 'the act') as on that date he had not attained the age of 16 years.

Held

It was held that the court should first consider the legality or otherwise of conviction of the accused and in case the conviction is upheld, a report should be called for from the trial court on the point as to whether the accused was juvenile on the date of occurrence and upon receipt of the report, if it is found that the accused was juvenile on such a date and continues to be so,

---

[93] (2005) 12 SCC 615.

[94] IPC, 1860, Section 307: Attempt to murder—Whoever does any act with such intention or knowledge, and under such circumstances that, if he by that act caused death, he would be guilty or murder, shall be punished with imprisonment of either description for a term which may extend to 10 years, and shall also be liable to fine; and if hurt is caused to any person by such act, the offender shall be liable either to [imprisonment for life], or to such punishment as is hereinbefore mentioned.

Attempts by life convicts—When any person offending under this section is under sentence of [imprisonment for life], he may, if hurt is caused, be punished with death.

he shall be sent to juvenile home. But in case it finds that on the date of occurrence, he was a juvenile but on the date when this court is passing the final order upon the report received from the trial court, he no longer continues to be juvenile, the sentence imposed against him would be liable to be set aside.

Sampurna Behura v. Union of India and Others[95]

Facts

In this Writ Petition under Article 32 of the Constitution, the court has been monitoring the implementation of the JJ Act, 2000 (for short 'the act'). The court has already passed several orders for constitution of JJBs under Section 4 of the act and CWCs under Section 29 of the act in different states and union territories and most of the states and union territories have taken steps to constitute the JJBs and the CWCs.

As there were complaints that in many districts CWCs were not operational or functional and even JJBs had not been constituted in the manner provided in the act, in our order dated 19 August 2011, the court requested the State Legal Services Authorities to coordinate with the respective Child Welfare Departments of the states to ensure that the JJBs and CWCs are established and are functional with the required facilities.

Held

To monitor the implementation of the provisions of the act relating to SJPU (Section 63 of the JJ Act, 2000)[96], the Home Departments and the Director Generals of Police of the states/union territories shall ensure that at least one police officer in every police station with aptitude is given appropriate training and orientation and designated as Juvenile or Child Welfare Officer, who would handle the juvenile or child in coordination with the police.

The required training would be provided by the District Legal Services Authorities under the guidance of the State Legal Services Authorities and Secretary, National Legal Services Authority would issue appropriate guidelines to the State Legal Services Authorities for training and orientation of police officers, who are designated as the Juvenile or Child Welfare Officers. The training

---

[95] Writ Petition (Civil) No. 473 of 2005.

[96] JJ Act, 2000, Section 63: Special juvenile police unit—

(1) In order to enable the police officers who frequently or exclusively deal with juveniles or are primarily engaged in the prevention of juvenile crime or handling of the juveniles or children under this Act to perform their functions more effectively, they shall be specially instructed and trained.

(2) In every police station at least one officer with aptitude and appropriate training and orientation may be designated as the 'juvenile or the child welfare officer' who will handle the juvenile or the child in coordination with the police.

(3) Special juvenile police unit, of which all police officers designated as above, to handle juveniles or children will be members, may be created in every district and city to coordinate and to upgrade the police treatment of the juveniles and the children.

and orientation may be done in phases over a period of 6 months to 1 year in every state and union territory.

The home departments and the Director Generals of Police of the states/UTs should also ensure that SJPU comprising all police officers designated as Juvenile or Child Welfare Officers is created in every district and city to coordinate and to upgrade the police treatment to juveniles and the children.

The matter is to be listed in the first week of January 2012 when the state governments and the UT would file an affidavit stating steps taken by them pursuant to this order.

Shashi Kumar Saini v. the State[97]

Facts

In this case, 100 grams of marijuana was recovered from the person of the juvenile/petitioner. The petitioner applied for bail under Section 12 of the JJ Act, 2000. The state opposed the bail on the ground that the petitioner would be exposed to moral danger if set free.

Held

The Delhi High Court held that the provisions of Section 12 of the JJ Act, were mandatory and had to be followed and the petitioner was required to be released on bail. After this observation, the court granted bail to the juvenile considering the Social Investigation Report (SIR).

Munney @ Rahat Jan Khan v. State of U.P.[98]

Facts

While challenging the order of High Court which upheld conviction under Section 302 read with Section 34 of the IPC and sentence of imprisonment of life imposed by first Additional Sessions Judge, the appellant also took a plea that he was a juvenile as on the date of incident which took place on 11 November 1978. The appellant was convicted by Ld. ASJ on 26 February 1980 and at that time Uttar Pradesh Children Act 1951 was applicable which afforded protection to a child and defined a child under Section 2(4) to be a person under the age of 16 years.

Held

The court considered the fact that appellant in his statement under Section 313 CrPC recorded on 19 January 1980 has given his age as 18 years and claimed to be studying in 12th class which

---

[97] 2005 VI AD Delhi 200.
[98] 2006 AIR (SC) 2902.

reflected his age to be nearly 17 years at the time of occurrence. No plea that appellant was child was taken during the course of trial or in appeal before the high court and hence it was concluded that the appellant was not a child at the time of commission of offence.

Master Niku Chaubey v. State[99]

Facts

A revision petition was directed against the order dated 03 March 2006 passed by the Additional Sessions Judge, Fast Track Court, Rohini, Delhi. By virtue of the said order, bail had been refused to the juvenile, Master Niku Chaubey on the ground that the release of the juvenile on bail is likely to bring him into association of bad company and expose him to moral and psychological danger. The state opposed the grant of bail on the ground that the alleged act committed by the juvenile was one of great moral degradation and the act in itself would demonstrate the perversity of the mind of the juvenile.

Held

The Delhi High Court observed that the nature of the offence is not one of the conditions on which bail can be granted or refused to the juvenile. It was held that bail in case of a juvenile has to be considered purely under the parameters of Section 12 of the said act which requires bail to be granted mandatorily unless the court feels that the release of the juvenile is likely to bring him into association of any known criminal or expose him to moral, physical, or psychological danger or that his release would defeat the ends of justice.

Murari thakur & Anr. v. State of Bihar[100]

Facts

Dhaneshwar Mishra, elder brother of the first informant Bhuneshwar Mishra was going for grazing his buffalo when he saw his deceased nephew Bal Krishna Mishra with the appellants going across the river in Parti land. When Dhaneshwar Mishra enquired from them where they were going, they all replied that they were on a stroll and they went towards east of the river. Dhaneshwar Mishra also went across the river with his buffalo. After sometime he heard the sound of gasping from the other side of a field of sugarcane and leaving his buffalo, he went towards the sugarcane field he found that on a ridge under the tree of Jamun (rose apple), appellant Murari Thakur had caught hold of the legs of deceased, appellant Sudhir Thakur was sitting on the back of the deceased holding both his hands, and the third accused Sunil Kumar (who is not before us) after pressing the neck of the deceased was cutting it with a sharp edged weapon. Dhaneshwar Mishra saw this incident from a distance of ten laggis, and he ran raising hulla and the appellants and Sunil Kumar fled away

[99] 2006 [2] JCC 720.
[100] 2007 AIR (SC) 1129.

towards west of the sugarcane field. When Dhaneshwar Mishra reached the place, he found that all the three appellants had already committed the murder of the deceased by cutting his neck. On hulla of Dhaneshwar Mishra, number of other persons came there and they saw the dead body of the deceased. Fard-e-bayan of the first informant was recorded at the place of the occurrence and a case under Section 302/34 of the IPC was registered against all the three appellants. The appellant for the first time in Supreme Court submitted that the appellants are entitled to the benefit of the JJ Act, 2000 as per the amendment of 2006.

Held

It was held in this case that the plea to claim benefit of the JJ Act, 2000 cannot be raised for the first time before Supreme Court as question of age is a question of fact on which evidence and cross examination are required; thus, therefore, it cannot be allowed to be taken up at a later stage.

Pawan v. State of Uttranchal[101]

Facts

Amar Singh was a migrant labourer from Nepal. He and his minor daughter Sushma aged 6 years were residing in the locality known as Raj Mahal Hotel Compound Mallital, Nainital. On 25 September 2003, Sushma left her home to ease herself. When she did not return for quite some time, she was looked for in the market, around the lake, and at all nearby places by her father, but to no avail. Despite frantic efforts, her whereabouts could not be known. The night became horrendously eventful for him and three migrant labourers from Nepal who were waiting for Sushma to return. At midnight, four persons came from the side of the road up to a vacant plot and were seen throwing the dead body of a girl from the gunny bag in that plot. The dead body was of Sushma. All the four accused were taken to the Police Station.

After medical evidence, it was proven, doubtlessly, that the victim died of homicidal death and that she was raped before being murdered. There was no eyewitness account and the case depended wholly upon circumstantial evidence. It was argued that two of the accused were 'juvenile' within the meaning of JJ Act, 2000 (for short 'the act, 2000') on the date of incident and the trial held under the CrPC was illegal. With regard to the age of one of the accused, reliance was placed on his statement recorded wherein his age has been recorded as 17 years and a school-leaving certificate indicating his date of birth. For the second accused, his school-leaving certificate which records his date of birth was relied upon.

Held

It was held that where the materials placed before the court by the accused, prima facie, suggest that the accused was 'juvenile' as defined in the act, 2000 on the date of incident, it may be

---

[101] (SC) 2009(2) RCR (Criminal) 451.

necessary to call for the report or an inquiry be ordered to be made. However, in a case where plea of juvenility is found unscrupulous or the materials lack credibility or do not inspire confidence and even, prima facie, satisfaction of the court is not made out, we do not think any further exercise in this regard is necessary. If the plea of juvenility was not raised before the Trial Court or the High Court and is raised for the first time before the Supreme Court, the judicial conscience of the court must be satisfied by placing adequate and satisfactory material that the accused had not attained age of 18 years on the date of commission of offence; such material that required any further inquiry into juvenality would be unnecessary.

Hari Ram v. State of Rajasthan[102]

Facts

The Appellant, Hari Ram, was arrested along with several others on 30 November 1998, for commission of offences under Sections 148, 302, 149, 323, and 325 of the IPC. After the case was committed for trial, the Additional Sessions Judge, Didwana, by his order dated 3 April 2000, determined the age of the accused to be below 16 years on the date of commission of the offence and after declaring him to be a juvenile, directed that he be tried by the JJB, Ajmer, Rajasthan.

This appeal has been filed against the order dated 7 December 2005, passed by the Jodhpur Bench of the Rajasthan High Court. The appeal filed by the state of Rajasthan was allowed holding that the Appellant was not a juvenile and the provisions of the JJ Act, 2000, were not, therefore, applicable to him.

According to the appellant's father, the appellant's date of birth was 17 October 1982 and offence was alleged to have been committed on 30 October 1998, which meant that at the time of commission of the offence, the appellant had completed 16 years and 13 days

Held

The Supreme Court held

the Explanation to section 20 of the Juvenile Justice Act, 2000, which was added in 2006, makes it very clear that in all pending cases, which would include not only trials but even subsequent proceedings by way of revision or appeal, the determination of juvenility of a juvenile would be in terms of Clause (l) of Section 2, even if the juvenile ceased to be a juvenile on or before 1st April, 2001, when the Juvenile Justice Act, 2000, came into force, and the provisions of the Act would apply as if the said provision had been in force for all purposes and for all material times when the alleged offence was committed. In fact, Section 20 enables the Court to consider and determine the juvenility of a person even after conviction by the regular Court and also empowers the Court, while maintaining the conviction, to set aside the sentence imposed and forward the case to the Juvenile Justice Board concerned for passing sentence in accordance with the provisions of the Juvenile Justice Act, 2000.

[102] (2009) 13 SCC 211.

The effect of the proviso to Section 7-A introduced by the Amending Act makes it clear that the claim of juvenility may be raised before any Court which shall be recognized at any stage, even after final disposal of the case, and such claim shall be determined in terms of the provisions contained in the Act and the Rules made thereunder which includes the definition of Juvenile in Section 2(k) and 2(l) of the Act even if the Juvenile had ceased to be so on or before the date of commencement of the Act.

Apart from the aforesaid provisions, Rule 98 of the Juvenile Justice Rules 2007 has to be read in tandem with Section 20 of the JJ Act, 2000, which provides that even in disposed of cases of JICL, the state government or the board could, either suo motu or on an application made for the purpose, review the case of a juvenile, determine the juvenility, and pass an appropriate order under Section 64 of the act for the immediate release of the juvenile whose period of detention had exceeded the maximum period provided in Section 15 of the act, that is, 3 years.

Sub-Section (1) of Section 49 vests the Competent Authority with power to make due inquiry as to the age of a person brought before it and for the said purpose to take such evidence as may be necessary (but not an affidavit) and shall record a finding as to whether the person is a juvenile or a child or not, stating his age as nearly as may be. Sub-Section (2) is of equal importance as it provides that no order of a Competent Authority would be deemed to have become invalid merely on account of any subsequent proof that the person, in respect of whom an order is made, is not a juvenile or a child, and the age recorded by the Competent Authority to be the age of the person brought before it, would, for the purpose of the Act, be deemed to be the true age of a child or a juvenile in conflict with law. Sub-Rule (3) of Rule 12 indicates that the age determination inquiry by the Court or Board, by seeking evidence, is to be derived from:

(i) the matriculation or equivalent certificates, if available, and in the absence of the same;
(ii) the date of birth certificate from the school (other than a play school) first attended; and in the absence whereof;
(iii) the birth certificate given by a corporation or a municipal authority or a Panchayat.

Sub-Clause (b) of Rule 12(3) provides that only in the absence of any such document, would a medical opinion be sought for from a duly constituted Medical Board, which would declare the age of the juvenile or the child. In case exact assessment of the age cannot be done, the Court or the Board or as the case may be, the Child Welfare Committee, for reasons to be recorded by it, may, if considered necessary, give benefit to the child or juvenile by considering his/her age on the lower side within a margin of one year.

The Supreme Court held that the High Court had erred in holding that the provisions of the JJ Act, 1986, would not be applicable to the appellant's case since he was allegedly 13 days above the age prescribed.

The Supreme Court further held that in view of Sections 2(k), 2(l), and 7A read with Section 20 of the said Act, the provisions thereof would apply to the Appellant's case and on the date of the alleged incident it would be held that he was a juvenile. The appeal was, therefore, allowed and the order passed by the High Court was set aside.

Dharambir v. State (NCT of Delhi)[103]

Facts

An appeal was directed against the final judgment delivered by the High Court of Delhi. By the impugned judgment, the high court has upheld the conviction of the Appellant for offences punishable under Sections 302 and 307 read with Section 34 of the IPC 1860, for committing murder of one of their close relatives and for attempting to murder his brother. The Appellant was sentenced to imprisonment for life under Sections 302/34 IPC and to rigorous imprisonment for a term of 7 years for offence under Section 307/34 IPC.

When the matter came up for hearing, the Appellant submitted that since at the time of commission of the said offences, he had not completed 18 years of age, he was a juvenile within the meaning of Section 2(k) of the JJ Act 2000, and an inquiry in terms of Section 7A of the act of 2000 had to be made so as to determine the age of the appellant. In support of the submission, the Appellant relied on his school-leaving certificate dated 2 December 2009.

Held

Proviso to sub-section (1) of Section 7A contemplates that a claim of juvenility can be raised before any court and has to be recognised at any stage even after disposal of the case and such claim is required to be determined in terms of the provisions contained in the Act of 2000 and the rules framed thereunder, even if the juvenile has ceased to be so on or before the date of the commencement of the Act of 2000. The effect of the proviso is that a juvenile who had not completed eighteen years of age on the date of commission of the offence would also be entitled to the benefit of the Act of 2000 as if the provisions of Section 2(k) of the said Act, which defines to mean a person who has not completed eighteenth year of age, had always been in existence even during the operation of the 1986 Act. It is, thus, manifest from a conjoint reading of Sections 2(k), 2(l), 7A, 20 and 49 of the Act of 2000, read with Rules 12 and 98 of the Juvenile Justice (Care and Protection of Children) Rules, 2007 that all persons who were below the age of eighteen years on the date of commission of the offence even prior to 1st April, 2001 would be treated as juveniles even if the claim of juvenility is raised after they have attained the age of eighteen years on or before the date of the commencement of the Act of 2000 and were undergoing sentences upon being convicted.

The Court further said that in the present case, as per the report of the Registrar submitted in terms of Section 7A of the act of 2000, the age of Appellant as on the date of commission of offences, that is, 25 August 1991, was 16 years, 9 months and 8 days. Therefore, the Appellant was held to be a juvenile as on the date of commission of the offences for which he was convicted and was therefore required to be governed by the provisions of the act of 2000.

---

[103] (2010) 5 SCC 344.

Gangaram Dushanna Dandil v. *the State of Maharashtra*[104]

Facts

The Applicant was convicted by the Sessions Court under Sections 395, 396 and 452 of IPC. The Applicant stated that at the time when the offence was committed, that is, on 28 May 2003, he was a juvenile. To support the submission, the Applicant relied on a bonafide certificate issued by the school where he was studying, a birth certificate issued by Tahasildar, District Adilabad. An ossification test was conducted on the Applicant by a radiologist. He opined that the age of the applicant was between 19 and 20 years. Thus, when the offence was committed on 28 May 2003, the applicant was below 18 years of age.

Held

Relying on Section 2(k), Section 2(l), Section 6, Section 7-A, and Section 15(g) of the JJ Act 2000 as amended by Juvenile Justice Amendment Act, 2006, the High Court opined that a JICL cannot be tried by an ordinary criminal court. Even if it is found that he has committed an offence he can be sent to a special home for a period of 3 years only.

In this case a plea of juvenility was not raised by the applicant in the Trial Court. The High Court held that since the Applicant did not raise the plea of juvenility, a wrong procedure was followed. His conviction itself was not sustainable. In view of the provisions of the JJ Act, the Applicant ought to have been referred to the board and if the board had come to a conclusion that he had committed the offence, the applicant could have been sent to a Special Home for a period of 3 years only. The Court then went on to modify the order of sentence and substituted the sentence of life imprisonment to a period of 3 years.

Shah Nawaz v. *State of U.P. & Anr.*[105]

Facts

The Appellant claimed to have born on 18 June 1989 in Muzaffarnagar, Uttar Pradesh. To substantiate this claim, he relied on the marksheet of his high school examination issued by the school authority and the school leaving certificate. The documents furnished clearly showed that the date of birth of the appellant had been noted as 18 June 1989.

Held

The Supreme Court relied on the date of birth reflected in the marksheet and the school leaving certificate to declare the accused a juvenile, and held that 'rule 12 of the Rules categorically envisages that the medical opinion from the medical board should be sought only when the

[104] 2010 (2) MAH.L.J(Cri) 170; 2010 ALL MR (CRI) 1380.
[105] (2011) 13 SCC 751.

matriculation certificate or school certificate or any birth certificate issued by a corporation or by any Panchayat or municipality is not available'.

It further stated:

We are satisfied that the entry relating to date of birth entered in the mark sheet is one of the valid proof of evidence for determination of age of an accused person. The School Leaving Certificate is also a valid proof in determining the age of the accused person.... In light of the above discussion, we hold that from the acceptable reports, the date of birth of the appellant is 18-6-1989, the Additional Sessions Judge and the High Court committed an error in taking a contrary view. While upholding the decision of the Board, we set aside the orders of the Additional Sessions Judge dated 13-1-2009 and the High Court dated 10-12-2012. Accordingly, the appellant is declared to be a juvenile on the date of commission of the offence and may be proceeded in accordance with law. The appeal is allowed.

A.K. Asthana v. Union of India and ANR[106]

Facts

This petition was filed as a PIL flags the issue of the media while disseminating news, disclosing the name and identity of CNCP, without seeking the permission of the CWC and in violation of Section 21 of the JJ Act, 2000.

The aforesaid Committee proposed 'Guidelines for Media Reporting on Children', which were approved by this Court with some modifications vide order dated 8 August 2012 and ordered to be implemented with immediate effect. However it was subsequently informed that the said Guidelines remained to be implemented as there was no circulation and publicity.

Held

In this case, the Court accordingly incorporated those Guidelines in its order dated 5 December 2012 and directed immediate implementation thereof. The Guidelines are as follows:-

A. For hospitals

1. It shall be the duty of the hospital or medical facility, where a child may be referred, admitted for treatment or being treated or which conducts any other medical examination/tests or provides any service to child, to ensure that no detail pertaining to identity and infringement upon privacy of such a child is made available to the media, unless ordered to do so by the JJB or CWC concerned or any other court.

2. Every hospital shall have a committee in place to inquire about cases of lapses regarding to breach of privacy or confidentiality of children's identity. The inquiry committee shall examine the reasons behind such a lapse and shall recommend appropriate action against those responsible for such lapses, as per law.

[106] Delhi High Court, W.P.(C) 787/2012.

3. The inquiry committee shall have three members, out of which one member shall be an external person from a registered child rights organization and it shall be headed by a chief medical officer of the hospital concerned. It shall be the responsibility of chief medical officer to initiate and inquiry committee meeting either on his/her own cognizance or on being complained about such a lapse having been committed. Complainant, as well as, adversely affected parties, shall be given reasonable opportunity of being heard in writing, before such a committee finalizes its findings. A copy of such findings shall be provided to affected parties. An inquiry shall be completed within a period of 3 months from the date of the incident being reported. The chief medical officer shall take action as per recommendation of the inquiry committee within one week from the conclusion of inquiry and shall intimate all members of the inquiry committee about action taken. A copy of the proceedings, copy of the complaint, findings along with an action-taken report shall be submitted to the State Commission for Protection of Child Rights or NCPCR (where State Commission for Protection of Child Rights does not exist) within one week from the implementation of the inquiry committee's recommendations. The commission concerned, upon receipt of the inquiry committee case papers, shall record its satisfaction to the inquiry and if not satisfied shall take cognizance and initiate its own inquiry as per provisions of the Commission of Protection of Child Rights Act, 2005.

4. In case, the person/s responsible for lapse are outside the authority of the hospital, the head of the inquiry committee shall mention so in his/her report to State Commission for Protection of Child Rights or NCPCR who in turn shall take up the matter with the authority appropriate to cause action to be taken.

5. 'Hospital' means any hospital which comes under the jurisdiction of the Medical Council of India and includes any pathology, clinic, or facility used for medical purposes.

B. **For courts**

1. Courts shall obliterate details leading to disclosure of identity of a child from judicial proceedings before issuing a certified copy or uploading them on the website.

2. Cause lists and case titles in the cases shall not mention the name of child. Instead pseudo names, that is, 'XYZ' or 'ABC' shall be used to refer to a child's name.

3. Registry/reader/alhmad of the court concerned shall not accept any application as may be filed by lawyers or in-person parties, if they contain reference to the name of the child, provided that in appropriate cases courts may permit so, after giving the reason in writing.

4. Inspection of judicial record shall be permitted only when an undertaking is given that the child's identity-related details shall not be disclosed to anyone else or be used for any other purpose except for legal representation in the case concerned or any other related case by the applicant applying for inspection.

5. Courts will ensure that names of children are not called at the time of hearing by the court staff.

6. After declaration of juvenility or child in any case, the court passing such an order shall obliterate the name- and identity-related details of such a person being declared a juvenile or child from its record. For the past court record, a direction to keep the record in a sealed

cover shall be passed and the application for inspection/certified copy shall be subject to Clause B1 and B4 in addition to orders passed by concerned court.

C. For competent authorities under the Juvenile Justice Act

1. Orders and cause list shall not mention name of child, as far as possible.
2. Calling of names of children or juveniles shall not be permitted.
3. It shall be the duty of the lawyer concerned, family members of the child, or probation officer or welfare officer from the child's home/observation home concerned to ensure that concerned child is produced when the matter is taken up for hearing and appropriate directions in this regard will be issued to all concerned so that child does not suffer in any way due to failing from appearing before authorities. Proactive efforts from JJB and CWCs are to be made in this regard and to ensure that child does not suffer in any way because of such procedural requirements.
4. Every JJB, CWC, institutions for JICL and CNCP shall have notice boards prominently visible stating that disclosure of identity of a child is punishable under Section 21 of the JJ Act, 2000 and those who happen to witness any proceedings before such competent authorities are deemed to have consented to abide by such condition.
5. The counsel for the NCPCR has also filed before us the report dated 2 September 2014 of the committee aforesaid inter alia to the effect that though guidelines pertaining to the police and lawyers have also been formulated by the committee but could not be finalized as the same need clarification from this court. It is stated that the Delhi Police Revised Standing Order No. Ops-47 with respect to missing persons read with Standard Operating Procedure drafted on the directions issued by this court in W.P.(Crl.) No. 249/2009 titled 'Court on Its Own Motion vs. State' provides for the police to immediately photograph every found/recovered child for the purposes of advertisement and to make people aware of the missing child and for such photographs of the recovered child to be published on the website and through the newspaper and even on the TV so that the parents of the missing child could locate their missing child and recover him or her from the custody of the police. It is stated that the said procedure is violative of Section 21 supra which prohibits any report in any newspaper, magazine, news-sheet, or visual media, of any inquiry regarding a JICL or CNCP under this act, from disclosing the name, address or school or any other particulars calculated to lead to the identification of the juvenile or child and publication of any picture of such juvenile or child without the permission of the CWC.
6. The counsel for the Central Government invites attention to the order dated 10 May 2013 of the Supreme Court in W.P.(C) No. 75/2012 titled 'Bachpan Bachao Andolan vs. Union of India' directing that every found/recovered child must be immediately photographed by the police for purposes of advertisement and to make people aware of the missing child and publication of the photographs of the recovered child on the website and through the newspapers and even on T.V. so that the parents could locate their missing child and recover him or her from police custody. He states that any prohibition imposed by this Court in the proposed guidelines would be in contravention of the said order of the Supreme Court.

7. Though it appears to us that in neither of the orders aforesaid the provisions of Section 21 mentioned earlier were considered but we have still enquired from the counsels whether not the aforesaid directions are necessary for immediately restoring the recovered child to his/her parents/guardians and that if it were not so, considerably more time would be taken in locating the parents/guardians and informing them and resultantly in the recovered child staying for longer periods in a juvenile home or otherwise away from his parents/guardians and which is likely to be not in his/her interest and may be more prejudicial to the child.

8. The counsel for the NCPCR and the petitioner appearing in person though not controverting the aforesaid, state that still, in view of the provisions of Section 21, a provision be made for obtaining the permission of the CWC.

9. We have enquired as to how much time is likely to be taken in obtaining the said permission.

10. The counsel for the NCPCR assures us that the said permission can be obtained within a day of recovery of the lost/missing/removed from the custody of parents/guardians child.

11. The counsel for the NCPCR at this stage states that he will be making an appropriate application to the Supreme Court for clarification of the order aforesaid in Bachpan Bachao Andolan petition.

The Court was also of the opinion that the same would be a more appropriate course.

Court on Its Own Motion v. Dept. of Women and Child Development & Ors[107]
Facts

International Bridges of Justice, while interacting with some young offenders at Central Jail, Tihar found that some young offenders who were shown as between age of 18 to 21 years were found to be juveniles. Hence, a writ Petition was filed raising the question that whether the juveniles subjected to adult criminal justice system in prison clearly amounted to violation of their fundamental rights and was contrary to provisions of the JJ Act, 2000. The Court, disposing of the writ petition held that the main object and purpose of JJ Act was that of juvenile's reformation and rehabilitation so that he also might have an opportunity to enjoy as other children. There could be no denial of fact that lodging juveniles along with hardened adult criminals could have drastic implications on physical and mental well-being of juvenile offender. Trying minors in adult courts and sentencing them in adult prisons was totally against the objective and purpose of the JJ Act. Even for hardened career criminals, jail could be dangerous place, but for the youth it could be especially dangerous as they were often vulnerable to prison victimization because of their size and age. Thus, the separate justice system for juveniles and that of adolescents which are different from adults are less responsible for their transgressions and more amenable to rehabilitation. Lodging juveniles in adult prisons amounts to deprivation of their personal liberty

[107] 2012 IVAD (Delhi) 641.

on multiple aspects. Hence lodging of juveniles in prisons clearly amounts to violation of their fundamental rights and contrary to provisions of the JJ Act, apart from adverse psychological impact on these children.

Held

The court issued directions to all appropriate authorities for compliance so as to prevent incarceration of children in conflict with law, in jails or their subjection to Adult Criminal Justice System. The Ratio Decidendi of this case was that 'lodging juveniles in adult prisons amounts to deprivation of their personal liberty on multiple aspects'.

The court accordingly directed:-

1. Those inmates in jail about whom investigations were made by the teams of NCPCR/Delhi Legal Services Authority (DLSA), among others, and who are suspected to be juvenile as per initial investigations, shall be kept by the superintendent of the Tihar Jail separately, insulated and segregated from all other prisoners. They shall be produced in batches before the JJB. Further enquiry into the matter to conclusively determine their age shall be conducted by the JJB. Those who are ultimately found to be juvenile shall be shifted from the jail to observation home by the JJB.
2. List of 19 such prisoners was submitted to the court, who may be juveniles though their ages are shown as above 18; some of those may be in the list of the prisoners investigated by NCPCR/DLSA. Enquiry into their ages shall also be conducted in a similar manner.
3. Teams of NCPCR/DLSA in a similar manner shall visit Tihar Jail. For those who appear to be juvenile, a procedure for ascertainment of their ages shall also be followed in a similar manner as by producing them before the JJB. These teams shall document the cases and forward the list to jail authorities as well as JJB.
4. The IOs, while making arrest shall reflect the age of the prisoner arrested in the Arrest Memo. It would be the duty of the police officer to ascertain the said age by making inquiry from the prisoner arrested if such prisoner is in possession of any age proof. In other cases, if the prisoner appears to be a juvenile and the police officer believes that the prisoner is a juvenile, he shall be produced before the JJB instead of criminal court.
5. The police authorities shall introduce age memo on the lines of an arrest memo. A concrete and well-thought scheme in this regard needs to be evolved by the SJPU to address the concern. We direct SJPU to evolve such a scheme and place before us on the next date of hearing.
6. As and when a young person is apprehended/arrested and he is produced before the Magistrate, it will be the duty of the Magistrate also to order ascertainment of age of such a person. The Magistrate shall, in all such cases, undertake this exercise if the young person from his/her looks appears to be below 18 years of age and also in all those cases where in the arrest memo age is stated to be 18–21 years. A preliminary enquiry in this behalf shall be undertaken of all these young persons whose age is stated to be up to 21 years.

In conducting the inquiry, the following points would need to be taken into consideration:

- The IO shall ask the person if s/he has received formal schooling at any point of time; if the child answers in an affirmative, the IO should verify the record of such a school at the earliest.
- If the parents of the person are available, this inquiry should be made to them. The IO should ask the parents whether they have got the date of birth of the child registered with the MCD or the gram pradhan as provided under law, and taken the answers/documents on record.
- Where no such document is found immediately and the IO has reasonable grounds to believe that such a document might be existing, he shall produce such persons before the board and should seek time for obtaining these documents.
- A preliminary inquiry can be made from the parents of such a person about the time of their marriage and the details of how many children do the parents have and after how long of the marriage were these children born.
- In addition to this, an inquiry of previous criminal involvement of the juvenile shall necessarily be made with the effort to find if there is any past declaration of juvenility. For this, the police should also maintain data of declaration of juvenility.
- The inquiry conducted in each case shall be recorded in writing and shall form a part on investigation report in each case where a child claims his/her age up to 21 years irrespective of whether s/he is found a juvenile or an adult.
- The SJPU shall set up a mechanism in place for necessary coordination and assistance to police officer who may require such information.
- An advisory/circular/standing order, as may be appropriate, be prepared by the The SJPU for the assistance of police officer/IOs/junior welfare officers for the purpose of assistance on matters related to age inquiry. Such advisory/circular/standing order shall also include the procedure which needs to be followed by the IOs in cases of transfer of cases from adult courts to JJB and vice versa.
- In each case, where a public officer arrests a person as adult and later on such person turns out to be a juvenile, DCP concerned shall undertake an inquiry to satisfy him/her that a deliberate lapse was not committed.

Directions for Commissioner of Police

1. Commissioner of police shall issue a standing order clarifying the roles and responsibilities of police officers.
2. Commissioner of police on receipt of half yearly report from nodal head of SJPU shall pass necessary directions to give effect to the recommendations and to address the concerns as may be raised in such reports. An action taken report of the same shall also be forwarded to the Juvenile Justice Committee of Honourable Delhi High Court.

For Deputy Commissioners of Police, In-charge of Districts Concerned

1. In case any person approaches the DCP with a complaint that Police is not taking notice of juvenility of any offender and is refusing to take on record the documents being provided to suggest juvenility and instead treating a child as adult, it shall be the duty of DCP concerned

to do an immediate inquiry into such complaint. Such an inquiry shall be completed within 24 hours of having received such complaint and if the complaint turns out to have merit and truth, DCP concerned shall give orders to the concerned police officers to immediately take corrective steps and shall also initiate disciplinary action against erring police official.

2. In cases where any action is taken against an erring police officer, a quarterly report of the same containing the nature and reasons of such lapse and details of action taken shall be furnished by the DCP concerned to the concerned JJB having jurisdiction over that district along with a copy to the nodal head of SJPU for their record and intimation.

3. DCPs shall, during the regular monthly meeting with all the SHOs and Inspector-Investigations, shall brief them about their responsibilities, any new judgment or order from JJBs and Courts, any practice direction etc. and shall ensure that their subordinate police officers don't show children as adults, take all necessary steps to verify the age of accused persons and are in overall compliance with the provisions of JJ Act & Rules.

4. DCPs shall also ensure that all the police stations under their jurisdiction put in place the required setup and required notice boards etc.

5. On being intimated by the JJBs about any lapse having been committed on age investigation, DCP concerned shall institute an inquiry and take such action as may be required or appropriate. An action taken report shall be submitted to the JJB by the DCP concerned within a month from the receipt of such intimation.

For Nodal Head/ In-Charge of Special Juvenile Police Unit

1. Nodal head of SJPU shall cause quarterly (once in three months) inspection of all the police stations through an official not below the rank of ACP in order to check that all the police stations have put in place the required setup and all the obligations required.

2. A report shall be prepared by such ACPs of such visits documenting the best practices or shortcoming noticed at the police stations and shall be submitted to the Nodal Head of SJPU within 10 days of such visit.

3. Nodal Head of SJPU shall make a report on half yearly basis and shall submit it to the Commissioner of Police with recommendations. A copy shall also be submitted to Juvenile Justice Committee of Honourable Delhi High Court.

4. District Level units of SJPU shall on a regular basis monitor the functioning of police stations of that district vis-à-vis implementation of JJ Act and Rules and direction of this Honourable Court and shall provide necessary guidance and trainings to the police.

For the Officer In-Charge of the Police Station

1. It shall be the duty of the officer in charge of the police station to ensure that police officers of his or her police station have taken all measures to ensure that proper inquiry or investigation on the point of age has been carried out and that all the required formalities, procedure have been carried out and required documents have been prepared in this regard.

2. Officer in charge shall also ensure that a notice board, prominently visible, in Hindi, Urdu, and English language informing that persons below the age of 18 years are governed under the provisions of JJ Act and cannot be kept in police lock up and jails and are not to be taken to

the Adult Criminal Courts. Such notice Board shall also contain the names and contact details of Juvenile Welfare Officers, Probation Officers and Legal Aid Lawyers of Delhi State Legal Services Authority (DSLSA).

For the Investigating Officer or Any Other Police Officer Acting under the Instruction of Investigation Officer

1. Every Police officer at the time of arresting/apprehending young offenders shall be under obligation to inform the alleged offender about his/her right to be dealt with under the provisions of JJ Act if s/he is below 18 years of age and a proper counselling shall be done on the point of age.

2. IO or any other police officer affecting the arrest/apprehension shall also prepare the Age Memo. A copy of such Age Memo shall also be delivered to the alleged offender and his parents/guardians/or relative who have been intimated about his/her arrest.

3. At the time of forwarding the copy of FIR to the Ilaka Magistrate within 24 hours, IO shall be under duty to file the preliminary age memo along with the FIR in case arrest/apprehension is made before forwarding the FIR.

4. On completion of age inquiry, which shall be done, preferably within one week of arrest/apprehension, the completed age memo be filed before the court concerned.

5. At the time of first production of an offender who is between 18 to 21 years of age as per the initial inquiry of the IO as above, before the Court, IO or the Police officer responsible for producing the offender before the Court, shall produce alleged offender, along with a copy of the FIR and age memo before the Secretary of respective District Legal Services Authority, irrespective of whether the alleged offender is being represented by a legal aid lawyer or not.

6. If the alleged offender claims to be a juvenile and age documents to support such claim are not readily available and it is not possible for IO to obtain such documents within 24 hours of arrest, accused shall be produced before JJB.

7. At the time of first production of offender before Court or JJB, it shall be the duty of IO to ensure that parents or relatives of such offender are duly informed about (1) date (2) time and (3) particulars of the court of such production and a copy of such intimation shall be produced before the Court at the time of first production.

For the Juvenile Welfare Officers

1. It shall be the duty of the Juvenile Welfare Officers (JWOs) or Child Welfare Officer to obtain the copy of age declaration done by JJB or CWC and to forward such copy to the SJPU for entry into the record and to obtain a certificate that such entry has been done with SJPU and a copy of such certificate shall be deposited to the JJB or CWC concerned.

2. It shall be the duty of the Juvenile Welfare Officer to ensure that any offender at the Police station who might be a juvenile is not treated as an adult and if he notices any such incident, he shall immediately report to the Officer in Charge of the Police Station concerned with intimation to District SJPU.

3. In case, any police officer is approached by any person alleging that some one who is a juvenile and has been treated as an adult by any officer of that Police Station, it shall be the duty of such police officer to record the statement of such complainant and then to register a Daily

Diary Entry to this effect immediately and take up the issue with the Juvenile Welfare Officer or Investigation Officer concerned or the Officer In Charge concerned and cause corrective steps to be taken by such police officer. JWO shall furnish a copy of such DD Entry to the aggrieved person/ complainant. A report about such complaint, copy of DD entry, details of action taken or proposed to be taken shall be forwarded to the District SJPU within 24 hours of receiving such complaint.

For Tihar and Rohini Jails

1. 'Visitors' boards' prescribed in Rule 12 and 13 of the Delhi Prison (Visitors of Prisons) Rules, 1988, shall specifically mention in their reports the status of young offender found in the jails and also recommend follow up action to be taken up by the Jail Authorities.
2. The jail authorities will not get the medical examination test done at the first instance on its own. Such cases will be immediately intimated to the DSLSA with complete details such as FIR No, Court name, next date of hearing and other required details to enable DSLSA to take appropriate follow up action.
3. Such persons who appear to be juveniles as per JJ Act, 2000 shall be segregated immediately from the other prisoners. If Jail authorities are of the view that any person brought in the Jail may be a probable juvenile, it should send a letter addressed to the Court concerned within 24 working hours, requesting for an age inquiry to be conducted. Copy of such letter shall also be attached with the Warrant of the prisoner. It should be the prerogative and responsibility of the Court concerned to initiate an age inquiry as per law and make a decision accordingly. Jail authorities can at the most bring the fact of possible juvenility to the notice of Courts by way of a proper communication.
4. Every jail shall display at a prominent place in all the wards, canteen, and visitor's area in Hindi, English, and Urdu languages notice boards informing inmates that persons who age are below 18 years at the time of commission of offense are not supposed to be in Jail and are entitled to kept in children Homes and be treated under the Provisions of Juvenile Justice Act and be dealt with by the JJB which make efforts for reformation and rehabilitation. Such Notification shall also inform the procedure to be adopted and the persons to be contacted within jail in case if they want to claim juvenility. Jail Authorities as well as Legal Aid Authorities shall be under duty to provide effective and speedy legal aid to every inmate who wants to put a claim of juvenility in the court.
5. Jail authorities/superintendent shall make available the details of each inmate, as maintained by them, to the panel visitors of NCPCR, which shall include but not be limited to name, address, age on record, previous history of institutionalization in jails, and medical reports.

For Juvenile Justice Boards

1. JJB shall conduct the proper age inquiry of each child brought before it as per the procedure laid down in Rule 12 of the Delhi JJ Rules, 2009.
2. On every occasion, when the case of a juvenile is transferred from the adult court to the JJB and the juvenile is transferred from jail to the concerned Observation Home, the JJB shall

interact with the juvenile and record his/her version on how s/he came to be treated as an adult. If from the statement of the juvenile and after appropriate inquiry from IO, it appears that the juvenile was wrongly shown as an adult by the IO, then the JJB shall intimate the concerned DCP. This intimation shall be done in all those cases which are received from the JJB by way of transfer from the adult court, and shall be done even in all those cases in which the declaration of juvenility has been done by the Adult Court.

3. JJBs shall determine the age of a person by way recording the evidence brought forth by the Juvenile and the prosecution/complainant and the parties shall be given an opportunity to examine, cross examine, or re-examine witnesses of their choice.

4. In case of medical age examination, the parties shall be given copies of the medical age examination report immediately by the JJBs. The parties shall have the right to file objection thereto, including the right to cross-examine before final age determination is done.

5. While declaring the age, the order of age declaration shall also state the age as nearly as possible as on the date of commission of the offence.

6. Before commencing the age inquiry, a notice thereof shall be served upon the complainant by the JJB or the Court concerned, which shall also accord opportunity to the complainant of being heard on the issue including producing evidence; however the age inquiry will be concluded within the stipulated time limit of one month.

7. It shall be the duty of Board to ensure that every juvenile in whose respect age inquiry is being conducted is being represented by a Counsel and in those cases, where there is no lawyer present before the board at the time of hearing of case; Board shall provide a Legal Aid Lawyer.

8. JJB shall give copy of age declaration to JWO to get it recorded with Nodal Officer of SJPU. A certified copy of the age declaration shall be mandatorily given to the juvenile or his/her parents on the same day along with a copy to the concerned Juvenile or Child Welfare Officer.

For National Commission for Protection of Child Rights

1. The NCPCR shall constitute a panel of at least 10 persons to make visits to various jails in Delhi in order to find out if there are any persons lodged in such jails who should have been the beneficiaries of the JJ Act. Members of such panel may visit various jails as per the schedule drawn in consultation with/ intimation to the Jail Authorities.

2. Reports of such visits along with the list of probable juveniles shall be forwarded to the Member Secretary of DSLSA, jail authorities, and the JJBs concerned for further action. The NCPCR shall devise a Performa which shall be used by such visitors and shall be supplied to all such visitors on the panel. Such filled up proformas will be used to compile a report.

3. Such persons shall be only those persons who are in a position to and are willing to visit various jails in Delhi at least once a month but it may conduct such visits more frequently if required.

4. NCPCR shall make arrangements to pay for a reasonable honorarium and incidental expenses on travel etc. to the members of this panel whose services would be obtained by NCPCR from time to time.

5. The NCPCR shall provide training and orientation to all the members of the panel on JJ Act, method of age inquiry, jail rules and discipline, and method of filling up the proforma etc.
6. Such panel may be revised as and when required by NCPCR.

For Legal Aid Lawyers and Delhi Legal Services Authority

1. Legal Aid Lawyers from Delhi State Legal Services Authority who are authorized to be the jail visiting lawyers shall visit jails on their schedule as may be prescribed and shall intimate the details of inmates who may be juveniles to the secretaries of the respective District Legal Services Authorities for further appropriate action.
2. Legal Aid Lawyers shall be entitled to make visit to the Mulahiza ward(New admission ward) of the adolescent and female jails and be allowed to freely interact with the inmates and shall not wait for inmates to approach them in the legal aid room.
3. Superintendent of each jail shall intimate to the DSLSA on a fortnightly basis about the names, case details, court and date of next hearing of those inmates who may be juveniles.
4. Whenever any offender of 18 to 21 years age is produced at the office of the Secretary of concerned District Legal Services Authority, the secretary himself/herself and in his/her absence the Front Office Lawyer will interact with the alleged offender to ascertain the facts as are relevant for determination of age such as date of birth, name of first attended school, names, number and date of birth of siblings, among others) while explaining the purpose of seeking such information and shall move applications where necessary and irrespective of the alleged offender being represented by private counsel to request the court to conduct an age inquiry.

For the Courts Concerned

1. Whenever an alleged offender is produced before a court, not being the JJB or CWC, it shall on the very first date of production question the offender about his/her age and shall inform such offender about the benefits of the JJ Act. If the offender claims or appears to be 18–21 years, it shall direct the IO to produce the alleged offender at the Office of the Secretary of District Legal Services Authority. The Court shall by way of an inquiry under Rule 12 of the Delhi JJ Rules 2009 satisfy itself that the offender is not a juvenile.
2. If the court concerned is of the view that the offender produced before it may be a juvenile, it shall order for immediate transfer to Observation Home and production of such offender before the JJB concerned, and shall direct the Alhmed to send the case file to JJB immediately.
3. If a claim of juvenility under Section 7A of the JJ Act is raised before any court at any point of time, the Court shall conduct an age inquiry as per the Rule 12 of the Delhi JJ Rules 2009 and if a person is established to be a juvenile, shall order for same day transfer to Observation Home (if offender is below 18 years as on the date of such order) and to the Place of Safety (if person has turned adult on the date of such order) and shall direct the Alhmed to send the case file complete in all respect including documents relating to Bail etc. to the JJB Concerned.
4. If there is an adult co-accused also, the copy of the judicial file shall be prepared by such Court and shall be forwarded to the JJB Concerned.

For the Government Hospitals and Medical Boards

1. All Government Hospitals shall constitute Medical Boards to carry out medical age examinations and shall give report not later than 15 days of request being made in this regard.
2. All the members of medical Board (Physiologist, Dental Examiner and Radiologist/ Forensic expert)shall give their individual reports based on their respective examinations and the same shall be mentioned in the report, based on which the Chairperson shall give the final opinion on the age within a margin of 1 year.

Guidelines for Legal Services in Juvenile Justice Institutions

1. When a child is produced before Board by Police, Board should call the legal aid lawyer in front of it, should introduce juvenile/parents to the lawyer, juvenile and his/her family/ parents should be made to understand that it is their right to have legal aid lawyer and that they need not pay any fees to anyone for this.
2. JJB should give time to legal aid lawyer to interact with juvenile and his/her parents before conducting hearing.
3. The JJB should mention in its order that legal aid lawyer has been assigned and name and presence of legal aid lawyers should be mentioned in the order.
4. Board should make sure that a child and his parents are given sufficient time to be familiar with legal aid counsel and get time to discuss about the case before hearing is done.
5. The JJB should make sure that not a single juvenile's case goes without having a legal aid counsel.
6. The JJB should issue a certificate of attendance to legal aid lawyers at the end of month and should also verify their work done reports.
7. In case of any lapse or misdeed on the part of legal aid lawyers, board should intimate the State Legal Services Authority and should take corrective step.
8. The JJB and the legal Aid lawyers should work in a spirit of understanding, solidarity and coordination. It can bring a sea-change.
9. Legal Aid Lawyer should develop good understanding of Juvenile Justice Law and of juvenile delinquency by reading and participating in workshops/trainings on Juvenile Justice.
10. Legal Aid Lawyer should maintain a diary at center in which dates of cases are regularly entered.
11. If a legal aid lawyer goes on leave or is not able to attend Board on any given day, he/she should ensure that cases are attended by fellow legal aid lawyer in his/her absence and that case is not neglected.
12. Legal Aid lawyer should not take legal aid work as a matter of charity and should deliver the best.
13. Legal Aid Lawyer should raise issues/concerns/problems in monthly meeting with State Legal Services Authority.
14. Legal Aid Lawyer should maintain file of each case and should make daily entry of proceeding.
15. Legal Aid lawyer should not wait for JJB to call him/her for taking up a case. There should be effort to take up cases on his/her own by way of approaching families who come to JJB.

16. Legal Aid Lawyer should inspire faith and confidence in children/ their families whose cases they take up and should make all possible efforts to get them all possible help.
17. Legal Aid lawyer should abide by the terms and conditions of empanelment on legal Aid Panel.
18. Legal Aid lawyer should tender his/her monthly work done report to JJB within one week of each month for verification and should submit it to concerned authority with attendance certificate for processing payments.
19. Legal Aid Lawyer must inform the client about the next date of hearing and should give his/ her phone number to the client so that they could make call at the time of any need.

Salil Bali v Union Of India & Anr[108]

Facts

Seven Writ petitions and one Transferred Case was taken up together for consideration in view of the commonality of the grounds and reliefs prayed for therein. A common prayer was of seeking declaration of JJ Act, 2000 as ultra vires to provisions of the Constitution and to take steps to bring change in said Act in conformity with provisions of Constitution and United Nations Standard Minimum Rules for administration of juvenile justice due to rising graph of criminal activity of juveniles below age of 18 years was made. The Court dismissed the writ petitions and held that the basis of fixing of the age till when a person could be treated as a child at 18 years in the JJ Act, 2000, was Article 1 of the Convention of the Rights of the Child. If what has come out from the reports of the Crimes Record Bureau, is true, then the number of crimes committed by juveniles comes to about 2% of the country's crime rate. In any event, in the absence of any proper data, it would not be wise to deviate from the provisions of the JJ Act, 2000, which represent the collective wisdom of Parliament. It may not be out of place to mention that in the JJ Act, 1986, male children above the age of 16 years were considered to be adults, whereas girl children were treated as adults on attaining the age of 18 years. In the JJ Act, 2000, a conscious decision was taken by Parliament to raise the age of male juveniles/children to 18 years. In recent years, there has been a spurt in criminal activities by adults, but not so by juveniles, as the materials produced before the Apex Court show.

Held

The age limit which was raised from 16 to 18 years in the JJ Act, 2000, is a decision which was taken by the Government, which is strongly in favour of retaining Sections 2(k) and 2(1) in the manner in which it exists in the Statute Book. The essence of the JJ Act, 2000, and the Rules framed thereunder in 2007, is restorative and not retributive, providing for rehabilitation and reintegration of children in conflict with law into mainstream society. The age of eighteen has been fixed on account of the understanding of experts in child psychology and behavioural patterns that till such

---

[108] AIR 2013 SC 3743.

an age the children in conflict with law could still be redeemed and restored to mainstream society, instead of becoming hardened criminals in future. There are, of course, exceptions where a child in the age group of sixteen to eighteen may have developed criminal propensities, which would make it virtually impossible for him/her to be reintegrated into mainstream society, but such examples are not of such proportions as to warrant any change in thinking, since it is probably better to try and reintegrate children with criminal propensities into mainstream society, rather than to allow them to develop into hardened criminals, which does not augur well for the future. This being the understanding of the Government behind the enactment of the JJ Act, 2000, and the amendments effected thereto in 2006, together with the Rules framed thereunder in 2007, and the data available with regard to the commission of heinous offences by children, within the meaning of Sections 2(k) and 2(1) of the JJ Act, 2000, which the Court did not think that any interference is necessary with the provisions of the Statute till such time as sufficient data is available to warrant any change in the provisions of the aforesaid Act and the Rules. On the other hand, the implementation of the various enactments relating to children, would possibly yield better results.

Ajahar Ali v. State of West Bengal[109]

Facts

Appellant was held guilty in trial for the offence punishable under Section 354 of IPC, 1860. Appellant contended that since the incident occurred more than 18 years ago and at that time the Appellant as well as the complainant were about 16 years of age, he should be given benefit under the provisions of Probation of Offenders Act, 1958 (Act 1958).

Held

It was held that in the instant case, appellant committed a heinous crime and with the social condition prevailing in the society and the modesty of a woman has to be strongly guarded. Noting the conduct of the Appellant in the instant case, it was not held to be appropriate for where benefit of the Act, 1958 could be given to the Appellant. As observed by High Court, that the Appellant was dealt with very leniently and it was a fit case for enhancement of sentence but considering the fact that the incident occurred long back, the High Court refrained to do so. Hence based on the same grounds the appeal accordingly was dismissed by the Supreme Court.

Dr. Subramanian Swamy & Ors. v. Raju Thr. Member Juvenile Justice Board & Anr.[110]

Facts

On 16 December, 2012 a young lady (23 years in age) and her friend were returning home after watching a movie in a multiplex located in one of the glittering malls of Delhi. They boarded a

[109] (2013) 10 SCC 31.
[110] AIR 2014 SC 1649.

bus to undertake a part of the journey back home. While the bus was moving, 5 persons brutally assaulted the young lady, sexually and physically, and also her friend. Both of them were thrown out of the bus. The young lady succumbed to her injuries on 29 December 2012. Five persons were apprehended in connection with the crime. One of five persons identified was below 18 years of age on date of commission of crime. His case referred for inquiry to JJB. Other accused were tried in regular sessions court. The interpretation of the provisions of the act for determination of the question whether offence(s) allegedly committed by juvenile is to be inquired into by JJB or juvenile is required to be tried in regular criminal court?

The JJ Act treated all under 18 as separate category for purpose of differential treatment so far as commission of offences are concerned. Contentions advanced by petitioners to the contrary on strength of thinking and practices in other jurisdiction. It was held, in instant case that there was no question of sending juvenile to face regular trial.

It was urged by the appellant that the relevant provisions of the JJ Act, must be read to mean that juveniles (children below the age of 18) who are intellectually, emotionally, and mentally mature enough to understand the implications of their acts and who have committed serious crimes do not come under the purview of the act Such juveniles are liable to be dealt with under the penal law of the country and by the regular hierarchy of courts under the criminal justice system administered in India. This is what was intended by the Legislature; a plain reading, though, shows an unintended omission which must be made up or furnished by the court. It was further urged that if the act is not read in the above manner the fall out would render the same in breach of Article 14 as inasmuch as in that event there would be a blanket/flat categorization of all juveniles, regardless of their mental and intellectual maturity, committing any offence, regardless of its seriousness, in one homogenous block in spite of their striking dissimilarities.

The petitioner contended, that a classification beyond what would be permissible under Article 14 inasmuch as the result of such classification does not further the targeted object, that is, to confer the benefits of the act to persons below 18 who are not criminally responsible in view of the low level of mental maturity reached or achieved. This, in substance, was also the argument of the learned counsel of the petitioner, who in addition, had contended that the act replaces the criminal justice system of the country by a scheme which is not even a poor substitute. The substituted scheme did not even remotely fit with constitutional tapestry woven by certain basic features namely the existence of a criminal justice system. Reading down the provisions of a statute cannot be resorted to when the meaning thereof is plain and unambiguous and the legislative intent is clear. The fundamental principle of the 'reading down' doctrine can be summarized as follows:

> Courts must read the legislation literally in the first instance. If on such reading and understanding the vice of unconstitutionality is attracted, the courts must explore whether there has been an unintended legislative omission. If such an intendment can be reasonably implied without undertaking what, unmistakably, would be a legislative exercise, the Act may be read down to save it from unconstitutionality.

Held

The Court dismissed the writ petition and held that if the Legislature had adopted the age of 18 as the dividing line between juveniles and adults and such a decision is constitutionally permissible the enquiry by the courts must come to an end. Even otherwise there is a considerable body of world opinion that all under 18 persons ought to be treated as juveniles and separate treatment ought to be meted out to them so far as offences committed by such persons are concerned. The avowed object is to ensure their rehabilitation in society and to enable the young offenders to become useful members of the society in later years.

Shabnam Hashmi v. Union Of India & Ors.[111]

Facts

The petitioner, Shabnam Hashmi had moved this court back in 2005 after she was told that she had only guardianship rights over a young girl she had brought home from an adoption home. Being a Muslim, she was subject to the Muslim Shariat Law which did not recognise an adopted child to be on par with a biological child. In her plea, Hashmi wanted the right to adopt and the right to be adopted to be recognized as Fundamental Rights.

Held

It was decided in this case that the JJ Act, 2000, as amended, is an enabling legislation that gives a prospective parent the option of adopting an eligible child by following the procedure prescribed by the act. Rules and the CARA guidelines, as notified under the act. The Act does not mandate any compulsive action by any prospective parent leaving such person with the liberty of accessing the provisions of the act, if s/he so desires. Such a person is always free to adopt or choose not to do so and instead follow what s/he comprehends to be the dictates of the personal law applicable to him. The JJ Act, 2000 is a small step in reaching the goal enshrined by Article 44 of the Constitution. Personal beliefs and faiths, though must be honoured, cannot dictate the operation of the provisions of an enabling statute. An optional legislation that does not contain an unavoidable imperative cannot be stultified by principles of personal law which, however, would always continue to govern any person who chooses to so submit himself until such time that the vision of a uniform Civil Code is achieved.

Further, the right of child to be adopted and that of prospective parents to adopt cannot be declared as fundamental right under Article 21 of the Constitution. It is not the appropriate time and stage where right to adopt and right to be adopted can be raised to status of fundamental right and/or to understand such right to be encompassed by Article 21 of the Constitution. Elevation of right to adopt or to be adopted to the status of fundamental right will have to await dissipation of conflicting thought processes in this sphere of practices and belief prevailing in country.

Suggestions for Law Reform

It is evident that there is a great disparity between what CNCP and conflict with law need, what they[112]have been promised by law, and what the reality of their situation is. Urgent and

---

[111] AIR 2014 SC 1281.

[112] Atiya Bose and Suparna Gupta, *Areal Opportrunity for Change – What Young Offenders Need and How Probation Officers Respond—A Study in Maharashtra* (Mumbai, India: Aangan Trust). Available at http://aanganindia.org/pdf/real-oppourtunity-for-change.pdf (accessed on 17 November 2016).

decisive action is needed in order for the crisis that the Juvenile Justice system faces to be ameliorated. The law reform needs to include the following action points:

Right of the Child to be Heard

This right imposes a clear legal obligation on states parties to recognize this right and ensure its implementation by listening to the views of the child and according them due weight. This obligation requires that states parties, with respect to their particular judicial system, either directly guarantee this right, or adopt or revise laws so that this right can be fully enjoyed by the child. There is a need for such child friendly mechanism in the JJBs and CWCs.

Diversion from Judicial Proceedings

Diversion means referring cases away from formal criminal justice proceedings towards community support to avoid the negative effects of being implicated in such proceedings. Diversionary measures can come into play at any stage—at the time of the arrest or immediately before the foreseen court hearing—either as a generally applicable procedure or on the decision of the police, prosecutor, court or similar body. The fundamental premise behind diversion is to hinder the negative effects of subsequent proceedings in juvenile justice administration for example the stigma of conviction and sentence. The alternative to formal adjudication must be compatible with the rights of the child which preclude measures such as corporal punishment. Diversion may involve a restorative justice component. Restorative justice is an approach that recognises how crime affects the victim, the community, and the offender. Its primary focus is to repair the damage caused by the offence, to make reparation to the community and to the victim, and to return the offender to a productive place in the community. For justice to be truly restorative, the community, the victim, and the offender must take active roles.

States shall seek to promote the establishment of measures for dealing with children in conflict with the law without resorting to judicial proceedings, provided that human rights and legal safeguards are fully respected (UNCRC, Article 40). The police, the prosecution, or other agencies dealing with juvenile cases shall be empowered to dispose of such cases, at their discretion, without recourse to formal hearings. Any diversion involving referral to appropriate community or other services shall require the consent of the juvenile, or her or his parents or guardian, provided that such decisions to refer a case shall be subject to review by a competent authority, upon application (Beijing Rules).

According to Article 40 (3) of UNCRC, the states parties shall seek to promote measures for dealing with children alleged as, accused of, or recognized as having infringed the penal law without resorting to judicial proceedings, whenever appropriate and desirable. Given the fact that the majority of child offenders commit only minor offences, a range of measures involving removal from criminal/juvenile justice processing and referral to alternative (social) services (that is, diversion) should be a well-established practice that can and should be used in most cases. Promoting measures for dealing with children in conflict with the law without resorting to judicial proceedings applies, but is certainly not limited to children who commit minor offences, such as shoplifting or other property offences with limited damage and first-time child offenders. Statistics in many states parties indicate that a large part, and often the majority, of offences committed by children fall into these categories. It is in line with the principles set out in Article 40(1) of UNCRC to deal with all such cases without resorting to criminal law procedures in court. In addition to avoiding stigmatization, this approach has good results for children, is in the interests of public safety, and has proven to be cost-effective. The state parties should take measures for dealing with children in conflict with the law without resorting to judicial proceedings as an integral part of their juvenile justice system, and ensure that children's human rights and legal safeguards are thereby fully respected and protected (Article 40(3)). A variety of community-based programmes have been developed, such as community service, supervision and guidance by, for example, social workers or probation officers, and family conferencing and other forms of restorative justice including restitution to and compensation of victims. Diversion (that is, measures for dealing with children, alleged as, accused of, or recognized as having infringed the penal law without resorting to judicial proceedings) should be used only when there is compelling evidence that the child committed the alleged offence, that s/he freely and voluntarily admits responsibility, no intimidation or pressure has been used to get that admission and, the admission will not be used against him/her in any subsequent legal proceeding. The child must freely and voluntarily give consent in writing to the diversion, a consent that should be based on adequate and specific information on the nature, content, and duration of the measure, and on the consequences of a failure to cooperate, carry out, and complete the measure. The JJ Act, 2000 does not contain any provisions for the diversion of children away from the formal system. All children who are arrested by the police are to be brought before the JJB for a formal determination of guilt and disposition. There must be a provision for diversion in the JJ Act.

Review of Guidelines for and Training of Staff and Personnel

A departmental review of recruitment guidelines for staff and personnel in the JJ system to ensure that appropriate personnel are hired for this position. This should include determining requisite qualifications, experience, and skills as well as detailing a job description according to the JJ Act and Rules Planning, a structured training program for them that includes training on key functions such as interview skills, writing the SIR, making a care plan, supervision and mentoring. Trainings should be continuously held, and the staff should be required to undergo periodic refresher trainings. A review should be held of caseload distribution and the corresponding staffing pattern across the state with the view to provide high-density districts.

Reform in Juvenile Justice Boards

The interpretations, procedures, and perceptions of juvenile justice system have today transformed the juvenile court from its original model as a social service agency into a deficient, second-rate, marginalized criminal court. Juvenile Courts have to be revitalized with the most expansive vision and based upon a deeper understanding of the psychological and social forces which bring children into court. There has to be a JJB that is sensitive to the developmental needs of juveniles in each case, flexible enough to respond to new discoveries in social science research, and willing to invest in and experiment with promising new interventions for offenders. JJBs should be vital community resources. A developmental perspective may be usefully employed in formulating legal responses.[113] Interventions in the JJBs should have educational, mental health, and social service components. It has been found that multisystemic therapy shows promise with young offenders.[114] Personnel in the JJBs are the key. Unless the JJBs can identify and train good people, juvenile justice systems will not realize their potential. Judges in JJBs should be especially trained to recognize the educational, social, and treatment needs of children and families in crisis. The orders cannot be passed in isolation; knowing and tapping the available services for such children should be the first priority.

It is significant to note that currently, there is too much reliance on plea bargaining. When a child is in an institution or before strangers, s/he is asked to choose between going to trial and pleading guilty. The deal is almost impossible to resist. A child's response to such an offer may not be voluntary. In a JJB , plea bargaining is particularly destructive. Children who are scared cannot understand the various forces at work. This negotiation does not further the interest of the child but furthers the interest of the system.[115] Pressures are generally applied by probation officers to encourage children to plead guilty. Children who are not guilty and who have to plead to something that he did not do, undermine the entire system. In future, plea bargaining need not be done without a representative of the child's best interest.

A JJB of the twenty-first century must have interdisciplinary connections with a variety of professions: law, medicine, psychiatry, psychology, and child welfare administration and management.

There should be speedy disposal of cases involving children in order to ensure that the developmental needs of the child are addressed and the child continues to attain his/her growth and development.

- Community-based correction includes activities and programmes within the community that have effective ties with local environment with employment, education, and social and clinical service delivery systems including drug abuse prevention services.
- Computerized facilities should be introduced for recording social histories and court records. Investigating social histories offer valuable perspectives. It is important to keep records of repeat offences. The traditional confidentially of juvenile court records and proceedings must be replaced by greater transparency and openness.
- The basic human rights of the child must be protected in the JJBs . In re Gault,[116] the Supreme Court of the USA laid down the following basic rights in a Juvenile Court:

---

[113] See Elizabeth S. Scott and Thomas Grisso, 'The Evolution of Adolescence: A Developmental Perspective on Juvenile Justice Reform', Journal of Criminal Law and Criminology, 88, no. 1, 1997.

Developmental models help to understand how we become the people we are. According to Professor Erikson's model, each period of life has its 'own particular challenges and hurdles and from the way each child resolves or facts to resolve these may come an enduring set of responses in the future. Each stage brings with it a new social role, a new set of tasks to be mastered, new patterns of interaction, and new emotions. Erikson's theory relates to identity development.

[114] See David Tate, N. Dickon Reppucci, and Edward P. Mulvey, 'Violent Juvenile Delinquents: Treatment Effectiveness and Implications for Future Action', 50 am Psychologist, 777, 779 (1995). This therapy is directed at solving the youth's multiple problems in many contexts—family, peers, schools, and neighbourhood.

[115] Thomas F. Geraghty, 'Justice for Children: How Do We Get There?' Journal of Criminal Law and Criminology, 88, 1997.

[116] In re Gault, 38 US 1 (1967).

- Notice of charges
- Right to counsel
- Right to confrontation and cross-examination
- Privilege against self-incrimination
- Right to a transcript of proceedings
- Right to appellate review
- The juvenile court should be able to supervise the control over services that are provided for the child. A court should be able to hold a state agency responsible for the treatment of children.

Juvenile treatment and correctional facilities are unlikely to perform well without the oversight of an independent ombudsman, as the children in their care are powerless.—

And finally, best interest of the child in juvenile justice must integrate and link the conduct of all who work in juvenile justice system—CWC members, social workers, prosecutors, defence lawyers, judges, mental health professionals, NGOs, and probation officers.

Legal Aid and Assistance in the Juvenile Justice System

Juveniles should have the right of legal counsel and be enabled to apply for free legal aid, where such aid is available, and to communicate regularly with their legal advisers. Privacy and confidentiality shall be ensured for such communications. As per Section 16 of Vienna Guidelines, Priority should be given to setting up agencies and programmes to provide legal and other assistance to children, if needed free of charge, such as interpretation services, and, in particular, to ensure that the right of every child to have access to such legal aid and assistance from the moment that the child is detained is respected in practice. The JJ Act allows the presence of a legal practitioner before the JJB.[117] However, in the case of CNCP, there is no such provison. This needs to be rectified.[118] There should be some support person to represent the views of children before the CWC. The legal aid lawyers must be provided special training to deal with cases of children

The law must be implemented in its true spirit. A Special Committee to be constituted immediately dispose of all cases pending before the JJBs and CWCs. Rehabilitation and Reintegration care plans of children to be included in orders of JJBs and CWCs. Separate homes for juveniles in conflict with law apprehended after they have turned 18 years of age.

Need to Develop the Concept of Restorative Justice in Juvenile Justice Jurisprudence

The word restorative means to restore or make restitution, that is to bring back to an original condition or to put someone back in a former position. Whereas justice means quality of being

[117] JJ Act, Article 28(1)(6).
[118] The amendment to Rule 6(33C)(3) of the Maharashtra Amended JJ Rules, 2011 wherein JJBs can appoint NGO partners to provide paralegal and other services provides the necessary framework.

just and equitable.[119] Restorative justice is a process whereby all the parties with a stake in a particular offense and its implication for future are brought together to face each other, inform each other about their crimes and victimization, and collectively reach an agreement on a penalty or sanction. It is centrally concerned with restoration of the victim, as well as restoration of the offender to a law. This process has emerged as a new form of justice in the criminal administration of justice. It may be seen as a criminal justice embedded in social context. In many countries around the world, juvenile justice legislations are guided by a balanced and restorative justice philosophy, 'the protection of the public interest, to provide for children committing delinquent acts programs of supervision, care, and rehabilitation that provide balanced attention to the protection of the community, the imposition of accountability for offenses committed, and the development of competencies to enable children to become responsible and productive members of the community'.

The juvenile justice statues in US generally lay down provisions 'to protect, restore, and improve the public safety ... provide the opportunity to bring together affected victims, the community, and juvenile offenders for restorative purposes'. Further, 'while holding paramount the public safety, the juvenile justice system shall take into consideration the best interests of the juvenile, the victims, and the community in providing appropriate treatment to reduce the rate of recidivism'.[120]

This is an emerging concept in Indian juvenile justice administration and jurisprudence in India. In the *State of Gujarat* v. *Raghavbai Vasrambhai and Ors*, the judge opines that 'in realm of victimology the decision is one of the aspect towards the fulfilling the design and desideratum and restorative justice to the victims of crime'. Again in the case of *Anupam Sharma* v. *NCT Delhi and Anr.*, the court observed: 'Restorative justice may be used as a synonym for mediation. The object and nature of restorative justice aims at restoring the interest of the victim. Involvement of the victim in the settlement process is wlcome in the process of restorative justice. It is a process of voluntary negotiation and concertaion girectly or indirectly between the offender and the victim'.

In the rules on JJ Act, 2007, the concept of restorative justice has been promoted. The definition of detention states that the detention in case of JICLs means 'protective custody' which is in line with principles of restorative justice. The principle of best interest of the child shall mean that the traditional objectives of criminal justice, retribution, and repression, must give way to rehabilitative and restorative objectives of juvenile justice.

There is a need to further develop this concept into juvenile justice.

[119] Karanshubh, 'Criminal Law, Restorative Justice and Weaker Sections: Role of Judiciary in the perspective of Delinquency Prevention', 6 April 2011. Available at http://www.legalservicesindia.com/article/article/restorative-justice-&-weaker-sections-623-1.html (accessed on 17 November 2016).

[120] Sandra Pavelka, 'Restorative Juvenile Justice Legislation and Policy: A National Assessment', *International Journal of Restorative Justice*, 4, no. 2, 2008. Available at www.crjcs.org (accessed on 17 November 2016).

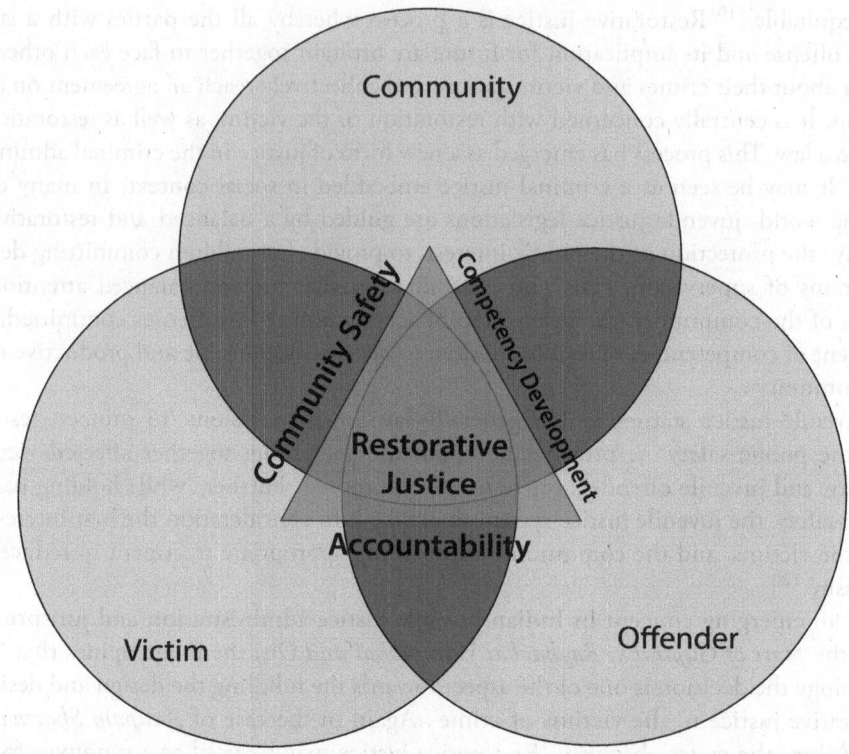

Figure 6.6 Restorative Justice Practices[121]

Juvenile Justice (Care and Protection of Children) Bill, 2014[122]

The JJ Act, 2000 has been amended twice in 2006 and 2011.[123] 23-year-old Nirbhaya, a paramedical student, was gang raped by six persons on a moving bus in Delhi and one of them was found to be a minor, just a few months short of turning 18. The teenager was found guilty of taking part in the gang rape. In fact, during the pendency of the trial, the juvenile accused attained majority. Yet, he was tried as a juvenile as the law treats a person as a juvenile if at the time of the commission of offence he/she was below 18 years of age. He was sent to a correctional home for 3 years as per JJ Act 2000. The case against the juvenile offender had sparked a lot of public outrage with demands being raised to bring down the age to be declared juvenile from 18 to 16 years. After this, the juvenile justice legislation after that has been

[121] Source: Division of Juvenile Justice, State of Alaska Department of Health and Social Services. Available at http://dhss.alaska.gov/djj/Pages/GeneralInfo/RJ.aspx (accessed on 23 June 2015).

[122] PRS Legislative Research. Available at http://www.prsindia.org/uploads/media/Juvenile%20Justice/Legislative%20Brief%20Juvenile%20Justice%20Bill.pdf (accessed on 12 June 2015).

[123] The act was amended twice in 2006 and 2011 to make it more child-friendly and to remove discriminatory references to children suffering from certain diseases.

subject to intense debate among academia, civil society, professionals, peoples' organizations, and the state.

The Ministry of Women and Child Development had introduced the JJ Bill, 2014 in the Lok Sabha on 12 August 2014. This draft bill provisions responded to the perceptions, articulated by a wide cross-section of society for the need to have an effective and strengthened system of administration of juvenile justice, care and protection. The proposed legislation, which would replace the existing JJ Act, 2000, clearly defined and classified offences as petty, serious and heinous, and defined differentiated processes for each category. Recognizing the rights of the victims as being equally important as the rights of juveniles, special provisions were proposed to tackle heinous offences committed by individuals in this age group. Further, a Parliamentary Standing Committee on Human Resource Development was set up for examination of the bill.

Significant Provisions of the 2014 Bill[124]

- The bill permits juveniles between the ages of 16–18 years to be tried as adults for heinous offences. Also, any 16–18 year old, who commits a lesser, that is, serious offence may be tried as an adult only if he is apprehended after the age of 21 years.
- The JJB and CWC will be constituted in each district. The JJB will conduct a preliminary inquiry to determine whether a juvenile offender is to be sent for rehabilitation or be tried as an adult. The CWC will determine institutional care for CNCP.
- Eligibility of adoptive parents and the procedure for adoption have been included in the bill.
- Penalties for cruelty against a child, offering a narcotic substance to a child, and abduction or selling a child have been prescribed.

The JJ Bill, 2014, has brought in changes which have raised several concerns. The bill is a violation of Constitution of India, Indian and international laws and norms. This bill violates the United Nations Convention on the Rights of the Child since it requires every child under 18 to be treated as equal. Article 14, that is, right to equality, can also be violated in that sense. Moreover, it seems to also violate the Article 20(1) of Indian Constitution for it is according higher penalty to the same offence if the adult is apprehended after 21 years of age.

Some of the principles that would be violated by its implementation are the best interest of the child, principle of fresh start, principle of equality and non-discrimination, principle of right to privacy and confidentiality. The provision that enables the JJB to transfer into the criminal justice system a child above 16 years of age who has committed a heinous offence has been made with no basic understanding of ground realities or research studies or documented evidence about the working of the system across the country. The other arguments against treating juvenile offenders are as follows:

[124] Apoorva Shankar and Tanvi Deshpande, 'Legislative Brief', Juvenile Justice (Care and Protection of Children) Bill, 2014, PRS Legislative Research, Institute for Policy Research Studies, New Delhi, 20 April 2015.

1. Vulnerability may be a result of factors like age, gender, caste, class, community, region, religion, natural calamities, dysfunctional families, poverty etc. Many children may be perceived as being in conflict with law when actually they may be in need of care and protection and vice-versa. The National Crime Record Bureau statistics from 2013 indicates that the number of FIRs filed against juveniles stand at 1.2 per cent of the total crimes committed. Also JICL alleged to have committed serious offences constitute a miniscule population. National Crime Records Bureau's Report reveals that the juvenile crimes accounted for only 0.5 per cent of total crimes committed in 2013.[125] The rationale for changing an entire legislation on the basis of these low numbers is untenable.

2. Children who are in conflict with the law have a lesser culpability than adults because they 'differ from adults in their physical and psychological development, and their emotional and educational needs'.[126] Even at ages 16 and 17, when compared to adults, juveniles on average are more impulsive, aggressive, emotionally volatile, likely to take risks, reactive to stress, and prone to focus on and overestimate short-term payoffs and underplay longer-term consequences of what they do.[127] The failed example of the USA's experiment with transferring adolescent offenders over 16 years into the adult criminal system has proved that it was a mistake to exclude these children from juvenile justice as they have been found to be more prone to reoffending than those who were not so transferred

3. The chances of reformation and reintegration of 16–18 years old convicted through the adult criminal justice system and released thereafter will be very slim as they will face stigma, societal isolation, and disqualification from many jobs.

4. Dr. Laurence Steinberg's research on the adolescent brain is that teenagers are not as mature in either brain structure or function as adults.[128]

5. The provision in Clause 7 of the bill[129]which mandates the trial of any person as an adult if apprehended after completing 21 years of age for committing any serious or heinous offence, when they were between 16 to 18 years, is against Article 20 and 20 (1) of the Constitution of India and the Supreme Court judgments.

6. Rehabilitation continues to be one of the weakest aspects of the proposed bill. Children in institutions are particularly affected by the lack of adequate rehabilitation options, thus affecting their social reintegration.

[125] National Crime Records Bureau, *Report: Crime in India, 2013.* Available at http://ncrb.gov.in/CD-CII2013/home.asp (accessed on 17 November 2016).

[126] Penal Reform International, 'The Minimum Age of Criminal Responsibility', Justice for Children Briefing No. 4, 2013. Available at http://www.penalreform.org/wp-content/uploads/2013/05/justice-for-children-briefing-4-v6-web_0.pdf (accessed on 17 November 2016).

[127] Teens' ability to consider what might happen later on is still developing. See L. Steinberg, E. Cauffman, J. Woolard, S. Graham, and M. Banich, 'Are Adolescents Less Mature Than Adults? Minors' Access to Abortion, the Juvenile Death Penalty, and the Alleged APA "Flip-Flop", *American Psychologist*, 64, 583–94 (2009).

[128] Michael F. Caldwell, 'Juvenile Sexual Offenders', in *Choosing the Future for American Juvenile Justice*, ed. Franklin E. Zimring and David S. Tanehaus. Available at http://nyupress.org/books/book-details.aspx-?bookid=12281#.U6ERT_IW4Wk (accessed on 17 November 2016).

[129] Clause 7: Trial as adults of children apprehended after completion of 21 years for committing serious or heinous offences.

7. The entire section on Aftercare has been omitted in the bill. Instead, the child leaving the institution on attaining 18 years of age is provided with a one-time financial assistance. The bill does not lay any responsibility on the state to provide aftercare facilities.
8. The JJ Bill 2014 has mandated the District Child Protection Unit (DCPU) as an implementation body. The DCPU is a branch of Integrated Child Protection Scheme (ICPS). In majority of the states, ICPS is implemented through a Society which appoints people on contractual basis. It is not a good strategy to put the entire responsibility of implementation of the provisions of the JJ Act on a body which runs on contractual staff.
9. Proposing to promote foreign adoption, is opening its doors to possibility of unethical practices. Another concern is also the impact that the shortened time frame of 30 days period of reconsideration for surrender and relinquishment of a child by birth-parents in compelling socio-economic situations

It is recommended that there is a need to strengthen the implementation of the existing Juvenile Justice system. Provide human resources, infrastructure, and protocols and ensure implementation of the existing Act through strict monitoring without reducing the age. The juvenile justice legislation must continue to have a socio legal approach. Governments need not succumb to the pressures being put by a section of the society to enact a new regressive law on juvenile justice and must instead think of ways to activate and implement the current legislation in its true letter and spirit.[130]

The 2014 Bill was referred to the Department related Parliamentary Standing Committee.[131] In their report of 25 February 2015, the Committee made several recommendations to further strengthen the bill. Most of the recommendations of the Committee have been accepted. Accordingly, the Ministry of Women and Child Development proposed to undertake Amendment to the said bill on the basis of the recommendations of the Committee.

The major recommendations of the Standing Committee to the 2014 Bill include:

- **Constitutional provisions:** The Committee noted that the 2000 Act recognises the sensitive age of 16–18 year old and is reformative and rehabilitative in nature. Subjecting juveniles to the adult judicial system would go against the principle of Articles 14 (unequal treatment of 16–18 year old) and 15(3) (against the objective of protecting children) of the Constitution. It also said that the bill was in violation of Articles 20(1) and 21 of the Constitution. It was also noted by the Committee that clauses 7[132] and 21[133] of the proposed legislation were also unconstitutional and contrary to the established principle of juvenile justice. It is the characteristics inherent in a child that requires child offenders to be treated differently from adult.

---

[130] Available at http://www.thehindu.com/news/national/karnataka/amendment-to-juvenile-justice-act-criticised/article7140406.ece (accessed on 12 June 2015).

[131] *Two Hundred Sixty Four Report*, Juvenile Justice (Care and Protection of Children), presented to the Rajya Sabha on 25 February 2015.

[132] Clause 7: Trial as adults of children apprehended after completion of 21 years for committing serious or heinous offences.

[133] Clause 21(1): Evaluation by children's court whether child has undergone reformation and can make meaningful contributions to society.

Therefore, it would be the age of the person on the date on which the offence was committed that would determine whether such person was to be dealt with under the juvenile justice system or the criminal justice system.

- **National Crime Records Bureau (NCRB) Data:** One of the reasons cited for the Bill's introduction is an increase in heinous offences committed by 16–18 year old. The Committee stated that this data compiled by NCRB is misleading as it is based on filing of FIRs and not actual convictions. It was pointed out that the percentage of juvenile crimes to total crimes in India has been a miniscule 1.2 per cent only and that the percentage of violent crimes committed by juveniles could even be smaller. It was 25 contended that there was misconception among the public that the number of children committing offences, more particularly violent offences, such as rape and murder, was on the increase.

- **Implementation:** The committee observed that the act is not being implemented well. It recommended better implementation and uniform establishment of systems and procedures, by all agencies.

Amendments to the Juvenile Justice (Care and Protection of Children) Bill, 2014

On 22 April 2015, the Union Cabinet, has approved the introduction of Amendment to the Juvenile Justice (Care and Protection of Children) Bill, 2014. [134]

The new proposed Act provides that in case a heinous crime has been committed by a person in the age group of 16–18 years it will be examined by the JJB to assess if the crime was committed as a 'child' or as an 'adult'. This assessment will take place by the board which will have psychologists and social experts, the trial of the case will accordingly take place as a juvenile or as an adult on the basis of this assessment.

The new legislation proposed to streamline adoption procedures for orphaned, abandoned and surrendered children. It establishes a statutory status for the CARA. The legislation further proposed several rehabilitation and social integration measures for institutional and non-institutional children. It also provided for sponsorship and foster care as completely new measures. It provided for mandatory registration of all institutions engaged in providing child care. New offences including illegal adoption, corporal punishment in child care institutions, the use of children by militant groups, and offences against disabled children were also incorporated in the proposed legislation.

Under this 2015 amendment, Juveniles of 16–18 years who commit heinous crimes like rape are to be 'transferred' and be treated as an adult. It is based on an assessment whether the crime was committed as a 'child' or as an 'adult'. The assessment would be done by psychologists and social experts of JJB. Secondly, any 16–18 year old, who commits a lesser, that is, serious offence, may be tried as an adult only if he is apprehended after the age of 21 years.

Reformation and rehabilitation as opposed to retribution is the essence of juvenile justice system. In 2014, in *Dr. Subramanian Swamy & Ors. Vs. Raju & Anr.*,[135]the Apex Court upheld

---

[134] Press Information Bureau, 'Amendments to the Juvenile Justice (Care and Protection of Children) Bill', Government of India, 22 April 2015. Available at http://pib.nic.in/newsite/PrintRelease.aspx-?relid=118528 (accessed on 17 November 2016).

[135] Criminal Appeal No. 695 of 2014.

the treatment of all persons 'under 18 as a separate category for the purposes of differential treatment so far as commission of offences are concerned' under the JJ Act, 2000. The Justice J.S. Justice Verma [Retd.] Committee, constituted by the then Government of India to examine the law regarding sexual assault against women, declined to recommend reduction of the age of juvenility to 16 years. While arriving at its conclusion, the Committee referred to the decreasing rates of recidivism, as also to 'the neurological state of the adolescent brain'. The Parliamentary Standing Committee that examined the bill has also submitted its detailed objections to waiver of juveniles into the adult system. Having found waiver as unconstitutional, the Committee recommended strengthening the implementation of the existing law. It also observed, '...there were provisions in the act of 2000 itself, that is, Section 16 to deal with children between 16–18 who have committed serious crime which were within the juvenile system and there was no need to push those children into adult criminal system, a move which could be described as retributive only'.[136] Hence there is no rational or scientific, or legal basis for excluding children from juvenile justice system. On the basis of the approval of the Cabinet, an amendment to the Juvenile Justice (Care and Protection of Children) Bill, 2014 will be introduced in the current session of Parliament. It is hoped that the parliamentarians are sensitive to the vulnerabilities of children and consider the rights of children.

We still have a long way to go in achieving full compliance with Constitutional provisions, international law like UNCRC and General Comment 10, for example, in the areas of procedural rights, the development and implementation of measures for dealing with children in conflict with the law without resorting to judicial proceedings, and the use of deprivation of liberty only as a measure of last resort. We need to strengthen the implementation of these provisions.

Juvenile Justice (Care and Protection of Children) Act, 2015

The JJ Act, 2015 came into force on 1 January 2016 after it received the President's assent on 31 December, 2015. It was passed on 7 May 2015 by the Lok Sabha and passed on 22 December 2015 by the RajyaSabha.[137] The passing of the act was prompted by a public outcry on the release of the minor involved in the gruesome 16 December 2012 gang-rape incident on completion of his 3-year term in a juvenile home. Four of the five co-accused who were adultsin that case are facing death penalty. The juvenile rapist in Nirbhaya case (of Delhi gangrape) who was only 17 years and few months from completing his 18 years of age, escaped jail and stiff punishment with his co-accused, lodged in jail and convicted. It was the sustained public pressure and outcry led by Nirbhaya's parents which compelled a stalled Rajya Sabha to debate and pass the law in one single day.[138]

---

[136] Available at http://thewire.in/2015/05/23/a-dislocation-of-the-juvenile-justice-system/ (accessed on 17 November 2016).

[137] Available at http://wcd.nic.in/sites/default/files/gazette%20notification_0.pdf (accessed on 20 February 2016).

[138] Available at http://www.hindustantimes.com/punjab/amended-juvenile-justice-act-is-a-message-for-society/story MJEUTpHKthryaLFkndJUpL.html (accessed on 20 February 2016).

Salient Features of the Juvenile Justice Act, 2015

The objectives of the act are to consolidate and amend the law relating to children alleged and found to be in conflict with law and CNCP by catering to their basic needs through proper care, protection, development, treatment, social reintegration, by adopting a child-friendly approach in the adjudication and disposal of matters in the best interest of children and for their rehabilitation through processes provided, and institutions and bodies established, under the act.[139]

'Child' means a person who has not completed 18 years of age;[140] new definitions such as orphaned,[141]abandoned[142] and surrendered[143]children, petty,[144] serious[145] and heinous[146] offences committed by children. There are three categories of offences under the act:

1. Petty offences includes the offences for which the maximum punishment under the IPC or any other law for the time being in force is imprisonment up to 3 years.
2. 'Serious offences' includes the offences for which the punishment under the IPC or any other law for the time being in force, is imprisonment between 3 and 7 years and
3. 'Heinous offences' includes the offences for which the minimum punishment under the IPC or any other law for the time being in force is imprisonment for 7 years or more

- The word juvenile has been replaced by the word child in the act[147] and the words alleged and found to be in conflict with law, instead of the term JICL.[148]

---

[139] JJ Act, 2015, Preamble.

[140] JJ Act, 2015, Section 2(12): 'Child' means a person who has not completed 18 years of age.

[141] JJ Act, 2015, Section 2(42): 'Orphan' means a child—

(1)   who is without biological or adoptive parents or legal guardian; or
(2)   whose legal guardian is not willing to take, or capable of taking care of the child.

[142] JJ Act, 2015, 'abandoned child' means a child deserted by his biological or adoptive parents or guardians, who has been declared as abandoned by the Committee after due inquiry.

[143] JJ Act, 2015, Section 2(60): 'Surrendered child' means a child, who is relinquished by the parent or guardian to the committee, on account of physical, emotional, and social factors beyond their control, and declared as such by the committee.

[144] JJ Act, 2015, Section 2(45): 'Petty offences' includes the offences for which the maximum punishment under the IPC or any other law for the time being in force is imprisonment up to 3 years.

[145] JJ Act, 2015, Section 2(54): 'Serious offences' includes the offences for which the punishment under the Indian Penal Code or any other law for the time being in force, is imprisonment between 3 and 7 years.

[146] JJ Act, 2015, Section 2(33): 'Heinous offences' includes the offences for which the minimum punishment under the IPC or any other law for the time being in force is imprisonment for 7 years or more.

[147] JJ Act, 2015, Section 2(13): 'Child in conflict with law' means a child who is alleged or found to have committed an offence and who has not completed 18 years of age on the date of commission of such offence.

[148] JJ Act, 2015, Preamble.

- There was no definition of abandoned child in the JJ Act 2000. In the 2015 Act, the CWC is required to declare child as abandoned after due inquiry.[149]
- There have been changes in understanding of CNCP which are to be dealt with by the CWCs. Under the 2015 Act:[150] The word "Or" has been added at the end of each category of CNCP.
- Establishment of CWC along with JJBs in each district.[151]
- The definition of Special Home has been revised. Special Home has been defined to mean an NGO, registered under Section 48, for housing and providing rehabilitative services to children in conflict with law, who are found, through inquiry, to have committed an offence and are sent to such institution by an order of the board.[152]
- Principle of family responsibility has been brought about.[153]It has been stated that 'itis the primary duty for families to care, to nurture, and protect the child whether they be the biological parents or adoptive or foster'. This law is also asking for 'all resources to be mobilized including those of family and community, for promoting the well being, facilitating development of identity and providing an inclusive and enabling environment to reduce vulnerabilities of children and the need for intervention under this Act'.[154] The school teacher, the community Pradhan, the neighbourhood watch group, the neighbours, the community NGOs, and more. This is one of the many Principles set out for care and protection of children. The Act also places the responsibility of prevention on families and the community, the neighbourhood watch group as a whole. This also means that reformation homes must associate community volunteers in bringing about reformation while they are inside correctional homes and not keep volunteers away. This law is saying clearly to seek out and collaborate and follow the participatory model.[155]

---

[149] JJ Act, 2015, Section 2(1): 'Abandoned child' means a child deserted by his/her biological or adoptive parents or guardians, who has been declared as abandoned by the committee after due inquiry.

[150] 'Categories of Children in Need of Care and Protection under JJ Act, 2015' prepared by Anant Kumar Asthana via googlegroups.com, dated 15 January 2016.

[151] JJ Act, 2015, Section 27.

[152] JJ Act, 2015, Section 2(56): 'Special home' means an institution established by a state government or by a voluntary or NGO, registered under Section 48, for housing and providing rehabilitative services to children in conflict with law, who are found, through inquiry, to have committed an offence and are sent to such institution by an order of the board.

[153] JJ Act, 2015, Section 3(v): Principle of family responsibility: The primary responsibility of care, nurture, and protection of the child shall be that of the biological family or adoptive or foster parents, as the case may be.

[154] JJ Act, 2015, Section 3(vii): Positive measures: All resources are to be mobilized including those of family and community, for promoting the well-being, facilitating development of identity and providing an inclusive and enabling environment, to reduce vulnerabilities of children and the need for intervention under this act.

[155] JJ Act, 2015, Section 49(1): The state government shall set up at least one place of safety in a state registered under Section 41, so as to place a person above the age of 18 years or child in conflict with law, who is between the age of 16 and 18 years and is accused of or convicted for committing a heinous offence.

- Permits trying of juveniles between the ages of 16 and 18 years as adults for heinous offences.[156] The JJB is given the option to transfer cases of heinous offences by such children to a children's court (court of sessions) after conducting preliminary assessment.[157] The Act provides for placing such 'offender children' in a 'place of safety' both during and after the trial till they attain the age of 21, after which his/her evaluation shall be conducted by the children's court. Empowers JJB to examine the nature of crime and decide whether it was committed as a child mind or as an adult mind. Based upon the preliminary inquiry of JJB, juvenile offender will be either sent for rehabilitation or will be tried as an adult. Most importantly juveniles committing heinous crimes such as of rape and or murder and are between the age 16–18 years of age can now be tried as adults if the JJB after due deliberations come to this assessment.[158]After the evaluation, the child is either released on probation and if not reformed, he/she will be sent to a jail for the remaining term.

[156] JJ Act, 2015, Section 19:

(1) After the receipt of preliminary assessment from the board under Section 15, the Children's Court may decide that (i) there is a need for trial of the child as an adult as per the provisions of the CrPC, 1973 and pass appropriate orders after trial subject to the provisions of this section and Section 21, considering the special needs of the child, the tenets of fair trial and maintaining a child friendly atmosphere and (ii) there is no need for trial of the child as an adult and may conduct an inquiry as a board and pass appropriate orders in accordance with the provisions of Section 18.

(2) The Children's Court shall ensure that the final order, with regard to a child in conflict with law, shall include an individual care plan for the rehabilitation of child, including follow up by the probation officer or the district child protection unit or a social worker.

(3) The Children's Court shall ensure that the child who is found to be in conflict with law is sent to a place of safety till he attains the age of 21 years and thereafter, the person shall be transferred to a jail, provided that the reformative services including educational services, skill development, alternative therapy such as counselling, behaviour modification therapy, and psychiatric support shall be provided to the child during the period of his/her stay in the place of safety.

(4) The Children's Court shall ensure that there is a periodic follow up report every year by the probation officer or the District Child Protection Unit or a social worker, as required, to evaluate the progress of the child in the place of safety and to ensure that there is no ill-treatment to the child in any form.

(5) The reports under Subsection (4) shall be forwarded to the Children's Court for record and follow up, as may be required.

[157] JJ Act, 2015, Section 18(3): Where the board after preliminary assessment under Section 15 pass an order that there is a need for trial of the said child as an adult, then the board may order transfer of the trial of the case to the Children's Court having jurisdiction to try such offences.

[158] JJ Act, 2015, Section 19:

(1) After the receipt of preliminary assessment from the board under Section 15, the Children's Court may decide that— (i) there is a need for trial of the child as an adult as per the provisions of the CrPC, 1973 and pass appropriate orders after trial subject to the provisions of this section and Section 21, considering the special needs of the child, the tenets of fair trial and maintaining a child friendly atmosphere; (ii) there is no need for trial of the child as an adult and may conduct an inquiry as a Board and pass appropriate orders in accordance with the provisions of Section 18.

(2) The Children's Court shall ensure that the final order, with regard to a child in conflict with law, shall include an individual care plan for the rehabilitation of child, including follow up by the probation officer or the District Child Protection Unit or a social worker.

- Empowers JJB to examine the nature of crime and decide whether it was committed as a child mind or as an adult mind. Based upon the preliminary inquiry of JJB, juvenile offender will be either sent for rehabilitation or will be tried as an adult. Most importantly, juveniles committing heinous crimes such as of rape and/or murder and are between the age 16–18 years of age can now be tried as adults if the JJB after due deliberations come to this assessment.[159]
- If the JJB is satisfied that the child brought before it has not committed any offence—it can pass an order to that effect. In case of CNCP, JJB could refer the child to the CWC with appropriate directions.[160]
- Community service should be under the supervision of an organization or person identified by JJB.[161]
- The functions of the JJB include ensuring informed participation of the child, protection of rights throughout, providing legal aid, interpreters, and translators. They must direct the PO/CWO/SW to submit the SIR within 15 days from the date of the first production to ascertain circumstances in which the alleged offence was committed. The JJB can transfer to the CWC matters concerning care and protection of a CICL. ICP for rehabilitation should be included in the final order along with follow-up by the PO/DCPU/NGO. They must conduct at least one inspection a month of residential facilities for CICLS and recommend action for improvement of quality of services to DCPU and state government. They must also regularly inspect jails meant for adults to check if children are lodged and take immediate measures for transferring the child to the OH. They can also direct the police to register FIR for offences against CICL/ CINCP.[162]

---

(3) The Children's Court shall ensure that the child who is found to be in conflict with law is sent to a place of safety till s/he attains the age of 21 years and thereafter, the person shall be transferred to a jail, provided that the reformative services including educational services, skill development, alternative therapy such as counselling, behaviour modification therapy, and psychiatric support shall be provided to the child during the period of his stay in the place of safety.

(4) The Children's Court shall ensure that there is a periodic follow up report every year by the probation officer or the District Child Protection Unit or a social worker, as required, to evaluate the progress of the child in the place of safety and to ensure that there is no ill-treatment to the child in any form.

[159] JJ Act, 2015, Section 19.

[160] JJ Act, 2015, Section 17: Orders regarding a child not found to be in conflict with law.

(1) Where a board is satisfied on inquiry that the child brought before it has not committed any offence, then notwithstanding anything contrary contained in any other law for the time being in force, the board shall pass order to that effect.

(2) In case it appears to the board that the child referred to in Subsection (1) is in need of care and protection, it may refer the child to the committee with appropriate directions.

[161] JJ Act, 2015, Section 18(1)(c): Order the child to perform community service under the supervision of an organization or institution, or a specified person, persons or group of persons identified by the board.

[162] JJ Act, 2015, Section 8(3)(k): Order the police for registration of first information report for offences committed against any child in conflict with law, under this Act or any other law for the time being in force, on a complaint made in this regard.

- JJBs have to ensure that the procedures are child-friendly and the environment is not intimidating and does not resemble regular courts.[163]
- Establishment of Children's Courts that can either try the child as an adult or conduct an inquiry and pass orders under Section 18(1) if it doesn't see the need for the trial as an adult. If it tries the child as an adult, it should consider the special needs of the child, tenets of fair trial, and maintain a child-friendly atmosphere.[164]
- The new Act 2015 mandates the treatment of persons who were apprehended after they attained the age of 18 years as per the JJ Act. Such persons should be kept in a 'place of safety'[165] if they haven't been released on bail.[166]

[163] JJ Act, 2015, Section 7: Procedure etc. in relation to board: (1) The board shall meet at such times and shall observe such rules in regard to the transaction of business at its meetings, as may be prescribed and shall ensure that all procedures are child friendly and that the venue is not intimidating to the child and does not resemble as regular courts.

[164] JJ Act, 2015, Section 19: Powers of Children's Court:

(1) After the receipt of preliminary assessment from the board under Section 15, the Children's Court may decide that—

    (a) there is a need for trial of the child as an adult as per the provisions of the CrPC, 1973 and pass appropriate orders after trial, subject to the provisions of this section and Section 21, considering the special needs of the child, the tenets of fair trial and maintaining a child friendly atmosphere;

    (b) there is no need for trial of the child as an adult and may conduct an inquiry as a board and pass appropriate orders in accordance with the provisions of Section 18.

(2) The Children's Court shall ensure that the final order, with regard to a child in conflict with law, shall include an individual care plan for the rehabilitation of child, including follow up by the probation officer or the District Child Protection Unit or a social worker.

(3) The Children's Court shall ensure that the child who is found to be in conflict with law is sent to a place of safety till s/he attains the age of 21 years and thereafter, the person shall be transferred to a jail, provided that the reformative services including educational services, skill development, alternative therapy such as counselling, behaviour modification therapy, and psychiatric support shall be provided to the child during the period of his/her stay in the place of safety.

(4) The Children's Court shall ensure that there is a periodic follow up report every year by the probation officer or the District Child Protection Unit or a social worker, as required, to evaluate the progress of the child in the place of safety and to ensure that there is no ill-treatment to the child in any form.

(5) The reports under Subsection (4) shall be forwarded to the Children's Court for record and follow up, as may be required.

[165] JJ Act, 2015, Section 49:

(1) The state government shall set up atleast one place of safety in a state registered under Section 41, so as to place a person above the age of 18 years or child in conflict with law, who is between the age of 16 to 18 years and is accused of or convicted for committing a heinous offence.

(2) Every place of safety shall have separate arrangement and facilities for stay of such children or persons during the process of inquiry and children or persons convicted of committing an offence.

(3) The state government may, by rules, prescribe the types of places that can be designated as place of safety under Subsection (1) and the facilities and services that may be provided therein.

[166] JJ Act, 2015, Section 6: Placement of persons, who committed an offence, when person was below the age of 18 years—

- Unlike the earlier act, chief metropolitan magistrates (CMMs) and chief judicial magistrates (CJMs) cannot be appointed as Principal Magistrates of JJBs. The Magistrate should have at least 3 years' experience. The selection procedure for the appointment of social workers should be prescribed by the state government. The JJ Board will comprise a Metropolitan Magistrate and two eminent social workers who are actively involved in health, education, or welfare activities for at least 7 years or practicing professionals with a degree in child psychology, psychiatry, sociology, or law.[167]

- A social worker appointed as a member of the board must have been actively involved in health, education, or welfare activities pertaining to children for at least 7 years or must be a practicing professional with a degree in child psychology, psychiatry, sociology, or law. The member of JJB must be a practicingprofessional with a degree in child psychology, psychiatry, sociology, or law.[168]

- Several new offences committed against children, which were so far not adequately covered under any other law, are included in the 2015 Act. These include: sale and procurement of children for any purpose including illegal adoption,[169] corporal punishment in child care institutions,[170] use of child by militant groups,[171] offences against disabled

---

(1) Any person, who has completed 18 years of age, and is apprehended for committing an offence when he was below the age of 18 years, then, such person shall, subject to the provisions of this section, be treated as a child during the process of inquiry.

(2) The person referred to in Subsection (1), if not released on bail by the board shall be placed in a place of safety during the process of inquiry.

(3) The person referred to in Subsection (1) shall be treated as per the procedure specified under the provisions of this act.

[167] Section 4(2)of the JJ Act, 2015: Board shall consist of a Metropolitan Magistrate or a Judicial Magistrate of First Class not being Chief Metropolitan Magistrate or Chief Judicial Magistrate (hereinafter referred to as Principal Magistrate) with at least 3 years' experience and two social workers selected in such manner as may be prescribed, of whom at least one shall be a woman, forming a bench and every such Bench shall have the powers conferred by the CrPC, 1973 on a Metropolitan Magistrate or, as the case may be, a Judicial Magistrate of First Class.

[168] JJ Act, 2015, Section 4(3): No social worker shall be appointed as a member of the board unless such person has been actively involved in health, education, or welfare activities pertaining to children for at least 7 years or a practicing professional with a degree in child psychology, psychiatry, sociology, or law.

[169] JJ Act, 2015, Section 81: Sale and procurement of children for any purpose.

[170] JJ Act, 2015, Section 82(1): Any person in-charge of or employed in a child care institution, who subjects a child to corporal punishment with the aim of disciplining the child, shall be liable, on the first conviction, to a fine of ten thousand rupees and for every subsequent offence, shall be liable for imprisonment which may extend to three months or fine or with both.

[171] JJ Act, 2015, Section 83:

(1) Any non-state, self-styled militant group or outfit declared as such by the central government, if recruits or uses any child for any purpose, shall be liable for rigorous imprisonment for a term which may extend to 7 years and shall also be liable to fine of five lakh rupees.

(2) Any adult or an adult group uses children for illegal activities either individually or as a gang shall be liable for rigorous imprisonment for a term which may extend to 7 years and shall also be liable to fine of five lakh rupees.

children[172], and, kidnapping and abduction of children.[173]There is a new clause dealing with children who are at risk of being made to marry by parents or other persons.[174] So if a child marriage is about to be performed, the CWC can intervene. Corporal punishment in child care institutions have been taken as a serious offence liable, on the first conviction, to a fine of ten thousand rupees and for every subsequent offence, shall be liable for imprisonment which may extend to three months or fine or with both.

- It is an offence against a child, under the 2015 Act, if a person gives or causes to be given, to any child any intoxicating liquor or any narcotic drug or tobacco products or psychotropic substance, except on the order of a duly qualified medical practitioner, shall be punishable with rigorous imprisonment for a term which may extend to 7 years and shall also be liable to a fine which may extend up to one lakh rupees.[175] This is a welcome provision as the use of tobacco is a prominent risk factor for 6 to 8 leading causes of death including cancers, cardio-vascular diseases and lung disorders are directly attributable to tobacco use. Studies report high prevalence of tobacco use among children and youth of the country. Children in institutions have access to tobacco and other drugs. The new provisions have been made for the underage people 16–18 years to prevent them from the harmful effects of smoking and tighten the noose around those selling or providing pan *masala, gutkha* and cigarettes to children.

- The definition of after care has been included.[176] After care means making provision of support, financial or otherwise, to persons, who have completed the age of 18 years but have not completed the age of 21 years, and have left any institutional care to join the mainstream of the society.

- For streamlined and more effective adoption procedures for orphaned, abandoned and surrendered children, the existing Central Adoption Resource Authority has been given statutory body status.[177] It has introduced concepts from the Hague Convention on Protection of Children

---

[172] JJ Act, 2015, Section 85: Whoever commits any of the offences referred to in this chapter on any child who is disabled as so certified by a medical practitioner, then, such person shall be liable to twice the penalty provided for such offence.

[173] JJ Act, 2015, Section 84: For the purposes of this act, the provisions of Sections 359 to 369 of the IPC, shall mutatis mutandis apply to a child or a minor who is under the age of 18 years and all the provisions shall be construed accordingly.

[174] JJ Act, 2015, Section 2(14)(xii): Who is at imminent risk of marriage before attaining the age of marriage and whose parents, family members, guardian, and any other persons are likely to be responsible for solemnization of such marriage.

[175] JJ Act, 2015, Section 77: Whoever gives, or causes to be given, to any child any intoxicating liquor or any narcotic drug or tobacco products or psychotropic substance, except on the order of a duly qualified medical practitioner, shall be punishable with rigorous imprisonment for a term which may extend to 7 years and shall also be liable to a fine which may extend up to one lakh rupees.

[176] JJ Act, 2015, Section 2(5): 'Aftercare' means making provision of support, financial or otherwise, to persons, who have completed the age of 18 years but have not completed the age of 21 years, and have left any institutional care to join the mainstream of the society.

[177] JJ Act, 2015, Section 68: The CARA existing before the commencement of this act, shall be deemed to have been constituted as the Central Adoption Resource Authority under this act to perform the following functions, namely—

and Cooperation in Respect of Inter-Country Adoption, 1993 which were missing in the previous act.[178] Separate chapter (VIII) on Adoption provides for detailed provisions relating to adoption and punishments for not complying with the laid down procedure. Processes have been streamlined with timelines for both in-country and inter-country adoption that include declaring a child legally free for adoption. The authorized foreign adoption agency has been defined.[179]

- The act introduces foster care in India. Families will sign up for foster care and abandoned, orphaned children, or those in conflict with the law will be sent to them. Such families will be monitored and shall receive financial aid from the state.[180] In adoption, disabled children and children of physically and financially incapable will be given priority. Parents giving up their child for adoption will get 2 months to reconsider, compared to the earlier provision of 1 month.[181]
- Several rehabilitation and social reintegration measures have been provided for children in conflict with law.[182]
- All child care institutions, whether run by state government or by voluntary or non-governmental organizations, which are meant, either wholly or partially for housing children, regardless of whether they receive grants from the government, are to be mandatorily registered

---

(1)   to promote in-country adoptions and to facilitate inter-state adoptions in coordination with state agency;
(2)   to regulate inter-country adoptions;
(3)   to frame regulations on adoption and related matters from time to time as may be necessary;
(4)   to carry out the functions of the central authority under the Hague Convention on Protection of Children and Cooperation in respect of inter-country adoption;
(5)   any other function as may be prescribed.

[178] JJ Act, 2015, Section 68(d): To carry out the functions of the central authority under the Hague Convention on Protection of Children and Cooperation in respect of inter-country adoption.

[179] JJ Act, 2015, Section 2(6): 'Authorised foreign adoption agency' means a foreign social or child welfare agency that is authorised by the Central Adoption Resource Authority on the recommendation of their central authority or government department of that country for sponsoring the application of non-resident Indian or overseas citizen of India or persons of Indian origin or foreign prospective adoptive parents for adoption of a child from India.

[180] JJ Act, 2015, Section 44(4): The state government, after taking into account the number of children, shall provide monthly funding for such foster care through District Child Protection Unit after following the procedure, as may be prescribed, for inspection to ensure well-being of the children.

[181] JJ Act, 2015, Section 35(3): The parents or guardian who surrendered the child, shall be given two months' time to reconsider their decision and in the intervening period the committee shall either allow, after due inquiry, the child to be with the parents or guardian under supervision, or place the child in a Specialised Adoption Agency, if he or she is below 6 years of age, or a children's home if he is above 6 years.

[182] JJ Act, 2015, Section 95(4): The committee or the board, as the case may be, receiving the transferred child will process for restoration or rehabilitation or social re-integration, as provided in this act.

under the act within 6 months from the date of commencement of the act. Stringent penalty is provided in the law in case of non-compliance.[183]

• It mandates induction and refresher training for all, be it magistrates, social workers, police officers, and all other experts engaged.[184]

A public interest litigation has been filed and admitted in the Supreme Court of India, under Article 32 of the Constitution, challenging the constitutional validity of the JJ Act, 2015 According to the petition, the new Act is unreasonable, arbitrary, and in violation of Article 14 (right to equality) of the Constitution. It challenges Section 15 of the new Act which says in case of a heinous offence alleged to have been committed by a child, who has completed or is above the age of 16 years, the JJB shall conduct a preliminary inquiry to determine whether a juvenile offender is to be sent for rehabilitation or be tried as an adult. The plea said the impugned amended Act is draconian and unconstitutional which instead of providing care and protection to children deems them as adult in cases where the alleged commission of crime by them is heinous in nature. The writ petition has also cited neuro scientific research that said teenagers' brains are not completely developed and they are incapable of understanding the consequences of their actions. It further said that the amendment goes against the letter and spirit of the UN Convention on the Rights of the Child and is against the protection accorded to Child and adolescent criminals since 1800s.[185]

[183] JJ Act, 2015, Section 41(1): Notwithstanding anything contained in any other law for the time being in force, all institutions, whether run by a state government or by voluntary or NGOs, which are meant, either wholly or partially, for housing CNCP or children in conflict with law, shall, be registered under this act in such manner as may be prescribed, within a period of six months from the date of commencement of this act, regardless of whether they are receiving grants from the central government or, as the case may be, the state government or not, provided that the institutions having valid registration under the JJ Act, 2000 on the date of commencement of this Act shall be deemed to have been registered under this act.

[184] JJ Act, 2015, Section 107:

(1) In every police station, at least one officer, not below the rank of assistant sub-inspector, with aptitude, appropriate training and orientation may be designated as the child welfare police officer to exclusively deal with children either as victims or perpetrators, in coordination with the police, voluntary and NGOs.

(2) To co-ordinate all functions of police related to children, the state government shall constitute SJPUs in each district and city, headed by a police officer not below the rank of a Deputy Superintendent of Police or above and consisting of all police officers designated under Subsection (1) and two social workers having experience of working in the field of child welfare, of whom one shall be a woman.

(3) All police officers of the SJPUs shall be provided special training, especially at induction as child welfare police officer, to enable them to perform their functions more effectively

[185] See also http://www.livelaw.in/new-juvenile-law-challenged-in-sc/ (accessed on 17 November 2016).

International Law and the Administration of Juvenile Justice

There have been several international developments in the administration of juvenile justice. It was not until the International Covenant on Civil and Political Rights, 1966 that specific provisions regulating the administration of juvenile justice were enshrined in a global treaty. The provisions on the administration of juvenile justice in the International Covenant are very specific. Article 10(2)(b) provides for the separation of accused juveniles from adults and for their speedy adjudication; Article 14(4) provides that the trial procedures for juveniles should take into account the age of juveniles and the desirability of promoting their rehabilitation.[186] These are provisions which, although useful, are limited as they only focus on narrow and specific aspects of juvenile justice. As an increasing number of states began to develop separate juvenile justice systems, the need became apparent on the international level for a complete framework which states could utilize for guidance in establishing and operating their own national juvenile justice systems. In 1980, the Sixth United Nations Congress on the Prevention of Crime and the Treatment of Offenders called for the preparation of minimum rules regulating the administration of juvenile justice.[187] In 1985, the General Assembly adopted the United Nations Standard Minimum Rules for the Administration of Juvenile Justice, known as the Beijing Rules.[188] They provide, as intended, a framework within which a national juvenile justice system should operate and a model for states of a fair and humane response to juveniles who may find themselves in conflict with the law.

The Beijing Rules

The Beijing Rules, which are divided into six parts, cover the whole range of juvenile justice processes:

- General Principles;
- Investigation and Prosecution;
- Adjudication and Disposition;
- Non-institutional Treatment;
- Institutional Treatment and Research and Planning;
- Policy Formulation; and
- Evaluation.

The Beijing Rules are not a treaty and they as an entire body of rules are nonbinding per se. But some of the rules have become binding on state parties by being incorporated into the Convention on the Rights of the Child. Others can be treated not as establishing new rights but as providing more details on the contents of existing rights. The Beijing Rules provide that:

---

[186] International Covenant on Civil and Political Rights in Van Beuren International Documents, 1993, Article 6(5).

[187] UN Doc. Resolution 4, *Sixth United Nations Congress on the Prevention of Crime and the Treatment of Offenders.*

[188] UN Doc A/RES/40/33.

- A comprehensive social policy is in place to ensure the well-being of juveniles.
- Reaction to juvenile offenders is always to be in proportion to the circumstances of both the offenders and the offence.
- Police officers who deal extensively with juveniles shall be specially instructed and trained.
- Detention pending trial is to be used as a measure of last resort and for the shortest possible period of time.
- The placement of a juvenile in an institution is always to be a disposition of last resort and for the minimum necessary period.
- Necessary assistance such as housing, vocational training, and employment is to be provided to facilitate the rehabilitative process.[189]

The Definition of Juvenile under Beijing Rules

In international law, the definition of child is generally directly or indirectly related to age. The term juvenile, however, does not necessarily correspond to the concept of 'child'. According to Rule 2(2)(a) of the Beijing Rules, 'A juvenile is a child or young person who under the respective legal system may be dealt with for an offence in a manner which is different from an adult.' It is the manner in which a child is treated for an offence which dictates whether a child is also a juvenile.

The definition of a juvenile is critical because the standards incorporated into the Beijing Rules, many of which are improvements on existing standards, only apply to juveniles and not to all children. Hence the definition enshrined in the Beijing Rules contains a gaping hole, because it allows the national legal system to define juvenile. In essence, the Beijing Rules say no more than that if a person is treated as a juvenile, s/he is a juvenile. The reason for the special protection and entitlements of children is because of their age and vulnerability, not because of the system of trial.

Although, the Beijing Rules were drafted by states so as to be applicable within the widest range of legal systems, this definition of a juvenile severely limits the application of the Rules. In some jurisdictions children who are accused of serious offences are treated as if they were adults and in such cases the Beijing Rules would not apply.[190] The drafters of the Beijing Rules did try partially to overcome this handicap by encouraging states to make efforts to extend the principles enshrined in the Beijing Rules to all juveniles in welfare and care proceedings but this does not affect children accused of serious offences. The Convention on the Rights of the Child has transformed some of the Beijing principles into binding law.

Basic Principles of International Law for a Juvenile Justice System in the Best Interest of the Child

International law incorporates a number of basic principles upon which a juvenile justice system should be based. They are based on the various covenants, conventions, and guidelines. They are broadly as follows:

---

[189] Mitra, *Policy and Law in Juvenile Justice.*
[190] In the United States, children who are accused of murder may be tried as adults.

- The well-being of the child in the administration of justice needs to be maintained.[191]
- Criminal responsibility should be related to age at which the children are able to understand the consequences of their action.[192]
- Diverting children from formal trial procedures.[193]
- Juveniles to be brought as 'speedily as possible' to adjudication.[194]
- The arrest, detention, or imprisonment should only be imposed on children as a measure of last resort.[195]
- The rights of children prior to the determination of charges include the duty to inform parents or guardians[196] and all children should be presumed innocent until proven guilty according to law.[197]
- The Convention on the Rights of the Child, the International Covenant on Civil and Political Rights, the regional human rights treaties, and the Beijing Rules provide the rights of children during the determination of criminal charges. They provide that the principles of natural justice are equally applicable to children. Right to counsel is important for children.[198]
- Specific forms of punishment like corporal punishment and imposition of death penalty are prohibited for children.[199] The children should be provided with alternatives to institutional care.[200]

Standards for the Prevention of Juvenile Delinquency

The United Nations Guidelines for the Prevention of Juvenile Delinquency, known as Riyadh Guidelines were adopted in 1990.[201] The guidelines focus on early protection and preventive intervention paying particular attention in situations of social risk. The term 'social risk' denotes children who are demonstrably endangered and in need of non-punitive measures because of the effects of their circumstances and situation on health, safety, and education as determined by a competent authority.

The underlying principle of the Riyadh Guidelines is that the prevention of juvenile delinquency should utilize both the child's family and the school. The principal aim of the Guidelines

---

[191]   Both the Beijing Rules and the Convention on the Rights of the Child emphasize this.

[192]   UNCRC, Article 40(3)(b) and Beijing Rules, Rule 4.

[193]   UNCRC, Article 40(3)(b) and Beijing Rules, Rule 11.1.

[194]   International Covenant on Civil and Political Rights, Article 10(2)(b) and Beijing Rules, Rule 20.

[195]   Rules for the Protection of Juveniles Deprived of Their Liberty, Rule 30. See also United Nations Standard Minimum Rules for Non-custodial Measures, Tokyo Rules adopted by GARes, 45/110 on 14 December 1990 [17(1)(c) of the Beijing Rules, 37(b) of UNCRC, and Rules for the Protection of Juveniles Deprived of Their Liberty].

[196]   International Covenant on Civil and Political Rights, Articles 9(4) and 15(1).

[197]   UNCRC, Articles 40(2)(b)(1) and International Covenant on Civil and Political Rights, Article 14(2).

[198]   A UN study found that the right to counsel can become more important because of the informality of juvenile proceedings.

[199]   UNCRC, Article 37(a), ICCPR, Article 7, and Beijing Rules, Rule 111.

[200]   UNCRC, Article 40(4).

[201]   Adopted by the General Assembly on 28 March 1991; UN Doc. A/RES/45/112.

is to help socialize and integrate children through the family and through the active involvement and support of the community.

The Guidelines also recommend that children should use schools as resource and referral centres for the provision of counselling, particularly for children with special needs and for the dissemination of information on the prevention of drug, alcohol, and substance abuse.[202]

A Comparative Survey of the Juvenile Justice Systems in Various Countries and the Developments

A survey of the Juvenile Justice Systems in some other countries reveal the following trends.

Prevention of Institutionalization

The traditional approach of institutionalization of CEDC deprives the child of basic human rights. The child is also separated from his/her family environment. These children are thus deprived of their family environment and experience several negative experiences in large, depersonalized institutions. Institutions generally tend to be destructive, unhealthy, and debilitating places. Some of the end products of such institutions are seen in the aftercare homes. Many of them have psychological and behavioural problems and inadequate skills, and feel unable to fit into the community. They have been stigmatized as 'losers'.

Of course, not all juvenile institutions are harsh, brutal, and cruel. But, they all, by nature, deprive children of their freedom to a greater or lesser degree and they are undesirable alternatives to keeping children in their own homes or communities whenever possible. Secondly, institutionalization is an expensive alternative.

Article 9 of the United Nations Convention on the Rights of the Child states that the child should ideally be brought up in a family environment that is secure and nurturing, and protects its rights. If the biological family is unable to look after the child, then there should be a substitute or alternative family for long-term or short-term care. These alternatives are the non-institutionalization services. They are the programmes for the rehabilitation and care of children outside the institution. They have to be integrated, community-based, family-oriented, and preventive.

The main objective of non-institutional services is that every child has a right to a family and therefore it is necessary to ensure the child's rights within a family. This can be achieved by strengthening the family as a unit, by providing counselling and support services. When the child's own family of origin cannot look after him, substitute foster care should be arranged. The final objective is to work towards de-institutionalization of the child.

There are several countries that have statutes for preserving and strengthening the families and thus preventing delinquency and institutionalization. The new child welfare provisions reveal language that essentially covers the entire range of governmental and legal actions aimed at families. Generally, institutionalization is resorted to in three instances.

- when a youth has committed an especially heinous crime,
- when a youth is a chronic and serious offender, or
- when a youth is dangerous to himself or others.

---

[202] Guidelines 25 and 26.

Rehabilitation within the Families and Communities

It is believed that the families of juveniles are necessarily dysfunctional because juvenile crime results from individual family and environmental factors. It is unwise to attempt to prevent juvenile crime by removing juveniles from conditions in which they will eventually return.

Because families and communities contribute significantly to juveniles' troubling behaviour, family counselling remains the most effective method for healing juvenile offenders.[203] Efforts conducted in community settings have been extremely effective in reducing institutionalization and attenuating the criminal activity of even serious offenders.

Public policy goals demand that policymakers consider the human benefits of avoiding institutionalization. Even if the costs and general efficacy of the punitive, out-of-home-community and rehabilitative, in-home-community options were equivalent and if states ignored the rights and treatment needs of children, basic values would dictate a preference for in-home rehabilitation. Obvious social benefits are derived from programmes that reduce crime because of the high human costs of victimization. Wise public policy demands supporting family integrity, minimizing restrictions on liberty and intrusions on the privacy of youth and their families.

De-institutionalization

Children are entitled to a decent, stable home environment. This entitlement is a human right memorialized in several International Declarations and Conventions. The significance of the family is reflected in the United Nations Declaration of 1994 as the International Year of the family. The year 1994 highlighted the importance of the family and its role in promoting healthy behaviour.[204] The United Nations Convention on the Rights of the Child 1989 also affirms this right.

In addition to recognizing the rights of duties of children and families, the United Nations also adopted the Riyadh Guidelines, which aimed at delinquency prevention. These guidelines demonstrate the international community's renewed focus on families and communities and its continued belief that young people should be institutionalized only as a last resort. The International Covenant on Civil and Political Rights explicitly protects families and proposes a justice system that contains special procedures for juveniles designed to promote their rehabilitation.

Examples of these approaches and trends can be seen in The Uniform Juvenile Court Act adopted by Georgia, North Dakota, and Pennsylvania that aim to achieve the foregoing purposes in a family environment wherever possible; separating the child from his/her parents only when necessary for his/her welfare or in the interests of public safety. The State of Oregon has, however, incorporated the Uniform Act's focus on Community Empowerment and has become a model. The objectives of Oregon's Community Juvenile Services Acts are as follows:

- The family unit shall be preserved.
- Intervention shall be limited to those actions, which are necessary and utilize the least restrictive and most effective and appropriate resources.

[203] See Levesque and Tomkins, 'Revisioning Juvenile Justice', *Journal of Urban and Contemporary Law*, 48, no. 87, 1995.

[204] See United Nations Convention on the Rights of the Child, 1989. The convention establishes children's right to a family environment, 'a full and decent life' and 'a standard of living adequate to the child's physical, mental, spiritual, moral, and social development' (at Preamble, Article 23, Article 27).

- The family shall be encouraged to participate actively in whatever treatment is afforded to a child.
- Treatment in the community rather than commitment to a State Juvenile Training School shall be provided whenever possible.
- Communities shall be encouraged and assisted in the development of alternatives to secure temporary shelter for children who are not eligible for secure detention.

The above programme had improved juvenile justice by decreasing the number of 'at risk' youth who enter the system. [See US Department of Justice Office of JJ and Delinquency Prevention OJJDP, The Juvenile Justice Bulletin, 1990.] The focus however has typically been on community involvement by providing more shelter, specialized foster care, runaway projects, and services for street youth.[205]

Maine's Family Support Services Act 1994, Oklahoma's Family Support Act 1993, and Louisiana's Community and Family Support Act 1995, all stress on providing in-home, family-based services for children and preventing or delaying 'out of home placement' of children with severe development disabilities, and providing social services to stabilize family life and to preserve family units.

This new international ethos in juvenile justice should be reflected in the approaches to the Juvenile Justice legislations. The Juvenile Justice legislation should provide that the act be liberally constructed so that each child under the jurisdiction of the juvenile Court shall receive, preferably in the child's own home, the care, guidance and control that will best serve the child's welfare and its best interests.[206] The goals of family preservation statutes must attempt to pre-empt juvenile and family problems, strive to serve the best interests of children and the community by improving parenting skills, and providing services in the least restrictive environment. The ultimate goal should be family preservation, reunification, or permanent alternative placement.

United Nations Rules for the Protection of Juveniles deprived of their Liberty, 1990 (Havana Rules)[207]

These Rules were adopted by the United Nations in 1990 and have come to be known as the JDL Rules or the Havana Rules since they were adopted in Havana, Cuba. It is important to note that

---

[205] Juvenile Justice: A New Focus on Prevention. Hearing before the sub-committee of the Senate Committee on the Judiciary on Juvenile Justice, 102nd Congress Session 32, 36 (1992) [testimony of Thomas R. English, Executive Director of the Oregon Council on Crime and Delinquency].

[206] IOWA Code Ann. (1994). The Nebraska Juvenile Court Code states: 'to achieve its purpose in the juveniles' own home whenever possible, separating the juvenile from his or her parent when necessary for his or her welfare or in the interest of public safety and when temporary separation is necessary, to consider the developmental needs of the individual juvenile in all placements and to ensure every reasonable effort to reunite the juvenile and his or her family.'

[207] *Working with Children in Conflict with Law*, A Summary Booklet for Professionals working in the Child Justice System in Eastern Caribbean, UNICEF Office for Barbados and Eastern Caribbean, 2009. See more at http://www.unicef.org/easterncaribbean/Working_with_children_in_conflict_with_the_law.pdf (accessed on 17 November 2016).

these Rules are not only applicable to custodial settings, but to police stations where children are often held in custody.[208] The major purpose of the Rules is to ensure that the rights of the detainee are respected at all times. Section III applies to children under arrest or awaiting trial 'who are presumed innocent and should be treated as such'. As a general rule, detention before trial should be avoided, and is limited only to exceptional circumstances. Rule 12 specifies that the 'deprivation of liberty should be effected in conditions and circumstances which ensure respect for the human rights of juveniles'. Section IV addresses the management of juvenile facilities. Emphasis is placed on the need to encourage social reintegration of offenders by allowing children to continue their education and/or vocational training in the community as far as possible, since receiving education in a place of detention usually has a stigma attached to it. Recreational activities are also encouraged for the well-being of the child in custody. Section V also addresses the need for cells to be in proper condition and for general hygiene to be maintained—clean bedding, adequate medical and health care to be provided. Importance is given to the need for the rights of the detained child to be respected and for them treated with dignity at all stages of the child justice system. As such, the application of physical force is restricted, and cruel and degrading treatment or punishment is prohibited. In an effort to monitor the treatment of children in custody, it is proposed that qualified, independent inspectors conduct inspections 'unannounced'. Qualified medical officers who are 'attached to the inspecting authority or the public health service' are also expected to participate in the inspections. Section VI addresses the need to have qualified personnel, and a sufficient number of specialists working at the facilities where children are held in custody. It calls on personnel to: minimise differences 'between life inside and outside the detention facility'; to respect the Rules and to report any violations to their superior officers or organs 'vested with reviewing or remedial power'; to ensure the full protection of the physical and mental health of children; and for personnel to continuously improve their knowledge and professional capacity by attending in-service training courses.[209]

These Rules are for any person under the age of 18, under deprivation of liberty, that is, any form of detention or imprisonment or the placement in a public or private custodial setting as a result of the penal law. The Rules are intended to counteract the detrimental effects of deprivation of liberty by ensuring respect for children's rights. Special emphasis is given to pretrial detention and to the respect of certain rules in arrest and police headquarters situations. This is of paramount importance, since this stage of the prodecure accounts for the most serious violations of children's rights reported in various countries.

Major Principles

1. Deprivation of liberty should be a disposition of last resort and for the minimum period;
2. minors cannot be deprived of their liberty without objective judicial grounds;

---

[208] *Working with Children in Conflict with Law*, a summary booklet for professionals working in the Child Justice System in Eastern Caribbean , UNICEF Office for Barbados and Eastern Caribbean, 2009. Available at http://www.unicef.org/easterncaribbean/Working_with_children_in_conflict_with_the_law.pdf (accessed on 17 November 2016).

[209] *Working with Children in Conflict with Law.*

3. the establishment of small open facilities must be encouraged;
4. juveniles deprived of their liberty should be prepared for release (educational programmes);
5. contacts with families must be maintained; and
6. the facilities management personnel must be trained.

United Nations Guidelines on Justice in matters involving Child Victims and Witnesses of Crime (2005) and Model Law on Justice in Matters Involving Child Victims and Witnesses of Crime[210]

Child victims and witnesses of crime in many cases are unable to testify or provide adequate information to prosecute perpetrators. They are also victimized, intimidated, or forced to act illegally under duress.[211] In its resolution 2005/20, the Economic and Social Council adopted the Guidelines on Justice in Matters involving Child Victims and Witnesses of Crime. The Guidelines filled an important gap in international standards in the area of the treatment of children as victims or witnesses of crime. The Guidelines, which represent good practice based on the consensus of contemporary knowledge and relevant regional and international norms, standards and principles, were adopted with a view to providing a practical framework to achieve the following objectives:[212]

- To assist in the review of national laws, procedures, and practices so that they ensure full respect for the rights of child victims and witnesses of crime and contribute to the implementation of the Convention on the Rights of the Child by parties to that convention.
- To assist governments, international organizations, public agencies, non-governmental and community-based organizations and other interested parties in designing and implementing legislation, policies, programmes, and practices that address key issues related to child victims and witnesses of crime.
- To guide professionals and, where appropriate, volunteers working with child victims and witnesses of crime in their day-to-day practice in the adult and juvenile justice process at the national, regional, and international levels, consistent with the Declaration of Basic Principles of Justice for Victims of Crime and Abuse of Power.
- To assist and support those caring for children in dealing sensitively with child victims and witnesses of crime.[213]

These Guidelines form part of the body of United Nations standards and norms in crime prevention and criminal justice, which are internationally recognized normative principles in that area as developed by the international community since 1950. The implementation of these guidelines requires legislation on key issues related to child victims and witnesses of crime, in particular the role of child victims and witnesses within the justice process. The Guidelines form

---

[210] Available at http://www.unicef.org/rightsite/files/cfjusticeguidelines.pdf (accessed on 17 November 2016).

[211] United Nations, 'Justice in Matters Involving Child Victims and Witnesses of Crime Model Law and Related Commentary', New York, 2009. Available at http://www.unodc.org/documents/justice-and-prison-reform/UNODC_UNICEF_Model_Law_on_Children.pdf (accessed on 17 November 2016).

[212] United Nations, 'Justice in Matters Involving Child Victims'.

[213] United Nations, 'Justice in Matters Involving Child Victims'.

part of the body of United Nations standards and norms in crime prevention and criminal justice, which are internationally recognized normative principles in that area as developed by the international community since 1950.[214]

The UNODC and UNICEF have developed a model law to help countries in adapting their national legislation on justice in matters involving child victims and witnesses of crime. The model law is intended as a tool for drafting legal provisions concerning assistance to and the protection of child victims and witnesses of crime, particularly within the justice process. Designed to be adaptable to the needs of each state, the Model Law was drafted paying special attention to the provisions of the above 2005 Economic and Social Council Guidelines on Justice in Matters involving Child Victims and Witnesses of Crime.[215]

In drafting the Model Law, care was taken to reflect the need to accommodate the specificities of national legislation and judicial procedures, the legal, social, economic, cultural, and geographical conditions of each country and the various main legal traditions. The Model Law allows informal and customary justice systems to use and implement its principles and provisions.[216]

UN Guidelines on the Alternative Care of Children, 2010[217]

The UNCRC seeks to protect children who are unable to live with their parents or remain in a stable family setting (Article 20).[218] However, the UNCRC does not describe in any depth what measures should be taken. Though the Resolution A/RES/64/142, dated 24 February 2010, the UN General Assembly adopted the document 'Guidelines for the Alternative Care for Children'. The Resolution considers the Guidelines as a set of appropriate guidelines which will contribute to orientate the policy and practice 'with the aim of promoting the application of the Convention on the Rights of the Child and other relevant regulations that are part of international tools related to the protection and wellbeing of children deprived of parental care or at risk of losing it'.

The Guidelines are intended to enhance the implementation of the Convention on the Rights of the Child and of relevant provisions of other international instruments regarding the protection and well-being of children who are deprived of parental care or who are at risk of being so. The guidelines aim :

---

214 United Nations, 'Justice in Matters Involving Child Victims'.

215 United Nations, 'Justice in Matters Involving Child Victims'.

216 United Nations, 'Justice in Matters Involving Child Victims'.

217 Available at http://www.unicef.org/protection/alternative_care_Guidelines-English.pdf (accessed on 17 November 2016).

218 Article 20, UNCRC:

(1) A child temporarily or permanently deprived of his/her family environment, or in whose own best interests cannot be allowed to remain in that environment, shall be entitled to special protection and assistance provided by the state.

(2) States parties shall in accordance with their national laws ensure alternative care for such a child.

(3) Such care could include, inter alia, foster placement, kafala of Islamic law, adoption or if necessary placement in suitable institutions for the care of children. When considering solutions, due regard shall be paid to the desirability of continuity in a child's upbringing and to the child's ethnic, religious, cultural, and linguistic background.

1. To support efforts to keep children in, or return them to, the care of their family or, failing this, to find another appropriate and permanent solution, including adoption and kafala of Islamic law;

2. To ensure that, while such permanent solutions are being sought, or in cases where they are not possible or are not in the best interests of the child, the most suitable forms of alternative care are identified and provided, under conditions that promote the child's full and harmonious development;

3. To assist and encourage governments to better implement their responsibilities and obligations in these respects, bearing in mind the economic, social, and cultural conditions prevailing in each state; and

4. To guide policies, decisions, and activities of all concerned with social protection and child welfare in both the public and the private sectors, including civil society[219]

   The Guidelines have been created to ensure respect for two basic principles of alternative care for children, namely:

   a) that such care is genuinely needed (the 'necessity principle'), and

   b) that, when this is so, care is provided in an appropriate manner (the 'suitability principle').[220]

The Guidelines are a non-binding international instrument. So, while their general merit for informing the approach to alternative care for children is clearly recognised, they comprise no obligations on the part of states or any other concerned parties

General Comment No. 10 of CRC Committee[221]

The Committee on the Rights of the Child[222] General Comment No. 10 (2007) gave detailed guidance on the principles in Articles 37[223] and 40[224] of the UNCRC in relation to juvenile

---

[219] Available at http://www.unicef.org/protection/alternative_care_Guidelines-English.pdf (accessed on 17 November 2016).

[220] Available at http://www.unicef.org/protection/alternative_care_Guidelines-English.pdf (accessed on 17 November 2016).

[221] UNCRC, *General Comment No. 10 (2007): Children's Rights in Juvenile Justice*, 25 April 2007, CRC/C/GC/10. Available at http://www.refworld.org/docid/4670fca12.html (accessed on 23 June 2015).

[222] The UNCRC is the body of 18 Independent experts that monitors implementation of the Convention on the Rights of the Child by its state parties. It also monitors implementation of two Optional Protocols to the Convention, on involvement of children in armed conflict and on sale of children, child prostitution, and child pornography. On 19 December 2011, the UN General Assembly approved a third Optional Protocol on a communications procedure, which will allow individual children to submit complaints regarding specific violations of their rights under the Convention and its first two optional protocols. The protocol entered into force in April 2014.

[223] UNCRC, Article 37: Detention and Punishment—No one is allowed to punish children in a cruel or harmful way. Children who break the law should not be treated cruelly. They should not be put in prison with adults, should be able to keep in contact with their families, and should not be sentenced to death or life imprisonment without possibility of release.

[224] UNCRC, Article 40: Juvenile Justice—Children who are accused of breaking the law have the right to legal help and fair treatment in a justice system that respects their rights. Governments are required to

justice.[225] In general Comment No. 10, the UNCRC Committee on the Rights of the child mentioned that many states parties still have a long way to go in achieving full compliance with the UNCRC, for example, in the areas of procedural rights, the development and implementation of measures for dealing with children in conflict with the law without resorting to judicial proceedings, and the use of deprivation of liberty only as a measure of last resort.[226] It laid down the following:

The leading principles of a comprehensive juvenile justice policy

States parties have to apply systematically the following general principles contained in articles 2, 3, 6, and 12 of UNCRC, as well as the fundamental principles of juvenile justice enshrined in articles 37 and 40.

- Non-discrimination (Article 2)
- Best interests of the child (Article 3)
- The right to life, survival and development (Article 6)
- The right to be heard (Article 12)
- Dignity (Article 40(1))

The Committee acknowledged that the preservation of public safety is a legitimate aim of the justice system. However, this aim is best served by a full respect for and implementation of the leading and overarching principles of juvenile justice as enshrined in UNCRC.

Core elements of a juvenile justice policy

The core elements of a juvenile justice policy must be the prevention of juvenile delinquency; interventions without resorting to judicial proceedings and interventions in the context of judicial proceedings; the minimum age of criminal responsibility and the upper age-limits for juvenile justice; the guarantee for a fair trial; and deprivation of liberty including pretrial detention and post-trial incarceration.

Age and children in conflict with the law—The minimum age of criminal responsibility

There is a need to provide the states parties with clear guidance and recommendations regarding the minimum age of criminal responsibility. Article 40 (3) of UNCRC requires states parties to

---

set a minimum age below which children cannot be held criminally responsible and to provide minimum guarantees for the fairness and quick resolution of judicial or alternative proceedings.

[225] General Comment No. 10, 2007, Children's Rights in Juvenile Justice, Committee on the Rights of the Child, Forty-Fourth Session, Geneva, 15 January–2 February 2007. Available at http://www2. ohchr.org/english/bodies/crc/docs/AdvanceVersions/GeneralComment10-02feb07.pdf (accessed on 17 November 2016).

[226] General Comment No. 10, 2007.

seek to promote, the establishment of a minimum age below which children shall be presumed not to have the capacity to infringe the penal law, but does not mention a specific minimum age in this regard. This minimum age means the following: Children who commit an offence at an age below that minimum cannot be held responsible in a penal law procedure. Even (very) young children do have the capacity to infringe the penal law but if they commit an offence when below MACR the irrefutable assumption is that they cannot be formally charged and held responsible in a penal law procedure. For these children special protective measures can be taken if necessary in their best interests.

Children at or above the MACR at the time of the commission of an offence (or infringement of the penal law) but younger than 18 years can be formally charged and subject to penal law procedures. But these procedures, including the final outcome, must be in full compliance with the principles and provisions of UNCRC. A minimum age of criminal responsibility below the age of 12 years is considered by the Committee not to be internationally acceptable. States parties are encouraged to increase their lower MACR to the age of 12 years as the absolute minimum age and to continue to increase it to a higher age level.

The right to be heard (Article 12). Article 12(2) of UNCRC requires that a child be provided with the opportunity to be heard in any judicial or administrative proceedings affecting the child, either directly or through a representative or an appropriate body in a manner consistent with the procedural rules of national law. It is obvious that for a child alleged as, accused of, or recognized as having infringed the penal law, the right to be heard is fundamental for a fair trial. Parents or legal guardians should also be present at the proceedings because they can provide general psychological and emotional assistance to the child.

Organization of Juvenile Justice

In order to ensure the full implementation of the principles and rights elaborated in Comment No. 10, it is necessary to establish an effective organization for the administration of juvenile justice, and a comprehensive juvenile justice system. As stated in Article 40 (3) of UNCRC, states parties shall seek to promote the establishment of laws, procedures, authorities, and institutions specifically applicable to children in conflict with the penal law. The privacy of these children and the confidentiality of their cooperation should be fully respected and protected. In this regard, the Committee refers the states parties to the existing international guidelines on the involvement of children in research.

Non-governmental Organization Interventions

There are several central and state government schemes and NGO interventions in the administration and implementation of the JJ Act, 1986. The interventions are in the areas of preventive, institutional, non-institutional, as well as rehabilitative work. Observation homes, juvenile homes, special homes, and aftercare homes are run by the government as well as by the NGOs. The government also provides grant-in-aid to the NGOs to run the homes. The services provided by these homes might include medical treatment, education, accommodation, vocational training, recreation, and job placement. The intake of children depends on the age and 'category' of the child. Some of these 'categories' are: street children, orphans, semi-orphans, girl children, non-court committed, court committed, children from broken families, children of unwed mothers, and school dropouts. The interventions seem to be concentrated within urban areas, prime cities, and in certain geographical areas. The NGOs appear to be working in an individu-alized, small-scale manner and their efforts are thus fragmented and confined to certain areas and to certain specified categories of children. It is alleged that some of the NGOs are 'choosy' about the children. Some of them want only 'good children'. A major area of concern is that there are inadequate homes for the disabled children and children affected by HIV/AIDS.

There are network organizations as well working with street children and other underprivileged children for their survival, protection, and development. A good example of evolving partnerships to reach out to children is the Childline intervention, a national 24-hour, free phone emergency outreach service, which tries to link CNCP to long-term services. Any child/adult concerned can call 10-98 (1098) free of charge. This includes regular follow-up. It is a project of the ministry of social justice and empowerment, Government of India, in partnership with NGOs, the UNICEF, and the corporate sector.

The SOS Children's Villages of India are an example of a good NGO intervention which needs to be emulated. These villages provide a home to orphaned and abandoned children. Children in SOS Villages grow up as children in an ordinary family. They live with a mother, brothers, and sisters in a family home. Siblings are not separated. An SOS Village is made up of ten to twenty houses, run by a team of efficient child care workers, who support and help the mothers in caring for the emotional and educational well-being of the children entrusted to their care. This type of child care is recommended as this is the closest alternative to a family and is in an integrated setting that balances the needs and develops relationships between the child, mother, family, and community. Institutional care provided by the government should be on the lines of a SOS Village.

HAQ: Centre for Child Rights

HAQ works towards the recognition, promotion, and protection of rights of all children and aims to look at the child in an integrated manner within the framework of the Constitution of India, and the UN Convention of the Rights of the Child, which India ratified in 1992. To carry forward its mandate, HAQ undertakes not only research and documentation but also is actively engaged in public education and advocacy of children's rights. It also seeks to serve as a resource and support base for individuals and groups dealing with children at every level. HAQ's work on juvenile justice began in 2005 with providing legal aid to the children in conflict with law. Over the years, HAQ with the support of other stakeholders was able to ensure the presence of legal aid lawyers in the JJBs. Since then, HAQ's intervention in the boards has been largely confined to providing counselling to the children in conflict with law. The children needing counselling are marked to HAQ through orders of the magistrates.[227] HAQ has worked closely with the judicial

---

[227] Available at http://www.haqcrc.org/our-work (accessed on 17 November 2016).

mechanisms to monitor and implement the law, is called upon to develop training materials and also train judicial officers, police, and other functionaries in the JJ system.[228]

Prayas Juvenile Aid Centre Society[229]

Prayas Institute of Juvenile Justice (under Prayas Juvenile Aid Centre Society) set up in the year 1999 with an objective to undertake and promote research in the thematic areas of Prayas including Juvenile Justice, Child Rights, and Child Protection. Prayas Institute of Juvenile Justice clearly focuses on the rights of the children across India and deeply imbibes the four basic rights of Children as mentioned in the UNCRC such as Survival Rights, Development Rights, Protection Rights, and Participation Rights. Prayas Institute of Juvenile Justice has conducted action-based research on Juvenile Justice System and Rights of Children in the states of Bihar and Delhi.

---

[228] Available at http://www.haqcrc.org/juvenile-justice (accessed on 17 November 2016).
[229] Available at http://www.prayaschildren.org/prayasresearch.html (accessed on 17 November 2016).

7

Right to Development
Education, Play, and Recreation

PART I: Right to Education

The Declaration on the Right to Development describes development as 'a comprehensive economic, social, cultural and political process, which aims at the constant improvement of the wellbeing of the entire population and of all individuals on the basis of their active, free and meaningful participation in development and in the fair distribution of benefits'.[1] The right to development includes access to information, education, play and leisure, cultural activities and the right to freedom of thought, conscience and religion. Development and provisional rights under the United Nations Convention on the Rights of the Child (UNCRC) guarantee children the right to an appropriate quality of life, medical care, social security, and education. By way of their right to a name, registration in a birth register, and a nationality, children are also guaranteed a personal identity and the legal status of a state citizen. A child's right to development includes:

- Right to education
- Right to learning
- Right to relax and play
- Right to all forms of development—emotional, mental, and physical

Elementary Education—The Right of Every Child

Right to education of every child is clearly a human right. Education is important as it enables the child to:

- develop and realize her/his full potential as a human being;
- develop the ability to think, question, and judge independently;
- develop a sense of self-respect, dignity, and self-confidence;

---

[1] Declaration on the Right to Development, 4 December 1986. The Declaration on the Right to Development was adopted by the General Assembly by Resolution 41/128 of 4 December 1986. Available at http://legal.un.org/avl/ha/drd/drd.html (accessed on 19 September 2015).

- develop and internalize a sense of moral values and critical judgment;
- learn to love and respect fellow human beings and nature;
- develop civic sense, citizenship, and values of participatory democracy; and
- enable decision making.

Education is a human right with immense power to transform. On its foundation rest the cornerstones of freedom, democracy, and sustainable human development. Education is desired for itself as it opens up a vast world of opportunities and ideas to the educated person. It is also of great instrumental value in the process of economic growth and development. Education plays a critical role in demographic transition; female education, in particular, is seen to be important in the process of economic growth and development.[2] Education also plays a critical role in the process of lowering fertility and mortality. Primary schooling is associated with better health outcomes. There is a strong correlation between literacy and life expectancy. The returns to education are large and positive. Schooling has been seen to have a positive impact on agricultural output. In political and social terms too, schooling creates an educated population and a more constructive citizenry. Education empowers and empowerment affects larger social processes.[3] In recent decades, the importance of education has been reflected in increased budgetary allocations to basic education, compulsory schooling legislation, and widespread media attention to education and development issues.

Millions of young people around the world grow up unable to build decent lives for themselves because they are denied their right to education. The *State of the World's Children, 2015* points out that nearly 9 in 10 children from the wealthiest 20 per cent of households in the world's least developed countries attend primary school—compared to only about 6 in 10 from the poorest households. The gap can be dramatic even in lower middle-income countries.[4]

Millions of girls around the world are still being denied an education. There are still 31 million girls of primary school age out of school. Of these, 17 million are expected never to enter school. There are 4 million fewer boys than girls out of school. There are also 34 million female adolescents out of school, missing out on the chance to learn vital skills for work. In 10 countries around the world, no more than half of poorest girls enter school, and in 10 countries, 9 out of 10 of the poorest young women have not completed school.[5] Denying girls their right to a quality education effectively denies them all other human rights and minimizes the chances of successive generations—particularly the chances of their daughters—to develop to their fullest potential.

Thus, as the world has become more complex, school systems have expanded in both size and complexity and in the challenges they face. People see growing disparities and gaps—in costs, quality, achievement, and certification—and this has led to a 'crisis of confidence' in public schooling throughout much of the world.

---

[2] United Nations Children's Fund (UNICEF), *The State of the World's Children* (New York, 1999).

[3] M. Swaminathan and V. Rawal, *Primary Education for All* (India Development Report, 2000), p. 68.

[4] UNICEF, *The State of the World's Children 2015: Executive Summary* (New York, USA, November 2014).

[5] UNESCO, *Education for All Global Monitoring Report*, October 2013. Available at http://www.unesco.org/new/fileadmin/MULTIMEDIA/HQ/ED/GMR/images/2011/girls-factsheet-en.pdf (accessed on 19 September 2015).

Basic education consists of a combination of indispensable competencies, knowledge, skills, and an attitude that serves as the foundation of any individual's lifelong learning. Although there will be differences in what constitutes 'basic education' from society to society, there are some fundamentals that are common across cultural, social, and political boundaries. Key competencies include reading, writing, and numeracy. Without these competencies it is difficult for an individual to pursue learning in modern times. Knowledge should be both theoretical and practical. An example is the area of basic science. Its content, for instance, is likely to vary according to the particular context, but it must provide learners with the basic scientific concepts and experience that will allow them to function on a daily basis in such areas as food, nutrition, water, and sanitation. Skill provides an individual with the ability to use knowledge effectively and easily. There are many different types of skills. Survival skills are those that are basic to survival, such as finding food and seeking protection. Life skills enable an individual to have access to a better life. These might include skills for work, problem-solving skills, communication, analysis, and logic. Attitudes are feelings about or positions towards certain purposes or aspects of life. These include self-esteem, tolerance, cooperation, and civic responsibility. Thus, basic education is a broad and complex concept. Although there is general agreement as to what the components are, there is plenty of room for each country and community to configure these components in ways that are most relevant to them. In operation, basic education occurs in a wide range of contexts and is not limited by structure, content, or participants.[6] Basic education meets the fundamental learning needs of children, youth, and adults, going beyond the confines of formal primary education. This expanded vision of basic education encompasses all ages and all modalities, focuses on learning and acquiring specific competencies rather than on institutional forms, and promotes a unified basic education system with mutually supportive and complementary components.

Primary education for children is the most important component of basic education, if only because the human life cycle requires that the basic competencies and life skills be acquired at an early age. The formal primary school is the principal vehicle for primary education, but other complementary non-formal and flexible approaches are needed to make primary education universal. Other programmes which support progress towards that goal, but which are also important in their own right, are 'second chance' primary education for youth and adults, adult education and literacy, early childhood programmes, and parents' education.

The absence of primary education of an acceptable quality remains a serious problem in most parts of the developing world. Early childhood development (ECD) and adult basic education serve as supporting efforts to primary education. The relative emphasis and mix of activities will vary from country to country.[7]

The net enrolment rate in primary education was estimated at 88 per cent in 2013–14. The annual drop-out rate in primary education has also shown a declining trend. Significant progress has also been made in bridging the gender and social category gaps in elementary education. The progress towards universalization of elementary education has brought about substantial increase in enrolment in secondary education. The past few years have also seen a huge increase in the

---

[6] Available at www.unicef.org visited on 4 July 2002.
[7] Available at www.unicef.org visited on 4 July 2002.

demand for higher education. There has also been a substantial increase in literacy rate since 2001.[8]

The United Nations Educational, Scientific and Cultural Organisation (UNESCO) has drafted a definition of literacy as the 'ability to identify, understand, interpret, create, communicate, compute and use printed and written materials associated with varying contexts. Literacy involves a continuum of learning in enabling individuals to achieve their goals, to develop their knowledge and potential, and to participate fully in their community and wider society.'[9]

The National Literacy Mission (NLM)[10] defines literacy as acquiring the skills of reading, writing, and arithmetic, and the ability to apply them to one's day-to-day life. The achievement of functional literacy implies:[11]

1. self-reliance in 3 R's,
2. awareness of the causes of deprivation and the ability to move towards amelioration of their condition by participating in the process of development,
3. acquiring skills to improve economic status and general well being, and
4. imbibing values such as national integration, conservation of environment, women's equality, observance of small family norms.

The working definition of literacy in the Indian census since 1991 is as follows:[12]

- *Literacy rate*: The total percentage of the population of an area at a particular time aged 7 years or above who can read and write with understanding. Here the denominator is the population aged 7 years or more.
- *Crude literacy rate:*[13] The total percentage of the people of an area at a particular time who can read and write with understanding, taking the total population of the area (including below 7 years of age) as the denominator.

India has made considerable progress in improving literacy rate among population aged 7 and more during the period 2001–11.[14] The literacy rate among the population aged 7 and above

---

[8] Ministry of Human Resource Development (MHRD), GoI, *Education for All towards Quality with Equity*, first edition (New Delhi, India: National University of Educational Planning and Administration, August 2014).

[9] UNESCO, 'E-Plurality of Literacy and Its Implications for Policies and Programmes', Education Sector Position Paper (Paris: UNESCO, 2004).

[10] The NLM (1988–2008): The NLM was launched in 1988 to impart functional literacy to non-literates in the age group 15–35 years in a time-bound manner.

[11] MHRD, *NLM, UNESCO & Literacy*, NLM (New Delhi, India: GoI). Available at http://www.nlm.nic.in/unesco_nlm.htm (accessed on 14 September 2015).

[12] K. Park, *Preventive and Social Medicine*, 19th edition (Jabalpur, India: Banarsidas Bhanot Publishers, 2007).

[13] Crude literacy rate = number of literate person divided by total population multiplied by 100.

[14] MHRD, *Education for All towards Quality with Equity*, 1st edition (India, New Delhi, India: National University of Educational Planning and Administration, GoI, August 2014).

increased from 64.84 per cent in 2001 to 72.99 per cent in 2011[15]. During the period 2001 to 2011, a total of 202.75 million persons (98.11 male and 104.64 female) were made literate.[16]

Table 7.1 Number of Primary Schools, Schools Imparting Upper Primary Education, and Schools Imparting Elementary Education (2000–01 to 2013–14)[17]

Year	Number of primary schools (schools with only primary section)	Number of schools imparting upper primary education	Number of schools imparting elementary education
2000–01	638,738	206,269	845,007
2001–02	664,041	219,626	883,667
2002–03	651,382	245,274	896,656
2003–04	712,239	262,286	974,525
2004–05	767,520	274,731	1,042,251
2005–06	772,568	288,493	1,061,061
2006–07	784,852	305,584	1,090,436
2007–08	805,667	445,108	1,250,775
2008–09	809,108	476,468	1,285,576
2009–10	809,974	493,838	1,303,812
2010–11	827,244	535,080	1,362,324
2011–12	842,481	569,697	1,412,178
2012–13	853,870	577,832	1,431,702
2013–14	858,916	589,796	1,448,712

Table 7.1 illustrates the availability of schools imparting primary/upper primary/elementary education in all parts of the country. During the period 2000–01 to 2013–14, the total number of primary schools (schools with only primary section) has increased by 34.5 per cent (from 638,738 to 858,916 schools). The total number of schools imparting upper primary education has increased by 185.9 per cent (from 206,269 to 589,796), while the total number of schools imparting elementary education (schools with primary or upper primary sections, schools with primary and upper primary sections, and secondary/higher secondary schools with primary and or upper primary section) has increased by 71.4 per cent (from 845,007 to 1,448,712) during the same period.[18]

The total number of schools in the country during the year 2013–14 was 1,518,160 (Unified District Information System for Education [U-DISE], National University of Educational Planning and Administration [NUEPA]). The total number of schools with primary section in 2013–14 was 1,200,772. The ratio of primary to upper primary sections was 2.04 in 2013–14,

[15] MHRD, *Education for All towards Quality with Equity*.
[16] MHRD, *Education for All towards Quality with Equity*.
[17] Source: Statistics of School Education, 2007–08, MHRD, GoI; and U-DISE, NUEPA.
[18] MHRD, *Education for All towards Quality with Equity*.

while the ratio of primary to secondary sections and that of secondary to higher secondary sections were 2.60 and 2.19 respectively.[19]

Out-of-School Children

The number of out-of-school children (OOSC) has declined steadily since 2001. The number of out-of school children in the age group 6–14 years was estimated at 32 million in 2001.[20] This represented 28.2 per cent of the population in the age group 6–14 years in 2005–06. A national-level study commissioned by the MHRD, GoI through an independent agency (Indian Market Research Bureau [IMRB]) conducted in 2005, estimated the number of OOSC at 13.45 million during the year 2005–06. According to this survey, the number of OOSC accounted for 6.94 per cent (4.34 per cent in urban and 7.8 per cent in rural areas) of the total number of children in the age group 6–14 years in 2005–06 (Table 7.2). The IMRB survey conducted in 2009 indicated that the number of OOSC declined from 13.45 million in 2005–06 to 8.15 million in 2009–10. These surveys indicated that the percentage of OOSC to total population in the age group 6–14 years has decreased from 6.94 per cent in 2005–06 to 4.28 per cent in the year 2009–10.[21]

Table 7.2   Percentage Distribution of All Children and OOSC by Gender[22]

	6–10 years		11–13 years	
	All children	OOSC	All children	OOSC
Boys	54.6	50.3	55.1	49.5
Girls	45.4	49.7	44.9	50.5
All	100.0	100.0	100.0	100.0

In Table 7.2, we have compared the distribution of child population and OOSC among different categories. Table 7.2 shows that there are more boys (54 per cent) than girls (46 per cent) in the child population whereas the proportions are reversed among OOSC, where around half are girls.[23]

The national goal of primary education for all children continues to be elusive. Three factors have been commonly acknowledged to be important obstacles to universal primary education (UPE). First, there is a problem of poverty. The poor, it is argued, cannot afford to send their children to school. In some cases, children may be employed as child workers and may contribute to the family's earnings. While it is children of the poor who work, there are important demand-side

[19] MHRD, *Education for All towards Quality with Equity.*
[20] *Census of India,* 2001.
[21] Ministry of Human Resource Development, *Education for all towards Quality with Equity.*
[22] Source: UNICEF: A Situational Study of India.
[23] UNICEF, *A Situational Study of India* (New Delhi: UNICEF India Country Office, UNICEF House, 2014).

factors which determine the pattern of child labour use. There is a growing demand for primary education for children, even among the poorest communities. Evidence suggests that poverty of income is not the reason why parents fail to enrol their children in school, or keep them there.

A second reason pertains to the quality of schooling and school infrastructure. In India, school infrastructure is woefully inadequate. For many children, the absence of a functioning school in the neighborhood is the main determinant of non-attendance. The problems of physical distance from a school are exacerbated by problems of social distance for children from underprivileged households.[24] Given that the average quality of schooling is very low, a frequently cited argument is that education of such poor quality is of little use. The low quality of education is blamed for low school enrolment and the high dropout rate. While these statements are valid, it is wrong to argue, as is often done, that without an improvement in quality, nothing much can be gained. While quality is very important, the case for universal education cannot be separated from that for raising quality. To put it differently, the struggle for more schools and for universal education must be made together with the struggle for better quality.

Lastly, there are problems of motivation, both among parents and children. These may be due to a range of factors including long years of deprivation, an environment in which there is no tradition of literacy, inadequate information about the returns to schooling, nutrition deprivation of children, low quality of school education, and so on. Empirical studies, however, indicate a high level of motivation among poor parents. Parents are willing to take on extra work to see that their children go to school. In other words, there is demand for schooling even among poor parents and poor children.

Apart from this, children were not in school for other reasons like lack of time in the morning and inability to get help with homework. Further, the initial enthusiasm for school often waned with the children's negative experience of school such as the absence of classroom activity and physical punishments.[25] Disciplinary practices are certainly a deterrent to schooling. Some teachers, most of them being overenthusiastic and some with uncontrollable anger, punish the children physically as well as mentally. A division bench of the Delhi High Court commented: 'Brutal treatment of children can never inculcate discipline in them. Obedience exacted by striking fear of punishment can make the child adopt the same tactics when he grows up for getting what he wants.'[26] The High Court banned corporal punishment in Delhi schools. Other deterrents include rigid admission and examination schedules, formalities, and procedures.

Educational Policy and Planning in India

Education occupies a strategic position in India's development priorities. Successive development policies and Five-Year national development plans have accorded high priority to education development. The key developments that guided the development of school education and literacy plans and programmes in India are indicated in Table 7.3.

[24] Public Report on Basic Education (PROBE) Team, *Public Report on Basic Education* (New Delhi: Oxford University Press, 1999).

[25] PROBE Team, *Public Report on Basic Education*

[26] *The Tribune*, 'HC Bans Corporal Punishment for School Children', vol. 120, no. 333, City edition, Chandigarh, 2 December 2000, p. 1.

Table 7.3 Key Developments That Guided the Development of Education in India[27]

Year	Key Developments
1986	National Policy on Education (NPE), 1986 adopted.
1987	Several large centrally-assisted schemes/programmes such as 'Operation Blackboard' (OB) and the 'scheme for restructuring and reorganization of teacher education' launched.
1988	NLM launched
1992	NPE, 1986 revised.
1994	District Primary Education Programme (DPEP) launched to universalize primary education in selected districts.
1995	Centrally-assisted National Programme of Nutritional Support to Primary Education, popularly known as the Mid-Day Meal Scheme (MDMS) launched.
1999	A separate Department of School Education and Literacy created within the Ministry of Human Resource Development, GoI.
2001	(i) Sarva Shiksha Abhiyan (SSA), the flagship programme for universalisation of elementary education, launched; (ii) Adoption of the National Policy on Empowerment of Women. The policy supported the provision of childcare facilities, including crèches at work places of women.
2002	(i) The Constitution (Eighty-Sixth Amendment) Act, 2002 inserted Article 21-A in the Constitution of India to provide free and compulsory education for all children in the age group of six to fourteen years as a Fundamental Right; (ii) Commitment to the provision of early childhood care and education to children below the age of six years reiterated. The Constitution (Eight-sixth Amendment) Act, 2002 envisaged substitution of new article for article 45. The substituted article 45 states 'The State shall endeavour to provide early childhood care and education for all children until they complete the age of six years'; (iii) The Tenth Five-Year Plan (2002–07) launched.
2003	National Youth Policy (NYP), 2003 formulated.
2004	(i) Education Cess introduced for raising additional financial resources needed to fulfill Government's commitment to universalize elementary education; (ii) EDUSAT (Educational Satellite), a satellite exclusively dedicated to education launched to harness modern technology for delivery of education of good quality to all, including hard-to-reach groups.
2005	National Curriculum Framework (NCF-2005) for school education formulated.
2007	Eleventh Five-Year Plan (2007–12) launched.
2009	(i) The Right of Children to Free and Compulsory Education (RTE) Act, 2009 enacted. The Act makes it incumbent on Governments to provide for free and compulsory education to all children of the age of six to fourteen years. Section 11 of the act also states, 'with a view to prepare children above the age of three years for elementary education and to provide early childhood care and education for all children until they complete the age of six years, the appropriate Government may make necessary arrangement for providing free pre-school education for such children'; (ii) The NLM

(Cont'd)

---

[27] Ministry of Human Resource Development, *Education for All towards Quality with Equity*.

Table 7.3   *(Cont'd)*

Year	Key Developments
	recast with a special focus on female literacy and the 'Sakshar Bharat' (Literate India) programme launched as the national adult education programme on 8 September 2009; (iii) The revised NCF for teacher Education formulated; (iv) The Rashtriya Madhyamik Shiksha Abhiyan (RMSA) launched in March 2009, with the vision of making secondary education of good quality available, accessible and affordable to all young persons in the age group 15–16 years; (v) Revised Centrally-sponsored Scheme of Inclusive Education for the Disabled at Secondary Stage approved; (vi) The Centrally-Sponsored Scheme 'Construction & Running of Girls' Hostel for Students of Secondary and Higher Secondary Schools approved.
2010	(i) The RTE Act 2009 came into force from 1 April 2010; (ii) All states/union territories (UTs) notified state RTE Rules. Central RTE Rules apply to UTs without legislation; (iii) The SSA Framework aligned to RTE Act; (iv) Revised Centrally-Sponsored Scheme of ICT@ Schools approved.
2011	The revised Centrally-Sponsored Scheme 'Vocationalisation of Higher Secondary Education' approved.
2012	The Twelfth Five-Year Plan (2007–12) launched;
2013	(i) National Early Childhood Care and Education (ECCE) Policy adopted; (ii) The Integrated Child Development Services, the flagship programme of the GoI for ECCE restructured and strengthened.
2014	National Youth Policy, 2014 adopted.

National Policy of 1968

The National Policy of 1968 marked a significant step in the history of education in post-independence India. It aimed to promote national progress, a sense of common citizenship and culture, and to strengthen national integration. It laid stress on the need for a radical reconstruction of the education system, to improve its quality at all stages, and gave much greater attention to science and technology, the cultivation of moral values, and a closer relation between education and the life of the people. Since the adoption of the 1968 Policy, there has been considerable expansion in educational facilities all over the country at all levels. More than 90 per cent of the country's rural habitations now have schooling facilities within a radius of 1 kilometre. There has been sizeable augmentation of facilities at other stages also. Perhaps the most notable development has been the acceptance of a common structure of education throughout the country and the introduction of the 10+2+3 system by most states. In the school curricula, in addition to laying down a common scheme of studies for boys and girls, science and mathematics were incorporated as compulsory subjects and work experience assigned a place of importance.

National Policy on Education, 1986

The NPE, 1986 was the second policy on education since Independence. It was regarded as a landmark. It redefined educational priorities and made a fresh attempt to cope with the three strands that have influenced educational policy in India, namely, issues relating to quantity, quality, and equity. The policy gave the highest importance to UPE.

The activities which foster and promote the all-round balanced development of the child in the age group of 0–6 years in all dimensions—physical, mental, social, emotional, and moral—have been collectively described in NPE, 1986 as ECCE. Both these components, care and education, are essential, since either by itself is inadequate. The ECCE is the birthright of every child.

The NPE, 1986 has explicitly recognized the importance of ECCE as a crucial input not only for human development but also for universalization of elementary education and women's development. It has, therefore, emphasized the need for large-scale investment in the development of the young child, both through the government and through voluntary organizations. It has recommended a holistic approach of providing ECCE programmes which should aim at fostering nutrition, health, and social, physical, mental, moral, and emotional development of the child. In this context the policy has clearly recommended that ECCE programmes should be 'child-oriented, focused around play and the individuality of the child. Formal methods and introduction of the three Rs will be discouraged at this stage.'[28]

Consistent with the thrust of the national policy, early childhood education programmes are being qualitatively and quantitatively strengthened both in the voluntary and in the government sectors. While early childhood education per se is being provided to children in the 3–6 age group under these schemes, there exist wide diversities in terms of curriculum, infrastructure, financial allocations, staff quality, clientele, etc. These diversities are evident not only in different schemes but often within the same scheme from one region to another.

Often, what is practiced in the name of pre-school education is not necessarily what has been envisaged in the national policy. Most ECCE programmes, based on curriculum, have become a downward extension of primary schools, wherein the basic philosophy and methodology of early childhood education are being generally ignored. The staff, in many cases, are not adequately qualified or trained in early childhood education and does not have the basic knowledge of child development. Particularly in urban settings, pre-schools are generally located in cramped, poorly ventilated areas, sometimes even in *barsatis*[29] on roof tops, with no safe, open space for children to play in. In rural areas, in addition to other constraints, the availability of suitable manpower is the major issue. Facilities in terms of equipment and material form another significant area of diversity. In view of the present scenario, provision of early childhood education of a good quality cannot be ensured. In this context a persistent recommendation emerging from major seminars/conferences over the years has been that there should be some system of licensing or accreditation of pre-schools/ECCE programmes. There is, therefore, a need to formulate certain prerequisites and standards which would ensure some uniformity within the diversities with respect to different aspects/components of an early childhood education programme.

[28] Department of Pre-school and Elementary Education, MHRD, GoI.

[29] *Barsati* means a one-room set of accommodation constructed adjacent to the entrance to the roof of any building.

With the specific objective of laying down these minimum prerequisites, the department of pre-school and elementary education developed a document—minimum specifications for pre-schools. An effort was made to specify these, keeping in mind the contextual realities of our country. While the minimum was specified as 'essentials', the 'desirables' were also included, provision of which would certainly enhance the quality of any ECCE programme. These specifications were categorized into several groups. The physical structure and facilities included details about the location, play areas, facility for drinking water, sanitary facilities, sleeping facilities, and storage space. Under equipment and material, details about the outdoor equipment, material for large muscle development, indoor equipment/material, and first-aid kit were provided. Also the safety precautions, age of admission, and admission procedure were given. Under the pre-school staff, the staff structure and adult-child ratio, qualifications of the teacher, qualifications of the helper, and salary structure were detailed out. The timings and content and methodology of the pre-school programme were also listed. It finally included the kind of records and registers to be maintained, namely, the admission records, the progress records, teachers' diary, and other registers. All this was specified in detail with a view to bringing uniformity all across.

Following the policy statement in 1986 on improving learning conditions, a number of national-level programmes were launched which have continued to contribute to improvement of school conditions in the 1990s. For instance, OB, launched in 1987 and continued and expanded in the 1990s, is one major programme under which learning conditions have been created and expanded to improve the quality of schooling at the primary stage. The OB has a wide coverage throughout the country. Some of the responses to policy changes in the years since the national policy chartered a new course of community-based education for development are being highlighted later in this chapter. These include initiatives of the central and state governments, as well as independent initiatives from educational institutions and voluntary organizations.[30]

National Policy on Early Childhood Care and Education, 2013

A National Policy on Early Childhood Care and Education was adopted in September 2013. The policy envisages promotion of inclusive, equitable, and contextualized opportunities for promoting optimal development and active learning capacity of all children below 6 years of age. The policy lays down the way forward for a comprehensive approach towards ensuring a sound foundation for survival, growth and development with focus on *care and early learning* for every child. The key goals of the policy include universal access with equity and inclusion; quality in ECCE; and strengthening capacity, monitoring and supervision, advocacy, research and review.[31]

National Youth Policy, 2003, 2014

The NYP, 2003 reiterated the country's commitment to the composite and all-round development of the youth and adolescents of India. The objectives of the NYP, 2003 included providing the

---

[30] M.S. Yadav and Meenakshi Bhardwaj, *Learning Conditions for Primary Education* (National Institute of Educational Planning and Administration, Ministry of Human Resource Development, GoI, April 2000).

[31] MHRD, *Education for All towards Quality with Equity*.

youth with proper educational and training opportunities and facilitating access to information in respect of employment opportunities and to other services, including entrepreneurial guidance and financial credit. The NYP, 2014 policy seeks to empower youth of the country to achieve their full potential. The main objectives of the policy are to:

1. create a productive workforce that can make a sustainable contribution to India's economic development;
2. develop a strong and healthy generation equipped to take on future[32] challenges;
3. instill social values and promote community service to build national ownership;
4. facilitate participation and civic engagement at levels of governance; and
5. support youth at risk and create equitable opportunity for all disadvantaged and marginalized youth. The priority areas of NYP, 2014 include education, employment and skill development, entrepreneurship, health and healthy lifestyles, sports, promotion of social values, community engagement, participation in politics and governance, youth engagement, inclusion and social justice. In the NYP, 2014 document, the youth age-group is defined as 15–29 years.

Five Year Plans and Elementary Education[33]

Five-year plans are an important development strategy in India. Five-year plans have repeatedly promised to take the nation towards achieving universalization of elementary education. Expenditure on education in the five-year plans has shown a rapid rise since the inception of the first five-year plan in the country, but an analysis of intra-sectoral allocation of resources during the plan period shows a lopsided emphasis on elementary education. In the first five-year plan, 56 per cent of the total plan resources to education were allocated to elementary education. The relative importance given to elementary education declined to 35 per cent in the second plan, to 34 per cent in the third plan, and gradually to 30 per cent in the sixth plan. It was only during the seventh and eighth plans that significant efforts were made to increase the allocation substantially, though the allocation in the eighth plan was still less than the corresponding one in the first plan in percentage terms. Elementary education was given a boost in the seventh plan. It also received a favourable response in the eighth plan.[34]

The Tenth Five Year Plan (2002–07) envisaged all children completing 5 years of schooling by 2007; reduction in gender gaps in literacy rates by at least 50 per cent by 2007; and increase in literacy rates to 75 per cent within the plan period.

The Eleventh Five Year Plan (2007–12) sought to reduce dropout rates in elementary education from 52.2 per cent in 2003–04 to 20 per cent by 2011–12; develop minimum standards of educational attainment in elementary school, and through regular testing monitor effectiveness of education to ensure quality; increase literacy rate for persons of age 7 years and above to 85

---

[32] MHRD, *Education for All towards Quality with Equity.*

[33] MHRD, *Education for All towards Quality with Equity.*

[34] Jandhyala B.G. Tilak, *Financing of Elementary Education in India* (New Delhi: National Institute of Educational Planning and Administration, MHRD, GoI, April 2000).

per cent; lower gender gap in literacy to 10 percentage points; increase the percentage of each cohort going to higher education from the present 10 per cent to 15 per cent by the end of the Eleventh Plan.

The Twelfth Five Year Plan (2012–17) has accorded high priority to the expansion of education, ensuring that educational opportunities are available to all segments of the society, and ensuring that the quality of education imparted is significantly improved. The Twelfth Plan targets for school education and literacy include:

1. ensuring universal access and, in keeping with the letter and spirit of the RTE Act, providing good-quality free and compulsory education to all children in the age group of 6 to 14 years;
2. improving attendance and reduce dropout rates at the elementary level to below 10 per cent and lower the percentage of OOSC at the elementary level to below 2 per cent for all socio-economic and minority groups and in all states/UTs;
3. increasing enrolments at higher levels of education and raise the gross enrollment ratio (GER) at the secondary level to over 90 per cent, at the higher secondary level to over 65 per cent;
4. raising the overall literacy rate to over 80 per cent and reducing the gender gap in literacy to less than 10 per cent;
5. providing at least one year of well-supported/well-resourced pre-school education in primary schools to all children, particularly those in educationally backward blocks (EBBs); and
6. improving learning outcomes that are measured, monitored and reported independently at all levels of school education with a special focus on ensuring that all children master basic reading and numeracy skills by Class II and skills of critical thinking, expression and problem solving by Class V.[35]

Laws Relating to Child Education in India

Evolution of Laws

The Indian Education Commission appointed in 1882, contained the proposal for adopting a law for universal compulsory education or at least for children employed in factories was mooted. This was also rejected due to financial and administrative difficulties. The first experiment of making primary education compulsory took place in 1893 when the ruler of the state of Baroda, Maharaj Sayajirao Gaekwad, introduced compulsory education in the Amreli division of his state; since the results were promising, he extended it to the entire state in 1906.[36]

Gopal Krishna Gokhale made the first definite demand for the official introduction of primary education in March 1910 when he moved a resolution in the Imperial Legislative Council, which was later withdrawn. Even as late as 1913, the British government was not prepared to accept the principle of compulsion, but wished to expand primary education on a 'voluntary basis'. However, in 1918, with the efforts of Vithalbhai Patel, Bombay passed a Primary Education

[35] MHRD, *Education for All towards Quality with Equity.*

[36] A. Mehendale, 'Compulsory Primary Education in India: The Legal Framework', *Lawyers Collective*, April 1998, pp. 4–5.

Act permitting municipalities to introduce compulsory education in their areas. Within a few years, other provinces also passed laws aimed at compulsory education. By the early 1930s, the principle of compulsory education was written into state law. But these laws, however, were not implemented satisfactorily due to many reasons, such as technical flaws, lack of experience, and unwillingness to make use of the power of prosecution under the acts.[37]

Constitution of India

In 1950, after Independence, the Constitution of India in Article 246 dealt with the subject matter of laws made by the Parliament and by the legislatures of states. Education, including technical and medical education, is placed in List III, that is, the Concurrent List of the Seventh Schedule of the Constitution of India.[38] Thus, the Parliament as well as the individual state legislatures can make laws on the subject of education. Such a scheme of distribution of legislative powers under the Constitution is a necessary component of a federal political structure.

The Constitution, in Article 45, made compulsory education a matter of national policy. The Constitution, in Article 45, lays down as a directive principle that every child up to the age of 14 shall receive free and compulsory education. Articles 39f, 46, and 47 lend further support to this constitutional directive. The founding fathers of the Constitution clearly intended to ensure that every child, irrespective of social or economic status of his/her parents, received care and education from birth up to the age of 14 years. This goal was to have been achieved 'within a period of ten years from the commencement of this Constitution'.

Article 28 of the Constitution is also relevant to education of children. It provides freedom as to attendance at religious instruction or religious workshop in certain educational institutes. The provision in this article protects the child from any information of religious instruction through educational institutions. Article 29 of the Constitution provides the right to admission to educational institutes (receiving state aid) without discrimination on the basis of religion, race, caste, and language. A related directive has been given in Article 41 of the Constitution, which states that the state shall, within the limits of its economic growth and development, make effective provisions for securing the right to work.

The Constitution of India lays down that the state legislature may by law endow the panchayats (Article 243g) and municipalities (Article 243w) with such powers and authority as may be necessary to enable them to function as institutions of self-government. Such a law may contain provisions for the devolution of powers and responsibilities with respect to:

- the preparation of plans for economic development and social justice; and
- the implementation of schemes for economic development and social justice as may be entrusted to them, including those in relation to the matters listed in the schedules.

[37] Mehendale, 'Compulsory Primary Education'.

[38] Education was a state subject whereby the state legislature had the exclusive jurisdiction of legislating in matters pertaining to education. In 1976, with the Constitution (Forty-Second Amendment) Act, education became a concurrent subject. As a result of this amendment, no part of the subject of education now belongs to the exclusive state list.

The Eleventh Schedule[39] of the Constitution recognizes the powers, authorities, and responsibilities of the panchayats in matters pertaining to education, including primary and secondary schools, technical training and vocational education, and adult and non-formal education.[40] The Twelfth Schedule[41] of the Constitution covers the powers, authorities, and responsibilities of the municipalities, which includes promotion of cultural, educational, and aesthetic aspects.[42] Thus, among the local bodies the panchayats have been given clear-cut powers for undertaking activities for the promotion of elementary education, whereas for the municipalities, this has not been spelt out clearly.[43] The Seventy-Third and seventy-fourth constitutional amendments have given a statutory basis to district planning by providing for a District Planning Committee to consolidate the plans prepared by panchayats and municipalities and to prepare a draft development plan for the district as a whole.

Universal free and compulsory education should have become a reality in India by 1960. Article 45 of the Indian Constitution says: 'The State shall endeavour to provide, within a period of ten years from the commencement of this Constitution, for free and compulsory education for all children until they complete the age of 14 years.' But that constitutional obligation was time and again deferred—first to 1970 and then to 1980, 1990, and 2000. Realizing the sluggish attitude and delaying tactics in implementing the Constitutional commitment, the Supreme Court of India, in the Unnikrishnan judgment in 1993, said: 'It is noteworthy that among the several articles in Part IV only Article 45 speaks of time limit, no other article does. Has it not significance? Is it a mere pious wish, even after 44 years of the Constitution?' The Tenth Five-year Plan visualizes that India would achieve universal elementary education by 2007. However, the Union Human Resource Development Minister recently announced that India would achieve this target by 2010.

Before the interpretation of Article 21 to include RTE till the age of 14 years,[44] every state had designed legislations to look into the affairs of free and compulsory education of weaker children whose parents could not secure to make them literate. However, these legislations remained more so in nature of enabling legislations as the onus of discharging the duty was left to the 'local authority' that was to decide the mode of implementation of the act. A number of legislations have been passed on free and compulsory education in India before and after Independence. Between 1918 and 1921, primary education acts were passed in eight provinces. All the acts were applicable to both the sexes except in the Central Provinces where the act was essentially for boys. After Independence, states have enacted legislations making elementary education compulsory. In the 1960s, most states framed their own laws on the model of the Delhi School Education Act, 1960. The provisions of the acts are similar to the provincial laws

[39]   Added by the Constitution (Seventy-Third Amendment) Act, 1993.
[40]   Entries 17,18, and 19 respectively.
[41]   Twelfth schedule has been inserted by the Constitution (Seventy-Fourth Amendment) Act, 1993.
[42]   Entry 13.
[43]   'Frequently asked questions on the Fundamental Right to Education', compiled by Centre for Child and the National Law School of India University, Bangalore, August 1998.
[44]   *Mohini Jain* v. *Union of India* (1992) 3 SCC 666 and later in *J.P. Unnikrishnan* v. *State of Andhra Pradesh* 1993 SCC (1) 645.

enacted during the British rule.[45] Compulsory education laws in India do not make education compulsory; they merely establish the conditions under which state governments may make education compulsory in specified areas. All these laws permit local authorities to introduce compulsory education.[46]

Table 7.2 shows the various state acts before the passing of RTE Act, 2009.

Table 7.2   Compulsory Education Acts in States/UTs of India[47]

S. No.	States	Name of the Act
1.	Delhi	The Delhi Primary Education Act, 1960 (Act No. 39 of 1960)
2.	Uttar Pradesh	United Provinces Primary Education Act, 1919 (Uttar Pradhesh Act No. 7 of 1919) United Provinces (District) Board Primary Education Act, 1926, adapted and modified by adaptation orders, 1950 (Uttar Pradesh Act No. 7 of 1926)
3.	Haryana	Punjab Primary Education Act, 1960
4.	Andhra Pradesh	Andhra Pradesh Education Act, 1962 (Act No. 1 of 1982)
5.	Assam	The Assam Elementary Education (Provincialisation) Act, 1974 (Assam Act No. 6 of 1975)
6.	Bihar	Bihar Primary Education (Amendment) Act, 1959 (Bihar and Orissa Education Act No. 1 of 19191) as amended by Bihar Act IV of 1959
7.	Goa	Goa Compulsory Elementary Education Act, 1995
8.	Jammu and Kashmir	Jammu and Kashmir Education Act, 1984 (Act No. XI of 1984)
9.	Gujarat	Gujarat Compulsory Primary Education Act, 1995 (Goa Act No. 4 of 1996)
10	Kerala	Kerala Education Act, 1958 (Act No. 6 of 1959) (as amended by Acts 35 of 1960, 31 of 1969, and 9 of 1985)
11.	Himachal Pradesh	Himachal Pradesh Compulsory Education Act, 1953
12.	Karnataka	Karnataka Education Act, 1983 (Karnataka Act No. 1 of 1995)
13.	Tamil Nadu	Tamil Nadu Compulsory Education Act, 1994 (Act No. 33 of 1985)
14.	West Bengal	West Bengal Primary Education Act, 1973 (West Bengal Act No. 43 of 1973)
15	Rajasthan	Rajasthan Primary Education Act, 1964 (Bangalore Act No. 1 of 1973)
16.	Madhya Pradesh	Madhya Pradesh Primary Education Act, 1964 (Act No. 33 of 1973)
17.	Maharashtra	Maharashtra Primary Education Act, 1947 (Bombay Act No. LXI of 1973) (as modified till 30 April 1986)
18.	Sikkim	Sikkim Primary Act, 2000 (Act No. 14 of 2000)
19.	Punjab	Punjab Primary Education Act, 1960 (Act No. 39)

[45] Mehendale, 'Compulsory Primary Education'.
[46] Mehendale, 'Compulsory Primary Education'.
[47] National Institute of Education Planning and Administration, New Delhi, India, March 2003.

The acts mentioned in Table 7.2 indicate that no fee shall be levied for any child attending an approved school under the management of the state government or local authority, or a school board. Education was not provided free of cost at schools managed by private bodies. In addition, the concept of 'free education' implied merely non-payment of fees and did not include expenses such as transport, school uniforms, and examination fees. Thus 'free education' was not actually free and families had to incur costs on education in addition to losing out on the meagre wage that the child would have otherwise brought home.[48]

The state acts had provided for attendance authorities. The attendance authorities were persons appointed under the various state primary education acts to ensure that children attend school as per the provisions of the acts. The acts stated that the state government may appoint as many persons as it was thought fit to be attendance authorities. It could also appoint as many persons as are considered necessary, to assist the attendance authorities in the discharge of their duties. There was a reliance on the bureaucracy to enforce the laws. In case the child was not sent to school, the attendance authority had to hold an inquiry. If no 'reasonable excuse' existed for non-attendance, an order against the parent had to be passed in a prescribed form. In the event of failure on the part of parents to send their children to school, judicial proceedings had to be initiated. In certain state rules as of Karnataka, exemption from school attendance was granted when the child's assistance was specially required by the parent or guardian to help his vocation. Thus, laws and rules themselves had left enough scope for defeating the object of child's right to education.[49]

All the state acts clearly indicated that parents were duty-bound to send the child to an approved school, unless a reasonable excuse for non-attendance existed. In case parents were unable to send their children to school, they are liable to be penalized. Compelling parents without providing any facilities for schooling or supportive measures for ensuring that children complete at least the minimum level of schooling, was meaningless. There was a legitimate fear that penal provisions could be used as a weapon to cause further harassment to poor families, already struggling for survival. All the acts stated that children of school-going age should not be employed. Any employer engaging a child who should be in school could be penalized under the state acts. However, child labour was rampant and it was evident that these provisions as also laws prohibiting child labour were not enforced. It was absurd to equate parents with employers.

All the state statutes on free and compulsory education did not impose any duty on the states to provide adequate and quality educational facilities. There was absolutely no mention of the quality of education in any of them. There was also no mention of the obligation towards others.

Common features of some of the state primary education acts from the states of Delhi, Karnataka, Assam, Andhra Pradesh, Rajasthan, Madhya Pradesh, Punjab, West Bengal, and Maharashtra were the following:

- The age group was generally 6–11 years or 6–14 years.
- Parents were duty-bound to send their child to an approved school unless there was a reasonable excuse.

---

48 Mehendale, 'Compulsory Primary Education', pp. 6–7.
49 Mehendale, 'Compulsory Primary Education', p. 7.

- All the state acts indicated that no fee shall be levied for any child attending an approved school under a state government or local authority but there was no definition of the word 'fee'. There was a need to define 'free education'. The word 'free' should have included fees as well as all ancillary expenses.
- Children of school-going age should not be employed. Such employer would be penalized. However, this was not enforced in practice as there were hardly any convictions.
- Many state acts come into effect by notification. Since there was no time limit within the acts, the states notified them as and when it pleased them.
- Reliance was placed on the bureaucracy as the implementing authority. There was a provision of attendance authorities.
- Exemption from school attendance was allowed if the child's assistance was required by parents/guardians.
- No duty was imposed on the state to provide adequate and quality educational facilities.
- There was no mention of quality of education, child rights, and citizenship education.

This history of compulsory primary education worldwide shows that legislation cannot play a positive role in ensuring universal education unless the social conditions are favourable. So, a strategy of mass mobilization and supportive services to bring children to school and a social recognition of the value of education is required for effective implementation of laws. When the legal basis of primary education is voluntary, enrolment in primary schools shows a rapid increase only up to a certain point. When this point is reached, enrolment slows down and almost reaches a standstill; rapid advance beyond this point is possible only if compulsion is introduced.

Compulsion has to be accompanied with measures to strengthen the socio-economic conditions of families. If families have the means to meet their basic necessities, primary education itself being a fundamental necessity, the notion of compulsion in universalizing education will become redundant.[50]

The effectiveness of law as a means to achieve 'education for all' has been limited. The state has not displayed the political will to create conditions for the implementation of laws dealing with the prohibition of child labour, extending school facilities for all, and improving the quality of education. Further, the law itself was outdated and divorced from ground realities. Also, there was very poor implementation of the education laws.

The enforcement of compulsory education laws in several developing countries was facilitated by the system of compulsory birth registration. Of course, the societal coalitions have proved to be crucial in introducing and extending compulsory education laws and banning the employment of children. Church groups, religious leaders, trade unionists, school teachers and educational officials, philanthropists, and social reformers have played significant roles.

Modern states regard education as a legal duty and not merely a right. The notion of the duty denies parents the right to choose. Parents are told by the state that no matter how great is their need for child labour or income, they must relinquish their child to school for a part of the day. The notion of duty also applies to the state. Education needs more of our funds, it also needs our creative thinking about how to develop schools relevant to the needs of actual and potential child

---

[50] Mehendale, 'Compulsory Primary Education', pp. 7–8.

workers. Schools must teach useful skills that are seen as relevant by both children and parents. The debate needs to shift to the rights of the child vis-à-vis the duty of the state.

In 1991 a book by Myron Weiner[51] highlighted the fact that existence of child labor and illiteracy of the children was more so prevalent due to non-empathy of middle class and state bureaucracy than alone the poverty. There were two landmark pronouncement of court judgments in *Mohini Jain* v. *Union of India*[52] and later in *J.P. Unnikrishnan* v. *State of Andhra Pradesh*,[53] that had held right to free and compulsory education a matter of right to life for all children of the country as per interpretation of Article 21 of the Constitution.

Thereafter, India ratified the UNCRC[54] and as part of Article 51(c)[55] of the Constitution, it was obliged to foster respect for international laws and treaties. Article 28 of the UNCRC obliges commitment from its member nations to bring their national legislations for securing the rights and justice of children in their country. According to Article 28 of the UNCRC[56]:

1. State parties recognize the rights of the child to education and with a view to achieving this right progressively and on the basis of equal opportunity, they shall in particular:

   a) make primary education compulsory and available free to all;
   b) encourage the development of different forms of secondary education, including general and vocational education, make them available and accessible to every child, and take appropriate measures such as the introduction of free education and offering financial assistance in case of need;
   c) make higher education accessible to all on the basis of capacity by every appropriate means;
   d) make educational and vocational information and guidance available and accessible to all children; and
   e) take measures to encourage regular attendance at schools and the reduction of drop-out rates.

2. States parties shall take all appropriate measures to ensure that school discipline is administered in a manner consistent with the child's human dignity and in conformity with the present convention.

3. States parties shall promote and encourage international cooperation in matters relating to education, in particular with a view to contributing to the elimination of ignorance and illiteracy throughout the world and facilitating access to scientific and technical knowledge and modern teaching methods. In this regard, particular account shall be taken of the needs of developing countries.

---

[51] Myron Weiner, *The Child and the State in India: Child Labor and Education Policy in Comparative Perspective* (Princeton University Press), p. 199.

[52] (1992) 3 SCC 666.

[53] 1993 SCC (1) 645.

[54] India acceded to the convention on 11 December 1992.

[55] Article 51(c), Constitution 1950: The state shall endeavour to foster respect for international law and treaty obligations.

[56] Article 28 of the UNCRC, 1989.

The 83rd Amendment bill was tabled in the Lok sabha in July 1997. The Constitution (83rd Amendment) Bill provided to make free and compulsory education to all citizens of the age group of 6–14 years, a fundamental right by inserting Article 21A in the Constitution.[57] Under this bill, Article 45[58] of the Constitution had to be omitted and in Article 51A[59] of the Constitution, after Clause (j) the following clause will be added, namely: Clause (k) to provide opportunities for education to a child between the age of 6 and 14 years of whom such citizen is a parent or guardian. This bill was replaced by the Constitution (Ninety-third Amendment Bill) 2001 which was passed by the Lok Sabha in November 2001.[60] Subsequently, this 83rd bill was reintroduced in the Parliament in 2001 via the 93rd Amendment Bill, 2001, which had the following provisions.[61]

The significant provisions of the 93rd amendment were:

- The amendment made education a fundamental right for children in the age group 6–14 years.[62]
- It provided that the state shall endeavor to provide early childhood care and education for all children until they complete the age of 6 years.[63]
- It shall be the fundamental duty of the parents and guardians to provide opportunities for education to their children or, as the case may be, wards between the age of 6 and 14 years.[64]

This amendment made the right to free and compulsory education for the children, a fundamental right. The fundamental right to free education had a paramount importance as it meant that the state was now under the legal obligation to provide free and compulsory education to all children between 6–14 years of age. If the state fails to fulfil its obligations, any person can seek constitutional remedies against the state for the violation of fundamental rights.[65]

---

[57] Article 21A: The state shall provide free and compulsory education to all children of the age of 6–14 years in such manner as the state may by law determine.

[58] Article 45: The state shall endeavour to provide early childhood care and education for all children until they complete the age of 6 years.

[59] Article 51A(k): Who is a parent or guardian to provide for opportunities for education to his child as the case may be, ward between the ages of 6–14 years.

[60] Juneia Nalini, *Constitutional Amendment to Make Education a Fundamental Right: Issues for Follow up Legislation* (New Delhi, India: National Institute of Education Planning and Administration, March 2003).

[61] The Ninety-Third Amendment Bill was passed by the Lok Sabha on 27 November 2001 and by the Rajya Sabha on 14 May 2002.

[62] Ninety-third Constitutional Amendment: After Article 21 of the Constitution the following article shall be inserted, namely: 'Article 21A. The state shall provide free and compulsory education to all children of the age of six to fourteen years in such manner as the State may, by law, determine.'

[63] For Article 45 of the Constitution, the following shall be substituted: 'Article 45. The state shall endeavour to provide early childhood care and education for all children until they complete the age of six years.'

[64] In Article 51A of the Constitution, after Clause (j) the following clause shall be added, namely: '(k) who is a parent or guardian to provide opportunities for education to his child or, as the case may be, ward between the age of six and fourteen years.'

[65] *Constitution of India*, Articles 226 and 32.

Later, by 73rd[66] & 74th Constitutional Amendment Act (CAA), [67] education for transferred under 11th & 12th schedules to Panchayati Raj institutions so as to broaden the horizon and outreach of RTE to lowest most strata of the society.

Critique of the 93rd Constitution Amendment Act

The amendment sought to make free and compulsory education a fundamental right only for the children in the age group of 6–14 years and not for the children in the age group of 0–6 years. However, in the *Unnikrishnan* judgment (1993), the Supreme Court of India gave the clear verdict that education is a fundamental right for all children up to 14 years. Therefore, this provision diluted the judgment and can be termed regressive. In fact it should provide free and compulsory education to all children till the age of 18 years. India has ratified the UNCRC wherein the child is defined as a person below 18 years of age.

In the amendment, the provision for ECCE for the age group of 0–6 years has been included in the directive principles of state policy. The directive principles are not enforceable. The age group of 0–6 years, should be a part of the fundamental right to education as it influences the most vital period of the child's development. Without the ECCE, the effort to provide free and compulsory education to children in the age group of 6–14 years cannot be successful.

The new Article 21A states: 'The State shall provide free and compulsory education to all children of the age of six to fourteen years in such manner *as the state may, by law, determine* (emphasis added).' This discretion will enable the government to justify cheap, low-cost alternatives in the name of education as the enjoyment of this right would depend upon the whims and fancies of the government. The government might resort to second-class alternatives such as single-teacher schools, education-guarantee scheme, and para-teachers. There have been alarming arbitrary trends of promoting a large variety of non-formal education centres. The non-formal stream is considered equivalent to school education. Adult literacy classes have been considered as school education. The term 'education' needs to be defined and qualified. It should be made the commitment of the GoI to provide quality education to all children, without any discrimination.

This act compels the parents to send their children to school by including it as a fundamental duty (Article 51A). There is an apprehension that the government would use this provision randomly against poor parents to shirk its responsibility of imparting free and compulsory education.

There is a provision for 'free and compulsory' education to all children. The word 'free' is not defined. Presently, it is claimed that government schools are giving free education to the students

[66] The 73rd Amendment inserted a new Part IX in the Constitution which contains Article 243 and Articles 243A to 243-O. Section 4 of the Amendment inserted a new Eleventh Schedule to the Constitution which deals with matters on which the panchayats may be devolved with powers and responsibility by the state legislatures by law.

[67] The 74th CAA requires the state governments to amend their municipal laws in order to empower urban local bodies (ULBs) 'with such powers and authority as may be necessary to enable them to function as institutions of self governance'. This amendment introduced the XII Schedule.

as they do not charge any fee. However, the poor parents have to bear other expenses pertaining to school uniforms, books, and examination fees. This implies that the parents still have to pay for the education. Thus the concept of free education is certainly a misnomer or a myth. Therefore, a clear definition of the expression 'free education' should be inserted to make this amendment meaningful.

The amendment was silent on the role of private schools which can still charge exorbitant fees, as they appear to be out of the purview of the act.

There have been strong demands from various child rights activists, educationists, and non-governmental organizations that the act be amended to:[68]

• Include free and compulsory education as a fundamental right up to the age of 18 years. The state cannot abdicate its responsibility of imparting free and compulsory education by transferring it to the parents under the alibi of a fundamental duty.
• Lay down that there should be an unambiguous provision of imparting equitable quality education for all children. There should not be any cheap, alternative education for the poor children.
• Allocate all necessary resources to achieve this right from the Consolidated Fund of the Union and states.
• Determine, by law, appropriate means to verify whether children up to 18 years are enjoying this right. In other words there should be a monitoring mechanism.
• Extend this right to all educational institutions, whether under state or non-state auspices.
• Establish accountability for implementing this law. Failure to provide conditions for the exercise and enjoyment of this right shall be an offence punishable by law.
• Provide special opportunities for the girl child, the disabled and other disadvantaged and vulnerable groups.

Right of Children to Free and Compulsory Education Act, 2009

The first draft of the RTE Bill was proposed in the Parliament in 2008 with the belief that values of equality, social justice and democracy and the creation of a just and humane society is possible only through provision of inclusive elementary education extending to children belonging to all sections of the society. This meant that right to free and compulsory education could no longer be enjoyed by those who can afford it, but children belonging to socially and educationally backward classes are equally entitled to the fruits of education. Subsequently it made the government realize that the importance of improving education is more than a directive principle of the state duty,[69] and extends on the shoulders of not merely schools run or supported by the

---

[68] Campaign against Child Labour, National Alliance for the Fundamental Right to Education, Bharatiya Jan Vigyan, and Forum for Crèche and Childcare Services, and other networks working on education have suggested many of the aforementioned amendments to the Ninety-Third Constitutional Amendment Bill.

[69] Article 45 of Constitution in 1950: 'The state shall endeavour to provide within a period of 10 years from the of commencement of this Constitution, for free and compulsory education of all children until they complete the age of fourteen years.'

appropriate governments, but is also a responsibility of schools which are not dependent on government funds[70]. The RTE Act, 2009 was passed by the Parliament in August 2009. After receiving Presidential assent, it was notified for implementation from 1 April 2010.

The landmark passing of the RTE Act, 2009 marked a historic moment for the children of India. The RTE Act, 2009 received the Presidential assent on 26 August 2009. For the first time in India's history, children have been guaranteed their right to quality elementary education by the state with the help of families and communities. Few countries in the world have such a national provision to ensure child-centered, child-friendly education to help all children develop to their fullest potential. There were an estimated 8 million 6 to 14-year-olds in India out-of-school in 2009.

The salient features of the RTE Act, 2009 are as follows:[71]

1. Free and compulsory education to all children of India in the 6 to 14 age group;[72]
2. No child shall be held back, expelled, or required to pass a board examination until completion of elementary education;[73]
3. A child above 6 years of age has not been admitted in any school or though admitted, could not complete his or her elementary education, then, he or she shall be admitted in a class appropriate to his or her age, provided that where a child is directly admitted in a class appropriate to his or her age, then, he or she shall, in order to be at par with others, have a right to receive special training, in such manner, and within such time limits, as may be prescribed, provided further that a child so admitted to elementary education shall be entitled to free education till completion of elementary education even after 14 years.[74]
4. Proof of age for admission: For the purposes of admission to elementary education, the age of a child shall be determined on the basis of the birth certificate issued in accordance with the provisions of the births. Deaths and Marriages Registration Act, 1856 or on the basis of such other document, as may be prescribed. No child shall be denied admission in a school for lack of age proof.[75]
5. A child who completes elementary education shall be awarded a certificate;[76]
6. Calls for a fixed student-teacher ratio: in primary schools—1:30 and in upper primary schools—1:35.[77]
7. Provides for 25 per cent reservation for economically disadvantaged children in admission to Class 1 in all private unaided schools of the country.[78]

---

[70] Clause 4 of the 'Statement of Objects and Reasons, Right of Children to Free and Compulsory Education Act 2009', GoI.

[71] The Right to Education Act (Act 21A of 2009), GoI.

[72] The Right to Education Act, 2009, Section 3(1): Every child of the age of 6 to 14 years shall have a right to free and compulsory education in a neighbourhood school till completion of elementary education.

[73] The Right to Education Act, 2009, Section 16.

[74] The Right to Education Act, 2009, Section 4.

[75] The Right to Education Act, 2009, Section 14.

[76] The Right to Education Act, 2009, Section 30(2).

[77] The Right to Education Act, 2009, Section 25.

[78] The Right to Education Act, 2009, Section 12(1)(c).

8. Mandates improvement in quality of education.[79]
9. School teachers will need adequate professional degree within 5 years or else will lose job.[80]
10. School infrastructure (where there is problem) to be improved in 3 years, else recognition cancelled.[81]
11. Financial burden will be shared between state and central governments.[82]

Model rules were provided by the centre.[83] Today, almost every state has its state education rules to the RTE Act, 2009. The state rules in general have not provided for adequate incentives especially to teachers who have a huge responsibility under the act. There is a need for social audits under the act. The role of civil society organizations is absent under the act and rules. Stakeholders under the act are not aware of their roles and responsibilities .

Implementation of the RTE Act, 2009

Indian children have the right to receive free and compulsory education from the age of 6 to 14 years of age. The government will bear all the expenditures of schooling. There has been tremendous progress since the enactment of the RTE Act in India:

• All states and UTs have notified RTE rules.
• Budgetary provision for the SSA has more than doubled between 2009–10 and 2014–15 and the SSA programme has been adapted to ensure that no child in this age group remains out of school, and that all children study in age appropriate grades.
• An additional 11.8 million children enroled from 2009–10 to 2012–13, making it 199.7 million.[84]

The act has mandated reservation of a minimum of 25 per cent of the seats at the entry level class for children belonging to economically weaker sections (EWS) and disadvantaged groups in all private unaided schools, excluding minority institutions. The cost of education of these children is to be reimbursed by the government to the extent of per child expenditure incurred by the state or the actual school fees, whichever is less. After the enactment of this RTE Act, 2009, the private unaided schools resisted compliance of their responsibility to admit students from weaker sections to the extent of 25 per cent in their classes from 1–8 as per Section 12(1)(c) of the RTE Act, 2009.[85] This provision was challenged by private schools in *Society for Unaided*

---

[79] The Right to Education Act, 2009, Section 8 and Section 9.
[80] The Right to Education Act, 2009, Section 23.
[81] The Right to Education Act, 2009, Section 19.
[82] The Right to Education Act, 2009, Section 7.
[83] The RTE Model Rules finalized in February 2010 provide guidelines to be followed by the states to implement the RTE Act.
[84] Department of School Education and Literacy, Ministry of Human Resource Development, GoI, National University of Educational Planning and Administration, DISE, New Delhi: 2009–2010 and 2012–2013.
[85] The Right to Education Act, 2009, Section 12(1): For the purposes of this act, a school—

(1) specified in Subclause (i) of Clause (n) of Section 2 shall provide free and compulsory elementary education to all children admitted therein;

Private Schools of Rajasthan v. *UoI*[86] as an infringement of their fundamental right under Article 19(1)(g) and by minority schools under Articles 29[87] and 30[88] of the Constitution. However, the Honourable Supreme Court upheld the validity of the act with the exception that minority unaided institution were exempt from admitting children as per Section 12 of the RTE Act, 2009. Hence Section 12(1)(c) became applicable.[89] The objective of this reservation was to put millions of children in private schooling but in practice there are certain concerns. There is no method is prescribed for selecting the 25 per cent poor students for admission into unaided private schools. In the absence of a viable provision, the private unaided (de facto commercial) schools can choose the 25 per cent poor children in a way that the choice would benefit the school. Each state has modified the model guidelines and framed its own set of implementation processes. Delhi defines EWS as the families from EWS having household income less than 1 lakh per annum while the disadvantaged groups include SC, ST, and non-creamy layer of OBC, orphans and physically and mentally challenged children. On the other hand, Rajasthan has set this income limit to

---

(2)   specified in Subclause (ii) of Clause (n) of Section 2 shall provide free and compulsory elementary education to such proportion of children admitted therein as its annual recurring aid or grants so received bears to its annual recurring expenses, subject to a minimum of 25 per cent.;

(3)   specified in Subclauses (iii) and (iv) of Clause (n) of Section 2 shall admit in Class I, to the extent of at least 25 five per cent of the strength of that class, children belonging to weaker section and disadvantaged group in the neighbourhood and provide free and compulsory elementary education till its completion, provided further that where a school specified in Clause (n) of Section 2 imparts pre-school education, the provisions of Clauses (a) to (c) shall apply for admission to such pre-school education.

[86]   AIR 2012 SC 3445: (2012) 6 SCC 1.

[87]   The Constitution of India 1949, Article 29: Protection of interests of minorities—

(1)   Any section of the citizens residing in the territory of India or any part thereof having a distinct language, script or culture of its own shall have the right to conserve the same

(2)   No citizen shall be denied admission into any educational institution maintained by the state or receiving aid out of state funds on grounds only of religion, race, caste, language or any of them

[88]   Constitution of India, 1949, Article 30: Right of minorities to establish and administer educational institutions—

(1)   All minorities, whether based on religion or language, shall have the right to establish and administer educational institutions of their choice

(1A)   In making any law providing for the compulsory acquisition of any property of an educational institution established and administered by a minority, referred to in Clause (1), the state shall ensure that the amount fixed by or determined under such law for the acquisition of such property is such as would not restrict or abrogate the right guaranteed under that clause

(2)   The state shall not, in granting aid to educational institutions, discriminate against any educational institution on the ground that it is under the management of a minority, whether based on religion or language

[89]   According to Section 12(1)(c) of the RTE Act, all specified category or private schools must reserve 25 per cent of their seats for children belonging to EWS from the neighbourhood and provide them admission from Class I onwards; wherever such a school provides pre-school education, these rules are to be applied to the pre-school section as well.

2.5 lakh per annum. A lot of states including Haryana, Kerala, Karnataka, and Tamil Nadu have specifically included human immunodeficiency virus (HIV)-affected children in this quota in addition to other categories. Uttar Pradesh has further conditioned admission under this section. A government order issued in Uttar Pradesh in 2012 stipulated that children from EWS sections could be admitted to private schools only after all seats in government or government-aided schools had been filled.

In many so called 'elite' schools, the children from marginalized sections of society are discriminated in the classroom on the basis of gender, caste, and ethnicity. Despite Indian constitution strictly prohibiting discrimination on the bases of caste and other social backgrounds and making it a punishable act yet children from marginalized sections are discriminated in schools. There are also concerns whether those enroled in private schools will cope and adjust with education system and culture of elite schools. There are many concerns like quality education, funding, poor infrastructure, and teacher skills.

The RTE Act will be implemented through National Commission for Protection of Child Rights (NCPCR) and in the states through State Commission for Protection of Child Rights (SCPCR). The NCPCR/SCPCR falls under the Ministry of Women and Child Development whereas the RTE Act, 2009 and free and compulsory education is a subject matter of Ministry of Human Resource Development. There is never convergence nor coordination between ministries. It is difficult. The NCPCR and SCPCR need to be strengthened. They are headless, and without members in many states, are merely recommendatory bodies without judicial powers. They do not have pedagogical expertise nor academic capability to deal with educational matters. The RTE Act needs to constitute a proper regulatory body so that it can effectively supervise and monitor the functioning of the schools and also examine whether the children are being provided with not only free and compulsory education, but quality education. The regulatory authority can also plug the loopholes, take proper and steps for effective implementation of the act, and redress the grievances of the children.

Other issues of concern that were raised on the RTE Act, 2009 related to confusion of admission of disabled children, neighbourhood clause, and formation of school management committee and provision of time period to update schools with all infrastructural facilities. Concerns have also been raised in various fora on the Continuous and Comprehensive Evaluation (CCE) and 'no detention' policy (NDP) in the context of 'no detention' provision in the RTE Act. Concerns have also been raised at various fora on the CCE and NDP in the context of 'no detention' provision in the RTE Act.

A study done on the implementation of the RTE Act, 2009 revealed the following findings:[90]

• The sample states/UTs[91] have implemented provisions of RTE Act, 2009 to a great extent.

---

[90] Soni R.B.L., Md. Rahman Atiqur, Status of Implementation of RTE Act-2009 in Context of Disadvantaged Children at Elementary Stage, Department Of Elementary Education National Council of Educational Research And Training Sri Aurbindo Marg, New Delhi, 2013. Available at http://www.ncert. nic.in/departments/nie/dee/publication/pdf/StatusreportRTE2013.pdf (accessed on 18 September 2015).

[91] Total sample of 84 schools from states/UTs and 402 respondents from different groups was selected. One state in each region (Uttarakhand in North, Andhra Pradesh in South, Orissa in East and Gujarat in West) was selected. Besides, two UTs were selected for the study. Two non-responding states were also selected for the study on the recommendation of experts

- There were very few cases of age appropriate admissions of disadvantage and children with disabilities.
- In most of the places, materials for training of children admitted that under-age appropriate placement in different classes were not available.
- State-, district-, and block-level functionaries and teachers were aware of provisions of RTE Act, 2009.
- Efforts were being made to implement various provisions of the act.
- Parents were not aware of various provisions of RTE Act.
- Shortage of teachers, alarming pupil-teacher ratio, other official duties assigned to teachers, busyness in training programmes, duties in block-level office, making Aadhar cards and voter identification cards, no training of regular teachers in education of children with disabilities, and non-availability of special teacher support on daily basis are challenges in the implementation of RTE.
- States/UTs have plans to increase scholarship amount for disadvantaged and children with disabilities, to implement various provisions of RTE Act and to carry out infrastructural modifications in school buildings for children with disabilities.
- States/UTs have very limited vision of arranging different types of educational materials for children with various disabilities.
- All states/UTs have taken initiatives in conducting community awareness programmes to bring all children, including children with disabilities, to schools.
- All states/UTs encourage parents of children with disabilities to bring them to Anganwadi centres.[92]

Another area of concern is that there is nothing in the act or its rules that will prevent unaided private schools from charging students for activities that are not mentioned in the act or rules. Examples would be laboratory fee, computer fee, building fee, sports fee, fee for stationery, fees for acttivities such as music, painting, pottery, and so on.

Norms for buildings, the number of working days, teacher workload, equipment, library, and extra-curricular activities are prescribed only for unaided schools, and not for other schools including government schools. Only an obligatory teacher-student ratio is prescribed both for government and unaided schools. This means that as long as the teacher-pupil ratio is maintained, the school would be considered as fit. Two arguments often given for continuing to have, or even encouraging, private unaided schools is that the government has no money to set up the needed schools, and that government schools cannot be run as well as private schools. There have been excellent studies and reports that show that the government can find money to adopt a common school system with a provision of compulsory and totally free education up to Class XII in the country over the next 10 years. Further, even today the best system of school education in the country is the central school (Kendriya Vidyalaya) system run by the government. The country needs 400,000 such schools, and India can afford it.[93]

[92] Anganwadi is a government sponsored child-care and mother-care centre in India. It caters to children in the 0–6 age group. The word means 'courtyard shelter' in Hindi. They were started by the Indian government in 1975 as part of the Integrated Child Development Services programme to combat child hunger and malnutrition.
[93] Pushpa Bhargava, 'RTE Act: Some Rights and Wrongs', *The Hindu*, 25 July 2010.

The RTE Act, 2009 was amended vide the RTE (Amendment) Act, 2012 and came into force from 1 August 2012 in order to rectify the concerns raised by the parents and stakeholders. The RTE (Amendment) Act, 2012 made a provision for home-based education for children with multiple disabilities and severe disability and also included children with disability in the definition of 'child belonging to disadvantaged group'. The RTE (Amendment) Act, 2009 also clarifies that this act shall not apply to madrasas, vedic pathshalas, and educational institutions that are primarily imparting religious instruction. The Amendment Bill of 2012 amended Section 1,[94] Section 2,[95] Section 3,[96]

[94] The Right to Education Act, 2009, Section 1 (as amended by 2012 Amendment Act): Short title, extent and commencement—

(1) This Act may be called the RTE Act, 2009.
(2) It shall extend to the whole of India except the state of Jammu and Kashmir.
(3) It shall come into force on such date as the Central Government may, by notification in the Official Gazette, appoint.
(4) Subject to the provisions of articles 29 and 30 of the Constitution, the provisions of this Act shall apply to conferment of rights on children to free and compulsory education
(5) Nothing contained in this Act shall apply to Madras as, Vedic Pathsalas and educational institutions primarily imparting religious instruction.

[95] Right to Education Act, 2009, Section 2 (as amended by 2012 Amendment Act)—

(d) child belonging to 'disadvantaged group' means [a child with disability or] a child belonging to the scheduled caste, the scheduled tribe, the socially and educationally backward class or such other group having disadvantage owing to social, cultural, economical, geographical, linguistic, gender or such other factor, as may be specified by the appropriate Government, by notification;...
(ee) 'child with disability' includes:

   (A) a child with 'disability' as defined in Clause (i) of Section 2 of the Persons with Disabilities (Equal Opportunities, Protection of Rights and Full Participation) Act, 1995,1 of 1996
   (B) a child, being a person with disability as defined in Clause (j) of Section 2 of the National Trust for Welfare of Persons with Autism, Cerebral Palsy, Mental Retardation and Multiple Disabilities Act, 1999; 44 of 1999
   (C) a child with 'severe disability' as defined in Clause (o) of Section 2 of the National Trust for Welfare of Persons with Autism, Cerebral Palsy, Mental Retardation and Multiple Disabilities Act, 1999.

[96] The Right to Education Act, 2009, Section 3(as amended by 2012 Amendment Act): Right of child to free and compulsory education—

(1) Every child of the age of 6 to 14 years, including a child referred to in Clause (d) or Clause (e) of Section 2, shall have the right to free and compulsory education in a neighbourhood school till the completion of his or her elementary education....
(3) A child with disability referred to in Subclause (A) of Clause (ee) of Section 2 shall, without prejudice to the provisions of the Persons with Disabilities (Equal Opportunities, Protection of Rights and Full Participation) Act, 1995, and a child referred to in Subclauses (B) and (C) of Clause (ee) of Section 2, have the same rights to pursue free and compulsory elementary education which children with disabilities have under the provisions of Chapter V of the Persons with Disabilities (Equal Opportunities, Protection of Rights and Full Participation) Act, 1995:1, provided that a child with multiple disabilities referred to in Clause (h) of Section 2 of the National Trust for Welfare of Persons with Autism, Cerebral Palsy, Mental Retardation and Multiple Disabilities Act, 1999 and a child with

Section 21,[97] Section 22,[98] Section 25,[99] and Section 39.[100]

---

severe disability referred to in Clause (o) of Section 2 of the National Trust for Welfare of Persons with Autism, Cerebral Palsy, Mental Retardation and Multiple Disabilities Act, 1999 may also have the right to opt for home-based education.

[97] The Right to Education Act, 2009, Section 21 (as amended by 2012 Amendment Act): School Management Committee—

(1) A school, other than a school specified in Subclause (iv) of Clause (n) of Section 2, shall constitute a School Management Committee consisting of the elected representatives of the local authority, parents or guardians of children admitted in such school and teachers, provided that at least three-fourth of members of such committee shall be parents or guardians, provided further that proportionate representation shall be given to the parents or guardians of children belonging to disadvantaged group and weaker section, provided also that 50 per cent of members of such committee shall be women.

(2) The School Management Committee shall perform the following functions, namely:-

(a) monitor the working of the school;
(b) prepare and recommend school development plan;
(c) monitor the utilisation of the grants received from the appropriate Government or local authority or any other source; and
(d) perform such other functions as may be prescribed.

These, provided that the School Management Committee constituted under Subsection (1) in respect of:

(1) a school established and administered by minority whether based on religion or language; and
(2) all other aided schools as defined in Subsection (ii) of Clause (n) of Section 2, shall perform advisory function only.

[98] The Right to Education Act, 2009, Section 22 (as amended by the 2012 Amendment Act): School Development Plan—

(1) Every School Management Committee, except the School Management Committee in respect of a school established and administered by minority, whether based on religion or language and an aided school as defined in Subclause (ii) of Clause (n) of Section 2, constituted] under Subsection (1) of Section 21, shall prepare a School Development Plan, in such manner as may be prescribed.

(2) The School Development Plan so prepared under Subsection (1) shall be the basis for the plans and grants to be made by the appropriate Government or local authority, as the case may be.

[99] The Right to Education Act, 2009, Section 25(as amended by 2012 Amendment Act): Pupil-teacher ratio—

(1) Within 3 years from the date of commencement of this act, the appropriate government and the local authority shall ensure that the pupil-teacher ratio, as specified in the schedule, is maintained in each school.

(2) For the purpose of maintaining the pupil-teacher ratio under Subsection (1), no teacher posted in a school shall be made to serve in any other school or office or deployed for any non-educational purpose, other than those specified in Section 27.

[100] The Right to Education Act, 2009, Section 39(as inserted by 2012 Amendment Act): Power of central government to remove difficulties—

A significant number of these amendments are concerned with the education of children with disabilities. The amendment of giving the choice of home-based education to children with multiple disabilities and to children with severe disabilities has been opposed as an extremely retrogressive step which will have huge negative repercussions on the rights of children in education. It is watering down of the fundamental right to education that every child has in our country and goes against the very spirit of the RTE Act which is formalizing education and building standards for quality. Such an option is likely to foster great social isolation, exclusion from community and peers and devaluation of the child. It is likely to exclude the child from many other entitlements and also to expose the child to a lack of protection that social isolation brings. The quality of life of any child will be seriously compromised if we isolate them in the home. The label of severe and profound disability on a child is a deeply questionable practice in our country. The UN Convention on the Rights of Persons with Disabilities, 2006 which India[101] has ratified rejects the purely medical parameters that India uses to label children and people with disabilities. All laws relating to persons with disabilities are being either amended or rewritten at this time even in our own country. It is unclear to us why the MHRD has chosen to use concepts and thinking that is now changing. By legitimizing home-based education we are legitimizing non-formal education for one set of children in the law that outlines a fundamental right in our country. This is being seen as a grave injustice to the right of the child to a legitimate education.[102]

The amendment also gives school management committees an advisory role in minority schools, both aided and unaided, and puts madarsas[103] and vedic schools and other institutions providing primarily religious instruction outside the mandate of the right to education act. As per the amendment, the school management committee will not have the final authority in all minority schools, its role will be advisory.

Section 16 of the RTE mandates that no child can be detained or held back in a class until the completion of his/her elementary education. The corollary of this is *continuous and comprehensive*

(1) If any difficulty arises in giving effect to the provisions of this act, the central government may, by order, published in the Official Gazette, make such provisions not inconsistent with the provisions of this act, as may appear to it to be necessary for removing the difficulty, provided that no order shall be made under this section after the expiry of three years from the commencement of the Right of Children to Free and Compulsory Education (Amendment) Act, 2012.

(2) Every order made under this section shall be laid, as soon as may be after it is made, before each House of Parliament.

[101] Ratified by India on 1 October 2007.

[102] Letter by Taneja Anjela, Head of Policy at Global Campaign for Education on 26 April 2012 to Kapil Sibal, then Honourable Minister for Human Resources Development, Ministry of Human Resources Development Government of India. Available at http://www.slideshare.net/anjelataneja/letter-on-rte-amendments-april-26th (accessed on 16 September 2015).

[103] 'Madrasa' (Islam) is defined as an educational institution, particularly for Islamic religious instruction. See William Collins Sons & Co. Ltd., *Collins English Dictionary—Complete & Unabridged 2012 Digital Edition* (HarperCollins Publishers, 2012).

evaluation prescribed in Section 29(h), more commonly known as CCE. These provisions have given a legal status to the principle of no detention and the development of a progressive and holistic evaluation framework, enunciated in the National Policy on Education, 1986 and also the NCF, 2005. In 2012, the MHRD stated its position on the NDP as follows:

'The 'no detention' provision is made because examinations are often used for eliminating children who obtain poor marks. Once declared 'fail', children either repeat grade or leave the school altogether. Compelling a child to repeat a class is demotivating and discouraging.'

It was also clarified that the CCE is 'a procedure that will be non-threatening, releases the child from fear and trauma of failure and enables the teacher to pay individual attention to the child's learning and performance'.

As asserted by several educationists and academics, the NDP and CCE are based on sound principles of pedagogy and assessment, recognized world-wide. They are thus a welcome change to the exam-centric culture prevalent in Indian schools. There are also very strong equity considerations behind the NDP policy, especially for children from low-income families, and girls. In fact, wastage in the schooling system due to high repetition and high dropout rates has been a major concern since the 1990s. The no-detention clause in the RTE Act seeks to address that concern.

Besides, research evidence indicates that detention of students by a year or more does not improve learning. Even the Geeta Bhukkal Committee—a sub-committee under the Central Advisory Board of Education (CABE)[104] set up to look into this matter—admits that there is no research anywhere in the world which establishes that repeating a year helps children perform better.[105] But research does say that repeating has adverse academic and social effects on the child.

A common misconception was that no-detention meant no assessment. This has since been clarified by the MHRD but it is possible that the message did not reach all ears. Guidelines for implementing CCE were issued at various points of time by the CBSE, NCERT and state-level bodies. In fact, CCE is the assessment system under RTE and should go hand in hand with the NDP. It allows for students to be assessed on non-cognitive as well as non-academic areas of learning. In this way, a child need not be 'failed' simply because of non-performance on a narrowly defined and rigid set of indicators. Here again, there was, and perhaps still is, a lack of awareness regarding the finer points of CCE as well as of its implementation.

Meanwhile, as learning outcomes continued to dip, the NDP and CCE policies came under attack. Some of the criticisms that came forth were: students become lackadaisical as there is no longer a fear of failure, parents are no longer strict with their children, teachers are struggling to maintain discipline, attendance has dropped, and so forth. Schools complained of poor performance in Class IX because of students becoming used to automatic promotions. Many states,

---

[104] *Report of Central Advisory Board of Education Sub-Committee for Assessment and Implementation of Continuous and Comprehensive Evaluation in the Context of the No Detention Provision in the Right of Children to Free and Compulsory/Education Act, 2009*, submitted by Geeta Bhukkal, Education Minister, Government of Haryana and Chairperson of Cabe Sub-Committee.

[105] *Report of Central Advisory Board of Education Sub-Committee*

including Bihar, Chhattisgarh, and Assam opposed the NDP at the 59th meeting of CABE in 2012. The Geeta Bhukkal committee reported, that no-detention demotivates students, and increases the burden on teachers. The aforementioned criticisms carry the assumption that students can only learn under the threat of failure. [106]

The phenomenon of poor learning outcomes is the product of many factors which influence learning, and should not be conveniently pinned to the NDP. There is a pressing need to acknowledge the failure of other key provisions of the RTE, for instance, the stipulated pupil-teacher ratio. Many government schools still face an acute shortage of qualified teachers.[107] There are huge vacancies of teachers. Many teachers in schools are temporary or para teachers and are ill paid and almost untrained in teachers' training. There are no monitorable indicators set for measuring the quality of child performance in the schools. The implementation of RTE Act will require a multi-pronged approach by educating and empowering the panchayats, school management committees, and civil society organizations. The government will require to appoint more than 1 million teachers. Para teachers are not the real solution for quality education. The adequate resources will be required for implementation of RTE Act.

Until the time an adequate number of teachers are recruited and the PTR is met, it is unreasonable to expect CCE and NDP to succeed. Moreover, there is a need to engage more deeply with teachers, as they are the ultimate executors of any learning-oriented reform. Teacher-training programmes must be revised in line with the requirements of CCE. In-service support should also be provided to ensure that teachers are equipped and motivated to drive learning outcomes without having to teach to a test. Meanwhile, more effort needs to go into designing a workable, accessible framework which meets the objectives of continuous and comprehensive assessment.[108]

There is a need to engage with the stake holders and prepare and make them ready for the CEE and NDP. There is an urgent need to provide access with a focus on equity, with special measures to bring in girls, children from disadvantaged groups and those with disabilities into schools. Despite the flaws in the way of RTE Act, it is very important to ensure proper implementation of the act.

According to the *ASER 2014 Report*[109] the overall situation with basic reading continues to be extremely disheartening in India.[110] The report is based on the survey in 577 districts and 16,497 villages covering 341,070 households and about 569,229 children in the age group 3–16.[111] The

---

[106] Shruti Ambast and Akriti Gaur, 'Don't Make the No-Detention Policy a Scapegoat for Poor Learning Outcomes, Research Fellows', Education Initiative, Vidhi Centre for Legal Policy. Available at http://thewire.in/2015/08/17/dont-make-the-no-detention-policy-a-scapegoat-for-poor-learning-outcomes-8637/ (accessed on 30 September 2015).

[107] Ambast and Gaur, 'Don't Make the No-Detention Policy a Scapegoat'.

[108] Ambast and Gaur, 'Don't Make the No-Detention Policy a Scapegoat'.

[109] The ASER is an annual household survey to assess children's schooling status and basic learning levels in reading and arithmetic. See *10th Annual Status of Education Report*, released by NGO Pratham on 13 January 2015.

[110] *ASER 2014: Annual Status of Education Report*, Facilitated by Pratham, Main Findings January 2015 (New Delhi: ASER Centre). Available at http://img.asercentre.org/docs/Publications/ASER%20Reports/ASER%202014/National%20PPTs/aser2014indiaenglish.pdf (accessed on 4 October 2015).

[111] *ASER 2014.*

report reveals that for 6 years in a row, school enrolment in India was 96 per cent or above for the 6–14 age group and India is close to universal enrolment in this age group. Nationally, the percentage of children out of school in the age group 6–14 remains at 3.3 per cent. This is the same as was in 2013.[112]

Highlights of the Report[113]

- The 25 per cent of Class 8 students cannot read a Class 2-level text.[114]
- Only one-fourth of all children in Class 3 can read a Class 2 text fluently in 2014. This number rises to just under half in Class 5.[115]
- Close to 75 per cent of Class 8 children can read Class 2-level text, which implies still 25 per cent children cannot read.[116]
- The proportion of Class 5 children who can at least read a Class 2-level text has raised from 46.8 per cent in 2012 to 47 per cent in 2013 and to 48.1 per cent in 2014.[117] 38.7 per cent of Class 3 children can read at least a Class 1 level text in 2012, which is slightly higher at 40.2 per cent in 2014.[118]
- Tamil Nadu has shown major gains in reading over 2013 for Class 5.[119]
- 30.8 per cent of children of age group 6–14 in rural India were enroled in private schools in 2014, which has increased in the number slightly from 29 per cent in 2013.[120]
- However, Mathematics continued to be a serious and major source of concern.[121]
- All India (rural) figures for basic arithmetic have remained virtually unchanged over the last few years.[122]
- 26.3 per cent of Class 3 children could do two digit subtractions in 2012 and this number is at 25.3 per cent in 2014. [123]
- For Class 5 children, the ability to do division has increased slightly from 24.8 per cent in 2012 to 26.1 per cent in 2014.[124]
- The percentage of children in Class 2 who still cannot recognize numbers up to nine has increased from 11.3 per cent in 2009 to 19.5 per cent in 2014.[125]

---

[112] *ASER 2014.*
[113] *ASER 2014.*
[114] *ASER 2014.*
[115] *ASER 2014.*
[116] *ASER 2014.*
[117] *ASER 2014.*
[118] *ASER 2014.*
[119] *ASER 2014.*
[120] *ASER 2014.*
[121] *ASER 2014.*
[122] *ASER 2014.*
[123] *ASER 2014.*
[124] *ASER 2014.*
[125] *ASER 2014.*

Court Judgments on Right to Education

Before the Constitution (93rd Amendment) Act 2001, the right to education was prescribed by Articles 41, 45, and 46 of the Constitution, all of which were directive principles of state policy, but the courts had interpreted the right to education as a fundamental right by incorporating it within the fundamental rights in Article 21. The trend has been to hold that the right to life under Article 21 and the dignity of the individual cannot be assured unless it is accompanied by the right to education and that the provisions in Parts III and IV of the Constitution are supplementary and complementary to each other.

Kharak Singh v. State of U.P & Ors.[126]

The Honourable Court held that educating a child requires more than a teacher and a blackboard, or a classroom and a book. The RTE is a comprehensive model that requires that a child studies in a quality school, and a quality school certainly should pose no threat to a child's safety.

University of Delhi v. Ram Nath[127]

Education seeks to build up the personality of the pupil by assisting his physical, intellectual, moral, and emotional development. Article 21 of the Constitution has been used by the courts to make RTE a fundamental right much before the 93rd CAA, 2001. The word 'life' in Article 21 has been interpreted in the widest possible manner. It does not simply mean physical life, but also covers other expressions of life. It is something more than a mere biological existence of a human body. Life also includes education, personality, and whatever is reasonably required to give expression to life, its fulfilment, and its achievements.

Km. Chitra Ghosh & Another v. Union of India[128]

The Honourable Supreme Court stated that treating education as a fundamental right of the citizens is part of the ideals of the founding fathers of the Constitution and hence, time has come when its importance must be realized by the government and conditions appropriate for its existence must be made in the society.

A.V. Chandel v. Delhi University[129]

The Delhi High Court observed that fundamental rights (also called human rights or basic rights) are of two kinds: (1) classical rights and (2) economic (and social) rights. Article 41 of the

[126] AIR 1963 SC 1295, Section 16
[127] (1964) 2 SCR 703 at p. 710: (AIR 1963 SC 1873 at p. 1875, Section 6).
[128] (1969) 2 SCC 228.
[129] AIR 1978 Del 308.

Constitution of India, therefore, provides that 'the State shall, within the limits of its economic capacity and development, make effective provision for securing the right to work, to education, etc.' even in the narrower sense, right to education would appear to be a fundamental right which can be spelt out if Subclause (a), (b), and (c) of Article 19(1) is read with Article 21 independent of Article 41 and the Delhi University Act.

Bandhua Mukti Morcha v. Union of India[130]

It was held that the RTE is implicit in and flows from the right to life guaranteed under Article 21 (related to the dignity of the individual).

Mohini Jain v. State of Karnataka[131]

In this petition under Article 32 of the Constitution of India, Mohini Jain had challenged the notification of the Karnataka government permitting the private medical colleges in the state of Karnataka to charge exorbitant tuition fees from the students other than those admitted to the 'Government seats'. It was held and declared that charging of capitation fee by the private educational institutions as a consideration for admission is wholly illegal and cannot be permitted. The Supreme Court first recognized the right to education as a fundamental right . The following was observed: 'Right to life' is the compendious expression for all those rights which the courts must enforce because they are basic to the dignified enjoyment of life. It extends to the full range of conduct which the individual is free to pursue. The right to education flows directly from right to life. The right to life under Article 21 and the dignity of an individual cannot be assured unless it is accompanied by the right to education. The state government is under an obligation to make an endeavour to provide educational facility at all levels to its citizens. The RTE is a fundamental right guaranteed under Article 21 of the Constitution and that dignity of individuals cannot be assured unless accompanied by right to education and that charging of capitation fee for admission to educational institutions would amount to denial of citizens' right to education and is violative of Article 14 of the Constitution.

Unnikrishnan J.P. and Others v. State of Andhra Pradesh[132]

The main question under consideration in this landmark case was whether the right to primary education as mentioned in Article 45 of the Constitution of India is a fundamental right under Article 21 of the Constitution of India. It was held that the RTE is not stated expressly as a fundamental right in Part III. This court has, however, not followed the rule that unless a right is expressly stated as a fundamental right, it cannot be treated as one. Freedom of the press is not expressly mentioned in Part III, yet it has been read into and inferred from the freedom of speech and expression. The right to education, which is implicit in the right to life and personal liberty

---

[130] AIR 1984 SC 802.
[131] AIR 1992 SC 1858.
[132] AIR 1993 SC 2178.

guaranteed by Article 21 must be construed in the light of the directive principles in Part IV of the Constitution.

A true democracy is one where education is universal, where people understand what is good for them and the nation, and know how to govern themselves. The three Articles—45, 46, and 41—are designed to achieve the said goal, among others. It is in the light of these articles that the content and parameters of the RTE have to be determined. The RTE, understood in the context of Articles 45 and 41, means:

- Every child/citizen of this country has a right to free education until he completes the age of 14 years, and
- After a child/citizen completes 14 years, his right to education is circumscribed by the limits of the economic capacity of the state and its development.[133]

In this case the Supreme Court narrowed the ambit of the fundamental right to education as propounded in the Mohini Jain case. The court observed:

> The right to education which is implicit in the right to life and personal liberty guaranteed by Article 21 must be construed in the light of the directive principles in Part IV of the Constitution. So far as the right to education is concerned, there are several articles in Part IV which expressly speak of it. Article 41 says that the 'State shall, within the limits of its economic capacity and development, make effective provision for securing the right to work, to education and to public assistance in cases of unemployment, old age, sickens and disablement, and in other cases of undeserved want'.

Delhi Abibhavak Mahasangh v. Union of India and Others[134]

The petition was filed by parents' association alleging that 30 recognized schools in Delhi city had hiked their tuition fees unreasonably and were 'indulging in large-scale commercialization of education'. The Honourable Supreme Court directed in its views:

> There has to be an element of public benefit in the running of the schools. The schools are to be run for public good and not for private gain. The object has to be service to the Society and not to earn profit. The public benefit and not private or benefit to a favored section of the Society has to be the aim. Keeping these aims and objects in view the schools are required to also follow and comply the provisions of the Delhi School Education Act (for short the 'act') and the Rules framed there under as also the affiliation Bye laws framed by Central Board of Secondary Education. The schools are also required to comply the conditions upon which the land may be allotted to it by a public authority on concessional rates for setting up of a school building and its playground etc.[135]

---

[133] This position has been reiterated in the following judgments after the Unnikrishnan case: *Murlidhar Kesekar* v. *Vishwanath Barde* (1995) Supp (2) SCC 549; *Ganapathi Nath Middle School* v. *M.D. Kannan* (1996) 6 SCC 464; *K. Krishnamacharyulu* v. *Sri Venkateswara Hindu College of Engineering* (1997) 3 SCC 571; *State of Himachal Pradesh* v. *Himachal Pradesh State Recognized and Aided Schools Managing Committee* (1995) 2 SCC 534; *N. Kunchichekku* v. *State of Kerala* (1995) Supp. 2 SCC 382.

[134] 1999 (49) DRJ 766.

[135] 1999 (49) DRJ 766.

Modern School v. Union of India & Ors[136]

The Honourable Supreme Court upheld the right of the director of education (DOE) of the Delhi state government to regulate tuition fees chargeable by private unaided schools. The court also prohibited the transfer of fees, funds, or surpluses of one school to another or to its parent trust or society though it permitted school managements to collect reasonable sums (up to 10–15 per cent of tuition fees) for capital expenditure to be credited into a separate development fund maintained in the name of the school.

T.M.A. Pai Foundation & Ors v. State of Karnataka & Ors[137]

A number of petitions were filled by the management of minority and non-minority educational institutes. Their contention that the government must get off their back, and that they should be allowed to provide quality education uninterrupted by unnecessary rules and regulations, laid down by the bureaucracy for its own self-importance. The private educational institutions, both aided and unaided, established by minorities and non-minorities, in their desire to break free of the unnecessary shackles put on their functioning as modern educational institutions and seeking to impart quality education for the benefit of the community for whom they were established, and others, have filed the writ petitions and appeals asserting their right to establish and administer educational institutions of their choice unhampered by rules and regulations that unnecessarily impinge upon their autonomy.

In the aforementioned case, the court specifically dealt with the issue whether in order to determine the existence of a religious or linguistic minority in relation to Article 30, the state or the country as a whole is to be taken as the unit. Of the 11 judges constituting the bench, Kripal C.J. delivered judgment for six of the judgments. There were three concurring and two dissenting judgments on the issue.

The majority view was that language being the basis for the establishment of different states, for the purpose of Article 30, a 'linguistic minority' will have to be determined in relation to the state in which the educational institution is sought to be established. The position with regard to the religious minority is similar, since both religious and linguistic minorities have been put in par in Article 30. Therefore the test for determining who are linguistic or religious minorities within the meaning of Article 30 would be one and the same either in relation to a state legislation or central legislation. Article 30(1) uses the terms 'linguistic' or 'religious' minorities. The word 'or' means that a minority may either be linguistic or religious and that it does not have to be both—a religious minority as well as linguistic minority. It is sufficient if it is one or the other or both. The Constitution of India provides for special rights to both linguistic and religious minorities 'to establish and administer educational institutions of their choice' under Article 30. Hence no such law can be framed as may discriminate against such minorities with regard to the establishment and administration of the educational institutions vis-à-vis other educational institutions. Article 30 is a special right conferred on the religious and linguistic minorities because of their numerical handicap

---

[136] Appeal (civil) 2699 of 2001.
[137] (2002) 8 SCC 481.

and to inspire in them a sense of confidence. While upholding these rights, the Supreme Court has, in the *TMA Pai* case, also endorsed the concept that there should be no reverse discrimination and opines that 'the essence of Article 30(1) is to ensure equal treatment between the majority and the minority institutions. No one type or category of institution should be disfavoured or, for that matter, receive more favourable treatment than another. Laws of the land, including rules and regulations, must apply equally to the majority institutions as well as to the minority institutions.

Social Jurist v. Government of National Capital Territory of Delhi & Ors[138]

The court ordered Delhi Development Authority (DDA) to take 'appropriate action' against 265 'recognized, private unaided' schools in the Delhi region which had been allotted land (by DDA) at concessional prices under the Master Plan of Delhi in 1962, on the condition that they would reserve a 25 per cent freeships quota for disadvantaged children, for breach of that condition.

Maharshi Mahesh Jogi v. State of M.P. & Ors[139]

The court in this judgment emphasized the need to cherish the realm of Article 26 of the Universal Declaration of Human Rights (UDHR) in the light of depleting learning standards of the children in the country: RTE at least in the elementary stages and education to promote general culture, abilities, judgment and sense of responsibility to become a useful member of society and opportunity to recreation, and play to attain the same purpose as of education.

Environment and Consumer Protection Foundation v. Delhi Administration and Others[140]

The aforementioned public interest litigation (PIL) sought to improve conditions in government and aided schools to give effect to Article 21A. Supreme Court sought affidavits from states on compliance with norms and standards in the RTE Act and disposed petition with directions to states to implement all requirements under RTE Act within 6 months stating that these standards were to apply to all schools '*whether State owned or privately owned, aided or unaided, minority or non-minority.*'

P.A. Inamdar and Others v. State of Maharashtra and Others[141]

The court held that education plays a cardinal role in accelerating the progress of the country in every sphere of national interest. Therefore, no sections of citizens can be ignored or left behind because it would hamper the progress of the country as a whole. Hence, it is the duty of the state to do all it can to educate every section of citizens who need a helping hand in marching ahead along with others.

[138] CW No. 3156 of 2002.
[139] AIR 2002 MP 196, Section 24–27
[140] WP (C) 631/2004 (12 October 2012).
[141] (2005) 6 SCC 537, Section 85.

Society for Un-aided Private Schools of Rajasthan v. UoI[142]

The case arose out of a series of petitions filed by several private aided and unaided schools, challenging the act and specifically Section 12(1)(c) that mandated private unaided schools to admit 25 per cent of their Class 1 strength with children from weaker and disadvantaged sections and provide them with free education.

The apex court in this landmark judgment upheld the constitutional validity of Section 12 of the RTE provision that requires private unaided schools to reserve 25 per cent seats for socially and economically weaker children. The judgment was a progressive child-centred decision that aimed to bring children from weaker section at par with rest of the children of the country. However, in its dissecting judgment by K.S. Radhakrishnan J., the court held that application of the RTE Act, 2009 to unaided minority schools is unconstitutional and violative of spirit of Article 30 of the Constitution of India. Affirming the laws laid down in *T.M.A. Pai Foundation* v. *State of Karnataka*,[143] it exempted minority institutions from the ambit of RTE.

Election Commission of India v. St. Mary's School & amp; Ors.[144]

The Honourable Court directed the state not to make teachers teaching in classroom to work unnecessarily and regularly engaged in polling duties unless absolutely required in some circumstances and that too ensuring that class hours of teaching and availability of teachers in schools for the children is not hampered and disturbed. While the democratic state has a mandate to conduct elections, the mundane demands of instruction superseded the state's need to staff polling places. A citizenry sufficient education is essential to understand civil rights and social duties of a developing and democratic country like India.

Society for Un-Aided Pvt School of Rajasthan v. UoI and Anr.[145]

This judgment was concerned with the constitutional validity and applicability of the RTE Act, 2009 qua unaided non-minority schools.

Explaining the scope of Article 21A, the court stated that the object of the said article is to provide for free and compulsory education to all children of the age of 6 to 14 years in such manner as the state may, by law, determine. Thus, under the said article, the obligation is on the state to provide free and compulsory education to all children of a specified age. However, under the said article, the manner in which the said obligation will be discharged by the state has been left to the state to determine by law. Thus, the state may decide to provide free and compulsory education to all children of the specified age through its own schools or through government aided schools or through unaided private schools. Dealing with the question that whether such a law transgresses any constitutional limitation, the court held that Section 12(1)(c) of RTE Act, 2009, inter alia,

---

[142] (2005) 6 SCC 537.
[143] (2002) 8 SCC 481.
[144] (2008) 2 SCC 390.
[145] (2012) 6 SCC 1.

provides for admission to Class 1, to the extent of 25 per cent of the strength of the class of the children belonging to weaker section and disadvantaged group in the neighbourhood and provide free and compulsory elementary education to them till its completion. The emphasis is on 'free and compulsory education'. Earmarking of seats for children belonging to a specified category who face financial barrier in the matter of accessing education satisfies the test of classification in Article 14. Further, Section 12(1)(c) provides for a level playing field in the matter of right to education to children who are prevented from accessing education because they do not have the means or their parents do not have the means to pay for their fees.

The court further held that there are a number of stakeholders including those who want to establish and administer educational institutions as these supplement the primary obligation of the state to provide for free and compulsory education to the specified category of children. Hence, Section 12(1)(c) also satisfies the test of reasonableness, apart from the test of classification in Article 14. Accordingly, the court held that the RTE Act, 2009 is constitutionally valid and shall apply to the following:

i.   a school established, owned or controlled by the appropriate government or a local authority;
ii. an aided school including aided minority school(s) receiving aid or grants to meet whole or part of its expenses from the appropriate government or the local authority;
iii. a school belonging to a specified category; and
iv. an unaided non-minority school not receiving any kind of aid or grants to meet its expenses from the appropriate government or the local authority.

The court further held that merely because the resources of the state in providing professional education are limited, private educational institutions, which intend to provide better professional education, cannot be forced by the state to make admissions available on the basis of reservation policy to less meritorious candidates. Unaided institutions, as they are not deriving any aid from state funds, can have their own admissions that are fair, transparent, non-exploitative, and based on merit. Examining whether the private unaided educational institutions have any obligations/ responsibilities in realization of children's rights, the apex court made the following observations:

1. Article 21A casts an obligation on the state to provide free and compulsory education to children of the age of 6 to 14 years and not on unaided non-minority and minority educational institutions.
2. Rights of children to free and compulsory education guaranteed under Article 21A and RTE Act can be enforced against the schools defined under Section 2(n) of the act, except unaided minority and non-minority schools not receiving any kind of aid or grants to meet their expenses from the appropriate governments or local authorities.
3. Section 12(1)(c) is read down so far as unaided non-minority and minority educational institutions are concerned, holding that it can be given effect to only on the principles of voluntariness, autonomy and consensus and not on compulsion or threat of non- recognition or non-affiliation.
4. No distinction or difference can be drawn between unaided minority and non-minority schools with regard to appropriation of quota by the state or its reservation policy under Section 12(1)(c) of the act. Such an appropriation of seats can also not be held to be a

regulatory measure in the interest of the minority within the meaning of Article 30(1) or a reasonable restriction within the meaning of Article 19(6) of the Constitution.

5. The appropriate government and local authority have to establish neighbourhood schools as provided in Section 6 read with Sections 8 and 9, within the time limit prescribed in the statute.

6. Duty imposed on parents or guardians under Section 10 is directory in nature and it is open to them to admit their children in the schools of their choice, not invariably in the neighbourhood schools, subject to availability of seats and meeting their own expenses.

7. Sections 4, 10, 14, 15 and 16 are held to be directory in their content and application. The concerned authorities shall exercise such powers in consonance with the directions/guidelines laid down by the central government in that behalf.

8. The provisions of Section 21 of the act, as provided, would not be applicable to the schools covered under Subsection (iv) of Clause (n) of Section 2. They shall also not be applicable to minority institutions, whether aided or unaided.

9. In exercise of the powers conferred upon the appropriate government under Section 38 of the RTE Act, the government shall frame rules for carrying out the purposes of this act and in particular, the matters stated under Subsection (2) of Section 38 of the RTE Act.

10. The directions, guidelines, and rules shall be framed by the central government, appropriate government and/or other such competent authority under the provisions of the RTE Act, as expeditiously as possible and, in any case, not later than six months from the date of pronouncement of this judgment.

11. All the state governments which have not constituted the State Advisory Council in terms of Section 34 of the RTE Act shall so constitute the Council within three months from today. The Council so constituted shall undertake its requisite functions in accordance with the provisions of Section 34 of the act and advise the government in terms of Clauses (6), (7), and (8) of this order immediately thereafter.

12. Central government and state governments may set up a proper regulatory authority for supervision and effective functioning of the act and its implementation.

13. Madrasas and vedic pathshalas which predominantly provide religious instructions and do not provide for secular education stand outside the purview of the act.

The Azim Premji Foundation Arguments in this Matter[146]

The team of Centre for Law and Policy Research (CLPR)[147] represented the Azim Premji Foundation as an Intervenor in this litigation, and submitted a detailed brief on its behalf.

---

[146] I.A. No. 7 in W.P. (C) No. 95/2010 .

[147] The CLPR is a non-profit organization based in Bangalore. The CLPR aims to promote public policy research, litigation and legal education. As part of its policy work, the CLPR has initiated projects in the form of pre-legislative recommendations to proposed legislations. The centre also undertakes intensive research tailored to author text books suitable for law students. The CLPR is also involved in certain litigation work in the High Court of Karnataka, Supreme Court and the sub-ordinate courts. As part of its litigation work, the centre has taken up matters, mainly by way of public interest, in the areas of disability law, environment, public health and urban infrastructure development law.

One of the important arguments made by CLPR in its written submissions to the court was about the horizontal application of fundamental rights. The horizontality of rights concept basically means that non-state private actors are also covered by fundamental rights obligations. This issue is really the core of the RTE Act, which mandates that all private unaided schools are also required to take in 25 per cent of children from disadvantaged groups and are required to follow the basic norms and standards set by the state for all schools. Although in India we have never had a direct application of fundamental and civil rights applying to non- state actors, the debate of horizontality of rights is not new. There are several articles in Part III which contains the fundamental rights which directly apply to non- state actors as well.

The Honourable Supreme Court held that private actors are not merely required to be perform negative duties of restraint from infringing on fundamental rights, but also to positively provide socio-economic rights guarantees such as the right to education.

Himangi v. GNCT of Delhi[148]

The Honourable High Court of Delhi, in this judgment examined the provision of Delhi School Education (Free seats for Students belonging to Economically Weaker Section and Disadvantage Group) Order, 2011.

'Clause 2(c) of the aforesaid order read: 'c) "Child belonging to weaker section" means a child whose parents have total annual income of less than one lakh rupees from all sources and who have been staying in Delhi for the last three years.'

Due to this clause, children belonging to parents of weaker sections who had not been staying in Delhi for the past 3 years were arbitrarily getting excluded from the ambit of RTE and in particular to the benefits under Section 12(1)(c) of the RTE Act. This despite being the law specifying the fact that parents whose income is less than 1 lac have a right to get their children admitted in schools as per RTE norms. The additional residence criteria of 3 years was proving to be a hindrance in way of child's admission and right to seek education and was directed by the court to be quashed.

Sau. Laxmibai Shantaram Doke Samajvikas Prathisthan v. The State of Maharashtra[149]

In the instant case the court held that the act of 2009 also applied to existing schools thereby making the following observations:

1. Right to establish an educational institution of its choice on permanent no grant basis, is a fundamental right guaranteed to all the citizens within the meaning of Article 19(1)(g) of the Constitution of India.[150].

---

[148] W.P.(C) 3168/2013.

[149] 2013(2)SCT612(Bombay).

[150] Constitution of India, Article 19: Protection of certain rights regarding freedom of speech, etc.—

(1) All citizens shall have the right

(a) to freedom of speech and expression;

(b) to assemble peaceably and without arms;

2. That fundamental right, however, cannot be confused with the right to ask for recognition of the school.

3. The proposals for recognition of the school to be established by the private management on 'permanent no grant basis and not receiving any other aid whatsoever' from the government, will henceforth have to fulfil the conditions specified, among others, in Sections 12,[151] 19,[152]

(c) to form associations or unions [or cooperative societies];

(d) to move freely throughout the territory of India;

(e) to reside and settle in any part of the territory of India; [and]

(g) to practise any profession, or to carry on any occupation, trade or business.

[151] The RTE Act, 2009, Section 12: Extent of school's responsibility for free and compulsory education—

(1) For the purposes of this act, a school—

(a) specified in Subclause (i) of Clause (n) of Section 2 shall provide free and compulsory elementary education to all children admitted therein;

(b) specified in Subclause (ii) of Clause (n) of Section 2 shall provide free and compulsory elementary education to such proportion of children admitted therein as its annual recurring aid or grants so received bears to its annual recurring expenses, subject to a minimum of 25 per cent.;

(c) specified in Subclauses (iii) and (iv) of Clause (n) of Section 2 shall admit in class I, to the extent of at least 25 per cent. of the strength of that class, children belonging to weaker section and disadvantaged group in the neighbourhood and provide free and compulsory elementary education till its completion, provided further that where a school specified in Clause (n) of Section 2 imparts pre-school education, the provisions of clauses (a) to (c) shall apply for admission to such pre-school education.

(2) The school specified in Subclause (iv) of Clause (n) of Section 2 providing free and compulsory elementary education as specified in Clause (c) of Subsection (1) shall be reimbursed expenditure so incurred by it to the extent of per-child-expenditure incurred by the state, or the actual amount charged from the child, whichever is less, in such manner as may be prescribed, provided that such reimbursement shall not exceed per-child-expenditure incurred by a school specified in Subclause (i) of Clause (n) of Section 2, provided further that where such school is already under obligation to provide free education to a specified number of children on account of it having received any land, building, equipment or other facilities, either free of cost or at a concessional rate, such school shall not be entitled for reimbursement to the extent of such obligation.

(3) Every school shall provide such information as may be required by the appropriate Government or the local authority, as the case may be.

[152] RTE Act, 2009, Section 19—Norms and standards for school

(1) No school shall be established,, or recognised, under Section 18, unless it fulfils the norms and standards specified in the Schedule.

(2) Where a school established before the commencement of this act does not fulfil the norms and standards specified in the schedule, it shall take steps to fulfil such norms and standards at its own expenses, within a period of three years from the date of such commencement.

25[153] read with Schedule of the act of 2009 and of the Rule 3.2 of the Code (for Secondary/ Higher Secondary School) or Rule 107 of the Rules of 1949 (for Primary School), as the case may be, and also in the recognition order itself.

4. Indeed, it will be open to the state to impose strictest terms and conditions including, inter alia, mentioned by us in Paragraph 67 above, fulfilment whereof can be made precondition for grant of recognition and continuation thereof, by the private schools to be established and run on no grant in aid basis and without receiving any other aid whatsoever from the government. The terms and conditions, however, will have to be reasonable restrictions and in the interests of the general public.

5. Initially provisional recognition shall be granted to the unaided private secondary/higher secondary school, if it fulfils the conditions specified in Act of 2009 and Rule 3.2 of the code for grant of recognition, as provided in Rule 4.1 of the Secondary Schools Code; and recognition shall be granted to unaided private primary school, if it fulfils the conditions specified in Act of 2009 and Rule 107 of the Rules of 1949, as provided in Section 39 of the act of 1947 read with Rule 107 of the Rules of 1949.

6. The pre-existence of a perspective plan or inclusion of the location in the perspective plan or School Development Plan, as the case may be, for considering the proposal for recognition of the 'private unaided schools' on permanent no-grant-in-aid basis or not receiving any other aid from the government whatsoever, cannot be a condition precedent.

7. We further hold that the provisions of the Secondary Schools Code relating to permission under Rules 2.1 to 2.14 of the Code and Rule 106 of the Rules of 1949 to start a school would apply only to the proposals for establishing a school on 'grant in aid basis or receiving any other aid' from the Government. However, even after grant of permission, such a school shall not function or run until the grant of recognition, as per Section 18 of the

---

(3) Where a school fails to fulfil the norms and standards within the period specified under Subsection (2), the authority prescribed under Subsection (1) of Section 18 shall withdraw recognition granted to such school in the manner specified under Subsection (3) thereof.

(4) With effect from the date of withdrawal of recognition under Subsection (3), no school shall continue to function.

(5) Any person who continues to run a school after the recognition is withdrawn, shall be liable to fine which may extend to one lakh rupees and in case of continuing contraventions, to a fine of ten thousand rupees for each day during which such contravention continues.

[153] RTE Act, 2009, Section 25: Pupil-teacher ratio—

(1) [Within three years] from the date of commencement of this act, the appropriate government and the local authority shall ensure that the pupil-teacher ratio, as specified in the schedule, is maintained in each school.

(2) For the purpose of maintaining the pupil-teacher ratio under Subsection (1), no teacher posted in a school shall be made to serve in any other school or office or deployed for any non-educational purpose, other than those specified in Section 27.

act of 2009[154]. Only on this interpretation the constitutional validity of the aforementioned provisions and the opening part of Rule 107(1) of the Rules of 1949 can be saved.

8. We also hold that the state shall forthwith consider the proposals of all the private institutions 'for grant of recognition' for Marathi medium school on permanent no-grant-in-aid basis and not receiving any other aid from the government whatsoever, in the given locality on its own merits and in accordance with law.

9. That be done expeditiously and the decision so taken be communicated to the concerned management, in any case, not later than 31 May 2010, so that, if recognition were to be granted, the concerned school can commence at the beginning of the academic year 2010–11, from June 2010.

Pramati Educational and Cultural Trust and Ors. v. Union of India (UoI) and Ors.[155]

Concerning the constitutional validity of the provisions of the RTE Act, 2009 ('RTE Act') that spells out this conceptual distinction between Article 19(1)(g) and Article 30, the court held that the RTE Act did not violate Article 19(1)(g) as regards non-minority unaided private schools, but did violate the enhanced protection accorded to minority institutions under Article 30. The discussion in the case makes it clear that the animating factor is the conceptual distinction between minority and non-minority schools. Unaided (and naturally, aided) private schools cannot thwart public regulation by the state in order to further a recognized constitutional objective. Specifically, the Supreme Court noted:

---

[154] RTE Act, 2009, Section 18: No school to be established without obtaining certificate of recognition—

(1) No school, other than a school established, owned or controlled by the appropriate government or the local authority, shall, after the commencement of this act, be established or function, without obtaining a certificate of recognition from such authority, by making an application in such form and manner, as may be prescribed.

(2) The authority prescribed under Subsection (1) shall issue the certificate of recognition in such form, within such period, in such manner, and subject to such conditions, as may be prescribed, provided that no such recognition shall be granted to a school unless it fulfils norms and standards specified under Section 19.

(3) On the contravention of the conditions of recognition, the prescribed authority shall, by an order in writing, withdraw recognition, provided that such order shall contain a direction as to which of the neighbourhood school, the children studying in the derecognised school, shall be admitted, provided further that no recognition shall be so withdrawn without giving an opportunity of being heard to such school, in such manner, as may be prescribed.

(4) With effect from the date of withdrawal of the recognition under Subsection (3), no such school shall continue to function.

(5) Any person who establishes or runs a school without obtaining certificate of recognition, or continues to run a school after withdrawal of recognition, shall be liable to fine which may extend to one lakh rupees and in case of continuing contraventions, to a fine of ten thousand rupees for each day during which such contravention continues.

[155] AIR 2014 SC 2114.

'When we examine the 2009 Act, we find that under Section 12(1)(c) read with Section 2(n)(iv) of the Act, an unaided school not receiving any kind of aid or grants to meet its expenses from the appropriate Government or the local authority is required to admit in class I, to the extent of at least twenty-five per cent of the strength of that class, children belonging to weaker section and disadvantaged group in the neighbourhood and provide free and compulsory elementary education till its completion. We further find that under Section 12(2) of the 2009 Act such a school shall be reimbursed expenditure so incurred by it to the extent of per-child expenditure incurred by the state, or the actual amount charged from the child, whichever is less, in such manner as may be prescribed. Thus, ultimately it is the state which is funding the expenses of free and compulsory education of the children belonging to weaker sections and several groups in the neighbourhood, which are admitted to a private unaided school These provisions of the 2009 Act, in our view, are for the purpose of providing free and compulsory education to children between the age group of 6 to 14 years and are consistent with the right under Article 19(1)(g) of the Constitution, and are meant to achieve the constitutional goals of equality of opportunity in elementary education to children of weaker sections and disadvantaged groups in our society. We, therefore, do not find any merit in the submissions made on behalf of the non-minority private schools that Article 21A of the Constitution and the 2009 Act violate their right under Article 19(1)(g) of the Constitution.'

Hence the court upheld the RTE Act.

Karthik Rao & Ors v. State of Karnataka & Ors[156]

The aforementioned petition filed by parents challenged schools' claim of minority status. Petition allowed by the court held:

- 'Self Serving assertion' of minority status is not permitted. No denial of admissions without declaration of minority status by a competent authority
- More non-minority students than minority.
- Declaration applies to school/college. Not the trust or society.
- Denying admission violation of children's fundamental right under Article 21A and also their human right.

State of Karnataka and Anr. v. Associated Management of (Government Recognized Unaided English Medium) Primary and Secondary Schools and Ors.[157]

In the aforementioned case, the court, while defining the expression 'mother tongue' as per Article 350A, stated that it means the mother tongue of the linguistic minority group in a partic-ular state and it is the parent or the guardian of the child who will decide what the mother tongue of child is. The court further held the following in this case:

1. Under Article 350A of the Constitution, it is provided that it shall be the endeavour of every state and of every local authority within the state to provide adequate facilities for instruction

---

[156] WP. 29061/2014.
[157] AIR 2014 SC 2094.

in the mother tongue at the primary stage of education to children belonging to linguistic minority groups. Article 350A cannot be interpreted to empower the state to compel a linguistic minority to choose its mother tongue only as a medium of instruction in a primary school established by it in violation of the fundamental right under Article 30(1). Therefore, state has no power under Article 350A of the Constitution to compel the linguistic minorities to choose their mother tongue only as a medium of instruction in primary schools.

2. The word 'freedom' in Article 19 of the Constitution means absence of control by the state and Article 19(1) provides that the state will not impose controls on the citizen in the matters mentioned in Subclauses (a), (b), (c), (d), (e) and (g) of Article 19(1) except those specified in Clauses 2 to 6 of Article 19 of the Constitution. In all matters specified in Clause (1) of Article 19, the citizen has therefore the liberty to choose, subject only to restrictions in Clauses (2) to (6) of Article 19.

3. Freedom or choice in the matter of speech and expression is absolutely necessary for an individual to develop his personality in his own way and this is one reason, if not the only reason, why under Article 19(1)(a) of the Constitution every citizen has been guaranteed the right to freedom of speech and expression.

4. A child, and on his behalf his parent or guardian, has the right to choose the medium of instruction at the primary school stage under Article 19(1)(a) and not under Article 21 or Article 21A of the Constitution.

5. The imposition of mother tongue affects the fundamental rights under Articles 19, 29 and 30 of the Constitution. A private unaided school which is not a minority school and which does not enjoy the protection of Articles 29(1) and 30(1) of the Constitution can choose a medium of instruction for imparting education to the children in the school.

6. Right to freedom of expression includes right of child/parent to choose medium of instruction. The government cannot impose the mother tongue on a linguistic minority for imparting primary education.

National Coalition for Education through Its National Convener, Rama Kant Rai v.
Union of India & Ors[158]

The aforementioned case was filed as PIL under Article 32 of Constitution of India in response to the numerous reports being filed against widespread violations of children's right to education across the country including various violations of specific legislative requirements contained in the RTE Act, 2009.

The petitioner[159] in this case was seeking the issuance of writ of mandamus or any other appropriate writ by the Honourable Court to direct the following:

---

[158] Writ Petition (C) No. 267 of 2014.

[159] The petitioner in this case, that is, the National Coalition for Education is a network of organizations committed to the Right to Education, including All India Primary Teachers Federation (AIPTF), All India Federation of Teachers Organization (AIFTO), All India Secondary Teachers Federation (AISTF), All India Association for Christian Higher Education (AIACHE), World Vision India, and People's Campaign for Common School System (PCCSS).

- All states shall finish mapping within 6 months of filing this PIL and that the new schools are constructed within 6 months of the completion of these mappings such that all neighbour-hoods have a primary school within 1 km and an upper primary within 3 km (as per RTE Model Rules Part IV Section 6); and that all single-classroom schools be upgraded to be in compliance with the RTE Act Schedule 2(i).
- The states and territories shall upgrade existing and construct new public-sector teacher train-ing centres so as to ensure the availability of required trained teachers.
- The panachayats and ULBs shall complete an identification and mapping of all school-age children in their areas taking special care to include migrant, nomadic, displaced, Dalit, deno-tified tribe, and other marginalized communities and to ensure that all of them are in RTE compliant schools within 6 months of filing this PIL.
- The states and UTs shall upgrade all deficient schools with the appropriate physical infrastruc-ture so as to be in compliance with the RTE Act.
- The states and UTs shall regularize and make permanent all contract teachers and para-teach-ers in the country.
- The states and UTs shall ensure that teachers are not assigned to prohibited non-education duties, including midday meal preparation.
- The states and UTs shall ensure that all schools have a properly constituted SMC with compo-sitions in compliance with RTE Act.
- The central government shall ensure that all schools running under the National Child Labour Project (NCLP) be brought in to compliance with the RTE Act, particularly with respect to physical infrastructure, teaching hours, and professionally trained teachers.
- The states and UTs shall ensure that all private schools are registered with the government to disclose the total number of students admitted under the EWS quota in the entire state.

The Honourable Supreme Court disposed of the aforementioned case holding, saying that it will not be possible for the Supreme Court to monitor the implementation of the prayers, even if they are granted and therefore it directed the petitioner to approach the appropriate high courts for specific prayers so that there is effective implementation of the RTE Act, 2009.

The Government of Andhra Pradesh and Ors. v. K. Hanmi Reddy and Ors.[160]

Honourable Court reiterating the importance of education in para. 99 and para. 100 of the case held the following:

Now it is not in dispute that primary education has become a fundamental right in view of Article 21-A of the Constitution of India and the Right to Education Act, 2009 has been enacted in further-ance of Article 21-A of the Constitution of India. The constitutional validity of Right to Education Act has been upheld by the Apex Court in the case between Society for Unaided Private Schools of Rajasthan's case.[161] Various schemes have been introduced to improve the elementary education and enhance the academic standard and to provide basic facilities to the students. Rashtriya Madhyamika

---

[160] 2015 (3) ALD 150.
[161] (2012) 6 SCC 102.

Siksha Abhiyan is one of the schemes introduced by the Government. The main object of the said scheme is to enhance standard of education. The state is under corresponding obligation to implement the provisions of Right to Education Act, 2009. Now there is sharing pattern of fund between the Central Government and the state Government in implementation of RTE Act and in view of the scheme of Sarva Siksha Abhiyan.

The standard of education cannot be expected unless the teachers are determined to enhance the standards. It is the teacher who observes the students and shapes the future of the children. If a teacher is unable to meet his/her basic needs and if he/she is under stress and strain due to financial difficulties, how can we expect him/her to utilise all his/her mental abilities and concentrate on his/her work. The basic needs of a teacher must be fulfilled. He would not have to bother about the future of his own children or for their basic requirements or his family's minimum necessities. Cost of living has been increasing day by day. Medical expenses have become a burdensome. A teacher who has no security and who cannot fulfil his basic needs cannot perform his duties as expected. Therefore, it is in the interest of the nation and society that everybody should think how to improve the life standard of a teacher and thereby develop the nation. In view of the latest developments in the policies of the central government and in view of the latest schemes introduced by the Central Government and enactment of Right to Education Act, 2009, it appears that it is the obligation of the state Government to provide basic facilities and regular scales of pay to the teachers.

Government Schemes and Programmes in the Field of Elementary Education in India

Sarva Siksha Abhiyan

The SSA is Government of India's flagship programme for achievement of Universalization of Elementary Education (UEE) in a time-bound manner, as mandated by 86th amendment to the Constitution of India making free and compulsory education to children in the age group of 6–14 years a fundamental right. The SSA is being implemented in partnership with state governments to cover the entire country and address the needs of 192 million children in 1.1 million habitations.

The programme seeks to open new schools in those habitations which do not have schooling facilities and strengthen existing school infrastructure through provision of additional classrooms, toilets, drinking water, maintenance grant, and school-improvement grants. Existing schools with inadequate teacher strength are provided with additional teachers, while the capacity of existing teachers is being strengthened by extensive training, grants for developing teaching-learning materials and strengthening of the academic support structure at a cluster, block, and district level. The SSA seeks to provide quality elementary education including life-skills. The SSA has a special focus on girls' education and children with special needs. The SSA also seeks to provide computer education to bridge the digital divide.[162]

---

[162] Ministry of Human Resources Development, Government of India. Available at http://ssa.nic.in/ (accessed on 3 October 2015).

The SSA, aiming at universalization of elementary education, has undoubtedly enhanced enrolment and retention rate of children in schools. But the changing scenario around the globe calls for urgent attention towards ensuring quality of education to meet the human resource demand for market and for the upliftment of the society in general. The Government of India is also now shifting its focus to quality of education. The RTE, 2009 is a step forward, which focuses on the quality of teaching and learning. This has led to substantial reforms and making concerted efforts in educational planning and management. The NCF, 2005 has made recommendations for children-centered pedagogy (constructivist approach), as well as curricular and examination reforms. Also, CCE is in place as per the Government of India's policy for over all development of students.

Barriers and Challenges to Right to Elementary Education

The challenges to the right to elementary education include:

- lack of infrastructure, facilities, materials and support systems for children
- inadequate conditions of work for teachers
- student-teacher ratio
- lack of adequate training aids and material for teachers
- curriculum detached from local language, needs, values and aspirations of children at risk of dropping out
- distance to school
- social/language barriers
- discrimination (gender, ethnicity, and disability, among others)
- early marriage
- inflexible scheduling
- fear of violence at, or on the way to, school
- over age out of school children
- documentation/ procedural

Besides these, there are two major barriers in promoting Right to Education

- corporal punishment in schools
- child labour

Corporal Punishment in Schools

Corporal punishment has been a form of punishment in schools in India for a long time and sadly, this form of punishment still continues to thrive today. Disciplinary practices are certainly a deterrent to schooling. Fear of corporal punishment discourages regular attendance at schools and increases dropout rate. This obviously hampers and obstructs education and affects their right to education, which is a fundamental right. Some teachers, most being overenthusiastic and some with uncontrollable anger, punish the children physically as well as mentally. Thus, corporal punishment in schools poses as one of the barriers to the right to education. The Ministry of Human Resource Development, Government of India made a connection between corporal punishment and children dropping out of school. This is an important admission.

The committee on the Rights of the Child in the General Comment No. 8 defines 'corporal' or 'physical' punishment as:

> any punishment in which physical force is used and intended to cause some degree of pain or discomfort, however light.[163] Most involves hitting ('smacking', 'slapping', 'spanking') children, with the hand or with an implement.... In the view of the Committee, corporal punishment is invariably degrading. In addition, there are other non-physical forms of punishment that are also cruel and degrading and thus incompatible with the Convention. These include, for example, punishment which belittles, humiliates, enigrates, scapegoats, threatens, scares or ridicules the child.

Corporal punishment is also defined as is the infliction of pain intended to change a person's behaviour or to punish them. Though it mainly refers to physical pain either through hitting or forcing the child to withstand in uncomfortable positions, an evolving definition also includes within its ambit wrongful confinement, verbal insults, threats and humiliation, which are used with impunity and in utter disregard to the law of land and principles of learning.[164]

The practice of abusing children verbally by attacking their psyche occupies the top rank in the list of punishments in school. As many as 81.2 per cent of the children were subjected to outright rejection by being told that they are not capable of learning, reports a recent study *Eliminating Corporal Punishment in Schools* by the NCPCR.[165] The study surveyed 6,632 students across seven states. According to the report:

> Three out of five school children, in the 3–5 age group—that's how early it starts—were beaten with a cane as a form of corporal punishment. An alarming 99 per cent had experienced some of corporal punishment—the four most common forms of physical punishment being beaten by cane, being hit on the back, getting boxed on the ears and being slapped.[166] The NCPCR study found that 99 per cent of 6,700 students surveyed in seven states had suffered some form of punishment at the hands of their teachers. Boys are marginally more likely to face physical abuse (73 per cent) than girls (65 per cent). Corporal punishment in both government as well as private schools is deeply ingrained as

---

[163] The Committee on the Rights of the Child in the General Comment No. 8, UNCRC, CRC General Comment No. 8, 2006: The Right of the Child to Protection from Corporal Punishment and Other Cruel or Degrading Forms of Punishment (Articles 19, 28, Para. 2, and 37, inter alia), 2 March 2007, CRC/C/GC/8. Available at http://www.unhcr.org/refworld/docid/460bc7772.html (accessed on 20 September 2015).

[164] NCPCR, *Protection of Children against Corporal Punishment in Schools and Institutions*, Report of Summary Discussions by the Working Group on Corporal Punishment, Delhi, December 2008. Available at http://harprathmik.gov.in/pdf/rte/corporal%20punishment%20ncpcr.pdf (accessed on 20 September 2015).

[165] NCPCR, *Protection of Children against Corporal Punishment in Schools and Institutions*.

[166] NCPCR, *Protection of Children against Corporal Punishment in Schools and Institutions*.

a tool to discipline children and as a normal action. But most children do not report or confide about the matter to anyone and suffer silently.[167]

Two out of three school-going children in India are physically abused, says the national report on child abuse by the Ministry of Women and Child Development in 2007. The crime is rampant in every single district of the country. Two out of three school-going children in India are physically abused says the national report on child abuse by the Ministry of Women and Child Development in 2007.[168] The crime is rampant in every single district of the country. Corporal punishment in both government as well as private schools is deeply ingrained as a tool to discipline children and as a normal action. But most children do not report or confide about the matter to anyone. Although the Supreme Court had banned corporal punishment in schools in 2000, the 'system' is still prevalent in several institutions.

Corporal punishment encourages violence. Even a little slap carries the message that violence is the appropriate response to conflict or unwanted behaviour. Aggression breeds aggression. Children subjected to physical punishment have been shown to be more likely than others to be aggressive to siblings; to bully other children at school; to take part in aggressively anti-social behaviour in adolescence; to be violent to their spouses and their own children and to commit violent crimes. National commissions on violence in America, Australia, Germany, South Africa, and the UK have recommended ending corporal punishment of children as an essential step towards reducing all violence in society. Corporal punishment can be emotionally harmful to children causing psychological damage.

Laws Relating to Corporal Punishment in India

Article 21 of the Constitution of India protects the 'right to life' of all citizens including children.[169] The right to life has been interpreted widely by the courts in India to guarantee a right to life with dignity and a life free from fear, cruelty, exploitation , violence and abuse. Articles 39(e) and 39(f) of the Directive Principles of State Policy also direct that the tender age of children is not abused and they should develop in conditions of dignity and freedom.[170]

---

[167] NCPCR, *Protection of Children against Corporal Punishment in Schools and Institutions.*

[168] L. Kacker, S. Varadan, and P. Kumar, 2007, *Study on Child Abuse: India, 2007*, national report on child abuse by the Ministry of Women and Child Development in 2007 (New Delhi: Ministry of Women and Child Development, Government of India).

[169] Constitution of India, Article 21: Protection of Life and Personal Liberty—No person shall be deprived of his life or personal liberty except according to procedure established by law, in the case of *Bandhua Mukti Morcha* v. *Union of India and Others* (1992 AIR 38) in respect of bonded labour and weaker section of the society. The following was laid down: 'Article 21 assures the right to live with human dignity, free from exploitation. The state is under a constitutional obligation to see that there is no violation of the fundamental right of any person, particularly when he belongs to the weaker section of the community and is unable to wage a legal battle against a strong and powerful opponent who is exploiting him.'

[170] Constitution of India, Article 39:

The state shall in particular direct its policy towards securing that the health and strength of workers, men and women, and the tender age of children are not abused·and that citizens are not forced by economic

Indian Penal Code, 1860

All children under the age of 7 are supposed to be exempted from criminal liability and any mistake they may have done cannot merit corporal punishment in schools in India as they are still in an age of innocence and they are incapable of understanding complex issues. According to the principles of *Doli Incapaxi*, children under the age of 7 cannot be given any form of punishment by any teacher.[171]

Currently, a number of legal provisions under the Indian Penal Code (IPC), 1860 can be used to prosecute someone who inflicts corporal punishment on a child in school or a custodial institution. These include abetment of suicide committed by a child,[172] voluntarily causing hurt,[173] or grievous hurt or causing hurt by dangerous weapons.[174] There have been several cases of suicides

---

necessity to enter avocations unsuited to their age and strength; f. that children are given the opportunities and facilities to develop in a healthy manner and in conditions of freedom and dignity and that childhood and youth are protected against exploitation and against moral and material abandonment.

[171] IPC, Section 82: Act of a child under 7 years of age—Nothing is an offence which is done by a child under 7 years of age.

[172] IPC, Section 306: If any person commits suicide, whoever abets the commission of such suicide, shall be punished with imprisonment of either description for a term which may extend to 10 years, and shall also be liable to fine.

[173] According to Section 319 of the IPC whoever causes bodily pain, disease or infirmity to any person is said to cause hurt. The definition of hurt contemplates causing of pain by a person to another so it is not necessary that there should be visible injury caused on the person. The causing of pain is sufficient. Causing disease and infirmity also come within the purview of this section. The essential ingredients of the offence of simple hurt are as follows:

(1) The offender voluntarily caused bodily pain , disease or infirmity to the victim ;
(2) The offender did so with the intention of causing hurt or with the knowledge that he would thereby cause hurt to the victim.

Sections 321 and 322 define what is meant by the expression 'voluntarily causing hurt' and 'voluntarily causing grievous hurt'. Whoever does any act with the intention to cause or knowledge that he is thereby likely to cause simple or grievous hurt to any person and causes the hurt so intended or known to be likely is said to voluntarily cause hurt or grievous hurt, as the case may be (Sections 321–22).

A person is not said voluntarily to cause grievous hurt if both the hurt intended or known to be likely and the hurt caused are not grievous, that is, for the offence of voluntarily causing grievous hurt it is necessary that (i) the hurt caused should be grievous; and (ii) the hurt intended should also be grievous.

The offence shall not be constituted if any of the two is simple. It does not matter or make any difference in case of grievous hurt if the grievous hurt caused is of a kind different from the grievous hurt intended to be caused.

Punishment for voluntarily causing hurt, i.e., simple hurt is imprisonment of either description upto one year, or fine upto Rs 1,000 or both (Section 323) and for voluntarily causing grievous hurt imprisonment upto 7 years and fine (Section 325).

[174] IPC, Section 320 states that the following eight kinds of hurt are designated as grievous—

(1) Emasculation.
(2) Permanent privation of the sight of either eye.

and attempted suicide throughout the country by children owing to corporal punishment in schools in India. A teacher can be booked under Section 306 of the IPC, 1860 if the infliction of corporal punishment leads a child to commit suicide.

Juvenile Justice (Care and Protection of Children) Act, 2000

Section 23 of the Juvenile Justice Care and Protection Act (JJ Act), 2000 criminalizes actions that may cause a child mental or physical suffering, punishable with an imprisonment for a term which may extend to 6 months, or fine, or with both. This provision does not clearly use the words corporal punishment but it is interpreted as cruelty to children. Though it is intended to punish cruelty by those in authority, it equally applies to parents and teachers. The law does not excuse teachers and parents and they are liable for assaulting or exposing a juvenile to unnecessary forms of punishment .[175]

Juvenile Justice (Care and Protection of Children) Rules, 2007[176]

The model rules also enunciate 'fundamental principles' of care and protection with regard to the juvenile justice process and institutional care in juvenile homes which explicitly prohibit corporal punishment and maltreatment of children within the juvenile institutional system and lay out duties for the state for protection of children from abuse within the juvenile system:

---

(3)   Permanent privation of the hearing of either ear.
(4)   Privation of any member or joint.
(5)   Destruction or permanent impairing of the powers of any member or joint.
(6)   Permanent disfiguration of the head or face.
(7)   fracture or dislocation of a bone or tooth.
(8)   Any hurt which endangers life or which causes the sufferer to be during the space of twenty days in severe bodily pain, or unable to follow his ordinary pursuits.

A person can not cause grievous hurt unless the hurt caused falls within one of the clauses specified in Section 320 of IPC.

[175]   JJ Act, 2006, Section 23:

Whoever, having the actual charge of or control over, a juvenile or the child, assaults, abandons, exposes or wilfully neglects the juvenile or causes or procures him/her to be assaulted, abandoned, exposed or neglected in a manner likely to cause such juvenile or the 13 child unnecessarily mental or physical suffering, shall be punishable with imprisonment for a term which may extend to six months, or fine, or with both. This section has no exceptions to exempt parents or teachers.

[176]   Rules under the JJ Act, 2000 (56 of 2000) (as amended by the Amendment Act 33 of 2006) to be administered by the states. Ministry of Women and Child Development Notification, New Delhi, 26 October 2007. Available at http://wcd.nic.in/childprot/juvenile%20justice%20_care%20and%20protection%20of%20children_%20rules%202%E2%80%A6.pdf (accessed on 21 November 2016).

Chapter II: Principle of dignity and worth (a) Treatment that is consistent with the child's sense of dignity and worth is a fundamental principle of juvenile justice.... Respect of dignity includes not being humiliated, personal identity, boundaries and space being respected, not being labeled and stigmatized, being offered information and choices and not being blamed for their acts.

Chapter VI: Principle of Safety (no harm, no abuse, no neglect, no exploitation and no maltreatment) (a) At all stages, from the initial contact till such time he remains in contact with the care and protection system, and thereafter, the juvenile or child or juvenile in conflict with law shall not be subjected to any harm, abuse, neglect, maltreatment, corporal punishment or solitary or otherwise any confinement in jails and extreme care shall be taken to avoid any harm to the sensitivity of the juvenile or the child. (b) The state has a greater responsibility for ensuring safety of every child in its care and protection, without restoring to restrictive measures and processes in the name of care and protection.

Rules 46 and 60 further specify the juvenile home as an 'abuse free' environment and outline mechanisms to ensure the creation of such an environment:

Rule 46: (3) The environment in an institution shall be free from abuse, allowing juvenile or children to cope with their situation and regain their confidence.

Rule 60: (1) Every institution shall have systems of ensuring that there is no abuse, neglect and maltreatment and this shall include the staff being aware of what constitutes abuse, neglect and maltreatment as well as early indicators of abuse, neglect and maltreatment and how to respond to these.

Juvenile Justice (Care and Protection of Children) Act, 2015

The Juvenile Justice (Care and Protection of Children) Act, 2015 came into force on 15 January 2016 and repealed the Juvenile Justice (Care and Protection of Children) Act, 2000. Under Section 2(24) of this act 'corporal punishment' means the subjecting of a child by any person to physical punishment that involves the deliberate infliction of pain as retribution for an offence, or for the purpose of disciplining or reforming the child. Under Section 82 of JJ Act, corporal punishment is prohibited in child care institutions The act states in Article 82 that any person in-charge of or employed in a child care institution, who subjects a child to corporal punishment with the aim of disciplining the child, shall be liable, on the first conviction, to a fine of Rs 10,000 and for every subsequent offence, shall be liable for imprisonment which may extend to 3 months or fine, or both. If a person employed in an institution is convicted of inflicting corporal punishment, such a person shall also be liable for dismissal from service, and shall also be debarred from working directly with children thereafter.

In case, where any corporal punishment is reported in an institution, the management of such institution does not cooperate with any inquiry or comply with the orders of the committee or the board or court or state government, the person in-charge of the management of the institution shall be liable for punishment with imprisonment for a term not less than three years and shall also be liable to fine which may extend to Rs 1,00,000.

Right of Children to Free and Compulsory Education Act, 2009

The RTE Act, 2009 explicitly prohibits physical punishment and mental harassment in schools of children aged between 6 and 14.[177] Sections 8[178] and 9[179] of the RTE Act place a duty on the

[177] RTE Act, 2009, which has come into force with effect from 1 April 2010, prohibits 'physical punishment' and 'mental harassment' under Section 17(1) and makes it a punishable offence under Section 17(2). These provisions read as follows: Section 17, Prohibition of physical punishment and mental harassment to child—

(1) No child shall be subjected to physical punishment or mental harassment.
(2) Whoever contravenes the provisions of Subsection (1) shall be liable to disciplinary action under the service rules applicable to such person.

[178] RTE Act, 2009, Section 8: Duties of appropriate government—
The appropriate government shall

(1) provide free and compulsory elementary education to every child, provided that where a child is admitted by his or her parents or guardian, as the case may be, in a school other than a school established, owned, controlled or substantially financed by funds provided directly or indirectly by the appropriate government or a local authority, such child or his or her parents or guardian, as the case may be, shall not be entitled to make a claim for reimbursement of expenditure incurred on elementary education of the child in such other school.
Explanation:
The term 'compulsory education' means obligation of the appropriate government to

(a) provide free elementary education to every child of the age of 6 to 14 years; and
(b) ensure compulsory admission, attendance and completion of elementary education by every child of the age of 6 to 14 years;

(2) ensure availability of a neighbourhood school as specified in Section 6;
(3) ensure that the child belonging to weaker section and the child belonging to disadvantaged group are not discriminated against and prevented from pursuing and completing elementary education on any grounds;
(4) provide infrastructure including school building, teaching staff and learning equipment;
(5) provide special training facility specified in Section 4;
(6) ensure and monitor admission, attendance and completion of elementary education by every child;
(7) ensure good quality elementary education conforming to the standards and norms specified in the schedule;
(8) ensure timely prescribing of curriculum and courses of study for elementary education; and
(9) provide training facility for teachers.

[179] RTE Act, 2009, Section 9:
Duties of local authority:
Every local authority shall:

(1) provide free and compulsory elementary education to every child, provided that where a child is admitted by his or her parents or guardian, as the case may be, in a school other than a school established, owned, controlled or substantially financed by funds provided directly or indirectly by the appropriate government or a local authority, such child or his or her parents or guardian, as the case may be, shall not be entitled to make a claim for reimbursement of expenditure incurred on elementary education of the child in such other school;

appropriate government and the local authority to 'ensure that a child belonging to the weaker section and the child belonging to disadvantaged group are not discriminated against and prevented from pursuing and completing elementary education on any grounds'. The RTE Act does not preclude the application of other legislation that relates to the violations of the rights of the child, for example, booking the offenses under the IPC and the Scheduled Caste and Scheduled Tribe Prevention of Atrocities Act of 1989.

State Amendments

The Goa Children's Act categorically states in Section 4(2) that 'corporal punishment is banned in all schools'. Many state education acts have been amended as well, particularly in Andhra Pradesh and Tamil Nadu, Maharashtra. The 'education departments' in many states have also issued orders and circulars.

National Commission for Protection of Child Rights Guidelines on Corporal Punishment, 2012[180]

In August 2007, the NCPCR also wrote to all chief secretaries with detailed guidelines recommending practical steps for the elimination of corporal punishment. In December of the same year, the Human Resource Development Ministry also wrote to all chief secretaries recommending that corporal punishment be prohibited in all schools in the jurisdiction of the state government as it 'severely affects the human dignity of the child, thereby reducing his/her self-esteem and self-confidence'.[181]

---

(2) ensure availability of a neighbourhood school as specified in Section 6;

(3) ensure that the child belonging to weaker section and the child belonging to disadvantaged group are not discriminated against and prevented from pursuing and completing elementary education on any grounds;

(4) maintain records of children up to the age of 14 years residing within its jurisdiction, in such manner as may be prescribed;

(5) ensure and monitor admission, attendance, and completion of elementary education by every child residing within its jurisdiction;

(6) provide infrastructure including school building, teaching staff, and learning material;

(7) provide special training facility specified in Section 4;

(8) ensure good quality elementary education conforming to the standards and norms specified in the schedule;

(9) ensure timely prescribing of curriculum and courses of study for elementary education;

(10) provide training facility for teachers;

(11) ensure admission of children of migrant families;

(12) monitor functioning of schools within its jurisdiction; and

(13) decide the academic calendar.

[180] NCPCR, *Guidelines for Eliminating Corporal Punishment in Schools* (New Delhi, 2012). Available at http://www.ncpcr.gov.in/view_file.php?fid=108 (accessed on 20 September 2015).

[181] No. NCPCR/Edu.1/ 07/39, 9 August 2007. Available at http://ncpcr.gov.in/view_file.php?fid=384 (accessed on 15 September 2015).

The guidelines laid down by the NCPCR state:

1. There is no room for corporal punishment in any deliberation with the child. All children are to be informed through campaigns and publicity drives that they have a right to speak against corporal punishment and bring it to the notice of the authorities. They must be given confidence to make complaints and not accept punishment as a 'normal' activity of the school.
2. Every school, including hostels, JJ homes, shelter homes, and other public institutions meant for children must have a forum where children can express their views. Such institutions could take the help of an NGO for facilitating such an exercise.
3. Further a box where children can drop their complaints, even if anonymous has to be provided for in each school.
4. There has to be a monthly meeting of the PTAs or any other body such as the SEC/VEC to review the complaints and take action.
5. The PTAs are to be encouraged to act immediately on any complaints made by children without postponement of the issue and wait for a more grave injury to be caused. In other words the PTAs need not use their discretion to decide on the grievousness of the complaint.
6. Parents as well as children are to be empowered to speak out against corporal punishment without any fear that it would have adverse effect on children's participation in schools.
7. The education department at all levels—block, district, and state—are to establish procedures for reviewing the responses to the complaints of children and monitoring the action taken on the same.

The National Charter for Children, 2003[182]

This charter acknowledges the principles and provisions of the Constitution and of the 1974 National Policy as comprising its guiding frame, and includes 'neglect' and 'degrading treatment' in its listing of conditions from which children must be protected. The charter states its intent to 'secure for every child its right to be a child and enjoy a healthy and happy childhood … and to awaken the conscience of the community in the wider societal context to protect children from all forms of abuse' and asserts that 'the state and community shall undertake all possible measures to ensure and protect the survival, life and liberty of all children.'

Article 7(f) of the Charter states: 'The state shall ensure that school discipline and matters related thereto do not result in physical, mental, psychological harm or trauma to the child.'

National Plan of Action for Children, 2005[183]

One of the core objectives of the National Plan of Action (NPA) is 'to protect all children against neglect, maltreatment, injury, trafficking, sexual and physical abuse of all kinds, pornography, corporal punishment, torture, exploitation, violence, and degrading treatment'.

---

[182] Department of Women and Child Development, *Gazette of India*, Part I, Section I (New Delhi: MHRD, Government of India, 9 February 2004).

[183] Department of Women and Child Development, MHRD, Government of India. Available at http://www.wcd.nic.in/napaug16a.pdf (accessed on 20 September 2015).

National Policy on Education (1986, modified 1992)[184]

The NPE, 1986 in Para. 5.6 provides for a child-centric approach. It states that a warm, welcoming and encouraging approach, in which all concerned share solicitude for the needs of the child, is the best motivation for the child to attend school and learn. A child-centered and activity-based process of learning should be adopted at the primary stage. First-generation learners should be allowed to set their own pace and be given supplementary remedial instruction. As the child grows, the component of cognitive learning will be increased and skills will be organized through practice. The NDP at the primary stage will be retained, making evaluation as disaggregated as feasible. Corporal punishment will be firmly excluded from the educational system and school timings as well as vacations adjusted to the convenience of children.

National Policy for Children, 2013

It states that in education, the state shall 'ensure no child is subjected to any physical punishment or mental harassment' and 'promote positive engagement to impart discipline so as to provide children with a good learning experience'. Law reform has gone some way to prohibiting corporal punishment in schools but is not yet complete.[185]

Guidelines by Ministry of Women and Child Development[186]

The Ministry of Women and Child Development had issued guidelines on corporal punishment. The guidelines provided for setting up child-rights cells in all schools where children can file a complaint. They, however, have remained only on paper so far.

Judgments on Corporal Punishment In Schools in India

M. Natesan v. State of Madras and Another[187]

It was a case where a boy of 15 years was sent with the progress report to get the signature of his parents in it. But he returned it with a thumb impression of another person, stating that the said thumb impression was that of his mother, which was proved to be wrong. The teacher got agitated and he beat the boy on his right palm with a stick. He did not cry. He, therefore, beat

184 The NPE (with modifications undertaken in 1992). Available at http://www.ncert.nic.in/oth_anoun/npe86.pdf (accessed on 20 September 2015).

185 Department of Women and Child Development, *National Policy for Children 2013* (MHRD, Government of India), para. 4.6(xv). Available at http://wcd.nic.in/childwelfare/npc2013dtd29042013.pdf (accessed on 20 September 2015).

186 National Commission for Protectionof Child Rights, *Guidelines for Eliminating Corporal Punishment in Schools* (Ministry of Women and Child Development and MHRD, Government of India). Available at http://www.ncpcr.gov.in/view_file.php?fid=108 (accessed on 26 September 2015).

187 AIR 1962 Mad 216.

him again, asking him why he did not cry. This resulted in causing three injuries, two superficial and one contusion. The Madras High Court laid down:

It cannot be denied that having regard to the peculiar position of a school teacher he must in the nature of things have authority to enforce discipline and correct a pupil put in his charge. To deny that authority would amount to a denial of all that is desirable and necessary for the welfare, discipline and education of the pupil concerned. It can therefore be assumed that when a parent entrusts a child to a teacher, he on his behalf impliedly consents for the teacher to exercise over the pupil such authority. Of course, the person of the pupil is certainly protected by the penal provisions of the Indian Penal Code. But the same code has recognised exceptions in the form of sections 88[188] and 89[189]. Where a teacher exceeds the authority and inflicts such harm to the pupil as may be considered to be unreasonable and immoderate, he would naturally lose the benefit of the exceptions. Whether he is entitled to the benefit of the exceptions or not in a given case will depend upon the particular nature, extent and severity of the punishment inflicted.

Ganesh Chandra Saha v. Jiw Raj Somani[190]

It was a case where a student lost his book and it was found to be stolen by another person of the school, by name the Samshi, of Class 7. Petitioner was the headmaster of the school. He beat Samshi, who committed theft of the book, with a cane and also gave him some fists and

---

[188] IPC, 1860, Section 88 : Act not intended to cause death, done by consent in good faith for person's benefit—

Nothing which is not intended to cause death, is an offence by reason of any harm which it may cause, or be intended by the doer to cause, or be known by the doer to be likely to cause, to any person for whose benefit it is done in good faith, and who has given a consent, whether express or implied, to suffer that harm, or to take the risk of that harm.

[189] IPC, 1860, Section 89: Act done in good faith for benefit of child or insane person, by or by consent of guardian:

Nothing which is done in good faith for the benefit of a person under twelve years of age, or of unsound mind, by or by consent, either express or implied, of the guardian or other person having lawful charge of that person, is an offence by reason of any harm which it may cause, or be intended by the doer to cause or be known by the doer to be likely to cause to that person, provided—

first, that this exception shall not extend to the intentional causing of death, or to the attempting cause death;

second, that this exception shall not extend to the doing of anything which the person doing it knows to be likely to cause death, for any purpose other than the preventing of death or grievous hurt, or the curing of any grievous disease or infirmity;

third, that this exception shall not extend to the voluntary causing of grievous hurt, or to the attempting to cause grievous hurt, unless it be for the purpose of preventing death or grievous hurt, or the curing of any grievous disease or infirmity;

fourth, that this exception shall not extend to the abetment of any offence, to the committing of whichoffence it would not extend.

[190] AIR 1965 Cal 32.

blows. He was charged for the offence under Section 323[191] of the IPC. The magistrate found him guilty and sentenced him to pay a fine of Rs 15,000 with default sentence. This was challenged before the High Court of Calcutta. The wound certificate showed that Samshi had some minor injuries, but one tooth was found loose, which could have been caused because of the blow inflicted on the student. Discussing on this aspect and also accepting the principle of law, recognized in England and schools therein, the Honourable Culcutta High Court observed thus:

> When a boy is sent by his parent or guardian to a School, the parent or the guardian must be said to have given an implied consent to his being under the discipline and control of the School authorities and to the infliction of such reasonable punishment as may be necessary for the purposes of School discipline or for correcting him. Then again when a boy over 12 years of age himself goes to a school it should be presumed that he gives an implied consent to subject himself to the discipline and control of the School authorities and to receive such reasonable and moderate corporal punishment as may be necessary for his correction or for maintaining school discipline. Under the Indian Penal Code consent can be given by a child not under 12 years of age [vide Section 90[192] of the Indian Penal Code]. The action of the petitioner in administering corporal punishment to the complainant is, therefore, covered by Section 88[193] of the Indian Penal Code.

Abdul Vahid v. State of Kerala & Another[194]

In this case, the petitioner—an Arabic teacher at Manikkal Madrassas—beat Sajad, a student learning Arabic, with a cane on his buttock. He cried and was taken to his house in the evening

---

[191] IPC, 1860, Section 323: Punishment for voluntarily causing hurt—

Whoever, except in the case provided for by section 334, voluntarily causes hurt, shall be punished with imprisonment of either description for a term which may extend to one year, or with fine which may extend to one thousand rupees, or with both.

[192] IPC, 1860, Section 90: Consent known to be given under fear or misconception—

A consent is not such a consent as it intended by any section of this Code, if the consent is given by a person under fear of injury, or under a misconception of fact, and if the person doing the act knows, or has reason to believe, that the consent was given in consequence of such fear or misconception; or

Consent of insane person—if the consent is given by a person who, from unsoundness of mind, or intoxication, is unable to understand the nature and consequence of that to which he gives his consent; or

Consent of child—unless the contrary appears from the context, if the consent is given by a person who is under twelve years of age.

[193] IPC, 1860, Section 88: Act not intended to cause death, done by consent in good faith for person's benefit—

Nothing which is not intended to cause death, is an offence by reason of any harm which it may cause, or be intended by the doer to cause, or be known by the doer to be likely to cause, to any person for whose benefit it is done in good faith, and who has given a consent, whether express or implied, to suffer that harm, or to take the risk of that harm.

[194] 2005 CriLJ 2054.

by two persons. He complained to his father that he has got pain. He was shown to a private hospital. As pain subsisted, he was taken to the S.U.T. Hospital, Thiruvananthapuram. Though the Juma-at office bearers promised to pay him the treatment expenses, they failed. Hence the case was filed. The court hence quashing the order of the trial court held:

> When a child is sent to Madrassa or a school, the parents of the said child give an implied authority to the master or the class teacher or Headmaster/Headmistress to enforce discipline and correct the students who commit errors in front of him or her or in the classes. If a corporal punishment is given by any of them, in the process of maintaining such discipline, and also to make him/her adhere to the prescribed standards of the school, which are necessary for the upliftment and development of the child, including the development of his character and conduct in and outside the school, so that he is trained to be aware of the good qualities of a citizen, it cannot be said to be an act intended to injure the student. In such a situation, if no intentional injury is caused, considering the age of the student, it cannot be said that the said school teacher has inflicted injury to harm him. But again, the act of the teacher on the student, in imposing corporal punishment, depends upon the circumstances of each case. If a teacher out of fury and excitement, inflicts injury which is harmful to the health of a tender aged student, it cannot be accepted as a right conferred on such a teacher to inflict such punishment, because of the express or implied authority granted by the parents of that student. Therefore, there cannot be any generalized pattern of principle in such situations. The acts of a teacher have to be appreciated and assessed depending upon the circumstances that are placed before the Court. In each case, it is the duty of the teachers to have a restrained and controlled imposition of punishments on the pupils under their care and charge. Unwieldy, uncontrolled, and emotional attacks or actions on their part cannot be accepted.

Hasmukhbhai Gokaldas Shah v. State of Gujarat[195]

On perusing the evidence and the material witnesses in the instant case, the court held in Para. 18 and Para. 19:

> Section 88[196] of the I.P. Code is in respect of an act not intended to cause death, done by consent in good faith for person's benefit while Section 89[197] of the I.P. Code speaks of an act done in good faith

---

[195] 2009 CriLJ 2919.

[196] IPC, 1860, Section 88: Act not intended to cause death, done by consent in good faith for person's benefit—

Nothing which is not intended to cause death, is an offence by reason of any harm which it may cause, or be intended by the doer to cause, or be known by the doer to be likely to cause, to any person for whose benefit it is done in good faith, and who has given a consent, whether express or implied, to suffer that harm, or to take the risk of that harm.

[197] IPC, 1860, Section 89: Act done in good faith for benefit of child or insane person, by or by consent of guardian—

Nothing which is done in good faith for the benefit of a person under twelve years of age, or of unsound mind, by or by consent, either express or implied, of the guardian or other person having lawful charge of that person, is an offence by reason of any harm which it may cause, or be intended by the doer to cause or be known by the doer to be likely to cause to that person, provided—

first, that this exception shall not extend to the intentional causing of death, or to the attempting cause death;

for benefit of child or insane person, by or by consent of guardian, the principle which is advanced is this is that when a child is sent to school, the guardian consents to reasonable corporal punishment to the child. Corporal punishment to child, in present days, with principle as advanced, is not recognized by law. It is an archaic notion that to maintain discipline, child can be punished physically by the teaching staff because of implied consent by the parents or guardian.

Global Context of Corporal Punishment in Schools

It is now globally recognized that punishment in any form or kind in school comes in the way of the development of the children. All educational institutions including schools and hostels, government as well as private, are custodians of children during the time the children are on their premises. It is thus the responsibility of the management/administration of the school/institution to ensure that children are safe from all forms of violence, including corporal punishment and they all must be held accountable for any violence.

A UNICEF Multiple Indicator Cluster Survey, which spanned five years from 2005–10, revealed that in selected countries in Eastern and Central Europe and Central Asia alone, more than 50 per cent of boys and girls aged 2–14 had been subjected to psychological or physical punishment by their parents or other adults of the household. These numbers were higher among most vulnerable groups such as the Roma and children with disabilities.[198]

The United Nations Secretary-General's *Study on Violence against Children* has been a global effort to paint a detailed picture of the nature, extent, and causes of violence against children, and to propose clear recommendations for action to prevent and respond to. This is the first time that an attempt has been made to document the reality of violence against children around the world, and to map out what is being done to stop it.[199] According to the study, violence perpetrated by teachers and other school staff, with or without the overt or tacit approval of education ministries and other authorities that oversee schools, includes corporal punishment, cruel and humiliating forms of psychological punishment, sexual and gender-based violence, and bullying.[200] Corporal

---

second, that this exception shall not extend to the doing of anything which the person doing it knows to be likely to cause death, for any purpose other than the preventing of death or grievous hurt, or the curing of any grievous disease or infirmity;

third, that this exception shall not extend to the voluntary causing of grievous hurt, or to the attempting to cause grievous hurt, unless it be for the purpose of preventing death or grievous hurt, or the curing of any grievous disease or infirmity;

fourth, that this exception shall not extend to the abetment of any offence, to the committing of which offence it would not extend.

[198] 'Ending Corporal Punishment of children'. Available at http://www.ohchr.org/EN/NewsEvents/Pages/CorporalPunishment.aspx#sthash.rO1vRS3O.dpuf (accessed on 20 September 2015).

[199] United Nations Secretary-General's Report on Violence against Children, *Global Initiative to End All Corporal Punishment of Children, Global Summary of the Legal Status of Corporal Punishment of Children*, 28 June 2006. Available at http://www.unicef.org/violencestudy/reports/SG_violencestudy_en.pdf (accessed on 20 September 2015).

[200] United Nations Secretary-General's Report on Violence against Children, *Global Initiative to End All Corporal Punishment of Children*.

punishment such as beating and caning is a standard practice in schools in a large number of countries. Violence in schools in the form of playground fighting and bullying of students also occurs. In some societies, aggressive behaviour, including fighting, is widely perceived as a minor disciplinary problem.[201] Bullying is frequently associated with discrimination against students from poor families or ethnically marginalized groups, or those with particular personal characteristics (for example, appearance, or a physical or mental disability). Sexual and gender-based violence also occurs in educational settings. Much is directed against girls, by male teachers and classmates. Violence is also increasingly directed against lesbian, gay, bisexual, and transgendered young people in many states and regions. Sexual and gender-based violence is facilitated by government's failure to enact and implement laws that provide students with explicit protection from discrimination.[202]

Numerous international and regional human rights institutions such as the UNCRC, the Convention against Torture and Other Cruel, Inhuman, or Degrading Treatment or Punishment, and the UDHR, have declared that some or all forms of school corporal punishment violate the human rights of children. Many nations have either restricted or have placed an explicit ban on corporal punishment in their schools.[203]

The UNCRC includes the Right to Protection of the Child against Abuse, which is categorized as an immediate right. Article 19 of the UNCRC requires states to protect children from 'all forms of physical or mental violence'.[204] During the first decade of the convention, the Committee on the Rights of the Child recommended to over 120 states to abolish all corporal punishment and develop public-education campaigns to promote positive, non-violent discipline in the family, schools, and other institutions. In 1999, the Committee on Economic, Social and Cultural Rights adopted a general comment on the RTE which stated that corporal punishment is inconsistent with the fundamental guiding principle of international human rights law enshrined in the Preambles to the UDHR and both Covenants.

The UNCRC requires states parties to take all appropriate measures to ensure that school discipline is administered in a manner consistent with the convention. The Global Initiative to End All Corporal Punishment of Children reports that 102 countries have banned corporal

---

[201] United Nations General Assembly, *Report of the Independent Expert for the United Nations Study on Violence against Children*. Available at http://www.unicef.org/violencestudy/reports/SG_violencestudy_en.pdf (accessed on 20 September 2015).

[202] United Nations General Assembly, *Report of the Independent Expert*.

[203] See generally *Human Rights Watch: Spare the Child, Corporal Punishment in Kenyan Schools*. Available at http://www.hrw.org/reports/999/kenyafmdex.htm (accessed on 20 September 2015).

[204] UNCRC, Article 19 states:

(1) State parties shall take all appropriate legislative, administrative, social and educational measures to protect the child from all forms of physical or mental violence, injury or abuse, neglect or negligent treatment, maltreatment or exploitation, including sexual abuse, while in the care of parent(s), legal guardian(s) or any other person who has the care of the child.

(2) Such protective measures should, as appropriate, include effective procedures for the establishment of social programmes to provide necessary support for the child and for those who have the care of the child, as well as for other forms of prevention and for identification, reporting, referral, investigation, treatment and follow-up of instances of child maltreatment described heretofore, and, as appropriate, for judicial involvement.

punishment in school, but enforcement is uneven.[205] The pace of reform is gathering momentum in light of the UN Study on Violence against children which recommended in its final report prohibition in law of all corporal punishment of children by 2009.[206]

The UNCRC, the highest authority for interpretation of the convention, emphasizes states' immediate obligation to prohibit and eliminate all corporal punishment and other forms of cruel or degrading treatment. Issuing its 2006 General Comment on the right of the child to protection from violent punishment, the committee explains that its purpose is 'to highlight the obligation of all states parties to move quickly to prohibit and eliminate all corporal punishment and all other cruel or degrading forms of punishment of children and to outline the legislative and other aware-ness-raising and educational measures that states must take'. The committee reiterates states' obligations to prohibit and eliminate corporal punishment in all settings of children's lives and states:

> Article 37 of the Convention requires States to ensure that 'no child shall be subjected to torture or other cruel, inhuman or degrading treatment or punishment'. This is complemented and extended by Article 19, which requires States to 'take all appropriate legislative, administrative, social and educational measures to protect the child from all forms of physical or mental violence, injury or abuse, neglect or negligent treatment, maltreatment or exploitation, including sexual abuse, while in the care of parent(s), legal guardian(s) or any other person who has the care of the child'. There is no ambiguity: 'all forms of physical or mental violence' does not leave room for any level of legalized violence against children. Corporal punishment and other cruel or degrading forms of punishment are forms of violence and States must take all appropriate legislative, administrative, social and educational measures to eliminate them.
>
> The Committee strongly recommends that the State party prohibit corporal punishment in the family, in schools and other institutions and undertake education campaigns to educate families, teachers and other professionals working with and/or for children on alternative ways of disciplining children.[207]

In 2006, the report of the *UN Secretary-General's Study on Violence against Children* was submitted to the UN General Assembly. Among its key recommendations was that all states should urgently prohibit all forms of violence against children, including all corporal punishment.

In the context of the almost universal ratification of the UNCRC, repeated recommendations from the committee on the Rights of the Child and other UN Treaty Bodies and follow-up to the UNSG's Study, there is now rapidly accelerating global progress. By October 2011, 31 states had achieved a complete ban on corporal punishment in all settings, including the home. A substantial majority of states (120) has banned all corporal punishment in schools.[208]

A majority of the Council of Europe member states have now committed themselves to put an end to all corporal punishment of children. Full prohibition in law has so far been adopted by 18 member states and at least 7 others have publicly pledged to do the same within the near future. The Commissioner for Human Rights has welcomed this development and urged other countries as well to consider moving towards prohibition and elimination of all corporal

---

[205] UNCRC, Article 19.
[206] The list of submissions is available at the website of the United Nations Secretary-General's *Study on Violence against Children*. Available at http://www.violencestudy.org (accessed on 20 September 2015).
[207] CRC/C/15/Add.228, *Concluding Observations on Second Report*, paras 44 and 45, 26 February 2004.
[208] For details of progress, see http://www.endcorporalpunishment.org (accessed on 20 November 2016).

punishment against children. This issue paper explains why and gives background information on steps already taken by the European Court of Human Rights and other international and European human rights mechanisms.[209]

Violence perpetrated by teachers and other school staff, with or without the overt or tacit approval of education ministries and other authorities that oversee schools, includes corporal punishment, cruel and humiliating forms of psychological punishment, sexual and gender-based violence, and bullying.[210] Corporal punishment such as beating and caning is standard practice in schools in a large number of countries. The UNCRC requires states parties to take all appropriate measures to ensure that school discipline is administered in a manner consistent with the convention. The Global Initiative to End All Corporal Punishment of Children reports that 102 countries have banned corporal punishment in school, but enforcement is uneven.[211]

The UN Global Study on violence against children, child rights was reviewed by experts global progress in prohibiting corporal punishment of children, and analysed the remaining challenges in fully respecting their dignity and physical integrity. According the UN Deputy High Commissioner for Human Rights, Kyung-wha Kang:

> Violence against children, including corporal punishment, is a violation of the rights of the child. It conflicts with the child's human dignity and the right of the child to physical integrity. It also prevents children from reaching their full potential, by putting at risk their right to health, survival and development. The best interests of the child can never be used to justify such practice. The need to promote non-violent values and awareness-raising amongst all those working with children is essential if we want this situation to come to an end.[212]

Kang was speaking at a side event of the current session of the Universal Periodic Review in Geneva, coorganized by the Permanent Missions of Finland, Tunisia, Uruguay, and a number of civil society organizations. Experts noted that corporal punishment was one of the issues raised during the examination of many states, adding that more than 80 had subsequently accepted recommendations to prohibit it.

Paulo Sérgio Pinheiro, the Independent Expert appointed by the UN Secretary-General to lead the UN Study on Violence against Children, acknowledged progress however stressing that such advancements were made mainly outside the family setting.[213] He stated: 'Only five per cent of the children of the world live in states which have extended the prohibition of assault to protect children from being hit in their homes and families and all other settings in their lives....

[209] Council of Europe, Commissioner of Human Rights, Children and Corporal Punishment, *The Right Not to Be Hit, Also a Children's Right*, CommDH/IssuePaper(2006)1REV, updated version 2008. Available at https://wcd.coe.int/ViewDoc.jsp?id=1237635 (accessed on 20 September 2015).

[210] United Nations Secretary-General's Report on Violence against Children, *Global Initiative to End All Corporal Punishment of Children*.

[211] United Nations Secretary-General's Report on Violence against Children, *Global Initiative to End All Corporal Punishment of Children*.

[212] For more information, see http://www.ohchr.org/EN/NewsEvents/Pages/CorporalPunishment. aspx#sthash.rO1vRS3O.dpuf (accessed on 20 September 2015).

[213] For more information, see http://www.ohchr.org/EN/NewsEvents/Pages/CorporalPunishment. aspx#sthash.rO1vRS3O.dpuf (accessed on 20 September 2015).

Most of the world's children can still be assaulted with impunity by those who purport to love and care for them.'

Law Reform Relating to Corporal Punishment in Schools

In practice, the current provisions as well as guidelines have failed to deter the use of corporal punished given how widely it is being used even today and how widely it is accepted as a method of discipline in India. One of the factor that deters many parents from complaining is retaliation and victimization of the child by the school authorities. The usual fears are that the child will have to continue in the same school, or the other siblings may suffer, or they may have to change the school. Also, many parents would not prefer to go through the lengthy and complex legal procedures.

The IPC, 1860 is supposed to protect children from being subjected to punishment in schools in India; however there are loopholes in the law that aids the use of such brutal punishments in school. According to IPC, Section 83, any child who has not done homework or has not dressed in an appropriate fashion should not incite any form of corporal punishment in schools in India.[214] However, this is hardly ever implemented in reality and most children are still be subjected to corporal punishment for the aforementioned faults.

The RTE Act, 2009 must be implemented in its proper spirit The grievance redressal mechanisms and school management committee must be active and perform their role. The states under their RTE rules have notified block-/district-level grievance redressal agencies under the RTE Act. This decentralized grievance redressal mechanism of each state/UT should be made publicly available and posted on all school, panchayat bulletin boards. The local authority can also provide for a system of registering grievances related to corporal punishments at both the district and sub-district levels. The NCPCR and SCPCRs have been entrusted with the task of monitoring children's right to education under the RTE Act, 2009.[215]

There are many contradictions that can be found in the law pertaining to corporal punishment as this is one of the main issues in the country. If headmasters are allowed to use brutal punishment on children up till a certain point, the headmaster himself becomes the judge of the extent to which he can carry on the penalty. Since the headmaster himself is the judge, the children are at his mercy and no other person is present to supervise the delivery of punishment and this dilutes the provisions in the law for the safety of children. At the same time, using excessive force and punishing a child for a cause that is not justifiable is prohibited under the Section 89 of the IPC. The law says that incidents outside the scope of good faith are prohibited.

The IPC, Section 88,[216] for example, protects an act which is not intended to cause death and is done by consent in good faith for person's benefit. A teacher/guardian who administers in good

---

[214] IPC, Section 83: Act of a child above 7 and under 12 of immature understanding—Nothing is an offence which is done by a child above 7 years of age and under 12, who has not attained sufficient maturity of understanding to judge of the nature and consequences of his conduct on that occasion.

[215] Under Section 32(3) and (4) of the RTE Act, the SCPCRs are the appellate authority to receive appeals from the aggrieved persons who would prefer such appeals when their grievances relating to children's right to education are not redressed by the designated local authorities under Section 32(2).

[216] IPC, Section 88: Act not intended to cause death, done by consent in good faith for person's benefit—

faith a moderate and reasonable corporal punishment to a pupil to enforce discipline in school is protected by this section and such an act is not even a crime under Section 323. Section 89 of the IPC protects an act by guardian or by consent of guardian done in good faith for benefit of child under 12 years, unless it causes death or grievous injury.[217] These provisions extend to teachers having quasi-parental authority that is, consent or delegation of authority from parents. Both these IPC sections therefore need to be amended so that it does not help in accused teachers going scot-free.

The IPC, Section 88 provides the headmaster or a guardian the freedom to inflict pain through corporal punishment in schools in India as long as the reason is justifiable. However, this protection does not last if a condition or problem like death occurs.[218] Sections 88 and 89 of the IPC provide immunity to a person inflicting corporal punishment on a child if such a punishment is inflicted in good faith for the child's benefit. Clearly, the defence under Sections 88 and 89 are incompatible with Constitution of India and obligations under the UNCRC, which protects children from torture and cruel, inhuman, and degrading treatment. Freedom from torture is an absolute right that cannot be qualified. Thus, Section 88 needs to be amended and Section 89 needs to be repealed as a necessary step towards protecting children from violence.

Nothing which is not intended to cause death, is an offence by reason of any harm which it may cause, or be intended by the doer to cause, or be known by the doer to be likely to cause, to any person for whose benefit it is done in good faith, and who has given a consent, whether express or implied, to suffer that harm, or to take the risk of that harm.

[217] IPC, Section 89: Act done in good faith for benefit of child or insane person, by or by consent of guardian—

Nothing which is done in good faith for the benefit of a person under 12 years of age, or of unsound mind, by or by consent, either express or implied, of the guardian or other person having lawful charge of that person, is an offence by reason of any harm which it may cause, or be intended by the doer to cause or be known by the doer to be likely to cause to that person, provided—

first, that this exception shall not extend to the intentional causing of death, or to the attempting to cause death;
second, that this exception shall not extend to the doing of anything which the person doing it knows to be likely to cause death, for any purpose other than the preventing of death or grievous hurt, or the curing of any grievous disease or infirmity;
third, that this exception shall not extend to the voluntary causing of grievous hurt, or to the attempting to cause grievous hurt, unless it be for the purpose of preventing death or grievous hurt, or the curing of any grievous disease or infirmity;
fourth, that this exception shall not extend to the abetment of any offence, to the committing of which offence it would not extend.

[218] IPC, Section 88: Act not intended to cause death, done by consent in good faith for person's benefit—

Nothing which is not intended to cause death, is an offence by reason of any harm which it may cause, or be intended by the doer to cause, or be known by the doer to be likely to cause, to any person for whose benefit it is done in good faith, and who has given a consent, whether express or implied, to suffer that harm, or to take the risk of that harm.

The Indian law does not cover mental trauma or emotional stress to the child. The concept of therapeutic jurisprudence must be included in Indian law to protect children. The IPC, Section 88,[219] for example, protects an act, which is not intended to cause death, done by consent in good faith for person's benefit. A teacher/guardian who administers in good faith a moderate and reasonable corporal punishment to a pupil to enforce discipline in school is protected by this section and such an act is not even a crime under Section 323. Section 89 of the IPC protects an act by the guardian or by the consent of the guardian done in good faith, for the benefit of child under 12 years, unless it causes death or grievous injury.[220]

These provisions extend to teachers having quasi-parental authority, that is, consent or delegation of authority from parents. Both these IPC sections therefore need to be amended so that it does not help in accused teachers going scot-free. However, contrary to Sections 88 and 89 of the IPC, the Gujarat High Court in its judgment in the case *Hasmukhbhai Gokaldas Shah* v. *State of Gujarat*, 17 November 2008,[221] has clearly stated that 'corporal punishment to child in present days … is not recognised by law'. This ruling by the Gujarat High Court in 2008 confirmed that where the law prohibits corporal punishment in schools, Section 89 of the Penal Code cannot be used as a legal defence for its use.

Further, India is a state party to the UNCRC. The standard of 'the best interests of the child' is now a part of domestic law. In 2006, the Committee on the Rights of the Child explained this obligation further when it reiterated, in General Comment No. 8 that 'the right of the child to protection from corporal punishment and other cruel or degrading forms of punishment'.

---

[219] IPC, Section 88: Act not intended to cause death, done by consent in good faith for person's benefit—

Nothing which is not intended to cause death, is an offence by reason of any harm which it may cause, or be intended by the doer to cause, or be known by the doer to be likely to cause, to any person for whose benefit it is done in good faith, and who has given a consent, whether express or implied, to suffer that harm, or to take the risk of that harm.

[220] IPC, Section 89: Act done in good faith for benefit of child or insane person, by or by consent of guardian—

Nothing which is done in good faith for the benefit of a person under twelve years of age, or of unsound mind, by or by consent, either express or implied, of the guardian or other person having lawful charge of that person, is an offence by reason of any harm which it may cause, or be intended by the doer to cause or be known by the doer to be likely to cause to that person, provided—

first, that this exception shall not extend to the intentional causing of death, or to the attempting to cause death;

second, that this exception shall not extend to the doing of anything which the person doing it knows to be likely to cause death, for any purpose other than the preventing of death or grievous hurt, or the curing of any grievous disease or infirmity;

third, that this exception shall not extend to the voluntary causing of grievous hurt, or to the attempting to cause grievous hurt, unless it be for the purpose of preventing death or grievous hurt, or the curing of any grievous disease or infirmity;

fourth, that this exception shall not extend to the abetment of any offence, to the committing of which offence it would not extend.

[221] 2009 CriLJ 2919.

Globally, there is growing recognition of students' rights to discipline that respects their dignity, and of the role of positive discipline in children's learning. Increasingly teachers are being instructed not to use physical or humiliating punishment, and to use positive discipline instead. Teachers' training must include positive disciplining methods.[222] The positive-discipline parenting and classroom-management model is based on the work of Alfred Adler and Rudolf Dreikurs originated in the 1920s.[223] It consists of a specific set of techniques for rewarding good behaviour and curtailing negative behaviour. It is a programme designed to teach children to become responsible, respectful, and resourceful, and it inculcates a spirit of self-discipline. It empowers children to make life decisions, based on their own experiences, and to utilize an internal system of reinforcement to weigh the values of the decisions that they have made.[224] To practice these skills, exercises are provided to help teachers put these principles into practice across a wide range of situations. Ultimately the use of positive discipline reduces the time teachers spend on behavioural issues, so they can spend more time on teaching.[225]

There is no doubt that the violence against children in schools has reached unacceptable levels. Further, despite the regular guidelines against corporal punishment by the government, court judgments declaring it illegal, constitutional provisions that protect children, sections under the IPC relating to physical harm and intimidation that can be used against offenders, the RTE Act—corporal punishment continues to be an accepted practice in India. A strong law is necessary—educational administration enables teachers to develop skills to deal with different situations without resorting to punishment. Going to courts now is an option but it is a long wait for justice. An ombudsman for students of schools to safeguard their rights along with a child helpline number that can immediately respond to a child and suspend the accused teacher during inquiry. Legal protections against corporal punishment must be speedy and sure to safeguard the rights of a child. However, in practice, legal options are usually resorted to only in case of extreme corporal punishment or as a last resort. Law against corporal punishment is required as a deterrence and will go a long way in making children feel safer in schools as they will know that they have a law to protect them. Simultaneously public education is crucial to accompany law reform. The process of law reform with provisions on corporal punishment itself has the potential to be educational if properly disseminated. Awareness workshops must be held in schools so that teachers and administrators know what the law says and how they could deal with routine issues in a child-friendly and humane manner. The law-reform process must go hand-in-hand with enhancing student-teacher ratio, improving infrastructure, and also sensitization and training of teachers of their child rights and to treat children with dignity and care. Above all, clear guidance must be laid down to teachers and pre-school staff, health personnel, social workers, police and other key professionals on their role in preventing such violations and how to respond in concrete situations when there are indications that a child may suffer violence and need help.

[222] Joan E. Durrant, *Positive Discipline in Everyday Teaching: Guidelines for Educators* (Thailand: Save the Children, 2010).

[223] For more information, see http://unicef.in/Story/197/All-You-Want-to-Know-About-Corporal-Punishment#sthash.DiwQBiXl.dpuf (accessed on 20 September 2015).

[224] For more information, see http://unicef.in/Story/197/All-You-Want-to-Know-About-Corporal-Punishment#sthash.DiwQBiXl.dpuf (accessed on 20 September 2015).

[225] Durrant, *Positive Discipline in Everyday Teaching*

Child Labour—A Barrier to Education

Second *National Labour Commission Report* (2002) established the link between child labour and education and stated:

> All out of school children must be treated as child labourers or those who have the potential to become child labourers. All work done by children, irrespective of where it is done, must be considered as child labour. Only then girls and children working within the family become a part of the strategy to eliminate child labour, and significant headway will be made towards achieving the goal of eliminating child labour.[226]

According to Article 21A of the Constitution of India education is a fundamental right for all children between 6 and 14 years. This has implications for fulfilment of the obligation of the state to ensure that every child between 6 and 14 years is in school. Article 24 of the Constitution of India states that children below 14 years cannot work in hazardous occupation or industry . This implies that children below 14 years can work in non-hazardous occupation or industries, implying a clear contradiction between these two constitutional provisions. If children below 14 years are allowed to work in non-hazardous occupations or industries, they cannot be in school. There is a need for constitutional reform in this area.

Any work that interferes with the child's schooling and his or her physical, mental, psychological and emotional being is considered hazardous as far as a child is concerned. No child must be permitted to work during school hours on school working days. A time-bound programme must be established for the complete abolition of child labour within the next 5 years. The law on education must include child labour abolition and vice versa. The dual policy of abolition and regulation in child labour must go. A firm and clear policy stand has to be taken so that all children are in school and not working. Schools should be made ready for first-generation learners. Distinction between hazardous and non-hazardous must be removed as it creates problems in law enforcement and it is not required as no child needs to work. The age of the child who cannot work must be 18 years.

A day should soon come when all children are in school, receiving good quality meaningful education, with the state giving their parents work so that they can look after their children. It is the responsibility of the union government—in fact, a legal duty. Poverty alleviation programmes and schemes must be extended to all families whose children work. Government must provide alternate employment and income generation programmes to these families and strengthen them so that their children remain in school .

The need of the hour is a comprehensive law on education and child labour and not fragmented or separate laws. Both education and child labour need to be addressed in one law. A legal framework is required to work towards a time-bound complete abolition of child labour in all forms of employment and to send all children below 18 years, who are presently working, to a full-time formal school. It should provide employment to adults in the family and include them in the poverty-alleviation schemes and programmes so that they are economically strengthened. There is a need for a legal and policy framework in support of child labour and education and

---

[226] Second National Commission on Labour, *Report of the Study Group on Women and Child Labour* (2002), Section viii: Recommendations, p. 220.

battle for schools from a rights-based perspective and against the gains of the market forces in perpetuating child labour. A clear policy must be enunciated so that no child works and every child attends full-time formal school up to 18 years of age. The age of 18 should be prescribed for the abolition of child labour and provision of compulsory education. Currently, there are two separate ministries dealing with child labour (Ministry of Labour) and education (Ministry of Human Resource Development). There needs to be a convergence in the two ministries.

The Global Context of Elementary Education

Globally there have been several initiatives and campaigns relating to the right to elementary education of children. Some of them are as follows.

World Declaration on Education for All, 1990

Article 1 of this declaration states that every person—child, youth, and adult—shall be able to benefit from the educational opportunities designed to meet their basic learning needs. These needs comprise both learning tools (literacy, oral expression, numeral proficiency, and problem solving) and basic learning content (knowledge, skills, values, and attitudes) required by human beings to be able to survive, develop their full capacities, live and work in dignity, participate fully in development, improve the quality of their lives, make informed decisions, and continue learning. The declaration recognized the diversity, complexity, and changing nature of the basic learning needs of children, youth, and adults necessitating broadening and constantly redefining the scope of basic education to include the following components:

- Learning begins at birth.
- The main delivery system for the basic education of children outside the family is primary schooling.
- The basic learning needs of youth and adults are diverse and should be met through a variety of delivery systems.
- All available instruments and channels of information, communication, and social action could be used to help convey essential knowledge and inform and educate people on social issues.[227]

Meeting these basic learning needs involves action to enhance the family and community environments for learning.[228]

Jomtien Declaration, 1990

In 1990, some 1,500 participants from 155 nations and dozens of non-governmental organizations (NGOs) and development agencies met in Jomtien, Thailand, to adopt the World

---

[227] Article 5.
[228] *Framework for Action to Meet Basic Learning Needs: Guidelines for Implementing the World Declaration on Education for All*, para. 10.

Declaration on Education for All (EFA). This declaration and its framework for action were remarkably insightful documents; they analysed the challenges and opportunities facing the last decade of the twentieth century and proposed that countries set targets for the year 2000 based on an 'expanded' vision of universal basic education. These were:

- expansion of early childhood care and development (ECCD) activities;
- universal access to, and completion of, primary education;
- improvement in learning achievement;
- reduction of the adult illiteracy rate to one half of its 1990 level;
- expansion in basic education and training in other essential skills required by youth and adults; and
- increased acquisition of the knowledge, skills, and values required for better living and sustainable development.[229]

Jomtien emphasized not only access to education, but equity and learning achievement through broadening the means and scope of basic education. According to the 1990 Jomtien Declaration, 'active and participatory approaches are particularly valuable in assuring learning acquisition and allowing learners to reach their fullest potential'. Encouraging the use of interactive, learner-centred methods is a priority in the promotion of quality basic education. These methods should be used deliberately to support learning aims that relate to the knowledge, skills, and attitudes of peace education. Research supports the idea that cooperative and interactive learning methods promote values and behaviours.

A child-friendly education system requires the development of child-friendly, child-centred systems. Schools, which are effective vehicles of learning, provide a healthy environment (physically and psychologically), and should be based on the principles of UNCRC. Child-friendly education systems recognize and respect children's rights and responsibilities, provide the enabling environment to realize these rights, and help ensure such an environment in the community and household.

Specifically, a child-friendly education system reflects and realizes the rights of every child; cooperates with other partners to promote and monitor the well-being and rights of all children; defends and protects all children from abuse and harm (as a sanctuary), both inside and outside the school.

The goals for children and development for the decade adopted at the World Summit for Children in September 1990 endorsed the Jomtien goals, emphasizing the priority to universal access to primary education, completion of the primary stage by at least 80 per cent of the children and reduction of the gender gap.

World Education Forum, Dakar, Senegal, 2000

One hundred eighty-two countries attended the World Education Forum, 2000 at Dakar in Senegal. The Dakar Framework of Action has been adopted by all of them. The framework

---

[229] World Conference on Education for All, *Framework for Action*, 1990.

- recognizes the right to education as a fundamental human right,
- reaffirms commitment to the expanded vision of education as articulated in Jomtien, and
- calls for renewed action to ensure that every child, youth, and adult receive education by 2015.

Education for All, 2000 Assessment, 2000[230]

The Education for All movement is a global commitment to provide quality basic education for all children, youth and adults. The movement was launched at the World Conference on Education for All in 1990 by UNESCO, UNDP, UNFPA, UNICEF and the World Bank. Participants endorsed an 'expanded vision of learning' and pledged to universalize primary education and massively reduce illiteracy by the end of the decade. Ten years later, with many countries far from having reached this goal, the international community met again in Dakar, Senegal, and affirmed their commitment to achieving Education for All by the year 2015. They identified six key education goals which aim to meet the learning needs of all children, youth and adults by 2015.

As the lead agency, UNESCO has been mandated to coordinate the international efforts to reach Education for All. Governments, development agencies, civil society, NGOs and the media are but some of the partners working toward reaching these goals.

The EFA goals also contribute to the global pursuit of the eight Millennium Development Goals (MDGs), adopted by 189 countries and world's leading development institutions in 2000. Two MDGs relate specifically to education but none of the eight MDGs can be achieved without sustained investment in education. Education gives the skills and knowledge to improve health, livelihoods and promote sound environmental practices.

Education for All Goals

Six internationally agreed education goals aim to meet the learning needs of all children, youth and adults by 2015.

Goal 1: Expand Early Children Care and Education

The goal calls for better and more possibilities to support young children, and their families and communities, in all the areas where the child is growing—physically, emotionally, socially, and intellectually. It also lays special emphasis on children who suffer disadvantage or who are particularly vulnerable, for example, those living in poverty, AIDS orphans, rural and minority children, and in some situations girls as a whole.

In a world context, major global disparities in provision continue to divide the world's richest and poorest children. In 2006, pre-primary GERs averaged 79 per cent in developed countries and 36 per cent in developing countries, falling as low as 14 per cent in sub-Saharan Africa. Global disparities are mirrored in wide gaps within countries, especially between the richest and poorest children.[231]

---

[230] Available at www.inruled.org (accessed on 19 September 2015).
[231] UNESCO, *Overcoming Inequality: Why Governance Matters*, EFA Global Monitoring Report 2009.

Goal 2: Provide Free and Compulsory Primary Education for All

The goal aims to allow children to go to school and finish primary education, by 2015. Primary schooling must be entirely free of charge and be compulsory for every child. Some groups of children need special attention, for instance those who belong to minority groups and those whose circumstances are particularly difficult.

In a the world context the average net enrolment ratios for developing countries have continued to increase since Dakar. Sub-Saharan Africa raised its average net enrolment ratio from 54 to 70 per cent between 1999 and 2006, for an annual increase six times greater than during the decade before Dakar. The increase in South and West Asia was also impressive, rising from 75 per cent to 86 per cent. In 2006, some 75 million children, 55 per cent girls, were not in school, almost half in sub-Saharan Africa. As per trends, millions of children were expected to be out of school in 2015—the target date for UPE. Projections for 134 countries accounting for some two-thirds of OOSC in 2006 suggest that some 29 million children will be out of school in 2015 in these countries alone.[232]

Goal 3: Promote Learning Skills for Young People and Adults

This goal places the emphasis on the learning needs of young people and adults in the context of lifelong learning. It calls for equitable access to learning programmes that are appropriate, and mentions life skills particularly. We should note too that EFA Goal 6 also refers to essential life skills as a desirable outcome of quality basic education.

In a world context, governments are not giving priority to youth and adult learning needs in their education policies. Meeting the lifelong needs of youth and adults needs stronger political commitment and more public funding. It will also require more clearly defined concepts and better data for effective monitoring.[233]

Goal 4: Increase Adult Literacy by 50 per cent

This goal calls for a certain level of improvement in adult literacy by 2015—it says that it should be 50 per cent better than it was in 2000. The needs of women should receive particular attention. In addition, all adults should have opportunities to go on learning throughout their lives.

In a world context, an estimated 776 million adults—or 16 per cent of the world's adult population—lack basic literacy skills. About two-thirds are women. Most countries have made little progress in recent years. If current trends continue, there will be over 700 million adults lacking literacy skills in 2015. Between 1985–1994 and 2000–2006, the global adult literacy rate increased from 76 per cent to 84 per cent. However, 45 countries have adult literacy rates below the developing country average of 79 per cent, mostly in sub-Saharan Africa, and South and West

---

[232] UNESCO, *Overcoming Inequality*.
[233] UNESCO, *Overcoming Inequality*.

Asia. Nearly all of them are off track to meet the adult literacy target by 2015. Nineteen of these countries have literacy rates of less than 55 per cent.[234]

Goal 5: Achieve Gender Parity by 2005, Gender Equality by 2015

This goal calls for an equal number of girls and boys to be enroled in primary and secondary school by 2005—this is what gender parity means (even though not all girls and boys may be enroled at this stage). It further aims to achieve gender equality in education by 2015. This is a more ambitious goal, meaning that all girls and boys have equal opportunity to enjoy basic education of high quality, achieve at equal levels and enjoy equal benefits from education.

Where the World Stands

In 2006, of the 176 countries with data, 59 had achieved gender parity in both primary and secondary education—20 countries more than in 1999. At the primary level, about two-thirds of countries had achieved parity. However, more than half the countries in sub-Saharan Africa, South and West Asia and the Arab States had not reached the target. Only 37 per cent of countries worldwide had achieved gender parity at secondary level.[235]

Goal 6: Improve the Quality of Education

This goal calls for improvement in the quality of education in all its aspects, aiming for a situation where people can achieve excellence. Everyone should be able to achieve learning outcomes that are recognized and can be measured, particularly with regard to literacy, numeracy and other skills essential for life.

In a world context international assessments highlight large achievement gaps between students in rich and poor countries. Within countries too, inequality exists between regions, communities, schools, and classrooms. These disparities have important implications not just in education but for the wider distribution of opportunities in society. In developing countries there are substantially higher proportions of low learning achievement. Many essential resources taken for granted in developed countries remain scarce in developing countries, including basic infrastructure such as electricity, seats, and textbooks. There are large national and regional disparities in pupil-teacher ratios, with marked teacher shortages in South and West Asia, and sub-Saharan Africa.[236]

Millennium Development Goal 2[237]

The MDG Goal 2 was to achieve UPE. *Every child has the right to go to school, but millions are still being left behind.* Universal primary education involves entering school at an appropriate

---

[234] UNESCO, *Overcoming Inequality.*

[235] UNESCO, *Overcoming Inequality.*

[236] UNESCO, *Overcoming Inequality.*

[237] At the Millennium Summit in September 2000 the largest gathering of world leaders in history adopted the UN Millennium Declaration, committing their nations to a new global partnership to reduce

age, progressing through the system and completing a full cycle. However, there are 72 million children still out of school. Nearly half of these children live in sub-Saharan Africa. On current trends, 56 million children could still be out of school by 2015. Of those students enroled in school, millions drop out or leave school without having gained the most basic literacy and numeracy skills. Additionally, pupil-teacher ratios in many countries are in excess of 40:1 and a severe teacher shortage exists. Many governments are neglecting the 'education poor'—those on the fringes of society, ranging from indigenous populations to street children, from the disabled to linguistic and cultural minorities. New approaches must be tailor-made for such groups—simply increasing opportunities for standard schooling is not enough. Unless we reach the children who are being left behind, the goal of education for all children will not be reached.[238]

Millennium Development Goal 3

The MDG Goal 3 was to promote gender equality and empower women by eliminating gender disparity in primary and secondary education. The following were the targets of the goal:[239]

- The developing countries as a whole have achieved the target to eliminate gender disparity in primary, secondary, and tertiary education.
- Globally, about three-quarters of working-age men participate in the labour force, compared to half of working-age women.
- Women make up 41 per cent of paid workers outside of agriculture, an increase from 35 per cent in 1990.
- The average proportion of women in the Parliament has nearly doubled over the past 20 years.
- Women continue to experience significant gaps in terms of poverty, labour market and wages, as well as participation in private and public decision-making.

Children in Emergency Situations

Another area of major international concern is the education of children in emergencies. Emergencies include natural disasters such as floods and earthquakes, and human-made crises

---

extreme poverty and setting out a series of time-bound targets, with a deadline of 2015, which are now known as the MDGs. The MDGs are the world's time-bound and quantified targets for addressing extreme poverty in its many dimensions—income poverty, hunger, disease, lack of adequate shelter, and exclusion—while promoting gender equality, education, and environmental sustainability. They are also basic human rights—the rights of each person on the planet to health, education, shelter, and security. For more information, see http://www.unmillenniumproject.org/goals/ (accessed on 22 November 2016).

[238] Available at http://www.unesco.org/new/en/education/themes/leading-the-international-agenda/education-for-all/education-and-the-mdgs/goal-2/ (accessed on 22 November 2016).

[239] Target 3A: Eliminate gender disparity in primary and secondary education, preferably by 2005, and in all levels of education no later than 2015.

such as civil strife and war, the latter also called 'complex emergencies'. Persistent poverty, the increasing number of children living on streets, and the HIV/AIDS pandemic are silent, chronic emergencies. All emergency situations have an adverse impact on education. Children, for example, especially girls, drop out of school during natural disasters and war. During droughts parents may not be able to pay the required school fees. Poverty and fighting disable students, hamper their ability to learn. War is a major psychosocial stressor with long-lasting effects that influence learning.[240]

The Convention on Human Rights and the UNCRC, among others, declare education to be an inalienable right. It is also an enabling right, in that it assists children and adults to access their other rights. It is the right of every child regardless of the circumstances in which she or he is thrust. Children in emergency situations must be able to participate in quality primary education that includes the same 'core' of skills, knowledge, competencies, values, and attitudes that constitute a basic education, and to which the world committed in 1990 at the Jomtien Conference on Education for All. In emergency situations, whether caused by human or natural forces, education serves many purposes. It plays a critical role in normalizing the situation for the child and in minimizing the psychosocial stresses experienced when emergencies result in the sudden and violent destabilization of the child's immediate family and social environment. It is essential to assist children to deal with their future more confidently and effectively, and can be instrumental in making it possible for them to develop a peaceful society. Furthermore, educational activities that include parents and other community members can play an important part in rebuilding family and community cohesiveness. The increasing use of children as fighters in conflict is most alarming. While stopping this trend will require coordinated effort, education must play a key role in demobilization. As with other educational responses in emergencies, this must have two aspects: the basic care that is every child's right, and a component tailored to the particular circumstances. The challenge is to tailor a programme that allows children to reassume the childhood that has been stolen from them.

Education for All Global Monitoring Report 2015[241]

According to Education for all Global Monitoring Report 2015:

- In 2012, nearly 58 million children of primary school age were not enroled in school. The reasons include demographic pressures, conflict situations, marginalization of various socio-economic groups, and a lack of adequate commitment in some countries with large out-of-school populations.[242] Despite these challenges, countries including Burundi, Ethiopia, Morocco, Mozambique, Nepal and the United Republic of Tanzania achieved substantial, albeit uneven,

---

[240] Available at www.unicef.org (accessed on 22 November 2016).

[241] UNESCO, *Education for All Global Monitoring Report*, Education for All 2000–2015: Achievements and Challenges (France, 2015). Available at http://unesdoc.unesco.org/images/0023/002325/232565e.pdf (accessed on 3 October 2015).

[242] UNESCO, *Education for All Global Monitoring Report*.

progress in reducing gender and income disparities in primary school access, and in increasing net enrolment ratios and attainment rates.[243]

- Net enrolment ratios improved substantially: Of the 116 countries with data, 17 increased primary net enrolment ratios by over 20 percentage points between 1999 and 2012. Bhutan, the Lao People's Democratic Republic, and Nepal provide examples of stellar improvement in net enrolment ratios in Asia. Latin America, El Salvador, Guatemala, and Nicaragua increased their net enrolment ratios by over 10 percentage points. In sub-Saharan Africa, Burundi's net enrolment ratio increased from less than 41 per cent in 2000 to 94 per cent in 2010.[244]
- Fewer children have never been to school: The percentage of children who have never been to school fell in the vast majority of countries. Among countries where at least 20 per cent of children did not go to school in 2000, 10 had more than halved the percentage by 2010. The percentage of children who had never been to school decreased by remarkable rates in Ethiopia (from 67 per cent in 2000 to 28 per cent in 2011) and the United Republic of Tanzania (from 47 per cent in 1999 to 12 per cent in 2010).[245]
- Large out-of-school populations remain in some countries: High-population countries continued to have substantial out-of-school populations in 2012. India increased its net enrolment ratio from 86 per cent to 99 per cent, but Nigeria and Pakistan made far less progress than expected, due partly to ethnic and religious strife, weak democracy and corrupt political leadership.[246]
- Most countries have a long way to go on primary completion, especially for the poorest people: Primary school completion increased in the vast majority of countries. Eight countries increased primary attainment rates by over 20 percentage points: Benin, Cambodia, Ethiopia, Guinea, Mali, Mozambique, Nepal and Sierra Leone. But progress has been far from adequate, signalling enduring problems of affordability, quality and relevance.[247]
- Progression varies among countries: Drop-out is a serious problem in low-income countries, especially among late entrants and poor children. Of the 139 countries with sufficient data, in 54 countries—mostly in Central Asia, Central and Eastern Europe, and Western Europe – almost all children who enroled in primary school were likely to reach the last grade by 2015. But in 32 countries, mostly in sub-Saharan Africa, at least 20 per cent of children are likely to drop out early.[248]
- Substantial progress was made in user fee abolition: Schooling is now free in most countries, in principle. In sub-Saharan Africa, 15 countries have adopted legislation abolishing school fees since 2000. Confirming the cost-related barriers to access, fee abolition had a strong positive impact on enrolment in the years after its implementation. Such progress was partly possible because of the increased finance available for education. Fee abolition was also motivated by domestic politics: it is a popular election agenda in low-income African countries. The sudden expansion of enrolment following user fee abolition can strain the primary education system,

---

[243] UNESCO, *Education for All Global Monitoring Report*.
[244] UNESCO, *Education for All Global Monitoring Report*.
[245] UNESCO, *Education for All Global Monitoring Report*.
[246] UNESCO, *Education for All Global Monitoring Report*.
[247] UNESCO, *Education for All Global Monitoring Report*.
[248] UNESCO, *Education for All Global Monitoring Report*.

as the experience of the 1990s showed. As a result, most countries have since used a sequenced approach. However, capitation grants provided through fee-abolition initiatives to expand education systems were often insufficient, poorly delivered, and inadequately targeted.[249]

- Some approaches succeeded by increasing demand: Schooling is rarely free despite legislative and policy commitments to fee abolition, as there are many other costs to families. Initiatives to increase family demand for primary schooling reduce financial burdens such as transport, school lunches and school uniforms. Social protection programmes include demand-side measures for improving education, such as cash transfers, school-feeding programmes, scholarships, stipends, and bursaries.[250]

- School feeding programmes: Food for education initiatives have reached 368 million children in 169 countries. Not only do school feeding programmes help ensure that children who attend school remain healthy, but also participants tend to have consistently better enrolment and attendance than non-participants.[251]

- Cash transfer programmes: Cash transfers to vulnerable households, pioneered in Latin America, have become prevalent in middle- and low-income Asian and sub-Saharan African countries. Most cash-transfer programmes have boosted enrolment and attendance, and reduced dropout. However, cash transfers do not always improve the education outcomes of vulnerable groups. There is debate about whether transfers should be conditional. Programmes may more easily find political support if they are conditioned on children attending school. Transfers that depend on attendance have a greater impact on education than unconditional cash transfers.[252]

- Supply-side interventions have helped increase primary school access: Infrastructure projects such as school and road construction have had strong effects on education access. There has been an increase in health interventions that can also have vital effects on education outcomes. Further, non-government institutions, such as private, community, and non-formal schools, are increasingly providing education alongside public schools.[253]

- School and classroom construction: The availability of a school building is often considered the first step to ensure that children can attend school. In Mozambique, for example, abolishing fees and tripling the number of primary and secondary schools between 1992 and 2010 substantially reduced the number of students who had never been to school.[254]

- Infrastructure and health sector improvements: Many countries have significantly improved road, electricity, and water infrastructure, thus increasing access to schools. Girls' enrolment is particularly sensitive to distance and infrastructure improvements, India being an important example.[255]

- Private and other non-government institutions have become important education providers: The role of private schooling in education has grown over the past two decades. In South Asia,

---

[249] UNESCO, *Education for All Global Monitoring Report.*
[250] UNESCO, *Education for All Global Monitoring Report.*
[251] UNESCO, *Education for All Global Monitoring Report.*
[252] UNESCO, *Education for All Global Monitoring Report.*
[253] UNESCO, *Education for All Global Monitoring Report.*
[254] UNESCO, *Education for All Global Monitoring Report.*
[255] UNESCO, *Education for All Global Monitoring Report.*

about one-third of 6- to 18-year-olds attend private schools. The private share of primary enrolment at least doubled in a wide range of countries in the Arab States, Central and Eastern Europe, and sub-Saharan Africa. Community schools are often more adaptable, cost-effective, student-focused, and relevant to local needs than government schools. Many provide schooling in areas underserved by the government, for instance, in Ghana, the United Republic of Tanzania, and Zambia. Non-formal education centres provide flexible, accelerated learning programmes as bridges to the formal system or for young children who have missed schooling. In Bangladesh, BRAC, a large NGO, operates thousands of non-formal schools. Religious schools fill a niche for many parents. In Afghanistan, Bangladesh, Indonesia, and Pakistan, Islamic schools—called madrasas—have long played an important role in providing education to underprivileged groups.[256]

- Reaching the marginalized is essential for UPE: Progress in legislation and policy has increased primary school participation for many disadvantaged groups. Marginalized groups, however, continue to experience barriers to education on the grounds of poverty, gender, caste, ethnicity and linguistic background, race, disability, geographical location and livelihood. Marginalized children often suffer from multiple disadvantages that reinforce each other.[257]

- Ethnic and linguistic minorities: In many countries, wide gaps exist in education participation and attainment between the ethnic majority population, which often speaks the dominant language, and minority groups that speak other languages. In some contexts mother tongue and bilingual instruction are seen as improving education access for ethnolinguistic minorities. However, serious questions remain about the quality of education provided in these different languages.[258]

- Working children: Child labour affects educational attainment and achievement. Availability of education and enforcement of education legislation can reduce child labour, thus improving education outcomes and reducing poverty. The number of children aged 5 to 11 in the labour force fell from 139 million in 2000 to 73 million in 2012. School children who work were found at age 13 to lag behind their non-working peers in grade progression in many countries.[259]

- Nomadic communities: Pastoralist populations remain among the most underserved by education globally. Since 2000, nomad-specific education plans have emerged in Ethiopia, Nigeria, Sudan, and the United Republic of Tanzania, but may not have increased enrolment. Pen and distance learning, potentially a useful model for nomadic communities, has remained limited.[260]

- Children affected by HIV and AIDS: Since Dakar, the growth in financing, policies, and support services related to children affected by HIV and AIDS has focused on their care, treatment and social welfare but has not prioritized education. The first policies to address education access for orphaned and vulnerable children emerged around the mid-2000s. Numerous

[256] UNESCO, *Education for All Global Monitoring Report*.
[257] UNESCO, *Education for All Global Monitoring Report*.
[258] UNESCO, *Education for All Global Monitoring Report*.
[259] UNESCO, *Education for All Global Monitoring Report*.
[260] UNESCO, *Education for All Global Monitoring Report*.

countries in sub-Saharan Africa and in South and West Asia have since created national action plans for such children.[261]

- Slum children: In 2000, most governments were ambivalent about providing education in slums. Since then, the issue of slum dwellers has become more critical with substantial migraion from rural areas. In the absence of adequate government policy and planning, NGOs and the private sector have played a significant role. Low-fee private schools have proliferated in slums in countries including India, Kenya, and Nigeria.[262]

- Children with disabilities: Between 93 million and 150 million children are estimated to live with disabilities, which increases their risk of being excluded from education. In developing countries, disability tends to be linked with poverty, and it hinders access to education even more than socio-economic status, rural location, or gender. Girls with disabilities can be especially marginalized. Disabled children's access to schooling is often limited by a lack of understanding about different forms of disability and the needs of disabled children, as well as a lack of teacher training and physical facilities, and discriminatory attitudes towards disability and difference. Many countries have begun including children with disabilities in mainstream education, although some still favour segregation. In practice, most countries have hybrid policies and are incrementally improving inclusionary practices. Approaches that involve the community, parents, and the children themselves are more likely to provide sustainable, relevant solutions and foster inclusion.[263]

- Education in complex emergencies is an evolving problem: Education in complex emergencies—such as warfare, civil disturbances and the large-scale movements of people—is an evolving problem, and a serious one. Emergency situations can lead to high numbers of school attacks, or sexual violence, further marginalizing already disadvantaged groups. Boys and girls are at risk of being forcibly recruited, sometimes from their classrooms, and exploited as front-line soldiers, spies, suicide bombers or sexual slaves. Girls are especially vulnerable in conflict situations. Since 2000, the Inter-Agency Network on Education in Emergencies has grown into a vast network of organizations and individuals in over 170 countries. Establishing minimum standards for education in emergencies in 2003 was a key step; a further one is the growing financial commitment for fragile states by the Global Partnership for Education. Despite such advances, however, the lack of funding for education within humanitarian aid budgeting remains a huge problem globally.[264]

International Laws on Right to Education

The right to basic education has been a key element of almost every international declaration on human rights since the UN was established (Figure 7.1). The UN Declaration of Human Rights, 1948, the 1959 Declaration of the Rights of the Child, the 1966 International Covenant

---

[261] UNESCO, *Education for All Global Monitoring Report.*
[262] UNESCO, *Education for All Global Monitoring Report.*
[263] UNESCO, *Education for All Global Monitoring Report.*
[264] UNESCO, *Education for All Global Monitoring Report.*

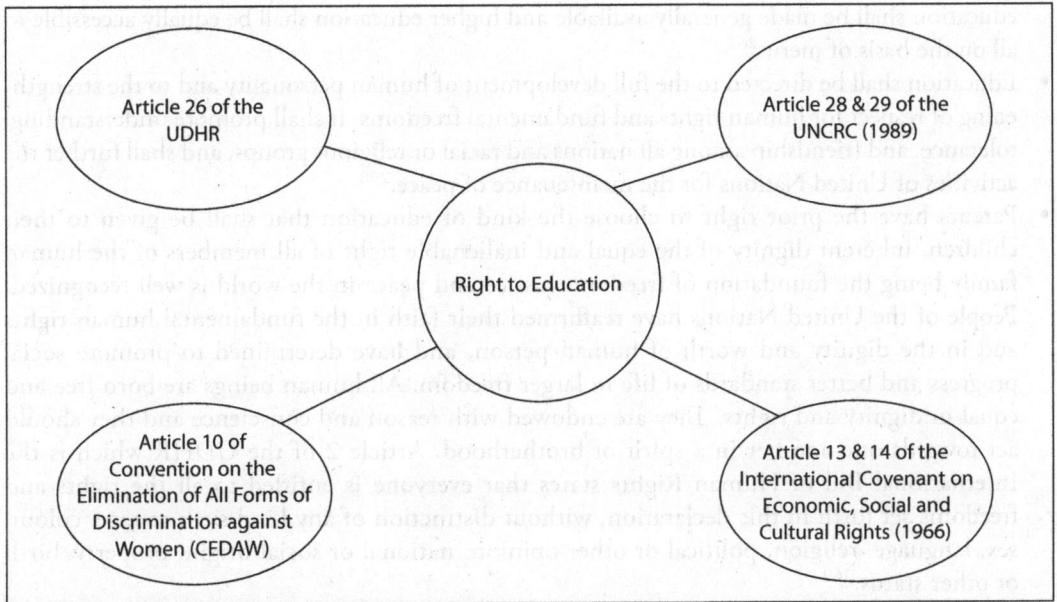

Figure 7.1   International Laws Related to the Right to Education[265]

on Economic, Social, and Cultural Rights, the 1989 UNCRC, the 1990 World Declaration on Education for All, the 1990 World Declaration on the Survival, Protection, and Development of Children, the 1995 Beijing Declaration, and the 1996 Amman Affirmation, all express a commitment to education as a right. Constitutions and laws in most countries recognize the child's right to education.

Universal Declaration of Human Rights, 1948

The Article 26 (UDHR, 1948) was proclaimed by the General Assembly as a 'common standard of achievement for all peoples and all nations' to the end that every individual and every organ of society, keeping this declaration constantly in mind, shall strive by teaching and education to promote respect for these rights and freedoms and by progressive measures to secure the universal and effective recognition and observance. The article provides:[266]

- Everyone has the right to education. Education shall be free, at least in the elementary and fundamental stages. Elementary education shall be compulsory. Technical and professional

---

[265] Source: Author's own.

[266] United Nations High Commissioner for Human Rights (OHCHR), Geneva, Switzerland. Available at http://www.ohchr.org/EN/UDHR/Pages/Introduction.aspx (accessed on 3 October 2015).

education shall be made generally available and higher education shall be equally accessible to all on the basis of merit.[267]

- Education shall be directed to the full development of human personality and to the strengthening of respect for human rights and fundamental freedoms. It shall promote understanding, tolerance, and friendship among all nations and racial or religious groups, and shall further the activities of United Nations for the maintenance of peace.[268]

- Parents have the prior right to choose the kind of education that shall be given to their children, inherent dignity of the equal and inalienable right of all members of the human family being the foundation of freedom. Justice and peace in the world is well recognized. People of the United Nations have reaffirmed their faith in the fundamental human rights and in the dignity and worth of human person, and have determined to promote social progress and better standards of life in larger freedom. All human beings are born free and equal in dignity and rights. They are endowed with reason and conscience and they should act towards one another in a spirit of brotherhood. Article 2 of the UDHR which is the International Bill of Human Rights states that everyone is entitled to all the rights and freedoms set forth in this declaration, without distinction of any kind such as race, colour, sex, language, religion, political or other opinion, national or social origin, property, birth or other status.[269]

International Covenant on Economic, Social, and Cultural Rights, 1976

Article 13(1) of the covenant provides that the state parties recognize the right of everyone to education. Article 13(2) recognizes that with a view to achieving full realization of the right to education, primary education should be made compulsory and available free to all and the development of a system of schools at all levels should be actively pursued. The article also respected the liberty of parents or legal guardians to choose their childrens' schools other than those established by public authorities and to ensure religious and moral education of their children.[270] Article 13(3) recognizes the liberty of individuals and bodies to establish and direct educational institutions which shall conform to such minimum standards as may be laid down by the state. Article 14 provides that each party to the Covenant, if it has not been able to secure within its jurisdiction free, compulsory, primary education within a period of two years, shall adopt a detailed plan of action for its progressive implementation.[271]

---

[267] OHCHR, Geneva, Switzerland. Available at http://www.ohchr.org/EN/UDHR/Pages/Introduction.aspx (accessed on 3 October 2015).

[268] OHCHR, Geneva, Switzerland. Available at http://www.ohchr.org/EN/UDHR/Pages/Introduction.aspx (accessed on 3 October 2015).

[269] OHCHR, Geneva, Switzerland. Available at http://www.ohchr.org/EN/UDHR/Pages/Introduction.aspx (accessed on 3 October 2015).

[270] OHCHR, Geneva, Switzerland. Available at http://www.ohchr.org/EN/UDHR/Pages/Introduction.aspx (accessed on 3 October 2015).

[271] OHCHR, Geneva, Switzerland. Available at http://www.ohchr.org/EN/UDHR/Pages/Introduction.aspx (accessed on 3 October 2015).

India is a signatory to the UDHR and has acceded to the International Covenants on Civil and Political Rights and on Economic, Social, and Cultural rights on 10 April 1979.[272] The civil and political rights were made subject to immediate realization, while the other group of economic, social, and cultural rights were sought to be progressively realized. Delicate balance between the political and civil rights and social and economic rights has been sought to be achieved in the Indian Constitution. Likewise, balance has been tried to be maintained between the individual rights and social needs. The holistic approach made in our Constitution to both categories of human rights, that is, (i) political and civil rights and (ii) social and economic rights, is highly appreciable.[273]

Political and civil rights are guaranteed in one form or the other under Chapter III of our Constitution. They are made fundamental and are enforceable though they are subjected to reasonable restrictions. Principles have been laid down in Chapter IV of the Indian Constitution under the directive principles of state policy, though not enforceable by any court of law. Nevertheless, they are fundamental in the governance of the country and it shall be the duty of the state to apply these principles in making laws.[274]

Convention on the Elimination of All Forms of Discrimination against Women, 1981[275]

The CEDAW is the most comprehensive human rights instrument to protect women from discrimination. It is the first international treaty to address the fundamental rights of women in politics, health care, education, economics, employment, law, property and marriage and family relations. Article 10 ensures equal access to education and vocational guidance for women, equal access to the same curricula, examinations and teaching quality, equal access to scholarships and study grants and finally, equal access to adult education including literacy programs.[276] India signed the Convention on 30 July 1980 and ratified it on 9 July 1993 with certain declarations.[277]

---

[272] OHCHR, Geneva, Switzerland. Available at http://www.ohchr.org/EN/UDHR/Pages/Introduction. aspx (accessed on 3 October 2015).

[273] OHCHR, Geneva, Switzerland. Available at http://www.ohchr.org/EN/UDHR/Pages/Introduction. aspx (accessed on 3 October 2015).

[274] Constitution of India.

[275] The CEDAW was adopted by the United Nations General Assembly in 1979. It entered into force on the 3 September 1981.

[276] UN Women Australia. Available at www.unwomen.org.au, www.genderequalityonline.org.au (accessed on 3 October 2015).

[277] Declarations are as follows:

(1) With regard to Articles 5(a) [elimination of prejudices and customary and all other practices which are based on the idea of the inferiority or the superiority of either of the sexes or on stereotyped roles for men and women] and 16(1) [appropriate measures to eliminate discrimination against women in all matters relating to marriage and family relations] of the Convention on the Elimination of All Forms of Discrimination against Women, the Government of the Republic of India declares that it shall abide by and ensure these provisions in conformity with its policy of non-interference in the personal affairs of any Community without its initiative and consent.

Convention on the Rights of the Child, 1989

Nearly every country in the world has ratified the UNCRC. Articles 28 and 29 of the UNCRC, 1989 deal with the right to education. Article 28(1) enjoins the state parties to make primary education free and compulsory to all and take measures to encourage regular attendance at schools and the reduction of dropout rates. It also states that particular steps should be taken to make educational and vocational information and guidance available and accessible to all children. Article 29 specifies that the education of the child shall be directed to development of mental and physical abilities and overall all-round development.[278]

Starting from a child-rights perspective, there are a number of overarching principles that relate to education. In the UNCRC:[279]

- Education is a right.
- Education is also an enabling right, a right that facilitates children and adults access many of their other rights throughout their lifetimes. In this regard, education has an important role to play in empowerment because it supports democratic action, is a means to promote child rights and social rights, and can equip individuals and groups with the skills to move on in their lives. Thus, education is a very profound right.
- Education must be available without discrimination.
- Children have a right to quality education that will serve as the basis for lifelong learning.
- Education must address the best interests and ongoing development of the complete child. This means that, in addition to being child-centred, education is much more than attention to cognitive development. It is also concerned with the child's social, emotional, and physical development. It also calls for more than the conventional integrated approach. Rather education must be conceptualized from the child's point of view and with an understanding of the interrelated nature of the child's needs, which vary according to the level of individual development.
- Education must accord dignity to every child. Thus, respect, as a value is critical.

In Article 28, the UNCRC established the right of all children, without discrimination, to education. The convention also provides a framework by which the quality of that education must be assessed. If children are required to sit in overcrowded classrooms or classrooms with no

---

(2) With regard to Article 16(2) [to specify a minimum age for marriage and to make the registration of marriages in an official registry compulsory] of the Convention on the Elimination of All Forms of Discrimination against Women, the Government of the Republic of India declares that though in principle it fully supports the principle of compulsory registration of marriages, it is not practical in a vast country like India with its variety of customs, religions and level of literacy.

[278] OHCHR, Geneva, Switzerland. Available at http://www.ohchr.org/EN/UDHR/Pages/Introduction.aspx (accessed on 3 October 2015).

[279] OHCHR, Geneva, Switzerland. Available at http://www.ohchr.org/EN/UDHR/Pages/Introduction.aspx (accessed on 3 October 2015).

teachers, their learning and developmental needs are clearly not being fulfilled. Article 29 guides us, therefore, towards a more child-centred model of teaching, one in which students participate actively, with proper classrooms and teachers, and developing the self-esteem that is essential for learning and decision making throughout life.[280] The UNCRC also establishes the indivisibility of rights. That is, we must address all rights equally, and it is here that there are significant further implications that go to the very core of the conduct of educational activities. In addressing education in a UNCRC framework, it means going far beyond Articles 27, 28, 29, and 32. Every other article needs to be considered in relation to those articles that specifically address the right to education. Furthermore, an added challenge is considering how education can and must address a child's right to protection[281].

There must be an enabling legislative framework that does more than paying lip service to guaranteeing children their right to education. It must facilitate these necessary changes in the education system, both at the macro and micro levels. The UNCRC calls for free compulsory education. It is recognized that this might not be possible immediately, especially as universality is not yet a reality in many countries, but plans must be put in place and immediate action initiated toward this end. In the short run, it is essential that any cost of education be equitable.[282]

Landmark International Judgments on Right to Education

Brown v. Board of Education[283]

The historic decision by US SC declared state laws that were discriminatory of establishing separate public schools for black and white students (that is, segregation based on racial discrimination) were unconstitutional and is against the principle of human dignity. It also held it to be violation of Equal Protection Clause of the 14th Amendment of the US Constitutional Amendment. Chief Justice Warren wrote—'To separate [some children] from others of similar age and qualifications solely because of their race generates a feeling of inferiority as to their status in the community that may affect their hearts and minds in a way unlikely ever to be undone'.

The court further observed in this case:

Education is perhaps the most important function of state and local governments.... It is the very foundation of good citizenship. Today it (education) is a principal instrument in awakening the child to cultural values, in preparing him for later professional training, and in helping him to adjust normally to his environment. In these days, it is doubtful that any child may reasonably be expected to succeed in life if he is denied the opportunity of an education. Such an opportunity, where the state has undertaken to provide it, is a right which must be made available to all on equal terms.

[280] UNICEF, *The State of the World's Children 1999*. Available at https://www.unicef.org/sowc99/sowc99e.pdf (accessed on 22 November 2016).

[281] OHCHR, Geneva, Switzerland. Available at http://www.ohchr.org/EN/UDHR/Pages/Introduction.aspx (accessed on 3 October 2015).

[282] OHCHR, Geneva, Switzerland. Available at http://www.ohchr.org/EN/UDHR/Pages/Introduction.aspx (accessed on 3 October 2015).

[283] 347 U.S. 483.

Sampanis and others v. Greece[284]

The group of children in Greece were denied admissions in the academic year due to enrolment difficulties of the school and were later admitted in a separate building as students of preparatory classes. The court holding the practice as violative of Article 14 of EDHR: prohibition of discrimination commented severely against this practice of diving and discriminating children and violating their right to seek quality education at a common platform.

Abbott v. Burke[285]-

A series of state Supreme Court rulings starting in 1985, continues to shape and reshape education—especially for New Jersey's poorest kids.

Key decisions and documents:

Abbott II (June, 1990): Court finds funding disparity between rich and poor districts violates constitutional guarantee of a 'thorough and efficient' system of education.
Abbott V (May 1998): Court orders preschool and school reforms and building construction and repairs.
Abbott XX (May 2009): Court finds existing School Funding Reform Act constitutional: Court orders the state to fully fund SFRA (School Funding Reform Act) for the Abbott districts.

The Abbott rulings remain one of the most important set of decisions on school equity in the country and are still a major force in New Jersey. Abbott decisions have been called the most important equal education rulings since Brown v. Board of Education. It was Abbott that led to *universal preschool* in the state's poorest districts, the state's massive *school construction and renovation* program, and the addition of *extra programs and funding for the disadvantaged* initiatives in and outside Abbott schools.[286]

CCJEF v. Rell[287]

This petition had highlighted the state's failure to adequately and equitably fund public schools that was failing in imparting quality education to children under the directive of right to education. On 22 November 2005, fifteen students and their families from across the state brought an action in the Hartford Superior Court challenging the constitutionality of Connecticut's broken education system. The Connecticut Coalition for Justice in Education Funding (CCJEF) helped bring the case to ensure that the interests of all schoolchildren, whether they attend large urban, urban-ring, suburban, or rural school districts, are similarly represented in this action.

---

[284] ECtHR, *Sampanis and Others v. Greece*, Application no. 32526/05, 5 June 2008. Available at http://cmiskp.echr.coe.int/tkp197/view.asp?action=html&documentId=836273&portal=hbkm&source=externalbydocnmber&table=?F69A27FD8FB86142BF01C1166DEA398649 (accessed on 3 October 2015).
[285] 199 N.J. 140 (2009) (Abbott XX).
[286] Available at http://www.edlawcenter.org/cases/abbott-v-burke.html (accessed on 3 October 2015).
[287] 295 Conn. 240 (2010).

The *CCJEF* v. *Rell* complaint alleged that the state's failure to suitably and equitably fund its public schools has irreparably harmed thousands of Connecticut schoolchildren by limiting their future ability to take full advantage of the nation's democratic processes and institutions, to secure meaningful employment in the competitive high-skills/high-wage global marketplace, and to successfully continue their education beyond high school. The state's failure to provide plaintiff schoolchildren with opportunities to meet the state's own learning standards has resulted in a system that fails Connecticut's students and offends the Connecticut constitution. The complaint also alleged that the state's systemic school funding failure disproportionately impacts African-American, Latino, and other minority students, in violation of the Connecticut constitution and federal law. In a 2010 pretrial ruling, the Connecticut Supreme Court affirmed the state's constitutional obligation and remanded the case back to the trial court for full trial on the merits of Plaintiffs' adequacy and equity claims.

Part II: Right to Play and Recreation[288]

Play is a fundamental right. It is a process and is freely chosen. It is the means by which children and young people explore their world, their roles and their relationships. It can be cooperative, competitive or solitary, destructive or creative. It can be escapist, imaginative, therapeutic, adventurous, quiet, messy, challenging, structured or spontaneous. Play empowers children, affirms and supports their right to make choices and discover their own solutions. It encourages healthy emotional and physical development. It is a natural instinct that needs to be nurtured. Play has both educational and social benefits in that, through it, children learn about complex relationships and more importantly, about themselves. It also provides a basis of conceptual understanding that allows them to succeed in formal education. However, play is also important for its own sake, it shouldn't have to have a reason or an end.

The UNCRC guarantees the right to play and recreational activities to all children. The UNCRC in Article 31 acknowledges the importance of play and recreation.[289] The article recognizes the right of the child to engage in play and recreational activities appropriate for the age of the child and to encourage the provision of appropriate and equal opportunities for cultural, artistic, recreational, and leisure activity. However, millions of children are denied this right, never experiencing this vital aspect of their development because of war, disease, and poverty, or because the importance of play has not been recognized or accepted, or because of misconceptions relating to play.

Play is an important vehicle for young people's development and an introduction to lifelong active living.[290] The involvement of children and youth in enjoyable physical recreation activities

---

[288] Available at www.UNICEF.org (accessed on 5 July 2002).

[289] UNCRC, Article 31 states:

(1) State parties recognize the right of the child to rest and leisure, to engage in play and recreational activities appropriate to the age of the child and to participate freely in cultural life and the arts.

(2) State parties shall respect and promote the rights of the child to participate fully in cultural and artistic life and shall encourage the provision of appropriate and equal opportunities for cultural, artistic, recreational and leisure activity.

[290] Available at www.SCY.org (accessed on 5 July 2002).

is a cornerstone of their health and well-being. Children and youth develop physically and socially through involvement in sport, and research shows a connection between physical fitness, academic ability, and positive behaviour generally. The healthy stress of the competitive situation, and participation with their peers, can help young people gain self-confidence and mature emotionally. Also, there is much evidence that participation in physical recreation programmes can have a very positive influence on children and youth at risk and that such programmes, if adapted to their needs, have the potential of engaging otherwise 'hard-to-reach' youth.

Natural outdoor play environments offer important opportunities for children to begin to value the environment. Through play, children explore cause and effect and gradually build a knowledge base that cannot be taught through structured learning activities. Play is a vehicle for the development of creativity and flexibility, invaluable qualities in human development.

Play can be a vehicle for children to pass on their culture for sharing between generations, and for children to communicate their feelings and ideas to adults. Through play, young children learn to become active participants in community. Play days and play festivals are a major form of celebration of culture and community around the world. Play has therapeutic value and is also a way for children to gain a sense of control over difficult circumstances as witnessed in hospital settings and in war zones.

Play is fundamental to all aspects of child development and is a key component in preserving community and culture, in the broadest sense.[291] Play is valuable in children's physical exercise and growth and in their development of motor skills. Children playing together present rich opportunities for social, moral, and emotional development and hence for the development of their personality and their ability to handle stress and conflict. It is in free play that children learn to understand and cooperate with others.

The importance of play to children is strongly supported by researchers from a range of disciplines including psychology, education, philosophy, anthropology, and recreation. In spite of this, society as a whole continues to view play as a frivolous pastime, at best useful for children to 'let off steam'. The reasons for this misunderstanding are many and varied. One reason is our difficulty in clearly defining play. Play is not synonymous with recreation, although there are many opportunities for play in recreation programmes and environments, and it does not include everything children do in their leisure time. Play is not created by adults for children but children initiate themselves. Play is spontaneous, self-motivated, controlled by the child.[292]

For reasons already outlined, specialists in children's play theory see play as fundamental to human development. *A concerted effort on the part of governments, organizations, and communities should be made to promote the fact that play and learning are not competing ideologies.* Parents and other decision makers must ensure a balance in children's lives both to avoid unhealthy levels of stress and to allow opportunities for informal play.

Schools, communities, and parents must work together to ensure a balance in children's lives through offering engaging and healthy alternatives to sedentary and isolated activities.

There are a number of issues that create barriers to children's play opportunities. While ensuring that safety is not compromised, there is a need for a paradigm shift in the way we think about playgrounds. Children need a wider range of play possibilities, which would be ensured through

---

[291] Available at www.ccy/scy (accessed on 5 July 2002).
[292] Available at www.ccy/scy (accessed on 5 July 2002).

a much greater variety of play material and by involving children in the planning process. Special consideration should be given to access for children with disabilities. Children play everywhere. Spontaneous or free play is important for children in both the natural and built environment. Open space is diminishing due to competition for urban land and commercial priorities for its use, and the built environment, such as, shopping malls, hotels, etc., do not always anticipate or plan for children playing.

Decision makers and planners should apply a 'child-friendly lens' to policy affecting young people in public space and involve children themselves as much as possible. Examples of things that may be considered are:

- preservation of undeveloped land,
- parks that are close to schools and jointly planned with schools,
- community gardens where children and youth can care for plants, and
- parks and open space that offer children and youth opportunities for climbing, challenge, and adventure. Planners should ensure a wide range of environments to encourage many kinds of children's play and ensure they are well situated, safe, and well maintained. A field action project[293] converted a dumping space into playground for children. Such initiatives have to be taken on a mass scale.

The challenge before us now is to make every child feel part of something special. To encourage policy planners to think creatively about how they can use sport as a tool in their policies. To build partnerships among governments, civil society, and the private sector to ensure the widest and most effective use possible of that tool. Child advocates must be vigilant in their protection of this right, for the twenty-first century offers serious threats to this seemingly natural and simple aspect of human development.[294]

Article 31 has often been overlooked as a stand-alone right, yet other convention rights also have a direct impact on play. For example, the UNCRC states that education should be directed to a broad range of developmental areas, including the child's personality, talents and mental and physical abilities (Article 29). Play and leisure activities can also play a vital role in meeting the child's right to 'the highest attainable standard of health' and to 'preventative health care' as set out in Article 24.[295]

The UN Committee on the Rights of the Child in its General comment No. 17 (2013) Relating to Right to Play[296]

The importance of play and recreation in the life of every child has long been acknowledged by the international community. Article 31 of the UNCRC sets out children's right to rest, leisure and play, cultural life and the arts (the 'Article 31 rights').

[293] A project of Tata Institute of Social Sciences, Mumbai.

[294] Available at www.scyofbc.org (accessed on 22 November 2016).

[295] UNCRC, Article 24.

[296] The UNCRC Committee elaborates its general comments with a view to clarifying the normative contents of specific rights provided for under the UNCRC or particular themes of relevance to the convention, as well as offer guidance about practical measures of implementation.

Widely acknowledged as central to children's health, development and happiness, nevertheless Article 31 rights have not routinely been given the level of attention they deserve.

In 2013 the UN Committee on the Rights of the Child published its 'General Comment' No. 17 on Article 31, a landmark document setting out both the importance of Article 31 to children and young people, and the obligations of governments to make progress in implementation.

Children's play is defined under General Comment No. 17 as 'any behaviour, activity or process initiated, controlled and structured by children themselves; it takes place whenever and wherever opportunities arise. Caregivers may contribute to the creation of environments in which play takes place, but play itself is non-compulsory, driven by intrinsic motivation and undertaken for its own sake, rather than as a means to an end. Play involves the exercise of autonomy, physical, mental or emotional activity, and has the potential to take infinite forms, either in groups or alone. These forms will change and be adapted throughout the course of childhood. The key characteristics of play are fun, uncertainty, challenge, flexibility and non-productivity. Together, these factors contribute to the enjoyment it produces and the consequent incentive to continue to play. While play is often considered non-essential, the Committee reaffirms that it is a fundamental and vital dimension of the pleasure of childhood, as well as an essential component of physical, social, cognitive, emotional and spiritual development.'[297]

The present general comment seeks to enhance the understanding of the importance of article 31 for children's well-being and development; to ensure respect for and strengthen the application of the rights under article 31, as well as other rights in the convention, and to highlight the implications for the determination of:

1. Consequent obligations of states in the elaboration of all implementation measures, strategies and programmes aimed at the realization and full implementation of the rights defined in Article 31;
2. The role and responsibilities of the private sector, including companies working in the areas of recreation, cultural and artistic activities, as well as civil society organizations providing such services for children;
3. Guidelines for all individuals working with children, including parents, on all actions undertaken in the area of play and recreation.

General Comment No. 17 highlights the fundamental importance of recognizing and facilitating this right for girls and boys of all ages. It emphasizes the role of play in providing opportunities for the expression of creativity, imagination, self-confidence, self-efficacy, and for the development of physical, social cognitive and emotional strength and skills. It further highlights that, through play, children explore and experience the world around them, experiment with new ideas, roles and experiences, and in so doing learn to better understand and construct their social position within the world.

The General Comment stresses that play is essential for the realization of other rights. For example, Article 31 itself recognizes the interrelationships between play, recreation, leisure, rest

---

[297] Brooker Woodhead, *The Right to Play*: Early Childhood in Focus 9 (United Kingdom: The Open University, 2013).

and participation in cultural life and the arts. Play is also a key dimension of education, necessary to achieve the best possible health, integral to the child's optimum development, and a valuable route to recovery and reintegration after trauma, loss, neglect or violence. Although children have a spontaneous urge to play and will seek out opportunities to do so in the most unfavourable environments, the Committee recognizes that certain conditions need to be assured if the right to play is to be fully realized. Children need to be free from harmful stress, violence, discrimination and physical dangers. They require appropriate time and space. They need access to natural environments, material resources and other children. They also need the key adults around them to recognize the importance and legitimacy of play, as well as support children in play activities. Governments must therefore act to promote and protect these conditions.[298]

Judgments on Right to Play, Leisure, and Recreation

Following are some of the judgments in which the importance of playground have been recognised by the court. This right to play, recreation, and leisure needs further recognition.

Division Bench in Holy Saint Education Society v. Venkataamana[299]

In the instant case the court held that a site reserved for children's playground under the scheme prepared under the City Improvement Act when came to be vested in the corporation, it was under a duty to retain it as such and it had no authority to divert it for any other use or grant it to a private person or organisation' held that the ratio was not helpful as, 'both under the provisions of the City Improvement Act and the BDA Act, the CIT or the BDA, as the case may be, had the authority to improve the scheme by making alteration in the scheme and in exercise of the said power, the purpose for which any space was reserved, could be changed and after such change is effected the land could be disposed of for the purpose for which it is earmarked after such change.

In Bangalore Medical Trust v. B.S. Muddappa[300]

In the instant case, the Bangalore Development authority allotted the open space to a hospital. This allotment was challenged by a writ petition filed by the residents of that locality on the ground that it is contrary to the provisions of the Bangalore Development Authority Act, 1976 and the scheme sanctioned there under, and the legislative intent to protect and preserve the environment by reserving open space for 'ventilation', recreation and play grounds and parks for the general public to invoke equity jurisdiction of the high court.

It was observed that

in fact, public spirited citizens having faith in rule of law are rendering social and legal service by espousing cause of public nature. They cannot be ignored or overlooked on technical or conservative yardstick of the rule of locus standi or absence of personal loss or injury. Present day development

---

[298] Woodhead, *The Right to Play.*
[299] ILR 1982 1 Karn 1.
[300] AIR 1991 SC 1902.

of this branch of jurisprudence is towards free movement both in nature of litigation and approach of the courts. Residents of Locality seeking protection and maintenance of environment of their locality cannot be said to be busy bodies or interlopers. Even otherwise, violation of rule of law either by ignoring or affronting individual or action of the executive in disregard of the provisions of law raises substantial issue of accountability of those entrusted with responsibility of the administration. It furnishes enough cause of action either for individual or community in general to approach by way of writ petition and the shelter under cover of technicalities of locus standi nor can they be heard to plead for restraint in exercise of discretion as grave issues of public concern outweigh such consideration.

It was further observed as under at para 36 of the instant case:—

Public Park as a place reserved for beauty and recreation was developed in 19th and 20th Century and is associated with growth of the concept of equality and recognition of importance of common man. Earlier, it was a prerogative of the aristocracy and the affluent either as a result of royal grant or as a place reserved for private pleasure. Free and healthy air in beautiful surroundings was privilege of few. But now, it is a, 'gift' from people to themselves.' Its importance has multiplied with emphasis on environment and pollution. In modern planning and development it occupies an important place in social ecology. A private nursing home on the other hand is essentially a commercial venture, a profit oriented industry, Service may be its moto but earning is the objective. Its utility may not be undermined but a park is a necessity not a mere amenity. A private nursing home cannot be a sub-stitute for a public park. No town planner would prepare a blue print without reserving space for it. Emphasis on open air and greenery has multiplied and the city or town planning or development acts of different states require even private house-owners to leave open. space in front and back for lawn and fresh air. In 1984 the BF Act itself provided for reservation of not less than fifteen per cent of the total area of the lay out in a development scheme for public parks and play grounds the sale and disposition of which is prohibited under Section 38A of the Act. Absence of open space and public park, in present day when urbanisation is on increase, rural exodus is on large scale and congested areas are coming up rapidly, may give rise to health hazard. May be that it may be taken care of by a nursing home. But it is axiomatic that prevention is better than cure. What is lost by removal of a park cannot be gained by establishment of a nursing home. To say, therefore, that by conversion of a site reserved for low lying park into a private nursing home social welfare was being promoted was being oblivious of true character of the two and their utility.

Court on Its Own Motion v. Union of India through Ministry of Urban Development & Ors[301]

This petition was registered taking cognizance of the letter dated 12 April 2014 of Honourable Justice Kurian Joseph, Judge Supreme Court of India regarding the deplorable state of affairs in the Children's Park near India Gate and the Lake Park near Sarojini Nagar/opposite Laxmi Bai Nagar, and suggesting that the Delhi Legal Services Authority addresses the issue, so that the human rights of the children to get a congenial atmosphere in these parks befitting their age and dignity are not violated.

Notice was issued to the Ministry of Urban Development, Government of India, Government of National Capital Territory of Delhi (GNCTD), Central Public Works Department, New Delhi

---

[301] W.P.(C) No.2345/2014 & CM No.5406/2015.

Municipal Council (NDMC), DDA, East Municipal Corporation of Delhi, North Municipal Corporation of Delhi, South Municipal Corporation of Delhi and Delhi Cantonment Board and vide order dated 16 April 2014 direction was issued to the NDMC to ensure that immediate steps are taken in repairing the broken/damaged playing equipments, swings and other facilities in the aforesaid two parks and for upgrading and maintaining the same.

The importance of play equipment or apparatus installed in children parks, which the governmental agencies concerned are treating so lightly and casually, also cannot be undermined. There is substantial research showing a clear link between play and brain development, motor-skills, and social capabilities. All learning—emotional, social, motor, and cognitive—is accelerated, facilitated and fuelled by the pleasure of play.

During the pendency of the present petition, there was a report of a child dying in a park in New Moti Nagar, Delhi due to injury on head and chest caused by the iron bar swing on which she was playing. Justice Kurian Joseph vide his letter dated 5 February 2014 to the learned Amicus Curiae drew attention to the said incident as well as to Article 39(f) of the Constitution of India imposing a duty on the state to secure that children are given opportunities and facilities to develop in a healthy manner as well as to the UNCRC adopted by the United Nations General Assembly Resolution on 20 November 1989 ratified by India on 11 December 1992 inter alia recognizing the right of the children to relax and play and to join in a wide range of activities.

The court observed in para 9 and 10 of the instant case:

> It appears to us that the agencies concerned have forgotten the importance of children parks and we need to remind them of the same.
>
> Parks are inherently attractive to children because they permit escape from the tight strictures of daily life. Such parks offer children the daily benefits of direct experience with nature, the motivation to explore, discover and learn about their world and to engage in health promoting physical activities. The parks have also been perceived as offering the children a sense of place, self-identity, and belonging, as an antidote to social alienation, vandalism, and violence. It is in the parks that children are able to engage in informal, experiential learning through play and shared experiences with peers, laying the foundation for effective formal education. Experts on the subject have opined that children do not learn effectively exclusively within a classroom; they need alternative, hands-on learning environment to match their varied learning styles. Parks are crucial antidote to the unhealthy trends of city life and test driven education mandates. Other studies have shown that not playing outdoors, diminution of recess, and the abandonment of outdoor play in schools is resulting in serious health effects and potentially diminishing the life spans of the present generation. Mental health experts, educationists and sociologists are beginning to suggest that when kids stop going out into the natural world to play, it can affect not just their development as individuals but society as well.

The court, while observing the important role which children parks play in developing the physical and cognitive capabilities of children, held that the policy dated 30 March 2015 for regular maintenance and upkeep of children's parks has been finalized and upon being approved by this court would be implemented qua all children's parks in Delhi, irrespective of the agency/municipality under which they may fall .

Accordingly, while disposing of this petition the court directed:

1. that the said policy be adopted by all the governmental agencies, whether party to this petition or not, within three months hereof; (we clarify that the fact that the policy has been prepared

under the directions of this court and has been approved by us, will not come in the way of the individual agency, if finding any other change to be made in the policy for better enforcement/implementation thereof, making such changes, without being required to approach this court);

2. that each of the agencies concerned within whose territorial jurisdiction or domain any of the parks/ children's park fall, to within the said period of three months, also designate an officer by rank, who will be personally responsible for enforcement/implementation of the said policy and who will be held responsible, in the event of any breach thereof being found;

3. each of the agencies concerned within whose territorial jurisdiction/domain any of the parks/ children parks fall, to prominently display the policy aforesaid on their respective websites as well as at all parks/children parks, together with the designation of the officer so nominated for implementation thereof and from time to time also display the name of the officer occupying the said post and the telephone number(s), email address(s) and address, where grievances/ complaints with respect to the implementation of the policy can be lodged, along with the address, email address(s) and telephone number(s) of the Delhi Commission for Protection of Child Rights (DCPCR) to which grievances of non-redressal of the complaints can be made;

4. each of the agencies concerned to devise a mechanism for time bound redressal of the grievances/complaints received;

5. DCPCR, to actively concern itself with the maintenance and upkeep of all children parks in Delhi, in accordance with the policy aforesaid and to from time to time have the parks inspected and to suggest to the governmental agencies concerned the steps to be taken for improvement thereof and to either on its own or on receipt of any complaint of failure to maintain the parks in terms of policy, enquire into same and take consequent action including of identifying the erring/ guilty officials and reporting the same for appropriate administrative action.

Law Reform Relating to Right to Play

It is very unfortunate to note that 'Play' is being denied to the children India because of the factors like wrongly conceived education policies, poverty, social customs, less importance to play in academics, attitude of teachers, parents and school administrators, urbanisation, mechanisation etc. and India is no exception to it. It is being observed that a majority of the children become adult without playing thus negatively effecting physical, mental and social aspects of their personality. Play is so important to optimal child development that it has been recognized by the UN High Commission for Human Rights as a right of every child. Play is an inevitable reality of life as well as a medium of education. The right to play is a global issue. Around the world children's play opportunities are threatened through war, poverty, fear, widening gap between the poor and rich and unbalanced importance given to academic pursuits. Although India is a signatory to the UNCRC, but the state fails to protect this fundamental right of its children to play due to different social, economic and cultural beliefs and gaps. One of the major and the most visible problem in the context of India, particularly the urban India is: Children from elite schools are overburdened with their home works and tuitions, hence find it difficult to find any time to play and parents of children often consider outdoor playing as a waste of time, so indulge in indoor games in computer, or listening to music for recreation. Children from disadvantaged backgrounds have no childhood. In the spare time they either engage themselves to increase the family earning or in domestic chores or in. In a metro city like Kolkata, multi-storied buildings and shopping malls have left very sibling care. The ever-widening socio-cultural- economic gap between the haves and have- not's in little space for the greens and meadows, leaving children confined in their flats/ rooms. this city prohibits them from mingling with each other The right to play must be made a fundamental right in the Constitution of India. It is as important as Right to education and we need a policy on right to play .

The right to play, recreation, rest, leisure and participation in cultural and artistic life is not only a fundamental right of every child, but its realization will bring significant individual and societal benefits.

Some NGOs working for promoting Right to Education in India

Pratham[302]

It is an innovative learning organization created to improve the quality of education in India. As one of the largest NGOs in the country, Pratham focuses on high-quality, low-cost, and replicable interventions to address gaps in the education system. Established in 1995 to provide education to children in the slums of Mumbai, Pratham has grown both in scope and geographical coverage. The mission to improve the quality of education in India and ensure that all children not only attend but also thrive in school is being accomplished by working in collaboration with the government, local communities, parents, teachers, volunteers, and civil society members. Pratham's programmes aim to supplement rather than replace governmental efforts. They are implemented on a large scale to not only reach as many children as possible, but also to create an adoptable demonstration model for state governments.

National Alliance for the Fundamental Right to Quality Education and Equity[303]

Here, CRY (Child Rights and You) along with other eight other NGOs formed the National Alliance for the Fundamental Right to quality Education and Equity (NAFRE) and has been the prime mover of this alliance. NAFRE today is an alliance of more than 2,000 grassroot voluntary organisations and thousands of individuals from all sections of society.

Its objectives are to:

* Strengthen micro-level initiatives for universalising education.
* Act as a critical link, transferring learning from these grassroot initiatives to the macro level
* Critically work with all levels of government, media and industry to make education a national priority

Largely with the eff orts of CRY, NAFRE is today recognized as a premier national alliance on education, influencing policy on the right to education. Also, CRY worked towards strengthening

---

[302] Available at http://pratham.org/about-us/about-pratham (accessed 2 October 2015).
[303] Available at http://www.cry.org/projects/storiesofhopen.html (accessed on 2 October 2015).

the efforts of 12 state Alliances of NGOs in education as well as establishing National level links between these state Alliances and NAFRE enabling all of them to together, build perspectives on the issue of universalisation of education, throughout their partner network and beyond. The NAFRE is also responsible for the 83rd amendment to make education a fundamental right.

National Coalition for Education[304]

The National Coalition for Education (NCE) strives to advocate the Right to Education as a justifiable right for every child on the basis of equal opportunity, gender equity, in a child friendly environment and with the participation of civil society and teachers A coalition of Teachers Unions and NGOs in India which act as a country counter part of GCE (Global Coalition for Education) which stands for the Right to Education. National Coalition for Education is a conglomeration of networks working on Right to Education, AIPTF; a union of more than 3 million primary teachers, All India Federation of Teachers' Organisations (AIFTO); a union of 1.2 million teachers, All India Association for Christian Higher Education (AIACHE); an association of 300 college principals, World Vision India; a foundation working for children education and development.

The networks have been working together on the issues of the Right to Free and Quality education, the eradication of child labour and the promotion of Child Rights since long independently and in collaboration with each other and with other civil society groups.

Some Non-governmental Organizations Working on Child's Right to Play

CINI[305] Kolkata, has been working relentlessly for a long time to ensure the rights of children of different strata. With the same objective, we have been organising an event for the last few years with the children of Kolkata. This is a unique opportunity of coming together of children from disadvantaged background and elite schools. This event promotes the long forgotten children's games of the country. As part of this initiative, CINI is organizing small events in different parts of the city to spread mass awareness and build network with like-minded organizations and government departments to advocate on children's 'Right to Play'. It's not only about outdoor games, it's about games, songs, dance, drama, music, karate, sounds, colours, flowers – an effort to ensure the children's recreation in their own way. Children from various socio-economic background, their parents, teachers, and government officials are invited to be involved and witness the enthusiasm and creative talents of the children. Goal of the programme: Advocate for recognizing 'play' as children's right by the government and mobilize resources to support that from all segments of the society. Objectives of the programme:

- to ensure children's access to the playgrounds
- to promote state specific indigenous traditional games
- to campaign for spaces, infrastructure and support for children to play

---

[304] Available at http://www.nceindia.org.in/ (accessed on 2 October 2015).
[305] Available at www.cini-india.org (accessed on 2 October 2015).

- integration of sports in education
- advocate importance of 'play' for out of school children
- advocate importance of ECD through 'play'

Strategies of the programme: The following strategies would be adopted to reach the above objectives:

- advocacy with government;
- mega event in the streets of Kolkata;
- promoting traditional street plays and games;
- networking with other NGOs;
- sensitization of parents;
- sensitization of local government and elite schools on right to play.

Future Challenges

The changing concept of development, from a narrow preoccupation with national income to a broader concern with people's well-being and their capacity to better themselves and to improve their environment, casts a new light on the importance of education. Human development interpreted as widening human choices in economic, political, social, and cultural terms assigns a critical role to education. The new vision of human development will remain an empty rhetoric until education enables people to understand and exercise the choices that are promised by this new vision. The recognition of the central importance of education in promoting human development has led to three areas of agreement on educational priorities. First, it is recognized that priority must be given to basic education since it is the foundation of a national educational system and because basic education contributes most substantially to overall economic and social development, including the reduction of poverty, fertility, and child mortality. Second, it is recognized that the core of basic education is primary education for children since they embody the future of a society. Third, the education of girls and women has emerged as the most precious investment that a society can make in its future. The beneficial impacts of education, especially of the education of girls, on social development are well recognized. The number of years of schooling of girls has been found to be closely related to the reduction of child mortality and morbidity, the improvement of family health and nutrition, and the slowing of population growth. A challenge before India as well as before other developing countries is the education of the girl child. In a culture that idolizes sons and dreads the birth of a daughter, to be born a female comes perilously close to being less than human. The girl child has to be made a priority in educational policies. Corporal Punishment must be banned completely and monitoring bodies established. There must be grievance redressal forums that are easily accessible. The IPC must be reviewed to remove the provisons that give defense to the accused.

Universal primary education is widely recognized as one of the most effective instruments for combating child labour. It is believed that no country can successfully eliminate child labour without first enacting and implementing compulsory education legislation. Quality basic education, particularly at the primary level, not only improves the lives of children and their families but contributes to the future economic growth and development of a country. Education and child labour laws should not only reinforce but also complement one another. Education laws and policies can reinforce child labour laws by keeping children in schools and away from the workplace. Child labour laws, in turn, can be a useful tool for retaining children in school, helping Governments achieve their universal basic education objectives. International Standards on child labour have made this link by encouraging countries to make admission into the workforce conditional on completion of compulsory education. ILO Convention No. 138 establishes the minimum age for employment at not less than the age for completing compulsory schooling and in no event less than fifteen years.

Education must be available to all children without discrimination. It should reach out to those who have been traditionally unreached including girls, the poor, working children, children affected by emergencies and HIV/AIDS, the disabled, and those with nomadic lifestyles. This right is one that transcends access alone and includes quality. Education must be provided from a rights perspective, recognizing the indivisibility of rights and the need for educational processes to respect all rights. Education can also be an 'enabling right'—a right that facilitates access to other rights throughout a lifetime.

In order for the world to survive and prosper in the new century, people will need to learn more and learn differently. A child entering the new century is likely to face more risks and uncertainties and will need to gain more knowledge and master more skills than any generation before. The challenges the world faces at the onset of the twenty-first century are an impressive lot: urbanization and globalization, population expansion and environmental deterioration, terrorism, sexism, fundamentalism, and authoritarianism—with the addition of ethnic conflict and political instability, corruption, disease, and poverty. But the end of the twentieth century has also brought with it technological and scientific development, at a faster rate than at any previous period in human history, in health, in agriculture, in industrial production, and notably in the fields of communication, mass media, and information. As the twenty-first century begins, the opportunities to learn have expanded in more ways than most people can imagine.

Schools will remain the most effective and efficient way to transmit the knowledge and skills, and promote the values, needed for the future. They must continue to be expanded in quantity and improved in quality. But given the increasing complexity of the world, and the increasing amount of learning that takes place outside of the classroom, a single focus on schools and even on the basic education system is no longer enough. Strengthening the other critical environments in which children learn—the family, the community—must also become a major and more explicit focus of development.

A new approach is needed where it is recognized that building and supplying more schools (with teachers, new curricula, and texts), though important tasks in themselves, do not automatically lead to more positive learning outcomes and that learning takes place not only in schools (in fact, not even mostly in schools) but also in other environments—in families and communities, with peers and through the media, in the playgrounds and other public places.

The basic right of the child is not only to education as in Article 28 of the UNCRC, but to learning and to the opportunity to learn, to have access to enabling and supportive learning environments, which will help children gain both access to other rights and to the knowledge, skills, competencies, attitudes, and values needed for continuing lifelong learning.

The 'expanded vision' of basic education which the Jomtien Declaration promotes includes universalizing access and promoting equity; focusing on learning acquisition; broadening the means and scope of basic education; enhancing the environment for learning; and strengthening partnerships within a supportive policy context, through mobilizing resources and strengthening international solidarity.

Learning should be to develop one's personality and be able to act with greater autonomy, judgment, critical thinking, and personal responsibility; to develop all aspects of one's potential—memory, reasoning, aesthetic sense, spiritual values, physical capacities, and communication skills; to make one healthy and enjoy play and sports; to value one's own culture; to possess an ethical and moral code; to speak for and protect oneself; to make one resilient.

The NDP, a key component of the RTE Act, was enforced on April 1, 2010 with an aim to ensure that every child between the age of 6 and 14 studies in school. The idea behind the policy was to minimise the number of students who drop out of the schooling system because of failure and are too embarrassed or de-motivated to repeat a year. This controversial policy of no detention and CEE is widely being blamed for deteriorating learning levels across schools in India. Many state education ministers, student and teacher groups have said that the policy should be reviewed, if not removed altogether. It should be a matter of concern to all those interested in the Indian education system that there is growing demand to bring back a pass-fail system in lieu of one that allows for non-threatening, holistic assessment. At the time when RTE targets remain largely unmet there is a need to have a strong political will and commitment to ensure elementary education to every child in India. The stake holders must be prepared for this much needed reform. There is no study or research to suggest that the quality of learning of the child improves if she or he is detained. In fact, more often than not failure can be a reason for the child abandoning school based learning altogether . Repeating a class does not give the child any special resources to deal with the same syllabus requirements for yet another year[306] School-imposed grade repetition is stressful for students and is associated with reduced self-esteem; impaired peer relationships; alienation from school and a sharply increased likelihood of eventual dropout.[307] The indirect consequences of moving from no detention to detention is likely to manifest as increase in child labour and incidences of child marriage[308] as well as, perhaps a lost opportunity for many children to have at least one nutritious meal in a day. The worst affected will be girl children and children with special needs. Restoring the examination system, detention policy, within the RTE framework will raise questions on some other important provisions within the RTE. For example, age appropriate admissions followed by special training for such children, whose learning level is below than required level; screening procedures for admission; and anytime admission in schools. [309]

Partnerships and networks are needed at all levels of the system. The promotion of such partnerships at the community level often produces little success if the major sectoral and political forces of

[306] The Right of Children to Free and Compulsory Education Act, 2009. Available at http://mhrd.gov.in/sites/upload_files/mhrd/files/upload_document/RTE_Section_wise_rationale_rev_0.pdf (accessed on 2 October 2015).

[307] Jere Brophy, *Grade Repetition*, The International Academy of Education, UNESCO, 2006. Available at http://unesdoc.unesco.org/images/0015/001520/152038e.pdf (last accessed on 2 October 2015).

[308] UNICEF, *Child Marriage in India: An Analysis of Available Data* (New Delhi, India, December 2012). Available at http://www.unicef.in/Itstartswithme/childmarriage.pdf (accessed on 2 October 2015).

[309] Ravi Prakash, '10 Reasons Why Rolling Back 'No Detention' Policy in RTE Act Would be a Bad Idea', *Education*, Oxfam India. Available at https://www.oxfamindia.org/education/10-reasons-why-rolling-back-No-detention-policy-in-RTE-act-would-be-a-bad-ideaee (accessed on 1 October 2015).

society do not support them, and likewise, sectoral collaboration at the top of the system does not necessarily translate into easy networking in fractious, heterogeneous communities. Mobilization and advocacy, at all levels, are essential. Policy makers, teachers, and parents, for example, must all understand the importance of good quality schooling and the indicators of successful learning.

It is important to obligate the state, the trustee of the nation, to provide education for all. Too often, compulsory education is seen as a legal frame-work that places parents and children in the negative role of criminal or victim. It is not to make children and families obligated to something they cannot achieve, but rather to place the burden on the states, to require the states to make quality primary education accessible to every child. Only after that is it appropriate to place the burden of proof on children and families. This will require dialogue and, sometimes, pressure, and advocacy for the border between family responsibility and state responsibility is not one that is well defined and may vary according to the context.

All advanced industrial countries and those contemporary developing countries that have made education compulsory regard education not as a right but as a duty. When education is made a duty, parents, irrespective of their economic circumstances and beliefs are required, by law, to send their children to school. It is also the legal obligation of the state to provide an adequate number of schools appropriately situated and to ensure that no child fails to attend school.[310]

If the right to education is to become meaningful, the process of education has to be one that equips children to face the challenges of life as they grow up to become adults. Seen in the context of the larger society, it has not only to prepare children for the challenges of tomorrow, but also to act as an agent of change, something that empowers them to play an active role in the creation of the world of tomorrow. The close links between basic education and key civic, economic, and social goals of communities lend a special urgency to the effort to fulfil the promise of basic education for all. There is an urgent need to provide access with a focus on equity, with special measures to bring in girls, children from disadvantaged groups and those with disabilities into schools.

The Right to play, recreation and leisure must be given equal importance. Children cannot be displaced from their homes, parks, and playgrounds . There must also be specially designed spaces for children with special needs with physical and mental disabilities to be able to play, safely.

[310] Weiner, *Child and the State in India.*

8 Right to Survival
Health, Nutrition, and Shelter

The right to survival of a child includes:

- access to healthcare services for children in emergency situation and for prevention of disease, through the existing healthcare network;
- access to shelter;
- provision of nutritional facilities for children in need of care and protection; and
- provision of an identity.

Right to Health

In 1946, the World Health Organization (WHO) defined health in its Constitution as 'a state of complete physical, mental, and social well-being and not merely the absence of disease or infirmity'.[1] The Constitution proclaimed that the enjoyment of the highest attainable standard of health is one of the fundamental human rights of every human being without distinction of race, religion, political belief, and economic or social condition. The Constitution also recognized that the health of all people is fundamental to the attainment of peace and security and is dependent upon the fullest cooperation of individuals and states. This was the vision shared by all the member states, including India.[2]

This vision was translated into a conceptual framework in the 'Health for All by 2000' Declaration of Alma Ata in 1978 (which meant the attainment by all citizens of the world, by the year 2000, of a level of health that would permit them to lead socially and economically productive lives).[3] The Alma Ata Declaration strongly reaffirmed that health, which is a state of complete

[1] WHO, 'Trade, Foreign Policy, Diplomacy and Health: Glossary of Globalization, Trade and Health Terms'. Available at http://www.who.int/trade/glossary/story046/en/ (accessed on 11 October 2015).

[2] 'Preamble to the WHO Constitution'. Available at http://www.who.int/governance/eb/who_constitution_en.pdf (accessed on 11 October 2015).

[3] WHO, 'Primary Health Care: Report of the International Conference on Primary Health Care. Alma-Ata, USSR, 6–12 September 1978', Geneva, 1978. Available at http://whqlibdoc.who.int/publications/9241800011.pdf (accessed on 11 October 2015).

physical, mental, and social well-being, and not merely the absence of disease or infirmity, is a fundamental human right and that the attainment of the highest possible level of health is one of the most important worldwide social goals, whose realization requires the action of many other social and economic sectors, in addition to the health sector. It also stated that primary healthcare (PHC) was the key to attaining health for all as part of overall development. It defined PHC as 'essential healthcare made universally accessible to individuals and families in the community by means acceptable to them, through their full participation and at a cost that the community and the country can afford'. The PHC is the first level of contact of individuals, the family, and the community, bringing healthcare as close as possible to where people live and work.[4]

The call for 'Health for All' was a call for social justice. It was not a single finite goal, but a strategic process leading to progressive improvement in the health of people. Despite many gains in the realm of health (such as increase in life expectancy, decreasing mortality, decline in infectious diseases, and reduction in child mortality and morbidity), progress towards Health for All in many countries has been hampered due to slow socio-economic development, lack of political commitment, failure to achieve equity in access to all PHC elements, inappropriate allocation and use of resources, low status of women, and other factors. Thus, Health for All still remains an unfulfilled dream. Recognizing this, the WHO renewed the health-for-all strategy and gave a call for Health for All in the twenty-first century.[5] The new policy highlights the need to apply national and international instruments that will advance the 'right to health'. The policy indicates how the quest for equity in health requires disaggregated data and an appreciation that improved access to health services will not yield the largest gains to equity in health. In addition, explicit attention is given in the policy to the increasing importance of ethics for a widening range of fundamental issues in medicine and public health, that extend from the beginning of life to death.[6]

International Human Rights Law

The WHO Constitution enshrines the highest attainable standard of health as a fundamental right of every human being. The right to health includes access to timely, acceptable, and affordable healthcare of appropriate quality. Yet, about 150 million people globally suffer financial catastrophe annually, and 100 million are pushed below the poverty line as a result of healthcare expenditure.[7] The right to health does not mean the right to be healthy. Vulnerable and marginalized groups in societies tend to bear an undue proportion of health problems. The right to health means that governments must generate conditions in which everyone can be as healthy as possible. Such conditions include ensuring availability of health services, healthy and safe working conditions, adequate housing, and nutritious food.[8]

[4] WHO, 'The Work of WHO 1973', Official Records of the WHO, No. 213, Geneva, 1973.

[5] Fernando S. Antezana, Claire M. Chollat-Traquet, and Derek Yach, 'Health for All in the 21st Century', *World Health Statistics Quarterly*, 51 (1998). Available at http://apps.who.int/iris/bitstream/10665/55721/1/WHSQ_1998_51_1_p3-6_eng.pdf?ua=1 (last accessed on 11 October 2015).

[6] Antezana et al., 'Health for all'.

[7] WHO, 'The Right to Health', WHO Fact Sheet No. 233, reviewed in November 2013. Available at http://www.who.int/mediacentre/factsheets/fs323/en/ (last accessed on 12 October 2015).

[8] WHO, 'The Right to Health'.

The right to health has been enshrined in international and regional human rights treaties as well as national Constitutions all over the world. Many of these international instruments do not focus primarily on children and their health, but do relate in significant ways to child health. The United Nations (UN) human rights treaties include:

- International Covenant on Economic, Social and Cultural Rights (ICESCR), 1966
- Convention on the Elimination of All Forms of Discrimination against Women (CEDAW), 1979
- United Nations Convention on the Rights of the Child (UNCRC), 1989

Some examples of regional human rights treaties are:

- European Social Charter (ESC), 1961
- African Charter on Human and Peoples' Rights (AHPHR), 1981
- Additional Protocol to the American Convention on Human Rights in the Area of Economic, Social and Cultural Rights (the Protocol of San Salvador), 1988

The ICRSCR, in Article 12, states that steps for the realization of the right to health include those that:

- reduce infant mortality and ensure the healthy development of the child;
- improve environmental and industrial hygiene;
- prevent, treat, and control epidemic, endemic, occupational, and other diseases; and
- create conditions to ensure access to healthcare for all.

General Comment on the Right to Health by the United Nations Committee on Economic, Social, and Cultural Rights[9]

To clarify and operationalize the above provisions, the United Nations Committee on Economic, Social, and Cultural Rights, which monitors compliance with the ICESCR, adopted a General Comment on the Right to Health in 2000. The General Comment stated that the right to health extended not only to timely and appropriate healthcare but also to the underlying determinants of health, such as access to safe and potable water and adequate sanitation, an adequate supply of safe food, nutrition, and housing, healthy occupational and environmental conditions, and access to health-related education and information, including on sexual and reproductive health.

According to the General Comment, the right to health contains four elements:[10]

---

[9] WHO, 'The Right to Health'.
[10] WHO, 'The Right to Health'.

1. *Availability*: A sufficient quantity of functioning public health and healthcare facilities, goods, and services, as well as programmes.
2. *Accessibility*: Health facilities, goods, and services accessible to everyone. Accessibility has four overlapping dimensions:

   a. non-discrimination;
   b. physical accessibility;
   c. economical accessibility (affordability);
   d. information accessibility.

3. *Acceptability*: All health facilities, goods, and services must be respectful of medical ethics and culturally appropriate, as well as sensitive to gender and life-cycle requirements.
4. *Quality*: Health facilities, goods, and services must be scientifically and medically appropriate and of good quality.

Further, according to the General Comment, the right to health also has a 'core content', referring to the minimum essential level of the right. Although this level cannot be determined in abstract, as it is a national task, key elements are set out to guide the priority setting process. Included in the core content are:

- essential primary healthcare;
- minimum essential and nutritious food;
- sanitation;
- safe and potable water;
- essential drugs.

Another core obligation is the adoption and implementation of a national public health strategy and plan of action. This must address the health concerns of the whole population; be devised, and periodically reviewed, on the basis of a participatory and transparent process; contain indicators and benchmarks by which progress can be closely monitored; and give particular attention to all vulnerable or marginalized groups.

State parties must move forward in line with the *principle of progressive realization*. This means that state parties should take deliberate, concrete, and targeted steps forward, using the maximum available resources. These resources include those within a state as well as resources available through international assistance and cooperation. In this context, it is important to distinguish the inability from the unwillingness of a state party to comply with its right to health obligations.[11] As part of the current reform process, the WHO has launched a new approach to promote and facilitate the mainstreaming of gender, equity, and human rights, building upon the progress that has already been made on these areas at all three levels of the organization. The WHO has been actively strengthening its role in providing technical, intellectual, and political leadership on the right to health. Overall, this entails:

---

[11] WHO, 'The Right to Health'.

- strengthening the capacity of WHO and its member states to integrate a human rights-based approach to health; and
- advancing the right to health in international law and international development processes.[12]

The right to health requires countries to do more than merely provide for comprehensive systems of healthcare delivery and insurance. It obligates them to undertake measures aimed at promoting individual and community health and at preventing diseases, to remove other external causes of morbidity and mortality, to eliminate health inequalities, and to improve the conditions that may hamper achievement of the highest attainable level of health. The right to health is interdependent with many other human rights. The human right to health includes:[13]

- The human right to the highest attainable standard of physical and mental health, including reproductive and sexual health.
- The human right to equal access to adequate healthcare and health-related services, regardless of sex, race, or other status.
- The human right to equitable distribution of food.
- The human right to access to safe drinking water and sanitation.
- The human right to an adequate standard of living and adequate housing.
- The human right to a safe and healthy environment.
- The human right to safe and healthy workplace, and to adequate protection for pregnant women in work proven to be harmful to them.
- The human right to freedom from discrimination and discriminatory social practices, including female genital mutilation, prenatal gender selection, and female infanticide.
- The human right to education and access to information relating to health, including reproductive health and family planning, to enable couples and individuals to decide freely and responsibly on all matters of reproduction and sexuality.
- The human rights of the child to an environment appropriate for physical and mental development.

The right to health is solidly embedded in international human rights law.[14] It is explicit in Article 25 of the Universal Declaration of Human Rights (UDHR) adopted by the United Nations General Assembly in 1948.[15] According to Article 25, everyone has the right to a standard of living that is adequate for the health and well-being of himself and his family, including food, clothing, shelter, housing, and other elements. Article 25 lays special emphasis on motherhood and childhood. Again in the ICESCR, which came into force in 1976, Article 11 states that the

---

[12] WHO, 'The Right to Health'.

[13] See *The People's Movement for Human Rights Learning*. Available at http://www.pdhre.org/ (last accessed on 11 October 2015).

[14] A. Hendriks, 'The Right to Health in National and International Jurisprudence', *European Journal of Health Law* 5, no. 4 (1998): 389–409.

[15] UN, 'Preamble to the Universal Declaration of Human Rights, 1948'. Available at http://www.un.org/en/documents/udhr/ (accessed on 11 October 2015).

state parties recognize the right of everyone to an adequate standard of living for himself and his family, including adequate food, clothing, and housing.

The CEDAW provides that the states shall eliminate discrimination against women in health-care and ensure, on the basis of equality of men and women, access to healthcare services, including those related to family planning, and further ensure appropriate services in connection with pregnancy.[16] It has to be ensured that women in rural areas have access to adequate healthcare facilities, including information counselling and services in family planning (CEDAW, Articles 10, 12, and 14). The CEDAW enjoins the states to eliminate racial discrimination and to guarantee the right of everyone, without distinction as to race, colour, or national or ethnic origin, to equality before law, the right to public health, medical care, social security, and social services.[17]

Numerous subsequent international and regional human rights treaties have given further definition to the right to health. Other international instruments recognizing the right to health include various conventions adopted within the context of the International Labour Organization (ILO) and, at the regional level, the ESC, the African Charter on Human and Peoples' Rights, and the Additional Protocol to the American Convention on Human Rights in the Area of Economic, Social, and Cultural Rights. The European Convention on Human Rights and Biomedicine also proclaims a right to equitable healthcare.

The UNCRC, in Articles 7, 24, and 27,[18] provides for the right to access child health. Article 7 of the convention specifies that every child shall be registered immediately after birth and shall have the right from birth to a name, the right to acquire a nationality, and as far as possible, the right to know and be cared for by his or her parents. Article 24 of the convention commits that the national governments are committed to diminish infant and child mortality, ensure the provision of necessary medical assistance and healthcare to all children with emphasis on the development of primary healthcare, combat disease and malnutrition, and ensure appropriate pre-natal and post-natal healthcare for mothers. Article 27 of the convention emphasizes on recognizing the rights of every child to a standard of living adequate for the child's physical, mental, spiritual, moral, and social development.[19] To address the three articles, the discussion on 'right to access child health' was divided into three parts, namely 'Birth Registration', 'Preventive Care—newborn care, child malnutrition and child immunization', and 'Curative Care—knowledge of oral rehydration salts (ORS) and use of ORS, and knowledge of danger signs of acute respiratory infections (ARIs)'.[20]

The heads of states and governments gathered in Rome at the World Food Summit at the invitation of the Food and Agriculture Organization (FAO) reaffirmed on 13 November 1996 the

---

[16] WHO, 'The Convention on the Elimination of All Forms of Discrimination against Women: The Convention in General'. Available at http://www.who.int/hhr/CEDAW.pdf (accessed on 11 October 2015).

[17] WHO, CEDAW.

[18] UNICEF, 'The Convention on the Rights of the Child—Survival and Development Rights: The Basic Rights to Life, Survival and Development of One are full potential'. Available at http://www.unicef.org/crc/files/SurvivalDevelopment.pdf (last accessed on 24 October 2015).

[19] UNICEF, 'The Convention on the Rights of the Child'.

[20] F. Ram, Abhishek Singh, and Usha Ram, 'Human Rights Approach to Maternal & Child Health: Has India Fared Well?', *Indian Journal of Medical Research* 137, no. 4 (April 2013): 721–27. Available at http://www.ncbi.nlm.nih.gov/pmc/articles/PMC3724252/ (accessed on 24 October 2015).

right of everyone to have access to safe and nutritious food, consistent with the right to adequate food and the fundamental right of everyone to be free from hunger. They considered it intolerable that more than 800 million people throughout the world, and particularly in developing countries, do not have enough food to meet their basic nutritional needs. They pledged their political will and their common and national commitment to achieving food security for all and to an ongoing effort to eradicate hunger in all countries. They formally renewed their commitment to the right to adequate food and recommended that the content of this right be defined more clearly and ways to implement it be identified.

The concept of nutrition rights originated in the context of the UNCRC and was developed by the United Nations Children's Fund (UNICEF), which defined nutrition rights as the combination of access to food, health, and necessary care. These three components are necessary to guarantee adequate nutrition to children. More and more non-governmental organizations (NGOs) are resorting to an explicit rights approach, especially in their work related to the Committee on the Rights of the Child, the committee which monitors state compliance with the UNCRC. On the international level, the World Alliance on Nutrition and Human Rights, a network of experts in the fields of nutrition and human rights, is strongly promoting the rights approach to the food and nutrition aspects of its work. Other organizations involved in issues such as breastfeeding, access to health facilities, and especially, child malnutrition, are increasingly working on a rights basis.

Health for All in the Twenty-First Century

Health for All remains the cornerstone of the WHO's institutional vision. Health for All in the Twenty-First Century is a continuation of the Health for All process. As a result, the 51st World Health Assembly has recognized Health for All in the Twenty-First Century as a framework for the development of future policy.

World Health Declaration[21]

The member states of the WHO reaffirmed their commitment to the principle enunciated in its Constitution that the enjoyment of the highest attainable standard of health is one of the fundamental rights of every human being; in doing so, the dignity and worth of every person is affirmed. The Declaration recognized that the improvement of health and well-being of people is the ultimate aim of social and economic development.

International Campaigns on Health

People's Health Assembly

The People's Health Assembly, an international multi-sectoral initiative, aims at bringing together individuals, groups, national and international organizations, networks, and civil society

---

[21] World Health Declaration, 'Health-for-All Policy for the Twenty-first Century', Fifty-First World Health Assembly, WHA51.7, Agenda item 19, 16 May 1998. Available at http://www.nszm.cz/cb21/archiv/material/worldhealthdeclaration.pdf (accessed on 9 October 2015).

movements that have been long involved in the struggle for health. The goal of People's Health Assembly is to re-establish health and equitable development as top priorities in local, national, and international policy making, with PHC as the strategy for achieving these priorities.

Global Health Assembly

The Global Health Assembly was convened during 4–8 December 2000 at Dhaka, Bangladesh. Ninety-two countries sent 1,453 participants to the assembly, which was the culmination of 18 months of preparatory action around the globe. The preparatory process elicited unprecedented enthusiasm and participation of a broad cross-section of people who had been involved in thousands of village meetings, district-level workshops, and national gatherings. At the Assembly, they reviewed their problems and difficulties, shared their experiences and plans, and formulated and endorsed the People's Charter for Health. The Charter is now the common tool of a worldwide citizen's movement committed to making the Alma Ata dream a reality.

Massive Effort Campaign against the Diseases of Poverty

The Massive Effort Campaign is a campaign to break the vicious cycle of poverty and disease. For the first time in history, the international community got together the financial means, the medications, and the know-how to take a stand against a small number of diseases that cause tremendous suffering and economic loss. This Massive Effort Campaign against the diseases of poverty, which unites partners in unique ways, is moving the world from word to action that can facilitate sustainable development, stimulate economic growth, ensure greater global public health security, and, most importantly, save human lives. This is a multi-sectoral initiative involving health networks, NGOs, ethical organizations, corporates, and others, to develop an integrated approach that combines preventive, curative, promotive, and rehabilitative aspects to address the diseases of poverty, namely malaria, tuberculosis (TB), and human immunodeficiency virus (HIV)/acquired immunodeficiency syndrome (AIDS). In recent times, the efforts to control communicable diseases are directed towards HIV/AIDS. The campaign seeks to bring about a policy change for concerted efforts to tackle the diseases of poverty. In India, the campaign is in its initial phase. The campaign planning has started off with a preparatory meeting of activists, corporates, social action groups, media persons, and others.[22]

Children's Health and Environment

Over the last 20 years there have been acknowledgements at the highest level of the need to protect the environment in order to underpin efforts to safeguard child health. As far back as 1989, states pledged in the UNCRC to 'combat disease and malnutrition ... taking into consideration

[22] The National Centre for Advocacy Studies hosted the meeting in Pune, Maharashtra. The Catholic Health Association of India in Secunderabad hosted the second planning meeting. In this meeting a National Campaign Team was constituted, and it was decided that the campaign would be launched in March 2002.

the dangers and risks of environmental pollution'.[23] The WHO held two international conferences on Children's Health and the Environment, the first in Bangkok in 2002, and the second in Buenos Aires in 2005, and both made commitments for further action in the area. In 2004, the WHO European Region developed a policy framework called the Children's Environmental Health Action Plan, which contains four regional priorities. The Busan Pledge for Action on Children's Health and the Environment (2009) called on the WHO to facilitate the development of a global plan of action to improve children's environmental health, and regularly monitor and report on its progress.[24]

- Child survival and development hinge on basic needs to support life; among these, a safe, healthy, and clean environment is fundamental. Children are exposed to serious health risks from environmental hazards. Environmental risk factors often act in concert, and their effects are exacerbated by adverse social and economic conditions, particularly conflict, poverty, and malnutrition. There is new knowledge about the special susceptibility of children to environmental risks; action needs to be taken to allow them to grow up and develop in good health, and to contribute to economic and social development.
- Each year, at least 3 million children under the age of five die due to environment-related diseases.
- The ARI annually kill an estimated 2 million children under the age of five. As much as 60 per cent of ARIs worldwide are related to environmental conditions.
- Diarrhoeal diseases claim the lives of nearly 1.5 million children every year. Eighty to 90 per cent of these diarrhoea cases are related to environmental conditions, in particular, contaminated water and inadequate sanitation.
- Environmental risks to children vary from region to region. Children in many countries still face the major traditional environmental hazards, including unsafe water, lack of sanitation, contaminated food, injuries, indoor air pollution from use of solid fuel, outdoor air pollution, and exposure to a myriad of toxic heavy metals, chemicals, and hazardous wastes that may be brought home from the workplace. However, other children live in adverse environments that are vastly different from those of generations ago. In addition to the traditional environmental hazards, due to rapid changes in economic structures, technologies, and demography, new or modern environmental hazards have appeared or been recognized, such as the increased use of

[23] UNCRC General Comment on the right of the child to the enjoyment of the highest attainable standard of health (Article 24).

[24] Busan Pledge for Action on Children's Health and the Environment, June 2009. The third WHO International Conference on Children's Health and the Environment was held in Busan, Republic of Korea (June 2009), hosted by the Korean Ministry of Environment, in collaboration with the Ministry of Health, Welfare and Family Affairs, and organized by WHO, jointly with national and international partners concerned about children's health and the environment. The conference addressed current and emerging trends, new scientific research findings, and the translation of research into policy to protect the children's health from environmental threats. Available at http://www.who.int/ceh/global_plan/en/ (accessed on 20 October 2015).

radiation in paediatric healthcare settings[25, 26]. These may be linked to global challenges such as uncontrolled urbanization, new technologies, industrialization in developing countries, ecosystem degradation, and the impacts of climate change. Developing regions carry a disproportionately heavy share of the environmental disease burden and children in developing nations have the highest death rates.[27]

Global Campaign Report, 2010

The United Nations Millennium Development Goals (MDGs) Summit 2010 and the UN Secretary-General's Special Session, which launched the Global Strategy for Women's and Children's Health, marked a turning point for improving maternal and child health. The Global Strategy urged countries to cultivate progress by addressing the root policy issues that impact women's and children's health. In response, 14 countries made legislative commitments to strengthen policies for Reproductive–Maternal–Neonatal–Child and Adolescent Health (RMNCH). The pledges range from embedding gender in national development agendas to enforcing laws on the minimum age of marriage and the endorsement of mortality audits. Eight countries committed to policy measures to improve their health systems, such as strengthening registration of vital statistics and developing community-based healthcare. Finally, six countries made commitments on cross-cutting policy approaches, which include enforcement of laws on human immunodeficiency virus (HIV)/AIDS and the adoption of best-practice policies for fighting malaria.[28]

Mental Health Action Plan, 2013–2020[29]

Mental health is an integral part of health and well-being, as reflected in the definition of health in the Constitution of the WHO: 'Health is a state of complete physical, mental and social well-being and not merely the absence of disease or infirmity.'[30] Mental health, like other aspects of health, can be affected by a range of socio-economic factors that need to be addressed through comprehensive strategies for promotion, prevention, treatment, and recovery in a whole-of-government

---

[25] WHO, 'WHO Global Plan of Action for Children's Health and the Environment (2010–2015)'. Available at http://www.who.int/ceh/cehplanaction10_15.pdf (accessed on 20 October 2015).

[26] WHO, 'WHO Global Plan of Action'.

[27] WHO, 'WHO Global Plan of Action'.

[28] UN, *The Global Campaign for the Health Millennium Development Goals 2010: Putting the Global Strategy for Women's and Children's Health into Action* (Oslo: Ministry of Foreign Affairs, Government of Norway, 2010). Available at http://www.who.int/pmnch/topics/mdgs/2010globalcampaign.pdf (accessed on 11 October 2015).

[29] In May 2012, the Sixty-Fifth World Health Assembly adopted resolution WHA65.4 on the global burden of mental disorders and the need for a comprehensive, coordinated response from health and social sectors at the country level.

[30] WHO, *Mental Health Action Plan 2013–2020*, [NLM classification: WM 101). Available at http://apps.who.int/iris/bitstream/10665/89966/1/9789241506021_eng.pdf?ua=1 (accessed on 11 October 2015).

approach.[31] The vision of the action plan is a world in which mental health is valued, promoted, and protected, mental disorders are prevented, and persons affected by these disorders are able to exercise the full range of human rights and access high-quality, culturally-appropriate health and social care in a timely way to promote recovery, in order to attain the highest possible level of health and participate fully in society and at work, free from stigmatization and discrimination. Its overall goal is to promote mental well-being, prevent mental disorders, provide care, enhance recovery, promote human rights, and reduce the mortality, morbidity, and disability for persons with mental disorders.[32] Children and adolescents with mental disorders should be provided with early intervention through evidence-based psycho-social and other non-pharmacological interventions based in the community, avoiding institutionalization and medicalization. Furthermore, interventions should respect the rights of children in line with the UNCRC and other international and regional human rights instruments.[33]

Some International Judgments on Health and Nutrition

Sawhoyamaxa Indigenous Community v. Paraguay[34]

The Sawhoyamaxa, an indigenous community in Paraguay, brought this case against the Paraguayan government for failing to ensure their ancestral property rights. The Sawhoyamaxa's claim for territorial rights had been pending since 1991. The lands at issue constituted their traditional habitat suitable for their subsistence activities, consisting of hunting, fishing, and gathering. The lands claimed were at the time owned by corporations, but were within the traditional lands the Sawhoyamaxa occupied prior to the non-indigenous possession of such lands in the nineteenth century. The state's failure to recognize the Sawhoyamaxa's title and possession of their lands had negative implications on their nutrition and health, and thus threatened their 'survival and integrity'. Waiting for the government to resolve their land claim, the Sawhoyamaxa were forced to live along the national road under extreme poverty, in non- hygienic conditions, and deprived from their traditional means of subsistence and basic services, such as access to healthcare and clean water. As result of their poor living conditions and the state's failure to take appropriate preventative measures, the Sawhoyamaxa experienced a number of deaths, particularly of children and the elderly, from diseases and epidemics such as tetanus, pneumonia, measles, bronchitis, serious dehydration, cachexia, and enterocolitis.

The Court found the State of Paraguay in violation of Article 4 (right to life) of the American Convention on Human Rights for failing to adopt the necessary measures to 'prevent or avoid risking' the right to life of the Sawhoyamaxa community. The Court held that the right to life is a fundamental and inalienable right and 'a pre-requisite for the enjoyment of other human rights'. Therefore, the right to life cannot be restricted, including in times of war, public danger, or other threats to the independence or security of the state. It is significant to note that the right to life cannot be restricted in war, public danger, and internal disturbances.

---

[31] WHO, *Mental Health Action Plan*.
[32] The Global Campaign, 'Putting the Global Strategy'.
[33] The Global Campaign, 'Putting the Global Strategy'.
[34] Inter-Am. Ct. H.R. (ser. C) No. 146 (29 March 2006).

In this case the court has stretched the fact that failure by the state to recognize the land claim of an indigenous community including children threatened their survival and integrity and was violative of the right to life as it had negative implications on their nutrition and health, and thus threatened their 'survival and integrity'.

BLAST and Anr. v. Government of Bangladesh[35]

The Petitioner, Bangladesh Legal Aid and Services Trust (BLAST), a public interest NGO, alleged that the Respondents (which included salt manufacturers and the Government) had violated the Iodine Deficiency Diseases Prevention Act, 1989. The act required edible salt to be iodized before sale, in order to combat iodine deficiency diseases such as goitre and cretinism among adults and children. However, on testing certain samples of salt manufactured by some of the Respondents, the Petitioner had found the iodine content to be lower than that mandated by the act. The Petitioner brought a case before the High Court, alleging a breach of the act by the salt manufacturers, and also brought a case against the Government for inaction in performing its monitoring duties under the act.

The Court noted that none of the Respondents had challenged the allegations or the validity of the rule, and as a result, accepted the allegations put by the Petitioner. It thus held that the salt manufacturers were defaulters under the act for not having produced salt with proportionate quantities of iodine. The Court also held the Government liable for not carrying out its mandated duties of regularly checking and testing salt samples. The Government was thus responsible for the consequences, such as an increase in iodine deficiency diseases, that followed from its inaction.

The Court directed the Government to perform its functions in accordance with the act and prosecute the offenders. The Government was also to ensure that unregistered edible salt manufacturers were penalized and not allowed to market or produce salt for human consumption. Further, the Government was to collect samples of edible salt currently in the market and test them for iodine content. The results of the same were to be submitted to the court twice a year.

This judgment held that in addition to the manufacturers, the Government was also responsible for not carrying out its mandatory duty of checking and testing the iodine content in the salt as iodine deficiency leads diseases such as goitre and cretinism among adults and children. It is significant in a country like India as well where there is iodine deficiency among pregnant woman and also new born children.

Yakye Axa Indigenous Community v. Paraguay[36]

The indigenous community of Yakye Axa, a traditional society of hunter-gatherers, was resettled as part of a development programme in Paraguay, which started in 1979. They were displaced to lands with a natural environment and resources that were different from the Yakye Axa's traditional territory, and incompatible with their traditional means of subsistence. They also faced poor living conditions. The lack of water and food in the settlement land caused the deaths of many children, youths, and elderly people in the community. In 1996, as part of their efforts

---

[35] 25 BLD (HDC) (2005) 83.
[36] Inter-Am. Ct. H.R. (ser. C) No. 125 (17 June 2005).

to reclaim their ancestral lands, the Yakye Axa left their settlement to reclaim their traditional lands, but were denied access to them. They resettled alongside a national road, facing the lands they attempted to resettle. They requested that the state legalize the ancestral lands for their community. At the temporary settlement, the Yakye Axa community also experienced 'extremely destitute' living conditions. The health of children and the elderly was particularly affected. They had no toilets or sanitary facilities, which created 'very deficient' hygienic conditions. The closest hospital for the community was about 70 kilometers away. Lack of adequate public transportation forced the Yakye Axa to travel 200 kilometers to reach the regional hospital. The community had no health centre or post and 'health promoters' did not visit the community on a regular basis. Upon the failure of the state to grant the rights of the Yakye Axa to these ancestral lands, the Yakye Axa filed petition before the Inter-American Commission on Human Rights. In turn, following the response of the state to the Report on the Merits issued by the Commission, the Commission submitted the case to the Inter-American Court of Human Rights.

The Court found the State of Paraguay in violation of Article 4 of the American Convention on Human Rights to the detriment of the Yakye Axa Community for failing to take the necessary measures to ensure them the 'possibility' of having a decent life. The Court recognized the right to life as 'crucial in the American Convention' on which other rights depend, and opined that restrictions on the right to life are inadmissible. The right to life guarantees every person not to be arbitrarily deprived of his/her life or subjected to conditions that 'impeded or obstruct access to a decent existence'. The state bears the duty as guarantor to create the 'minimum living conditions' that ensure human dignity and uphold the right to life. The state is expected to take 'positive, concrete measures' to fulfill the right to life, especially of those who are vulnerable and at risk, and 'whose care becomes a high priority'.

The deaths of children and elderly occurred due to lack of water and food in the community. This was due to displacement by the state and resettlement in a place with no access to minimum living conditions, which was violative of the right to life. It was held that the right to life guarantees every person not to be arbitrarily deprived of his/her life or be subjected to conditions that 'impeded or obstruct access to a decent existence'. This was another judgment in which the right to life had been held to be supreme and it implies that during displacement and resettlement of the children and families, the state must take the necessary measures to ensure for them the 'possibility' of having a decent life.

Children's Health Scenario in India

Some of the key indicators of children's health are as follows:[37]

- During 2009–10, majority of the states/union territories (UT) showed significant decline in Infant Mortality Rate (IMR), while only a few states where IMR was comparatively low, remained at the same level (Lakshadweep: IMR 25, Puducherry: IMR 22) or even showed

[37] Social Statistics Division, Central Statistics Office, Ministry of Statistics and Programme Implementation, 'Children in India 2012—A Statistical Appraisal', Government of India. Available at http://mospi.nic.in/Mospi_New/upload/Children_in_India_2012.pdf (accessed on 9 October 2015).

increase by one point (Kerala: IMR 13 in 2010 from 12 in 2009). IMR in 2010 was lowest in Goa (10), followed by Kerala (13) and Manipur (14). The states of Madhya Pradesh (62), Orissa (61), Uttar Pradesh (61), Assam (58), Meghalaya (55), Rajasthan (55), Chhattisgarh (51), Bihar (48), and Haryana (48) reported IMR above the national average (47). However, among these states, Bihar, Madhya Pradesh, Odisha, Rajasthan, and Uttar Pradesh have recorded noteworthy progress in bringing down their high IMR by 12 or more points since 2005.[38]

- The Under-Five Mortality Rate (U5MR) is the probability (expressed as a rate per 1,000 live births) of a child born in a specified year dying before reaching the age of five, if subjected to current age-specific mortality rates. Among children aged 0 to 4 years, the main causes of death are: certain infectious and parasitic diseases (A00–B99) (23.1 per cent), diseases of the respiratory system (16.1 per cent), diseases of the nervous system (12.1 per cent), diseases of the circulatory system (7.9 per cent), injury, Poisoning, and other factors (0.9 per cent), and other major causes (33.9 per cent).

- U5MR at the national level has declined during the last decade. Sample Registration System (SRS)-based U5MR in India for the year 2010 stands at 59 and varies from 66 in rural areas to 38 in urban areas. Within a span of the last 2 years, U5MR has declined by 10 percentage points as against a drop of 5 points in the preceding 3 years. The U5MR is higher for females than males, as in 2010, it stood at 64 for females against 55 for males.

- The male–female gap in U5MR was more in rural areas than in urban areas.[39]

- As per SRS Report 2010,[40] at the national level, the death rate (deaths per thousand) in 5–14 years age group is estimated to be 0.9. Rural–urban differentials exist, with the urban areas registering significantly lower death rates (0.6) as compared to those in rural areas (1.0). Among the bigger states, the lowest death rate in this age group is registered in Kerala (0.3), followed by Tamil Nadu, (0.5), Punjab (0.5), and Maharashtra (0.5), while the highest rate is observed in Jharkhand (1.4), followed by Odisha (1.3), and Uttar Pradesh (1.3). Other bigger states figure in between these states.[41]

  - The coverage evaluation survey 2009 (UNICEF and the Government of India) reveals the immunization coverage rates for each type of vaccination, according to either immunization card or mother's recall. The analysis of vaccine-specific data indicates higher coverage of each type of vaccine in urban areas than in rural areas. According to the primary immunization schedule, the child should be fully vaccinated by the time he/she is 12 months old. Full immunization includes one dose of BCG (Bacillus Calmette-Guerin), three injections of DPT (diphtheria, pertussis, and tetanus), three dozes of polio, and one injection of measles.[42]

- At the national level, 61 per cent of the children aged 12–23 months have received full immunization. The coverage of immunization was higher in urban areas (67.4 per cent), compared to that in the rural areas (58.5 per cent). It is a matter of concern that nearly 8 per cent

---

[38] Ministry of Statistics and Programme Implementation, 'Children in India 2012'.

[39] Ministry of Statistics and Programme Implementation, 'Children in India 2012'.

[40] SRS.

[41] SRS.

[42] Ministry of Statistics and Programme Implementation, 'Children in India 2012'.

children did not receive even a single vaccine. Nearly 62 per cent of the male children aged 12–23 months have received full immunization, while among the females it was nearly 60 per cent. It is shocking to note that the birth order of the child still continues to affect the immunization coverage. While 67.4 per cent of first-birth order children are fortunate enough to receive full immunization, only 40.4 per cent in the category of birth order 4 and above are covered under full immunization.[43]

- Mother's education also has a significant role in ensuring full immunization coverage to their children. The full immunization coverage of children aged 12–23 months stood at 76.6 per cent for mothers with education of 12 or more years, whereas for mothers who had no education, only 45.3 per cent of children got full immunization.[44]
- The full immunization coverage of children aged 12–23 months is highest in Goa (87.9 per cent), followed by Sikkim (85.3 per cent), Punjab (83.6 per cent), and Kerala (81.5 per cent). The full immunization coverage is lowest in Arunachal Pradesh (24.8 per cent).[45]
- An attempt is made in the Coverage Evaluation Survey 2009 to analyse at what stage the children dropped out and did not get all vaccines. The BCG–measles drop-out rate is found to be 14.7 per cent and 17.7 per cent children dropped out between BCG and DPT3, 10.3 per cent between DPT1 and Measles, and 13.3 per cent between DPT1 and DPT3. The data further reveals that drop out rate increases with birth order, and decreases with better education of the mother and better economic conditions of the family. Drop out rate is more among rural children (15.8 per cent) than among urban children (12.2 per cent).[46]
- It was evident from the 2008/09 HIV estimates (latest Sentinel surveillance rounds) in 2009 that the number of HIV infections has decreased from 2.442 million in 2008 to 2.395 million in 2009. However, the percentage distribution of HIV infections for the age group 0–15 years has increased from 4.2 per cent in 2008 to 4.36 per cent in 2009, indicating increased number of HIV-infected children in 2009, which is a matter of concern.[47]

In spite of the recent progress in the health sector, as exhibited by the above-mentioned statistical indicators, the situation is not adequate to ensure a bright future for the children of India. This is a multifaceted problem which is directly linked, to a large extent, to the mother's health conditions and safe delivery conditions, and also to the socio-economic conditions of the family, along with the country's healthcare system. Over time, the nation has implemented a number of child-centric programmes, but much remains to be done to guarantee better health conditions to the children.[48]

National Policies, Charters, and Action Plans

National health policies, strategies, and plans play an essential role in defining a country's vision, priorities, budgetary decisions, and course of action for improving and maintaining the health of

[43] Ministry of Statistics and Programme Implementation, 'Children in India 2012'.
[44] Ministry of Statistics and Programme Implementation, 'Children in India 2012'.
[45] Ministry of Statistics and Programme Implementation, 'Children in India 2012'.
[46] Ministry of Statistics and Programme Implementation, 'Children in India 2012'.
[47] Ministry of Statistics and Programme Implementation, 'Children in India 2012'.
[48] Ministry of Statistics and Programme Implementation, 'Children in India 2012'.

its people. Most countries have been using the development of national health policies, strategies, and plans for decades to give direction and coherence to their efforts to improve health. Until 1983, India did not have a formal national health policy (NHP). The health sector was developed through the discussions of the Central Council of Health and Family Welfare, the Planning Commission, and the occasional committees constituted by the central government.

National Health Policy, 1983

In its first NHP, India was committed to attaining the goal of 'Health for All by the Year 2000' through the universal provision of comprehensive PHC services. The main focus was the formulation of an integrated and comprehensive approach towards future development of health services. The policy aimed at a thorough overhaul of the existing approaches to education and training of medical and health personnel and reorganization of health infrastructure. It envisaged the complete integration of all plans for health and human development with the overall national socio-economic development process, integrating all health-related sectors. With multi-sectoral approach, the policy sought to provide universal, comprehensive PHC services relevant to the actual needs and priorities of the community at a cost which the people can afford, ensuring that the planning and implementation of the various health programmes are through the organized involvement and participation of the community, adequately utilizing the services being rendered by private voluntary organizations active in the health sector. Accordingly, the goals were set to achieve 'Health for All by 2000'.

In the realm of primary healthcare, the Policy recognized the need for comprehensive PHC with special emphasis, besides the curative aspect of health, on preventive, promotive, and rehabilitative aspects of health. It also focused on decentralized primary healthcare with people's involvement in the identification of their health needs and priorities and in the implementation and management of the various health programmes.

Government initiatives in the public health sector have recorded some noteworthy successes over time. Smallpox and Guinea worm disease have been eradicated from the country; polio is on the verge of being eradicated; leprosy, kala-azar, and filariasis can be expected to be eliminated in the foreseeable future. There has been a substantial drop in the Total Fertility Rate (TFR) and IMR. The success of the initiatives taken in the public health field are reflected in the progressive improvement of many demographic/epidemiological/infrastructural indicators over time,[49] as may be seen from Table 8.1.

In respect of TB, the public health scenario has not shown any significant decline in the pool of infection among the community, and there has been a distressing trend in the increase of drug resistance to the type of infection prevailing in the country. A new and extremely virulent communicable disease, HIV/AIDS, has emerged on the health scene since the declaration of the NHP 1983. As there is no existing therapeutic cure or vaccine for this infection, the disease constitutes a serious threat not merely to public health but to economic development in the country. The common waterborne infections—gastroenteritis, cholera, and some forms of hepatitis—continue

[49] Available at http://childlineindia.org.in/CP-CR-Downloads/National_Health_policy_2002.pdf (accessed on 12 October 2016).

Table 8.1 Achievements through the Years: 1951–2000[50]

Demographic indicator	1951	1981	2000
Life expectancy	36.7	54	64.6
Crude birth rate	40.8	33.9	26.1
Crude death rate	25	12.5	8.7
IMR	146	110	70

to contribute to a high level of morbidity in the population, even though the mortality rate may have been somewhat moderated.

Another area of grave concern in the public health domain is the persistent incidence of macro and micro-nutrient deficiencies, especially among women and children. In the vulnerable sub-category of women and the girl child, this has a multiplier effect through the birth of low-birth-weight babies and serious ramifications of the consequential mentally and physically retarded growth.[51]

National Nutrition Policy, 1993[52]

The Nutrition Policy of 1993 outlines the nutritional status of children in India. In 1993 there were already a number of mechanisms in place to address the issue of malnutrition and under-nutrition, such as the Integrated Child Development Services (ICDS) scheme, Special Nutrition Programme, the Wheat Based Nutrition Programme, and others. The policy outlines a few additional provisions to ensure proper nutrition of all populations.[53]

Under the direct, short-term services section, the policy calls for the need to expand the ICDS and similar programmes to cover the actual population of children in India. It is also required that mothers be given the proper information and support to provide for their children by growth monitoring for effective nutrition. Adolescent girls and expecting mothers also need to be taken into the purview of programmes. Food provided to society needs to fortify against nutrient loss, low-cost nutritious food needs to be produced for poorer families, and programmes should attempt to address and prevent nutrient deficiencies especially among women, expecting and nursing mothers, and children.[54]

Under indirect long-term and structural changes, the policy calls for the establishment of food security reserves. The dietary patterns of people need to be adjusted for better health by producing healthier food, increasing agriculture input to yield high-nutrient foods, and aligning

---

[50] Source: SRS, SRS Bulletin Vital Statistics, Registrar General of India (RGI).

[51] Jan Swasthya Sabha, *Whatever Happened to Health for All by 2000?* (Chennai: National Co., 2000).

[52] Department of Women and Child Development, MHRD, *National Nutrition Policy 1993*, Government of India, New Delhi, 1993. Available at http://www.childlineindia.org.in/National-Nutrition-Policy-1993.htm (accessed on 15 October 2015).

[53] MHRD, *National Nutrition Policy 1993*.

[54] MHRD, *National Nutrition Policy 1993*.

the food and agricultural policies to the nutritional needs of the nation. There is a need for poverty alleviation programmes and a functional public distribution system to ensure that poor families are capable of buying food. There is need for basic land reforms to address the needs of the landless poor. Health services under the Health and Family Welfare Ministry also tie into the nutritional needs of the population and hence should be strengthened. Awareness about basic health and nutrition is vital to a healthier population. There is also a need to strengthen surveillance of nutrition especially of children, adolescent girls, and pregnant mothers. Other areas that require government implementation, intervention, and assistance are monitoring of programmes, administrating minimum wage, insuring effective community participation, and education.[55]

To ensure its implementation, the Policy outlines the need for inter-ministerial coordination through the establishment of a committee, the constitution of a National Nutrition Council, various tasks for the state governments, and proper monitoring of children's nutritional status.[56]

National Health Policy, 2002

The NHP, 1983, in a spirit of optimistic empathy for the health needs of the people, particularly the poor and underprivileged, had hoped to provide 'Health for All by 2000' through the universal provision of comprehensive PHC services. The NHP, 2002 has attempted to set out a new policy framework for the accelerated achievement of public health goals in the socioeconomic circumstances currently prevailing in the country.

The NHP, 2002 has been formulated taking into consideration the ground realities in regard to the availability of resources. In the period when centralized planning was accepted as a key instrument of development in the country, the attainment of an equitable regional distribution was considered one of its major objectives. Despite this conscious focus in the development process, the attainment of health indices has been very uneven across the rural–urban divide.

The NHP, 2002 also envisages giving priority to school health programmes which aim at preventive health education, providing regular health check-ups, and promotion of health-seeking behaviour among children. The school health programmes can gainfully adopt specially designed modules in order to disseminate information relating to 'health' and 'family life'. This is expected to be the most cost-effective intervention as it improves the level of awareness not only of the extended family, but of the future generation as well.

It is widely accepted that school and college students are the most impressionable targets for imparting information relating to the basic principles of preventive healthcare. The policy will attempt to target this group to improve the general level of awareness in regard to 'health-promoting' behaviour.

Social, cultural, and economic factors continue to inhibit women from gaining adequate access even to the existing public health facilities. This handicap has an adverse impact on the health, general well-being, and development of the entire family, particularly children. This policy

---

[55] MHRD, *National Nutrition Policy 1993*.
[56] MHRD, *National Nutrition Policy 1993*.

recognizes the catalytic role of empowered women in improving the overall health standards of the community, including children.[57]

Efforts made over the years for improving health standards have been partially neutralized by the rapid growth of the population. The government has separately announced the 'National Population Policy 2000' (NPP 2000). The principal common features covered under the NPP, 2000 and NHP, 2002 relate to the prevention and control of communicable diseases, giving priority to the containment of HIV/AIDS infection, the universal immunization of children against all major preventable diseases, addressing the unmet needs for basic and reproductive health services, and supplementation of infrastructure. The synchronized implementation of these two policies—the NPP, 2000 and the NHP, 2002—will be the very cornerstone of any national structural plan to improve the health standards of children in the country.

National Population Policy, 2000

The NPP, 2000 recognizes the link between high infant mortality and excessive population growth. The policy statement committed the nation to a reduction of the IMR to under 30 per 1,000 by the year 2010. This necessitates a rapid reduction in neonatal deaths, which form a major component of infant mortality. The policy also aimed to achieve 80 per cent deliveries in institutions and 100 per cent deliveries by trained personnel by the year 2010. In pursuance of the NPP, 2000, the government has constituted the National Technical Committee on Child Health with a view to harnessing professional inputs regarding implementation of programmes for child survival, with special focus on newborn health.

National Plan of Action for Children, 2005

The NPAC, 2005 is the most comprehensive planning document concerning children. Its value is that it clearly outlines goals, objectives, and strategies to achieve the objectives outlined and recognizes the needs of all children up to the age of 18. It is divided into four basic child right categories as per the UNCRC: child survival, child development, child protection, and child participation.[58]

The NPAC, 2005 is divided into the following four sections; and all categories of rights apply to all age groups, including before birth.[59]

- Child survival;
- Child development;

[57] Ministry of Health and Family Welfare, 'Draft National Health Policy, 2001', Government of India. Available at www.mohfw.nic.in (accessed on 2 February 2017).

[58] ChildLine India Foundation, 'Child Protection & Child Rights, National Mechanisms Child Related Policies, National Plan of Action 2005', Mumbai, India. Available at http://www.childlineindia.org.in/National-Plan-of-Action-2005.htm (accessed on 10 October 2015).

[59] Ministry of Women and Child Development, 'National Plan of Action for Children, 2005', Government of India, New Delhi. Available at http://www.wcd.nic.in/NAPAug16A.pdf (accessed on 10 October 2015).

- Child protection;
- Child participation.

The guiding principles of the NPAC, 2005 are:[60]

- To regard the child as an asset and a person with human rights.
- To address issues of discrimination emanating from biases of gender, class, caste, race, religion, and legal status in order to ensure equality.
- To accord utmost priority to the most disadvantaged, poorest of the poor, and least served child in all policy and programmatic interventions.
- To recognize the diverse stages and settings of childhood, and address the needs of each, providing to all children the entitlements that fulfill their rights and meet their needs in each situation.

The plan identifies 12 key areas, keeping in mind priorities and the intensity of the challenges that require utmost and sustained attention in terms of outreach, programme interventions, and resource allocation, so as to achieve the necessary targets and ensure the rights and entitlements of children at each stage of childhood.[61] These are:

- Reducing IMR.
- Reducing Maternal Mortality Rate (MMR).
- Reducing malnutrition among children.
- Achieving 100 per cent civil registration of births.
- Universalization of early childhood care and development, and quality education for all children, achieving 100 per cent access and retention in schools, including pre-schools.[62]
- Complete abolition of female foeticide, female infanticide, and child marriage, and ensuring the survival, development, and protection of the girl child.
- Improving water and sanitation coverage in both rural and urban areas.
- Addressing and upholding the rights of Children in Difficult Circumstances.
- Securing for all children all legal and social protection from all kinds of abuse, exploitation, and neglect.[63]
- Complete abolition of child labour with the aim of progressively eliminating all forms of economic exploitation of children.
- Monitoring, review, and reform of policies, programmes, and laws to ensure protection of children's interests and rights.
- Ensuring child participation and choice in matters and decisions affecting their lives.

[60] Ministry of Women and Child Development, 'National Plan of Action for Children, 2005'.
[61] Ministry of Women and Child Development, 'National Plan of Action for Children, 2005'.
[62] Ministry of Women and Child Development, 'National Plan of Action for Children, 2005'.
[63] Ministry of Women and Child Development, 'National Plan of Action for Children, 2005'.

National Vaccine Policy, 2011[64]

Universal childhood immunization has been accepted by world public health leaders as both an affordable and cost-effective strategy not only for child survival but also for promoting PHC. This document covers all categories of vaccine, vaccines being used in Universal Immunisation Programme (UIP),[65] vaccines available but not part of UIP (both new and underutilized), and those vaccines which are likely to become available in the future. The document also touches the aspects related to vaccine security in the country and vaccination programme in broader framework of the NHP. The National Vaccine Program (NVP) will be widely disseminated among policy makers and programme managers. This document will be utilized for the drafting of the strategies and operational plans. This will be key document which will be utilized for harmonizing other policy and planning documents. For each area, a number of monitoring indicators will be prepared and progress on this document will be monitored accordingly. This will include a summary of progress, identified areas where progress is lagging, and proposal for corrective actions, where needed. There are multiple stakeholders, including national and state governments and development partners, in the immunization programme in India. The Union and state governments are involved in all aspects of the programme, while the role of development partners most often comprise providing technical assistance and support, rather than direct implementation. While the policy implementation will be monitored on a regular basis, this policy will be reviewed after periodic intervals, allowing changes to be made, which respond to the reality of the-then health policy environment in the country.[66]

Child Health in the Twelfth Five Year Plan (2012–17)

The Twelfth Plan suggested the following reforms in public health system with regard to children:[67]

- Full immunization among children under 3 years of age, and pregnant women.[68]
- Full antenatal, natal, and post-natal care.[69]

[64] Ministry of Health and Family Welfare, 'National Vaccine Policy', Government of India, April 2011. Available at http://mohfw.nic.in/showfile.php?lid=900 (accessed on 11 October 2015).

[65] The UIP is a vaccination programme launched by the Government of India in 1985. It became part of Child Survival and Safe Motherhood Programme in 1992 and is currently one of the key areas under the National Rural Health Mission (NRHM) since 2005. The programme consists of vaccination for seven diseases: TB, diphtheria, pertussis (whooping cough), tetanus, poliomyelitis, measles, and Hepatitis B. Hepatitis B was added to UIP in 2007. Thus, UIP has seven vaccine-preventable diseases in the programme. In 2014, it was announced that four vaccines will also be added to the programme, namely rotavirus, rubella, and Japanese encephalitis, as well as the injectable polio vaccine. Ministry of Health and Family Welfare, 'Universal Immunization Program', Government of India. Available at http://mohfw.nic.in/WriteReadData/l892s/Immunization_UIP.pdf (accessed on 3 March 2017).

[66] Ministry of Health and Family Welfare, 'National Vaccine Policy', Government of India, April 2011. Available at http://mohfw.nic.in/showfile.php?lid=900 (accessed on 11 October 2015).

[67] Planning Commission, Government of India, *Twelfth Five Year Plan (2012–2017): Social Sectors*, Volume III (New Delhi: SAGE Publications India Pvt. Ltd). Available at http://planningcommission.gov.in/plans/planrel/12thplan/pdf/12fyp_vol3.pdf (accessed on 10 October 2015).

[68] Planning Commission, *Twelfth Five Year Plan*.

[69] Planning Commission, *Twelfth Five Year Plan*.

- Skilled birth attendance with a facility for meeting needs for emergency obstetric care.
- Iron and folic acid supplementation for children, adolescent girls, and pregnant women.
- Regular treatment of intestinal worms, especially in children and reproductive-age women.
- Universal use of iodine and iron fortified salt.[70]
- Vitamin A supplementation for children aged 9 to 59 months.[71]
- Access to a basket of contraceptives and safe abortion services.[72]
- Preventive and promotive health educational services, including information on hygiene, hand-washing, dental hygiene, use of potable drinking water, avoidance of tobacco, alcohol, high calorie diet and obesity, need for regular physical exercise, use of helmets on two-wheelers and seat belts; advice on initiation of breastfeeding within one hour of birth and exclusively up to 6 months of age, and complimentary feeding thereafter, adolescent sexual health, awareness about Reproductive Tract Infection (RTI)/Sexually Transmitted Infection (STI); and the need for screening for non-communicable diseases (NCDs) and common cancers for those at risk.[73]
- Home-based newborn care, and encouragement for exclusive breastfeeding till 6 months of age.[74]
- Community-based care for sick children, with referral of cases requiring higher levels of care.[75]
- HIV testing and counselling during antenatal care.[76]
- Free drugs to pregnant HIV-positive mothers to prevent mother-to-child transmission of HIV.[77]
- Malaria prophylaxis, using Long Lasting Insecticide Treated Nets (LLIN), diagnosis using Rapid Diagnostic Kits (RDK), and appropriate treatment.[78]
- School check-up of health and wellness, followed by advice, and treatment if necessary.
- Management of diarrhoea, especially in children, using ORS.[79]
- Diagnosis and treatment of TB and leprosy, including drug and multi-drug resistant cases.[80]
- Vaccines for Hepatitis B and C for high risk groups.[81]
- Patient transport systems including emergency response ambulance services of the 'dial 108' model.[82]

---

[70] Planning Commission of India, *Twelfth Five Year Plan.*
[71] Planning Commission of India, *Twelfth Five Year Plan.*
[72] Planning Commission of India, *Twelfth Five Year Plan.*
[73] Planning Commission of India, *Twelfth Five Year Plan.*
[74] Planning Commission of India, *Twelfth Five Year Plan.*
[75] Planning Commission of India, *Twelfth Five Year Plan.*
[76] Planning Commission of India, *Twelfth Five Year Plan.*
[77] Planning Commission of India, *Twelfth Five Year Plan.*
[78] Planning Commission of India, *Twelfth Five Year Plan.*
[79] Planning Commission of India, *Twelfth Five Year Plan.*
[80] Planning Commission of India, *Twelfth Five Year Plan.*
[81] Planning Commission of India, *Twelfth Five Year Plan.*
[82] Planning Commission of India, *Twelfth Five Year Plan.*

Health Outcome Goals Established in the Twelfth Five Year Plan

- Reduction of IMR to 25 per 1,000 live births by 2017.
- Reduction in MMR to 100 per 100,000 live births by 2017.
- Reduction in TFR to 2.1 by 2017.

National Policy for Children, 2013[83]

The National Charter for Children, 2003, adopted on 9 February 2004, underlined the intent to secure for every child its inherent right to be a child and enjoy a healthy and happy childhood, to address the root causes that negate the healthy growth and development of children, and to awaken the conscience of the community in the wider societal context to protect children from all forms of abuse, while strengthening the family, society, and the nation. To affirm the government's commitment to the rights-based approach in addressing the continuing and emerging challenges in the situation of children, the Government of India adopted the Resolution on the National Policy for Children, 2013.[84]

Survival, health, nutrition, development, education, protection, and participation are the undeniable rights of every child and are the key priorities of this policy. This policy suggested the following measures to the states with regard to the health of children:[85]

1. Improve maternal healthcare, including antenatal care, safe delivery by skilled health personnel, postnatal care, and nutritional support.[86]
2. Provide universal access to information and services for making informed choices related to birth and spacing of children.[87]
3. Secure the right of the girl child to life, survival, health, and nutrition.[88]
4. Address key causes and determinants of child mortality through interventions based on continuum of care, with emphasis on nutrition, safe drinking water, sanitation, and health education.[89]
5. Encourage focused behaviour change communication efforts to improve new born and childcare practices at the household and community level.[90]
6. Provide universal and affordable access to services for prevention, treatment, care, and management of neonatal and childhood illnesses and protect children from all water-borne, vector-borne, blood-borne, communicable, and other childhood diseases.[91]

---

[83] Ministry of Women and Child Development, 'The National Policy for Children, 2013', Government of India. Available at http://wcd.nic.in/childwelfare/npc2013dtd29042013.pdf (accessed on 10 October 2015).

[84] Ministry of Women and Child Development, 'The National Policy for Children, 2013'.

[85] Ministry of Women and Child Development, 'The National Policy for Children, 2013'.

[86] Ministry of Women and Child Development, 'The National Policy for Children, 2013'.

[87] Ministry of Women and Child Development, 'The National Policy for Children, 2013'.

[88] Ministry of Women and Child Development, 'The National Policy for Children, 2013'.

[89] Ministry of Women and Child Development, 'The National Policy for Children, 2013'.

[90] Ministry of Women and Child Development, 'The National Policy for Children, 2013'.

[91] Ministry of Women and Child Development, 'The National Policy for Children, 2013'.

7. Prevent disabilities, both mental and physical, through timely measures for prenatal, perinatal and postnatal health and nutritional care of mother and child, provide services for early detection, treatment, and management, including interventions, to minimize and prevent further disabilities, prevent discrimination faced by children with disabilities (mental and physical), and provide services for rehabilitation and social support.[92]

8. Ensure availability of essential services, supports and provisions for nutritive attainment in a life-cycle approach, including infant and young child feeding (IYCF) practices, special focus on adolescent girls and other vulnerable groups, and special measures for the healthcare, and nutrition, including nutrition education, of expectant and nursing mothers.[93]

9. Provide adolescents access to information, support, and services essential for their health and development, including information and support on appropriate lifestyle and healthy choices and awareness on the ill effects of alcohol and substance abuse.[94]

10. Prevent HIV infections at birth and ensure that infected children receive medical treatment, adequate nutrition, and after-care, and are not discriminated against in accessing their rights.[95]

11. Ensure that only child-safe products and services are available in the country and put in place mechanisms to enforce safety standards for products and services designed for children.[96]

12. Provide adequate safeguards and measures against false claims relating to growth, development, and nutrition.[97]

India Newborn Action Plan, 2014

The India Newborn Action Plan (INAP) is India's committed response to the global Every Newborn Action Plan (ENAP), launched in June 2014 at the 67th World Health Assembly, to advance the Global Strategy for Women's and Children's Health. The ENAP sets forth a vision of a world that has eliminated preventable newborn deaths and stillbirths.[98]

The INAP lays out a vision and a plan for India to end preventable newborn deaths, accelerate progress, and scale up high-impact yet cost-effective interventions. The INAP has a clear vision supported by goals, strategic intervention packages, priority actions, and a monitoring framework. For the first time, INAP also articulates the Government of India's specific attention on preventing stillbirths.[99]

India's continuous commitment and ongoing efforts to reduce child mortality and morbidity have resulted in a 59 per cent reduction in U5MR since 1990. India has proven that it can reach

[92] Ministry of Women and Child Development, 'The National Policy for Children, 2013'.
[93] Ministry of Women and Child Development, 'The National Policy for Children, 2013'.
[94] Ministry of Women and Child Development, 'The National Policy for Children, 2013'.
[95] Ministry of Women and Child Development, 'The National Policy for Children, 2013'.
[96] Ministry of Women and Child Development, 'The National Policy for Children, 2013'.
[97] Ministry of Women and Child Development, 'The National Policy for Children, 2013'.
[98] Child Health Division, Ministry of Health and Family Welfare, 'India Newborn Action Plan' (INAP), Government of India, New Delhi, September 2014. Available at http://www.newbornwhocc.org/INAP_Final.pdf (accessed on 10 October 2015).
[99] Child Health Division, 'INAP'.

even the most hard-to-reach and vulnerable children with affordable life-saving interventions, as is also evident from its polio eradication strategies. The INAP aims for the following:[100]

- Building on existing commitments under the National Health Mission and 'Call to Action' for child survival and development.[101]
- Alignment with the ENAP; defining commitments based on specific contextual needs of the country.[102]
- Attaining Single Digit Neonatal Mortality Rate by 2030, 5 years ahead of the global plan.[103]
- Emphasizing on strengthened surveillance mechanism for tracking stillbirths.[104]
- Focusing on ending preventable newborn deaths, improving quality of care, and care beyond survival.[105]
- Prioritizing those babies that are born too soon, too small, or sick, as they account for majority of all newborn deaths.[106]
- Aspiring towards ensuring equitable progress for girls and boys, rural and urban, rich and poor, and between districts and states.[107]
- Identifying major guiding principles under the overarching principle of Integration: Equity, Gender, Quality of Care, Convergence, Accountability, and Partnerships.[108]
- Defining six pillars of interventions: Pre-conception and antenatal care; care during labour and child birth; immediate newborn care; care of healthy newborn; care of small and sick newborn; and are beyond newborn survival.[109]
- Serving as a framework for states/districts to develop their own action plan with measurable indicators.[110]

National Mental Health Policy, 2014:[111]
This policy recognizes the following concerns relating to children:

- The mental health of children in institutions and rescue homes under Juvenile Justice (Care and Protection) Act (JJ Act), 2000 due to the deprivation of their liberty in custody.

[100] Child Health Division, 'INAP'.
[101] Child Health Division, 'INAP'.
[102] Child Health Division, 'INAP'.
[103] Child Health Division, 'INAP'.
[104] Child Health Division, 'INAP'.
[105] Child Health Division, 'INAP'.
[106] Child Health Division, 'INAP'.
[107] Child Health Division, 'INAP'.
[108] Child Health Division, 'INAP'.
[109] Child Health Division, 'INAP'.
[110] Child Health Division, 'INAP'.
[111] Department of Health and Family Welfare, Ministry of Health and Family Welfare, 'National Mental Health Policy 2014', Government of India. Available at http://www.mohfw.nic.in/index1.php?lang=1&level=2&sublinkid=4723&lid=2964 (accessed on 11 October 2015).

- The children of persons with mental health problem are vulnerable and their needs must be adequately addressed. It also recognizes that if the caregiver is no more, the children lack critical support system.

Draft National Health Policy, 2015 for India

The draft NHP, 2015 comes at a critical juncture in India's development trajectory. Since the formulation of the last NHP in 2002, there have been significant achievements in eradicating polio, arresting the spread of HIV and AIDS, raising the proportion of safe deliveries, reducing U5MR, expanding health service delivery infrastructure, and increasing human resources for health, among others. At the same time, however, private provision and utilization of healthcare services has increased, resulting in very high out-of-pocket share in total health expenditure. India still has a long way to go to provide quality health services and reduce the financial burden of health expenditure, especially on the poor. Therefore, India's health system, especially the financing and delivery of healthcare services, needs radical reform to achieve the objectives of universal health coverage that have, in large part, motivated the draft NHP, 2015.[112]

Significant Provisions of the Draft National Health Policy, 2015[113]

- The draft NHP 2015 has proposed a target of raising public health expenditure to 2.5 per cent from the present 1.2 per cent of the gross domestic product (GDP). It also notes that 40 per cent of this would need to come from central expenditure.[114]
- The draft policy suggests making health a fundamental right similar to education, the denial of which should be punishable. The Centre shall enact, after due discussion and on the request of three or more states, a National Health Rights Act, which will ensure health as a fundamental right, whose denial will be justiciable.[115]
- As per the draft document, the government plans to rely mostly on general taxation for financing healthcare expenditure. With the projection of a promising economic growth, the fiscal capacity to provide this level of financing should become available.[116]
- The government is also keen to explore the creation of a health cess on the lines of education cess for raising money needed to fund the expenditure the policy would entail. Other than general taxation, this cess could mobilize contributions from specific commodity taxes such

[112] Anit Mukherjee, 'Comments on India's Draft National Health Policy 2015', Center for Global Development, Washington, DC, February 2015. Available at http://www.cgdev.org/sites/default/files/NHP_CGD%20Comments_25Feb15.pdf (last accessed on 10 October 2015).

[113] Ministry of Health and Family Welfare, 'National Health Policy 2015: Draft', Government of India. Available at http://www.mohfw.nic.in/showfile.php?lid=3014 (last accessed on 10 October 2015). The draft policy has been placed in the public domain until 28 February 2015 for public consultation. The new policy is being introduced almost 13 years after the last health policy was drafted.

[114] Ministry of Health and Family Welfare, 'National Health Policy 2015: Draft'.

[115] Ministry of Health and Family Welfare, 'National Health Policy 2015: Draft'.

[116] Ministry of Health and Family Welfare, 'National Health Policy 2015: Draft'.

as the taxes on tobacco and alcohol, from specific industries, and innovative forms of resource mobilization.[117]

• While there is intent to increase expenditure on healthcare, the draft policy also stresses on the role of the private sector. While the public sector is to focus on preventive and secondary care services, the document recommends contracting out services like ambulatory care, imaging and diagnostics, and tertiary care, down to non-medical services such as catering and laundry, to the private sector.[118]

As mentioned earlier, India's health systemneeds radical reform to achieve the objectives of universal health coverage that have, in large part, motivated the draft NHP 2015. States should be given the primary responsibility of implementing NHP and be provided with adequate funds to do so NHP-2015 should propose incentive-based payment for performance at the state level.

Government of India Programmes and Schemes

Integrated Child Development Services Scheme, 1975[119]

Children in the age group 0–6 years constitute around 158 million of the population of India (2011 Census). Launched on 2 October 1975, the ICDS Scheme is one of the flagship programmes of the Government of India and represents one of the world's largest and unique programmes for early childhood care and development. It is the foremost symbol of the country's commitment to its children and nursing mothers, as a response to the challenge of providing pre-school non-formal education on one hand, and breaking the vicious cycle of malnutrition, morbidity, reduced learning capacity, and mortality on the other. The beneficiaries under the Scheme are children in the age group of 0–6 years, pregnant women, and lactating mothers.[120] Objectives of the scheme are:

• To improve the nutritional and health status of children in the age group 0–6 years;
• To lay the foundation for proper psychological, physical, and social development of the children;[121]
• To reduce the incidence of mortality, morbidity, malnutrition, and school dropout;
• To achieve effective coordination of policy and implementation among the various departments to promote child development; and
• To enhance the capability of the mother to look after the normal health and nutritional needs of the child through proper nutrition and health education.[122]

---

[117] Ministry of Health and Family Welfare, 'National Health Policy 2015: Draft'.
[118] Ministry of Health and Family Welfare, 'National Health Policy 2015: Draft'.
[119] Ministry of Women and Child Development, 'Integrated Child Development Scheme', Government of India. Available at http://wcd.nic.in/icds/icds.aspx (accessed on 12 October 2015).
[120] Ministry of Women and Child Development, 'Integrated Child Development Scheme'.
[121] Ministry of Women and Child Development, 'Integrated Child Development Scheme'.
[122] Ministry of Women and Child Development, 'Integrated Child Development Scheme'.

The ICDS Scheme offers a package of six services, namely:[123]

- supplementary nutrition;
- pre-school non-formal education;
- nutrition and health education;
- immunization;
- health check-up; and
- referral services.

In 2001, the Supreme Court directed that ICDS be 'geographically universalized', that is, there must be an Anganwadi in each settlement.[124] In order to address various programmatic, management, and institutional gaps, and to meet administrative and operational challenges, the government has approved the Strengthening and Restructuring of ICDS Scheme during the Twelfth Five Year Plan.[125] Key features of Strengthened and Restructured ICDS include:

- Repositioning the Anganwadi Centre (AWC) as a 'vibrant Early Childhood Development Center (ECDC) centre', to become the first village outpost for health, nutrition, and early learning, minimum of six hours of working, among others
- Construction of AWC building and revision of rent, including upgradation, maintenance, improvement, and repair.
- Strengthening Package of Services—strengthening ECCE, focus on under-3s, care and nutrition counselling service for mothers of under-3s, and management of severe and moderate underweight children.
- Improving Supplementary Nutrition Programme with revision of cost norms.
- Management of severe and moderate underweight children—identification and management of severe and moderate underweights through community-based interventions, Sneha Shivirs, and so on.
- Strengthening training and capacity, as well as technical human resource and other resources..
- Enhancing the budgets.

To give a good start to a child, there is a need to focus further on the 0–2 age-group. For this, the outreach activities must be strengthened to ensure the ICDS functionaries do not miss out on the critical 0–2 age group and the families in their homes. There is also a need for promoting decentralization of administration, ensuring quality, participation of women's/mother's groups, and strengthening convergence with related schemes.[126]

---

[123] Ministry of Women and Child Development, 'Integrated Child Development Scheme'.

[124] *PUCL* v. *Union of India & Others*, Writ Petition (Civil) No. 196/2001. Anganwadi is a government sponsored child-care and mother-care centre in India. It caters to children in the 0–6 age group.

[125] Ministry of Women and Child Development, 'Strengthening and Restructuring of Integrated Child Development Services Scheme', Communication No. 1-8/2012-CD-1, dated 22 October 2012, Government of India.

[126] Ministry of Women and Child Development, 'Integrated Child Development Scheme'.

National Health Mission, 2013[127]

The National Health Mission (NHM) encompasses its two Sub-Missions, the NRHM and the National Urban Health Mission (NUHM). The main programmatic components include Health System Strengthening in rural and urban areas— reproductive–maternal–neonatal–child and adolescent health (RMNCH+A), and communicable diseases and NCDs. The NHM envisages achievement of universal access to equitable, affordable, and quality healthcare services that are accountable and responsive to people's needs.

Outcomes for NHM[128] in the 12th Plan are synonymous with those of the 12th Plan. The endeavor would be to ensure achievement of the following indicators:

1. Reduce MMR to 1/1,000 live births;
2. Reduce IMR to 25/1,000 live births;
3. Reduce TFR to 2.1;
4. Prevention and reduction of anaemia in women aged 15–49 years;
5. Prevent and reduce mortality and morbidity from communicable diseases, NCDs, injuries, and emerging diseases;
6. Reduce household out-of-pocket expenditure on total healthcare expenditure;
7. Reduce annual incidence and mortality from TB by half;
8. Reduce prevalence of leprosy to less than 1/10,000, and incidence to zero in all districts.

According to this mission:[129]

Specific goals for the states will be based on existing levels, capacity, and context. State-specific innovations will be encouraged. Process and outcome indicators will be developed to reflect equity, quality, efficiency, and responsiveness.

Targets for communicable diseases and NCDs will be set at the state level, based on local epidemiological patterns and taking into account the financing available for each of these conditions.[130]

One of the key components of the NRHM is to provide every village in the country with a trained female community health activist—ASHA, or Accredited Social Health Activist. Selected from the village itself and accountable to it, the ASHA will be trained to work as an interface between the community and the public health system.

[127] Ministry of Health and Family Welfare, 'A Strategic Approach to Reproductive, Maternal, Newborn, Child and Adolescent Health (RMNCH+A) in India', Government of India, January 2013. Available at http://nrhm.gov.in/nhm.html (accessed on 15 October 2015).

[128] The Union Cabinet, vide its decision dated 1 May 2013, has approved the launch of National Urban Health Mission (NUHM) as a Sub-mission of an over-arching NHM, with NRHM being the other sub-mission of NHM.

[129] Ministry of Health and Family Welfare, 'National Health Mission', Government of India. Available at http://nrhm.gov.in/nhm/about-nhm/goals.html (accessed on 15 October 2015).

[130] Ministry of Health and Family Welfare, 'National Health Mission'.

Janani Suraksha Yojana, 2005[131]

Janani Suraksha Yojana (JSY) is a safe motherhood intervention under the NRHM, being implemented with the objective of reducing maternal and neonatal mortality by promoting institutional delivery among poor pregnant women. The JSY encourages women to make use of public health facilities for safe delivery by providing cash assistance of Rs 1,400 in rural areas and Rs 1,000 in urban areas to cover wage loss and other expenses in the states of Bihar, Jharkhand, Rajasthan, Madhya Pradesh, Chhattisgarh, Odisha, Uttar Pradesh, Uttarakhand, Assam and Jammu and Kashmir. In the remaining states, pregnant women are entitled to Rs 700 in rural areas and Rs 600 in urban areas for giving birth in public health facilities. It also provides cash incentives to female community health workers for promoting safe care in pregnancy and facilitating access to institutional care.

Janani–Shishu Suraksha Karyakram, 2011[132]

Government of India has launched this cashless scheme on 1 June 2011 with utmost emphasis on entitlements and elimination of out of pocket expenses for both pregnant women and sick neonates.

Reproductive, Maternal, Newborn, Child and Adolescent Health RMNCH+A, 2013[133]

The RMNCH+A approach has been launched in 2013 and it essentially looks to address the major causes of mortality among women and children as well as the delays in accessing and utilizing healthcare and services. The RMNCH+A strategic approach has been developed to provide an understanding of 'continuum of care' to ensure equal focus on various life stages.[134] Priority interventions for each thematic area have been included in this to ensure that the linkages between them are contextualized to the same and consecutive life stage. It also introduces new initiatives like the use of Score Cards to track performance, the National Iron Plus Initiative to address the issue of anaemia across all age groups, and the Comprehensive Screening and Early interventions for defects at birth, diseases and deficiencies among children and adolescents. The RMNCH+A appropriately directs the states to focus their efforts on the most vulnerable population and disadvantaged groups in the country.[135] It also emphasizes on the need to reinforce efforts in those poor-performing districts that have already been identified as high focus districts.[136]

---

[131] Ministry of Health and Family Welfare, 'National Health Mission', Government of India. Available at http://nrhm.gov.in/nrhm-components/rmnch-a/maternal-health/janani-suraksha-yojana/background.html (accessed on 15 October 2015).

[132] Ministry of Health and Family Welfare, 'National Health Mission', Government of India. Available at http://nrhm.gov.in/janani-shishu-suraksha-karyakram.html (accessed on 15 October 2015).

[133] Ministry of Health and Family Welfare, 'A Strategic Approach to Reproductive, Maternal, Newborn, Child and Adolescent Health (RMNCH+A) in India', Government of India, February 2013. Available at http://rmncha.in/upload/Content/101.pdf (accessed on 15 October 2015).

[134] Ministry of Health and Family Welfare, 'A Strategic Approach'.

[135] Ministry of Health and Family Welfare, 'A Strategic Approach'.

[136] Ministry of Health and Family Welfare, 'A Strategic Approach'.

Laws on Child Health in India

The Constitution of India envisages the establishment of a new social order based on equality, freedom, justice, and dignity of the individual. It aims at the elimination of poverty, ignorance, and ill health, and directs the state to regard the raising of the level of nutrition and the standard of living of its people and the improvement of public health as among its primary duties. The provision of healthcare services is the responsibility of the state governments. The Ministry of Health and Family Welfare at the Centre is responsible for policy formulation and allocation of funds for certain health programmes.

Constitution of India and Right to Health

The right to health is not included directly as a fundamental right in the Indian Constitution. The Constitution makers imposed this duty on the state to ensure social and economic justice. Part four of the Constitution, which contains the Directive Principles of State Policy (DPSP), imposed the duty on the states. The Constitution of India does not provide for the right to health as a fundamental right. It directs the states to take measures to improve the condition of healthcare of the people.[137] Thus, the Preamble to the Constitution of India, inter alia, seeks to secure for all its citizens justice—social and economic. It provides a framework for the achievement of the objectives laid down in the Preamble. The Preamble has been amplified and elaborated in the DPSP.[138]

The Constitution of India, in Articles 39(e) and (f), provides that the state shall, in particular, direct its policy towards securing the health of children. Further, in Article 47,[139] the state is

[137] Article 39 in the Constitution of India: Certain principles of policy to be followed by the state: The state shall, in particular, direct its policy towards securing:

(e) that the health and strength of workers, men and women, and the tender age of children are not abused and that citizens are not forced by economic necessity to enter avocations unsuited to their age or strength;

(f) that children are given opportunities and facilities to develop in a healthy manner and in conditions of freedom and dignity and that childhood and youth are protected against exploitation and against moral and material abandonment.

[138] *Preamble to the Constitution of India:* We, the people of India, having solemnly resolved to constitute India into a [sovereign, socialist, secular, democratic, republic] and to secure to all its citizens:

Justice, social, economic and political;
Liberty of thought, expression, belief, faith and worship;
Equality of status and of opportunity;
and to promote among them all
Fraternity assuring the dignity of the individual and the [unity and integrity of the Nation];
in our Constituent Assembly this twenty-sixth day of November, 1949, do hereby adopt, enact and give to
ourselves this constitution.

[139] Article 47 of the Constitution of India is one of the Directive Principles which directs the state to raise the level of nutrition and the standard of living and to improve public health as among its primary

directed to raise the level of nutrition and the standard of living of its people. The improvement of public health is mentioned as among its primary duties and, in particular, the state is directed to endeavour to bring about prohibition of the consumption of intoxicating drinks and of drugs which are injurious to health, except for medicinal purposes. Unfortunately, in the Constitution of India, health is not a fundamental right of citizens and, therefore, cannot be justiciable in courts. The provision of healthcare is contained in the directive principles and it is a duty of the state to raise the level of nutrition and the standard of living, and to improve public health. Article 38[140] imposes liability on the state for securing a social order for the promotion of welfare of the people; but without public health, we cannot achieve it. This means that without public health, welfare of the people is impossible. Article 41[141] imposes the duty on the state for providing public assistance for those who are sick and disabled. Article 42[142] makes provisions to protect the health of infants and mothers through maternity benefit. Article 48A ensures that state shall endeavour to protect and improve pollution-free environment for good health.[143]

Some other provisions relating to health fall under the DPSP.[144] Article 47 of the Constitution states that it is the duty of the state to also raise the level of nutrition and the standard of living and to improve public health.

---

duties and, in particular, the state shall endeavour to bring about prohibition of intoxicating drinks and drugs which are injurious to health.

[140] Article 38 in the Constitution of India: State to secure a social order for the promotion of welfare of the people:

(1) The state shall strive to promote the welfare of the people by securing and protecting as effectively as it may a social order in which justice, social, economic, and political, shall inform all the institutions of the national life;

(2) The state shall, in particular, strive to minimize the inequalities in income, and endeavour to eliminate inequalities in status, facilities, and opportunities, not only among individuals but also among groups of people residing in different areas or engaged in different vocations.

[141] Article 41 provides the right to assistance in case of sickness and disablement. It runs thus: 'The state shall within the limits of its economic capacity and development, make effective provisions for securing the right to work, to education and to public assistance in case of unemployment, old age, sickness and disablement and in other cases of undeserved want.'

[142] Article 42 give the power to state to make provision for securing just and humane conditions of work and for maternity relief and for the protection of the environment, same as given by Article 48A; and the same obligation is imposed on Indian citizens by Article 51A(g).

[143] Article 48A in the Constitution of India: Protection and improvement of environment and safeguarding of forests and wild life: The state shall endeavour to protect and improve the environment and to safeguard the forests and wild life of the country.

[144] Article 39(e) in the Constitution of India: that the health and strength of workers, men and women, and the tender age of children are not abused and that citizens are not forced by economic necessity to enter avocations unsuited to their age or strength;

Article 39(f) in the Constitution of India: that children are given opportunities and facilities to develop in a healthy manner and in conditions of freedom and dignity and that childhood and youth are protected against exploitation and against moral and material abandonment.

The state shall, in particular, direct its policy towards securing health of workers. The state organized village panchayats and gave them powers and authority to function as units of self-government. This Directive Principle has now been translated into action through the 73rd Amendment Act, 1992 whereby Part IX of the Constitution, titled 'The Panchayats', was inserted. The panchayat system has significant implications for the health sector.[145] Not only the state, but the panchayat and the municipalities are also responsible for improving and protecting public health. Article 243G says, ' ... the Legislature of a state may, by law, endow the Panchayats with necessary power and authority ... in relation to the matters listed in the Eleventh Schedule'.[146]

The DPSP are only directives to the state. These are non-justifiable. No person can claim compensation for the state not fulfilling these directives. However, the Supreme Court has brought the right to health under the purview of Article 21 of the Constitution. Article 21 deals with

---

Article 42 in the Constitution of India: Provision for just and humane conditions of work and maternity relief: The state shall make provision for securing just and humane conditions of work and for maternity relief.

[145] Article 243 in the Constitution of India: Definitions: In this part, unless the context otherwise requires,

(a) district means a district in a state;
(b) gram sabha means a body consisting of persons registered in the electoral rolls relating to a village comprised within the area of panchayat at the village level;
(c) intermediate level means a level between the village and district levels specified by the governor of a state by public notification to be the intermediate level for the purposes of this part;
(d) panchayat means an institution (by whatever name called) of self-government constituted under article 243B, for the rural areas;
(e) panchayat area means the territorial area of a panchayat;
(f) population means the population as ascertained at the last preceding census of which the relevant figures have been published;
(g) village means a village specified by the governor by public notification to be a village for the purposes of this part and includes a group of villages so specified.

Article 243A in the Constitution of India: Gram sabha: A gram sabha may exercise such powers and perform such functions at the village level as the legislature of a state may by law, provide.

[146] The entries in this schedule having direct relevance to health are as follows:

5: Water supply for domestic industrial and commercial purpose.
6: Public health, sanitation conservancy, and solid waste management.
9: Safeguarding the interest of weaker sections of society, including the handicapped and mentally retarded.
11: Drinking.
16: Vital statistics including registration of births and deaths.
17: Regulation of slaughter-houses and tanneries.
23: Health and sanitation including hospitals, primary health centres, and dispensaries.
24: Family welfare.
25: Women and child development.
26: Social welfare, including welfare of the handicapped and mentally retarded.

'Right to Life', which is a fundamental right and justiciable in courts. The Supreme Court has observed 'that the right to life includes the right to live with human dignity and what goes along with it, namely, the bare necessaries of life such as adequate nutrition, clothing and shelter.'[147]

The Fundamental Right to Life, as stated in Article 21 of the Indian Constitution, guarantees to the individual her/his life and personal liberty except by a procedure established by law.[148] The scope of this provision is very wide. It prescribes for the right of life and personal liberty. The concept of personal liberty comprehends many rights related indirectly to life or liberty of a person, as well as the right to health. Thus, the right to health, along with numerous other civil, political, and economic rights, is afforded protection under the Indian Constitution.

Article 21 has been expanded by the Courts. The judiciary has clearly read into Article 21, the Right to Life, and the right to health. In fact, it has gone deeper into the meaning of health and has substantiated the meaning of the right to life. The Fundamental Right to Life, as stated in Article 21 of the Indian Constitution,[149] guarantees to the individual her/his life which or personal liberty except by a procedure established by law.

The Supreme Court has widely interpreted this fundamental right and has included in Article 21 the right to live with dignity and 'all the necessities of life such as adequate nutrition, clothing … .' It has also held that an act which affects the dignity of an individual will also violate her/his right to life. The Constitution incorporates provisions guaranteeing everyone's right to the highest attainable standard of physical and mental health. Article 21 guarantees protection of life and personal liberty to every citizen.

The Supreme Court, in *Bandhua Mukti Morcha* v. *Union of India*,[150] has held that the right to live with human dignity, enshrined in Article 21, is derived from the DPSPs, and therefore includes protection to health. In *Vincent Panikulangara* v. *Union of India*,[151] the Supreme Court of India observed on the right to healthcare: 'Maintenance and improvement of public health have to rank high as these are indispensable to the very physical existence of the community and on the betterment of these depends the building of the society of which the Constitution makers envisaged. Attending to public health in our opinion, therefore is of high priority—perhaps the one at the top.' In a historic judgment in *Consumer Education and Resource Centre* v. *Union of India*,[152] the Supreme Court has held that the right to health and medical care is a fundamental right under Article 21 of the Constitution, as it is essential for making the life of the workmen meaningful and purposeful with dignity of person. Right to Life in Article 21 includes protection of the health and strength of the worker. The expression 'life' in Article 21 does not connote mere animal existence. It has a much wider meaning which includes right to livelihood, better standard of life, hygienic conditions at the workplace, and leisure. The court held that the state, be it the Union or state government, or an industry, public or private, is enjoined to take all such action which will promote health, strength, and vigour of the workers during the period of employment,

---

[147] *Francis Coralie Mullin* v. *The Administrator, Union Territory of Delhi and others*, (1981) 1 SCC 608.

[148] Article 21 in the Constitution of India: Protection of life and personal liberty: No person shall be deprived of his life or personal liberty except according to procedure established by law.

[149] Article 21 in the Constitution of India.

[150] AIR 1997 SC 2218.

[151] (1987) 2 SCC 165.

[152] (1995) 3 SCC 42.

and leisure and health even after retirement, as basic essentials for a healthy and happy life. The right to life with human dignity encompasses within its fold some of the finer facets of human civilization which makes life worth living.

In *Kirloskar Brothers Ltd* v. *Employees' State Insurance Corpn.*,[153] The Supreme Court, following the Consumer Education and Research Center's case, has held that 'right to health' is a fundamental right of the workmen. The Court also held that this right is not only available against the state and its instrumentalities but even private industries to ensure to the workmen to provide facilities and opportunities for health and vigour of the workers, as assured in the provisions of Part IV of the Constitution, which are an 'integral part of right to equality under Art 14 and right to invigorated life under Article 21 which are fundamental rights to the workmen.

Further in, *State of Punjab and Others* v. *Mohinder Singh Chawala*,[154] 'it has been held that right to health is integral to right to life. Government has a constitutional obligation to provide health facilities'. Similarly, the court has upheld the state's obligation to maintain health services. Apart from recognizing the fundamental right to health as an integral part of the Right to Life, there is sufficient case law both from the Supreme and High Courts that lays down the obligation of the state to provide medical health services. The issue of adequacy of medical health services was also addressed in *Paschim Banga Khet Mazdoor Samity* v. *State of West Bengal*.[155] The question before the court was whether the non-availability of services in the government health centres amount to a violation of Article 21. It was held that that Article 21 imposes an obligation on the state to safeguard the right to life of every person. Preservation of human life is thus of paramount importance. Therefore, the failure of a government-run health centre to provide timely treatment is violative of a person's right to life. Further, the court ordered that PHC centres be equipped to deal with medical emergencies. It has also been held in this judgment that the lack of financial resources cannot be a reason for the state to shy away from its constitutional obligation. The Court ruled that a Public Interest Petition for maintenance of approved standards for drugs in general and for the banning of import, manufacturing, sale, and distribution of injurious drugs is maintainable. A healthy body is the very foundation of all human activities, hence the adage 'Sariramadyam Khalu Dharma Sadhanam". In a welfare state, it is the obligation of the state to ensure the creation and sustaining of conditions congenial to good health. Again, in *Mahendra Pratap Singh* v. *State of Orissa*,[156] the Court reiterated that right to life includes the right to PHC. In this case, on the basis of demands of the local people and public at large, the Department of Health and Family Welfare of the Government of Orissa decided to open certain primary health centres in different areas for the year 1991–92, subject to fulfilment of certain conditions. The government, however, failed in opening the healthcare centres.

The court held the following in the aforementioned cases:

> In a country like ours, it may not be possible to have sophisticated hospitals but definitely villagers within their limitations can aspire to have a Primary Health Centre. The government is required to assist people get treatment and lead a healthy life. Healthy society is a collective gain and no Government should make any effort to smother it. Primary concern should be the primary health centre and technical fetters cannot be introduced as subterfuges to cause hindrances in the establishment of health centre. .

---

153 (1996) 2 SCC 682.
154 AIR 1997 SC 1225.
155 (1996) 4 SCC 37.
156 AIR 1997 Ori 37.

The Court further stated that 'great achievements and accomplishments in life are possible if one is permitted to lead an acceptably healthy life'. Thereby, there is an implication that the enforcing of the right to life under Article 21 is a duty of the state and that this duty covers the ensuring of the right to PHC. This implies that the right to life includes the right to PHC.

Some Important Judgments on Right to Health in India

The Indian judiciary has interpreted the right to health in many ways. There have been several public interest litigations (PILs) as well as litigation arising out of claims that individuals have made on the state, with respect to health services and other issues. As a result, there is various substantial case law in India, which shows the gamut of issues that are related to health.

Parmanand Katara v. Union of India[157]

The petitioner, a human rights activist, filed this application under Article 32 of the Constitution, asking for a direction to the Union of India that every injured citizen brought for treatment should instantaneously be given medical aid to preserve life, and only thereafter should the procedural criminal law should be allowed to operate, in order to avoid death due to medical negligence; and in the event of breach of such direction, apart from any action that may be taken for negligence, appropriate compensation should be admissible. He appended to the writ petition a report entitled 'Law Helps the Injured to Die', published in the *Hindustan Times*. In the said publication it was alleged that a person driving a scooter was knocked down by a speeding car. Seeing the profusely bleeding person on the scooter, a person who was on the road picked him up and took him to the nearest hospital. The doctors refused to attend on the injured and told the man that he should take the patient to a different hospital located some 20 kilometres away, which was authorized to handle medico-legal cases. The Samaritan carried the victim, lost no time to approach the other hospital, but before he could reach, the victim succumbed to his injuries.

In the aforementioned case, the court held:

> Every doctor whether at a Government hospital or otherwise has the professional responsibility to extend his services for protecting human life. The Doctor does not infringe the law of the land by proceeding to treat the injured victim on his appearance before him either by himself or being carried by others. Courts will not summon a medical professional to give evidence unless the evidence is important and even if he is summoned, the men in this profession should not be made to wait and waste time unnecessarily.

Common Cause v. Union of India and Others[158]

In the above case, a petition was filed under Article 32 of the Constitution. The petitioner highlighted the serious deficiencies and shortcomings in the matter of collection, storage, and supply of blood through the various blood centres operating in the country and prayed that an

---

[157] (1989) 4 SCC 286.
[158] Writ Petition (civil) 91 of 1992.

appropriate writ order or direction be issued, directing the Union of India, the states, and the UTs, who had all been impleaded as respondents in the petition, to ensure that proper positive and concrete steps in a time-bound programme are immediately initiated for obviating the malpractices, malfunctioning, and inadequacies of the blood banks all over the country, and to place before the Court a specific programme of action aimed at overcoming the deficiencies in the operation of blood banks.

> The Supreme Court, while recognizing that blood donation is considered as a great life-saving service to humanity, held that it must be ensured that the blood that is available with the blood banks is healthy and free from infection, and laid down a system of licensing of blood banks.

Citizens and Inhabitants of Municipal Ward v. Municipal Corporation[159]

The court in the instant case deliberated on the question whether the state machinery was bound to assure adequate conditions necessary for health. The case involved the maintaining of sanitation and drainage facilities by municipal corporations. It was held that the state and its machineries (in the instant case, the Muncipal Corporation) were bound to assure hygienic conditions of living, and therefore, health.

From the aforementioned judgments the following legal principles are applicable to the child's right to health:

- Every doctor, whether at a government hospital or otherwise, has the professional responsibility to extend his services for protecting human life.
- The PHC centres should be equipped to deal with medical emergencies. It has also been held in the judgments that the lack of financial resources cannot be a reason for the state to shy away from its constitutional obligation.
- It must be ensured that the blood that is available with the blood banks for use is healthy and free from infection.
- The state and its machineries (for example, the muncipal corporation) are bound to assure hygienic conditions of living, and therefore, health.

Javed and others v. State of Haryana[160]

Facts

The Haryana Panchayati Raj Act was passed by the Haryana State Assembly in 1994. It laid down that a person with more than two living children could not become or continue as sarpanch, up-sarpanch, or panch of a panchayat (head or deputy head of village council), or member of a panchayat samiti or zilla parishad. However, anyone with more than two children at the time of the enactment and up to the expiry of 1 year from commencement would not be deemed disqualified. The act also declared that if an already-elected person has another child 1 year after

[159] AIR 1997 MP 33.
[160] (2003) 8 SCC 369.

commencement, and exceeds the norm of two living children during the term for which he/she is elected, then he/she will be disqualified and the post will become vacant. The 1-year exemption was granted in case of conception just before or around the time of commencement. Under the provisions of the act, several persons, including women, were disqualified or proceeded against for disqualification either from contesting elections or from continuing in the office of *panch/ sarpanch*. The constitutional validity of Sections 175 (1) (q) and 177 (1) of the act, which spelt out the disqualification, was challenged on the grounds that it was arbitrary, discriminatory, and violative of the fundamental rights to equality under Article 14, life and liberty under Article 21, and freedom of religion under Article 25 of the Constitution. It was also contended that the number of children a person has does not affect his/her capacity, competence, or quality to serve in any office of a panchayat, and that the disqualification has no connection with the purpose sought to be achieved by the Panchayati Raj Act, 1994.

Held

The Supreme Court observed in the above case that reasonable classification based on intelligible differentia, which distinguishes persons or things grouped together from others left out of the group, was permissible for the purpose of legislation. However, the parameters chosen must have a rational relation to the objective sought to be achieved by the legislation. Applying this criterion, the court held that persons with more than two living children were clearly distinguishable from persons not having more than two living children, and the classification was thus based on intelligible differentia. The court then considered whether the disqualification had any nexus or connection with the purpose sought to be achieved by the legislation. The judgment took note of the provisions of Article 243G of the Constitution, which empowers the legislature of a state to endow panchayats with powers and the authority necessary to function as institutions of self-government. Clause (b) of Article 243G provides that village panchayats be entrusted with the power to implement schemes for economic development and social justice and in relation to matters listed in the Eleventh Schedule of the Constitution. Entries 24 and 25 of the Eleventh Schedule are on 'family welfare' and 'women and child development', respectively.

Exercising the powers given to state legislatures, the Haryana legislature enacted the Haryana Panchayati Raj Act, 1994. Section 21 of the act mentioned the functions and duties of panchayats, and Clause XIX (1) specified 'public health and family welfare—(1)'implementation of family welfare programme'. Family welfare was held by the court to include family planning as well. The court observed that to carry out the purpose of the act as well as the mandate of the Constitution, the legislature had made a provision making a person with more than two living children ineligible for the post of *panch* or sarpanch. The disqualification was held to have a nexus with the purpose sought to be achieved by the act, and was declared valid as family planning, as a part of family welfare, was part of the functions and duties of panchayats. The court also refused to strike down the provision on grounds that a similar disqualification was not present for other elective offices or state legislatures and Parliament.

Dealing with the challenge to the provision on the grounds that it violates life and liberty under Article 21, the court put forward a long discourse about the 'torrential increase in the population of the country'. Sprinkling it with selective quotes like 'population explosion is more dangerous than (a) hydrogen bomb', the Court, rather than engaging with the socio-economic realities as to why people have children, targeted population as the root of all ills in society. Unemployment, congestion in urban areas, slums, and non-attainment of goals spelt out in the Constitution were all attributed to the increase in population. In fact, the judgment referred approvingly to a National Planning Committee set up by the Congress in 1940, that recommended, along with the establishment of birth-control clinics, other necessary measures such as raising the age of marriage and 'a eugenic sterilisation programme'. Lack of social welfare measures, infant and child mortality, children as economic security, especially to people from lower socio-economic backgrounds, were concepts that did not seem to matter to the Court while examining the issue of population and forming opinions and judgments. The Court observed that the disqualification was conceptually devised in the national interest, and it was futile to urge that the impugned legislation violated the right to life and liberty under Article 21.

Rights of the Unborn Child and Rights during Early Childhood

One of the most controversial debates in current legal issues involves the legal status of the unborn. The UDHR, adopted by the UN General Assembly in 1948, has inspired all subsequent human rights conventions and declarations. The preamble of UDHR provides for 'equal and inalienable rights of all members of the human family'. Article 3 states that 'everyone has the right to life'. Whether the unborn is included in this Declaration is unsure. Discussing the legal status of the unborn in international law, Flood is of the opinion that 'all members of the human family' can only mean all members of the human species.[161]

In the case of *Vo v. France*,[162] the court observed that since the unborn has the capacity to become a person and is protected in some states, it requires 'protection in the name of human dignity, without making it a "person" with the "right to life" for the purposes of Article 2'.[163,164]

In 1968, the UN International Covenant on Civil and Political Rights explicitly provided that 'Every human being has the inherent right to life' and that the death penalty shall not be carried out on pregnant women. Prenatal care, therefore, is given for the benefit of both the child and the mother, and the well-being of each is tied to the wellbeing of the other'.[165]

In Article 24 of the UNCRC, the Right to Health expressly gives children rights during the entire prenatal period, as elaborated next.[166]

[161] Flood J. Patrick, 'Is International Law on the Side of the Unborn Child?', *National Catholic Bioethics Quarterly* 7 (2007): 75–76.

[162] *Vo v. France*, 53924/00, Eur. Ct. H.R., 8 July 2004.

[163] Article 2 of the European Convention on Human Rights protects the right to life.

[164] Rosamund Scott, 'The English Fetus and the Right to Life', *European Journal of Health Law* 11 (2004): 352.

[165] International Covenant on Civil and Political Rights, adopted by the General Assembly of the United Nations on 19 December, 1966. Available at https://treaties.un.org/doc/Publication/UNTS/Volume%20999/volume-999-I-14668-English.pdf (accessed on 28 October 2015).

[166] 'Convention on the Rights of the Child: Adopted and Opened for Signature, Ratification, and Accession' by General Assembly resolution 44/25 of 20 November 1989, entry into force 2 September 1990. Available at http://www.ohchr.org/en/professionalinterest/pages/crc.aspx (accessed on 28 October 2015).

1. States parties recognize the *right* of *the child* to the enjoyment of the highest attainable standard of health.
2. States parties shall pursue full implementation of *this right, in particular,* shall take appropriate measures: [...] (d) To *ensure* appropriate *pre-natal ... health care* for mothers.

The UN Committee on the Rights of the Child has not only called on states to introduce and strengthen 'prenatal care for children' but has also explicitly condemned selective abortion (on the ground of sex, ethnic origin, social and cultural status, or disability) as a 'serious violation' of the rights of the child. The UN Convention on the Rights of Persons with Disabilities 2007 provides that 'every human being' has the right to life. Thus, international law protects the rights of an unborn child.[167]

Children need special protection and care during the entire prenatal period.[168] In India the healthcare scenario for an average citizen is in a grim situation.[169] Even the most basic antenatal healthcare programme does not receive priority over other health schemes. In this situation, it is almost impossible to provide good antenatal services to the unborn child.[170]

Child Sex Ratio in India

It is a matter of deep concern that the child sex ratio (CSR), which is the number of girls per thousand boys in the 0–6 age group, has been declining in India. The ratio has fallen from 945 in 1991 to 927 in 2001. The CSR had earlier declined by 17 points from 962 in 1981 to 945 in 1991. In 2011, the ratio had further declined to 914. So, overall in the 0–6 age group, the ratio had declined from 976 in 1961 to 914 in 2011. It is significant to note that in 2011, the CSR was 902 in the urban areas and in rural areas it is 919. This problem is not limited only to metropolitan regions now, but has spread to even smaller towns, as represented in Table 8.2.

Table 8.2   Child Sex Ratio (0–6 Years) in India, 1991–2011[171]

Census	Total	Rural	Urban
1991	945	948	935
2001	927	933	906
2011	914	919	902

[167] John Keown, 'International Human-Rights Law and the Unborn Child', *National Review*. Available at http://www.nationalreview.com/bench-memos/247662/international-human-rights-law-and-unborn-child-john-keown (accessed on 28 October 2015).

[168] 'Convention on the Rights of the Child'.

[169] Ravi Kanojia, 'Rights of an Unborn Baby versus the Social and Legal Constraints of Parents: Birth of a New Debate', *Journal of Indian Association of Pediatric Surgeons*, 13, no. 3 (2008): 92–93.

[170] Kanojia, 'Rights of an Unborn Baby'.

[171] Source: Population Totals, Census 2011.

Femicide

Femicide, which includes female infanticide, sex-selective abortions, sex selection of embryos, and other methods of averting the natural formation of a female foetus (sperm separation), takes place everyday in every corner of this country. During the late 1970s, cases of abortion of female foetuses were reported from many of the major cities of India. The practice continues to this day with more invasive techniques of sex determination like ultrasonography having replaced amniocentesis and chronic villus sampling. In the states of Punjab and Haryana in north-western India, mobile ultrasound units regularly visit the rural areas. Abortion of female foetuses is no longer an urban phenomenon in these parts of India.

According to the 1991 Census, the overall sex ratio[172] of the country was 929 women per 1,000 men. This sex ratio is becoming more skewed day by day. Medical and scientific procedures are becoming more efficient and consequently it is becoming easier to get rid of a female child. With a population count of 1,027 million, the census[173] also showed the male population as 531 million and female population as 496 million. The sex ratio of 933 females per 1,000 males showed an overall improvement of 6 points from the sex ratio of 927 per 1,000 males in 1991. In 2011, the country had a low sex ratio of 943 females per 1,000 males, which has shown slight improvement during the last decade (Figure 8.1). Among the states, the sex ratio is lowest for Haryana, while among the UTs, Daman and Diu lags behind. Kerala tops the list with the highest sex ratio.[174]

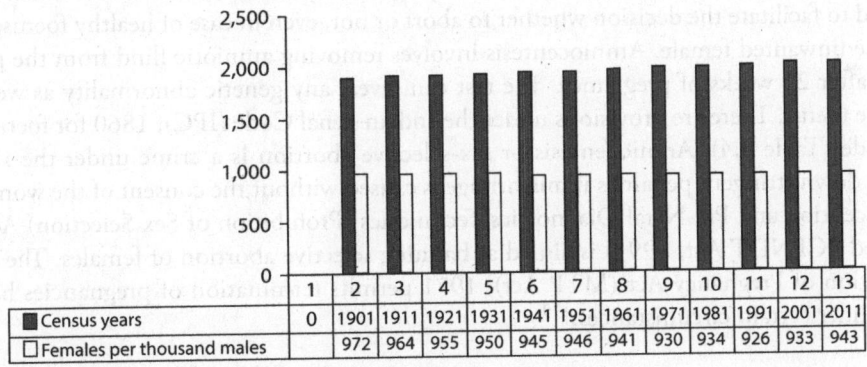

	1	2	3	4	5	6	7	8	9	10	11	12	13
■ Census years	0	1901	1911	1921	1931	1941	1951	1961	1971	1981	1991	2001	2011
▢ Females per thousand males		972	964	955	950	945	946	941	930	934	926	933	943

Figure 8.1   Sex Ratio Trends: Implications for Girls[175]

[172] Sex ratio is number of females per thousand males.

[173] *Census of India*, 1991.

[174] Central Bureau of Health Intelligence, Directorate General of Health Services, Ministry of Health and Family Welfare, 'National Health Profile 2012 (January–December)', Government of India. Available at http://cbhidghs.nic.in/index2.asp?slid=1256&sublinkid=1163 (accessed on 10 October 2015).

[175] Ministry of Health and Family Welfare, 'National Health Profile 2012 (January–December)'. Available at http://cbhidghs.nic.in/index2.asp?slid=1256&sublinkid=1163 (accessed on 10 October 2015).

According to India's 2011 Census, while the overall female–to–male ratio has improved marginally as compared to the last Census, fewer girls were born than boys. A UN study titled 'Sex Ratios and Gender Biased Sex Selection: History, Debates and Future Directions' (Table 8.3) found that the northeastern states such as Manipur and Nagaland have shown a sharp decline in the CSR between 2001 and 2011. In contrast, the ratio in Punjab improved from 798 to 846 and in Haryana from 819 to 834 in the same period. The report has also mentioned that the dwindling number of girls is fuelling increase in crimes such as kidnapping and trafficking.[176]

Table 8.3   Decline in Child Sex Ratio and Overall Sex Ratio[177]

	Decline in CSR and OSR						
	1951	1961	1971	1981	1991	2001	2011
Overall sex ratio (OSR)	-	−5	−11	4	−7	6	10
CSR	-	−7	−12	−2	−17	−18	−9

Amniocentesis was brought into India in 1975, as a measure of detecting genetic disorders and abnormalities. Unfortunately, this invention of medical science has resulted in 'quickening the pace of death of the female child from the born to the unborn stage'.[178] It is being used to get rid of the girl child before birth. Amniocentesis in India has become synonymous with the sex determination test, which has led to sex-selective abortions. The advancement of science and invention of sophisticated equipment has now made it easy to identify the sex of the foetus much ahead of birth and to facilitate the decision whether to abort or not, even in case of healthy foetuses, to get rid of the unwanted female. Amniocentesis involves removing amniotic fluid from the pregnant woman after 20 weeks of pregnancy. The test can reveal any genetic abnormality as well as the sex of the foetus. There are provisions under the Indian Penal Code (IPC), 1860 for foeticide and infanticide (Table 8.4). Amniocentesis or sex-selective abortion is a crime under the IPC. The IPC lays down stringent penalties if miscarriage is caused without the consent of the woman. The Pre-Conception and Pre-Natal Diagnostics Techniques (Prohibition of Sex Selection) Act, 1994 (amended PCPNDT Act, 1994) is aimed at banning selective abortion of females. The Medical Termination of Pregnancy Act (MTP Act), 1971 permits termination of pregnancies before 20 weeks, under certain circumstances.[179]

Indian Penal Code, 1860

The relevant provisions of IPC are as follows:

[176] Mary E. John, 'Sex Ratios and Gender Biased Sex Selection: History, Debates & Future Directions', *UN Women Multi-Country Office for India, Bhutan, Maldives & Sri Lanka*, New Delhi, 2014. Available at http://www.global-sisterhood-network.org/content/view/2919/59/ (accessed on 2 February 2017).

[177] Source: John, 'Sex Ratios and Gender Biased Sex Selection'.

[178] Anand Grover, 'Amniocentesis or Female Foeticide', *The Lawyers* (March 1986): 3.

[179] Asha Bajpai, *The Girl Child and the Law: Rights of the Child* (NLSIU/UNICEF, 1990).

Table 8.4   Relevant Provisions of IPC for Foeticide and Infanticide[180]

Section	Offence	Punishment
312	Causing miscarriage voluntarily.If the woman be quick with child (quick with child is not defined under the act but it can be interpreted to mean a child capable of being born alive).	Imprisonment for 3 years or fine or both. Imprisonment for 7 years and fine.
313	Causing miscarriage without the woman's consent.	Imprisonment for life or imprisonment for 10 years and fine.
314	Death caused by an act done with intent to cause miscarriage.If the act is done without the woman's consent.	Imprisonment for 10 years and fine. Imprisonment for life or as above.
315	Act done with intent to prevent a child being born alive or to cause it to die after its birth.	Imprisonment for 10 years or fine or both.
316	Causing death of a quick unborn child by an act amounting to culpable homicide.	Imprisonment for 10 years.
318	Concealment of birth by secret disposal of dead body.	Imprisonment for 2 years or fine or both.

According to 'Crime in India Report 2014', a total of 121 'infanticide' cases were reported under section 315 of the IPC in the country during 2014. The incidents increased by 47.6 per cent in the year 2014 over 2013 (from 82 cases in 2013 to 121 in 2014). Most of the cases were reported in Rajasthan (33 cases), followed by Madhya Pradesh (14 cases) and Maharashtra (12 cases). Total numbers of victims were 121 in 121 cases. The conviction rate under the crime head 'infanticide' (42.9 per cent) was highest during the year 2014.[181]

A total of 107 cases of 'foeticide' were reported under sections 315 and 317 of the IPC in the country during 2014, as compared to 221 cases in the year 2013, indicating a decline of 51.6 per cent. Madhya Pradesh, Rajasthan, Uttar Pradesh, and Punjab reported 30 cases, 24 cases, 11 cases, and 10 cases respectively. The total number of victims was 107 in 107 cases. Out of 107 victims of foeticides, 53 were males, 50 were females, and sex of 4 foetuses was not known. Crime rate was negligible at the all-India level under this head, with Chandigarh (0.3), Himachal Pradesh (0.2), Haryana, Madhya Pradesh, Punjab, Rajasthan, and the UT of Delhi with 0.1 each.[182]

A total of 983 cases of exposure and abandonment were reported under section 317 of the IPC during 2014, as compared to 930 cases during 2013, showing an increase of 5.7 per cent during the year 2014. Maharashtra reported the highest number of such cases (225 cases), followed by Rajasthan (213 cases). The total number of victims was 989 in 983 cases. Crime rate was 0.2 at the all-India level under this head, with the highest rate in Daman and Diu (1.1), followed by

[180]   Source: Compiled by the author.

[181]   National Crime Records Bureau, Ministry of Home Affairs, 'Crime in India, 2014', Government of India, New Delhi. Available at http://ncrb.gov.in/ (accessed on 25 October 2015).

[182]   Ministry of Home Affairs, 'Crime in India, 2014'.

Chandigarh (0.8). The lowest charge sheet rate was found in cases of 'exposure & abandonment' (17.8 per cent).[183]

The Pre-Conception and Pre-Natal Diagnostics Techniques (Prohibition of Sex Selection) Act, 1994

The decline in sex ratio is a matter of great concern and is the result of preference for male children in the Indian society. The practice of sex-selective abortion (or social sex selection) has been the cause of skewed sex ratios. Maharashtra was the first state in the country to enact a related law—the Maharashtra Regulation of Use of Pre-Natal Diagnostics Techniques Act—in 1988, prohibiting the use of new scientific techniques for sex-determination and sex selection. This was followed by several other states like Goa and Gujarat.[184] In 1994 the Government of India passed the Pre-Natal Diagnostic Techniques (Regulation and Prevention of Misuse) Act, 1994 (PNDT Act. Though this act was passed on 20 September 1994, it came into force from 1 January 1996. The objective of the act was to provide for the regulation of the use of prenatal diagnostic techniques[185] for the purpose of detecting genetic or metabolic disorders or chromosomal abnormalities or certain congenital malformation or sex-linked disorders, and for the prevention of the misuse of this techniques for the purpose of prenatal sex determination leading to female foeticide.[186] There were lot of loopholes under this act and there were hardly any convictions. A writ petition was filed under Article 32 of the Constitution of India by the Centre for Enquiry into Health and Allied Themes (CEHAT), Mahila Sarvangeen Utkarsh Mandal (MASUM), and Dr Sabu M. George.[187] The PIL sought to accomplish the following objectives:

- To activate the central and state governments for rigorous implementation of the central legislation, and
- To interpret the legislation and/or to demand amendments to ensure that the techniques that use pre-conception or during-conception sex selection are also brought under the purview of the act.

According to the petitioners, the PNDT Act, for all its intents and purposes, was a toothless piece of legislation. The problem was the interpretation of this act by the ultrasonologists, the abortionists, the doctors, and most importantly, the government. Despite the intent and purpose of the act being wide and all-encompassing, it was being interpreted to exclude prenatal sex selection. Thereby, there were widespread advertisements by various clinics providing prenatal sex selection. It was further alleged that a narrow interpretation of the act was being forwarded,

[183]   Ministry of Home Affairs, 'Crime in India, 2014'.

[184]   Shalini Phansalkar Joshi 'Compilation and Analysis of Case-Laws on Pre-Conception and Pre-Natal Diagnostics Techniques (Prohibition of Sex Selection) Act, 1994', United Nation Population Fund.

[185]   PNDT Act 1994, Section 2(j): 'Prenatal diagnostic techniques' include all prenatal diagnostic procedures and prenatal diagnostic tests.

[186]   The Preamble to the PNDT Act, 1994.

[187]   In the Supreme Court of India, extraordinary original jurisdiction. Writ Petition [C] No. 301 of 2000, Equivalent Citation: (2001) 5 SCC 577.

which gave licence to all doctors to conveniently adopt this technique without fear of the law. This technique has been condemned by the Beijing Convention as violation of human rights and ethical medical practices, and India is a signatory to the same from as early as 1995; and the same is binding on India.

The petitioners further contended that by ultrasonography and amniocentesis, the sex of the foetus is determined during the pregnancy of the woman and the foetus is aborted if found to be a female. These tests were carried out even by compounders and doctors without the necessary qualifications. At times, the ultrasonologist and abortionist were one and the same person, but no one really cared as families wanted to get rid of their female children and the medical professionals (abortionists) wanted to make money. Another method which had increasingly become popular was sperm separation or Ericsson's technique. In this technique, men's sperm was taken and tested in a laboratory to separate the XX and XY sperms, and only XY sperms which can produce boys were used to artificially inseminate the women. Thus, sex selection took place prenatally; in this instance, even before conception. The latest genetic technique, which was primarily used for sex determination, was Prenatal Genetic Diagnosis (PDG).

After filing of this petition, the Court issued notices to the concerned parties on 9 May 2000. It took nearly 1 year for the various states to file their affidavits in reply/written submissions. Prima facie, it appeared that despite the PNDT Act being enacted by the Parliament 5 years back, neither the state governments nor the central government had taken appropriate actions for its implementation. The Supreme Court, therefore, issued the following directions for the proper implementation of the act:

- The central government was directed to create public awareness against the practice of pre-natal determination of sex and female foeticide through appropriate releases/programmes in the electronic media. This was also to be done by the Central Supervisory Board (CSB), as provided under Section 16(iii) of the PNDT Act.
- The central government was directed to implement with all vigour and zeal the PNDT Act and the Rules framed in 1996. Rule 15 provided that the intervening period between two meetings of the Advisory Committees constituted under Subsection (5) of Section 17 of the PNDT Act to advise the appropriate authority shall not exceed 60 days. It would be seen that this rule was strictly adhered to.
- Meeting of the CSB would be held at least once in six months [refer proviso to Section 9(1)]. The constitution of the CSB was provided under Section 7. It empowered the central government to appoint 10 members under Section 7(2)(e), including eminent medical practitioners, eminent social scientists, and representatives of women welfare organizations. It was hoped that this power would be exercised so as to include those persons who could genuinely spare time for the implementation of the act.
- The CSB was to review and monitor the implementation of the act [refer Section 16(ii)].
- The CSB should issue directions to the appropriate authorities in all states and UTs to furnish quarterly returns to the CSB, giving a report on the implementation and working of the act. These returns should inter alia contain specific information about:

  ◆ Survey of bodies specified in Section 3 of the act.
  ◆ Registration of bodies specified in Section 3 of the act.

♦ Action taken against non-registered bodies operating in violation of Section 3 of the act, inclusive of search and seizure of records.

♦ Complaints received by the appropriate authorities under the act and action taken pursuant thereto.

♦ Number and nature of awareness campaigns conducted and results flowing therefrom.

- The CSB should examine the necessity to amend the act keeping in mind emerging technologies and difficulties encountered in implementation of the act, and to make recommendations to the central government (refer Section 16).

- The CSB should lay down a code of conduct under Section 16(iv) of the act, to be observed by persons working in bodies specified therein, and to ensure its publication so that public at large can know about it.

- The CSB would require medical professional bodies/associations to create awareness against the practice of prenatal determination of sex and female foeticide, and to ensure implementation of the act.

This judgment was hailed as a positive step in the implementation of the PNDT Act.

The PNDT Act and Rules were amended keeping in view the emerging new technologies for selection of sex before and after conception, problems faced in the working of implementation of the PNDT Act, and certain directions of the Supreme Court after the above-mentioned PIL was filed in May, 2000 on slow implementation of the act. These amendments came into operation with effect from 14 February 2003. The government passed the new act called Pre-Conception and Pre-Natal Diagnostics Techniques (Prohibition of Sex Selection) Act (PCPNDT Act), 1994.

Important Provisions of the Pre-Natal Diagnostics Techniques (Prohibition of Sex Selection) Act

The preliminary object of the PCPNDT Act was to put a check on female foeticide with the intent to prohibit prenatal diagnostic techniques for determination of the sex of the foetus,[188] which led to female foeticide. The few basic requirements of the act are:[189]

---

[188] Section 6 in the PCPNDT Act: Determination of sex prohibited—On and from the commencement of this act—

(1) no Genetic Counselling Centre or Genetic Laboratory or Genetic Clinic shall conduct or cause to be conducted in its Centre, Laboratory or Clinic, pre-natal diagnostic techniques including ultrasonography, for the purpose of determining the sex of a foetus;

(2) no person shall conduct or cause to be conducted any pre-natal diagnostic techniques including ultrasonography for the purpose of determining the sex of a foetus;

(3) no person shall, by whatever means, cause or allow to be caused selection of sex before or after conception.

[189] Anita Bhaktwani, 'The PC-PNDT Act in a Nutshell', *Indian Journal of Radiology and Imaging* 22, no. 2 (April–June 2012): 133–4. Available at http://www.ncbi.nlm.nih.gov/pmc/articles/PMC3498638/ (accessed on 15 October 2015).

1. Registration under Section (18) of the PCPNDT Act.[190]
2. Written consent of the pregnant woman and prohibition of communicating the sex of the foetus under Section 5 of the act.[191]
3. Maintenance of records as provided under Section 29 of the act.[192]

[190] Section 18 in the PCPNDT Act: Registration of Genetic Counselling Centres, Genetic Laboratories or Genetic Clinics—

(1) No person shall open any Genetic Counselling Centre, Genetic Laboratory or Genetic Clinic, including clinic, laboratory, or centre having ultrasound or imaging machine or scanner or any other technology capable of undertaking determination of sex of foetus and sex selection, or render services to any of them, after the commencement of the Pre-natal Diagnostic Techniques (Regulation and Prevention of Misuse) Amendment Act, 2002 unless such centre, laboratory, or clinic is duly registered under the act.

(2) Every application for registration under Subsection (1), shall be made to the Appropriate Authority in such form and in such manner and shall be accompanied by such fees as may be prescribed.

(3) Every Genetic Counselling Centre, Genetic Laboratory, or Genetic Clinic engaged, either partly or exclusively, in counselling or conducting pre-natal diagnostic techniques for any of the purposes mentioned in section 4, immediately before the commencement of this Act, shall apply for registration within 60 days from the date of such commencement.

(4) Subject to the provisions of Section 6, every Genetic Counselling Centre, Genetic Laboratory, or Genetic Clinic engaged in counselling or conducting pre-natal diagnostic techniques shall cease to conduct any such counselling or technique on the expiry of six months from the date of commencement of this Act unless such Centre, Laboratory, or Clinic has applied for registration and is so registered separately or jointly or till such application is disposed of, whichever is earlier.

(5) No Genetic Counselling Centre, Genetic Laboratory, or Genetic Clinic shall be registered under this Act unless the Appropriate Authority is satisfied that such Centre, Laboratory, or Clinic is in a position to provide such facilities, maintain such equipment and standards as may be prescribed.

[191] Section 5 in the PCPNDT: Written consent of pregnant woman and prohibition of communicating the sex of foetus—

(1) No person referred to in Clause (2) of section 3 shall conduct the pre-natal diagnostic procedures unless—

(a) he has explained all known side and after effects of such procedures to the pregnant woman concerned;

(b) he has obtained in the prescribed form her written consent to undergo such procedures in the language which she understands; and

(c) a copy of her written consent obtained under Clause (b) is given to the pregnant woman.

[(2) No person including the person conducting pre-natal diagnostic procedures shall communicate to the pregnant woman concerned or her relatives or any other person the sex of the foetus by words, signs, or in any other manner.]

[192] Section 29 in the PCPNDT: Maintenance of records—

(1) All records, charts, forms, reports, consent letters, and all the documents required to be maintained under this act and the rules shall be preserved for a period of 2 years or for such period as may be prescribed, provided that, if any criminal or other proceedings are instituted against any genetic

4. Creating awareness among the public at large by displaying a signboard declaring prohibition of sex determination.
5. The act mandates compulsory registration of all diagnostic laboratories, all genetic counselling centres, genetic laboratories, genetic clinics, and ultrasound clinics.[193]

The act penalizes all the errant parties, either involved in sex determination or non-maintenance of records.[194] The act is legislated in a manner that it should be a deterrent for those indulging in sex determination. The unfortunate decline in the male–female sex ratio has necessitated stringent measures; there is suspension of registration, filing of criminal cases, and sealing of machines. Besides, criminal prosecution will also lead to suspension and cancellation of registration[195] granted by the State Medical Council.[196] Remedies like filing an appeal before the appellate authority[197] and getting the machines released from the court of law are also provided, but all these remedial measures are time-consuming and bring the career of an individual to a standstill, thus acting as a deterrent.[198]

---

counselling centre, genetic laboratory, or genetic clinic, the records and all other documents of such centre, laboratory or clinic shall be preserved till the final disposal of such proceedings.
(2) All such records shall, at all reasonable times, be made available for inspection to the appropriate authority or to any other person authorised by the appropriate authority in this behalf.

[193] Section 18 in the PCPNDT Act.
[194] Bhaktwani, 'The PCPNDT Act'.
[195] Section 20 in the PCPNDT Act: Cancellation or suspension of registration—

(1) The appropriate authority may suo moto, or on complaint, issue a notice to the genetic counselling centre, genetic laboratory or genetic clinic to show cause why its registration should not be suspended or cancelled for the reasons mentioned in the notice.
(2) If, after giving a reasonable opportunity of being heard to the genetic counselling centre, genetic laboratory, or genetic clinic and having regard to the advice of the advisory committee, the appropriate authority is satisfied that there has been a breach of the provisions of this act or the rules, it may, without prejudice to any criminal action that it may take against such centre, laboratory or clinic, suspend its registration for such period as it may think fit or cancel its registration, as the case may be.
(3) Notwithstanding anything contained in Subsection (1) and (2), if the appropriate authority is of the opinion that it is necessary or expedient so to do in the public interest, it may, for reasons to be recorded in writing, suspend the registration of any genetic counselling centre, genetic laboratory or genetic clinic without issuing any such notice referred to in Subsection (1).

[196] Section 20 in the PCPNDT Act.
[197] Section 21 in the PCPNDT Act: Appeal—
The genetic counselling centre, genetic laboratory, or genetic clinic may, within 30 days from the date of receipt of the order of suspension or cancellation of registration passed by the appropriate authority under Section 20, prefer an appeal against such order to—

(1) the central government, where the appeal is against the order of the central appropriate authority; and
(2) the state government, where the appeal is against the order of the state appropriate authority, in the prescribed manner.

[198] Section 21 in the PCPNDT Act.

The most effective precautionary measures are to maintain records scrupulously, fill the Form-F as provided in the act[199] accurately and correctly, and submit the records to the appropriate authority within the stipulated time; then there would be nothing to worry about.[200]

Under the PCPNDT Act, no prenatal diagnostic techniques shall be conducted except for the purposes of detection of any of the following abnormalities, namely:[201]

1. Chromosomal abnormalities;
2. Genetic metabolic diseases;
3. Haemoglobinopathies;
4. Sex-linked genetic diseases;
5. Congenital anomalies;
6. Any other abnormalities or diseases as may be specified by the CSB.[202]

---

[199] Form F: Form for Maintenance of Record in Respect of Pregnant Woman by Genetic Clinic/Ultrasound Clinic/Imaging Centre.

[200] Bhaktwani, 'The PC-PNDT Act'.

[201] Section 4 in the PNDT Act.

[202] Section 7 in the PCPNDT Act: Constitution of Central Supervisory Board—

(1) The central government shall constitute a board to be known as the Central Supervisory Board to exercise the powers and perform the functions conferred on the board under this act.

(2) The board shall consist of—

    (a) the minister in charge of the ministry or department of family welfare, who shall be the chairman, ex officio;

    (b) the secretary to the Government of India in charge of the Department of Family Welfare, who shall be the vice-chairman, ex officio;

    [(c) three members to be appointed by the Central Government to represent the Ministries of Central Government in charge of Women and Child Development, Department of Legal Affairs or Legislative Department in the Ministry of Law and Justice, and Indian System of Medicine and Homoeopathy, ex officio;]

    (d) the director general of health services of the central government, ex-officio;

    (e) ten members to be appointed by the central government, two each from among—

        (i) eminent medical geneticists;

        (ii) eminent gynaecologist and obstetrician or expert of stri-roga or prasuti-tantra;

        (iii) eminent paediatricians;

        (iv) eminent social scientists; and

        (v) representatives of women welfare organisations;

    (f) three women Members of Parliament, of whom two shall be elected by the House of the People and one by the council of states;

    (g) four members to be appointed by the central government by rotation to represent the states and the UTs, two in the alphabetical order and two in the reverse alphabetical order, provided that no appointment under this clause shall be made except on the recommendation of the state government or, as the case may be, the UT;

    (h) an officer, not below the rank of a Joint Secretary or equivalent of the central government, in charge of family welfare, who shall be the member-secretary, ex officio.

Authorities under the Act

Under the act, the central government has to appoint one or more appropriate authorities for the UTs and the state government has to appoint appropriate authorities for the state. The important aspect here is that the appointment is through notification in the official gazette (Table 8.5).[203] The appropriate authority shall have powers in respect of the following matters:[204]

[203] Section 17 in the PNDT Act: Appropriate authority under the act—

(1) The central government shall appoint, by notification in the Official Gazette, one or more appropriate authorities for each of the UTs for the purposes of this act.

(2) The state government shall appoint, by notification in the Official Gazette, one or more appropriate authorities for the whole or part of the state for the purposes of this act having regard to the intensity of the problem of pre-natal sex determination leading to female foeticide.

(3) The officers appointed as appropriate authorities under Subsection (1) or Subsection (2) shall be,—

   [(a) when appointed for the whole of the state or UT, consisting of the following three members:—
      (i) an officer of or above the rank of the joint director of health and family welfare—chairperson;
      (ii) an eminent woman representing women's organisation; and
      (iii) an officer of law department of the state or UT concerned, provided that it shall be the duty of the state or UT concerned to constitute multi-member state/UT level appropriate authority within three months of the coming into force of the Pre-natal Diagnostic Techniques (Regulation and Prevention of Misuse) Amendment Act, 2002, provided further that any vacancy occurring therein shall be filled within three months of the occurrence;

   (b) when appointed for any part of the state/UT, of such other rank as the state government, as the case may be, may deem fit.

(4) the appropriate authority shall have the following functions, namely:—

   (a) to grant, suspend or cancel registration of a Genetic Counselling Centre, Genetic Laboratory or Genetic Clinic;
   (b) to enforce standards prescribed for the Genetic Counselling Centre, Genetic Laboratory and Genetic Clinic;
   (c) to investigate complaints of breach of the provisions of this act or the rules made thereunder and take immediate action;
   (d) to seek and consider the advice of the advisory committee, constituted under Subsection (5), on application for registration and on complaints for suspension or cancellation of registration;
   [(e) to take appropriate legal action against the use of any sex selection technique by any person at any place, suo motu or brought to its notice and also to initiate independent investigations in such matter;
   (f) to create public awareness against the practice of sex selection or pre-natal determination of sex;
   (g) to supervise the implementation of the provisions of the act and rules;
   (h) to recommend to the board and state boards modifications required in the rules in accordance with changes in technology or social conditions;
   (i) to take action on the recommendations of the advisory committee made after investigation of complaint for suspension or cancellation of registration].

[204] Section 17A of the PCPNDT Act.

1. Summoning of any person who is in possession of any information relating to violation of the provisions of this act or the rules made thereunder;
2. Production of any document or material object relating to Clause (a);
3. Issuing search warrant for any place suspected to be indulging in sex selection techniques or prenatal sex determination; and

The initiatives undertaken by Government of India to strengthen effective implementation of the PCPNDT Act include the following:

- The National Inspection and Monitoring Committee has been reconstituted, and apart from inspections, has been further empowered to oversee follow-up action by Appropriate Authorities against organizations found guilty of violations under the act during inspections.[205]
- Operational guidelines for PNDT–NGO Grant in Aid Scheme have been revised to ensure targeted use of resources for effective implementation of the act.[206]
- States have been asked during appraisal of the annual Programme Implementation Plan (PIP) to take advantage of funding available under NRHM for strengthening infrastructure and augmentation of human resources required for effective implementation of the PCPNDT Act.[207]

In 2012, Rule 11 (2) of the PCPNDT Rules, 1996 was amended to provide for confiscation of unregistered machines and further punishment of organizations which fail to register themselves under the act.[208] In 2014 the Central Government[209] inserted Rule 18A relating to the code of conduct to be observed by Appropriate Authorities[210] notified under the act, including the state, district, and sub-district. The authorities under the act were notified inter-alia to observe and implement the provisions of the act and Rules in a balanced and standardized manner in the course of their work.

Table 8.5   Offences and Penalties under the PCPNDT Act, 1994[211]

Offences	Penalties
Any medical geneticist, gynaecologist, registered medical practitioner, or any person who owns a	Punishable with imprisonment for a term which may extend to 3 years and with fine which may

(Cont'd)

[205] Ministry of Health and Family Welfare, Press Information Bureau, 'Implementation of PC & PNDT Act', Government of India, 25 November 2011. Available at http://pib.nic.in/newsite/PrintRelease.aspx?relid=77581 (accessed on 18 October 2015).

[206] Ministry of Health and Family Welfare, 'Implementation of PC & PNDT Act'.

[207] Ministry of Health and Family Welfare, 'Implementation of PC & PNDT Act'.

[208] Ramesh Rachna Kale and Bhosale Swapnali, 'Missing Girls in India: A Need for Social Marketing Initiatives', *International Journal of Research in Computer Application & Management* 5, no. 5 (May 2015). Available at www.ijrcm.org.in (accessed on 18 October 2015).

[209] Government of India, Ministry of Health and Family Welfare (PNDT) Section, Notification No: V.11011/8/2013-PNDT, New Delhi, 24 February 2014.

[210] Section 17 of the PCPNDT Act, 1994.

[211] Source: Compiled by the author.

Table 8.5   (Cont'd)

Offences	Penalties
Genetic Counselling Centre, a Genetic Laboratory, or a Genetic Clinic or is employed in such a Centre, Laboratory, or Clinic and renders his professional or technical services to or at such a Centre, Laboratory, or Clinic, whether on an honorary basis or otherwise, and who contravenes any of the provisions of this Act or rules made thereunder.	extend to Rs 10,000 and on any subsequent conviction, with imprisonment which may extend to 5 years and with fine which may extend to Rs. 50,000 [PCPNDT Act, Section 23 (1)].
No person or organization shall publish, distribute or cause to be published or distributed any advertisement regarding facilities for prenatal determination of sex.	Punishable with imprisonment for a term which may extend to 3 years and with fine which may extend to Rs. 10,000 [PNDT Act, Section 22(3)].
Any medical geneticist, gynaecologist, registered medical practitioner, or any person who owns a genetic counselling centre, laboratory, or clinic or is employed in them and renders his professional or technical services and contravenes the provisions of this act or rules made there under.	Punishable with imprisonment for a term which may extend to 3 years and with fine which may extend to Rs. 10,000 and on any subsequent conviction with imprisonment which may extend to 5 years and with fine which may extend to Rs. 50,000 [PCPNDT Act, Section 23(1)]. The name of the registered medical practitioner shall be reported by the Appropriate Authority to the State Medical Council concerned for taking necessary action, including suspension of the registration if the charges are framed by the court and till the case is disposed of, and on conviction, for removal of his name from the register of the Council for a period of 5 years for the first offence and permanently for the subsequent offence [PCPNDT Act 1994, Section 23(2)].
Any person who seeks the aid of any Genetic Counselling Centre, Genetic Laboratory, Genetic Clinic or ultrasound clinic or imaging clinic or of a medical geneticist, gynaecologist, sonologist or imaging specialist or registered medical practitioner or any other person for sex selection or for conducting prenatal diagnostic techniques on any pregnant woman for the purposes other than those specified in the act.	Imprisonment for a term which may extend to 3 years and with fine which may extend to Rs. 50,000 for the first offence and for any subsequent offence with imprisonment which may extend to 5 years and with fine which may extend to Rs. 100,000 [Section 23(3)].
Penalty for contravention of the provisions of the act or Rules for which no specific punishment is provided.	Punishable with imprisonment for a term which may extend to three months or with fine, which may extend to Rs. 1,000 or with both, and in the case of continuing contravention, with an additional fine which may extend to Rs. 500 for every day during which such contravention continues after conviction for the first such contravention [Section 25 of the PCPNDT Act].

(Cont'd)

Table 8.5   *(Cont'd)*

Offences	Penalties
When any offence under this act is committed by a company.	Every person who, at the time the offence was committed, was in charge of and was responsible for the conduct of business and was aware of the offence shall be deemed to be guilty and proceeded against and punished accordingly [PCPNDT Act, Section 26].

Implementation of the Pre-Natal Diagnostics Techniques (Prohibition of Sex Selection) Act

As part of an effort to understand the reasons for such lax implementation of a crucial social legislation, the NHRC and the United Nations Population Fund (UNFPA) jointly requested the Public Health Foundation of India (PHFI) to undertake a study[212] to assess the status of implementation of the PCPNDT Act (hereafter referred to as the act) across 18 states in the country, where skewed sex ratios are a major problem and interventions are required on priority, as recognized by NHRC and UNFPA. The 18-state study aimed to understand the barriers to this legal process by reviewing available cases registered by the states under the act and identifying bottlenecks in the implementation of the act, with the idea that remedial measures to make the law more effective may be found through a more in-depth understanding of these bottlenecks and impediments.[213]

Specifically, the study has attempted to address the following key objectives:[214]

- To identify difficulties faced by implementing authorities in their actions with regard to implementing the act, including understanding current levels of knowledge as regards legal processes involved in effective management of cases, and taking necessary steps to ensure conviction.
- To map challenges of effective case law documentation, including loopholes/weaknesses from the evidentiary and prosecution side, that contribute to non-conviction.[215]
- To better understand processes that lead to successful convictions.

---

[212] The study was carried out by a partnership of organizations: The Centre for Youth Development and Activities (CYDA), Pune, Prayatn, Jaipur, Adithi, Patna, Vimochana, Bengaluru; and PHFI, New Delhi, in Andhra Pradesh, Assam, Bihar, Delhi, Goa, Gujarat, Haryana, Jharkhand, Karnataka, Madhya Pradesh, Maharashtra, Odisha, Punjab, Rajasthan, Tamil Nadu, Uttarakhand, Uttar Pradesh, and West Bengal, between 2008 and 2009.

[213] CYDA, Pune, Prayatn, Jaipur, Adithi, Patna, Vimochana, Bengaluru; and PHFI, New Delhi, supported by the NHRC and UNFPA, 'Implementation of the PCPNDT Act In India: Perspectives and Challenges', April 2010. Available at http://countryoffice.unfpa.org/india/drive/IMPLEMENTATIONOFTHEPCPNDTACTININDIAPerspectivesandChallenges.pdf (accessed on 18 October 2015).

[214] CYDA et al., 'Implementation of the PCPNDT Act'.

[215] CYDA et al., 'Implementation of the PCPNDT Act'.

In most states under study, implementation structures have been constituted as per the act; the identified gap, however, lies in their optimal functioning and effective delivery of operations as mandated. This is made evident through several findings of the report, salient among them being:[216]

- Relevant bodies/authorities do not meet regularly as mandated; the level of rigour of these meetings in terms of content and thoroughness with a focus on the task at hand is also sub-optimal.
- The responsibility of handling the act and all activities as required is invariably an additional duty for individuals within implementing authorities, particularly the Appropriate Authorities; it is commonly perceived as difficult to handle against overlapping and conflicting priorities.
- There is a gap between the availability of funds and their effective utilization because of lack of clarity/awareness about the exact procedure involved in utilization.[217]
- It is mandatory to include NGO representatives in the committees constituted under the act. However, in some states, inappropriate NGO representatives, that is, those who do not have relevant knowledge, are sometimes included as members of the committees.[218]

Intensified effective implementation of the PCPNDT Act was carried out. Inspections by the National Inspection and Monitoring Committee (NIMC) have been scaled up. Details of total conviction, from the Ministry of Health and Family Welfare, Government of India, as per reports submitted by states/UTs, are given in Table 8.6.[219]

Table 8.6   Statewise Total Convictions under PCPNDT Act (up to December 2014)

S. No.	States/ UTs	No. of Convictions
1.	Andhra Pradesh, Arunachal Pradesh, Assam, Chhattisgarh, Goa, Jharkhand, Karnataka, Kerala, Manipur, Meghalaya, Mizoram, Nagaland, Sikkim, Tamil Nadu, Tripura, Uttarakhand, West Bengal, Andaman and Nikobar Islands, Chandigarh, Dadra and Nagar Haveli, Daman and Diu, Lakshadweep, Puducherry.	0
2.	Bihar	11
3.	Gujarat	6
4.	Haryana	54
5.	Himachal Pradesh, Jammu and Kashmir, Uttar Pradesh, Delhi	1

(Cont'd)

[216] CYDA et al., 'Implementation of the PCPNDT Act'.
[217] CYDA et al., 'Implementation of the PCPNDT Act'.
[218] CYDA et al., 'Implementation of the PCPNDT Act'.
[219] Press Information Bureau, Ministry of Health and Family Welfare, 'Effective Implementation of PNDT Act', Government of India, 3 March 2015. Available at http://pib.nic.in/newsite/PrintRelease.aspx-?relid=116303 (accessed on 8 October 2015).

Table 8.6 *(Cont'd)*

S. No.	States/ UTs	No. of Convictions
6.	Madhya Pradesh	2
7.	Maharashtra	61
8.	Odisha	3
9.	Punjab	28
10.	Rajasthan	37
	Total	**206**

There are zero conviction in nearly 20 states and only one conviction in a state like UP where there is blatant and obvious preference for male children and huge violations of the act. As per Table 8.7, maximum convictions have happened in Maharashtra, followed by Haryana and Rajasthan. But overall implementation is still very poor, as violations of the act are rampant. There are zero convictions in majority of the states. Stringent enforcement and swift and tough action against the violators is the need of the hour. There are complex social behaviours and attitudes that deeply influence sex ratios in India. Preference for male children is still one of the major factors. The devalued status of women in our societies is another major factor. Law is an important tool for social change. It is required to enhance the effectiveness of existing implementation structures and systems through a national plan of action, intensive especially legal training, and sensitization of the implementing authorities and concerned stakeholders, with a focus on efficiency and monitoring. Aaccountability of the implementing authorities must also be built in and action should be taken against erring officials. Radiologists/sonologists/gynecologists have to play a major role towards prevention of female foeticide and implementation of the PCPNDT Act. There is a need for strengthening of ethical medical practice and inclusion of child rights and gender justice in the medical school curriculum. School curriculum and teacher training must also include child rights and the values of equality and non-discrimination must be embedded firmly in the minds of students and teachers.

Important Judgments under the PCPNDT Act, 1994[220]

Vinod Soni and Anr. v. Union of India[221]

Facts

The petitioners were a married couple seeking to challenge the constitutional validity of the PCPNDT Act.

[220] Joshi, 'Compilation and Analysis of Case-Laws'.
[221] 2005 Cr LJ 3408, 2005 (3) Mh LJ 1131.

The petition contained basically two challenges to the enactment:

1. First, that it violated Article 14 of the Constitution;
2. Second, that it violated Article 21 of the Constitution.

The petitioners contended in this petition that the provision of Article 21 has been gradually expanded to cover several facets of life, pertaining to life itself and personal liberties which an individual has, as a matter of his fundamental right. Several judgments of the Supreme Court of India were relied upon to argue that personal liberty includes the liberty of choosing the sex of the offspring. Thus, it was contended that the couple was entitled to undertake any such medicinal procedure which provides for determination or selection of sex, so that they can exercise the right of deciding the nature of their family.

Held

The Bombay High Court observed that 'right to personal liberty cannot be expanded by any stretch of imagination to liberty to prohibit to coming into existence of a female or male fetus which shall be for the nature to decide'. After making reference to the decisions of the Supreme Court, which explain that Article 21 includes the right to food, clothing, decent environment and even protection of cultural heritage, the High Court held that 'these rights, even if, further expanded to the extremes of the possible elasticity of the provisions of Article 21, cannot include right to selection of sex, whether preconception or post-conception'.

It was further observed by the High Court that 'this Act is factually enacted to further the right of the child to full development as given under Article 21. A child conceived is, therefore, entitled under Article 21 to full development, whatever be the sex of that child.' Accordingly, the High Court dismissed the petition by holding that it does not even make a prima facie case for violation of Article 21 of the Constitution.

M/s Malpani Infertility Clinic Pvt. Ltd. & Others v.
Appropriate Authority, PNDT Act & Others[222]

Facts

This writ petition was filed by M/s Malpani Infertility Clinic Pvt. Ltd. in the High Court of Bombay, challenging the order, passed by the Appropriate Authority, suspending the registration of the petitioner's diagnostic centre under the PNDT Act. The main contention raised was that show-cause notice, as contemplated under Section 20(1), an opportunity of hearing, as contemplated under Section 20(2), and sufficient reasons, as required under Section 20(3) of the act, were not given to the petitioners before taking the action of suspending their registration; hence the order was bad as per law.

[222] AIR 2005 Bom 26, 2005 (1) Bom CR 595, (2005) 107 BOM LR 737.

Held

Considering the peculiar facts of the case, the Bombay High Court rejected the petitioners' contention and pointed out that the petitioners had joined as Respondent No. 38 in Writ Petition (Civil) No. 301/2001, filed by Center for Enquiry into Health and Allied Themes (CEHAT) before the apex court, and also filed an affidavit therein, defending the sex determination tests on the ground of 'family balancing'. Though subsequently the petitioners had filed another affidavit tendering apology, they knew that they were prosecuted for criminal offence under the provisions of the act. It was held that, as the Appropriate Authority has, after referring to that criminal prosecution, issued the order of suspension, there was sufficient notice to the petitioners and there was also sufficient mention of the reasons by the Appropriate Authority in the suspension order. It was further held that, 'when the reasons are required to be given in writing it is not necessary that there ought to be a detailed discussion'. As regards the contention that Section 20(3) provides only for cancellation and not for suspension of the registration, it was pointed out that such power has to be read in to the Section, otherwise the provisions of a welfare enactment will be rendered nugatory. In the words of High Court, 'where there is a conflict of private interest, to carry on a particular activity which the Public Authority considered as damaging to the social interest, surely the power under the Statute has to be read as an enabling power'.

Radiological and Imaging Association (State Chapter-Jalna), through Dr. Jignesh Gokuldas Thakker, its PCPNDT Coordinator for the Indian Radiological and Imaging Association v. Union of India (UOI), through its Secretary, Ministry of Health and Family Welfare, State of Maharashtra through its Secretary, Ministry of Health and Family Welfare, and Mr. Laxmikant Deshmukh, Collector and District Magistrate[223]

Facts

In a series of landmark decisions delivered by the Bombay High Court towards effective and meaningful implementation of the provisions of the act, one must say this judgment constitutes a major milestone. It once again proves that the judiciary is one step ahead of legislature and executive in acting as catalyst for social change. This writ petition under Article 226 of the Constitution was filed by the Radiological and Imaging Association, challenging two actions initiated by the Collector of Kolhapur District. One was the circular dated 14 January 2011 issued by him, requiring the radiologists and sonologists in the district to transmit Form F online within 24 hours of conducting sonography. The challenge was on the ground that the said circular is without authority of law because under the PCPNDT Rules, Form F is required to be submitted by up to the fifth day of the next month and not immediately within 24 hours, and not online. The Collector and Civil Surgeon strongly supported the circular on the ground that Kolhapur district was having the worst sex ratio of 838 females per 1,000 males, and one of the causes for the same was found to be the illegal use of sonography centres for sex selection tests, resulting in sex determination. It was found that there were two blatant violations of the act, namely under-reporting and false reporting of sonography tests. Moreover, as Kolhapur alone had 250 sonography centres and more than 12,000 sonography tests were being conducted on pregnant women each month, considering the magnitude of the work and the volume of manpower required to monitor the submission of Form F and its analysis for necessary action under the act and rules, it was submitted that with online submission of Form F, the said task had become easy, less time consuming, and effective for taking prompt action. Moreover, it was in consonance with the spirit and object of Rule 9(4), which already required the sonography centres to submit Form F every month.

Held

The High Court found considerable substance in these submissions as it noticed four distinct advantages in the online submission of Form F when such large number of sonographies —15,000 per month—are performed. First, the entire information in Form F had to be filled up during online submission, otherwise the Form was not accepted by online system. Second, the work of submitting information in Form F had to be completed on a day-to-day basis, which led to the third advantage for the district administration—carrying out meaningful scrutiny and analysis to zero in on cases where sex selection was resorted to after sex determination. Fourth, it would enable the Appropriate Authority to take immediate action in case of breach of provisions of the act and rules. The High Court, therefore, found that the circular to submit Form F online within 24 hours was in keeping with the letter and spirit of Section 17(4).

Sadhu Ram Kusla v. Ranjit Kaur and Ors.[224]

Facts

In this case the acquittal of the respondents by the trial court for the offences punishable under Sections120 B, 312, 315 of the IPC, and Section 23 of the act was challenged. The allegations against the respondents were to the effect that respondent no. 3, Dr. Kamlesh Jindal, who was running her Nursing Home at Rampura, had conducted sonography test on respondent no. 1, who was 14 weeks pregnant. The test was allegedly conducted to determine 'foetus well being' and the result was found to be normal. However, respondent no. 1 had a miscarriage on the same night. Hence, it was contended by the petitioner that the sonography test was in fact conducted to determine sex of the foetus, and the pregnancy was terminated on finding the foetus to be female. It was argued that if the foetus was found to be normal in the sonography test, a miscarriage could not have occurred on the same night by alleged excessive bleeding, as contended by the respondents. Respondent no. 2 was the husband of respondent no. 1, and respondent no. 4 was Dr. Laxmi, who had terminated the pregnancy of respondent no. 1. During trial, evidence was laid both by the prosecution and defence. As per respondent no. 1, she had continuous bleeding and pain for two days and therefore had gone for ultrasound scan to respondent no. 3, to know the condition of the foetus. She was told by respondent no. 3 that there was risk of abortion and she should get herself admitted. However, as no male member was accompanying her, she refused to get admitted and had the miscarriage the same night. The trial court accepted the defence case and acquitted all the four accused.

---

[224] Criminal Misc. No. 337–MA of 2007.

Held

In appeal, the High Court also concurred with the decision of the trial court by holding that there was practically no case made out. It was opined by the High Court that the mere fact that there was miscarriage on the same night on which sonography test was conducted, ipso facto does not establish that sex of the foetus was detected and disclosed. It was further held that there is no legal basis for the presumption that since there was an abortion, the foetus was female. There was also no evidence to prove that the foetus was of a female.

Vijay Sharma and others v. Union of India[225]

Facts

This writ petition was filed under Article 226 of the Constitution of India, by Mr. Vijay Sharma and others, challenging the validity of the act on the ground that it violates the principle of 'equality of law' enshrined in Article 14 of the Constitution. The petitioners were a married couple having two female children, and were desirous of having a male child. According to them, by doing so, they could then enjoy the love and affection of both son and daughter, and their daughters could enjoy the company of their own brother while growing up. According to them, couples who already have children of one sex should be allowed to make use of the prenatal diagnostic techniques at pre-conception stage to have a child of the opposite sex. It was further argued that under the provisions of the MTP Act, termination of pregnancy is allowed under certain circumstances; hence there is no reason to impose a blanket ban on determination of sex at the pre-conception stage. An innovative plea was raised to the effect that, if anguish caused by unwanted pregnancy is recognized as ground for termination of the pregnancy under the MTP Act, why the anguish caused to a mother who conceives a female or male child for the second or third time is not considered under the PCPNDT Act. Since the act thus discriminates between two women situated in similar positions, it violates Article 14 of the Constitution, it was argued.

Held

The High Court, after elaborately dealing with the Object, Reasons, and Provisions of the Act, held that there can be no comparison between the two legislations, namely the MTP Act and the PCPNDT Act. The two Acts have different objectives. The MTP Act does not deal with sex selection before or after conception. Anguish of a mother who does not want to bear a child of a particular sex cannot be equated with a mother who wants to terminate the pregnancy not because of the sex of child but for other circumstances. Thus, by process of comparative study, the High Court held that provisions of the act cannot be called as discriminatory and hence violative of Article 14 of the Constitution.

The High Court had, in this case, taken note of the frightening figure showing imbalance in sex ratio in various parts of India, and expressed its concern for the same. The High Court was also aghast at the shocking arguments in the petition, proclaiming that if the country was

---

[225] AIR 2008 Bom 29, (2007) 5 Bom CR 710, 2007 (6) ALL MR 336.

economically and socially backward, it was better that female children were not born. The court, in its strong and harsh words, held that 'such tendency affects the dignity of women. It undermines their importance. It insults and humiliates womanhood. It violates woman's right to life. Sex selection is therefore against the spirit of the law and Constitution.' Thus rejecting all the challenges raised to the constitutional validity of the act, the court dismissed the petition and directed the state to take all expeditious steps to prevent misuse of the diagnostic techniques.

Hemanta Rath v. Union of India and Others[226]

Facts

This writ petition was filed in public interest by Hemanta Rath, a social activist, under Article 226 of the Constitution of India in the High Court of Orissa, seeking directions for the effective implementation of the PCPNDT Act in the state. The said PIL was filed following publication of a series of news items in the newspapers and in the electronic media to the effect that hundreds of skeletons, skulls, and body parts of children had been recovered from different parts of the state. The petitioner asserted that recovery of such body parts had shocked the common man, and it was clear from the news reports that the recoveries were made from an area close to various nursing homes and clinics. There were strong allegations that the practice of sex selection and prenatal sex determination was still rampant.

Therefore, the complaint in the petition raised the contention that there was total inaction both on the part of the state government and the central government in the matter of implementing the provisions of the said act, which was enacted for preventing infanticide and foeticide. It was contented in this petition that neither the appropriate authorities were appointed as contemplated under Section 17(1) of the act, nor did the state constitute any advisory committee. Hence, it was urged by the petitioner that the provisions of Section 28 of the act had become nugatory without constitution of the Appropriate Authority.

The state of Orissa, in its reply, stated that in view of the report in the newspapers, immediate steps were taken by lodging cases and the cases had been handed over to the state crime branch, as a result of which, doctors and some of the members of the staff of the concerned nursing homes and ultrasound clinics had been arrested.

Held

After referring to the object of the act and constitutional principles, the High Court stressed both the statutory and constitutional obligation of the state to implement the provisions of the act. The High Court also took note of the delayed response of the state in the formation of the State Advisory Committee, which was constituted only in 2007. This also was not in accordance with the provisions of the act.

The High Court gave explicit directions to the state government to appoint Appropriate Authorities and Advisory Committees within six weeks and further directed the Committees to

---

[226] AIR 2008 Orissa HC 71, (2008) I OLR 916.

take strict measures to implement the provisions of the act. The court observed that the act had come into existence in order to protect an appropriate male and female ratio in society so that there would be no social imbalance.

Suhasini Umesh Karanjkar v. Kolhapur Municipal Corporation & Ors[227]

Facts

This decision was landmark in more than one sense, and also a long and much awaited decision. It overruled the earlier decision delivered by the two-judge Aurangabad Bench of the Bombay High Court in Writ Petition No. 1587 of 2009, filed by Dr Dadasheb Popatrao Tarte against the state of Maharashtra through the Minister for Health and Family Welfare, and decided on 14 August 2009. In that writ petition, seizure of ultrasonography machines was challenged on the ground that Section 30 of the act did not empower the Appropriate Authority to seize such machine used in genetic clinics. The High Court had accepted the said contention, holding that reading of Section 30 and Rule 12 of the act does not empower the Appropriate Authority to seize the ultrasonography machines used in the genetic clinics. The High Court had, therefore, set aside the seizure of ultrasonography machines and directed their return to the petitioner. However, it was clear that while arriving at this conclusion, Explanation (2) of Rule 12, which defines material object to include machines, and Explanation (3), which states that 'seize' and 'seizure' would include 'seal' and 'sealing' respectively, were not brought to the notice of the High Court.

The result of the said decision was, however, to the effect that the Appropriate Authority could not seize sonography machines and because of this decision, machines already seized had to be released and returned. When this anomalous position was brought to the notice of the High Court in Writ Petition No. 7896 of 2010, filed by Dr Mrs Suhasini Umesh Karanjkar against the Kolhapur Municipal Corporation and others, dated 23 December 2010, it was held that this part of the decision required reconsideration and the matter deserved to be heard by a larger Bench. Accordingly, the matter was considered in detail by the Full Bench which, in its decision dated 12 June 2011, positively and conclusively held that the analysis of the provisions of the act was sufficient to hold that the expression 'material object', in respect of which the power to seize and seal is conferred upon the Appropriate Authority/authorized officer, included ultrasound machines, other machines, and equipment used for prenatal diagnostic techniques or sex selection techniques, and hence it can be held as settled law that the Appropriate Authority has power to seize the ultrasound machines used in genetic clinics.

Held

In this case, before parting with the matter, the High Court also made a reference to the disturbing figures of the declining national CSR over the previous five decades, to which its attention was brought by the learned Additional Government Pleader, reflecting that in the census of 2011, the national female CSR had fallen to 914, whereas in Maharashtra, it had gone down from 913

---

[227] 2011 (4) AIR Bom R 326, 2011 (4) Mh LJ 21, (2011) 4 Bom CR 293.

in 2001 to 883 in 2011. It had gone down to as low as 801 in Beed district. In Kolhapur district, where the offence in question was registered, it was 839. The High Court also felt distressed by the fact that a number of cases on offences registered under the act were pending in Courts of the Judicial Magistrate First Class for a long period, sometimes up to 6 years, and in a few cases as long as 6 to 8 years. The High Court, therefore, directed that all cases under the act be taken up on top priority basis and the Metropolitan Magistrates, Mumbai and the Judicial Magistrates (First Class) in other districts try and decide such cases with utmost priority, preferably within 1 year. Criminal cases instituted in the year 2010 and prior thereto should be tried and decided by 31 December 2011. The High Court gave further directions to circulate the copy of the judgment to all the courts in Maharashtra for timely compliance.

Dr Vandana Ramchandra Patil v. the State of Maharashtra & Anr[228]

Facts

This case was filed by the appellant for the offences punishable under the provisions of the PCPNDT Act, and during the pendency of the trial, his clinic and the sonography machine used by him were sealed, along with the suspension of his license for medical practice. The appellant filed this case before the High Court for opening the seal of the ultrasonography machine so that it could be used.

Held

After hearing both the parties, the Court held that as the offence was committed under the PCPNDT Act essentially with the use of the ultrasonography machine, and as the machine was the most important component in the crime which was repetitive in nature, the prevention of the crime was best achieved by sealing the machine. If the seal was opened, the accused in the case would be facilitated to repeat the crime. Once a case was made out, the repetition of such a crime had to be prevented and cannot be allowed to proliferate. Accordingly, the Court ordered the machine to be shifted to the hospital of the Corporation and the seal to be retained till it was shifted until the trial was over.

Voluntary Health Association of Punjab v. Union of India and Ors[229]

Facts

This writ petition was filed in 2006 since the directions of the Supreme Court for proper implementation of the PCPNDT Act, given as early as 2001 and 2003 in the case of *CEHAT* v. *Union of India*, were not complied with by the various states. The petition came up for hearing before the apex court on 4 March 2013.

In this ptition, the apex court had to express its concern again about Indian society's discrimination towards the girl child because of various reasons and prejudices which have their roots

---

[228] Writ Petition No. 4399 of 2012.
[229] AIR 2013 SC 1571, (2013) 4 SCC 1.

in social behaviour , and due to the evils of the dowry system still prevailing in the society. The Court noted the decline in the female child ratio across the country, caused by the misuse of prenatal diagnostic techniques and the improper implementation of the act meant to prevent such misuse. In this petition, therefore, the personal attendance of the health secretaries of the states of Punjab, Haryana, NCT Delhi, Rajasthan, Uttar Pradesh, Bihar, and Maharashtra was secured to examine what steps they had taken for the proper and effective implementation of the provisions of the act, as well as the various directions issued by the Court.

Held

The Court took notice of the Census figure of 2011, which showed a decline in female CSR in many states of India from 2001 to 2011. The Court also took notice that there was a lack of proper supervision and effective implementation of the act by various states except for the state of Maharashtra. It was also found that the ultrasound machines used for such sex determination in violation of the provisions of the act were seized and, even if seized, they were being released to the violators only to facilitate repetition of the crime. Moreover, very few cases resulted in conviction and were pending disposal for several years in many courts. Many of the ultrasonography clinics did not even maintain any record in respect of the pregnant women, as per rules. Many of the clinics were totally unaware of the amendments in the act and Rules. Therefore, the apex court, again issued various directions in this petition, as follows:

- The CSB and the State and Union Territories Supervisory Boards should meet at least once in six months, so as to supervize the effective implementation of the act.
- The State Advisory Committees and District Advisory Committees should gather information relating to the breach of the provisions of the act and the Rules and take steps to seize records, seal machines, and institute legal proceedings in case they notice violation of the provisions of the act.
- The said Committees should report the details of the charges framed and the conviction of the persons under the act to the State Medical Councils for proper action, including suspension of the registration of the unit and cancellation of licence to practise.
- The authorities should ensure also that all records and forms are maintained in accordance with Rule 9(8).
- They should further ensure that manufacturers and sellers of ultrasonography machines do not sell any machine to any unregistered centre, and disclose, on a quarterly basis, a list of persons to whom the machines have been sold.
- Steps should also be taken by the state governments and other authorities under the act for mapping of all registered and unregistered ultrasonography clinics in three months' time.
- A Special Cell should to be constituted by the state governments and the UTs to monitor the progress of various cases pending in the courts under the act, and take steps for their early disposal.
- To seize and, if necessary, confiscate the machines which are used illegally and incontravention of the provisions of the act.
- To communicate this order to the Registrars of various courts to take appropriate follow-up action with due intimation to the concerned courts.

Abortion and Rights of a Child

Abortion[230] is one of the subjects that have been discussed extensively at both national and international levels. It is a controversial issue all over the world. The right to life is a very broad concept and is the most fundamental of all rights. Religious, moral, and cultural perceptions and sensibilities continue to influence abortion laws throughout the world. The right to life, the right to liberty, and the right to security of person are major issues of human rights that are sometimes used as justification for the existence or the absence of laws controlling abortion. In this debate, arguments presented in favour of or against abortion focus on either the moral permissibility of an induced abortion, or justification of laws permitting or restricting abortion. The issue of the foetus' life raises the question whether one person's desire for autonomy can extend to ending another's existence. Besides, killing is a crime and the foetus is an innocent life. Aborting foetuses because they may be disabled might imply a rejection of people with disabilities. Another argument is that an embryo (or, in later stages of development, a foetus) is a human being, entitled to protection from the moment of conception, and therefore has a right to life that must be respected.[231] If abortion is banned, or just more restricted, we would return to the days of 'back-street abortions'. Wwomen would resort to unhygienic measures or approach quacks to abort the foetuses. Another argument in favour of abortion is that when the act of abortion is necessary to save the mother's life, the rationale is not that the foetus is seen to have less value than the mother, but that if no action is taken, both will die. If abortion is banned, a woman who does not want to carry her pregnancy would carry it and then abandon the new-born child.[232] This would be more dangerous to the life of the baby. Thus, it is better to terminate the pregnancy at an earlier stage. Many countries in which abortion is legal require that certain criteria be met in order for an abortion to be obtained, often, but not always, using a trimester-based system to regulate the window in which abortion is still legal to perform. There is this dilemma whether a mother has a right to terminate her pregnancy at any time she wishes, or whether an unborn child has a right to life.[233]

---

[230] Abortion is the termination of a pregnancy by the removal or expulsion from the uterus a foetus or embryo resulting in or causing its death. Abortion can be classified into two types:

(1) Spontaneous abortion—An abortion which results due to the complications during pregnancy and that occurs unintentionally is called spontaneous abortion. It is also termed as miscarriage.
(2) Induced abortion, which has also been divided into two types:

    (a) Therapeutic abortion—An abortion which is induced to preserve the health of the mother when her life is in danger or when it is found that the child, if born, will be a disabled one is termed as therapeutic abortion.

    (b) Elective abortion—An abortion induced for any other reason is known as elective abortion.

Both embryo and foetus mean unborn child.

[231] Sai Abhipsa Gochhayat, 'Understanding of Right to Abortion under Indian Constitution', *Manupatra*. Available at http://manupatra.com/roundup/373/Articles/PRESENTATION.pdf (accessed on 18 October 2015).

[232] Gochhayat, 'Understanding of Right to Abortion'.

[233] Gochhayat, 'Understanding of Right to Abortion'.

According to Ronald Dworkin, who made a detailed study on the issue of abortion,[234] a foetus has no interest before the third trimester.[235] A foetus cannot feel pain until late in pregnancy, because its brain is not sufficiently developed before then. The scientists have agreed that foetal brain will be sufficiently developed to feel pain from approximately the 26th week.[236] Thus, whether abortion is against the interest of a foetus must depend on whether the foetus itself has interests, not on whether interests will develop if no abortion takes place. Something that is not alive does not have interests. Once a foetus can live on its own, it may have interests. This is only after the third trimester.[237]

In the USA, the entire issue of abortion has been the centre of intense debate. It is viewed as part of the rights of women to abort. In the leading decision on *Roe* v. *Wade*,[238] the US Supreme Court recognized the constitutional right of a woman to decide whether or not to terminate her pregnancy. This decision was altered in *Webster* v. *Reproductive Health Service*,[239] which allowed the state to impose greater restrictions on the availability of abortion and of doctor–patient communication with respect to abortion. In response to *Roe* v. *Wade*, several states enacted laws limiting abortion, including laws requiring parental consent for minors to obtain abortions, parental notification laws, spousal consent laws, spousal notification laws, laws requiring abortions to be performed in hospitals but not clinics, laws barring state funding for abortions, and laws banning most very-late-term abortions. The Supreme Court struck down several state restrictions on abortions in a long series of cases stretching from the mid-1970s to the late 1980s.

In the Supreme Court of Canada, interpreting Article 7 of the Canadian Charter guarantees an individual's right to life, liberty, and freedom and security of a person. In the leading case of *Morgentalor Smoling and Scott* v. *R*,[240] the Court focused on the bodily security of pregnant women. The Criminal Code of the country required a pregnant woman who wanted an abortion to submit an application to a therapeutic committee, which resulted in delays. The Supreme Court found that this procedure infringed the guarantee of security of a person. This subjected the pregnant women to undue psychological stress. The court further observed that the state's interest in protecting the foetus was legitimate, but the right to security of the person of a pregnant woman was infringed more than was required to achieve the objective of protecting the foetus. Also, the Abortion Act, 1967 of the UK, in its Article 2, does not confer an absolute right to life to the unborn, as was held in *Paton* v. *United Kingdom*.[241] Abortion is permitted if the continuance of the pregnancy involves risk. The right to life of the foetus is subject to an implied limitation, allowing pregnancy to be terminated in order to protect the life of a mother. The same was upheld in *H* v. *Norway*.[242]

Abortion is severely condemned in Vedic, Upanishadic, the later puranic (old) and smriti literature. Paragraph 3 of the Code of Ethics of the Medical Council of India says: 'I will maintain

---

[234] Ronald Dworkin, ed., *Freedom's Law: The Moral Reading of the American Constitution* (Oxford University Press, 1999), 90.

[235] Dworkin, *Freedom's Law*, 90. He says that 'not everything that can be destroyed has an interest in not being destroyed'.

[236] See Clifford Grobstein, *Science and the Unborn: Choosing Human Futures* (Basic Books, 1988), 13.

[237] Dworkin, *Freedom's Law*.

[238] 410 US 13 (1973).

[239] 492 US 490 (1989).

[240] (1988) 44 DLR (4th) 385.

[241] (1980) 3 EHRR 408.

[242] (1992) 73 DR 155.

the utmost respect for human life from the time of conception'. The Supreme Court has said that the right to privacy is implicit in Article 21 of the Constitution and a right to abortion can be read from this right.

In India, right to life has been recognized under Article 21 of the Constitution, which says that 'No person shall be deprived of his life and personal liberty except according to the procedure established by law'. 'Person' here includes both man and woman. Among various rights which are available to a woman, the right to abortion is also believed to be one of the most essential and fundamental rights. Right to abortion has been recognized under right to privacy, which is a part of right to personal liberty, and which emanates from right to life.[243] Indian law allows abortion, if the continuance of pregnancy would involve a risk to the life of the pregnant woman or grave injury to her physical or mental health. Abortion was being practised earlier by many. Because it was illegal, it was practised in a clandestine manner. The passing of the act made medical termination of pregnancy legal, with certain conditions for safeguarding the health of the mother. The MTP Bill was passed by both the Houses of the Parliament and received the assent of the President of India on 10 August 1971. It came on the Statute Book as the 'The MTP Act, 1971'. This law guarantees the right of women in India to terminate unintended pregnancy by a registered medical practitioner in a hospital established or maintained by the government or a place approved for the purpose of this act by the government.

Medical Termination of Pregnancy Act, 1971

Under the MTP Act, all abortions require the consent of the woman and all abortions after 20 weeks of conception are illegal. Section 3 of the act mentions the provisions for medical termination of pregnancy. The conditions under which abortions can be conducted under the act are depicted in Figure 8.2.

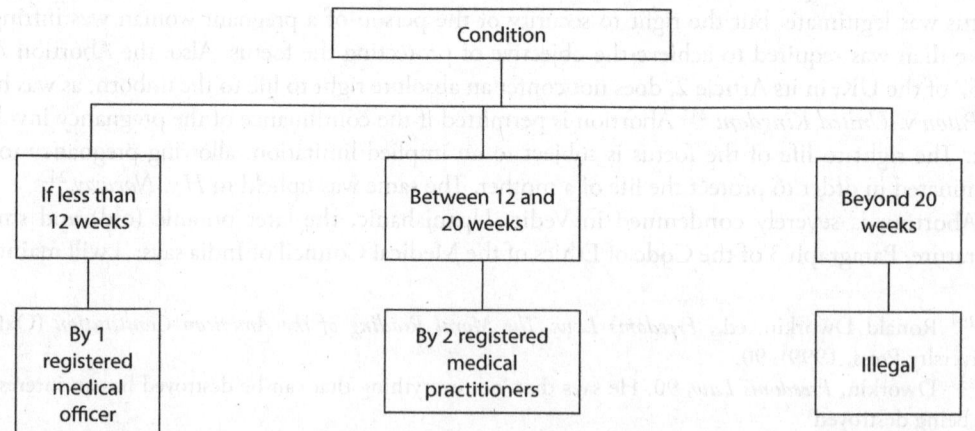

Figure 8.2 Termination of Pregnancy under the MTP Act[244]

---

[243] *Roe* v. *Wade*, 410 US 113 (1973).
[244] Source: Compiled by the author.

If any of the above conditions are satisfied, the termination of pregnancy is allowed with the consent of the woman, as a health measure, on humanitarian grounds, and on eugenic grounds. The pregnancies can be terminated only at government hospitals or a place for the time being approved for the purpose of this act by the government or a District Level Committee constituted by that government[245] under the following circumstances:[246]

- Pregnancy would involve a risk to life of the pregnant woman or cause a grave injury to her physical or mental health.
- If there is substantial risk that the child, if born, would suffer from such physical or mental abnormalities as to be seriously handicapped.
- If the pregnancy is alleged to have been caused by rape, the anguish caused by such pregnancy shall be presumed to cause a grave injury to the mental health of the pregnant woman.
- Where any pregnancy has occurred as a result of failure of any device or method used by any married woman or her husband for the purpose of limiting the number of children, the anguish caused by such unwanted pregnancy may be presumed to constitute a grave injury to the mental health of the pregnant woman.
- In case of a minor below 18 years or a mentally ill person, the pregnancy shall be terminated with the consent in writing of her guardian.

Under the MTP Act, the pregnancy can be terminated by a registered medical practitioner and if it is done by anyone who is not a registered medical practitioner, it would be an offence punishable with rigorous imprisonment for a term which shall not be less than 2 years but which may extend to 7 years under the IPC.[247]

The MTP Act also plays a 'guilty' role by sanctioning abortions up to 20 weeks. A woman can be brought into the acceptable categories defined in Section 4 of the MTP Act. On the finding of a female foetus, she can easily have her pregnancy terminated. The PCPNDT Act permits diagnostic tests to find out whether there is any chromosomal abnormality, congenital anomaly, sex-linked genetic disorder, or any other abnormality justifying termination of the pregnancy. Such tests would disclose the sex of the foetus. These techniques are thus largely misused to determine the sex and not the abnormalities, not out of curiosity but with the object of destroying the female foetus. The constitutional validity of sex determination followed by abortion is doubtful. In law, an unborn child can be considered a person as such within the meaning of Articles 14, 15, and 21 of the Constitution, with several statutory rights. Abortion being resorted to in the case of female children only would make them violate Articles 14 and 15. The right to an abortion is essential to a woman to ensure her control over her reproductive process. But the decisions as to whether she wants the child or not must be taken regardless of the sex of the unborn child. But in practice, in a majority of the cases, the issue is not of the reproductive rights of the woman or

---

[245] MTP Act, Section 4 amended by the Medical Termination of Pregnancy Amendment Act, 2002 (No. 64 of 2002). The committee with the chief medical officer or district health officer as the chairperson of the said committee, provided that the district level committee shall consist of not less than three and not more than five members including the chairperson.

[246] MTP Act, Section 3.

[247] MTP Act, 2002.

her choice but of the sex of the unborn child. Abortion preceded by sex determination is totally illegal and a criminal act on the part of the doctor.[248] To overcome this, doctors specify any of the grounds available under the MTP Act for carrying out abortions. There is no method to check that the reasons specified are true. These certificates have to be forwarded to the government. The government, being concerned only with its family planning programme 'targets', is thus a willing party to this legalized female foeticide.[249]

Important Judgments relating to the Medical Termination of Pregnancy Act

D. Rajeswari v. State Of Tamil Nadu And Ors[250]

Facts

This case is of an unmarried girl of 13 years who approached the Court praying for issue of a direction to terminate the pregnancy of the child in her womb, on the ground that bearing the unwanted pregnancy of the child of three months made her mentally ill and the continuance of pregnancy caused great anguish in her mind, which would result in a grave injury to her mental health, since the pregnancy was caused by rape.

Held

The. Court observed that unless the pregnancy of the petitioner is terminated, not only would mental shock and anguish be caused, but an irreparable and irremediable loss would be caused to her, and therefore granted permission to terminate the pregnancy.

Dr. Nisha Malviya and Anr. v. State of M.P.[251]

Facts

In the above case, there were five accused, including two doctors, facing trial. It was alleged that one of the accused committed rape on a minor girl aged about 12 years and made her pregnant. The other two co-accused then took the minor girl to Bhopal and terminated her pregnancy. It was contended on behalf of the prosecution that the pregnancy was terminated to conceal or destroy the evidence of rape, as pregnancy was certainly an evidence of sexual intercourse having been committed on her.

Held

The Court held that the act of miscarriage was done to destroy evidence of rape and hence all the accused were guilty of termination of pregnancy without the consent of the mother/girl.

[248] Grover, 'Amniocentesis or Female Foeticide', 6.
[249] Peter Borne, ed., *Medicine, Medical Ethics and the Value of Life* (London: John Wiley & Sons), 145.
[250] 1996 Cr LJ 3795.
[251] 2000 Cr LJ 671.

Shri Bhagwan Katariya and Others v. *State of M.P.*[252]

Facts

In the above case the complainant, Smt. Anita, was married to Navneet. The applicants were the younger brothers of Navneet. After the complainant conceived, the husband and the other family members took an exception to it, took her for abortion, and got the abortion done without her consent. The complainant, even before she conceived the child, had on several occasions written a number of letters to her parents, wherein she reflected her pathetic condition. After conceiving, she wrote certain letters to her parents, wherein she showed that she was hale and hearty and was happy with the events. She, however, wrote in the letters that the husband and the other family members were not happy with the said condition. Thereafter, she also wrote thatthe abortion was effected contrary to her wishes. Thereafter, the matter was reported to the police. The police, after making proper investigations, arrested the persons accused in the matter.

Held

The Court opined that if we refer Section 3 of the MTP Act, a doctor is entitled to terminate the pregnancy under particular circumstances and if the pregnancy is terminated in accordance with the provisions of law, it must be presumed that it could not be done without the consent of the woman. In the present case, a permanent scar had been carved on the heart and soul of the woman by depriving her of her child.

The above case law shows that a woman has an absolute right to abortion and no one can take away this right from her. The judiciary has been playing a vital role in securing these rights to women. Right to abortion has been regarded as a fundamental right of privacy.

Amendments to the Medical Termination of Pregnancy Act, 1971

Enacted in 1971, the MTP Act does not recognize a woman's right to abortion and instead legalizes the conduct of abortions under the liberal conditions stipulated therein. The MTP Act was enacted on the impetus of the Central Family Planning Board as a measure to control fertility and to protect doctors from penalization for terminating pregnancies for medical reasons.[253] There is now a need for using a rights-based approach to abortion.

Though abortion has been legal in India for over 40 years now, every two hours a woman dies because of abortion related causes. Statistics reveal that unsafe abortions are the third largest cause of maternal deaths in India and account for 8 per cent of maternal mortalities because women do not have access to safe abortion services.[254] One of the main reasons for women not receiving

[252] (2001) 4 MPHT 20 CG.

[253] Indira Jaising, C. Sathyamala, and Asmita Basu, *Lawyers Collective (Women's Rights Initiative): From the Abnormal to the Normal—Preventing Sex Selective Abortions through the Law* (New Delhi: Lawyers Collective [Women's Rights Initiative], 2007).

[254] Aarti Dhar, 'Court Ruling on Abortion for Rape Survivor Is Reminder of Need to Amend the Law', *The Wire*, 31 July 2015. Available at http://thewire.in/2015/07/31/court-ruling-on-abortion-for-rape-survivor-is-reminder-of-need-to-amend-the-law-7629/ (accessed on 23 October 2015).

MTP services on site is non-availability of doctors. In comparison, mid-level providers (which include nurses and doctors of the Department of Ayurveda, Yoga and Naturopathy, Unani, Siddha and Homoeopathy [AYUSH][255]) are not only available at all levels of the health system but global experiences suggest that these cadres of trained providers can safely offer abortion services. The NPP 2000 had also identified permitting mid-level providers to offer abortion services as one of the strategies to remove barriers to women's access to safe abortion services.[256]

At the time of the passage of the MTP Act in 1971, Dilation and Curettage (D and C) was the only available technology. Now, there are new technologies like manual vacuum aspiration (MVA) and medical methods of abortion (MMA) which are very safe. Experts say there is no evidence that increasing the gestation limit for abortion leads to an increase in the abortion rate—a major argument used by those opposing the MTP amendments. Whether abortion is legally more restricted or available on request, a woman's likelihood of having an unintended pregnancy and seeking induced abortion is about the same. However, legal restrictions, together with other barriers, mean many women induce abortion themselves or seek abortion from unskilled providers.[257]

Globally, out of 60 countries with abortion laws that specify a gestation limit within their law, 34 countries allow abortion anytime for more indications than saving the life of mother. These indications include foetal impairment, rape, economic, and social reasons.[258] In 2004, Ethiopia approved a new law which legally prohibits abortion but allows it under certain conditions including when the pregnancy results from rape or incest, in case of foetal abnormalities, for women with physical or mental disabilities, and for minors who are physically or psychologically unprepared o raise a child.[259] It is important to note the provision that if minors are not prepared to raise a child, they can abort.

Nikita Mehta was an educated, middle-class woman who was equipped with sufficient information on the foetus' health condition and apparently did not face any coercion from her family. She wanted to terminate a pregnancy which had a high probability of resulting in a miscarriage or the birth of a child with a serious heart defect. This could have been a routine decision, had it not been for the fact that Nikita's pregnancy had advanced beyond the 20 weeks deadline during which medical termination of pregnancy is permitted in India.[260] Rather than resort to an illegal abortion, Nikita and her husband, along with the specialist who diagnosed a congenital anomaly in the foetus, filed a petition at the Mumbai High Court asking for permission for an abortion in the 23rd week, which was when the problem was detected.

1. The argument was that in several countries including the United Kingdom, there is no gestational age limit set for abortion in the case of foetal abnormalities.

[255] L. Patel, T.A. Bennett, C.T. Halpern, H.B. Johnston, and C.M. Suchindran, 'Support for Provision of Early Medical Abortion by Mid-level Providers in Bihar and Jharkhand, India', *Reproductive Health Matters* 17 (2009): 70–79.

[256] Patel et al., 'Support for Provision of Early Medical Abortion'.

[257] Dhar, 'Court Ruling on Abortion'.

[258] Dhar, 'Court Ruling on Abortion'.

[259] Dhar, 'Court Ruling on Abortion'.

[260] Neha Madhiwalla, 'The Niketa Mehta Case: Does the Right to Abortion Threaten Disability Rights?' *Indian Journal of Medical Ethics* V, no. 4 (October–December 2008). Available at http://issuesinmedicalethics.org/index.php/ijme/article/view/456/1111 (accessed on 18 October 2015).

2. Nikita's personal reason for wanting an abortion was that she did not want to give birth to a severely disabled infant and witness its suffering.
3. The trauma caused to her and her family was an additional reason.

Section 5 of the MTP Act allows for abortion beyond the stipulated time and at non-designated places when it is to be done immediately in order to save the life of the pregnant woman. In Nikita Mehta case, the child's severe abnormal condition was detected only after 20 weeks of conception. The high Court did not allow it, so she approached the Supreme Court to terminate the foetus as the law did not permit so. The Supreme Court, in her case, disallowed the abortion. Mehta subsequently had a miscarriage. Nikita's case raised several ethical dilemmas related to abortion, disability, and the role of medical intervention and again revived the amendments to the MTP Act.

The Ministry of Health and Family Welfare released a draft of the MTP Bill, 2014,[261] which proposes to improve access to abortion through steps that will expand the healthcare providers' base and simultaneously reduce women's dependency on healthcare providers during the process of seeking abortion. The bill proposes to train and allow non-allopathic and mid-level healthcare providers to perform abortions. It also outlines the methods of abortion more clearly than the 1971 MTP Act, recognizing medical termination of pregnancy as a separate and legal technique of abortion. While these steps will improve women's access to care for abortion, other changes proposed by the bill will liberalize the law, making it more inclusive than the 1971 Act. First-trimester abortion will be considered a matter of the woman's choice and a physician's opinion will no longer be required. A woman will require only one physician's opinion in the second trimester. The amendment bill also explicitly extends abortion care to unmarried women and aims at ensuring privacy for women seeking abortion. The gestational limit for abortion will be extended from 20 to 24 weeks, and in addition, abortion will be provided for specific foetal anomalies after this period.

Significant Proposed Amendments to Medical Termination of Pregnancy Act

The revised law establishes that poverty and other social factors may be grounds for reducing the criminal penalty for abortion and that in case of rape or incest, no proof is required beyond the women's statement that it has occurred. The amendments proposed to the MTP Act include the following clauses:

• Increasing the gestation limit from 20 to 24 weeks for special categories of women (rape victims, women with disabilities—to be defined in the rules) and making first-trimester abortions available on request by removing the requirement of a doctor's approval up to 12 weeks of gestation. The clause is important since certain foetal abnormalities that are incompatible with life are detected only after 20 weeks of gestation.[262]

---

[261] Shweta Krishnan, 'MTP Amendment Bill, 2014: Towards Re-magining Abortion Care', *Indian Journal of Medical Ethics*. Available at http://www.issuesinmedicalethics.org/index.php/ijme/article/view/2179/4663 (accessed on 15 October 2015).

[262] Ministry of Health and Family Welfare, Government of India, Notification No: 12015/49/2008-MCH, Draft Medical Termination of Pregnancy (Amendment) Bill, 2014.

- Under the existing MTP Act provisions, an abortion can only be performed by a Registered Medical Practitioner (RMP).[263] The Ministry's proposed amendments will replace the requirement of an RMP with that of a Registered Health Care Provider (RHCP)— who could be a healthcare provider qualified under the Indian Medicine Central Council Act and entered into the Central Register or State Register of Indian Medicine (Ayurveda, Unani and Siddha), a qualified general nurse, or a qualified auxiliary nurse midwife.[264]
- If termination of pregnancy is performed by a person who is not a registered healthcare provider, he/she shall be punishable with imprisonment for a term not less than 2 years, which may extend to 7 years.[265]
- The proposal in the new bill, to allow persons other than just doctors to perform abortions, has been criticized by the Indian Medical Association. 'MTP is a procedure meant to be conducted by an allopathic doctor only and cannot be conducted by the paramedical staff on their own as they are not at all well equipped to handle critical medical conditions arising out of excessive bleeding especially during incomplete abortions as a result of procedures provided by unauthorised medical or paramedical professionals during and after MTPs.

While a section of the Indian medical community is suspicious of both non-allopathic systems and the notion that anyone less than a doctor can perform an abortion, the WHO has said that involving health workers can help reduce the number of deaths arising from the 22 million unsafe abortions that take place worldwide each year, almost all in low and middle-income countries. The WHO has now come up with a new guideline, 'Health Worker roles in providing safe abortion care and post-abortion contraception', that aims to help break down one critical barrier which limits access to safe abortion care—the lack of trained providers. The WHO guideline is the first to make an evidence-based recommendation on the safety, effectiveness, feasibility, and acceptability of involving a range of health workers in the delivery of recommended and effective interventions for providing safe abortion and post-abortion care, including post-abortion contraception.

The Supreme Court recently gave a landmark verdict on allowing a minor rape survivor to abort her more than 24-week-old foetus—following clearance from medical doctors. The Bench of Justices Anil R. Dave and Kurian Joseph took note of the fact that the foetus has a life now and questioned if 'killing the child will solve everything'. But since a 14-year-old girl cannot be asked to bear a child and such a situation will not only lead to immense physical and mental agony, but may also compel her to take an 'extreme step', the Court permitted her to abort. This decision is likely to give a push to the proposed amendments to the MTP Act, which seek to allow termination of pregnancy beyond 20 weeks.[266]

[263] The RMP, under the MTP Act, is defined as 'a medical practitioner who possesses any recognised medical qualification as defined in Clause (h) of Section 2 of the Indian Medical Council Act, 1956, (102 of 1956) whose name has been entered in a State Medical Register and who has such experience or training in gynaecology and obstetrics as may be prescribed by rules made under this Act'.

[264] Ministry of Health and Family Welfare, Draft MTP (Amendment) Bill, 2014.

[265] Ministry of Health and Family Welfare, Draft MTP (Amendment) Bill, 2014.

[266] Utkarsh Anand, 'Supreme Court: A 24-week Pregnant Teen Can Abort if Doctors Permit', *Indian Express*, 30 July 2015. See more at http://indianexpress.com/article/india/india-others/sc-quashes-hc-order-allows-minor-rape-victim-to-abort-foetus-after-medical-permissions/#sthash.r4XApxyX.dpuf (accessed on 2 February 2017).

Rights during Early Childhood

Registration of Birth

Under Article 7 of the UNCRC, the child shall be registered immediately after birth and shall have a name and the right to acquire a nationality. Birth registration allows a child to have a nationality and an identity, which in turn allows the child to get a passport, open a bank account, obtain credit, vote, and find employment. It also helps a child get access to basic health and education rights. Having a record of a child's birth is also essential in ensuring that the child is accounted for in the protection system. It prevents a child from hazardous child labour, allows for proper age determination in case of juvenile conflicts, avoids recruiting of children into the military, makes countering child marriage more efficient, and helps keep a record of the child and his/her family in case of runaways or lost children.

The enactment of the Registration of Births and Deaths Act (RBD Act), 1969 was an important landmark, which made the registration of births, deaths, and still births compulsory across the country.[267]

This act provides for:[268]

- uniform law across the country on the registration of births and deaths;
- compulsory reporting and registration of all births and deaths;
- implementation of the act is the responsibility of the state governments;
- rules framed by the state governments are based on a model set of rules provided by the central government (Registrar General, India).

It has been made the duty of the following persons to give the information to the registrar of births orally or in writing (Section 8):

- in respect of births in a house, by the head of the household and in his/her absence the oldest adult male member;
- in respect of birth in a hospital, health centre, maternity or nursing home, and other such facilities, the medical officer in charge;
- in respect of births in a jail, the jailor in charge;
- in respect of birth in a hostel, boarding house, lodging house, or public place, the person in charge;
- in respect of any newborn child deserted in a public place, the headman of the village or the officer in charge of the police station;
- in respect of births in plantation (Section 9), the superintendent of the plantation.

It has been made the duty of the midwife or any other medical or health attendant at a birth or any other person specified by the state government to notify the birth to the registrar (Section 10). If the birth of any child has been registered without a name, the parent or guardian of such

---

[267] The Registration of Births and Deaths Act 1969, Section 2(a).

[268] UNICEF India, 'Birth Registration—the Picture in India'. Available at http://unicef.in/Story/1133/Birth-Registration-the-picture-in-India (accessed on 23 October 2015).

a child has to give the name to the registrar either orally or in writing and then the registrar will enter the name (Section 15). In case of a child born outside India, the parents should get the birth of the child registered under this act within 60 days from their date of arrival in India (Section 20). If any person fails to give the information or issue any certificate which he is bound to do under the act, without any reasonable cause, he shall be punishable with a fine which may extend to Rs 50 (Section 23).

This act is difficult to enforce. Registration of births is not a widely prevalent practice in India. Easy access and facilities for registration are required. The panchayats and the local bodies set up under the seventy-second and seventy-third constitutional amendments may be utilized to perform the functions of registration.

An estimated 26 million births and about 9 million deaths take place in the country every year. Together, approximately 35 million vital events have to be registered every year. The current registration level of births and deaths in the country is about 58 per cent for births and 54 per cent for deaths. Each year about 42 per cent of births go unregistered, which amounts to about 10 million births. There are five major low performing states (Uttar Pradesh, Bihar, Rajasthan, Andhra Pradesh, and Madhya Pradesh) that have problems of low registration, with registration ranging from 20 per cent to 57 per cent, which is affecting the overall registration level in the country because these five states also account for approximately 25 per cent% of the annual births and are among the most populous states in the country. Registration level in the rural areas is lower when compared to the urban areas.[269]

Key issues and challenges in registration of births are as follows:[270]

- low priority accorded to registration and general apathy;
- lack of inter-departmental coordination;
- inadequate budget allocation by the states for civil registration work;
- low levels of knowledge among registration functionaries about the processes and procedures of registration, reporting, and management of data;
- lack of regular monitoring and supervision of civil registration work in the states;
- lack of awareness about the need and importance of registration.

While there is much to be done to achieve universal birth/death registration in India, many positive steps have been taken too, as mentioned next.[271]

- A National Campaign on Birth Certificates was initiated in November 2003 with the objective of clearing the backlog on issuance of birth certificates accumulated over the previous 10 years. During the first phase of the campaign, approximately 30 million birth certificates were issued in a span of 1 year. The Second Phase of the National Campaign was launched in April 2005 and according to the Office of the Registrar General, India, approximately 9.3 million birth certificates have been distributed during this phase.[272]

---

[269] UNICEF India, 'Birth Registration'.
[270] UNICEF India, 'Birth Registration'.
[271] UNICEF India, 'Birth Registration'.
[272] UNICEF India, 'Birth Registration'.

- The government has also initiated the review process of the RBD Act after a span of 37 years, to look into legal and administrative procedures and bottlenecks so as to make the law more citizen-friendly.[273]

Let us take a look at a landmark judgment on the RBD Act next.

Committee for Legal Aid to Poor v. Union of India & Ors[274]

Facts

This writ petition was filed by an NGO with the grievance that registration of births in India is at a low, that very few children are provided with birth certificates, and that the provisions of the RBD Act are not being implemented. Under Section 3 of the act, the Central Government is required to appoint a Registrar General and other such officers to coordinate and unify the activities of the Chief Registrars of the states and submit an annual report to the Central Government on the working of the act. The main grievance of the writ petitioner was that the relevant provisions of the act were not being implemented.

Held

The Court disposed off the writ petition and gave the following directions:

- All states/UTs were directed to notify ASHAs,[275] Aanganwadi workers, dais, and headmasters of government schools under Section 10[276] of the RBD Act.
- All states/UTs are directed to switch over to a uniform format for birth certificates, as suggested by the Registrar General, with the national emblem on the said certificates.

Immunization

Immunization remains the single most feasible and cost-effective way of ensuring that all children enjoy their rights to survival and good health. India still lacks a robust system to track

---

[273] UNICEF India, 'Birth Registration'.

[274] Writ Petition (Civil) no. 37 of 2009.

[275] One of the key components of the NRHM is to provide every village in the country with a trained female community health activist—ASHA, or Accredited Social Health Activist.

[276] Section 10 of the RBD Act, 1969: Duty of certain persons to notify births.—

(1) It shall be the duty of

  (a) the midwife or any other medical or health attendant at a birth or a death,

  ...

  (c) any other person whom the state government may specify in this behalf by his designation, to notify every birth or death or both at which he or she attended or was present, or which occurred in such areas as may be prescribed, to the Registrar within such time and in such manner as may be prescribed.

vaccine-preventable diseases. Vaccination coverage varies considerably from state to state, with the lowest rates in India's large central states. Differences in uptake are geographical, regional, rural–urban, poor–rich, and gender-related. On average, girls receive fewer immunizations than boys and higher birth order infants have lower vaccination coverage.[277]

Let us have a look at some significant statistics on immunization up to the year 2015:[278]

- Nine million routine immunization (RI) sessions are organized in India each year.
- These target 26 million children and 30 million pregnant women.
- The sessions are served through a massive 27,000 cold chain stores.
- The national average for full immunization is 61 per cent, and 72 per cent for DPT-3 coverage.
- The number of districts with less than 80 per cent DPT-3 coverage stand at 403 out of 601, amounting to 67 per cent, or two-thirds of the total.
- India has the biggest number of children not immunized with DPT-3—7.4 million.
- Each National Immunization Day, 172 million children are immunized for polio.
- India's polio vaccination campaigns cover 800 million children a year.
- A 3-year campaign to ensure children receive the second measles vaccination is targeting 135 million children, with 70 million children covered in 2012–13 alone.
- In a special drive in 2012–13, 15.35 million doses of vaccine were administered to children who had earlier been missed.
- Rural children are least likely to have complete vaccination, and this inequity is most pronounced in states like Madhya Pradesh, Rajasthan, Chhattisgarh, Jharkhand, and Uttar Pradesh.
- The highest inequity between rural and urban areas exists in Kerala, followed by Chhattisgarh and Haryana.

Vaccination Act, 1880[279]

The Vaccination Act, 1880 gives power to prohibit inoculation and to make the vaccination of children compulsory in certain municipalities and cantonments. According to the act, inoculation is prohibited in any place to which the act applies. There is also a provision for the vaccination of unprotected children. An unprotected child is a child who has not been protected from smallpox by having had that disease either naturally or by inoculation, or by having been successfully vaccinated, and who has not been certified under this act to be un-susceptible to vaccination. The act has various other provisions relating to vaccination, such as the procedures to be adopted when vaccination is unsuccessful or when vaccination is successful or when the child is unfit for vaccination. The act also provides for the giving of certificates. This is an outdated legislation not in tune with the present-day health scenario.

---

[277] UNICEF India, 'Immunization'. See more at http://unicef.in/Whatwedo/3/Immunization#sthash.lbTh5wLk.dpuf (accessed on 25 October 2015).

[278] UNICEF India, 'Immunization'.

[279] The Vaccination Act, 1880, Act No. 13 of 1880 (9 July 1880).

Nutrition

It is a well-established fact that the good health of the mother has a distinct and direct bearing on that of the child, effecting the store of nutrients in the foetus, a full-term well-developed baby at birth, a risk-free delivery, and breast milk of good quality during the lactation period. The period of pregnancy demands a support system that ensures additional dietary allowances, systematic antenatal care, life free from stress and risk, and a positive attitude from family and society. This is extremely important as it has long-term effects on the birth and development of the child.[280]

The first National Guidelines on Infant and Young Child Feeding were formulated by Ministry of Women and Child Development (Food and Nutrition Board) in 2004, and the same guidelines were revised in 2006. By the end of 2009, nutritional achievement goals did not make for happy reading. There was a necessity to revise the existing guidelines and have more viable and scientifically accepted national guidelines on IYCF.[281]

Some of the highlights of the guidelines are:

- Early initiation of breastfeeding, and exclusive breastfeeding for the first six months of life, followed by continued breastfeeding for up to 2 years and beyond with adequate complementary food, is the most appropriate feeding strategy for infants and young children.
- Adequate nutrition and anaemia control for adolescent girls and pregnant and lactating mothers is also advocated.[282]

Table 8.7 reveals that as per the National Family Health Survey (NFHS–3) data, the nutritional status of children aged 0–5 months exclusively breastfed is only 46.3 per cent and children under 3 years with stunted growth is 38.4 per cent.

Table 8.7   Child Feeding Practices and Nutritional Status of Children in India (Percentage) (2005–06)

| Key indicators for India from NFHS–3 (percentage) | NFHS-3 (2005–6) | Residence | | Education | | | | NFHS-2 (1998–9) | NFHS-1 (1992–3) |
		Urban	Rural	No education	<8 years complete	8–9 years complete	10 years complete and above 4		
Children under 3 years breastfed within 1 hour of birth	23.4	28.9	21.5	15.9	27.2	31.7	33.0	16.0	9.5

(Cont'd)

---

[280] M. Swaminathan, 'The Continuum of Maternity and Childcare Support', paper presented at the Sixth Conference of the Indian Association for Women's Studies, Mysore, 31 May–2 June 1993.

[281] Ministry of Human Resource Development, Department of Women and Child Development (Food and Nutrition Board), Government of India, 'Infant and Young Child Feeding Guidelines of 2010'.

[282] Ministry of Human Resource Development, 'Infant and Young Child Feeding Guidelines of 2010'.

Table 8.7   *(Cont'd)*

Key indicators for India from NFHS–3 (percentage)	NFHS-3 (2005–6)	Residence		Education				NFHS-2 (1998–9)	NFHS-1 (1992–3)
		Urban	Rural	No education	<8 years complete	8–9 years complete	10 years complete and above 4		
Children aged 0–5 months exclusively breastfed	46.3	40.3	48.3	48.1	46.7	38.0	31.7	Na	Na
Children aged 6–9 months receiving solid or semi-solid food and breast milk	55.8	62.1	53.8	49.1	51.5	58.4	69.6	Na	Na
Children under 3 years who are stunted[283]	38.4	31.1	40.7	46.7	38.0	31.7	20.8	45.5	Na
Children under 3 years who are wasted	19.1	16.9	19.8	21.7	19.1	16.7	13.8	15.5	Na
Children under 3 years who are underweight	45.9	36.4	49.0	55.2	44.6	40.1	26.3	47.0	51.5

Source: Key Indicators for India from NFHS–3

[283] A stunted child has a height-for-age z-score that is at least 2 standard deviations (SD) below the median for the WHO Child Growth Standards. Chronic malnutrition is an indicator of linear growth retardation that results from failure to receive adequate nutrition over a long period and may be exacerbated by recurrent and chronic illness.

Malnutrition and Anaemia Rates among Children in India

The three indices of nutritional status, namely weight for age, height for age, and weight for height still indicate a high prevalence of malnutrition among children under 3 years of age. The rate of malnutrition is decreasing at only 1 per cent per year. Malnutrition is much higher in rural areas and in children from disadvantaged groups in urban areas.[284]

Malnutrition among under-five children is a major public health problem in India. This is reflected by the fact that the prevalence of under-weight children in India is among the highest in the world, and is nearly double that of sub-Saharan Africa.[285]

The nutritional status of Indian children, based on NFHS–3 data, is as follows:[286]

- 38.4 per cent of children under age three are stunted, that is, too short for their age, and 46 per cent are underweight, that is, too thin for their age. Both indicators have only slightly improved from 1998–99.[287]
- Wasting, defined as an abnormally low weight for the child's height, affects 19 per cent of children under age three, with a slight deterioration from 1998–99.[288]
- Overall, girls and boys are equally likely to be undernourished. Under-nutrition is higher in rural areas and is strongly correlated with the level of maternal education, showing a two-fold difference between non-educated mothers and those with 10 years or more of education. This may be linked to a stark difference in access to nutritious diet and complementary feeding at 6–9 months.[289]
- Most children under age three are anemic (79.2 per cent). The prevalence is slightly higher in rural areas and among non-educated mothers. High prevalence of anaemia may be linked to poor variety of diet, poor hygienic conditions, and limited access to iron supplementation.[290]

Improvements Needed in Infant and Child Feeding and Micronutrient Intake

While breastfeeding is nearly universal in India, less than half the children (46 per cent) are fed only breast milk for the first six months, as recommended. Exclusive breastfeeding is slightly higher among the non-educated mothers and in rural areas. Work conditions and access to

[284] 'India Report on the World Summit for Children 2000', Department of Women and Child Development, Ministry of Human Resource Development, Government of India.

[285] World Bank. 'India, Undernourished Children: A Call for Reform and Action'. Available at http://web.worldbank.org/WBSITE/EXTERNAL/COUNTRIES/SOUTHASIAEXT/0,content MDK:20916955~pagePK:146736~piPK:146830~theSitePK:223547,00.html (accessed on 23 October 2015).

[286] 'National Family Healthy Survey (NFHS–3) 2005–2006 India National Reports'. Available at http://motherchildnutrition.org/india/overview-india.html (accessed on 11 October 2015).

[287] 'National Family Healthy Survey (NFHS–3) 2005–2006 India National Reports'.

[288] 'National Family Healthy Survey (NFHS–3) 2005–2006 India National Reports'.

[289] 'National Family Healthy Survey (NFHS–3) 2005–2006 India National Reports'.

[290] 'National Family Healthy Survey (NFHS–3) 2005–2006 India National Reports'.

breast milk substitutes may impact the feeding pattern among urban and better educated mothers.[291]

Only 23.4 per cent of children are breastfed within one hour of birth and the prevalence is significantly lower among the non-educated mothers and in rural areas. However, there has been an overall improvement from 9.5 per cent in 1992–3 to 16 per cent in 1998–9.[292]

Only 55.8 per cent of children aged 6–9 months receive solid or semi-solid food and breast milk. Although the percentage is significantly lower among non-educated mothers and in rural areas, the prevalence in urban areas and among well-educated mothers is still less than 70 per cent, making complementary feeding a high priority that needs to be addressed.[293]

Only 44 per cent of breastfeeding children aged 6–23 months are fed at least the minimum recommended number of times per day (twice a day for children aged 6–8 months and thrice for children aged 9–23 months) and only 36 per cent are given food from at least three food groups, as recommended to ensure adequate diversity in their diet.[294]

Just 25 per cent of children aged 6–35 months received vitamin A supplements in the six months before the survey. The Government of India recommends biannual vitamin A supplements for children aged 6–59 months.[295]

India's performance on the nutrition front is poor overall. According to the NFHS –3 (up to 2005–6), almost half of the children under 5 years of age (48 per cent) are stunted, that is, too short for their age—an indicator of chronic malnutrition; 43 per cent are underweight. The proportion of severely undernourished children is also notable—24 per cent are severely stunted and 16 per cent are severely underweight. It also shows that among children under 3 years of age, 45.9 per cent are underweight. The last NFHS round in 1998–9 showed the percentage of underweight children under three at 46.7. The improvement in 7 years is therefore only negligible. The NFHS–3 also points to a rise in anaemia among children in the 6–35 months age group, from 74.2 per cent since the last round to 79.1 per cent in the latest. These two important indicators of child malnutrition present an alarming picture of child health in the country.

Artificial Milk Substitutes and Malnutrition

Breastfeeding is recognized as the single most important strategy in infant survival. The superiority of breast milk over any other food in promoting the optimum growth of the newborn and in combating infections has been clearly established. The WHO recommends that breastfeeding should begin as early as possible, be maintained exclusively for the first 4–6 months of life, and continued with supplementary food at least up to the second year of life. Of late, much concern is being expressed worldwide over the declining trend in breastfeeding, largely attributed to the aggressive marketing strategies adopted by manufacturers of baby food. The World Health Assembly, on 21 May 1981, adopted an International Code of Marketing of

[291] 'National Family Healthy Survey (NFHS–3) 2005–2006 India National Reports'.
[292] 'National Family Healthy Survey (NFHS–3) 2005–2006 India National Reports'.
[293] 'National Family Healthy Survey (NFHS–3) 2005–2006 India National Reports'.
[294] 'National Family Healthy Survey (NFHS–3) 2005–2006 India National Reports'.
[295] 'National Family Healthy Survey (NFHS–3) 2005–2006 India National Reports'.

Breast Milk Substitutes[296] for the proper nutrition and health of children. The aim of the Code is to contribute to the provision of safe and adequate nutrition for infants by the protection and promotion of breastfeeding and by ensuring the proper use of breast milk substitutes, when these are necessary, on the basis of adequate information and through appropriate marketing and distribution.[297] The Code also lays down in Article 4 that governments should have the responsibility to ensure that objective and consistent information on IYCF is provided, for use by families and those involved in the field of IYCF. This responsibility should cover the planning, provision, design, and dissemination of information or their control. India was a signatory to this International Code and the Government of India responded through the Ministry of Health by adopting the 'Indian National Code for Protection and Promotion of Breastfeeding' in 1983.

The Executive Board of the WHO, at its 101st session in January 1998, called for a revitalization of the global commitment to appropriate infant and young child nutrition, and in particular, breastfeeding and complementary feeding.[298] Subsequently, in close collaboration with the UNICEF, WHO organized a consultation (Geneva, 13–17 March 2000) to assess IYCF practices, review key interventions, and formulate a comprehensive strategy for the next decade. WHO and UNICEF jointly developed the Global Strategy for Infant and Young Child Feeding.[299] The Global Strategy was based on the evidence of the significance of nutrition in the early months and years of life, and of the crucial role that appropriate feeding practices play in achieving optimal health outcomes. Lack of breastfeeding, and especially lack of exclusive breastfeeding during the first half-year of life, are important risk factors for infant and childhood morbidity and mortality that are only compounded by inappropriate complementary feeding. The life-long impact includes poor school performance, reduced productivity, and impaired intellectual and social development.[300]

In India, breastfeeding is deep-rooted culturally, and studies in the country record the fact that breastfeeding is universal and is accepted as a natural function. But in spite of this, studies reveal declining trends in urban areas. There is evidence of malnutrition and mortality in children because of artificial milk-food substitutes in the absence of strong legal interventions.[301] Artificial milk substitutes are being promoted through the healthcare system and aggressive advertising and marketing.

The Infant Milk Substitutes, Feeding Bottles and Infant Foods (Regulation of Production, Supply and Distribution) Act, 1992 (IMS Act) sought to provide for the prohibition of advertisements, incentives, donation, and promotion of artificial milk-food substitutes and to promote, protect, and support breastfeeding.

The objectives of the IMS Act are:

---

[296] 20 ILM 1004 (1981).

[297] WHO, 'International Code of Marketing of Breast Milk Substitutes', Article 1.

[298] WHO, 'Global Strategy for Infant and Young Child Feeding', (NLM classification: WS 120), Geneva: 2003. Available at http://apps.who.int/iris/bitstream/10665/42590/1/9241562218.pdf (accessed on 24 October 2015).

[299] WHO, 'Global Strategy for Infant and Young Child Feeding'.

[300] WHO, 'Global Strategy for Infant and Young Child Feeding'.

[301] Chidananda Reddy, 'The Infant Government's Anti-Infant Policy', *The Lawyers* (June 1990).

- To regulate the production, supply, and distribution of infant milk substitutes,[302] feeding bottles,[303] and infant foods;[304] and
- To promote breastfeeding and ensure proper use of infant foods.

Prohibitions under the Infant Foods, Breast Milk Substitutes and Feeding Bottles Act, 1992

Under the IMS Act, there are certain prohibitions in relation to infant milk substitutes, feeding bottles, and infant foods. The prohibitions are:

- It prohibits any person from taking part in publication of any advertisement [IMS Act 1992, Section 2(a)][305] or taking part in the promotion or use or sale or giving an impression or creating a belief that the milk substitutes or infant foods are equivalent to or better than mother's milk [IMS Act 1992, Section 3[306]].
- It prohibits any person from giving incentives or inducement or any other articles as gifts for the use or sale of infant milk substitutes or feeding bottles or contacting any pregnant woman or the mother of an infant for giving the above incentive or inducement [IMS Act 1992, Section 4][307].
- Donations or distribution of infant milk substitutes or feeding bottles can be done only to an orphanage or through the healthcare system [IMS Act Section 5(a)][308].

[302] IMS Act, 1992, Section 2(g): 'Infant milk substitute' means any food being marketed or otherwise represented as a partial or total replacement for mother's milk, whether or not it is suitable for such replacement.

[303] IMS Act, 1992, Section 2(c): 'Feeding bottle' means any bottle or receptacle used for the purpose of feeding infant milk substitutes, and includes a teat and a valve attached or capable of being attached to such bottle or receptacle.

[304] IMS Act, 1992, Section 2(f).

[305] Section 2(a) of the IMS Act, 1992, amended in 2003: 'Advertisement' includes any notice, circular, label, wrapper or any other documents and also includes any visible representation or announcement made by means of any light, sound, smoke, or gas or by means of electronic transmission or by audio or visual transmission.

[306] Section 3 of the IMS Act, 1992, amended in 2003: No person shall

(1) advertise, or take part in the publication of any advertisement, for the distribution, sale or supply of infant milk substitutes feeding bottles or infant foods;
(2) give an impression or create a belief in any manner that feeding of infant milk substitutes and infant foods are equivalent to, or better than, mother's milk; or
(3) take part in the promotion of infant milk substitutes, feeding bottles, or infant foods.

[307] Section 4 of the IMS Act, 1992 amended in 2003: No person shall

(1) supply or distribute samples of infant milk substitutes or feeding bottles or infant foods gifts of utensils or other articles;
(2) contact any pregnant woman or the mother of an infant; or
(3) offer inducement of any other kind, for the purpose of promoting the use or sale of infant milk substitutes or feeding bottles or infant foods.

[308] Section 5(a) of the IMS Act, 1992amended in 2003: Subject to the provisions of Subsection (4) of Section 8, no person shall donate or distribute.

- No informational or educational equipment or material relating to infant milk substitutes or feeding bottles can be donated or distributed except through the healthcare system [IMS Act 1992, Section 5(b)][309].

Provisions as to Information to be Included on the Containers and Labels [Section 6]

The act lays down that every container [IMS Act 1992, Section 2(b)] or any label [IMS Act 1992, Section 2(c)] affixed to the container must clearly and conspicuously indicate an important notice giving the following particulars:

- the statement 'MOTHER'S MILK IS BEST FOR YOUR BABY' in capital letters;
- the statement that infant milk substitute or infant food should be used only on the advice of a health worker as to the need for its use and the proper method of its use;
- a warning that infant milk substitute or infant food is not the sole source of nourishment of an infant;
- the instructions for its appropriate preparation and a warning against the health hazards of its inappropriate preparation;
- the ingredients used;
- the composition or analysis;
- the storage conditions required;
- the batch number, date of manufacture, and the date before which it is to be consumed, taking into account the climatic and storage conditions of the country; and
- such other particulars as may be prescribed.

The act also prescribes that the container or label should not have the following [Section 6(2)]:

- Pictures of an infant or a woman or both;
- Pictures or other graphic material or phrases designed to increase the saleability of infant milk substitutes or infant food;[310]
- The word 'humanized' or 'materialized' or any other similar word; or
- Such other particulars as may be prescribed.

Particulars to be Provided on Educational and Other Materials
Relating to Feeding of Infants [Section 7]

The following clear information on infant milk substitutes[311] and feeding of an infant should be included on every educational or other audio or visual communication, including advertisements

---

(1) infant milk substitutes or feeding bottles or infant foods to any other person except to an orphanage.

[309] Section 5(b) of the IMS Act, amended in 2003: Subject to the provisions of Subsection (4) of Section 8, no person shall donate or distribute

(2) any informational or educational equipment or material relating to infant milk substitutes or feeding bottles or infant foods.

[310] Section 6 of the IMS Act, 1992 amended in 2003.
[311] Section 7 of the IMS Act, 1992, amended in 2003.

or material relating to promotion of infant milk substitutes,[312] with the intention of the information reaching pregnant women or mothers of infants:

- the benefits and superiority of breastfeeding;
- the preparation for, and the continuance of breastfeeding;
- the harmful effects on breastfeeding due to the partial adoption of bottle feeding;
- the difficulties in reverting to breastfeeding of infants after a period of feeding by infant milk substitute;
- the financial and social implications in making use of infant milk substitutes and feeding bottles;
- the health hazards of improper use of infant milk substitutes and feeding bottles; and
- the date of printing and publication of such material and the name of the printer and publisher.[313]

Directions Regarding Health Workers and the Healthcare System [Section 8]

The healthcare system cannot be used for the display or distribution of placards or posters relating to the promotion or use or sale of infant milk substitutes or feeding bottles or infant foods. There are two exceptions to this direction:

- donation or distribution to orphanages; and
- dissemination of scientific, educational, and factual information and material to health workers.[314]

Only a health worker shall demonstrate feeding with infant milk substitutes or infant foods to a mother of an infant and also clearly explain the hazards of its improper use [IMS Act, Section 8(3)]. No person who works in the healthcare system can be paid for promoting the use or sale of such substitutes or bottles or foods by the producer, supplier, and distributor of these products [IMS Act, Section 8(2)]. No commission or remuneration to the employees can be fixed based on the volume of sale [IMS Act, Section 9(2)].[315] Only an institution or an organization engaged in healthcare for mothers can distribute infant milk substitutes or feeding bottles to a mother who cannot resort to breastfeeding [IMS Act, Section 8(4)].

Standards of Infant Milk Substitutes, Feeding Bottles, or Infant Foods

Infant milk substitutes or infant foods or feeding bottles should conform to the standards laid down under the Prevention of Food Adulteration Act (PFA Act), 1954 or the Bureau of Indian

---

[312] Section 7 of the IMS Act, 1992 amended in 2003.

[313] Section 7(f)(a) of the IMS Act, 1992 amended in 2003.

[314] IMS Act, Section 2(e): 'Health worker' means a person engaged in healthcare for mothers, infants, or pregnant women.

[315] Section 9(2) of IMS Act, 1992 amended in 2003: No producer, supplier or distributor referred to in Subsection (1), shall offer or give any contribution or pecuniary benefit to a health worker or any association of health workers, including funding of seminar, meeting, conferences, educational course, contest, fellowship, research work, or sponsorship.

Standards Act, 1986,[316] or else, should have the approval of the Central Government [IMS Act, Section 11].

Powers Relating to Enforcement of the Act

Sections 12–20 of the act lay down the provisions relating to the enforcement of the act. The provisions of the Code of Criminal Procedure 1973 (CrPC) relating to search and seizure are applicable. Any food inspector appointed under Section 9 of the PFA, or any authorized officer not below the rank of a Class I officer, can enter and search at any reasonable time any premises or any place if there are reasons to believe that any provision under this act have been violated.[317] The food inspector has the following powers:

- He can take any sample and send the sample for analysis.
- He can inspect any place where any article of food is manufactured or stored for sale.
- He can seize or carry away or keep the article under safe custody.
- If the article of food is unfit for human consumption, he may destroy it after giving notice.
- He can break open any package or door if the person in charge refuses to open the package.
- He can seize the books of accounts or other documents and return them within a period of thirty days.
- He can seize the milk substitute or feeding bottle or infant food or container [IMS Act, Section 13].

Penalties under the Act

Contravention of Sections 3, 4, 5, 7, 8, 9, 10, or 11(2) of the act[318] will entail imprisonment for a term which may extend to 3 years or fine which may extend to Rs. 5,000, or both. For contravening Section 11(1) [IMS Act, Section 20(2)], the punishment is imprisonment for a term not less than six months, but which may extend to 3 years, and fine which may not be less than Rs. 2,000. The court may, for special reasons to be mentioned in the judgment, impose a sentence of imprisonment for a term which shall not be less than three months but which may extend to 2 years, with fine which shall not be less than Rs. 2,000. Where an offence under this act has been committed by a company, every person who at the time when the offence was committed was in charge of the company shall be deemed to be guilty of the offence [IMS Act, Section 22].

Cognizance of Offences under the Act

The offences under this Act[319] are bailable and cognizable [IMS Act, Section 23]. A complaint in writing can be made by:

---

[316] The Bureau of Indian Standards Act, 1986, Section 3.

[317] IMS Act, 1992, Section 12.

[318] IMS Act, 1992, Section 20(1): (1) Any person who contravenes the provisions of Sections 3, 4, 5, 7, 8, 9, 10, or Subsection (2) of Section 11 shall be punishable with imprisonment for a term which may extend to 3 years, or with fine which may extend to five thousand rupees, or with both.

[319] IMS Act, 1992, Section 21.

- A person authorized under the PFA;[320]
- An officer authorized by the government;
- A representative of such voluntary organizations that are engaged in the field of child welfare, development, and child nutrition.

Child Nutrition and the National Food Security Act, 2013 (Right to Food Act)[321]

The National Food Security Act (NFSA), 2013 aims to provide subsidized food grains to two thirds of India's 1.2 billion people and includes the Midday Meal Scheme, the ICDS scheme, and the Public Distribution System (PDS). Further, the NFSA recognizes maternity entitlements. The act has a special focus on nutritional support to women and children. Besides providing for meals to pregnant women and lactating mothers during pregnancy and six months after child birth, the act states that such women will also be entitled to receive maternity benefit of not less thanRs. 6,000.[322] Children up to 14 years of age will be entitled to nutritious meals as per the prescribed nutritional standards.[323] In case of non-supply of entitled food grains or meals, the beneficiaries will receive food security allowance. The Midday Meal Scheme and the ICDS are universal in nature, whereas the PDS will reach about two-thirds of the population (75 per cent in rural areas and 50 per cent in urban areas). Section 2(11) of the act states that a meal means a hot-cooked meal or pre-cooked and heated meal or take-home ration, as may be prescribed by the Central Government. Children aged six months to 14 years will get take-home rations or hot cooked food. One of the major challenges in the implementation of the NFSA is the issue of access to the entitlements. Monitoring mechanisms should be streamlined at the block, district, state, and the central levels for its proper implementation.

Landmark Judgments on Right to Nutrition of Children in India

The urgent need to tackle the vital issues of child survival, growth, and health, which in India are turning into a serious developmental crisis, has also been emphasized by several important judicial interventions in recent years. The Supreme Court of India, in interim orders in November 2001, April 2004, and October 2004, moved to safeguard the entitlements of children through the ICDS.[324] The order in 2001 was the first significant one, taking forward the notion that the right to food is part of the fundamental right to life, as enshrined in Article 21 of the Constitution. By calling for the 'universalization' of the ICDS, the Court also underlined the importance of a rights perspective to the issue. This means that the ICDS is not just a welfare scheme but the

---

[320] The Food Adulteration Act, 1954, Section 20.

[321] The National Food Security Act, 2013. Available at http://indiacode.nic.in/acts-in-pdf/202013.pdf (accessed on 24 October 2015).

[322] Section 4(b) of the NFSA.

[323] Section 5(1) of the NFSA.

[324] *People's Union for Civil Liberties* (PUCL) v. *Union of India & Others*, Writ Petition (Civil) No. 196/2001.

entitlement of every child under six and every pregnant mother. The implication is that if the basic food and health needs of infants and children are not met by the state, it is tantamount to a violation of their fundamental human rights, including their right to life. By placing poverty issues in a rights perspective, the Court firmly holds governments responsible and accountable for the condition of the most vulnerable sections of the population.

Suo Moto Writ Petition on the Reports Published in Various Marathi Newspapers about the Untimely Death of Many Children Due to Malnutrition within Two Months in Dhule and Nandurbar District v. State of Maharashtra & Ors[325]

On 20 September 2006, the Bombay High Court issued the following interim orders:

1. The state government shall make functional additional 12,684 Anganwadi Centres as per the Government of India guidelines, as set out in the affidavit dated 4 October 2005, by 31 October 2006. Failure to do so shall expose the Principal Secretary, Women and Child Development Department, Mumbai, to an action under the Contempt of Courts Act, 1971.
2. The state government shall initiate the mission 'Bal Mrutyu Mukta Maharashtra', (by whatever name called) as suggested by the Dr. Abhay Bang Committee and, accordingly, modify 'Rajmata Jijau Maternal Child Health and Nutrition Mission', started from 11 March 2005, to ensure that the IMR due to malnutrition is reduced to almost nil within 5 years from the day of the judgment. In other words, the state government shall ensure that the IMR due to malnutrition is brought down to almost nil in tribal as well as non-tribal areas by 30 September 2011.
3. To begin with, the state government shall, as suggested by the Dr. Abhay Bang Committee, identify malnutrition-free villages and maternal death and child death-free villages and felicitate such villages. To ensure that more and more villages are malnutrition-free and maternal death and child death-free, the state government shall give responsibility and funds to panchayats and self-help groups.
4. The state government shall involve the local panchayats, self-help groups, and NGOs for control of child deaths and malnutrition.
5. While reviewing the assessment of the officers/workers working in the Health Department—officers and workers who have contributed in controlling child deaths and malnutrition and in prevention of child mortality—adequate incentives shall be given to such officers and workers.
6. The scheme 'Rajmata Jijau Maternal Child Health and Nutrition Mission', be adequately modified by providing more facilities, adequate medicines, and kits to Anganwadis, which may help in eradicating malnutrition deaths.
7. The state government, as far as possible, may involve Tribal Gram Sabha (tribal village committee) where tribal areas are concerned, for the development programme planning.
8. The Female Pada volunteers who have been appointed in the districts must be suit- ably trained for management of common childhood problems and also for home-based neonatal care. Training programme must start, if not started so far, by 1 January 2007.

[325] Suo Motu Writ Petition No. 5629 of 2004.

9. For emergency referral of pregnant women, transport should be made available or the provision for delivery vans should be made.

10. As per IMR and severe malnutrition, high risk areas should be identified and these areas should be provided with additional budget and requisite re- sources. If necessary, the Nav Sanjivani Programme initiated by the state government should be modified to ensure that it has the desired impact.

11. The state government shall issue instructions to the Collectors of 15 tribal districts to spend minimum of two days in a month in the tribal villages of the district where there is high rate of infant mortality and severity of malnutrition, and during their stay there, the Collectors shall coordinate with all agencies, including NGOs, involved in the mission. If there is no substantial improvement in combating the child deaths due to malnutrition in a particular district, the poor performance in this regard must be reflected in the service record of the concerned Collector.

12. The Chief Secretary shall ensure that every single rupee allocated in the state budget to the various schemes for the purposes of combating child mortality and malnutrition gets issued timely and percolates down to the needy.

13. The state government shall ensure the availability of the doctors and the emergency obstetrics centres not only in district hospitals but also in small places.

People's Union for Civil Liberties v. Union of India & Others (Right to Food Petition)[326]

In April 2001, the PUCL filed a writ petition on the right to food in the Supreme Court. This petition was filed at a time when the country's food stocks reached unprecedented levels while hunger in drought-affected areas intensified. Initially, the case was brought against the Government of India, the Food Corporation of India (FCI), and six state governments, in the context of inadequate drought relief. Subsequently, the case was extended to the larger issues of chronic hunger and under-nutrition, and all the state governments were added to the list of respondents. The above PIL initiated by the PUCL petition is known as the 'right to food petition.

The first major interim order of the Supreme Court in this PIL was issued on 28 November 2001. This order focused on eight food-related schemes: (1) PDS; (2) Antyodaya Anna Yojana (AAY); (3) National Programme of Nutritional Support to Primary Education, also known as 'Midday Meal Scheme';[327] (4) ICDS; (5) Annapurna; (6) National Old Age Pension Scheme (NOAPS); (7) National Maternity Benefit Scheme (NMBS); and (8) National Family Benefit

---

[326] Writ Petition (Civil) No. 196/2001.

[327] The scheme is undertaken by the Department of School Education and Literacy under the Ministry of Human Resource Development, New Delhi. Mid Day Meal in schools has had a long history in India. In 1925, a Mid Day Meal programme was introduced for disadvantaged children in Madras Municipal Corporation. By the mid 1980s, three states, namely Gujarat, Kerala, and Tamil Nadu, and the UT of Pondicherry had universalized a cooked Mid Day Meal Programme with their own resources for children studying at the primary stage. By 1990–91 the number of states implementing the Mid Day Meal programme with their own resources on a universal or a large scale had increased to 12. More than 25.70 lakh cook-cum-helpers were engaged by the states/UTs during 2013–14 for preparation and serving of midday meals to children in elementary classes. Available at http://mdm.nic.in/ (accessed on 18 October 2015).

Scheme (NFBS). Essentially, the interim order of 28 November 2001 converted the benefits of these eight schemes into legal entitlements.

Further, the Supreme Court directed the Central and state governments to implement the (ICDS in full and to ensure that every ICDS disbursing centre in the country provides:

- 300 calories and 8–10 grams of protein forach child up to 6 years of age;
- 500 calories and 20–25 grams of protein for each adolescent girl;
- 500 calories and 20–25 grams of protein for each pregnant woman and each nursing mother;
- 600 calories and 16–20 grams of protein for each malnourished child; and
- that it has a disbursement centre in every settlement.

This order, however, received very little attention for several years. Virtually nothing was done to implement it. In April 2004, several marathon hearings on the ICDS were held in the Supreme Court and detailed orders were issued, consisting, inter-alia, of the following:

- The Supreme Court directed the Government of India to increase the number of Anganwadis[328] from 600,000 to 1.4 million habitations, and to 'file within three months an affidavit stating the period within which it proposes to increase the number of AWCs so as to cover the 14 lakh habitations'.
- 'All the State Governments/UTs shall allocate funds for the ICDS on the basis of one rupee per child per day, 100 beneficiaries per AWCs and 300 days feeding in a year, that is, on the same basis on which the centre makes the allocation.'
- All Scheduled caste and Scheduled Tribe (SC/ST) habitations should have an Anganwadi 'as early as possible'. Until the SC/ST population is fully covered, all new Anganwadis should be located in habitations with high SC/ST populations.
- 'All state/UTs shall make earnest effort to cover the slums under the ICDS.'
- ICDS services should never restrict to BPL families ('BPL shall not be used as an eligibility criteria for ICDS').
- 'Contractors shall not be used for supply of nutrition in Anganwadis and preferably ICDS funds shall be spent by making use of village communities, self-help groups and Mahila Mandals for buying of grains and preparation of meals.'
- ICDS funds provided by the Central Government under the Pradhan Mantri Gramodaya Yojana (PMGY) should be fully utilized by the state governments. Further, these funds should supplement, and not substitute, ICDS funds provided by the state governments.
- 'The Central Government and states/UTs shall ensure that all amounts allocated are sanctioned in time so that there is no disruption whatsoever in the feeding of children.'
- 'All state governments/UTs shall put on their websites full data for the ICDS schemes including where AWCs are operational, the number of beneficiaries category-wise, the funds allocated and used and other related matters.'

[328] Anganwadi is a government-sponsored childcare and mother-care centre in India. It caters to children in the 0–6 age group. The Hindi word means 'courtyard shelter' in English. The Anganwadi centres were started by the Indian government in 1975 as part of the ICDS programme, to combat child hunger and malnutrition.

• Local women's self-help groups and Mahila Mandals should be encouraged to supply the supplementary food distributed in Anganwadi centres. They can make purchases, prepare the food locally, and supervise the distribution.

On 13 December 2006, immediately thereafter, the Supreme Court made a series of orders on the ICDS. This landmark judgment, which was the culmination of a long series of Court hearings on ICDS, clearly ordered the government to ensure 'universalization with quality' in a time-bound manner. This order also specified the monetary allocation to be made per beneficiary under the ICDS scheme. The court instructed all state governments and UTs to fully implement the ICDS scheme by, inter alia, (i) allocating and spending at least Rs. 2 per child per day for supplementary nutrition, out of which the Central Government shall contribute Re. 1 per child per day; (ii) allocating and spending at least Rs. 2.70 for every severely malnourished child per day for supplementary nutrition, out of which the Central Government shall contribute Rs. 1.35 per child per day; (iii) allocating and spending at least Rs. 2.30 for every pregnant woman and nursing mother/adolescent girl per day for supplementary nutrition, out of which the Central Government shall contribute Rs. 1.15 per child per day. Chief Secretaries of all state governments/UTs were directed to submit affidavits, giving details of the steps that have been taken with regard to the order of the Court of 7 October 2004, directing that 'contractors shall not be used for supply of nutrition in Anganwadis and preferably ICDS funds shall be spent by making use of village communities, self-help groups and Mahila Mandals for buying of grains and preparation of meals'. Chief Secretaries of all state governments/ UTs must indicate a time-frame within which the decentralization of the supply of Supplementary Nutrition Programme (SNP), through the local community, shall be done. On 22 April 2009, an affidavit dated 2 March 2009 was presented in the Supreme Court on behalf of the Ministry of Women and Child Development, agreeing to increase the allocations under the ICDS Scheme.

Uday Foundation v. Union of India[329]

Facts

The pertinent issue of food safety and junk food was brought before the Delhi High Court in this case. The three applications were filed by the Retailers Association of India, the All India Food Processors Association, and the National Restaurants Association of India, pleading that The Food Safety and Standards Act, 2006 does not contemplate regulation of what we may call 'junk food'. The petition, under Article 226 of the Constitution of India, was filed in public interest, flagging the issue of easy availability of junk food and carbonated drinks to children, and its harmful effects. The petition sought a ban on junk food and carbonated drinks in schools and initiation of measures to develop a comprehensive school canteen policy with emphasis on health and nutrition. The lack of definition for 'junk food' and absence of pertinent guidelines on this issue was highlighted by the Delhi High Court.

Held

After considering the pertinent need to regulate junk food in schools across the country, the Delhi High Court asked the Food Safety and Standards of India (FSSAI) to come up with strong

[329] WP (C) 8568/2010, Delhi High Court, decided on 29 October 2013.

regulations and to consider banning the sale of junk food in schools. The Court also asked the Central Board of Secondary Education (CBSE) to consider the need to ban junk food in all its affiliated schools.

The IMS Act is a little-known Act. Even many professionals in the field are unaware of this law. The law needs to be implemented stringently and greater awareness has to be created by the government. The Cable, Television Networks (Regulation) Act, 1995 was amended. According to Sections 6 and 7 of this Act, 'no advertisement shall be permitted which is not in conformity with prescribed advertising code and which promotes directly or indirectly production, sale or consumption of infant milk substitute, feeding bottles or infant foods', through a cable service. Section 16 of the act provides the following punishment for contravening the provisions of this act (i) for the first offence, imprisonment up to 2 years or a fine of Rs. 1,000 or both, and (ii) for every subsequent offence, imprisonment up to 5 years or a fine of Rs. 5,000/-. After this amendment there were no advertisements of baby foods on television channels. Further amendments are needed to implement this Act. There are no stringent rules to tackle the issue of sponsoring of scientific sessions, inducements, and other gifts by infant food manufacturers.[330] There should be a plan for baby-friendly hospitals and medical store initiatives. Under this plan, those medical shop owners who will (i) have posters and write-ups highlighting benefits of breastfeeding in their shop, and (ii) not promote sale of bottles, milk substitutes, and baby foods in their shops, will be appreciated. The medical profession should also resist commercial promotion of baby foods, refuse growth charts with brand names and logos, and refuse free gifts, samples, and sponsorships from infant milk and baby food companies.[331] The implementation of the NFSA needs to be monitored.

Rights of the Child and Working Mothers

Even though the government has passed the legislation of IMS Act, regulating the sale and marketing of infant foods and feeding bottles, attention has not been paid to the role of mothers as working women. Women with full-time jobs face difficulties while breastfeeding. The primary needs, both nutritional and psychic, of the mother–child dyad at this stage are close proximity and constant interaction. This can be achieved by a working mother only by either abstaining from full-time work away from home or by keeping the infant near the workplace in a crèche or day-care centre. Keeping in mind the inherent health hazards and standards of hygiene involved in group care of young children, the possible health hazards in a workplace environment, the difficulties of transportation to and from the workplace, and the child's need for close one-to-one interaction, the women either leave their jobs or have a tendency to wean the child away from breastfeeding. The role of the working mother needs to be kept in view while forming necessary provisions, so that this issue does not affect the development of children adversely.

[330] Satish Kamtaprasad Tiwari, Pushpa Chaturvedi, 'The IMS Act 1992: Need for More Amendments and Publicity', *Indian Pediatrics* (2003): 743–46.

[331] Tiwari and Chaturvedi, 'The IMS Act 1992'.

Article 42[332] of Constitution of India contains the directive that the state shall make provisions for securing just and humane conditions of work and maternity benefits. Additionally, in order to regulate the employment of women in certain establishments for certain periods before and after childbirth and to provide for maternity benefits and certain other benefits, the Parliament enacted the Maternity Benefits Act (MBA), 1961. The objective of maternity benefits is to protect the dignity of 'Motherhood' by providing complete healthcare to a woman and her child when she is not able to perform her duty due to her health condition. The MBA applies to every factory, mine, and plantation, and any shop or establishment which has had 10 or more employees on any given day over the preceding year. Employees must also have worked in the establishment for 80 days in the 12 months preceding the date of delivery. They should inform their employer of the leave period at least seven weeks before the delivery date, and name the person to whom payment should be made in the case of absence or death.

The Employees' State Insurance (ESI), a self-financing social security and health insurance scheme for workers, may be an alternative source of maternity benefits to employees earning Rs. 15,000 or less per month, with the employer contributing 4.75 per cent and the employee contributing 1.75 percent. Those who qualify may receive maternity benefits under the ESI scheme instead of the MBA. The Employees State Insurance Act (ESI Act), 1948, which applies to factories, shops, hotels, restaurants, newspapers, and road and motor establishments, provides similar benefits to certain categories of employees not falling within the purview of the MBA. This means that a woman cannot claim benefits under the ESI Act and the MBA simultaneously. This automatically restricts the scope of the act to large establishments, leaving out those who are employed in small establishments, self-employed, contractual workers, casual labour, temporary and seasonal workers, family labour, and other such workers, with the exception of beedi workers, who are covered by a separate Act.

Relevant Provisions of the Maternity Benefit Act, 1961

The MBA prohibits employment of women in any establishment[333] for a period before and after childbirth,[334] and provides for payment of maternity benefits to them. The act provides that a woman (who has actually worked for a period of not less than 80 days immediately preceding the date of her expected delivery [Maternity Benefit Act, 1961, Section 5(2)[335]] shall be entitled

---

[332] The Constitution of India, Article 42: Provision for just and humane conditions of work and maternity relief—The state shall make provision for securing just and humane conditions of work and for maternity relief.

[333] MBA, Section 3(e).

[334] MBA, Section 3(b): 'Child' includes a still-born child.

[335] Section 5(2) of the MBA: No woman shall be entitled to maternity benefit unless she has actually worked in an establishment of the employer from whom she claims maternity benefit, for a period of not less than [80 days] in the 12 months immediately preceding the date of her expected delivery, provided that the qualifying period of [80 days] aforesaid shall not apply to a woman who has immigrated into the state of Assam and was pregnant at the time of the immigration. Explanation—For the purpose of calculating under the subsection the days on which a woman has actually worked in the establishment 3 [the days for which she has been laid off or was on holidays declared under any law for the time being in force to be

to maternity benefit for a period not exceeding three months (usually six weeks preceding and including the day of delivery and six weeks immediately following that day) [Maternity Benefit Act 1961, Section 5(3)[336]]. This obviously restricts exclusive breastfeeding to a period ranging from six weeks at worst to ten weeks at best, since most women would prefer to take some part of the leave before childbirth.

Under Section 10 of the MBA, a woman is also entitled to an additional period of leave with wages up to a maximum of one month if she is suffering from illness arising out of pregnancy, delivery, premature birth, or miscarriage. This clause is intended to safeguard the mother's health but cannot be used to extend the period of breastfeeding. Section 11 provides for two nursing breaks of fifteen minutes duration each in the course of the mother's working day. If the crèche is not attached to the workplace she can take not less than five or not more than fifteen minutes time for travel. This assumes that the mother has access to a crèche or some other facility near enough for her to avail of the nursing breaks.

Qualitatively, the law practically debars healthy mothers from exclusively breastfeeding their infants for more than six to 10 weeks and more or less compels them to resort to supplementary milk food, thus running counter to the intention of the act regulating the sale of infant food and breast milk substitutes, and illustrating the manner in which a haphazard approach leads to laws which cancel each other out.

Hence, the single most important step from the point of view of promotion of breastfeeding is the amendment of the MBA along lines more sensitive to the needs of the mother and child, as suggested below:

- Maternity leave as such should be calculated from the day of childbirth and should be for a period of four months.
- Mothers may have the option of extending leave for a further period, at first on half pay and then without pay, but without loss of other service benefits, seniority, and other facilities.
- Leave from two to four weeks may be taken during the final stages of pregnancy as medically advised and should not be treated as maternity leave.
- Women should not be transferred or subjected to other punitive actions or suffer loss of benefits during the basic maternity leave period of four months.
- Nursing breaks should be of minimum 40 minutes duration each—20 minutes for feeding and 20 minutes for travel—and may be allowed till the child reaches the age of 12 months.

---

holidays with wages] during the period of twelve months immediately preceding the date of her expected delivery shall be taken into account.

[336] Section 5(3) of the MBA: [The maximum period for which any woman shall be entitled to maternity benefit shall be 12 weeks of which not more than six weeks shall precede the date of her expected delivery], provided that where a woman dies during this period, the maternity benefit shall be payable only for the days up to and including the day of her death, provided further that where a woman, having been delivered of a child, dies during her delivery or during the period immediately following the date of her delivery for which she is entitled for the maternity benefit, leaving behind in either case the child, the employer shall be liable for the maternity benefit for that entire period but if the child also dies during the said period, then, for the days up to and including the date of the death of the child.

The last rule should be applicable only:

- When there is a crèche facility, statutory or otherwise, at or 'near' the workplace, defined as ten minutes travel time each way.
- When there is any arrangement, individual or organized, by which the mother can go to the child or the child can be brought to the mother within this period. In the latter case, nursing space should also be provided.

There is great need to improve the implementation of the act with regard to access to medical bonus and nursing breaks. In practice, the provision of nursing breaks has been rendered useless in the absence of rest rooms and crèches at the workplace. Establishments must be directed and assisted in setting up crèches in their premises so that nursing breaks can be made use of by breastfeeding mothers effectively and easily.

The suggested legislation is applicable only to the organized sector. The low level of utilization of home-based women beedi workers under the Beedi and Cigar Workers (Conditions of Employment) Act, 1966, which attempts to imitate the organized sector legislation, illustrates the futility of enforcing such laws in the unorganized sector. In the unorganized sector, maternity benefits must become the direct responsibility of the state, as well as autonomous boards and corporations that stand in an employer relationship to women artisans and labourers. As far as funding is concerned, devices can be found to oblige employers to share the financial burden.[337] Labour welfare funds can also be drawn upon for this purpose, as in the case of beedi workers. A National Maternity Fund needs to be created to ensure workers' rights in the unorganized sector and outsourced contractual workers also need to be included.

The implementation of the MBA is poor in the unorganized sector. In an attempt to protect the welfare of these workers, the Unorganized Workers' Social Security Act, 2008 was passed. This includes coverage of hospitalization expenses and maternity benefits.[338]

Important Judgments on Maternity Benefit Act, 1961

Shah v. Presiding Officer, Labour Court, Coimbatore and others[339]

Issues Before the Court

The question before the Supreme Court was whether in calculating the maternity benefit for the period covered by Section 5, Sundays, being wage-less holidays, should be excluded.

Held

- The apex court, in holding that Sundays must also be included, applied the beneficial rule of construction in favour of the woman worker and observed that the benefit conferred by the

[337] National Commission on Self-Employed Women and Women in the Informal Sector, 'Shram Shakti Report', 1988.

[338] Section 3 of the Unorganised Worker's Social Security Act, 2008.

[339] (1977) 4 SCC 384.

Act, read in the light of Article 42 of the Constitution, was intended to enable the woman worker not only to subsist but also to make up her dissipated energy, nurse her child, preserve her efficiency as a worker, and maintain the level of her previous efficiency and output.

- During pregnancy not only cannot she work for her living, but in fact needs extra income for her medical expenses. In order to enable the woman worker to subsist during this period and to preserve her health, the law makes a provision for maternity benefit so that the woman can play her productive and reproductive roles efficiently.

- Performance of the biological role of child-bearing necessarily involves withdrawal of a woman from the workforce for some period.

F.M. Kolia and Anr. v. Manager, The Tiles and Pottery Works Ltd and Ors[340]

Facts

The petitioner applied for maternity leave pay under the MBA, but her claim was contested on the ground that she had attended work only for 143 days. The establishment was a seasonal factory which worked for only 8 months in a year, and consequently, the petitioner was 'prevented' from working during the rainy season as the factory remained closed. The respondent submitted that during the 12 months of her employment period, she should have worked for a period of 160 days at least, and since she worked for 143 days only, she was not entitled to the benefit.

Held

The Court held in this particular case that the establishment was a seasonal factory which worked for only 8 months in a year. Hence, during monsoon days, the petitioner was prevented from working on account of the factory remaining closed.

Therefore, in view of the facts of the case, it remained undisputed that the petitioner had completed 160 days and qualified herself for benefits as provided by the MBA. Hence, allowing the petition, the Court directed the respondent to pay to the petitioner her maternity leave pay as provided for under the MBA.

Rattan Lal and Ors v. State of Haryana and Ors[341]

Facts

Grievance of the teachers appointed on ad hoc basis by the state of Haryana with regard to non-payment of salary during the summer vacations, and denial of other privileges such as casual leave, medical leave, maternity leave, and others, came to be considered in this case.

Held

These benefitspaid summer vacations and all other privileges such as casual leave, medical leave, and maternity leave,which are available to all government servants, the Court observed, were

[340] (1981) 22 GLR 528.
[341] 1985 (3) SLR 548; 1985 (2) SLJ 437 (SC).

denied to the ad hoc teachers unreasonably on account of the pernicious system of appointment adopted by the state government. Strongly deprecating the policy of the state government under which ad hoc teachers were being denied salary and allowances for the period of the summer vacations, the apex court ordered the payment of the above-mentioned privileges, including maternity and medical leave, to those entitled to it.

Municipal Corporation of Delhi v. Female Workers[342]

Facts

In this case the union of female workers who were not on regular rolls, but were treated as temporary workers and employed on the muster roll, claimed that they should also get maternity benefits like regular workers.

Held

The court held that the provisions of the act would indicate that they are wholly in consonance with the DPSP, as set out in Article 39 and in other Articles, especially Article 42. A woman employee, at the time of advanced pregnancy, cannot be compelled to undertake hard labour as it would be detrimental to her health and also to the health of the foetus. It is for this reason that the act provides that she would be entitled to maternity leave for certain periods prior to and after delivery. Hence, the female workers who were not on regular rolls were entitled to the maternity benefits just like the regular workers, the Court ordered.

Division Bench of the Punjab & Haryana High Court in the case of Raj Bala v. State of Haryana and Ors[343]

Facts

The state government contended that several mistresses, teachers, and lecturers appointed in different schools and colleges in the states were not entitled to maternity leave on the ground that they were contractual appointees.

Held

The Court directed the state government to grant the benefit of maternity leave to the petitioners. The Court further observed, '... there is hardly any distinction between an ad hoc employee and a contractual employee. Both are engaged for a definite term as may be specified in the letter of appointment. So far as they are performing the same duties and functions and are holding the same post, it will be very difficult to draw the fine line of distinction between these two classes.'

---

[342] (2000) SCC 224.
[343] 2002 (3) RSJ 43.

Ms Sonika Kohli and Anr v. Union of India and Ors[344]

Facts

The applicants were appointed as school teachers by the Chandigarh Administration on contract basis for a specific period. In view of the various decisions of the apex court, High Court, and this Tribunal the contract appointees were allowed to continue in service till such time when they were replaced by the teachers duly selected and appointed in accordance with the Chandigarh Education Service (School Cadre) Group 'C' Recruitment Rules, 1991. The District Education Officer issued an advertisement dated 9/10 August 2002, inviting applications for appointment on contract basis, with a view to replace the earlier contract appointees.

An almost new point of controversy which was raised in this case was with regard to the admissibility of maternity leave to female teachers appointed on contract basis. The respondents denied the benefit of maternity leave to the contract female employees on the ground that maternity leave was not admissible to contract employees as they were not covered by the Punjab Civil Services Rules, Vol. I, Part-I.[345] The respondent contended that the benefit of maternity leave with pay was payable to permanent/regular female employees and that the Chandigarh Administration was justified in carving out a distinction between the regular female teachers and the teachers appointed on part-time or contract basis.

Held

The Court opined that the claim for maternity leave was founded on grounds of fair play and social justice. Before the advent of the Constitution and for a sufficiently long time thereafter, it was customary or say traditional for women to stick to their homes, but now they seek various jobs so as to attain economic independence by utilizing their talent, education, and industry. Sometimes they take up jobs to overcome economic hardship. For a woman, to become a mother is the most natural phenomenon in her life. Whatever is needed to facilitate the birth of a child to a woman who is in service, the employer has to be considerate and sympathetic towards her and must realize the physical difficulties which a working woman would face in performing her duties at the work place while carrying a baby in the womb or while rearing a child after birth. Our Constitution, which, in its Preamble, promises social and economic justice, enshrines certain radical provisions in the form of Articles 42 and 43, which deal with the just and humane conditions of work and maternity relief as well as living wage, conditions of work ensuring a decent standard of life, and full enjoyment of leisure and social and cultural opportunities. These principles are required to be followed by the state as enjoined by Article 39. Against the backdrop of these Articles, the Parliament has enacted the MBA with a view to regulate the employment of women in certain establishments for certain periods before and after child birth, and to provide for maternity benefit and certain other benefits. The act also provides that a female worker would be entitled to maternity leave for certain periods prior to and after delivery. Hence, the Court held, the female teachers appointed on contract basis shall be entitled to maternity leave with pay in accordance with the rules applicable to the regular teachers.

---

[344] 2004 (3) SLJ 54 (CAT).
[345] Rules Relating to Pay and Allowances, Leave, Passage and Other General Conditions of Services.

Seema Gupta v. *Guru Nanak Institute of Management*[346]

Facts

The petitioner filed a writ petition against the order by which her services were terminated on grounds of unauthorized leave/absence within two months of extended maternity leave. The correspondence between the parties to the petition revealed that the petitioner's request for leave was on account of her 'erratic and indifferent health condition as well as that of her infant child'.

Even though the petitioner did not request for one full year's leave initially, she did so after rejoining her duties. She made an application for the purpose after she was served with repeated show cause notices which alleged habitual absenteeism.

Held

The court held that the case falls into what may be justly described as a 'horizontal' application of fundamental right. Fundamental rights are ordinarily enforceable against state or state agencies, or those 'authorities' acting as instruments of the state. Yet, once the object of a fundamental right, such as for instance, the equality clause, or protective legislation relating to gender, is sought to be given shape through some statute, and made applicable to non-state 'actors", such intervention is known as horizontal application of the concerned fundamental right.

If exigencies of service were upheld as a valid justification for denying or rejecting the valuable right to claim extended maternity leave up to 1 year, such special rights would be rendered meaningless, existing only on paper. The respondent did not pay attention to the peculiarities of the case or the special nature of the right involved. Thus impugned, the termination letter could not be sustained; it was held illegal and the respondent was directed to reinstate the petitioner to her post.

N. Mohammed Mohideen and Sahna v. *The Deputy Commissioner of Labour (Inspection) (Beedi and Cigar Establishments Chief Inspector—Appellate Authority under the Maternity Benefit Act, 1961) and Inspector of Labour (Women) (under the Maternity Benefit Act, 1961)*[347]

Facts

The facts of the case were that the respondent used to roll beedis in the petitioner's establishment. She sought for maternity leave with pay for her third delivery, under provisions of the Beedi and Cigar Workers (Conditions of Employment) Act, 1966. The question which came up before the Hon. Court was whether the object of the MBA was to restrict the maternity leave with wages.

Held

The Court held that one of the basic human rights contained in the UDHR is special care and assistance for motherhood. In pursuance of its world-wide programme regarding provisions for maternity protection, the ILO has adopted Convention 3 and Recommendation 95 concerning maternity protection. Even though India has not ratified the convention, it does subscribe to the

---

[346] 135 (2006) DLT 404.
[347] (2009) ILLJ 177 Mad.

principles contained therein, and one of the DPSPs of the Indian Constitution is that there should be provision for maternity relief. The Court observed: 'There is no provision under the M.B. Act fixing any ceiling on the number of deliveries made by a female worker. So long as Article 42 of the Constitution read with the provisions of the M.B. Act is available, every female worker covered by the act is entitled to claim maternity benefits without any ceiling on the number of deliveries made by them. That will be the correct interpretation which will be in tune with the judgment of the Supreme Court rendered in *B. Shah* v. *Labour Court, Coimbatore and others*.[348]

Vandana Kandari v. *University of Delhi*[349]

Facts

The petitioners were students of different semesters in the Law Faculty, University of Delhi. They sought relaxation in the shortfall of their attendance in all those lectures which they could not attend because of the advanced stage of their pregnancy. The petitioners were detained from appearing in the semester examination and hence they filed the petition.

Held

The Court held that withholding relaxation to these students was equivalent to making motherhood a crime. The apex court, discussing the case of *Lata Singh* v. *State of U.P AIR*,[350] held that live-in relationships and premarital sex were not offences and their legal validity should be recognized. The Court further stated that: 'The society today is changing at a rapid pace and we must be in tune with the realities and not hold on to archaic social mores. Once such a right, however unpopular, is recognized then it cannot be ruled out that there can be more cases of girl students proceeding on maternity leave when while they are still in college.' Therefore, a female student cannot be deprived of her student status or be detained in any semester due to her inability to attend classes because of her pregnancy.

Analysing the above judgments, it is clear that the Courts in India have reiterated while pronouncing judgments that the MBA, being a piece of welfare legislation which aims at protecting the health of the pregnant mother and her foetus, must necessarily be given a broad interpretation in favour of the woman worker, by applying the beneficent rule of construction. Thus, in various judgments, the courts have clearly laid down that the mode of payment, nature of appointment, or service, in the form of contractual, regular or nonregular, permanent or temporary, cannot be made grounds for denying maternity benefit to female employees. The courts have emphasized through several case laws that mere technicalities must not be allowed to defeat the purpose of the MBA, which is to allow women to efficiently balance their reproductive as well as productive roles, through special care and assistance for motherhood. Therefore, the provisions of the MBA ought to be construed in the light of broader principles enshrined in our Constitutions, the UDHR, the CEDAW, among others.[351]

[348] 1977 (2) LLN 606.
[349] 170 (2010) DLT 755.
[350] AIR 2006 SC 2522.
[351] Shashi Bala, *Implementation of Maternity Benefit Act*, NLI Research Studies Series No. 099/2012 (Noida: V.V. Giri National Labour Institute, 2008). Available at http://www.vvgnli.org/sites/default/files/publication_files/099-2012_Shashi_Bala.pdf (accessed on 1 November 2015).

Amendments to Maternity Benefit Act, 1961

The MBA needs amendment. Firstly, the duration of leave must be extended in order to allow a mother to fully recover and recuperate as well as efficiently nurse her new-born child. Besides, the duration of postnatal period must be extended keeping in mind factors like rise in number of late marriages, caesarean births, nuclear families, and increasing urbanization. In the 44th Indian Labour Conference, held in February 2012, it has been recommended that maternity leave under the MBA be increased from the present level of 12 Weeks to 24 Weeks.[352] Currently, the entire responsibility of the act rests with the employer. Placing the entire burden of providing maternity benefit on the employer may deter the employer from employing women. Thus, the cost of maternity protection should be shared among different agencies through some form of social insurance scheme or general taxation. There could be sector-wise or region-wise responsibility in case of small organizations and industries. The MBA completely disregards the role of the father in a child's upbringing. Paternity leave could be an important opportunity for men to nurture their children and support new mothers with the physical and emotional demands related to childbirth. It should also be noted that the right to paternity leave could be crucial for changes in the relationships and perceptions of parenting roles in the long run. Thus, the MBA should include such a provision to benefit the society at large. The responsibility of childcare is often singularly put upon women. This reinforces patriarchal notions and stereotypes and also enhances the discrimination they face from employers. In order to reduce these factors, the act should also make a provision for paternity leave and follow a more egalitarian approach. Also, the act must specifically provide protection to persons who adopt children.[353]

Day Care and Crèche Facilities

The provisions for crèches for children of working mothers is obligatory under certain labour laws in the organized sector. Laws with reference to crèches exist primarily in relation to the organized sector. The Factories Act, 1948, the Mines Act, 1950, and the Plantations Act, 1951 make it obligatory for the employer to provide crèches for children aged 0–6 years wherever more than a stipulated minimum number of women are employed in factories, mines, and plantations. Modelled on those of industrialized countries, these laws have not been amended to keep pace with the changing economic situation, and are largely irrelevant to the present-day working conditions, besides being applicable to only a small minority of working women. This becomes evident when it is noted that any similar legislation has not been passed for the benefit of women working in the tertiary sector (services, trades, and professions) in whose numbers there has been a spectacular increase in the last three decades. Provisions in relation to crèches in various legislations in India are summarized in Table 8.8.

---

[352] Law is Greek, 'Maternity Benefits: What are your Legal Rights?'. Available at http://lawisgreek.com/maternity-benefits-what-are-your-legal-rights/ (accessed on 4 November 2015).

[353] Bala, *Implementation of Maternity Benefit Act.*

Table 8.8 Legislation Relating to Crèches[354]

	Factories Act, 1948 (Section 48)	Plantation Labour Act, 1951 (Section 12)	Beedi and Cigar Workers (Conditions of Employment) Act, 1966 (Section 14)	Contract Labour (Regulation and Abolition) Central Rules, 1971 [Clause (vi)(d) of sub-rule (2) of rule 25]	Inter State Migrant Workmen (RECS)[355] Central Rules, 1980 (Rule 44)	The Building And Other Construction Workers (RECS)[356] 1996 (Section 35)
No. of women workers	More than 30	More than 50	More than 30	More than 20	More than 20, and employment to continue for three months or more	More than 50
No. of children (including women workers employed by the contractor)	–	More than 20	–	–	–	–
Age of Children	Till 6 years	Below 6 years	Below 6 years	Below 6 years	Below 6 years	Below 6 years
Provision	A suitable room or rooms for the use of children	A suitable room or rooms for the use of children of such workers	A suitable room or rooms for the use of children	Two rooms to be provided for children. One playroom and the other as a bedroom. Creche should be located within 50 metres of every establishment	Two rooms to be provided for children. One playroom and the other as bedroom for the children	Suitable room or rooms for the use of children
Authority to make rules	The state government may make rules relating to location and standards of construction	The state government may make rules prescribing location, standards of construction, equipment, and amenities.	The state government may make rules prescribing location and standards in respect of construction, accommodation, furniture, and so on.	The chief labour commissioner may prescribe the standard of construction and maintenance of crèches	–	The appropriate Government may, by notification, make rules under the act

354 Source: Compiled by the author.

355 The Inter-state Migrant Workmen (Regulation of Employment and Conditions of Service) Act, 1979.

356 The Building and Other Construction Workers (Regulation of Employment and Conditions of Service) Act, 1996.

One of the detailed labour law regulations about crèche is the Mines Crèche Rules, 1966; where rules elaborate on standards of crèche, including the structure of the room, ventilation, flooring, sanitation, latrines and bathrooms for children, provision of staff, medical arrangement, diet of children, and so on. The Rules also require the crèche to be open while the women are at work, irrespective of day or night, with adequate staff. The problem remains that these laws providing for crèche facilities are exclusive and limiting as they only provide facilities for children of women employees involved in certain specified establishments and the primary providers continue to be the owners of such establishments.[357]

Analysis of the laws reveal several lacunae, chief among which is the insistence on a minimum number of women workers for the law to become applicable. This not only makes it easy for evasion by various simple strategies, but even assuming no evasion is attempted, this makes it of limited applicability, since it omits certain categories of workers such as those employed in small establishments, temporary and casual workers, contract workers, and others. Employers evade this responsibility by under-reporting of the number of female workers in the muster rolls. Further, if one considers childcare as a fundamental right of women and children, the question of stipulating numbers or their use and misuse becomes irrelevant. Within the broader framework of the Constitution, which allows equality to all citizens with no discrimination, every child has a right to holistic care and development and every mother the right to demand such facilities, irrespective of what she contributes to the national statistics. Another shortcoming is the placing of administrative as well as financial responsibility on employers, who may lack the willingness and expertise to run crèches, rather than on professionals or agencies specialized for the purpose. This only results in reducing attention to the quality and nature of day care, focusing instead on numerical targets.

The unorganized sector comprises a major part of the Indian economy. Those enterprises and employments are involved in the unorganized sector which are unregistered under any legal provision. More than 90 per cent manpower contributes to the unorganized sector globally. In the Indian scenario, 86 per cent of human resource is employed in the unorganized sector. Ninety-one per cent of women workers are rendering their services in the unorganized sector. Women are exempted from maternity benefit and childcare facilities in this sector.[358] It becomes necessary to consider the Rajiv Gandhi National Crèche Scheme for the Children of Working Mothers[359] since women are denied the benefit of statutory crèche facilities. Under the Scheme, the state provides assistance to NGOs for running crèches for infants. This scheme was brought forth with the view that working mothers from poor families require institutional support for young children, with the objective of providing day care services for the children of working women in the organized and unorganized sectors. This scheme specifically provides for participation of 50

---

[357] Law Commission of India, Report No. 259, 'Early Childhood Development and Legal Entitlements', August 2015. Available at http://lawcommissionofindia.nic.in/reports/Report259.pdf (accessed on 24 October 2015).

[358] Arti and Rajesh Kumar Shastri, 'Role, Problems and Challenges of Women Workers in Unorganized Sector', *New Man International Journal of Multidisciplinary Studies* 1, no. 12 (December 2014). Available at http://www.newmanpublication.com/admin/issue/br/18%20nm.pdf (accessed on 24 October 2015).

[359] Ministry of Human Resource Development, Department of Women and Child Development, Government of India, Rajiv Gandhi National Crèche Scheme for the Children of Working Mothers.

per cent of children from below-poverty-level (BPL) families. However, the scheme specifies users fee of Rs. 20 per child per month to be collected from children from BPL families and Rs. 60 per child per month. The minimum number of women workers required to call in this facility stands at fifty or more, under both the Building and Other Construction Workers (RECS) Act, 1996 and the Plantation Labour Act, 1951. This was enacted by the Central Government as per power conferred under Section 58 (d) of the Mines Act, 1952. This provision must be reconsidered by the state as providing for young children should be a state responsibility and the payment of this fee might be difficult for single mothers and widows of poor families, considering the abysmally low payment in the unorganized sector and the inflated cost of living in the current scenario.[360]

Linking crèches to the number of women workers does not allow the development of an egalitarian society as it further reinforces the stereotype that childcare is the predominant concern of the woman. It is pertinent to mention that there is no need for a minimum number of workers to be employed in order for a crèche to be set up by an employer. Even if one worker, either man or woman, has a child, it is the duty of the employer to provide childcare assistance in the form of crèches. The focus should be on the developmental rights of children and not on the number of female employees. Childcare is not only the responsibility of the mothers. The very presence of employees, whether male or female, who have children, should be the sole criterion for providing crèche facilities.

Law Reform Relating to Crèches

The Law Commission, in its 259th Report, has suggested that every child under six should have an unconditional right to crèche and day care provided and regulated by the state.[361] The Commission suggested that a new article, 24A, be inserted in Part III of the Constitution to ensure that the child's right to basic care and assistance becomes an enforceable right. The Commission said that the provision of crèches should be made the responsibility of the state, not of the employer, especially in the unorganized sector. In Finland, after the enactment of the act on Children's Day Care of 1973, the obligation to organize day care for children under school age rests with the local authorities. The local authorities may provide day care either in day care centres or in the form of family day care. Since 1990, parents have enjoyed an unconditional right to day care for children under 3 years of age either in municipal day care or by receiving child home care allowance in order to care for their children at home. Since August 1997, it has been possible for families to receive private child-care allowance for providing their children with private care.[362] The introduction of statutory right to childcare provides equal opportunity for all young children to be in an institutional system of care arranged for by the state and is required to be done by a welfare state.

---

[360] Law Commission of India, 'Early Childhood Development and Legal Entitlements'.

[361] Law Commission of India, 'Early Childhood Development and Legal Entitlements'.

[362] 'Early Childhood Education and Care Policy in Finland', background report prepared for the OECD Thematic Review of Early Childhood Education and Care Policy, May 2000. Available at http://www.oecd.org/finland/2476019.pdf (accessed on 24 November 2016).

Government Programmes and Schemes for Child Health and Development

A number of childcare programmes for improving the health status of children are being implemented.

Integrated Child Development Services Scheme[363]

Children in the age group 0–6 years constitute around 158 million of the population of India (2011 census). These children are the future human resource of the country. The Ministry of Women and Child Development is implementing various schemes for welfare, development, and protection of children. Launched on 2 October 1975, the ICDS Scheme is one of the flagship programmes of the Government of India and represents one of the world's largest programmes for early childhood care and development. The beneficiaries under the scheme are children in the age group of 0–6 years, pregnant women, and lactating mothers. The objectives of the scheme are:

- to improve the nutritional and health status of children in the age group 0–6 years;
- to lay the foundation for proper psychological, physical, and social development of the child;
- to reduce the incidence of mortality, morbidity, malnutrition, and school dropout;
- to achieve effective coordination of policy and implementation among the various departments to promote child development; and
- to enhance the capability of the mother to look after the normal health and nutritional needs of the child through proper nutrition and health education, day care programmes, and schemes.

Indira Gandhi Matritva Sahyog Yojana—Conditional Maternity Benefit[364]

The Indira Gandhi Matritva Sahyog Yojana (IGMSY)—Conditional Maternity Benefit (CMB) envisages providing cash directly to pregnant and lactating women in response to the individuals fulfilling specific conditions. The scheme attempts to partly compensate for wage loss of pregnant and lactating women both prior to and after delivery of the child. The objectives of the scheme are to improve the health and nutrition status of pregnant, lactating women and infants by:

- Promoting appropriate practices, care, and service utilization during pregnancy, safe delivery, and lactation;
- Encouraging the women to follow (optimal) IYCF practices including early and exclusive breast feeding for six months;
- Contributing to a better enabling environment by providing cash incentives for improved health and nutrition to pregnant and nursing mothers.

---

[363] Ministry of Women and Child Development, Government of India. See more at http://wcd.nic.in/icds/icds.aspx (accessed on 25 October 2015).

[364] Ministry of Women and Child Development, Government of India, Notification No.9-5/2010-IGMSY, New Delhi, 2010. Available at http://wcd.nic.in/SchemeIgmsy/IGMSYscheme.pdf (accessed on 25 October 2015).

Reproductive and Child Health Programme, 2005

The second phase of the Reproductive and Child Health Programme, 2005, that is, RCH–II, has commenced from 1 April 2005. The main objective of the programme is to bring about a change in mainly three critical health indicators—reducing TFR, IMR, and MMR—with a view to realizing the outcomes envisioned in the MDGs, the NPP 2000, the Tenth Plan Document, the NHP 2002, and Vision 2020 India.

Salient Features of RCH–II Programme

1. Adoptions of sectorwide approach which effectively extends the programme reach beyond RCH to the entire family welfare sector.
2. Building state ownership by involving states and UTs in development of the programme from the outset.
3. Decentralization through development of district and state level need-based plans.
4. Flexible programming with a view to moving away from prescriptive scheme-based micro planning and instead allowing states to develop need-based work plans with freedom to decide upon programme inputs.
5. Capacity building at the district, state and the Central level to ensure improved programme implementation. In particular, the emphasis being on strengthening financial management systems and monitoring and evaluation capabilities at different levels.
6. Adoption of the logical framework as a programme management tour to support and outcome driven approach.
7. Performance-based funding to ensure adherence to programme objectives, reward good performance, and support weak performers through enhance technical performance.
8. Pool financing by the development partners to simplify and rationalize the process of assessing external assistance.
9. Convergence, both inter-sectoral and intra-sectoral, to optimize utilization of resource as well as infrastructural facilities.

Rajiv Gandhi National Crèche Scheme for the Children of Working Mothers, 2006[365]

The scheme provides day care services to children (0–6 years) of working mothers, including holistic care for the physical, mental, and emotional development of these children, and delivers the following services:

- every crèche cares for approximately 25 children;
- each crèche managed by a crèche worker and a helper;
- supplementary nutrition, immunization, and healthcare facilities;
- recreation;
- non-formal pre-school education to children.

[365] Department of Women and Child Development, Ministry of Human Resource Development, 'Rajiv Gandhi National Crèche Scheme for the Children of Working Mothers', Government of India. Available at http://wcd.nic.in/rajivgandhicrechescheme.pdf (accessed on 24 October 2015).

Beti Bachao, Beti Padhao Programme (2015)[366]

Census (2011) data showed a significant declining trend in the CSR, with an all-time low of 918 in 2011, from 976 in 1961. It reflected both pre-birth discrimination manifested through gender-biased sex selection, and post-birth discrimination against girls. The decline is widespread across the country and has expanded to rural as well as tribal areas. Alarmed by the sharp decline, the Government of India introduced the Beti Bachao, Beti Padhao (BBBP) programme to address the issue in 100 gender-critical districts. Coordinated and convergent efforts are needed to ensure survival, protection, and education of the girl child. The overall goal of the BBBP Scheme is to celebrate the girl child and enable her education . The objectives of the Scheme are to prevent gender-biased sex selective elimination, to ensure survival and protection of the girl child, and to ensure education of the girl child. The BBBP initiative has two major components: i) Mass Communication Campaign; and ii) Multi-sectoral action in 100 selected districts (as a pilot project) with adverse CSR, covering all states and UTs.

Special Health Issues Relating to Children

Children Affected by HIV/AIDS

India has an estimated 202,000 children infected by HIV/AIDS.[367] Using a conservative vertical transmission rate of 30 per cent, a new cohort of approximately 56,700 HIV infected infants is added every year. As of September 2006, the programme has about 45,000 individuals on ART[368] through public, private, and NGO-supported ART centres.[369] There are 2,300 children who are currently receiving ART in India,[370] however half of HIV-positive children die undiagnosed before their second birthday.[371]

The Existing Situation in India

The global, regional, and India estimates are as follows:[372]

[366] Ministry of Women and Child Development, Government of India. Available at http://wcd.nic.in/BBBPScheme/About_BBBP_Scheme.pdf (accessed on 2 November 2015).

[367] Sue Armstrong, Chris Fontaine, and Andrew Wilson, 'Report on the Global AIDS Epidemic', July 2004. Available at http://data.unaids.org/Global-Reports/Bangkok-2004/unaidsbangkokpress/gar-2004html/gar2004_00_en.htm (accessed on 25 October 2015).

[368] Antiretroviral Treatment.

[369] Ministry of Health and Family Welfare, National AIDS Control Organisation (NACO), Government of India, 'Technical Report on India HIV Estimates—2006'. Available at http://naco.gov.in/upload/Surveillance/Reports%20&%20Publication/Technical%20Report%20on%20HIV%20Estimation%202006.pdf (accessed on 25 October 2015).

[370] NACO, 'Technical Report on India HIV Estimates—2006'.

[371] NACO, 'Guidelines for HIV Care and Treatment in Infants and Children', November 2006. Available at http://www.iapsmgc.org/userfiles/4Guidelines_for_HIV_care_and_treatment_in_Infants_and_children.pdf (accessed on 25 October 2015).

[372] UNICEF India, 'Latest Stories: HIV/AIDS'. See more at http://www.unicef.in/Story/1123/HIV-AIDS (accessed on 25 October 2015).

- An estimated 33.4 million people worldwide were living with HIV (2008).
- Approximately 2.1 million children under 15 were living with HIV (2007).
- An estimated 2.1 million people died of AIDS-related causes (2007).
- An estimated 290,000 children under 15 died of AIDS-related causes (2007).
- India has a low HIV prevalence of 0.34 per cent. Yet in terms of individuals infected,
- India is home to the third largest number of people living with HIV in the world.
- The vast majority of HIV infections in India occur through sexual transmission (85.6 per cent).
- Nearly five per cent of infections are attributable to parent-to-child transmission.
- The epidemic disproportionately affects women, who account for 40 per cent of the total infections in the country.
- In India, the epidemic is more pronounced in urban areas than rural ones and decreases with increasing education levels.

In India, mother-to-child transmission of the virus during pregnancy, labour, and delivery or breastfeeding is called parent-to-child-transmission, to emphasize the role of the father in both the transmission of the virus and management of the infected mother and child. Nearly five per cent of infections are attributable to parent-to-child-transmission. It is estimated that out of 27 million pregnancies every year, nearly 49,000 occur in HIV-positive mothers. In 2009, only 11,489 of an estimated 49,000 pregnant women living with HIV received ART treatment to prevent parent-to-child transmission. This is because of multiple factors including social customs, lack of family support, and financial barriers, which constrain women from availing of institutional care necessary for administering treatment. Prevention of Parent to Child Transmission (PPTCT) services have also not been scaled up in remote areas with lower HIV prevalence.[373]

One of the best practices in PPTCT in India is the outreach approach used by the Integrated Counselling and Testing Centres (ICTCs) to ensure that HIV-positive women who are tested are followed-up before, during and after an institutional delivery, and provided with ART prophylaxis.[374] The core principle of this approach rests on the continuum of care for women, children, and their families—a chain of interventions that begin before pregnancy and continue through pregnancy, labour, and delivery, and subsequently as part of routine or specialized chronic care services after the child is born.[375] It is estimated that 70,000 children below the age of 15 are living with HIV in India and 21,000 children are infected every year through parent-to-child transmission. A small proportion are also infected by unsafe injections and blood transfusions. Most children are infected with the virus while still in the womb, during birth, or while breastfeeding.[376]

[373] UNICEF India, 'Latest Stories: HIV/AIDS'.

[374] UNICEF India, 'Latest Stories: HIV/AIDS'.

[375] WHO, 'New Guidance on Prevention of Mother-to-Child Transmission of HIV and Infant Feeding in the Context of HIV, 2010'. Available at http://www.who.int/hiv/pub/mtct/PMTCTfactsheet/en/ (accessed on 5 November 2015).

[376] The National Pediatric Antiretroviral Treatment (ART) Initiative was launched in 2006. A total of 40,000 children living with HIV will be provided ART by the end of NACP–III. A total of 375 ART centres shall be equipped to offer paediatric ART in the country. Follow-up of HIV-exposed infants, according

It is a dreaded disease and more than the lack of awareness about it, the attitude towards it is still a big problem. In such a scenario, a child, with its own limitations of understanding, facing the rejection of elders and society at large, has to go through a lot of emotional trauma. Also, the onus of the problem does not lie on any specific institution—the government, AIDS societies, NGOs, or people.

There are many categories of children living with AIDS who may or may not have family/community support or may not have it. They include:

- Children who are confirmed as infected by HIV;
- The infections may be from mother to child;
- Needing blood transfusion due to illnesses;
- Drug abuse—intravenous drug (IVD) users;
- Sexually abused;
- Affected by the epidemic: where parents or siblings are HIV positive;
- Vulnerable to HIV (in high-risk communities);
- Living under the shadow of the epidemic, being born, growing, and becoming sexually active in a world having added risk of infection.

Impact on Children Living with AIDS

Children with HIV/AIDS in a developing or poor country face many more problems than the children of developed countries due to lack of funds and proper healthcare services. This is reflected in the duration of survival of an infected child from these countries. Very often, they are seen only as added burdens on already scarce resources. Many a times, a child affected with the infection does not get the required attention from the family or immediate social circle due to lack of funds on their part. Heavy healthcare costs and lack of government support create difficult situations. Children also are seen not getting enough nutrition to fight against the disease.

On the other hand, the children having infected parents or siblings have other types of problems. They do not get outside support to take care of their parents. Very often, they have to take the burden of taking care of their parents and younger siblings. This might also affect their education. The parents' capacity to earn reduces, leading to malnourishment of the children. They might also have to resort to earning due to financial pressures. While the death of male members and increase of women-headed households create a negative impact on their growth, the death of both parents leads to being an orphan with no one to take care of them and their siblings. These children might have to take help of their grandparents or might also suffer from loss of inheritance, or might be forced to migrate. All these situations create emotional and physical vulnerability for children.

---

to the Indian Guidelines, begins at six weeks. The 'Road to Health' card for these children includes information on maternal HIV status, co-trimoxazole prophylaxis, infant HIV diagnosis, and infant feeding information. To reach more mother–infant pairs and to provide for and incorporate HIV care into the package of services for mothers and children, the Reproductive and Child Health (RCH) programme is linked to the PPTCT and Pediatric HIV programme. (UNICEF India, 'Latest Stories: HIV/AIDS')

The 'Rights' Approach to Children Infected and Affected by HIV/AIDS

India is a signatory to the UNCRC. However, children are suffering from discrimination, exploitation, and abuse. Infected children face several denials or limitations of their rights. Some of the violations of their rights are:[377]

- right to education;
- health and social services—as a result of inadequate or inaccessible health services;
- treatment, care, education, and social programmes;
- societal and family abandonment and rejection;
- children and mothers being forced to live on the streets;
- lack of nutrition to fight against infection;
- children's proneness to infection/epidemics related to their own communities;
- right to family being affected from challenge to immediate family environment and support through sickness, disability, and premature death from AIDS of one or both parents;
- reduced ability of infected parents to sustain their livelihood and care for them;
- school dropout due to need for caring for parents and younger siblings and need to earn;
- right to information, education, and services; and
- understanding of circumstances that make them especially vulnerable to sexual exploitation and abuse.

Based on the UNCRC, the following standards should be established and affirmed for children living with HIV/AIDS:

- Children have a right to survival and development. Therefore, realization of all rights must be protected from the impact of HIV/AIDS. Children have a right to health services/non-discrimination in health services. The medical personnel including doctors need to be sensitized on this issue.
- Children have a right to information and opportunities to develop life skills. Therefore, children should have access to HIV/AIDS prevention education, information, and the means for prevention, including attention to the ability to negotiate safer sex practices. Media should be encouraged to disseminate information of social and cultural benefits to children, taking into account their linguistic needs.[378]
- Voluntary testing and counselling must be available in antenatal clinics to provide information on what women can do if they are HIV positive and given their situation, what acceptable alternatives to breastfeeding exist.
- Children have a right to a safe and supportive environment free from exploitation and abuse. Therefore, special measures should be taken by governments to prevent and minimize the impact of HIV/AIDS caused by such factors as sexual abuse and trafficking, forced prostitution, sexual exploitation, use of illicit drugs, and harmful traditional practices. Sexual

---

[377] UNICEF India, 'Latest Stories: HIV/AIDS'.

[378] Sandie Blanchet, 'The Rights Approach to HIV/AIDS', presentation at the Media Workshop on HIV/AIDS and Child Rights, Gujarat, 13–14 August 1999, supported by UNICEF, Gujarat.

exploitation of girls of all ages is fuelled by the AIDS fear and is taking a heavy toll. Sexual abuse within the family also needs to be addressed. Educating the parents and reaching out directly to the children is essential in preventing the exploitation.[379]

- Children have a right to be protected from discrimination and exploitation, irrespective of their own HIV/AIDS status or that of members of their families. In relation to HIV/AIDS, to which a strong stigma is attached, protection from non-discrimination is particularly important. No discrimination should be suffered by children on any grounds, including in education, leisure, recreation, sports, and cultural activities because of their HIV/AIDS status. Children have a right to access health and social services on an equitable basis, irrespective of their own HIV/AIDS status or that of members of their families. All infected children should be provided with adequate HIV/AIDS treatment and care. Attention must be paid to ensure that orphans receive adequate support services.
- Children have a right to be heard and to have their aspirations, views, and needs reflected in decisions affecting them and their future.
- Children's right to privacy and confidentiality should be protected. The identity of the child and of his family should always be protected in the media.

National AIDS Prevention and Control Policy[380]

During the Eighth Five Year Plan (1992–97), the NACO was established under the Ministry of Health and Family Welfare to implement the programme which consists of five components: strengthening of management capacity for prevention and control of HIV/AIDS; improving public awareness; improving blood safety and rational use of blood; building surveillance and clinical management capacity; and controlling sexually transmitted diseases. In Thailand, a high-level commitment of the government, a multi-pronged approach to HIV/AIDS awareness, and a 100 per cent condom policy had considerably brought down the rate of spread of the disease. The issues that need to be examined in this connection are: respect for the rights of sex workers; their empowerment, so that they have a choice and they do not have to resort to prostitution; and above all, improving the status of the girl child.[381]

The available surveillance data clearly indicates that HIV is prevalent in almost all parts of the country. In the recent years it has spread from urban to rural areas and from individuals practising risk behaviour to the general population. Studies indicate that more and more women attending antenatal clinics are testing HIV-positive, thereby increasing the risk of perinatal transmission. The attributable factors for such rapid spread of the epidemic across the country today are labour migration and mobility in search of employment from economically backward to more advanced regions, low literacy levels leading to low awareness among the potential high-risk groups, gender

---

[379] Blanchet, 'The Rights Approach to HIV/AIDS'.

[380] Ministry of Health and Family Welfare, National Health Portal, 'National AIDS Prevention Policy', Government of India. Available at http://www.nhp.gov.in/national-aids-prevention-and-control-policy (accessed on 25 October 2015).

[381] Doris Grote, 'HIV/AIDS Situation in India and in Gujarat', presentation on HIV/AIDS at the Media Workshop on HIV/AIDS and Child Rights, Gujarat, 13–14 August 1999, supported by UNICEF, Gujarat.

disparity, and STI/RTI among both men and women. The social stigma attached to sexually transmitted infections also holds good for HIV/AIDS. The effects of stigma are devastating.[382] The general objective of the policy is to prevent the epidemic from spreading further and to reduce the impact of the epidemic not only upon the infected persons but upon the health and socio-economic status of the general population at all levels. The policy envisages effective containment of the infection levels of HIV/AIDS in the general population in order to achieve zero-level of new infections by 2007. The specific objectives of the policy are:

1. To reiterate strongly the Government's firm commitment to prevent the spread of HIV infection and reduce personal and social impact.
2. To generate a feeling of ownership among all the participants both at the government and non-government levels, like the Central Ministries and agencies of the Government of India, state governments, city corporations, industrial undertakings in public and private sectors, panchayat institutions, and local bodies, to make it a truly national effort.
3. To create an enabling socio-economic environment for prevention of HIV/AIDS; to provide care and support to people living with HIV/AIDS; to ensure protection/promotion of their human rights, including right to access healthcare system, right to education, employment, and privacy; and to mobilize support of a large number of NGOs/Community Based Organizations (CBOs) for an enlarged community initiative for prevention and alleviation of the HIV/AIDS problem.
4. To decentralize the HIV/AIDS control programme to the field level with adequate financial and administrative delegation of responsibilities.
5. To strengthen programme management capabilities of the state governments, municipal corporations, panchayat institutions, and leading NGOs participating in the programme.
6. To bring in horizontal integration at the implementation level with other national programmes like the RCH, the Revised National Tuberculosis Control Program (RNTCP), the ICDS, and the PHC system.
7. To prevent women, children, and other socially weak groups from becoming vulnerable to HIV infection by improving health education, legal status, and economic prospects.
8. To provide adequate and equitable provision of healthcare to the HIV-infected people and to draw attention to the compelling public health rationale for overcoming stigmatization, discrimination, and seclusion in society.
9. To constantly interact with international and bilateral agencies for support and cooperation in the field of research in vaccines, drugs, emerging systems of healthcare and other financial and managerial inputs.
10. To ensure availability of adequate and safe blood and blood products for the general population through promotion of voluntary blood donation in the country.[383]
11. To promote better understanding of HIV infection among people, especially students, youth, and other sexually active sections to generate greater awareness about the nature of its transmission and to adopt safe behavioural practices for prevention.[384]

---

[382] Ministry of Health and Family Welfare, 'National AIDS Prevention Policy'.
[383] Ministry of Health and Family Welfare, 'National AIDS Prevention Policy'.
[384] Ministry of Health and Family Welfare, 'National AIDS Prevention Policy'.

Judgments on Right of HIV/AIDS Affected and Infected

A. v. Medical Superintendent, Smt. Sucheta Kriplani Hospital & Anr[385]

Facts

The family of the victim belonged to Bihar and was living below the poverty line. Both husband and wife were HIV-positive and had faced harassment at their native place on grounds of their HIV status. The woman faced denial of treatment during her advanced pregnancy stage, after which they came to Delhi on 12 December 2010. The woman, who was nine month pregnant, got admitted in the Lady Hardinge Medical College on 24 December. Since her haemoglobin was below normal, she was asked to procure one unit of blood in order to facilitate the caesarean surgery. Her husband informed the hospital that as he was also HIV positive, he could not donate blood and there was no other family member in Delhi or in nearby areas to help them as donors.

The hospital did not take this situation into consideration and again on 3 January 2011, the hospital authorities asked her husband to arrange for blood for the surgery. Wherein, he again expressed his inability to donate the blood. The hospital also asked him to provide clothes, gloves, masks, and a kit of universal precaution, knowing well that he could not afford them at all.

After facing a series of denials and harassment, the husband moved the Delhi High Court for denial of basic human rights and pleaded for justice so that his wife's pregnancy could proceed with dignity and without any discrimination. A case was filed for seeking access to blood and treatment under the right to health, right to dignity, and rights to equality and for poor HIV-positive pregnant women.

Held

The High Court heard the matter and gave immediate directions to the Lady Hardinge Hospital, saying, 'There is an urgent need to issue direction to ensure the protection of the right to health and life of the woman and her foetus. A direction is accordingly issued to the Medical Superintendent, Lady Hardinge Medical College and Smt. Sucheta Kriplani Hospital immediately to arrange one unit of blood and further quantity of blood as may be required, from any of the authorized blood banks.

Law Reform Relating to Rights of Children Affected/infected by HIV/AIDS

There is a need for a child rights-based approach law to prevent discrimination against children and assure them of their rights to health, education, and nutrition. The process of drafting the HIV/AIDS Bill started with the International Policy Makers Conference on HIV/AIDS, held in May 2002 in New Delhi, where the need for a law on HIV was highlighted. An advisory working group was formed, chaired by the Project Director of the NACO, under the Ministry of Health and Family Welfare.[386]

---

[385] Writ Petition (C) of 2011, order dated 14 January 2011.

[386] The responsibility of drafting the HIV/AIDS Bill was given to Lawyers Collective HIV/AIDS Unit, a non-profit organization. The Bill was prepared after extensive research and nationwide consultations with

The HIV/AIDS Bill, 2007[387]

The AIDS Bill provides for protection and prevention of HIV epidemic in India. This bill contains specific rights for women, children, and people in the care and custody of the state in order to counter the wide-ranging societal discrimination faced by them. The bill embodies principles of human rights and seeks to establish a humane and egalitarian legal regime to support India's prevention, treatment, care, and support efforts vis-à-vis the epidemic. The key provisions of the HIV/AIDS Bill 2007[388] are:

- *Prohibition of discrimination:* The bill provides protection against discrimination in employment, education, healthcare, travel, and insurance in both the public and private sectors.
- *Informed consent for HIV testing, treatment, and research:* The bill mandates the provision of non-coerced, written consent after giving full details about the risks, benefits, and alternatives.
- *Non-disclosure of HIV-related information:* The bill recognizes a person's right to privacy and confidentiality of HIV status with certain exceptions.
- *Access to treatment:* The bill requires that the state provide free of cost access to comprehensive HIV-related treatment including ART drugs, diagnostics, and nutritional supplements.
- *Right to a safe working environment for doctors, healthcare workers, and other persons whose occupation may put them at risk of exposure to HIV:* The bill imposes an obligation on healthcare institutions to provide necessary universal precautions and prophylaxis.
- *Promotion of risk reduction strategies for groups at higher risk of HIV infection:* Targeted interventions like the promotion of condoms among sex workers and men who have sex with men, and distribution of clean needles to people who inject drugs, have proven to prevent HIV transmission. Certain criminal laws, however, impede these services by threatening providers and recipients with prosecution. The bill provides legal immunity to risk reduction programmes, thus strengthening efforts to prevent HIV.
- *Information, education, and communication:* The bill obliges the government to make HIV-related information accessible to all. It also mandates the government to create Information, Education, and Communication (IEC) material with community inputs, showing sensitivity across gender and age. These resources should be multilingual, easily understood, and regularly updated.
- *Implementation mechanisms*, including institutional grievance redressal, Health Ombudsman, and HIV/AIDS authorities. These will be supported by special procedures to be followed in

---

stakeholders including HIV-positive people, high-risk groups, women and children's groups, healthcare service providers, employers and employee organizations, lawyers, and civil society organizations. The HIV/AIDS Bill was submitted to NACO in August 2006. Presently, the health ministry is in discussion with the law ministry regarding some provisions of the bill. The bill is still to be tabled in Parliament.

[387] Ministry of Law and Justice (Legislative Department), the HIV/AIDS Bill, 2007, published in *The Gazette of India*, New Delhi.

[388] See Lawyers Collective HIV/AIDS Unit, 'The HIV/AIDS Bill 2009', New Delhi. Available at http://www.lawyerscollective.org/wp-content/uploads/2010/11/Parliamentarians.pdf (accessed on 1 November 2015).

courts, including suppression of identity and expeditious hearing, to make justice accessible to HIV-affected persons.

There is a need for a specific law to safeguard the rights of children and hold the service providers accountable.

Children and Disability

As per the WHO, disability is an umbrella term covering impairments, activity limitations, and participation restrictions.[389] Thus, disability is a complex phenomenon, reflecting an interaction between features of a person's body and features of the society in which he or she lives.[390] The United Nations Convention on the Rights of Persons with Disabilities[391] (CRPD), the first legally binding disability-specific human rights convention adopted by the UN, gives two descriptions of disability. The Preamble to the Convention states that 'Disability results from the interaction between persons with impairments and attitudinal and environmental barriers that hinder their full and effective participation in society on an equal basis with others'" Again, it emphasizes that 'Persons with disabilities include those who have long term physical, mental, intellectual or sensory impairments which in interaction with various barriers may hinder their full and effective participation in society on an equal basis with others'.[392]

The 'World Report on Disability' estimates that there are more than one billion people living with disability.[393] Prevalence is believed to be highest in the poorest parts of the world, and among the poorer sections of society.[394] UNICEF estimated in 2005 that 150 million children live with a disability globally, and that the majority of these are in low or middle income countries (LMICs), with estimates of childhood disability prevalence varying from 0.4–12.7 per cent.[395] They face many barriers to their inclusion and participation in everyday activities.[396] UNICEF argues that for these children, many of their deprivations stem from and are perpetuated by their

---

[389] Impairment is a problem in body function or structure; an activity limitation is a difficulty encountered by an individual in executing a task or action; while a participation restriction is a problem experienced by an individual in involvement in life situations.

[390] Geeta Chopra, *Child Rights in India: Challenges and Social Action*, Department of Human Development and Childhood Studies, Institute of Home Economics, University of Delhi (New Delhi: Springer India, 2015).

[391] The CRPD and its Optional Protocol (A/RES/61/106) was adopted on 13 December 2006 at the United Nations Headquarters in New York, and was opened for signature on 30 March 2007.

[392] Natasha Graham, 'Children With Disabilities', UNESCO Institute for Statistics (UIS), Montreal, 2014. Available at http://allinschool.org/wp-content/uploads/2015/01/OOSC-2014-Children-with-Disabilities-final.pdf (accessed on 25 October 2015).

[393] WHO, 'World Report on Disability 2011', WHO Press, Geneva, Switzerland. Available at http://www.unicef.org/protection/World_report_on_disability_eng.pdf (last accessed on 25 October 2015).

[394] Kuper et al., 2008 and Rischewski et al., 2008

[395] UNICEF, 'The State of the World's Children', United Nations Children's Fund, New York, USA, May 2013. Available at http://www.unicef.org/sowc2013/files/SWCR2013_ENG_Lo_res_24_Apr_2013.pdf (accessed on 5 November 2015).

[396] WHO, 'World Report on Disability 2011'.

invisibility, and the report calls for ways in which they can be rendered visible through sound data collection and analysis (UNICEF, 2013). Two recent key influential resource documents on disability have been the first ever WHO and World Bank 'World Report on Disability',[397] and UNICEF's 'State of the World's Children' report on children with disabilities.[398] The former report concludes: 'People with disabilities have generally poorer health, lower education achievements, fewer economic opportunities and higher rates of poverty than people without disabilities. This is largely due to the lack of services available to them and the many obstacles they face in their everyday lives.'[399,400]

The 2013 UNICEF 'State of the World's Children' report[401] focuses on the experiences of children with disabilities, and their families. It highlights that children who live in poverty and have a disability are even less likely to attend the local school or health service, are likely to be vulnerable to violence, and their families more likely to be poorer. One of the key recommendations is to promote approaches which remove the physical, cultural, economic, communication, mobility, and attitudinal barriers that impede the realization of the child's rights.[402]

International Instruments on Persons with Disability

UN Declaration on the Rights of Mentally Retarded Persons, 1971[403]

The principles contained in the United Nations Declaration on the Rights of Mentally Retarded Persons, 1971 [G.A. Res. 2856 (XXVI) of 20 December, 1971] are reproduced as follows:[404]

1. The mentally retarded person has, to the maximum degree of feasibility, the same rights as other human beings.
2. The mentally retarded person has a right to proper medical care and physical therapy and to such education, training, rehabilitation, and guidance as will enable him to develop his ability and maximum potential.
3. The mentally retarded person has a right to economic security and to a decent standard of living. He has a right to perform productive work or to engage in any other meaningful occupation to the fullest possible extent of his capabilities.
4. Whenever possible, the mentally retarded person should live with his own family or with foster parents and participate in different forms of community life. The family with which he lives

---

[397] The 'World Report on Disability' is a comprehensive document which illustrates the great need for improved data, policies, and programmes to address disability. A recurrent theme in the report is the connection between disability and poverty. Subgroups that are identified as particularly vulnerable include women, older people, children, and persons with mental health disabilities.

[398] UNICEF, 'The State of the World's Children'.

[399] WHO, 'World Report on Disability 2011'.

[400] Graham, 'Children with Disabilities'.

[401] UNICEF, 'The State of the World's Children'.

[402] Graham, 'Children with Disabilities'.

[403] 'Declaration on the Rights of Mentally Retarded Persons, Proclaimed by General Assembly resolution 2856 (XXVI) of 20 December 1971'.

[404] 'Declaration on the Rights of Mentally Retarded Persons'.

should receive assistance. If care in an institution becomes necessary, it should be provided in surroundings and circumstances as close as possible to those of normal life.

5. The mentally retarded person has a right to a qualified guardian when this is required to protect his personal well-being and interests.

6. The mentally retarded person has a right to protection from exploitation, abuse, and degrading treatment. If prosecuted for any offence, he shall have a right to due process of law with full recognition being given to his degree of mental responsibility.

7. Whenever mentally retarded persons are unable, because of the severity of their handicap, to exercise all their rights in a meaningful way, or should it become necessary to restrict or deny some or all of these rights, the procedure used for that restriction or denial of rights must contain proper legal safeguards against every form of abuse. This procedure must be based on an evaluation of the social capability of the mentally retarded person by qualified experts and must be subject to periodic review and to the right of appeal to higher authorities.

UN Conventions on Disability

Children with disabilities are doubly disadvantaged, being marginalized and discriminated against both because of their age and their disability. The two key conventions which detail guiding principles for work with children with disabilities are:

1. the UNCRC, and
2. the United Nations Convention on the Rights of Persons with Disabilities (UNCRPD).

Within the UNCRC, specific reference to disability includes Article 19[405] on children with disability,[406] and non-discrimination is one of the important principles (Article 2)[407] of the

---

[405] UNCRC, Article 19:

(1) States parties shall take all appropriate legislative, administrative, social, and educational measures to protect the child from all forms of physical or mental violence, injury or abuse, neglect or negligent treatment, maltreatment or exploitation, including sexual abuse, while in the care of parent(s), legal guardian(s), or any other person who has the care of the child.

(2) Such protective measures should, as appropriate, include effective procedures for the establishment of social programmes to provide necessary support for the child and for those who have the care of the child, as well as for other forms of prevention and for identification, reporting, referral, investigation, treatment, and follow-up of instances of child maltreatment described heretofore, and, as appropriate, for judicial involvement.

[406] Plan International, *Include Us! A Study of Disability among Plan International's Sponsored Children: Full Report* (Woking, UK: Plan International, 2013). Available at http://disabilitycentre.lshtm.ac.uk/files/2013/12/Include-us-full-report.pdf (accessed on 25 October 2015).

[407] UNCRC, Article 2:

(1) States parties shall respect and ensure the rights set forth in the present convention to each child within their jurisdiction without discrimination of any kind, irrespective of the child's or his or her parent's

UNCRC.[408] All countries that have ratified the UNCRC, therefore, have a responsibility to be inclusive of children with disabilities. A recent monitoring report of the UNCRC acknowledged that 'the challenges faced by children with disabilities in realizing their right to education remain profound' and that they are 'one of the most marginalized and excluded groups in respect of education'.[409] Children with disabilities are less likely to start school, have lower rates of school attendance, and lower transition rates to higher levels of education.[410] A gap for school attendance at primary level between children with disabilities and their non-disabled peers exists, and this gap widens for attendance at the secondary level.[411] Additionally, while enrolment may have increased for some types of impairment groups in a few LMICs, and some progress has been made with building the capacity of teachers on inclusive teaching practice, the overall quality of educational experiences for disabled children remain rather poor and exclusionary.[412]

United Nations Convention on the Rights of Persons with Disabilities, 2008

The CRPD is an international human rights treaty of the UN, intended to protect the rights and dignity of persons with disabilities. The convention has served as the major catalyst in the global shift from viewing persons with disabilities as objects of charity, medical treatment, and social protection, towards viewing them as full and equal members of society, with human rights. It was adopted on 13 December 2006 at the UN Headquarters in New York. The convention follows decades of work by the UN to change attitudes and approaches to persons with disabilities. The purpose of the convention is to promote, protect, and ensure the full and equal enjoyment of all human rights and fundamental freedoms by all persons with disabilities, and to promote respect for their inherent dignity.

The CRPD came into force in 2008. As of October 2015, it has 160 signatories and 159 parties, including 158 states and the European Union.[413] It sets out clearly the obligations on

---

or legal guardian's race, colour, sex, language, religion, political or other opinion, national, ethnic or social origin, property, disability, birth, or other status.

(2) States parties shall take all appropriate measures to ensure that the child is protected against all forms of discrimination or punishment on the basis of the status, activities, expressed opinions, or beliefs of the child's parents, legal guardians, or family members.

[408] Plan International, 'Include Us!'.

[409] WHO, 'World Report on Disability 2011'.

[410] WHO, 'World Report on Disability 2011'.

[411] UNICEF, *Children and Young People with Disabilities Fact Sheet* (New York, USA: UNICEF, May 2013). Available at http://www.unicef.org/disabilities/files/Factsheet_A5__Web_NEW.pdf (accessed on 25 October 2015).

[412] N. Singal, R. Jeffery, A. Jain, and N. Sood, 'The Enabling Role of Education in the Lives of Young People with Disabilities in India: Achieved and Desired Outcomes', *International Journal of Inclusive Education* 15, no. 10 (2011): 1205–18.

[413] UN, 'UN Treaty Collection: Parties to the Convention on the Rights of Persons with Disabilities: List of Parties'. Available at https://treaties.un.org/Pages/ViewDetails.aspx?src=TREATY&mtdsg_no=IV-15&chapter=4&lang=en (accessed on 28 October 2015).

states to promote, protect, and ensure the rights of persons with disabilities. states ratifying the CRPD have a range of general obligations. Among other things, they undertake to:

- Adopt legislation and other appropriate administrative measures where needed;
- Modify or repeal laws, customs, or practices that discriminate directly or indirectly;
- Include disability in all relevant policies and programmes;
- Refrain from any act or practice inconsistent with the CRPD;
- Take all appropriate measures to eliminate discrimination against persons with disabilities by any person, organization, or private enterprise.[414]

India ratified the CRPD on 1 October 2007.[415] The CRPD, the first legally binding disability-specific human rights convention adopted by the UN, gives two descriptions of disability. The Preamble to the convention states that 'Disability results from the interaction between persons with impairments and attitudinal and environmental barriers that hinder their full and effective participation'.[416] It emphasizes that 'Persons with disabilities include those who have long term physical, mental, intellectual or sensory impairments which in interaction with various barriers may hinder their full and effective participation in society on an equal basis with others'. Both the expressions reflect a shift from a medical model to a social model of disability. In the medical model, individuals with certain physical, intellectual, psychological, and mental impairments are considered disabled. According to this model, disability lies in the individual as it is equated with restrictions of activity with the burden of adjusting with environment through cures, treatment, and rehabilitation. In contrast, in the social model the focus is on the society, which imposes undue restrictions on the behaviour of persons with impairment. In this model, disability does not lie in individuals, but in the interaction between individuals and society. It advocates that persons with disabilities are rights holders and are entitled to strive for the removal of institutional, physical, informational, and attitudinal barriers in society. In India, different definitions of disability conditions have been introduced.[417]

Among the 50 articles in the convention, Article 7 is dedicated specifically to children with disabilities:[418]

1. States parties shall take all necessary measures to ensure the full enjoyment by children with disabilities of all human rights and fundamental freedoms on an equal basis with other children.
2. In all actions concerning children with disabilities, the best interests of the child shall be a primary consideration.

---

[414] WHO, 'World Report on Disability 2011'.

[415] UN Department of Economic and Social Affairs, 'Convention and Optional Protocol Signatures and Ratifications'. Available at http://www.un.org/disabilities/countries.asp?id=166 (accessed on 5 November 2015).

[416] CRPD.

[417] Ministry of Statistics and Programme Implementation, Government of India, 'Disability in India—A Statistical Profile', Chapter 3, Pune, March 2011. Available at: http://mospi.nic.in/Mospi_New/upload/disablity_india_statistical_profile_17mar11.htm (last accessed on 5 November 2015).

[418] CRPD.

3. States parties shall ensure that children with disabilities have the right to express their views freely on all matters affecting them, their views being given due weight in accordance with their age and maturity, on an equal basis with other children, and to be provided with disability and age-appropriate assistance to realize that right.

In addition, there are several references to children with disabilities throughout the text of the convention:

- Article 4 refers to the need to consult children with disabilities in the development and implementation of legislation and policies implementing the convention;[419]
- Article 8 covers the need to raise awareness and foster among children respect for the rights and dignity of persons with disabilities, particularly within the education system;[420]
- Article 16 highlights the need for child-focused legislation and policies;[421]
- Article 18 underscores the need for children with disabilities to be registered immediately after birth, and reinforces the right to have a name from birth, acquire a nationality, and the right to know and be cared for by their parents;[422]
- Article 23 refers to the right of children with disabilities to retain their fertility and their right to equal respect of family life; and states that children are not to be separated from parents with disabilities against their will;[423]
- Article 24 states that persons with disabilities should be guaranteed the right to inclusive education at all levels, regardless of age, without discrimination, and on the basis of equal opportunity, and children with disabilities shall not be excluded from free and compulsory primary education, or from secondary education on the basis of disability;
- Article 30 talks about ensuring that children with disabilities have equal access with other children to participation in play, recreation, and leisure and sporting activities, including those activities in the school system.[424]

Most of the 50 articles are of relevance to children with disabilities, and Article 7 specifically articulates the responsibility of the governments towards children with disabilities. The convention incorporates a social development perspective, and emphasizes the need to ensure that international development programmes are inclusive of and accessible to persons with disabilities.

United Nations Convention on the Rights of the Child

India has ratified the UNCRC.[425] The provisions relating to disabled children in the convention are as follows:

---

[419] Article 4(1)(a) of CRPD.
[420] Article 8(1)(b) of CRPD.
[421] Article 16 of CRPD.
[422] Article 18(2) of CRPD.
[423] Article 23(1)(c) of CRPD.
[424] Article 30(1) of CRPD.
[425] India ratified the UNCRC.

- Article 6 states that every child has the inherent right to life and the state has an obligation to ensure the child's survival and development.
- All children have the right to a decent standard of living adequate for their total development. Article 27 states that every child has the right to a standard of living adequate for his or her physical, mental, spiritual, moral, and social development.[426]

A disabled child deserves special care, education, and training to be of help to the society.

- Article 23 of the UNCRC says that a mentally or physically disabled child should enjoy a full decent life, in conditions which ensure dignity, promote self reliance, and facilitate the child's active participation in the community.[427]
- Article 24 says that a child has the right to the highest standard of health and medical care attainable.[428]
- Article 26 states that a child has the right to benefit from social security, including social insurance.

WHO Mental Health Action Plan 2013–20[429]

Mental well-being is a fundamental component of the WHO's definition of health. Good mental health enables people to realize their potential, cope with the normal stresses of life, work productively, and contribute to their communities. Mental health matters, but the world has a long way to go to achieve it. Many unfortunate trends must be reversed—neglect of mental health services and care, and abuses of human rights and discrimination against people with mental disorders and psycho-social disabilities. This comprehensive action plan recognizes the essential role of mental health in achieving health for all people. It is based on a life-course approach, aims to achieve equity through universal health coverage, and stresses the importance of prevention. The four major objectives of the action plan are to:[430]

1. Strengthen effective leadership and governance for mental health;
2. Provide comprehensive, integrated, and responsive mental health and social care services in community-based settings;

---

[426] The state's duty is to provide material assistance and support programmes, particularly with regard to nutrition, clothing, and housing.

[427] It also mentions the responsibility of the government in extending assistance in terms of the disabled child's access to education, training, healthcare services, and rehabilitation opportunities in a manner conducive to the child's achieving the fullest possible social integration and individual development. Children with disability shall include mentally retarded, physically handicapped, emotionally disturbed, and severely mentally ill children.

[428] States shall place special emphasis on the provision of primary and preventive healthcare, public health education, and the reduction of infant mortality. They shall encourage international cooperation in this regard and strive to see that no child is deprived of access to effective health services.

[429] WHO, *Comprehensive Mental Health Action Plan 2013–2020* (Geneva, Switzerland: WHO, 2013). Available at http://apps.who.int/iris/bitstream/10665/89966/1/9789241506021_eng.pdf?ua=1 (accessed on 25 October 2015).

[430] WHO, *Comprehensive Mental Health Action Plan 2013–2020*.

3. Implement strategies for promotion and prevention in mental health;
4. Strengthen information systems, evidence, and research for mental health.

Each of the four objectives is accompanied by one or two specific targets, which provide the basis for measurable collective action and achievement by member states towards global goals. A set of core indicators relating to these targets as well as other actions have been developed and are being collected via the Mental Health Atlas project on a periodic basis.[431]

National Laws Relating to Disabled Children in India

India has 2.042 million disabled children in the 0–6 years age group. Around 71 per cent of them—1.452 million—are in rural areas. There are 590,000 disabled children in cities. Of the total disabled children in the country, 1.104 million are male and 938,000 are female. Among them, 149,000 children have multiple disabilities. Children with hearing and eyesight disabilities form the lion's share among them. All age groups put together, there are more than 4.1 million children with eyesight problems, and 4.7 million children.[432]

The Constitution of India accords rights to children, including disabled children, as citizens of the country, and in keeping with their special status, the state has even enacted special laws [Article 15(3)] upholding various rights, as mentioned next:

• Right to free and compulsory elementary education for all children in the 6–14 years age group (Article 21 A);
• Right to be protected from any hazardous employment till the age of 14 years (Article 24);
• Right to be protected from being abused and forced by economic necessity to enter occupations unsuited to their age or strength [Article 39(e)];
• Right to equal opportunities and facilities to develop in a healthy manner and in conditions of freedom and dignity; and right to guaranteed protection of childhood and youth against exploitation and against moral and material abandonment [Article 39 (f)]; and
• Right to early childhood care and education to all children until they complete the age of 6 years (Article 45).

Besides, disabled children also have these rights as equal citizens of India, just as any other adult male or female:

• Right to equality (Article 14);
• Right against discrimination (Article 15);
• Right to personal liberty and due process of law (Article 21);
• Right to being protected from being trafficked and forced into bonded labour (Article 23);
• Right of minorities for protection of their interests (Article 29);

[431] WHO, *Comprehensive Mental Health Action Plan 2013–2020*.

[432] Ministry of Home Affairs, 'Population Enumeration Data (Final Population): Data on Disability'. Available at http://www.censusindia.gov.in/2011census/population_enumeration.html (accessed on 1 November 2015).

- Right of weaker sections of the people to be protected from social injustice and all forms of exploitation (Article 46); and
- Right to nutrition and standard of living and improved public health (Article 47).

The JJ Act, 2015 has come into force on 15 January 2016. It replaces the JJ Act, 2000. The 2015 Act includes a child who is mentally ill or mentally or physically challenged as a child in need of care and protection to be produced before the Child Welfare Committee. Under Section 53 of the act, the services that shall be provided, by the institutions registered under this act in the process of rehabilitation and re-integration of children, may include equipment such as wheel-chairs, prosthetic devices, hearing aids, braille kits, or any other suitable aids and appliances as required, for children with special needs and also appropriate education, including supplementary education, special education, and appropriate education for children with special needs. Under section 59 of JJ Act, 2015, children with physical and mental disability, may be given preference over other children for inter-country adoption. Under Section 75 of the act, whoever, having the actual charge of, or control over, a child, assaults, abandons, abuses, exposes or wilfully neglects the child or causes or procures the child to be assaulted, abandoned, abused, exposed or neglected in a manner likely to cause such child unnecessary mental or physical suffering, shall be punishable with imprisonment for a term which may extend to 3 years or with fine of Rs 1 lakh or with both. The act also provides that if on account of the aforesaid cruelty, if the child is physically incapacitated or develops a mental illness or is rendered mentally unfit to perform regular tasks or has risk to life or limb, such person shall be punishable with rigorous imprisonment, not less than 3 years but which may be extended up to 10 years and shall also be liable to fine of Rs 5 lakh.[433] The Child Welfare Committee (CWC) is the competent authority to deal with the issues.[434]

There are three laws in India that cover the area of disability. They are as follows:

1. Rehabilitation Council of India Act, 1991;
2. Persons with Disabilities Act (Equal Opportunities, Protection of Rights and Full Participation) Act, 1995; and
3. National Trust for the Welfare of Persons with Autism, Cerebral Palsy, Mental Retardation and Multiple Disabilities Act, 1999.

Rehabilitation Council of India Act, 1992

This act was passed by the Parliament to regulate the manpower development programmes in the field of education of children with special needs. Earlier in 1986, the government had decided to set up a Rehabilitation Council of India (RCI) under the Ministry of Social Justice and Empowerment as an autonomous body. Later, it got the assent from the President and became an act in 1992, and the Council came into force with effect from June 1993. The major objectives of the RCI Act are:

- To regulate the training policies and programmes in the field of rehabilitation of people with disabilities.

---

[433] The JJ Act.
[434] Section 29 of the JJ Act.

- To standardize training courses for rehabilitation professionals/personnel dealing with people with disabilities and ensure uniformity in various training centres throughout the country.
- To prescribe minimum standards of education and training institutions in the field of rehabilitation uniformly throughout the country.
- To recognize institutions/universities running degree/diploma/certificate courses in the field of rehabilitation of the disabled and to withdraw recognition wherever the facilities are not satisfactory.
- To recognize and equalize foreign degree/diploma/certificate in the field of rehabilitation awarded by universities/institutions.
- To maintain a Central Rehabilitation Register of persons possessing the recognized rehabilitation qualification.
- To collect information on a regular basis on education and training in the field of rehabilitation of people with disabilities, from institutions in India and abroad.
- To encourage continuing rehabilitation education by way of collaboration with organizations working in the field or rehabilitation of persons with disabilities.

The RCI has so far developed more than 50 courses and recognized more than a hundred institutions to offer special education and rehabilitation manpower development programmes in India. Out of these courses, nine are pertaining to visual impairment. Recently, RCI introduced a fully sponsored manpower development scheme so as to enable universities and colleges in the country to conduct need-based courses. This scheme will enable the most difficult regions in the country to initiate teacher preparation programmes in education of children with special needs. The enactment of the RCI Act goes a long way in accrediting special education manpower development programmes in the country.

Persons with Disabilities (Equal Opportunities, Protection of Rights and Full Participation) Act, 1995

This act came into force on 7 February 1996. It is a comprehensive legislation and the main purpose of the act is to define the responsibilities of the Central and state governments with regard to the services for disabled persons. The act also ensures full life to disabled individuals so as to make full contribution in accordance with their disability conditions. Blindness,[435] low vision,[436] leprosy-cured,[437], hearing impairment,[438] loco motor disability,[439] and Mental illness[440] are the seven disability conditions covered under the act. A person with disability means a person suffering from not less than 40 per cent of any disability as certified by a medical authority.[441]

---

[435] PWD Act, Section 2(b).
[436] PWD Act, Section 2(u).
[437] PWD Act, Section 2(n).
[438] Section 2(l).
[439] Section 2(o).
[440] Section 2(q), and mental retardation [Section 2(r)].
[441] PWD Act, Section 2(f).

Important Provisions of the Act

Chapter II of the act deals with the Central Coordination Committee and the Central Executive Committee, to be set up by the central government under the act. Chapter III provides for the setting up of the State Coordination Committees and the State Executive Committees by the state governments.

Chapter IV deals with prevention and early detection of disabilities through surveys, investigations, and research conducted concerning the cause, occurrence, and prevention of disabilities. Provisions are also made for creating awareness and training and taking measures for prenatal, perinatal, and postnatal care of the mother and child.[442]

Chapter V deals with education. As per the act, the central and state governments shall ensure that every child with disability has access to free and adequate education till the age of 18 years. It also indicates that integrated education and special schools will have to be set up to meet the educational needs of children with disabilities. Introduction of non-formal education, functional literacy schemes, provision of aids and appliances, education through open schools and universities, and other such moves are also stressed in the act. It also indicates that the government should create adequate teacher-training facilities to prepare teachers for special and integrated schools. Development of research on assistive devices and other areas of disability, and financial incentives to universities for taking researchers are also envisaged in the act.[443]

Chapter VI of the act provides for employment of the disabled. The appropriate governments have been enjoined upon:

- To identify posts in establishments reserved for persons with disabilities.[444]
- To reserve 1 per cent posts each for persons with blindness or low vision, hearing impairment, and loco motor disability or cerebral palsy.[445] If vacancies are not filled, they have to be carried forward.
- To create a special employment exchange.[446]
- To develop schemes for ensuring employment.[447]
- To reserve 3 per cent seats in all educational institutions.[448]
- To keep vacancies reserved in poverty alleviation schemes.[449]
- To give incentives to employers to ensure 5 per cent of the workforce is composed of persons with disabilities.[450]

---

[442] PWD Act, Section 25.
[443] PWD Act, Sections 26–30.
[444] PWD Act, Section 32.
[445] PWD Act, Section 33.
[446] PWD Act, Section 34.
[447] PWD Act, Section 38.
[448] PWD Act, Section 39.
[449] PWD Act, Section 40.
[450] PWD Act, Section 41.

Chapter VII is for affirmative action for the disabled. Under this the government shall prepare schemes for providing aids and appliances to persons with disabilities, and schemes for preferential allotment of land at concessional rates to the disabled.[451]

To provide equal opportunities and full participation to the disabled, as far as it is economically possible, roads, buildings, constructions, structures, transport, and employment should be so adapted that they are accessible to the persons with disabilities.[452] The act also provides for certification of institutions for the disabled.[453]

Chapter XIII deals with social security and rehabilitation of persons with disabilities. There is a provision for payment of unemployment allowance to the disabled. But these social security measures have to be undertaken within the economic capacity of the state governments.[454]

National Trust for Welfare of Persons with Autism, Cerebral Palsy, Mental Retardation and Multiple Disabilities Act, 1999 (National Trust Act)

The enactment of the National Trust Act aims to fulfill a common demand of families seeking reliable arrangement for their severely disabled wards. The National Trust has been set up under the National Trust Act specifically for persons with four disabilities, namely autism, cerebral palsy, mental retardation, and multiple disabilities. One of the objects of the Trust is to promote independent living among these four groups of persons and to support organizations that provide facilities for persons with the said four disabilities. The specific objectives of the act are:

- To enable and empower persons with disabilities to live as independently and as fully as possible, within and as close as possible to the community to which they belong;
- To promote measures for the care and protection of persons with disabilities in the event of death of their parent or guardian; and
- To extend support to registered organizations to provide need-based services during the period of crisis in the families of disabled individuals covered under this Act.

Important Case Laws on Disability Rights

The issue of the condition of inmates at mental healthcare institutes has been before various courts, and various directions have been passed in this connection, including by the apex court.

The following is a summary of relevant cases and the directions issued therein:

Sheela Barse (II) v. Union of India[455]

Facts

This case related to the rehabilitation of mentally retarded, abandoned, or destitute children, lodged in various jails of the country, for safe custody.

---

[451] PWD Act, Sections 42 and 43.
[452] PWD Act, Sections 44–47.
[453] PWD Act, Chapter X, Sections 50–55.
[454] PWD Act, Chapter XIII.
[455] (1986) 3 SCC 632.

Held

It was observed by the Court that a child is a national asset and it is the duty of the state to look after the child with a view of ensuring full development of its personality. Towards this end, state governments are to set up necessary remand homes and observation homes where children accused of offences can be lodged, pending trial. Children should be released on bail if the state government has insufficient accommodation in its remand homes or observation homes. The Court gave other such directions to ensure the protection of children in criminal trials.

The Court also clarified that the right to a speedy trial is a fundamental right under Article 21 and as such the Union Government should endeavour to enact a central act for the protection and welfare of children. It should specifically ensure the social, economic, and psychological rehabilitation of children who are abandoned, destitute, or lost. Although the Court had already called upon the state governments by its order dated 5 August 86 to bring into force and to implement vigorously the provisions of the Children's Act enacted in various states, it observed that it would be desirable if the Central Government initiates parliamentary legislation on the subject in order to bring about uniformity with regard to various provisions relating to children.

Chandigarh Administration v. Nemo[456]

Facts

The Petition was filed by the Chandigarh Administration in public interest, seeking permission for the medical termination of the pregnancy of a mentally retarded girl. The girl in question was an orphan and an inmate of a home for the mentally challenged, in Chandigarh. During her stay in the home, pursuant to complaints of nausea and abdominal pain from the girl, the Medical Social Worker and the staff nurse conducted a pregnancy test on her, which turned out to be positive. It was alleged that the girl had been raped by the guard posted at the said institute.

Subsequently, a reference was made to the Director-Principal of the Government Medical College and Hospital, who constituted a three-member Medical Board to evaluate the mental status of the victim, which in turn opined that she was in the category of 'mild mental retardation'. The Board submitted its opinion, recommending medical termination of the pregnancy of the victim, inter-alia, on the grounds that there was no doubt that the pregnancy was an outcome of rape and that the mental retardation in presence of bony abnormalities in her could have a genetic basis and could be inherited by the baby, and hence, continuation of pregnancy could be associated with complications considering her age, mental status, and previous surgery. Further, being mildly mentally retarded, she would be unable to look after herself and would not be able to mother a child.

Held

The Court issued directions regarding the administration of welfare institutes in Chandigarh subsequent to the incident. The question of medical termination of her pregnancy was also decided by the Court (this was subsequently overturned by the apex court).

[456] CWP No. 8760 of 2009, Chandigarh High Court.

The Court expressed its anguish at the manner in which institutions like Nari Niketan or Ashreya were being run. It noted that the fact that a hapless, mentally retarded inmate of one of the petitioner's institutes had been allegedly raped by none else than one of the guards of the institute, told the tale of criminal and administrative negligence, callousness, and an indifferent attitude of those who are at the helm of affairs in these institutions. The Court strongly deprecated the manner and the mechanism with which the state-helped welfare institutions were being run or managed. It noted that if the allegations were found to be true, it would need to be an eye opener for the high echelons of the Administration to introspect and carry out sweeping administrative reforms towards the objects sought to be achieved by such institutions.

The moot point which was placed for the Court's consideration was whether the pregnancy of the victim was liable to be terminated, and if so, who could be the competent person to give consent for such termination. Directions in respect of administration of such institutes were also passed. The following directions were passed by the Court:

1. A Medical Board was notified and directed to visit and examine each and every inmate of government-run/aided institutions every fortnight and submit its periodical report to the Secretary, Department of Health, UT Administration.

    a) The periodical examination of the inmates of such institutions was required to necessarily include examination as to whether or not the inmate had been subjected to any sexual abuse.

    b) It was directed that in case the medical board found any inmate to be a victim in terms of the direction (2) above, the matter should be reported to the local police forthwith.

    c) The petitioner, Chandigarh Administration, was directed to provide the best medical treatment to all the inmates of the government-run/aided institutes without any plea or pretext of the financial constraints or non-availability of adequate funds.

    d) It was further directed that a Monitoring Committee be constituted, consisting of at least five members which would include not less than three NGO workers/social workers of high repute in the specialized field, and preferably be headed by an NGO worker/social worker only, along with two members who would be responsible officers of the Chandigarh Administration, and who were empowered to accord necessary sanction for the day-to-day expenditure, as may be incurred to provide basic amenities to the inmates of all the government-run/aided institutes.

    e) The Home Secretary of the Chandigarh Administration was directed to notify a list within one month of NGOs, social workers, human right activists, and volunteers, including lawyers, inclined to provide free legal aid services, who would be given visiting rights not less than once a week to all the welfare institutions. It was further directed that any report submitted by such a visitor regarding poor/malfunctioning or on improvement thereof, would be considered and acted upon by the Competent Authority of the Chandigarh Administration within one month.

    f) The description and the particulars of each inmate, along with photographs, if possible, and their latest status of educational pursuit, were directed to be displayed on the website of the Department concerned and/or the Chandigarh Administration, and such list was to be updated from time to time.

g) It was directed that the petitioner, Chandigarh Administration, start a community kitchen in all the government-run/aided institutions, and if the inmates included females, by employing the female staff only. The Administration, with the approval of the Monitoring Committee constituted as per the Court order, was directed to involve the inmates in the cooking process by ensuring that no risk was caused to their mental and physical health. It was further directed that all the inmates be provided nutritious, healthy, and adequate food. It was further directed that the Monitoring Committee as well as the NGOs/Social Workers to whom visiting rights were provided were expected to test the quality of the food.

h) It was further directed that the Administration not keep/employ male employees for the internal functioning of the institutions unless all the inmates were only male. The Administration was directed to explore the feasibility of employing retired lady police officers/officials or ex-army personnel for the outer security purposes of such institutions.

Mumbai Mirror v. the Secretary[457]

The Court took suo moto cognizance of an article which appeared in the *Mumbai Mirror* on 24 August 2010, on the inhuman condition in which the inmates of a Children's Home at Shahpur in the District of Thane lived. This PIL is ongoing and some of the major policy reforms brought in by this PIL relating to intellectually challenged children are as follows:

1. The Directorate of Health Services is involved to provide regular health check-ups for children in mentally disabled children's (MDC) homes across the state.
2. The norms for the participation of mentally challenged, hearing and speech impaired children in criminal trials have been prepared.
3. The Government of Maharashtra hs agreed to provide compensation to both mentally challenged boys and girls under the Manodharya Scheme.

Payel Sarkar v. Central Board of Secondary Education and Ors[458]

Facts

The petitioner, a student, was not allowed to sit for the All India Senior School Certificate Examination because of frequent absence from school. The Court accepted that her poor attendance record was attributable to a "special learning disability". A provision in the school by-laws allowed for exemptions from school attendance policies for blind, physically handicapped, and dyslexic students.

Issue

Are students suffering from serious diseases, including students living with HIV and those with special learning disabilities, exempt from the strict enforcement of school attendance policies?

---

[457] PIL 182/2010, Mumbai High Court.
[458] AIR 2010 Calcutta 74.

Held

The Court reviewed the school by-laws and stated that the head of the school 'must make arrangements for special remedial teaching' for children 'belonging to the weaker sections of the community' and those with 'special learning disabilities or … who require specialized psychoeducational counselling'. The Court declared that the current grouping of students who qualified for exemption from school attendance policies was not inclusive enough. The Court held that the 'rigidity of attendance should be relaxed' for students with special learning disabilities and others "in exceptional circumstances created on medical grounds, such as candidates suffering from serious diseases like cancer, AIDS, T.B. or similar serious diseases requiring long period of hospitalization'.

Policies, Plans, and Schemes in India Relating to Disability

National Policy on Education, 1986

The NPE is implemented to achieve the goal of providing education to all, including the disabled. The objective of the policy is to integrate the physically and mentally handicapped with the general community as equal partners to prepare them for normal growth and to enable them to face life with courage and confidence. It envisages that wherever possible, children with motor and other mild handicaps will be educated with others. Special schools with hostels will be provided as far as possible at district headquarters for severely handicapped children.

Deendayal Disabled Rehabilitation Scheme to Promote Voluntary Action for Persons with Disabilities, 2009[459]

The following model projects are supported under the scheme:

1. *Project for Pre-School and Early Intervention and Training:* The primary objective is to prepare infants and children up to 6 years of age for schooling in special schools and/or integration at the appropriate stage in regular schools. The project also provides for therapeutic services, day care, and counselling of parents.
2. *Special Schools:* Special school projects for the mentally challenged, the hearing and speech impaired, and the visually challenged are supported. The main thrust of special education is to develop communication skills and other sensory abilities, with the end objective varying from acquiring daily living skills to integration in regular institutions of learning and society in general. Residential facilities can also be covered under the grant. Continuing projects for special schools for orthopaedically handicapped children are being funded, but there is no model project.
3. *Project for Cerebral Palsied Children:* The objective is similar to projects for special schools, with more emphasis on catering to the therapy needs of the individual.
4. *Home Based Rehabilitation Programme/Home Management Programme:* The objectives of this project include guidance and provision for mobility skills, development of basic communication

[459] Ministry of Social Justice and Empowerment, Government of India, effective from 1 April 2009. Available at http://socialjustice.nic.in/ddrs.php (accessed on 1 November 2015).

skills and daily living skills, and training and sensitization of families of children with disabilities in the context of the home environment.

Assistance to Disabled Persons for Purchase/Fitting of Aids and Appliances (ADIP Scheme)[460]

The main objective of this scheme is to assist the needy, disabled persons, including disabled children, in procuring durable, sophisticated, and scientifically manufactured, modern, standard aids and appliances to promote physical, social, psychological rehabilitation by reducing the effects of disabilities and at the same time enhancing their economic potential.

Impact of Cochlear Implants in Children with Hearing Impairment under ADIP Scheme[461]

Hearing impairment has a significant impact on the child and his family. This impact is seen on every aspect of life including cognitive, communication, psycho-social, educational, and personality development, as well as on financial condition of the family. Considering the wide ranging impact of hearing impairment, early identification and intervention during the critical learning years has been found to be very important in minimizing the impact of the hearing impairment in the child's overall development.

Group Home and Rehabilitation Activities Under National Trust Act for Disabled Adults[462]

The National Trust was setup in the context of parents' worries about the future of their children with special needs when they will be no more. In order to provide a sustainable solution to this rather difficult problem, Group Home and Rehabilitation Activities under National Trust Act for Disabled Adults (GHARAUNDA)—a scheme of lifelong shelter and care—is conceived with the following objectives:

1. To provide an assured minimum quality of care services throughout the life of the persons with autism, cerebral palsy, mental retardation, and multiple disabilities.
2. To encourage assisted living with independence and dignity.
3. To facilitate establishment of requisite infrastructure for the assured care system throughout the country.
4. To provide care services at an affordable price on a sustainable basis.

---

[460] 'Scheme of Assistance to Disabled Persons For Purchase/Fitting of Aids/Appliances (ADIP Scheme)', (applicable w.e.f. 1 April 2014) Government of India, Ministry of Social Justice and Empowerment, New Delhi. Available at http://socialjustice.nic.in/pdf/adiprevised010414.pdf (accessed on 1 November 2015).

[461] Cochlear Implant under ADIP Scheme of Government of India Implemented by Ali Yavar Jung National Institute for the Hearing Handicapped, Mumbai. Available at http://adipcochlearimplant.in/ (accessed on 1 November 2015).

[462] Ministry of Social Justice and Empowerment, Government of India, National Trust for the Welfare of Persons with Autism, Cerebral Palsy, Mental Retardation and Multiple Disabilities. Available at http://www.thenationaltrust.co.in/nt/images/stories/Gharaunda/gharaunda_eng.pdf (accessed on 1 November 2015).

Niramaya[463]

In order to enable and empower persons with disability to live as independently and as fully as possible, health services and their access to persons with disabilities assume a very significant role. In this context, the health insurance facility becomes important, but presently, such products are not easily available for persons with disabilities. In such a situation, a health insurance scheme—Niramaya—is conceived with the following objectives:

- To provide affordable health insurance to persons with autism, cerebral palsy, mental retardation, and multiple disabilities.
- To encourage health services-seeking behaviour among persons with disability.
- To improve the general health condition and quality of life of persons with disabilities.

Law Reform Relating to Disability

In October 2007, India ratified the United Nations Convention for Rights of Persons with Disability (PWD). Since then, the advocates of PWD rights have been calling for an amendment of the PWD Act so that it better aligns with the provisions of the PWD Convention, thus leading to the formation of the Right of Persons with Disabilities Bill, 2014.[464]

Highlights of the Bill[465]

The Right of Persons with Disabilities Bill replaces the erstwhile PWD Act. Instead of seven disabilities specified in the act, the bill covers 19 conditions, as follows:

- Persons with at least 40 per cent of a disability are entitled to certain benefits such as reservations in education and employment, preference in government schemes, and so on.
- The bill confers several rights and entitlements to disabled persons. These include disabled-friendly access to all public buildings, hospitals, modes of transport, polling stations, and so on.
- In case of mentally ill persons, district courts may award two types of guardianship. A limited guardian takes decisions jointly with the mentally ill person. A plenary guardian takes decisions on behalf of the mentally ill person, without consulting him.
- Violation of any provision of the act is punishable with imprisonment up to six months, and/or fine of Rs 10,000. Subsequent violations carry a higher penalty.

---

[463] Ministry of Social Justice and Empowerment, National Trust for the Welfare of Persons.

[464] The bill was introduced in the Rajya Sabha on 7 February 2014 by the Minister of Social Justice and Empowerment, Mallikarjun Kharge. The bill was referred to the Standing Committee on Social Justice and Empowerment, chaired by Ramesh Bais, on 16 September 2014. The committee was scheduled to submit its report during the Budget Session 2015.

[465] *PRS India*, 'Legislative Brief of the Rights of Persons with Disabilities Bill, 2014'. Available at http://www.prsindia.org/billtrack/the-right-of-persons-with-disabilities-bill-2014-3122/ (accessed on 1 November 2015).

- In 'extraordinary situations', district courts may appoint plenary guardians for mentally ill persons. The bill does not lay down principles for such determination, in a consistent manner, across various courts.

The bill is being brought in to fulfill obligations under an international treaty. Violation of any provision in the act will attract imprisonment and/or fine. Given the widespread obligations (such as making all polling booths accessible to the disabled), many acts of omission or commission could be interpreted as criminal offences. The question is whether it is appropriate for Parliament to impose legal and financial obligations on states and municipalities with regard to disability, which is a state list subject. The Financial Memorandum does not provide any estimate of the financial resources required to meet obligations under the bill. The bill overrides the Mental Health Act, 1987 but the safeguards against misuse of powers by guardians are lower. The bill is inconsistent with other laws in some cases. These include conditions for termination of pregnancy and the minimum penalty for outraging the modesty of a woman.

Studies have shown that children with disabilities are disproportionately vulnerable to violence, neglect, and abuse as a result of exclusion and discrimination. An increasing body of evidence shows that many children with disabilities lack access to protection, and medical, psychosocial, and legal services.[466] These children are often more isolated, and may have little possibility for reporting or receiving support.[467] Key recommendations to improve protection for this vulnerable group include: (i) the need to tackle social and structural discrimination which affects children with disabilities; (ii) greater investment in high-quality, free services that prevent and respond to sexual violence against children and young people with disabilities; (iii) support greater participation of children with disabilities by rendering them more visible, for example, conducting more research on issues that affect them; and (iv) increase in advocacy activities.[468]

The Rights of Persons with Disabilities Bill, 2016 was passed by both Houses of Parliament on 17 December 2016. It will replace the Persons with Disabilities Act 1995 and make the law more compliant with the UN Convention on the Rights of Persons with Disabilities Some of the salient provisions of the new Act are:

1. disability has been defined based on an evolving and dynamic concept and the types of disabilities have been increased from existing seven to 21. It also defines Persons with benchmark disabilities as those with at least 40 per cent of any of the above specified disabilities. Speech and Language Disability and Specific Learning Disability have been added for the first time. Acid Attack Victims have been included. The Centre will have the power to add

---

[466] UNICEF, 'Annual Report 2005, Covering 1 January 2005 through 31 December 2005', June 2006. Available at http://www.unicef.org/about/annualreport/2005/pdf/Unicef2005ar.pdf (accessed on 1 November 2015).

[467] Handicap International, 'Out from the Shadows: Sexual Violence against the Children with Disabilities' (London: Save the Children, 2011). Available at http://www.ohchr.org/Documents/HRBodies/CEDAW/HarmfulPractices/HandicapInternationalandSavetheChildren.pdf (accessed on 1 November 2015).

[468] WHO, 'World Report on Disability'.

more types of disabilities to it. The types of disabilities now include mental illness, autism spectrum disorder, cerebral palsy, muscular dystrophy, chronic neurological conditions.

2. The PWDs shall have the right to equality. They shall not be discriminated against on grounds of their disability. Rights include protection from inhuman treatment and equal protection and safety in situations of risk, humanitarian emergencies, natural disasters and armed conflict. All existing public buildings shall be made accessible for disabled persons.

3. At least 5 per cent seats in all government institutions of higher education and those getting aid from the government are required to reserve seats for persons with benchmark disabilities. Earlier it was only 3 per cent.

4. every child with benchmark disability between the age group of 6 and 18 years will have the right to free education

5. The union and state governments will ensure that at least 4 per cent of the vacancies in identified establishments are filled by persons or class of persons with at least 40 per cent of any of the disabilities. The reservation must be computed on the basis of total number of vacancies in the strength of a cadre. Government can exempt any establishment from this provision of reservation.

6. Disabled persons have the equal right to own and inherit movable and immovable property, as well as control their financial affairs in par with others. Guardianship: The district court may order guardianship to the disable person if found a mentally ill person and not capable of taking care of himself or of taking legally binding decisions.

7. District level committees will be constituted by the state governments to address local concerns of PWDs.

8. Special Courts will be designated in each district to handle cases concerning violation of rights of PWDs.

9. Central and state advisory boards on disability will be constituted central and state governments respectively. They will advise governments on policies and programmes on disability. They will also review the activities of organisations dealing with disabled persons.

10. National and state fund will be created to provide financial support to the persons with disabilities. The existing national fund for PWDs and the Trust Fund for Empowerment of PWDs will be subsumed with the national fund.

11. It provides for imprisonment ranging from 6 months to 2 years, along with a fine ranging from Rs 10,000 to Rs 5 lakh, for discriminating against differently abled persons.

12. It also strengthens the office of chief commissioner and state commissioners for persons with disabilities which will act as regulatory bodies.

13. Makes assaulting, insulting, intimidating, denying food to a person with disability, or sexually exploiting a differently-able woman and performing a medical procedure on such women without consent that may lead in termination of pregnancy a penal offence with a jail term up to 5 years.

14. Any person who contravenes any provision of the act will be punishable with a maximum fine of Rs 5 lakh.

Children as Victims of Drugs

Children, because of their tender age, are particularly prone to be swayed into addiction under unhealthy influences and to be used as instruments in drug trafficking. There is a widespread use of illicit drugs among street children. Even among children in institutions, use of drugs is increasing. There are innumerable documented instances to show that poor children are introduced and addicted to drugs only to be manipulated as tools in drug trafficking by organized criminal syndicates. If a child is less than 7 years of age, Section 82 of the IPC is applicable and the act committed by the child is not treated as an offence. If the child is above 7 years and below 12 years, depending on his/her maturity of understanding, the criminal liability will be decided.[469] If above 12 years, the child will be dealt with under the juvenile justice system. The Narcotic Drugs and Psychotropic Substances Act (NDPS Act), 1985 declares illegal the production, possession, transportation, purchase, and sale of any drug enumerated in the schedule to the act. A general rule of penal policy envisaged under the act is that an offender, be he an addict or a trafficker, is subject to punishment which includes imprisonment as well as fine. Possession of drugs is in itself an offence under the NDPS Act. It does not matter whether the possession is for personal consumption or for any other purpose. The punishment depends upon the quantity of drugs possessesed. However, if the offender is charged with either possession of small quantities of drugs or with consumption of drugs and he voluntarily seeks to undergo medical treatment for de-addiction at a hospital or institution maintained or recognized by the government or a local authority, he shall not be liable for prosecution. This immunity from prosecution may be withdrawn if he does not undergo the complete treatment for de-addiction.Under the JJ Act, it is an offence to give or cause to be given to any juvenile or child any intoxicating liquor or any drug or psychotropic substance except upon the order of a duly qualified medical practitioner or in case of sickness. The punishment for this offence is imprisonment for a term which may extend to 3 years, and fine.[470] The JJ Act will override the NDPS Act.

The interventions of the NGOs in this area include running detoxification centres, advocacy, developing community mobilization strategies, and networking.

Children's Right to Shelter/Housing

Here are a few recent reports on some instances that affected the child's right to shelter/housing:

- The settlement of Babrekar Nagar was razed to the ground in 1997. An area of around 30 hectares belonging to the Collector and 10 hectares belonging to the Maharashtra Housing and Area Development Authority (MHADA) was cleared. A total of 12,842 families were displaced, which amounted to approximately 26,000 children exposed to violence and the traumatic experience of eviction.
- Children in 18 villages of Tamil Nadu were uprooted by the State Industries Promotion Corporation of Tamil Nadu (SIPCOT). Among the approximately 36,000 people to be involuntarily evicted with no place to go, are 13,000–14,000 children. These children will lose the

[469] Section 83, IPC.

[470] Section 25 in the JJ Act: Penalty for giving intoxicating liquor or narcotic drug or psychotropic substance to juvenile or child—Whoever gives, or causes to be given, to any juvenile or the child any intoxicating liquor in a public place or any narcotic drug or psychotropic substance except upon the order of duly qualified medical practitioner or in case of sickness shall be punishable with imprisonment for a term which may extend to 3 years and shall also be liable to fine.

stability of a house and rural surroundings, because it will be very hard for the immigrants, once in the city of Chennai (the most likely place to go for most of them once evicted) to find, build, and keep a stable home. Certainly, a large number of them will, from sheer necessity, end up in the streets, on pavements, or in a slum.

- The Sanjay Gandhi Nagar Demolition is one of the largest ever demolitions conducted in urban India. The Sanjay Gandhi National Park, Mumbai, has an area of 103.09 square kilometres and contains about 86,000 huts, that is, about 450,000 people. Bombay Environmental Action Group, an environmental group, filed a petition before the Mumbai High Court for clearing Sanjay Gandhi National Park. Fifty-six thousand families, that is, about 300,000 people, have been evicted without being provided with an alternative site. Only those families having their names included in the electoral roll of 1 January 1995 are entitled to a patch of land measuring 15' x 10', for which they have to pay a sum of Rs 7,000 per family. The alternative site is offered outside the city limits, in an adjoining district, and about 13 km away from the railway station. Many do not have the financial capacity to pay Rs. 7,000 and others apprehend that this reloca-tion will severe them from their means of livelihood and will disturb their children's schooling.
- In a survey conducted in 2005, the Punarvasan Sangharsh Samiti found that in the Akkalkuwa block—one of the areas affected by the Sardar Sarovar dam—98 children had died. Of these, 71 were malnourished, and 45 were found to be in the second stage of malnourishment.[471]
- Between March 2012 and September 2015, information compiled by Housing and Land Rights Network (HLRN)[472] reveals that over 42,000 families or more than 230,000 people have suffered from forced evictions in urban India, without due process or rehabilitation, and lost their homes as a direct result of state-sponsored demolition drives.[473]
- In January 2013, Bruhat Bengaluru Bangalore Mahanagara Palike (BBMP), a civic body responsible for providing infrastructure and services in the Greater Bangalore Metropolitan area, demolished 1,200 homes and evicted over 5,000 people living in economically weaker section (EWS) quarters in Ejipura/Koramangala, Bangalore. The demolition affected around 1,200 women and 2,000 children. The four-day demolition drive razed around 900 tin sheds that were built at the site more than 11 years ago. The BBMP did not follow any due process for the eviction. The demolition was carried out in the presence of a large police force that allegedly used force against the residents.

Even though India has the largest population of street children in the world, there is no authentic data in India on street children. Street children are an extremely vulnerable group because of the way they are forced to live, homeless, out on the streets. Their mobility is high, they are without any parental guidance and without any form of family love or affection, and

---

[471] HAQ: Centre for Child Rights, 'Handbook on Children's Right to Adequate Housing', New Delhi, 2008.

[472] HLRN, *The Human Rights to Adequate Housing and Land in India: Report for the United Nations Human Rights Council on Implementation of UPR Recommendations* (New Delhi: HLRN, 2015). Available at http://hlrn.org.in/documents/UPR_Recommendations_Housing_and_Land_India_HLRN_Sept_2015.pdf (accessed on 5 November 2015).

[473] Youth for Unity and Voluntary Action (YUVA) Report, 'Mumbai Evictions (December 2004–March 2005): An Analysis of Impact in Twenty Eight Communities', YUVA , Mumbai 2005.

hence, are subjected to the grimness of an existence not suitable for their physical and emotional stage of development. They have to work to make a living and are constantly exposed to the dangers and the unhealthy life of the city and the streets. Due to their distrust and even hatred against all forms of authority (created by their daily experiences with them), it is hard to reach this specific group of children. While engaged in various trades and services which directly/indirectly benefit the city dwellers, they do not have sufficient access to even the basic services required for their healthy growth and development. The significance of such forced demolitions cannot be understated, and the impact of this on families and especially the children cannot be forgotten. Majority of the people said that they come to large cities in search of work and to support their families. In such an event, it often happens that needs of children often go neglected. The right to development and survival of children in such situations is often not appropriately met.

Lack of adequate housing has long-term deleterious effects, including severe psychological impact on children. Children suffer the most from forced evictions and displacement which often result in loss of education, and in the absence of adequate rehabilitation, homelessness. Street children, in particular, face extreme conditions of violence, abuse, harsh weather conditions, injury, malnutrition, exploitation, and lack of security. Despite the existence of several programmes, the plight of street children continues to be dismal.[474]

The above case studies[475] present the displacement of children and the consequent gross violation of their basic human rights to housing and to live in dignity. The right to housing is defined as follows: 'The human right to a place to live is an inalienable right closely linked to the right to live, in all of its spiritual and material aspects. All children, women and men have the right to a safe and decent place to live in peace with dignity ... The right to a place with dignity is not limited exclusively to a physical structure, a house. It is conceived in a broader sense that integrates housing—shelter and habitat—environment as a whole. This includes the cultural, historic, social, economic, political, legal, environmental, physical, and territorial dimensions.'[476]

In its essence, housing as a living impulse creates roots entailing security. The house is to be seen as the home—the one stable point in the child's life where she/he can return to, where she/he will find love and peace: 'Nurturing families, in all their forms, are the primary institution and the best environment for protecting and promoting the rights and well-being of children. Whenever possible, children must be able to live with their families in adequate, secure housing.[477] Adequate housing includes legal security of tenure, including protection from forced eviction and displacement; availability of services, materials, facilities, and infrastructure; affordability, habitability, accessibility, and location. Essential to the survival of families is their capacity to support themselves in ways which do not undermine family life. When families are unable to provide adequately for their children, states have the obligation to assist and support them.'[478]

---

[474] HLRN, *The Human Rights to Adequate Housing and Land in India*.

[475] '"The Child in Search of the State", Alternate Report to the India Country Report on the Implementation of the Right to Housing as Enshrined in the Convention on the Rights of the Child', submitted by Human Rights Foundation (HRF), LAYA's and YUVA, September 1998.

[476] The Habitat International Coalition, in coordination with other international voluntary organizations and community-based organizations, have defined this right.

[477] In the words of the Expert Seminar on Children's Rights and Habitat organized by the UNICEF, the United Nations Centre for Human Settlement (UNCHS)/Habitat in February 1996.

[478] UNCRC, HRF, LAYA, YUVA, 'The Child in Search of the State'.

Laws Relating to Right to Adequate Housing

The Constitution of India and the Right to Housing

There is no explicit or specific provision of the right to adequate housing in the Constitution of India. There are several laws related to housing and land rights through which land may be acquired, evictions may take place, and compensation and rehabilitation provided. Besides, there are several court judgments that have defined housing rights.[479] Article 21[480] of the Constitution of India deals with the right to life and includes the right to housing and shelter. In the case of *Francis Coralie Mullin, Petitioner* v. *The Administrator, Union Territory of Delhi and others*,[481] it was held that the right to life enshrined in Article 21 cannot be restricted to mere animal existence. It means something much more than just physical survival. The right to life includes the right to live with human dignity and all that goes along with it, namely the bare necessaries of life such as adequate nutrition, clothing, and shelter over the head, and facilities for reading, writing, and expressing oneself in diverse forms, freely moving about, and mixing and commingling with fellow human beings. Article 39(f) of the Constitution of India also deals with the necessity of the appropriate conditions for the overall development of children. In *Olga Tellis* v. *Bombay Municipal Corporation*,[482] the Supreme Court held that the right to life of dignity under Article 21 of the Constitution is impossible without the basic necessities such as food, clothing, and shelter.

In the case of *Prabhakaran Nair* v. *State of Tamil Nadu*,[483] the Supreme Court held that shelter is one of our fundamental rights. Again, in *M/s Shantistar Builders* v. *Narayan Khimalal Totame*,[484] the Supreme Court dealt with the concept of suitable accommodation. 'Basic needs of man have traditionally been accepted to be three—food, clothing, and shelter. The right to life is guaranteed in any civilized society. This right would take within its sweep the right to food, the right to clothing, the right to decent environment and a reasonable accommodation to live in. The difference between the need of an animal and a human being for shelter has to be kept in view. For the animal it is bare protection of the body; for a human being it has to be a suitable accommodation which would allow him to grow in every aspect—physical, mental, and intellectual. The Constitution aims at ensuring fuller development of every child. That would be possible, only if the child is in a proper home …'

Despite the constitutional provisions and the provisions in the ICESCR and the UNCRC, demolitions are conducted all over the country by the state and under orders of the higher judiciary, namely the Supreme Court and the High Courts. The Supreme Court has, in *Almitra H. Patel* v. *Union of India and Others*,[485] stated that providing a slum-dweller with alternative accommodation is like rewarding a pickpocket. There has been a marked change in the attitude

---

[479] HAQ: Centre for Child Rights, 'Handbook on Children's Right'.

[480] Article 21: Protection of life and personal liberty.

[481] AIR 1981 SC 746.

[482] AIR 1986 SC 180, 193.

[483] AIR 1987 SC 2117.

[484] AIR 1990 SC 630.

[485] (2000) 2 SCC 678.

of the courts during the last decade, the concentration being on clearing cities of its 'dirt' and on assisting the rich and the middle class to lead a comfortable life.

Upholding the importance of the right to a decent environment and a reasonable accommodation, in *Shantistar Builders* v. *Narayan Khimalal Totame*,[486] the Court held that 'The right to life would take within its sweep the right to food, the right to clothing, and the right to decent environment and a reasonable accommodation to live in. The difference between the need of an animal and a human being for shelter has to be kept in view. For the animal it is the bare protection of the body, for a human being it has to be a suitable accommodation which would allow him to grow in every aspect - physical, mental and intellectual. The Constitution aims at ensuring fuller development of every child. That would be possible only if the child is in a proper home. It is not necessary that every citizen must be ensured of living in a well-built comfortable house but a reasonable home particularly for people in India can even be mud-built thatched house or a mud-built fireproof accommodation.'

In *Chameli Singh* v. *State of UP*,[487] a Bench of three judges had considered and held that the right to shelter is a fundamental right available to every citizen, and it was read into Article 21 of the Constitution as encompassing within its ambit the right to shelter, to make the right to life more meaningful. In paragraph 8 it has been held that 'In any organised society, right to live as a human being is not ensured by meeting only the animal needs of man.[488] It is secured only when he is assured of all facilities to develop himself and is freed from restrictions which inhibit his growth. All human rights are designed to achieve this object. Right to live guaranteed in any civilised society implies the right to food, water, decent environment, education, medical care and shelter. These are basic human rights known to any civilised society. All civil, political, social and cultural rights enshrined in the UDHR and convention or under the Constitution of India cannot be exercised without these basic human rights.' Emphasizing further on the right to shelter, the Court in this case held that, 'Shelter for a human being, therefore, is not a mere protection of his life and limb. It is home where he has opportunities to grow physically, mentally, intellectually and spiritually. Right to shelter, therefore, includes adequate living space, safe and decent structure, clean and decent surroundings, sufficient light, pure air and water, electricity, sanitation and other civic amenities like roads etc. so as to have easy access to his daily avocation. The right to shelter, therefore, does not mean a mere right to a roof over one's head but right to all the infrastructure necessary to enable them to live and develop as a human being. Right to shelter when used as an essential requisite to the right to live should be deemed to have been guaranteed as a fundamental right. In a democratic society as a member of the organised civic community one should have permanent shelter so as to a physically, mentally and intellectually equip oneself to improve his excellence as a useful citizen as enjoined in the Fundamental Duties and to be a useful citizen and equal participant in democracy. The ultimate object of making a man equipped with a right to dignity of person and equality of status is to enable him to develop himself into a cultured being. Want of decent residence, therefore, frustrates the very object of the constitutional animation of right to equality, economic justice, fundamental right to residence, dignity of person and right to live itself.'

[486] (1990) 1 SCC 520; AIR 1990 SC 630.
[487] (1996) 25 CC 549 132.
[488] (1996) 25 CC 549 132 (SCC pp. 555–6).

In *P.C. Gupta* v. *State of Gujarat and Ors*, in 1994, the Court went further, holding that the right to shelter in Article 19(1)(g), read with Articles 19(1)(e) and 21 of the Constitution of India, included the right to residence and settlement. Protection of life, guaranteed by Article 21, encompasses within its ambit the right to shelter to enjoy the meaningful right to life. The right to residence and settlement was seen as a fundamental right under Article 19(1)(e) and as a facet of inseparable meaningful right to life as available under Article 21.

In *Ahmedabad Municipal Corporation, Appellant* v. *Nawab Khan Gulab Khan And Others*,[489] the Court observed that 'Article 19(1)(e) accords right to residence and settlement in any part of India as a fundamental right. Right to life has been assured as a basic human right under Article 21 of the Constitution of India. Article 25(1) of the UDHR declares that everyone has the right to a standard of living adequate for the health and well-being of himself and his family; it includes food, clothing, housing, medical care and necessary social services. Article 11(1) of the ICESCR lays down that state parties to the Covenant recognise that everyone has the right to standard of living for himself and his family including food, clothing, and housing and to the continuous improvement of living conditions.'

International Law Relating to Right to Adequate Housing

The provisions relating to right to housing in international laws are as follows:

International Covenant on Economic, Social and Cultural Rights

The states parties to the ICESCR recognize the right of everyone to an adequate standard of living for himself and his family, including adequate food, clothing, and housing, and to the continuous improvement of living conditions. The states parties will take appropriate steps to ensure the realization of this right, recognizing to this effect the essential importance of international cooperation based on free consent.[490]

General Comment 3, General Comment 4, and General Comment 7 of the United Nations Committee on Economic, Social, and Cultural Rights[491]

General Comment 3

THe ICESCR provides for progressive realization and acknowledges the constraints due to the limits of available resources; it also imposes various obligations which are of immediate effect. Of these, two are of particular importance in understanding the precise nature of states parties' obligations. Thus, for example, a state party in which any significant number of individuals is

---

[489] AIR 1997 SC 152.

[490] Article 11(1) of the ICESCR.

[491] United Nations Committee on Economic, Social and Cultural Rights, General Comments 3, 4, and 7.

deprived of essential foodstuff, essential PHC, of basic shelter and housing, or of the most basic forms of education is, prima facie, failing to discharge its obligations under the Covenant.[492]

General Comment 4

In its General Comment No. 4 (1991), the Committee observed that all persons should possess a degree of security of tenure which guarantees legal protection against forced eviction, harassment, and other threats. It concluded that forced evictions are prima facie incompatible with the requirements of the Covenant. Having considered a significant number of reports of forced evictions in recent years, including instances in which it determined that the obligations of states parties were being violated, the Committee was in a position to seek to provide further clarification as to the implications of such practices in terms of the obligations contained in the Covenant.

1. *Legal security of tenure.* Tenure takes a variety of forms, including rental (public and private) accommodation, cooperative housing, lease, owner-occupation, emergency housing, and informal settlements, including occupation of land or property. Notwithstanding the type of tenure, all persons should possess a degree of security of tenure which guarantees legal protection against forced eviction, harassment, and other threats. States parties should consequently take immediate measures aimed at conferring legal security of tenure upon those persons and households currently lacking such protection, in genuine consultation with affected persons and groups.

2. *Availability of services, materials, facilities, and infrastructure.* An adequate house must contain certain facilities essential for health, security, comfort, and nutrition. All beneficiaries of the right to adequate housing should have sustainable access to natural and common resources, safe drinking water, energy for cooking, heating, and lighting, sanitation and washing facilities, means of food storage, refuse disposal, site drainage, and emergency services.

3. *Affordability.* Personal or household financial costs associated with housing should be at such a level that the attainment and satisfaction of other basic needs are not threatened or compromised. Steps should be taken by states parties to ensure that the percentage of housing-related costs is, in general, commensurate with income levels. States parties should establish housing subsidies for those unable to obtain affordable housing, as well as forms and levels of housing finance which adequately reflect housing needs. In accordance with the principle of affordability, tenants should be protected by appropriate means against unreasonable rent levels or rent increases. In societies where natural materials constitute the chief sources of building materials for housing, steps should be taken by states parties to ensure the availability of such materials.

4. *Habitability.* Adequate housing must be habitable, in terms of providing the inhabitants with adequate space and protecting them from cold, damp, heat, rain, wind, or other threats to health, structural hazards, and disease vectors. The physical safety of occupants must be guaranteed as well. The committee encourages states parties to comprehensively apply the Health Principles of Housing prepared by the WHO, which view housing as the environmental factor most frequently associated with conditions for disease in epidemiological analyses; inadequate and deficient housing and living conditions are invariably associated with higher mortality and morbidity rates;

---

[492] United Nations Committee on Economic, Social and Cultural Rights, General Comment 3.

5. *Accessibility*. Adequate housing must be accessible to those entitled to it. Disadvantaged groups must be accorded full and sustainable access to adequate housing resources. Thus, such disadvantaged groups as the elderly, children, the physically disabled, the terminally ill, HIV-positive individuals, persons with persistent medical problems, the mentally ill, victims of natural disasters, people living in disaster-prone areas, and other groups should be ensured some degree of priority consideration in the housing sphere. Both housing law and policy should take fully into account the special housing needs of these groups. Increasing access to land by landless or impoverished segments of the society should constitute a central policy goal of the states parties. Discernible governmental obligations need to be developed, aiming to substantiate the right of all to a secure place to live in peace and dignity, including access to land as an entitlement.

6. *Location*. Adequate housing must be in a location which allows access to employment options, healthcare services, schools, childcare centres, and other social facilities. This is true both in large cities and in rural areas where the temporal and financial costs of getting to and from the place of work can place excessive demands upon the budgets of poor households. Similarly, housing should not be built on polluted sites or in immediate proximity to pollution sources that threaten the right to health of the inhabitants.

7. *Cultural adequacy*. The way a house is constructed, the building materials used, and the policies supporting these must appropriately enable the expression of cultural identity and diversity of housing. Activities geared towards development or modernization in the housing sphere should ensure that the cultural dimensions of housing are not sacrificed, and that, inter alia, modern technological facilities, as appropriate, are also ensured.

General Comment 7[493]

Whereas some evictions may be justifiable, such as in the case of persistent non-payment of rent or of damage to rented property without any reasonable cause, it is incumbent upon the relevant authorities to ensure that they are carried out in a manner warranted by a law which is compatible with the Covenant and that all the legal recourses and remedies are available to those affected.

Forced eviction and house demolition as a punitive measure are also inconsistent with the norms of the Covenant. Likewise, the Committee takes note of the obligations enshrined in the Geneva Conventions of 1949 and Protocols thereto of 1977 concerning prohibitions on the displacement of civilian population and destruction of private property, as these relate to the practice of forced eviction.

States parties shall ensure, prior to carrying out any evictions, and particularly those involving large groups, that all feasible alternatives are explored in consultation with the affected persons, with a view to avoiding, or at least minimizing, the need to use force. Legal remedies or procedures should be provided to those who are affected by eviction orders. States parties shall also see to it that all the individuals concerned have a right to adequate compensation for any property, both personal and real, which is affected. In this respect, it is pertinent to recall Article 2.3 of the International Covenant on Civil and Political Rights (ICCPR), 1966, which requires states

[493] See Paragraph 11–16 of General Comment 7 of the United Nations Committee on Economic, Social and Cultural Rights.

parties to ensure 'an effective remedy' for persons whose rights have been violated and imposes the obligation upon the 'competent authorities [to] enforce such remedies when granted'.

In cases where eviction is considered to be justified, it should be carried out in strict compliance with the relevant provisions of international human rights law and in accordance with general principles of reasonableness and proportionality. In this regard, it is especially pertinent to recall General Comment 16 of the Human Rights Committee, relating to Article 17 of the ICCPR, which states that interference with a person's home can only take place 'in cases envisaged by the law'. The Committee observed that the law 'should be in accordance with the provisions, aims and objectives of the Covenant and should be, in any event, reasonable in the particular circumstances'. The Committee also indicated that 'relevant legislation must specify in detail the precise circumstances in which such interferences may be permitted'.

Appropriate procedural protection and due process are essential aspects of all human rights but are especially pertinent in relation to a matter such as forced eviction, which directly invokes a large number of the rights recognized in both the ICCPR and the ICESCR. The Committee considered that the procedural protections which should be applied in relation to forced evictions include: (i) an opportunity for genuine consultation with those affected; (ii) adequate and reasonable notice for all affected persons prior to the scheduled date of eviction; (iii) information on the proposed evictions, and, where applicable, on the alternative purpose for which the land or housing is to be used, to be made available in reasonable time to all those affected; (iv) especially where groups of people are involved, government officials or their representatives to be present during an eviction; (v) all persons carrying out the eviction to be properly identified; (vi) evictions not to take place in particularly bad weather or at night unless the affected persons consent otherwise; (vii) provision of legal remedies; and (viii) provision, where possible, of legal aid to persons who are in need of it to seek redress from the courts.

Evictions should not result in individuals being rendered homeless or vulnerable to the violation of other human rights. Where those affected are unable to provide for themselves, the state party must take all appropriate measures, to the maximum of its available resources, to ensure that adequate alternative housing, resettlement, or access to productive land, as the case may be, is available.

Violation of the Rights of the Child under the United Nations Convention on the Rights of the Child

Children's housing rights imply more than the mere concept of a shelter. Adequate housing is of particular importance for children whose physical and intellectual development is closely linked to the environment where they grow up and the living conditions they confront. Article 27[494]

---

[494] Article 27, UNCRC:

1. States parties recognize the right of every child to a standard of living adequate for the child's physical, mental, spiritual, moral, and social development.
2. The parent(s) or others responsible for the child have the primary responsibility to secure, within their abilities and financial capacities, the conditions of living necessary for the child's development.
3. States parties, in accordance with national conditions and within their means, shall take appropriate measures to assist parents and others responsible for the child to implement this right and shall in case

of the UNCRC addresses the right of the child to adequate shelter. Homeless children, migrant children, runaway and abandoned children are all children whose right to shelter is violated.

The right to privacy[495] and the right to a secure and permanent home are often the most important aspects of privacy. Though urban slum pockets often face the problem of overcrowded homes, such homes at least provide some kind of personal space and protection, which is very essential for the child's overall development. A home for most children is primarily the existence of a warm, intimate, social climate. Such a climate is vital not only for the quality of life of children but also for their future adult lives. All children have the right to live with their closest relatives in an atmosphere characterized by love and understanding and the state has the obligation to support parents in child raising. The right to housing is one necessary condition to fulfill this obligation.[496]

Children's right to adequate housing cannot be interpreted in a narrow or restrictive sense but is rather understood to encompass living in security, peace, and dignity. This concept is interrelated to and interdependent with nearly every other right in the UNCRC. The gross violation of the right to housing of a child has an adverse impact on the other rights to shelter, nutrition, clean water, sanitation, education, health, and a safe environment, as listed next:

- The right to privacy, family, and home [UNCRC, Article 16.1]. The right to information, access, and support of health, hygiene, and sanitation [UNCRC, Article 24.2(e)];
- The right to appropriate measures to combat disease and malnutrition;
- The right to the highest attainable standard of health and the right to appropriate measures to combat disease and malnutrition;
- The right to provisions of primary needs such as clean drinking water [UNCRC, Article 24.2(c)];
- The right to protection from the illicit use of narcotic drugs and psychotropic substances [UNCRC, Article 33];
- Right to education [UNCRC, Articles 28.1, 2, and 3];
- The right to play, recreation, and cultural life [UNCRC, Article 31];
- The right to a name and nationality [UNCRC, Articles 7.1 and 2].

---

of need provide material assistance and support programmes, particularly with regard to nutrition, clothing, and housing.

4. States parties shall take all appropriate measures to secure the recovery of maintenance for the child from the parents or other persons having financial responsibility for the child, both within the state party and from abroad. In particular, where the person having financial responsibility for the child lives in a state different from that of the child, state parties shall promote the accession to international agreements or the conclusion of such agreements, as well as the making of other appropriate arrangements.

[495] Article 16, UNCRC:

1. No child shall be subjected to arbitrary or unlawful interference with his or her privacy, family, or correspondence, nor to unlawful attacks on his or her honour and reputation.
2. The child has the right to the protection of the law against such interference or attacks.

[496] M. Subramaniam, 'Civil Rights of Children and the CRC', a paper presented at the Maharashtra state-level workshop on the Convention on the Rights of the Child, 18–19 January 2001.

- The right to an identity [UNCRC, Articles 8.1 and 2];
- The right to be cared for by a (legal) guardian [UNCRC, Articles 18.1, 2, and 3];
- The right to survival and development [UNCRC, Article 6.2];
- The right to protection from the law against interference and attacks [UNCRC, Article 16.2];
- The right to protection from physical and mental violence [UNCRC, Articles 19.1 and 2];
- The right to protection from economic exploitation [UNCRC, Articles 32.1 and 2];
- The right to protection from sexual exploitation and abuse [UNCRC, Article 34].

Recommendations for the Protection of the Rights of the Child[497]

The following recommendations should be followed in order to avoid violation of the rights of the child in forced eviction cases:

1. The state should not undertake forced evictions unless it can provide adequate rehabilitation.
2. A grievance redressal mechanism must be set up for cases of any violation of human rights.
3. In the event of an eviction becoming unavoidable either due to risk to the settlement or for a stated development purpose:

   a) Evictions must be announced at least one month before the actual demolition.
   b) Assistance must be offered to those who need it the most, like elderly people, women, and families with (young) children.
   c) Arrangements for proper and complete resettlement must be made. Transit accommodation must be created for the interim period prior to resettlement.
   d) The government must be responsible for providing food supplements, education, healthcare, and leisure to the affected children.
   e) There must be extra care for the children of working parents during the transit period so that these children can feel safe and secure while their parents go out to work.
   f) The resettlement must be within the vicinity of the old one, so that the social structure of the child's life, like school, friends, playgrounds, and simple familiarity is not disrupted.
   g) All the evicted children must be registered and given new identification cards.
   h) All the aforementioned provisions and services should be continued once the people have been resettled and not end after the transit period.[498]

Institutionalized mechanisms for participatory planning, including participation of children in the process of need assessment, planning, implementation, evaluation, and monitoring in urban and rural human settlement programmes, should become an essential prerequisite to child-centred habitat.[499]

The government has given a low priority to the provision for shelter, as reflected in the declining direct public investment on housing in the successive Five Year Plans, from 16 per cent in the first to 1.5 per cent of the out-lay in the seventh plan. In the Eighth Five Year Plan, though emphasis had been placed on social housing schemes and the public sector outlay had increased from Rs. 14.91

---

[497] UNCRC, HRF, LAYA, and YUVA, 'The Child in Search of the State'.
[498] UNCRC, HRF, LAYA, and YUVA, 'The Child in Search of the State'.
[499] UNCRC, HRF, LAYA, and YUVA, 'The Child in Search of the State'.

billion in the seventh plan to Rs 48.23 billion in the eighth, it failed even to propose any viable alternative for providing and improving the housing condition of the homeless people in the country.

Children are the worst affected because of lack of housing policy. While it is certain that commercial interests and market forces will not care for the interests of the poor and the children in the present context of globalization, liberalization, structural adjustments, and privatization of essential services, the struggle for ensuring the housing rights of the poor and marginalized sections like the children is one of the most crucial needs.

Concluding Recommendations on Child's Right to Housing by the United Nations Committee on the Rights of the Child[500]

The UN Special Rapporteur on adequate housing has defined the human right to adequate housing as: 'The right of every woman, man, youth and child to gain and sustain a safe and secure home and community in which to live in peace and dignity'.[501] The Committee on the Rights of the Child, in its Concluding Observations in July 2014,[502] raised concerns about the forced displacement of a large number of children and their families and the loss of their ancestral lands owing to manufacturing operations, in particular families and children living in the area of the POSCO steel plant[503] and port facilities in the state of Odisha.[504] It also raised concerns at the lack of information about safeguards to guarantee compliance with the UNCRC and international human rights standards. The Committee recommended that the state party take appropriate measures to give effect to its commitments made at Habitat II in 1996 regarding children's access to housing.[505] In light of the Commission on Human Rights resolution 1993/77 on forced evictions, the Committee on the Rights of the Child recommended that India must prevent any occurrence of forced relocation, displacement, and other types of involuntary population movements. The Committee further recommended that resettlement procedures and programmes include registration, facilitate comprehensive family rehabilitation, and ensure access to basic services. The Committee was concerned with the large and increasing number of children living and/or working on the streets, who were among the most marginalized groups of children in India. The Committee recommended that mechanisms be established to ensure that these children are provided with identity documents, nutrition, clothing, and housing. Moreover, it must be ensured that these children have access to healthcare; rehabilitation services for physical, sexual, and substance abuse; services for reconciliation with families; education, including vocational and life-skills training; and access to legal aid. The Committee recommended also that cooperation from the civil society must be taken in this regard.[506]

---

[500] HLRN, *The Human Rights to Adequate Housing and Land in India*.
[501] HLRN, *The Human Rights to Adequate Housing and Land in India*.
[502] HLRN, *The Human Rights to Adequate Housing and Land in India*.
[503] HLRN, *The Human Rights to Adequate Housing and Land in India*.
[504] HLRN, *The Human Rights to Adequate Housing and Land in India*.
[505] HLRN, *The Human Rights to Adequate Housing and Land in India*.
[506] HLRN, *The Human Rights to Adequate Housing and Land in India*.

Campaigns and Initiatives

The Committee for Right to Housing (CRH) was a precursor to the Campaign for Housing Rights. It emerged in 1985 as a direct response to the Supreme Court judgment of July 1985 which sought to re-empower the government/Bombay Municipal Corporation to continue with demolitions/evictions of slums and pavement dwellers. CRH was a collective of 16 voluntary organizations working with slum and pavement dwellers of Mumbai. Simultaneously, at the national level, the National Campaign for Housing Rights (NCHR) was initiated in 1986 with the support of various individuals, organizations, mass-based groups, and trade unions.

Campaign for Housing Rights has been one of the most planned and organized advocacy efforts that succeeded in developing a public argument for advocating the fundamental rights of millions of homeless people to have adequate housing. The campaign helped channelling and coordinating the efforts of hundreds of social action groups, voluntary organizations, and individuals at the national, regional, and grass-roots level to bring forth housing into the centre stage of public advocacy and policy priorities. The NCHR began in August 1986 and emerged as an all-India organization with a fairly widespread membership and units in more than 20 states. The problem of housing in India was analysed and addressed by the campaigners in a holistic manner, taking it as an issue related to human rights, socio-economic rights, environment, gender equality, distributive justice, and paradigms of development.

Indira Awas Yojana, 1985[507]

Indira Awaas Yojana (IAY) is the biggest and most comprehensive rural housing programme ever taken up by the Government of India. It has its origin in the wage employment programmes of National Rural Employment Programme (NREP), which began in 1980, and the Rural Landless Employment Guarantee Programme (RLEGP), which was started in 1983, as construction of house was permitted under these programmes. However, there were no common norms. It was in June 1985 that the IAY was launched as a sub-scheme of RLEGP by earmarking a part of the fund for construction of houses for SCs/STs and freed bonded labourers. When Jawahar Rozgar Yojana (JRY) was launched in April 1985, 6 per cent of the funds was allocated for housing for the SCs/STs and freed bonded labourers. In 1993–4, the coverage was extended to non-SC/ST families by increasing the earmarked fund for housing under JRY to 10 per cent and allowing the use of the additional 4 per cent for this category of beneficiaries. The IAY was made an independent scheme with effect from 1 January 1996. It is now a flagship programme of the Ministry of Rural Development as part of the larger strategy of rural poverty eradication, aimed at reducing the rigours of poverty and providing the dignity of an address to the poor households to enable them to access different rural development programmes. Beneficiaries under IAY include SCs, STs, freed bonded labourers, minorities in the BPL category, and other BPL families. Under the scheme, financial assistance is provided for new construction in the form of a grant of Rs. 70,000 per dwelling unit in the plains and Rs 75,000 for hilly/difficult areas.

---

[507] Department of Rural Development, Ministry of Rural Development, 'Indira Awas Yojana, Guidelines', Government of India, June 2013. Available at http://iay.nic.in/netiay/IAY%20revised%20 guidelines%20july%202013.pdf (accessed on 1 November 2015).

Towards Right to Survival for All Children

Right to survival is a prerequisite for the realization of all other rights including social, economic, cultural, civil, and political rights. Right to health is a right to life, right to live with dignity, and right to livelihood. But poverty, undernourishment, ill health, rural–urban divide, regional variations and disparities among different socio-economic groups, and various other factors contribute to an uneven attainment of health of the people. There is a need for the Government to undertake proactive measures to upgrade and provide quality healthcare services for the poor. The new healthcare policy acknowledges that the present concept of PHC covers hardly 20 per cent of the health needs and that heavy out-of-pocket health expenditure is pushing nearly 63 million people into poverty every year.[508] The government has, consequently, broadened the definition of PHC to include more services related to reproductive and child health as well as several infectious diseases and NCDs. But although bringing down medical expenses has been listed among the major objectives of the new policy, there are no concrete measures as to how this will be implemented or operationalized. The new policy needs to lay down clearly the measures to regulate the private healthcare sector. The Centre and states must expand public healthcare infrastructure, recruit more doctors and paramedical staff, set up new diagnostic laboratories, and revamp procurement, stocking, and distribution of drugs.

An area of concern is that the Health Ministry guidelines on the regulation of assisted reproductive technology (ART) clinics fail to address the issue of breastfeeding for surrogate children.[509] India's surrogacy industry is presently governed by the Health Ministry-approved National Guidelines for Accreditation, Supervision and Regulation of ART Clinics, 2005. As of now, these guidelines do not address the issue of breastfeeding for children born out of surrogacy but once the ART (Regulation) Bill is passed, the central government will be empowered to frame rules and address the issue of breastfeeding. Childless couples from all over the world bring home babies with help from India's mushrooming ART centres. But commissioning parents tend to overlook the infant's need for mother's milk, despite the fact that is has been scientifically established that mother's milk is a critical source of nutrition for the infant. It is, therefore, surprising and disturbing to note that the Health Ministry guidelines on the regulation of ART clinics do not address the issue of breastfeeding for surrogate children. This concern needs to be addressed. While surrogacy may be changing the world for many parents, the long-term health of the child requires that arrangements be made for breastfeeding. Unless the woman is not lactating, no reason is good enough to deny mother's milk to a child. Today, with better testing and refrigeration facilities, the milk bank option is growing popular. An example is the establishment of thousands of human milk banks in Brazil, where women volunteer milk donations.

Under Article 21 of the Constitution, Right to Life and Personal Liberty is not merely a right to protect one's body, but the guarantee under this provision contemplates a larger scope.

[508] 'A Misguided Approach; New National Health Policy a Step in the Wrong Direction', *Business Standard*, 6 January, 2005, New Delhi, India. Available at http://www.business-standard.com/article/opinion/a-misguided-approach-115010601238_1.html (accessed on 1 November 2015).

[509] Tripti Nath, 'Surrogate Children in India Deprived of Mother's Milk', *The Hindu*. Available at http://www.thehindu.com/sci-tech/health/diet-and-nutrition/surrogate-children-in-india-deprived-of-mothers-milk/article4917720.ece (accessed on 1 November 2015).

Right to Life means the right to lead a meaningful, complete, and dignified life. It does not have a restricted meaning. It is something more than survival or animal existence. The meaning of the word life cannot be narrowed down and it will be applicable for every citizen of the country. Therefore, the state must guarantee to a pregnant working woman all the facilities and assistance that she requires while protecting her employment, as well as her own and her child's health. Since the bearing and rearing of children is a social responsibility that women undertake in society, it is only fair that the entire society supports women in this task. The state should, therefore, devise means by which this support can be given to all women through the formation of a national maternity fund which the government, employers, and maybe employees (regardless of sex) can contribute to. Employers and employees may be given incentives in the form of tax exemptions for their contribution.[510] The coverage of maternity protection should include health coverage and wage payment so that there is a fall in infant mortality and maternal mortality. Maternity leave cannot be limited based on number of children or number of working days. The enforcement of the concerned Act, Maternity Benefits Act, 1961, is still poor. Even though the act mentions two mandatory nursing breaks of limited time during the course of work (after the mother comes back to work from maternity leave), this has been poorly implemented. If this act is properly implemented, lots of childhood morbidity and mortality can be averted.

Closely associated with health are the issues of nutrition and clean drinking water, which must be available throughout the year. Over one billion people in the world lack access to clean water and more than twice that many lack access to basic sanitation.[511] Inadequate water and sanitation services, the second most common cause underlying medical conditions that lead to child mortality, impose considerable illness and coping costs on households in developing countries.

Children's health includes the study of possible environmental causes of children's illnesses and disorders, as well as the prevention and treatment of environmentally mediated diseases in children and infants. Children are highly vulnerable to the negative health consequences associated with many environmental exposures. They receive proportionately larger doses of environmental toxicants than adults, and the fact that their organs and tissues are rapidly developing makes them particularly susceptible to chemical injuries. Research in children's health looks at the effects of air pollution on respiratory diseases such as allergies and asthma, the impact of lead, mercury, and other environmental contaminants on cognitive development and behaviour, and the influence of prenatal and early-life exposures on growth and development.[512]

The PCPNDT Act regulates the provision of pre-conception and prenatal diagnostic services. History of both these laws is that while the PC & PNDT Act was passed pursuant to a demand

---

[510] 'Minutes and Recommendations of the National Consultation on the Maternity Benefit Act', held on 2 July 2013, Vigyan Bhawan Annexe, New Delhi. Available at http://nmew.gov.in/WriteReadData/1892s/4875392939Minutes%20and%20Recommendations%20of%20the%20National%20Consultation%20on%20the%20Maternity%20Benefit%20Act,%20held%20on%20July%202nd%202013,%20Vigyan%20Bhawan%20Annexe,%20New%20Delhi.pdf (accessed on 27 October 2015).

[511] United Nations Development Programme (UNDP), 'Beyond Scarcity: Power, Poverty and the Global Water Crisis', *Human Development Report 2006* (New York: UNDP, 2006).

[512] See National Institute of Environmental Health Sciences (NIEHS), North Carolina. Available at http://www.niehs.nih.gov/health/topics/population/children/ (accessed on 1 November 2015).

made by the women's movement to stop sex-selective abortions. Section 312 of the IPC becomes redundant after the passing of the PCPNDT Act. This needs to be reviewed.

India is also a signatory to the UDHR and the ICESCR, which declare and establish housing as a universally recognized fundamental human right. Several court judgments in India have enjoined the state to make the right to housing a fundamental right. In spite of these proclaimed stands, the Indian government is yet to recognize the right to housing as a fundamental right. Lobbying for an amendment to Articles 19 and 21 of the Constitution of India, declaring housing an explicit fundamental right, there is a need to advocate and campaign for a comprehensive people's bill of housing rights with a perspective of child rights. There is a need for a housing policy so that child rights are not violated. Above all, the government must urgently address the broader structural issues that lead to forced migration of children from rural areas to cities in need of subsistence. The state must create more and better equipped long-term homes to meet the special needs of street children, in particular children who are orphans and abandoned and disabled, which focus on their holistic and all-round development, including education, housing, and health.

A lot remains to be done in order to protect the rights of the children with disabilities and to achieve their inclusion in educational programmes and full participation in the community. In order for change to occur, governments must work together with stakeholders at different levels through a rights-based and child-centred approach to implement the laws and establish mechanisms to ensure accountability.

The Land Acquisition Act should be amended, or new legislation adopted, to recognize a justiciable right to resettlement and rehabilitation for all displaced or evicted persons, including women and those without formal land titles. Dams, mining, and infrastructure projects must not be implemented if this entails displacement and irreversible destruction of people's livelihoods and shelter. Such projects should only be carried out with the consent of communities and on the condition that due legal process, proper resettlement, rehabilitation (under the 'land for land' principle), and compensation to all victims is guaranteed.

The Recommendations of the 259th Report of the Law Commission of India, on 'Early Childhood Development and Legal Entitlements', must be implemented.[513]

The Law Commission of India felt that it is the right time to position the rights of young children within the development agenda and create appropriate legal entitlements as per early childhood development. The Law Commission said that despite several recommendations, the welfare of under-six children—who constitutes 16 per cent of the population—remains 'locked in Part IV of the Constitution" under the DPSP, which are not justiciable in courts of law. The Commission, on 27 August 2015, recommended to amend the Constitution so as to make sure that education for children below 6 years of age becomes mandatory and these children are offered protection from all forms of neglect, harm, and exploitation. Currently, only elementary education—for children in the 6–14 age group—is a legal entitlement under the The Right of Children to Free and Compulsory Education Act, 2009 (RTE Act). The Law Commission has recommended that early childcare, including crèche and day care facilities, be made a legal

513 Law Commission of India, Ministry of Law and Justice, 'Early Childhood Development and Legal Entitlements', Government of India. Available at http://pib.nic.in/newsite/PrintRelease.aspx?relid=126379 (accessed on 1 November 2015).

entitlement. Apart from amending the RTE Act to provide early childhood care and education for 3–6 year olds, the Commission has also called for a new Article, 24A, to be inserted into Part III of the Constitution to make a child's right to basic care and assistance a fundamental and an enforceable right. Also, the Commission has called for amending the MBA to double maternity leaves from three months and make it mandatory for every state to ensure that it covers all women, including those working in the unorganized sector. As for crèches, the Commission has said that every child under six should have an unconditional right to crèche and day care facilities regulated and operated by the state.

According to the Law Commission Report, early childhood development period spans from the time the child takes birth till he/she attains the age of 6 years. It is the period in every child's life when the most rapid growth and development of the entire life span takes place. In this period, the foundations of cognitive, physical, and socio-emotional development, language, and personality are laid. This is the period of maximum vulnerability in which deprivation can seriously impact a child's health and learning potential.

The following points should be amended, keeping in mind the needs of the children who are under 6 years of age:

• All children of this age group should have the Right to Care and Assistance. Their basic necessities should be fulfilled and they should not suffer from any sort of neglect, harm, and exploitation.
• Free and compulsory education should be offered to all children by the state as per the norms laid down by the law.
• It is also the fundamental duty of parents or guardians to send their children to school so that they receive elementary education.
• The children who are above 3 years are eligible to receive elementary education and childhood care till they attain the age of 6 years, and the respective government should make necessary arrangements to provide free education to such children.
• The maternity benefits should be increased from 12 weeks to 180 days.
• It has also been suggested that the government should come up with such policies in which the women working in private sectors are also entitled to enjoy maternity leave benefits.
• A statutory authority or Council for Early Childhood Development should be set up so as to make sure that early childhood developments is promoted in the best possible manner.
• The teacher recruited to provide pre-school education should be given adequate training.
• Every child in the age group of 0–6 years has the right to crèche and day care facilities.[514]

The above recommendations need to be implemented and relevant laws amended.

Earlier, in 1983, the Indian government had adopted the Indian National Code for Protection and Promotion of Breastfeeding. Sadly, despite having the best laws in place, the law was violated time and again. The Association for Consumers Action on Safety and Health (ACASH) is one of three voluntary organizations which have been authorized, by a government notification, to

---

[514] Law Commission of India, 'Early Childhood Development and Legal Entitlements'.

report violations of the act.[515] ACASH has been studiously keeping an eye out for negligence on part of baby food manufacturers. Thanks to this vigilance, Johnson and Johnson faced legal proceedings at two metropolitan magistrate courts in Bombay for violating the act. ACASH and the Maharashtra Food and Drug Administration filed the complaints, alleging that the company had advertised silicone nipples for their bottles and offered discounts on the bottle, thereby undermining breastfeeding. Such vigilance on the part of a British group, Baby Milk Action, ensured that Nestlé is facing a boycott in 17 countries, including the UK, Germany, Switzerland, Norway, Finland, and Italy. The Maharashtra-based Breast Feeding Promotion Network of India suggested in 1996 that India join the international boycott.[516] Nestlé was given 1 year to change its approach to marketing. The group's conclusion was that Nestle had not conformed to the requirements of the act and had recommended the use of cereal-based food at a very early age. In India, Nestlé's milk-food packaging does not have labels in languages that Indian mothers can understand. In 1997, the Indian Academy of Pediatrics adopted a resolution not to accept sponsorship or financial assistance from companies that manufacture and market baby food and feeding bottles. The pressure and the temptations, however, continue. If there is anything that can beat the onslaught mounted by baby food manufacturers, it is education about the negative effects of infant milk substitutes and the benefits of breast milk to both mother and baby.[517]

In the Constitution of India, health is still not recognized as a fundamental right of citizens. The fundamental right to health would mean making the right to healthcare a legally enforceable entitlement. In the Alma Ata declaration, provision of universal, comprehensive PHC was seen as the key to attaining health for all as part of overall development. Poverty contributes to undernourishment and ill health, and ill health perpetuates poverty. Thus, there is a need to see health as being central to sustainable human development and it would be necessary to formulate an NHP with a detailed plan and timetable for realization of the core right to healthcare. Investment in health is one of the major steps towards poverty alleviation, and improved health is a key factor for human development. Health has to become an integral part of the development agenda.[518] The judiciary in India has clearly read the right to health into Article 21 on Right to Life. The case law reflects the ability of the courts to read the meaning of 'health' in a very wide sense (everything from the responsibility of the municipal corporation to provide sanitation facilities, down to access to emergency medical treatment has been interpreted in the right to health) An amendment to the Constitution, which will declare health as a fundamental right, is desirable. Enumerated rights have an edge over wider interpretations of existing rights, as states can be held accountable for violations.

Therefore, there is a need for renewed campaign initiatives to make health a fundamental human right for all children till the age of 18 years, to take the Health for All strategy to the new

---

[515] Panchali Das, 'A Conceptual Review of Advertising Regulation and Standards: Case Studies in the Indian Scenario', International Marketing Conference on Marketing & Society, 8–10 April 2007, IIMK. Available at http://dspace.iimk.ac.in/bitstream/handle/123456789/597/743-752.pdf?sequence=1&isAllowed=y (accessed on 24 October 2015).

[516] Das, 'A Conceptual Review'.

[517] Das, 'A Conceptual Review'.

[518] Ashish Bose, 'Health for All: Broken Promises', Economic and Political Weekly 36, no. 11 (2001): 905–07.

millennium, to force the government to commit for Health for All in the Twenty-First Century. All health networks, NGOs, people's organizations, social action groups, nd other concerned parties., must come together to realize the vision of Health for All in the Twenty-First Century into a reality, through networking, grass-roots mobilization, and policy advocacy.

The campaign must strive for the following charter of demands:[519]

- Making basic healthcare a fundamental, constitutional right of every citizen;
- Ensuring provision of basic prerequisites for a healthy life;
- Allocation of 5 per cent of GDP towards health;
- Ensuring comprehensive primary healthcare to all;
- Making provision of good-quality secondary and tertiary services;
- A comprehensive policy on education of professionals in the health sector;
- Social and self-regulation of the private medical sector;
- Rational and people-centred drug policy;
- Support to traditional healing systems;
- Democratization of the process of health policy making;
- Ecological and social measures to check resurgence of communicable diseases;
- Child-centred health initiatives;
- Special measures relating to occupational and environmental health;
- Comprehensive measures to promote mental health;
- Special measures to promote the health of the physically and mentally disadvantaged and disabled;
- Universal availability of birth control measures.

The right to health must be guaranteed as a fundamental right like the right to education. Any amendment guaranteeing the right to health should have a focus on PHC, which is preventive and curative. It should also have specific focus on the health of women—more specifically, reproductive health, children, and the disabled—both physically and mentally.

Non-governmental Organizations Working on Health, Nutrition, Housing, and Disability Rights of Children, Children Affected by HIV/AIDS, Infant Milk Substitutes, and PCPNDT Act

Centre for Enquiry into Health and Allied Themes[520]

The CEHAT is the research centre of Anusandhan Trust. It is involved in research, training, service, and advocacy on health and allied themes. Socially relevant and rigorous academic health research and health action at CEHAT is aimed at well-being of the disadvantaged masses, strengthening people's health movements, and realizing the right to health and healthcare. The CEHAT acts as an interface between progressive people's movements and academia. Its strategies are:

---

[519] Anand Phadke, *Towards Health Care for All* (Allahabad: Indian Academy of Social Sciences, 1999), 33–38.

[520] See Centre for Enquiry Into Health and Allied Themes (CEHAT). Available at http://www.cehat.org/go/AboutCehat/Home (last accessed on 1 November 2015).

- To undertake socially relevant research and advocacy projects on various socio-political aspects of health.
- To establish direct services and programmes to demonstrate how health services can be made accessible, equitably and ethically.
- To disseminate information through databases and relevant publications.

The CEHAT is a multidisciplinary team with training and experience in medicine, life sciences, economics, social sciences, social work, journalism, library and information, science, and law.

Society for Nutrition, Education and Health Action[521]

The Society for Nutrition, Education & Health Action's (SNEHA's) Child Health and Nutrition Programme launched its Aahar (a word which means food in Hindi) project in October 2012 in Dharavi, one of the largest slums in Asia. The project aims to improve the health and nutrition status of children under 3 years of age through:

- Rigorous screening and early identification of malnourished children;
- Combinations of hospital care, community-based management of acute malnutrition (CMAM), and referrals; and
- Regular follow-up and monitoring.

The project covers an estimated population of 300,000 in Dharavi, and is implemented in partnership with the World Bank-financed ICDS Scheme and the Municipal Corporation of Greater Mumbai (MCGM).

Housing and Land Rights Network India[522]

The HLRN India, works for the recognition, defence, promotion, and realization of the human rights to adequate housing and land, which involves ensuring a safe and secure place for all individuals and communities, especially marginalized communities, to live in peace and dignity. The HLRN was established in 1999 in New Delhi to address the growing need for research, education, and advocacy on housing and land rights in the region. A particular focus of its work is on promoting and protecting the equal rights of women to adequate housing, land, property, and inheritance. The HLRN aims to achieve its goals through advocacy, research, human rights education, and outreach through network building at local, national, and international levels. The office is located in New Delhi, India, providing a useful platform for linking members with other networks, regional and international NGOs, and with the UN system. As part of the Habitat International Coalition, HLRN helps build solidarity with and contributes to global processes related to housing and habitat issues. HLRN's objective is to promote economic, social, and cultural rights, especially for the most marginalized and

---

[521] See SNEHA, Mumbai. Available at http://www.snehamumbai.org/our-work/ngo-child-health-and-nutrition-sneha-mumbai.aspx (accessed on 1 November 2015).

[522] See HLRN, India. Available at http://hlrn.org.in/about-us (accessed on 1 November 2015).

discriminated groups and communities. Specifically, their work focuses on the practical application of the human right to adequate housing (HRAH) as a legal framework articulated in international and, where applicable, domestic law. They are also involved in efforts to promote and gain legal recognition of the right to land as a human right.

ASTHA India[523]

AARTH (Action, Advocacy, Research and Training in Disability) is an initiative of ASTHA and has grown out of understanding of the issues that are arising in the field of disability that are evolving and changing at a fast pace at the national and the global level. AARTH functions as a centre for resources, housing materials, information, and good practices focusing on disability and development. AARTH is an information and resource provider for children and persons with disability, their families, communities, and other stakeholders. It promotes a rights-based approach by advocating for disability-related issues and how they are linked to other developmental issues. It also runs a help-line reaching out to children and families with disability.

Committed Communities Development Trust, Mumbai[524]

Since 1990, Committed Communities Development Trust (CCDT) has been actively associated with marginalized communities in the slums of Mumbai and its suburbs. Over the years, health and education emerged as the two major domains of its interventions, with a special focus on family and children infected and affected by HIV/AIDS. In 1995, when interventions were limited to prevention, CCDT recognized the urgency for home-based care and was the first in India to develop a comprehensive home-based care program for HIV/AIDS infected/affected families. They were first in the country to make HIV/AIDS prevention and care an integrated community programme, including education, livelihood, self-care, nutrition, counselling, and psychological support—to minimize the overall vulnerability of the child and the family.

Forum against Sex Selection[525]

The Forum against Sex Selection (FASS) is a Mumbai-based network working to renew the campaign against sex selective abortions which is responsible for the appallingly skewed sex ratio in India, and in particular, the state of Maharashtra. The FASS is a network with over 50 members including NGOs, individual activists, lawyers, and teachers. The FASS is also in dialogue with the Maharashtra state government and the state health minister to ensure the implementation of the PCPNDT Act. The FASS has conducted interactive workshops to discuss its perspective and plan strategies to take its campaign forward and to understand challenges to implementing the

[523] See Astha, India. Available at http://asthaindia.in/aarth.asp#1 (accessed on 1 November 2015).

[524] See Committed Communities Development Trust, Mumbai. Available at http://ccdtrust.org/introduction/ (accessed on 1 November 2015).

[525] See FASS, Mumbai. Available at https://fassmumbai.wordpress.com/about/ (accessed on 1 November 2015).

PCPNDT Act. Apart from improving the sex ratio, the main thrust of the FASS campaign is to strengthen the overall position of women in India and to enable women to live with dignity, in a non-discriminatory environment.

Association for Consumer Action on Safety and Health[526]

The Association for Consumer Action on Safety and Health (ACASH) is an independent, non-profit, voluntary organization addressing health-related consumer issues and advocating for the rights of the consumers and the general public. The ACASH was founded in 1986 by a group of doctors, lawyers, and other concerned individuals. It serves as an information centre to educate, guide, and disseminate information in the field of health and safety issues. The ACASH has been appointed by the Government of India, Ministry of Human Resources Development (Department of Women and Child Development) to monitor and report violations of the IMS Act.

Disability Rights Initiative[527]

The Disability Rights Initiative provides legal aid, takes up PIL, provides access to the legal system, and campaigns to improve facilities for persons with all types of disabilities. It engages in out-of-court advocacy and has initiated extensive work on law reform for people with disabilities. This stems from the obligation of the state to bring all its laws, policies, and rules in conformity with the UN CRPD, which has been signed and ratified by India. Some of the issues of concern include:

- Disability as a reason for discrimination;
- Lack of education opportunities both at the primary and higher levels;
- Lack of employment and livelihood opportunities;
- Lack of physical access to the built infrastructure;
- Lack of access to information in accessible formats.

---

[526] See Association for Consumers Action on Safety and Health (ACASH), Mumbai. Available at http://www.acash.org/ (accessed on 1 November 2015).

[527] HRLN, Socio-Legal Information Centre (SLIC), 'Disability Rights'. Available at http://www.hrln.org/hrln/disability-rights.html#ixzz3qFOycDhD (accessed on 1 November 2015).

9   Making Child Rights a Reality

The Paradigm Shift

Children have a special place in all the wisdom and traditions of the world. Sri Ramana Maharishi, looking at a child in the prayer hall, reportedly remarked: 'One can attain the bliss of Brahman only when the mind becomes pure and humble, like the mind of this child.' The gospel of St. Luke says that people brought their children to Jesus, asking him to place his hands on them in blessing. When his disciples tried to prevent the people from approaching their teacher, Jesus said: 'Let the children come to me, do not stop them because the Kingdom of God belongs to them.' Rabindranath Tagore had stated: 'Every child when born brings with it the hope that God is not yet disappointed with man.' There is thus a societal recognition of the fact that children constitute the most fundamental and valuable resource of any society, and any developmental activity has to include the child rights perspective. Development projects and priorities must be made accountable to the rights of the child.

The Constitution of India gives a special status to children and provides affirmative action in their favour. To translate the vision of the child embodied in the Constitution, various legislations, policies, and programmes have been taken up. In the field of international law, India has ratified several protocols in the twenty-first century—(i) the Optional Protocol to the Convention on the Rights of the Child on the Involvement of Children in Armed Conflict (OPAC), in November 2005;[1] (ii) the Optional Protocol to the Convention on the Rights of the Child on the Sale of Children, Child Prostitution and Child Pornography (OPSC), in August 2005;[2] (iii) the Convention on the Rights of Persons with Disabilities, in October 2007;[3] and (iv) the Convention

---

[1] *Optional Protocol to the Convention on the Rights of the Child on the Involvement of Children in Armed Conflict*, New York, 25 May 2000, ratified by India on 30 November 2005. Available at http://www.ohchr.org/EN/ProfessionalInterest/Pages/OPACCRC.aspx (accessed on 22 February 2016).

[2] *Optional Protocol to the Convention on the Rights of the Child on the Sale of Children, Child Prostitution and Child Pornography*, entered into force on 18 January 2002, ratified by India on 16 August 2005. Available at http://www.ohchr.org/EN/ProfessionalInterest/Pages/OPSCCRC.aspx (accessed on 22 February 2016).

[3] *Convention on the Rights of Persons with Disabilities*, New York, 13 December 2006, ratified by India on 1 October 2007. Available at http://www.ohchr.org/Documents/Publications/AdvocacyTool_en.pdf (accessed on 24 November 2016).

against Transnational Organized Crime[4] and the Protocol to Prevent, Suppress and Punish Trafficking in Persons, especially Women and Children[5] (referred to as the Trafficking Protocol); as well as the Protocol against the Smuggling of Migrants by Land, Sea and Air[6] (referred to as the Smuggling Protocol), which supplements the Convention against Transnational Organized Crime, in May 2011.[7] Some recent policy initiatives include the National Early Childhood Care and Education (ECCE) Policy[8] and the National Policy for Children, 2013.[9]

It has now been more than 25 years since the United Nations Convention on the Rights of the Child (UNCRC), 1989 was adopted.[10] The importance of the UNCRC is now widely accepted and recognized. The UNCRC has been described as nothing short of 'the cornerstone of a new moral ethos for children', 'beginning of a new child rights jurisprudence', and an instrument stressing that 'respect for and protection of children's rights is the starting point for the full development of the individual's potential in an atmosphere of freedom, dignity and justice'. Once ratified, the UNCRC makes it a binding duty for the states to implement its provisions

[4] *United Nations Convention against Transnational Organized Crime and the Protocols Thereto*, New York, 15 November 2000. Ratified by India on 5 May 2011. Available at https://www.unodc.org/documents/middleeastandnorthafrica/organised-crime/UNITED_NATIONS_CONVENTION_AGAINST_TRANSNATIONAL_ORGANIZED_CRIME_AND_THE_PROTOCOLS_THERETO.pdf (accessed on 24 November 2016).

[5] *Protocol to Prevent, Suppress and Punish Trafficking in Persons, Especially Women and Children, Supplementing the United Nations Convention against Transnational Organized Crime*, 15 November 2000, New York, ratified by India on 5 May 2011. Available at http://www.osce.org/odihr/19223?download=true (accessed on 24 November 2016).

[6] *Protocol against the Smuggling of Migrants by Land, Sea and Air, Supplementing the United Nations Convention against Transnational Organized Crime*, 15 November 2000, New York, ratified by India on 5 May 2011.

[7] The ECCE policy was adopted in India on 27 September 2013.

[8] The 86th Constitutional Amendment, 2002 lays down that the state shall endeavour to provide ECCE for all children until they complete the age of 6 years (Article 45). Again, Section 11 of the Right of Children to Free and Compulsory Education Act (RTE Act), 2010 states: 'With a view to prepare children above the age of three years for elementary education and to provide early childhood care and education for all children until they complete the age of six years, the appropriate government may make necessary arrangement for providing free pre-school education for such children'. The policy resolved to promote inclusive, equitable, and contextualized opportunities for promoting optimal development and active learning capacity of children below 6 years (early childhood).

[9] The government adopted the new National Policy for Children, 2013 on 26 April 2013. The policy recognizes every person below the age of 18 years as a child and covers all children within the territory and jurisdiction of the country. It recognizes that a multisectoral and multidimensional approach is necessary to secure the rights of children. The policy has identified four key priority areas survival; health and nutrition; education and development; and protection and participation for focused attention. As children's needs are multisectoral, interconnected, and require collective action, the policy calls for purposeful convergence and coordination across different sectors and levels of governance.

[10] 20 November 2014 marked 25 years since the adoption of the UNCRC at the UN General Assembly in New York. On this day, for the first time in an international treaty, children were recognized as rights holders. It marked the transition from addressing children's issues through charity alone, to galvanizing the move towards advocacy that would bring about systemic change for the realization of children's rights.

by adopting relevant legislative and administrative measures. Further, governments must report on the measures adopted and progress made in advancing children's rights in their countries in the form of a report submitted to the Committee on the Rights of the Child,[11] appointed by the United Nations (UN) as per Article 44 of the convention.[12]

India signed the UNCRC in the year 1989 and ratified it in 1992, thereby committing itself to safeguard the rights of children enshrined in the convention. As a signatory to the UNCRC, the Ministry of Women and Child Development (MWCD), the nodal ministry for women and children, has the obligation to submit a country report every 5 years to the UN Committee on the UNCRC, on the progress and initiatives undertaken by the Government of India in securing children's rights, and the issues and challenges faced. India also ratified two optional protocols to the UNCRC, as elaborated next.[13]

Optional Protocol on the Sale of Children, Child Prostitution and Child Pornography[14]

India ratified this Optional Protocol on 16 August 2005. The OPSC deals with three main forms of violence, including sale of children, child prostitution, and child pornography. Governments that ratify the OPSC agree that acts such as the sale of children, child prostitution, and child pornography are very serious crimes. The OPSC asks governments to make sure that these acts are considered serious crimes and that anyone who commits them is punished, including people who try to commit them or help to commit them. Sometimes, a private company (for instance, a

---

[11] The UNCRC is the body of 18 independent experts that monitors implementation of the convention by its state parties. It also monitors implementation of two optional protocols to the convention, on involvement of children in armed conflict and on sale of children, child prostitution, and child pornography. All state parties are obliged to submit regular reports to the committee on how the rights are being implemented. States must initially report 2 years after acceding to the convention, and then every 5 years. The committee examines each report and addresses its concerns and recommendations to the state party in the form of concluding observations. Available at http://www.ohchr.org/EN/HRBodies/CRC/Pages/CRCIndex.aspx (accessed on 22 February 2016).

[12] UNCRC, Article 44:

(1) State parties undertake to submit to the committee, through the secretary-general of the United Nations, reports on the measures they have adopted which give effect to the rights recognized herein and on the progress made on the enjoyment of those rights:

   (a) within 2 years of the entry into force of the convention for the state party concerned;
   (b) thereafter every 5 years.

(2) Reports made under the present article shall indicate factors and difficulties, if any, affecting the degree of fulfilment of the obligations under the present convention. Reports shall also contain sufficient information to provide the committee with a comprehensive understanding of the implementation of the convention in the country concerned.

[13] Optional protocols are created to complement an existing convention and recognize new commitments governments need to respect, and once ratified by a government, carry the same strength as a convention and can be used in the same way.

[14] Adopted and opened for signature, ratification, and accession by the General Assembly resolution A/RES/54/263 of 25 May 2000.

hotel, a club, a bar) is involved in these crimes. For this reason, the OPSC asks countries to make sure private companies can also be made responsible. When this happens, it is important that child victims receive help to make sure they feel safe and understand what is going on. The OPSC also describes how child victims should be protected and supported during the legal process and in court cases. Governments who sign on to the OPSC also agree that child victims have the right to seek 'compensation for damages from those legally responsible'. This means that child victims should be able to start legal action against whoever is responsible for the crime committed against them, and get compensation for what happened. Compensation can include money or other things (for example, medical care or social support) that can help a victim heal and recover from the harm suffered.[15]

Optional Protocol to the Convention on the Rights of the Child on the Involvement of Children in Armed Conflict[16]

The OPAC is a multilateral treaty whereby states agree to

1. prohibit the conscription of children under the age of 18 into the military; and
2. ensure that military volunteers under the age of 18 are exempted from taking a direct part in hostilities.

The protocol requires the ratifying governments to ensure that while their armed forces can accept volunteers below the age of 18, they cannot be conscripted, and 'states parties shall take all feasible measures to ensure that members of their armed forces who have not attained the age of 18 years do not take a direct part in hostilities'. Non-state actors and guerrilla forces are forbidden from recruiting anyone under the age of 18 for any purpose. India ratified this optional protocol on 30 November 2005.[17]

Optional Protocol to the Convention on the Rights of the Child on a Communications Procedure[18]

On 19 December 2011, the UN General Assembly approved a third optional protocol on a communications procedure, which will allow individual children to submit complaints regarding specific violations of their rights under the convention and its first two optional protocols. This third Optional Protocol to the Convention on the Rights of the Child on a Communications Procedure (OP3CRC) sets out an international complaints procedure for child rights violations.

---

[15] Available at http://srsg.violenceagainstchildren.org/sites/default/files/children_corner/RaisingUnderstanding_OPSC.pdf (accessed on 22 February 2016).

[16] Adopted and opened for signature, ratification and accession by General Assembly resolution A/RES/54/263 of 25 May 2000, entry into force 12 February 2002.

[17] Available at https://treaties.un.org/Pages/ViewDetails.aspx?src=IND&mtdsg_no=IV-11-b&chapter=4&lang=en (accessed on 29 February 2016).

[18] *Optional Protocol to the Convention on the Rights of the Child on a Communications Procedure*, 19 December 2011, New York. Entry into force on 14 April 2014, in accordance with Article 19(1).

It entered into force in April 2014, allowing children from states that have ratified to bring complaints about violations of their rights directly to the UN Committee on the Rights of the Child, if they have not found a solution at the national level.[19]

There has been a paradigm shift in approaches towards children. The shift in focus is from the welfare to the developmental approach (Table 9.1).

Table 9.1 Approaches towards Children[20]

Earlier Approach	Present Approach
Needs	Rights
Welfare	Development
Institutional and residential care	Family-based alternatives and non-residential
Custodial care	Holistic development
Segregation and isolation	Inclusion in mainstream
Beneficiary and recipient	Participant and partner

Country Reports on Convention of the Rights of the Child of India to the Committee on Rights of the Child

First Country Report

The Government of India submitted its first *Country Report on the Convention of the Rights of the Child* in February 1997. The report reviewed the situation of children in the country with reference to the articles of the convention. The priority issues that the *Country Report* focused on included the measures of implementation, civil rights and freedom, and special measures of protection. The first *India Country Report* on the UNCRC stated:

> Unless the life of the child in the family and community improves, all development efforts would be meaningless. There is, therefore, a need to raise awareness and create an ethos of respect for the rights of the child in society to meet his or her basic developmental needs. Advocacy and social mobilization are two crucial processes which are being emphasized to achieve this end. With India's ratification of the UN convention on the Rights of the Child, the 'rights approach' to child development is gradually gaining importance and will henceforth form the basis of Government's strategy towards child development.[21]

Some major recommendations of the UNCRC Committee were the following:[22]

---

[19] Available at http://www.ohchr.org/EN/HRBodies/CRC/Pages/CRCIndex.aspx (accessed on 29 February 2016).

[20] Source: Compiled by the author.

[21] Government of India, *India Country Report on the Convention on the Rights of the Child*, 1997. Available at http://www.childlineindia.org.in/CP-CR-Downloads/UNCRC%20India%20periodic%20 report%202001.pdf (accessed on 24 November 2016).

[22] At its 589th to 591st meetings (see CRC/C/SR.589-591), held on 11 and 12 January 2000, the Committee on the Rights of the Child considered the initial report of India (CRC/C/28/Add.10), which

- To pursue efforts to ensure full compatibility of its legislation with the convention, taking due account of the general principles of the convention, and consider adopting a code for children.
- To take all necessary measures, including the allocation of the required resources (that is, human and financial), to ensure and strengthen the effective implementation of existing legislation.
- To provide adequate resources and to take all other necessary steps to strengthen the capacity and effectiveness of national human rights institutions, including the National Human Rights Commission, National Commission for Women, and Scheduled Castes and Scheduled Tribes Commission.
- To adopt a comprehensive national plan of action, based on a child rights approach, to implement the convention.
- To develop a comprehensive system for collecting disaggregated data as a basis to assess progress achieved in the realization of children's rights and to help design policies to be adopted to implement the convention.
- To empower the statutory National Commission for Children (NCC) and make it independent to receive and address complaints of violations of child rights, including those with respect to the security forces.
- To develop an ongoing programme for the dissemination of information regarding the implementation of the convention among children and parents, civil society, and all sectors and levels of government.
- To develop systematic and ongoing training programmes on the provisions of the convention for all professional groups working with children (judges, lawyers, law enforcement officials, civil servants, local government officials, personnel working in institutions and places of detention for children, teachers, health personnel including psychologists, and social workers).
- To review legislation with a view to ensuring that age limits conform to the principles and provisions of the convention, and take greater efforts to enforce those minimum-age requirements.
- To take concerted efforts at all levels to address social inequalities through a review and reorientation of policies, including increased budgetary provision for programmes targeting the most vulnerable groups.
- To take steps to ensure states abolish the discriminatory practice of 'untouchability', prevent caste- and tribe-motivated abuse, and prosecute state and private actors who are responsible for such practices or abuses.
- To ensure full implementation of the Scheduled Castes and Scheduled Tribes (Prevention of Atrocities) Act, 1989, Scheduled Castes and Scheduled Tribes Rules (Prevention of Atrocities) Act, 1995, and Employment of Manual Scavengers Act, 1993.
- To develop skills-training programmes in community settings for teachers, social workers, and local officials in assisting children to make and express their informed decisions and to have their views taken into consideration.
- To make greater efforts to ensure the timely registration of all births, in accordance with Article 7 of the convention, and take training and awareness-raising measures as regards registration in rural areas.

---

was submitted on 19 March 1997, and at the 615th meeting, held on 28 January 2000, adopted the concluding observations. For more information, see http://www.un.org/documents/ga/docs/55/a5541.pdf (accessed on 18 February 2016).

- To implement the recommendations made by the National Police Commission in 1980[23] and the Parliamentary Committee in 1996,[24] which call for a mandatory judicial inquiry in cases of alleged rape, death, or injury of persons in police custody; establishment of investigative bodies; and payment of compensation to people who have been victims of custodial abuse.
- Amendment to the Juvenile Justice (Care and Protection of Children) Act is recommended to provide for complaints and prosecution mechanisms for cases of custodial abuse of children. In addition, the committee recommends the amendment of Section 197 of the Code of Criminal Procedure (CrPC), which requires government approval for prosecution of law-enforcement officials when complaints of custodial abuse or illegal detention are alleged; and Section 43 of the Police Act, so that police cannot claim immunity for actions while executing a warrant in cases of illegal detention or custodial abuse.
- To review the legislative framework of domestic and inter-country adoption. The committee recommends that the state party become a party to the 1993 Hague Convention on Protection of Children and Co-operation in Respect of Intercountry Adoption, 1993 (referred to as the Hague Convention later in the chapter).
- To take legislative measures to prohibit all forms of physical and mental violence, including corporal punishment and sexual abuse of children in the family, schools, and care institutions.
- To increase the capacity of institutions for the rehabilitation of children with disabilities and improve access to services for such children living in rural areas.
- To take all necessary steps to adapt, expand, and implement the Integrated Management of Child Illness strategy, and to pay particular attention to the most vulnerable groups of the population.
- To strengthen the existing National Reproductive and Child Health programme, targeting the most vulnerable groups of the population.
- To take appropriate measures to give effect to the commitments made at Habitat II in 1996 regarding children's access to housing.
- To establish mechanisms to ensure that street children are provided with identity documents, nutrition, clothing, and housing.
- To implement measures designed to comply with Article 45 of the Constitution, which mandates free and compulsory education for all children up to 14 years of age.
- To adopt comprehensive legislation to ensure adequate protection of refugee and asylum-seeking children, including in the field of physical safety, health, education, and social welfare, and to facilitate family reunification.
- Respect for human rights and humanitarian law aimed at the protection and care of children in armed conflict.

---

[23] The National Police Commission, Government of India, Fourth Report, June 1980. See Available at http://bprd.nic.in/writereaddata/linkimages/8939843683-FOURTH%20REPORT.pdf (accessed on 28 February 2016).

[24] *Twenty-Eighth Report (1996) of the Committee on Home Affairs on the Criminal Law (Amendment) Bill, 1994*, introduced on 9 May 1994. *The Report of the Department-Related Parliamentary Standing Committee on Home Affairs*, 28 February 1996. Available at http://rajyasabha.nic.in/rsnew/annual_report/2001/bill.pdf (accessed on 28 February 2016).

- To abolish the requirement of governmental permission for criminal prosecutions or civil proceedings against members of the security forces.
- To amend the Child Labour (Prohibition and Regulation) Act (CLPRA), 1986 so that household enterprises and government schools and training centres are no longer exempt from prohibitions on employing children, and coverage is expanded to include agriculture and other informal sectors. The Factories Act, 1948 should be amended to cover all factories or workshops employing child labour. The Beedi and Cigar Workers (Conditions of Employment) Act (Beedi Act), 1966 should be amended so that exemptions for household-based production are eliminated. Employers should be required to have and produce on demand proof of age of all children working on their premises.
- To simplify court procedures so that responses are appropriate, timely, and child-friendly; and to vigorously pursue enforcement of minimum-age standards.
- To ratify International Labour Organization (ILO) Convention No. 138 concerning the Minimum Age for Admission to Employment, and No. 182, concerning the Prohibition and Immediate Action for the Elimination of the Worst Forms of Child Labour.
- To develop rehabilitation services for children who are victims of substance abuse.
- To ensure that laws concerning the sexual exploitation of children are gender neutral; provide civil remedies in the event of violations; ensure that procedures are simplified so that responses are appropriate, timely, child-friendly, and sensitive to victims; include provisions to protect from discrimination and reprisals those who expose violations; and vigorously pursue enforcement.
- To consider raising the age of criminal responsibility and ensure that persons under 18 years are not tried as adults. Section 2(h) of the 1986 JJ Act should be amended to ensure that boys under 18 years are covered by the definition of juvenile, as girls already are.[25]

The Second Periodic Report on the United Nations Convention on the Rights of the Child

The *Second Periodic Report* was submitted by India in 2001, which was reviewed by the UNCRC Committee in February 2004.[26] The following are some major recommendations of the committee for the implementation of the convention:[27]

- To take all necessary measures to adopt, in consultation with all relevant partners including the civil society, a new Plan of Action for Children that covers all areas of the convention, includes the Millennium Development Goals, and fully reflects 'a world fit for children'; to allocate the necessary human and financial resources for its full implementation; and provide for a coordination and monitoring mechanism.
- To expedite the adoption of the National Charter for Children and make sure that the Charter adopts a child-rights–based approach and covers all the rights and principles of the convention.

[25] Available at http://www.un.org/documents/ga/docs/55/a5541.pdf (accessed on 29 February 2016).

[26] Available at http://wcd.nic.in/sites/default/files/childobserv.pdf (accessed on 29 February 2016).

[27] The UN Committee considered the second periodic report of India at its 932nd and 933rd meetings, held on 21 January 2004, and adopted it, at the 946th meeting held on 30 January 2004.

- To establish an independent NCPCR in accordance with the Paris Principles relating to the status of national institutions.[28]
- To involve non-governmental organizations (NGOs) in a more systematic and coordinated manner in all stages of the convention's implementation, including policy formulation at the national, state, and local levels, and in the drafting of future periodic reports.
- To develop a system of data collection and indicators consistent with the convention and disaggregated by gender, age, social status (scheduled castes and tribes, or religious community), and urban and rural area, and make it publicly available. This system should cover all children up to the age of 18, with specific emphasis on those who are particularly vulnerable.
- To strengthen efforts to disseminate the principles and provisions of the convention, and make those efforts systematic in order to sensitize society about children's rights through social mobilization. To undertake systematic education and training on the provisions of the convention for all professional groups working for and with children, in particular, judges, lawyers, law-enforcement officials, civil servants, municipal and local workers, personnel working in institutions and places of detention for children, teachers, health personnel including psychologists, and social workers.
- To implement the Scheduled Castes and Scheduled Tribes (Prevention of Atrocities) Act, 1989; the Scheduled Castes and Scheduled Tribes Rules (Prevention of Atrocities), 1995; the Employment of Manual Scavengers and Construction of Dry Latrines (Prohibition) Act, 1993; and the Pre-conception and Pre-natal Diagnostic Techniques (Prohibition of Sex Selection) Act (PCPNDT Act), 1994.
- To promote, within the family, schools, institutions, as well as in judicial and administrative proceedings, respect for the views of children, especially girls, and facilitate their participation in all matters affecting them.
- To ensure the timely registration of all births by the year 2010.
- To ratify the convention against Torture and Other Cruel, Inhuman or Degrading Treatment or Punishment, set up child-sensitive mechanisms to receive complaints against law enforcement officials regarding ill-treatment during arrest, questioning, and police custody and in detention centres.
- To prohibit corporal punishment in the family, in schools, and other institutions and undertake education campaigns to educate families, teachers, and other professionals working with and/or for children on alternative ways of disciplining children.
- To ensure recognition and implementation of the principle that both parents have common responsibilities for the upbringing and development of their child.
- To review the legal framework for domestic adoption and take all necessary measures, including the adoption of new guidelines by the central authority, to implement the newly ratified 1993 Hague Convention and ensure that adoption is possible for children of all religions.

---

[28] General Assembly Resolution No. 48/134 and the Committee's General Comment No. 2 on national human rights institutions, to monitor and evaluate progress in the implementation of the convention at the federal and at the state levels. Available at http://wcd.nic.in/sites/default/files/childobserv.pdf (accessed on 24 November 2016).

- To adopt new legislative measures and amend outdated legislation to prohibit all forms of physical and mental violence, including sexual abuse of children in the family, in schools, and in institutions.
- To reinforce efforts in developing effective policies and programmes to improve the health situation of children.
- To increase efforts to prevent HIV/AIDS and uphold the rights of children. To strengthen various measures to prevent mother-to-child transmission, by combining and coordinating them with the activities meant to reduce maternal mortality, and take adequate measures to address the impact upon children of the HIV/AIDS-related deaths of parents, teachers, and others, in terms of children's reduced access to family life, adoption, emotional care, and education.
- To establish a comprehensive policy for children with disabilities.
- To enforce the Dowry Prohibition Act, 1961 and the Karnataka Devadasis (Prohibition of Dedication) Act, 1982 and Rules, 1982—to take legislative and awareness-raising measures to prohibit and eradicate all kinds of traditional practices harmful to the health, survival, and development of children, boys as well as girls.
- To take all necessary steps to implement the Child Marriage Restraint Act, 1929—to strengthen educational and awareness programmes, in cooperation with NGOs and community leaders, with a view to preventing early and forced marriage; and strengthen sexual and reproductive health education, mental health, and adolescent-sensitive counselling services, and make them accessible to adolescents.
- To provide support and material assistance to economically disadvantaged families and to guarantee the right of children to an adequate standard of living.
- To prevent any occurrence of forced relocation, displacement, and other types of involuntary population movements.
- To introduce human rights, including children's rights, into the school curricula. To strengthen efforts to progressively ensure that that all girls and boys in urban, rural, and least developed areas, and children belonging to scheduled castes and tribes, have equal access to educational opportunities.
- To provide the necessary human and financial support for the establishment and reinforcement of toll-free 'childlines' in all districts.
- To ensure respect for human rights and humanitarian law aimed at the protection, care, and physical and psycho-social rehabilitation of children affected by armed conflict, notably, regarding any participation in hostilities by children.
- To adopt comprehensive legislation to ensure adequate protection of refugee and asylum-seeking children, including in the fields of physical safety, health, education, and social welfare, and to facilitate family reunification.
- To ensure the full implementation of the CLPRA, the Bonded Labour (System Abolition) Act, 1976, and the Employment of Manual Scavengers and Construction of Dry Latrines (Prohibition) Act, 1993—to amend the CLPRA so that household enterprises and government schools and training centres are no longer exempt from prohibitions on employing children. To promote community-based programmes for the prevention of child labour; ratify ILO Conventions No. 138 concerning the Minimum Age for Admission to Employment, and No. 182 concerning the Prohibition and Immediate Action for the Elimination of the Worst Forms of Child Labour.

- To extend the scope of the Immoral Traffic (Prevention) Act, 1956 to all forms of trafficking of children and ensure that all trafficked children are always treated as victims.
- To strengthen and extend the Integrated Programme for Street Children to address the large and increasing number of street children, with the aim of protecting these children, especially girls, and of preventing and reducing this phenomenon, in particular, through assistance to families and the provision of adequate housing and access to education.
- To implement a juvenile justice system that is in conformity with the convention, in particular Articles 37,[29] 40,[30] and 39,[31] and with other UN standards in this field, such as the United Nations Standard Minimum Rules for the Administration of Juvenile Justice (the Beijing Rules),[32] the United Nations Guidelines for the Prevention of Juvenile Delinquency (the Riyadh Guidelines),[33] the United Nations Rules for the Protection of Juveniles Deprived of their Liberty,[34] and the Vienna Guidelines for Action on Children in the Criminal Justice System.[35]

Combined Third and Fourth Periodic Report[36]

India submitted the 'Combined Third and Fourth Periodic Report on the UNCRC, 2008' and the two Optional Protocols to the Convention on the Rights of the Child—on Sale of Children, Child Prostitution and Child Pornography; and Children Affected by Armed Conflict, ratified by India in 2005.[37] The *Third and Fourth Combined Periodic Report on the Convention on the Rights of the Child* was a product of extensive consultations with all stakeholders. The combined report presented the major initiatives that had been taken to ensure the rights of children. It also highlighted the current status of children, efforts made to address their concerns, and the

[29] UNCRC, Article 37: Detention and punishment—No one is allowed to punish children in a cruel or harmful way. Children who break the law should not be treated cruelly. They should not be put in prison with adults, should be able to keep in contact with their families, and should not be sentenced to death or life imprisonment without possibility of release.

[30] UNCRC, Article 40: Juvenile justice—Children who are accused of breaking the law have the right to legal help and fair treatment in a justice system that respects their rights. Governments are required to set a minimum age below which children cannot be held criminally responsible and to provide minimum guarantees for the fairness and quick resolution of judicial or alternative proceedings.

[31] UNCRC, Article 39: Rehabilitation of child victims—Children who have been neglected, abused, or exploited should receive special help to physically and psychologically recover and reintegrate into society. Particular attention should be paid to restoring the health, self-respect and dignity of the child.

[32] Adopted by General Assembly Resolution No. A/Res/40/33 of 29 November 1985.

[33] Adopted by General Assembly Resolution No. A/RES/45/112 of 14 December 1990.

[34] Adopted by the General Assembly on 14 December 1990.

[35] Elaborated by an expert group in Vienna on 23–25 February 1997, these guidelines were approved by the United Nations Economic and Social Council through resolution ECOSOC Res. 1997/30 of 21 June 1997.

[36] Ministry of Women and Child Development, *Third and Fourth Combined Periodic Report on the Convention on the Rights of the Child 2011* (New Delhi: Government of India). Available at http://www.utsahassam.org/pdf/resource/INDIA-periodic-Report-CRC.pdf (accessed on 29 February 2016).

[37] Ministry of Women and Child Development, *Third and Fourth Combined Periodic Report* (New Delhi: Government of India).

challenges which were yet to be overcome. The *Third and Fourth Combined Periodic Report* took into consideration a period between 2001 and 2008. During this period, ongoing flagship programmes for employment, education, health, nutrition, rural infrastructure, and urban renewal were consolidated. New flagship programmes for food security and skill development were introduced or were in the process of being initiated.[38] The report included the following major efforts to strengthen the framework for protection of child rights:

- Adoption of the National Food Security Act (NFS Act), on 10 September 2013; Protection of Children from Sexual Offences Act (POCSO Act), on 14 November 2012; and (c) Right of Children to Free and Compulsory Education Act (RTE Act), in August 2009.
- Establishment of the NCPCR in 2007, to safeguard and enforce the rights of all children in the country.
- Launch of a universal Integrated Child Protection Scheme (ICPS) in 2009–2010, based on the principles of 'protection of child rights' and 'best interest of the child'.
- Expansion of the Midday Meal Scheme. The progress of the Integrated Child Development Services (ICDS) into the third phase of expansion. Revamping of the rural public health infrastructure and rapidly expanding social protection net through insurance schemes and pensions are some of the initiatives taken to ensure the survival, development, care, and protection of our children.
- Amendment of the Persons with Disabilities (Equal Opportunities, Protection of Rights and Full Participation) Rules (PWD Rules), 1996, in 2009, so as to (i) simplify and decentralize the process of issue of disability certificates, and (ii) make more detailed provisions regarding eligibility for appointment of Chief Commissioner for Persons with Disabilities, with terms of appointment. Detailed guidelines have been issued to state governments, requesting them to make similar changes in the state rules.

Some of the major recommendations of the UNCRC Committee on the report were the following:[39]

- To undertake a revision of all legislation related to children to ensure the coherent and consistent harmonization of the legislative framework on children's rights with the principles and provisions of the convention at the federal and state levels, and to ensure that they are applied in the same way to all children in the territory of the state party.
- To ensure that the MWCD has sufficient authority to coordinate all activities related to the implementation of the convention at the inter-ministerial level as well as at the federal and state levels, and that the National Coordination Action Group[40] (NCAG) functions effectively at all levels.

[38] Ministry of Women and Child Development, *Third and Fourth Combined Periodic Report* (New Delhi: Government of India).

[39] Committee on UNCRC, *Concluding Observations on the Consolidated Third and Fourth Periodic Reports of India*, 13 June 2014, CRC/C/IND/CO/3–4. Available at http://www.refworld.org/docid/541bee3e4.html (accessed on 28 February 2016).

[40] NCAG, formed by the Ministry of Women and Child Development, Government of India, mandated to monitor the implementation of the National Policy for Children.

- To improve the data collection system: The data should cover all areas of the convention and should be disaggregated by age, sex, geographic location, ethnic, national, and socio-economic background, in order to facilitate analysis of the situation of all children, particularly those in situations of vulnerability.
- To ensure the independence of the NCPCR and all other commissions at all levels, including with regards to their funding, mandate, and immunities.
- Training of law enforcement officials, judges, prosecutors, teachers, media persons, health workers, social workers, personnel working in all forms of alternative care, and migration authorities.
- To establish a clear regulatory framework for the industries operating in the state party to ensure that their activities do not negatively affect human rights or endanger environmental and other standards, especially those relating to children's rights.
- To ensure that children who are in marginalized or in disadvantaged situations, such as children from scheduled castes and scheduled tribes, children with disabilities, children with HIV/AIDS, and asylum-seeker and refugee children, have access to basic services and enjoy their rights under the convention.
- To take immediate legal, policy, and awareness-raising measures to prevent female infanticide and abandonment of girls, including addressing of factors that reinforce cultural norms and practices that discriminate against girls.
- To ensure the effective implementation of the PCPNDT Act so as to prevent sex-selective abortions and strengthen regulatory mechanisms.
- To develop procedures and criteria to provide guidance to all relevant persons in authority for determining the best interests of the child in every area and for giving it due weight as a primary consideration.
- To take measures to ensure the effective implementation of legislation recognizing the right of the child to be heard in relevant legal proceedings, including CRC/C/IND/CO/3-4, by establishing systems and/or procedures for social workers and courts to comply with.
- To expedite the adoption of the amendments to the Registrations of Births and Deaths Act (RBD Act), 1969, make it accessible to the population, and guarantee both birth registration and the prompt issuance of a birth certificate.
- To take all appropriate measures in order to ensure that every child, whatever his or her parents' religion is, has the right to enjoy freedom of religion.
- To explicitly prohibit all forms of corporal punishment against children under 18 in all settings throughout its territory.
- To establish mechanisms, procedures, and guidelines to ensure mandatory reporting all of cases of child sexual abuse (CSA) and take necessary measures to ensure the proper investigation, prosecution, and punishment of perpetrators.
- To ensure the effective implementation of the Prohibition of Child Marriage Act, 2006 (PCMA), including by clarifying that the PCMA supersedes the different religious-based Personal Status Laws. The UNCRC Committee also recommended that the state party take the necessary measures to combat dowry, child marriage, and the devadasi custom, including by conducting awareness-raising programmes and campaigns with a view to changing attitudes, as well as counselling and reproductive education, to prevent and combat child marriages, which are harmful to the health and well-being of girls.

- Implementation of the ECCE Policy of 2013, which would enable parents to take better care of young children.
- To review legislation on adoption with a view to harmonizing it in line with the UNCRC and the Hague Convention—to ensure the effective implementation of the Guidelines Governing the Adoption of Children, 2011, establish effective monitoring mechanisms and accreditation of all individuals and entities dealing with adoptions directly or as intermediaries, consider limiting their number, and ensure that domestic and inter-country adoption processes do not result in financial gains to any party.
- To ensure that the Assisted Reproductive Technology Bill (ART Bill), 2014 or other legislation to be developed contains provisions which define, regulate, and monitor the extent of surrogacy arrangements and criminalizes the sale of children for the purpose of illegal adoption, including the misuse of surrogacy. This should include ensuring that action is taken against all those who have undertaken illegal adoptions.
- To ensure that best interests of the child are taken into account as a primary consideration when sentencing parents, whereby avoiding, as far as possible, sentences for parents which lead to their separation from their children.
- To develop a national plan of action for children with disabilities which integrates all provisions of the UNCRC as well as indicators to measure outcomes and ensure effective coordination among relevant ministries for its implementation.
- To ensure that appropriate resources be allocated to the health sector, with particular attention to specific maternal and child healthcare policies, programmes, and schemes to improve the health situation of children, in particular to respond to high rates of acute respiratory infections, malnutrition, and diarrhoea.
- To ensure the effective implementation of the NFS Act which contains provisions aiming at combating children's undernourishment.
- To enhance efforts to promote exclusive breastfeeding practices, including the promotion of breastfeeding from birth, complementary feeding strategies with or without provision of food supplements as well as micronutrient interventions for mothers; and ensure the effective implementation of, and compliance with, the International Code of Marketing of Breast-milk Substitutes, and establishment of a monitoring and reporting system to identify violations of the code, and to ensure that stringent measures are taken in all situations of violations of the code.
- To adopt the Human Immunodeficiency Virus and Acquired Immune Deficiency Syndrome (Prevention and Control) Bill, 2014 and ensure that it contains specific provisions addressing the needs of children infected with HIV/AIDS in line with the convention.
- To strengthen efforts to fully implement the RTE Act at the federal and state levels, including inter alia, by developing RTE compliant school development plans.
- To strengthen existing child protection systems, including the ICPS, with the aim to identify and provide assistance to children in need of protection, especially unaccompanied refugee and asylum-seeking children, and consider acceding to the Convention Relating to the Status of Refugees, 1951 and its 1967 Protocol.
- To expedite the adoption of the Child Labour (Prohibition and Regulation) Bill, 2012 and develop a comprehensive strategy to prevent and eliminate all forms of child labour, including sanctions against individuals involved in child labour—to consider ratifying ILO Conventions

No. 138 concerning the Minimum Age for Admission to Employment, No. 182 concerning the Prohibition and Immediate Action for the Elimination of the Worst Forms of Child Labour, and No. 189 (2011) concerning Decent Work for Domestic Workers.

- To avoid, in all situations, treating children in street situations as criminals.
- To give effect to the Juvenile Justice Rules (JJ Rules) of 2007, establishing the minimum age of criminal responsibility at 18 and maintaining it at an internationally acceptable level.[41]

In the aforementioned recommendations of the UNCRC Committee, there are certain concerns that are repeatedly being brought up in the concluding points. These include establishment of minimum age of criminal responsibility as 18, elimination of all forms of child labour, protection of street children, non-discrimination of children so that all children, irrespective of their religious background or scheduled castes or scheduled tribes background, enjoy the whole range of rights enshrined in the convention, implementation of various laws, ratification of international instruments relating to children, ensuring adequate budgetary allocations for children, strengthening monitoring and evaluation systems and structures, dissemination of the convention, and capacity building of the stakeholders.

Major Concerns and Obstacles in Realizing the Rights of the Child

A large number of children in India still live much below the standards set by the constitution and national and international law. They suffer an array of threats to their development, well-being, and survival. They suffer from poverty, diseases, famine, and war, and they also suffer from acts and omissions by their own caretakers, guardians, and parents. Primary education is far from universal.

Poor Care and Services for Disabled Children

There is poor level of access to care and service for children with physical and mental disabilities. Disabled and abandoned children are in many instances put to work as beggars or they languish in remand homes with no special facilities for them.

The Concept of Legitimacy in Indian Laws

An area of concern is the perpetuation of the offensive term 'illegitimate' in the legal system in referring to a child born to parents not married to each other. An innocent child is still stigmatized by this reference. Statutes need to be amended to remove such age-old terms which are offensive in our present-day society.[42] The modern law has tried to improve the position of illegitimate children by raising their status to legitimate children in certain matters. But a vast majority of

---

[41] Committee on UNCRC, 'Concluding Observations'. Available at http://www.indianet.nl/pdf/CRC_CO_India_140613.pdf (accessed on 28 February 2016).

[42] From Washington, Supreme Court Judge Charles Smith in *Guard* v. *Beeston* (1997) 940 P. 2d 642, 668.

children still remain unaffected. 'To be designated as an illegitimate child in preadolescence is an emotional trauma of lasting consequence.'[43]

In Indian law, or in the personal law of any community of India, legitimization by subsequent marriage of parents is not recognized. All laws in India make a distinction between legitimacy and illegitimacy. The Hindu Marriage Act (HMA), 1955 [as amended by the Marriage Laws (Amendment) Act, 1976][44] and the Special Marriage Act (SMA), 1954 confers a status of legitimacy on the child of annulled, voidable, and void marriage.[45] But an inferior status has been conferred on such children in as much as it has been laid down that such children can inherit the property of the parents alone, and of none else.[46] However, children of bigamous Hindu marriages can inherit the property of their father (Section 16, HMA). Such a child cannot get any right to inherit the property of other parental relatives or be a 'coparcener'. This is done by the introduction of the doctrine of fiction in the HMA. On the other hand, a child born to a mother with whom the father has not gone through a form of marriage cannot inherit from him.

The SMA also recognizes the right of the children born of void marriages to inherit from both the parents (Section 26, SMA). Parsi, Muslim, and Christian children, if illegitimate, cannot inherit from their father according to their personal laws. Section 21 of the Indian Divorce Act, 1869 (IDA), applicable to Christians, however, provides that children of such marriages shall be entitled to succeed to the estate of the parents only when the marriage is annulled (i) on the ground that another spouse was living at the time of the marriage but that the subsequent marriage was contracted in good faith and with full belief of the parties that such other spouse was dead, or (ii) on the ground of insanity of any of the parties. Section 21 does not make any provision for the children when the marriage is annulled on any other ground, for example, on the ground of the parties being within the degree of prohibited relationship or on the ground of any of the parties being idiot. When compared with the provisions of Section 16 of the HMA or Section 26 of the SMA, the provisions of Section 21 of the IDA are obviously discriminatory, and since the IDA applies to the parties solely on the ground of their professing Christian religion, the discrimination would appear to be based on religion and thus violative of Article 15 of the Constitution. Similarly, the provisions of Section 3 of the Parsi Marriage and Divorce Act, 1939 thus appear to be much less comprehensive than the analogous provisions in Section 26 of the SMA and Section 16 of the HMA and would, therefore, result in denial of equality before the law and equal protection of the laws[47] to children of different religions.

Under Muslim law, a status of legitimacy may be conferred on a child by acknowledgement of paternity. The Muslim doctrine applies to cases where the legitimacy of a child is uncertain. If he is known to be an illegitimate child, the doctrine does not apply. In other words, it applies only to

---

[43] *Mississippi Code of 1972* (as amended). From the Alaska Supreme Court in *BEB* v. *BEB* (1999) 979, P. 2d 514, 517.

[44] Section 16, as amended by the Marriage Laws (Amendment) Act, 1976. Before the amendment, the status of legitimacy could be conferred only on the children of those void marriages which were declared null and void.

[45] Section 26: The language of Section 16, HMA, and this section is identical.

[46] Proviso to Section 16, HMA.

[47] Paras Diwan, *Law of Adoption, Minority, Guardianship and Custody* (Delhi: Universal Law Publishing Co. Pvt. Ltd., 2000).

cases where either the fact or the exact time of the alleged marriage is a matter of uncertainty that is neither proved nor disproved.[48] It is required that the acknowledgement must be not merely as a child but as a legitimate child, the age of the child and the person acknowledging should be such as to admit being the father of the child, the child must not be known to be the child of another, and the acknowledgement must not be repudiated by the child.[49]

Under the scheme of the Indian Succession Act, 1925, illegitimate children cannot be deemed to be included within the ambit of the expressions used in describing the heirs of Class I of the schedule to the act. These expressions have to be taken to refer to legitimate 'son' and 'daughter' born out of the union of a subsisting marriage. The act does not expressly equate illegitimate children to legitimate children. In the matter of inheritance and succession under the act, the two do not stand on par but stand apart. The act separates and distinguishes the two and excludes the illegitimate from any right to intestate succession except to the extent expressly enacted in the proviso to Section 3(1)(j) of the act. For the purpose of succession to the property of a male Hindu dying intestate, the Hindu Succession Act, 1956 clearly intends only a legitimate relationship with the father unlike with the mother, with whom a special fictional legitimacy and consequent heritability flowing therefrom is established. This outdated concept of legitimacy as far as children are concerned should be abolished.

Child Labour

Child labour denies a child the 'right to childhood'. Any work done by children that harms them, exploits them either physically, mentally, or morally, or blocks their access to education can be termed as child labour. There are several loopholes in the CLPRA.

Institutionalization

In practice, institutions have become 'hostels' where children are being placed for food, clothing, shelter, and education due to the inability of their parents to look after them. Such institutionalized children suffer from the 'institutional child syndrome' and are victims of excessive routinization and regimentation, physical and sexual abuse and trauma, low self-esteem, segregation and isolation from society, and low education and skills. They do have difficulty in joining the main stream and adjusting in society. Institutionalization seems to be the rule rather than an exception. Non-institutional and family-based alternatives are not adequate. There are still disparities in the interpretation and implementation of adoption procedures which causes undue delays. The general impression is that legal adoption is time-consuming and tedious. Unethical practice of buying and selling babies violates the child's dignity and sense of self-worth. After-care services are almost non-existent.

Child Custody

There does not seem to be any consideration of the concept of the best interest of child in lower courts. The records of the lower courts do not reveal the reasons why a particular order was given

[48] Baillie 406; *Hedaya*, 439; *Md Allabad* v. *Muhammad* (1888) 10 All 289.
[49] Baillie 408; *Hedaya*, 408; *Habibur Rehman* v. *Altaf Ali* (1921) 48 IA 114.

by a judge.[50] Children are 'dragged' to the courts dealing with matrimonial disputes as ancillary to the main matter. The trauma of the child in a matrimonial dispute is not considered. The child's interest needs to be represented and protected in such matters.

Violation of the Right to Survival

In cities like Mumbai, nearly 70 per cent of the population reside in slums and on pavements under the most difficult circumstances. These slum dwellers include children and they are constantly under the threat of forced eviction. Demolitions and forced evictions from homes disrupt the social structure of the child's life to survival including the right to shelter, nutrition, school, playground, and friends.

Child Marriages

There are still thousands of child marriages reported throughout the country. Early marriages are a form of CSA and a violation of a child's freedom to enjoy childhood. Implementation of the PCMA is very poor.

Child Witnesses and Victims

The POCSO Act needs to be implemented in its true spirit. Child-friendly courtrooms hardly exist in some cities. There is a need for more such court rooms. The infrastructure of children's courts needs to be developed. Mandatory reporting needs more training of the doctors, nurses, police, social workers, and civil society in general.

Mental Health of Children

In India, 15 per cent of children have serious emotional disturbances.[51] The facilities for healing are inadequate and majority of the children are never identified. The legal system has no provision to consider the mental-health perspective or to deal with the trauma of children who come in contact with the system either as victims or as offenders.

Challenge of New Technology

The digital revolution, the global spread of computers and the Internet, and the electronic revolution have made pornography more accessible to children. Statistics reveal that paedophiles (adults engaged in sexual crimes against children) have an access to children through the Internet.

[50] Asha Bajpai, 'Children and Courts', unpublished study supported by the Board of Research Studies, Tata Institute of Social Sciences, 2000.

[51] World Health Organization, *World Health Organization Report, 2001*. Available at http://www.who.int/whr/2001/en/ (accessed on 24 November 2016).

Research has established that online pornography plays an accessory role in negative social issues such as child abuse, youth crime, promiscuity, and sexually transmitted diseases.[52]

Status of the Girl Child

Child marriages, amniocentesis, female feticide, child trafficking, child sexual exploitation and abuse, infant and maternal mortality rates, and dowry demands and deaths are all evils linked in some way or the other to the low status of the girl child in India. There appears to be an utter powerlessness of the girl child against the ideological onslaught of patriarchal forces perpetuated through customs and traditions, proverbs and myths, and folklore and folk songs. In a culture that idolizes sons and dreads the birth of a daughter, the girl child suffers special disadvantages. Today the 'rejection' of the unwanted girl can begin even before her birth; prenatal sex determination tests followed by quick abortions eliminate thousands of female foetuses. This has led to the growing disparity between male and female infant mortality rates. As per the 2011 Census, the child sex ratio (0–6 years) has shown a decline from 927 females per thousand males in 2001 to 919 females per thousand males in 2011.[53] These 'unwanted' and 'unwelcome' girls are born in indifference and reared in neglect. A girl is likely to be breastfed less often and for shorter periods than a boy is. A number of studies indicate that in children under the age of 5, girls suffer from malnutrition more often than boys do. Not only are more girls malnourished, the degree of their malnutrition is also greater. The root cause is not so much as the lack of food but the lack of 'value' attached to the girl child. Eating less than her brother, a girl does twice as much work, not only at home but also in the fields. The temporary nature of the girl's membership in her family, coupled with her low economic worth, ensures a minimum investment in her development. The girl child's labour is as continuous as it is unrecognized, unpaid, and unrewarded. She is denied education and training and this denies her many basic skills or information that would equip her to earn a living or fight for her rights both within the home and outside it. Child marriages, though prohibited by law, are still prevalent. Although the family and the larger economic order exploit the labour of young children of both sexes in different ways, girls are worse off. Their work is either not visible enough or is accorded such low value that they are viewed merely as an economic liability. The girl child's status should be enhanced by empowering her through education and providing her with skills to make herself reliant and economically independent.

Poverty and Exclusion among Urban Children

Cities represent some of the most serious obstacles to children's development and the enjoyment of their rights. Children from cities face chronic poverty, marginalization, violence, and exploitation. They lack a secure home, access to health services, shelter, and education and have no space for play. They have to face air pollution, high noise levels, and difficulty in sleeping.[54]

---

[52] Available at http://netsafety.nic.in/internet.htm (accessed on 22 August 2002).

[53] Press Information Bureau, Ministry of Health and Family Welfare, *Decline in Child Sex Ratio* (Government of India, 11 February 2014). Available at http://pib.nic.in/newsite/PrintRelease.aspx?relid=103437 (accessed on 29 February 2016).

[54] UNICEF, 'Poverty and Exclusion among Urban Children', *Innocenti Digest* 10 (November 2002).

Non-participation of Children

Unfortunately, children's participation at any level is considered least important in India. As a cultural practice, children are always told to obey elders without questioning. Children are always told not to express their opinions in front of the elders. They are always told that they do not have the capacity to think on their own and they are not capable of taking any decision on their own. This culture also reflects in the education system. The same culture persists in the society where efforts to understand children's views, even on the issues of their concern, are never taken into consideration. Against a historical and cultural legacy of 'children being seen and not heard', children's voices have been unheard, silenced, ignored, or at best interpreted. Children and young people have been largely ignored as active participants in decision-making processes. However, in recent years, evidence of children's 'invisibility in decision making processes' has begun to accumulate from different sectors of the world community.[55] Such awareness is acting as a catalyst for change.

Non-enforcement of Laws

Legislation is one of the main weapons for empowering children and providing them with justice. If laws could guarantee their own enforcement there would never be any injustice. On paper, there are laws and policies, but there is a need for mechanisms and structures to ensure that the rights of the child do not remain on paper and get translated into action. This is a great challenge.

Lack of Coordination

There is no coordination or sharing of information among the government, the ministries, law enforcers and implementers' community, and civil society organizations.

Action Plan and Strategies for Realizing the Rights of the Child

Eliminating the obstacles will help realize the rights of the child. The action plan has to be multifaceted and multidimensional and with diversity of approach, as the problems are complex and deep-rooted. Several underlying issues need to be addressed; the child's perspective, context, and environment must be incorporated. There are several challenges ahead.

Awareness Campaigns

A campaign must be launched to promote awareness of the UNCRC, the constitutional provisions, and the situation of children in India. The campaign should focus on information dissemination on child rights at the state and national levels. It should also demand the implementation of the commitments made by the Government of India. The campaign must undertake initiatives at the national level, through awareness building, networking, and child-centred policy advocacy,

---

[55] Oxfam, 1985, Save the Children, 1995; Johnson, Hill and Ivan-Smith, 1995; Quortrup, 1996, Butler and Williamson, 1994.

for building a conducive institutional environment wherein all the internationally agreed and accepted child rights are fully practised and promoted. One of the objectives of the campaign must be to mobilize public opinion for the protection and promotion of child rights through information dissemination, awareness, and sensitization activities. School children, children in institutions, law enforcers, teachers, doctors, lawmakers, and policy planners should all be made aware of the rights of the child.

Recommendations for Legislative Reform in Support of Children

Legislation is one of the main weapons for empowering children and providing them with justice. The Indian legal system has to evolve a great deal in securing the rights of the child. First, there has to be some synchronization of the upper age limit for childhood if the rights of childhood have to be realized. The UNCRC creates, for the first time, a balanced and clearly articulated framework for determining the rights that a child has under international law. Even with its inherent problem of enforcement, the convention can be a catalyst for legal reform since it sets out the rights a child should be able to claim at some point in the national legal system. This multilateral treaty has given a new dimension to the concept of child rights that must be appreciated at the national level if domestic legal systems are to incorporate this holistic perception of rights. The criticism in South Asia—that legal systems are irrelevant to social problems—results from the practice of engaging in ad hoc law reform without any attention to creating adequate support systems for implementation. The balanced and holistic approach to child rights in the convention encourages law reform to be integrated with basic changes in government policy and other initiatives, so that there is a concerted effort to have an impact on social practice and the lives of citizens.[56] Any reform in law should be strategic and aimed at systemic change.

Commission for Protection of Child Rights Act, 2005

The main weakness of the NCPCR is that its directives are only recommendatory in nature and the bodies lack any powers to enforce their own recommendations. The implication is that the commission can call for records, summon, and record evidence and submit its report to the government. But if the government refuses to send a report or appear before it, there is nothing that the commission can do except chastise the government. It has been noted that even the strictures and awards of compensation by the National Human Rights Commission (NHRC) are only recommendatory and very rarely have its directions ever been carried out by the state governments.

Further, the same bureaucracy and police who are often the main violators and abusers of children's rights conduct the inspections, inquiries, and investigations. Very often, inspections and inquiries are reduced to 'calling for reports' from central or state agencies and if the commission is satisfied 'either that no further inquiry is required or that the required action has been initiated or taken by the concerned government or authority, it may not proceed with the complaint and

---

[56] Savitri Goonesekere, *Children, Law and Justice: A South Asian Perspective* (New Delhi: UNICEF, Sage Publication, 1998), pp. 92–93.

inform the complainant accordingly'. It is not obliged to hear the versions of all concerned, such as the child, children's groups, parents, others in the community, or anyone else. The inquiries should be carried out by trained and sensitized investigators, either by the commission's own investigators or by an independent body with persons from civil society as members, who may be assisted by a government official.

There is no prescribed time frame within which the NCC should initiate inquiries upon receiving complaints and complete inquiries and investigations.

There is a need to include the provision for mandatory enforcement of the orders of the commission, and the commission should be given powers to initiate contempt proceedings against those not complying with its orders within a time frame.

There is no provision for any form of participation by children. This is not in conformity with the UNCRC's right to participation. Some activists have suggested that there should be an 'advisory body' of children (consultative body may be more appropriate) whose opinions are taken and valued before any decisions or actions are taken by the NCC.[57]

The NCC/NCPCR is not an independent body. Section 4 of the Commission for Protection of Child Rights Act, 2005 states that the chairperson of the NCPCR should be appointed on the recommendation of a three-member selection committee constituted by the Central Government under the chairmanship of the minister-in-charge of the Ministry or Department of Women and Child Development. There are no legal provisions detailed to ensure proper selection of the chairperson and members by the Selection Committee. Further, due to such lacuna in the legal provisions, the appointment of members to the NCPCR has been challenged in *Association for Development* v. *Union of India*,[58] on the grounds that the appointments were not based on objective criteria or qualification

The NCC should be so structured at the central, state, district, taluk, and panchayat levels that anyone—even a child or children's group—access to it and is able to interact and influence its functioning panchayat-level upwards.

Child Labour (Prohibition and Regulation) Act, 1986

The UN Committee on the Rights of the Child, in its concluding observations in all the three reports submitted by India, has recommended that the CLPRA, should be amended so that household enterprises, government schools, and training centres are no longer exempt from

---

[57] Human Rights Advocacy and Research Foundation (HRARF) and the Child Rights and You (CRY) consultations.

[58] 2010 (115) DRJ 277. The appointment of two members of the NCPCR was challenged before the Delhi High Court on the ground that they did not possess the requisite qualifications specified in Section 3 of the Commission on Protection of Children Act (CPCR Act), 2005. Since the term of the members was to expire shortly, the high court refrained from looking into the appointments. Instead, the court proceeded to consider the process to be followed for future appointments. On behalf of the Government of India, the Solicitor General submitted that the Selection Committee shall comprise of at least one independent expert of eminence in the field of child rights or welfare. Further, after the completion of the selection process and 30 days before the notification of appointment, the details of the Selection Committee as well as the candidates, along with their qualifications, shall be put up on the website of the Ministry of Human Resources Development.

prohibitions on employing children and coverage is expanded to include agriculture and other informal sectors. The act should also address issues related to rehabilitation, education, and family income generation schemes. There should be stricter law enforcement in cases of child labour, with more incentives for exemplary enforcement personnel. Besides, there is a need for a legislative ban on employment of children below a certain age. Currently, there is no lower age limit in the law for employment of child labour. The invisible hidden child labour in the unorganized, informal sector should be brought within the purview of the act. Child labour in domestic work has already been included as a hazardous occupation.[59] A mandatory registration of the child domestic worker and the employers, and development of helplines and outreach programmes are required to protect the child domestic workers. There is need for legislation that will protect their rights. Illegal or undocumented child labourers should get greater protection. Child labour in agricultural employment must be included as a hazardous occupation. Rehabilitation and reintegration of all child labourers should be included in the provisions of the act. Employment of a child in contravention with the law should be made accountable and stringent punishment must be included. The offences must be made non-bailable .

The district-level vigilance committees should be strengthened to identify and eliminate bonded child labour. The Factories Act, 1948 should be amended to cover all factories or workshops employing child labour. The Beedi Act should be amended so that exemptions for household-based production are eliminated. Employers should be required to have, and produce on demand, proof of age of all children working on their premises.

The current CLPRA is not aligned to the RTE Act as it permits employment of children below 14 years of age in occupations and processes not prohibited by law. Article 21A and Article 23 of the Constitution of India contradict each other.[60] There is a need for constitutional amendment here. The CLPRA is not in conformity with the ILO Conventions 138 and 182, which provide for minimum age of entry into employment and prohibition of employment of persons below 18 years, in work which is likely to harm health, safety, and morals. It is also violative of Article 32 of the UNCRC. India's reservation on Article 32 of the UNCRC must be withdrawn now.[61]

---

[59] Inserted by SO 1724(E) on 10 October 2006 (w.e.f. 10 October 2006).

[60] The CLPRA prohibits employment of a child in 18 occupations and 65 processes and regulates the conditions of working of children in other occupations/processes. As per this act, a child means any person who has not completed 14 years of age. The act provides punishment for the offence of employing or permitting employment of any child in contravention of the provisions of the act. The RTE Act enjoins the state to ensure free and compulsory education to all children in the age group of 6–14 years. This implies that if a child is in the work place, he would miss school.

[61] The Government of India ratified the UNCRC in 1992. It deposited its instrument of accession to the aforementioned conventions on 11 December 1992 to the United Nations Secretary-General. That instrument contains the following declaration:

While fully subscribing to the objectives and purposes of the Convention, realising that certain of the rights of the child, namely those pertaining to the economic, social and cultural rights can only be progressively implemented in the developing countries, subject to the extent of available resources and within the framework of international co-operation; recognising that the child has to be protected from exploitation of all forms including economic exploitation; nothing that for several reasons children of different ages do work in India; having prescribed minimum ages for employment in hazardous occupations and in certain other areas; having made regulatory provisions regarding hours and conditions of employment; and being

The Union Cabinet, chaired by Prime Minister Narendra Modi, has given its approval for moving official amendments to the Child Labour (Prohibition and Regulation) Amendment Bill, 2012 on 13 May 2015.[62] The Official Amendments, along with the Amendment Bill, proposes to make certain salient amendments to the CLPRA, as discussed next.

1. Employment of children below 14 years has been prohibited in all occupations and processes and age of prohibition of employment has been linked to age under the RTE Act.
2. A new definition of 'adolescent' has also been introduced in the amendment and employment of adolescents (14 to 18 years of age) has also been prohibited in hazardous occupations and processes. However, an exception has been made

   a) where the child helps his family or family enterprises, which is other than any hazardous occupations or processes set forth in the schedule, after his school hours or during vacations; and
   b) where the child works as an artist in an audio–visual entertainment industry, including advertisement, films, television serials, or any such other entertainment or sports activities except the circus, subject to such conditions and safety measures, as may be prescribed and provided that such work does not affect the school education of the child.[63]

These exceptions in the new bill will again lead to misuse by employers as is happening with the current act, and must be removed. All labour by children below 18 years must be abolished and right to free and compulsory education for preschool children and 14–18 year olds must be ensured. The ambiguous definition of family, the term 'helping family', and lack of monitoring

---

aware that it is not practical immediately to prescribe minimum ages for admission to each and every area of employment in India-the Government of India undertakes to take measures to progressively implement the provisions of Article 32, particularly paragraph 2(a), in accordance with its national legislation and relevant international instruments to which it is a state party.

Article 32 of the UNCRC, which has been mention in the instrument of accession, reads as follows:

(1) States parties recognize the right of the child to be protected from economic exploitation and from performing any work that is likely to be hazardous or to interfere with the child's education, or to be harmful to the child's health or physical, mental, spiritual, moral or social development.
(2) States parties shall take legislative, administrative, social and educational measures to ensure the implementation of the present article. To this end, and having regard to the relevant provisions of other international instruments, states parties shall in particular:

   (a) provide for a minimum age or minimum ages for admission to employment;
   (b) provide for appropriate regulation of the hours and conditions of employment;
   (c) provide for appropriate penalties or other sanctions to ensure the effective enforcement of the present article.

[62] Press Information Bureau, Government of India, Cabinet, 'Approval to Move Official Amendments to the Child Labour (Prohibition & Regulation) Amendment Bill, 2012'. Available at http://pib.nic.in/newsite/PrintRelease.aspx?relid=121636 (accessed on 29 February 2016).

[63] Press Information Bureau, 'Approval to Move Official Amendments'.

mechanisms to check if children are attending schools also increase vulnerability to trafficking.[64] Child labour and right to education are interlinked. The law on child labour must include the right to education and the rehabilitation of those rescued. A provision for interim compensation and final compensation must be included.[65] Accountability of agencies and time-bound implementation, too, must be included. Children in the entertainment industry also need to be protected as many a times they are forced to work by their parents and it affects their right to education, development, and health.[66] It will be difficult to ensure that the child is working in a non-hazardous family enterprise and that s/he is doing so only after school hours. The offences under the bill are cognizable but they must be made non-bailable and punishment must be made more stringent. The provision in the bill, for the constitution of Child and Adolescent Labour Rehabilitation Fund for one or more districts for the rehabilitation of the children or adolescents rescued, is welcome. The bill itself, when enacted, will provide for a fund to carry out rehabilitation activities, which is much needed. This will give a legislative mandate to the *M.C. Mehta* judgment.[67]

The Child Labour (Prohibition and Regulation) Amendment Act, 2016 received the assent of the President on 29th July, 2016. The Act came into force in order to amend Child Labour (Prohibition and Regulation) Act, 1986. The Act prohibits employment of children below 14 years of age in all occupations. But it allows adolescents (those between 14 and 18 years of age) to work in non-hazardous occupations and processes. They can work in family-run establishments after school hours and during vacations. The government justified the exceptions to strike 'a balance between the need for education for a child and reality of the socio-economic condition and social fabric in the country'. But how will this be implemented. It is time to take a stand to completely abolish all child labour for all children.

Law Reform for Juvenile Justice

The concept of juvenile justice is composed of two important ideas, namely fairness or justness to children and an alternative justice system. The age of criminal responsibility is 7 years.[68] This is considered very low by international standards. This age needs to be raised to 18 years.

[64] Bachpan Bachao Andolan (BBA), 'National Consultation Held for Strengthening the Amendments to the Child Labour Act', 23 November 2015. Available at http://www.bba.org.in/?q=content/national-consultation-held-strengthening-amendments-child-labour-act#sthash.vx2E7NKv.dpuf (accessed on 29 February 2016).

[65] BBA, 'National Consultation'.

[66] BBA, 'National Consultation'.

[67] *M.C. Mehta* v. *State of Tamil Nadu & Ors* [1996] RD-SC 1576 (10 December 1996). The Supreme Court ordered that employers employing children illegally must pay Rs 20,000 into a fund known as the Child Labour Rehabilitation-cum-Welfare Fund, to be used only for the benefit of that child. The court also ordered the government to either (a) provide employment for an adult member of every family with a child who is employed in a factory or mine or other hazardous work or, if not possible to provide an adult family member with a job, (b) contribute Rs 5,000 to the Child Labour Rehabilitation-cum-Welfare Fund for each child employed in a factory or mine or other hazardous employment. Adults who are offered jobs in this way would also have a duty to ensure that their children entered full-time education and did not continue to work.

[68] IPC, Section 82: Act of a child under 7 years of age—Nothing is an offence which is done by a child under 7 years of age.

The JJ Act, 2015 has come into force on 15 January 2016, after the president of India gave his assent to the bill on 31 December 2015. This act repealed the JJ Act, 2000. The JJ Act, 2015 provides for strengthened provisions for both children in need of care and protection and children in conflict with the law. Some of the key provisions include change in nomenclature from 'juvenile' to 'child' or 'child in conflict with law' across the act to remove the negative connotation associated with the word 'juvenile'; inclusion of several new definitions such as orphaned, abandoned, and surrendered children and petty, serious, and heinous offences committed by children; clarity in powers, function, and responsibilities of the Juvenile Justice Board (JJB) and the Child Welfare Committee (CWC); clear timelines for inquiry by the JJB; special provisions for heinous offences committed by children above the age of 16 years; and a separate new chapter on adoption to streamline adoption of orphan, abandoned, and surrendered children.

Several rehabilitation and social reintegration measures have been provided for children in conflict with the law and those in need of care and protection. Under institutional care, children are provided with various services including education, health, nutrition, de-addiction, treatment of diseases, vocational training, skill development, life-skill education, counselling, and others, to help them assume a constructive role in society. The variety of non-institutional options include sponsorship and foster care, including group foster care, for placing children in a family environment which is other than their biological family, which is to be selected, qualified, approved, and supervised for providing care to children.

Several new offences committed against children, which are so far not adequately covered under any other law, are included in the act. These include sale and procurement of children for any purpose including illegal adoption, corporal punishment in child care institutions, use of children by militant groups, offences against disabled children, and kidnapping and abduction of children.

Under Section 15 of the JJ Act, 2015, special provisions have been introduced regarding punishment of child offenders committing heinous offences in the age group of 16–18 years. The act further states:

> The Children's Court shall ensure that the child who is found to be in conflict with law is sent to a place of safety till he attains the age of twenty-one years and thereafter, the person shall be transferred to a jail, provided that the reformative services including educational services, skill development, alternative therapy such as counselling, behaviour modification therapy, and psychiatric support shall be provided to the child during the period of his stay in the place of safety.

Regarding place of safety, they are non-existent in several states. The essence of the Juvenile Justice law is reformation of the child who has committed an offence but the provision of treating the child in conflict with law who is between 16–18 years with harsher punishment goes against the spirit of the law. Societies that inflict violence on children also experience violence by children. This law has the potential for misuse by the framing of false cases against most vulnerable children, especially where they are involved in elopement/consensual sex. Children living in conflict areas would be the worst affected.

The definition of children in need of care and protection has been expanded in the 2015 Act. Street children must be considered as children in need of care and protection and must not be treated as 'criminals' or children in conflict with the law.

The UNCRC recognizes the right of every child alleged as, accused of, or recognized as having infringed the penal law to be treated in a manner consistent with the promotion of the child's sense of dignity and worth, so as to reinforce the child's respect for human rights and fundamental freedoms of others, taking into account the age of the child and the desirability of promoting his or her social reintegration, and his or her assumption of a constructive role in society.[69] The UNCRC encourages the establishment of a separate justice system specifically applicable to children;[70] anticipates measures to deal with the child without resorting to judicial proceedings, provided that human rights and legal safeguards are fully respected;[71] and foresees a variety of dispositions to ensure that children are dealt with in a manner appropriate to their well-being and proportionate both to their circumstances and to the offence.[72]

Currently, 'criminal retributive' justice in the Indian juvenile justice system has come to be seen as the only response to violent crimes by juvenile offenders. In 1985, the Beijing rules stated that consideration shall be given, wherever appropriate, to dealing with juvenile offenders without resorting to formal trial by the competent authority.[73] These rules became a legal obligation, vide Article 40, para 3(b), for all state parties who had ratified the UNCRC. They shall, whenever appropriate and desirable, take measures for dealing with juvenile offenders without resorting to judicial proceedings, with the important condition that human rights and legal safeguards are fully protected.[74] This diversion is meant to avoid the child being dealt with and sentenced by the juvenile court. One of the orders under the JJ Act is community service. But its implementation is a challenge. There are no guidelines for it. The implementation of diversion requires a well-trained service, such as probation or social service, as well as rules relating to responsibilities of these services. In the Netherlands, of all the cases of alleged offences by children, 40 per cent are diverted by police and from the remaining 60 per cent, two-thirds are diverted by the prosecutor; and ultimately only 20 per cent of all juvenile offenders are dealt with by the juvenile court.[75]

Restorative justice processes have emerged in different parts of the world as a framework that responds to the victims' need to be heard and healed. Restorative justice means that justice should be done by restoring/repairing the damaged relationship between the offender and the victim and/or community. It acknowledges the role of the community in the justice process. Restorative justice involves victims, offenders, and community members in an effort to put things right. The primary objective of restorative justice is to attend to victim's needs, thereby making the offender responsible for repairing harm.

There is a need for development and implementation of diversion and restorative justice in the Indian juvenile justice system. A strategy or policy needs to be developed for incorporating these processes. Legislation needs to clearly provide law enforcement, judiciary, and prosecutors with options for diverting children away from the criminal justice system. Standard operating procedures (SOP) and guidelines must be developed for its implementation.

[69] UNCRC, Article 40(1).

[70] UNCRC, Article 40(3).

[71] UNCRC, Article 40(3)(b).

[72] UNCRC, Article 40(4).

[73] United Nations Standard Minimum Rules for the Administration of Juvenile Justice (Beijing Rules), 1985, Rule 11.1.

[74] Jaap E. Doek, 'Understanding Diversion and Restorative Justice: Setting the Context', International Colloquium on Juvenile Justice, New Delhi, 16–18 March 2013.

[75] Doek, 'Understanding Diversion and Restorative Justice'.

Non-institutionalization

The traditional approach of custodial care in an institution is undergoing a change and all child welfare activities must try and ensure that the physical, social, emotional, and educational needs of the child are met in a secure, nurturing, family environment. On 5 February 2016, the Supreme Court of India sent a notice to the Secretary, MWCD, Government of India, returnable on 14 March 2016. The purpose of issuance of the notice to the Ministry was to require a manual to be prepared by the Ministry, that will take into consideration the living conditions and other issues pertaining to juveniles who are in Observation Homes or Special Homes or Places of Safety in terms of the JJ Act, 2015.[76] A Model Prison Manual is necessary for children's institutions in India. This Manual is a detailed document that deals with a variety of issues including custodial management, medical care, education of prisoners, vocational training and skill development programmes, legal aid, welfare of prisoners, after care and rehabilitation, Board of Visitors, prison computerization, and so on and so forth. It is a composite document that needs to be implemented in all homes under the juvenile justice system.[77]

The emphasis in the future should be on non-institutionalization and improving the quality of childcare in residential institutions, ensuring participation of children and simultaneously developing family-based alternatives. There should be a genuine attempt to develop a consolidated and comprehensive package of the various schemes and grants of the various ministries to develop non-institutional services and prevent institutionalization, so that more and more children are rehabilitated through family-based alternatives. The family should be strengthened as a unit to prevent family disintegration and institutionalization of the child. The right to family and home should include the right to shelter.

Organizations working with children in need of care and protection and with families at risk should expand their activities to initiate preventive, community-based, family-oriented, non-institutional services for the vulnerable child. There should be uniform social and legal practices for governing adoption throughout the country. A uniform law on adoption needs to be secured so that the children of all religious communities can be adopted.

Child Trafficking

During 2002 and 2012, the National Crime Records Bureau (NCRB) data shows an increase in instances of child trafficking for the crimes of 'procuration of minor girls', 'importation of girls from foreign country', 'selling of girls for prostitution', and 'buying of girls for prostitution'. Cases under these crime heads collectively increased from 214 to 991 in the period.[78] Child trafficking could be for reasons including sexual exploitation, forced labour, child labour, camel jockeying, marriage, begging, illegal adoptions, and child soldiers. Children who go missing may be trafficked, exploited, and abused for various purposes, from camel jockeys in the Gulf countries to victims of organ trade and even grotesque cannibalism, as reported at Nithari village in Noida. All forms of

---

[76] 'Re—Inhuman Conditions in 1382 Prisons', in the Supreme Court of India Civil Original Jurisdiction Writ Petition (CIVIL) no. 406/2013.

[77] 'Re—Inhuman Conditions in 1382 Prisons'.

[78] NCRB, 'Crime Statistics 2000–2012'.

trafficking must be prohibited and prevented. India has ratified the United Nations Convention against Transnational Organised Crime, 2000 in 2011.[79] Supplementing this is the UN Protocol to Prevent, Suppress and Punish Trafficking in Persons, Especially Women and Children, 2000 (Trafficking Protocol).[80] Article 9 of the Trafficking Protocol deals with prevention of trafficking in persons. It requires state parties to establish comprehensive programmes and other measures to not only prevent trafficking, but also protect victims of trafficking from re-victimization.[81] India needs to amend the laws to include the prevention aspect. Even the Immoral Traffick (Prevention) Act (ITPA), 1986 does not include the prevention provisions. Some prevention is done in ITPA through closure of brothels and sealing of premises.[82] The ITPA mostly deals with rescue[83] and repatriation,[84] without assessing and addressing the concerns of prevention and re-trafficking.

[79] *United Nations Convention against Transnational Organized Crime*, New York, 15 November 2000, ratified by India on 5 May 2011.

[80] *Protocol to Prevent, Suppress and Punish Trafficking in Persons, Especially Women and Children.*

[81] Trafficking Protocol, Article 9: Prevention of trafficking in persons—

(1)   States parties shall establish comprehensive policies, programmes and other measures:

    (a)   to prevent and combat trafficking in persons; and

    (b)   to protect victims of trafficking in persons, especially women and children, from revictimization.

(2)   States parties shall endeavour to undertake measures such as research, information and mass media campaigns and social and economic initiatives to prevent and combat trafficking in persons.

(3)   Policies, programmes and other measures established in accordance with this article shall, as appropriate, include cooperation with non-governmental organizations, other relevant organizations and other elements of civil society.

(4)   States parties shall take or strengthen measures, including through bilateral or multilateral cooperation, to alleviate the factors that make persons, especially women and children, vulnerable to trafficking, such as poverty, underdevelopment and lack of equal opportunity.

(5)   States parties shall adopt or strengthen legislative or other measures, such as educational, social or cultural measures, including through bilateral and multilateral cooperation, to discourage the demand that fosters all forms of exploitation of persons, especially women and children, that leads to trafficking.

[82] Trafficking Protocol, Article 9.

[83] The ITPA, Section 18: Closure of brothel and eviction of offenders from the premises—(1) A magistrate may, on receipt of information from the police or otherwise, that any house, room, place or any portion thereof within a distance of two hundred metres of any public place referred to in Subsection (1) of Section 7 is being run or used as a brothel by any person, or is being used by prostitutes for carrying on their trade, issue notice on the owner, lessor or landlord or such house, room, place or portion or the agent of the owner, lessor or landlord or on the tenant, lessee, occupier of, or any other person in charge of such house, room, place, or portion, to show cause within seven days of the receipt of the notice why the same should not be attached for improper use thereof, and if, after hearing the person concerned, the magistrate is satisfied that the house, room, place or portion is being used as a brothel or for carrying on prostitution, then the magistrate may pass orders,—(a) directing eviction of the occupier within seven days of the passing of the order from the house, room, place, or portion.

[84] The ITPA, Section 16: Rescue of person—

(1)   Where a magistrate has reason to believe from information received from the police or from any other person authorized by state government in this behalf or otherwise, that any person is living, or is carrying, or is being made to carry on, prostitution in a brothel, he may direct a police officer not below

The ITPA needs to be amended in these aspects to bring it to the international standards of the instruments ratified by India. The ITPA, Indian Penal Code (IPC), and other anti-trafficking laws must be comprehensive enough to cover all offences listed in the Optional Protocol to the UNCRC.[85] Child Welfare Committees under the JJ Act play an important role in child trafficking. They must be trained, empowered, and provided resources to deal with such issues. At least some members of the CWCs must be full-time members.

The issue of child trafficking is linked with missing children. Registration of a First Information Report (FIR) in cases of missing children is now mandatory, by virtue of the judgment of the Hon'ble Supreme Court in *Bachpan Bachao Andolan* v. *Union of India*.[86] Thus, any complaint of a missing child must be forthwith registered as an FIR (under Section 154 CrPC),[87] with the initial presumption of either abduction or trafficking of the child (unless, the same is proved otherwise in the investigation).

In its judgment dated 13 January 2015 and 20 February 2015, directed that Standard Operating Procedures on Missing Children be formulated.[88] The SOP encompasses detailed procedures for state and non-state individuals and institutions involved in tracing, tracking, and rehabilitating missing/found/traced children. The SOP determines specific roles and responsibilities of primary stakeholders responsible for investigation, tracing, rehabilitation, and preventive work. This includes the police, CWCs, the JJB, district child protection unit within the ICPS,[89]

---

the rank of a sub-inspector to enter such brothel, and to remove therefrom such person and produce her before him.

(2) The police officer, after removing the person shall forthwith produce her before the magistrate issuing the order.

85 ITPA, Section 16.

86 W.P. (Civil) No. 75 of 2012 (10 May 2013).

87 CrPC, Section 154: Information in cognizable cases—

(1) Every information relating to the commission of a cognizable offence, if given orally to an officer in charge of a police station, shall be reduced to writing by him or under his direction, and be read over to the informant; and every such information, whether given in writing or reduced to writing as aforesaid, shall be signed by the person giving it, and the substance thereof shall be entered in a book to be kept by such officer in such form as the state government may prescribe in this behalf.

(2) A copy of the information as recorded under Subsection (1) shall be given forthwith, free of cost, to the informant.

(3) Any person aggrieved by a refusal on the part of an officer in charge of a police station to record the information referred to in Subsection (1) may send the substance of such information, in writing and by post, to the superintendent of police concerned who, if satisfied that such information discloses the commission of a cognizable offence, shall either investigate the case himself or direct an investigation to be made by any police officer subordinate to him, in the manner provided by this code, and such officer shall have all the powers of an officer in charge of the police station in relation to that offence.

88 'Model Standard Operating Procedures on Missing Children', submitted by the Tata Institute of Social Sciences to the Supreme Court, 10 April 2015 (unpublished).

89 The ICPS, a flagship scheme of the Government of India, aims to strengthen existing systems, structures, and services to address present situations of children facing violence, exploitation, abuse, and neglect, as well as create preventive mechanisms to avoid possible scenarios of vulnerability. The scheme also envisages creating a safety network for children at all levels—state, local, district, and the village level. The

and other stakeholders. According to the SOP, the investigating officer in each case of missing children must ensure that the data available in each missing children's file, details of efforts made, and progress in the case should be uploaded weekly on the computer maintained at the police station and linked to www.trackthemissingchild.gov.in.[90] This information should also be provided to the parents/guardians, upon request, at the police station. Even for found/traced children, all relevant angles should be examined, such as the involvement of organized gangs, application of provisions of the Bonded Labour Act, ITPA, and such other relevant acts while investigating a case. Whenever an organized gang is found involved, the matter shall be referred to Anti Human Trafficking Units (AHTU)/Special Task Forces (STF)/Crime Investigation Department (CID) for further investigation and to ensure prosecution of the offenders.[91] The SOP, if implemented properly, will be immensely helpful in tracking missing children and preventing their trafficking and exploitation.

Rehabilitation is very important to children rescued from the trade. A more critical area is the formulation of a well-thought-out policy that would clearly focus on prevention of child trafficking for exploitation. The problem of child prostitution has to be addressed not merely through rehabilitation but with greater emphasis on prevention. There are backward villages and districts that are the source areas for traffickers. The brothels in the cities are a symptom of that problem. NGOs working towards rural development should target such poor families that are forced to send their children to earn. The poverty alleviation and development programmes should target such families that are at risk.[92] It is necessary that integration be established between various agencies, NGOs at the grass roots, and state-/city-level NGO networks to ensure a substantial impact on the problems of children in prostitution.

There is a need for development of bilateral and interstate control and reintegration and advocacy programmes to prevent the exploitation of children in forced prostitution and trafficking. Immediate steps should be taken to enforce extraterritorial laws and initiate appropriate action to ensure that no offending foreign tourist escapes punishment by leaving the country. Appropriate legislation should be immediately initiated to make sexual abuse and commercial sexual exploitation of children a very serious crime and to impose very severe and deterrent punishment on the offenders, both Indian and foreign. The laws should be gender-neutral and ensure that procedures are simplified and child-friendly, and responses are appropriate, timely, and sensitive to victims. There should be victim support services to protect the victims from

---

emphasis of ICPS is on building strong inter-sectoral linkages and the critical role of the state towards the fulfilment of the same.

[90] TrackChild is a national portal developed by the Ministry of Women and Child, Government of India which not only has data on 'missing' children but also has a live database to monitor the progress of the 'found' children who are availing various services in different Child Care Institutions (CCIs) under the ICPS and the JJ Act. It facilitates data entry and matching of missing and found children, and also enables follow-up of the progress of children who are beneficiaries of the ICPS.

[91] AHTU/STF/CID.

[92] Gerry Pinto, 'Agenda for the NGOs', presentation at the National Consultation on Child Prostitution, 18–20 November 1995, New Delhi, organized by the Young Men's Christian Association (YMCA), End Child Prostitution and Trafficking (ECPAT), and UNICEF.

discrimination and reprisals and also to protect those who expose violations and vigorously pursue enforcement. A mechanism to monitor implementation and enforcement should be laid down. In case of sex tourism, extradition and other arrangements must be promoted to ensure that a person who exploits a child for sexual purposes in another country (the destination country) is prosecuted either in the country of origin or in the destination country. There should be a provision for confiscation or seizure of assets and profits and other sanctions against those who commit sexual crimes against children in destination countries. Relevant data should be shared among different countries.

Custody and Guardianship

The trauma of the child has to be taken into consideration in custody battles between parents. It is absolutely necessary that experienced and able judges preside over custody and guardianship disputes. They should be trained in handling such sensitive matters and be child friendly. Beside the judges, the other staff and personnel of the courts should also be sensitized to be child friendly.

Legal custody gives a parent the right to make medical, educational, and religious decisions for their children, and to give consent for a minor child to marry or enter the armed services. Joint legal custody means that both parents share these decisions. Parents who agree to joint custody generally continue to play a full and active role in providing a sound social, economic, educational, and moral environment for their children. Joint legal custody means that both parents have the responsibility for raising the children and carrying out the tasks of guiding, disciplining, supporting, and caring for the children. Joint custody can allow parents to provide individual guidance to their children while collaborating on child rearing skills. Both parents will care for their children at separate times. Joint custody encourages parents to be consistent in managing daily routines and activities. The Supreme Court recently held that there should not be automatic presumption that the mother alone is preferred to retain custody and such generalization is not in the welfare of the child. It was suggested that the family court judges have to be trained so that they can decide on the importance of shared parenting as a necessary option when both the parents are in position to take care and live in the same city. 'Shared parenting', in legal terms, usually means there will be a 'presumption' that when the parents separate, children should spend an equal or nearly equal amount of time with both parents—a 50-50 split. This aspect needs to be included and practical hurdles in implementation considered and addressed.

Therefore, changes are required in the substantive law of guardianship and custody, non-adversarial dispute resolution processes, and the law on child abduction. In relation to guardianship and custody, there should be a statutory checklist of factors to assist the judge in determining custody disputes, and to ensure that the child's best interests are of paramount consideration. The custody orders ought to include 'residence', 'contact', 'specific issue', and 'prohibited steps' orders, which will focus more on practical arrangements for the child. The child's views should be obtained in all guardianship and custody disputes. In respect of dispute resolution, priority listing of custody cases and a Case Management Practice Direction should be given by the court to encourage efforts to resolve disputes at an early stage. Children must be separately represented in any proceedings affecting them. There must be a representative of the child to represent the child's views and interest. The best interest of the child must always be the primary consideration and must be spelt out in the orders.

Law on Child Abduction

The number of cases of either the father or the mother abducting the child and fleeing the country of stay are increasing. India must sign the Hague Convention on International Child Abduction 1980[93] and also legislate on it. The multilateral treaty provides for an expeditious method to return a child taken from one member-nation to another. It seeks to protect children internationally from the harmful effects of their removal or retention and to establish procedures to ensure their prompt return to the state of their habitual residence, as well as to secure protection for the rights of access.

Amendment to the Prohibition of Child Marriage Act, 2006

The enforcement of this law should be taken up on a priority scale. Medical and community facilities are to be provided to help children and their families. Emphasis should be placed on family-based and community-based rehabilitation rather than state institutionalization. Child marriages are prejudicial to the developmental needs of very young parents and their children. A change in the legal value system on the age of marriage must also be reflected in the age for expression of sexual consent in the laws regulating rape and other sexual offences.[94] This will require reform in the penal codes as well. The following amendments are required in the PCMA:

- Uniform age of marriage of 18 years for both boys and girls.
- A dedicated cadre of officers exclusively dealing with prohibition and prevention and enforcing the PCMA, along with the child protection committees.
- Establishing Child Protection Committees along with the Child Marriage Prohibition Officers (CMPO) and civil society groups to empower community groups to play a key role in preventing and prosecuting child marriages.
- The PCMA, which is the national law against child marriage, does not allow the question of consent in case of minors and treats child marriage as a punishable offence. However, there is some confusion in the act since it declares some marriages void and some others voidable.
- Marriage of a minor solemnized by use of force, fraud, deception, enticement, selling and buying or trafficking, is deemed a void marriage, while all other child marriages are voidable at the option of the parties to the marriage, and hence valid marriages, until they are nullified by the court.
- If the law does not attribute consent to a child, it must render all child marriages void, as all child marriages then become marriages that have taken place either through some form of coercion or use of fraud, trafficking, and such other illegal means, or by influencing the mind of the child.
- There is need for a National law to ensure compulsory registration of marriages.
- Birth certificates are most authentic documents of identity, hence 100 per cent birth registration should be ensured, along with ensuring that birth registration necessarily leads to

---

[93] Hague Convention on the Civil Aspects of International Child Abduction, 25 October 1980, T.I.A.S. No. 11, 670, 1343 U.N.T.S. 89.

[94] Goonesekere, *Children, Law and Justice.*

possession of a birth certificate also. This alone can help people access benefits of the existing programmes and schemes without hindrance, and will also go a long way in ensuring people their other fundamental rights. The Registration of Births and Deaths (Amendment) Bill, 2012 was introduced in the Rajya Sabha on 7 May 2012, after a series of efforts being made since 2007 primarily to include the registration of marriages within its purview. This bill needs to be pursued and passed.

- Child brides and grooms to should be treated as children in need of care and protection.
- Special Juvenile Police Units, mandated under the JJ Act, 2000 are meant to be created to engage with children who need care and protection under this law. The functions of a Unit are also important in preventing child marriages. They are specifically trained and created to deal with children in need of care and protection. They should coordinate with the regular police and make sure that children rescued from child marriages are taken to the CWC or Judicial Magistrate of First Class, as the case may be.
- Members of the village panchayats should be educated to secure the help of the prohibition officer in cases involving child marriages. Such grams sabhas (village councils) should be targeted and made accountable where there is evidence that child marriages are rampant.
- It is important to create child helpline centres across various levels where it the need for child protection is felt.
- Under Section 366 of the IPC, kidnapping/abduction of a woman to compel her into marriage or for illicit intercourse and use of criminal intimidation or any other method of compulsion is a punishable offence. Section 496 makes going through the marriage ceremony with fraudulent intention a punishable offence. With an amendment to the criminal law in April 2013, Section 370 of the IPC now contains specific provisions to deal with human trafficking for purposes of sexual exploitation, slavery, and servitude. This provision can be used to book a case of trafficking for marriage also, though marriage is not mentioned in it explicitly.
- The PCMA seeks to prohibit the solemnization of marriages of girl below the age of 18 years and boys below the age of 21 years. The act prescribes penalties for the solemnization, promotion, and allowing of child marriages. A male above 18 years of age can be punished under the act for contracting a marriage with a girl under 18 years. The act is, however, silent on sexual relations in a child marriage. It extends legitimacy to children born of child marriages, thus indirectly acknowledging sexual intercourse within a child marriage. Under the IPC, sexual intercourse by a man with his wife above 15 years of age is an exception to rape. The Criminal Law Amendment Act, 2013 (CLA Act) raised the age of consent to 18 years but did not disturb this exception. Sexual intercourse with a wife above 15 years of age and below 18 years of age will not amount to rape under the IPC. The POCSO Act was enacted to protect children from offences of sexual assault, sexual harassment, and pornography and to provide a child-friendly system for the trial of these offences. Under the POCSO Act, the term 'child' has been defined to mean 'any person below the age of eighteen years'. The act does not recognize sexual autonomy of children in any form. Children can also be held liable for committing sexual offences under the act. As a result, sexual interactions or intimacies among or with children below the age of 18 years constitute an offence. These contradictions in the various laws need to be addressed .
- The IPC provides for a marital rape exception which states that '[s]exual intercourse or sexual acts by a man with his own wife, the wife not being under fifteen years of age, is not rape'. No such exception has been grafted into the POCSO Act, under which an act of sexual intercourse

with a person under 18 is an offence irrespective of the gender or age of the victim or the accused. The offence of marital rape must be recognized and included in the IPC.

- Further, one of the grounds of aggravated penetrative sexual assault is penetrative sexual assault by 'a relative of the child through blood or adoption or marriage or guardianship or in foster care or having a domestic relationship with a parent of the child or who is living in the same or shared household with child commits penetrative sexual assault on such child'. This is punishable with a fine and a minimum term of 10 years imprisonment, which may extend to life imprisonment. It is clear that under the POCSO Act, a spouse of a person below the age of 18 years can be prosecuted. Irrespective of whether the marriage has been contracted voluntarily, a person having sexual contact with a person under 18 years can be punished.

- It is now mandatory for those who have information about the commission of a sexual offence to report it to the local police under the POCSO Act, and information on child marriages may also be communicated and reported under mandatory reporting.

Law Reform—Protection of Children from Sexual Offences Act, 2012

The POCSO Act defines a 'child' to mean 'any person below the age of eighteen years' and raised the age of consent from 16 years under the IPC to 18 years. Under the POCSO Act, sexual activity with children below the age of 18 years has come to be treated as a crime, the question of consent has no meaning in the case of children, and even in a case of a 'valid child marriage', the boy can be penalized under the provisions of the POCSO Act.

The CLA Act of 2013, drafted after the 16 December 2012 gang rape case in Delhi, causes confusion on the question of consent and sexual activity between minors in a valid marriage. On one hand it makes consent immaterial in the case of victims of rape below the age of 18 years, on the other hand it declares sexual intercourse by a husband with his wife as statutory rape only if the wife is below the age of 15 years. When these laws were being drafted several groups had raised concerns that the age of sexual consent be lowered to 16 years so that consensual sexual activity among young people does not get criminalized. Even the fact that a child marriage is per se valid under the PCMA, and therefore sexual activity between young married couples should be not criminalized, went unheard.[95] These confusions must be removed to ensure that protections required by young people are not denied because of confusion in existing laws.

Section 42A,[96] read with the definition of child and the offences under the act, has the potential to lead to unintended consequences—the most severe of which could be the resort to child

---

[95] Enakshi Ganguly Thukral and Bharti Ali, 'Child Marriage in India: Achievements, Gaps and Challenges—Response to Questions for OHCHR Report on Preventing Child, Early and Forced Marriages for Twenty-Sixth Session of the Human Rights Council, Submission by HAQ: Centre for Child Rights', Delhi. Available at http://www.ohchr.org/Documents/Issues/Women/WRGS/ForcedMarriage/NGO/HAQCentreForChildRights1.pdfhttp://www.ohchr.org/Documents/Issues/Women/WRGS/ForcedMarriage/NGO/HAQCentreForChildRights (accessed on 29 February 2016).

[96] POCSO Act, Section 42A: Act not in derogation of any other law—The provisions of this act shall be in addition to and not in derogation of the provisions of any other law for the time being in force and, in case of any inconsistency, the provisions of this act shall have overriding effect on the provisions of any such law to the extent of its inconsistency.

marriage in order to evade criminal prosecution. Since the passing of the PCMA, a child marriage is voidable at the instance of the child who was party to the marriage. The option to annul the marriage can be exercised by a child who was a party to the marriage within 2 years of attaining majority. Section 12 of the PCMA stipulates the circumstances under which a child marriage will be void. These include being taken or enticed out of the keeping of the lawful guardian or being forced or compelled by deceitful means to go from any place. There have been a sizeable number of cases in which girls between the ages of 16 and 18 years have left their homes on their own, with a man of their choice. In such cases, it is routine for the parents of the girl to slap a case against the man alleging kidnapping from lawful guardianship, rape, and sexual assault.[97] The NCPCR Bill, 2010 proposed that any consensual sexual act that may constitute penetrative sexual assault should not be an offence when it is between two children who are both above 14 years of age and are either of the same age or the difference in age is not more than 3 years. It is imperative that the POCSO Act be amended to address this anomaly and abuse. Mandatory reporting under the act will be successful only after proper orientation and training to doctors, nurses, teachers, principals, parents, social workers, and the police.

Area for Law Reform—Separate Law for Raping Infants below 10 Years[98]

On 11 January 2016, the Supreme Court asked the Parliament to enact a separate law providing for harsh punishment to criminals raping infants and children below 10 years of age. The Supreme Court asked the Government to consider introducing a separate provision to define rape of girl children and to impose rigorous imprisonment for the offenders.[99]

Referring to the rape of a 28-month-old baby and several cases of sexual atrocities on girl children aged between 2 and 10 years, narrated in a public interest litigation (PIL) filed by Supreme Court Women Lawyers' Association (SCWLA), the Bench of Justices Dipak Misra and N.V. Ramana asked the Centre to carve out a separate offence under IPC Section 376 dealing with rape of girl children. At present, Section 376(I) covers acts of rape committed on minors who are defined as women aged below 16 years.[100]

The bench said: 'A child, though a minor, may stand in a different category. The pain visited to a child who knows nothing about sex or rape is a brutal assault.' The PIL sought castration of offenders who commit rape on girl children below the age of 10 years. Due to the sharp rise in

---

[97] 'Child Marriage and the Protection of Children from Sexual Offences Act, 2012', Centre for Child and the Law (CCL), National Law School of India University (NLSIU), 2013. This note has been prepared by Swagata Raha, with inputs from Anuroopa Giliyal from the Centre for Child and the Law, NLSIU, Banagalore, India. Available at https://www.nls.ac.in/ccl/justicetochildren/poscoact.pdf (accessed on 29 February 2016).

[98] *The Pioneer*, 'SC for Harsher Laws against Child Rape', New Delhi, 12 January 2016. Available at http://www.dailypioneer.com/todays-newspaper/sc-for-harsher-laws-against-child-rape.html (accessed on 29 February 2016).

[99] *The Pioneer*, 'SC for Harsher Laws against Child Rape'.

[100] *Supreme Court Women Lawyers Association (SCWLA)* v. *Union of India & Anr.* Writ Petition (Civil) no. 4 of 2016.

such cases, it was contended that whenever a society moves in this direction, a fear psychosis must be created in the minds of criminals in order to put a curb on such crimes.

The bench said: 'We want to make it clear that courts do not create offences or introduce punishment'. Citing the Vishaka case where the apex court had identified the crime of sexual harassment faced by women at workplace, Justice Misra said: 'The issue pertained to facet of Article 32 of Constitution where women required to be treated with dignity at workplace.[101] The present case deals with dignity of child.'

The court suggested to the centre to consider defining 'child' within the offence of sexual assault and to prescribe rigorous punishment for this category of offences. It said that a thought has to be thought of by Parliament that may think of defining child in context of rape and further prescribe rigorous imprisonment for persons accused of such acts. This area of law reform needs to be considered.

Banning of Child Pornography Sites[102]

On 26 February 2016, the Supreme Court directed the Centre to block all child pornography websites, and told the government that the excuse of technical difficulty in banning such sites would not be accepted as a ground for failure to comply with its order.[103] A Bench of Justices Dipak Misra and Shiva Kirti Singh also said people could not be allowed to watch pornography websites at public places in the name of freedom of speech and expression, and that such persons should be booked for obscenity. Expressing concern about the internet hosting multiple child pornography websites 'which are being deliberately run with perversity to make money', the Bench directed the government to sit with information technology experts to find out ways to block them. The Bench further said: 'Innocent children cannot be made prey to these kind of painful situations, and a nation, by no means, can afford to carry any kind of experiment with its children in the name of liberty and freedom of expression.' The court said what is obscene for one person could be a matter of art for another and the government had to draw a fine line. It, however, said that there could not be divergent views on child pornography and it must be banned.[104]

Children Affected and Infected by HIV/AIDS

Children affected and infected by HIV/AIDS face discrimination in education, healthcare, nutrition shelter, housing, and development. The Human Immunodeficiency Virus and Acquired Immune Deficiency Syndrome (Prevention and Control) Bill, 2014 was introduced in the Rajya Sabha on 11 February 2014. The bill sought to prevent and control the spread of HIV and AIDS, prohibited discrimination against persons with HIV and AIDS, provided for informed consent and confidentiality with regard to their treatment, placed obligations on establishments to safeguard

---

[101]   *SCWLA* v. *Union of India & Anr.*
[102]   'SC Orders Ban on Child Porn Sites, Says "Want No Excuse"', *Times of India*, Delhi, 27 February 16. Available at http://timesofindia.indiatimes.com/india/SC-orders-ban-on-child-porn-sites-says-want-no-excuse/articleshow/51162251.cms (accessed on 29 February 2016).
[103]   *Times of India*, 'SC Orders Ban'.
[104]   *Times of India*, 'SC Orders Ban'.

their rights, and created mechanisms for redressing their complaints. The bill listed the various grounds on which discrimination against HIV-positive persons and those living with them is prohibited, which included denial, termination, discontinuation, or unfair treatment with regard to (i) employment, (ii) educational establishments, (iii) healthcare services, (iv) residing or renting property, (v) standing for public or private office, and (vi) provision of insurance (unless based on actuarial studies). The requirement for HIV testing as a pre-requisite for obtaining employment or accessing healthcare or education is also prohibited. Every HIV infected or affected person below the age of 18 years had the right to reside in a shared household and enjoy the facilities of the household. The bill also prohibited any individual from publishing information or advocating feelings of hatred against HIV-positive persons and those living with them.[105] This bill has lapsed, but there is a need for a law to protect child rights with a child rights approach.

Also, HIV/AIDS should be included in Reproductive Child Health Programmes. Rehabilitation options should be worked out through child-centred policies, special support programmes, and placement of affected children in adoptive homes and acceptance by children's homes. Further, HIV/AIDS should be viewed in the context of total quality of health, education, care, and support services.

Children with Disabilities

More institutions should be set up and the capacity increased in the existing institutions for the education and rehabilitation of children with disabilities and to improve access to services for those children living in homes and rural areas. Awareness campaigns which focus on prevention, inclusive of education, family care, and promotion of the rights of children with disabilities, need to be undertaken. The carers who have to look after disabled children should be given special assistance in terms of financial support and their right to education and employment. Education, vocational training, and capacity building of children with disabilities must be undertaken. The Sarva Shiksha Abhiyan must be expanded to cover education of children with disabilities. Teachers, principals, parents, and children themselves must be sensitized to the rights of disabled children.

In 2001, while deliberating on the Right to Food case, the Supreme Court of India declared the Integrated Child Development Services Scheme[106] (ICDS) to be a legal entitlement of children of India in the 0–6 age group. It has given orders for the universalization of the ICDS.[107] Unfortunately, in practice, this right relating to childhood malnutrition is not designed to include children with disabilities in all their activities. If this issue is clarified or suitably modified and linked to Ministry of Social Justice, it could act as a preventive measure

[105] The Human Immunodeficiency Virus and Acquired Immune Deficiency Syndrome (Prevention and Control) Bill, 2014. Available at http://www.prsindia.org/billtrack/the-human-immunodeficiency-virus-and-acquired-immune-deficiency-syndrome-prevention-and-control-bill-2014-3126/ (accessed on 29 February 2016).

[106] *People's Union for Civil Liberties (PUCL)* v. *Union of India & Ors.*, Civil Original Jurisdiction at the Supreme Court of India, Writ Petition (Civil) No. 196 of 2001.

[107] Yamini Jaishankar and Jean Drèze, *Supreme Court Orders on the Right to Food: A Tool for Action*, 2005, order dated 28 November 2001, on page 19. Available at http://www.righttofoodindia.org/data/scordersprimeratoolforaction.pdf (accessed on 29 February 2016).

for children with disabilities by providing early intervention services, including nutrition to children with disabilities, at a time when they need it the most. There are several schemes for children with disabilities from the Ministry of Social Justice, Government of India, but there is lack of awareness and accessibility of these schemes. Getting a disability certificate to avail these schemes is also a cumbersome process.

The RTE Act applies to all children in India, including disabled children. The Persons with Disabilities (Equal Opportunities, Protection of Rights and Full Participation) Act (PWD Act), 1995 legitimizes a whole range of educational options, including non-formal options, for children with disabilities. But in practice, there are barriers to inclusive education for disabled children. The teachers, principals, staff, students, and parents all need to be oriented to accept inclusive education. There is further confusion since two Ministries deal with disabled children's education—the Ministry of Social Justice and the Ministry of Human Resource Development. There is a need for coordination between these two ministries.

The Rights of Persons with Disabilities Bill (RPwD) was passed in both the Rajya Sabha and Lok Sabha on December 16 2016. This new Act replaces the now redundant 1995 law based on a medical model. Disability has been defined based on an evolving and dynamic concept. The types of disabilities have been increased from existing 7 to 21 and the Central Government will have the power to add more types of disabilities. Speech and Language Disability and Specific Learning Disability have been added for the first time. Acid Attack Victims have been included. Dwarfism, muscular dystrophy have has been indicated as separate class of specified disability. The New categories of disabilities also included three blood disorders, Thalassemia, Hemophilia and Sickle Cell disease. Additional benefits such as reservation in higher education, government jobs, reservation in allocation of land, poverty alleviation schemes etc. have been provided for persons with benchmark disabilities and those with high support needs.. Every child with benchmark disability between the age group of 6 and 18 years shall have the right to free education. Government funded educational institutions as well as the government recognized institutions will have to provide inclusive education to the children with disabilities. Reservation in vacancies in government establishments has been increased from 3% to 4% for certain persons or class of persons with benchmark disability. The 2016 Act provides for grant of guardianship by District Court under which there will be joint decision—making between the guardian and the persons with disabilities.There is a creation of National and State Fund to provide financial support to the persons with disabilities. Special Courts will be designated in each district to handle cases concerning violation of rights of PwDs. It also strengthens the office of chief commissioner and state commissioners for Persons with Disabilities which will act as regulatory bodies. Section 3(3) allowing discrimination against a disabled person if it is "a proportionate means of achieving a legitimate aim' needs to clearly specify that no person with disability shall be discriminated on the grounds of disability. The 2016 Act highlighting the social security needs of the disabled. It states that the government will help the disabled by providing aids and appliances, disability pensions, allowances for care givers and a comprehensive insurance scheme. But that instead of allocating a specific amount for this, the proposed law says "the appropriate government shall within the limits of it's economic capacity and development" fund such schemes. This provision may help governments to escape this responsibility. The increase in job reservation needs to be more and even the private sector must be made liable.

National Right to Food Security Act, 2013

Right to food is a human right and means access to adequate food at all times with dignity. Both Articles 25 and 27 of the UNCRC include the right of children to food and nutrition. Article 25 of the UNCRC recognizes the right of children to the highest attainable standard of health and Article 27 recognizes the right to a adequate standard of living. The Constitution of India, in Article 39(f), directs the right to equal opportunities and facilities to develop in a healthy manner and in conditions of freedom and dignity and guaranteed protection of childhood and youth against exploitation and against moral and material abandonment.[108] Article 47 of the Constitution of India, dealing with right to nutrition and standard of living and improved public health, is also applicable to children.[109]

India has a large number of children suffering from under-nutrition. In 2013, the government of India put in place a massive food safety net program. Beginning as an ordinance passed in July and then as an act of Parliament in September, the National Food Security Act seeks, according to its preamble, to 'provide for food and nutritional security ... by ensuring access to adequate quantity of quality food at affordable prices to people'.[110] Although the act has created several mechanisms to reduce leakage and ensure effective monitoring, it remains to be seen how transparent and cost-effective the proposed institutional frameworks will be. Along with this, the state and central governments of India to experiment with other mechanisms (such as direct cash transfers or food stamps, wherever appropriate).[111]

India has been slow to implement the World Health Organization's International Code of Marketing of Breastmilk Substitutes. The Essential Newborn Care programme has been implemented nationwide, which provided that trained midwives or health workers as well as appropriate equipment were present at every birth in a health institution.

Special Newborn Care clinics have been established. Efforts were ongoing to improve maternal and post-maternal care and reduce the maternal mortality rate.[112]

---

[108] Constitution of India, Article 39(f): Certain principles of policy to be followed by the state—The state shall, in particular, direct its policy towards securing: (f) that children are given opportunities and facilities to develop in a healthy manner and in conditions of freedom and dignity and that childhood and youth are protected against exploitation and against moral and material abandonment.

[109] Constitution of India, Article 47: Duty of the state to raise the level of nutrition and the standard of living and to improve public health—The state shall regard the raising of the level of nutrition and the standard of living of its people and the improvement of public health as among its primary duties and, in particular, the state shall endeavour to bring about prohibition of the consumption except for medicinal purposes of intoxicating drinks and of drugs which are injurious to health.

[110] Avinash Kishore, Pramod Kumar Joshi, and John F. Hoddinott, 'India's Right to Food Act: A Novel Approach to Food Security', *2013 Global Food Policy Report*, eds Andrew Marble and Heidi Fritschel (Washington, D.C.: International Food Policy Research Institute [IFPRI], 2014), Chapter 3, pp. 29–42. Available at http://ebrary.ifpri.org/cdm/ref/collection/p15738coll2/id/128046 (accessed on 29 February 2016).

[111] Kishore, Joshi, and Hoddinott, 'India's Right to Food Act'.

[112] 'Committee on Rights of Child Examines Reports of India under the Convention and Protocols on Children in Armed Conflict, Sale of Children'. Available at http://www.ohchr.org/en/NewsEvents/Pages/DisplayNews.aspx?NewsID=14663&LangID=E#sthash.vrlsi32z.IdlL5cM1.dpuf (accessed on 29 February 2016).

In April 2001, a writ petition was filed in the Supreme Court of India by the Peoples' Union for Civil Liberties to seek legal enforcement of the Right to Food.[113] The interim orders in this case have become critical. In an interim order on 28 Novemeber 2001, the Supreme Court converted most food and employment related schemes into 'legal entitlements'. This implies that the central and state governments cannot change the schemes without the permission of the Supreme Court. The orders on universalizing access to food, especially for children—related to mid-day meals and the ICDS—have been landmarks. On 28 December 2001, the Supreme Court directed state and central governments to universalize the mid-day meals and provide hot cooked meals to all primary school children in India. The interim order also universalized the ICDS programme, making it mandatory for the government to provide supplementary nutrition and other services under ICDS to all children below six, all pregnant women, nursing mothers, and adolescent girls.

Law on Commercial Surrogacy

The ART Bill, that seeks to regulate the surrogacy industry, must be made into a law. The bill would regulate assisted reproductive technology clinics in order to prevent the misuse of reproductive technology, including surrogacy. It would also protect the best interests of the child and ensure that every child has the inherent right to lead a healthy life. Currently, as per the Supreme Court directive, India does not support commercial surrogacy.

Protection of Children from Cyber Crimes

Concerning internet security and measures to protect children from cyber-crimes, legislation is in place to prohibit cyber stalking and cyber bullying, as well as identity theft, hacking of emails, and exposure to illicit or non-appropriate online content.[114] Another piece of legislation criminalized online child pornography.[115] Internet safety tips have been issued to children, and teachers in schools have been taught cyber security.

Improving the Status of the Girl Child

A holistic approach is required in improving the girl child's overall status. Extending the reach of the health and education infrastructure—both quantitatively and qualitatively—and deploying the media wisely are essential if we are to create a climate in which girls can develop to their full potential. The ICDS network is clearly one effective response to the problem of early neglect of the girl child. Through its immunization, nutritional supplementation, and pre-school education

---

[113] *PUCL v. Union of India & Ors.*, Writ Petition (Civil) 196 of 2001. This case, popularly known as the Right to Food Case, has since become a rallying point for trade unions, activists, grass-roots organizations, and NGOs to make the right to food a justiciable right.

[114] 'Committee on Rights of Child Examines Reports of India under the Convention and Protocols on Children in Armed Conflict, Sale of Children'. Available at http://www.ohchr.org/en/NewsEvents/Pages/DisplayNews.aspx?NewsID=14663&LangID=E#sthash.vrlsi32z.IdlL5cM1.dpuf (accessed on 29 February 2016).

[115] 'Committee on Rights of Child Examines Reports of India'.

components, it can offset the discrimination a girl faces at home and can lay the foundation for healthy physical and mental development. It is also necessary to enlarge the scope of the ICDS to address the needs of the children in the 6–14 years age group. This is an important period in a girl's life when major biological, psychological, and social changes take place and the girl child is seriously affected by the absence of suitable legislative protection. The girl child has hardly any time to play or to be a child. She requires freedom from domestic drudgery and in many cases freedom from the tyranny of her family. She requires both physical and mental solace to grow. Laws must be enacted to ensure provision of crèches and *balwadi*s in the countryside where women work on land. Medical services and welfare services must be expanded. As with the right to be born, their right to remain alive can only be enforced if parents, family, and society at large value their daughters. There must be effective implementation of the PCPNDT Act so as to prevent sex-selective abortions and strengthen regulatory mechanisms.

Early Childhood Care

The Law Commission of India, in its 259th report titled *Early Childhood Development and Legal Entitlements*, highlights the issues relating to the rights of children under the age of 6 years. The Commission proposes that if the child receives favourable environmental inputs of health, nutrition, learning, and psychosocial development, the chances of the child's brain developing to its full potential are considerably enhanced. It has further proposed that the Maternity Benefits Act, 1961 be amended in consonance with the forward-looking provisions in the Central Civil Services (Leave) Rules, 1972, whereby maternity benefits should be increased from 12 weeks to 180 days. This should be made obligatory on the state and not left to the will of the employers and should cover all women, including women working in the unorganized sector. The provision for unconditional right to crèches and day care has also been made the responsibility of the state and not the employer. Furthermore, the Commission has advocated the formulation of policy guidelines laying down minimum specifications of paid maternity leave to women employed in the private sector. Three Constitutional amendments have been recommended by the Law Commission of India (LCI). The LCI has suggested the insertion of a new Article, 24A, to Part III of the Constitution of India, to ensure that the child's right to basic care and assistance becomes an enforceable right. LCI has also suggested an amendment to Article 21A of the Constitution of India, which deals with the Right to Education. Lastly, the fundamental duty of the parent or the guardian to provide education has been recommended to be extended to children between the ages of six and 14, by amending Article 51A(k).[116]

The Government of India has firmed up plans to increase the maternity leave for working women from the existing 12 weeks to 26 weeks. Besides, there are plans to provide for 12 weeks of maternity leave to commissioning mothers who use surrogates to bear a child as well as to working women adopting a baby below the age of 3 months.[117]

---

[116] '259th Report of the Law Commission of India'. Available at http://www.livelaw.in/law-commission-of-india-suggest-to-make-right-to-childhood-care-a-fundamental-right/ (accessed on 29 February 2016).

[117] 'Govt Plans to Increase Maternity Leave to 26 Weeks', *Live Mint*, 6 March 2016. Available at http://www.livemint.com/Politics/T8WypxXXCcPyLHZDE3jo2H/Govt-plans-to-increase-maternity-leave-to-26-weeks.html (accessed on 29 February 2016).

Right to Participation

Participation of children has been described as the present-day 'buzzword'.[118] Human rights instruments on children's rights stress 'participation' as a core value along with survival, protection, and development. The concept of participation rights involves a value system on the child's personal autonomy that has to be worked out within the important relationship with the child, the parents, and the state. Participation rights require the recognition of many civil rights already incorporated into national Constitutions. Since participation rights give a new priority to constitutionally guaranteed civil rights, the UNCRC can help to strengthen the enforcement of these rights and foster the perception that children must have these rights.

These rights reflect a growing awareness of the need to listen to children's views and to facilitate their participation in decisions which affect them. In recent years, there have been significant developments in national and international policies in relation to children and young people. National laws in Norway and the United Kingdom, which also had their roots in a strong concept of parental rights, have already articulated this change in new legal concepts. Children are no longer seen merely as recipients of adult care and protection but are recognized as actors in their own lives, as individuals whose views and options should be exposed and seriously listened to. Article 12[119] of the UNCRC clearly establishes that the children have a right to be involved in decisions which affect them.

This right extends from decisions affecting them as individuals to decisions which affect them as a body. Yet, making a reality of children's participation presents an enormous challenge to society. Participation rights may be the most difficult to recognize because they can be perceived as a challenge to parental and state authority. There is now a recognition that children's participation creates a new challenge for social development.

Children who participate effectively will be aware of societal processes and their rights and responsibilities, be sensitive towards rights violations of others in the society, develop capacity to think, question, and judge, and accordingly be prepared to take action for bringing about change in the society. This will facilitate a process of empowerment of the child's mind. There should be programmes aiming at empowering children through creating awareness about children's rights and responsibilities in relation to their environment. India should develop skills-training programmes in community settings for teachers, social workers, and local officials in assisting children to make and express their informed decisions and to have these views taken into consideration.

The JJ Act and the custody laws provide for the views of the child being recognized by the courts, but the other laws must also bring in this aspect of child participation and taking the views of the child in every decision affecting them. Besides, other structures like schools, child rights commissions, and administrative bodies must also take the child's views into consideration.

Child Witness Code

Testimony from children is often essential to prove that abuse occurred, to identify the perpetrator of abuse, and to prove other crimes. Thus, children often have to testify in legal proceedings. The

---

[118] Hank Van Beers, 'A Plea for a Child-Centred Approach to Research and Street Children', *Childhood* 3, no. 2 (1996): 90–105.

[119] UNCRC, Article 12.

physical infrastructure in majority of the courtrooms in India are not designed with children in mind and the formal nature of proceedings that occur there cause fear and anxiety that interferes with some children's ability to provide full and accurate testimony. Testifying in courts is also very stressful for many children. A child witness code is required to ascertain the truth, reduce trauma to children, and create conditions that will allow children to provide reliable and complete evidence, increase the number of children who are able to testify in legal proceedings, and also to protect the rights of persons accused of crimes. This code could be based on the UN model law relating to Justice in Matters involving Child Victims and Witnesses of Crime.[120]

Representation of the Child's Interest

The child's future is at stake but his/her interests are never separately represented in Indian courts. The child's interests are considered to coincide with the parents' or as the court thinks fit, relying on the probation or welfare officer's or counsellor's report. There is a need to introduce the concept of a guardian *ad litem*, or child's legal counsel, or a child's representative, involved throughout the court proceedings in which children are involved. This is especially required as child-friendly court procedures and personnel have yet to be evolved. To protect the children best, independent child advocates must be appointed by the courts. These advocates will not only represent the children but also hear their problems and concerns, work with their families, and prepare them for the court proceedings. Because the child's own interests may be in conflict with the courts' judgment, specially trained child advocates are required to play the roles of fact finder, legal representative, case monitor, mediator, and information and resource persons.

This principle of the best interest of the child applies not only to courts but also to all decisions relating to children, including parents, local and administrative authorities, and children themselves. To determine the best interest of the child, the least detrimental solution must be found. Considerations must be weighed against each other. The best interest of the child should be a paramount consideration in anything related to the child. Today, the best principle universally applies not only in the context of legal and administrative proceedings or in other narrowly defined contexts of custody and guardianship in family law, but in relation to all actions concerning children. The National Policy for Children, 2013 states that the principle of best interest of the child must be applied.[121] Procedures and criteria must be developed to provide guidance to all relevant persons in authority in courts of law, administrative authorities and legislative bodies, public and private social welfare institutions, as well as traditional and religious leaders and the

[120] United Nations Office on Drugs and Crime, Vienna, United Nations, New York, 2009. In its resolution 2005/20 of 22 July 2005, the Economic and Social Council adopted the Guidelines on Justice in Matters involving Child Victims and Witnesses of Crime. The guidelines form part of the body of UN standards and norms in crime prevention and criminal justice, which are internationally recognized normative principles in that area, as developed by the international community since 1950. The concept of protection of child victims, as used in the Model Law, includes the protection of children not willing or not able to testify or provide information, and child suspects or perpetrators who have been victimized, intimidated, or forced to act illegally, or who have done so under duress. Available at https://www.unodc.org/documents/justice-and-prison-reform/UNODC_UNICEF_Model_Law_on_Children.pdf (accessed on 29 February 2016).

[121] Ministry of Women and Child Development, National Policy for Children (Government of India, 2013), adopted on 26 April 2013.

public at large for determining the best interests of the child in every area and for giving it due weight as a primary consideration.

Legal Aid and Services

Under Section 12(c) of the Legal Services Authorities Act, 1987, a child who has to file or defend a case shall be entitled to free legal services. Legal aid and legal literacy programmes can be used to further children's rights. These programmes need to be linked to community awareness programmes. Legal counselling could be included in these programmes. Clinical legal education programmes focusing on children's issues need to be developed in law schools. Law school curriculum should also include child rights and laws. Non-formal dispute resolutions like *Lok Adalat*s could also be used to settle disputes involving children in a manner which is informal and which has a non-adversarial environment. The *Panchayati Raj* institutions can be involved in these services. These programmes could also involve paralegal training programmes among adult social workers. Legal Services Authorities can play an important role in providing justice to the child. .They can help in providing lawyers to represent children's interests and also help in providing compensation to the children whose rights have been violated.

There is scope for NGOs to play a role as paralegal professionals in JJBs, CWCs, and to assist specific groups such as street children, child labourers, disabled children, among others.

Role of Media

The work of the media affects children's lives. It influences decisions made about them and the way in which they are regarded by the rest of the society. The media can inform the public about child rights, draw attention to violations, give children a voice, and expose shortcomings in the system, highlighting the achievements of children—their aspirations and the risks they face. The media has a responsibility to ensure that children are not inadvertently exposed while reporting on them. In the context of HIV/AIDS, this responsibility is crucial to prevent discrimination of affected children. The functions of the media should be to inform, to educate, and to entertain, in that order.

Community Participation

Protecting children is as much a part of community responsibility as that of the system. Community participation could be included in the areas of decision making, priority setting, planning, implementation, services delivery system, evaluation of programmes, consolidation of benefits of development, and sharing of financial responsibility.

Role of Non-governmental Organizations

The NGOs have significant roles and crucial tasks in the struggle for the realization of the rights of children and in elaboration and further development of the standards and rights affirmed by the national and international laws, in developing more effective implementation by monitoring resource allocation, and in child development programmes and projects by undertaking evaluation thereof, helping develop participatory, community-level structures for delivering resources and services to meet the basic needs of children. Advocacy and lobbying will also be necessary in support of proposals for law reform and setting of standards. Rights are of limited value unless they can be effectively asserted. The NGOs have an important role to ensure effective assertion of rights. The Mathura rape case, involving the rape of a girl in custody, led to the reform in rape laws. Additional tasks include critiquing national reports prepared by governments and, where appropriate, preparing alternative NGO reports on the subject. The NGOs will also have to play important roles to ensure effective assertion of the rights of the child. At the regional level, NGOs will also need to explore ways of using regional human rights machinery and instruments to address regional specificities and disparities and developing regional positions and strategies regarding issues relating to children.[122] At the international level, NGOs' vital role will include identifying specific areas for international cooperation and technical assistance to realize the rights of the child. The challenge for child rights NGOs lies in applying a participatory empowerment approach to the development of the rights of the child.

Training, Sensitization, and Capacity Building

Training, sensitization, and capacity building are an important part of the strategy to protect the rights of the child. Effective child protection and development depends on skills, knowledge, and judgment of all professionals, personnel, and staff working with children. It is important that people in direct contact with children receive training to raise their awareness of the issues and concerns of laws and rights relating to children. The various agencies involved in the childcare system, that is, the JJBs and CWCs members, lawyers , school teachers, government officials from various ministries like the Ministry of Human Resources, Development, Department of Women and Child Development, Ministries of labour, finance, social justice and empowerment, and the Planning Commission, need to be trained to protect the interests of the child. There is a necessity to train functionaries of the children's institutions, including the superintendents, the probation officers, the caretakers, cooks, teachers, and medical officers, to sensitize and humanize them. The bureaucracy needs to be sensitized. Training of law-enforcing agencies, police, judiciary, lawyers, doctors and paramedics, health workers, social workers, media, prosecutors, and NGOs is necessary. The police force needs to be trained to handle the needs of child victims, which requires awareness of law, methodologies of handling child victims, administration, and reaching out to NGOs. Border police, registration officials, visa and passport and immigration authorities should all be provided with detailed guidelines to deal with children. Railway police and authorities, including all senior government servants, and Indian Administrative Services (IAS) and Indian Police Service (IPS) officers should be sensitized for empathy building and replacing hostile attitudes. The UNCRC must be disseminated to all stakeholders including school teachers, parents, school children, and children in institutions.

---

[122] Clarence Dias, 'The Child in the Developing World: Making Child Rights a Reality', Report of the Seminar on Rights of the Child, sponsored by National Law School of India University and UNICEF, NLSIU, Bangalore, 1990.

Monitoring Bodies and Ombudsperson

Passing of orders by the courts or enacting child-friendly laws is not the end of the matter. These laws and orders have to be monitored and violators held accountable. Directions of the courts should not remain on paper as far as children are concerned. For compliance of court orders, the Mumbai High Court, in the case of *Krist Pereira* v. *State of Maharashtra and Others*,[123] constituted a permanent body called the Maharashtra State Monitoring Committee, consisting of a retired judge of the High Court, two secretaries including the Secretary of the Dapartment of Women and Child Development, and three experts in the field, out of whom two should be female members. The Committee makes appropriate recommendations to the state government for proper functioning of the juvenile justice system. In *Prerana* v. *State of Maharashtra*,[124] the court constituted a Monitoring and Guidance Committee under the Deputy Secretary, Department of Women and Child Ddevelopment, and whose members consist of representatives of NGOs specializing in different fields. The Committee has been authorized to supervise the functioning of rehabilitation home and ensure proper rehabilitation of rescued girls. This is one of the effective methods of implementing court orders. Besides, there are legislations wherein there are provisions for monitoring bodies, boards of control, and advisory bodies. These bodies should be activated and strengthened. In the case of *Mumbai Mirror* v. *Department of Women and Child, Government of Maharashtra*, the Mumbai High Court is monitoring the compliance of its directions through a High Court-appointed Coordination Committee.[125]

Another strategy is the appointment of the ombudsperson for children. Such an ombudsperson first appeared in the early 1980s in Sweden and Norway.[126] In order to really be the voice of children, the ombudsperson must be an independent body and be able to express freely his/her opinion on actions undertaken by the public administration, reprimanding—where necessary—the lack of a system. The ombudsperson should be able to promote authoritatively the best interests of children. If children are to be given valuable help, they must be clearly told whom to get in touch with and must be given the appropriate means to do so. The ombudsperson must direct the child to a kind of help tailored to meet his or her needs and then monitor the specific handling of the case and the quality of the service offered to the child. It is of utmost importance for the ombudssperson to have a direct link with the children and to become, for them, *the* ultimate point of reference.

The ombudsperson must imperatively be free from any bond and external influence, in order to keep his/her distance. There are two essentials models: a public and a private one. In the first one, the office of the ombudsperson is situated at a governmental or, even better, at a parliamentary level. In Norway and Flanders, the Parliament is accountable for the seriousness of the office; it acknowledges children as a special category of citizens and allows this function to be performed in the most democratic way. This is known as the Scandinavian model. The

---

[123] Criminal Writ Petition No. 1107 of 1996, Mumbai High Court.

[124] Criminal Writ Petition No. 1332 of 1999, Mumbai High Court.

[125] PIL 182/2010 of Mumbai High Court.

[126] Dominick Luquer and Massimo Toschi, 'New Tools for the Protection of Children in Europe: A Comparison of Experiences of National Ombudspersons for Children', *European Conference Report*, Milano, 1997.

second model is the non-governmental one, found in the Anglo-Saxon tradition. In this case, the ombudsperson's office is run by a private initiative, by NGOs acting generally through 'class actions'.[127] To begin with, the chosen model of ombudsperson needs to have an official status in order to be able to express publicly the specific issues of children and to guarantee the respect of their needs. The 'acknowledgement' is also necessary to guarantee the stable and permanent nature of this office.

Child-friendly Justice

Child-friendly justice refers to justice systems which guarantee the respect and the effective implementation of all children's rights at the highest attainable level, and give 'due consideration to the child's level of maturity and understanding the circumstances of the case'. Courts can play a very important role in promoting justice to children. Public interest litigation has been used beneficially to realize the protection rights of children. Courts have ensured the implementation of progressive laws and interpretation of restrictive laws in the best interest of the child. Courts have used innovative methods to ensure justice to the child. In the Bhiwandi remand home case in Mumbai,[128] the courts permitted the inspection of institutions and then formulated an expert committee to visit all the children's institutions in Maharashtra and submit a report.

As far as possible, children must not be involved in adversarial court proceedings. Alternate dispute resolution methods like mediation, conciliation, diversion, and restorative justice must be used. The infrastructure in the Courts must be child-friendly and in keeping with the POCSO Act and the various related Supreme Court judgments. Delhi has now become the first city in the country to have its own 'Vulnerable Witness Deposition Complex' which has been designed 'to provide protection, privacy, confidentiality and comfort to vulnerable witnesses in an in-camera atmosphere' in cases of sexual offences. Extensive guidelines have been laid down by the Supreme Court as well as the Delhi High Court in several judgments with regard to every stage of a criminal investigation as well as trials. for recording of evidence of vulnerable witnesses. In Goa, matters related to sexual abuse are dealt with in-camera so as to protect the victim from the alleged offender. The atmosphere in the court room is free and informal, the President does not wear a black coat or a gown, and advocates and police appear in civil dress. Such court rooms must be designed at other places as well.

Working Together Approach

The 250-plus legislations relating to children have to be harmonized and interlinked. For instance, the JJ Act, 2015 needs to be linked to the Probation of Offenders Act 1958, the CLPRA, the education laws, , the adoption laws, the child marriage laws, and the PWD Act. The different ministries dealing with different issues and concerns of children have to work in coordination. The ministries of labour, social justice and empowerment, finance, and human resources development

---

[127] Luquer and Toschi, 'New Tools for the Protection of Children in Europe'.

[128] *Krist Pereira* v. *State of Maharashtra and Others*, Criminal Writ Petition No. 1107/1996, *Mumbai Mirror*, 24 August 2010. *Rescue Sham* v. *The State of Maharashtra*, PIL 182/2010, Mumbai High Court.

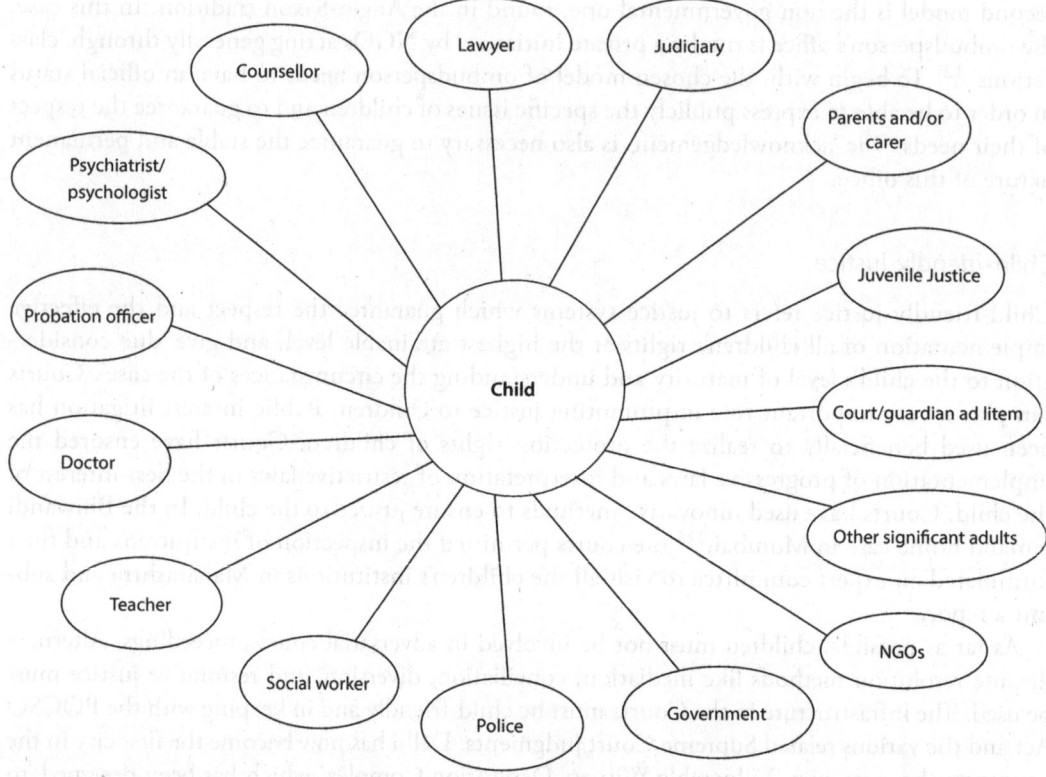

Figure 9.1   Working Together Approach[129]

deal with different legislations. None of these legislations can work in isolation. Multidisciplinary and interdisciplinary teams and partnerships have to work together. A partnership between many actors and stakeholders can work together to realize the rights of the child. The judiciary, different ministries, bureaucrats, medical professionals, agencies and NGOs, legal activists, police, teachers, lawyers, counsellors, parents, mental health professionals, and all those citizens who are concerned with the rights of the child need to have a coordinated and a partnership approach. Figure 9.1 depicts a graphic presentation of the Working Together Approach for the protection of child rights.

Ratification of International Instruments

International human rights treaties, conventions, covenants, and declarations are powerful tools to realize the rights of the child. India has ratified the UNCRC. Article 73 of the Constitution

---

[129]   Source: Compiled by the author.

of India states, 'Subject to the provisions of the Constitution, the executive power of the Union, shall extend—

- to the matters with respect to which Parliament has power to make laws; and
- to the exercise of such rights, authority and jurisdiction as are exercisable by the Government of India by virtue of any treaty or agreement. . . .'.

This power covers the conventions ratified by the country or any decision made at any international conference, association, or other body

Therefore, international conventions like the UNCRC can be enforced in Indian courts without a statute. This was clearly laid down in the case of *Mayanbhai Ishwarlal Patel* v. *Union of India*.[130] Again in the case of *Vishaka* v. *State of Rajasthan*,[131] the Supreme Court reiterated the principle that in the absence of a domestic law the contents of international conventions and norms are significant for the interpretation of fundamental rights. Any international convention not inconsistent with the fundamental rights given in the Constitution of India and in harmony with its spirit must be read into those international provisions to enlarge their meaning and content and to promote the object of the Constitutional guarantee.[132] Therefore, the provisions of the UNCRC can be enforced without a statute if they are in consonance with the fundamental rights.

India needs to ratify the ILO Convention 182on Words Forms of Child Labour 1999, the ILO Minimum Age Convention 1973, the Hague Convention on International Child Abduction, General Assembly Resolution on Early, Child and Forced Marriage,[133] and the OP3CRC.

A wide range of stakeholders and reform agents need to be brought together, including relevant actors from outside the legal, judicial, and human rights area, to jointly address issues in a strategic way. Given the diversity and the disparities in the country, perhaps regional networks or strategic alliances on specific issues may be more workable. Initiatives have to be taken by various people's organizations, community leaders, advocacy groups, child rights activists and public interest professionals, civil society, and governments working towards the goal of translating the dream of child rights into reality. Socio-eco-political-legal change cannot be sustained in isolation. Alliances have to be built with other movements for change, such as women's rights, environment, labour, housing, health, education rights, and with organizations, individuals, parents, and other civil society organizations involved in child rights issues. Interventions should be made at the level of government programmes and policy directives towards establishing an agenda to ensure the rights of the child.

Children can no longer be considered as passive recipients of services. Governments and civil society must accept children as partners and facilitate their participation in matters which affect their lives. The challenge is, therefore, to change the mindset and establish that children can no

---

130 AIR 1969 SC 783.

131 (1997) 7 SCC 323.

132 *Vishaka* v. *State of Rajasthan*, AIR 1997 SC 3011.

133 General Assembly Resolution on Early, Child and Forced Marriage (A/C.3/69/L.23), United Nations General Assembly Sixty-Ninth Session Agenda Item 65(a). Available at http://www.right-to-education.org/news/un-adopts-resolution-early-child-and-forced-marriage (accessed on 15 October 2016).

longer be objects of charity, philanthropy, and welfare. They have rights and the government, civil society, and NGOs are obliged to provide for them. There must be legislative, administrative, and judicial support to implement the policies, plans, and legislations in the interest of the child. The ideals and norms set forth in our Constitution, national laws and case laws, international conventions, regulations, policies, and practices have addressed norms and issues relating to children and have contributed considerably towards the betterment of children. We also need other means—political, psychological, managerial, economic, social, and financial—to implement the best interest of the child. Public interest litigation has been used beneficially to realize the protection of rights of children. The Supreme Court of India has, in recent years, used the directive principles of state policy so as to expand fundamental rights to include socio-economic rights.

It is now more than a quarter of century since the UNCRC has been adopted. The rights perspective has been incorporated in several laws and policies in India. What is now required is the harmonization of all child related laws with the UNCRC and other international human rights instruments and standards. Several law reform initiatives have been taken, some bills are pending, and some areas of law reform are still to be taken up. The major challenge is the implementation of child friendly-laws in their true spirit. The significance of the UNCRC is that it represents a commitment to improving the situation of children in India. Thus, it can be used by public advocates to force the government to take action on child issues. As the government has already agreed that these standards should be met, advocates need to bring instances of the violation of children's rights to the attention of the government and the public, and demand change. However, the efforts have not been utterly inadequate. Although law, in the form of international conventions or national legislation, can contribute considerably towards child rights, what matters is how laws are actually implemented and what is done to reach the ideals contained in these laws. Ways must be found, therefore, to enforce their implementation and to ensure that children experience true childhood.

There is a dire need for correcting legal perspectives, both substantive and procedural, and to foster, adopt, and create child-centered approaches and institutions. Accountability has to be fixed for non-implementation of legislation. Legal education and research should include child rights advocacy. All this requires reallocation of resources for children. It is essential that the children are placed high on the political agenda of development. Bodies like the NITI Aayog (National Institution for Transforming India Aayog)[134] have to provide adequate financial allocation for children and greater economic aid to villages. It is also imperative that such resource allocation be

---

[134] The Union Government of India announced formation of the National Institution for Transforming India (NITI) Aayog on 1 January 2015, and the first meeting of NITI Aayog was held on 8 February 2015. The NITI Aayog is a group of people including experts, with authority entrusted by the government to formulate/regulate policies in social and economic issues. It replaced the 65-year-old Planning Commission with a body that will give state governments a much larger say in crucial decisions. The new NITI will act more like a think tank or forum. One of its functions includes evolving a shared vision of national development priorities, sectors, and strategies with the active involvement of states in the light of national objectives. 'NITI Blogs', which provide public access to articles, field reports, and work in progress as well as the published opinions of NITI officials, are available to the public on the Aayog website. Available at http://www.niti.gov.in/ (accessed on 29 February 2016).

accompanied by the creation of participatory delivery mechanisms and structures for the effective utilization of these resources. Quality control and a set of indicators need to be developed to assess the implementation of child rights. Beside the parents, teachers and other members of the adult community and the civil society have to be educated on the rights of the child. And giving children a voice, through the creation of a forum empowering their opinion, may accelerate the progress towards realizing the rights of the child. India should develop resources—intellectual, ideological, institutional, and ecological—for sustained child rights advocacy.

Realization of the rights of the child calls for a well-defined, child-friendly, national movement involving individuals and masses, peoples and societies, families and communities, states and nations. Awareness of the rights of children is crucial. We all have an obligation to give a *first call on resources for children*, and above all, create and sustain an environment in which children's rights can be realized. Such a child-friendly movement will include families, schools, media, work-places, homes, communities, neighbourhoods, cities, and nations. Timely allocation of sufficient human, technical, and financial resources for the effective operationalization of the laws and policies must be ensured. Budgetary allocations must adequately take into consideration child protection needs. This must be based on reliable data to be made available. The budget allocation for child protection, health, and primary education must be substantially increased. A budgeting process must be established that includes a child rights perspective. This must be complemented by effective monitoring and evaluation systems. There must be coordination between ministries dealing with child rights issues. And finally, good governance has a central role to play to ensure that children are at the centre of a development agenda that guides policy decisions and budgetary allocations, as well as monitors progress. Good governance and the full enjoyment of children's right are mutually reinforcing.[135]

---

[135] UNICEF, 'Poverty and Exclusion among Urban Children'.

Index

Abbott II (June 1990), 692
Abbott V (May 1998), 692
Abbott v. Burke, 692
Abbott XX (May 2009), 692
ABC v. The State (The NCT of Delhi), 216–18
Abdul Vahid v. State of Kerala & Another, 665
Abhivday Ashram, 489
abortion: criminal penalty, 777; death of women
   in India, 775, 778; elective, 770n230; of female
   foetuses, 747; first-trimester, 777; to protect
   life of mother, 776; right of child, 770–72,
   770n230; right of women, 771; spontaneous,
   770n230; therapeutic, 770n230
Accredited Social Health Activist (ASHA), 735
Action, Advocacy, Research and Training in
   Disability (AARTH), 860
Action against Trafficking and Sexual Exploitation
   of Children (ATSEC), 490
Action Aid, 490–91
action plan and strategies, for preserving rights of
   children, 881
Action for Social Development (ASD), 85
Act of Parliament, 40
acute respiratory infections (ARI), 712
Additional Protocol to the American Convention
   on Human Rights in the Area of Economic,
   Social and Cultural Rights (San Salvador
   Protocol, 1988), 709, 712
ad litem, 905
adolescent, defined, 885
adopted child, natural guardianship of, 256–58,
   265
adoption leave, 100
adoption of children: adoption leave, 100;
   adoptive parents, eligibility of, 97–98, 577;

Andhra Pradesh adoption scandal, 85–88;
biological parents, legal status of, 169; Central
Adoption Resource Agency (CARA), 63,
83–84, 88, 122, 141, 165; Child Adoption
Resource Information and Guidance System
(CARINGS), 15; child legally available for,
80; in Christian community, 52–53; common
secular and uniform law on, 166–71; concept
and practice of, 50; critique of laws and practice
relating to, 73; documents required for, 98;
effects of marriage on prior, 61; estimated
number of, 54; follow up of progress of, 101;
by foreign parents, 78; under Guardians
and Wards Act (1890), 61–64; guidelines
enabling, 15, 66, 101–02; Hague Convention
on Intercountry Adoption (1993), 31; Hindu
Adoptions and Maintenance Act (HAMA,
1956), 55–61, 70; under Hindu Minority
and Guardianship Act (1956), 64; in Hindu
mythology, 48–49; by a Hindu woman, 58; in
history, mythology, and religion, 47–54; inter-
country adoption (ICA), 77–106; international
laws relating to, 114–28; judgments relating
to, 127–55; under Juvenile Justice (Care and
Protection of Children) Act (2000), 71; law
reform in, 159–72; laws in India, 55–77; legal
effects of, 59–61; under Maharashtra Adoption
Act (1995), 168; malpractices in, 63; meaning
of, 530; in Muslim community, 50–51; natural
guardianship and, 64; orphaned, abandoned,
and surrendered children, procedures for, 94; in
Parsi community, 50–52; permitted by court,
56n38; present status of, 53–54; prospective
adoptive parents (PAPs), 15; registration of a
deed of, 101; scandals in, 82–87; succession

About the Author

Asha Bajpai is founder dean and professor of law at the School of Law, Rights and Constitutional Governance, Tata Institute of Social Sciences, Mumbai, India. She is a PhD in law with specialization on child rights. She has been involved in teaching, research, training, and legislative reform for more than two decades. Bajpai recently became India's first chair of the United Nations Convention on the Rights of the Child Policy Center.